MTV

Italy

1st Edition

by
Sylvie Hogg
Brad Archer, Taryn Firkser, Anne Laurella,
Andre Legaspi, John Moretti
with Nina Kontas

Sylvie Hogg

Native Californian **Sylvie Hogg** (Lead writer, The Basics, Rome & Lazio, Florence & Tuscany, Umbria, Bologna/Emilia-Romagna, Venice & the Veneto, Naples & Campania, Sicily chapters) moved to Rome after graduating from Dartmouth and spent five fabulous years working as a tour guide and travel writer. She now lives in New York City and writes about Italy for several publications in the US and UK. She loves rock n' roll, and is always planning her next trip. She is the author of *Frommer's Irreverent Guide to Rome* and *Frommer's Rome Day by Day.*

Brad Archer

Brad Archer (The Basics) lives in New York City, where he currently does International Marketing for MTV and can be found singing with the Juilliard Choral Union, daydreaming by the Hudson, or out on the live music circuit.

Taryn Firkser

South African-Canadian **Taryn Firkser** (Venice & the Veneto, Liguria & the Italian Rivera, Naples & Campania chapters) has a Bachelor's degree in Geography and a Master's degree in Tibetan Studies and hopes to one day make a career of traveling the world.

Anne Laurella

Budget-airline jetsetter **Anne Laurella** (Bologna & Emilia-Romagna, Sicily chapters) divides her time between her native Stockholm, Sweden, and Rome. She can be spotted lounging on the beach in Sicily or eating prosciutto with her partner-in-crime, Sylvie. Anne recently launched her own editorial company.

Andre Legaspi

Andre Legaspi (Florence & Tuscany, Umbria, Bologna & Emilia-Romagna chapters) was born and raised in Queens, New York and attended McGill University in Montreal, where he wrote CD reviews and covered the music scene.

John Moretti

John Moretti (Florence & Tuscany, Venice & the Veneto, Milan & the Lakes chapters), has written for *The International Herald Tribune, The Independent on Sunday, Italy Daily, New York Sun*, The Associated Press, and FT Online. He's also the author of *Frommer's Florence, Tuscany & Umbria*.

Published by:
Wiley Publishing, Inc.
111 River St.
Hoboken, NJ 07030-5774

ISBN-13: 978-0-7645-8771-9

ISBN-10: 0-7645-8771-4

Editor: Kathleen Warnock

Production Editor: Ian Skinnari

Cartographers: Andrew Murphy, Guy Ruggiero

Cover & Interior Design: Eric Frommelt

Production by Wiley Indianapolis Composition Services

For information on our other products and services or to obtain technical support, please contact our Customer Care Department within the U.S. at 800/762-2974, outside the U.S. at 317/572-3993 or fax 317/572-4002.

Wiley also publishes its books in a variety of electronic formats. Some content that appears in print may not be available in electronic formats.

Manufactured in the United States of America

5 4 3 2 1

Table of Contents

CONTENTS

List of Maps

LIST OF MAPS

Acknowledgments

Sylvie Hogg would like to thank: my awesome family, all my friends from Rome, my Classics professors, Frank Bruni, Kathleen Warnock—and, last but not least—the Rolling Stones, the Go! Team, and Sam Cooke, for getting me through many a late night of writing this book. The editor would like to thank Melinda Quintero and Megan Murray for their assistance with the maps; the rest of the Frommer's/MTV editorial team: Kelly Regan, Naomi Black, Alexis Lipsitz, Jennifer Reilly, and Caroline Sieg for the brainstorming and ideas; Ian Skinnari for his eyes and his humor; Frommer's Classic authors Darwin Porter & Danforth Prince, for their guidance, inspiration, and research (particularly in Sicily), and the wonderful folks at MTV Books, particularly Lollion Chong and Jacob Hoye.

An Invitation to the Reader

In researching this book, we discovered many wonderful places—hotels, restaurants, shops, and more. We're sure you'll find others. Please tell us about them, so we can share the information with your fellow travelers in upcoming editions. If you were disappointed with a recommendation, we'd love to know that, too. Please write to:

MTV Italy, 1st Edition
Wiley Publishing, Inc.
111 River St.
Hoboken, NJ 07030-5774

An Additional Note

Please be advised that travel information is subject to change at any time—and this is especially true of prices. We therefore suggest that you write or call ahead for confirmation when making your travel plans. The authors, editors, and publisher cannot be held responsible for the experiences of readers while traveling. Your safety is important to us, however, so we encourage you to stay alert and be aware of your surroundings. Keep a close eye on cameras, purses, and wallets, all favorite targets of thieves and pickpockets.

A Note on Prices

The MTV Guides provide exact prices in each destination's local currency. The rates of this exchange as this book went to press are listed in the table below. Exchange rates are constantly in flux; for up-to-the-minute information, consult a currency-conversion website such as www.oanda.com/convert/classic.

Euro €	US $	UK £	Canadian $	Australian $	New Zealand $
1€ equals	$1.20	£0.68	C$1.35	A$1.60	NZ$1.75

Star Ratings, Icons & Abbreviations

Every hotel, restaurant, and attraction listed in this guide has been ranked for quality, value, service, amenities, and special features using a star-rating system. Hotels and restaurants are rated on a scale of zero (recommended) to three stars (exceptional). Attractions, shopping, and nightlife are rated according to the following scale: zero stars (recommended), one star (highly recommended), two stars (very highly recommended), and three stars (must-see). In addition to the star-rating system, we also use three feature icons that point you to great deals, in-the-know advice, and unique experiences. Throughout the book, look for:

 The most-happening restaurants, hotels, and things to do—don't leave town without checking these places out

 When cash flow is at a trickle, head for these spots: no-cost museums, free concerts, bars with complimentary food, and more

 Savvy advice and practical recommendations for students who are studying abroad

The Best of Italy

Passionate, gorgeous, generous Italy is bursting with "bests." The abbreviated list here includes the sights, places, tastes, and moments in our Italian travels that have made us smile the most. From laying eyes on the Colosseum at night, to slurping gelato on a sweltering summer day, to feeling the electricity in the stadium during a big Italian soccer match, these have been our most stimulating experiences and the fondest memories, the things we've spent hours at the local Internet cafe e-mailing home about, and the stories we'll tell for years to come.

For each destination that we've covered in this book, you'll find individual city and regional "bests" that meet the same criteria: Whether they're famous tourist attractions or more under-the-radar cultural experiences, these are the aspects of this wonderful boot-shaped country that have lodged themselves in our hearts (and in some cases, on our hips), and that we most look forward to repeating on our next trip.

With her glamorous good looks, illustrious history, and in-your-face passion for life, the sun-kissed, sea-washed *bel paese* has something for everyone, and then some. In Italy, the hits just keep on comin', and there are still plenty to be discovered. *Buon viaggio,* and here's to creating your own amazing travel experiences!

Most Awesome Ancient Ruins

The power and the glory of the Roman Empire are best summed up in the towering travertine arcades of the mighty **Colosseum,** where gladiators and wild animals tore at each other before 65,000 crazed spectators for over 400 years. Nearby, the marble and brick skeletons of downtown ancient Rome haunt the historic valley of the **Roman Forum.** The fragmentary columns, arches, and walls can be difficult to read, but we've given you a comprehensive guide to the Forum (p. 152) that should help you make sense of it all. Both the Colosseum and Forum take on an other-worldly splendor after dark, when they're illuminated by dramatically placed flood-lights. For a fascinating, hands-on look at the way the ancient Romans lived, the vast archaeological site of **Pompeii** (p. 618) is always amazing, visit after visit. In this once-wealthy Roman town that was buried by the apocalyptic eruption of Mt. Vesuvius in A.D. 79, you can explore the remarkably modern-seeming vestiges of sumptuous villas, baths, theaters, even a brothel. For those who can't make it down to Pompeii, the ruins at **Ostia Antica** (p. 204), the port town of ancient Rome, offer an equally interesting (and much less crowded) encounter with sophisticated public and private buildings from imperial times. **Hadrian's Villa** (p. 204) in Tivoli is another great day trip from Rome, where emperor Hadrian tricked out his country estate with fake canals and islands and other inventive design features that today's hottest architects only wish they'd thought of first. For a truly mystical, transporting experience, don't miss the **Valley of the Temples** (p. 683) in Agrigento, Sicily. The evocative amber-toned skeletons of these six Greek temples, situated along a dramatic rocky ridge, dotted with olive and almond trees, are among the most memorable archaeological ruins in the world.

All-Star Churches

From a lineup of thousands of hopeful houses of God, we've picked three Hall-of-Famers: No matter where you travel on the planet Earth, you'll never find a more impressive church than **St. Peter's Basilica** in the Vatican (Rome; p. 180). While we admit the exterior of St. Peter's is a bit of a cliché, the vastness of the interior catches everyone by surprise. It's the biggest church in the world, and it's filled with incomprehensible amounts of gold, bronze, and marble, including Michelangelo's justly celebrated *Pietà*. In the case of the **Duomo in Florence** (p. 257), it's all about the exterior: Brunelleschi's massive dome is like a red-skinned monster that looms over the quintessential Renaissance city. Catching a glimpse of the candy-striped marble walls of the immense cathedral, down a narrow alley, when you least expect it, is one of the most breathtaking sights in all of Italy. A view of **St. Mark's Basilica** (p. 487) in Venice is enhanced by the romantic mist that often hangs over the Venetian lagoon, but on a clear day, when the afternoon sun hits the basilica, the gilded domes and façade shimmer like a mirage, and the interior of St. Mark's is filled with near-horizontal shafts of light.

Best Carbs

Screw Dr. Atkins and the South Beach Diet: If you're coming to Italy, you eat flour and sugar, or you miss out big time. In Ravenna, Rimini, and Riccione, don't miss a chance to taste a fresh-baked *piadina* (flatbread made with pork lard). In Rome, indulge in the regional pasta specialties of *rigatoni alla carbonara* (with egg, *pecorino* cheese, and pancetta) and *bucatini all'amatriciana* (tomato, pancetta, and onion). Campania is the birthplace of **pizza** and mozzarella, and a dough pie is de rigueur when you're in Naples. For dessert, spike your blood sugar with **cannoli** in Sicily, or **gelato** anywhere in Italy.

Best Party Zone

Champagne spray-downs, beach volleyball tournaments, sand-castle contests, bonfires, and all-night dance parties await summer revelers in the anything-goes Riviera Romagnola towns of **Rimini** and **Riccione,** on the Adriatic Coast (east of Florence and Bologna). A word to the wise, however: This is a sporty, sun-loving scene, so show up toned and tanned, or you'll feel like a fish out of water. Speaking of fish out of water, the leaping bottlenose dolphins at the Rimini Delfinario put on one hell of a show. See "Rimini & Riccione: Partying On Italy's Adriatic Beaches."

Best Secret Island Getaways

If only they were a little easier to get to, the islands of **Ponza** (off the Roman coast; p. 206) and **Panarea** (in the Aeolian Islands, off the north coast of Sicily; p. 705) would have been exploited by international tourism long ago. As it is, they're just small enough and remote enough that they've stayed insider, yet totally happening, Italian vacation spots—and that's how we like them. With just a bit of planning, you can work in a detour to either one (Ponza from Rome or Naples; Panarea from Naples or Milazzo, in Sicily). When you get there, rent a small motorboat—there's nothing quite as fabulous as a DIY island circumnavigation, with on-board picnic and frequent dips in spectacular coves, in the middle of the Mediterranean.

Best College Towns

You might be surprised at the young, international vibe that reigns on the medieval streets of **Perugia,** the capital of Umbria, but Perugia's Università per Stranieri has long been the most effective (and most fun) place in Italy for foreigners to study the Italian language. Crack open a Peroni and mix with Swedish, Japanese, and Italian students around the fountain at the end of Perugia's main drag, Corso Vannucci. See our Umbria chapter. Even more venerable than Perugia, hip and elegant **Bologna** is home to the oldest university in Europe, with all the lively pubs, cultural happenings, and heated intellectual discussions you'd expect from such a well-established college town. In the 17th-century campus of the university, you can visit the Anatomical Theater, an ornate chamber where medical students dissected thousands of cadavers on a fancy marble slab. Read about Bologna in the "Bologna & Emilia-Romagna" chapter.

Best Bars for Abandoning All Pretense of Blending In

When, in the course of your Italian vacation, you just want to party 'til you, well . . . (you know), look no further than the **Drunken Ship** (p. 131) in Rome and the **Red Garter** (p. 243) in Florence, where body shots and Power Hour drink specials are only the beginning of a trip down memory lane to spring breaks and frat basements past. . . .

Best Bars, Period

Whether it's the fun-loving clientele, the laid-back atmosphere, the great tunes, or the hook-up potential that draws us there, we've plunked down many a euro on the wooden counters of these watering holes. At the **Vineria Reggio** (p. 132), on Campo de' Fiori in Rome, glasses of wine start at 1.50€ and the mood at *aperitivo* time is always festive. Grab a table on the cobblestones for great people-watching on Rome's party piazza par excellence. **Rock Castle** (p. 335) in Perugia is an awesome place to hang out and drink with the international student population, and the music on the PA never lets you down. **Corto Maltese** (p. 389) is a funky, divey Bologna institution, whose dance floor, pool table, and crowded bar are all eminently fertile zones for sowing the seeds of love (or a hook-up, anyway) with a local. In Milan, where most bars and lounges are busy trying to woo high-roller fashionistas and financiers, **Bar Magenta** (p. 546) is a more down-to-earth choice, where Motown, rock, and R&B classics play on the speakers. It's also the first stop for any scarf-wearing *tifoso* headed toward San Siro for an Inter or AC Milan soccer game. Late at night, soak up that superfluous pint with Magenta's legendary sandwiches crafted by old men and an even older, hand-cranked meat slicer.

Most Jaw-Dropping Natural Scenery

The waterfront of **Lake Como** is the only place in the world where palm trees flourish at the base of the foothills of the Alps. The fact that George Clooney hangs out here (he has a villa in Laglio) only adds to the visual

THE BEST OF ITALY

splendor of this preposterously gorgeous place. See "Milan & the Lakes." In Liguria, the hikes between the five villages of the **Cinque Terre**—with sweeping sea views and dense woods along the way—are a wonderful way to get back to nature. Just watch out for the flailing "hiking sticks" of the middle-aged tour groups who often monopolize the trails. (See "Cinque Terre: Five Breathtaking Towns" in the Liguria chapter). For all out Mediterranean fabulousness, there's a good reason why **Capri** and the **Amalfi Coast** (see Naples chapter) are as famous as they are. Verdant cliffs plunge vertiginously to the sea, and the water is a shade of cerulean blue that you probably didn't know Nature had in her box of crayons.

Best Piazzas for Hanging Out

By day, **Campo de' Fiori** in Rome (p. 128) is a picturesque fruit, vegetable, and trinket market; by night, it's drink central. Almost every other shop front on the cobblestoned pedestrian square is an alcohol purveyor of some kind, so whether you're in the mood for raucous American-themed pubs, or more chill, sophisticated wine bars, or back-to-basics open container with the punk kids on the steps of the statue, the possibilities are endless. The de facto living room of Bologna is the L-shaped **Piazza Maggiore** (p. 390), surrounded by imposing medieval palaces and towers; along one edge of the piazza, the Sala Borsa is a library, cafe, and general meeting point; on the opposite side, the draped arcades of the gorgeous portico known as the Pavaglione offer shopping and shade. You won't be the first one to have made **Piazza San Marco** (p. 483) your hangout in Venice. Its eternal popularity means prices are steep, but it's worth having at least one drink here for the legendary setting and view of St. Mark's Basilica. A more under-the-radar choice in Venice, **Campo San Giacometto** (p. 476) has cool restaurants and wine bars frequented by hip locals. A few of the bars here have outdoor seating on an astonishingly bare esplanade facing the Grand Canal. In student-ruled Perugia, it all goes down on **Piazza IV Novembre** (p. 322). By early evening, everybody who's anybody convenes around the fountain at the end of Corso Vannucci for several rounds of drinks. A friendly bar nearby will give you a plastic cup for your beer and let you use their bathroom, even if you're not a paying customer. Amid the chaotic and sometimes seedy streets of Naples, **Piazza Gesù Nuovo** has emerged as a hip hangout; the square and its immediate side streets are home to some of the most popular bars and lounges in town. It's not really a piazza, but in Milan, **Corso Como** is the strip of restaurants and nightclubs where models, moguls, and wannabes (i.e., you and I) come to strut their stuff.

Best Hostels

You're guaranteed to meet fellow English-speaking travelers and receive a warm welcome at **Archi Rossi** (p. 225) in Florence, **The Beehive** (p. 91) and **Colors** (p. 95) in Rome, and **Hostel of the Sun** (p. 604) in Naples.

Best Museums

We're not talking yawn-inducing galleries that we're telling you to visit just because you "should." The collections in these world-class halls of art are important *and* highly entertaining. The mile-long galleries of the **Vatican Museums** (p. 185) in Rome are crowded and hot in summer, but the treasures of ancient statuary and Michelangelo's eye-popping frescoes in the Sistine Chapel make it worth the trouble. At the **Capitoline Museums** (p. 190), also in Rome, you can commune with hauntingly realistic portraits of emperors and gods and take in spectacular vistas over the Roman Forum from the 78 B.C. Roman archive hall, the Tabularium, which has recently been incorporated into the museums. Many argue that Rome's best museum is the small but star-studded

Galleria Borghese, (p. 191) where Bernini's extraordinary sculpture of *Apollo and Daphne* defies the physical properties of marble, and Caravaggio's strident paintings seem to want to jump out of their frames and pick a fight with you. When you're in Naples, before or after you've visited Pompeii (or even if you don't make it to Pompeii), a visit to **Museo Archeologico Nazionale** (p. 613) is a must. All the best artifacts from Pompeii ended up here, from everyday kitchen utensils, to monumental mosaics, to a very racy trove of ancient erotica in the Gabinetto Segreto wing of the museum. The main museum of Venice is the **Accademia** (p. 490), which is worth your euros and time as much for the vivid Venetian paintings on the walls as for the sumptuous setting itself—in a grand palace that gives you a wonderful sense of the utter opulence of Venice in its heyday. At the **Uffizi** (p. 254) in Florence, there are enough Madonna and Child paintings to make your head spin, but you might just levitate when you lay eyes on Botticelli's babes—not to mention a slew of Michelangelos, Da Vincis, and Caravaggios. Just be sure to book your visit in advance, or brave a bitch of a line to get in.

Most Fun Touristy Excursions

Just because they're hackneyed and overpriced, don't shy away from these truly enjoyable, totally worthwhile rites of Italian tourism passage: on Capri, board an old-school rowboat and lean back as your captain whisks you through the narrow opening to the **Blue Grotto,** where the gorgeous natural spectacle of pilot-light-colored water (and the boatmen who sing off-key sea chanteys inside the grotto) will have you grinning from ear to ear (p. 656). The best evening activity in nightlife-challenged Venice is a **gondola ride** (p. 466), which is more than romantic—it's sublime, and it's perhaps the most deservedly hyped European traditions. Yeah, it's expensive, but if you skip dinner

that night and bring a few friends, the cost isn't so bad. Just make sure you go at night, when the canals are virtually empty, and, if you're lucky, your gondolier might let you row a few strokes on the Grand Canal. Bring booze, because you'll want to toast the sweetness of life over and over.

Best Climbable Sights Worth Climbing

Don't be suckered into climbing more steps in Italy than you already have to; not every tower or church dome is worth the money and physical effort, but some should not be missed. At the top of the list, the **Leaning Tower** (p. 305) is an absolute must if you're going to Pisa, but it's not for the weak of stomach—the climb itself isn't terribly strenuous, but the spiral steps that wind around the off-kilter column do a number on your equilibrium. Advance booking is essential in high season, and watch your alcohol intake the night before, as puking off the Leaning Tower is a no-no. For views of Florence and Tuscany that keep going, and going, and going . . . you should definitely make the trek to the top of Brunelleschi's dome at the **Duomo in Florence** (p. 257). The most central panorama in Rome is at the top of the locally ridiculed **Vittoriano** (aka "The Wedding Cake"; p. 144), which is free to climb. In Bologna, a less famous leaning tower, the medieval **Torre Asinelli** (p. 392), gives you a great perspective over the city's wagon-wheel street plan. There's an elevator that goes to the top of the **Campanile in Venice** (p. 487), so you won't really exert yourself, but the views over the lagoon will take your breath away. Bad-asses who want to get up close and personal with belching and hissing volcanoes can hike to the craters of **Mt. Vesuvius** (Naples; p. 624) and **Mt. Etna** (Sicily; p. 702). Vesuvius is considered "safe," but before climbing Etna, it's imperative that you check with local officials to find out the status of the volcano. If you sneak up on Etna when it's in the middle of a bad bout of acid reflux, *arrivederci!*

Best Place to See Real Modern Italian Culture

Churches and monuments are fine, but the real shrines of modern Italy are the **soccer** stadiums. It doesn't matter what team you see, or what city you see them in, but if you're in Italy during the *calcio* season (Aug–June), do yourself a favor and get tickets to a game. The passion of the fans is electric but rarely violent, and after the first 5 minutes of stadium choruses, you'll be chanting along with them and taunting the other teams' supporters with juvenile insults and hand gestures. There might even be a few sandwiches thrown. It's awesome. In this book, there are several cities where you can catch a Serie A (premier league) match: in Rome, **AS Roma** and **SS Lazio** (see box, p. 198) play at the Stadio Olimpico; in Milan, **Inter** and **AC Milan** (p. 550) play at Stadio Meazza in San Siro; in Florence, **La Fiorentina** (p. 263) plays at Stadio Artemio Franchi; in Genoa, **Sampdoria** plays at Stadio Ferraris; **Bologna FC** plays at that city's Stadio Renato dall'Ara; **FC Parma** plays at Stadio Tardini (see box, p. 440); and **Verona Hellas** and **Chievo Verona** play at Stadio Bentegodi.

Best Regions for Road Tripping

Renting a car and driving around Italy can be an absolute blast, but some regions are more scenic and automobile-friendly than others. The rolling hills of **Tuscany** and **Umbria,** for instance, are best explored with your own wheels, since many of the most picturesque little towns are not easily accessible by train or bus. Furthermore, you don't need to spend much time in any one place, so having your own car gives you the freedom to move on when you're bored. You'll also be served well by a car on **Sicily**—as long as you steer clear of central Palermo!—the island's distances are manageable, the highways are well maintained and scenic, and there are a ton of worthwhile detours off the main bus and train routes that are really best reached by your trusty Fiat. In general, driving in Italy is less crazy than you've heard (once you're out of the cities, anyway). Signs are explicit and uniform throughout the country, and you'll get the hang of the fast-lane etiquette after your first day on the *autostrada.* Italian roads are not well lit, however, so don't get behind the wheel at night.

Most Relaxing Small Towns

The classic tourist trifecta of Rome-Florence-Venice can take its toll on your nerves. For a mellow overnight stop between Rome and Florence, consider recharging your batteries in **Orvieto** (p. 357), a medieval hill town with Etruscan grottoes, cozy wine bars, and splendid *duomo.* On the main train line between Florence and Venice (about an hour north of Bologna), **Ferrara** (p. 441) is an elegant little Renaissance city with a picture-perfect castle (with moat!), extensive bike paths (bikes are available for rent everywhere), and pumpkin ravioli in every restaurant!

Best *Vino*

In Rome, white **Falanghina** is supposed to bring good luck to all who drink it (and it goes wonderfully with all the fresh vegetables and seafood you'll be eating in summer). Medium-bodied red **Sangiovese** and **Lambrusco** are the perfect pairing for the comfort food of Emilia-Romagna. You may think that **chianti** is old news, but I swear it tastes a hundred times better in its native land, Tuscany. In the Bay of Naples region, drop a few peach slices in a glass of white **Lacryma Christi** for the quintessential Campanian summer quencher.

Best Next-Big-Thing Destinations

First, there was Tuscany; a few years later, international tourists started coming to

Umbria. In Italy, the hits just keep on coming, so pretty soon, another region is bound to be discovered, right? When you visit **Bologna** and its region, **Emilia-Romagna,** you'll scratch your head and wonder why they're not more known to tourists. The towns are lovely, the people are warm, and the food is outta control. (The shopping is some of the best in Italy, too.) **Sicily** is also amazingly undervisited for how much it has to offer a foreign tourist. There's sun and sea, ancient ruins, and again, warm people and fantastic food—the flavors of vegetables and seafood that you find in Sicily are simply not found anywhere else in the world. Sicily shyness is partially explained by its separation from mainland Italy, and by people's irrational fear of the Mafia. Hogwash! Sicily is an easy hop from Rome, Venice, and Milan, and chances are Don Corleone will not order a hit on you for eating gelato made by a rival "family" in Siracusa. Who knows? Maybe Emilia-Romagna and Sicily will never be big tourist destinations—indeed, it's probably better than way!—but they have all the right stuff.

The Basics

So, you're going to Italy. Lucky you! By now, you've started daydreaming about all the beautiful things you'll see, all the amazing food you'll eat, all the booze you'll consume, and all the romantic things that will happen to you. Guess what? In all likelihood, all of the above will come true without your planning a damn thing. After all, going to Italy is hardly the most hardcore, extreme travel you'll do—it's one of the most developed countries in the world, it's friendly, it's safe, and it's seen centuries of travelers. Italy might be foreign to you, but as a tourist, you're not foreign to Italy. We want you to be wild and carefree in your approach to travel in Italy, but to a point. There are plenty of things you should think about and be aware of—from the logistical to the cultural—before you board that jet plane to *bella Italia!* We'll start with some overall planning suggestions, and take it down to the nitty-gritty. Read on, and you'll minimize those "I can't believe I didn't think of that" moments that can stress you out and throw a wrench into your otherwise *dolce viaggio*.

The Regions in Brief

Italy is about the size of the U.S. state of Arizona, but the peninsula's shape gives you the impression of a much larger area; the ever-changing seacoast contributes to this feeling, as do the large islands of Sicily and Sardinia. Bordered on the northwest by France, on the north by Switzerland and Austria, and on the east by Slovenia (formerly part of Yugoslavia), Italy is a land largely surrounded by the sea.

Two areas within Italy's boundaries aren't actually part of Italy: the **State of Vatican City** and the **Republic of San Marino.** Vatican City's 44 hectares (109 acres) were established in 1929 by a concordat between Pope Pius XI and Benito Mussolini, acting as head of the Italian government; the agreement also gave Roman Catholicism special status in Italy. (The Republic of San Marino, with a capital of the same name, strides atop the slopes of Mt. Titano, 23km/14 miles from Rimini. It's small and completely surrounded by Italy, so it still exists only by the grace of Italy.)

Here's a brief rundown of the cities and regions covered in this guide:

Rome & Latium

The region of **Latium** is dominated by **Rome,** capital of the ancient empire and the modern nation of Italy, and **Vatican City,** the independent papal state. Much of the civilized world was once ruled from here, going back to the days when Romulus and Remus are said to have founded Rome in 753 B.C. For generations, Rome was referred to as *caput mundi* (capital of the world). It remains a timeless city, ranking with Paris and London as one of the top European destinations. There's no place with more artistic monuments—not even Venice or Florence.

Florence & Tuscany

Tuscany is one of the most culturally and politically influential provinces—the development of Italy without Tuscany is simply unthinkable. It was Tuscany, with its sun-warmed vineyards and towering cypresses, that inspired the artists of the Renaissance. Nowhere in the world is the impact of the Renaissance still felt more fully than in its birthplace, **Florence,** the repository of artistic works left by Leonardo and Michelangelo. Since the 19th century, travelers have been flocking to Florence to see the Donatello bronzes, the Botticelli smiles, and all the other preeminent treasures. Alas, it's now an invasion, so you run the risk of being trampled underfoot as you explore the historic heart of the city. To escape, head for the nearby Tuscan hill towns, former stomping ground of the Guelphs and Ghibellines. The main cities to visit are **Lucca, Pisa,** and especially **Siena,** Florence's great historical rival with an inner core that appears to be caught in a time warp. We also profile **Elba, Chianti,** and **Arezzo,** as well as **San Gimignano,** northwest of Siena, celebrated for its medieval "skyscrapers."

Umbria

Pastoral, hilly, and fertile, **Umbria** is similar to Tuscany, but with fewer tourists. Its once-fortified network of hill towns is among the most charming in Italy. Crafted from millions of tons of gray-brown rocks, each town is a testament to the masonry and architectural skills of generations of craftsmen. Cities particularly worth a visit are **Perugia, Gubbio, Assisi, Spoleto** (site of the world-renowned annual arts festival), and **Orvieto,** a mysterious citadel once used as a stronghold by the Etruscans. Called the land of shadows, Umbria is often covered in a bluish haze that evokes an ethereal painted look. Many local artists have tried to capture the province's glow, with its sun-dappled hills, terraced vineyards, and miles of olive trees. If you're short on time, visit Assisi to check out Giotto's frescoes at the Basilica di San Francesco (they've been repaired after the 1997 earthquakes), and Perugia, the largest and richest of the province's cities. In addition (even though it's not really in Umbria, but rather across the border in The Marches), we also give you a glimpse of **Urbino,** where students from around the world have gone (or will go) for a semester abroad.

Bologna & Emilia-Romagna

Italians seem to agree on only one thing: The food in **Emilia-Romagna** is the best in Italy. The region's capital, **Bologna,** boasts a stunning Renaissance core with plenty of churches and arcades, a fine university with roots in the Middle Ages, and a populace with a reputation for leftist leanings. The region has one of the highest standards of living. When not dining in Bologna, you can take time to explore its artistic heritage. Other art cities abound—none more noble than Byzantine **Ravenna,** still living off its past glory as the one-time capital of the declining Roman Empire.

If you can visit only one more city in the region, make it **Parma,** to see the city center with its Duomo and baptistery and to view its National Gallery. This is the home of Parmigiano-Reggiano cheese and prosciutto. We also swing by **Ferrara,** and then hang out for awhile at the Adriatic resorts of **Riccione** and **Rimini.**

Venice & the Veneto

Northeastern Italy is one of Europe's treasure troves, encompassing **Venice** (arguably the world's most beautiful city), the surrounding **Veneto** region. The Veneto, dotted with rich museums and some of the best architecture in Italy, sprawls across the verdant hills and flat plains between the Adriatic, the Dolomites, Verona, and the edges of Lake Garda. For many generations, the fortunes of the Veneto revolved around Venice, with its sumptuous palaces, romantic waterways, Palazzo Ducale, and Basilica di San Marco. Aging, decaying, and sinking into the sea, Venice is so alluring we almost want to recommend visiting it even if you have to skip Rome and Florence. Nearby is **Treviso,** and we also give you a glimpse of three fabled art cities in the "Venetian Arc": **Verona,** of Romeo and Juliet fame; **Vicenza,** to see the villas of Andrea Palladio where 16th-century aristocrats lived; and **Padua,** with its Giotto frescoes.

Milan, Lombardy & The Lake District

Flat, fertile, prosperous, and politically conservative, **Lombardy** is dominated by **Milan** just as Latium is dominated by Rome. Lombardy is one of the world's leading commercial and cultural centers, and it has been ever since Milan developed into Italy's gateway to northern German-speaking Europe in the early Middle Ages. Although some people belittle Milan as an industrial city with a snobbish contempt for the poorer regions to the south, its fans compare it to New York.

Milan's cathedral is Europe's third largest, its La Scala opera house is world-renowned, and its museums and churches are a treasure trove, with one containing Leonardo's *Last Supper.* However, Milan still doesn't have the sights and tourist interest of Rome, Florence, and Venice. Also competing for your time will be the gorgeous lakes of **Como, Garda,** and **Maggiore,** which lie near Lombardy's eastern edge.

Liguria & Genoa

Comprising most of the **Italian Riviera,** the region of **Liguria** incorporates the steeply sloping capital city of **Genoa,** charming medieval ports like **Portofino,** and five traditional coastal communities **(Cinque Terre).** There's also a series of beach resorts (including **Rapallo** and **Santa Margherita**) that resemble the French Riviera. Although overbuilt and overrun, the Italian Riviera is still a land of great beauty.

Naples & Campania

More than any other region, **Campania** reverberates with the memories of the ancient Romans, who favored its strong sunlight, fertile soil, and bubbling sulfurous springs. It encompasses both the anarchy of **Naples** and the elegant beauty of **Capri** and the **Amalfi Coast.** The region also contains many sites specifically identified in ancient mythology (lakes defined as the entrance to the Kingdom of the Dead, for example) and some of the world's most renowned ancient ruins (including **Pompeii**). Campania is overrun, overcrowded, and over everything, but it still lures visitors. Allow at least a day for Naples, which has amazing museums and the world's worst traffic outside Cairo. Those seeking fun in the sun head for Capri or Portofino. The leading resorts along the Amalfi Drive (even though they're not exactly undiscovered) are **Ravello** (not on the sea) and **Positano** (on the sea). **Amalfi** and **Sorrento** and island **Ischia** also have beautiful seaside settings.

Italy: The Big Picture

Sicily

The largest Mediterranean island, **Sicily,** is a land of beauty, mystery, and world-class monuments. It's a bizarre mix of bloodlines and architecture from medieval Normandy, Aragonese Spain, Moorish North Africa, ancient Greece, Phoenicia, and Rome. Since the advent of modern times, part of the island's primitiveness has faded, as thousands of cars clog the narrow lanes of its biggest city, **Palermo.** Poverty remains widespread, yet the age-old stranglehold of the Mafia seems less certain because of the increasingly vocal protests of an outraged Italian public. On the eastern edge of the island is Mt. Etna, the tallest active volcano in Europe. Many of Sicily's larger cities are relatively unattractive, but areas of ravishing beauty and eerie historical interest include **Syracuse, Taormina,** and **Agrigento.** Sicily's ancient ruins are rivaled only by those of Rome itself. The Valley of the Temples is worth the trip here. You can also reach the **Aolean Islands** from here.

The Stuff You Need to Figure Out Before You Go

- **You need to get there.** For the best airfare and flight structure, get to know the big travel websites and shop around. In our experience booking flights to Italy online, Kayak, Orbitz, and Priceline have always had the best prices and the most flights to choose from. In general, try to book your flights well in advance—at least a month before you depart, more for summer travel. While Italy airfares do occasionally go on sale at the last minute, the savings are hardly more than $50 or so—which is hardly worth the anxiety of wondering if you'll get a seat.

- **You need a place to sleep.** In a perfect world, you would book your hotel reservations in Italy even before you booked your flight there—during high season, it can be tough to find good-value accommodations on the spot. However, it's not a perfect world. You'll probably end up changing your travel plans somewhat while abroad, and furthermore, some hostels don't accept reservations until the day before your intended arrival. So, even if you can't book all your accommodations before you leave home, you'll find plenty of helpful tips in the "Staying There" section, later in this chapter, which will give you a feeling for the lay of the land, accommodations-wise, in Italy.

- **Know what to expect at different times of the year.** Italian tourism has a rather entrenched seasonal cycle, and depending on when you go, you're likely to have quite different experiences. Weather, of course, is the most obvious variable. There are also significant differences in traveler demographics during the year: droves of North American college kids come in the summer, while older, more budget-oriented travelers tend to come in the off-peak months of February and November.

- **Pay attention to opening hours.** The majority of Italian museums are closed on Monday. The Vatican Museums are closed half of Saturday and all of Sunday and keep short weekday hours in winter. We'll also give you advice about the best days of the week and the best times of day to visit different sights. Where possible (at such top attractions as the Uffizi in Florence), book your tickets online in advance.

- **Embrace the cultural differences.** You won't find all the conveniences of home in Italy, and the language barrier can be frustrating, but part of why you flew thousands of miles to get here was to experience something different, right? Even with plenty of quirks that will strike you as odd, Italy is nevertheless a bedrock of Western culture and a democracy not so different from ours in many respects. Contrary to what you might have heard about train strikes, laziness, and general national dysfunction, Italy is not a third-world country. Okay, parts of the south might cause you to raise your eyebrows at that statement, but for all the talk you may have heard, the country and its services function pretty well.

○ **Be realistic about how much you can do on your trip.** Time flies when you're having fun, and you'll be having a lot of fun in Italy. Don't rush through the country in your quest to send postcards from 10 different cities. Leave the *veni vidi vici* to Julius Caesar, and allow yourself some idle *dolce vita*.

How Much Time Do I Need in Italy?

To get a sense for the best that Italy has to offer, we recommend you spend at least 2 weeks. If you're content to visit only a few cities or regions, a week to 10 days is great. If you're only visiting one city, you'll probably find that a long weekend is quite satisfying. However long you stay, wherever you go, you'll leave wanting more. Also, when you factor in travel time between destinations, checking in at hotels, arriving at the train station in time for your next train out, etc., you lose a lot of valuable hours that you might have originally dedicated to hanging out, sightseeing, or partying. Moral of the story: You need more time than you think.

We especially recommend that you resist the temptation to do a whirlwind Rome-Florence-Venice-in-a-week scenario. Lots of people do it, but it's far more fun to spend more time in each place and get your bearings before you pack up and head for the next city. Unless you're an experienced traveler,

OKKIO! (Watch Out)

Throughout this book, you'll find boxes with the heading *"Okkio,"* which denotes a fact or warning you need to know about (such as legal, cultural, and personal advice) gained from hard-won experience. Not knowing these things could hinder or derail your trip.

you'll be wiped out and overwhelmed if you try to see too much too quickly. At a bare minimum, you need 3 full days in Rome, 2 full days in Florence, 2 full days in the Bay of Naples, and 1 day (including 1 night) in Venice.

Try to spend a few days in less touristy places like Bologna or Perugia, both of which have charming medieval centers and lively student populations. In warm weather, definitely dedicate at least 1 full day, if not several, to a beach or island. Allow 1 full "buffer day" at the start of your trip to recover from jet lag, and remember that you won't be doing or seeing much of anything on the day of your return flight since you'll most likely be heading to the airport in the morning.

WHEN TO GO

Late April, all of May, early June, late September, and early October are the all-around most agreeable times to visit Italy. The weather is mild to warm, and crowds, while not exactly light, are much more manageable than they are in sticky summer.

Summer remains a popular season for overseas visitors, because that's when most people in the Northern Hemisphere can take a long vacation, but this means airfares and hotel rates all go up from June to early September. If you can spend a significant amount of time at the beach, a lake, or a swimming pool, summer in Italy—specifically June and July—can be fantastic, too. Summer is also fun because it's the season when the

THE BASICS

most young people are traveling through Europe, and most cities have some kind of summer-long festival with concerts and other special events under the stars. For the traditional tourist destinations of Rome, Florence, and Venice, summer can be trying, as these cities get uncomfortably hot and humid from June through August (imagine Washington, D.C., Chicago, or New York, without air-conditioning), forming a bad first impression on many first-time visitors.

Italy is all about being outside, walking around, and enjoying the open-air sights that are everywhere, but even the splendors of ancient Rome and Renaissance Tuscany quickly lose their luster when you're battling sunstroke and—let's be realistic—a bad hangover. August is still very much Italy's national holiday month and a terrible time to visit any Italian city—the streets are depressingly deserted, many shops and restaurants are closed, and it can be brutally hot. If you're just headed for seaside or mountain resorts, however, August is great.

The Case for Not Going to Italy in Summer

- It can cost 50% more to fly to Italy in summer than it does in late spring and early fall. Hotels also jack up their prices in June and July.
- Air-conditioning does not exist in Italy—at least, not as you know it. Those establishments that do have it don't turn it on high enough, or turn it on for useless 15-minute spurts at random times throughout the day.
- The canals of Venice heat up and spread their toxic stink all over the lagoon (which makes it very hard to see anything romantic about this extraordinary city).
- Thinking of going to an indoor place like the Vatican to escape the heat? Think again. In summer, the museums turn into a sauna, which might be good for your

pores, but it can't be good for those 500-year-old frescoes in the Sistine Chapel.

If summer's the only time you can travel, however, never fear. You can still have a very good time, and here are some tips to make things cooler in the hot, hot sun:

The Case for Going to Italy in Summer

- Get thee to the beach! This is how everyone, from ancient Latin tribes to modern Italians, survives their sweltering cities—by taking a break from them and heading to the sea, so be sure to incorporate one or more beach, lake or island days into your trip. (And the way Italy is shaped, you're never too far from a place to swim.) That bracing dip in the Med off Capri will more than make up for the day before, when you almost died of asphyxiation in the 100°F (38°C) heat of Pompeii.
- Get to know the treasures of Italy's churches (they're usually free, and they stay cool year-round), and when you have to tour shadeless ruins like the Roman Forum, avoid the deadly blazing heat of midday by sticking to the early morning or late afternoon. Don't get too ambitious with the sightseeing, and stay hydrated.
- Take advantage of summer festivals, like Perugia's *Umbria Jazz* or Rome's *Estate Romana*. Monitor your city's information websites and local newspaper listings for summer-only rock and hip-hop shows at open-air venues. More big names in the music world are making it to more parts of Italy than ever before.
- In August, avoid the cities. Seriously, it's miserable. During this month, residents flee Rome, Florence, and Milan in droves, sapping these normally lively places of all their energy. Italy's beaches and islands are where the party's at in August.
- Gelato, gelato, gelato!

La Bella Figura: Being Cool in Italy

The concept of *la bella figura* is one of the cornerstones of Italian society. Translated literally into English, it means "fine figure," which might imply that you have to look glamorous to fit in here. Not at all: *Bella figura* is much more about courtesy, politeness, and not embarrassing yourself in public than wearing head-to-toe Armani or having your hair perfectly done. Part of why this country is so civilized is that everyone in Italy, even without being actively aware of it, strives to achieve a *bella figura* (at least in public) at all times. Indeed, *la brutta figura*—the "ugly" and dreaded polar opposite of *bella figura*—is mortifying to Italians. Unfortunately, many Italians have come to expect rude and obnoxious or arrogant *brutta figura* behavior from a certain kind of tourist (who tend to be young, alcohol-loving, and from larger countries). You can still be yourself and have fun—just be cool in public, be respectful of the country that's hosting you, look respectable, and remember the niceties that are part of Italians' cultural DNA, and you will maintain your *bella figura*.

→ Saying hello to everyone when you walk into a coffee bar
Bella figura

→ Going on a rowdy pub crawl through the *centro storico* of Rome or Florence
Brutta figura

→ Saying thank you when you leave a shop, even if you haven't bought anything
Bella figura

→ Wearing flip-flops to dinner
Brutta figura

→ Giving up your seat on the bus to an old lady
Bella figura

→ Taking pictures in museums when photography is clearly not permitted
Brutta figura

→ Mastering a few basic phrases in Italian, even if your pronunciation sucks
Bella figura

→ Freaking out and raising your voice when a local doesn't understand English
Brutta figura

And because there is also an undeniably phony component to the whole thing:

→ A-list name-dropping (e.g., "I babysit for Brad and Angelina")
Bella figura

→ Carrying around your ratty clothes in a Prada shopping bag
Bella figura

→ Carrying around your Prada clothes in a ratty backpack
Brutta figura

THE BASICS

Italy's Average Daily Temperature & Monthly Rainfall

Rome	Jan	Feb	Mar	Apr	May	June	July	Aug	Sept	Oct	Nov	Dec
Temp. (°F)	49	52	57	62	72	82	87	86	73	65	56	47
Temp. (°C)	9	11	14	17	22	28	31	30	23	20	13	8
Rainfall (in.)	2.3	1.5	2.9	3.0	2.8	2.9	1.5	1.9	2.8	2.6	3.0	2.1

Florence	Jan	Feb	Mar	Apr	May	June	July	Aug	Sept	Oct	Nov	Dec
Temp. (°F)	45	47	50	60	67	76	77	70	64	63	55	46
Temp. (°C)	7	8	9	16	19	24	25	21	18	17	13	8
Rainfall (in.)	3	3.3	3.7	2.7	2.2	1.4	1.4	2.7	3.2	4.9	3.8	2.9

Naples	Jan	Feb	Mar	Apr	May	June	July	Aug	Sept	Oct	Nov	Dec
Temp. (°F)	50	54	58	63	70	78	83	85	75	66	60	52
Temp. (°C)	9	12	14	17	21	26	28	29	24	19	16	11
Rainfall (in.)	4.7	4	3	3.8	2.4	.8	.8	2.6	3.5	5.8	5.1	3.7

Passports, Visas & *Permesso*

For up-to-date passport requirement info for American citizens, visit the passport Web page of the U.S. State Department at **http://travel.state.gov**. This site will be your key to updated travel advisory information and passport requirements/application downloads.

If you don't have a passport yet, allow *plenty* of time before your trip to get one; passport processing in the U.S. normally takes 3 weeks but can take longer during busy periods (especially spring). And keep in mind that if you need a passport in a hurry, you'll pay a higher processing fee.

No matter what country you're traveling from, before your trip, make a few copies of the critical front pages of your passport, with your photo, passport number, and issuing agency info. Keep one copy with you, in a separate place from the passport itself—e.g., the bottom of your suitcase—and leave a copy with a trusted friend or family member at home. If you lose your passport, you'll need to visit the nearest consulate or embassy of your native country as soon as possible for a replacement. Replacement passports will be issued much more quickly if you have a photocopy of the vital info passport page handy. Note that there are varying requirements to obtain a passport for travelers under the age of 14 and depending on whether you are renewing your passport or applying for one for the first time.

When traveling between destinations (on planes, trains, boats, etc.), safeguard your passport in an inconspicuous, inaccessible place like the inside pocket of your handbag or daypack. When you've arrived at your destination, it's best to stow your passport in the hotel safe. Even if your individual room doesn't have a safe, the reception desk usually does—ask for the *cassaforte*.

Italian law requires all hotels and hostels to register their guests with the police station, so you must have your passport (or European Union ID card, for European citizens) with you whenever you're checking

OKKIO! Being Deported Is Not Cool

While it's tempting to extend your time in Italy by taking a job at a bar or a sketchy tour company, we know of several young Americans and Australians who've been caught without the proper paperwork and deported—not the *arrivederci* they were imagining, we can assure you.

THE BASICS

into a new hotel. So, don't leave your passport at the hotel safe in Florence if you're taking an overnight road trip to Siena.

When you clear customs and immigration at any Italian airport, your passport should be stamped with an entry date. (I say "should," because sometimes booth staff at immigration is too busy checking out the new female arrivals on Alitalia Flight 611 from JFK to fuss with bureaucratic details.)

From the date that's stamped in your passport, most foreign citizens are automatically given a 3-month "tourist visa." If you're arriving by train from within the European Union, however, the start of your 3-month visa will be the date of your first check-in at a hotel or hostel, which, as mentioned previously, are required by law to register all guests with the local police.

If you arrive by train and stay in a private home or apartment, there will be no official record of your arrival in Italy. Just make sure someone—family and friends at home, or the U.S. consulate in Italy—knows your whereabouts in case of emergency.

For Residents of Australia: You can pick up an application from your local post office or any branch of Passports Australia, but you must schedule an interview at the passport office to present your application materials. Call the **Australian Passport Information Service** at ☎ **131-232,** or visit the government website at www.passports.gov.au.

For Residents of Canada: Passport applications are available at travel agencies throughout Canada or from the central **Passport Office,** Department of Foreign Affairs and International Trade, Ottawa, ON K1A 0G3 (☎ **800/567-6868;** www.ppt.gc.ca).

For Residents of Ireland: You can apply for a 10-year passport at the **Passport Office,** Setanta Centre, Molesworth Street, Dublin 2 (☎ **01/671-1633;** www.irlgov.ie/iveagh). Those under age 18 and over 65 must apply for a €12 3-year passport. You can also apply at 1A South Mall, Cork (☎ **021/272-525**) or at most main post offices.

For Residents of New Zealand: You can pick up a passport application at any New Zealand Passports Office or download it from their website. Contact the **Passports Office** at ☎ **0800/225-050** in New Zealand or 04/474-8100, or log on to www.passports.govt.nz.

For Residents of the United Kingdom: To pick up an application for a standard 10-year passport (5-yr. passport for children under 16), visit your nearest passport office, major post office, or travel agency or contact the **United Kingdom Passport Service** at ☎ **0870/521-0410** or search its website at www.ukpa.gov.uk.

WHAT IF I WANT TO STAY LONGER?

If your plans do change midstream (e.g., you started out in Italy with purely touristic intentions but then decided to stay longer for Italian language classes or dental school or

Planning for a Longer Stay . . . Before You Leave

If you're planning to stay in Italy for more than 3 months, and you want to do it legally, you'll need a proper *permesso di soggiorno* (stay permit). To get one of these, you must appear in person at an Italian consulate in your home country with required documentation (Italian government-approved letters of employment, or letters of enrollment in Italy-based study programs) to obtain either a work visa (*permesso di lavoro*) or a study visa (*permesso di studio*), good for anywhere from 3 months to 2 years. Visit **www.italyemb.org** or contact your local Italian consulate for further information on obtaining a visa.

What Kind of Traveler Are You?

One of the most important questions to consider is, "What kind of traveler am I?" Even if you have not had a lot of experience with travel, this is something that shouldn't be too difficult to determine based on your daily life and your expectations for your trip. Take a moment to think about the statements below, and you'll pinpoint your traveling persona.

The *Turistissimo*

I feel like I must see everything I possibly can while in Italy.

I am less focused on historical details, and more interested in grabbing that photo and heading onto the next major attraction.

I am likely to be the first one up in the morning, ready to grab my espresso, and hit the Duomo.

I am likely to plan out my stay prior to arriving to maximize my travel route, excursions, and attractions.

If I could have it my way, I would ski the Italian Alps, shop in Milan, hike along Cinque Terre, grab a souvenir at the Ponte Vecchio, swing past Greve for a glass of wine, take a photo holding up the Leaning Tower of Pisa, hit a modern art museum in Bologna, parade past the Colosseum, hit the beach, and end my trip with a panoramic shot of Mt. Vesuvius.

I would feel as though I was missing out if I were to have a 3-hour dinner. After resting my feet for a few minutes, I would be anxious to hit the road again and see and do more sights.

The *Studente*

I am likely to study the history behind major Italian attractions.

When visiting an attraction I ask questions and explore the architect/painter/sculptor behind it all.

When in a museum, I rent the audio tour that explains what I'm seeing.

I am likely to buy a book and read about what I saw upon returning home.

I would prefer to see fewer attractions and hear more details.

I am more likely to study a few paintings that grab me in a museum than skip over them all to get to the statue of *David*.

I prefer to see the city by way of guided tours.

I am likely to wake up early and spend the first hour of my day with a leisurely espresso while planning the day ahead.

I must have a travel book with me so that I can read up on the attractions as I see them.

I prefer to see fewer cities/regions of Italy and spend more time in each.

I'll rent a car to travel to a nearby city, and enjoy the countryside on my way. I can always come back!

The Sensory Wanderer

I am less likely to read up on my city prior to arriving.

I am more focused on the aesthetics of a city and its treasures than its details and history.

I can spend a day in a museum enjoying painting after painting, without the need to memorize who painted them.

I am looking forward to capturing the feel of my destination as opposed to the best photos of its tourism icons.

When choosing a restaurant I walk around in the less touristy part of town until I see something that inspires me.

I would enjoy spending an afternoon of my trip with a bottle of wine and a book in a Renaissance garden.

I like to get out of the *centro* and explore the outer limits of the city.

I would like to take a leisurely drive through the Chianti region with no particular agenda besides enjoying the countryside.

I am not likely to wait on line at the Accademia for 4 hours to see the statue of *David*.

I am more likely to shop when I stumble upon an outdoor market than to hunt down the nearest Prada store.

The Partier

The first thing I look for in a travel guide is hot clubs and bars.

When packing, I think mostly about what I will be wearing at night.

I would rather stay out late and sleep in. I can see the attractions in the afternoon.

I plan on getting drunk on the plane ride over! I'm on vacation!

I'll have more money for the cover at the club if I don't spend money on entrance to this museum.

I really want to hook up with an Italian guy/girl!

The Italophile

I didn't speak Italian, but started studying when I decided to go to Italy.

I really want to make Italian friends and let them show me around.

I don't want to go to bars that are going to be filled with Americans.

What do Italians do on the weekend?

How do I get away from the tourists?

I would hate to be in an Italian city in August when everyone is on holiday.

I would prefer a home-stay setup over a hotel of my own.

I would rather eat in an ancient family-owned restaurant and have dinner for hours than swing by a hot spot in the *centro*.

The Fashionista

Where's Gucci?

Is there a gift shop here?

Is this on sale?

Will you come down 10€ on the price?

I would rather take the bus out to the Versace outlets outside of Florence than read a book by the Arno.

Now that you've determined the type of travel you will be doing, it's important to think about *who* you will be traveling with. Choosing a travel buddy is a lot like finding a new roommate. Traveling with your closest friend always seems like the best option, but make sure he/she wants to do the same of types of things that you do and has the same type of travel style! Your time may be limited, so minimizing potential for debate and conflict is a great way to maximize your experience.

U.S. & Canadian Embassies and Consulates in Italy

ROME: U.S. Embassy, via Vittorio Veneto 12, 00187 ROMA ☎ **06/46741;** fax 06/4674-2244; http://rome.usembassy.gov. **U.S. Citizen Services** Mon–Fri 8:30am–12:30pm.

MILAN: U.S. Consulate General, via Principe Amedeo, 2/10, 20121 MILANO ☎ **02/290-351;** fax 02/290-3573; http://milan.usconsulate.gov. **U.S. Citizen Services** Mon–Fri 8:30am–noon.

FLORENCE: U.S. Consulate General, Lungarno Vespucci, 38, 50123 FIRENZE ☎ **055/266-951;** fax 055/215-550; http://florence.usconsulate.gov. **U.S. Citizen Services** Mon–Fri 9am–12:30pm.

NAPLES: U.S. Consulate General, Piazza della Repubblica, 80122 NAPOLI ☎ **081/583-8111;** fax: 081/583-8275 or 081/761-1804; http://naples. usconsulate.gov. **U.S. Citizen Services** Mon–Fri 8am–noon.

GENOA: Consular Agency, via Dante 2, 16121 GENOVA ☎ **010/584-492;** fax 010/5533-033. **U.S. Citizen Services** Mon–Thu 11am–3pm.

TRIESTE: Consular Agency, via Roma 15, 34132 TRIESTE ☎ **040/660-177;** fax 040/631-240. **U.S. Citizen Services** Mon–Fri 10am–noon.

PALERMO: Consular Agency, via Vaccarini 1, 90143 PALERMO ☎ **091/ 305-857;** fax 091/625-6026. **U.S. Citizen Services** Mon–Fri 9am–12:30pm.

The **Canadian Consulate** and passport service is in Rome at Via Zara 30 (☎ **06/445-981**). The **Canadian Embassy** in Rome is at Via G. B. de Rossi 27 (☎ **06-445-981;** fax 06/445-982912). The Canadian Consulate in Milan is at V.V. Pisani 19 (☎ **02/67581**).

whatever), you should apply for a *permesso di soggiorno* at the main police station *(questura)* of the nearest major city. The immigration line at the *questura* is bureaucracy at its most convoluted—and filled with remarkable real immigrants who just brought the whole family from Bangladesh in hopes of a better life. In your quest for a *permesso,* you'll end up making several early-morning trips back to the *questura,* as no one can ever seem to assemble all the required documentation on their first try.

For your *permesso* to be processed, you'll also need to purchase the necessary government-issued *bolli* (tax stamps), available at any *tabacchi* store. If the almighty *questura* agents do give you the seal of approval, the actual *permesso* can take up to a week to spool out of the dot-matrix printer that issues them; in the meantime, they'll give you a chitlike temporary *permesso*. Note that work permits are almost impossible to obtain unless you have a local employer sponsoring you. Study permits are a bit easier to come by, but you'll still have to produce *molti documenti* proving your enrollment in a legitimate international study program or locally recognized school.

For additional information about entry and stay regulations, contact the Italian Government Tourist Board (in the U.S., ☎ 212/245-5618; www.italiantourism.com).

Customs Info

WHAT CAN I TAKE WITH ME?

When entering Italy, your luggage is subject to search and held to specific import Customs regulations. As a general rule, you are allowed to bring all personal items duty-free including clothes, cameras, and means for entertainment such as music, sporting equipment, computer, etc., as long as they will not be sold once in Italy. They also have strict guidelines that define those quantities of alcohol, tobacco, coffee, etc., which can be brought into the country duty-free. Please make sure to check with the Italian State Tourist Board for any inquiries at www.italiantourism.com/regulat.html.

WHAT CAN I BRING HOME WITH ME?

Returning U.S. citizens who have been away for at least 48 hours are allowed to bring back, once every 30 days, $800 worth of merchandise duty-free. You'll pay a flat rate of duty on the next $1,000 worth of purchases. Any dollar amount beyond that is subject to duties at whatever rates apply. On mailed gifts, the duty-free limit is $200. Be sure to keep your receipts or purchases accessible to expedite the declaration process. *Note:* If you owe duty, you are required to pay on your arrival in the United States—either by cash or check, and, in some locations, a Visa or MasterCard).

To avoid paying duty on foreign-made personal items you owned before your trip, bring along a bill of sale, insurance policy, jeweler's appraisal, or receipts of purchase. Or you can register items that can be readily identified by a permanently affixed serial number or marking—think laptop computers, cameras, and iPods—with Customs before you leave. Take the items to the nearest Customs office or register them with Customs at the airport from which you're departing. You'll receive, at no cost, a Certificate of Registration, which allows duty-free entry for the life of the item.

For specifics on what you can bring back and the corresponding fees, download the invaluable free pamphlet *Know Before You*

OKKIO! That Knockoff Could Cost You

Italian law allows for fines of up to 10,000€ for those caught purchasing counterfeit items in Italy. Yup, this includes that fake Prada bag you picked up on the street in Milan.

Go online at **www.cbp.gov**. (Click on "Travel," and then click on "Know Before You Go! Online Brochure.") Or contact the **U.S. Customs & Border Protection (CBP),** 1300 Pennsylvania Ave. NW, Washington, DC 20229 (☎ **877/287-8667**) and request the pamphlet.

Canadian Citizens

For a clear summary of Canadian rules, write for the booklet *I Declare,* issued by the **Canada Border Services Agency** (☎ **800/461-9999** in Canada, or 204/983-3500; **www.cbsa-asfc.gc.ca**).

U.K. Citizens

For information, contact **HM Customs & Excise** at ☎ **0845/010-9000** (from outside the U.K., 020/8929-0152), or consult their website at **www.hmce.gov.uk**.

Australian Citizens

A helpful brochure available from Australian consulates or Customs offices is *Know Before You Go*. For more information, call the **Australian Customs Service** at ☎ **1300/363-263**, or log on to **www.customs.gov.au**.

New Zealand Citizens

Most questions are answered in a free pamphlet available at New Zealand consulates and Customs offices: *New Zealand Customs Guide for Travellers, Notice no. 4*. For more information, contact **New Zealand Customs,** The Customhouse, 17–21 Whitmore St., Box 2218, Wellington (☎ **04/473-6099** or 0800/428-786; **www.customs.govt.nz**).

THE BASICS

What to Bring . . . and What to Put It In!

"Backpacker" is a figurative term. You can be a young, carefree, budget-oriented traveler even if you drag a rolling suitcase. In most cases, a rolling bag is just as convenient to carry around as a backpack, if not moreso, and it can be easier to keep organized. However, when it comes to climbing stairs and covering longer distances on foot, the classic backpack can't be beat.

To maximize the space in any bag, the key words are **rolling** and **compartmentalizing**. Rolling your clothes will keep you more space-efficient and you'll fit more. As for compartmentalizing, you want to be able to access those things that you need most, more readily, and others not so much. Put toiletries, etc., near the top or in their compartment. Keep film, camera, etc., in a separate compartment that is easily accessible, and make sure you have a separate compartment for dirty clothes. Another thing to keep in mind is that **you don't have to look like a schlep to be a backpacker!** Nice(r) clothes don't necessarily take up more room, so ditch the hiking boots and pack some wrinkle-free clothes so that you can look presentable when you hit the town.

The reality is, unless you're taking an adventure/eco-tourism trip, you won't *really* be hiking too much. Mostly, you'll be traipsing around cities where the locals look effortlessly chic year-round.

Lastly, we all know that shoes can take up the most room in our bags. Keep in mind when choosing a backpack that there are straps on the outside for larger items such as shoes, sweatshirts, coats, and blankets. Regardless of whatever else you pack, you'll want that favorite, flattering pair of jeans; sneakers (comfortable but cool); comfy, nonskimpy sleepwear (for those shared hostel rooms); and a pair of rubber flip-flops for the shared bathrooms and showers you'll encounter at hostels and other budget hotels.

Keep the inside of your bag free for anything fragile that you might need to protect. And remember: Since you may want to bring a few things home, it doesn't hurt to leave a few compartments empty or pack an extra, empty bag for the goodies. And if you arrive in Italy and realize you forgot to pack socks, never fear: There are plenty of places to shop here!!

What to Bring

→ Clothes that suit the season and your activities. Check the weather, but the key here is comfortable city clothes, not summer camp gear (unless you're hiking the Alps or spending the trip on the beach).

→ Comfortable shoes and sandals. You'll be doing a ton of walking.

→ Camera and memory card. Film and batteries can be easily purchased in Italy.

→ Extra bag to bring stuff home in.

→ Electrical plug adapter (for computers and iPod and cellphone chargers).

→ Basic medicine kit (p. 40).

→ Copies of your prescriptions for medicines you take regularly.

→ Sunblock, sunglasses, and hat.

→ A change of clothes in your carry-on bag. (Luggage frequently misses its flight when you're connecting through another European airport.)

→ Passport (and visa if necessary).

→ ATM and/or credit cards, and some cash to keep you going upon arrival.

Money Money Money Money (Money!)

First, there was the ancient Roman *denarius*. In the Renaissance, you had old-school coins like ducats, doubloons, and florins. Then Italy got down to basics with the lira. Since 2002, the official currency of Italy has been the boring euro (€), which is the standard currency in all European Economic Community countries—for more information, visit **http:// europa.eu.int/euro/entry.html**.

Yes, the lira has been phased out completely, so forget about using those thousands of lire left over from your parents' 1995 trip to Italy! There are eight euro coins in circulation, ranging from 1 cent pieces to 2€ coins, as well as seven different euro bills from 5€ to 500€. Every country in the European Economic Community mints its own euro coins (which are standardized in color and shape, but differentiated by images of national landmarks or historical figures on the reverse), so you might come across a French or German 2€ coin here and there, but for the most part, euro coins tend to stay in their country of origin. All euro coins, regardless of the country where they were minted, are good throughout the EEC. At this writing, US$1 is approximately .82€; and 1€ is $1.22. This will fluctuate, of course, so make sure to check the exchange rates at **www.oanda.com/convert/classic** to see how your money will hold up during your stay in Italy. Europe is not exactly cheap right now, so make sure you budget accordingly. It is all too easy to think that US$1 is

THE BASICS

From Cheap to Splurge . . . From Low Rent to Top Euro

Throughout the book we divide the hostels/hotels and restaurants by price range, from "Cheap" to "Doable" to "Splurge."

You know what your budget is, and what's important for you to experience on your trip, so you can plan accordingly.

And even if most of your nights will be spent in hostels or budget hotels, and your meals consist of pizza and panini, we also think you should budget for, and treat yourself, to something deluxe you *know* you will enjoy, whether it's a meal at a world-class restaurant, or a night in a grande dame hotel. A constant stream of second-class travel, shared bathrooms, and meals consumed standing up can wear you out, and keep you from enjoying *la dolce vita* in the country that invented it.

Here is a very general price range for each category (and prices can, of course, vary widely depending upon what city or town you are in, the season, and even the day of the week):

Accommodations
Hostel: Dorm-style, 20€–25€; single/double/triple, 30€–75€
Cheap: Single, 65€–100€; double 75€–150€, triple/quad 100€–300€
Doable: Single, 75€–120€; double, 100€–200€; triple/quad/suite, 150€–250€
Splurge: Single, 150€–220€; double, 200€–350€; triple/quad/suite, 300€–1,000€ and (way) up.
Eating (not including wine):
Cheap: 5€–12€
Doable: Lunch 7€–15€; dinner 10€–25€
Splurge: Lunch 10€–25€; dinner 25€–50€ and up

What Things Cost in Italy

As you'll see in this handy box, the cheapest way to fill your stomach is with pizza, and the cheapest way to get drunk is with wine. As an added bonus, a ton of world-class art and architecture can be seen for free.

Cappuccino + pastry	2€
Bus/metro ticket	1€
Major monuments/museums	Free; or 6€–10€
Lesser monuments/museums	Free; or 2€–5€
Small bottle of water	1€
Can of soda	1.50€
Slice of pizza or panino (take-out)	2€–3€
Whole, 15-inch thin-crust pizza	4€–8€
Plate of pasta or risotto*	5€–10€
Main meat or fish dish*	9€–15€
Gelato cup or cone	1.50€–3€
Pint of beer	3€–4€
Glass of wine*	1.50€–4€
Cocktails*	4€–8€
Postcard + int'l postage	1.15€

(*prices can go a **lot** higher at fancy establishments)

more or less equal to 1€ and get yourself into trouble. Those decimals make a big difference.

Cash

Except at high-end hotels, fancier restaurants, and mass retailers, cash is still the preferred method of payment throughout Italy. Most smaller hotels, restaurants, and boutiques will accept credit cards (or debit cards with the Visa or MasterCard symbol), and they're used to dealing with tourists who only have plastic, but they'll love you forever if you can flash some cash. They'll often offer a modest discount for cash payment, too. However, carrying mass quantities of cash in heavily touristed Italian cities is neither smart nor practical. So, use your card where you can—just be prepared for a little attitude from time to time (as well as the all-too-common "our credit card machine is out of order" line).

That said, you will definitely need to have cash on hand for the following: local public transportation (including buses and taxis);

OKKIO! It's Not a Handful of Change, Its a LOT of Money!

With common denominations like .50€, 1€, and 2€, those euro coins in your pocket can add up to a lot of "real" money. It's certainly a beautiful thing that you can pay for a glass of wine in many places with a single 2€ coin, but if let yourself be brainwashed into thinking, "It's just a coin." You might suddenly find that you've spent the next several days' food budget. Take it from us: It can happen alarmingly fast when happy hour has no clear start or end time!

museum and monument admissions; on-the-go snacks and drinks; and other small incidentals like postcards and postage. When you do get cash from the Italian ATM (see next section), try to break down the 50€ and

Getting Money from Home (Quickly!)

If your pocket is picked, if you blow your budget, or if you just need more money in a hurry, you can have funds sent to you by a money-wiring service like **Western Union** (often attached to phone or Internet centers that serve the city's immigrant population) or a financial services institution like **American Express**, which has offices in major Italian cities. For Western Union, scan the streets around the train station for a shop front bearing the Western Union sticker, and go in and inquire about the procedure, which you can then relay to your parents (or whomever), by phone or e-mail from that same shop. Below are the addresses for American Express locations in Italy:

Rome   Piazza di Spagna 38, ☎ 06/67641

Florence   Piazza Cimatori/Via Dante Alighieri 22/r, ☎ 055/50981

Venice   Salizzada San Moisè, San Marco 1471, ☎ 041/520-0844

Milan   Via Larga 4, ☎ 02/721041

100€ notes into smaller bills as soon as possible. (Museum admissions and restaurant checks are good for this.) The quickest way to piss off a small business cashier is to present a 50€ bill when paying for a 2€ cappuccino. Yes, it's the banks' own fault for not stocking their ATMs with smaller denomination bills, but bars (and other places where nothing costs more than a few euros) hate to be in the business of making change for tourists. If you have no choice, just be as apologetic as you can, and they'll accommodate you (albeit begrudgingly).

ATMs

The easiest and best way to get cash when you're in Italy is from a local ATM (or

bancomat, as they're called here). ATMs are all over Italy, and nearly every bank card in the world can be used to withdraw cash as long as you have a compatible PIN code (many ATMs in Europe require a four-digit PIN). If you're unsure, check with your bank, and while you're at it, inquire about your daily withdrawal limit. Truth be told, we've never changed money before landing on Italian turf, and the first Italian ATM we've encountered has usually worked fine, but you can spare yourself that unpleasant suspense of wondering whether your ATM card will work abroad by exchanging at least some money—just

OKKIO! Dear Visa, I'm Off to Capri . . .

Banks and credit card companies often freeze accounts for suspicious activity (e.g., a 250€ withdrawal from the Banca di Roma at Fiumicino airport when your last activity was a $3.25 Starbucks charge in San Francisco), so before you leave home, make sure you call your bank or credit card company and let them know of your upcoming trip. Have the phone rep make a detailed note of when and where you'll be abroad so that your card doesn't get denied when you're trying to buy that amazing pair of boots in Florence. (I once spent a brutal, cashless 48 hours in Rome when I failed to make this simple, 5-minute toll-free call before leaving home.) If you don't call your credit card company in advance, you can still call the card's toll-free emergency number if a charge is refused—provided you remember to carry the phone number with you—but it usually takes 24 hours for your account to be reactivated. Perhaps the most important lesson here is to carry more than one card so you have a backup.

enough euros to cover airport incidentals and transportation to your hotel—before you leave. (Just don't expect the exchange rate to be ideal). If you decide to go that route, you can exchange dollars for euros at your local American Express or Thomas Cook office, or at your bank.

American Express also dispenses traveler's checks and foreign currency via www.americanexpress.com or ☎ **800/807-6233,** but they'll charge a $15 order fee and additional shipping costs. You can also just bring $100 or so cash in your wallet, so that if—God forbid—all your cards get demagnetized or your bank's computer system crashes, you can exchange U.S. dollars for euros at the airport to tide you over. If you never need the $100, you'll be that much richer when you get back to the States.

Because your bank will impose a fee of $5 or more every time you withdraw from an international ATM (and the bank from which you withdraw cash may charge its own fee), be strategic about how much you withdraw and how often. (The minimum withdrawal is usually 50€; the maximum is usually 300€.) Start by withdrawing, say, 200€ or 250€ at the airport or train station, and see how much of that you're spending on average per day. If you're using a credit or debit card to pay for your bigger-ticket expenses like hotel bills and restaurant meals, you may well find that you only need to make two or three trips to the ATM (spending $15 to $25 in fees) over the course of a 10-day trip to Italy.

Change Is Good!

When you change money, ask for some small bills (5€, 10€, and 20€) or loose change (1€ and 2€ coins). Petty cash will come in handy all the time in Italy. Consider keeping the smaller bills separate from your larger bills, so that they're readily accessible and you'll be less vulnerable to pickpockets.

You can also use your credit card to receive cash advances at foreign ATMs, again, provided you have a compatible PIN (see "Credit Cards" section below). And do keep in mind that you'll pay interest from the moment of your withdrawal, even if you pay your monthly bills on time.

Credit Cards

Credit cards are another safe way to carry money. They also provide a convenient record of all your expenses, and they generally offer relatively good exchange rates. You can also withdraw cash advances from your credit cards at banks or ATMs, provided you know your PIN. If you don't know yours, call the number on the back of your credit card and ask the bank to send it to you. It usually takes 5 to 7 business days, though some banks will provide the number over the phone if you tell them your mother's maiden name or the last four digits of your Social.

MasterCard, Visa, and American Express cards are commonly accepted in Italy, and as in the U.S., most storefronts will post the logos of the cards they accept in the windows. Do note, however, that small businesses in Italy (even in big cities) far prefer cash payment and will often lie about their credit card machine being out of order if they sense that you have enough cash to cover the purchase. If you'd really rather use the card, stand your ground, and you'll be amazed how quickly these credit card machines can spontaneously fix themselves! Deep down, shopkeepers know that the rest of the world's money is card-based, and they'd rather not lose the sale altogether.

Keep in mind that many banks now assess a 1% to 3% "transaction fee" on all charges you incur abroad (whether you're charged in local currency or U.S. dollars). But credit cards still may be the smart way to go when you factor in things like exorbitant ATM fees and the higher exchange rates and service fees you'll pay with traveler's checks.

Traveler's Checks

Back before international ATMs and global bank networks, and when Pan Am was still in business, there were these quaint things called traveler's checks. (Ask your grandparents to explain.) When you had an upcoming trip abroad (or even out-of-state), you'd go to your bank or American Express office and buy these checks in set denominations (of $20 or $50, usually), and then bring them with you on vacation. You could use them to pay for things like train travel and hotel bills, or you could trade them in for cash at the local bank or Amex office in your destination. Because the traveler's checks were numbered and protected, even if you lost them or they were stolen, your money would be protected.

Well, guess what? Good ol' traveler's checks are still out there!! Nowadays, they're less widely accepted at hotels and other businesses, but the fundamental idea behind traveler's checks is still a good one: You can cash them as you go along, and your money is protected in case of loss or theft of the checks. And given the fees you'll pay for ATM use at banks other than your own, this old-fashioned method of carrying money on the road isn't such a crazy idea.

You can get traveler's checks at almost any bank. **American Express** offers denominations of $20, $50, $100, $500, and (for cardholders only) $1,000. You'll pay a service charge ranging from 1% to 4%. You can also order American Express traveler's checks over the phone by calling ☎ **800/221-7282;** Amex gold and platinum cardholders who use this number are exempt from the 1% fee.

Traveler's Checks Tip

If you do choose to carry traveler's checks, the key is to keep a record of their serial numbers *separate* from your checks in the event that they are stolen or lost. You'll get a refund faster if you know the numbers.

Take It to the Bank (Not!)

Banks are all over the cities of Italy, but they're usually closed. To catch them in a rare moment of openness, try Monday to Friday from 8:30am to 1:30pm and then from 3 to 4pm (or something arbitrary like 2:45 to 4:50pm on alternate Thurs). It is our sincere wish, however, that you never actually have to go inside an Italian bank. There's usually only one teller working (and he/she will often disappear at random intervals for appallingly long cigarette breaks) and about 20 people in line. Trust us, this is one "authentic cultural experience" you can pass up. (As a colorful portrait of Italian bureaucracy at its finest, the post office beats the bank any day.) If, however, you do need the services of a bank teller, just bring some patience and a good book.

Visa offers traveler's checks at Citibank locations nationwide, as well as at several other banks. The service charge ranges between 1.5% and 2%; checks come in denominations of $20, $50, $100, $500, and $1,000. Call ☎ **800/732-1322** for information. **AAA** members can obtain Visa checks for a $9.95 fee (for checks up to $1,500) at most AAA offices or by calling ☎ **866/339-3378.** **MasterCard** also offers traveler's checks. Call ☎ **800/223-9920** for a location near you.

Foreign currency traveler's checks might be useful when traveling to Italy as they're accepted at locations where dollar checks may not be, such as bed and breakfasts, and they minimize the currency conversions you'll have to perform while you're on the go. American Express, Thomas Cook, Visa, and MasterCard offer foreign currency traveler's checks. You'll pay the rate of exchange at the time of your purchase (so it's a good

Before You Leave: The Checklist

Here are a few things you might want to do before you walk out the door to ensure to the most efficient and drama-free trip to Italy. We all love the idea of packing a bag and heading to *paradiso,* but it never hurts to take a moment and check into the details.

→ Do you have the address and phone number of Italy's U.S. embassy and consulates? There are consulates in Milan, Florence, and Naples and a U.S. embassy in Rome. There's a list of addresses/phone numbers of the consulates on p. 17, earlier in this chapter, or you can visit www. usembassy.it/acs.

→ Do you need to book any museum, theater, or special travel in advance? Almost all tourist attractions have websites—it never hurts to check 'em out!

→ How's the weather? Is it 100°F (38°C) in Florence? Is it raining in Sicily? Pack accordingly.

→ Did you check to make sure all of your favorite hot spots and tourist destinations are open? Is *David* being restored? Is the Leaning Tower still standing? Mt. Vesuvius planning on erupting any time soon? You never know!

→ Have you checked the current exchange rate? (www.oanda.com/convert/classic)

→ Did you find out your daily ATM withdrawal limit? Do you have your credit card PIN numbers? If you have a five- or six-digit PIN, did you obtain a four-digit number from your bank?

→ Did you notify your bank/credit card companies that you will be traveling overseas to avoid automatic account freezes for suspicious activity?

→ Do you have the credit card with which your ticket was purchased? Do you have your frequent flyer card?

→ If you purchased traveler's checks, have you recorded the check numbers, and stored the documentation separately from the checks?

→ Did you pack your camera, an extra set of batteries, and enough film/memory?

→ Do you have an international power converter to charge your iPod?

→ Do you have a safe, accessible place to store money?

→ Did you bring any ID cards that could entitle you to discounts, such as student ID cards, ISIC cards, etc.?

→ Did you bring emergency drug prescriptions and extra glasses and/or contact lenses? (See "Your Portable Medicine Cabinet," p. 40)

→ Did you leave a copy of your itinerary with someone at home?

→ If using a mobile phone from the U.S., did you check to make sure it can make/receive calls to/from Italy? Did you check into international long-distance rates with your carrier?

idea to monitor the rate before you buy), and most companies charge a transaction fee per order (and a shipping fee if you order online).

Getting There

With its central position in the Italian peninsula, Rome's **Fiumicino** airport (FCO) is the most common destination for tourists flying to Italy. If your trip is going to start in northern Italy, you can fly into Milan's **Malpensa** airport (MXP). There are also a few nonstop flights between North America and Venice's **Marco Polo** airport (VCE).

All major airline flights from North America to continental Europe are overnight flights; flight time from anywhere on the East Coast of the U.S. is about 8 hours. Because most hotels and hostels won't let you check in until lunchtime or later, try to book a flight that arrives in Italy in the mid- or late morning. If you arrive at 7 or 8am, you'll have several uncomfortable hours before you can shower, change, and freshen up. As for the trip back, flights from Italy to the U.S. depart in the late morning or early afternoon. Do your best to book a return flight that leaves at 10am or later—the only way to get to the airport in the early morning is by taxi, which is much more expensive than the airport train or bus services, which start running at 6:30am or so.

Airfare to Italy is highest in the summer (June–Aug) and lowest from November to March (with the exception of the Christmas and Easter periods). As an example, in 2006, the same round-trip flights from New York's JFK airport to Rome cost $868 in April, $1,049 in July, and $728 in November. From San Francisco to Rome, the same round-trip flights cost $992 in April, $1,312 in July, and $810 in November. (A year earlier, fares were $200 cheaper on average, but have since spiked because of rising fuel costs.)

Daily nonstop flights to Italy depart from New York (Newark and JFK), Philadelphia, Washington, D.C. (Dulles), and Atlanta.

There are no nonstop flights from the West Coast or the Midwest to Italy. If you're coming from the West or Midwest, common practice is to change planes at one of those airports on the Eastern seaboard before crossing the Atlantic to Rome or Milan.

A better idea to get to Italy from the Midwest or West is to get the long leg of your trip out of the way first by flying across the Atlantic to one of the European hubs that can be reached nonstop from Los Angeles, San Francisco, Chicago (or wherever)—British Airways to London, Air France to Paris, KLM to Amsterdam, etc.—and then taking a short, 2-hour connecting flight to the Italian city of your choice. Whatever you do, you'll want to **maximize your time on international flights,** since they're where the movies and the alcohol are free, the cabins are more comfortable, and the flight attendants are cooler and better looking.

For those whose trips originate on the East Coast, keep in mind that nonstop flights to Italy don't cost much more than flights that connect through a European hub like London, Paris, Frankfurt, Amsterdam, or

THE BASICS

Building a Multi-city Itinerary

If you're planning to visit several cities or regions in Italy, multi-city flight structures (e.g., flying into Rome and out of Venice) are a great option. All the big online travel agencies have a function that allows you to build a multi-city itinerary. Best of all, multi-city trips are priced about the same as regular round-trips—great news, since you used to pay quite a premium for this convenience.

OKKIO! Who's Got Your Ticket?

....

Most airline tickets to Europe are paperless e-tickets these days—meaning you present your passport or a credit card when you check in, and the computer pulls up your travel records—but a few airlines and online agencies still issue paper tickets from time to time. If you do book a paper-ticketed itinerary, *remember to bring the paper ticket with you to the airport,* or you will not be allowed to check in. Period.

Munich. So, if at all possible, we recommend that you go nonstop from the U.S.: You'll obviously get there faster (and get a decent night's sleep, if sleeping on planes is one of your talents), and you'll eliminate the risk of your luggage not making its connection at Heathrow or something (all too common, unfortunately).

Booking Your Flight Online

Of the big online travel agencies—Expedia. com, Travelocity, and Orbitz—we've had the best experience with **Orbitz.** (Priceline has also come through for us more than once.) We also like **Kayak.com,** an under-the-radar travel-booking site that uses a sophisticated search engine (developed at MIT). Each has different business deals with the airlines and many offer different fares on the same flights, so take the time to shop around. Open several Web browsers at once and do side-by-side searches for the same destination and dates, and you'll get a feel for how different sites behave. A nice feature of Expedia.com, Kayak, and Travelocity is that you can sign up for e-mail notification when a cheap fare becomes available to your favorite destination.

Also remember to check the individual websites for those carriers that fly from the U.S. to Italy—Alitalia (www.alitalia.com),

American (www.aa.com), Continental (www. continental.com), Delta (www.delta.com), United (www.united.com), and US Airways (www.usairways.com)—whose fares are sometimes not listed on travel agency websites. (The fares at the airlines' own sites can often be shockingly high, too. If you come across a $2,000 fare, don't give up hope; the same flight on Orbitz might only cost $700.)

If you want to get really creative (and you don't mind changing planes several times), you can scout out low-fare carriers such as Southwest (www.southwest.com), JetBlue (www.jetblue.com), AirTran (www.airtran. com), WestJet (www.westjet.com), easyJet (www.easyjet.com), or Ryanair (www.ryanair. com), which can take care of your short hops in North America and Europe but not the trans-Atlantic leg of your trip.

Great last-minute deals (e.g., half of what you'd pay by booking in advance) are often available through free weekly e-mail services provided directly by the airlines. Most of these are announced on Tuesday or Wednesday and must be purchased online. Most are only valid for travel that weekend, but some (such as British Airways) can be booked weeks or months in advance. Sign up for weekly e-mail alerts at airline websites or check megasites that compile comprehensive lists of last-minute specials, such as **Smarter Travel** (www.smartertravel.com). For last-minute trips, **www.site59.com** and **http://us.lastminute.com** often have amazing air-and-hotel package deals, for much less than the major-label sites (however, 90% of the hotels they offer are located miles from the heart of town).

If you're willing to relinquish some control over your flight details, use what is called an "opaque" fare service like **Priceline**'s "Name-Your-Own-Price" feature (www.priceline.com). Opaque travel sites offer rock-bottom prices in exchange for travel on a "mystery airline" at a mysterious time of day, often with a mysterious change of planes en route. The mystery airlines are all major, well-known carriers.. And, if you're not as flexible (or daring) with your travel plans, Priceline does offer specific fares for specific flights. If you do decide to see how low you can go, first visit, **BiddingForTravel** (www.biddingfortravel.com) an online forum of experienced travel bidders that help demystify Priceline's inner workings and offer strategic advice on how to get the best fare.

Other Cash-Saving Travel Ideas

◑ Keep an eye on local newspapers for promotional specials or fare wars, when airlines lower prices on their most popular routes. You rarely see fare wars at peak travel times, but if you can travel in the off-peak months, you may snag a bargain.

◑ Several reliable consolidators are worldwide and available online. **STA Travel** (☎ **800/781-4040**; www.statravel.com) is the world's top consolidator for students, but their fares are competitive for travelers of all ages. **ELTExpress** (☎ **800/ TRAV-800**; www.flights.com) has excellent fares worldwide, particularly to Europe. They also have "local" websites in 12 countries.

ECONOMY-CLASS SURVIVAL TIPS

Air travel is one of the last bastions of segregation—if you stop and think about it, the blatant classism in the skies is really pretty shocking. While expense accounters and hip-hop artists are maxin' and relaxin' up in the front of the plane, the rest of us are stuck in coach or economy—mere euphemisms for the cramped, stuffy, and downright inhumane conditions airlines subject the unwashed masses (i.e., me and you) to. Okay, I'm exaggerating, but unless you're flying first or business class, you will feel like a faceless wretch in an airborne herd of cattle on long-haul flights. But with a little advance planning, you

OKKIO! Travel in the Age of Bankruptcy

Airlines sometimes go bankrupt, so protect yourself by buying your tickets with a credit card, as the Fair Credit Billing Act guarantees that you can get your money back from the credit card company if a travel supplier goes under (and if you request the refund within 60 days of the bankruptcy). Travel insurance can also help, but make sure it covers against "carrier default" for your specific travel provider. And be aware that if a U.S. airline goes bust midtrip, U.S. law requires other carriers to take you to your destination (albeit on a space-available basis) for a fee of no more than $25, provided you rebook within 60 days of the cancellation.

can make an otherwise unpleasant experience almost bearable.

◑ **Know the layout:** Your choice of airline and airplane will affect your comfort and amenities. Boeing 747s and 777s are much roomier than 767s, for example. All passengers on 777s have their own TV screen and controls for movies and games. Older aircraft models only have a few TV screens hung every 10 rows or so in the center aisle, which makes for difficult viewing. Find more details at **www.seat guru.com**, which has extensive details about almost every seat on six major U.S. airlines. For international airlines, research firm Skytrax has posted a list of average seat pitches at www.airline quality.com.

◑ **Emergency exit seats** and **bulkhead** seats typically have the most legroom. Emergency exit seats are usually left unassigned until the day of a flight (to ensure that someone able-bodied fills them); it's worth getting to the ticket counter early to snag one of these spots for a long flight. Many passengers find that bulkhead seating (the row facing the walls at the front of each cabin section) offers more legroom, but keep in mind that bulkheads are where airlines often put baby bassinets, so you may be sitting next to a screaming infant for 9 hours while you enjoy all that extra legroom.

○ To have **two seats for yourself** in a three-seat row, try for an aisle seat in a center section toward the back of coach. If you're traveling with a companion, book an aisle and a window seat. Middle seats are usually booked last, so chances are good you'll end up with three seats to yourselves. And in the event that a third passenger is assigned the middle seat, he or she will probably be more than happy to trade for a window or an aisle.

○ If you're intent on getting some **sleep,** avoid the last row of any section or the row in front of an emergency exit, as these seats are the least likely to recline. Avoid seats near highly trafficked and potentially smelly toilet areas. Avoid seats in the back of many jets—these can be narrower than those in the rest of coach. You also may want to reserve a window seat so you can rest your head and avoid being bumped in the aisle. If you have trouble falling asleep on planes, ask your doctor for a sleeping pill (like Ambien or Lunesta) or sedative (like Valium or Xanax) to help you chill out (be sure to bring a prescription with you as well if you are staying a while and might need a refill). As a sleep and jet-lag aid, melatonin caplets—available over-the-counter at any drug store or herbalist— also work well for many travelers.

○ **Get up, walk around, and stretch** every 60 to 90 minutes to keep your blood flowing. This helps avoid deep-vein thrombosis, or "economy-class

OKKIO! DRINKING & FLYING DON'T MIX

As tempting as it is to kick off your vacation by hitting the airport pub for beers and tequila shots, there are a number of reasons you should keep the alcohol intake to a minimum on travel days. A celebratory cocktail or glass of wine with your meal, great, but save the binge drinking for when you're on *terra firma.*

—Too much merriment at the airport pub can cause you to miss your flight.

—No one on the plane wants to be stuck next to your liquor breath for hours.

—Altitude lowers your tolerance; turbulence messes with your stomach.

—The midflight hangover onset— 'nuff said.

syndrome," a potentially deadly condition caused by sitting in cramped conditions for too long. Other preventive measures include drinking lots of water and avoiding alcohol. See "Avoiding 'Economy Class Syndrome'" box under "Health & Safety," p. 39.

○ **Hydrate.** Drink water before, during, and after your flight to combat the lack of humidity in airplane cabins—which can be drier than the Sahara. Bring a bottle of water on board, and make frequent trips aft to the galley (the airplane's rear kitchen) where most airlines have a self-service mineral water and orange juice station set up for passengers throughout the flight.

○ **Detox.** Eat healthy, light portions (i.e., about half of what they serve you) and minimize your alcohol and caffeine intake. Air travel is stressful enough without having to deal with bloating and

When Your Body's Still in Another Time Zone . . .

Jet lag is a pitfall of traveling across time zones, not just spending 9 hours in an airplane (which is why jet lag is not acute when traveling north-south). When you travel east-west or vice versa, your body becomes thoroughly confused about what time it is, and everything from your digestion to your brain feels out of whack. Traveling east, say from Atlanta to Rome, is more difficult on your internal clock than traveling west, say from Venice to New York, because most peoples' bodies are more inclined to stay up late than fall asleep early. Italy, as with the rest of mainland Europe, is on Greenwich Mean Time +1 hour, which means it's 6 hours ahead of (later than) Eastern Time, 7 hours ahead of Central time, 8 hours ahead of Mountain time, and 9 hours ahead of Pacific time. Just like most of North America, Italy observes Daylight Savings Time *(ora legale)* from late March/early April to late October.

Tips for Avoiding Jet Lag

→ Exercise and sleep well for a few days before your trip.

→ Drink lots and lots of water before, during, and after your flight. Avoid alcohol.

→ Reset your watch to your destination time before you board the plane. Think in that time zone before you even get there.

→ Daylight is the number-one key to resetting your body clock. As soon as you arrive at your hotel, ditch your bags and go for a long, invigorating orientation walk around town. Stay outside, in the sun, for as much of that first day as possible.

→ Get on the local clock right away. As tired as you might feel, resist midday naps, as they will only screw you up even further. Keep moving, eat at the normal local meal times, and drink as much caffeine as you need to stay up until at least 10pm your first night.

→ Over-the-counter melatonin caplets can work wonders in helping you adjust quickly to a new time zone. Start by taking one the night of your flight, and then take one each following night at bedtime.

THE BASICS

palpitations. Think of your flight as a healthy detox, and you'll arrive at your destination feeling surprisingly fresh even if you're somewhat sleep-deprived.

○ **Roll the dice for an upgrade.** At check-in, turn on the self-deprecating charm and ask about any free upgrades to business class they might feel like offering little old you. Hey, don't laugh—I've gotten lucky twice using this strategem. Rome is not an especially big business destination, so many of those VIP seats in the front of the plane need to be filled at the last minute. (This is less likely to happen on flights to Milan, which are always filled with fashionistas and financiers.)

Staying There

Read this section carefully: Knowing the lay of the accommodations land in Italy (and being a bit anal about it) will be one of the most important factors in making your trip a stress-free success. Some key points to keep in mind:

OKKIO! When Your Luggage Misses Its Flight

If your luggage doesn't immediately show up on the ol' baggage carousel, try not to freak out. Busy airports like London Heathrow and Paris–Charles de Gaulle are notorious about not getting checked bags to their connecting flights on time, so if you've flown through one of those cities, there's actually a better-than-we'd-like-to-admit chance that your luggage might not have made it onto your flight. The good news is, your bags aren't really "lost," just delayed. File a report at the office in the baggage claim hall—be prepared to give an address where your stuff can be delivered, and a phone number where you can be reached, when it does arrive in Rome (usually 6–10 hr. later). It sounds sketchy, I know, but this has happened to me several times, and someone from the airline has always shown up with my bag at the specified address later that afternoon or evening. If you have any problems, you can call the Fiumicino airport luggage handling office at ☎ 06/6595-4252 24 hours a day.

○ **It pays to book early.** We can't stress this enough. Italy is popular year-round and the good, affordable beds go fast. If you know you'll be traveling to Italy in 3 months, get on the Internet *now* and starting sending e-mails to prospective hotels and hostels. You can always cancel, penalty-free, if your plans change.

○ **Reconfirm** all bookings several days before you arrive, and **carry documentation** (i.e., a print-out of the e-mail the hotel sent you) to prove your reservation exists.

○ **What cheap sleeps?** We'll be blunt: Hotel prices are high in Italy's major tourist destinations. Even those that we categorize as "cheap" in this book (e.g., 80€ for a no-frills double room with shared bath down the hall) might strike you as pricey if you're used to what similar lodging costs in Colorado or Cambodia. Know what to expect and plan accordingly, and you won't be blindsided by your cumulative hotel expenses, which may be anywhere from 25% to 50% of your daily budget.

○ **Playing the hostel game.** With prices starting at 18€ per night, dorm beds in hostel-style accommodations are the cheapest way to go in Italy's top tourist destinations. However, most hostels do not accept reservations more than 12 or 24 hours before your planned check-in time. (This is not because they're deliberately being pains in the ass—it's because they don't know how many beds they'll have free until their current guests inform them that they're moving out.) The best way to handle this is to call the hostel a few days before you're thinking of staying there, and get a clear understanding of how their reservations system works. Often, they'll ask you to call back at 9pm the night before your arrival to make a reservation, and then arrive by 3pm the next day to pay for your bed. Play by their rules, and everybody wins. If you're a member of **Hostelling International** (www.hihostels.com) you can often book days or even weeks in advance, but many private hostels/backpackers don't offer the same service.

○ **Location, location, location.** We're all for saving money, but we're also for living the Italian dream, which often means forking over a little extra cash for a room in a great location. It doesn't have to be fancy, but life's too short to sleep by the train station when you could wake up next to the Pantheon. Believe us, it makes a big difference in your quality of life. So even if you're traveling on a tight budget, try to plan for at least one "splurge."

○ **Skip the breakfast club.** Most Italian hotels offer some kind of continental buffet breakfast, at no extra charge, to their guests. This is not necessarily a good thing, as most breakfast rooms are depressing salons of tourists talking in too-soft voices, noshing on wooden croissants and sipping burnt coffee. Instead, get your day going the authentic Italian way—at the local coffee bar. These bars are on every corner in Italy, and for about 2€, you can take a cappuccino and pastry (standing up) alongside bright-eyed and boisterous locals.

○ **Consider short-term apartment rentals.** As more and more Italian city-dwellers move out of the *centro storico* and into the more livable and affordable suburbs, there are more vacant apartments in the hearts of cities like Rome and Florence than ever before. Most of these apartments are rented out as (furnished) short-term tourist accommodations. These properties, which were probably someone's family home for generations, can be booked through tourism and accommodations agencies easily found online. Simple Internet searches (e.g., Google "Florence apartments") will yield hundreds of results, with pictures and prices clearly posted.

Booking Your Hotel Online

Shopping online for hotels is generally done one of two ways: by booking through the hotel's own website or through an independent booking agency (or a fare-service agency like Priceline; see below). These Internet hotel agencies have multiplied in mind-boggling numbers, competing for the business of millions of consumers surfing for accommodations around the world. This competitiveness can be a boon for those who have the patience and time to shop and compare the online sites for good deals—but shop they must, for prices can vary considerably. And keep in mind that hotels at the top of a site's listing may be there for no other reason than that they paid money to get the placement. In our experience, most hotels offered in package deals to Italy are soulless chain-style monstrosities far removed from the city center.

Of the "big three" sites, **Expedia.com** offers a long list of special deals and "virtual tours" or photos of available rooms so you can see what you're paying for (a feature that helps counter the claims that the best rooms are often held back from bargain booking websites). **Travelocity** posts unvarnished customer reviews and ranks its properties according to the AAA rating system. **Trip Advisor** (www.tripadvisor.com) is another excellent source of unbiased user reviews of hotels. While even the finest hotels can inspire a misleadingly poor review from picky or crabby travelers, the body of user opinions, when taken as a whole, is usually a reliable indicator.)

Other reliable online booking agencies include **Hotels.com** and **Quikbook.com.** An excellent free program, **TravelAxe** (www.travelaxe.net), can help you search multiple hotel sites at once, even ones you may never have heard of—and conveniently lists the total price of the room, including the taxes and service charges. Another booking site, **Travelweb** (www.travelweb.com), is partly owned by the hotels it represents (including the Hilton, Hyatt, and Starwood chains) and is plugged directly into the hotels' reservations systems—unlike independent online agencies, which have to fax or e-mail reservation requests to the hotel, a good portion of which get misplaced in the shuffle. More than once, travelers have arrived at the hotel, only to be told that they have no reservation. To be fair, many of the major sites are improving in service and ease

OKKIO! When Is a Star Not a Star?

When booking a hotel through an online agency, keep in mind that star ratings are subjective, and that comments in the feedback section are often listed by the hotels themselves. Although a picture is worth a thousand words, it can also be very deceiving. We're not saying that these hotels are fleabag inns full of junkies, but they may have posted photos of the one room that's been renovated, giving you a skewed sense of the overall quality of the place. A bigger issue is that you'll never get a sense of how well located a hotel is from these websites, because everyone will advertise that their hotel is "steps from the Colosseum" or "minutes from the Duomo." How many steps? How many minutes? You'll find us repeating it often in this book: Hotel location is key in Italian cities. More often than not, you get what you pay for—and if that online hotel deal seems too good to be true, it probably is.

habit of showing up in without a reservation, you'll inevitably get stuck paying more than what you'd planned on spending. After all, the best-value accommodations in good locations tend to be fairly well known. We've listed the best budget hotel and hostel options in this book, but many of them are small, with fewer than 20 rooms. If you wait too long to call or e-mail for a reservation, these rooms (and others in the same price range) could be all gone, and all that's left might cost 50% to 100% more, or have an inconvenient location.

○ **Book online.** Many of the hotels we've listed in this book offer Internet-only discounts, so check their websites for the most advantageous rates and special seasonal offers. Conversely, other hotels supply rooms to Priceline, Hotwire, or Expedia.com at rates lower than the ones you can get through the hotel itself. Shop around. And if you have special requests—a quiet room, a room with a view—call the hotel directly and make your needs known after you've booked online.

○ **Stay near the train station** or the outskirts of town. There's no getting around it: You will always save some money if you're willing to settle for a bed away from the charming heart of an Italian city. And in smaller cities like Florence and Venice, the neighborhood near the train station really isn't so bad. In Rome, Milan, and Naples, however, the train station area is seedy and ugly and a considerable distance (i.e., not easy walking range) from the real heart of town—an all-around buzzkill, trust us. So, in those larger cities, we strongly urge you to cough up the extra dough for a better location.

○ **Remember the law of supply and demand.** Resort hotels are most crowded, and therefore most expensive,

of use, and Expedia.com will soon be able to plug directly into the reservations systems of many hotel chains—none of which can be bad news for consumers. In the meantime, you should definitely get a confirmation number and bring along a printout of any online booking transaction.

SAVING ON ACCOMMODATIONS BEFORE YOU GO

The rack rate is the maximum legal rate that a hotel can charge for a room. Hardly anybody pays this price, however, except in peak season or on holidays. To lower the cost of your room:

○ **Book early**—as in, as soon as you know you'll be taking the trip. If you make a

Check Out Apartment Living

If you're staying in town 3 nights or more, consider booking a self-catering apartment. (Most apartment rentals have a 3-night minimum stay.) While this isn't the most sociable option, it can allow you to stay in a prime location for a fraction of what a hotel room would cost. (For example, there are four-person apartments near the Spanish Steps in Rome that rent for under 200€ a night, whereas you'd probably pay twice that for two double rooms in a hotel in the same neighborhood.) Furthermore, apartments have kitchens, which allow you the fun and money-saving option of shopping for groceries at the local market, butcher shop, etc., and cooking some of your own meals.

on weekends, so discounts are more available for midweek stays. Business hotels in downtown locations are busiest during the week, so you can often expect discounts over the weekend. Almost all Italian hotels have high-season and low-season prices, and booking the day after "high season" ends can mean big discounts.

SAVING MONEY WHEN YOU'RE THERE

○ Before you start dialing away on the in-room phone, find out from hotel staff how much they charge per call. Some hotels charge astronomical rates, while other, more honest hotels only charge you what the phone company charges them—i.e., a humane .10€–.20€ for a local call. In the former case, use prepaid phone cards, pay phones, or your own cellphone instead of dialing direct from hotel phones.

○ If your hotel offers Internet access (in-room broadband or WiFi, or a public terminal in a common area), find out if there's a charge for using it. Some hotels don't disclose that they charge 10€ an hour for online access, so you stay logged on for hours, and then they slap you with an outrageous bill upon checkout.

○ In summer, if your hotel has air-conditioning, be sure to find out upfront if there's an additional charge for using it. (At smaller, budget hotels, it's usually something like 10€–15€ per day.)

○ Stock the minibar yourself. If, like us, you can't resist the siren song of the minibar, just remember that hotels charge through the nose for water, potato chips, and those little bottles of Jack Daniels. If you want to keep food and drink in the room, buy your own snacks and drinks and store them in the minibar. (But do it on the sly; most hotels don't condone this behavior.) Otherwise, if you drink a can of Coke from the minibar, just remember to go out and

Getting the Best Room

Always ask if there's a corner room available. They're often larger and quieter, with more windows and light, and often cost the same as standard rooms. When you make your reservation, ask if the hotel is renovating; if it is, request a room away from the construction. Ask about nonsmoking rooms, rooms with views, rooms that face an interior garden (versus rooms that face a busy street). Ask for a room that has been most recently renovated or redecorated.

If you aren't happy with your room when you arrive, politely ask for another one. Most lodgings will be willing to accommodate you if they have something else available.

THE BASICS

Questions to Ask About Your Accommodations

··

→ Will I be sharing a room with someone (as with most hostels)?

→ Will I be sharing a bathroom?

→ Are there safes for my personal valuables?

→ Is there a curfew (a few hostels or small hotels still have lock-in or lock-out)?

→ Is there air-conditioning or ceiling fans? (From June–Aug, this is key.)

→ Does the hotel serve breakfast, and if so, is there an extra charge?

→ Are there airport transfers to and from my hotel?

→ How far is the hotel from the train station? If it's not walking distance, how will I get there?

→ What is check-in/check-out time? Is there an hour after which they'll cancel my reservation if I haven't arrived yet?

→ Do they have Internet access—either a public terminal in the lobby or Wi-Fi throughout the property?

buy a new can at the cafe down the street and replace it before you check out.

○ Always ask about local taxes and service charges, which can increase the cost of a room by 15% or more. Smaller, family-run hotels include the tax (IVA) in the room charge, while larger, more expensive hotels often tack the IVA charge on top of the already exorbitant room rate, so check it out before you check in.

○ If a hotel insists upon tacking on any surprise charges that weren't mentioned at check in or prominently posted in the room, or a "resort fee" for amenities you didn't use, you can often make a case for getting it removed. You can always take any accommodations-related complaints to the local tourism board—mention that to an ornery hotel staffer, and they're sure to back down.

Health & Safety

Staying Well

Most illnesses experienced by travelers are caused by food and water that your digestive system isn't accustomed to—loosely translated as: Bring diarrhea medicine! Italians have extremely high standards of culinary hygiene, and the tap water is perfectly safe to drink—in fact, it's some of the best water in the world—but there are always going to be those miniscule microbes in the local tomatoes, etc., that can throw off your foreign gastrointestinal system for a few hours. In all likelihood, if you experience any, uh, *discomfort* from Italian food, it will probably be mild and pass in less than 24 hours.

Although there are no required vaccinations when entering Italy, it is important that you are up-to-date with all immunizations as defined by the Advisory Committee on Immunization Practice (ACIP). Major vaccinations include tetanus, hepatitis B, MMR, and chickenpox if necessary. It is also always a good idea to see your doctor 4 to 6 weeks prior to your departure for a regular checkup and to make sure you have enough prescription medications to last your entire stay.

For more information, contact the **International Association for Medical Assistance to Travelers (IAMAT)** (☎ 716/ 754-4883 or in Canada 416/652-0137;

www.iamat.org) for tips on travel and health concerns in the countries you're visiting, and for lists of local, English-speaking doctors. The United States **Centers for Disease Control and Prevention** (☏ 800/311-3435; www.cdc.gov/travel) provides up-to-date information on health hazards by region or country and offers tips on food safety. The website **www.tripprep.com**, sponsored by a consortium of travel medicine practitioners, may also offer helpful advice on traveling abroad. You can find listings of reliable clinics overseas at the **International Society of Travel Medicine** (www.istm.org).

If you suffer from a chronic illness, consult your doctor before your departure. For conditions like epilepsy, diabetes, or heart problems, wear a **MedicAlert identification tag** (☏ 888/633-4298; www.medicalert.org), which will alert doctors to your condition and give them access to your records through MedicAlert's 24-hour hot line.

Pack **prescription medications** in your carry-on luggage, and carry prescription medications in their original containers, with pharmacy labels—otherwise they may not make it through airport security. Also carry copies of your prescriptions in case you lose your pills or run out. Know the generic name of prescription medicines, just in case a local pharmacist is unfamiliar with the brand name.

It's also a good idea to pack an extra pair or two of **contact lenses** or **prescription glasses.** If you need new contact lenses or saline solution, or you need to repair a broken pair of glasses, stop in at any *ottica* (optician's shop). Italian opticians will sell you contacts without a doctor-issued paper prescription as long as you can tell them the strength, base curve, etc., of your prescription. They carry all the major name brands (Johnson & Johnson, Bausch & Lomb) for 20€–25€ a box.

OKKIO! Avoiding "Economy-Class Syndrome"

Deep-vein thrombosis, or as it's known in the world of commercial aviation, "economy-class syndrome," is a blood clot that develops in a deep vein. It's a potentially deadly condition that can be caused by sitting in cramped conditions—such as an airplane cabin—for too long. During a flight (especially a long-haul flight), get up, walk around, and stretch your legs every 60 to 90 minutes to keep your blood flowing. Other preventative measures include frequent flexing of the legs while sitting, drinking lots of water, and avoiding alcohol and sleeping pills. If you have a history of deep-vein thrombosis, heart disease, or another condition that puts you at high risk, some experts recommend wearing compression stockings or taking anticoagulants when you fly; always ask your physician about the best course for you. Symptoms of deep-vein thrombosis include leg pain or swelling, or even shortness of breath.

What If I Get Sick?

Any foreign consulate can provide a list of area doctors who speak English. If you get sick, consider asking your hotel concierge to recommend a local doctor—even his or her own. The emergency room (*pronto soccorso*) at the local hospital is also a great bet, since they're pretty loose about what constitutes an "emergency," and all care in the Italian ER is free. If your symptoms aren't too acute, go to a pharmacy—Italian pharmacists love to dispense medical advice. Tell them your symptoms (or what medication you'd normally take under similar circumstances at

THE BASICS

Your Portable Medicine Cabinet

The following is a list of medications and health aids to bring with you when traveling to Western Europe, as suggested by the CDC:

→ **Sunblock** (as well as sunglasses and a wide-brimmed hat) during summer months

→ Enough **prescription medication** to last your entire trip and a copy of your prescription(s)—Italian pharmacists can fill almost all foreign prescriptions, on the spot, and at a very low cost

→ **Antidiarrheal** medication

→ **Stomach-calming** medication like Pepto-Bismol or Gaviscon

→ **Insect repellent** containing DEET during the summer

→ A **pain reliever** like aspirin, acetaminophen, or ibuprofen

→ **Antifungal** or **antibacterial** cream or ointment

With the exception of high-SPF waterproof sunblock, all of the above are readily available at Italian supermarkets and pharmacies, but do you really want to be in the position of having to track down some Imodium AD when you're about to climb the Leaning Tower of Pisa? Pack a small medicine kit with some basics, and you'll always be prepared.

home), and they'll hook you up with the right Italian equivalent. (They're not supposed to do it, but they'll often offer up prescription-only meds like antibiotics.)

LA FARMACIA

If you need a pharmacy while in Italy, look for the neon green cross sign. In addition to being the place where you get prescriptions filled, the *farmacia* can also hook you up with tampons, over-the-counter painkillers like ibuprofen or aspirin, and sunblock. Note that the *farmacia* does not stock contact lens items—for that, head to the *ottica*.

Pharmacies are all over the cities in Italy, and are normally open Monday to Saturday from 8am to 8pm, sometimes breaking for the midday *riposo* from 2 to 4pm or so. In every city, pharmacies take turns staying open late and on Sundays, so if you find a pharmacy and it's closed, look for the sign in the window indicating the nearest pharmacy on duty for that particular shift. In big cities like Rome and Milan, there are 24-hour pharmacies, usually near the main train station. Italian pharmacists are happy to fill foreign

prescriptions, although packaging (e.g., drops instead of pills) and name brands of prescription drugs are often different from what you're used to back home. Prices for prescription drugs are regulated by the Italian government, which keeps pharmaceutical costs remarkably low all over the country.

Pronto Soccorso

The emergency room at Italian hospitals is known as the *pronto soccorso*. If you are ever in a situation where you are being rushed to the hospital or need to go to the emergency room, bring your ID and any relevant medical documents. Regardless of your insurance status, care at the *pronto soccorso* is free, proof once again that Italy is often a kinder and gentler place than the U.S. I once crashed my scooter in Rome and had to spend 3 nights at the hospital, undergoing CAT scans, EEGs, and EKGs. My hospital bill as an uninsured American citizen? 0.00€.

OKKIO! EWW. JUST EWW.

Never put a thermometer in your mouth, as Italians always put them in the armpit.

Definitely note that Italian *farmacisti* will often give you higher doses of medication than what you're taking in the U.S. (e.g., 500mg instead of 200mg). The sometimes lax attitude of Italian pharmacists also means that they've been known to dispense pre-scription meds like Valium to people without paper proof of the prescription (!).

Playing Safely

With so many young, good-looking natives (and fellow backpackers) on the loose, hooking up is as time-honored a tradition on Italian vacations as seeing the masterpieces of the Renaissance. If you're going to par-take, just remember they have STDs and sperm in Italy, too. And that Dutch hottie from the hostel in Rimini might be a walking gonorrhea case. *Always* use a latex condom (or polyurethane if you're allergic) when engaging in sexual activity abroad (or any-where for that matter).

Condoms that are not latex are less effec-tive against disease transmission and preg-nancy and should be avoided. If you are unsure as what the condom is made of or it is not clearly marked, it's not worth the risk. Latex condoms (*preservativi*) are widely available in Italy at supermarket check-out lines or any pharmacy—Settebello and Jeans are common brands.

When the mood hits late at night, a lot of pharmacies have vending machines set up in their closed storefronts where you can buy single condoms—a refreshing reminder that Italy is Catholic in name but frequently not in deed. But since condoms take up almost no room, the simplest solution might just be to pack some condoms from home.

As with any destination, you should always avoid shared needles for tattoos, piercings, or injections of any kind. Always make sure that you watch the establishment open a fresh needle—again, it's not worth the risk.

Covering Health Care Costs

As the Italian National Health system is run by the government, Italy does not have a system to cover U.S. citizens. Emergency care at Italian hospitals is free to everyone, regardless of insurance status, but you will be charged for other office visits and exami-nations. That being said, it is always good to make sure that you have a U.S. health insur-ance policy and that you have checked with them to see how they may or may not cover medical attention in Italy. Most health plans (including Medicare and Medicaid) do not provide coverage, and the ones that do often require you to pay for services upfront and reimburse you only after you return home. As a safety net, you may want to buy travel medical insurance, particularly if you're trav-eling to a remote or high-risk area where emergency evacuation is a possible scenario.

Health Checklist

→ Have I packed all necessary medications suggested above?

→ Have I visited my doctor to dis-cuss access to prescription medications?

→ Have I packed my drugs in their original containers in my carry-on luggage?

→ Do I have copies of my pre-scriptions, the names of their generic versions, and a letter from my doctor for any injected medications or controlled sub-stances?

→ Have I packed condoms and any other birth control I might need?

THE BASICS

Safety Tips

→ Never give out your credit card information unless you're using it to pay for something.

→ Solo travelers, beware of those who are very eager to befriend you in a crowded tourist area. Just as in the U.S., if someone seems abnormally nice or generous, you should smell a rat.

→ Always stay by your drink. It's rare, but we've heard a few stories about someone being slipped a roofie or other substance in their drink and having their stuff stolen (or worse). Stay aware.

→ Watch how much you drink. Being drunk makes you an even easier target.

→ Stay in well-lit, populated areas at night. Walking around Italian cities at night is quite safe, but you don't want to find yourself alone and far off the beaten path.

→ Keep your money, *permesso,* and passport in a secure location, preferably on your body and not in a secondary bag or backpack.

→ Always keep copies of your passport, visa, *permesso,* etc. in a location other than that of the originals. These are the only documents you have that prove your (legal) presence in Italy.

→ Use common sense.

THE BASICS

If you require additional medical insurance, try **MEDEX Assistance** (☎ 410/453-6300; www.medexassist.com) or **Travel Assistance International** (☎ 800/821-2828; www.travelassistance.com; for general information on services, call the company's Worldwide Assistance Services, Inc., at ☎800/777-8710).

Personal Safety

On the whole, Italy is very safe. The main thing you need to watch out for is petty theft—unfortunately, **pickpockets** and **bag-snatchers** are a very real problem in the bigger cities, and especially Rome and Naples. The streets and public transportation in Italian cities are crawling with petty criminals and other sleight-handed miscreants, but locals rarely get pickpocketed. How is this? The city's petty thieves prey on you, the unwitting *Americano,* who is naive enough to leave your wallet in your jeans pocket. Gypsies (called *zingari* or *rom* here) make up the majority of the pickpocket population, and

they're pretty easy to recognize. Young women with disheveled hair, wearing loose, mismatched floral garments, try to distract you with their babes-in-arms, pleas for charity, or newspapers, under which their hands work deftly at undoing your money belt or reaching into your pocket. The other street thieves are plainclothes pickpockets, who might be dressed like respectable businessmen, but whose "business" is riding crowded metro trains and buses and slipping away with wads of tourists' cash.

In addition to working the crowded tourist areas and public transportation, many thieves are so bold as to steal bags from crowded bars and restaurants. Anyone eating or drinking alfresco is a target for thieves on the prowl, so be sure to keep your bags and other valuable (cameras, etc.) well away from the side of the table that faces the open piazza or street. Truly ballsy types have been known to go inside a crowded, casual restaurant (like a lively pizzeria) and take handbags that have been hung on the back of dining chairs. The good news is that these thieves aren't violent, and it's a good bet that no one will ever "mug" you in Italy. Because gypsies have such a predictable M.O. (everything you need to know about how they work is in these two paragraphs), they're quite easy to deflect. Just keep your bags close to your body—no need for paranoid clutching—and an I-am-not-a-victim attitude about you, and you'll likely make it through your visit without having to cancel your credit cards. If you do catch a hand in your pocket or relieving you of your bag, you should have no qualms

about screaming at them in the language of your choice, with all the expletives you like, and repeatedly shouting *"Polizia!"* (The mention of the police tends to disperse the pickpockets faster than anything else.)

As with any part of the world, you should also keep an eye out for other scams and use common sense to avoid any situations that could sacrifice your safety.

Keep in mind that Italy is not quite the melting pot that the U.S. prides itself on being. There may be some anti-American or anti-Bush sentiments—in the form of graffiti or political demonstrations—that may make you uncomfortable. Remember that you are a guest in their country, and be respectful of their opinions. For further information regarding female and minority travelers, see the relevant sections later in this chapter.

Most importantly, maintain respect for the country and its moral and legal statutes. Americans may have reputations as partiers, but that does not give us *carte blanche* to behave like idiots, nor does it exempt us from being held accountable for our actions under a law that may be different from our own.

THE BASICS

Getting Wired

Whether or not you bring your own computer, you'll have many opportunities to check your e-mail, update your travel blog, tweak your MySpace page, etc., while in Italy. If you feel like toting your PowerBook along, you'll find Wi-Fi coverage in a lot of places, and broadband cable connections in some hotels, but chances are your backpack is stuffed enough without having to squeeze in your laptop (and worry about its theft). If you don't bring your own computer, you'll still find plenty of Internet points (the local term for Internet cafes and kiosks) in Italy.

If you don't already have one, you may want to open a free, Web-based e-mail account with Yahoo!, Hotmail, or Gmail,

which you can access from any computer in the world with an Internet connection. If you already have an AOL account, you can log onto www.aol.com and check your AOL mail from there.

Without Your Own Computer

Almost all hostels and some budget hotels have at least one Internet terminal set up for guests' use. Some places offer this service for free; others charge up to 5€ an hour. (Whatever you do, avoid logging on at any large hotel's business center—their rates for Internet use are ridiculously high, and usually not very well posted.)

If your hotel does not have a public computer, you'll need to track down an Internet

OKKIO! You Need ID to Surf the 'Net

Italy passed an anti-terrorism law in 2005 that requires you to present a valid international ID (i.e., your passport) before you can log on at public Internet terminals (that is, at hotels' public computers, Internet points, and libraries).

cafe, or "point." In larger cities, a good place to start your search is at the train station, where there is often a small office-like space with several public terminals. Otherwise, you can canvas the area immediately around the train station, where there are usually a bunch of telecom centers set up to serve budget travelers (whose hotels are usually nearby) and an immigrant population that needs to communicate easily and cheaply with home. Any city's tourist-heavy *centro storico* is also full of Internet spots. This is especially true of Florence, which has a huge student population. Another idea is to stop in at the local bar or pub—those with an expat clientele, especially, are likely to have a computer hooked up to the Internet for patrons' convenience. For each destination in this book, we've listed the addresses of some of the better and more popular Internet points. As you might expect of any computer that's touched by dozens of hands daily, the keyboards are sticky, the mouse often doesn't work, etc., so make sure you sit down at a decently functioning terminal before you waste valuable minutes trying to get the space bar to work.

Most major airports now have Internet kiosks scattered throughout their terminals. These kiosks, which you'll also see in hotel lobbies and tourist information offices around the world, give you basic Web access for a per-minute fee that's usually higher than regular Internet cafe prices. The kiosks' clunkiness and high price means you should avoid them whenever possible.

With Your Own Computer

If you're going to haul along your laptop, make sure that at least some of the places you'll be staying offer in-room broadband connections or Wi-Fi coverage on the property. Hotels that offer Wi-Fi often have some convoluted password-protected network that may be down half the time; in fact, hotels that offer the somewhat more old-fashioned broadband/Ethernet cable connection are often more reliable. If you have a wireless card, just open your laptop and see what

OKKIO! Remember a Converter

Italy uses 220-volt electricity, whereas the U.S. uses 110-volt. Using any appliances with the wrong voltage can fry them. Hairdryers are a classic casualty of this common traveler's mistake, but most lower-voltage electronics (like laptops and iPods and cellphone chargers) will do just fine with 220-V electricity. That being said, it's still a good idea to check with the manufacturer to see how your appliances will handle the voltage switch. If they're at risk, then be sure to use a **voltage converter.** (Those are the clunky, boxy contraptions you can buy at gadget stores like Brookstone.) Smaller, simpler **adaptors** change a plug from American flat prongs to European round prongs, but do not work as electrical converters. Adaptors can be purchased at almost any hardware store *(ferramenta)* in Italy for a few euros. Converters are harder to find in Italy, so if you need one, buy a converter before you leave home.

happens. With so many unprotected wireless networks in such close proximity, you'll often be able to get online automatically. We've been in many a nonwired hotel where we've managed to poach off a neighboring network (from the apartment across the street or law offices next door) that wasn't password-protected.

Although they're not nearly as widespread as in the U.S., there are more and more Wi-Fi "hot spots" cropping up at cafes and bars throughout Italy. In 2005, the city of Rome launched free Wi-Fi access in over 20 public parks and piazzas throughout the city. Logging on in one of these hot spots requires a simple, one-time registration.

The website **wifi411.com** has a remarkably comprehensive list of all the wireless Internet networks throughout the world (including Italy); select your desired city, and then select "All Networks" and "All Locations," and you'll get dozens of results.

Some airports also have wireless hot spots where access costs $6.95 per day—of course, you only end up using it for an hour, so it ends up being a bit of a rip-off.

Mobile Phones

Yes, you can totally get through your trip without having a cellphone, but let's face it—it's incredibly handy to have at least one between you and your traveling companions for when you need to make hotel reservations, coordinate travel plans with other people, and, of course, for when you meet someone cute at the *discoteca* and need to exchange numbers!

Italy, like most of the world, is on **GSM (Global System for Mobiles),** a big, seamless network that makes for easy cross-border cellphone use throughout Europe and dozens of other countries worldwide. In the U.S., T-Mobile, AT&T Wireless, and Cingular use this quasi-universal system; in Canada, Microcell, and some Rogers customers are GSM, and all Europeans and most

Australians use GSM. If your cellphone is on a GSM system, and you have a world-capable multiband phone such as many Sony Ericsson, Motorola, or Samsung models, you can make and receive calls across civilized areas around much of the globe, including Italy. Just call your wireless operator and ask for "international roaming" to be activated on your account. Unfortunately, per-minute charges can be high—usually $1 to $1.50 in western Europe. When you speak to your service provider, make sure you check to see if there is a per-month charge for international calling capability. T-Mobile, for example, doesn't charge you a per-month fee; Cingular does. If your provider does charge you for this service, remember to call and cancel it when you return from your trip.

If you don't have a GSM phone, you can always **rent a mobile phone** for your trip. There are dozens of cellphone rental outfits on the Web—including www.planetfone. com, www.worldcell.com, www.cellhire.com, www.cellularabroad.com, and www.rentcell. com—which are all pretty competitive with each other. You'll fill out an online form (or call their toll-free customer service line) and

Take Off the Earbuds!

Whatever you do about phone use in Italy, try to keep the chitchat with friends and family back home to a minimum. Don't get so caught up with being in touch with the U.S. that you don't step out of your comfort zone and let yourself really experience Italian culture. The same goes for iPods and portable game devices—they're great for the plane ride over and long train rides, but stow them away when you're on a city bus and walking around town. Enjoying Italy is all about stimulating all your senses, which is why you'll never see locals walking around with white earbuds in their ears.

Telephone Tips: From Your Cell or a Payphone

To call Italy from the United States, dial the **international prefix, 011;** then Italy's **country code, 39;** and then the city code (for example, **06** for Rome and **055** for Florence), which is now built into every number. Then dial the actual **phone number.**

A **local phone call** from a payphone in Italy costs around .10€. **Public phones** accept coins, precharged phone cards (*scheda* or *carta telefonica*), or both. You can buy a *carta telefonica* at any *tabacchi* (tobacconists; most display a sign with a white T on a brown background) in increments of 5€, 10€, and 20€. To make a call, pick up the receiver and insert .10€ or your card (break off the corner first). Most phones have a digital display that'll tell you how much money you've inserted (or how much is left on the card). Dial the number, and don't forget to take the card with you after you hang up.

To **call from one city code to another,** dial the city code, complete with initial 0, and then dial the number. (Note that numbers in Italy range from four to eight digits in length. Even when you're calling within the same city, you must dial that city's area code—including the zero. A Roman calling another Rome number must dial 06 before the local number.)

To **dial direct internationally,** dial **00,** then the country code, the area code, and the number. The country code for the United States and Canada is 1.

Italy has recently introduced a series of **international phone cards** *(scheda telefonica internazionale)* for calling overseas. They come in increments of 50, 100, 200 and 400 *unita* (units), and they're available at *tabacchi* and bars. Each *unita* is worth .15€ of phone time; it costs 5 *unita* (.65€) per minute to call within Europe or to the United States or Canada. You don't insert this card into a payphone phone; just dial ☏ 1740 and then *2 (star 2) for instructions in English, when prompted.

To call the free **national telephone information** (in Italian) in Italy, dial ☏ 12. **International information** is available at ☏ 176 but costs .60€ a shot.

To make **collect or calling-card calls,** drop in .10€ or insert your card and dial one of the numbers here; an American operator will come on to assist you The following calling-card numbers work all over Italy: AT&T ☏ 172-1011, **MCI** ☏ 172-1022, and **Sprint** ☏ 172-1877.

provide your credit card number, and they'll ship you a box that contains your rental cellphone, extra battery, charger, and dorky cordura cases, to the address of your choice. When you've returned from your trip, you just put everything back in the same packaging and ship it back to them in the preaddressed and prepaid FedEx or UPS package. The whole process couldn't be easier—just remember to do it at least a week in advance of your trip. Phone rental isn't cheap, however. You'll usually pay around $50 per week,

plus airtime fees of anywhere from 15¢ to a dollar a minute. (Most have free incoming calls, however.) The bottom line: Shop around for the best deal.

While you can rent a phone from any number of overseas sites, including kiosks at airports and at car-rental agencies, we suggest renting the phone before you leave home. That way you can give loved ones and business associates your new number, make sure the phone works, and take the phone wherever you go—especially helpful for

Emergency Numbers

Another very important phone detail to master is the emergency numbers in Italy—the numbers that are comparable to 911 in the U.S. (Note that these numbers do not have a prefix; they're the same no matter where in Italy you're dialing from. These numbers will work from any phone—land line, payphone, or cell—even if you have no credit on a calling card.)

Ambulance (medical emergencies) **118**

Fire department *(vigili del fuoco)* **115**

Carabinieri (army police, general emergencies) **112**

Polizia (state police, general emergencies) **113**

overseas trips through several countries, where local phone-rental agencies often bill in local currency and may not let you take the phone to another country.

For trips of more than a few weeks, **buying a phone** makes more economic sense than renting one, as Italy has a number of cheap, prepaid phone systems. Once you arrive, stop by a local cellphone shop—Vodafone, TIM, and Wind are the big names in cellular service in Italy—and ask about the cheapest package; you'll probably pay less than $100 for a phone and a starter calling card. Most providers have plans where calls to land lines and text messages are as low as 10¢ per minute, and all incoming calls, even from outside Italy, are free. When your starter calling card runs out, you can buy more time with a *ricarica* card, sold in denominations of 10€ and up at any *tabacchi* or cellphone store and some newsstands. Note that your *ricarica* card must be the same brand as the provider (Vodafone, TIM, or Wind) you signed up with.

If you don't plan on taking a mobile phone with you or renting one while abroad, you can still make phone calls from a public telephone on the street. Pick up a phone card at any *tabacchi*, and many newsstands and coffee bars. If you plan on calling the States a lot, this can get rather pricey.

Getting Around Italy

By Train

Italy's national train system, while not as clean as the Swiss or as fast as the Japanese, functions quite well and will probably be the only method of transportation you need use while touring the mainland. Most of Italy is accessible by one of the major rail lines. For train timetables and fare information, visit the handy official site of Italian train travel at **www.trenitalia.com**. There are a bunch of different train types (that make more stops, cost more, etc.) so consider which is the right train for your needs.

If you have a **Eurailpass** (see box below), you can use it for second-class travel on any train in Italy, except Eurostar (ES) and Cisalpino (CIS) trains, without paying a supplement.

If you don't have a Eurailpass, you can buy individual tickets on an as-needed basis from city to city. With the exception of ES and CIS trains, which must be booked 24 hours in advance, you can usually buy your ticket the day of your train travel. Tickets can be purchased at most travel agents around town (look for those displaying the blue-and-green TRENITALIA or FS—*Ferrovie dello Stato* emblem), and at any train station.

THE BASICS

Behold! The Legendary Eurailpass!

Many travelers to Europe take advantage of one of the great travel bargains of our time, the **Eurailpass,** which permits unlimited rail travel in any country in western Europe (except the British Isles) and Hungary in eastern Europe. Oddly, it doesn't include travel on the rail lines of Sardinia, which are organized independently of the rail lines of the rest of Italy.

The advantages are tempting: There are no tickets; simply show the pass to the ticket collector, then settle back to enjoy the scenery. Seat reservations are required on some trains (see box below). Many trains have couchettes (sleeping cars), for which an extra fee is charged. Obviously, the 2- or 3-month traveler gets the greatest economic advantages. To obtain full advantage of a 15-day or 1-month pass, you'd have to spend a great deal of time on the train.

Eurailpass holders are also entitled to considerable reductions on certain buses and ferries as well. You'll get a 20% reduction on second-class accommodations from certain companies operating ferries between Naples and Palermo or for crossings to Sardinia and Malta.

In **North America,** you can buy these passes from travel agents or rail agents in major cities such as New York, Montreal, and Los Angeles. Eurailpasses are also available **Rail Europe** (☎ 877/272-RAIL; www.raileurope.com). No matter what everyone tells you, you *can* buy Eurailpasses in Europe as well as in America (at the major train stations), but they're more expensive. Rail Europe can give you information on the rail/drive versions of the passes.

A **Eurailpass** is $605 for 15 days, $785 for 21 days, $975 for 1 month, $1,378 for 2 months, and $1,703 for 3 months. If you're under 26, you can buy a **Eurailpass Youth** entitling you to unlimited second-class travel for $394 for 15 days, $510 for 21 days, $634 for 1 month, $897 for 2 months, and $1,108 for 3 months. Even more freedom is offered by the Eurailpass **Saver Flexi,** which is similar to the Eurail Saverpass, except that you are not confined to consecutive-day travel. For travel over any 10 days within 2 months, the fare is $608; any 15 days over 2 months, the fare is $800.

Eurailpass Saver, valid all over Europe for first class only, offers discounted 15-day travel for groups of three or more people traveling together from April to September, or two people traveling together from October to March. The price is $513 for 15 days, $668 for 21 days, $828 for 1 month, $1,173 for 2 months, and $1,450 for 3 months.

The **Eurailpass Flexi** allows you to visit Europe with more flexibility. It's valid in first class and offers the same privileges as the Eurailpass. However, it provides a number of individual travel days you can use over a much longer period of consecutive days. That makes it possible to stay in one city and yet not lose a single day of travel. There are two passes: 10 days of travel in 2 months for $715, and 15 days of travel in 2 months for $940.

Having many of the same qualifications and restrictions as the Flexipass is the **Eurailpass Youth Flexi.** Sold only to travelers under 26, it allows 10 days of travel within 2 months for $465, and 15 days of travel within 2 months for $612.

These prices are valid as of Summer 2006; please check www.raileurope.com to confirm current prices.

THE BASICS

Train Routes Through Italy

Another possibility is a **kilometric ticket,** which is good for multiple travelers up to a certain total distance—ask about the *biglietto chilometrico* at a local travel agency.

Unless you have a very specific question (or you need to book an overnight sleeping compartment), *you do not need to wait in the long lines to see a ticket-window agent* at the train station. All Italian train stations are equipped with **self-service ticketing machines** with touch-activated screens, which take credit cards (or debit cards with the Visa or MasterCard symbol) and cash. These yellow machines are pretty self-explanatory and user-friendly; follow the on-screen prompts until you've created your desired itinerary, and then choose your form of payment. You can even use these machines to book Eurostar tickets if you book at least 24 hours in advance.

OKKIO! Stamp Your Ticket

It's not enough to simply buy a train ticket; for it to be valid for travel, you must **time-stamp** your ticket before you board Italian trains. Yellow *convalida* time-stampers are located throughout the train station and always at the end of platforms. Tons of travelers forget this detail, and while train conductors may never check your ticket, it's not worth the *brutta figura* of appearing to ride the train for free. Validated train tickets must be used within 6 hours of being stamped, so in your zeal to comply with the rules, don't stamp your ticket earlier than you need to! Eurostar tickets do not need to be stamped, as they're already printed with a specific unchangeable date and time.

Eurostar or Intercity, What's the Difference?

To summarize: The Eurostar is a modern train with bright interiors and clean upholstery. The **Intercity** is definitely more shopworn, with seating compartments that carry a faint reek of cigarettes and old food. No-smoking cars in the Eurostar really *are* smoke-free, whereas this rule isn't always strictly respected on the Intercity. Also, A/C in the Eurostar always works, while A/C in the Intercity *usually* works (otherwise, open windows do the trick). The food quality is the same in both lines: there are decent (but never great) snacks in the café car, and there's a full-service restaurant car (serving lunch and dinner only at set meal times) on most trains— Eurostar and Intercity—that travel for more than 4 hours or so. One final advantage to traveling on Eurostar trains is that they're not affected by national train strikes, which happen about once per month in Italy. As for the Intercity, only trains with a final destination outside Italy (e.g. Munich, Paris, Vienna) are immune to the strikes.

Text-Message Ticketing: If you have a cellphone while you're in Italy, and it's capable of receiving Italian text messages, you can buy your train tickets online at www.trenitalia.com, and they'll send you a confirmation SMS (text message) with your booking number. When the conductor comes through the train to check tickets, you'll literally open up your cellphone and flash him that screen with the confirmation message. As bizarre as it sounds, this slick new system has gained huge popularity in Italy since it was introduced a few years ago.

From Eurostar to Regionale

Types of Italian Trains

→ **ES Eurostar.** Italy's fastest and most expensive trains only stop in big cities and important rail hubs. The cars are modern and air-conditioned; some seats are provided with electrical supply (European voltage and outlet) and all have tray-tables suitable for laptops. There's a dining car and snack bar at the center of the train. If you're using a Eurailpass, you'll have to pay a supplement to ride the Eurostar. Reservations (seat assignments) are required and must be made at least 24 hours in advance. This means if you book a ticket for the 2pm Eurostar to Bologna, you can't just use that ticket to hop on the 3pm Eurostar to Naples.

→ **IC Intercity.** A good compromise, and the most common train type in Italy, IC trains make more stops than Eurostars, but they're less expensive. They are air-conditioned, but most have food and drink stains dating back to the 1980s. Most IC trains also have a dining car and snack bar. There is no supplement for Eurailpass holders. Seats may be reserved, but it's not required, which gives you the flexibility of changing your travel plans at the last minute. For instance, if you booked a ticket for the 4pm IC to Florence, you can use it for any IC to Florence—later that day, or several days later. (Seat assignments, of course, will not be kept if you choose to take a different IC train.)

→ **EC Eurocity.** For all intents and purposes, these are the same as IC trains; the only difference is that they originate or end up in a city outside Italy, such as Munich, Vienna, or Paris. If you're traveling on an overnight EC (Euronight, or EN), be sure to book your sleeping compartment or seat assignment 24 hours in advance.

→ **CIS Cisalpino.** These trains are operated by a joint venture between the Italian and Swiss rail companies. Service is similar to IC trains, and the routes connect the main cities of central and northern Italy with the main cities of Switzerland. Eurailpass holders pay a supplement on CIS trains, and reservations are required. Dining cars on these trains are great for watching the passing Alpine scenery.

→ **EXPR Espresso.** These slow "express" trains, also notated as "E," are often on night service, providing both regular seats and sleeping cars. No supplement is charged to Eurail holders, and reservations are not necessary. Food and drink service is available on some trains as indicated on schedules.

→ **DIR Diretto.** Don't let the name fool you. These are *direct* trains, but they're slow as molasses. If your city is served by an IC, take the IC; some smaller towns are only served by DIR trains, however. DIR trains have modern, commuter-type cars, with second-class seating only, and are uncrowded during off-peak hours.

→ **IR Interregionale and REG Regionale.** Take an IR or R only if you're traveling to a local destination that can't be reached by IC. Check the timetable carefully, as IR or R trains departing at different times to the same station do not necessarily make all the same stops en route. Like DIR Diretto trains, IR Interregionale and REG Regionale are usually uncrowded during off-peak hours. Some have air-conditioned cars, but no dining service is offered.

THE BASICS

Travel Times Between the Major Cities

Cities	Distance	Train Travel Time
Florence to Milan	298km/185 miles	2½ hr.
Florence to Venice	281km/174 miles	4 hr.
Milan to Venice	267km/166 miles	3½ hr.
Rome to Florence	277km/172 miles	2½ hr.
Rome to Milan	572km/355 miles	5 hr.
Rome to Naples	219km/136 miles	2½ hr.
Rome to Venice	528km/327 miles	5¼ hr.
Rome to Genoa	501km/311 miles	6 hr.

By Car

Road-tripping by car in Italy is great if you plan to delve into the country's rural areas that aren't well served by rail (e.g., smaller hill towns of Tuscany); otherwise, you'll probably find the train an easier beast to tame. Driving in urban areas is a nightmare, but once you're outside the city, the highways and state roads are well marked and easy to use. The main highways (**autostrade,** or A, indicated by green signs) that connect Italy's major cities aren't particularly exciting, but they're usually the fastest way from point A to point B. Lesser roads (**strade statali,** or SS)—anywhere from two to four lanes—are slower but usually more scenic. SS roads are indicated by blue signs and often involve stoplights when they pass through towns. None of Italy's roads is particularly well-lit at night, which is nerve-wracking if you have to drive in the dark. As in the U.S. and the rest of mainland Europe, Italians drive on the right side of the road.

U.S. and Canadian drivers don't need an **international driver's license** to drive a rented car in Italy. However, if you're driving a private car, you need such a license. You can apply for an International Driver's License at any **American Automobile Association (AAA)** branch. You must be at least 18 and have two 2×2-inch photos and a photocopy of your U.S. driver's license with your AAA application form. The actual fee for the license can vary, depending on where it's issued.

RENTING A CAR

To rent a car in Italy, a driver must have nerves of steel, a sense of humor, a valid

Sciopero! Train & other Transit Strikes

Transit strikes are all too common in Italy—whether it's the Alitalia pilots' or Venice *vaporetto* drivers' union, someone in the transportation sector goes on strike about once a month. The good news is that most of these strikes are announced days or weeks in advance, which should leave you enough time to make alternative arrangements. Note that *EuroStar (ES) trains are not affected by general national train strikes.* The official site that announces strikes is in Italian only www.commissione garanziasciopero.it, but you can get the info you need from these sites: www.summerinitaly.com and www.seekitaly.com. Hotel and hostel staff are also quite good about alerting guests to impending strikes that will affect local travel.

Italian Train Tips

➔ Keep your schedule somewhat flexible: Italian trains often run late, and announced transit strikes are not uncommon.

➔ Most train trips in Italy are under 4 hours, but if you're going to be covering a long distance on a particular trip (say, from Naples to Milan, or from Venice to Rome), consider booking your train travel overnight. This will help you maximize your daylight time in Italy and save you money that you'd otherwise have spent on a night's lodging. Overnight train trips must be booked at least 24 hours in advance to guarantee a seat or sleeping compartment.

➔ Italian trains have smoking sections, so if you're going to smoke, be sure to smoke in the special smoking cars only, not just in the corridor of a nonsmoking car with the window open.

➔ If you're trying to hoard your cash, banish all thoughts of the faster and cleaner Eurostar trains from your mind. Intercity trains are covered by rail passes, and they're not that much slower than Eurostars.

➔ Unfortunately, theft can be a problem on trains. Keep your bags near you at all times, and if you're going to sleep, make sure you have a hand or arm on valuables.

➔ If you have any other questions about schedules and fares, **www.trenitalia.com** is a wonderful resource. (There's a link for the English version of the site at the top left-hand corner of the homepage).

driver's license, and a valid passport and (in most cases) be over 25.

For booking rental cars online, the best deals are usually found at rental-car company websites, although all the major online travel agencies also offer rental-car reservations services. Priceline and Hotwire work well for rental cars, too; the only "mystery" is which major rental company you get, and for most travelers the difference is negligible. Another great online resource for car rental is **EasyCar** (www.easycar.com), which has many rental locations throughout Italy.

You can also rent a car on the spot when you get to Italy. Big agencies like Hertz (www.hertz.com), Avis (www.avis.com), and Maggiore (www.maggiore.it, an affiliate of National and Alamo, who often beats Hertz's and Avis's rates) all have offices at Italian airports and major train stations. The best deals are sometimes with smaller, independent agencies, but these usually require you

to return the car to the same place you picked it up, which might not be convenient in every case.

Keep in mind that gas *(benzina)* is expensive in Italy—two to three times what it costs in the U.S., if you can believe that! We're talking $6 a gallon as of Spring 2006. As a general rule, gas stations are open from 7:30am to 2pm and 3:30 to 7:30pm. **Autogrill** (restaurant/cafe/service stations) along the *autostrada* are open 24/7, however.

OKKIO! Take the Long Way Home

Cities that appear to be close to each other on a map might involve inconvenient train changes and slow regional lines—for the best connections, travel through big train hub cities like Rome, Florence, Bologna, or Milan.

OKKIO! The Left-Lane Rule

Only use the left lane if you are passing someone. If you and your little Fiat hatchback make the mistake of hanging out in the left lane, you'll find an endless convoy of black BMW SUVs crawling up your ass (at about 90 miles an hour). If that's too subtle an indication that someone wants you to pull over, he'll also flash his headlights at you until you get out of the way. Obnoxious, yes, but this will happen to you over and over, so get used to it.

By Bus

BETWEEN CITIES

Coach travel between Italian regions and cities is pretty unheard of as a means of tourist transport, but there are a few regional bus lines that serve daytrip destinations (that aren't accessible by train) from major cities like Rome and Florence. See the relevant regional or city chapters for more information on getting around.

IN THE CITIES

Once you're in a city, the most efficient and cost effective way to get around, other than using your own two feet, is by bus, metro, or tram. Pick up a public transit map and head on out. Bus lines are named by numbers and the piazza, street, or landmark that is their final destination. Choose the destination that lies in your desired general direction, and get on that bus—it's usually that simple. Even though different local agencies operate each city's public transit system, no matter where you are, bus tickets can be purchased at a *tabacchi* shop or a newsstand, and they all cost 1€ for a ride in one direction (they cannot be purchased on board). Make sure you validate your bus ticket as soon as you get on the bus. Just stick it in the timer, as you'll see others doing. Often times, your bus trip becomes invalid after 1 hour or 75 minutes. Bus authorities do random checks and if you're caught without a ticket, you're in for a *bruttissima figura* moment: You'll get a hefty fine and heaps of public embarrassment.

For Travelers With Special Interests or Needs

Student Travelers

Before you leave, get an **International Student Identity Card** (ISIC), which offers substantial savings on rail passes, plane tickets, and many entrance fees. It also provides you with basic health and life insurance and a 24-hour help line. The card is available for $22 from **STA Travel** (☎ **800/781-4040** in North America; www.sta.com or www.statravel.com). If you're no longer a student but are under 26, you can get an **International Youth Travel Card (IYTC)** for the same price from the same people, which entitles you to some of the same discounts. **Travel CUTS** (☎ **800/667-2887** or 416/614-2887; www.travelcuts.com) offers similar services for both Canadians and U.S. residents.

OKKIO! Hope You Can Drive Stick . . .

When renting a car in Italy, make sure that you have a valid driver's license and remember that most rental cars are manual transmission (stick shift). Automatic transmission can be prohibitively expensive, or not available at all. A bustling Italian city flooded with *motorini* and pedestrians is definitely not the place to learn how to drive a manual.

Almost all of Italy's monuments and museums offer reduced rates to students—the trouble is, many of these reductions are reserved for EU citizens only. Still, bring along your regular university ID, which often works just as well.

Once in Italy, if you decide you want one, you can get an ISIC or IYTC card at **CTS** (www.cts.it), which is the national student travel agency, with offices in every city you're likely to visit. Staffed by friendly young Italian students, CTS is also a great one-stop shop for booking train tickets, ferry tickets, and cheap flights—within Italy, to other parts of Europe, or overseas. Most CTS offices are open Monday to Friday, from 9:30am to 1pm, and from 2:30 to 6:30pm, and on Saturday from 9:30am to 1pm.

There are hundreds of CTS offices in Italy; start with these:

○ **Rome:** Via Genova 16, ☎ **06/462-0431,** and Corso Vittorio Emanuele II 297, ☎ 06/687-2672
○ **Florence:** Via dei Ginori 25/r, ☎ **055/289-570**
○ **Venice:** Ca' Foscari, Dorsoduro 3252, ☎ **041/520-5660**
○ **Bologna:** Largo Respighi, 2/f, ☎ **051/261-802**
○ **Milan:** Corso Porta Ticinese 100, ☎ **02/837-2674**

At a less official level, many pubs and bars offer discounted drink prices for students, and some clubs will waive a cover if you can produce a valid student ID.

Single Travelers

Solo travelers can have a grand old time in Italy. You can choose your own adventure and follow your own itinerary, without the tension that inevitably arises from making sure your traveling companions want to do exactly what you want to do, and without the distraction of your friends' constant chit-chat that can keep you from fully absorbing the local sights and sounds.

Safety issues concerning solo travelers are minimal in Italy. Believe it or not, a foreign woman walking alone is less likely to be harassed than two foreign women walking together (for what to expect if you're a woman going solo, see "Women Travelers" below).

If you stay at hostels and go on group walking tours, bike tours, etc., you're bound to meet a ton of young, like-minded people, whom you can join for dinner and nights on the town, etc. In every major city, there are also plenty of bars and pubs that have a high backpacker or expat quotient. We've listed the best ones in each city chapter in this book. Don't feel weird about hitting the town on your own—it'll give you an exhilarating sense of freedom, and you might stumble into adventures that never would have happened if you'd just stayed at the hostel reading a book.

Italians are incredibly open and are more likely to strike up a conversation with you if you're by yourself. (So, if part of your plan in Italy is to meet some fine young locals, going around solo can be a great strategy!) One exceedingly common pitfall of traveling for too long on your own, however, is that when you do finally interact with people, you're so relieved for the human contact that you tend to talk too much. Don't let this happen to you—you'll come off as a crazy person, even if you're not!

To save money as a solo traveler, always stay in hostels, as single rooms in budget hotels usually cost almost as much as double rooms.

Travelers with Disabilities

Many travel agencies offer customized tours and itineraries for travelers with disabilities. **Flying Wheels Travel** (☎ 507/451-5005; www.flyingwheelstravel.com) offers escorted tours and cruises that emphasize sports and private tours in minivans with lifts. **Access-Able Travel Source** (☎ 303/232-2979; www.access-able.com) offers extensive

THE BASICS

access information and advice for traveling around the world with disabilities. **Accessible Journeys** (☎ 800/846-4537 or 610/521-0339; www.disabilitytravel.com) caters specifically to slow walkers and wheelchair travelers and their families and friends.

Avis has an "Avis Access" program that offers such services as a dedicated 24-hour toll-free number (☎ 888/879-4273) for customers with special travel needs; special car features such as swivel seats, spinner knobs, and hand controls; and accessible bus service.

Organizations that offer assistance to disabled travelers include **MossRehab** (www.mossresourcenet.org), which provides a library of accessible-travel resources online; the **American Foundation for the Blind (AFB)** (☎ 800/232-5463; www.afb.org), a referral resource for the blind or visually impaired that includes information on traveling with Seeing Eye dogs; and **SATH (Society for Accessible Travel & Hospitality)** (☎ 212/447-7284; www.sath.org; annual membership fees: $45 adults, $30 seniors and students), which offers a wealth of travel resources for all types of disabilities and recommendations on destinations, access guides, travel agents, tour operators, vehicle rentals, and companion services.

For more information specifically targeted to travelers with disabilities, the community website **iCan** (www.icanonline.net/channels/travel) has destination guides and several regular columns on accessible travel. Also check out the quarterly magazine *Emerging Horizons* (www.emerginghorizons.com; $14.95 per year, $19.95 outside the U.S.); and *Open World* magazine, published by SATH (see above; subscription: $13 per year, $21 outside the U.S.).

Gay & Lesbian Travelers

As a general rule, Italy is not unlike many other countries when it comes to gay and lesbian travel. Metropolitan areas seem to have more gay bars and clubs than outlying towns

and villages. Rome, Milan, and Florence all have active gay scenes, but the gay culture is not very overt. You won't see a lot of same-sex couples walking hand-in-hand, but the Italian attitude towards homosexuality is very laissez-faire. It is rarely discussed, but judgment and harassment seem to be less prevalent than in some parts of the U.S. Homosexuality is a more personal rather than public issue in Italian culture. This is evident in that many gay venues for entertainment are off the beaten track and usually not in a city's *centro.*

Since 1861, Italy has had liberal legislation regarding homosexuality, but that doesn't mean it has been looked on favorably in a Catholic country. Homosexuality is much more accepted in the north than in the south, especially in Sicily, although Taormina has long been a gay mecca. However, all major towns and cities have an active gay life, especially Florence, Rome, and Milan, which considers itself the "gay capital" of Italy and is the headquarters of **ARCI Gay,** the country's leading gay organization with branches throughout Italy. Capri is the gay resort of Italy, rivaled only by the gay beaches of Venice.

In general, gender lines are not quite as rigid within its cultural confines. You will often see men being very affectionate with each other, but this has little reflection on their sexuality. All this being said, if you are gay, and looking to hit up the scene in Italy, here are some valuable resources to make it happen:

Since you've already picked up one of our guides, we'd like to recommend *Frommer's Gay & Lesbian Europe* (Wiley Publishing, Inc.), which is an excellent travel resource for the top gay & lesbian cities and resorts in Europe, and includes chapters on Rome and Florence.

The International Gay and Lesbian Travel Association (IGLTA) (☎ 800/448-8550 or 954/776-2626; www.iglta.org) is the trade association for the gay and lesbian travel industry, and offers an online directory of gay- and lesbian-friendly travel businesses; go to their website and click on "Members."

Many agencies offer tours and itineraries specifically for gay and lesbian travelers. **Above and Beyond Tours** (☎ 800/397-2681; www.abovebeyondtours.com) is the exclusive gay and lesbian tour operator for United Airlines. **Now, Voyager** (☎ 800/255-6951; www.nowvoyager.com) is a well-known San Francisco–based, gay-owned and -operated travel service. **Olivia Cruises & Resorts** (☎ 800/631-6277; www.olivia.com) charters entire resorts and ships for exclusive lesbian vacations and offers smaller group experiences for both gay and lesbian travelers.

Gay.com Travel (☎ 800/929-2268 or 415/644-8044; www.gay.com/travel or www.outandabout.com), is an excellent online successor to the popular *Out & About* print magazine. It provides regularly updated information about gay-owned, gay-oriented, and gay-friendly lodging, dining, sightseeing, nightlife, and shopping establishments in every important destination worldwide. It also offers trip-planning information for gay and lesbian travelers for more than 50 destinations, along various themes, ranging from Sex & Travel to Vacations for Couples.

The following travel guides are available at many bookstores, or you can order them from any online bookseller: *Spartacus International Gay Guide* (Bruno Gmünder Verlag; www.spartacusworld.com/gayguide) and *Odysseus: The International Gay Travel Planner* (Odysseus Enterprises Ltd.), both good, annual, English-language guidebooks focused on gay men; and the *Damron* guides (www.damron.com), with separate, annual books for gay men and lesbians.

Women Travelers

Ladies, if your ego needs a shot in the arm, you've come to the right country. Anyone

with a pulse and an X-chromosome is bound to be bombarded with flattery and romantic lines galore. Indeed, Italian men are very whimsical with professions of love, and if you get close enough, they'll sweep you off your feet before you know it. It can be great, but there's also a point at which the Italian fervor for women becomes annoying and can even feel threatening.

As a rule, the farther south you go in Italy, the more liberal the men get about flexing their machismo, which often translates to harassment. Note that blondes and anyone dressed skimpily are often a greater target for harassment or negative attention. The sensibility among Italian men sometimes characterizes foreign (and particularly American) women as "easy." When fraternizing with local boys, make sure you keep this in mind. As crass as it sounds, most Italian men are not interested in a female backpacker's intellect. That said, Italian men are not physically aggressive toward women, and if you are ever in a situation that makes you feel uncomfortable, feel free to walk away from it. The guy might not love the rejection, but he's not going to come and stalk you.

There's also a huge upside to being a female traveler in Italy—in addition to the ego boosting, you'll also benefit from male waiters offering you free after-dinner drinks, male service agents being really nice to you, and—this happened quite recently to a single female friend of mine—male cab drivers giving you a purely platonic, four-hour private tour of Rome, including gelato, and only charging you for gas.

As for general safety precautions, women should always use common sense when walking alone at night, just as you would in any metropolitan area.

Minority Travelers

Even though Italian society is not nearly as ethnically heterogeneous as the U.S., minority travelers shouldn't really encounter any problems. One thing that can take some getting used to is how ignorant/curious Italians are about how integrated other ethnicities are in other countries. While Italy has an ever-growing immigrant population, there is still major segregation between, say, Albanians, Ukrainians, and Bangladeshis and ethnic Italians. Also, for some reason, Italians have a hard time thinking of Asians as "Americans" even if, like so many Chinese- or Indian-Americans, they were born and bred in the U.S.A. And if you're African-American, you might find people asking you about "what that's like," and assuming you are an aspiring hip-hop artist or something. This curiosity isn't meant to be offensive, so take it as an opportunity to educate them—as their own population grows more diverse, Italians could certainly use some enlightenment on this front.

On the Net, there are a number of helpful travel sites for African-American travelers in particular: **Black Travel Online** (www.blacktravelonline.com) posts news on upcoming events and includes links to articles and travel-booking sites. Agencies and organizations that provide resources for black travelers include: **Rodgers Travel** (☎ **800/825-1775;** www.rodgerstravel.com), is a Philadelphia-based travel agency with an extensive menu of tours in destinations worldwide, including heritage and private-group tours.

Then there are the following collections and guides: ***Go Girl: The Black Woman's Guide to Travel & Adventure*** (Eighth Mountain Press), a compilation of travel essays by writers including Jill Nelson and Audre Lorde, with some practical information and trip-planning advice; ***Travel and Enjoy Magazine*** (☎ **866/266-6211;** www.travelandenjoy.com; subscription: $38 per year), which focuses on discounts and destination reviews; and the more narrative ***Pathfinders Magazine*** (☎ **877/977-PATH;** www.pathfinderstravel.com; subscription: $15 per year), which includes articles on everything from Rio de Janeiro to Ghana as well as information on upcoming ski, diving, golf, and tennis trips.

THE BASICS

MTV U Italian Language Study

If you want to get fluent and have fun doing it, the best-value and most effective program in Italy to learn Italian is the lively medieval town of Perugia, in the heart of Umbria. Italian language classes at Perugia's **Università per Stranieri** (www.unistrapg.it) start at 400€ for a 1-month, intensive course (accommodations and other living expenses are not included). Also home to a university for Italians, Perugia is full of students from all over the globe year-round. For more information, see the Perugia section in this book.

Alternatively, the venerable **Dante Alighieri** language school (www.dantealighieri.it), which is based in Florence, has affiliated locations in Rome, Bologna, Milan, Siena, and Venice. Dante Alighieri has flexible class structures; for example, an intensive 1-week, 20-hour course starts at 195€; a part-time 4-week, 40-hour course starts at 295€.

If you want to brush up on your Italian before heading across the ocean, check into what language schools may be available in your local area. You won't necessarily get fluent this way, but you'll get more out of your time in Italy if you can master some basic verb conjugations and useful expressions. If your goal is to get fluent, there is no substitute for full-immersion, and for that, studying in a place like Perugia can't be beat.

Eco-Tourists

If you're leaning more on the green side of things, Italy is flowing with eco-tourism options. A visit to **www.responsible travel.com** (whose motto is "holidays that give the world a break") shows trips on offer for all over Italy, ranging from cycling in Sardinia to farmstays in Tuscany. They are a UK-based site, but accept bookings from all over the world.

The International Ecotourism Society (TIES) defines eco-tourism as "responsible travel to natural areas that conserves the environment and improves the well-being of local people." You can find eco-friendly travel tips, statistics, and touring companies and associations—listed by destination under "Travel Choice"—at the TIES website, **www.ecotourism.org**.

Ecotravel.com is part online magazine and part eco-directory that lets you search for touring companies in several categories (water-based, land-based, spiritually oriented, and so on). Also check out **Conservation International** (www.conservation.org)—which, with National Geographic Traveler, annually presents World Legacy Awards (www.wlaward.org) to those travel tour operators, businesses, organizations, and places that have made a significant contribution to sustainable tourism.

Surf the Turf!

Useful & Necessary Sites to Check Out

Here's a list of sites you might want to bookmark as you plan your trip to Italy, and to call up as you sit at the Internet point in Bologna, figuring out which club you want to go to that night.

GOVERNMENT

○ **United States Diplomatic Mission to Italy:** Information regarding U.S. embassies, consulates, and travel information for U.S. citizens in Italy: **www.usembassy.it/acs**

○ **U.S. Department of State Website:** Information regarding passports, visas (including forms and applications), travel advisories and much more! **http://travel.state.gov**

OFFICIAL TOURIST BOARDS

○ **Italian State Tourist Board:** Multilingual, with links to the official sites for individual cities and regions. **www.enit.it** or **www.italiantourism.com**

○ *Azienda Provinciale di Turismo Roma* **(Rome Tourist Board): www.romaturismo.it**

○ *Azienda per il Turismo di Firenze* **(Florence Tourist Board): www.firenzeturismo.it**

○ **Tourism in Tuscany:** Offers itineraries, calendar of events. **www.turismo.toscana.it**

○ *Venizia:* Offers information from museums to beaches, and everything in between. **www.turismovenizia.it**

TRANSPORTATION

○ *Ferrovie dello Stato:* Official site for the national train system, Comprehensive timetable, prices, and online booking. **www.trenitalia.com**

○ *Autrostrade:* Official site of the well-run national highway system; with interactive route maps, with up-to-the-minute information on travel times, weather, traffic jams, and tolls. **www.autostrade.it/en**

MONEY

○ **X-Rates:** a good site to see how far your U.S. dollar will take you! **www.x-rates. com/calculator.html**

THE BASICS

Frommers.com—the Complete Travel Resource

For an excellent travel-planning resource, we highly recommend **Frommers.com** (www.frommers.com), voted Best Travel Site by *PC Magazine*. We're a little biased, of course, but we guarantee that you'll find the travel tips, reviews, monthly vacation giveaways, bookstore, and online-booking capabilities thoroughly indispensable. Among the special features are our popular Destinations section, where you'll get expert travel tips, hotel and dining recommendations, and advice on the sights to see for more than 3,500 destinations around the globe; the Frommers.com Newsletter, with the latest deals, travel trends, and money-saving secrets; our Community area featuring Message Boards, where Frommer's readers post queries and share advice (sometimes even our authors show up to answer questions); and our Photo Center, where you can post and share vacation tips. When your research is finished, the Online Reservations System (www.frommers.com/book_a_trip) takes you to Frommer's preferred online partners for booking your vacation at affordable prices.

Travel Blogs & Travelogues

More and more travelers are using travel web logs, or **blogs,** to chronicle their journeys online. You can search for other blogs about *Italy* at **Travelblog.com** or post your own travelogue at **Travelblog.org.** For blogs that cover general travel news and highlight various destinations, try **Writtenroad.com** or Gawker Media's snarky **Gridskipper.com.** For more literary travel essays, try Salon. com's travel section (**Salon.com/wander lust**), and **Worldhum.com**, which also has an extensive list of other travel-related journals, blogs, online communities, newspaper coverage, and bookstores.

For smaller blogs exclusive to Italy, check out a search on http://dir.blogflux.com/country/italy.html or http://www.blogfinds.com/italy. These can be a great resource in finding out what people like *you* are doing. Listen to your fellow travelers and take their advice!

Embracing *La Dolce Vita*

Before you head off to Italy, you might want to treat yourself to some Italian culture to whet your appetite, and we also have some suggestions for living "the sweet life," Italian-style when you get there.

Italy on the Big Screen

Italy's stunning architecture and rolling countryside have made it a popular choice for movie locations. Take a look at the list below, and perhaps add a few to your Netflix queue. You may get lots of ideas for places you want to see for yourself.

- ○ *The Bicycle Thief* (1948)—Rome
- ○ *The Bourne Identity* (2002)—Liguria, Rome
- ○ *Casanova* (2005)—Venice
- ○ *Cinema Paradiso* (1989)—Palermo province, Sicily
- ○ *The English Patient* (1996)—Montepulciano, Arezzo, Pienza, Siena
- ○ *Gladiator* (2000)—Tuscany
- ○ *The Godfather* (1972)—Outside Taormina (Sicily)
- ○ *The Italian Job* (1969)—Trento, Turin, Valle d'Aosta
- ○ *The Italian Job* (2003 remake)—Venice, Trento, Genoa, Rome

THE BASICS

- *The Lizzie McGuire Movie* (how could we forget??) (2003)—Rome
- *The Merchant of Venice* (most recent version, 2004)—Venice
- *Nights of Cabiria* (1952)—Rome
- *Ocean's Twelve* (2004)—Lake Como, Rome, Trapani (Sicily)
- *Roman Holiday* (1953)—Rome
- *A Room With a View* (1985)—Florence and Fiesole
- *Stealing Beauty* (1996)—Siena province, Tuscany
- *The Talented Mr. Ripley* (1999)—Ischia, Rome, Naples, Venice
- *Tea With Mussolini* (1999)—San Gimignano
- *Under the Tuscan Sun* (2003)—Tuscany

Modern Italian Cinema

La Dolce Vita and those Sophia Loren movies from the '60s are great, but they're dated. Below are some more current Italian films worth checking out for a bit of insight into modern Italian society. (All available at Netflix and well-stocked video stores.)

- **Caterina in the Big City** (*Caterina Va in Città*): (2005) A high school student moves from a rural town to Rome and gets caught up with fast-living friends from political extremes. Funny, paradoxical, and very honest.
- **But Forever in My Mind** (*Come Te Nessuno Mai*): (1999) Adorable coming-of-age film about high school students in Rome going through experiences for the first time and thinking they're totally unique to them—like we all did. Almost like an Italian *American Pie*, but smarter and more tasteful.
- **Facing Windows** (*La Finestra di Fronte*): (2003) A young woman stuck in a dull marriage "escapes" by caring for the Holocaust survivor who walks in their life, and by beginning a strange relationship with the handsome man who lives across from

her apartment. Surreal and full of lush cinematography that captures the irresistible beauty of Rome.

- **The Last Kiss** (*L'Ultimo Bacio*): (2001) Couple in their late 20s get pregnant, triggering a crisis when the guy isn't quite ready for this commitment. Set in Rome, and full of beautiful-people types that are drawn straight from reality.
- **Remember Me, My Love** (*Ricordati di Me*): (2003) A middle-aged couple have lost their passion. While their relationship is threatened by extramarital affairs, their teenage daughter will do anything to get a job as a showgirl on TV, and their son is spot-on portrait of the angst and idealism in youth.
- **The Son's Room** (*La Stanza del Figlio*): (2001) Oscar-winning director Nanni Moretti's wrenching, bittersweet drama about a Ligurian family that must cope with the drowning accident of their teenage son, and the psychoanalyst father's guilt over what he could have done to prevent it.

Priceless Italian Experiences (Cheap!)

Some of the most memorable things you can do when traveling in Italy won't cost you a dime. The Italians don't capitalize on their attractions as we would in the U.S., which means that many of the most important artistic and architectural attractions in Italy are readily visible just by walking down the street. If you're on a tight budget, try to avoid getting sucked into trendy clubs. Instead, spend your night drinking wine on a piazza—it'll be more authentic and certainly a hell of a lot cheaper.

Most attractions will offer discounts to college students and the like. Always mention any discount cards that you may have. ISIC Cards, AAA, college IDs, etc., can save you a bundle.

What Do I Do When Everything's Closed?

→ **Wander . . .** Sometimes the best experiences in Italy can be those that are uncharted and unplanned. Wander the city you're in, and enjoy this sense of mystery, but always make sure you know how to get home!

→ **Angels in the Architecture . . .** Find the major architectural attractions in your city and go on a treasure hunt. Many of Italy's most famous pieces of art are scattered through its streets. There is no charge to look, so keep your eyes open and discover that which defines the beauty of so many Italian cities.

→ **People-Watching . . .** Some of the best people-watching in Italy is right in the middle of a piazza. Sit back, relax, and enjoy the view. There is plenty to see! This is also a perfect opportunity to study your travel guide and chart out your next adventure.

→ **Get on the Bus, Gus . . .** It doesn't have to be an official tour. Just take a public bus through the city. You'll get a great view at very little expense (1€ or so). Just make sure to validate your ticket, as authorities do ticket checks and give out fines at random.

→ **Church Hopping . . .** Italy is known for its unlimited supply of *chiesas* that are almost always open during the day. You will find some of the most amazing medieval and Renaissance architecture and experience the true essence of Italy in these churches, as the Italian state is still very integrated with the rule of the Church.

→ **Go to Mass . . .** Even if you are not Catholic, you can still appreciate the spirituality in an Italian Catholic mass. These masses are very much the same way they were hundreds of years ago and will help you feel connected to the Italian culture and history.

→ **Go on a Photo Hunt . . .** Wait for that moment when the sun sets behind the Arno or the Colosseum illuminates! It's worth a thousand words, and the memory is priceless.

FOOD & DRINK

○ Order the house wine by the half bottle or bottle. It is usually the most inexpensive wine on the menu, but not at the expense of taste. You'll find the most delicious wines in Italy are already on the table.

○ Buy a bottle of wine and take it with you. Yes, open containers are permitted on the streets in Italy. Sitting on a bench with a pal and a bottle of wine can a good way to pass hours of downtime. Just remember to be respectful, as this is a privilege of the Italian culture and should not be abused.

○ A trattoria is a less expensive version of the standard *ristorante*. If you eat every meal at a trattoria, your taste buds won't complain. Most Italian food is made fresh with vegetables that would laugh at the preservatives we use in the U.S. if they could. Except in the densest tourist areas, it's hard to find a bad meal in Italy.

○ Grab some fruit, vegetables or a nice focaccia at one of Italy's endless outdoor markets—this makes for a satisfying and cheap snack or meal.

○ Stop in at a deli *(alimentari)* and have them make up a sandwich for you. Prosciutto, mortadella, and salami, as well as

Don't Get Bogged Down in the Bathroom!

When nature calls, whether in your hotel, restaurant or a public place, you might think you know what to do . . . but there are cultural differences between North American "restrooms" and Italian *bagnos*. For example:

→ Many bathroom light switches in Italy are set to timers. Make sure you know where the switch is located in case you find you're suddenly doing business in the dark!

→ Many toilets in Italy are flushed by pulling down on a cord. Make sure you hold it down long enough and let gravity do its thing.

→ Toilet seats in Italy are often narrower than those in the U.S., leaving more room for error. 'Nuff said.

→ The toilets in Italy don't fill up with water the same way they do here in the U.S. Neglecting the details, let's just say you should be respectful of the next user and use a toilet brush when necessary!

→ Sometimes there will be notes instructing you not to put paper in the toilet—although it may not be what you're used to, definitely put your paper waste in the trash as requested, or risk triggering an international incident.

a whole slew of cheeses, make great fillings for a picnic lunch.

SHOPPING, SIGHTSEEING, ETC.

○ Don't be afraid to bargain in one of Italy's outdoor markets. You'll find everything from leather coats to Italian trinkets, all for a negotiable price.

○ Don't phone home; use the 'net to keep in touch with friends and family. Although there is a fee for using the Internet at a cybercafe, the rates are much cheaper than an international mobile phone. Save yourself time and send a mass e-mail, bcc'ing the recipients—your friends and family will understand! You can also post a blog about your adventures abroad. You can even get crazy and send postcards!

○ **Walk!** The cheapest and often most enjoyable way to get around is to walk. It might be a novel idea for some Americans, but it's a great way to enjoy all that Italian cities have to offer.

Festivals & Holidays: What's Open? Santo *Who?*

You're in Catholic country now, so keep in mind that on local feast days, many shops, museums, and government offices close down completely, and in many cases, have a great big party that's a lot of fun. See the list below to make sure you're in the right city at the right time.

HOLIDAYS

Offices and shops in Italy are closed on the following **national holidays:** January 1 (New Year's Day), Easter Monday, April 25 (Liberation Day), May 1 (Labor Day), August 15 (Assumption of the Virgin), November 1 (All Saints' Day), December 8 (Feast of the Immaculate Conception), December 25 (Christmas Day), and December 26 (Santo Stefano).

Closings are also observed in the following cities on **feast days** honoring their patron saints: Venice, April 25 (St. Mark); Florence, Genoa, and Turin, June 24 (St. John the Baptist); Rome, June 29 (Sts. Peter and

THE BASICS

The Most Important Planning You'll Do:

→ Plan to spend a day walking through the city without a map. Plan to wander and you will discover the kinds of treasures that only Italy can hide.

→ Plan to order a house wine with dinner, let your taste buds dance, and stay there for hours.

→ Plan to shorten your stride and slow down your pace. You're in no rush, so act like an Italian and enjoy life at its slowest.

→ Plan to meet Italians. One of the easiest ways to learn about a country is to spend time with its people. Italy's people are its warmest and finest assets.

→ Plan to stare out the window as you travel by train. There's no better front row seat to some of the most beautiful countryside in the world.

→ Plan to take pictures, but not too many. Italians live in the moment. Forget about the future or the past, take heed and enjoy your present as much as possible.

→ Plan to eat.

→ Plan to fall in love. Be it with an Italian, a city, or a meal, you can't help but feel the love that dominates this culture.

→ Plan to come back again!

Paul); Palermo, July 15 (St. Rosalia); Naples, September 19 (St. Gennaro); Bologna, October 4 (St. Petronio); Cagliari, October 30 (St. Saturnino); Trieste, November 3 (St. Giusto); Bari, December 6 (St. Nicola); and Milan, December 7 (St. Ambrose).

Convince Them You're Italian!

○ Don't wait for your waiter to bring you a check. The Italians will never rush your meal, so take your time, enjoy your food, and remember you must **ask for the check when you are ready.**

○ **Wear tight jeans**—boys, that means you too! Italians wear their designer jeans with little room for error. Lose those baggy Abercrombies and pull on the more snug alternative.

○ **Drink lots and lots of wine.** Common knowledge reminds us that wine is a standard accompaniment to a fine meal in Italy. Order the house wine, and you'll be right on par with the native Italians. Be

merry, but remain civilized. The Italians love their wine, but you rarely see a mass of drunken debauchery in the street. A drunken display will always give you away as a tourist!

○ **The double kiss:** When greeting your fellow Italians, dive right into a kiss on their right and a kiss on their left. Men greet each other this way as well, so don't be afraid to let go of your machismo and start kissing!

○ **Take a breather and grab an *aperativo*.** Many Italians enjoy an aperativo after work and before dinner. Stop for a cocktail and some light appetizers (usually free during this time). Dinner is late in Italy, so this will tide you over!

○ Just because you're American, doesn't mean you need to travel with a Jansport or American Tourister bag! **Pick up an Invikta bag,** and take the Italians for a ride.

Rome & Lazio

Rome is tough to sum up in words, but when Italians talk about Rome, the word they use over and over is *fascino*. *Fascino* is a noun—derived from the Latin verb "to bind"—that doesn't translate perfectly into English, but it's a sort of cross between fascination, captivation, charm, and wonder—something that transcends beauty and inexplicably tugs on your heart.

First of all, Rome is the most visually impressive city in the world—it's an AK-47 of art and architecture that never stops firing ruins, fountains, churches, sculptures, frescoes, or spectacular green vistas into your sightlines. The Eternal City has been around for 2,800 years, after all, and you'd better believe she has a lot to show for it. That the splendors of Rome are all a bit rough around the edges only adds to the romance. Anyone with an ounce of nostalgia for the days of chariot races and gladiators will reel before the ruins of imperial Rome. The churches and fountains of Renaissance and baroque Rome amaze and delight all with their sheer scale, inventiveness, and richness of material.

Between the postcard sights, modern Roman life is played out on cobblestoned piazzas and narrow alleys. Sexy women flash by on Vespas, and gorgeous men pause to smoke a cigarette and read the newspaper, both aware of their place in the urban tableau. Coffee, food, and wine are at every turn, and the low-attitude bars and restaurants of Rome will welcome you. In its aesthetic and hedonistic generosity, there's a sunniness—a smiling, offhand manner—to Rome that gets under your skin the more time you spend here. The undulating topography of the seven-hilled city reverberates with history and the ensemble of so many sensory impressions rocks your soul like early U2.

Rome is sublime, but for many who travel here, it's not love at first sight. Beyond the glories of ancient Rome and the treasures of the Renaissance and baroque, Rome is still a metropolis of three million. The traffic, chaos, and grit that go along with being a big city are enough to turn off plenty of people who whisk through Rome, stopping only to snap pictures at the obligatory sights, and then board a train out of town. As hectic as it seems on the surface, the soul of the city is laid-back (some might even say lazy)—the Romans don't particularly like how stressful their city can be, so they take measures to offset it. You should, too. Go for an *aperitivo* at an outdoor cafe before dinner, and spend a long time at the table once you get to your restaurant. Make an effort to adopt a Roman rhythm during your days here, and you'll get much more out of your visit than you would if you spent every last waking minute trying to tick off must-see monuments. The Vatican isn't going anywhere anytime soon, so if you miss the Sistine Chapel this time around, you can always come back. Most people do.

The Best of Rome

Best Example of Mad Engineering Skills

With its 43m-wide (141-ft.) hemispherical dome of poured concrete, the astonishing 1,900 year-old **Pantheon** (temple to all the gods) is the best preserved ancient building in all the European, Asian, and African lands that used to make up the Roman Empire. See p. 169.

Best "Take Me Back to Ancient Times" View

The ruins of Rome at night are truly, disarmingly spectacular. Gazing over the floodlit marble columns, arches, and walls of the Roman Forum, Palatine Hill, and Colosseum from the terraces of the **Capitoline Hill (Campidoglio)** is one of the most memorable moments you can have in all of Italy. See p. 144.

Best Pizzeria

For overall fun and food quality, I head for loud and lively **La Montecarlo** (p. 116) when I'm in Rome. As for the best-tasting pies in town, that prize goes to **Dar Poeta** (p. 115) in Trastevere—also a lot of fun, but expect a wait!

Best Place to Party

Every night, from 6:30 on, the indoor-outdoor wine bars and pubs on **Campo de' Fiori** (p. 128) fill up with young local and international revelers. The American bars on the Campo offer drink specials every night, and the Italian enotecas have glasses of wine that start at 1.55€. If clubs are more your scene, head for **Testaccio** (p. 137), where Via Galvani, Via di Monte Testaccio, and Via Zabaglia are packed to the gills with lounges and discos for all musical tastes and sexual orientations.

Best Cheap Hotel

The **Albergo Sole al Biscione,** near Campo de' Fiori, is where I stayed when I was a student, and it's still where I choose to stay today. It's not fancy, but it overflows with Roman charm—interior rooms have shutters that open onto a multilevel courtyard with pink stucco walls, plants, and faux antique statuary. Hang out on the terrace, catch up on postcards, and soak up the rays of the Roman *sole.* See p. 97.

Best Hotel for Pretending You're in *The Great Gatsby*

The scene at the subtly glamorous **Hotel Locarno** is like a time warp back to the early 20th century. The furnishings are stylish Art Nouveau pieces, and when you park your bicycle in the garden or stop at the hotel bar for a coffee, you'll rub elbows with the other fashionable guests, all of whom seem to be writers, artists, or directors. See p. 105.

Best Place to Knock Back a Brewsky

Touring the Vatican can be a stressful experience, but the good news is, they do sell beer at the museum snack bar. Before you walk into the Sistine Chapel to contemplate Michelangelo's world-famous ceiling, take the edge off at the **Bar Sistina** (p. 187) and crack open a can of Tuborg.

Best *Bella Gente* Bars

When you need a break from the boisterous masses at Campo de' Fiori, but you still want to go out and drink, put on some clean clothes and cool accessories and head for **Société Lutèce** (p. 133), near Piazza Navona, or Salotto 42 (p. 133), near the Pantheon. These relatively new bars have rapidly established themselves as the hippest *centro storico* hangouts for the *bella gente* ("beautiful people").

Best Street

A few kilometers south of the Colosseum, the old **Appian Way (Via Appia Antica)** offers a welcome glimpse of the rustic Rome that lies just outside the chaos of the *centro.* Visit the catacombs, breathe the rural air of ancient farmland mixed with the scent of pine trees, and tread the 2,300-year-old basalt flagstones of the "Queen of Roads." See p. 172.

Most Fun Modern Cultural Activity

Chances are, you'll spend most of your time staring at the remnants of ancient or Renaissance society, but to get a sense of what Romans are like today, you can't beat the soccer games of **AS Roma** and **SS Lazio** at the Stadio Olimpico. The fans' unbridled passion and theatrics make a day at the stadium a truly electric event that'll have you beaming from ear to ear (especially if the home team wins). See box, p. 198.

Best Day Trip

I could give you more offbeat suggestions (and I have), but **Tivoli** (p. 204) is still the most satisfying single-day trip you can take to escape the urban chaos of Rome. Just be sure to hit *both* of Tivoli's main attractions, the Renaissance fountain-frenzy of **Villa d'Este,** and the imperial playground-estate of **Hadrian's Villa,** with its inventive architecture and fantastic water features.

ROME & LAZIO

Getting There

By Air

Delta, Continental, and Alitalia all offer nonstop overnight flights from major airports on the East Coast of the U.S. to Rome. Other international carriers such as British Airways, Air France, Lufthansa, KLM, and Iberia offer service from the U.S. to Rome, with connections in London, Paris, Amsterdam, and Madrid, respectively. For phone numbers and websites, see the Planning chapter.

If you're coming to Rome from Milan or Venice, flying with an economy airline like **Air One** (☎ **199/207080;** www.flyairone.it) is only slightly more expensive than taking the train, and it's faster. From Sicily, air is the only sensible option into Rome. All major airline flights into Rome (even those from within Italy) arrive at the city's main airport, **Roma-Leonardo da Vinci** (known to most as **Fiumicino,** or FCO; 24-hr. flight info ☎ **06/65951**), on the coast, about 30km (19 miles) west of central Rome.

If you're originating your trip to Rome from within Europe, there are a number of discount airlines—RyanAir (www.ryanair.com) from London; easyJet (www.easyjet.com) from several airports in the U.K., Ireland, Germany, and Switzerland—that fly into Rome's smaller airport, **Roma-Ciampino (CIA),** about 20km (12 miles) south of central Rome.

The website for both airports, **www.adr.it**, provides all kinds of practical information including flight schedules, ground transportation options, and duty-free shopping opportunities. Rome's major airport, Fiumicino, is modern and airy and not as busy as you might think, which makes the whole arrivals process much more manageable than at other large European hubs. In true provincial fashion, however, most planes don't have jetways to get passengers into the terminal, but shuttle buses that meet the flights somewhere on the tarmac. (The unexpected benefit of this system, however, is that in the time it takes you to board one of these shuttles and be driven to the terminal, your checked bags will probably be waiting for you at the baggage carousel.) Once you've gotten your luggage, the Customs and immigration process is as casual as can be—bat your eyelashes at the checkpoint officers if you're cute or think you are, and you'll likely be waved through without even having to show your passport. (Women will notice that this is a theme during your trip with Italian law enforcement.)

If you've arrived in Rome without accommodations lined up (which we do not recommend), the **Hotel Reservation** office at Fiumicino, just outside the Customs area, is open from 7am to 10pm daily (☎ **06/699-1000**).

Getting into Town from the Airport

FROM FIUMICINO
By Taxi

The easiest way to get into town, of course, is by taxi. Official, metered taxis have the SPQR city emblem on their doors and must wait in a queue on the airport drive directly outside the terminal. Anyone offering you a "taxi" inside the terminal is an illegal tout who will probably end up charging you a good deal more than what an official cab will cost. The metered fare from Fiumicino to most destinations in central Rome should be around 40€, with a small supplement for each large piece of luggage (although some drivers waive this fee). Tip the driver exactly 5€. If you're in a group of two or three, you might as well spring for a cab, since three separate train-plus-other-transport fares will cost you almost as much.

By Train

Rail can also be a convenient way to get into town, and it's much cheaper than cab fare if you're by yourself. From the arrivals hall, follow the bilingual signs to the RAILWAY STATION, or FS. This will lead you through a number of corridors and escalators over the airport drive and parking lots to Fiumicino's indoor train station, which feels a bit like a Habitrail with its transparent wall panels and giant yellow hoops over the tracks. There are two train lines that connect Fiumicino with not-quite-downtown Rome—taxi or private transfer is the only way to get directly into the heart of town.

The most popular line with tourists is the **Leonardo Express,** which is a nonstop train to Rome's main train station, Roma-Termini,

OKKIO! When Your Luggage Misses Its Flight . . .

If your luggage doesn't immediately show up on the ol' baggage carousel, try not to freak out. Busy airports like London Heathrow and Paris–Charles de Gaulle are notorious about not getting checked bags to their connecting flights on time, so if you've flown through one of those cities, there's actually a better-than-we'd-like-to-admit chance that your luggage might not have made it onto your flight. The good news is, your bags aren't really "lost," just delayed. File a report at the office in the baggage claim hall—be prepared to give an address where your stuff can be delivered, and a phone number where you can be reached, when it does arrive in Rome (usually 6–10 hr. later). It sounds sketchy, I know, but this has happened to me several times, and someone from the airline has always shown up with my bag at the speci-fied address later that afternoon or evening. If you have any problems, you can call the Fiumicino airport luggage handling office at ☎ **06/6595-4252**, 24 hours a day.

on the eastern end of the city center. The trip takes 31 minutes and costs 9.50€, with trains departing every 20 minutes from 6:30am to 11:30pm. The other line, the **FM1** to **Fara Sabina** or **Orte,** is a nicer double-decker train used mostly by commuters and other locals but very few tourists. This train has a flat fee of 5€ and departs every 20 minutes from 6am to 11:30pm, making stops at several suburbs on its way toward the city center; in town, it stops at several of the city's secondary train stations but not Roma-Termini.

For either the Leonardo Express or the FM1, buy your tickets from the newsstand/ *tabacchi* at the airport train station, from the train station ticket window agents, or from the yellow self-service machines. Validate (time-stamp) your tickets at the little yellow stamping machines in front of the tracks. If you're staying at a hotel in the *centro storico* or Trastevere, take the FM1 train to Roma-Trastevere (22 min) and then take a cab to your hotel (6€–8€) or tram 8 (1€) to Largo Argentina—it'll be faster and almost cer-tainly cheaper than going through Termini station and backtracking. (Roma-Trastevere is kind of a crappy station, though, so watch out for junkies.) If you do take the Leonardo Express train to Termini, you can only walk

to your hotel from there if you're staying in the immediate area (which is seedy but cheap); otherwise you'll have to take a bus (no. 40 cuts through the *centro storico*), the metro (see "Getting Around," later in this chapter), or a taxi. The trains from the air-port take you past Rome's ugliest suburbs, which can be disheartening—but trust us, the scenery will get a *lot* better once you're off the train and in the thick of old Rome.

FROM CIAMPINO

Rome's secondary airport, Ciampino, is a tiny, single-runway affair with few amenities beyond a sometimes-open snack bar.

If you've flown into Ciampino, the easiest way to get into town is with the coach serv-ice run by **Terravision** (☎ **06/7949-4572;** www.terravision.it), whose schedule coin-cides with all RyanAir, easyJet, etc., arrivals. The bus drops you off on Via Marsala, on the north side of Termini train station. Tickets cost 8€ and can be purchased from the Terravision desk or uniformed staff inside the arrivals hall at Ciampino. The only down-side to the Terravision service is that they wait until everyone gets their luggage, so if you've only brought carry-on bags, you might have to wait an hour or so to get out of the airport.

ROME & LAZIO

Public transportation from Ciampino to central Rome is a two-part deal: first, take a blue **COTRAL** bus (1€) to Anagnina metro station, then take **metro Line A** (another 1€) from Anagnina to Termini or wherever you happen to be headed. (For more information about areas served by the metro, see "Getting Around," later in this chapter.)

By Train

If you're traveling to Rome from within mainland Italy (that is, not Sicily), rail is the most economical, efficient, and hassle-free option. Rome's principal train station, **Roma-Termini,** is a busy rail hub through which most of Italy's main train lines pass. There are also daily direct trains to Roma-Termini from Paris, Munich, and Vienna. Termini's location, on the less-than-gorgeous eastern end of town, makes for an unfortunate introduction to the city, but then again, when have you ever been to a train station that was in a nice part of town?

Keep in mind that it's not unusual for Italian trains (especially the regional lines) to run a few minutes to an hour behind schedule. The exception to this is the Eurostar, which almost always runs on time—Mussolini would have been proud. While trains that arrive and depart perfectly on schedule are also quite common, it's a good idea to build an extra hour or two into your schedule to accommodate such potential setbacks.

See the table below for an example of travel times and second-class prices to Rome from other popular Italian cities (times and prices also valid vice versa).

For more information about the national train system, see the Planning chapter, or consult Trenitalia's extremely handy multilingual website, **www.trenitalia.com**.

INFORMATION FOR RAIL PASS USERS

European rail passes are good for second-class travel on Italian **Intercity (IC)** trains as well as the sluggish *regionale* **(R)** and *diretto* **(D)** trains, but if you want to travel on Italy's express service, the **Eurostar (ES)**, you'll have to pay a supplement—consult the literature that comes with your pass for more details. Note also that all Eurostar tickets must be booked at least 24 hours in advance, which gets you an assigned seat.

By Car

Whereas Joe Average Ancient Roman could pull his horse-drawn chariot right into the city walls and park it next to the Colosseum, modern drivers will encounter more challenges—traffic rules have tightened up in the last 2,000 years. If you're driving into Rome, park your car at a lot several kilometers outside the heart of the old city.

Rome can be reached quite easily, via the *autostrada* (toll expressway, with green signs) or *strade statali* (SS, slower state highways, with blue signs), from any direction in Italy. Like spokes on a wheel, the 12 ancient *vie consolari* (consular roads) lead out from the city at every compass point. Just to name a few: the Via Aurelia (SS 1) goes west toward the coast and southern Tuscany; the Via

From	Fast Train/Price	Next Fastest Train/Price
Florence	ES 1 hr 40 min, 30€	IC 2 hr 30 min, 22€
Venice	ES 4 hr 30 min, 45€	IC 6 hr, 39€
Milan	ES 4 hr 30 min, 47€	IC 6 hr, 41€
Bologna	ES 2 hr 45 min, 37€	IC 4 hr, 31€
Naples	ES 1 hr 45 min, 22€	IC 2 hr, 17€

Termini: Station of Dreams

Throughout the year 1999, seedy Termini was shrouded in scaffolding and plastic sheeting as the station underwent its extreme makeover for the new millennium. Marketing banners over the station's main entrances promised that the new Termini would be "more beautiful than a rose," but locals were skeptical. But when work wrapped up in 2000, the miracle was revealed: What used to be a vagrants' squat had become a gleaming concourse—full of restaurants, shopping, and even a tanning salon—where you actually wouldn't mind hanging out. Among its many retail attractions, Termini boasts an excellent, three-level **Benetton**, a **Nike** shop, **Sephora, Foot Locker,** music and book stores, **Optissimo** (for great sunglasses), and a supermarket. There are 14 restaurants/cafes at the station: on the upper level, **Ciao-Autogrill** is good for no-frills Italian; on the Ala Termini side, **Moka Café** has a sleek lunch buffet. If you're down for some hot wings and a rib-eye steak, head for the **Roadhouse Grill,** on the Via Marsala side. We don't necessarily recommend Chinese fast food in Italy, but if you're looking for it, you'll find **Wok** on the lower level. Coolest of all, the **McDonald's** on the lower level has sizeable ruins of 5th-century B.C. Roman walls in its dining area. To see all that the radically revamped station has to offer, check out www.romatermini.it. Now, if they could only make the surrounding neighborhoods as beautiful as a rose, too. . . .

ROME & LAZIO

Flaminia (SS 3) goes north to Umbria and Romagna; the Via Tiburtina (SS 5) goes east to Tivoli; and the famous Via Appia (SS 7) goes south toward Naples and Campania.

Rome also lies a few kilometers west of the A1 *autostrada* that runs vertically through much of Italy, from Naples in the south to Milan in the north. Rome is also the western terminus of the A24 *autostrada,* which runs east across the mountains to Abruzzo, the Gran Sasso d'Italia national park, and the city of L'Aquila. Running north from the Rome, the A12 *autostrada* connects the Eternal City with the port of Civitavecchia to the north, where cruise ships and other industrial vessels dock.

Whether you're coming into Rome from the *autostrada* or the state highways, exit where you see the ROMA CENTRO signs. Once you're on city streets, always keep your eyes peeled for the white, bull's-eye CENTRO signs and drive slowly—if you miss a turn, it can be murder trying to pick up the trail again. Then again, it can be murder even if you do follow

all the signs correctly, so if you have a Valium or other nerve-calmer left over from the flight, now would be the time to take it. After a few kilometers of inching closer to the *centro,* you really need to start thinking about ditching that car, because you won't find a place to park it in the old city. Furthermore, you won't be allowed to drive your car into the old city due to heavy restrictions on nonresident traffic. On the south side of Termini, the **ES** lot at Via Giolitti 267 (☎ 06/4470-4073) charges 13€ for 24 hours. You'll also find a few large parking structures in the Via Veneto area (a bit west of Termini): the underground **ParkSì** lot at Villa Borghese, Viale del Galoppatoio (☎ 06/322-5934) charges 15€ per day; nearby, **Parking Ludovisi,** Via Ludovisi 60, off Via Veneto (☎ 06/474-0632), charges 18€ per day. On the other side of town, pricey **Terminal Gianicolo,** Piazza Rovere, near the Vatican (☎ 06/684-0331), charges 26€ for 24 hours, but it's convenient to the *centro storico* and Trastevere. There are also unattended *parcheggio di scambio* lots near the Tiburtina, Ponte Mammolo, and Rebibbia metro stations (all on the eastern outskirts) where you can leave your car (for 5€ per day) and then take the metro into central Rome, but the lots are not in the nicest parts of town. Whatever you do, get rid of that car and have someone hide the keys from you until you're ready to leave Rome for good.

How about driving a car *outside* the city? Well, that's another matter entirely. There are a number of great little day trips you can take from Rome (see "Road Trips: All Roads Lead from Rome . . .," at the end of this chapter), some of which are most conveniently reached by car. If you're traveling alone or with one other person, consider renting the popular Smart car, mainland Europe's smaller and more cartoonish analogue to the Mini Cooper (they have those here, too). Two-seater Smarts are tiny, fuel-efficient, and shockingly chic. On the south side of Termini station, **Happy Rent,** Via Farini 3, at Via Cavour (☎ 06/481-8185; www.happyrent. com), will rent you a Smart for 75€/24 hours. A slightly more economical option, Fiat hatchbacks are available for 50€ from 9am–7pm. The **Maggiore** rental car agency (www.maggiore.it; worldwide partner of Alamo and National) has an office at Termini station at Via Giolitti 34 (☎ 06/488-0049; Mon–Fri 7am–8pm, Sat 8am–6pm, and Sun 8am–1pm) and at Fiumicino airport (☎ 06/ 6501-0678; daily 7am–midnight). All the other major players, like **Avis** (www.avis. com; ☎ 06/6501-1531) and **Hertz** (www. hertz.com; ☎ 06/6501-1553), have offices at

Fiumicino airport, Termini station (Avis: Via Giolitti 34, ☎ 06/481-4373; Hertz: Via Giolitti 34, ☎ 06/474-0389). Both agencies also have offices near Via Veneto (Avis: Via Sardegna 38A, ☎ 06/4282-4728; Hertz: Via Sardegna 35, ☎ 06/4290-4022). Hertz is also at the Villa Borghese underground parking lot (Viale del Galoppatoio 33; ☎ 06/321-6886).

By Bus

There's really no reason to take a bus to Rome, as every Italian city is connected to Rome by train, which is always more comfortable, faster, and more affordable. If, for some reason, you do get on some kind of national or international coach to Rome, it'll most likely drop you off at Tiburtina train station, on the eastern outskirts. From here, take metro Line B toward the center (in the direction of Laurentina) or bus 492.

The only other reason you might take a bus to Rome is if you're coming from a small town in Lazio or the Roman countryside. Regional bus service is operated by COTRAL (www.cotralspa.it); in the city, COTRAL terminals are outside several metro stations. From Lepanto metro station (Line A), near the Vatican, there are buses to the Etruscan necropolis of **Cerveteri** and the castle and low-key beach at **Santa Marinella;** from Cornelia metro station (Line A), you can catch a bus to the beach resort of **Fregene.** From Ponte Mammolo metro station (Line B), you can take a bus to **Tivoli** (Hadrian's Villa and Villa d'Este), and from Laurentina metro station (Line B), there are buses south to chic beach destinations like **Sabaudia** and **San Felice Circeo,** both of which are impossible to reach by train.

Rome Orientation

For a Roman, the *centro* is a much larger area than the average visitor needs to be concerned with. Most of the sights you'll want to see are within a rather compact swath of land that doesn't have a name that anyone agrees

on but stretches somewhat amorphously from the Vatican in the west to Termini station in the east, and from Piazza del Popolo and Villa Borghese in the north to the archaeological park of the Baths of Caracalla in the south. The five major roads in this zone—Via del Corso, Via Nazionale, Via dei Fori Imperiali, Via del Teatro di Marcello, and Corso Vittorio Emanuele—converge at Piazza Venezia, the busy traffic roundabout at the geographic center of Rome.

Most of historic Rome lies on the east side of the Tiber river, which snakes its way from north to south, crossed by 12 bridges, in the *centro*. The medieval Trastevere neighborhood, Vatican City, and Castel Sant'Angelo lie on the west side of the river. The *centro storico* is a confusing term, since most of Rome is "historic;" but the *centro storico* proper is the mostly flat territory between the eastern bank of the Tiber's C-shaped bend and Via del Corso, and includes such famous places at Piazza Navona, the Pantheon, Campo de' Fiori, and the Jewish Ghetto.

South of Piazza Venezia, the tangled and narrow streets of the *centro storico* give way to the open boulevards and green hills of ancient Rome's archaeological sites, including the Roman Forum and the Colosseum. North of the *centro storico* and east of Via del Corso is the so-called Tridente (Italians don't really use this term), the poshest part of central Rome, where you'll find the Spanish Steps and Piazza del Popolo. On the hill northeast of the Tridente is the Villa Borghese, central Rome's largest public park; south of it is Via Veneto and its luxury hotels. The Viminale and Quirinale hills, between Piazza Venezia and Termini, are less picturesque, with smog-stained offices and government buildings. The areas immediately surrounding Termini station are the seediest, least charming parts of central Rome, but they're also where you'll find most of the budget accommodations. Halfway down the Esquilino hill, south of Termini, is the delightful medieval Monti neighborhood, which ends at the Colosseum.

Within the areas described above, the longest distance you might cover in any one stretch, from Termini train station in the east to the Vatican in the west, for instance, is about a leisurely 1-hour walk. Major sights are so close to each other, however, that you'll often be walking less than a quarter of a mile between stops.

The Breakdown: What to Expect in Each 'Hood

➜ *Centro Storico* Despite the name, and the fact that it's one of the most artistically rich square miles in the world, this isn't actually the most touristy part of Rome (though it's up there). Nestled within the eastern curve of the Tiber's C-shaped bend, and crudely severed by the fascist-era Corso Vittorio Emanuele, the *centro storico* is a picturesque network of crooked, uneven cobblestone streets and ochre-washed palazzi that occasionally open up to magnificent public spaces like Piazza Navona or awesome ancient monuments like the Pantheon. Many of the backstreets here are slightly unkempt, which is an appealing contrast to the well-groomed blocks of the Tridente (Spanish Steps) area to the northeast. Every other business in the *centro storico* is a down-to-earth bar or neighborhood trattoria, although there are plenty of chic boutiques and more upscale bars and restaurants have joined the fray in recent years. The area around Campo de' Fiori, with its daytime produce market and evening "meat market," is more rough-and-ready than the more gentrified Piazza Navona and Pantheon areas, north of Corso Vittorio Emanuele. East of Via Arenula is the old Jewish Ghetto, which is a quieter, more residential zone where you can sample Roman Jewish cuisine. The *centro storico* is also the best place in town to get in on Rome's infectious, easygoing nightlife; the casual alfresco bars around Campo de' Fiori and the streets west of Piazza Navona are humming with young locals 7 days a week.

➜ **Spanish Steps (aka the Tridente)** This is the high-rent slice of the *centro,* home to

Rome Neighborhoods

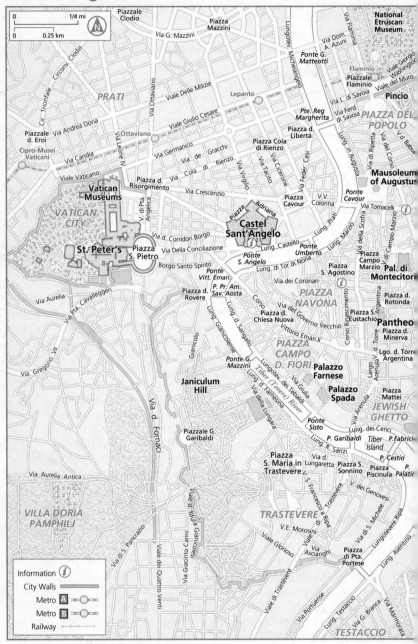

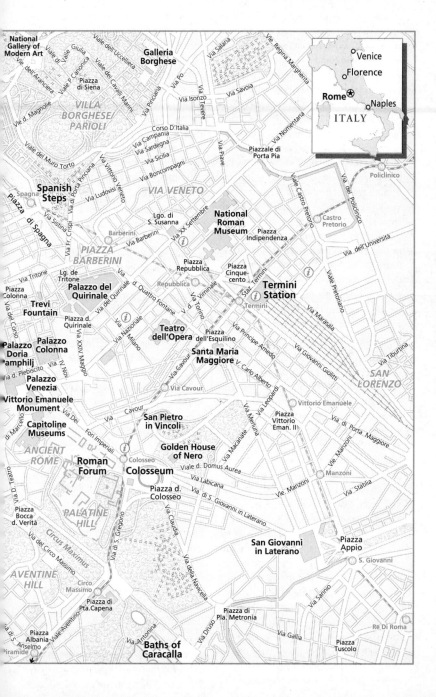

National
Gallery of
Modern Art

Galleria
Borghese

Viale dell'Uccelliera
Viale P. Canonica
Viale di Villa Giulia
Viale dei Cavalli Marini
Viale dell'Aranciera
Vie dell'Aranciera

Piazza
di Siena

Via Salaria

Via Po

Via Pinciana

Viale Regina Margherita

Via Savoia

Via Nomentana

Via d. Magnolie

VILLA
BORGHESE/
PARIOLI

Corso D'Italia

Via Campania
Via Sardegna
Via Sicilia

Piazzale di
Porta Pia

Policlinico

Viale del Muro Torto

Via Boncompagni

Via Piave

Viale Castro Pretorio

Via del Policlinico

Spanish
Steps

Spagna

Piazza
di Spagna

Via di Porta Pinciana
Via Vittorio Veneto
Via Ludovisi

VIA VENETO

Lgo. di
S. Susanna

Via XX Settembre

National
Roman
Museum

Piazza
Indipendenza

Via dell'Università

Via Fr. Crispi
Via Sistina

Barberini

Via Barberini

(i)

Via dei Pretoriano

Castro
Pretorio

PIAZZA
BARBERINI

Piazza
Repubblica

Piazza
Cinque-
cento

(i)

Via Tritone

Lg. de
Tritone

Via d. Quattro Fontane

Repubblica

Via Viminale

Termini
Station

Viale Pretoriano

Piazza
Colonna

Trevi
Fountain

Palazzo del
Quirinale

Via del Quirinale

Via del Corso

Piazza d.
Quirinale

(i)

Via Nazionale

Via Torino

Termini

Via Marsala

Palazzo
Doria
amphilj

Palazzo
Colonna

Via XXIV Maggio

Via Milano

Teatro
dell'Opera

Piazza
dell'Esquilino

Via Principe Amedo

Via Giovanni Giolitti

Via Tiburtina

Via d. Plebiscito

Via N. Nov.

Palazzo
Venezia

Santa Maria
Maggiore

V. Carlo Alberto

SAN
LORENZO

Vittorio Emanuele
Monument

Via Dei

Cavour

Via Cavour

Vittorio Emanuele

Via Cavour

di Marcello

Capitoline
Museums

Via

Fori Imperiali

Piazza
Vittorio
Eman. II

Via di Porta Maggiore

Vie. Manzoni

ANCIENT
ROME

(i)

San Pietro
in Vincoli

Via Merulana

Via Macanate

Manzoni

Via Statilia

Roman
Forum

Colosseo

Golden House
of Nero

Colosseum

Viale d. Domus Aurea

Vie. Manzoni

Via D. Teatro

Piazza
Bocca
d. Verità

Piazza d.
Colosseo

Via Labicana

Via di S. Giovanni in Laterano

Manzoni

PALATINE
HILL

Via di S. Gregorio

Via Claudia

Via della Navicella

Circus Maximus

San Giovanni
in Laterano

Piazza
Appio

Via del Circo Massimo

AVENTINE
HILL

Circo
Massimo

S. Giovanni

Viale Aventino

Piazza di
Pta.Capena

Via Sannio

Via di S.
Anselmo

Piazza
Albania

Piazza di
Pla. Metronia

Re Di Roma

Piramide

Via Antonina

Baths of
Caracalla

Via Druso

Via Gallia

Piazza
Tuscolo

Venice

Florence

Rome ✺

Naples

ITALY

the vast, sun–drenched squares of Piazza del Popolo and Piazza di Spagna (the Spanish Steps), and between them, all the designer boutiques you could possibly imagine. The southwestern part of the Tridente is essentially an extension of the *centro storico,* with wonderful dog-legging alleys that feel like a time warp to the 16th century. The area south of Via del Tritone is hopelessly tourist-infested, thanks to the presence of the magnificent Trevi Fountain. The Tridente is not particularly strong on dining or partying options; the best bets are on the west side of Via del Corso, on the cafe-filled Piazza San Lorenzo in Lucina, and especially at the trendy 'Gusto conglomerate of bars and restaurants on Piazza Augusto Imperatore. (Note that the name "Tridente," derived from the three streets that extend like a pitchfork south of Piazza del Popolo, is not used by locals. They refer to this area by its major squares—Piazza di Spagna, Piazza del Popolo, Piazza Augusto Imperatore.)

➜ **Trastevere**   Derived from the Latin *trans tiberim* ("across the Tiber"), this is the pocket of old Rome that lies south of the Vatican on the western side of the river's S-shaped curve. It has the same ochre-washed, ivy-covered walls and cobblestoned streets as the *centro storico* but fewer large piazzas and almost no famous monuments, as well as an independent, community atmosphere that gives it extra charm. Piazza Santa Maria in Trastevere is the heart of Trastevere; from here to Piazza Trilussa (Ponte Sisto) is the most picturesque section, with tons of places to eat and drink heartily—in fact, Trastevere gets almost too crowded in the evenings! West of busy Viale Trastevere is the quieter, more workaday part of Trastevere. Although it has plenty of modern influences, Trastevere is still the place in Rome where you can come and feel like you're in a different era—especially by day, when old men haul around carts of fruit, and when you can peek in the open doors of old-world workshops where

carpenters craft table legs by hand and marble workers restore ancient-looking sculptures. If you're born a *trasteverina,* you marry a *trasteverino,* and you probably live your whole life in the same building no more than a block from your parents, if not in the same building. The tree-lined ridge to the west of low-lying Trastevere is the Gianicolo (Janiculum Hill), de rigueur for its panoramic views back over the *centro.* Beyond it lies the enormous Villa Pamphilj, the city's largest public park, great for hiking, picnicking, and relaxing with real Romans.

➜ **Ancient Rome, Monti & the Celio** South and east of busy Piazza Venezia, you'll find a mix of phenomenally impressive ancient ruins, gorgeous green hills, and cozy medieval streets (in the Monti district, north of Via dei Fori Imperiali). Between Via dei Fori Imperiali and Via del Circo Massimo is the monumental archaeological zone where you'll no doubt spend several hours climbing over fallen columns in the Forum, over crumbling brick walls on the Palatine, or up the stairs of the *vomitoria* at the Colosseum. Make sure you return to this staggeringly history-soaked part of town at night, when the glories of ancient Rome are spectacularly floodlit (but not in a cheesy, *son-et-lumière* show way). Just northeast of here, Monti straddles either side of ugly Via Cavour and is home to the best expat-frequented pubs in Rome, making it a good nighttime destination if you just want to speak English, drink some beer, and watch a European football game. The Celio, which is the hill directly south of the Colosseum, has a grid of streets with some lively eateries (including Isidoro, our favorite pasta-sampling joint) and a few pubs; the rest of the Celio is occupied by rustic ancient churches and the lovely "green lung" of Villa Celimontana park.

➜ **Termini/Esquilino**   The area around the train station is a popular place to crash because it's home to (a) about 75% of the city's hotels, and (b) almost all of the budget sleeps.

Trouble is, it's downright seedy (where drunk vagrants far outnumber real Romans), and its grimy blocks are so far removed from the charm of the Rome we know and love that, if you stay here, you'll likely walk away from Rome with the wrong impression of what the city and its people are all about. We strongly suggest you pay a little extra to be closer to the heart of things, which means heading west from the station. While there are tons of accommodations options around Termini, strangely, there are almost no authentic places to eat. (You'll find curry and shawerma and other kinds of fastfood purveyors galore, however.) The northern side of the station is slightly nicer than the southern side (Esquilino), but the advantage of the southern side is that the seediness gives way relatively quickly to the more attractive and authentic Monti neighborhood (around the bottom of Via Cavour) and the sights of ancient Rome.

→**Via Veneto & the Quirinale** The wide, slalom curve of tree-lined Via Veneto descends from the Villa Borghese park to the traffic and public transportation hub of Piazza Barberini. In the 1950s and 1960s, fabulous Hollywood types partied at the Art Nouveau cafes here, and their decadent lifestyle inspired Federico Fellini's classic film *La Dolce Vita.* Roman showbiz has-beens and the wealthy tourists who check into the luxury hotels here are desperately trying to hang onto some of that glamorous mystique, but for the most part, Via Veneto is beautiful but vapid, like a Jessica Simpson who's past her prime. At the bottom of the street is the church of Santa Maria della Concezione, famous for the bizarre and macabre Crypt of the Capuchin Monks. The Quirinale hill, just south of here, is mostly government buildings, with several interesting baroque churches, but little in the way of eating or drinking until you reach the western edge, which leads down to the Trevi Fountain.

→**The Vatican & Prati** The western side of Ponte Vittorio Emanuele, right across the river from the *centro storico,* marks the beginning of Via della Conciliazione, the bombastic fascist-era boulevard that leads straight to Piazza San Pietro. St. Peter's is the only part of the Vatican that greets the city with open arms; the rest of the papal state is a recluse within fortresslike 16th-century brick walls. The only other major monument on this side of the river is Castel Sant'Angelo, whose massive rotund form presides over the Tiber like a barrel-chested security guard. Between Castel Sant'Angelo and the Vatican is the medieval Borgo district, a small lattice of streets with some cute, if touristy, bars and restaurants. North of here begins the Prati district, where many upper-middle-class Romans who can't deal with the nonsense of the historic center choose to live. Prati has wider streets, block after block of repetitive 19th-century *palazzi,* and all the good shops and services that you'd expect in a more well-to-do residential area. Via Cola di Rienzo is the main commercial drag, with department stores and smaller fashion boutiques, a supermarket, and some of the city's best delis. There are also a number of reasonably priced accommodations options in Prati and some excellent live music venues. Restaurants and pubs aren't the first thing that come to mind when you think of Prati, but there are actually some good spots to be found—with few exceptions, the nightlife scene is pretty mellow.

→**Roma Nord: Parioli & Flaminio** Venture north of Piazza del Popolo, and boldly go where no tourists (or at least very few) have gone before. Tram 2 plies the Via Flaminia from Piazzale Flaminio almost as far as the ancient Ponte Milvio (site of the A.D. 312 battle where Constantine, guided by the sign of the cross, killed his co-emperor Maxentius and later legalized Christianity). Along the way, there are several refreshingly modern cultural attractions to visit, including the new 21st-century art space, MAXXI (not open at presstime but you can still walk in and check out its progress), and the much-hyped Auditorium, an impressive new center for the performing arts. Across the pedestrian-only Ponte Milvio, north of the Tiber, is the no-frills drink shack known as the Chioschetto (p. 131), one of Rome's hottest gathering places for young locals. A bit downriver, on the west side of the Tiber, is the Stadio Olimpico, where you can (and absolutely should) catch a Roma or Lazio soccer game if they're in town. Moving eastward, onto the rolling hills north of Villa Borghese, you'll find Rome's most prestigious

residential area, Parioli, a rare pocket of town where SUVs outnumber Fiat hatchbacks and Smarts. Non-Romans might not get why it's so fabulous to be from here, as parts of it are frankly ugly, but a Parioli address is the ultimate status symbol in this city. (If you live here, it goes without saying that you have a *Filipina* maid and a summer house in Sardinia.) The main street, Viale Parioli—referred to by some as "the new Via Veneto"—has some very chic boutiques and a few restaurants that are great fun, including Duke's and Celestina.

Getting Around

By Motor Scooters *(Motorini)*

Rome is the ultimate *motorino* city. Renting a Vespa or other model scooter while in town is an activity I cannot recommend highly enough. While most distances in the tourist center are easily covered on foot, a *motorino* gives you near-instant access to farther-flung sights. Furthermore, the weather is usually so pleasant and the boulevards so scenic that riding a scooter in Rome is not only a practical but a ridiculously fun way to get around. Most outsiders, however, take one look at the traffic situation in the city and abandon any Vespa fantasies they might have been nurturing. However, it's really not as dangerous as it looks.

Motorini are light and easily maneuverable—you'll get the hang of it after a little practice—and you can always just go slowly on the side of the road until you're feeling more confident. Best of all, there are just so many *motorini* on the streets of Rome that if you're ever in doubt about driving etiquette, you can just let the *motorino* in front of you clear the path. Technically, there are parking laws in Rome that apply to *motorini,* but you can pretty much park anywhere—again, follow the example of locals and see where they're parking.

Before you set out, practice parking—rolling and lifting the bike onto its kickstand takes some strength, but it's more about finesse. Don't drive in the rain; when water mixes with the oil on the roads, the cobblestones get precariously slippery. Finally, have someone at the rental agency mark the nearest gas stations on your map—you'll need to bring the bike back with a full-ish tank.

Rental outfits provide helmets (which you are required by law to wear), chain locks (always a good idea, unless you're just stopping for a few minutes somewhere), and insurance (leave the documents in the compartment beneath the seat—you'll need to show them in the unlikely event you have a run-in with the police).

My favorite *motorino* rental agency in Rome is **Roma Rent,** Vicolo dei Bovari 7a (☎ **06/689-6555**), near Campo de' Fiori. Ask for one of the orange Vespas—not only are they cool looking, but their bright color will make you more visible in traffic, and they don't have the agency name embarrassingly emblazoned all over the chassis (as at some other rental agencies). Rates for a 50cc scooter start at 35€ a day (9am–7pm); and 42€ per 24-hour period. On the north side of Termini, **Eco Move Rent,** Via Varese 48–50, near Via Marghera (☎ **06/4470-4518;**

Where to Get Off When Your Destination Doesn't Have Its Own Stop

It seems like Rome's most famous piazzas and fountains do not lie directly on any bus, tram, or metro line; instead, they're in medieval neighborhoods where the streets are too narrow for buses or trams. However, these sights are usually only a few blocks from streets or piazzas where public transport is plentiful:

Campo de' Fiori: Take bus 30 Express, 40 Express, 87, or 492, or tram 8 to Largo Argentina; take bus 64 or 571 to the "Navona" stop on Corso Vittorio Emanuele (in front of McDonald's); or take bus 23, 271, or 280 to Lungotevere dei Vallati or Lungotevere dei Tebaldi (or Lungotevere della Farnesina, and walk across Ponte Sisto).

Pantheon: Take bus 30 Express, 40 Express, 64, 70, 87, 492, or 571, or tram 8 to Largo Argentina; or take bus 85 or 175 to the "Minghetti" stop on Via del Corso. Alternatively, the 116 electric minibus stops right in front of the Pantheon.

Piazza Navona: Take bus 40 Express to Largo Argentina; take bus 30 Express, 70, 87, 116, or 492 to Corso Rinascimento; or take bus 64 or 571 to the "Navona" stop on Corso Vittorio Emanuele (in front of McDonald's).

Trevi Fountain: Take bus 116, 175, or 492 to Via del Tritone; or take bus 85, 175, or 492 to the "Minghetti" stop on Via del Corso.

Trastevere: None of the interior of this charming neighborhood across the Tiber is served by public transportation, but you can still get pretty close. Tram 8, bus 780, and bus H travel on Viale Trastevere, the busy avenue that divides Trastevere into northern and southern halves. Buses 23, 271, and 280 travel on the *lungotevere* (riverside drive) that runs along Trastevere's eastern edge. If you're traveling south, on the western side of the Tiber river, get off at Lungotevere Farnesina/Trilussa for the action of northern Trastevere; get off at Lungotevere degli Alberteschi/Piscinula for the sleepier southern side of Trastevere. If you're traveling north, on the eastern side of the river, take buses 23, 271, or 280 and get off at Piazza di Monte Savello, then cross Tiber Island to southern Trastevere; or get off at Lungotevere dei Vallati and cross Ponte Sisto to the northern part of Trastevere.

www.ecomoverent.com), has easy-to-drive 50cc Vespas, MBK Ovettos, and Aprilia Habanas. Rates are 25€ for 4 hours, or 37€ for a 24-hour period. On the south side of Termini, **Happy Rent,** Via Farini 3, off Via Cavour (☎ **06/481-8185;** www.happyrent. com), has 50cc scooters for 33€ a day (9am–7pm) or 38€ per 24-hour period. If you're going to get a motorino, you might as well keep it for a few days, as it can be a hassle when you're worrying about getting it

back on time. At any agency, if you're renting for several days and/or you can pay in cash, ask about any discounts they might have.

By Public Transportation

Buses, trams, and the *metropolitana* subway (aka *la metro*) are run by ATAC (www.atac. roma.it). If you're staying in the *centro storico,* you'll be able to walk to most sights and restaurants, but chances are you'll need to take a bus, tram, metro, or some combination thereof, during your stay in Rome. If your

The Cemetery Express

Almost all buses in Rome are known by their route numbers, but a few have letters of the alphabet. The "H" bus (for hospital) connects the western suburbs with Stazione Termini, stopping at several major medical centers en route. In a depressing illustration of what sometimes happens to those who check into hospitals, Rome recently launched a new set of "C" bus lines—nine in all—which serve all the major cemeteries in town!

hotel is not in the heart of town, you'll be utilizing public transportation quite a bit, so get familiar with how it works. First of all, bear in mind that Rome is not London, New York, or Paris, where efficient underground systems get you within blocks of everywhere you want to go. Instead, Rome is a bus town, with a few handy and scenic tram lines thrown into the mix. Yes, Rome does have a subway, but it's a dinky two-line system, and getting in and out of the stations—especially Termini—can be unpleasant and time-consuming, so **wherever possible, we recommend you take the bus or tram instead of the metro.** In general, the stations along metro Line B are less of a hassle than on Line A. When the ATAC workers aren't on strike, the system actually runs quite well. Once you master a few key route numbers, you'll be able to get around comfortably and relatively quickly. All bus and tram lines do basically the same route in reverse, although some are modified by a few blocks due to one-way traffic restrictions.

USEFUL BUS LINES

Express buses are green, double-length, air-conditioned vehicles; most other buses are red and also air-conditioned. When buses are orange, they're bumpy and without A/C.

30 Express Runs from EUR in the south to Prati in the north, by way of Piramide and Via Marmorata (for Testaccio), Via Petroselli (for the Jewish Ghetto, the Mouth of Truth, and the Circus Maximus), Largo Argentina (for the Pantheon and Campo de' Fiori), Corso Rinascimento (for Piazza Navona), and Piazza Cavour (about a 15-min. walk to the Vatican).

40 Express Runs from Termini to St. Peter's, by way of Via Nazionale, Piazza Venezia, Largo Argentina (for the Pantheon and Campo de' Fiori), Corso Vittorio Emanuele (for Piazza Navona), and Castel Sant'Angelo. This double-length bus is a favorite of tourists, religious pilgrims, and anyone else who needs to travel east-west in the heart of Rome. "Express" means it makes only about a third of the stops that regular buses on the same route make. Air-conditioned.

64 Does pretty much the same route as the 40 Express, but makes many more stops and is almost always packed (i.e., you won't get a seat) with gypsies and perverts and smelly people. Only take the 64 in a pinch, and watch your back!

87 Connects the San Giovanni area with Prati (near the Vatican), by way of the Colosseum, Piazza Venezia, Largo Argentina (Pantheon and Campo de' Fiori), and Corso Rinascimento (Piazza Navona).

175 Runs from Termini to Stazione Ostiense, by way of Via del Tritone (for the Spanish Steps and Trevi Fountain), Via del Corso, the Colosseum, Circus Maximus, the Aventine, and Piramide (for Testaccio and trains to the beach at Ostia). The old orange buses need new shocks, but they're usually empty except for a few cute old people, and you can see a bunch of monuments as you ride. Not air-conditioned.

492 Runs from Stazione Tiburtina to Cipro metro station, by way of San Lorenzo, Castro Pretorio, Termini, Piazza Barberini (for Via Veneto), Via del Tritone (for the Spanish Steps and Trevi Fountain), Piazza

Rome *Metropolitana*

Battistini · Cornelia · Baldo degli Ubaldi · Valle Aurelia · Cipro-Musei Vaticani · Ottaviano-San Pietro · Lepanto · Flaminio

Rebibbia B
P. Mammolo
S.M. Soccorso
Pietralata

Spagna · Barberini · Repubblica

Bologna

A

Policlinico
Castro Pretorio
Tiburtina
M. Tiburtini

Termini
Cavour

Manzoni · S. Giovanni · Re di Roma · Ponte Lungo · Furio Camillo · Colli Albani · Arco di Travertino · P. Furba-Quadraro · Numidio Quadrato · Lucio Sestio · Giulio Agricola · SubAugusta · Cinecittà · Anagnina

Colosseo

Vittorio Emanuele

Circo Massimo

Piramide ○ — ○ Ostiense

Magliana □ · Garbatella

Muratella □ · Basilica S. Paolo

L. da Vinci
Aeroporto · Marconi

EUR Magliana

Fiumicino

Tor di Valle · Vitinia · Casal Bernocchi · Acilia · Ostia Antica

EUR Palasport · EUR Fermi · Laurentina B

Lido Nordo · Lido Centro · Stella Polare · Castel Fusano · C. Colombo

A

M METRO LINE A
Anagnina-Ottaviano

M METRO LINE B
Laurentina-Rebibbia

Fiumicino-Ostiense

Piramide-C. Colombo (Ostia)

Venezia, Largo Argentina, Corso Rinascimento (for Piazza Navona), and Piazza Risorgimento (for the Vatican Museums and St. Peter's).

23   Runs from the church of San Paolo Fuori le Mura in the south to the Vatican area, by way of Piramide and Testaccio, along the river past the Aventine, Jewish Ghetto, and *centro storico,* and Piazza Risorgimento (for the Vatican Museums and St. Peter's). Travels on the western (Trastevere) side of the river when doing the reverse route. Not too crowded in the middle of the day; gets packed heading south in the later afternoon.

75   Runs from Piazza Indipendenza (near Termini) to Monteverde, across the river in the west, by way of Via Cavour, Via dei Fori Imperiali, the Colosseum, Circus Maximus, Piramide and Via Marmorata (for Testaccio), and Viale Trastevere.

USEFUL TRAM LINES

Most are green and air-conditioned. A few are older, orange cars without A/C.

3   From Villa Borghese to Stazione Trastevere, by way of San Lorenzo, San Giovanni, the Colosseum, Circus Maximus, Testaccio, and Porta Portese. Slow, but handy and quite scenic.

8   From Largo Argentina to Viale Trastevere and Stazione Trastevere. The easiest way to get from the *centro storico* to Trastevere on public transportation.

Culture 101: Fitting In

Language: Most Romans speak very little English, but staff at restaurants and bars in the center are fluent enough to handle food and drink orders. People on the street might only know a few words in English, but this shouldn't be a hindrance. Between their genuine desire to help and the power of hand motions, you should be able to understand each other just fine. Nevertheless, you should treat your time in Rome as a chance to master a few key words and phrases in the most fun, musical, and romantic language in the world. Everyone will know that you're a foreigner, but you can make a *bellissima figura* (great impression) if you say *per favore* (please) when you're asking for something; *grazi* (thank you)—Italians use it profusely, and you can, too; and greet people (anyone) with a *buon giorno* (hello, until 3pm) or *buona sera* (hello, after 3pm) when you walk into their shop, bar, or restaurant, or if you stop to ask someone something on the street. When you leave, *arrivederci* is the proper formal salutation, but it's a hard word to pronounce (but if you can manage it, more power to you).

Dress: Roman dress is casual but pulled-together year-round. Jeans, not khakis, should be the foundation of your travel wardrobe while in Rome (or anywhere in Italy, for that matter). This is a cosmopolitan city, so there are no modesty concerns when it comes to dress, but shorts (and especially short-shorts or miniskirts), worn anywhere but the beach or in your hotel room, are just plain bad taste in Rome. Girls, don't worry about dressing up too much to go out; all you need are your favorite jeans (Citizens, Antik, etc., are like gold in Italy) and some cool accessories, but definitely no heels. Walking the cobblestones in stilettos is best left to the more experienced local women. (If you must, the trick is putting all your weight on the toe.) The other important thing to keep in mind is that Romans are very strict about what they wear in what season. Even though it never really gets that cold, and there are warm and sunny days in October and March, you'll never see locals bust out open-toed shoes between the end of September and mid-May. It's also a good idea to leave any expensive jewelry at home. Diamond engagement rings,

19 From Piazza Risorgimento (near the Vatican) to the eastern suburbs, by way of Villa Borghese.

USEFUL METRO STOPS

Line A

Ottaviano-San Pietro for the Vatican Museums and St. Peter's (handier than the stop called Cipro-Musei Vaticani)

Flaminio for Piazza del Popolo, the Pincio, and Via del Corso shopping

Spagna for the Spanish Steps, Via Condotti shopping, and Via Veneto

Barberini for Via Veneto and the Crypt of the Capuchin Monks

Termini for the main train station and only point of transfer to metro Line B

San Giovanni for the church of St. John Lateran and the Holy Stairs

Anagnina for bus connections to Ciampino airport

Line B

Colosseo for the Colosseum and Roman Forum ruins

Circo Massimo for the Circus Maximus, Baths of Caracalla, and Aventine hill pearls, and such are pretty alien to young Romans, but pickpockets may be tempted by your bling.

Drinking: The city is remarkably tolerant of alcoholic excess, but there's a big difference between the way Romans drink and the way many tourists do. Some Romans can be out all night and only have a few drinks (boring, right?); others will have multiple bottles of wine over dinner, then multiple cocktails at a club; but this is not a binge-drinking culture, so you'll rarely see Romans getting loud, obnoxious, or belligerent. At worst, they'll be boisterous and slur their words and one of their friends will give them a ride home. As for you, you can still drink plenty (wine is cheap—we know you will) but if you want to fit in, don't get too wasted. And for heaven's sake, do not join one of the many pub crawls that are pitched at the international backpacker set. We know it's tempting, and we know you want to meet people and maybe hook up, blah blah blah, but a group of 50 people screaming and vomiting from bar to bar in the *centro storico* is downright offensive to Rome and its people. Save the pub-crawling for Dublin.

Open containers are technically allowed everywhere, but should only be brought to piazzas (such as Campo de' Fiori or Piazza Trilussa), where other (nonderelict) locals are doing it, too. As long as you keep it low key and relatively hidden (e.g., in plastic cups), you can bring wine and beer to parks, viewpoints, and other lookout points. But if you're the only ones around and there's a cop in the area, expect to get hassled.

Having said all of this, you'll never fit in 100% (I lived in Rome for 6 years but was always pegged as a foreigner), nor should you want to (it's fun to be the token foreigner!). But as the token foreigner, don't go around acting superior or, God forbid, condescending. The Roman way of doing things might annoy you as often as it charms you, but you're on their turf: Stay cool, and don't treat this historic city as your personal playground. As long as you're courteous, respectful, and patient, you'll be a great ambassador for whatever country you call home.

ROME & LAZIO

Piramide for Testaccio and Ostia-Lido trains to Ostia Antica and the beaches at **Ostia.**

EUR-Fermi for the fascist-era monuments and museums of EUR

Ponte Mammolo for bus connections to Tivoli

By Taxi

Taxis come in handy when you have to get from the train station to your hotel with a lot of luggage and when you find yourself not wanting to deal with the bus at the end of a long day of sightseeing (e.g., in front of St. Peter's at 5pm). Unless you can score a ride with a local, you'll also need taxis to get to and from any of the nightlife spots outside the *centro.* A few taxi rules to keep in mind: You can't hail a cab on the street. By law, free cabs must proceed to the nearest taxi stand and pick up new fares there. (When it's raining or during rush hour, there will be a long queue of people at those taxi stands; when it's sunny and quiet, there'll be dozens of cabs dying to take you.)

There are taxi stands on three sides of Termini station, in front of the Colosseum metro station, at Piazza Venezia, the Spanish Steps, Piazza del Popolo, the Pantheon, Largo Argentina, Palazzo Madama (on Corso Rinascimento, just east of Piazza Navona), at Piazza San Pietro (Vatican City), in Piazza Risorgimento, near the Vatican Museums, and off Piazza G.G. Belli in Trastevere. You can also call for a cab (in Italian or very clear, elementary English) at ☎ **06/3570,** 06/4994, 06/6645, 06/5551, or 06/4157. The company at 3570 has the widest network of cabs, so call them first.

When the operator picks up, state the street address of your location as clearly as possible, and after a few moments and hold music that hasn't been changed in 10 years, a recorded voice will tell you the *sigla* (medallion number) of the taxi they're sending—if there's a cab available, that is. All too often (again, during rainy or busy nights downtown), they'll tell you they have no availability. When you do get the *sigla,* it's usually a city or river name, followed by a number (e.g., Pisa 35). Most hotels will call a cab for you, but performing this task yourself will make you feel like the Italian language pro you are.

By Bicycle

Bicycling in Rome is only advisable if you're sticking to the parks; or on Sundays, when there's hardly any traffic in the *centro storico;* or if you're on a guided bike tour, such as that offered by **Enjoy Rome,** Via Marghera 8/a (☎ **06/445-1843**). Otherwise, biking in Rome is a harrowing affair involving bumpy cobblestones, swarms of Vespas, and careening buses. It's not worth the stress— instead of renting a bike, consider renting a *motorino,* or save your money and walk.

Tourist Offices & Information

The **visitor center** of the Rome APT (Azienda di Promozione Turistica di Roma) is at Via Parigi 5 (off Piazza della Repubblica; ☎ **06/ 488-991;** www.romaturismo.com) and open Monday to Saturday 9am to 7pm. The APT also has a desk at Fiumicino airport, Terminal B, open daily from 8am to 7pm. You can also get information from the APT's **call center,** ☎ **06/8205-9127,** in operation every day from 9am to 7pm.

Throughout the city center, there are also **green kiosks,** run by the APT, where you can get brochures and maps, and ask touristy questions. You'll find kiosks at Termini station, Castel Sant'Angelo, Via dei Fori Imperiali, Piazza Cinque Lune (near Piazza Navona), Largo Goldoni, Via Minghetti (near the Trevi Fountain), Via dell'Olmata (near Santa Maria Maggiore), and in Trastevere at Piazza Sonnino. The illustrated city map published by the tourist board is compact and quite good, with all the major attractions in the *centro* well marked, so be sure to pick one up when you visit one of their offices. It's greenish and comes from a placemat-sized pad of tearsheets.

For info about other Italian cities and regions, you can also visit the office of **ENIT,** the **Italian state tourist board,** which is headquartered at Via Marghera 2/6 (a few blocks north of Termini; ☎ **06/49711;** www. enit.it).

For a more personal touch, stop in at **Enjoy Rome,** Via Marghera 8/a, a few blocks north of Termini (☎ **06/445-1843;** www. enjoyrome.com), where a staff of friendly Italians and native English speakers will give you free maps and pamphlets and answer questions. They're open Monday to Friday from 8:30am to 6:30pm, and Saturday from 8:30am to 2pm. Enjoy Rome also runs fantastic walking tours, a seasonal bike tour, and bus tours to the catacombs and Pompeii.

ROME & LAZIO

Playlist: Rome

Download these essential Eternal City tunes before your trip and you'll score huge points with the locals.

→ **Er Piotta, "Supercafone"** "Er Piotta" is Roman dialect for "Fitty Bucks" (well, close enough), and his super-catchy, quasi hip-hop tune from 1999 is a tongue-in-cheek celebration of the *coatto* or *cafone,* the stereotypical Roman "guido" who thinks he's God's gift to women, wears baby oil at the beach—and tons of gold chains, though he may be unemployed—and is constantly flexing his muscles. This one is so much fun to sing along to, it's worth downloading the lyrics: www.ipercafone.com/cantanti-supercafone.htm.

→ **Lando Fiorini, "La Società dei Magnaccioni"** A true Roman classic, "The Big Eaters' Club" is a table-slapping ode to gluttony and sloth that will come in handy when you're downing multiple flasks of *vino* and platefuls of hearty *cacio e pepe* with the salty old-timers of Testaccio and Trastevere.

→ **Flaminio Maphia, "Ragazze Acidelle"** From local hip-hop duo G-Max and Rude MC, this is a more obscure but catchy number that rails against snobby Roman chicks. The verses go pretty fast, but all can sing along to the chorus: *Oh ee, oh ee, oh ee, 'sta ragazza qui e' un po' acidella.* ("This chick is a little acidic.")

→ **Antonello Venditti, "Roma Roma Roma" and "Grazie Roma"** The former is the song everyone at the stadium sings at the start of AS Roma soccer games. The latter is the one you sing at the end of the game when Roma wins. Neither is a particularly great song, but it's the spirit that counts.

→ **Renato Zero, "Cercami (Live at the Stadio Olimpico)"** Renato is a skinny, aging, melodramatic Italian rocker, and "Look for Me" is his overproduced, Andrew Lloyd-Webber–style power ballad. The belted and whispered lyrics are slow enough that you can start to sing along—as Italians of all ages do—after you hear it a few times.

Recommended Websites

(Most of these homepages are in Italian; click on the British flag icon to bring up the English version of the site.)

○ **www.romaturismo.com** The official website of the Roman tourist board is bright, clean, and user-friendly. There are comprehensive accommodations listings, sightseeing and transportation info, and an events calendar, as well as suggested itineraries for 48- or 96-hour stays. Coolest of all is the Brochures feature, which allows you to download some substantial (and informative) full-color booklets and pamphlets (in PDF) about the Colosseum, the Appian Way, the fountains of Rome, and more.

○ **www.vatican.va** In addition to putting more archived papal speeches at your fingertips than you ever thought possible, the official website of the Holy See provides practical information and an abridged virtual tour of the Vatican Museums. To skip straight to the Vatican Museums info, go to **http://mv.vatican.va/3_EN/pages/MV_Home.html**.

○ **www.atac.roma.it** Official website of Rome's public transportation system. It's in Italian, but you can still feel your way through it. At the top of the page, the *Calcola Percorso* feature (Calculate Route) lets you enter the address of your origin and the address of your destination and tells you which buses and trams you need to take to get there. The *trovalinea* function allows you to search schedules and route maps by entering a bus or tram number. Click on *mappe* to download a handy, zoomable PDF map of the system.

○ **www.adr.it** All about Rome's airports, Fiumicino (Leonardo da Vinci, FCO) and Ciampino (CIA).

Rome Nuts & Bolts

ATMs Cash machines (called *bancomat* in Italy) are everywhere in this well-touristed town, but you probably won't need to carry around a ton of euros while you're in Rome, since credit and debit cards are accepted almost everywhere. A few things you will need cash for: refreshments at the local cafe, monument admissions, drinks, and buses, if you choose to take them. As always, plan your cash withdrawals carefully: The exchange rate is favorable through foreign ATMs, since the banks trade in large volume, but you're hit with fees of more than $5 (depending on your bank) every time you take out money while abroad.

Embassies & Consulates Visit your country's embassy or consulate to file for a replacement passport, apply for a marriage license, etc. Most are open Monday to Friday from 9am to noon; call for exact hours, and to find out exactly what documents you should bring with you to expedite your appointment.

Embassy and Consulate of the U.S.A.: Via Veneto 119A/121 (☏ 06/46741). Metro Barberini. Bus: 52, 53, 63, 95, 116, or 630.

Embassy of Canada: Via Zara 30, off Corso Trieste, northeastern suburbs (☏ 06/445-981). Bus: 36 or 60.

Embassy of the United Kingdom: Via XX Settembre 80, at Porta Pia (☏ 06/4220-0001). Bus: 36, 60, or 62.

Embassy of Australia: Via Alessandria 215, off Corso Trieste, northeastern suburbs (☏ 06/852-721). Bus: 36 or 60.

Embassy of New Zealand: Via Zara 28, off Corso Trieste, northeastern suburbs (☏ 06/440-29-28). Bus: 36 or 60.

Emergencies In an emergency, call the *polizia* at ☏ 113; for nonemergencies (like lost or stolen property), use ☏ 06/46861, or visit the main police station *(questura)* at Via di San Vitale 15 (at Via Genova, north of Via Nazionale). You can also turn to Italy's Army police force, the **Carabinieri** (who wear red-striped trousers designed by Valentino), to report emergencies or other disturbances of the peace. Call the Carabinieri at ☏ 112 for emergencies only; for nonemergencies, ☏ 06/6758-2800. Their central station *(caserma)* is at Via Cesare Battisti 6 (Piazza Venezia). If your pocket gets picked, turn to the multilingual **tourist aid helpline** at ☏ 06/422-371. To report a fire, a gas leak, or a grandma stuck in an elevator, dial ☏ 115 for the *vigili del fuoco* (fire department).

For medical emergencies, call an ambulance at ☏ 118, or visit the *pronto soccorso* (emergency room, where you will not be charged for treatment, regardless of your insurance status) at the nearest hospital: **Fatebenefratelli** (on Tiber Island; ☏ 06/6821-0828),

Santo Spirito (Lungotevere in Sassia 1, near the Vatican; ☎ 06/68351), **San Giacomo** (Via Canova 29, near Piazza del Popolo; ☎ 06/36261), **San Giovanni** (Via dell'Amba Aradam 8, south of the Colosseum; ☎ 06/77051). The **Polizia Municipale,** who handle dog bites and other petty crimes, are at ☎ 06/6769-4700, and the **Vigili Urbani,** who write parking tickets and tow cars and are regarded as general *rompipalle* (pains in the ass) by every Italian driver, are at Via della Consolazione 4 (on the south side of the Forum, off Vico Jugario; ☎ 06/67691).

Internet/Wireless Hot Spots In addition to the Internet cafes listed below, you can often get online at pubs with a large expat clientele, and most hostels and budget hotels have an Internet terminal set up in the lobby, which guests can use for free or for a nominal fee. And there's a new federal law you need to remember—bring your ID when you need to use a public terminal.

Easy Internet, Piazza Barberini 2–16, 8am–2am. 250 PCs and Subway sandwich shop inside. Rates from 3€/hr.

Easy Internet, Piazza in Piscinula 15 (Trastevere), daily 10am–8pm. 25 PCs. Rates from 3€/hr.

Internet Train/Verba, Via delle Fratte di Trastevere 44/b (off Viale Trastevere), ☎ 06/583-4033. Daily 9am–9pm. 15 PCs. So friendly. Sent many a Frommer's file from here—threw the ol' laptop on the *motorino* and plugged 'er in!! Rates from 4€/hr.

The NetGate, Piazza di Firenze 25 (near the Pantheon), ☎ 06/689-3445. 25 PCs. Rates about 5€ per hour..

TreviNet Place, Via in Arcione 103, ☎ 06/6992-2320. Rates about 3.50€ an hour.

Terrazza Barberini, Via Barberini 16, ☎ 06/4201-45962. 95€/hr.

Laundromats **Onda Blu** has two locations south of Termini, at Via Principe Amedeo 70/b and Via Lamarmora 12, both open daily 8am to 10pm. **Wash&Dry** is in Trastevere at Via della Pelliccia 35 (at Piazza de' Renzi) and near Piazza Navona at Via della Chiesa Nuova 15/16; both are open daily from 8am to 10pm. At either Onda Blu or Wash&Dry, 3.50€ will get you one load washed, another 3.50€ will get you 20 minutes in the dryer.

Caution: Always be sure to check the temperature settings of washers and dryers; hot is very hot, so unless you are looking to shrink your wardrobe so that it'll fit better in your backpack, choose a lower setting.

Most loads take 60 minutes to dry, so think carefully about how much you really need to wash, otherwise you might end up blowing the day's food budget on hot air. (If you're only doing undergarments and socks, the hotel sink and a travel bottle of Woolite is a time-honored cost-cutting technique. Washing larger garments in the room is frowned upon, and let's be honest, you'll never get those Juicy pants really clean by sloshing them around in the bathtub.)

Alternatively, seek out the local *tintoria* (full-service laundry/dry cleaner's) where they'll wash, dry, and fold your load for a bit more than it would cost to do it yourself, but at least you won't be wasting valuable Rome time hauling dirty laundry across town and waiting for the spin cycle to be over.

Luggage Storage If you need to ditch any bags for a few hours or even a few days, the luggage storage *(deposito bagagli)* service at Termini station (on the underground concourse, on the Via Giolitti side, near track 24; ☎ 06/4782-5543; daily 6am–midnight) will store your stuff for 3.80€ per piece for the first 5 hours. Each successive hour (6–12 hr.) is .60€ per piece per hour. After 12 hours, the hourly rate goes all the way down to 0.20€ per piece. A bargain, indeed! This is a great option for when you have to check out of your hostel/hotel early in the morning, but your train out of Rome doesn't leave until the afternoon or evening.

Postage & Shipping   **Postage stamps** *(francobolli)* are sold at all *tabacchi;* they ask you how many postcards you're sending and where, and you tell them—it's a simple transaction. Postage for postcards and letters to anywhere in Europe or the Mediterranean basin is 0.52€; for the rest of the world, it's 0.62€. Red post boxes are on the sides of buildings in Rome; drop your postcards in the *"tutte le altre destinazioni"* (all other destinations) slot, as opposed to the *"città"* slot. Some hotels also have a mail drop.

When you're in the Vatican area, you can also send your postcards home via the ***Poste Vaticane*** (the Vatican mail). Postage rates are the same as with the Italian mail, and Vatican stamps are as artistic as anything you'll find on the walls of the Sistine Chapel. The Vatican mail has a reputation for being faster and more reliable than the Italian mail—all outgoing mail is blessed by a special postal priest. The only drawback is that you can only mail your postcards and letters from the Vatican. There are two post offices in St. Peter's Square, along the Charlemagne Wing (left side) and just beyond the colonnades on the right side. Items must have Vatican postage and be mailed from the Vatican. There is also a Post Office in the Vatican Museum. Hours are 8:30am to 7pm Monday through Friday, and 8:30am to 6pm Saturday.

When you start to accumulate too many souvenirs, or you realize that you're never going to wear those hiking boots you packed, the easiest thing to do is ship 'em home. For that, you'll need to seek out the nearest post office, a glorious bureaucratic institution where you can not only mail things, you can rub shoulders with retirees waiting on line to cash their pension checks. There are several branches of the Poste Italiane (Italian **post office**) throughout Rome: look for the yellow and blue pt signs. Just west of Termini, the branch at Via Terme di Diocleziano 30 (☎ 06/4888-6920) is open Tuesday through Friday 8am to 7pm and Saturday 8am to 1:15pm. In the centro storico, a few blocks west of the Pantheon, there's a branch at Via Monterone 1 (☎ 06/6840-2520) open Tuesday through Friday 8am to 7pm and Saturday 8am to 1:15pm. Near the Spanish Steps, the post office at Piazza San Silvestro 19 (☎ 06/6973-7232) is open Tuesday to Friday 8am to 7pm and Saturday 8am to 5pm. In Trastevere, the branch at Largo San Giovanni de Matha, just west of Viale Trastevere (☎ 06/589-9079), is open Tuesday to Friday 8am to 2pm and Saturday 8:30am to 1pm. In the Vatican area, there's a branch of the Poste Italiane at Via di Porta Angelica 23 (☎ 06/6840-4843) that's open Tuesday through Friday 8am to 7pm and Saturday 8am to 1:15pm. The post office sells nifty yellow boxes and any other packaging supplies you might need. There are a few forms to fill out for parcels going overseas, but for all the bad press Italian government agencies get, the national mail system is actually quite hassle-free nowadays, with an excellent delivery record.

If you have important documents to send or need to get souvenirs to relatives securely and quickly, and you don't want to chance it with Italian bureaucracy, go to **Mail Boxes Etc.,** and see what brown can do for you. Ship your stuff via UPS from the

MBE branches at Via Barberini 3, near Piazza Barberini (☎ 06/4287-4288; Mon–Fri 9:30am–6pm); Via Leonina 38€–41, near Via Cavour (☎ 06/4782-4139; Mon–Fri 8:30am–2pm and 3–6pm, Sat 9am–noon); Via dei Mille 36€–40, north of Termini (☎ 06/446-1945; Mon–Fri 9am–7pm, Sat 9am–1pm); and Via della Scrofa 16, near the Pantheon (☎ 06/6830-0575; Mon–Fri 9am–2pm and 3–7pm, Sat 9am–1pm).

Restrooms   When you're out and about and nature calls, you should have no qualms about stopping in the nearest bar/cafe or restaurant and politely asking the management if you can use their *bagno.* This is standard practice throughout Italy—unlike in the U.S., Italian bathrooms are *not* for customers only. Drinking and eating establishments are required by law to allow anyone to use their toilet, although strung-out and derelict types are often told, "Sorry, the bathroom is out of order." So, as long as you're polite and not brandishing hypodermic needles, you'll be pointed to the restroom, which is usually a not-very-clean stall and almost invariably *in fondo a destra* (in the back, to the right). There are also public restrooms in the train station that charge a fee, but they're mostly used by tourists who don't know the trick we've just told you about, and by junkies who got turned away at all the bars and restaurants.

Safety   Rome is probably the safest large city you'll ever encounter. Walking around at night in any of the central neighborhoods is a nonissue; the only crime you'll need to be aware of in crowded tourist areas, at the train station, or on public transportation is pickpocketing (see box below). At night and on Sundays, the area around Termini train station fills up with unsavory types; it can be unpleasant navigating your way through these hordes of derelicts and the beer bottles they toss on the ground, but it's unlikely anyone will "attack" you. Everything else is common sense: Stay out of unpopulated parks at night, and beware of strangers (especially non-Italians) who are too friendly, as this can lead to a variety of bizarre and costly scams involving nightclubs, champagne tabs, and leather jackets . . . believe me, you don't want to go there. For more information on safety in Italy, see the Planning chapter.

Telephones   There are public pay phones *(cabina)* at the train station, in major piazzas and bus terminals, and at certain coffee bars (look for the white-and-red phone sign out front or the sticker in the window). Italian pay phones take a prepaid plastic card, called a *scheda telefonica,* which is issued by Telecom Italia and which must be purchased at a *tabacchi* store. Cards are sold in denominations of 2.50€, 5€, and 10€; in order for them to work, you must break off the perforated tab on the corner of the card. (A common rookie mistake is failing to break off the tab and then, when the card doesn't work, getting all huffy with the person who sold you the "defective" card—we don't want you to be a rookie.) Local calls (anything with a "06" prefix) are pretty cheap—maybe 0.20€ for a short call, as are calls to land lines in other Italian cities (0.50€ for a short call to book a hotel in your next city, for example). Be aware, however, that calls from Italian land lines to Italian cell phones (three-digit prefixes beginning with "3," such as that given you by Ilaria, the chick you met at Accademia '90 last night) are horrendously expensive and will probably bleed your *scheda telefonica* dry in a matter of seconds.

Calls from Italian pay phones to overseas phone numbers aren't as pricey as you might think, especially after 7pm Italian time, so as long as you can keep it somewhat brief, a call home shouldn't run you more than a few euros. If you're going to be chatting for a while, however, it does add up. The best bet, if you need to call home frequently, are international phone cards (anywhere from 5€–20€, available at newsstands or *tabacchi*) issued by a number of private companies that often have more advantageous rates for calling abroad. These private phone cards usually have a PIN code that you reveal by scratching off a gray bar on the back, and a series of access numbers to call before you're connected with Mom and Dad. Keep in mind that you will still need a dial tone to use one of these cards, and to get a dial tone at a pay phone, you always need to insert a Telecom Italia *scheda telefonica*. Moral of the story? Use the phone at your hotel, where the dial tone is free, when you need to call home. If dialing direct from your hotel phone (that is, without any PIN codes or phone cards), always ask hotel staff upfront what their charges are. Some hotels make a sizeable profit off of guest phone use; other more honest souls only charge you what the phone company charges them, with no mark-up whatsoever.

Tipping   In Rome, as in the rest of Italy, there are no hard and fast rules about tipping, but at the very least, all Romans tip the *barista* at their local coffee bar. You'll make a *bella figura* (good impression) and usually get faster service if you leave an extra 10 to 20 *centesimi* on the counter when you're having a *caffè* or cappuccino. For good service at restaurants, feel free to add a few euros (in cash only) to the bill as gratuity—it may be less than 10%, but it's plenty in this culture—but feel free, too, to withhold the extra change if service has been crappy. If you take a cab, round the fare up to the next whole euro amount: If the fare is 8.30€, give the driver 9€. If you're taking a cab to or from the airport, give the driver exactly 5€ as gratuity.

Sleeping

If you don't plan ahead, it can be very tough to find a desirable, cheap place to stay in Rome. "Cheap" is relative, and even with advance booking, you should expect to spend more on lodging here than anywhere else in Italy. We've created a carefully edited list of the best cheap places to stay in the best neighborhoods. Most of Rome's cheap hotels are on the seedy streets near Termini, but we only recommend three Termini-area accommodations, two of which are hostels. (It's not that Termini isn't safe; it's just ugly.)

Location is a huge key to enjoying your time in Rome, and you're generally much better off seeking lodging that's central, even if it means paying a premium for it. All the hotels we've listed have websites; definitely check and see what special web-only discounts they might be offering.

As for nuts and bolts, A/C is an important feature to look for in a hotel from June through August. If you're a light sleeper, try for a back room—they're quieter than those facing the street. When older properties have some rooms with private bath and some with toilet and shower across the hall, you're usually better off taking the room with the shared bath—they're cheaper and usually much bigger (the other rooms lost precious square footage when their bathrooms were installed). Just pack a pair of flip-flops for the trip to the shower, and you're good to go.

What Neighborhoods?

In the heart of the *centro storico*, **Campo de' Fiori** and **Piazza Navona** are the best all-around zones for eating and drinking, with street life that doesn't stop from sunrise to

OKKIO! Gypsies & Pickpockets

We don't want to scare you, but we do want to prepare you: Pickpockets—many of whom are gypsies, or *rom*—are a problem in Rome. No, you do NOT need to carry a dorky money belt, but on buses, metro trains, or anywhere there are crowds and tourists (busy piazzas, museum lines, etc.), you should always be vigilant about your bags, money, and other valuables. This is also true of any cafe or restaurant with outside seating or any especially busy bar or pizzeria where a thief could easily walk in and out unnoticed. Over the years, countless handbags, wallets, and backpacks have been stolen—in broad daylight—souring many travelers' experience in Rome. Depending on where you hang out or how you get around, you may never encounter them, but chances are you will. On the bright side, all you need to do to protect yourself is to be aware of them and their ways; once you've learned about their tricks, you can avoid being a victim and perhaps even save others around town.

Gypsies can be easy to spot: they often wear loose, mismatched floral garments and travel in gaggles of two to four women, half of whom carry babies in fabric slings across their chests. There are some gypsy children—usually girls—who work the streets alongside the older women, but they're more often beggars, not proactive pickpocketers.

The pickpockets have a common M.O.: They prey on anyone who's distracted or disoriented, which means crowds and tourists. You'll see them working the line to get into the Vatican Museums, asking tourists for money; what they're really doing is scoping the crowd for open pockets, backpacks, and handbags—when they find their victim, they'll sneak their hands in and snatch whatever they can, and when you realize what's happening, they're already running down the street.

The pickpockets are most often nonviolent; they won't physically assault you for your valuables, but if they can grab something on the sly, they'll do it.

the wee hours, and you'll be able to walk pretty much everywhere. Another great area for charm and vitality is **Monti,** the medieval neighborhood just north of Ancient Rome. For posh surroundings but relatively quiet nightlife, head for the **Spanish Steps,** which is also convenient to most monuments. For an old-fashioned village-y feel by day and energetic vibe by night, stay in **Trastevere,** but it's a bit more removed from the sights. The **Vatican** area has some great value accommodations in more modern buildings, but you're in for a bus ride or a decent hike to get to most sights and the action of the *centro storico.*

Hostels

MTV Best → **The Beehive** ★★ TERMINI
If you have to crash in the train station area, by all means, get a bed at this self-styled "hotel and art space" run by a friendly American couple who gave up their Los Angeles careers 8 years ago and came to Rome to open a hostel. If you didn't think hostels could get in on the whole "lifestyle" design game, guess again. Steve and Linda have poured a ton of taste and creativity into making their budget inn a cool place. Furnishings are modern and soothing, with vintage surf-inspired fabrics in the rooms and stylish, contemporary light fixtures casting a flattering glow throughout. There's also a small lounge,

Sleeping in Rome

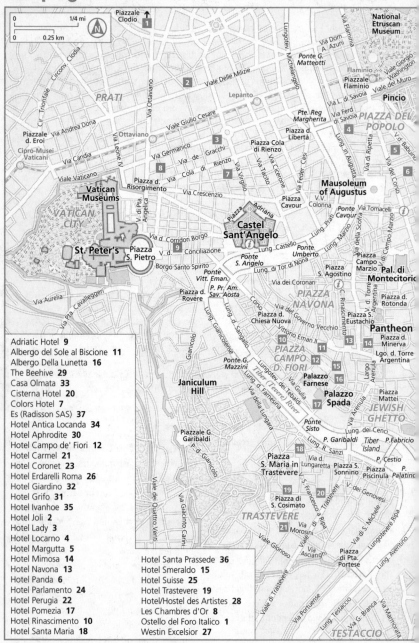

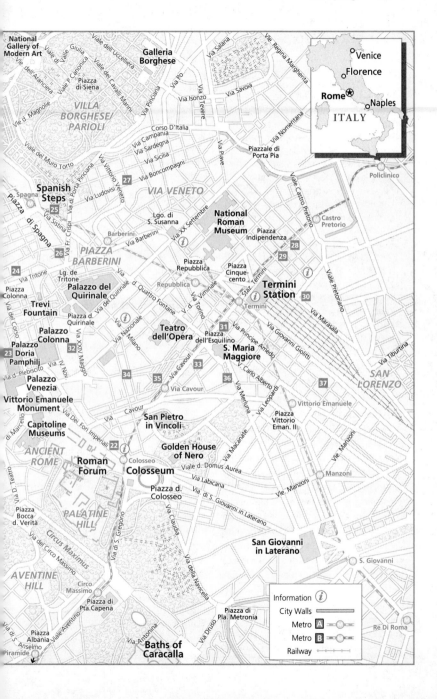

National Gallery of Modern Art

Galleria Borghese

Venice
Florence
Rome
Naples
ITALY

Viale dell'Uccelliera
Viale P. Canonica
Viale dei Cavalli Marini
Piazza di Siena
Via Po
Via Pinciana
Via Isonzo
Via Savoia
Viale di Valle Giulia
Viale della Magnolie
Viale del Muro Torto
Viale d. Aranciera

VILLA BORGHESE/ PARIOLI

Corso D'Italia
Via Campania
Via Sardegna
Via Sicilia
Via Boncompagni

Via Piave
Via Nomentana

Piazzale di Porta Pia

Policlinico

Spagna
Spanish Steps
Piazza di Spagna
Via Sistina
Via Fr. Crispi
Via Porta Pinciana
Via Vittorio Veneto
Via Ludovisi

27

VIA VENETO

Via XX Settembre

Via Regina Margherita
Via Salaria
Vie Castro Pretorio

Castro Pretorio

25
26
PIAZZA BARBERINI
Via Barberini
Barberini
Via Tritone
Lg. di S. Susanna

National Roman Museum
Piazza Indipendenza

28
29

24
Via Tritone
Lg. de Tritone
Piazza Colonna
Palazzo del Quirinale
Via del Quirinale
Via d. Quattro Fontane

Piazza Repubblica
Piazza Cinque- cento
Repubblica
Termini Station
Staz. Termini
Termini

i
30

Trevi Fountain
Piazza d. Quirinale
Via Milano
Via Nazionale
Via Viminale
Via Torino

Via Principe Amedo
Via Giovanni Giolitti

Via Marsala

Palazzo Colonna
Palazzo Doria Pamphilj
Via XXIV Maggio
Via IV Nov.
32

Teatro dell'Opera
Piazza dell'Esquilino
31
S. Maria Maggiore

Via Tiburtina

SAN LORENZO

23
Palazzo Venezia
Via d. Plebiscito
34
35
Via Cavour
33
Via Cavour
36
Via C. Carlo Alberto
Via Merulana
Via Leopardi
37

Vittorio Emanuele Monument
Via Dei Fori Imperiali

Piazza Vittorio Eman. II
Vittorio Emanuele
Via Manzoni

Capitoline Museums
Via Cavour

San Pietro in Vincoli

Piazza Vittorio Eman. II

Vle. Manzoni

ANCIENT ROME
Roman Forum
22
Colosseo
Colosseum

Golden House of Nero
Viale d. Domus Aurea
Via Macanate

Manzoni
Vle. Manzoni

Via D. Teatro
Piazza Bocca d. Verità
PALATINE HILL
Piazza d. Colosseo
Via Labicana
Via di S. Giovanni in Laterano

Circus Maximus
Via del Circo Massimo
Via di S. Gregorio
Via Claudia

San Giovanni in Laterano
Via della Navicella
S. Giovanni

AVENTINE HILL
Circo Massimo
Viale Aventino
Piazza di Pta.Capena
Via Druso
Piazza di Pla. Metronia

Re Di Roma

Piazza Albania
Via di S. Anselmo
Piramide

Via Antonina
Baths of Caracalla

Information
City Walls
Metro A
Metro B
Railway

ROME & LAZIO

Staying a Little Longer in Rome

As we mentioned in the "Basics" chapter, if you're staying awhile (three nights or more) in Rome, a furnished apartment might end up being a bargain compared to a hotel room. The web site **Rentalinrome. com** (☎ 06/990-5513) is surprisingly transparent with exact locations, exact rates, and multiple pictures of apartments. Their website lists over 400 properties—from studios to elaborate penthouses—in prime locations in the heart of Rome. Prices start at 80€ a night for "low-cost" apartments and 150€ a night for "luxury" apartments. Units sleep anywhere from 2 to 6 people and have fully equipped kitchens. Minimum stay is 3 nights, and they also have properties available for as long as a year.

as well as an outdoor "living room" where you can chill, eat, or drink amid fig and lemon trees, vines, and herbs. (Note that the Beehive is a very chill hostel—so if you're intent on doing the obnoxious pub-crawl thing, you should stay elsewhere.) The entire property is on a Wi-Fi network, which is available to all guests for free. The Beehive's one dorm room has four bunk beds; each of the eight beds is equipped with its own adjustable reading light, so you don't have to blind your roommates while you read this book. The other rooms at The Beehive are private rooms, which can be booked as doubles or triples. While there's no A/C, all rooms have ceiling fans and screens for keeping the mosquitoes out in summer (a feature overlooked by all too many Italian inns). Private rooms have a sink in the room; none of the rooms has its own private full bathroom. You can also make free calls to land lines within Italy; shower gel and shampoo are provided in the common bathrooms; and towels available on request for dorm guests. The on-site cafe serves organic, vegetarian food at breakfast, lunch, and dinner (and plenty of wine), and—proof that they've really thought of everything—they'll pack lunches for you to take with you in your backpack on long sightseeing or travel days. *Via Marghera 8.* ☎ *06/4470-4553. www.the-beehive.com. Dorm bed 20€–22€, double 70€–75€, extra bed 25€. Meals not included.*

→ **Casa Olmata** ★ SOUTH OF TERMINI/ MONTI   One of the better budget accommodations options in the south-of-Termini

Finding a Room in Rome

Showing up in Rome during high season without a hotel reservation is an unadulterated Bad Idea, but if you haven't booked anything, all hope is not lost. In Termini station (opposite platforms 4 and 20) and at Fiumicino airport, stop by the **Hotel Reservation** desk and see if they can hook you up with something. The service has a database of hundreds of hotels in Rome, which sell their rooms at hugely discounted rates at the last minute—meaning, you could potentially score a government-rated four-star room in a great location for 100€, or less than half the rack rate. Last-minute rooms at two- and three-star hotels near the train station can be as low as 50€. You can book through Hotel Reservation in person, on the phone (☎ 06/699-1000), or online (www.hotelreservation. it), but be sure you find out the exact location of the hotel before you put any money down, as some of the properties are in the boonies.

Crashing the Pool at the Hilton

If you find yourself in Rome in the middle of the summer, you'll be dying for a place to cool off. Soaking your feet in the hotel bidet can provide some relief, sure, but the surroundings are hardly atmospheric. The Trevi Fountain, while mighty tempting, is not a viable bathing option, either. The good news is, there are several government-rated four- and five-star hotels in the greener 'hoods of Rome where nonguests can pay a fee and use the swimming pool. For anywhere from 15€–40€ daily, you can live the fab poolside life at the modern **Es** hotel (p. 105) as well as at the following properties, all of which have cafes where you can get light meals and drinks:

In the Villa Borghese: **Hotel Parco dei Principi,** Via Frescobaldi 5 (☎ 06/854-421; www.parcodeiprincipi.com). Expect to mingle with business travelers and Roman families at the Parco dei Principi's basilica-shaped pool, immersed in the greenery of the Villa Borghese.

Above Trastevere: **Grand Hotel del Gianicolo,** Viale delle Mura Gianicolensi 107 (☎ 06/5833-5522; www.grandhotelgianicolo.it). The poolside crowd here is almost exclusively local Roman sunbathers who couldn't make it to the beach that day, so there'll be glares if you stand too long in anyone's sun line. The tranquil spot is surrounded by palm trees and umbrella pines.

In the hills above the Vatican: **Cavalieri Hilton,** Via Cadlolo 101 (☎ 06/35091; www.rome.hilton.com). There's a good mix here—package tour blue-hairs, Roman rich kids, cocktail-sipping expats. The Hilton has the most resort-y feel of Rome's hotel pools, the best locker room facilities, and the best food and drink.

Before you show up with your Coppertone and floaties, it's a good idea to call and make sure they haven't drained the pool for maintenance or something. Also, be aware that most Italian public pools require you to wear a bathing cap, which the hotels listed here all sell on-site for about 5€ or so.

---

zone. Just off Piazza Santa Maria Maggiore, in one of the few pockets of charm near Rome's main train station, this is a great setup, with friendly service and rooms ranging from economical private doubles to six-person (mixed) dorms. Unusual for hostel-style accommodations, every room has a TV. The neighborhood is clean and safe, full of pubs and pizzerias frequented by other backpackers and resident expats. In fact, if you stay here, you'll probably become a fixture at Fiddler's Elbow Irish pub, which is right next door. Guests at Casa Olmata have access to the building's fantastic rooftop terrace, with 360-degree views over the heart of the city. The hostel also sponsors a Spaghetti Party for its guests every other night—optional, but it can be a great way to meet and exchange travel tips with other young people from all over the world. Rates below are valid from April 1 to October 31 and include breakfast, bed linens, use of a fully equipped kitchen, and 30 minutes of Internet access each day (their server, however, seems to be down a lot). Prices go down by 15% in the off season. *Via dell'Olmata 36.* ☎ *06/483-019. www. casaolmata.com. Dorm 20€–22€, double 54€–58€, triple 75€, quad 92€–120€. Metro: Termini or Cavour. Bus: 75.*

🎵 Best → **Colors** ★★ VATICAN I worked for the owners of this hotel/hostel, Pierluigi and Fulvia, for 5 years. They love Rome with all their hearts, and they'll do everything in their power to make sure you have a great time in their beloved city. Furthermore, they know backpackers better than you know yourself and will anticipate your every need. In short, they rock. Intimate and lovingly kept, their hotel has private rooms (some with private bath, some with shared bath) and dorm rooms, all of which are painted in bright, tasteful colors like tangerine and lime. Colors attracts a lot of young, independent travelers, and you can hang out with fellow guests in the fully equipped, eat-in kitchen or on the terrace outside. You don't even need to do any cooking, because one of Rome's best take-out delis, Franchi, is 2 blocks away. While Colors doesn't formally serve breakfast, they do stock the kitchen with cornflakes, coffee, tea, and jam. When Pierluigi or Fulvia aren't there, Colors is staffed by energetic, helpful young English speakers who can also help you organize your time in Rome and book you on the excellent walking tours that Colors is affiliated with. There's no curfew, but you'll need to leave a deposit for a night key. *Via Boezio 31, at Via Terenzio.* ☎ *06/687-4030. www.colorshotel.com. Dorms 18€ Nov–Mar, 25€ Apr–Oct; double 70€–115€. Metro: Ottaviano. Bus: 23, 81, 87, 271, or 492.*

→ **Hotel/Hostel des Artistes** ★ TERMINI On a quiet street 4 blocks north of Termini, Des Artistes is just far enough away from the sleaze of the train station and quite popular with young international travelers. You should only stay here, however, if you're going to stay in their "hostel" accommodations. (Their private rooms are lovely, but if you're going to spend that much for a double, find a hotel in the *centro storico!*) The three youngish brothers who run the place are friendly, helpful, and clued-in about what's going on, from classical music to clubs. Linens and blankets are included in the dorm accommodations, and bathrooms have hair dryers and plenty of hot water. The common room has several high-speed Internet terminals (which guests can use free of charge). The hotel-filled neighborhood here is frankly flavorless, but the proximity of two hassle-free

public transportation options (bus no. 492 and the Castro Pretorio metro station) means you can reach the *centro storico* or the heart of ancient Rome pretty quickly. *Via Villafranca 20, at Via Vicenza.* ☎ *06/445-4365. www.hostelrome.com or www.hoteldesartistes. com. Some rooms have shared bath. Dorm 12€–23€, double from 140€. Metro: Castro Pretorio. Bus: 492.*

→ **Ostello del Foro Italico** NORTHERN SUBURBS In a 1930s white travertine building well northwest of the city center, right next to the Foro Italico, best known for its Fascist-era sports facilities, this 334-bed hostel has little in the way of charm, but it does have its pluses. Yeah, it's a hike from most of the sights, but if you're a sporty type, this isn't such a bad option. The adjacent Foro Italico is a big hangout for professional and amateur athletes—you can catch a water polo game at the indoor pool or just go for a run around the track at the Stadio dei Marmi. Best of all, the Stadio Olimpico, also here, is where Rome's two Serie A soccer teams, Roma and Lazio, play their home games. The downside to this location is that it's quite isolated from the pulse of everyday Roman life—even neighborhoody coffee bars are a 5-minute walk away, across busy roads. The hostel does have its own **bar** (daily 10am–10pm) and **restaurant** (daily 12:30–2:30pm and 6:30–9:30pm; meals are 9€). While you're up here, might as well take advantage of the quirky transportation options you have: Under the Ponte Duca d'Aosta bridge nearby, you can hop on the Battelli di Roma (p. 197) boat service and ride down the river to the *centro storico.* The hostel also has bikes available for rent, which you can use on the *pista ciclabile,* a paved walking and biking path that runs along the river all the way to the Vatican. (If you do rent a bike, we recommend you keep to the *pista.*) *Viale delle Olimpiadi 61.* ☎ *06/323-6267. www.ostellionline.org. Dorm bed 18€. Bus: 32, 280, or 628.*

Cheap

→ **Adriatic Hotel** ★ VATICAN A longtime budget favorite near Castel Sant'Angelo, the Adriatic is located in a rather unhospitable-looking 20th-century building, but once you're inside the hotel (the reception is on the second floor), the situation improves greatly. Outgoing, courteous staff offers guests a warm welcome and will do their best to ensure you have a pleasant stay. The colorful, comfortable, and carpeted rooms are among the most spacious you'll find in Rome at this price. Rooms at the cheaper end of the price ranges listed below have shared bath; the others have full private facilities. In all rooms, there's a 10€-per-day supplement for A/C. Some rooms have private terraces, but all guests have access to a communal terrace with equal parts shade and sun, and mismatched Mediterranean patio furniture. The Adriatic doesn't serve breakfast, but there's a bar/cafeteria right across the street from the property where you can get your morning cappuccino and pastry for under 2€. With such a handy location and great value accommodations, the Adriatic is recommended by many guidebooks and gets a lot of word-of-mouth business, so try to book as early as possible. *Via Vitelleschi 25. 06/6880-8080. www. adriatichotel.com. Single 60€–90€, double 90€–120€, triple 120€–150€, quad 180€.*

→ **Albergo Della Lunetta** ★ CENTRO STORICO/CAMPO DE' FIORI It might be the uptight stepsister of the more charming Sole, located right next door, but the affordable Lunetta has the same to-die-for location, near Rome's party piazza par excellence, Campo de' Fiori. You might wish some of the energy from the streets outside seeped up into the hotel, but the rooms are spotless, with spartan decor and exposed beam ceilings, and the front desk people are friendly. There's also a small roof terrace with views of the surrounding jumble of church domes and red-tile rooftops. Not all rooms have private bath, but all have at least a sink. It's nothing to sneeze at for night owls on a budget—when your fellow backpackers are trying to figure out what bus to take from Termini to get to Campo de' Fiori at *aperitivo* time, you'll only have to walk 100m (328 ft.) over the cobblestones to join the locals for happy hour. *Piazza del Paradiso 68, at Via del Biscione.* ☎ *06/686-10-80. www.albergo dellalunetta.it. Single 60€–70€, double 70€–120€, triple 100€–150€, quad 150€–180€. Bus: 30, 40, 46, 62, 64, 70, 87, 116, 492, or 571.*

📺 **Best** → **Albergo Sole al Biscione** ★★ CENTRO STORICO/CAMPO DE' FIORI *O Sole Mio!* I can't even begin to tell you how much I love this place. I lived at this peach-walled hotel, a block from Campo de' Fiori, when I was a student, and it's still where I stay whenever I travel to Rome. Dating back to the 15th century, the Sole is the oldest hotel in the city, with four floors that wrap around a multilevel interior garden where you can drink wine and write postcards. The rooms that overlook the courtyard garden are the best, so definitely request a *camera sul giardino* at the time of booking—you can open your shutters and take in all the romance of the surrounding ochre-washed walls, faux antique statuary, and greenery, and hear the church bells from Sant'Andrea della Valle several times daily. The cheaper rooms have a sink only (toilets and showers are down the hall and shared by very few other guests), but I actually prefer them to the cramped rooms with full private bath, which put beds and toilets too close for comfort, if you know what I mean. The hotel is a popular choice for university groups, so there are usually a bunch of students running around or studying in their rooms with their doors open. There's nothing fancy about the Sole—it's cash only, and there's no Internet or A/C—but it's overflowing with the kind of rough-around-the-edges charm that epitomizes Rome, and Piera, Adamo, Paolo and Nicola at the front desk will make you feel like family (tell 'em

Sylvie sent you). All rooms have a telephone and huge terry bath towels (hard to find in cheap Italian hotels!), and most have TV. The Sole doesn't serve breakfast, but hang a left outside the hotel's front door, and you'll find Caffè dell'Arte, where the Mazza family will hook you up with an awesome cappuccino. At night, all the bars and restaurants of Campo de' Fiori are a minute away. *Via del Biscione 76, at Piazza del Paradiso. ☎ 06/6880-6873. www.solealbiscione.it. No credit cards. Single with shared bath 65€, with private bath 85€; double with shared bath 95€, with private bath 110€–150€. Bus: 30, 40, 46, 62, 64, 70, 87, 116, 492, or 571. Tram: 8.*

→ **Hotel Aphrodite** ★ TERMINI   As you walk into the soothing reception area of this new government-rated three-star, you might wonder, is the Aphrodite a hotel or a day spa? Opened in 2003, this place is an amazing oasis of tranquility right across the street from the grime and chaos of Termini station. Modern rooms feature spotless wide-plank wood floors, bland furniture in light, calming tones, and boldly painted canvases above the beds. The quality of the bathrooms, considering the price, is also remarkable: sinks have luxurious polished travertine counters, and the walls are done up in colorful mosaics. The California-style rooftop terrace, which faces the white 1930s arcades of the station, does its best to channel a *Sunset Magazine* shoot (albeit on a lower budget), with redwood chaises, benches, tables, white canvas umbrellas, and boxes of geraniums. Unlike other accommodations in the area, which are typically crammed in along with five other sketchy hotels into the same ugly palazzo, the Aphrodite is the sole occupant in its recently restored building, which helps keep the atmosphere mellow and serene. Prices are way lower here than at other similarly appointed government-rated three-stars around town, so if you want to get a good night's rest, with a few extra amenities, and be able to roll out of bed and onto your train,

definitely check out the Aphrodite. *Via Marsala 90, at Via Milazzo. ☎ 06/491-096. www. accommodationinrome.com. Double 90€– 120€, triple 90€–150€, quad 110€–130€. Metro: Termini.*

→ **Hotel Carmel** TRASTEVERE   Of the few hotels in Trastevere, the Hotel Carmel is one of the best deals. The 20th-century building where the Carmel is located might not be the atmospheric 16th-century palazzo of your Roman dreams, but it's actually a good example of the kind of digs that most real Romans call home. Note that this location, a bit south of Piazza San Cosimato, is not the most charming part of Trastevere, but it's lively and plenty safe; a 5-minute downhill walk puts you in the thick of all the restaurants and village-y atmosphere of the neighborhood. The hotel's singles, doubles, and triples are decorated with richly colored bedspreads with stripes and florals that clash with Oriental throw rugs, which, in turn, clash with black and white checkerboard floor tiles. When you trudge back to the hotel after a long day of sightseeing, there's a roof garden with vines trained over a metal pergola and a bird's-eye view of the surrounding neighborhood. Surprise feature: The hotel also has a deal with a kosher kitchen—perhaps the only hotel in all Rome with such an arrangement— that will prepare Shabbat meals on request. *Via Goffredo Mameli 11 (extension of Via Morosini, north of Viale Trastevere). ☎ 06/ 580-9921. www.hotelcarmel.it. Single 85€, double 90€–100€, triple 140€. Bus: 75, 780, or H. Tram: 8.*

→ **Hotel Erdarelli Roma** ★ SPANISH STEPS   The bright and streamlined decor at this popular government-rated two-star pensione has a dorm-y, almost maritime feel that might remind you of your berth on *Semester at Sea.* Each room also has dark-green carpeting where, if you happened to bring along your golf irons, you can practice putting. That's where the "frills" end. The Erdarelli is a basic inn, but extremely friendly and well run, and an excellent budget choice in the otherwise pricey Spanish Steps zone—Via Due Macelli isn't the most gorgeous street, but other tourists are ponying up as much as 500€ a night to be in this 'hood. If you're in a group, you can snag a quad here and pay only a bit more than what it would cost to be in a dorm room near the train station. Twenty-two rooms have full private bathroom; six have shared bathrooms down the hall. A few rooms have their own small balcony, and all rooms have direct-dial telephone and A/C (10€ per day). The Erdarelli also serves a continental breakfast, included in the nightly room rate, in its bright but characterless dining room. *Via Due Macelli 28 (off Via del Tritone).* ☎ *06/ 679-1265. www.erdarelliromehotel.com. Single 50€–100€, double 70€–145€, triple 100€– 180€, quad 120€–230€. Metro: Barberini. Bus: 62, 63, 95, 175, or 492.*

➜ **Hotel Giardino** ⭑ ANCIENT ROME/VIA NAZIONALE   Trying to get over a bout of nausea from that airplane food? This inn just up the hill from Trajan's Markets ought to soothe your stomach, since it looks like it's been doused in several hundred bottles of Pepto-Bismol. There's pink paint on the walls, pink coverlets on the beds, and pink upholstery on the chairs and sofas. Rosy tones aside, this is a very pleasant place to stay, with larger-than-average rooms (owing to its being in a 19th-century palazzo instead of a 16th-century one!) and hardwood floors that lend a warm touch. All rooms have A/C, TV, and telephone. The relaxing roof terrace and adjacent, partially enclosed solarium have potted and hanging plants galore and a few simple chairs and tables where you can hang out and read or have a drink (BYOB). The location, at the bottom (western end) of Via Nazionale puts you within easy walking distance of ancient Rome, the Trevi Fountain, and the pubs of Monti, but watch out for traffic as you cross the busy streets around the hotel. Breakfast is included in the rate, but you might be better off seeking out your own cappuccino at one of the authentic Roman bars nearby, frequented by Carabinieri who patrol the Piazza del Quirinale just up the road. *Via XXIV Maggio 51 (off Largo Magnanapoli, at the western end of Via Nazionale).* ☎ *06/679-4584. www.hotel-giardino-roma.com. Single 60€–100€, double 90€–145€. Bus: 64, 70, 170, or H.*

➜ **Hotel Grifo** ⭑ ANCIENT ROME/MONTI Similar to the Ivanhoe, below, and even a bit nicer, the "Gryphon" is a good, under-the-radar budget choice in the medieval Monti quarter. It's also one of many Roman inns that inexplicably crams in all the clashing stripes, florals, and other patterned upholstery imaginable, with bedspreads that look like your favorite J. Crew madras shirt and elaborate Oriental rugs that warm the otherwise cold marble tile floors. The basic but perfectly functional cherry-stained furniture also gives the rooms a little extra coziness. All rooms have TV, telephone, hair dryer, minibar, safe, and A/C (included in the room rate). While all rooms have their own full private bath, some rooms' private shower is actually on the hall outside—a quirk of the hotel's past as a *casa di tolleranza*. If you've brought your 'puter, you can get online with the hotel's Wi-Fi network. Wrapping around the fifth floor of the building, an all-weather (covered) terrace offers views of Monti's narrow cobblestoned streets. Buffet breakfast is included in the rates, and the small, on-site bar will pour you a glass of excellent Italian wine as a post-sightseeing or pre-dinner *aperitivo*. In the immediate side streets, there are also a ton of cafes and bars where you can grab snacks and drinks. *Via del Boschetto 144 (at Via Panisperna).* ☎ *06/ 482-7596. www.hotelgrifo.com. Doubles 90€– 130€. Metro: Cavour. Bus: 75.*

➜ **Hotel Ivanhoe** ⭑ ANCIENT ROME/MONTI On a cute ochre-walled *piazzetta* in charming Monti, a yellow neon sign, in Arabian-Nights-style font, heralds your arrival at the Hotel Ivanhoe. Inside, the friendly brunette manning the reception desk may not be as hot as Lady Rowena, but she'll give you a map and answer your questions. As for the rooms themselves, bipolar decor includes dark, 1960s Communist-chic modular furniture and fanciful striped bedding that evokes the Swiss Guards' uniforms, if not Ivanhoe's jousting doublet itself. All rooms have private bath, TV, telephone, A/C, minibar, and hair dryer. Breakfast is included, but this bohemian neighborhood is so chock-full of characteristic Roman coffee bars, we recommend you grab your morning meal with locals outside the hotel. Nearby, you'll also find plenty of pubs where you can mix with Italians and expats, and it's only a short (downhill) walk from here to the Roman Forum. *Via de' Ciancaleoni 49 (at Via Urbana).* ☎ *06/486-813. www.hotelivanhoe.it. Single 80€–120€, double 100€–160€, triple 120€–192€. Metro: Cavour. Bus: 75.*

→ **Hotel Joli** VATICAN Dowdy floral wallpaper at this Vatican-area inn may remind you of your gramma's house, but there are new hardwood floors, it's clean, and hey, the price is right. (However, you should try for a room at the Lady, below, first.) All rooms have telephone and TV; and all except the cheapest single have private bath. Breakfast is included, but A/C costs 8€ extra. *Via Cola di Rienzo 243 (near Via Terenzio).* ☎ *06/324-1854. www.hoteljoliroma.com. Single 57€–72€, double 97€–108€, triple 135€, quad 165€–190€. Metro: Ottaviano. Bus: 23, 81, or 492.*

→ **Hotel Lady** ★ VATICAN Oh, she's a lady, all right. This hotel is surprisingly elegant for such a low price. Ceilings with big, dark exposed wood beams and iron curtain rods create an old-world feel; and warm, parlor-style light fixtures and knotty pine doors and armoires give it a cozy, cabin-in-the-woods vibe. The rooms aren't exactly big, but they work. The cheapest rooms have a sink only; some have a shower; only a few doubles (the most expensive) have full bathrooms. There's an extra charge for A/C, and

breakfast isn't included. Nearby is the non-touristy Via Cola di Rienzo, one of the better mainstream shopping streets in Rome, with plenty of coffee bars where you can grab your cappuccino. St. Peter's Square and the entrance to the Vatican Museums are an easy, short walk away. *Via Germanico 198 (near Via Fabio Massimo).* ☎ *06/324-2112. www.hotellady roma.it. Single 50€–90€, double 70€–150€, triple 90€–145€. Metro: Ottaviano or Lepanto. Bus: 70 or 81.*

→ **Hotel Margutta** ★ PIAZZA DEL POPOLO/SPANISH STEPS This 24-room inn, just down the street from Gregory Peck's apartment in *Roman Holiday,* is an unbelievable bargain in the poshest part of town. The picturesque street—between the hordes at the Spanish Steps and the gorgeous green heights of the Pincio—provides a dreamy atmosphere that may well convince you to drop everything and move to Rome. (Don't expect too much excitement in this elegant neighborhood at night, but the bars and cafes of Via della Croce are a short walk away.) Rooms are simply but graciously furnished, with white walls and linens, delicate wrought-iron headboards, and slender, Empire-style chairs and tables. Rooms on the top floor have delightful views over Roman rooftops. All rooms have private bath, TV, and air-conditioning. *Via Laurina 34, at Via Margutta.* ☎ *06/322-3674. www. hotelmargutta.it. Single 75€–125€, double 90€–160€. Metro: Flaminio.*

→ **Hotel Mimosa** ★ CENTRO STORICO/PANTHEON A ridiculously affordable hotel right near the Pantheon? What's wrong with this picture? Nothing—the Mimosa is run by a noble family who couldn't care less about making any money off tourists. What small profits they do make from the hotel are donated to charity. Interiors are a bit tired and institutional feeling, but everything's clean and comfortable, and all rooms have A/C (included in the rates below). The Mimosa is small and well known to the budget travel world, so be sure to book here as early as possible. *Via di Santa Chiara 61 (off Via di Torre Argentina).* ☎ *06/6880-1753. www.hotel mimosa.net. Double 60€–85€. Bus: 30, 40, 46, 62, 64, 70, 87, 116, 492, or 571.*

➔ **Hotel Panda** ★ SPANISH STEPS It's no secret that this pensione on lively Via della Croce is the best value hotel in the Spanish Steps area, and its 20 rooms get booked up quickly. Rooms are spare, but not without a bit of old-fashioned charm, like characteristic Roman *cotto* (terra-cotta) floor tiles and exposed beam ceilings with light-colored wood. The cheaper singles and doubles do not have a private bathroom; the triples are with full private bath only. The en-suite bathrooms tend to be cramped, however. Right outside your doorstep, there are several great cafes and wine bars (including the beloved Enoteca Antica,) where you can start or end your night, but you'll probably want to hit the *centro storico* or Trastevere for dinner. *Via della Croce 35, at Via Belsiana.* ☎ *06/678-0179. www.hotelpanda.it. Single 45€–68€, double 65€–98€, triple 124€–130€. Metro: Spagna.*

➔ **Hotel Perugia** ★ ANCIENT ROME/MONTI On a postcard-perfect street, whose ochre-walled buildings frame a dramatically cropped shot of the Colosseum (150m/492 ft. away), the Perugia has 13 perfectly functional but strangely decorated rooms. Some feel like dental exam rooms into which some bedroom furniture has been randomly thrown, but the prices are pure Novocaine, especially considering that all come with full private bath. Rooms are spread out over four floors, and there's no elevator, so you might want to try for a room on a lower floor. (The fourth-floor double, billed as having its own private balcony with splendid Colosseum views, only looks out onto a splendid clump of trees.) In summer, ask about A/C, as only a few rooms have it. Breakfast is served, but as always, we recommend you get it at the local coffee bar instead. The hotel has an Internet terminal available for guests in the reception area, and

there's also has a small bar stocked with Fanta and beer. Right down the street is the **Shamrock** (p. 135), one of Monti's more popular Irish-style pubs, where you can grab a beer after sightseeing or watch an Italian soccer game along with the regular clientele. *Via del Colosseo 7 (south of Via Cavour, at Via Cardelli).* ☎ *06/679-7200. www.hperugia.it. Single 40€–100€, double 75€–135€, triple 135€–180€, quad 145€–200€. Metro: Line B, Colosseo.*

➔ **Hotel Pomezia** ★ CENTRO STORICO/CAMPO DE' FIORI Along with the Sole, Smeraldo, and Lunetta, this is another great no-frills budget find in the Campo de' Fiori area. Room sizes and paint jobs vary widely, and decor is bland modular fare, but everything is kept meticulously clean, making it perfect for anyone who doesn't care about charm or amenities and just wants an excellent location in the dining and partying heart of the *centro storico*. Some rooms have a TV (with Italy's six national stations only); all have a direct-dial telephone. You won't find an elevator or A/C. A decent continental breakfast, with pastries from a nearby bakery, is included in rates, but be sure to visit one of the myriad *romanissimo* coffee bars nearby during your stay. *Via dei Chiavari 13, near Vicolo dei Chiodaroli.* ☎ *06/686-1371. www. hotelpomezia.it. Single 50€–105€, double 75€–125€, triple 90€–150€. Bus: 30, 40, 46, 62, 64, 70, 87, 116, 492, or 571. Tram: 8.*

➔ **Hotel Santa Prassede** TERMINI On a side street near Santa Maria Maggiore, the Santa Prassede is a very comfortable, good-value option on the northern fringe of the Monti district. Recently restructured rooms are on the boring, conservative side, but everything is immaculate, and there's enough room for you to unpack your luggage a bit (a novelty, you'll find, in Italian budget hotels). All rooms have full private bath, A/C, minibar, safe, and telephone, plus satellite TV, so you can catch up on *Anderson Cooper 360* on CNN International. *Via Santa Prassede 25, off Via Merulana.* ☎ *06/481-4850.*

www.hotelsantaprassede.it. Single 60€–100€, double 85€–140€, triple 100€–180€, quad 140€–220€. Bus: 70, 75, or 84.

➔ **Hotel Smeraldo** ★ CENTRO STORICO/ CAMPO DE' FIORI   In the tangle of cobble-stoned streets south of Campo de' Fiori, the Smeraldo is the priciest of the "cheap" inns in this neighborhood, mostly because all rooms have private bath and A/C—an important feature to keep in mind from June through August. The warm and almost elegant decor (the result of a recent refurbishing job) also help justify the extra euros. All rooms have TV and telephone with Internet connection capability. Definitely don't be suckered into the hotel's breakfast—there's a ridiculous 8€ charge for it, and you'll find a ton of great cafes across the street from the hotel where you can get your piping hot espresso and fresh *cornetto*. *Vicolo dei Chiodaroli 9, at Via dei Chiavari.* ☎ *06/687-5929. www.smeraldo roma.com. Single 75€–105€, double 110€– 140€, triple 135€–170€. us: 30, 40, 46, 62, 64, 70, 87, 116, 492, or 571. Tram: 8.*

➔ **Hotel Trastevere** ★ TRASTEVERE   The Antico Albergo Manara reopened its restored doors as Hotel Trastevere in 1998 to meet the demand for accommodations in this pictur-esque neighborhood on the west side of the Tiber. This little gem has fresh, bright bed-rooms with immaculate *cotto* (terra-cotta) tiles and comfortable, albeit boring furniture. Most of the rooms are spacious and look out onto the market square of Piazza San Cosi-mato. All of the bathrooms have been reno-vated and contain showers, although they're small. A few blocks downhill, you'll find all the streetlife of Trastevere; head up the hill, and you'll reach one of Rome's most glorious viewpoints, the Gianicolo (Janiculum Hill). All rooms have A/C, TV, Internet cable con-nections, and hair dryer. *Via Luciano Manara 24–25 (2 blocks up the hill from Via di San Cosi-mato).* ☎ *06/581-4713. www.hoteltrastevere. net. Single 80€, double 103€–105€, triple 130€, quad 155€. Bus: H, 44, 75, or 780. Tram: 8.*

Doable

➔ **Cisterna Hotel** TRASTEVERE   After the Santa Maria, below, this is the best-located of the Trastevere hotels, and right in the heart of the neighborhood's boisterous streetlife, which doesn't stop from dawn to the wee hours (i.e., light sleepers should probably stay away!). Staid, pink-toned rooms could use a rejuvenating treatment or two, but they're spacious and clean, and all have pri-vate bath. All rooms also have international satellite TV, A/C, telephone, radio, minibar, and safe. Breakfast is included in the room rates, but it would be a crime to miss out on having your morning coffee with the colorful characters of Trastevere at one of the neigh-borhood bars downstairs. *Via della Cisterna 8.* ☎ *06/581-7212. www.cisternahotel.it. Double 120€–130€. Tram: 3, 8; Bus: 75, 780, H.*

➔ **Hotel Antica Locanda** ★★ ANCIENT ROME/MONTI   A fantastic find in medieval Monti, the Antica Locanda is especially suited for couples not only because of its romantic decor, but because almost all rooms here are "matrimonial" doubles (not twin beds). Each of the 13 rooms is named for a different artist or composer: the Puccini is a cozy lair with a wrought iron bedstead, buttercream walls, exposed beam ceiling, and Oriental rugs on the handsome terra-cotta tile floor. The Rossini is homey and elegant, like the guest-room in your favorite relative's house, with a blue floral coverlet, brass bedstead, and dark-wood floors. Loveliest of all is the Mascagni Suite, which starts at a reasonable 155€ in the low season. No matter which room you get, you'll be tempted to sleep in well past breakfast, which is served in the roof garden in warm weather. In the bohemian neighborhood, you'll find a number of excel-lent places to eat and drink (including Rome's bastion of Indian restaurants on Via dei Ser-penti), and sights like the Roman Forum are only a short walk down the hill. All rooms have private bath, TV, telephone, hair dryer, minibar, and A/C. Breakfast is included in room rate. *Via del Boschetto 84 (at Via Panisperna).* ☎ *06/484894. www.antica-locanda. com. Double 130€–210€, Mascagni Suite 155€– 250€. Metro: Cavour. Bus: 40, 64, 70, or 75.*

→ **Hotel Campo de' Fiori** ✭ CENTRO STORICO/CAMPO DE' FIORI In an ivy-smothered building in the prime Campo de' Fiori zone, this government-rated two-star is just a shade more comfy than the nearby Sole, Smeraldo, and Pomezia (see "Cheap," earlier in this chapter), but priced about 50€ higher. Room decor—and comfort level—are all over the place in the hotel's 28 rooms, running the gamut from grandma's-house baby blue florals in bright and spacious top-floor rooms to cramped and dark, cabin-y doubles with tiny private bathrooms. If you have a choice of multiple rooms when you check in, it pays to see what your options are. All guests have access to the hotel's panoramic roof terrace, with great views of the dome of Sant'Andrea della Valle. Continental breakfast is included in the room rate and served in a classy subterranean dining room. With all these floors to cover, your knees better be in good shape—there's no lift. If the hotel's rooms are all booked, ask about the 15 short-term apartments they also rent, all located in the immediate vicinity of Campo de' Fiori. *Via del Biscione 6, off Campo de' Fiori.* ☎ *06/6880-6865. www.hotelcampodefiori.com. Double 150€–180€, triple 190€–220€, quad 210€– 250€. Bus: 30, 40, 46, 64, 70, 87, 116, 492, or 571.*

→ **Hotel Coronet** CENTRO STORICO/PANTHEON Dated decor at this Pantheon-area inn, occupying part of one floor of the massive noble Palazzo Doria-Pamphilj, may transport you back in time to the fussy 1800s, but there are modern conveniences like A/C, and some of the rooms (namely 34, 35, and 45) are huge, almost suitelike, with sitting areas. Ten of the 13 rooms have full private bath (on the small side, with fixtures in need of an update); the other three rooms have shower down the hall. Some rooms overlook the private urban garden of the Doria Pamphilj

family. *Piazza Grazioli 5 (off Via del Plebiscito).* ☎ *06/679-2341. www.hotelcoronet.com. Double 75€–170€. Bus: 30, 40, 46, 64, 70, 85, 87, 95, 116, 175, 492, or 571.*

→ **Hotel Navona** ✭✭ CENTRO STORICO/ PIAZZA NAVONA It's hard to believe this wonderfully lived-in, historic inn between Piazza Navona and the Pantheon is only a government-rated one-star hotel. From the elegant entryway to the spacious and well-lit, tastefully decorated rooms, it's also hard to believe that the Australian family that runs the place has kept prices so low. The Navona is continuously being restored, but with careful attention to preserving its antique character, so rooms get more comfortable every year, with soft lighting and relaxing green bedding, while cozy period touches, like exposed beam ceilings, remain intact. The Romantic poets Keats and Shelley were once boarders on the upper floors, and there are ancient ruins are in the basement. If you can score a room here, you'll definitely want to come back. All rooms have private bath and A/C, but there's a 15€ per-day charge for the latter. *Via dei Sediari 8, off Corso Rinascimento.* ☎ *06/686-4203. www.hotelnavona. com. Single 90€–110€, double 125€–140€, triple 160€–185€. Bus: 30, 40, 46, 62, 64, 70, 87, 116, 492, or 571.*

→ **Hotel Parlamento** ✭✭ SPANISH STEPS Equidistant from the Spanish Steps, the Trevi Fountain, and the Pantheon, the Parlamento is an old-fashioned but bright and clean inn, housed in a 16th-century, elevator-equipped palazzo. The Chini family, who manage the hotel, pride themselves on being especially helpful to guests, and they are; the concierge desk not only books tours and airport transfers but stocks a good range of wines that you can take to your room or the roof garden. If you make a reservation here, ask if any of the rooms with Jacuzzi tubs are available—there's nothing like coming back to a hydro-massage after a long day of Roman sightseeing! The roof garden, where you can have breakfast or just hang out in the sun, is a delightful mini-piazza in the sky. All rooms have TV, telephone, hair dryer, and safe. A/C is 12€ extra per day. *Via delle Convertite 5 (off Via del Corso).* ☎ *06/6992-1000. www.hotelparlamento.it. Single 80€–124€, double 90€–170€, triple 120€–195€, quad 132€–230€. Bus 62, 85, 96, 175, 492. Metro Barberini.*

➜ **Hotel Rinascimento** ⋆ CENTRO STORICO/CAMPO DE' FIORI If you can look past the grim entryway and accept the fact that many of the rooms are cramped, this is actually an excellent choice on a prime, non-touristy *centro storico* street north of Campo de' Fiori. The Rinascimento's location is really cool—on the nearby side streets, there are old-world craftsmen's shops, where local characters play card games on tables on the cobblestones, and of course, hundreds of great restaurants and pizzerias, and the action of Campo de' Fiori, within a 5-block radius. Amenities include full private bath, TV, telephone, minibar, and A/C. All rooms are wired for Internet connection; if you didn't bring your own computer, the hotel also has a public Internet terminal in the lobby. Check for special offers on their website, as there are often huge discounts available. *Via del Pellegrino 122.* ☎ *06/687-4813. www.hotelrinascimento.com. All rooms have private bath, A/C, TV, telephone. Breakfast included. Double 115€–180€, triple 165€–220€, quad 185€–240€. Bus: 30, 40, 46, 64, 70, 87, 116, 492, or 571.*

➜ **Hotel Santa Maria** ⋆⋆ TRASTEVERE Hidden off a tiny alley in the very best part of Trastevere, the Santa Maria is quite a surprising treat to behold. It's a one-story property, with rooms arranged almost motel-like, on porticoed halls around a lovely courtyard with orange trees. The rooms, which range from singles to bi-level suites, aren't exactly palatial, but they're fresh and comfy, with simple oak furniture, *cotto* tile floors, and sunny bedspreads, and the suites are a good-value option if you're traveling in a group. All rooms have full private bath, TV, telephone, minibar, and A/C, and there's an Internet point in the reception building off the courtyard. Don't plan to have a loud night in your room—the romantic Santa Maria is a quiet hotel—but this incredibly nightlife-friendly location means you can hit the surrounding bars and eateries and have an easy commute back to your bed. In additional to its orange trees, the central garden has tables and chairs where an ample breakfast is served in warm weather; otherwise, you eat breakfast in a converted artisan's workshop. This is an absolute treasure in a hotel-starved neighborhood. *Vicolo del Piede 2, between Piazza Santa Maria in Trastevere and Via della Pelliccia.* ☎ *06/589-4626. www.htlsantamaria.com. Single 135€–165€, double 155€–210€, triple 200€–250€, 4-person suite 250€–320€, 6-person suite 350€–450€. Bus: 23, 271, or 280. Tram: 8.*

➜ **Hotel Suisse** ⋆ SPANISH STEPS Near the Spanish Steps but hidden away from its madding crowd, the family-run Suisse is not an inn for party animals, but it is a great place to spend a few extra euros when you want some peace and quiet but still want to be close to the action of the *centro.* True to the hotel's name, cozy rooms are more Nordic than Latin in vibe, with small throw-rugs carefully placed over beautiful herringbone parquet floors, and functional but spare Empire-style furnishings that seem to have been drawn from the home of a Zurich playwright. (The Latin vibe isn't completely missing, however—the white-and-navy-pinstriped bedspreads make you feel like you're shacking up with Alex Rodriguez or Derek Jeter.) All 12 rooms have satellite TV and private bathrooms (shower, no tub) with brand-new fixtures, and 10 of the rooms are equipped with A/C (the use of which costs an extra 9€ per day); the other two rooms have ceiling fans. Breakfast, included in the room rate, is served in your room. Another bonus is that it's a short walk from here to the relaxing green parks of the Villa Borghese and panoramic Pincio terraces beyond. *Via Gregoriana 54 (at Via Capo le Case).* ☎ *06/678-3649. www.hotelsuisserome.com. Single 85€–100€, double 135€–158€. Metro: Barberini. Bus: 62, 63, 95, 175, or 492.*

➔ **Les Chambres d'Or** VATICAN Recently renovated rooms at this government-rated three-star right behind Piazza Risorgimento are comfortable and immaculately kept—like a 19th-century Best Western—with upholstery in saturated colors, small side tables and chairs, and dark blue patterned carpeting. Bathrooms are spacious, with proper shower stalls (not just a drain in the floor, as at some other moderate Roman inns), and plenty of counter space where you can spill out the contents of your beauty products bag. Their peak season rates are on the pricey side, but in the off season they'll usually sell rooms at well below the rack rate. All rooms have A/C, satellite TV, minibar, and radio. Breakfast is included in the rates and served at the downstairs Cafe Rendezvous, a real Roman bar with indoor and alfresco tables. *Via dei Gracchi 32 (at Via Ottaviano).* ☎ *06/390-8161. www.leschambresdor.com. Double 100€–190€, triple 130€–220€, quad 170€–260€, quintuple 180€–280€. Metro: Ottaviano. Bus: 23, 81, or 492.*

Splurge

➔ **Es (Radisson SAS)** ★★ ESQUILINO/TERMINI If you're the kind of person whose stylistic preferences skew toward edgy video installations instead of the treasures of the Vatican, you'll probably love the Es. When this behemoth of a "minimalist" hotel opened in 2002, it heralded the dawn of a new era of modern design in Rome. With an imposing, striated exterior that gives the building the look of a gigantic cruise ship, the Es communicates little with its neighborhood, the seedy southern side of Termini. Instead, the hotel is a glassy, metallic vessel unto itself. Uncluttered by fussy furniture and lit by huge

windows (which turn pink, yellow, or green at night), guest rooms feel larger than they are, and are priced well below what you'd pay at other government-rated five-stars around town. The cool, *Robinson Crusoe*–inspired "Raft"-style standard rooms have sink, shower, wardrobe, and queen bed on a single, raised platform of mahogany. Technological amenities include flat-screen TVs and high-speed Internet in every room, and, of course, those chameleonic windows. The star feature at the Es, however, is the rooftop terrace, where a full-service spa and outdoor swimming pool are located. The poolside cafe, Zest, which has hypnotic views over the 1930s arches of Termini station and its abacus-like railyard, is a surrealist-chic hipster hangout. (Anyone is welcome at the poolside bar; but nonguests have to pay a fee to use the pool itself—call the hotel for prices.) Rates include continental breakfast and A/C. *Via F. Turati 171, at Via Rattazzi.* ☎ *06/444841. www.radissonsas.com. Doubles from 260€. Metro: Vittorio. Bus: 70.*

MTV **Best** ➔ **Hotel Locarno** ★★ PIAZZA DEL POPOLO/SPANISH STEPS Sashay back in time to the glamorous 1920s at this fabulously stylish, understatedly hip hotel near Piazza del Popolo. The Locarno is like a bashful, slightly melancholy peacock that only shows its feathers to those who come inside—the exterior of the hotel gives no indication of how wonderful this place is. If you're going to cough up the extra dough to stay here, the "deluxe" double rooms and suites in the east wing of the building are where you want to be; these are the *Great Gatsby* rooms, the breathtaking period pieces with original Art Nouveau furniture, walls washed in sumptuously fading colors, and high, intricately coffered ceilings. The dark and cramped standard and "superior" doubles in the main building are not nearly as interesting (some are frankly depressing). All guests have access to a small, attractive patio in the back. Overall, the nostalgic, romantic atmosphere

When in Rome . . . Breakfast as the Romans Do

The majority of Italian hotels throw in some kind of continental breakfast involving stale croissants, weak coffee, and—randomly—cheese, but you can and should get a much better, more authentic Roman breakfast at the nearest coffee bar, which are everywhere in Rome—just look for the words "bar" or "caffetteria." Breakfast is the one meal in Italy that isn't a lingering, sit-down affair. A typical *colazione* is taken standing up at your neighborhood bar and consists of cappuccino and a pastry (just one, so the carbs won't kill you) from the bar's glass counter. The simplest pastry is the *cornetto,* a denser, sweeter version of a croissant, which comes in plain *(semplice)* or whole-grain *(integrale)* varieties, or you can choose from a bunch of Danish-type pastries filled with fruit, ricotta, chocolate, or Nutella. Cappuccino is the overwhelming favorite morning coffee drink, but you can also get a *caffellatte* (don't ask for just a "latte," unless all you want is a glass of warm milk), or a plain old *caffè* (espresso) if you don't want any milk at all. Taken standing up, your drink and pastry should cost a whopping 2€, but you'll pay about double that if you sit down (Italians don't). If you like OJ in the morning, all Roman bars will squeeze you a fresh orange *spremuta* for about 2€. Until you become a regular, it's a good idea to pay first (there's usually a separate cashier), and always lay down a .10–.20€ tip on the counter when you place your order with the barista.

of the Locarno has made it a favorite with visiting filmmakers, poets, and other artistic types. All rooms have full private bath, international satellite TV, telephone, A/C, minibar, and safe. *Via della Penna 22, off Via Ripetta.* ☎ *06/361-0841. www.hotellocarno.com. Single 140€, double 210€–310€, suite 450€–650€. Metro: Flaminio.*

→ **Westin Excelsior** ★★ VIA VENETO When you want to indulge in some full-blown Italianate fabulousness, this landmark 19th-century palazzo has the kind of over-the-top glitz that would make Donald Trump feel right at home. By far the flashiest grande dame on the Via Veneto luxury hotel corridor, the Excelsior is like a Hollywood actress dolled up for Oscar Night, year-round. Not surprisingly, it's Rome's most popular spot with celebrities (the kind who don't shy away from the paparazzi) and other professional partyers. The bling begins in the marble-wainscoted lobby—windows are festooned with drapery thicker than your grandma's lasagna, and ridiculously elaborate chandeliers cast their twinkling reflections on gilt Rococo mirrors and overstuffed, chintz-upholstered furniture—and continues right up to the Villa La Cupola suite (which the management claims is the largest hotel room in Europe), a frescoed folly with its own private swimming pool and panoramic patio. "Deluxe" rooms (aka the ones you might be able to afford) are equally lavish, with plush settees, lacquered desks, intricate crown mouldings, and wall panels of beet-red chintz. Bathrooms are glossy, 1930s-glam affairs, with tropical plants and plenty of black marble. Smart guests should prowl the halls and listen for where the parties are—there are always a few at the Excelsior worth crashing, and if you happen to stumble upon some famous person's in-room rager, you can always snap a photo and sell it to the tabloids, thereby reclaiming the small fortune it takes to spend the night here. *Via Vittorio Veneto 125, at Via Boncompagni.* ☎ *06/47081. www. excelsior.hotelinroma.com. Rates include breakfast. Metro: Barberini. Bus: 52, 53, 63, 116, or 490. A/C, TV, Internet. Double from 350€.*

Eating

Rome's casual, high-quality dining scene is one of the city's most attractive qualities. All over town, you can just walk in and have an amazing meal with free-flowing wine in a fun, authentic place for less than 15€ per person. While finding and paying for hotels in Rome might stress you (and your wallet) out, the good news is, eating and drinking in Rome won't—the trick is to steer clear of restaurants that are right on the main squares, as they tend to be way-overpriced tourist traps.

In general, the best areas for down-home Roman cooking and lively atmosphere are the backstreets of the *centro storico,* Monti, and Trastevere. For a young, social atmosphere and really cheap tab, sit-down pizzerias are your best bet. If you manage to befriend any locals, the weekend-night out-of-town meal, at a rustic osteria in one of the countless hill towns around Rome, is a favorite pastime of fun-loving types and a classic experience you'll not soon forget.

On the Menu

Roman cuisine is traditional and simple. You won't find a whole lot of variety, but you will find time-tested, intensely flavorful and satisfying pastas, a selection of grilled or roast pork, beef, or seafood dishes, and a variety of tasty vegetable side dishes *(contorni)* to keep vegetarians or health-conscious types happy. If you're looking for poultry, you're in the wrong town. Chicken—and turkey, especially—is almost unheard of in Roman kitchens. Start your meal off with a *bruschetta* (pronounced *brusketta,* not *brushetta*)—toasted bread with garlic and whatever else smeared on top—and end it with whatever *dolce fatto in casa* (homemade dessert) they're offering. *Panna cotta* (cooked cream), tiramisu, *crème caramel,* or a simple *macedonia* (fresh fruit cup, with lemon juice squeezed on top) are all widely available.

As for drinks, the standard combo is *vino* (of course!) and *acqua minerale* (mineral water); you can request *liscia* (still), *frizzante* (sparkling), or, locals' favorite compromise, *Ferrarelle* (this is a brand name but is also understood to mean water with just a touch of fizz). Do opt for the mineral water, as it does wonders for your digestion and helps mitigate your hangover from what will probably be a high *vino* intake each and every night. All but the simplest restaurants have some kind of wine list, but the *vino della casa* (house wine) is what you'll be ordering most of the time; it costs 7€ a liter and tastes just fine. If you like cocktails with your dinner, too bad; it's simply not done in Rome. Note that very few Roman restaurants, unlike their counterparts in other world cities, have a bar area where you can just come and have a drink either before or totally separate from your meal—that's what the *aperitivo* is for.

OKKIO! The Quinto Quarto

Traditional Roman cuisine makes heavy use of slaughterhouse leftovers—aka hot dog ingredients—and the old-fashioned trattorias and osterias of Trastevere and Testaccio are still serving up the *quinto quarto* (the "fifth quarter," or innards) of cows and pigs to eager audiences. If you don't want any UFOs (unidentified farm-animal organs) floating around on your plate, steer clear of the following words on the menu: *pajata* (red sauce with intestines from an unweaned calf—yep, mother's milk still inside), *trippa* (tripe), *animelle* (a medley of fried glands), and *coratella* (heart, and who the hell knows what else).

PASTA ALLA ROMANA

On almost every menu in town, you'll find some or all of the following pasta sauces, which originated in Rome or the surrounding countryside hundreds of years ago. Though many are widely imitated around the world, you'll never find them tasting as good as they do right here in the Eternal City:

○ *Carbonara* Yummy but rich, this mixture of egg yolk, pancetta, pecorino romano, and pepper is kind of like a bacon-and-eggs breakfast served over pasta.

○ *Amatriciana* There's nothing better on a cold day than this hearty, tomato-based sauce with *guanciale* (pig cheek, like bacon), onions, and garlic.

○ *Arrabbiata* An awesomely flavorful option that also happens to be vegetarian, *arrabbiata* ("angry") sauce consists of tomato, garlic, and peperoncino.

○ *Cacio e pepe* Heaps of grated pecorino romano and pepper—simple but exquisite.

Coffee Bars & Gelaterias

When it comes to settling on a gelato place, make sure you're getting the good stuff. Almost all gelaterias will advertise *produzione propria* ("made in-house") or *artigianale* ("homemade") even if they're not, so it always pays to do the **banana gelato color test:** If their banana flavor is a muddy, brownish beige (the color of a very ripe banana), it's all natural, and you're good to go. If it's too yellow, it means there are probably artificial colors and other weird chemicals present in all the other flavors at that gelateria, so move on! (One final grammatical point: If you're getting a cup or cone of ice cream, it's *un gelato*, not *gelati!!*)

As for coffee, we've listed a few particularly famous (and touristy) Roman bars below, but if you're looking to mix with locals, hit one of the hundreds of unassuming little coffee places all over the city. (Just look for the word "bar"—they're on every block.) No matter where you go for your

Vino Dei Castelli

You might think of Rome as an ancient and modern world capital, but the stereotypical *romano de' roma* is not a city slicker but a fun-loving, coarse-tongued, and big-hearted country bumpkin. As such, real born-and-bred Romans are not a people who care to spend a lot of money on wine. Good for them, and for you, the Castelli Romani hill towns south of Rome (like Frascati and Albano) produce giant casks of cheap and drinkable table wine that is served in every trattoria and osteria in the city. A liter carafe of white or red *vino dei castelli* will set you back about 7€. For the full cultural experience, get an old-timer to teach you a few bars of "La Società dei Magnaccioni," a classic, table-slapping Roman anthem about sloth and gluttony.

espresso and cappuccino, you really can't go wrong when it comes to quality. If you start to cultivate a brand loyalty, all bars have a sign outside indicating what brand of espresso they serve: I'm partial to Danesi, Illy, and Lavazza, but some locals swear by Mauro and Negresco. See for yourself! See also "When in Rome . . . Breakfast as the Romans Do," in the Sleeping section (p. 106).

→ **Blue Ice Gelateria** ★ CENTRO STORICO/ GELATO It may lack the institutional cred of such historical gelaterias as Giolitti (below), but the Blue Ice chain, with six locations, has a lot going for it. It's cheap, efficient, tasty, and open late (for when that 1am craving hits, and believe me, it will). For the lactose intolerant and/or health freaks, they also have *sorbetto,* soy gelato, and frozen yogurt. *Near Campo de' Fiori: Via dei Baullari, at Piazza della Cancelleria.* ☎ *06/687-6114. Bus: 40, 46, 62, 64, 70, 81, 87, 116, 492, 571, or 628. Near the Trevi Fountain: Via delle Muratte 19.*

☎ 06/679-6762. Bus: 62, 85, 95, 175, or 492. No credit cards. Daily 9am–2am.

→ **Da Quinto** ★★ CENTRO STORICO/
GELATO & SMOOTHIES   Truth be told, the gelato at this hole in the wall west of Piazza Navona ain't that great—too icy, and kind of flavorless—but their enormous fruit smoothies are amazing! For about 3.50€, you'll get a blender full of berries, melon, banana, milk, honey, whatever you want. The portions are big enough to share (they're happy to split the smoothie into two cups), or you can ask them to pour your leftovers into your empty water bottle (they have funnels just for this, so they're happy to do it). The blonde girl behind the counter has been wearing the same pink plastic apron for years, but hey, if it ain't broke . . . Via di Tor Millina 15, at Via dell'Anima. ☎ 06/686-5657. No credit cards. Daily 10am–1am. Closed in Jan. Bus: 30, 40, 46, 62, 64, 70, 81, 87, 492, 571, or 628.

→ **Giolitti** ★★ PANTHEON/GELATO   A de rigueur stop on the tourism shuffle through the *centro storico,* this Roman institution (pronounced "joe-*leet*-tee") is the city's oldest combination *gelateria-pasticceria* and packed with locals and tourists alike. Don't be put off by the cashier lady in front, whom you have to pay before approaching the ice cream cases—she's gruff, but harmless. The men who scoop the gelato in back are much more service-oriented (especially when it comes to young females), but you really have to assert yourself in line here or you'll never get served. Some of their better flavors (among about a hundred choices) are After Eight (mint-chocolate-chip), *fiordilatte* (a simple, exquisite sweet cream), and *lampone* (raspberry). Via degli Uffici del Vicario 40, near Via di Campo Marzio. ☎ 06/679-42-06. www. giolitti.it. No credit cards. Daily 8am–2am. Bus: 62, 85, 95, 116, 175, or 492.

→ **Old Bridge** ★★ VATICAN/GELATO   If you ask me, the best thing about Old Bridge is the owner's poster-sized photograph of himself, underwater, with a great white shark. The draw, however, for all the Prati kids who flock here every night and brave huge lines for a scoop of something sweet, is that it's such a reliable social scene—where you show up in the hopes that the boy you have a crush on will also happen to be there at the same time so that you can ignore him. A great slice of Roman teen and 20-something life, and the gelato happens to very tasty, too. Try the chocolate—it's creamy and intensely flavorful but not too rich. (We're still not clear what the Old Bridge refers to, as there's no water in sight, but the Vatican Museums are only 3 minutes away.) *Viale dei Bastioni di Michelangelo 5 (Piazza Risorgimento). Apr–Oct Daily 11–1am, Nov–Mar Daily 11am–midnight. Metro Ottaviano; Bus 23, 492; Tram 19.*

→ **Pellacchia** ★ VATICAN/GELATO   Gelaterias abound in the Vatican area, but traditionalists in the know come to Pellacchia, an intimate, old-fashioned combo coffee bar/ gelateria right on the shopping strip of Via Cola di Rienzo. Not only is their gelato some of the best in the neighborhood, but staff is super-friendly and will let you try flavors before you place your final order. They don't have a ton of flavors to choose from, but there's always a chocolate, a cream, and a fruit of some kind. *Via Cola di Rienzo 103, at Piazza Cola di Rienzo. ☎ 06/321-08-07. No credit cards. Tues–Sun 10am–10pm (midnight in summer). Metro: Lepanto. Bus: 81 or 280.*

→ **Sant'Eustachio** ★★ CENTRO STORICO/
COFFEE   Sant'Eustachio's is by far the most celebrated espresso in the city, so if you're a coffee snob, you'd better make a pilgrimage to this classy little spot just west of the Pantheon. Look for the blue neon sign opposite the church (Sant'Eustachio) with the tape-recorded bells, and get in line. Your first stop is the cashier on the right, where everyone in front of you will be ordering *un grancaffè, per favore. The grancaffè* is Sant'Eustachio's specialty—it's a larger, creamier, and more

ROME & LAZIO

Eating in Rome

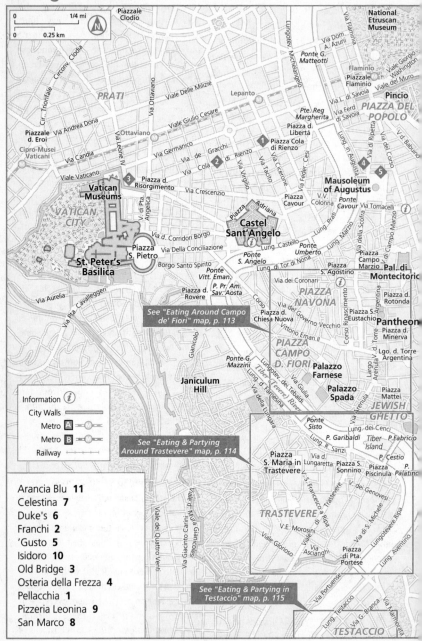

Arancia Blu **11**
Celestina **7**
Duke's **6**
Franchi **2**
'Gusto **5**
Isidoro **10**
Old Bridge **3**
Osteria della Frezza **4**
Pellacchia **1**
Pizzeria Leonina **9**
San Marco **8**

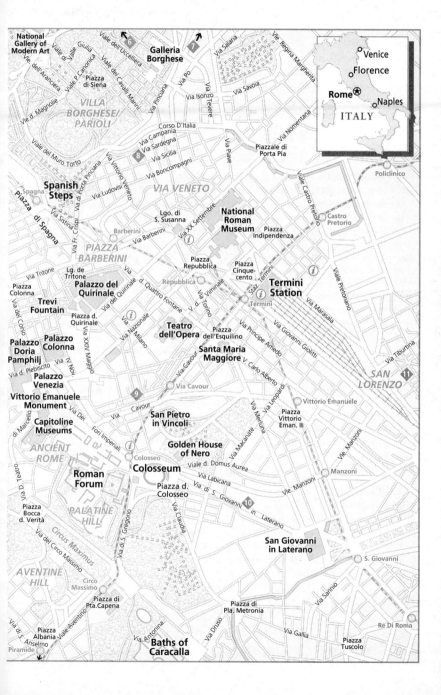

expensive version of an espresso shot, but before you get peer-pressured into ordering one, know that you can get a regular *caffè normale* (espresso) or cappuccino here, too, and they're just as good. Take your receipt to the Art Deco bar on the left, greet the *baristi*, say what you're having (they won't act like they're listening, but they are), and plunk down your .20€ tip on the zinc counter. All Sant'Eustachio drinks are served presweetened unless you request otherwise, so if you don't like sugar in your coffee, specify *amaro* (bitter) or *senza zucchero* (without sugar) with the barista. Sant'Eustachio also sells packaged whole beans and other inexpensive items that make good souvenirs for your coffee fiend friends back home. *Piazza Sant'Eustachio 82, at Piazza dei Caprettari. ☎ 06/656-13-09. No credit cards. Daily 8:30am–1am. Bus: 40, 46, 62, 64, 70, 87, 116, 492, 571, or 628.*

➜ **Tazza d'Oro** ★ PANTHEON COFFEE Facing the Pantheon, on the northeast corner of Piazza della Rotonda, this is a big and atmospheric coffee bar, with burlap sacks of roasted espresso beans that fill the entire square with a powerful coffee aroma (although the grease stench from McDonald's, a few doors down, can be stiff competition). There's always a long line at the single cashier, but it moves quickly. The sheer number of people they serve every day have left the *baristi* a bit surly, but even though they might not be as smiley as your local Starbucks staffers, these guys are lifers who know a thing or two about pulling coffee drinks. In summer—or anytime you're dragging from too much sightseeing—do not miss a chance to cool down and jolt up with their *granita di caffè*, a petite, clear plastic cup filled with crushed frozen espresso, interspersed with layers of full-fat whipped cream. It's the best 1.30€ you'll ever spend, I swear. Whole-bean or ground coffee in colorful canisters makes a great souvenir. *Via degli Orfani 84, at Piazza della Rotonda. ☎ 06/678-9292. No credit cards. Mon–Sat 8am–8pm. Bus: 30, 40, 46, 62, 64, 70, 87, 116, 492, or 571.*

A Hot Spot for Drinks & Sandwiches

Admittedly, some of the *bella gente* (Roman beautiful people) who made **Taverna del Campo** ★ a Campo de' Fiori hot spot have moved on to make way for the tourists, but the Taverna is still cool, especially on Sunday afternoons. You won't find any pasta or meat dishes here, but what you will find is a boatload of wine by the glass or bottle, pizza-bread sandwiches stuffed with marinated veggies, deli meats and cheese, and a ton of garlic. They also provide free peanuts (in the shell, which explains the elephant-cage look of the cobblestones around here). *Hint:* Taverna del Campo's casual food offerings make it a great place for a light lunch, but during the week, you'll find fewer tourists after 7pm, when the piazza fills up with locals on the prowl for the *aperitivo*/mating hour. Campo de' Fiori 16, at Via dei Baullari. ☎ **06/687-44-02.** Sandwiches 3€–4€. No credit cards. Tues–Sun 9am–2am.Bus: 30, 40, 46, 62, 64, 70, 81, 87, 492, 571, or 628. Tram: 8.

Delis & Snacks

These are our top recommendations, though any deli (*alimentari*) will make up basic (and cheap) sandwiches with whatever meats and cheeses they have, but they don't do condiments or vegetables. *Alimentari* citywide are closed Thursday afternoons, as well as Saturday afternoons in summer, and they're never open on Sundays.

➜ **Franchi** ★★ VATICAN/DELI Foodie heaven near the Vatican. Behind the deli

Eating Around Campo de' Fiori

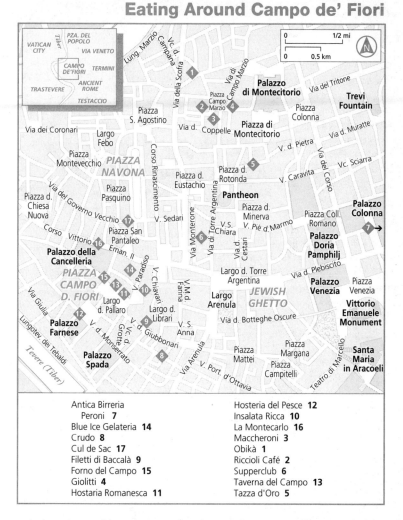

Pza. del Popolo • Vatican City • Via Veneto • Termini • Campo de' Fiori • Ancient Rome • Trastevere • Testaccio

Palazzo di Montecitorio

Piazza Campo Marzio

Piazza S. Agostino

Piazza di Montecitorio

Piazza Colonna

Trevi Fountain

Via dei Coronari

Largo Febo

Piazza Montevecchio

PIAZZA NAVONA

Piazza Pasquino

Piazza d. Chiesa Nuova

Piazza d. Eustachio

Piazza d. Rotonda

Pantheon

Piazza d. Minerva

Piazza Coll. Romano

Palazzo Colonna

Piazza San Pantaleo

Palazzo della Cancelleria

PIAZZA CAMPO D. FIORI

Largo d. Pallaro

Largo d. Librari

Largo d. Torre Argentina

Largo Arenula

JEWISH GHETTO

Palazzo Doria Pamphilj

Palazzo Venezia

Piazza Venezia

Vittorio Emanuele Monument

Palazzo Farnese

Palazzo Spada

Piazza Mattei

Piazza Margana

Piazza Campitelli

Santa Maria in Aracoeli

Antica Birreria Peroni **7**	Hosteria del Pesce **12**
Blue Ice Gelateria **14**	Insalata Ricca **10**
Crudo **8**	La Montecarlo **16**
Cul de Sac **17**	Maccheroni **3**
Filetti di Baccalà **9**	Obikà **1**
Forno del Campo **15**	Riccioli Café **2**
Giolitti **4**	Supperclub **6**
Hostaria Romanesca **11**	Taverna del Campo **13**
	Tazza d'Oro **5**

cases in the main part of the store is a mouth-watering array of the finest cheeses and cured meats from all over Italy and select regions of France, Spain, and northern Europe, as well as jars of rare truffles and other gourmet goods with eye-popping price tags. Save your drool for the stuff you can afford, which is the prepared food counter over on the right-hand corner of the store. Here, a well-heeled but ravenous lunch crowd jockeys for space in front of a tantalizing line-up of pastas, vegetables, roasted meats, fish plates, and fritters galore. Among Franchi's fried products, its 1€ *supplì*—fried rice balls, bound together by tomato sauce and mozzarella—are famous citywide. Since there's nowhere to sit at Franchi, everything can be packaged to-go in handy foil trays. Eat your picnic up the street in Piazza Risorgimento, amid the tourist traffic near the Vatican, or hike a little farther to Castel Sant'Angelo, where the castle's moat has

Eating & Partying Around Trastevere

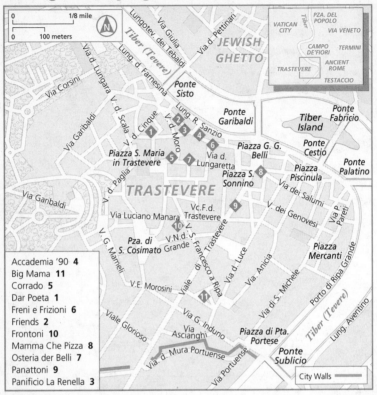

Accademia '90 **4**
Big Mama **11**
Corrado **5**
Dar Poeta **1**
Freni e Frizioni **6**
Friends **2**
Frontoni **10**
Mamma Che Pizza **8**
Osteria der Belli **7**
Panattoni **9**
Panificio La Renella **3**

been converted into a grassy park. *Via Cola di Rienzo 204, at Via Terenzio.* ☎ *06/6874651. www.franchi.it. Mon–Sat 9am–7:30pm. Bus: 23, 81, 271, 280, or 492.*

➔ **Frontoni** ★★ TRASTEVERE/DELI I have cured many a hangover (or tried to) with the marvelous pizza-bread sandwiches of Frontoni. You pick the size of pizza bread you want, and you can get as many fillings as you want—mortadella, mozzarella, salmon, basil, sun-dried tomatoes, roasted eggplant, all manner of condiments—and the white-haired men who work behind the counter will sing the names of the ingredients as they lovingly assemble your sandwich. Just be sure they slather it with plenty of olive oil and salt it generously—*mmm mmm!* Perhaps the most

exquisite choice here is the traditional *bresaola* (cured beef), arugula, and *parmigiano* sandwich—although, come to think of it, the ricotta and mushroom is pretty darn good, too. The *Maga Circe*, with salmon, artichoke, and mozzarella, is a favorite on beach days. Even if you don't make it to the beach, grab one of Frontoni's creations and head up to the Gianicolo, where you can plop down in the grass with your picnic and enjoy a glorious view. Besides the sandwiches, Frontoni has hot and cold plates also suitable for take-out. *Viale Trastevere 52, at Via San Francesco a Ripa.* ☎ *06/581-2436. www.frontoni.it. Sandwiches priced by ingredients and size, about 3.50€–5€. No credit cards. Mon–Sat 10am– 11pm; Sun 5–11pm. Bus: 75, 780, or H. Tram: 8.*

Eating & Partying in Testaccio

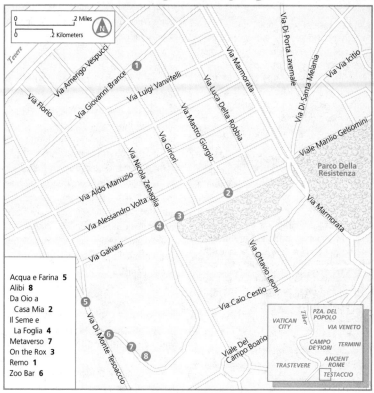

0 — .2 Miles
0 — .2 Kilometers

Tevere

Via Florio
Via Amerigo Vespucci
Via Giovanni Brance
Via Luigi Vanvitelli
Via Mastro Giorgio
Via Girori
Via Luca Delta Robbia
Via Marmorata
Via Di Porta Lavernale
Via Di Santa Melania
Via Icitio
Viale Manlio Gelsomini
Parco Della Resistenza
Via Nicola Zebaglia
Via Aldo Manuzio
Via Alessandro Volta
Via Galvani
Via Marmorata
Via Ottavio Leoni
Via Caio Cestio
Via Di Monte Tesoaccio
Viale Del Campo Boario

Acqua e Farina **5**
Alibi **8**
Da Oio a
  Casa Mia **2**
Il Seme e
  La Foglia **4**
Metaverso **7**
On the Rox **3**
Remo **1**
Zoo Bar **6**

❶ ❷ ❸ ❹ ❺ ❻ ❼ ❽

VATICAN CITY | PZA. DEL POPOLO
Tiber | VIA VENETO
CAMPO DE'FIORI | TERMINI
TRASTEVERE | ANCIENT ROME
| TESTACCIO

Pizza

⬛️ **Best** → **Dar Poeta** ★★★ TRASTE-
VERE   To get to the yummiest pizza in all
Rome, your navigational skills will be tested,
and you might have to wait for an hour to get
a table, but all aggravation is forgotten once
you sink your teeth into one of these heavenly pies. The trick to finding the place is
knowing that Vicolo del Bologna is a tiny, Y-
shaped street that hits Via della Scala, Vicolo
del Cinque, and Via Benedetta; Dar Poeta is
on the right fork of the Y, between Via
Benedetta and Via della Scala. Our time-
tested technique for a night at Dar Poeta goes
something like this: Arrive at about 8:30pm,
look for the bald guy with the clipboard, put
your name down, and let him know if you

have any preferences for an indoor versus
outdoor table. However long he tells you the
wait is, it'll be accurate to within 1 minute. If
the wait is under 30 minutes, find a nearby
motorino, sit on it, and watch the excitement
build as more and more parties of young
Romans arrive and try to wangle their way
onto some kind of friends-of-the-manager
list. If the wait is longer than 30 minutes, head
to Artù pub or Ombre Rosse cafe in Piazza
Sant'Egidio, a few blocks away, and have a
drink while you pass the time. Once you're
back at Dar Poeta and seated, start off with
the *bruschetta mista,* which features broiled
slices of bread, rubbed in garlic and oil and
topped with marinated vegetables, *ciauscolo*
(a type of *salame*), or delicious tuna pâté. As

Pizza Party

The cheapest way to fill your stomach in Rome is with pizza. (No, it's not just an American myth—they really do eat a lot of pizza in Italy.) Roman pizzas are thin-crusted and priced anywhere from 4€ for a basic margherita to 8€ for pizzas with more gourmet toppings, like *mozzarella di bufala* and *funghi porcini*. In Rome, as in the rest of Italy, pizzas come in one size only (about 14 inches in diameter) and are not meant to be shared. The Roman pizzeria is its own category of restaurant, with a young clientele and energetic vibe, and is usually open for dinner only; those that are open at lunch are probably tourist traps and should be avoided. Throughout the day, you can hit up your local *pizza al taglio* (by-the-slice) place for a cheap and delicious snack.

for your pizza order, branch out and sample their creative pies, like the *fior di salmone* (with smoked salmon and zucchini tops), or pumpkin and pancetta. One of the most popular pizzas here, the *campagnola* (with fresh cherry tomatoes, *mozzarella di bufala*, and basil), tends to sell out as the night wears on, so try to order it early. I always seem to get the *taglialegna* (the "lumberjack," with sausage and veggies), which never disappoints. If you can still find room after all that, their Nutella-filled calzone is a decadent dessert. Dar Poeta's Naples-style crust is already thicker than most Roman pies, but you can get extra-thick crust for 1€ more by ordering *doppio impasto*. Beer, as opposed to wine, is the preferred accompaniment here. *Vicolo del Bologna 45, near Via della Scala.* ☎ *06/588-0516. Reservations taken for 7:30–8:30pm only. Pizzas from 6€. Daily for dinner only. Bus: 23, 271, or 280.*

MTV Best → **La Montecarlo** ★★★

PIAZZA NAVONA If I'm traveling through Rome and only have 1 night for dinner, this is where I'm coming, with all my friends, for *bruschetta*, pizza, wine, and *limoncello*—that's how much I love this place. Loud, lively, and super-friendly, La Montecarlo really does feel like a party—there's always an energetic crowd of 20- and 30-somethings waiting for a table, but host extraordinaire Carlo (always in his dark, button-down shirt) will seat you in a flash if you stride confidently to the front of the line and pretend to be a regular. Seating in the original back room is far preferable to the sterile new dining room. There are also a bunch of rickety tables under an awning outside, making alfresco dining possible almost year-round. The pizza is thin-crusted, piping hot, and slightly misshapen, with toppings unevenly distributed—just how we like it. For how close it is to Piazza Navona, it's virtually tourist-free, and for how busy it gets, service is ridiculously fast but never rushing. They'll let you stay as long as you want as long as you keep eating and drinking, and you should savor your time here. When the time does come for the check (which you'll have to ask for), your waiter tallies it in his head and writes it on the paper tablecloth. It usually comes out to less than 10 euros *a cranio* ("per cranium"). **Nota bene:** They're one of few Roman pizzerias open for lunch, but it's a totally different scene—quieter and more touristy—by day. *Vicolo Savelli 11, at Corso Vittorio Emanuele II.* ☎ *06/686-1877. www.sevoinapizzadillo.net. Pizzas from 5€. Tues–Sun for lunch and dinner. Bus: 40, 64, or 571.*

→ **Panattoni** ★ TRASTEVERE The food and atmosphere are not as good as at Dar Poeta, but Panattoni (aka I Marmi) is nevertheless one of Trastevere's most popular pizzerias—it's certainly a hell of a lot easier to find. Its long, white marble-slab tables and bright lighting have earned Panattoni the nickname *"l'Obbitorio"* (the morgue), so don't go here expecting an intimate meal, but you'll be so crammed in with your tablemates that you're sure to make friends with some locals. Start with some fried appetizers (the *filetti di baccalà*, or battered and deep-fried cod fillets, are excellent), and then move onto your pizza, which is very thin-crusted and baked in a wood-fired oven here. There aren't many choices on the pizza menu besides a few Roman basics (like the *capricciosa*—the "kitchen sink" pizza, with artichoke, prosciutto, mushrooms, olives, and egg), but you definitely won't leave hungry. Wash it all down with some beer or a local *vino dei castelli. Viale Trastevere 53, between Piazza Sonnino and Piazza Mastai. ☎ 06/580-0919. Pizzas from 5€. Thurs–Tues for dinner only. Bus: 75, 780, or H. Tram: 3 or 8.*

➔ **Remo** ★★ TESTACCIO   If you tell a local you're going to get a pizza in Testaccio—the neighborhood most famous for its slaughterhouse (which was closed in the 1970s) and Monte Testaccio, a 35m-high (115-ft.) pile of broken ancient Roman bottles—it goes without saying that you're going to Remo. The pizza here is classic, thin-crusted Roman, with your standard array of simple earthy toppings (such as fresh local veggies, prosciutto, or the tomato-and-mozzarella standard margherita) and dirt cheap. Clientele is almost strictly regulars who live within 4 blocks of here, so you might be gawked at for the outsider tourist you are, but in a friendly way. The no-frills dining room consists of just a few rickety tables, so expect to wait at least 15 minutes for a table. (To pass the time, lean against the nearest *motorino* and flip through the pages of the local sports newspaper, *Corriere dello Sport,* to get up to speed on the latest soccer standings.) Over the course of your meal, you're bound to get an earful of colorful Roman dialect—the chief topic of discussion being AS Roma soccer team captain Francesco Totti's latest hamstring injury. Note that while Remo is a great slice of real workaday Roman life, it's not the place to

come and spend hours over wine and beer. The tiny, family-oriented dining room is more suited for fueling up and moving on to the clubs nearby, or whatever else the night might have in store. *Piazza Santa Maria Liberatrice 44, at Via R. Gessi. ☎ 06/574-6270. Pizzas from 4€. No credit cards. Mon–Sat for dinner. Closed Aug. Bus: 23, 30, 75, 95, 170, 271, or 280. Tram: 3.*

AND FOR A LITTLE SOMETHING DIFFERENT. . .

➔ **Acqua e Farina** ★ TESTACCIO   If traditional, round pizza seems a little too been-there-done-that for you, this trendy Testaccio joint is the perfect remedy. Acqua e Farina ("water and flour") takes the basic ingredients of pizza and twists them up into unique packets of dough topped with everything from goat cheese and radicchio to walnuts and sundried tomatoes. For purists, there's also plenty of mozzarella and ham. If the menu is unintelligible to you, don't worry—Italians aren't familiar with these new-fangled pizzeria terms, either. Just remember that everything has a regular dough base, so you only really need to pay attention to the toppings. In cold weather, head for the tables inside the warm and lively dining room; the rest of the year, sit in the charming little alfresco area, under a canopy of sycamore trees, on the cobblestones right opposite the old slaughterhouse. (Only in Testaccio do we use "charming" and "slaughterhouse" in the same sentence!) All year, this is packed with large parties of young Romans carbing up and getting a buzz on before hitting the nightclub strips of Via Galvani and Via di Monte Testaccio (both in the immediate vicinity). *Piazza O. Giustiniani 2 (at Via Galvani). ☎ 06/574-1382. "Mini pizzas" from 4€. Daily for dinner. Metro: Piramide. Bus: 23, 30, 75, 95, 170, 271, or 280. Tram: 3.*

. . . AND BY THE SLICE

These casual joints usually have a couple of no-frills tables where you can sit down and

ROME & LAZIO

eat, but it's more fun to get your order to-go and picnic on a bench in a nearby piazza.

→ **Forno del Campo** ★ CAMPO DE' FIORI Technically, this mainstay at the northwest corner of Campo de' Fiori is a bread and sweets bakery, but it also happens to churn out the most hyped *pizza bianca* in Rome. How a simple recipe of flour, water, and a little olive oil and salt can taste this good remains a mystery, but it really is worth the hype. Eating your *pizza bianca* plain is perfectly divine, but in our professional opinion, you'd be crazy not to make a Nutella-and-banana sandwich out of it. (Pick up a jar of Nutella at one of the nearby minigroceries, and grab a banana from the produce market in the middle of the square. Just be sure to bring something to spread and slice with.) *Campo de' Fiori 22.* ☎ *06/6880-6662. www. fornocampodefiori.com. Pizza bianca 0.50€– 1€. Mon–Sat 7am–6pm. Bus: 40, 46, 64, or 571.*

→ **Mamma Che Pizza** ★ TRASTEVERE Okay, so the name—"Mom, what pizza!"—is a little dorky, but with so many gourmet topping combos to choose from at this by-the-slice joint, we can hardly be critical. Whether you're in the mood for prosciutto with rosemary, *provola* with truffle oil, or just a big ol' slab of gorgonzola, you can't go wrong. (And, if you favor thicker, softer dough, you're in the right place.) The shop is tiny, with only a few high stools to sit on along the walls, but there are several benches right outside where you can rest and enjoy your pizza. They also provide free mineral water and cups to their customers. *Piazza Sonnino 52, at Via della Lungaretta.* ☎ *06/580-0341. Pizza sold by weight and ingredients, usually 1€–3€ for a medium-sized slice. No credit cards. Daily 11am–11pm. Bus: 23, 271, 280, 780, or H. Tram: 8.*

→ **Pizzeria Leonina** ★★ COLOSSEUM Without a doubt, the best *pizza al taglio* between the Colosseum and Termini station, and among the best in the entire city. At the lunchtime rush, locals crowd around the

cases of freshly made, rectangular pizza topped with dozens of different combinations of cheeses, vegetables, and meats. Indicate how much you want, and they'll cut it and reheat it in the oven for a few minutes. There are even dessert pizzas with apples and cinnamon, Nutella, or ricotta and honey. *Via Leonina 84.* ☎ *06/482-7744. Pizza sold by weight and ingredients, usually 1€–3€ for a medium-sized slice.*

→ **Panificio La Renella** ★ TRASTEVERE Furnishing fresh loaves of basic Italian bread to all the restaurants and households in the neighborhood, this bakery is a cornerstone of community life in the northern part of Trastevere. They also make up slabs of pizza, topped with fresh tomatoes, olives, specialty cheeses and hams, that you can buy by the slice throughout the day, making it a great place to take a load off when you're walking around on this side of the river. Eat your snack at a stool along the back counter, and read the community message board, where longtime expats have been advertising their English-teaching services and posting their housing needs for decades. In addition to pizza squares, you can also buy all the rolls, twists, and partial or full loaves your little carb-loving heart desires. *Via del Moro 15–16, between Via della Pelliccia and Piazza Trilussa.* ☎ *06/581-7265. Pizza sold by weight and ingredients, usually 1€–3€ for a medium-sized slice. Daily 8am–8pm.*

Cheap

Note that all the pizza places listed above fall into the "cheap" category.

→ **Antica Birreria Peroni** ★★★ PIAZZA VENEZIA/ITALIAN & MEATS Despite its location on the heavily trafficked tourist route between ancient Rome and the Trevi Fountain, this hugely popular lunch and dinner spot remains a locals' favorite. Sure, plenty of tourists end up here, too, but the overriding mood is fun, boisterous, and authentically Roman—though there are plenty of hearty dishes here that can pass as American comfort food (good to know when you're hung over). As the name suggests, beer is the drink of choice here, so ask for a pitcher as soon as you sit down, or else you'll piss off your waiter. In fact, there are quotes all over the walls praising the virtues of beer: "Beer is proof that God loves us" (Ben Franklin), or "Work is the curse of the drinking class" (Oscar Wilde). With such a loving attitude toward drinking, it should come as no surprise that the cuisine ain't fancy here—the kitchen at Birreria Peroni is all about simple, time-tested, and filling regional specialties done right, like spaghetti *all'amatriciana* and rigatoni *cacio e pepe,* a mind-boggling array of *wurstel* (from hot dogs on up to fancier German sausages), and meat secondi like *bistecca alla fiorentina* with home fries. The restaurant's claim to fame is an elusive sausage known as The Kilometer, strictly for the hardcore meat-eater. We won't ruin the surprise, but the hype on the *birreria*'s website is enough to pique anyone's curiosity about the Kilometer: "You can eat it, you can look at it, you can joke about it." You can even download a short .wmv clip about it. . . . For cool but hard-to-transport souvenirs, the restaurant also sells beer mugs and ceramic wine jugs for 6€–12€. *Via San Marcello 19, off Piazza Santi Apostoli. ☎ 06/679-5310. www.anticabirreriaperoni.com. Mon–Sat for lunch and dinner. Primi from 5€; secondi from 8€.*

→ **Arancia Blu** ★ SAN LORENZO/VEGETARIAN Gourmets and health freaks can meet each other halfway at this hip spot in the ugly but lively San Lorenzo university district. The "Blue Orange" disproves the theorem that haute vegetarian food must, by definition, consist of at least 50% soy, and have weird texture and a flavor that only ruminants really enjoy. This is Italy, after all, so even though there's no meat at Arancia Blu, you'll find dishes—including awesome handmade ravioli—made with enough amazing vegetables, garlic, and olive oil to satisfy even the hungriest appetite. (I'm a huge carnivore, and I enjoy this place.) A few plates are safe for vegans, but most feature eggs or cheese in some form or another. The room is a very handsome take on textbook trattoria decor, with hundreds of bottles of wine lining one wall, dark-wood tables and chairs, terracotta tile floors, and subtle lighting. Taking advantage of an Italian tax loophole, Arancia Blu is not technically a *ristorante* but a social club, which explains the (free) membership card you have to fill out before dining. *Via dei Latini 65, at Via dei Sabelli. ☎ 06/445-4105. No credit cards. Dinner daily; open for lunch Sun only. Bus: 71 or 492. Tram: 3 or 19.*

→ **Corrado** ★ TRASTEVERE/ROMAN On one of the more picturesque streets in Trastevere, Corrado is the real deal: an authentically Roman, awesome (but no-frills) choice when you just want to fill up on hearty food and pay Costco-style prices for it. Other restaurants in the 'hood court passing tourists with folksy printed menus out front, or waiters in matching outfits, but not Corrado. Massimo Conti, who runs the operations here, is a smudged T-shirt and jeans kind of guy, and the menu is one of those black boards with the white plastic insertable letters. There's never a whole lot to choose from, but count on a few Roman pastas, side dishes of green vegetables, and roasted meats. If they're offering anything with roasted potatoes with rosemary, order it—these potatoes, their browned edges glistening with olive oil, are the bomb. Shop owners and craftsmen in the area frequently order lunch from here, but old-school Corrado doesn't have any "to-go" containers; they'll just hand you your meal, on heavy white dinnerware, which you're expected to bring back, washed, after you've eaten. In fact, I used to live right above this place and probably still have some of their plates somewhere. *Via della Pelliccia 39, near Piazza de' Renzi. ☎ 06/580-6004. Mon–Sat for dinner;*

Tues–Sat for lunch. Primi from 5€; secondi from 8€. Bus: 23, 271, 280, 780, or H. Tram: 8.

→**Cul de Sac** ★★ CENTRO STORICO/WINE BAR & SMALL PLATES   The rambling, unique menu at this old standby off Piazza Navona gives you the chance to sample all kinds of unfamiliar (but not scary) European cheeses and deli meats without making an expensive commitment. With other small-portion a la carte items like couscous, salads, and stews, you have a ton of choices and can make your meal as light or as hearty as you wish. (Note that if you start ordering like crazy, this isn't such a cheap place after all.) Just be sure to pair it all with a bottle or two of wine: Cul de Sac is, first and foremost, an *enoteca*, and waiters are great about suggesting excellent, affordable vintages most wine snobs have never even heard of. There are a few tables on the small dais outside, but it's really more fun to eat inside, at one of the cozy wooden booths that line either side of an aisle that's as narrow as a ship's galley (there's even nautical netting on the upper shelves to keep the wine in place). Deft (and rather cute) waiters do-si-do with other staff and patrons to get their orders out, making flirtation and accidental contact an inevitability, if that's what you look for in a restaurant. Cul de Sac is eternally popular with locals (and some tourists) of all ages, so call ahead, or prepare to wait for up to half an hour. *Piazza Pasquino 73, at Via di San Pantaleo. ☎ 06/688-01-094. Small plates from 4€. Lunch Tues–Sun; dinner daily. Bus: 40 Express, 62, 64, 70, 81, 87, 492, or 628.*

→**Da Oio a Casa Mia** ★ TESTACCIO/ROMAN   Just up the street from Testaccio's monumental (defunct) slaughterhouse, this paper-tablecloth trat keeps it real with no-nonsense *cucina romana* (read: they do a mean fried esophagus and have no time for squeamish tourists). Oio also prepares Roman classics that *don't* involve calf brains, but vegetarians will not find much to order beyond bread and wine. (With the high volume of animal parts sloshing around in the kitchen, I wouldn't trust them to prepare a fully meat-free anything, even if they advertised such a dish on the menu.) In warm weather, there are a few outdoor tables on the sidewalk of Via Galvani; in cooler months, it's the spit-and-sawdust wood-paneled dining room, which suits this hearty fare perfectly. *Via Galvani 43–45, at Via Mastro Giorgio. ☎ 06/578-2680. No credit cards. Primi 6€–8€; secondi 8€–12€. Lunch and dinner Mon–Sat. Bus: 23, 30, 75, or 280. Tram: 3.*

→**Filetti di Baccalà** ★ CAMPO DE' FIORI/FISH & SNACKS   Sometimes, a deep fryer is all you need. As any Brit can tell you, few things help a hangover like fish and chips, and this is Rome's chippie. Dar Filettaro di Santa Barbara, as the place is properly called, is a one-trick pony; all they have are fillets of cod (*filetti di baccalà*), deep-fried and salted, and potatoes, also deep-fried and salted. The picnic tables here, in a tiny square off Campo de' Fiori, are piled high with butcher-paper tablecloths and "napkins" (also butcher paper) to absorb some of the grease, but you still might want to ask your doctor about getting started on Lipitor after you've eaten here. *Largo Librari 88, at Via Giubbonari. ☎ 06/686-4018. No credit cards. Cod and potatoes: 4€–6€. Dinner Mon–Sat. Closed Aug. Bus: 30, 40, 46, 62, 64, 70, 87, 116, 492, or 571.*

→**Hostaria Romanesca** ★ CAMPO DE' FIORI/ROMAN   Rome's market square par excellence is more of a drinking and snacking spot, but if you want a real meal with a view of the action on Campo de' Fiori, Romanesca's your best bet. Especially strong menu items include the ravioli (stuffed with ricotta, in a creamy tomato sauce), and the astonishingly juicy *pollo ai peperoni* (stewed chicken with bell peppers and tomato sauce), but all the food is solid, if not especially creative. Only come here if it's nice weather and you can get an outside table; the kitchen is not well ventilated, meaning it belches its hot air out onto inside diners, causing you to perspire uncomfortably throughout your meal. *Campo de'*

Fiori 40, along east side of square. ☎ 06/686-4024. No credit cards. Primi 6€–8€; secondi 8€–12€. Lunch and dinner Tues–Sun. Bus: 40, 62, 64, 70, 87, 116, 492, or 571.

➔ **Il Seme e La Foglia** ★★ TESTACCIO/SALADS & SANDWICHES   In one of the most typical Roman neighborhoods, a decidedly atypical place to eat: "The Seed and the Leaf" is a sit-down salads and sandwiches spot on the corner opposite Monte Testaccio (ancient Rome's amphora dump). The small tables and relaxed vibe are great for lingering over lunch while you read your guidebook and sip some wine or beer—plenty of solo eaters hang out here—and enjoy the fact that you're at least a mile from the nearest tour bus, but still in a very happening part of town. It's open until 1:30am, so the cafe is also a popular destination for the club-going set, who stop in here for a quick refuel before or after hitting the discoteche on Via Galvani and Via di Monte Testaccio. Via Galvani 18, at Via Zabaglia. ☎ 06/574-3008. Salads and sandwiches from 4.50€. Mon–Sat 8am–1:30am; Sun 6pm–1:30am. Bus: 23, 30, 75, or 280. Tram: 3.

➔ **Insalata Ricca** ★ CAMPO DE' FIORI/SALADS   When you can't bear the thought of one more pasta or pizza carb-fest, breathe easy and make your way to this wildly popular lunch and dinner spot, where the menu features dozens of meal-sized salads. (The name means "rich salad," and that's exactly what you get.) The lettuce is strictly—you guessed it—romaine, but the toppings run from surf to turf to garden patch to dairy farm, with crab meat, bresaola (cured beef), artichoke hearts, and fresh mozzarella di bufala among the ingredients. Salad-phobes (you know who you are) can also have a fine time here, as there are also plenty of pastas and meat dishes to choose from. Everyone, however, should order the bruschetta alle melanzane (garlic-rubbed toast with marinated roasted eggplants) as a starter. Divine! Don't let the crowds throw you off—there's a huge inside seating area in addition to all the tables outside, so seats tend to become available pretty quickly. The success of the Insalata Ricca idea has spawned the opening of several other branches around town, none of which holds a candle to the flagship here, a few blocks from Campo de' Fiori. Largo dei Chiavari 85, at Corso Vittorio Emanuele II. ☎ 06/6880-3656. www.linsalataricca.it. Salads from 7€. Daily for lunch and dinner. Bus: 30, 40, 46, 62, 64, 70, 81, 87, 116, 492, 571, or 628. Tram: 8.

➔ **Isidoro** ★★ COLOSSEUM/PASTA   From the outside, this looks like just another traditional Roman osteria, and it does have a full menu, but Isidoro is all about the kick-ass pasta sampling menu. Order the assaggini misti, get your partitioned, school-cafeteria type plate in position, and then let the games begin. New batches of pasta emerge from the kitchen every 8 minutes or so—penne with walnut-nutmeg-cream sauce, gnocchi with gorgonzola, tagliolini with mushrooms and asparagus . . . the hits just keep on coming, so see how many rounds you last until you are KO'd by the carbs. On some nights, you can also specify the assaggini misti di pasta al pesce, in which all the pastas are seafood based. Our pro tip: Go easy on the water, as that will unnecessarily fill your stomach at a place like this; do order a flask of wine, as it will give you the courage to go more rounds than you would if you were sober. (By now, you've gathered that Isidoro will blow your Atkins/South-Beach/whatever diet out of the water, but you're in Italy, damn it!—work it off by doing a few laps around the Colosseum, just down the street, after dinner. Via di San Giovanni in Laterano 59–61–63, near Via dei Querceti. ☎ 06/700-82-66. Assaggini misti from 8€, depending on how many rounds you last. Daily for lunch and dinner. Metro: Colosseo. Bus: 60, 85, 87, 117, 175, 271, or 571. Tram: 3.

➔ **Osteria der Belli** ★★ TRASTEVERE/SARDINIAN   Just off Piazza Santa Maria in Trastevere, this always-lively indoor-outdoor spot serves up Sardinian pasta and seafood dishes at great prices (scuppering the theory that you have to pay an arm and a leg for high-quality fish in Rome). If you don't get seated right away, it can be a challenge to remain on the waiters' radar—keep making eye contact with them whenever you can so that they know you're still there. Some of the star menu items include the fantastically garlicky *sauté di cozze e vongole* (sauté of mussels and clams, which you have to pick out of their shells—a good sign of freshness) and any of the seafood-based pastas (*alla pescatora*, or the shrimp-based risotto *alla crema di scampi*). If you want some real entertainment, come here on a Friday night (remember, this is a Catholic country, and Friday is fish night) and try to get a table near the boozy old-timer regulars; before dessert comes, they're into their fourth liter of wine and singing *trasteverino* drinking songs, and they may well invite you to join them. The piazza here is always busy with passing street musicians, but do keep an eye on your bags if you're eating outside, as gypsies tend to pass through as well. *Piazza Sant'Apollonia 9–11, at Via della Lungaretta.* ☎ *06/580-37-82. Primi 6€–9€; secondi 7€–12€. Tues–Sun for lunch and dinner. Bus: 23, 271, 280, 780, or H. Tram: 8.*

→ **San Marco** ★ VIA VENETO/ITALIAN It might not be in the most happening part of the town, but this hybrid pasta-pizza-meat-*enoteca* is an untouristed gem (so, don't tell 'em I sent you here). The sleek modern aesthetic in the front bar room is a refreshing break from all the rustic, tavern-y decor you'll be seeing in Italy, but traditionalists will love the cozy, library-ish back room. Especially popular with the young professionals who work in the office buildings on nearby Via Veneto and around Piazza Barberini, San Marco is packed in the early evening (from the *aperitivo* hour of 7pm until 8:30pm or so), but the crowds tend to dwindle later on (unlike most restaurants in the *centro storico*, which peak at 9:30pm). *Via Sardegna*

38/d, near Via Lucullo. ☎ *06/4201-2620. Mon–Sat for lunch and dinner. Bus: 52, 53, 63, or 116.*

Doable

→ **Celestina** ★★ PARIOLI/ITALIAN When Italian TV personalities, soccer stars, and other celebs you wouldn't recognize want a good traditional meal (in an environment where they're sure to get publicity), they come to this down-to-earth joint/hot spot in the posh Parioli neighborhood. For how varied the menu is, "La Celestina" really does a good job on all of it: between traditional meat- and veggie-based pastas, meat and fish secondi, and even some truly outstanding pizzas, you can't go wrong no matter what you order. While Celestina stays pretty attitude-free despite its continuous celeb clientele, make no mistake, you should not show up here looking like a schlep. Rock some hot jeans and a funky accessory or two, and the paparazzi who stop by nightly might even mistake you for visiting Hollywood royalty. *Viale Parioli 184, near Piazzale della Rimembranza.* ☎ *06/807-8242. Primi 8€–12€; secondi 10€–16€; pizzas from 6€. Daily for lunch and dinner. Bus: 52 or 53.*

EAT, SEE & BE SEEN: RESTAURANT HOT SPOTS

All these restaurants have a scene to them as well as their wine and cuisine; all are considered "Cheap/Doable" except for Supperclub and Hosteria del Pesce, which are "Splurges."

→ **Crudo** ★ CAMPO DE' FIORI/FUSION & RAW Opened in 2004, stylish Crudo brings a bit of the New York or London scene to a tiny cobblestoned alley near Campo de' Fiori. Perhaps it takes its name and eponymous ethos ("raw") a bit too seriously, staunchly refusing to cook anything, but the striking space—a vast garagelike salon, with unfinished cement walls and floors, 1960s furniture upholstered in white and red leather, and a huge mural of a snarling wolf—is always packed with Romans 20- and 30-something scenesters having an *aperidinner* (i.e., stopping in for a drink, and then noshing on enough oysters, sushi, and carpaccio to call it a meal). The food can be outstanding; it can also be just plain weird (e.g., unidentifiable and seemingly unnecessary sauces), but it's always beautifully presented and impeccably fresh—and of course, it gives Romans an excuse to throw around the word *wasabi*, an asset for trendiness in this image-conscious town. *Via degli Specchi 6, at Via Monte di Farina.* ☎ *06/683-8989. www.crudoroma.it. Small plates from 7€. Aperitivi and dinner daily. Bus: 23, 30, 40, 46, 62, 64, 70, 81, 87, 116, 271, 280, 492, or 571. Tram: 8.*

➔ **Duke's** ★★ PARIOLI/CALIFORNIAN & MEDITERRANEAN   Ever wanted to mix with hot Italian sailors from the Prada *Luna Rossa* sailing team (and their coed groupies)? (Umm, is the pope Catholic?) Well, look no further than the bar at Duke's, in the posh Parioli district north of the *centro*. This breezy, California-style restaurant (named after legendary surfer Duke Kahanamoku), attracts the well-groomed, well-dressed, and well-off young creatures of Rome's northern suburbs with its sexy, surf-inspired indoor-outdoor setup and tantalizing menu of seafood tartare, light pastas, grilled fish—and, rarity of all rarities in Rome—chardonnay! There's always a wait for a table, even if you've called ahead, but it's all the better for chatting up that tanned skipper in the red chinos while you sip your fruity cocktail at the bar. It's a bit of a trek up here, but it's always a fun night out, and there are no tourists in sight. (*Tip:* If you don't want to do the whole California cuisine thing, you can just have a drink here, and then eat Italian food at Celestina down the block.) *Viale Parioli 200.* ☎ *06/8066-2455. www. dukes.it. Primi 11€–15€; secondi 15€–18€. Tues–Sat 8:30pm –midnight. Bus: 53 from Piazza San Silvestro.*

➔ **'Gusto** ★★ PIAZZA DEL POPOLO/ITALIAN   The 'Gusto gourmet triumvirate occupies an imposing, fascist-era building on the northern side of Piazza Augusto Imperatore. (See also Osteria della Frezza, below.) 'Gusto itself is a modern restaurant and pizzeria (two different dining rooms with two different menus and festivity levels) in a buzzy, soaring space slightly reminiscent of high school wood shop, with blocky, unfinished wooden tables, white paper table liners, and industrial-looking ducts overhead. Black-clad staff is friendly (and much better looking than most customers), and there's a ton to choose from on the reasonably priced pizzeria menu; the restaurant menu is more expensive and eclectic (the atmosphere is also more uptight). For either, it's a good idea to make reservations. The attached book and gift shop sells cookbooks and great Italian kitchen stuff that makes great presents for foodie friends back home. *Piazza Augusto Imperatore 9, off Via Ripetta.* ☎ *06/322-6273. www.gusto.it. Pizzeria: pizzas from 7€; restaurant: primi from 9€, secondi from 14€. Tues–Sun for lunch and dinner. Metro: Flaminio or Spagna. Bus: 913.*

➔ **Maccheroni** ★★ PANTHEON/ITALIAN   There's nothing too flashy about the restaurant itself, but this is a favorite of stylish young locals who work in TV, film, or finance, who come here for dinner in huge groups before laying siege to the equally hip and laid-back bars and clubs of the *centro*. The fare at Maccheroni, as the name would suggest, is simple but perfectly executed, and reasonably priced, considering how frequently we use the term "heavenly" to describe it. The pasta *alla gricia* (with pecorino romano cheese, black pepper, and pancetta) is a heavenly plate of steaming, cheesey, bacon-y goodness (and somehow not as rich as it sounds). A long list of secondi includes a heavenly and oh-so-tender *tagliata di manzo con rughetta* (grilled beef strips on a bed of arugula) and good ol' fashioned *polpettine al sugo* (meatballs in red sauce). One of the more perfect spots in the *centro storico* for getting a little drunk (hello, the house wine is

3€/liter!!), eating great food, and being in the company of some of the chicer citizens of Rome. *Via delle Coppelle 44, at Via degli Spagnoli.* ☎ *06/6830-7895. Primi 8€–14€; secondi 10–15€. Tues–Sun for dinner. Bus: 30, 40, 46, 62, 64, 70, 81, 87, 116, 492, 571, or 628. Tram: 8.*

➔ **Obikà** ★ PANTHEON/MOZZARELLA & LIGHT FARE   If you ask an Italian, mozzarella isn't even cheese: it's its own class of dairy product hovering in the limbo between milk and cheese, and *mozzarella di bufala campana DOP* is the highest form of it. The menu at this sleek and innovative "mozzarella bar" near the Pantheon features endless permutations of *mozzarella di bufala* served with toasted bread, spicy Calabrese pâtés, prosciutto and other meats, salads, you name it. If you decide to try this place out, it's great for brunch or lunch but not dinner—it's a cool gimmick, and the place is pretty lively, but you'll want to save your precious Roman evenings for a more convivial, traditional Roman environment. In any case, *mozzarella* is one of the most incorrectly used Italian culinary terms in the world—when you taste the real thing here (or anywhere they serve it in Italy), you'll never go back to that massproduced, over-compressed stuff they sell in U.S. supermarkets. One of the more unique and successful creations to be spawned by Rome's modern restaurant craze, the Obikà franchise has now gone on to open branches in Milan and London. *Via dei Prefetti, at Piazza Firenze.* ☎ *06/683-2630. Small plates 6€–10€. Daily noon–midnight. Bus: 70, 87, 116, or 492.*

➔ **Osteria della Frezza** ★★ PIAZZA DEL POPOLO ROMAN/*APERITIVO*   Tacked onto the back of the 'Gusto conglomerate of trendy restaurants set in fascist-era buildings, this *osteria* with black-and-white tile and brown leather decor makes a very chic backdrop for at least part of your evening. The cramped and sometimes lifeless back room is where you can have a real sit-down meal, but we far prefer the sexy 1930s scene in the front parlor area (enter from Via della Frezza). Grab a seat

on one of the leather-upholstered chairs and start out with a dish of olives and a glass of something splurge-y, like Barolo in a big grown-up glass, and then let that party of dashing captains of industry in the corner buy the next round. Continue nibbling on tapas-style munchies, hundreds of cheeses, and small-plate versions of pastas and meat dishes—with this setup, drinks can easily turn into a full meal, which is great, as long as you're okay with forgoing a proper seat and table to eat your food on. Otherwise, just hit Osteria della Frezza for your predinner snacks, and then move on to a more traditional restaurant. (Note that this is not a normal *aperitivo* place in that there's no free buffet spread; you pay for whatever munchies you order, along with whatever you drink.) *Via della Frezza 16, at Via Corea.* ☎ *06/322-62-73. Bus: 81, 628, or 913. Daily for aperitivo and dinner. Small plates from 4.50€.*

➔ **Riccioli Café** ★ PANTHEON OYSTER BAR Create a light, free-form meal of oysters (fresh from Brittany), fish kebabs, and other seafoody nibbles at this sleek, modern spot in the hip restaurant zone north of the Pantheon. Their *aperitivo* hour is popular with trendy locals, so you can also just stop in here for some predinner drinks and snacks, or a post-dinner cocktail at one of their outdoor tables. (Around the corner from Riccioli is its parent restaurant, La Rosetta, one of the most famous and expensive seafood restaurants in Rome, but hardly a swanky night out.) *Piazza delle Coppelle 10A, at Via delle Coppelle.* ☎ *06/6821-0313. www.larosetta.com. Small plates 6€–11€. Mon–Sat for aperitivo, dinner, and after-dinner drinks. Closed Aug. Bus: 70, 81, 87, 116, 571, or 628.*

➔ **Supperclub** ★★ PANTHEON/GLOBAL For a transporting experience into modern Euro-fabulousness, check out this übertrendy spinoff of the original joint in Amsterdam. Its white interiors strike quite a contrast with its location, near the 1,900-year-old Pantheon, but just like the ancient Romans, here you eat lying down, get a massage, are served by half-naked waiters, and listen to great music (only nowadays of the chill-out variety; no lyre-strumming). Dinner is prix fixe and actually delicious for such a themed place—expect several courses of creative, Mediterranean- and Asian-inspired dishes that are light, flavorful, and relatively easy to eat in a reclining position. After dinner, Supperclub is like a Habitrail for hipsters, with long, narrow tunnels that terminate in various play areas—dining rooms with broad white sofas, cagelike bars, or swank dance floors (but no hamster wheel, darn it all). Note that reservations should be made several days in advance for dinner; if they're booked, you can always come by around 11:30pm, when it morphs into a nightclub. *Via de' Nari 14, at Via Monterone.* ☎ *06/6880-7207. www.supperclub.com. Prix-fixe dinner 75€.*

➜ **Hosteria del Pesce** ★★ CAMPO DE' FIORI/SEAFOOD With its bright lights and huge bin of ice and fish, the tiny vestibule at Via Monserrato 32 looks like the back room of a fish market, not the entrance to a potentially pricey seafood restaurant. Inside, the atmosphere improves dramatically: Lights are low, and walls are painted in the same reds and turquoises that grace many an Italian fishing boat's hull. This is not the kind of place where you'll be mixing with other diners or bantering with your waiters—who are clearly much more socialized with fish than with people—so if you're only a few people, you may not enjoy this place as much as you could. It's best to come here in a group of four or more, where you can make your own party and just rejoice over how good the food is, because most of it is truly exquisite. My favorite thing on the menu here, the *bis* or *tris di pasta,* is a sampling of two or three different kinds of seafood pastas, great for sharing, and relatively easy on the wallet. If you go the whole fish route, be sure to ask your waiter what the approximate price will be—whole fish are priced according to weight (e.g., 10€ per *etto,* or 10g), and if you're not careful, you could end up with serious sticker shock (as in, 100€ for a freakin' flounder) when the bill comes! Because wine is also by the bottle here (and on the expensive side), you'd be wise to do a little preloading at one of the myriad 2€/glass wine bars on Campo de' Fiori, 5 minutes away. *Via Monserrato 32, at Via Barchetta.* ☎ *06/686-5617. Reservations recommended. Bus: 23, 116, 271, or 280. Primi from 12€; seafood secondi from 24€.*

Partying

Club snobs dismiss Rome as a provincial place to party. Let them thumb their noses. If partying means having fun, not stressing about what you're doing or where you're going, drinking cheaply, and being able to change courses quickly, then Rome is in fact one of the best places to party in the world. (But if you're looking for cutting-edge DJs and über-sophisticated lounges, well, not so much. . . .)

Because dinner is still a sacrosanct event around which an evening is built, nightlife in Rome has a definite rhythm to it; there's the *aperitivo* before your meal, the after-dinner drinks, and the nightclubs. (This is not the same as Milan, for instance, where eating out is so expensive that many treat the *aperitivo* buffet as dinner.) Only at Rome's Irish-style pubs can you sit and drink from 5pm till close without looking like a loser/weirdo. Most bars are open until 2 or 3am, and with the exception of Monday, which is slow throughout Italy, there are tons of people out every night of the week. The other nice thing about Rome is that, unlike New York or London, places that are cool stay cool for longer than 6 months. Bars that are hot right now will probably still be hot in 2010.

Because so many of the best bars and pubs are right in the heart of the *centro storico* (and within a 5-min. walk of each

Partying in Rome

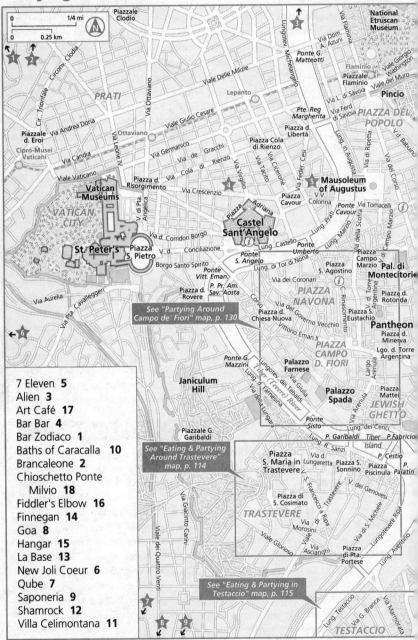

7 Eleven **5**
Alien **3**
Art Café **17**
Bar Bar **4**
Bar Zodiaco **1**
Baths of Caracalla **10**
Brancaleone **2**
Chioschetto Ponte
  Milvio **18**
Fiddler's Elbow **16**
Finnegan **14**
Goa **8**
Hangar **15**
La Base **13**
New Joli Coeur **6**
Qube **7**
Saponeria **9**
Shamrock **12**
Villa Celimontana **11**

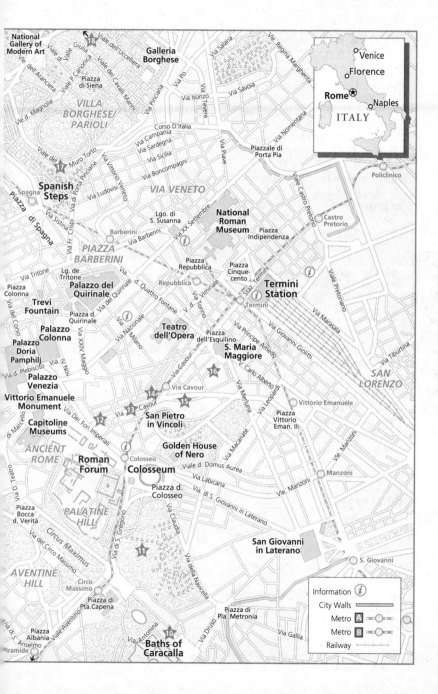

National Gallery of Modern Art

18

Viale dell'Uccelliera

Galleria Borghese

Via Salaria

Via Regina Margherita

Venice

Florence

Rome ✪

Naples

ITALY

Via di Valle Giulia

Viale P. Canonica

Viale dei Cavalli Marini

Piazza di Siena

Via Pinciana

Via Po

Via Isonzo

Via Savoia

Via Nomentana

Vle. dell'Aranciera

Vle. d. Magnolie

VILLA BORGHESE/ PARIOLI

Corso D'Italia

Via Campania

Via Sardegna

Via Sicilia

Via Boncompagni

Via Plave

Piazzale di Porta Pia

Via Castro Pretorio

Policlinico

Viale del

Muro Torto

Via di Porta Pinciana

Via Vittorio Veneto

Via Ludovisi

VIA VENETO

Via Nazionale

Spanish Steps

Spagna

Piazza di Spagna

Via Sistina

Via Fr. Crispi

Via Barberini

Lgo. di S. Susanna

Via XX Settembre

National Roman Museum

Piazza Indipendenza

Castro Pretorio

Viale Pretoriano

Barberini

PIAZZA BARBERINI

Lg. de Tritone

Via Tritone

Palazzo del Quirinale

Via d. Quattro Fontane

Piazza Repubblica

Repubblica

Piazza Cinque-cento

Piazza Republica

Termini Station

Staz. Termini

Termini

Via Marsala

Piazza Colonna

Trevi Fountain

Via del Corso

Piazza d. Quirinale

Via del Quirinale

Via Nazionale

Via Milano

Teatro dell'Opera

Via Torino

Via Vimmale

Piazza dell'Esquilino

Via Principe Amedeo

Via Giovanni Giolitti

Via Tiburtina

SAN LORENZO

Palazzo Colonna

Palazzo Doria Pamphilj

Via d. Plebiscito

Via XXIV Maggio

Via IV Nov.

Palazzo Venezia

Via Cavour

S. Maria Maggiore

16

V. Carlo Alberto di

Via Merulana

Vittorio Emanuele

Piazza Vittorio Eman. II

Vle. Manzoni

Vittorio Emanuele Monument

Via Dei Fori. Imperiali

12

14

15

Via Cavour

15

San Pietro in Vincoli

Via Macarate

Via Leopardi

Manzoni

Vle. Manzoni

Capitoline Museums

di Marcello

ANCIENT ROME

Roman Forum

i

Colosseo

Golden House of Nero

Colosseum

Viale d. Domus Aurea

Via Labicana

Via di S. Giovanni in Laterano

Piazza d. Colosseo

Via Claudia

Piazza Bocca d. Verità

PALATINE HILL

Via del Circo Massimo

Circus Maximus

Via di S. Gregorio

11

Via della Navicella

San Giovanni in Laterano

S. Giovanni

Via di D. Teatro

AVENTINE HILL

Circo Massimo

Piazza di Pta.Capena

Viale Aventino

Via Antonina

10

Via Druso

Piazza di Pla. Metronia

Via Gallia

Piazza Albania

Piramide

Via di S. Anselmo

Baths of Caracalla

Information ⓘ

City Walls

Metro Ⓐ

Metro Ⓑ

Railway

where to Find out what's on

The weekly events guide, *Roma C'è* (available at newsstands) is the best single resource for concerts and club events. It's in Italian, but with common words like "house" and "underground," you'll get the gist. Word of mouth is also key to finding out what's on in Rome, and if you make a few acquaintances at your hotel or hostel, or even with the young sales clerk at some trendy boutique, you might get invited to an amazing private party at a villa on the Appian Way. Where available, check bars' and clubs' websites for nightly specials, live music calendars, or DJ sets.

other), you don't need to worry too much about making a plan. Just start at one place and see where the night takes you. If you get a hankering for club-going, beware: It gets spendy in a hurry. In addition to the cab fare it'll take to get to most of Rome's discos, all the clubs charge a cover of 10€–20€, and drinks are usually 7€–10€.

Photocopy these pages and stash them in your pocket so that you'll know where to go—naturally, you'll look like a bit of a tool carrying the whole book around with you.

What to Wear

While Roman nights don't demand formal attire, khakis and flip-flops are a no-no unless you're going to one of the city's mostly expatriate Irish pubs. On the flipside, don't overcompensate by hitting the town in a black suit or a hussy outfit with big hair and too much makeup—no one will talk to you if they think you're part of the Russian mafia. Clean jeans, with hems that barely graze the ground, and a T-shirt can work fine as long as you've piled on plenty of accessories (more than you

think you need). Shoes can be whatever you want—even sneakers—as long as they're fashionable and you can walk in them. Ladies, if you wear stilettos, you're asking for an embarrassing heel-snaring incident on the cobblestones.

Mating Ground

📺 **Best** *It is nightfall in Rome. On motorini and Fiats from every corner of the city, the natives make their ritualistic journey to Campo de' Fiori in hopes of finding companionship. Some will take seats at outdoor cafes and try out their English on foreign tourists; some will simply mill about in the center of the square, shyly hoping a male specimen from a nearby herd will notice them.*

The evening scene at **Campo de' Fiori**—produce and fish market by day, pick-up central and playa's piazza by night—is like an Animal Planet documentary on Roman mating habits. Meat market factor aside, this is by far the most happening square in Rome (though not the most cutting-edge), and a perfectly contained (and traffic-free) world of bars, cafes, and restaurants that locals migrate to every single night. Whether or not you're looking to hook yourself your own "catch of the day," you could easily spend every night of your stay in Rome hanging out here—as long as you don't mind crowds. By 6:30pm, gaggles of young Romans have filled the chairs at the alfresco bars for an *aperitivo*. Some stay for dinner, but most eat elsewhere, so there's a bit of a lull from 8 to 10pm or so. After dinner, the crowds return and the Campo swells once again into one big outdoor party in the heart of Rome that doesn't shut down until housewives in their bathrobes appear at their apartment windows above, screaming at everyone to shut up and go home, which usually happens at around 1:30 or 2am.

There are literally dozens of places where you can eat, drink, and be merry on Campo de' Fiori, but in general, you'll find a younger, more anything-goes scene in the northern half of the square, and a quieter, more middle-aged scene in the southern half. Some of our recommendations:

○ **Vineria Reggio**   Popular with young and old and cheap-cheap-cheap, "La Vineria" is the most democratic (and centrally located) spot on the square. See full listing below.

○ **Taverna del Campo**   Similar to its next-door neighbor, the Vineria, but with some occasional unnecessary attitude, this is especially recommended on Sunday afternoons, when many of the other bars are closed. Piazza Campo de' Fiori 16, ☎ **06/687-4402.**

○ **The Drunken Ship**   Spring break meets frat party. For many Americans on study programs in Rome, it doesn't get much better than this. See full listing below.

○ **I Giganti**   Loud music thumps inside, while pods of barstools and high tables on the cobblestones outside make for a more pubby atmosphere. The in spot for Romans aged 18 to 25 (which, in American years, is more like 14–21). Piazza Campo de' Fiori 26. ☎ **06/687-4182.**

○ **Il Nolano**   There's a mellower vibe and older demographic at this *bottiglieria* (e.g., a bar that takes its wine pretty seriously) that offers prime viewing of the action from its old-school wooden cinema chairs on the western side of the square. Piazza Campo de' Fiori 11. ☎ **06/687-9344.**

○ **Caffè dell'Arte**   Okay, so it's not really on Campo de' Fiori, but open containers are allowed in the middle of the square, and you can get bottles of wine (have them open it and give you cups) and beer to go at this coffee bar for cheaper than what they'll cost at a real bar on the Campo itself. Via del Biscione 80 (off the southeast side of the square).

How to Get In

→ Be female. (If male, show up at the club *with* several females.)
→ Look decent.
→ Name drop. Every party-promoter/bouncer/club-owner in Rome seems to be named Dario, so it can't hurt to say that you are an *amico di Dario* if you get any resistance at the door. (If you get a blank stare, try *Claudio*.)

Bars & Lounges

When in Rome a drink costs . . . around 2€ up to 8€ for a glass of wine, depending on how fancy the place is; about 4 or 5€ for a pint of beer (so work those Happy Hours), and 4 or 5€ for a cocktail in a more laid back place, 7 to 10€ in trendier spots.

→ **7 Eleven** VATICAN   Only entertain the idea of coming to this late-night-only den if you meet the following criteria: You're in a fun group, and you're already three sheets to the wind. In that case, 7 Eleven (no relation to the convenience store chain) can be a grand old place to stretch out your evening. Fight fatigue with a cocktail of cranberry juice and Red Bull, but curb the temptation to order anything from the pub-grub food menu. The kitchen is a bit iffy, and that cheeseburger that seemed like such a good idea at 4am might well come back to haunt you the next day, when you're trying to make it through the Vatican Museums. *Via Pierluigi da Palestrina 22/a (off Piazza Cavour). Bus: 81, 87, or 492.*

→ **Accademia '90** ★ TRASTEVERE   Every night, the cobblestoned streets of Trastevere are a continuous stream of festivity, as Romans from all over town flood the neighborhoods bars and restaurants. Among them, one of the best for a casual, lively night out is Accademia '90, a bit away from the

Partying Around Campo de' Fiori

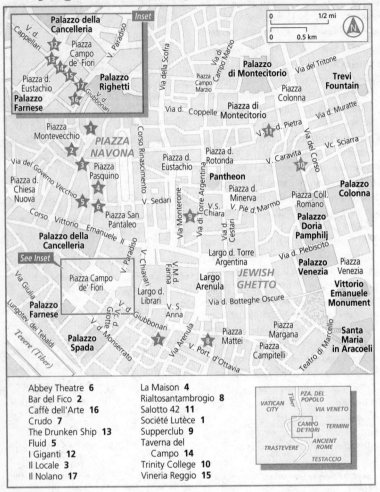

Abbey Theatre **6**	La Maison **4**
Bar del Fico **2**	Rialtosantambrogio **8**
Caffè dell'Arte **16**	Salotto 42 **11**
Crudo **7**	Société Lutèce **1**
The Drunken Ship **13**	Supperclub **9**
Fluid **5**	Taverna del
I Giganti **12**	Campo **14**
Il Locale **3**	Trinity College **10**
Il Nolano **17**	Vineria Reggio **15**

pedestrian crush around Piazza Santa Maria in Trastevere. You can get wine, but beer and cocktails are the drinks of choice here. In warm weather, you can sit under the stars on the bar's rooftop terrace. When Roma and Lazio are playing, their games are showed on several screens. Clientele is young, good-looking, and there to have a good time—not to prove to anyone how hip they are. *Vicolo della Renella 90, off Via del Moro.* ☎ *06/589-6321. Bus: 23, 280, 780, or H. Tram: 8.*

→ **Bar Bar** ★★ VATICAN With a dark, cascading entrance that feels like a rabbit hole, and a long and winding bar full of psychedelic '60s colors and design elements, Bar Bar is like an updated and trendy version of Wonderland itself. It's also quite an exercise in vanity, as several TV screens throughout display slideshows of the bar's most beautiful regulars, caught in the act of having a fabulous time, baby! Nevertheless, this is a pretty fun place, with a steady flow of all the pop music you know by heart, and a sociable and hip crowd of 20-somethings who are usually only too willing to strike up a conversation with the fish-out-of-water *americano* (though not in a sleazy, meat-market way—these kids are too self-consciously cool for that). Sunday nights are extremely popular for the free *aperitivo* buffet you get with your drink purchase. *Via Ovidio 17.* ☎ *06/6830-8435. Cover 5€–10€ Fri–Sat. Bus: 23, 81, 87, or 492.*

→ **Bar del Fico** ★ PIAZZA NAVONA "Il Fico" is as hallowed an institution in Rome as the Catholic church, but to lay eyes on it during the day, you'd never know: it just looks like a regular cafe, albeit one with a huge fig tree *(fico)* growing out of the cobblestones out front. At night, this is the bar where all the cool people end up (because *fico* is also slang for cool) when no other evening plans materialize. Well, truth be told, Bar del Fico is not as popular as it used to be—the days when you could spot Matt Dillon sipping a drink here, or when Lenny Kravitz would come by and buy everyone a round, may be gone, but there are still some summer nights when this little piazzetta and its namesake bar are without a doubt *the* place to be. *Piazza del Fico 26.* ☎ *06/686-5205. Bus: 30, 70, 81, 87, 492, or 628.*

→ **Chioschetto Ponte Milvio** ★★ NORTHERN SUBURBS It takes the best part of an hour to get here from the *centro,* and decor consists of little more than a gravelly expanse on the side of the road, some plastic tables and chairs, and a bar inside a shack, but this is no ironic boondocks boite. This totally alfresco "kiosk" is where the young and beautiful people of affluent Roma Nord come for a drink when they don't feel like dressing up and dealing with the hassle of parking their Range Rovers and BMWs in the *centro storico*—which is more often than not. As long as the weather is decent, you'll find huge, easy-going crowds here, sipping mojitos, beer, or even coffee. Immediately adjacent is the pedestrianized and rather

atmospheric Ponte Milvio, the ancient Milvian Bridge, where Constantine vanquished Maxentius in A.D. 312; today, it's where lots of *chioschetto* patrons sneak off for make-out sessions. A few hundred meters downriver is the Stadio Olimpico, so if you're going to see Roma or Lazio play, you can combine it with a post-game drink up here. *Piazzale Ponte Milvio 44, at Lungotevere Maresciallo Diaz.* ☎*06/333-3461. Bus: 32 from Piazza Risorgimento (Vatican area), 53 from Piazza San Silvestro (Via del Corso), then cross Ponte Milvio. Tram: 2 from Piazzale Flaminio, then cross Ponte Milvio.*

📺 Best → **The Drunken Ship** CAMPO DE' FIORI There's nothing Roman about it, but the American-run Ship knows how to party like no other. My hypocritical side wants to file this under "if you must . . ." but who am I to judge? I was a total fixture here during my student days! Most nights feature some kind of special (Sun is Ladies' Night, with half-price drinks for girls 8–11pm; Tues is College Night, with 1€ shots and beers for students 8–9pm). My personal favorite is Power Hour (Wed), where 5€ and a valid student ID gets you all the Peroni beer you can drink from 9 to 10pm. Indeed, if you don't take advantage of these deals, it's almost like you're *losing* money! Clientele, as you can imagine, is overwhelmingly American and college-aged—steer clear of the sleazy hangers-on that are always here, looking to hit on foreign women. Music, spun by a DJ from a treelike platform near the door, is heavy on current hip-hop (and whatever else is on iTunes' top 10 list), with the occasional classic Duran Duran song thrown in to keep the party going. *Campo de' Fiori 20/21.* ☎*06/6830-0535. www.drunkenship.com. Daily 4pm–2am. Bus: 30, 40, 46, 62, 64, 70, 81, 87, 116, 492, 571, or 628. Tram: 8.*

→ **Fluid** ★ PIAZZA NAVONA Who knew Windex could be such a trendy design element? The embodiment of this bar's name, the back wall features greenish-blue fluid that drips in viscous streams down a rectangular glass panel. Hot. We make fun, but on a street that's otherwise occupied by medieval-looking wine bars and trattorie and boho boutiques, this is a welcome (if discordant) breath of fresh air. You can come early (6:30–8pm) for the free *aperitivo* buffet (and snag a seat on one of the ottomans that look like giant ice cubes), but the best scene is arguably later at night, when the narrow space is filled with after-dinner revelers. *Via del Governo Vecchio 46/47.* ☎ *06/683-2361. Bus: 30, 40, 46, 62, 64, 70, 81, 87, 116, 492, 571, or 628. Tram: 8.*

➔ **Friends** ★ TRASTEVERE   This cheerful cafe (pronounced *freends* in local parlance) has brushed chrome accents and colorful plastic chairs that combine to make the place look a little bit like a carnival ride—one in which Fashion TV is constantly playing on overhead screens. With its outdoor tables on Trastevere's Piazza Trilussa, this is a great place to go for *aperitivo* (free buffet with your drink purchase), but you'll find a more unwound, sillier atmosphere (in which drunk Romans outnumber resident expatriates) later at night. If you find yourself near the Pantheon, check out their branch at Via della Scrofa 59; north of Termini station, try the location at Via Piave 69/73. *Piazza Trilussa 34 (Lungotevere Raffaello Sanzio, opposite Ponte Sisto).* ☎ *06/581-6111. Bus: 23, 280, 780, or H. Tram: 8.*

Trinity College ★ PANTHEON   Ahhh, good ol' Trinity College. No young person's first stay in Rome is complete without a trip to this old standby, where the American university program coeds are naive and the Roman boys are horny (and as an added bonus, they also tend to be of the hot, water-polo-playing variety). The bartenders think they're Tom Cruise in *Cocktail*, so you might as well order something elaborate like a strawberry *caipiroska*, since even draft beers are subjected to a longwinded glass-flipping routine before they're served. It's always a party *al*

Trinity, and the music—a high-energy mix of the greatest hits of right now—helps to drive that point home. *Via del Collegio Romano 6 (off Via del Corso).* ☎ *06/678-6472. Bus: 40, 46, 62, 64, 85, 95, 116, or 492.*

MTV **Best** ➔ **Vineria Reggio (aka La Vineria)** ★★★ CAMPO DE' FIORI   An old Roman saying goes, "when the Colosseum falls, so too shall Rome." To hell with that—it's when the Vineria falls that Rome may well cease to exist. This unassuming wine bar on the west side of Campo de' Fiori is an integral part of the true Roman experience. Zero pretense despite a fairly fashionable clientele, quick and friendly service, tables on the piazza and a cozy indoor bar, and glasses of wine that start at 1.50€—what more could you ask? Note that it costs a bit more to sit down at one of the tables outside, and while you're welcome to drink your wine standing up on the cobblestones outside the door, you'll have to transfer your drink into a plastic cup. Start off with a toast of *prosecco,* and then have a glass of Falanghina—Roman superstition says that this local white wine brings a fun night to all who drink it. *Piazza Campo de' Fiori 15.* ☎ *06/6880-3268. Closed Sun. Bus: 30, 40, 46, 62, 64, 70, 81, 87, 116, 492, 571, or 628. Tram: 8.*

THE HOT SPOTS: COOLEST BARS & CLUBS

➔ **Crudo** ★ CAMPO DE' FIORI   This garage-like lounge, with bold art on the walls, cement floors, and 1960s-style leather furniture, is technically a restaurant (see listing in "Eating" section), but plenty of people just come for drinks before or after dinner. *RI Via degli Specchi 6.* ☎ *06/683-8989. www.crudoroma.it. Bus: 23, 30, 40, 46, 62, 64, 70, 81, 87, 116, 271, 280, 492, or 571. Tram: 8.*

➔ **Freni e Frizioni** ★★ TRASTEVERE   Ever since the popes reconsecrated pagan temples as Christian churches, the Romans have been very into reclaiming and reusing spaces for a completely different function. In the case of this new bar, "Brakes and Clutches," it's a former automotive repair garage that's been converted into a super-happening nightspot. Come howling wind or pouring rain, throngs of good looking young locals congress here nightly for a great *aperitivo* buffet, interesting cocktails, and a friendly atmosphere. The party always overflows to the pavement outside (you can't quite call it a congenial piazza, but no one cares). Barely sheltered from the rushing traffic of the riverside drive, with parked *motorini* used as makeshift seats, crumbling medieval walls around and sycamore trees nearby, it's quintessential *Rome. Via del Politeama 4–6, off Piazza Trilussa and Lungotevere Raffaello Sanzio.* ☎ *06/5833-4210. Bus: 23, 280, 780, or H. Tram: 8.*

➜ **Rialtosantambrogio** ✶ GHETTO   What once seemed like an illegal rave inside an abandoned school has now gone legit. It's cheap and always packed with an alternative crowd. *Via Sant'Ambrogio 4.* ☎ *06/6813-3640. Bus: 23, 63, 170, 280, 630, or 780. Tram: 8.*

➜ **Supperclub** ✶✶ PANTHEON   Supperclub is a full night's entertainment, where you eat your prix-fixe dinner while reclining somewhat awkwardly on white divans, and then avail of one of the club's many bars or dance floors to party with the other guests. It's fabulous but gimmicky, the kind of place where you go once and never really need to go back again, but try telling that to a Roman. Even if they don't want to cough up the dough to eat here, tons of locals flock here every night around midnight, when the place opens up as a sort of disco for the general public. See also "Eating" section. *Via de' Nari 14 (off Via di Torre Argentina).* ☎ *06/6880-7207. www.supperclub.it. Bus: 30, 40, 46, 62, 64, 70, 81, 87, 116, 492, 571, or 628. Tram: 8.*

📺 Best ➜ **Salotto 42** ✶✶ PANTHEON   When you want to pretend you're cooler and more worldly than you really are, don your asymmetrical skirt and slouchy boots, prepare some remarks about the latest exhibitions at the Venice Biennale, and head to this 3-year-old "book bar" opposite the ruins of Hadrian's Temple. It sounds pretentious, but Salotto 42 is not—it's just really that sophisticated. Created by two very nice and very hip 30-somethings (Damiano Mazzarella, a Roman New Yorker, and his wife, Malin Persson, a slight and low-key Swedish model), the "salon" consists of a single, rectangular space that feels like the artsy living room you'll probably never have, with plush velvet armchairs that feel lived in even though they're immaculate, and books galore (that you are welcome to browse while you nurse your drink). In the back, there's a bar and small kitchen that serves up a smorgasbord of Scandinavian small plates. This is also a great place to while away a few hours during the day: the classical music and comfy chairs are sure to soothe the nerves of any stressed-out traveler. (Especially for women who seek asylum from the ever present stares of Italian men!) On Saturday and Sunday, a fantastic international buffet brunch is served. *Piazza di Pietra 42.* ☎ *06/678-5804. www.salotto42.it. Tues–Sat 10am–2am; Sun 10am–6pm. Bus: 40, 46, 62, 64, 85, 95, 116, or 492.*

📺 Best ➜ **Société Lutèce** ✶✶ PIAZZA NAVONA   Definitely the coolest bar to open in Rome in a while, this spin-off of the Torino's ultra-chic Brasserie Société Lutèce is well hidden from the average tourist, on a cobblestoned and ochre-washed corner only 5 minutes from Piazza Navona. What really differentiates this place from the other "acceptable" hip-people bars in Rome is that the vibe makes everyone feel at home. The other novelty is that they haven't overdone it with the design: exposed brick walls are painted white, and you sit on red velvet banquettes at small wooden tables, creating an atmosphere of pared-down French chic. There's an *aperitivo* buffet as well as an all-night menu of small plates to accompany the Hemingway-ish classic cocktails. For how hip

ROME & LAZIO

and cool all of this is, the scene remains energetic and fun. *Piazza Montevecchio 17 (off Via dei Coronari).* ☎ *06/6830-1472. Daily 6:30pm to 2am. Bus: 30, 70, 81, 87, 492, or 628.*

Pubs

→ **Abbey Theatre** ★ PIAZZA NAVONA Just because you're in Rome doesn't mean you have to miss out on all your favorite NBA, NFL, MLB, NCAA, and NHL games—international and Italian sports fans unite at this Irish-style pub just down the road from Piazza Navona. The lively front room (where the beer taps and most of the action are) has barstools, small tables, and constant sports on the TV—from the Norwegian curling finals to the Super Bowl. The homey back room is filled with wooden booths and tables perfect for kicking back over several pints and good conversation. To remind you even more of home, the bartender is happy to make up Car Bombs and Flaming Dr. Peppers for you. Happy hour is from 3pm to 8pm, and there's plenty of bar food to be had, from baked potatoes to hot dogs to more Italian options like meat and cheese *antipasti.* When the pub is showing a Roma or Lazio soccer game, expect boisterous crowds, and reserve well in advance if you want to get a seat (on big game nights, there's a cover charge of 5€–10€, which can be applied to anything you order to eat or drink). Avoid the upstairs room (where the bathroom is)—it's a dark and somewhat depressing no man's land. *Via del Governo Vecchio 51–53 (at Via del Teatro Pace).* ☎ *06/686-1341. www.abbey-rome.com. Sun–Thurs 11am–2am; Fri–Sat 11am–3am. Bus: 30, 40, 46, 62, 64, 70, 87, 116, 492, 571, or 628.*

→ **Fiddler's Elbow** ★ TERMINI/ANCIENT ROME In the zone south of Termini, where the neighborhood has just turned from seedy to charming, this is an Italian-owned venerable hangout of serious-drinking resident Irish expats and jovial Romans. (Some patrons, to be honest, are creepy barflys, so be careful which barstool you choose!) If you

feel like busting out your *Riverdance* jig, there's a live Irish band (with fiddles!) on most Wednesday nights. Guests from the hostel next door, Casa Olmata, always end up here sooner or later, so it's usually easy to meet fellow travelers here. In the back, there are darts and a pool table; in the front, there's entertaining banter at the bar, and a computer where you can check your e-mail (when the server isn't down, that is). *Via dell'Olmata 43 (off Piazza Santa Maria Maggiore).* ☎ *06/487-2110. www.thefiddlerselbow.com. Daily 5pm–2am. Metro: Cavour. Bus: 75.*

→ **Finnegan** ★★ ANCIENT ROME If the cast of *Braveheart* had to choose one Roman drinking establishment in which to consume 10 pints of Guinness in one sitting, it would be Finnegan, the only Irish-owned and -managed Irish pub in Rome! Apart from natives of the Emerald Isle, clientele is big on beefy Kiwis, Scots, Aussies, and South Americans (and those Romans who strive to be them), which guarantees a good mood and boisterous atmosphere every night. Note that this doesn't mean girls or non-meathead guys will feel any less welcome—Finnegan has a way of making everyone feel at home. For sports fans, the pub shows all English football games. To see this pub at its best, come when the two Roman games of the Six Nations Rugby Tournament are played (Feb or Mar)—between the televised match and the shenanigans that ensue afterward, it's a jolly good time. *Via Leonina 66 (off Via dei Serpenti).* ☎ *06/474-7026. www.finneganpub.com. Daily 3pm–2am. Metro: Cavour. Bus: 75.*

→ **On the Rox** ★★ TESTACCIO Open till 5am, this zero-attitude cocktail pub is where you stumble in after all the nearby clubs on Via di Monte Testaccio have closed. Danish owners Anas and Christian indulge ill-advised sambuca orders and prompt drunken singalongs with their knowingly cheesy music selections. "Billie Jean," anyone? Earlier in the night, it's more relaxed but always busy, and there are usually lots of English speakers here—not backpackers so much, but northern Europeans who live here, or Americans who are in the Army and based in Rome. On Fridays and Saturdays, there are proper DJs playing a fun mix of rock, pop, disco and dance tunes you know by heart, and everyone gets up and shakes their booty at some point in the night. A great way to sample the buzz of Testaccio nightlife without signing up for the velvet ropes and cover charges at the discos in the 'hood. *Via Galvani 54 (near Via Zabaglia).* ☎ *06/574-6013. Daily 8pm–5am. Metro: Piramide. Bus: 23, 75, 95, 175, or 280.*

➜ **Shamrock** ★ ANCIENT ROME When you've just spent a hot and sweaty day traipsing through the ruins of ancient Rome, this Irish-in-name pub right above the Imperial Fora is the perfect place to settle into a pint or four. Happy Hour goes from 5 to 8pm, by which time the pub is packed to the gills with fun-loving young Romans and the odd resident expat. The Shamrock is also one of the better places in the city to watch a televised football (soccer) match—tensions in the bar run high during big games, and the unbridled shouts of agony or glee are priceless interactive theater. (To get a seat when games are shown, arrive at least 30 min. before kickoff.) The kitchen serves surprisingly excellent hot dogs *(wurstel)* and other pressed panini, and there's a dartboard in the back room. *Via del Colosseo 1/c (off Via Cavour).* ☎ *06/679-1729. Daily 3pm–2am. Metro: Cavour. Bus: 75.*

Live Music

➜ **Big Mama** ★★★ TRASTEVERE Descend the stairs into this subterranean rock, blues, and soul joint and you're immediately greeted by the reassuring stink of old cigarette smoke and beer. In fact, Big Mama is the closest thing Rome has to a honky tonk, with a surprisingly sophisticated, mixed crowd that really knows its music (and how to shake it when a good band plays, which is of ten). I've come here tired, hungover, and heartbroken, and always left at the end of

the night feeling like life is beautiful again—that's the kind of place this is. Management has high standards, and everyone who gets booked here is unbelievably talented. The absolute best act you can catch here is called Più Bestial Che Blues, a Sam Cooke/ Prince/Rolling Stones/Carole King/etc. harmonica-playing cover band fronted by Davide Gentili, my former dentist and a dead-ringer for George Clooney. When the drummer, Antonio Santirocco (known to all as *Il Sindaco*, "the mayor") goes up to the mike to do "Mannish Boy," he puts that Taylor Hicks kid from *American Idol* to shame with his fabulous jerking motions. Such a great time! The club is small, with big piers that block the view of the stage from some side tables, so you want a good view of the show, call and book a table at least a day in advance. *Vicolo di San Francesco a Ripa 18 (at Via San Francesco a Ripa).* ☎ *06/581-2551. www.big mama.it. Concerts are held almost every night Sept–May. Doors open at 9pm; shows start at 10:30; club closes at 1:30am. Cover charge (monthly pass) 8€. Bus: 23, 271, 280, 780, or H.*

➜ **Il Locale** ★★ PIAZZA NAVONA Feel like an insider as you watch relatively unknown Roman or Anglo bands take to the stage of this intimate, energetic rock venue on a tiny cobblestoned alley near Piazza Navona. Whether or not the "talent" puts on a great show, the socializing between sets, and especially after the performance, is a ton of fun. Typical of small music clubs, there's a diverse, cool, and unpretentious crowd that keeps drinking and dancing to music on the stereo until Roman ordinance laws force them to call it a night. Many happy memories, indeed. *Vicolo del Fico 3.* ☎ *06/687-9075. Tues–Sun 9pm–2am. Cover 5€–10€. Bus: 30, 40, 46, 62, 64, 70, 87, 116, 492, 571, or 628.*

Nightclubs

➜ **Alien** ★★ NORTHERN SUBURBS Some Roman kids are participating in Communist demonstrations by the time they're 18; the less activist, more carefree youth of the city just come to Alien. You won't find a jaded soul at this bubble of harmless indulgence, so check your cool-factor cares at the door, and rock out to Backstreet Boy anthems, Beyonce club mixes, even Bananarama's "Cruel Summer" along with 900 other smiling club-goers. With space-age decor and the requisite *cubisti* (cage dancers), it's a carbon copy of every commercial disco on the planet, but you know what? It's still pretty fun. You won't find many people over 25 here, so get in while you're still young. Tuesday is usually the best night in terms of manageable crowds and music mix. (Some historical background for the rose-tinted review: I came here on my first date with Marco, my adorable first Italian boyfriend.) Note that Alien relocates to the beach at Fregene in the summer. *Via Velletri 13–19. ☎ 06/841-2212. www.aliendisco.it. Tues–Sun 11pm–4am. Cover 10€–20€. Bus: 63. Fregene: Piazzale Fregene 5, ☎ 06/6656-4761.*

➔**Art Café** ★ VILLA BORGHESE For the average Roman, vacationing in Sardinia—specifically, the jet-setter resort of Porto Cervo—is the ultimate in aspirational luxury. No wonder, then, that the city's 20- and 30-somethings love the 1980s glamour of the Art Café, which looks and feels exactly like one of the megaferries that sail from Rome to Sardinia, except that it's on land—underground, in fact, moored securely next to a Hertz rental agency in the Villa Borghese's subterranean mall/parking lot. In summer, it transfers out of its dated underground environs and into Piazza di Siena in the Villa Borghese park directly above, which is lined with umbrella pines and gorgeous lighting—quite fabulous, really. When you can't make it to the emerald waters off Porto Cervo, there's even a VIP area with a wading pool. *Viale del Galoppatoio 33 (at the top of Via Veneto, in Villa Borghese). ☎ 06/3600-6578. Tues and Thurs–Sun 9pm–4am. Cover 15€–20€; early arrivals*

and women can sometimes get in free. Metro: Spagna. Bus: 52, 53, 95, or 116.

➔**Brancaleone** ★ EASTERN SUBURBS Founded in 1990 as a social outlet for marginalized and at-risk youth in an ugly part of town, Brancaleone began life as a squat in an abandoned building and has since become one of the coolest *centri sociali* in Rome, with a strong and varied line-up of music nights every week. For dancehall, come on Thursday for *One Love Hi Pawa*. For electronic and other genres you feel deep in your soul, *Agatha* (Friday night) is probably the best-loved Roman DJ night for people who really know their dance music. On Saturday, it's house. The only drawback (and the reason why I haven't given it more stars) is that it's a serious trek out here, but if you can make it, you'll have a great time, far from the tourist masses. While bus 60 Express (from the Colosseum or Piazza Venezia) gets you within 500m (1,640 ft.) of the club, the bus only runs until midnight, meaning you have to find a cab (not easy out there) or hitch a ride home (usually safe, but no guarantees) at the end of the night. *Via Levanna 11, off Via Nomentana, in the Montesacro district. ☎ 06/8200-4382. www.brancaleone.it. Wed–Sat 10:30pm–5am. Cover 5€. Bus: 60 Express to Piazza Sempione, then 5-min. walk farther along Via Nomentana; Via Levanna will be on your right. (You can also take metro Line B to Rebibbia, and then bus 311, but this is a bit of a sketchy proposition at night.)*

➔**La Maison** ★ PIAZZA NAVONA The exclusive Roman club that isn't really that exclusive, which is why it still works now, several very successful years since its opening. While the aging glitterati—film has-beens, sleazy politicos, and the like—party at god-awful places like Gilda or Jackie O—the *bella gente* of Rome who still have their original boobs and faces come to La Maison. Lucky for you, it's right in the heart of the *centro storico*, and there's usually little

In Da Club: Nightlife in Testaccio & Ostiense

The overwhelming majority of Rome's dance clubs are in the districts of Testaccio and Ostiense, just south of the center. Testaccio, where the streets Via di Monte Testaccio and Via Galvani skirt a rustic "mountain" made of pottery (this is where ancient Romans tossed all their used jugs), is the easier option, since it's well connected to the center by bus and metro, and there are dozens of clubs lined up to choose from. Farther south of Testaccio is Ostiense (specifically the area around Via Libetta); more of a pain to reach by public transport, but its clubs tend to be slightly more sophisticated (as in, less bridge-and-tunnel), but not by much.

In Testaccio, I like to hit up **Metaverso** (Via di Monte Testaccio 38/a; ☎ 06/574-4712; www.metaverso.com) for the sheer variety of offerings: Wednesday night is Reggae Night; on alternate Friday nights, DJs Pol Gee and Bob Corsi spin a blender of all kinds of musical genres for "Come As You Are;" and some nights feature live musical acts. For a real hoot, come on Saturdays at 4pm for the hip-hop open mic event, when the aspiring Eminems of Rome bust their rhymes (dare you to count how many times the final syllable is o.) A few doors down, the '80s child in me is also a sucker for **ZooBar** (Via di Monte Testaccio 22; ☎ 339/272-7995 [cell]; www.zoobar.roma.it), where The Clash, Depeche Mode, and New Order are on heavy rotation most nights. To reach Testaccio, take metro B to Piramide, or bus 23, 75, 95, 170, or 280 to Via Marmorata, or tram 3 to Via Marmorata.

In Ostiense, Goa (Via Libetta 13; 1 06/574-8277) has been doing the nebulous Indian/African/Asian ethno house thing for a while, but it's still very popular with the caftan-wearing, just-got-back-from-a-yoga-retreat-but-I'm-still-smoking-and-drinking set. For some good old-fashioned *discoteca* fare (i.e., commercial music), I've never been bored at Saponeria (Via degli Argonauti 20; 1 06/574-6999), popular with Roman jocks and their cute-as-a-button female cohorts. To reach Ostiense, take metro B to Garbatella, and then it's a 10-minute walk around the block; or take metro B to Piramide and then hop on bus 23 south (in the direction of Pincherle) to Via Ostiense/Via Garbatella (Via Libetta is off to the east).

problem getting in, as long as you dress the part (doesn't have to be fancy, just chic) and don't act like a stupid American. On nights when big international celebs are here (like the time Naomi Campbell and Usher came to party here after the MTV Europe VMA's), it's a bit more of a challenge getting past the bouncer. The club isn't huge, but its plush decor (velvet couches, ornate chandeliers, and dark red walls) gives it a classy look that offsets the pure bacchanalia that takes place here every night. Hang out with your friends on one of the divans up front and try to chat up one of the professional soccer players (there are always at least a few in-house), and then make your way through the tangle on the dancefloor to the bar, where a simple vodka lemon (an Italian nighttime staple—vodka and lemon soda water) will set you back 10€. Sunday nights here can be great, since they get started a bit earlier, and the resident DJ Flavia Lazzarini creates a laidback vibe with her ethno-house sets. *Vicolo dei Granari 3, off Via del Teatro Pace, near Via dell'Anima.* ☎ *06/683-3312. Cover 10€–20€; can be free if you are female and pretend to know someone. Tues–Sun 10pm–4am. Bus: 30, 40, 46, 62, 64, 70, 87, 116, 492, 571, or 628.*

A Summer Festival

ESTATE ROMANA

To keep its citizens from going crazy from the heat—and from the excruciating pause in the soccer calendar—the city of Rome puts on an impressive lineup of nocturnal entertainment from June through early September. The 3-month-long festival, which includes open-air cinemas, classical concerts in church courtyards or monumental ancient ruins, outdoor discos, and a ton of live rock and pop shows, is known as collectively known as the *Estate Romana* ("Roman summer"). There are tons of events all over town every night; check the weekly listings guide, *Roma C'è* (at newsstands), or the festival's website, www.estateromana.it, for details. Some of our favorites for all-around fun and fabulousness:

○ **Cornetto Free Music Festival** ★. Italy's biggest packaged ice cream brand, Algida, sponsors three huge free concerts (one in Rome, one in Milan, one in Naples) every summer. In recent years, Duran Duran, Beck, Velvet, and James Blunt played

Rome, Avril Lavigne and the Black Eyed Peas played Milan, and Jamiroquai, Joss Stone, and Morcheeba played Naples. In Rome, the concert has taken place at Piazza San Giovanni, the Circus Maximus, and in the Villa Borghese. Best of all, they give out a *Cornetto* (Algida's yummy top seller, like a Nestlé Drumstick) to all who show up. www.cornettoalgida.com.

○ **Jazz & Image** ★★★. It doesn't matter if you like jazz: (a) half the acts that play this festival aren't really jazz, and (b) the park where this takes place, the Villa Celimontana, above the Colosseum, is such a gorgeous place to pass an evening that you won't care what kind of music is on. Each year, Jazz & Image gets better, and there are now miniature versions of some of Rome's hottest restaurants (like the Riccioli Café oyster bar) that are set up around the festival, serving food and plenty of drinks to concert-goers. Some of my more memorable, *Dolce Vita* nights have been here. Piazza della Navicella. ☎ **06/589-7807.** www.villacelimontana jazz.com. Metro: Colosseo. Bus: 75, 81, 85, 87, 175, 271, 571, or 628. Tram: 3.

○ **Baths of Caracalla** ★★★. The ruins of the city's best-preserved ancient Roman baths are turned into a venue for full-scale symphony and opera performances

Makin' Out *alla romana*

Girls, if you find romance in Rome, I guarantee you the following: The guy'll take you up to **Bar Zodiaco**, on Monte Mario, north of the Vatican, for a cocktail and sweeping views of the city, and later, you'll end up at the **Gianicolo Hill**, Rome's lookout point par excellence. Yeah, it'll seem super-romantic, but trust us, it's as time-honored a tradition as throwing coins in the Trevi Fountain—Romans are nothing if not conformist.

A more romantic spot for a smooch session, though it's hardly undiscovered, is the **Pincio** terrace, at the far western end of Villa Borghese, overlooking Piazza del Popolo. From here, there are great views of the gorgeously illuminated dome of St. Peter's, and ivy-covered parapets where you easily imagine Renaissance maidens and courtiers meeting for trysts, and the occasional knave showing up, dagger glinting in the moonlight 'neath his doublet, for a good ol' fashioned double-crossing.

in July and August. The towering walls and umbrella pines are spectacularly floodlit—as long as you live, you'll be hard-pressed to find a more dramatic, powerful, or monumental setting for high *cultcha*. For opera, visit the Teatro dell'-Opera's website, **www.operaroma.it**. For the symphony, see the Accademia di Santa Cecilia's site, **www.santacecilia. it**. To get to the Baths of Caracalla, take metro Line B to Circo Massimo, or bus 118 to Viale delle Terme di Caracalla.

More Live Music & Other Stuff

➔ **Auditorium** ★★ NORTHERN SUBURBS Violin concertos, African vocalists, Brazilian jazz artists . . . there's a bit of everything at this cool new, Renzo Piano–designed center for the arts. Though much of the calendar is dedicated to classical or new-agey stuff, there are also film screenings (with cast and directors sometimes present), and the summer season tends to bring in more recognized international names from the world of pop and rock to Auditorium's outdoor amphitheater. *Viale Pietro di Coubertin, off Via Flaminia.* ☎ *06/8024-1281. www.auditorium.com. Ticket prices vary. Bus: M, 53, 217, or 910. Tram: 2.*

Gay & Lesbian

For more info about gay and lesbian nightlife, check out the website for the **Circolo di Cultura Omosessuale Mario Mieli** (center for GLBT culture; www.mariomieli.org), which is affiliated with **Muccassassina** (www. muccassassina.com), the city's most venerable gay disco night, held Fridays at **Qube** in the southeastern suburb of Portonaccio, Via di Portonaccio 212 (☎ **06/541-3985** or ☎ 06/438-5445; tram: 5).

➔ **Alibi** ★★ TESTACCIO Not only the best gay disco in Rome, but one of the best, period, on the Monte Testaccio strip (in a field of 20 or so, that ain't bad). It's cruisy, with a clientele of queens, muscle men, and straight-acting

For the Late Night Munchies . . .

La Base ANCIENT ROME/TERMINI Slightly reminiscent of Bob's Big Boy, with loads of American kitsch all over the walls, this place is as much a Roman institution as the Colosseum or the Sistine Chapel. If you're out late at the clubs and want a plate of penne at 4:30am, there's only one option: La Base. (And at that hour, you'll hardly notice that it's the most disgusting pasta you've ever eaten.) In any case, you'll feel right at home—for some random reason, all the pastas and pizzas are named after American sports teams. Via Cavour 274. ☎ **06/474-0659.** Daily 8pm–5am.

gays preening for each other on the club's multiple levels. Best of all is the roof terrace, which becomes the third dance floor in summer, against the rustic slopes and sycamore trees of Monte Testaccio. *Via di Monte Testaccio 39.* ☎ *06/574-3448. Metro: Piramide. Cover 10€. Bus: 23, 75, 95, 175, or 280.*

➔ **Hangar** ★ TERMINI/ANCIENT ROME Having survived since 1984, the Hangar is a landmark on the gay nightlife scene and a good place to socialize, and get the lay of the land for gays in Rome. Women are welcome any night except Monday, when the club features videos and entertainment for men. The busiest nights are Saturday, Sunday, and Monday, when as many as 500 people cram inside. *Via in Selci 69.* ☎ *06/488-1397. Wed–Mon 10:30pm–2:30am. Closed 3 weeks in Aug. No cover, but there's a 7€ "membership fee." Metro: Cavour. Bus: 75.*

➔ **New Joli Coeur** ★ EASTERN SUBURBS Just for lesbians, this bar/lounge/disco is only open on Saturdays or for special parties or theme evenings. The space is divided up into three rooms: one for board games and video games (how social!), one for live music and cabaret, and one for dancing. *Via Sirte 5, off*

Viale Eritrea. ☎ *06/574-3448. Sat 10pm–4am. Cover 10€. Bus: 38, 80, or 86.*

Sightseeing

If the sights of Rome don't impress you, there's something wrong with you. That's all there is to it. Of course, Rome is most famous for its showstopping ancient ruins, which lie in the majestic green hills and valleys of the urban archaeological zones south of the *centro storico.* The other headlining act is the Vatican, where St. Peter's, the Vatican Museums, and the Sistine Chapel suck thousands of tourists west across the river and into the tiny, 0.44 sq km (1/4 sq. mile) city-state daily. (Because of its temperamental opening hours and crowds situation, the Vatican is also the one sight that requires a tiny bit of planning on your part.)

In the cobblestoned alleys of Rome's *centro storico,* baroque churches, fountains, and theatrical piazzas lurk around every corner. Everything is so close together and so highly concentrated that if you simply walk for 10 minutes in any direction, you'll hit at least 10 world-famous, postcard-worthy monuments or public spaces along the way. Rome is so rich in art and architecture that the entire *centro* has been declared a UNESCO World Heritage Site. If you've ever taken an art history class, you'll have a lot of "so, *that's* what this looks like in person" moments. Owing to its almost 3,000-year history, the cityscape keeps you tuned in with a fascinating mix of ancient, medieval, Renaissance, baroque, neoclassical, and fascist sights. (This will come as a relief if you've just come from Florence, where the museums play like a broken record of Madonna and Child paintings.)

The other very cool thing about Rome is that you can see all the most impressive and "important" sights for about 20€. The Sistine Chapel, which is part of the Vatican

Museums, costs 10€, and the Colosseum costs 10€. Other than that, the Roman Forum, St. Peter's, the Trevi Fountain, the Pantheon, and countless churches and open-air ruins, monuments, and fountains are free of charge.

The Stuff You Need to See

The average first-time visitor in Rome stays for about 2.5 days, which is a travesty. However, if you plan your days carefully, you can still see a lot. Before you get too overwhelmed by the task before you, remember this: The city is incredibly compact and chock-full of treasures at every turn, and you'll end up seeing more than you planned to anyway—in most cases, "seeing" the sights on the lists below is as simple as walking by and staring for 5 or 10 minutes, and then moving on. Another helpful feature of Rome is that most of the monuments are perfectly visible (and often more impressive) all night long. If you're staying in Rome for 1 day, hit the blockbuster sights, but realize that you're not getting the full picture. There's more to Rome than crazy traffic and hordes of tourists at Colosseum! If you have a few days in the city, see the iconic attractions—just spend more time there and learn something—and mix it up with some of the less-famous, equally fascinating sights that make Rome so special.

○ **You *must:*** Colosseum, Roman Forum, Capitoline Hill, Pantheon, St. Peter's Basilica, Vatican Museums and Sistine Chapel

○ **You really should:** Piazza Navona, Trevi Fountain, Castel Sant'Angelo, Appian Way, backstreets of the *centro storico* or Trastevere, Pincio or Gianicolo (for a view)

◦ **Nice, but Overrated:** Spanish Steps, Mouth of Truth, Michelangelo's *Moses*

◦ **Under the Radar but Off the Charts:** Galleria Borghese, Crypt of the Capuchin Monks, the Foro Italico

ONE (VERY BUSY) DAY IN ROME:

This is an ambitious itinerary, but as long as you're not too hungover (and it's not blistering hot), you can do it. Everything on this tour is free except for the Vatican Museums and Sistine Chapel.

In the morning, start at the **Colosseum.** You don't have time to go inside, but you can get a good look at it by walking around its exterior. From here, head up the street to the **Roman Forum.** Walk through the Roman Forum and climb out of it via the ancient road that leads to the **Capitoline Hill.** Past Piazza del Campidoglio, take the *cordonata* ramp down to Piazza Venezia. From here, walk north to the **Trevi Fountain,** or save the Trevi for later that night and head straight to the **Pantheon** instead. (You need to see the Pantheon during the day because it's closed at night.)

From the Pantheon, head west to **Piazza Navona,** and get **lunch** at one of the lively, less-touristy trattorias in the side streets west of Piazza Navona. After lunch, hightail it over to the **Vatican Museums;** last entry is at 3:20pm. You won't have time to see much, so zip through the galleries of ancient art and head straight for the **Sistine Chapel.** Exit the Sistine Chapel via the door that leads directly to **St. Peter's Basilica.** Now, you've earned yourself a break. Head back to your hotel (if you have one), freshen up, and hit **Campo de' Fiori** around 7pm for an *aperitivo* with all the young locals who party there every night. Eat **dinner** somewhere in the vicinity, and then walk over to **Castel Sant'Angelo** to see how magnificent it (and its bridge) looks under the floodlights. From here, if you have any energy at all left

in you, you're pretty close to **Piazza del Popolo** and the **Spanish Steps,** which are also lively and quite pretty to see at night. If you're still trucking late-night, go to the Trevi Fountain. It's at its most spectacular after 1am, when all the tourists have finally gone home.

Note: The Vatican Museums and Sistine Chapel are not open on Sundays, and have morning-only hours on Saturdays (and daily from Nov–Feb), so you'll have do the Vatican in the morning (when it's more crowded and stressful, unfortunately) if you're visiting Rome on a Saturday or in the off-season. In that case, you might just want to leave the Vatican until next trip!

Hanging Out

THE BEST VIEWS IN & OF ROME

For overall panoramas, these three spots are your best bets:

◦ **Pincio** ★★   The romantic stone parapets at the western edge of the Villa Borghese look out over the terra-cotta rooftops and domes of the *centro storico* to the Vatican. See also "Makin' Out *alla romana*" (p. 138). Piazzale Napoleone. Metro: Flaminio. Bus: 117 or 119.

◦ **Gianicolo** ★★   Romans' other favorite lookout and make-out point is the Janiculum Hill, a tree-lined ridge above Trastevere. Depending on where you stand along the Gianicolo, the view takes in different parts of the city: From the northern stretch, you can see the dome of St. Peter's and Castel Sant'Angelo; the middle offers a good comprehensive *centro storico* overview; stand on the southern stretch and you can see the green hills and red-brick ruins of ancient Rome, from the Palatine to the Colosseum to the Baths of Caracalla. Passeggiata del Gianicolo. Accessible on foot from Trastevere (turn right up the hill at the top of Via Garibaldi); or take bus 115 or 870.

Major Sights in Rome

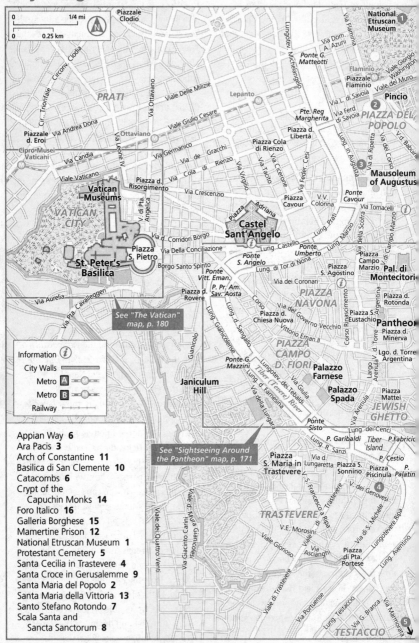

0 ——— 1/4 mi
0 ——— 0.25 km

Piazzale Clodio

National Etruscan Museum ❶

Via Flaminia

Lungotev. Michelangelo

Via Dom. A. Azuni

Ponte G. Matteotti

Viale Delle Milizie

Lepanto

Flaminio

Piazzale Flaminio

Viale Giorgio Washington

Viale del Muro

Pincio

PRATI

Via Ottaviano

Pte. Reg Margherita

Piazza d. Libertà

Via Ferd di Savoia

Via L. di Savoia

❷ PIAZZA DEL POPOLO

Viale Giulio Cesare

Piazzale d. Eroi

Via Andrea Doria

Ottaviano

Via Leone IV

Via Germanico

Piazza Cola di Rienzo

Via Cicerone

Lung. in Augusta

Via di Ripetta

Via del Babuino

Via del Corso

Cipro–Musei Vaticani

Via Candia

Via de' Gracchi

Via de Cola di Rienzo

Via Tacito

Via Feder. Cesi

❸ Mausoleum of Augustus

Viale Vaticano

Piazza d. Risorgimento

Via Cola di Rienzo

Via Virgilio

Piazza Cavour

V.V. Colonna

Ponte Cavour

Via Tomacelli ⓘ

Vatican Museums

V. di Pta. Angelica

Via Crescenzio

Piazza Adriana

Ponte Prati

Lungotev. Marzio

Via della Scrofa

Lungotev. in Sassia

Via di Campo Marzio

Piazza Campo Marzio

Pal. di Montecitori

VATICAN CITY

Castel Sant'Angelo

ⓘ

Ponte S. Angelo

Lung. Castello

Ponte Umberto

Piazza S. Agostino

Piazza Nicosia

Ⓘ

St. Peter's Basilica

Piazza S. Pietro

Via d. Corridori Borgo

Via Della Conciliazione

Lung. di Tor di Nona

Via dei Coronari

Piazza S. Eustachio

Pantheon

Piazza d. Rotonda

Borgo Santo Spirito

Ponte Vitt. Eman.

PIAZZA NAVONA

Piazza d. Minerva

Via Aurelia

Borgo Santo Spirito

Piazza d. Rovere

P. Pr. Am. Sav. Aosta

Corso Vittorio Eman.II

Piazza d. Chiesa Nuova

Via del Governo Vecchio

Corso Rinascimento

Via d. Torre Argentina

Lgo. d. Torre Argentina

Via Pta Cavalleggeri

Gianicolo

Lung. Gianicolense

PIAZZA CAMPO D. FIORI

Palazzo Farnese

Largo Arenula

Piazza Mattei

See "The Vatican" map, p. 180

Ponte G. Mazzini

Tiber (Tevere) River

Via Giulia

Palazzo Spada

JEWISH GHETTO

Information ⓘ

City Walls ▬▬▬

Metro Ⓐ ━◉━◉━

Metro Ⓑ ━◉━◉━

Railway ┄┄┄┄┄

Janiculum Hill

Lung. d. Farnesina

Via della Lungara

Ponte Sisto

Lung. dei Cenci

Tiber Island

P. Fabricio

P. Cestio

Lung. R. Sanzi

Lung. P. Garibaldi

See "Sightseeing Around the Pantheon" map, p. 171

Piazza S. Maria in Trastevere

Via d. Lungaretta

Piazza S. Sonnino

Piazza Piscinula

P. Palatin

❹

Appian Way **6**
Ara Pacis **3**
Arch of Constantine **11**
Basilica di San Clemente **10**
Catacombs **6**
Crypt of the
  Capuchin Monks **14**
Foro Italico **16**
Galleria Borghese **15**
Mamertine Prison **12**
National Etruscan Museum **1**
Protestant Cemetery **5**
Santa Cecilia in Trastevere **4**
Santa Croce in Gerusalemme **9**
Santa Maria del Popolo **2**
Santa Maria della Vittoria **13**
Santo Stefano Rotondo **7**
Scala Santa and
  Sancta Sanctorum **8**

Viale delle Mura di Porta S. Pancrazio

Viale di Quattro Venti

Via Giacinto Carini

Via G. Mameli

TRASTEVERE

V.E. Morosini

Via S. Francesco a Ripa

Viale Glorioso

Via Asciangh

Lungotevere Ripa

Via di S. Michele

Via dei Genovesi

Piazza di Pta. Portese

Via di Trastevere

Lung. Aventino

Via Aventino

Via Portuense

Lung. Testaccio

Via G. Branca

Via Marmorata

TESTACCIO ❺

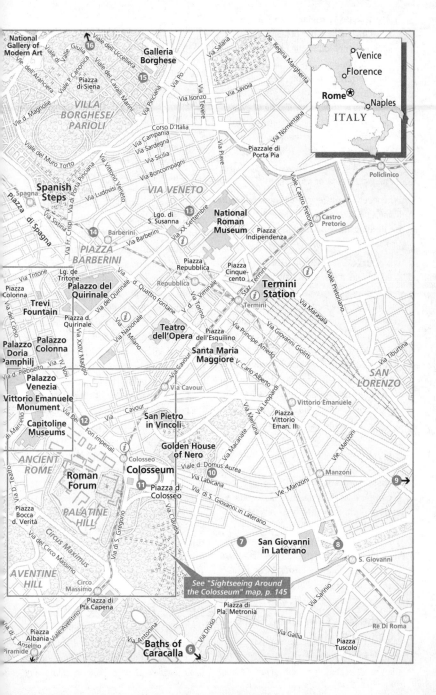

National
Gallery of
Modern Art

Viale dell'Uccelliera

16

Viale di Valle Giulia

Viale P. Canonica

Viale dei Cavalli Marini

**Galleria
Borghese**

15

Piazza
di Siena

Via Po

Via Pinciana

Via Salaria

Via Regina Margherita

Via Nomentana

Viale dell'Aranciera

Viale d. Magnolie

**VILLA
BORGHESE/
PARIOLI**

Corso D'Italia

Via Isonzo

Via Savoia

Policlinico

Viale del Muro Torto

Via Campania

Via Sardegna

Via Sicilia

Via Piave

Piazzale di
Porta Pia

Viale Castro Pretorio

Via Boncompagni

**Spanish
Steps**

Spagna

Piazza
di Spagna

Via Sistina

Via di Porta Pinciana

Via Vittorio Veneto

Via Ludovisi

VIA VENETO

Lgo. di
S. Susanna

13

Via XX Settembre

**National
Roman
Museum**

Piazza
Indipendenza

Castro
Pretorio

Viale Pretoriano

Via Fr. Crispi

14 Barberini

Via Barberini

ⓘ

**PIAZZA
BARBERINI**

Lg. de
Tritone

Piazza
Repubblica

Piazza
Cinque-
cento

ⓘ

Via Tritone

Piazza
Colonna

**Palazzo del
Quirinale**

Repubblica

ⓘ

Via del Quirinale d. Quattro Fontane

Viminale

Staz. Termini

**Termini
Station**

Via Marsala

**Trevi
Fountain**

Via del Corso

Piazza d.
Quirinale

ⓘ

Via Nazionale

Via d. Torino

Termini

Via Giovanni Giolitti

**Palazzo
Doria
Pamphilj**

**Palazzo
Colonna**

Via IV Nov.

Via XXIV Maggio

Via Milano

**Teatro
dell'Opera**

Piazza
dell'Esquilino

Via Principe Amedo

**Palazzo
Venezia**

**Santa Maria
Maggiore**

V. Carlo Alberto

**SAN
LORENZO**

Via Tiburtina

**Vittorio Emanuele
Monument**

Via Cavour

Vittorio Emanuele

Piazza
Vittorio
Eman. II

Vle. Manzoni

**Capitoline
Museums**

12

Via Cavour

Via Merulana

Via Macanate

Via di Teatro

**ANCIENT
ROME**

Fori Imperiali

ⓘ

**San Pietro
in Vincoli**

Piazza
Vittorio
Eman. II

Manzoni

9 →

Colosseo

**Golden House
of Nero**

10

**Roman
Forum**

Colosseum

11

Piazza d.
Colosseo

Viale d. Domus Aurea

Via Labicana

Vle. Manzoni

**PALATINE
HILL**

Piazza
Bocca
d. Verità

Via Claudia

Via di S. Giovanni in Laterano

Circus Maximus

Via del Circo Massimo

Via di S. Gregorio

**AVENTINE
HILL**

Circo
Massimo

7

**San Giovanni
in Laterano**

8

S. Giovanni

See "Sightseeing Around
the Colosseum" map, p. 145

Piazza di
Pta.Capena

Piazza di
Pla. Metronia

Via Sannio

Re Di Roma

Piazza
Albania

Viale Aventino

Via Rntonina

Via Druso

Via Gallia

Piazza
Tuscolo

Piazza S. Anselmo

Piramide

**Baths of
Caracalla**

6

ITALY

Venice

Florence

Rome✱

Naples

ROME & LAZIO

⊙ 📺 (Best) **Vittoriano** ★★ As much as we love to hate this behemoth of white marble on the south side of Piazza Venezia, nothing beats the upper terraces of the Vittoriano for a bird's-eye view of the most famous monuments of Rome. Here, you're right in the middle of everything, so you'll have great views of the Pantheon, St. Peter's, the Roman Forum, the Colosseum, and the Palatine. Piazza Venezia. Bus: 30, 40, 62, 64, 70, 85, 87, 95, 170, 175, 271, 492, or 571.

Whenever I want to impress newcomers in Rome, I take them to one of these two perches for thrilling, more zoomed-in views of a particular section of town:

⊙ 📺 (Best) **Capitoline Hill** ★★★ It doesn't get much more sublime than the vertiginous view over the Roman Forum from the railings on the south side of the Campidoglio. Saunter up here at night, with a little wine and you, and the floodlit spectacle of the marble ruins, which stretch majestically throughout the length of the Forum valley to the Colosseum, will definitely be a highlight of your trip. Piazza del Campidoglio (the terraces are at the end of the short walkways on either side of the bell-towered Palazzo Senatorio). Bus: 30, 40, 62, 64, 70, 85, 87, 95, 170, 175, 271, 492, or 571.

⊙ **Castel Sant'Angelo** ★★ The windblown ramparts at the summit of Rome's mausoleum-turned-fortress-turned-papal-hideout-turned-prison offer dramatic perspectives down the street to St. Peter's, and across the Tiber to the *centro storico*. Lungotevere Castello. For admission and hours, see full listing (p. 175). Bus: 23, 40, 62, 64, 70, 87, 271, 280, or 492.

Things You Can't Just Tell By Looking at Her

Rome's sights are beautiful to look at, but they hardly speak for themselves. To help them come alive, I've written especially lengthy descriptions about the most important monuments. If you're too lazy to read everything in these pages, you can also take a guided tour of the sights.

Do be aware, however, that not all tours are created equal. Bus tours are overpriced and have unintelligible guides—stick to walking tours. When it comes to picking a guide, steer clear of Italians (even if they're English-speaking): because their cultural bar is so much higher when it comes to art and architecture, they tend to assume you already know the basics and will start rattling off names and terms that will go in one jet-lagged ear and out the other. The best tours are those given by native English-speakers (Americans, Brits, Aussies, etc.) who are more like teachers than information-reciters and understand that most tourists are a clean slate when it comes to all this "imperial" and "baroque" stuff.

There are dozens of walking tour companies that employ these local expats, who focus on educating you while they entertain you. There's definitely a huckster factor, however, as hardly any of these guides are the bona fide academic experts ("archaeologists," "Ph.D. candidates") they claim to be. Many are just globetrotting backpackers who've landed in Rome for a few years, and ancient storytelling is a great gig—but you'll still learn something. The tours combine basic history, keys for understanding ruins and works of art, and titillating anecdotes. Most of these outfits offer a **free promotional tour** at St. Peter's or the Forum, and then they'll try to get you to sign up for another (paid) tour of another area the next day.

Ancient Ruins & Monuments

If this section is rather comprehensive, it's because I am a classics dork. Deal with it. Nothing sparks the imagination or fuels a nostalgic journey quite like the physical remains

Sightseeing Around the Colosseum

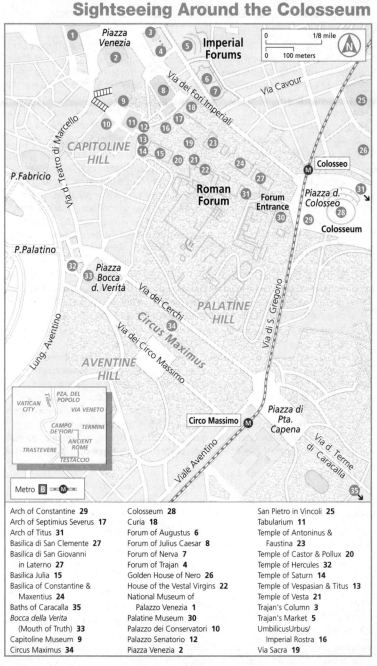

Lego Land: The Building Blocks of Rome

In Latin, *lego* means "I connect." And if you look around the city, there's been a lot of big-time connecting of blocks over the years. From 753 B.C. on down to the present day, almost everything in Rome is made of blocks of one of three primary building materials: tufa, travertine, and brick. Also, if it weren't for Roman cement, none of the vaulting and domes so prevalent in the imperial ruins would have been possible. All of these quintessential materials are forever hallowed in the world of architecture for what the Romans were able to achieve with them, and how well many of them still hold up, some after more than 2,000 years.

→ **Tufa** (*peperino* or *tufo*) is a local volcanic rock, reddish or grayish, depending on the source. A soft stone, tufa is easy to cut but prone to crumbling, meaning its surfaces are rough-hewn, never smooth or polished. The "workhorse" of Roman materials, tufa was one of the most widely used stones in the Republican era (before the 1st century B.C.), but it was not considered attractive by the emperors. You'll find it in Rome's earlier ruins (such as the temples at the Area Sacra of Largo Argentina, or in the Tabularium on the Capitoline Hill), and in the building foundations of some imperial Roman monuments, where it would have been covered by a more "presentable" sheeting of marble. Where it was purely functional, and out of sight of the general public (such as when it was used in the construction of aqueducts out in the countryside), tufa went naked.

→ **Travertine** (*lapis tiburtinus*) is the MVP of Roman materials, a white, calcareous, and incredibly durable limestone that is everywhere in the city, over all time periods. The Colosseum, St. Peter's Basilica, and the Trevi Fountain, plus countless palazzi and fountains, are all made of travertine, which is often erroneously called marble. The gaping travertine quarries in Tivoli (18km/11 miles east of Rome along the Via Tiburtina) are still very active today, furnishing kitchen and bathroom tiles to wealthy homeowners around the globe. In the fascist era, Mussolini had monuments built all over the city to showcase the glories of ancient Rome, and developed his own "third Rome" (after that of the emperors and the popes) in the EUR

of the glory days of ancient Rome. Since there's so much more to Roman ruins than meets the eye—from how they were built, to some of the crazy stuff they were used for—I've given you the back stories that will hopefully make these fallen buildings come alive. Happy reading!

Most of the major ancient sights are in the archaeological areas that spread out south of Piazza Venezia; a few other biggies, like the Pantheon, are nestled among other buildings in more modern parts of the city. A good place to start is at the Colosseum,

which is accessed by metro Line B (Colosseo stop); you can also get there on bus 60, 75, 85, 87, 175, 271, or 571, or tram 3.

MTV **Best** → **Colosseum** ★★★ ANCIENT ROME   As barbaric as they were spectacular, gladiator and wild-animal fights—known as "games" to the blood-and-guts-loving ancient Roman masses—were held in this famous arena for more than 4 centuries. The Colosseum is by far the mightiest surviving monument of imperial Rome, even though it's only half intact. It's also bigger in district, south of the city. Almost everything constructed in the 1920s and '30s is made of highly polished, icy-looking white travertine.

➔ **Bricks** (*opus latericium* or *opus testaceum*) are the unsung heroes of Roman architecture. Made of reddish-orange clay and baked in the sun, most Roman bricks were triangular in shape; the pointed side stuck into the center of the wall, which was then filled with a mixture of rubble and mortar (*opus caementicium,* a form of concrete). Another cool thing about Roman bricks is that they were all stamped with a manufacturer's seal, which archaeologists can use to date a building that otherwise provides no clues about its age. Large brick tiles called *bipedales* (because of their size, "two feet" square) were used to make the suspended floors in Roman baths; hot air circulated underneath them, and heat was conducted up through the tiles to the spaces above. In the center of Rome, you'll see brick ruins everywhere—at Trajan's Markets, the Palatine Hill, and the Baths of Caracalla, just to name a few—but remember that brick walls, pretty as they are to look at today, would have been covered by stucco or marble in ancient times. Sadly, the bricks of Rome are too exposed to the elements these days. When rain seeps in, the bricks expand, and when they're too swollen, brick walls can crumble within minutes. Recently, entire stretches of wall from the imperial palaces on the Palatine Hill have given way under heavy rainfall.

➔ **Cement** *(opus caementicium).* The Romans didn't invent it, but they perfected it. By about 100 B.C., Roman engineers had refined their signature blend of cement (two parts *pozzolana* ash, one part lime, add water) to the point where they could pour it over wooden forms of arches and vaults, and when it dried, it stayed put. Roman cement could even set while underwater. The largest scale and most astonishing use of cement in a Roman building is the 43m-wide (141 ft.) hemispherical dome of the Pantheon, still standing, with no steel reinforcements to counter its tensile forces, after almost 1,900 years.

real life than it looks in photographs. Properly known as the Amphitheatrum Flavium, the 65,000-spectator-capacity arena was a gift to the citizens of Rome from the emperors Vespasian and Titus (father and son, of the Flavian dynasty) and built in just 8 years (A.D. 72–80) by about 60,000 slaves. (The Colosseum's late 1st-century date means that it did not exist during the time of some of Rome's more famous rulers, like Julius Caesar, Augustus, Claudius, and Nero.) The building's three concentric, elliptical rings—a template for modern stadium design—are made of huge blocks of travertine (a porous white limestone, not marble), quarried in the nearby town of Tivoli. Each of the 80 arches around the base of the building) was a numbered entrance, whose number (I through LXXX) corresponded with that on the *tessera,* or clay ticket, given out to Roman citizens when games were held. Games—always state-sponsored—were held whenever there was an official Roman holiday. By the height of the Empire, 180 days of the year had been declared holidays, whether to honor Venus, or to celebrate the emperor's horse's birthday. Do the mathematics: There were games every other day of the year!

Tickets were free, but seating was strictly regulated according to social status. The richer classes sat lower to the action in the ring; the women and slaves had to settle for the nosebleed standing-room-only section at the very top of the building (equivalent to row ZZ at Madison Square Garden). The tunnels and stairwells that connected each of the 80 entrances to its particular seating section were called *vomitoria*. Contrary to popular belief, this is not where Romans came to puke when the action in the ring got too graphic; it was the *vomitoria's* own ability to spew out 65,000 people efficiently (about 8 minutes) at the end of the day that earned them their name. You'll see gutters in some *vomitoria;* again, these aren't puke drains, but remnants of the public lavatories located throughout the Colosseum. With roving snack vendors to boot, it really wasn't so different from sports stadiums of today. The Colosseum also had a retractable sunshade, the *velarium,* which was made of sails *(velae),* and hoisted by hundreds of elite seamen from the naval base of Misenum, near Naples. (It was Fleet Week every day at the Colosseum—how awesome is that?)

As for the games that were staged here, well, they make modern-day boxers, wrestlers, and bullfighters look like a bunch of sissies. The events at the Colosseum were known as *ludi* and divided into *munera* (gladiatorial contests—man on man), and *venationes* (wild-animal "hunts"—man on animal), which frequently (but not always) ended in death or dismemberment. The action in the arena was carefully choreographed and controlled from a complex series of underground passageways, still visible today. The arena floor was equipped with dozens of trap-doors and elevator shafts (also preserved) through which contestants, sharper weapons, or scenery could be lifted to the stage. When someone died,

an attendant performed the ol' death verification test (as gladiators often faked being dead to get out of the wretched gig), prodding the corpse with a hot iron. If the subject remained motionless, he was really dead and dragged off to the *spoliarium* (mass grave), just south of the Colosseum. If the subject yelped or flinched under the poker, he was still alive—but not for long: to punish his fakery, the attendant whacked the gladiator over the head with a blunt object. When the arena got too bloody, they would rake away the soiled sand (sand was called *arena* in Latin), and spread a fresh new layer of sand to soak up the next round's carnage—kind of like a Zamboni machine clearing the ice at a hockey game.

In the first decade of so of the Colosseum's history, they were able to remove the wooden floor and flood the substructures of the arena with water from the nearby Aqua Claudia aqueduct. This was essential for the staging of another beloved Roman pastime, the *naumachia,* or mock naval battle. What a show this would have been—they even created waves! Reduced-scale Roman triremes (warships) were built expressly for the *naumachia* event, and slaves were made to fight as imperial sailors on the high seas. The ship that stayed afloat, or whose crew didn't drown—these guys weren't the greatest swimmers—won the competition. When it was over, they opened up the drain that ran to the city's main sewer, the Cloaca Maxima, and whatever flotsam (living or dead) was left in the water was flushed out into the Tiber river. The *naumachiae* were time-consuming to set up, however—not the most efficient use of the Romans' valuable slaughter time!—and the organizers of the games decided to focus on dry-land events only from about A.D. 100 on.

The wild animals that fought in the Colosseum were captured and transported from all over the Empire: elephants, lions, and crocodiles came from the African provinces; tigers came from Asia; bears came from northern and eastern Europe. Baffled and angry, the beasts savaged their opponent, the human *venator*, as often as they were slain by him. (The Grizzly Man wouldn't have lasted 5 minutes in here, to say nothing of Roy Horn, whose sparkly outfits probably would have offended the animals.) The old notion that they fed Christians to the lions here is true; but Christians were considered enemies of the state until A.D. 315, and all captured enemies of state (traitors, thieves, and heretic—which included anyone who didn't worship the Roman gods) could be given the *damnatio ad bestias* death sentence: at intermission on a game day, the prisoners were dumped, unarmed, into the middle of the arena, and the hungry imperial menagerie turned loose among them. Even with this cheap diet of prisoner chow, acquiring and keeping big game was a costly enterprise, and with the budget constraints that came with the decline of the Empire, the Romans had to make do with chickens pecking each other to death in the middle of the Colosseum. A sad day, indeed—in its heyday, the Colosseum had seen hippos take on pumas in the ring. Man-on-man fights were phased out in the 5th century A.D.—a full century after the legalization and spread of Christianity in Rome—while a few pathetic *venationes* lingered on for another hundred years. They finally stuck a fork in it in 523 A.D., the date of the last recorded *ludus* at the Colosseum. From then on, the only group activity Romans had to look forward to was church on Sundays—not quite the same.

In the 1,500 years that have passed since the last games here, the Colosseum has seen its vicissitudes. The pockmarks evident between the travertine blocks today are the result of lead and iron clamps being pillaged from the Colosseum by metal-hungry Lombards in the Middle Ages. In the 14th century, an earthquake shook Rome and a third of the Colosseum came tumbling down.

In the 16th century, the fallen travertine blocks were carted off in papal wheelbarrows to the building site of the new St. Peter's Basilica at the Vatican. To make up for the theft, Pope Gregory XVI replaced the broken western wall of the Colosseum with a brick one in the 18th century. By the 19th century, the Colosseum was overgrown with exotic vegetation—plant spores, carried in the feces of the wild animals, had lodged in the stones and thrived here for centuries. All of that was torn out during Rome's "archaeological awakening" of the late 19th century. Today, the biggest threats to the Colosseum's preservation are pollution and—more alarmingly—the palpable vibrations from metro Line B, which rumbles beneath the ground here hundreds of times a day.

If you're budget is really tight, you can see most of the Colosseum from the outside, but if you can swing the price of admission, a visit inside the Colosseum is a memorable experience you won't regret. Via the original stone stairways, you can climb as high as the middle ring, which is still pretty high (about 25m/82ft. above the ground), and walk all the way around for a great Roman's-eye view of the arena below. The arena itself lost its original wooden floor long ago, but there's a modern wooden catwalk that allows you to tread on the same level as gladiator and animal did, and peer down to the subterranean level, where you can make out the vestiges of 32 elevator shafts. The design of the Colosseum, with its elegant superimposed arcades, was much more decorative than it needed to be from a functional standpoint, but creating visual grandeur was what Roman architecture was all about; by looking the way it did, the Colosseum spread propaganda to all who visited it, to all who heard about it throughout the Empire, that Rome was a glorious and powerful place. Well guess what? It has the same effect today. For a dramatic first vision of the Colosseum, take metro Line B to

"Colosseo" and emerge from the underground station to see the enormous, 15-story northern wall of the amphitheater looming before you. *Piazza del Colosseo.* ☎ *06/700-42-61. Metro: Colosseo. 8€ (ticket also good for admission at the Palatine Hill); 10€ when there are special exhibitions inside the Colosseum. Daily 9am to 1 hr. before sunset. Closed Jan 1, May 1, and Dec 25. Bus: 60, 75, 85, 87, 117, or 175. Tram: 3.*

→ **Arch of Constantine** ✶✶ ANCIENT ROME The triumphal arch of Constantine, which stands fenced in the middle of the cobblestoned esplanade between the Colosseum and the Palatine, was erected in A.D. 315 to commemorate the Battle of the Milvian Bridge of A.D. 312 (see box "Goodbye Pagans, Hello Jesus!," below), in which Constantine defeated his co-emperor aided by the Christian cross. I say "erected" in A.D. 315, because most of the stuff on the arch was actually created much earlier, for other emperors' victory monuments, and stolen by Constantine. By the 4th century, Roman sculpture—once so elegant and realistic—had gone seriously downhill: human figures started looking like pudgy little dwarves, and everything (people, horses, fortress walls) was depicted at the same height. So, with this embarrassing state of the arts, no wonder Constantine preferred to dismantle earlier emperors' monuments—where the sculptures were something you could be proud of—to decorate his arch. The round panels in the attic (upper level) are from Hadrian (A.D. 117–138); the rectangular reliefs are from Antoninus Pius (A.D. 161–180), and the friezes on the inside of the arch are from Trajan (A.D. 98–117). Constantine did employ some sculpture from his era, and it sticks out like a sore thumb. The narrow bands of relief that run above the smaller lateral arches are prime, even comical examples of 4th century loss of realism. If you stand facing the southern side of the arch (with the Colosseum ahead and to the right), the sculptural strip above the left lateral arch is particularly entertaining: in this scene, Constantine's army is sieging Verona; the city "walls" however, are about waist-height, making the whole thing look like Playskool's "My Li'l Siege" set. The horses, whose stature is also reduced, look like innocuous Shetland Ponies—hardly steeds worthy of battle. One unfortunate Veronese soul is shown flopping over the wall, legs akimbo, like a gymnastic feat gone horribly awry. In any case, everything on the Arch of Constantine is in an outstanding state of preservation, owing to its being associated with the triumph of Christianity over paganism and thus protected by the Church. Piazza del Colosseo/Via di San Gregorio. Bus: 60, 75, 85, 87, 117, or 175. Tram: 3.

Colosseum Insider Tips

Expert tip: In high season, the lines to get into the Colosseum can be long. When they are, head down the street to the entrance of the Palatine Hill, on Via di San Gregorio. Buy your ticket there (there's usually no line), as the ticket for the Palatine is the same one that gets you into the Colosseum. Ticket in hand, you can walk straight past all the people in line to buy their tickets at the Colosseum and right to the turnstiles, under the arcades on the northern side of the building. *Super insider secret:* Not that we endorse this, but it is possible to sneak into the Colosseum in the middle of the night. There are bars in one of the arches that don't go all the way down to the ground, meaning that a reasonably fit person can slip right underneath. Having said that, climbing all over the ruins of Rome's greatest ancient monument in the glow of moonlight is illegal and can be dangerous, so, um, you should probably forget you ever read this.

The Domus Aurea

A Palace Fit for a Raving Lunatic

In December 2005, due to excessive rainwater seeping into the walls of the ruins of Nero's "Golden House," the archaeological superintendent of Rome closed the site indefinitely. Whether or not it reopens in time for your visit (the cultural ministry is saying 2008 at the earliest), the Domus Aurea is still a fascinating part of ancient Rome.

When the great fire of A.D. 64 conveniently destroyed half of the city, emperor Nero appropriated the more devastated parts of Rome and built his dream home—the Domus Aurea, or "Golden House"—which stretched from the Palatine Hill, across the valley where the Colosseum is today, and up the Esquiline hill, toward modern-day Termini station. When it was finished, in A.D. 68, the new imperial estate occupied an entire third of the city of Rome. The Domus Aurea was not so much a unified palace as a series of pavilions, galleries, secret passageways, and porticoes surrounded by a sprawling park, at the center of which sat a man-made lake, the *Stagnum Neronis* (where the Colosseum now stands). A 45m-high (148-ft.) bronze-and-gold statue of Nero (portrayed as the sun god, with a radiate crown like the Statue of Liberty) presided over the whole thing.

Designed by imperial architects Severus and Celer, the Domus Aurea was filled with ingenious spaces and flights of architectural fancy. The famed octagonal dining room, where Nero entertained his most important guests, had a rotating floor that was powered by water jets from the aqueducts. A wanna-be spelunker who was in fact afraid of real caves, Nero also had his men build several grottoes on the property, complete with faux stalactites and atmospheric dripping water. Naturally, opulent frescoes, mosaics, and sculptures filled every room. The "golden" part of the name came from the fact that strategically placed windows and skylights flooded the halls with golden light, and the fact that many of the surfaces of the Domus Aurea were in fact covered in gold leaf.

When Nero committed suicide in A.D. 68 (less than a year after the palace was completed) and left no heir, a new dynasty of emperors, the Flavians, replaced the long-reigning Julio-Claudians, whose rule of Rome had begun with Julius Caesar. Vespasian, the first Flavian emperor, wanted to be known as the "emperor for the people," so instead of moving into the Domus Aurea, he tore most of it down. He even had the man-made lake drained, and on the dry lake bed, a few years later, his son Titus began construction on the Colosseum: the ultimate monument for the people of Rome rose in what was once the center of Nero's maniacal egotism. One of the few elements of the Domus Aurea to be preserved for a while was the "colossus"—that enormous statue of Nero with the radiate crown. Later emperors simply redid the face in their own likenesses, but the statue stayed intact for centuries (it was finally melted down for its bronze and gold in the Middle Ages). The Amphitheatrum Flavium ("Flavian double theater") came to be known as the Colosseum since it stood near the statue—*colosseum* literally means "place of the colossus."

What's left of the Domus Aurea (and what is unfortunately closed to the public for the time being) is a few hundred rooms of the Esquiline wing, now underground, beneath the Colle Oppio park.

Goodbye Pagans, Hello Jesus!

The A.D. 312 Battle of the Milvian Bridge, for which the triumphal Arch of Constantine was built, was significant for two reasons: first of all, by the end of the 200s A.D., when it became clear that the Empire had grown too large for one emperor to govern, the Romans decided to divvy up rule of the provinces among four emperors, or tetrarchs. Well, that didn't work so well; all the tetrarchs wanted to be sole ruler, so they started killing each other. In A.D. 312, it was down to Constantine and Maxentius; and at the Battle of the Milvian Bridge, Constantine killed Maxentius and won his dream of sovereign control over Rome. The legend of how Constantine won the battle, however, is what's most significant in the annals of history.

According to tradition, Constantine was addressing his troops the night before the battle when all of a sudden, he had a vision of the Christian cross. At this point in history, Christianity, like all monotheistic religions, was still illegal since it meant renouncing worship of the pagan gods that Romans believed protected the state. However, Constantine, a good practicing pagan, saw this apparition of the cross and heard a voice accompanying it say "In this sign, you will win."

Whether or not that was just James Earl Jones playing a joke on him, Constantine (as all Romans) was deeply superstitious, so if he had to win his battle under the sign of this "cult religion," it didn't matter—he just had to win. The next day, he rigged a makeshift cross atop the battle standards of his legions (above the traditional Roman wartime symbol of the eagle), and sure enough, he won the skirmish, routing Maxentius and killing thousands of his infantry. Constantine didn't need much more convincing than that, and the following year, he issued the Edict of Milan, which legalized Christianity throughout the Empire and ended centuries of religious persecution. Constantine did not personally convert to Christianity until his dying day, in A.D. 337, hoping to cash in on the possibility of the Christian afterlife. From the 4th century A.D. on, paganism gradually waned and Christianity took hold, and—if the presence of the Vatican in Rome is any evidence of just how dramatically the tide turned—the rest is history.

📺 Best FREE → **Roman Forum**
★★★ ANCIENT ROME The vast ruin-filled pit at the center of Rome's archaeological zone is hardly the most well preserved of the city's ancient monuments, but there is no place more important to the history of the Roman Republic and Empire than the Roman Forum. Incoherent though it may be today, the Forum was the center of commercial, political, and religious life in the capital city of the most powerful civilization in the Western world for over 700 years. (Sort of like Washington, D.C., combined with Manhattan, and about 500 years more long-lived.)

Other Italian cities have their one principal civic square (e.g., the omnipresent Piazza del Duomo), but in Rome, no piazza, however grand, has supplanted the symbolic importance of the Roman Forum; this graveyard of former glory will be the hallowed center of Rome for eternity.

In the earliest days of Rome, the area that would become the Forum—the valley between the Palatine, Capitoline, and Esquiline hills—was a swampland. The Romans thought it was a shame to let such central real estate go to waste (the mosquitos were annoying, too), so, in the 7th century

B.C., they engineered an elaborate sewer system, the Cloaca Maxima ("main drain"), to get rid of the excess moisture in the valley. As soon as the ground dried out, the Romans started building temples, basilicas, and markets in the newly reclaimed space, which came to be known as the *Forum* ("outdoor place"), and the rest is history. (The Cloaca Maxima still works today, channeling rainwater from the Forum underground and into the Tiber river, about 500m/1,640 ft. away.)

The Forum remained Rome's most important meeting place (aside from the massively popular Colosseum and Circus Maximus) for nearly a millennium. The oldest structures here are from about 500 B.C., while the newest were built in the mid-4th century A.D. When the Roman Empire decisively fell in 476 A.D., the Roman Forum was gradually abandoned. The barbarians carted off most of the bronze and gold statuary in the Middle Ages, and the popes scavenged the defunct pagan temples for their marble, which would be used to embellish Christian churches throughout the city. By the 15th century, the Forum had filled with so much dirt and debris that it had turned into a common cow pasture (Campo Vaccino) where animals grazed alongside the humbled skeletons of the once great and powerful Roman civilization. In fact, the Roman Forum was known as the Campo Vaccino until the end of the 1800s—just over a century ago!—when archaeology and scientific excavation and preservation (as opposed to greedy pilfering) finally came into vogue. To expose the original ground level of the Roman Forum, archaeologists had to remove about 7m (23 ft.) of dirt from throughout the valley.

WALK THIS WAY: A TOUR OF THE FORUM

The best place to begin your tour of the Forum is from the southeastern entrance, near the Colosseum.

The processional route of the ancients, a basalt flagstone road called the **Via Sacra** ("sacred way"), climbs from the valley of the Colosseum northwest toward a single marble arch, the triumphal **Arch of Titus** ✶. The Romans erected these monumental arches whenever they celebrated a *triumph,* a parade for a military victory in which they killed at least 5,000 of their enemies. If you only got 4,999, there was no triumph, and no arch. (Alright, so that was a technicality; they usually gave themselves the benefit of the doubt when it came to casualty counts.) The arch here was built to commemorate the Roman sack of Jerusalem in A.D. 70. Then a general in the Roman province of Judea, Titus led the Romans to victory and later became emperor, the second of the Flavian dynasty, ruling from A.D. 79–81. The relief sculptures along the inside of the passageway (usually gated off) depict the triumphal parade into Rome that followed the campaign in Jerusalem. On the south side, the relief panel shows Roman soldiers carrying some of the spoils from the Jewish wars, including the seven-branched candlestick looted from the temple of Herod. On the north side, the goddess of Victory (always recognizable by her wings) flies over the emperor in his chariot. Now, look up at the vaulted ceiling *(intrados)* of the arch. In the center panel, there's an eagle flying to the heavens, with a rather large human passenger peeking over its wing (it's a pretty sweet picture); this represents the apotheosis of Titus, who was deified and worshipped as a Roman god when he died in A.D. 81.

From the Arch of Titus, the Via Sacra dips down and to the right, under a bower of **laurel trees** (snap off some of the fragrant leaves, break them up in your hand, and dab your pulse points for some instant *eau d'emperor*). The next major monument in the Forum to look out for is the **Basilica of Maxentius** ✶✶, which is up a gravel path, out of the trees, to the right. Three barrel vaults made of brick and cement, representing less than a third of the building, are all

Fly Like an Eagle

Roman emperors and their family members could be apotheosized (deified, or turned into gods) when they died. The only prerequisite was that someone had to witness the spirit of the deceased being flown to the heavens on the back of an eagle. Given the lack of an eagle population in urban Rome 2,000 years ago, it's safe to say that imperial hopefuls probably bribed a few "witnesses" over the years. However, bird activity in general was a big deal in ancient Rome. The augurs or *auspices* were a college of priests whose sole job it was to monitor the flight of birds, whose behavior was believed to communicate portents, or divine will. If the birds did something troubling, it meant that the gods were expressing their displeasure with Rome, and the augurs could cancel an election or postpone a military campaign, thereby often wielding more power than the emperors themselves. The art of the augurs was called *auspicium*, from which the English word "auspicious" is derived.

that remain. The vaults are enormous, however, giving a great sense of just how formidable a structure this would have been in its heyday. In its purest form, a Roman basilica was rectangular and roofed, and functioned as a law court or general assembly hall. The basilica here, built by emperors Constantine and Maxentius in the early 4th century A.D., consisted of one central nave and two side aisles. The ruins here are of just one of the side aisles. Imagine three symmetrical vaults on the opposite side of the gravel area here, and an even higher and wider cross-vault arching over the space, spanning the main nave where most of the people would be gathered. Unfortunately, these missing elements of the basilica fell down in an earthquake. The tiny holes in the brick walls are evidence that there was marble revetment (cladding) here—thin marble slabs were affixed to walls by means of short metal hooks, which were looted by barbarians and made into weapons and ammo in the Middle Ages. The marble revetment itself is also long gone, pillaged by popes in the Renaissance and reused in the decoration of Catholic churches. This monumental "recycling program" was quite well implemented throughout the city, so whenever you see tiny holes in Roman ruins, you'll know someone stole its metal and/or marble.

Leaving the Basilica of Maxentius, return to the Via Sacra and follow it down (past more brick ruins) to where the terrain flattens out and the vistas open up. This is the heart of the Roman Forum, where the most important buildings used to stand, and where most of the tour groups congregate today. Off to the right, look for the six-columned *(hexastyle)* façade of the **Temple of Antoninus Pius and Faustina** ★★. (There are some nondescript ruins right in front of it where you can sit while you read up.) "Tony" Pius was emperor from A.D. 138–161 (his rule fell right between that of Hadrian and Marcus Aurelius), and when he died, his spirit was seen flying up to the heavens on the back of an eagle, and he was officially declared a Roman god. His wife, the empress Faustina, had died much earlier in A.D. 141 and was also deified. Antoninus had this temple built in the A.D. 140s and worshipped before the cult statue of his wife for 20 years. Upon his own death and apotheosis, the Romans saw fit to have Antoninus join Faustina in the temple. Take a good look at the architectural elements of this temple, because it's the best preserved example of one you'll see in the Roman Forum. As with all Roman temples, it was raised up on a high podium so as to signify the "elevated" function of the structure. In the middle of the brick staircase that approaches the front of the temple, there's a sacrificial altar (restored) where you would leave your offering to the god—a sort of admission fee you had to pay before gaining access to the *cella,* or cult chamber, of the temple. (Note that not every offering at the sacrificial altar was a lamb with its jugular sliced—at its Latin root, the verb "sacrifice" simply means "perform sacred rites," which could be something as simple and nonviolent as leaving a few coins . . . but there were plenty of dead animals, too.)

At the top of the stairs are six monolithic (single-piece) columns of *cipollino* marble, so called because of its onionlike appearance (*cipolla* is "onion" in Italian). Near the tops of the columns, there are deep, slanting furrows in the marble; in the Renaissance, the popes were at it again and wanted these columns for themselves, so they carved grooves in the marble and fixed ropes around the columns, and then tugged, huffed, and puffed, hoping the temple would tumble down. It never did, partly because about a third of the columns' length was buried under all the debris that had filled in the Forum over time. (By the 1500s, the ground level in the Roman Forum had risen about 6m/20ft.) When the popes failed to tear down the Temple of Antoninus Pius and Faustina, they decided just to build a church on top of it—the basilica of San Lorenzo in Miranda, built in the 1600s, is still here today. The "bat wings" on top of the temple are a dead giveaway that it's a baroque building from the 17th-century. The door of the church, halfway up the wall, floats in midair with no apparent way to access it— but when the church was built, the bottom of the doorway corresponded to the level of the ground outside. Full-fledged archaeological excavations in the Forum only got going in the late 1800s.

Now, with your back to the Temple of Antoninus Pius and Faustina, walk ahead and to the left (toward the tall honeycombs of brick walls of the Palatine Hill). Nestled beneath the slope of the Palatine are some low brick ruins and a grassy courtyard, filled with marble statues of female figures that belonged to the **House of the Vestal Virgins.** (The courtyard is closed off to visitors, but you can see well enough from the fence.) The Vestal Virgins and the head priest of Rome, the *pontifex maximus,* were the only people who actually lived in the Forum. The job of the Vestals was to tend to the flame in the **Temple of Vesta** ★ (goddess of the hearth), a tiny round temple nearby that's been restored with part of its curved wall and a few columns. Since the perpetuity of the flame in the temple signified the eternal prosperity of Rome, the Vestal Virgins bore a tremendous responsibility. So that they would not be distracted from their task, the Vestals took a vow of chastity, which could only be broken when they finished their 30-year terms of service. Since most Vestals were drafted into the cult between the ages of 6 and 10, they were discharged when they were about 40 (that Steve Carell movie might have resonated with them) and rather "mature" by Roman longevity standards. It's unlikely they had explosive sex lives in their golden years.

The Vestal Virgins spent the first 10 years of their assignment just watching their elders and learning everything there was to know about the flame arts; the middle 10 years were when they were actually on duty at the temple; and during the final 10 years, they imparted all their wisdom to the new inductees. A bit of a drawn-out process, yes, but hey, Rome's very livelihood depended on it. Over the centuries, there were a few instances where the Vestals got so overzealous at their craft of nurturing the flame that the wooden roof of the temple caught fire! Conversely, there were times when the Vestals slacked on the job and let the flame go out. That was not cool, and the offending Vestals were publicly flogged here in the Forum (but then allowed to go back to work). Worse still was the punishment that awaited any Vestal who was caught having lapsed in the "Virgin" part of her title. The *pontifex maximus* also acted as head gynecologist for the Vestals and conducted annual exams on them; if any of the women was discovered to have lost her virginity, she was buried alive.

On that uplifting note, let's move on to the **Temple of Castor and Pollux** ★, whose three conjoined columns are some of the most romantic and photographed ruins in the Forum. The 5th-century-B.C. temple was one of the largest in the Forum, with 8 columns (*octastyle*) across the front (east) and back (west) and 11 columns down the north and south sides. The columns that stand here today, carrying a small length of architrave, were part of the southern colonnade. Unlike the columns in the Temple of Antoninus Pius and Faustina, which are monolithic, the columns at the Temple of Castor and Pollux are made up of shorter lengths of marble, called drums, which are stacked on top of each other. Instead of being polished smooth, the columns here are fluted, a Roman decorative convention that emphasized verticality and also helped camouflage the fact the columns were not all one piece. The iron clamps that fixed one column drum to another were pillaged away in the Middle Ages, hence the gouge holes evident at the seams between the drums today.

The center of the Forum valley is a sea of mostly unrecognizable ruins—stumps where columns used to be, nondescript platforms where temples used to sit—but this is also where some of the most famous episodes in Roman history took place, so bear with it, and use your imagination. In the summer, this part of the Forum can be brutally hot, so find a spot in the shade and get your bearings before pressing on. At the southeastern end of the Forum square, there's a rather ravaged temple podium made of brown tufa, brick, and cement, about 2m (6½ ft.) high, with a low-pitched (modern) green roof. These paltry remains are all that's left of the **Temple of Divus Julius** ★ dedicated to Julius Caesar in 29 B.C. by his adopted heir, Augustus (Octavian). Caesar was assassinated in 44 B.C. at the Curia Pompei, the Senate House of Pompey (near Largo Argentina), not in the Forum, but his funeral took place here. Mark Antony delivered his famous speech—"Friends, Romans, Countrymen," or something like it—from the Rostra at the western end of the Forum (see discussion of the Rostra, below). The city's grief at the untimely death of Caesar was so acute that Roman citizens heaped enough of their personal burnables (chairs, tables, finery, etc.) on the pyre of Caesar to keep it burning for 7 days straight. After the seventh day, a comet was seen flying across the sky— the augurs interpreted this as the spirit of Caesar, flying to the heavens on the back of an eagle. In the minds of the Romans, he had become a god only a week after his death, but 15 years would pass before his temple was built. Caesar's adopted son, Octavian Augustus, became the first emperor of Rome in 29 B.C., and the Temple of Divus Julius was one of the first public building projects he commissioned as emperor. The temple was in fact built over the altar of Caesar, the very spot where Caesar's pyre had been placed. Some Romans still honor Julius Caesar by placing flowers over the altar of the temple, a few rounded blocks of tufa protected by the green roof here today. Even though nothing's left of the temple itself, archaeologists know that it was *hexastyle* because they found a Roman coin that depicts it as such; in many cases, ancient coins are the forensic photographs that help archaeologists piece together the past when there are few other clues about a structure's former appearance.

Just northwest of the Temple of Divus Julius is the main **Forum Square,** a large and mostly empty, paved rectangular area (closed off to visitors by a low iron fence). This was the only part of the Forum where there weren't temples and basilicas. It provided an open space where people could gather to hear speeches and merchants could hawk their wares; of course, it also provided a vantage point from which to admire the splendor of all the monuments in the Forum. Like an Italian piazza, it's what made the Forum a civic showcase, not just a purely functional set of buildings. The major structures on the long sides of the Forum Square were law courts, the **Basilica Julia** (on the southwest side of square) and **Basilica Emilia** (179 B.C., on the northeast side of square). All that remains of both basilicas are their footprints, some column stumps, and a few severed walls, but they once towered over the Forum Square, with heights of over 30m (98 ft.) and sumptuous marble-clad arcades. The Via Sacra continues along the northeast side of the square, but before continuing along it, make your way around to the southwest side of the Forum.

Near the western corner of the Forum Square, the travertine paving slabs are interrupted by a slightly sunken area surrounded by a low fence. This is the **Lacus Curtius** ("lake of Curtius"), one of the most humble-looking but sacred parts of the Forum. Legend has it that a thunderbolt cracked the ground open here in the 5th century B.C., resulting in a deep chasm. This was a terrible hazard, considering how many people walked through the Forum every day. The oracles believed that the only way to close up the chasm (and appease Jupiter, who had thrown the thunderbolt) was to throw "Rome's greatest treasure" into it. The colorful tale goes on to relate that one day, a Roman knight, Marcus Curtius, came galloping through the Forum, shouting, "Rome has no greater treasure than a brave citizen!"

Trees Company

A small enclosure in the center of the Forum Square contains modern incarnations of the three sacred plants of Rome: the fig tree, the olive tree, and the grapevine. In antiquity, these were the only flora in the otherwise paved, marble-clad, bronzed, and gilded Forum.

and rode his horse right into the chasm, which promptly resealed itself, leaving just a small basin where rain water collected. (A marble relief sculpture at the site illustrates the heroic ride of Curtius.) Thereafter, citizens tossed coins into the sacred basin as a way of safeguarding the health of Rome.

The long, low wall of brown tufa that runs along the northwestern side of the Forum Square is the **Rostra,** or speaker's platform, where many famous orators, such as Cicero and Mark Antony, paced back and forth, delivering their rousing speeches to the masses in the Forum Square below. The holes across the front wall of the platform are where iron hooks were placed to affix the metal ramming prows *(rostra)* of enemy ships captured in the naval battle of Antium (modern Anzio) in 338 B.C.

Back to the Via Sacra: In the northern corner of the Forum, just northeast of the Rostra, is a tall brick building with three windows and a bronze door. This is the **Curia Julia** ★★, or Senate house (29 B.C.), and the most intact structure in the Forum, though not everything here is original to the ancient period. First of all, the bronze doors here are fascist-era copies of the original ancient doors, which still exist—they're now the central doors to the cathedral of St. John Lateran (San Giovanni in Laterano), about a mile south of here. In any case, the modern bronze doors at the Curia are usually open, allowing you a peek inside the place where Rome's 300-member Senate used to meet.

ROME & LAZIO

On the floor, the 3rd-century-A.D. poly-chrome marble paving is almost perfectly preserved, as are the three stepped plat-forms on either side of the hall where the senators' chairs were placed. Most of the interior walls in the Curia are exposed brick, but against the back wall, a few fragmentary slabs of white marble are left from what would have been a full revetment (cladding) of every square inch, except for the ceiling. The flat wooden ceiling in the Curia is mod-ern, but it's a good restoration of what Roman wooden ceilings would have looked like. In large part, the Curia Julia owes its excellent condition to the fact that it was reconsecrated as a church (Sant'Adriano) in the 7th century A.D. The church was disman-tled, however, in the early 20th century, when the Forum excavations were well underway. If you look at the front façade of the Curia, you'll see body-sized horizontal niches on either side of the door. Now, look at the ground level of the baroque church, Ss. Luca e Martina, immediately adjacent and about 6m (20 ft.) higher. Until the 19th cen-tury, all parts of the Forum that stood below this level—including the lower third of the Curia—were underground. So, those body-sized niches on the lower part of the Curia were tombs, where people were buried when the building was a church. When archaeolo-gists discovered the bodies, they exhumed them and buried them elsewhere! Also on the façade of the Curia, there are beam-sized holes above the door; these holes are evi-dence of the Curia's ancient portico, or front porch, which was supported by wooden beams that stuck into the front wall. In the Republican era, before the Curia was built, the Senate used to assemble in any old consecrated *templum,* and they were a sig-nificant and respected governing body. Ironically, by the time they got their own proper meeting place in the Forum, in 29 B.C., the Senate had lost most of its power to the burgeoning figure of the emperor. To

demonstrate how meaningless the Senate had become, the emperor Caligula conferred the title of Senator on his favorite horse, Incitatus, in A.D. 39.

The Rostra and Curia Julia mark the end of the flat valley of the Roman Forum; from here, the topography slopes up to the north-west, to the Capitoline Hill. Before making its sharp left turn, the Via Sacra passes under-neath the triple-bayed triumphal **Arch of Septimius Severus** ★★. Like the Arch of Titus (p. 153), this marble arch was erected to commemorate a major Roman war vic-tory; in this case, it was the conquest of Parthia (Persia, or modern-day Iran), led by Septimius Severus, in A.D. 203 Septimius Severus was an emperor who had been born in Roman Tripolitania (modern Libya) and always spoke Latin with an African accent. All over the monument, relief sculptures (some very worn) depict various key episodes in the campaigns against the Parthians. On the bases that support the detached columns on either side of the arch, there are sculptural panels where prisoners are chained and led by their Roman captors. Notice the prisoners' Smurf-like hats; in antiquity, cultures from the near East wore floppy hoods, so the Roman sculptors who created these panels used that distinctive headgear, called a Phrygian cap, as short-hand for their ethnicity. In the attic level of the arch (the top section, above the central passageway), the six-line Latin inscription is wonderfully preserved; it basically con-gratulates Septimius Severus and his son, Caracalla, for being bad-asses and for expanding the Roman Empire all the way to Iran. Septimius Severus had another son, Geta, who shared the Empire with Caracalla after their father died in A.D. 211. Caracalla didn't like sharing, however, so he killed his brother in A.D. 212 and pronounced the *damnatio memoriae* on Geta, which meant that wherever poor Geta's name or likeness existed, it had to be wiped out from the

Roman Art as a Logo: Just Do It!

In Greece, she was called *Nike;* in Rome, she was *Victory* or *Victoria.* In either case, she was the goddess of winning, and in classical art, she is always depicted with a streamlined set of wings. You'll see Victory in the spandrels of the triumphal arches of Titus and Septimius Severus in the Roman Forum. If you take one of her wings and turn it on its side, it looks just like the world-famous "whoosh" logo of a certain athletic shoe company. Aaahh, the unexpected ways in which Roman culture has been passed down to us!

public record. Geta's name was originally mentioned on the fourth line of the inscription above the arch, but when Caracalla had him whacked, the fourth line was rewritten to say "to the best and strongest of princes"—meaning Caracalla. You can still make out the holes where the original bronze lettering was affixed. Atop the arch, there would have been a bronze-and-gold statue, long lost, of a *quadriga* (four-horse chariot) driven by the emperor.

After passing underneath the Arch of Septimius Severus, the Via Sacra curves sharply to the left and begins its climb toward the Capitoline Hill. The last major monument in the Roman Forum is the **Temple of Saturn** ✶✶, whose six frontal and two lateral columns, in monolithic pink and gray granite, are among the most evocative and imposing ruins in the Forum, and certainly the most gorgeous single structure in the Forum to behold under the floodlights at night. Equivalent to Kronos in Greek mythology, Saturn was one of the more senior Roman gods, the father of Jupiter (Greek Zeus), so as soon as the Forum area was drained and developed (in the 7th century B.C.), the Romans dedicated a temple to Saturn here. While the original temple dates back as far as 597 B.C. (that's 60 years *older* than the Parthenon in Athens, to give you some perspective on ancient dates), most of it was destroyed by a fire and subsequently rebuilt. The columns and architrave of the Temple of Saturn, as they appear today, are

from 42 B.C.—not too shabby after 2,050 years! The straightforward Latin inscription (also from 42 B.C.) above the columns reads SENATVS POPVLVSQVE ROMANVS INCENDIO CONSVMPTVM RESTITVIT, or "Restored by the Senate and People of Rome After a Fire Consumed It." Every year in December, Romans celebrated one of their favorite holidays, the week-long Saturnalia, at this temple. During Saturnalia, all societal conventions and rules of moral conduct went out the window. Slave boys made love with noble women, noble men dressed as slaves, and the whole thing usually turned into one big alcohol-soaked orgy. Everyone walked around greeting each other with a *Yo, Saturnalia!* ("Hey, praise to Saturn"). In its purer, earlier form, Saturnalia was a single day of merriment (Dec 17) on which Romans celebrated with their families and gave each other gifts. Many historians believe that in the Christian era, Church fathers settled upon the date of December 25 to celebrate Christ's birth so that the people would have something to look forward to in December, since Saturnalia had been such a festive period in pagan times.

As you're facing the Temple of Saturn, there's a nondescript, rounded brick ruin off the left side of the Via Sacra. Okay, so there's not much to look at, but this "monument" was the **Umbilicus Urbis Romae,** the sacred "belly-button of Rome." It was the very point from which distances were reckoned on all the famous roads that led to Rome in

The Most Romantic View in Rome

The gates to the Roman Forum lock down at sunset, but returning to the terraces overlooking the Forum at night is one of the most sublime things you can do in all of Italy (especially if you've had a little wine beforehand). On either side of Piazza del Campidoglio (Capitoline Hill), there are stunning, haunting vistas over the floodlit columns and arches. Sit and stare for a few minutes or an hour—in the dark, when the Fcrum is deserted, the noise of the modern city is silenced, and an irrepressible nostalgia for that forever-dead Golden Age of Rome swells in your heart and imagination. (I want my ashes scattered over the Forum at night, so let's hope my grandkids read this.)

antiquity. Under the Umbilicus Urbis Romae is the **Mundus** (not visible). The Mundus was the pit that, according to legend, Romulus dug when he founded the city in 753 B.C. All new citizens or immigrants to Rome were required to toss a handful of dirt from their homeland into the Mundus. The Mundus was also regarded as a gate to the underworld, which was opened three times a year so that the spirits of the underworld could breathe, but the Romans had to be especially careful not to let them escape!

The massive, arcaded gray tufa wall to the right of the Via Sacra—forming the northwest boundary of the Forum and the southeast slope of the Capitoline Hill—is the **Tabularium** ★★, or archives hall, built in 78 B.C. The interior of the Tabularium is still in near-perfect condition and is open to the public (it's part of the Capitoline Museums; see listing below), offering splendid views from its ancient galleries over the Forum below.

Immediately below and to the left (south) of the Tabularium are three white marble columns, which is all that remains of the 80 A.D. (ca.) **Temple of Vespasian and Titus**. Of the three Flavian emperors—Vespasian, Titus, and Domitian—only the first two, Vespasian (A.D. 69–79) and his eldest son, Titus (A.D. 79–81), were deified upon their deaths. (And for good reason; they gave the

Romans the Colosseum, after all!) Domitian (Titus's brother, who ruled from A.D. 81–96) was not quite as popular, and when he was assassinated in his bedroom by his own household staff, he was given the *damnatio memoriae* (a Senatorial decree ordering all mentions and images of him to be destroyed), which kind of ruined his chances of becoming a Roman god.

Climbing out of the Forum along the Via Sacra toward the Capitoline Hill, stop about halfway up (about 20m/66 ft. past the Temple of Saturn) and turn back around; this makes for a great **photo op** ★★. Stop snapping away at inanimate objects for a change, and have someone take your picture in front of the fence that overlooks the Forum here. If the photographer has any sense of compositon at all, you'll get a perfectly framed picture with you at the center, and imposing ruins flanking you on either side. Gorgeous!

Main entrance at Largo Romolo e Remo, Via dei Fori Imperiali. Four other entrances are at the Arch of Titus; the Arch of Septimius Severus (stairs in front of the church of Ss. Luca and Martina); Via di Monte Tarpeo (southern end of Capitoline Hill); and Via di San Teodoro (southwestern side of the Forum). ☎ **06/699-0110.** Free admission. Daily 9am to 1 hr. before sunset. Closed Jan 1, May 1, and Dec 25. Metro: Colosseo. Bus: 60, 75, 84, 85, 87, 117, 175, 271, or 571.

Good Places to Chill: The Seven Hills

Starting in the north and moving around the city clockwise, the famous seven hills of ancient Rome were the **Capitoline** (Campidoglio), the **Quirinal,** the **Viminal,** the **Esquiline,** the **Caelian** (Celio), the **Aventine,** and the **Palatine.** The Quirinale and the Esquilino have long been covered by modern buildings, and the Viminale isn't even recognizable as a hill anymore. The other four, however, still retain a great ancient-feeling atmosphere. A spur of red tufa, the Capitoline (Campidoglio, to modern Italians) was the citadel of Rome and perch for the city's most sacred temples (to Jupiter, Juno, and Minerva); it also formed the northern boundary of the Roman Forum. The Tarpeian Rock, on the steep western slope of the hill, was the precipice from which traitors were hurled to their death from ancient times right through the 1500s.

The Capitoline lost most of its ancient appearance when it was extensively embellished in the 16th century by none other than Michelangelo, who designed the outstanding public square here (Piazza del Campidoglio) and the pink buildings that surround it (the Capitoline Museums and Palazzo Senatorio, or city hall). The travertine steps around Piazza del Campidoglio are a great place to get some sun and write postcards, but don't forget to check out the breathtaking views from the terraces that overlook the Forum on either side of Palazzo Senatorio. At the far end of the Forum, south of the Colosseum, the Celio hill is one of my favorite under-the-radar spots in all of Rome. With crumbling ruins and overgrown vegetation and some great old sunbaked churches, it has that strange but fabulous Roman quality of feeling more like it's out in the country than in the middle of a three-million-person city.

The Celio's main attraction is its public park, the Villa Celimontana (bus: 81), which makes for great picnicking and chilling out after hitting the ancient sites. From the Celio, the green swath of archaeological parkland continues south to the Baths of Caracalla. West of the Celio (across the Circus Maximus), the Aventino was the favored residential area of the nonimperial wealthy citizens of ancient Rome, and it's still one of the most desirable (and leafiest) neighborhoods in central Rome today. Check out the Aventine's Giardino degli Aranci park (bus: 175) for wonderful views over the river and Trastevere. Finally, the hill that's stayed truest to its ancient roots is the Palatine, forming the southwestern boundary of the Roman Forum. The Palatine is now a tree- and grass-filled archaeological site where you can climb all over extensive but rather confusing ruins of imperial palaces (the 8€ ticket also gets you into the Colosseum).

➜ **Trajan's Markets and Forum** ★★
ANCIENT ROME   You'd better believe that the greatest city of the ancient world had an awesome shopping center. The most dominant feature in Trajan's Forum, which sits at the northern end of the "downtown" area of the Imperial Fora and Roman Forum, is the massive, concave-fronted, brick structure known as **Trajan's Markets.** Built on three levels, the markets were the world's first mall, housing 150 shops and commercial offices. In the monumental brick remains of the markets, you can clamber over stairs and hallways on three levels and wander into the wonderfully preserved individual shops. The outer terraces have a rampartlike feel, with tremendous views down Via dei Fori Imperiali. Elsewhere in Trajan's Forum, the **Basilica Ulpia** was an immense public meeting hall, now reduced to an outline of a

few columns on the ground. For its artistic importance and amazing state of preservations, the greatest single treasure in Trajan's Forum is **Trajan's Column** ★★★ (best seen from the pedestrian area above the excavations). Majestic and overtly phallic, the 40m-high (131-ft.) marble column was dedicated in A.D. 113 to commemorate the Romans' victory over Dacia (modern Romania). It is said that to make room for Trajan's Forum, the slope of the Quirinal hill (to the north) had to be cut away, and the Trajan's Column marks the height of the Quirinal before they brought in the bulldozers. The ascending spiral band of sculptured reliefs on the column depicts all stages of the military campaign, down to the finest detail of Romans hacking the Dacians' heads off. Trajan (A.D. 98–117) was the emperor responsible for extending the Roman Empire to its greatest geographical extent; when he died, the Romans bestowed on him the extraordinary honor of placing his ashes in the base of the column—tombs and mausolea were normally outlawed inside the city.

While we recommend an up-close-and-personal walk through the site, the view of these monuments from the street is fine if you're pressed for time. The main hall of Trajan's Markets was temporarily closed as this guide went to press, but much of the exterior, including the large semicircular building where most of the individual shops and offices were located, is still open to the public, for the reduced admission price of 3.20€. *Via IV Novembre 94, at Via Magnanapoli.* ☎ 06/679-00-48. *Admission 3.20€. Tues–Sun 9am–6pm (Apr–Oct), 9am–4pm (Nov–Mar); last admission 1 hr. before closing. Bus: 40, 60, 64, 70, 75, or 170.*

→ **Imperial Fora** ★★ ANCIENT ROME Showcased along either side of the Mussolini-era Via dei Fori Imperiali, which runs from Piazza Venezia in the north to the Colosseum in the south, are the ruins of the public squares that were grafted onto the Roman Forum to accommodate the growing population of the city—and to stroke the egos of the men who had them built. The dictator Julius Caesar and the emperors Augustus, Nerva, and Trajan all sponsored the construction of monumental *fora* (the proper plural of "forum") that would bear their names. Collectively, these public spaces are known as the Imperial Fora (in Italian, Fori Imperiali) and cover an area of nearly 3 sq. km (1 sq. mile). Because there's now a six-lane, heavily trafficked boulevard that runs roughshod over large sections of them, the Fori Imperiali can be difficult to understand. As you try to make sense of the sites, just keep in mind that they were all interconnected, and together with the Roman Forum, they were used for the same "downtown" purpose: social gathering (political or informal), shopping, and worshipping the pagan gods.

The ruins of the Imperial Fora, which were excavated in the 1920s and 1930s, lie well below street level. Only one of the areas, the Forum of Trajan, is regularly open to the public (see individual listing for Trajan's Markets and Forum); the other areas (Forum of Caesar, Forum of Augustus, Forum of Nerva) are usually closed, but it doesn't matter—they're all easily visible (for free) from the pedestrianized viewing platforms along either side of Via dei Fori Imperiali.

→ **Forum of Julius Caesar** ★ Julius Caesar was the first Roman leader who took it upon himself to build his own personal forum. The only major section of the Imperial Fora to lie on the southwestern side of Via dei Fori Imperiali, the 1st-century-B.C. ruins of Caesar's rather modest public square are closed to the public (except for those who prearrange a special visit), but what there is to see is perfectly visible from the railings that surround the site, which lies approximately 7m (23ft.) below street level. The best vantage point is from the north, looking south over the sunken enclosure. The most notable remains here are three columns, resting on a high podium, from the **Temple of Venus Genetrix**

Boulevard of Mussolini's Broken Dreams

As the leader of fascist Italy, Benito Mussolini believed that he had personally inherited the glories of the Roman Empire and missed no opportunity to draw parallels between the achievements of the ancient emperors and his own ambitions (invasion of Ethiopia, occupation of Albania, war on Greece . . .) The fascists had their problems, but they sure knew how to work architecture as a form of propaganda. The most brilliant example of this was the construction of the street—first called Via dell'Impero (street of the Empire), now called Via dei Fori Imperiali—that he had created to run dead-straight through the ruins of the Imperial Fora. At one end of the street is the balcony at Palazzo Venezia, where Mussolini used to deliver his rousing speeches over the crowds gathered below him; at the other end of the street is the Colosseum. Between them, Mussolini's urban planners placed bronze copies of ancient Roman statues of emperors along the sidewalks and planted dozens of umbrella pines—the iconic Roman tree—to heighten the monumentality and splendor of it all. Fascist marches and parades were held up and down the broad boulevard, while Mussolini boomed rhetoric from his balcony: "Look at what our ancestors achieved! We will do the same!" Well, Il Duce's dreams of being the next emperor of Rome didn't quite come true—he was stripped of his power in 1943, executed by partisans in 1945 while on the run with his mistress near Lake Como, and strung up by his feet in Milan—but he did endow Rome with an undeniably dramatic avenue.

(46 B.C.). Caesar was part of the Julio-Claudian family, who believed they were descended from the goddess of love, hence the dedication of the temple to "Venus the Family-Maker." Along the southwestern side of the Forum of Caesar are the two-story remains of the shops *(tabernae)* where the ancient bronze and silver market was located. The little road, *Clivus Argentarius,* that runs above the shops is exposed and open to pedestrians, and one of few honest-to-goodness ancient roads left in the city. If you look carefully at the black basalt stones that make up the ancient roadway, you'll notice tiny Vs engraved in the rock; these are archaeologists' marks that indicate that these are "real" *(vero)* stones from the 1st century B.C., not modern replacements.

➜ **Forum of Augustus** ✫ Across Via dei Fori Imperiali from (northeast of) the Forum of Julius Caesar, this is the second of the "annexes" to the greater Roman Forum area. Look for the lateral columns and the white

marble steps of the **Temple of Mars Ultor** (Mars the Avenger), dedicated by Augustus in 2 B.C. to remind the people that he had avenged the assassination of Julius Caesar when he and Mark Antony defeated Cassius and Brutus at the Battle of Philippi (Macedonia) in 42 B.C. But beyond the ruins of the temple, the most striking feature of all in the Forum of Augustus is the 33m-high (108-ft.) **rear wall,** which still bears the triangular roof outlines of the temple and other buildings that have long since fallen. More importantly, the enormous wall, made of blocks of gray tufa, also acted as a firewall between the marble-clad, bronzed, and gilded Forum of Augustus and the low-rent Suburra neighborhood immediately behind it. (The Suburra was the "red-light district" of ancient Rome, full of brothels, taverns, and sweat-shops, where the streets were dangerous, and violent crime was common. No wonder Augustus wanted to build a towering wall to separate his Forum from the slums!) The Forum of

Augustus was paved with slabs of precious Italian and imported marbles, many of which are preserved (though sun-faded and cracked) *in situ* today.

➔ **Forum of Nerva** Just south of the Forum of Augustus, Nerva's Forum (aka Forum Transitorium) is the most slender of the Imperial Fora. There's not a whole lot to see here, but you can get pretty up close and personal (from the pedestrian viewing platform above) with two marble columns left over from the portico that ran along the south side of the forum. Underneath the ground level of the Forum of Nerva, archaeologists have found the remains of cells where prisoners or slaves would have been kept.

➔ **Maps of the Roman Empire** ★ As part of his grand rhetorical plan to convince the Italian public that he was going to revive the glory days of the Empire, Mussolini put up five slate-and-travertine maps on the brick wall on the southwest side of Via dei Fori Imperiali, near the Colosseum end. The maps chart the growth of Rome in antiquity: The first shows the city back in the day of Romulus and Remus, 753 B.C., when Rome was no more than a settlement on the Palatine Hill; the second shows Rome after the Punic Wars (146 B.C.), when the Roman civilization had grown to include the Italian peninsula and Carthage (modern-day Tunisia) in North Africa; the third map is the empire at the time of the death of Augustus (A.D. 14); the fourth map is Rome as it looked under the reign of emperor Trajan (A.D. 98–117), the very height of the Roman Empire. By the time of Trajan's death,

the Roman world had spread to Portugal in the west, Hadrian's Wall in the north, Iran (Parthia) in the east, and well into northern Africa in the south. The fifth map in the series, of the budding "Fascist Empire," with Albania, Greece, and Ethiopia highlighted, has since been removed. Via dei Fori Imperiali.

➔ **Palatine Hill** ★★ ANCIENT ROME Chances are, you've heard the story about Romulus and Remus and the foundation of Rome. Well, the Palatine Hill is where it all went down. What began as a humble, grassy promontory on the east bank of the Tiber, where Romulus killed Remus in 753 B.C., morphed over the centuries into the Beverly Hills of the ancient world. Today, it's a sprawling perch of grass, trees, and brick ruins where you can escape the chaos of the city. As Rome grew, the Palatine became the residential enclave of the rich. By the 1st century A.D., any nonimperial, wealthy citizens of Rome living on the Palatine were displaced to the Aventine hill; the Palatine was now for emperors only. In period movies or TV shows, such as HBO's *Rome,* that are set in Roman antiquity, all the private scenes (usually involving hedonistic banquets or depraved behavior on the part of the emperor) take place on the Palatine. The ruins on this pretty, grassy hill on the southwest side of the Roman Forum include the extensive 2,000-year-old palaces, the Domus Augustana, built by Augustus (27 B.C.–A.D. 14), and the Domus Flavia, built by Domitian (A.D. 81–96), which had extravagant nymphaea (water gardens) and a stadium. Unfortunately, very little on the Palatine is signposted, which can be frustrating, and some of the better preserved wings of the palaces are closed to the public unless you arrange a special visit through the archaeological superintendent. Nevertheless, there's plenty to marvel at as you wander around the vast site, including the utterly incomprehensible honeycomb of brickwork that made up the imperial palaces.

For all the Fora...

Start at Via dei Fori Imperiali. ☎ 06/679-77-86. www.capitolium.org (great info on the life and times of ancient Romans). Metro: Colosseo. Bus: 60, 75, 84, 85, 87, 117, 175, or 571.

Brokeback Forum?

Long before there were Heath Ledger and Jake Gyllenhaal, there were the Forum of Augustus and the Forum of Julius Caesar. What am I talking about? Take a look at a map, and notice how these *Fora* are laid out. The Forum of Augustus, with its long rectangular public square and its two semicircular lateral recesses, has a rather phallic look to it. The western tip of the Forum of Augustus grazes the flank of the Forum of Julius Caesar, which stretches out perpendicular on the other side of Via dei Fori Imperiali. Were imperial architects trying to say something about a lustful relationship between Augustus and his adoptive father, Julius Caesar? Who knows—but one of my classics professors had a whole theory on this, and certainly, stranger sexual things happened in ancient Rome.

Sadly, much of the brickwork is falling apart under heavy rains and improper drainage, and a huge section of wall up here collapsed in the winter of 2005. There are impressive city views off the western terrace of the Palatine, which is where the emperors used to sit, in a special box seat called the *pulvinar*, to watch the chariot races in the Circus Maximus below. The modern gray building on the Palatine is the Palatine Museum (admission included with Palatine Hill/Colosseum ticket), which has some interesting finds from the palaces (marble decoration, statues, etc.), and a mock-up of the wattle-and-daub hut where Romulus lived 2,800 years ago. *Entrance on Via di San Gregorio or via the Forum.* ☎ 06/699-01-10. 8€ *(10€ when special exhibitions are held; ticket also good for admission at the Colosseum). Daily 9am to 1 hr. before sunset. Metro: Colosseo. Bus: 60, 75, 85, 87, 117, 175, or 571.*

FREE ➔ **Circus Maximus** ★★ ANCIENT ROME Once the entertainment capital of the Empire, Rome's old chariot race track is little more than a valley, the size of six football fields laid end on end, of half-dead grass today. Still, the Circo Massimo is a must-see, for its legendary place in Roman history, and for the powerful views of the Palatine Hill, just northeast of here. Strangely enough, the vast footprint of the circus has never been

encroached upon or built over, so you still get a perfect sense of just how big it was. In today's wide world of sports, we have nothing that comes even close to the scale and heart-pounding excitement and sheer testosterone levels of Roman chariot racing—it makes NASCAR look like a Shriner's parade. In any given race, up to 12 *quadrigae* (four-horse rigs) would be held in the starting gates *(carceres)* at the northwestern end of the circus. At the race official's signal, the barriers dropped, and 48 horses and their 12 charioteers surged forth to the thundering roars of the crowd. To win, all the charioteer had to do was be the first to complete seven laps around the *spina* (spine, or central ridge). It was usually over in less than 10 minutes. There were no rules, and if you've ever seen the movie *Ben-Hur*, you know that every race featured spectacular carnage, particularly at the treacherous "clubhouse turn," at the southeastern end of the track, as the teams raced for the homestretch beneath the imperial box on the Palatine Hill. Deaths, both human and animal, were commonplace, but any charioteer who managed to survive and win a few races became an instant celebrity, the ultimate stud that every Roman woman, poor or high-born—and some men, even—lusted after. Indeed, the races were all about glorifying the core Roman value of *virtus* (literally, manliness).

Those Crrraaazy Emperors

A Chronological Who's Who of Nutjobs in Roman History

In the United States, you have to be 35 and a native citizen to be president; in the cases of most Roman emperors, the requirements seem to have been more stringent. You had to be an inbred megalomaniac—or just plain sick and twisted. You don't believe me? Check out the lurid stories in *The Twelve Caesars,* by Latin biographer Suetonius (in the Penguin Classics section of your local bookstore).

Julius Caesar (d. 44 B.C.)—Named dictator for life, but never emperor, Caesar let the power go to his head. He proposed diverting the course of the Tiber river to go behind where the Vatican is now located, and he named a month after himself (July). Caesar veered too close to calling himself "king" for the Romans' comfort—the god Jupiter was the one and true king—and on that fateful day, the Ides of March, in 44 B.C., Caesar was aerated at the Senate, sustaining 23 stab wounds.

Tiberius (14 B.C.– A.D. 38)—Notorious for his perverse sexuality and abhorrent body odor, the dirty old man trained little boys to be "minnows" that would swim with him and nibble between his legs. One of Tiberius' favorite torture methods was to make his prisoners drink copious amounts of wine, and then tie a rope around their genitalia, cutting their flesh and preventing them from urinating.

Caligula (A.D. 38–41)—At the age of 26, Caligula (Gaius) embarked upon a reign of terror and depravity that makes Saddam Hussein look like the Easter Bunny by comparison. As if the thousands of completely arbitrary executions he ordered weren't enough, Caligula prayed for a military catastrophe, famine, plague, fire, or earthquake so that history would have something to remember him by. He had incestuous relationships with each of his three sisters and habitually ravished high-ranking, married women at banquets. He also made his favorite horse a senator.

Claudius (A.D. 41–54)—Not nearly as bad as Tiberius, Caligula, and Nero, but definitely a weird guy. When Claudius got angry about something, he slobbered and snotted uncontrollably. He also suffered from schizophrenia; he'd invite someone over to the palace for a game of dice, then randomly have the guy executed, and then get mad when the guy didn't show up for the game of dice. Claudius was also the only emperor to introduce an initiative to make farting acceptable at the dinner table.

The high banks on the north and south sides of the circus are where wooden and brick stands once stood, with a capacity for 300,000 spectators! Again, there's not much to see besides the outline of the Circus Maximus, but hike up to the top of the southeastern bank, sit down and take in the view across the valley of the track to the brick ruins of the Palatine Hill. If you have any imagination at all, it's hard not to get high before this extraordinary panorama of imperial Rome. Perhaps because of the mind-altering vista, this is locals' favorite spot for smoking joints. You'll also find American students eager to keep up an exercise regimen jogging around the track or kicking a soccer ball here—just watch out for the broken glass and doggy doo. *Via del Circo*

Nero (A.D. 54–68)—Aahh, the Black Prince! Where do we begin? Truth be told, Nero wasn't nearly as despicable as popular legend would have you believe, but he was a character. When the fire of A.D. 64 broke out and proceeded to destroy two-thirds of the city, Nero watched the conflagration from his perch on the Palatine Hill; lyre in hand, full stage costume on, he strummed and sang the *Sack of Ilium,* poetically observing the similarity between the burning of Rome and the burning of Troy. After the flames died down, Nero built his dream house, the Domus Aurea, to occupy a third of the city, and renamed Rome "Neropolis." To deflect accusations that he didn't do enough to prevent the fire, Nero blamed it on an upstart religious group, the Christians. He killed his mother, Agrippina, because she didn't like his girlfriend. He later kicked that girlfriend, Poppaea Sabina, to death while she was pregnant. Ever the "artist," Nero forbade anyone to leave the theater when he was performing in a play. On A.D. June 9, 68, Nero committed suicide, plaintively uttering *"qualis artifex pereo"* ("what an artist dies in me!") before he slit his throat.

Commodus (A.D. 180–192)—You probably know him better as "the guy Joaquin Phoenix played in *Gladiator,*" but this nutjob was no Hollywood invention. He fancied himself a modern-day Hercules and often appeared in the Colosseum, staging combats against wild animals as reenactments of the feats of the mythological hero. He also liked to fight as a gladiator, and whenever he had a contest in the arena, he charged the city of Rome 1 million sesterces (a lot of money) as his fee! Commodus was strangled to death in his bathtub in A.D. 192 by a wrestler named Narcissus.

Caracalla (A.D. 211–217)—Another charming head of the Roman state, Caracalla inherited the imperial throne along with his brother Geta when their father, Septimius Severus, died in A.D. 211. Caracalla never was one for sharing, so he killed Geta (while he slept in his mother's arm, no less—okay, weird family), and issued the *damnatio memoriae* on him, meaning that wherever Geta's name or likeness appeared in public, it had to be scratched out. (See the Arch of Septimius Severus, in the Roman Forum). Caracalla was not a political idiot, however; he increased soldiers' pay and extended Roman citizenship to all free residents of the Empire. In A.D. 212, he had luxurious baths (Terme di Caracalla) built in Rome, south of the Aventine Hill. Caracalla's imperial bodyguards murdered him in A.D. 217—a fine how-do-you-do, considering the pay raise he had given them.

Massimo. Free admission. Metro: Circo Massimo. Bus: 60, 75, 175, or 628. Tram: 3.

→ **Baths of Caracalla** ★★ AVENTINE Occupying a grassy, tree-filled space 400m long (1,312 ft.) and 330m wide (1,082 ft.), the towering brick ruins of this imperial bath complex make for a wonderful oasis of peace and quiet today, but this was quite the happening hangout in ancient times. Since most people didn't have running water in their homes, Roman baths were a part of daily life, provided by the state free of charge to citizens. These baths were built in the 3rd century A.D. by the emperor Caracalla, one of the bigger nutjobs ever to rule Rome, but at least he gave the city one hell of a tricked-out spa, with a capacity for 1,600 people. The Roman bathing ritual followed a precise order: first was the *caldarium* (hot water bath, in the back of the central bathing block), then the *tepidarium* (lukewarm water), then you'd finish up in the *frigidarium* (cold-water plunge bath) to seal your pores. The best-preserved area here is the *natatio*, or large swimming pool, which used to be surrounded by opulent marble statuary (look for the rounded niches in the brick). You could also get massages and pedicures at the baths, and there were workout areas (*palestre*, preserved on either side of the main bathing block) where you could get in an intense game of toss-the-ball-back-and-forth. (When it came to sports, Romans were better spectators than athletes.) The baths were also hotbeds of hedonism; stories abound of sexual deviance in the massage rooms, or underneath the bubbling surface of the *caldarium*. While extensive and atmospheric, the ruins here are not well marked, so prepare to use your imagination; even if you don't feel like doing a thorough tour, the 5€ admission is well worth it for the green and tranquil surroundings. There are fallen granite columns, shaded by umbrella pines, in the back garden area that make for perfect lounging and napping on a summer day. *Viale delle Terme di Caracalla 52.*

☎ *06/575-86-26. Admission 5€. Tues–Sun 9am–sunset; Mon 9am–2pm. Closed Jan 1, May 1, and Dec 25. Metro: Circo Massimo. Bus: 60, 75, 118, 175, or 628. Tram: 3.*

MEANWHILE, BACK IN THE CENTRO STORICO . . .

The sights below are in what was formerly the northern part of the ancient city, and what is today the heart of Renaissance and baroque Rome. Keep in mind that only about 35% of ancient Rome has been excavated—a whole other world still lies beneath the *palazzi* and *piazze* of the *centro storico*.

FREE ➜ **Area Sacra** ★ PANTHEON/ GHETTO   This sunken area right in the middle of a busy intersection contains the ruins of four Republican-era temples and a colony of several hundred cats. The generic name of the site, "Sacred Area," is due to the fact that when the area was excavated (in the 1930s—more on that below), archaeologists could tell that these were temples—the raised platforms on which the columns rest are a dead giveaway—but they weren't sure to whom they were dedicated. They still don't know, so the temples are known by the letters A, B (the round one), C, and D. Stand on

---

Archaeological Terms You Can Use to Impress People!

Opus Reticulatum: masonry laid out in a neat fishnet pattern. (*Opus Quasi Reticulatum* is an irregular fishnet, like a drag queen wearing stretched-out hosiery.)

Hexastyle: having six columns across the front (Temple of Antoninus Pius and Faustina, Temple of Saturn)

Intrados: the underside of an arch, vault, or dome

Octastyle: with eight columns across the front

Peripteral: a building (e.g., Roman temple) with columns around all four sides (Temple of Castor and Pollux)

Prostyle: having columns only across the front (as most Roman temples)

Vomitoria: tunnels and stairwells that connected each of the Colosseum's 80 arched entryways with a specific seating area

Romulus & Remus

Back in the 8th century B.C., a woman named Rhea Silvia gave birth to twin boys. Problem was, she was supposed to be a virgin priestess. Defending herself, she claimed that Mars, the god of war, had knocked her up; the gods weren't too pleased with this publicity, so they pulled an Enron and made the boys disappear, placing the newborns in a basket on the Tiber River, where water or the elements would surely kill them—or so they thought. As it happened, heavy rains upstream caused the river to swell and deposit the basket on the slopes of the Palatine Hill, where a local she-wolf *(lupa)* noticed the basket and its unusual cargo. Instead of eating them, the lactating she-wolf suckled the babies to health in her cave, the *lupercal*. Later, a shepherd named Faustulus adopted the boys and raised them as his own. The warm and fuzzy story quickly degenerates, however. Romulus and Remus were quarrelsome teenagers and each wanted control over the Palatine, and they mustered armies to help them. One day, the horseplay got out of control, and Romulus killed Remus for stepping over his imaginary "boundary." On that day, April 21, 753 B.C. (still celebrated as the birthday of Rome today), the city of Roma, instead of Rema, was born. That their glorious civilization started with a fratricide is something the Romans hasten to gloss over; additionally, few acknowledge the possibility that the friendly *lupa* who saved Romulus and Remus was a prostitute, not a wolf, as *lupa* was Latin slang for "whore."

the eastern wall for the best view, and then walk around to the northwest corner of the square (near Café Brek), and look down. You'll see some stone gutters left over from a *vespasiano* (ancient Roman slang for a pay toilet).

The Area Sacra's other claim to fame is that there is one large gray stone block here (on the western edge of the excavations) from the Curia Pompei, the senate house where Julius Caesar was stabbed on the Ides of March in 44 B.C. (The actual site of the assassination is buried beneath the no. 8 tram terminus here.) As for the cats lazing about in the Area Sacra, they are part of a government-protected colony of cats living in ruins all over Rome; there's a veterinary clinic and volunteer office built into the south wall of the excavations. Until the 1920s, all of this was underground, and apartment buildings and churches used to stand where the sunken Area Sacra ruins are now. Mussolini ordered the buildings to be razed in 1926 (tenants had to find housing

elsewhere), and the excavation began. When they raised a colossal marble head of a female goddess from here in 1930, the photo op made it all worth it as far as the Duce was concerned. (The head is now in the ACEA-Centrale Montemartini museum). *Largo di Torre Argentina. Lower part of ruins accessible by appointment only; call ☎ 06/6710-3819 or fax 06/689-2115. Bus: 30, 40, 46, 62, 64, 70, 87, 492, or 571. Tram: 8.*

🅼🆅 Best FREE → **Pantheon** ★★★
CENTRO STORICO Surrounded by Renaissance palazzi 1,400 years its junior, the ancient Pantheon (temple of all the gods) holds its own in the heart of the *centro storico*. It's the best-preserved Roman building anywhere in Europe, Asia Minor, or North Africa—what used to be the Roman Empire. Conveniently, it happens to be in Rome. The structure of the Pantheon, which was built from A.D. 118 to 125, under the emperor Hadrian, is a perfectly hemispherical, poured cement dome, sitting on top of a hollow cylindrical masonry base. It continues

to flabbergast modern engineers and cement workers, who can't quite figure out (a) how the Romans had the technology to build it in the first place, 1,900 years ago, and (b) that it's still here. The first thing most people see, approaching the Pantheon from Piazza della Rotonda, is its **porch** (in archaeology-speak, *pronaos*) of 16 gargantuan, monolithic granite columns. The porch is impressive enough as it is, but you have to keep in mind that the cobblestones on the piazza here today are about 7m (23 ft.) higher than ancient ground level. The Pantheon, like all Roman temples, was raised off the ground on a high podium, and there would have been a monumental stairway leading to the temple entrance. If you look carefully, the columns that make up the porch are mismatched—some are gray granite, and some are pink (well, pink-toned) granite. The first, uniform set of columns for the Pantheon was shipped from Egypt (the source of all ancient Roman granite), but the ship sank on its way to Rome. A replacement set had to be hewn and finished in a hurry, so they ended up with some pink columns and some gray ones.

Above the columns, the entablature is intact, though the bronze letters of the **inscription** are restored. The inscription says M AGRIPPA L F COS TERTIUM FECIT ("Marcus Agrippa, Son of Lucius, Consul for the Third Time, Made This")—a rather boring and misleading proclamation, since Hadrian, not Marcus Agrippa, built the Pantheon. Marcus Agrippa had built a pantheon (i.e., a temple to all the gods) on this site in 27 B.C., but his rectangular, wooden-roofed temple was completely destroyed by fire in the 80s A.D. When, in the early 2nd century A.D., Hadrian came along and decided to build a new pantheon on this spot, he kept the original inscription, crediting Agrippa. That the Romans had any interest at all in dedicating a temple to all the gods may have been a gesture of inclusion to all the rapidly absorbed cultures in the Roman Empire who didn't

necessarily believe in the Roman gods (most of whom were Greek gods who assumed Latinized names).

The triangular face of marble above the inscription is called the **pediment,** and it's riddled with holes. These holes are evidence that iron hooks were once drilled into the pediment and used to hang decorative marble, bronze, or gold sculpture. The sculptures, and the iron dowels that held them, are long gone, pillaged away by barbarians or possibly the pagan-hating Catholic Church. Speaking of which, it's thanks to the Church that the Pantheon is still in such good shape. In A.D. 609, not long after the fall of the Western Roman Empire, the Byzantine emperor Phocas donated the Pantheon to the popes, who reconsecrated the old pagan temple as a Christian place of worship, calling it Santa Maria ad Martyres. The Pantheon has been a church ever since, which spared it from being dismantled, and its continuous use over the centuries meant that it was always well maintained. (The fact that it's a church is also why it's free to visit today.)

Inside the Pantheon is where jaws really start to drop. Crossing the threshold—through the immense, original 2nd century A.D. **bronze doors**—your eyes are drawn up to the underside of the dome. Free of decoration, except for the elegantly telescoping coffers (square recesses) that also serve to lighten the load of the masonry, the gray **dome** measures 43m (141 ft.) in diameter, and 43m (141 ft.) in total height; that is, if you spun the dome around upside down inside the Pantheon, you'd have a perfect sphere. There is nothing like this design in the world. At the center of the dome is a 9m-wide (30-ft.) opening called the **oculus** ("eye"). Some romantics believe the oculus was meant to permit communication between the ancient worshipper and the gods in the heavens, but the Romans were not spiritual when it came to religion. (There was no "praying" involved; you came, you made your sacrifice,

Sightseeing Around the Pantheon

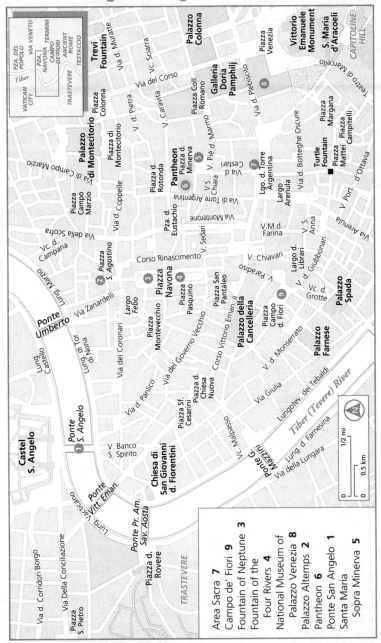

Area Sacra **7**
Campo de' Fiori **9**
Fountain of Neptune **3**
Fountain of the
  Four Rivers **4**
National Museum of
  Palazzo Venezia **8**
Palazzo Altemps **2**
Pantheon **6**
Ponte San Angelo **1**
Santa Maria
  Sopra Minerva **5**

and you hightailed it out of there and went to the Colosseum.) Instead, the builders of the Pantheon left the oculus open for two principal reasons: (1) so that the building would not collapse—the engineers were already pushing their luck with a dome of this size; and (2) *fiat lux*— to let light in.

The oculus also lets the rain in, and if you want a magical experience, come to the Pantheon during one of Rome's more angry thunderstorms (common on many summer afternoons), or better yet, a hailstorm. In the center of the floor, you'll see small, teardrop-shaped holes in the marble, which are ancient **drains** that still work today. Throughout the Pantheon's interior there are slabs of beautiful **colored marble,** almost all of which are original. The purple granite (porphyry) came from Egypt, as did the green *serpentine* marble; the yellow marble *(giallo antico)* came from Carthage (modern Tunisia). All over the floor, the marble is cut into circles and squares, which are the shapes that govern the form of the Pantheon as a whole. The ancient architect Vitruvius wrote that the circle and square were the spaces that the human body most naturally occupies when his limbs are extended. It was this notion that inspired the design of the Pantheon.

Over 1,000 years later, Leonardo da Vinci turned the concept into his famous drawing, *The Vitruvian Man.* In the walls of the Pantheon, there are marble statues (none particularly remarkable) of Christian saints and martyrs where cult statues of the Roman gods and deified emperors, like Augustus and Claudius, used to be. As the Pantheon is technically a church today, you can bury people here. The most famous permanent resident is the Renaissance painter Raphael. As a member of the secret society Virtuosi del Pantheon, Raphael had a key to a special side door and would come here at night and study the architecture by candlelight. Raphael died of syphilis (an unfortunate

result of too many amorous pursuits) in 1520 at the age of 37 and was buried in the Pantheon. His tomb is in the southeast part of the circular wall (to the back and to the left, as you walk in the door). The fancier tombs here, with honor guards and fresh flowers daily, belong to the 19th-century Savoy monarchs, king Vittorio Emanuele II (first king of unified Italy), his wife, Queen Margherita (she of the pizza), and their son, King Umberto I. Visit the Pantheon many times during your stay—it's free, and the light creates dramatically different effects depending on what time of day you're here or how bright the sun is shining. It never gets old. *Piazza della Rotonda.* ☎ *06/6830-0230. Free admission. Mon–Sun 9am–7pm; public holidays 9am–1pm. Closed Jan 1, May 1, and Dec 25. Bus: 30, 40, 62, 64, 70, 87, 116, 492, or 571.*

CATACOMBS & APPIAN WAY

Few places in Rome transport you to ancient times as well as the 📺 ⓫**Best** **Via Appia Antica (Appian Way)** ★★★, whose black basalt cobblestones, still bearing the wheel ruts of ancient cart traffic, run south of the city from Porta San Sebastiano. A few miles from the city walls, a rustic, agrarian landscape opens up on either side of the 4th-century-B.C. highway; the scenery is scattered with imposing or modest remains of ancient tombs and villas, and shepherds drive flocks of sheep from pasture to pasture, right across the "Queen of Roads." Even the scent of the Appian Way is rank with antiquity: Once you smell it, the combination of bright notes of umbrella pine needles, musty sunbaked brick and marble, and acrid pungency of leaves burning in farmyards becomes indelible in your memory.

The major tourist draw here are the **catacombs**, which are certainly very interesting, but it's the atmosphere along the ancient road itself that makes a trip out here so worthwhile. Past the catacombs are the picturesque ruins of the **Villa and Circus of Maxentius** (an emperor's country house and chariot race-track) and the picturesque white cylinder of the **Tomb of Cecilia Metella.** For information, contact Parco Regionale Dell'Appia Antica at Via Appia Antica 42 (☎ **06/512-63-14;** www.parcoappiaantica.org). Admission is free to the park and churches; entrance fees are 2€ to 5€ for the archaeological sites and catacombs. To get to the Appian Way by public transportation, take metro Line B to Circo Massimo or Piramide, and then bus 118. Hop off at the entrance to the *Catacombe di San Callisto* (if you're not sure, ask the driver), and then walk south from there to the most interesting sights.

Rome's most famous underground tourist attractions, the **catacombs,** are outside the city walls, as ancient Roman law forbade burials within the sacred *pomerium,* or city boundary. Of Rome's 65 known catacombs—sophisticated networks of hand-dug tunnels that became massive "dormitories" for the dead—most were Christian, a few were Jewish, and only a handful are open to the public.

→**Catacombs of San Callisto** ★★
Twelve miles and four levels of hand-dug tunnels make up the underground network of Rome's largest catacombs, home to the tombs of half a million Christians, buried here from the 1st to the 4th centuries A.D. Deep within the complex, a labyrinth of 10m-high (33-ft.) tunnels, whose walls are perforated up to the ceiling with *loculi* (tomb niches), is especially impressive (and uncannily reminiscent of college library stacks). *Via Appia Antica 110€–126, at Via Ardeatina.* ☎ *06/513-01-580. www.catacombe.roma.it. Admission 5€. Thurs–Tues 8:30am–noon and 2:30–5:30pm (until 5pm Oct–March). Closed Feb. Bus: 118.*

Nearby, the **Catacombs of San Sebastiano** are more intimate and incorporate a fascinating cluster of subterranean pagan tombs that once stood at street level. Visits to the catacombs are accompanied by guides, who take groups down at 10-minute intervals for a 35- to 40-minute tour. The guides are well meaning, but their English is spotty, so if you want to understand what they're talking about, stay close to the front of the group so that you can ask questions. Via Appia Antica 136, at Vicolo della Basilica. ☎ **06/788-70-35.** Admission 5€. Mon–Sat 9am–noon and 2:30–5:30pm (until 6:30pm May–Sept). Closed Nov.

Monuments & Public Spaces

→**Ara Pacis** ★★ PIAZZA DEL POPOLO
The sacrificial altar inside this brand-new glass-concrete-and-travertine museum is only about 12m by 11m (39 by 36 ft.), but physical stature aside, the Ara Pacis is a very big deal, (a) for the quality of the 2,000-year-old sculpture on it, and (b) for the fact that it even exists today. This little altar has had an interesting couple of millennia. Back in 13 B.C., upon returning from the newly pacified provinces of Gaul (France) and Spain, the emperor Augustus promised to build an "Altar of Peace" (Ara Pacis) in Rome. It was dedicated 4 years later, on January 30, 9 B.C. The finest sculptors of the day were hired to decorate the marble screens that surrounded the central altar with scenes from mythology and real life that would sum up, in a propagandistic way, the virtue of Augustus and his reign. The most striking thing about the sculptures here—which are considered by most scholars to be the finest surviving examples of Roman art—are the exquisitely rendered portraits of the imperial family and entourage. They're so highly detailed, with such careful attention paid to individual hairstyles and drapes and folds of togas, that they look like marble photographs.

The Ara Pacis originally stood at the point where the ancient Via Flaminia met the Campus Martius district. This corresponds with modern-day Via in Lucina, just off Via del Corso, several blocks from where the Ara Pacis is located now. How it ended up here

ROME & LAZIO

today is quite an epic story. When the Roman Empire fell, the Ara Pacis disappeared under the debris of the Middle Ages and remained hidden until the 16th century, when Renaissance relic hunters found some pieces of it and shipped them off to the Vatican, the Uffizi in Florence, and the Louvre in Paris. In the late 19th century, even more fragments were found under a building called Palazzo Fiano (which stood over the ancient site of the Ara Pacis). Because of the delicacy of excavating such intricately sculpted stone, those fragments were not immediately removed but kept under archaeologists' surveillance.

By 1937, an underground river had gathered strength near the Ara Pacis site and threatened to wash away, or at least erode, the precious marble. Lucky for the Ara Pacis and archaeologists, this was the fascist era, and there was nothing Mussolini liked better than resurrecting and showcasing ancient Roman glories. So, they somehow figured out a way to freeze the waterlogged ground under Palazzo Fiano and extract the rest of the Ara Pacis. Mussolini then ordered a pavilion to be built for the reconstructed Ara Pacis opposite the ruins of the Mausoleum of Augustus. (The square here, Piazza Augusto Imperatore, is done up in textbook fascist style, with harsh-looking palazzi of white travertine.) Eventually, most of the pieces of the Ara Pacis that had been dispersed around the museums Europe made their way back home, but some pieces were never recovered. The fascist-era pavilion was dismantled in 1999, and American architect Richard Meier was commissioned to create the modern museum that houses the Ara Pacis today. Meier, who also designed the new Getty Museum in Los Angeles, was ridiculed at first for designing a "Texas gas station" to house this most important work of Roman art, but the critics have since piped down. After 7 years of being closed to the public, the Ara Pacis will reopen in its bright and shiny new

digs—the only post-fascist structure in the *centro storico*, period—in 2006. *Lungotevere in Augusta, at Piazza Augusto Imperatore. www.arapacis.it. Admission 6.50€; 3€ with int'l student ID card. Tues–Sun 9am–7pm; Dec 24 and Dec 31 9am–2pm; closed Jan 1, May 1, Dec 25.*

FREE → **Bocca della Verità (Mouth of Truth)** ★ ANCIENT ROME What is actually kind of a cool ancient relic is now just a dumb tourist trap, but if you're in the vicinity of the Circus Maximus, you might as well line up and get your picture taken at the Mouth of Truth. According to popular legend, the Mouth of Truth was an ancient sewer cover whose surface was sculpted in the shape of a face—one that bears an uncanny resemblance to Barry Gibb of the Bee Gees in his full Afro-and-beard period. The mouth itself is a hole that goes all the way through to the other side of the huge marble disk. At some hazy point in the medieval period, the sewer cover was set up against the side of a building and became known as a lie detector. When they suspected their partners of cheating, men would bring their wives or mistresses to the Mouth of Truth and ask them if they'd been faithful; the suspect had to answer while placing her hand inside the hole in the mouth. Meanwhile, the inquisitor (who believed to know the awful truth already) would have hired a goon to stand behind the marble disk and chop off the woman's hand if she said "yes." Nowadays, there's no fingers being chopped off; just a continuous stream of tourists eager to snap that dorky photo of themselves sticking their hand in the old sewer cover. (For a more glamorous version of the ritual, check out the film *Roman Holiday*, with Audrey Hepburn and Gregory Peck. She's a princess, he's a reporter, they fall in love . . . awwww). *In the front porch of the Church of Santa Maria in Cosmedin, Piazza della Bocca della Verità 18. ☎ 06/678-14-19. Free admission. Daily 9am–1pm and 2:30–6pm, until 5pm in winter. Bus: 30 or 170.*

→ **Castel Sant'Angelo** ★★★ VATICAN Presiding over the western bank of the Tiber like a big ol' medium-rare hamburger of history, Castel Sant'Angelo has had quite a checkered past. It began its existence not as a castle but as the mausoleum of the emperor Hadrian (d. A.D. 138), which explains its squat, cylindrical shape. In ancient times, the mausoleum was ringed with opulent statuary, and a mound of earth sat on top of it, planted with cypress trees. In the late 3rd century A.D., the emperor Aurelian incorporated the mausoleum's formidable bulk into his fortification walls, the Mura Aureliane. To fend off one particularly bad barbarian invasion, the Romans sought refuge on top of the mausoleum and started using the old statues there as artillery, hurling marble heads and forearms at the barbarians who tried to scale the walls. From then on, the mausoleum became a fortress of sorts and began to be fortified with some of the battlements and ramparts you see here today. Castel Sant'Angelo didn't get its current name, "Castle of the Holy Angel," until A.D. 590, when a terrible plague was ravaging the city. One night, the Romans were praying in the streets for the plague to stop, when lo and behold, the archangel Michael flew down from the heavens and landed on top of the mausoleum, sheathing his sword, which signifed (the Romans would determine later) the end of the pestilence.

In the 13th century, the popes decided to appropriate the fortress for their own use and built themselves lavish apartments on the upper level. They also had the crenellated passageway known as *il passetto* constructed to link the castle with the apartments at the Vatican. In 1527, Pope Clement VII had to scurry down the *passetto* and hide out in Castel Sant'Angelo for 7 months during the siege of Rome by Holy Roman Emperor Charles V. Later, the popes kept their own prisoners here. (In Puccini's *Tosca*, this is where Cavaradossi was locked up. For her part, Tosca took a suicidal swan dive from one of the castle ramparts.) The visit of the castle begins with the heliocoidal (that's archaeo-jargon for "spiral") staircase (original to Hadrian's mausoleum), which climbs through the bowels of the structure to the terraces where the prison cells and ammunition storage magazines were located. From there, stairs lead to the elaborately frescoed papal quarters; at this higher level, there's a nice cafe and a covered gallery that goes all the way around the monument, affording great views of the city. The most commanding view, however, of the *centro storico* and the river below, is from the castle's highest point, the windy Terrazza dell'Angelo, where there's a bronze replica of the archangel sheathing his sword and sparing Rome from calamity. Even if you don't have the time or money to go inside, Castel Sant'Angelo is one of the more magnificent monuments in Rome to see by night, so try to make it part of one of your boozy evening walking tours. The bridge leading up to the castle, Ponte Sant'Angelo, is lined with fabulous marble statues of swooning angels, designed by baroque superstar Gianlorenzo Bernini. *Lungotevere Castello.* ☎ *06/687-50-36. Admission 5€. Tues–Sun 9am–7pm; closed public holidays. Bus: 23, 40, 46, 62, 64, 271, 280, or 571.*

FREE → **Foro Italico** ★★★ NORTHERN SUBURBS Underrated and undervisited!! This massive 1930s sports complex below Monte Mario, on the western bank of the Tiber a few kilometers north of the *centro,* is Mussolini's gloriously over-the-top paean to the cult of athleticism. The esplanades are covered with hugely entertaining black-and-white **mosaics** ★ of good little fascists doing virtuous fascist things—gymnasts performing difficult stunts like the "Iron Cross"; sporty guys doing calisthenics in their tighty whiteys; soldiers riding on tanks tagged with *Viva Mussolini* graffiti. The mosaics are in an amazing state of preservation, considering the fact that they get trampled every weekend

ROME & LAZIO

by the crowds who attend the Serie A soccer games of AS Roma and SS Lazio at the **Stadio Olimpico** ★ here. (See "Roma & Lazio Soccer Games: The Most Fun You Can Have on a Sunday in Italy" box, p. 198, for more info about attending a game.) The Stadio Olimpico is closed to the public except when games or concerts are held here, but to the immediate north of here is the fabulously campy **Stadio dei Marmi** ★★★, the crown jewel of fascist art in the Foro Italico.

The track and field arena is ringed by 60 white Carrara marble statues of athletes, each of whom represents a different city or region of Italy. The athletes hold sports equipment ranging from volleyballs to crossbows (and, bizarrely, a meat tenderizer) and strike ridiculously vain, almost balletic poses as they flex their butt cheeks and *Testosterone Monthly* cover-model facial expressions. Derek Zoolander, eat your heart out. The Foro Italico also has an indoor pool *(piscina)*, done up in fascist motifs of valiant divers and backstrokers, where you can often catch water polo games. Mmmm . . . Speedos. There's also a basic snack bar in the pool building. In May, the Italian Open is held at the tennis center here. Plenty of umbrella pines and the lush green slope of Monte Mario make this a refreshing place to spend an hour or two. *Largo de Bosis, at Lungotevere Maresciallo Cadorna. Free admission. Bus: 32, 271, or 280. Tram: 2.*

FREE → **Isola Tiberina** ★★ GHETTO/ TRASTEVERE Building on an ancient Roman myth, early city architects constructed a travertine platform around the island so that it would resemble a ship. Port and starboard, fore and aft, the "decks" today are great for sunning. Long associated with healing, Isola Tiberina has its own hospital and small church. *Free admission. Bus: 23, 63, 271, 280, 780, or H. Tram: 8.*

→ **Mamertine Prison** ★ ANCIENT ROME The dank and oppressive torture and execution chamber for Rome's most formidable enemies from the Republic through the Empire is not for the claustrophobic! Underneath the church of San Giuseppe dei Falegnami, the low-ceilinged prison cells hewn into the dark-gray tufa rock here are where St. Peter was supposedly imprisoned prior to his martyrdom at the Circus of Caligula in A.D. 64. There's not a lot to see, but it's an interesting detour while you're visiting the Roman Forum, immediately adjacent. *Clivo Argentario 1, at Via del Tulliano. ☎ 06/679-29-02. 1€–2€ donation expected. April–Sept daily 9am–noon and 2:30–6pm; Oct–March daily 9am–noon and 2–5pm. Bus: 60, 75, 85, 87, 117, 175, or 571.*

FREE → **Piazza Venezia** ★ Though it's hardly deserving of the name piazza (which normally denotes a public square that is welcoming of human beings), this is the most central point of old Rome, the heart where major traffic arteries Via del Corso, Via Nazionale, Via dei Fori Imperiali, Via del Teatro di Marcello, and Via del Plebiscito meet, carrying a continuous, fluid exchange of *motorini*, buses, and cars over the bumpy cobblestones. By far, the most prominent feature of Piazza Venezia is the 19th-century **Vittoriano** (Monument to Vittorio Emanuele II, the first king of unified Italy), which looms like a monumental exercise in bad taste at the southern side of the square. This garish heap of white marble is festooned with so much gaudy sculptural detail that it has been nicknamed the "wedding cake" by disparaging locals. Nevertheless, the enormous Vittoriano is a tourist favorite, and you'll always see groups of camera-wielding foreigners risking life and limb amid the maelstrom of traffic here to snap that perfect photo. The Vittoriano is open daily from 10am to 6pm; admission is free, and there's an outdoor snack bar, Caffè Italia, halfway up the monument on the left (east) side. The **view** ★★★ from the very top is the best comprehensive panorama of central Rome.

More important historically, the 15th-century **Palazzo Venezia** (on the west side of the square) became the headquarters of the fascist regime in 1929; Mussolini delivered his rousing speeches from the balcony that overlooks the piazza. Not coincidentally, there is a perfect, gun-barrel view of the Colosseum from here: Mussolini ordered everything that blocked his view of that ultimate monument of ancient Roman glory razed to the ground and paved Via dell'Impero (now called Via dei Fori Imperiali) to connect his balcony with the Colosseum, showcasing the ruins of the Imperial Fora (then, being excavated for the first time) on either side. There's a museum inside Palazzo Venezia, but don't expect access to Mussolini's old war room or anything; most of the fascist-era offices in the palace (including the room that opens up to the famous balcony) are closed to the public. Instead, what you're allowed to see is a mostly disappointing collection of decorative arts from the 14th to 17th centuries, and the occasional temporary exhibition. For the most part, the museum's a snooze—save your 4€ for a beer. *Piazza Venezia. Museum admission 4€; Tues–Sat 9am–7:30pm. Bus: 30, 40, 62, 64, 70, 85, 87, 95, 170, 175, 492, or 571.*

FREE → **Campidoglio (Capitoline Hill)** ★★★ ANCIENT ROME The citadel of ancient Rome and seat of modern city government is one of the best places to come early in your visit to get your bearings in Rome. The Campidoglio is several sights in one: the piazza itself, whose Michelangelo-designed star-shaped pavement has become an icon of the city, is a glorious and mighty Renaissance space. The salmon-toned *palazzi* (also Michelangelo) on either side of the square house the city's stupendous collection of ancient art in the Capitoline Museums. The ramp that leads up from Piazza Venezia to the Capitoline is another Michelangelo creation, the *cordonata*, at the top of which are colossal marble statues of Castor and Pollux that were excavated near Campo de' Fiori in the 16th century.

As highly dressed as the Campidoglio is, there's a wonderfully thrown-together look to it that is quintessentially Roman. The formal aspect of the Campidoglio really turns rustic on the southern and western sides of the hill, where wild vegetation flourishes on primordial slopes of red tufa bedrock. (The western slope was the site of the infamous Tarpeian Rock, where traitors were hurled from the summit of the Capitol to the brambles below.) On either side of Palazzo Senatorio (the bell-towered building that functions as the mayor's office today), there are terraces with heart-stopping views over the Forum. The ancient name of the hill, Capitolium, was derived from the fact that in very distant antiquity, a human head had been found up here. The head was believed to have belonged to a farmer named Olius, so they named the place Capitolium, from *caput olii* ("head of Olius"). Capitolium had become the more garbled Campidoglio by the medieval period. *Piazza del Campidoglio. Free admission to square and terraces; Museum admission (both) 7.80€, free on last Sun of each month. Hours: Tues–Sun 9am–8pm.. Bus: 30, 40, 46, 62, 64, 70, 87, 170, or H.*

FREE → **Piazza Navona** ★★★ Rome's grandest baroque square is the stage for an architectural smack-down between Francesco Borromini and Gianlorenzo Bernini. Weighing in on the western side of the oblong piazza is Borromini's **Sant'Agnese in Agone** (1653–57), a small church whose proud bearing is enhanced by its telescoping bell towers, oversized dome, and concave façade—a popular baroque feature, designed to draw in passersby (except on Mondays, when it's closed). In the center of the square, Bernini's action-packed, obelisk-crowned **Fountain of the Four Rivers** (1651) is a feisty competitor, with four reclining figures representing the

ROME & LAZIO

Danube, Plata, Ganges, and Nile. The fountain's base is a mass of travertine, hewn in the pre-weathered, organic style so favored in the 17th and 18th centuries. And any baroque sculptor worth his salt would sooner be caught dead than design a fountain that didn't include cavorting animals—today, overheated tourists and mentally unstable locals splash (illegally) alongside Bernini's "hippopotamus" (which is just a horse, wading) and river serpents. Between Borromini and Bernini, who wins? After 350 years, the jury is still out—but if you look up at the left bell tower of the church, a devastatingly *superb* statue of St. Agnes, placed there after the fountain's completion, seems to have the last laugh. Inside the Church of Sant'Agnese, check out the chapel on the left (through the door marked SACRA TESTA DI SANT'AGNESE): the chimpanzee-sized "skull of St. Agnes" is preserved inside a silver reliquary.

Piazza Navona got its shape, and its name, from the ancient **Stadium of Domitian**, ruins of which still exist below the ground here (visible from the outside of the north side of the piazza). The track and field events held at the stadium were called the *agones*, hence Piazza Navona, a corruption of the medieval name for the area, Platea in Agonis ("place of competition"). The square is at its best before 10am, when the tourist hordes and trinket sellers start to descend, so come for a morning cappuccino to enjoy an unspoiled view. Cafes and restaurants abound on Piazza Navona, but you'll never find locals dining here. Instead, head for one of the popular bars or restaurants in the action-packed nightlife area to the west of the piazza. *Piazza Navona. Free admission. Bus: 30 Express, 40, 62, 64, 70, 81, 87, 492, or 628.*

FREE → **Piazza del Popolo** ★★ A massive, 4,000-year-old pink granite Egyptian obelisk with wonderful hieroglyphics presides over this grand, newly pedestrianized expanse at the top of the Tridente. At no. 12,

on the north side of the piazza, the church of **Santa Maria del Popolo** ★ (☎ 06/361-08-36; Mon–Sat 7am–noon and 4€–7pm; Sun 8am–2pm and 4:30–7:30pm; free admission) is a trove of art treasures, including two fine paintings by Caravaggio; to the south, the façades of seemingly twin churches make for pretty pictures. Romans and tourists alike bask in the late afternoon sun that floods this vast, traffic-free oval space. The two cafes on either side of the square, Canova and Rosati, are touristy but lovely. Wonderfully uncluttered, the "square of the people" is perfect for idling and gelato licking, and a fitting introduction to the good-life Tridente district that spreads out pronglike to the south. To the east are the glorious green terraces of the Pincio hill, one of the most romantic spots in the city. *Free admission. Metro: Flaminio. Bus: 117 or 119.*

→ **Protestant Cemetery** ★★ TESTACCIO One of the most peaceful and unexpected sights in Rome is the Cimitero Acattolico (non-Catholic cemetery), separated from the furious traffic of Piazzale Ostiense by a tall, ancient brick wall. This green, slightly unkempt haven is the final resting place of the Romantic poets John Keats and Percy Bysshe Shelley, the founder of the Italian Communist Party, Antonio Gramsci, and other non-Catholics. At the grave of William Wetmore Story, a 19th-century American sculptor who lived in Rome for many years, a marble angel—his own work—slumps in grief over the tombstone, her neck collapsed in exhausted resignation. It's one of the most moving funerary monuments in the world. *Via Caio Cestio 6, near Piazzale Ostiense. ☎ 06/574-19-00. 1€–2€ donation expected. Tues–Sun 9am–6pm (until 5pm Oct–March). Last admission 30 min. before closing. Metro: Piramide. Bus: 23, 30, 60, or 95. Tram: 3.*

FREE → **Spanish Steps (Scalinata di Spagna)** ★★ Fortunately, the sweeping beauty of the Scalinata di Piazza di Spagna transcends the sometimes ugly crowds of tourists that populate the square day and night. The climb to the high terrace covers 12 curving flights of steps of varying width—watch where you're walking, or else risk an embarrassing faceplant—but the view from the top, where you can finally look away from your feet, is exhilarating. Come between 2 and 6am, and you'll enjoy that rarest of Roman treats—having the fabulous stage of the Spanish Steps to yourself. Called "Spanish" because the Spanish embassy to the Vatican is located opposite, the steps were actually designed by a Frenchman, De Sanctis, and built by Italians.

In summer, the Roman fashion commission puts on a sadistic fashion show here, in which models are forced to walk down the bumpy, slippery steps (in stilettos) as if they're on a runway! At the base of the steps is the **Fontana della Barcaccia** ("bad boat fountain") designed by Pietro Bernini, father of the great Gianlorenzo Bernini, in the early 16th century. According to legend, the fountain immortalizes a river boat that washed up and wrecked in Piazza di Spagna (having been buffeted through the streets all the way from the Tiber!) during a particularly heavy flood. The water that flows from the spigot here is ice cold and great to drink. Because Romans love to make up traditions, they say that if you drink from here, you will have eternal youth. Might as well give it a try. Rome's highest-end shopping is all located right in this vicinity, Via Condotti being the main road that leads straight to credit card debt. *Piazza di Spagna. Free admission. Metro: Spagna. Bus: 117 or 119.*

FREE ➔ **Trevi Fountain (Fontana di Trevi)** ★★★ TREVI If they had Sea World in the 18th century, this is probably what Shamu's tank would have looked like. An ingeniously sculpted travertine base of faux boulders and "fallen" building cornices gives rise to a dynamic pageant of mythological figures, over which thousands of gallons of water per minute thunder to the inviting, swimming-pool-blue basin below. In spite of the tourist swarms, Nicola Salvi's fountain (1732–62) is a monumental feast for the eyes that never fails to delight—and to surprise, given its location in such a tiny, hidden piazza. Rome is the most theatrical, cinematic city in Italy, and the Trevi is a wonderfully self-conscious piece of Rococo drama: the steps that surround it are thinly disguised theater seats, the pool is the orchestra, and the extravagantly sculpted façade is the stage set from which Neptune and his team of headstrong seahorses surge forth. Tradition says that if you want to come back to Rome, you should throw a coin into the Trevi Fountain. There's even a prescribed coin-pitching choreography: With your back to the fountain, take a coin in your right hand and throw it over your left shoulder (crossing your heart—awww).

Before the coin thing caught on, visitors to Rome used to swallow palmfuls of water from the Trevi to ensure their return to the city. I wouldn't do that today, but the spigots below the railing on the southeast side of the square are still fed by the Aqua Virgo aqueduct and are perfectly potable. For the best Trevi experience, come between 2 and 7am. It's 100% safe (there are police here around the clock making sure no one goes for a swim), and you can recline on the travertine slabs and bliss out to the roar of the water. *Fontana di Trevi. Bus: 52, 53, 62, 95, 116, 175, or 492.*

The Vatican

As the headquarters of the Catholic Church and the world's smallest, richest city-state, the Vatican has plenty of intrigue. However, most of the 10,000-plus visitors who cycle through Vatican City each day won't see the pope or sit in on any *Da Vinci Code*-esque secret meetings. Instead, what you'll do at the Vatican is see its incredible legacies of art and architecture—in the Vatican Museums, the Sistine Chapel, and St. Peter's Basilica and Square.

The Vatican

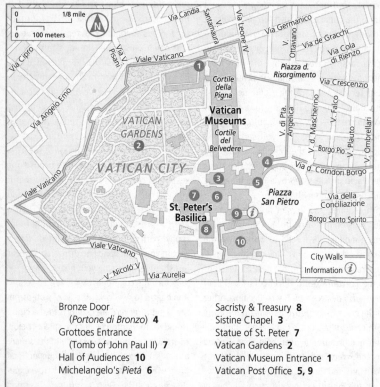

Bronze Door	Sacristy & Treasury **8**
(*Portone di Bronzo*) **4**	Sistine Chapel **3**
Grottoes Entrance	Statue of St. Peter **7**
(Tomb of John Paul II) **7**	Vatican Gardens **2**
Hall of Audiences **10**	Vatican Museum Entrance **1**
Michelangelo's *Pietá* **6**	Vatican Post Office **5, 9**

FREE ➜ **St. Peter's Square (Piazza San Pietro)** ★★★ Designed from 1656 to 1667 by Bernini to mimic a human embrace, this sweeping quadruple colonnade of 300 travertine piers is the gateway to the largest church in the world and one of the most recognizable images of the Vatican. In the center of the grand square stands an Egyptian obelisk that once served at a turning post in the Circus of Caligula, where St. Peter was martyred in A.D. 64. Along the south wall of the square are official Vatican souvenir and bookshops and a branch of the Vatican post office. On Sundays and Catholic holidays, Mass is celebrated in the square, and the pope often appears at his window in the Apostolic Palace (above the northern arm of the colonnade) to bless the faithful.

TV Best FREE ➜ **St. Peter's Basilica (Basilica di San Pietro)** ★★★ Confession (how appropriate!): I lived in Rome for a year before I bothered to go inside St. Peter's. I caught glimpses of it every day and thought to myself, yeah, it's big and important, but with that same image of the dome plastered all over every postcard rack in town, it seemed like a pompous cliché I didn't need to experience up close. (As Italian tourism clichés went, I thought the Colosseum and the Leaning Tower of Pisa were much cooler.) Then, one day, I went inside St. Peter's and literally lost my breath when I took that first step over the threshold. The magic of St. Peter's is the interior of the preposterously enormous basilica, and it blows you away.

In the Beginning . . .

To understand how Vatican City came to be the religious and tourist machine that it is today, we must rewind to ancient times and the story of St. Peter. In A.D. 64, the "Great Fire" destroyed about two-thirds of the city of Rome, and the people blamed then-emperor Nero for not doing more to prevent it. Nero needed a scapegoat, and who better than an upstart group of monotheistic cult members, the Christians? As the first pope and head of the Christian church in Rome, Peter was the first to be targeted under Nero's persecutions. He was sentenced to crucifixion at the Circus of Caligula, a chariot racetrack that stood on the Ager Vaticanus (the site of modern-day St. Peter's Square). Saying that he did not deserve to die in the same way Christ had been killed, Peter insisted that his crucifixion be upside-down. The Roman persecutors granted him his wish and nailed him to a cross, raising it to its inverted position before the delighted masses at the circus, in A.D. 64 or 65. Members of the Christian community saw to it that after the crowds had left the scene Peter got a proper burial. His tomb was placed in an existing *necropolis* (city of the dead) alongside the circus.

Over the next few centuries, Christians continuously visited his tomb and kept it from being vandalized. When, in A.D. 313, Constantine issued the Edict of Milan and legalized Christianity in the Roman Empire, the Christians could finally build physical churches over their holy places of worship. The first church in Rome was St. John Lateran (San Giovanni in Laterano, which is still the cathedral of Rome), which was built over the relics of St. John, south of the Colosseum. Shortly thereafter, on the Ager Vaticanus, construction began on a church that would sit right on top of Peter's tomb: it was called St. Peter's Basilica. The ambitious architectural program to convert the Vatican hill from a place of terrible Christian persecution into a monument to the glory of the Church would continue for almost 1,500 years: a bigger and better Renaissance basilica to St. Peter would rise over the relatively humble 4th century church, and countless sums of Church money would be paid to obtain the best materials and the best artists to embellish the papal stronghold.

The strongest single symbol at the Vatican of the Church's triumph in Rome is the obelisk at the center of St. Peter's Square. The Egyptian granite monolith was originally imported to Rome by the emperor Caligula to stand at the center of his circus—the same place where Peter was put to death. The obelisk eventually fell and lay in the dirt off to the side of St. Peter's for centuries, but in the 1580s, it was moved to its present location and crowned with a huge bronze cross, as if to say, "Who's your daddy *now,* pagans?"

St. Peter's was built from 1506–1626, in the shape of a Latin cross, over the basilica that the emperor Constantine had dedicated to St. Peter in the 4th century A.D. The 16th and 17th centuries in Rome were a time of huge artistic patronage, when the popes were not so much pious men but princes of noble descent who threw a ton of money into embellishing the city—and making sure their names appeared on any monuments they paid for. (This was nothing new; the ancient Roman emperors did the exact same thing.) St. Peter's Basilica and St. Peter's Square are the ultimate expression of that patronage—it

Read This Before You Visit the Vatican!

→ Allow the best part of **3 hours** to see the highlights of the Vatican, and accept that it's crowded. The Vatican is the one sight in Rome that subjects you to spending several hours cooped up indoors with little escape from other tourists. But you gotta do it.

→ In general, **the best times to go** to the Vatican Museums (which include the Sistine Chapel) are after 1pm from March to October; and after 10:30am from November to February (the museums have shorter hours in winter). The **best days to go** are Tuesday through Friday. Mondays get all the crowds who couldn't come on Sunday, when it's closed; Saturdays get all the weekend traffic, and the situation is worsened by the fact that the museums are only open until 12:45pm on Saturdays. Visits to the Vatican Museums and Sistine Chapel cannot be booked in advance—so depending on when you go, you could wait in line for 2 hours, or you could walk right in.

→ It's best to **visit the Vatican Museums first,** then exit them by way of the **right rear door of the Sistine Chapel,** which funnels you directly down to the entrance of St. Peter's. Then you'll be free to roam St. Peter's Square, send postcards through the Vatican mail, etc.

→ St. Peter's has a strictly enforced **dress code:** Men and women in shorts, above-the-knee skirts, or bare shoulders will not be admitted to the basilica. Charm does not work on the gray-suited thugs who patrol the entrance—cover up, or you will be turned away. Period.

→ For most tourists' intents and purposes, **the Vatican is closed on Sundays.** The Vatican Museums and Sistine Chapel are open on the last Sunday of the month for free, but you should avoid this like the plague. It's crowded beyond belief (as in, 2-hour lines to get in), and people get aggressive. If, on the other hand, you want to get elbowed in the groin by 4-foot-tall southern Italian ladies as you try to make your way to the Sistine Chapel, be my guest.

→ **Photography is allowed** everywhere in the public areas of the Vatican *except* for the Sistine Chapel. You can use flash inside St. Peter's but not on any paintings or tapestries in the Vatican Museums.

may be papal egotism disguised as religious devotion, but it's why we have such amazing monuments to visit here today.

A star-studded lineup of A-list architects and artists, including Michelangelo, Raphael, Donato Bramante, Giacomo della Porta, Carlo Maderno, and Gianlorenzo Bernini, worked on the design and decoration of St. Peter's. Michelangelo originally wanted a church with a shorter, Greek cross floor plan; his plans were scrapped by later architects who wanted to make St. Peter's the longest church in the world. Indeed, at 211m (692 ft.) in length, St. Peter's is the longest, and overall largest, church in Christendom, with an area of 23,000 sq. m (247,569 sq. ft.) and capacity for 60,000 people during Vatican conferences or important Masses. It's also the tallest building in Rome, with Michelangelo's dome crowning the skyline like a 136m-tall (446-ft.) papal tiara.

A TOUR OF ST. PETER'S

Once you've entered the basilica, walk to the central nave and take some time to soak it all in. Every square inch of the basilica's interior is covered with marble, bronze, or gold. Altarpieces that look like paintings are actually mosaics, made up of thousands of tiny chips of colored stone. The gold and lapis lazuli lettering of the Latin inscription that runs around the inside of the basilica is 2m (6¹/₂ ft.) tall. The marble cherubs holding the holy water fonts are twice the size of a normal human being. Throughout the basilica, there are over 1,100 columns and 500 statues.

Before you walk toward the main dome, turn back toward the way you came in; in the first chapel on the right is **Michelangelo's Pietà** ★★★, which he sculpted in 1499, at the age of 24. Second only in fame to his *David* (at the Accademia in Florence), the *Pietà* depicts Mary cradling the limp body of Jesus in her lap. The exaggerated proportions of Mary's lower body gives the sculpture a pyramidal form that keeps the composition from feeling top-heavy, but Michelangelo also meant for the heavy foundation to symbolize the Virgin Mary as the solid rock on which Christianity rests. Although there are tears on Mary's face, she is not consumed by grief; Michelangelo rendered her eyes in such a way as to suggest that she is cognizant of what her son's death will mean to humanity. Unfortunately, the *Pietà* is behind a heavy pane of bullet-proof glass—in 1972, when it was unprotected, a hammer-wielding madman attacked the *Pietà* and broke off part of Christ's foot—so you can't get very close to it, and you'll also have a hard time getting any good photos (definitely turn off your flash, otherwise you'll just get a reflection off the glass).

Now, head back to the central nave, and begin walking toward the dome. Along the floor, you'll find **bronze inscriptions** with the names and lengths of other, lesser churches of the world inlaid in the marble. Near the front door are the markers for the Florence Duomo and St. Paul's of London; closer to the dome, you'll find the marker for

the relatively tiny St. Patrick's Cathedral of New York ("Neo Eboracem").

In the main nave, as you near the dome, there's a **bronze statue of St. Peter,** made by Florentine sculptor Arnolfo di Cambio in the 13th century. Catholic pilgrims rub the foot of this statue to give thanks for having arrived in Rome safely.

The four-legged creature that crouches under the dome of St. Peter's is Gianlorenzo Bernini's splendid **baldacchino** ★★★. This fantastically over-the-top baroque canopy was cast in the mid-17th century from bronze that Pope Urban VIII stole from the porch of the Pantheon. Urban VIII's family name was Barberini, prompting the popular joke, "What the barbarians didn't do, the Barberini did." All in all, the *baldacchino*'s bronze weighs in at 30,000 kg (66,000 lb.), or 10 Ford F-150 trucks. If you look carefully at the *baldacchino*'s corkscrew legs, there are tiny gold and bronze bumblebees here and there. The bee was the family symbol of the Barberini family, so whenever you see the bees around Rome (and there are a lot of them), you'll know that Pope Urban VIII was the patron behind that work of art or architecture. Bernini's *baldacchino* marks the

Don't Call It a Cathedral!

Not all big churches are cathedrals. St. Peter's, for one, is just a basilica. What's the difference, you ask? Well, *basilica* is a general architectural term, roughly interchangeable with the Italian word *chiesa* (church). *Cathedral* is a technical term, meaning "seat church" (*cathedra* is the Greek word for "chair" or "seat"), or the head church of the bishop. Each diocese has one bishop, and each bishop has one "seat church." In the diocese of Rome, the only cathedral is the church of St. John Lateran (San Giovanni in Laterano).

ROME & LAZIO

The Keys to the Kingdom of Heaven

In the most famous 8-minute song in the history of rock 'n' roll, Led Zeppelin sang of "a lady who's sure all that glitters is gold, and she's buying a stairway to heaven." However, a stairway to heaven is useless if there's no one to open the gates when you get there. That's where the Vatican comes in.

Papal insignias—those coats of arms with the keys and the papal tiara floating overhead—are all over Rome, but especially prevalent in the Vatican (obviously). But what's with the keys? When Jesus made Peter the first pope (or "vice Christ"), he said "You are Peter, and upon this rock, I will build my church, and I will give you the keys to the kingdom of heaven." Inside the basilica, the inscription around the base of the dome is the Latin translation of that message: TU ES PETRUS ET SUPER HANC PETRAM AEDIFICABO ECCLESIAM MEAM ET TIBI DABO CLAVES REGNI CAELORUM. In Latin, the name *Petrus* (Peter) is so linguistically similar to the word *petram* (rock) that the inscription is saying that Peter is the rock upon which the church is built. All popes are the spiritual heirs of Peter, so all popes are symbolic "key-holders" to the kingdom of heaven.

Whether you can buy your way in—the issue raised by Robert Plant and Jimmy Page—is debatable: but considering all the gold and glitter they've poured into St. Peter's, the popes sure seem to think so.

holiest part of the basilica. Under the *baldacchino* is the papal altar, where only the pope may celebrate Mass; straight beneath that, about 10m (33 ft.) down, is the site of St. Peter's tomb, accessible only by prearranged tours of the excavations (*scavi*) of the necropolis of St. Peter's.

In the rear apse, at the very end of the basilica's Latin-cross floorplan, there's a bronze chair suspended on the wall; this is another Bernini-for-Urban-VII monument, the **Cathedra Petri** (chair of Peter, 1666). It's not actually his real chair (Peter's was a modest wooden number), just a symbolic way to indicate that Peter still presides over the Church from this high, all-seeing position. Above the Cathedra Petri is another Bernini creation, a gorgeous stained-glass **window** ★★, at the center of which a dove, representing the Holy Spirit, hovers in flight. To remind you of just how big everything is inside St. Peter's, the dove's wingspan is 2m (6½ ft.)!

Another cool Bernini sculpture worth checking out is the **tomb of Alexander VII** ★

(1667), near the short, left "arm" of the church. The monument is a mass of colored marble, at the top of which the pope sits with hands clasped in prayer. Underneath him, a "cloak" of rose-colored marble drapes over a service entrance to the basilica. A bronze and gold winged skeleton emerges from below, pushing the "cloak" out of the way. This figure—which is uncannily reminiscent of early Guns n' Roses album art, minus Slash's top hat—is Death personified, and his head is covered to signify that Death is faceless. In his hand, Death raises a golden hourglass aloft as if to make a morbid toast to Alexander's time running out.

Underneath the basilica (accessible by stairs in the piers that support the dome, free admission) are the **Vatican grottoes,** where the tombs of dozens of popes, including the **tomb of Pope John Paul II,** are. Contrary to a fancy marble shrinelike area behind glass that is marked SEPOLCRO DI SAN PIETRO, St. Peter's tomb is not on this level; it's a few meters deeper, in the even more ancient Vatican necropolis (see below).

To climb the **dome** ★ ★ of St. Peter's, exit the basilica to the left and follow the signs to the cupola. It costs 5€ to take the elevator to the halfway point of the church; from there, there are a few hundred more steps to the viewing platform around the lantern. If you wanna be a bad-ass and walk up the whole way, from the ground to the lantern, the Vatican still charges you 4€. There's a cafe at the midway point. As a side note, the dome of St. Peter's is not the absolute best place for a comprehensive view of Rome. It's the highest point in the city, but it's so far west of everything that you can't really get a good look at the monuments you'd recognize (e.g., the Colosseum), although you do get a great view of St. Peter's Square. (In other words, if you're feeling lazy, you can skip the dome.) If you are going to do it, however, keep in mind that the lines are shortest right after the dome opens (8–9:30am) and right before it closes (5:30pm Apr–Oct; 4:30pm Nov–Mar). *Piazza San Pietro.* ☎ *06/698-84-466 or 06/698-84-866. Free admission to basilica and grottoes (crypt); dome 4€–5€. Daily 7am–7pm; grottoes 7am–6pm (until 5pm Oct–March); dome 8am–6pm (until 5pm Oct–March). Metro: Ottaviano. Bus: 23, 40, 46, 62, or 64. Tram: 19.*

→ **Vatican Necropolis (Tomb of St Peter)** ★ ★ A haunting descent beneath the massive basilica takes you into the ancient level where bones believed to be St. Peter's were found in the 1940s. The atmospheric catacomb-like excavations and the spine-tingling archaeological story (that the priest-guides relate in a reverential whisper) give even non-Catholics the chills. *Città del Vaticano, along south wall of St Peter's.* ☎ *06/698-85-318. Fax 06/698-85-518. uff.scavi@fabricsp.va. Admission 9€. Mon–Sat by appointment only. Fax or e-mail request at least 1 month in advance. Metro: Ottaviano.*

VATICAN MUSEUMS & SISTINE CHAPEL

The richest museum in the world is enthralling in its quantity and quality, aggravating in its utter lack of explanatory signage. As a rule, the important stuff is where the crowds are, but try to resist the riptide of tour groups that washes headlong toward the Sistine Chapel, because you'll miss a ton of fabulous art along the way. The museum guidebook—or, better yet, the CD-ROM audioguide—can make your meander through these masterpiece-packed halls vastly more meaningful. (The museums' website, http://mv.vatican.va, is also an excellent source of background information.) For the best understanding of the Sistine Chapel, consider a guided tour. Near the entrance of the museums, there's a full-service restaurant and cafeteria, gift shops galore, and a branch of the Vatican post office. There's also a bag-check, but don't leave anything here unless you absolutely have to (they make you check pocket knives, large umbrellas, and other large packs)—you'll probably be exiting the museums by way of the Sistine Chapel, and coming all the way back to the entrance to pick up your stuff is a serious detour. If you rent an audioguide, however, you'll have to come all the way back to return it and collect your ID, which you have to leave as collateral. For tips on the best days of the week and times to visit the museums, see "Read This Before You Visit the Vatican!," p. 182.

The Highlights of the Vatican Museums

Near the entrance of the museums is the Vatican **Pinacoteca** (picture gallery). In addition to the standard Italian lineup of Holy Family triptychs, the Pinacoteca is home to Raphael's *Transfiguration* (1520, his last painting), in Room 8; Leonardo's enigmatic *St. Jerome* (1482), in Room 9; and Caravaggio's eerie, green-fleshed *Deposition* (1604), in

Room 12. Across the Cortile della Pigna (Courtyard of the Pine Cone, named for an ancient bronze pine cone at one end of the open square), head up the stairs to the Pio-Clementine Museums of classical statuary, which consists of room after room of Roman busts, full statues, and wonderful fragments. The first major ancient sculptures acquired by the Vatican are in the **Octagonal Courtyard.** The highlights in the Octagonal Courtyard include the exquisite marble **Apollo Belvedere** ★★ (a 2nd-century- A.D. copy of a 5th-century-B.C. original), a paragon of classical composure and ideal, unruffled beauty. In radical stylistic contrast, the terribly dramatic 1st-century- A.D. **Laocoön** ★★★ (Lay-ah-koh-on) captures the very height of human vulnerability. Done in the moving Hellenistic style—with struggling sinews and faces wrenched with despair—the sculpture depicts the fate of a Trojan priest who was suspicious of the Trojan horse and asked his people to "beware of Greeks bearing gifts." The Greek-favoring gods, angered, sentenced him to death by sea serpents. The Laocoön was discovered near the Colosseum, by a farmer plowing his field, in the early 1500s and was quickly snatched up by the popes. Michelangelo studied the sculpture in depth and copied certain anatomical elements of the Laocoön in the Sistine Chapel frescoes.

In the indoor gallery just beyond the Octagonal Courtyard, you'll find the expressive, though fragmentary, **Belvedere Torso** ★ (1st century B.C.), which inspired Michelangelo's rendering of Christ in the Last Judgment, in the Sistine Chapel. The torso is believed to be from a statue of Hercules because there are traces of a lion skin (common iconography for Hercules, whose most famous labor was the killing of the Nemean lion) visible on the base of the sculpture. The next major room is the Sala Rotonda (Round Room), where there is a fantastically preserved 1st-century-B.C. bronze statue of **Hercules** ★ (with lion skin

and the club he used to kill it—sorry, Simba). In the center of the Sala Rotonda, there's also an enormous **porphyry bowl** ★ (8m/26 ft. in diameter); this purple granite bowl came from the Emperor Nero's Golden House, where it was probably used as a bird bath. The floor of the Sala Rotonda is a finely detailed 3rd-century-A.D. Roman mosaic, which, incredibly, visitors are allowed to walk on. In the next room, the **Sala a Croce Greca** (Room of the Greek Cross), there are two porphyry sarcophagi (4th century A.D.) that were the tombs of members of the Emperor Constantine's family.

Upstairs, the **Etruscan Museum** ★ is well worth checking out—if it's open—for its knockout gold breastplates and pins from a 2,500-year-old tomb. The long hall at the top of the stairs is the **Gallery of the Candelabras,** which has even more "minor" Roman sculptures, which unfortunately collect dust and are ignored by many visitors but would fetch hundreds of thousands of dollars apiece if auctioned at Christie's today. The next room you hit is the **Gallery of the Tapestries,** which is dark and not very exciting unless you are into 16th- and 17th-century tapestries.

From here, the Vatican Museums morph into fresco heaven. The 32 brightly colored frescoes in the **Gallery of the Maps** ★ are a wonderfully detailed, frame-by-frame cartographical record of 16th-century Italy. After the Gallery of the Maps, you are funneled into the Sala Sobieski, named for the gigantic painting (by Jan Mateiko) here that depicts King Sobieski of Poland fighting off the Turks. Next up is the Sala dell'Immacolata (Room of the Immaculate Conception), which is where the traffic heading for the Sistine Chapel really begins to bottleneck. Make your way through the dawdling cruise-ship groups here, and head down the exterior passageway that leads to the Sala dei Chiaroscuri. Keep going. In the **Sala di Costantino** ★ (Hall of Constantine), pink-tinged frescoes by

Giulio Romano (1522–25) are a tribute to Christianity's triumph over paganism. The fresco by Tommaso Laureti in the center of the ceiling is a literal depiction of the theme; a pagan statue topples and breaks while a gilt Christian cross remains upright in the background.

In the famed **Stanze di Raffaello (Raphael Rooms)** ★★ (1506–17), exquisite frescoes like *The School of Athens* ★★★ (in the Stanza della Segnatura) and *The Liberation of St. Peter* ★★ (in the Stanza di Eliodoro) display the harmony of color and balance of composition that were the hallmark of High Renaissance classicism and Raphael's mastery as a painter. You don't have to be an art history geek to appreciate how good Raphael was—the sheer clarity, vivid details, dynamism, use of perspective, and punchy color are as accessible today as they would have been 500 years ago. There are multilingual explanatory panels in each room to fill you in on the specific historical or fantasy events depicted in the painting. There are also a number of very good tour guides in here that you can eavesdrop on for all kinds of interesting factoids. After the Raphael Rooms, a wrong turn and confusing signs can take you downstairs to the Vatican's dreadful modern art collection (noooo!!); keep to the left for the direct route to the Sistine Chapel—you're almost there.

Before entering the Sistine Chapel, however, I suggest you take a quick pit stop. Head down the stairs past the entrance of the chapel to a little outdoor cafe. Don't miss 📺 (Best) **Bar Sistina** ★, where Paolo, the rotund, bald guy who runs the cafe, has some premade sandwiches and packaged ice creams that'll hit the spot after a few hours in the Vatican Museums. He also has beer, which is even more refreshing on a hot day in the museums. To get the most out of your Sistine Chapel experience, I highly recommend cracking open a can or two of Tuborg and chilling out for a second on one of the plastic chairs here; when you do head back upstairs to the chapel, you'll have a bit of a buzz, which makes Michelangelo's awesome frescoes that much more impressive. (Just don't actually bring your beer *into* the chapel; that's frowned upon.)

The Sistine Chapel

Michelangelo's spectacular frescoes—covering more than 1,000 sq. m (10,764 sq. ft.) in all—very much live up to the hype, and after the thorough wipe-down they received in the 1980s and '90s, they're more eye-popping than ever. On the ceiling (1508–12), Michelangelo's stories of creation, Adam and Eve, and Noah are told in nine frames, surrounded by faux architectural elements and medallions. Michelangelo's *Last Judgment* (1535–41) is on the altar wall. In all, Michelangelo spent about 9 years in this room, permanently ruining his eyesight and screwing up his back beyond any chiropractor's repair, so that you could come in and gawk at his work for 10 minutes. So, you'd better enjoy it!

The lateral walls (the first part of the chapel to be decorated) are covered with 15th-century frescoes of the **life of Moses** and the **life of Christ,** including celebrated works by early Renaissance masters Luca Signorelli, Sandro Botticelli, and Perugino, but not Michelangelo.

The Ceiling

In the **first frame** (nearest the altar wall), God (in a purplish-pink bodysuit) twists through the heavens, separating light from darkness. In the **second frame,** God flies on across the sky, creating the sun and moon simply by pointing at them. (Note also how tight his butt is in that bodysuit!) In the **third frame,** God is supposed to be separating land from water, although it's not obvious that this is what's happening.

The **fourth frame** is the really famous one, the **Creation of Adam** ★★★. In this scene, God leans down from his cloud, right arm outstretched toward the naked body of

Adam, who reclines on the curved green surface of the Earth. Everything about the way Michelangelo has painted Adam convinces us that Adam is nothing more than the sum of his flesh and bones; there is no spark of life in him. His limp left hand awaits the electrical current from God's index finger. Back in the cloud, God has his left arm around Eve, who looks over at Adam with trepidation, as if she knows she's about to be created, too, and when they get together, there could be trouble. In the **fifth frame,** Eve is shown climbing out of Adam's side (a metaphorical representation of her being created from Adam's rib). Notice how bulky her body is—Michelangelo never could bring himself to depict women as they really are (softer and more rounded); instead, he gave women all the well-developed and articulated muscles that were part of his ideal (male) anatomy. The **sixth frame** is the Original Sin, in which Adam and Eve give into their temptation to eat of the forbidden fruit in the Garden of Eden and subsequently fall from grace. Notice how the serpent in the tree, offering the fruit to the couple, has breasts. Is Michelangelo saying that women are evil temptresses? Most historians concur that the artist was a bit of a misogynist.

In the seventh, eight, and ninth frames, we leave Adam and Eve behind and enter the life of Noah. The **seventh frame** is the Sacrifice of Noah; the **eighth frame** is the flood and Noah's ark; and the **ninth frame** is the Drunkenness of Noah. In this final scene, the Biblical patriarch is shown passed out and naked on the ground in front of a huge vat of wine, while his three sons (also naked, probably also drunk) confusedly go about covering him with strips of cloth.

The Prophets & Sibyls

Between the main ceiling and the chapel walls, the ethereal feel and delicate coloration of the Creation, Adam and Eve, and Noah frescoes is countered by massive, sculptural-looking Hebrew **prophets** and pagan **sibyls,** whose arbitrary poses and bodily bulk are typical of Michelangelo's habit of exploring and exalting the masculine form even when his figures were female.

The Last Judgment

On the altar wall, the swirling *Last Judgment* (1535–41) is much more fire-and-brimstone than his earlier work on the ceiling, reflecting the anger and disappointment of Michelangelo's later years. Against a field of electric blue (a pigment created from lapis lazuli dust), a muscle-bound and clean-shaven Christ sends the damned to hell with his right hand, following them with his gaze until they reach wild-eyed and oar-brandishing Charon, whose overcrowded ferry across the river Styx is losing passengers to tentacled demons. On the right half of the fresco, Christ's downturned left palm draws the blessed to the heavens with little fanfare. The *Last Judgment* is a crowded fresco, and it's full of fascinating details; just above the door where visitors enter the chapel, look for the frantic figure whose genitals are being bitten off by an angry snake. This is a portrait of Biagio da Cesena, a contemporary of Michelangelo's who complained that all the nudity in the Sistine Chapel frescoes was filthy and lewd and insisted that the naked figures be covered. Michelangelo eventually got so fed up with Biagio's complaints that he painted him into the lower right hand corner of the *Last Judgment* (in the cave of hell) and covered up Biagio's "filthy" naked parts with the biting mouth of a snake! Later, an artist named Daniele Da Volterra was hired to paint over all of Michelangelo's exposed genitalia with breechcloths; however, when the restoration of the frescoes was carried out in the 1980s, most of Da Volterra's breechcloths washed right off, since they were only superficially applied to the wall, not redone in fresco.

Tip: When you are finished getting a neckache at the Sistine Chapel, you can exit

The Fresco Technique

To create the highly durable "fresco" paintings in the Sistine Chapel (and much of Italy), artists began by applying a fresh (fresco) layer of wet plaster to the wall or ceiling they needed to decorate. While the plaster was still wet, they mixed their required pigments with limewater and applied the color to the wall or ceiling surface. Lime plaster took about a day to dry, so the artists had to apply fresh plaster every morning to the areas of their fresco that they hoped to complete that day. Each plaster patch in a fresco is called a *giornata,* because it took a "day" of work. There are 450 *giornate* in Michelangelo's *Last Judgment.*

the Vatican Museums via the right rear door (the one marked GROUPS WITH GUIDE ONLY) of the Sistine Chapel to go straight to St. Peter's. The remaining sections of the museum beyond the left door are not nearly as interesting as the sections you will have walked through to get to the Sistine Chapel. Exit the chapel via the left door *only* if you have rented a Vatican Museums audioguide, which must be returned at the museum entrance, which is about a 15-minute walk in the opposite direction of St. Peter's. *Città del Vaticano.* ☎ *06/6988-3333. http://mv. vatican.va. Admission 12€, 8€ students; free (and ridiculously crowded) on last Sun of month. March–Oct Mon–Fri 8:45am–4:45pm, Sat 8:45am–2:45pm; Nov–Feb Mon–Sat 8:45am–1:45pm; last Sun of month 8:45am–1:45pm. From Christmas to Epiphany Sunday (early Jan), hours are as from March–Oct; on Sat that fall around holidays or holiday weekends, the museums are open until 4:45pm. (For the exact schedule, which changes slightly from year to year, check the museums' website.) Last* admission 1 hr 25 min before closing. Closed Jan 1, 6; Feb 11; Mar 19; Easter and Easter Monday; May 1; Ascension Thursday; Corpus Christi Day; June 29; Aug 15–16; Nov 1; Dec 8; Dec 25, 26. Metro: Ottaviano.

VATICAN CITY FAQ

○ **Is the Vatican its own country?** Yes. For hundreds of years, the Rome-based popes held sway over most of the city-states that we know as Italy today. When Italy became a single, unified country in 1870, however, the Church lost its power over the peninsula. In 1929, the papal secretary and Prime Minister Benito Mussolini signed the Lateran Treaty, which created the 0.44 sq. km (¹/₄ sq. mile) sovereign state of Vatican City, representing a significant concession on the part of the Church. The Vatican did get its own postage stamps and license plates out of the deal—they're imprinted with the letters "SCV," for *Stato della Città del Vaticano.*

○ **How many people live in Vatican City?** Approximately 500 people, including the 120-member Swiss Guard, plus priests and nuns, and the pope and his household staff, are Vatican citizens, but only about 250 people live here full-time. The men and women who work at the Vatican Museums are Italian citizens who live in Rome and commute to the Vatican every day.

○ **Where exactly does the pope live?** The blocky, gray-stone building above the north side of St. Peter's Square is called the Apostolic Palace. Within the palace are the Papal Apartments, which are the pope's actual living quarters. When the pope greets the public from the Apostolic Palace (as he does on Sundays at noon to deliver the *Angelus* blessing), it's from the third window from the right, on the second-highest floor.

ROME & LAZIO

○ **Will I see the pope?** On an average day at the Vatican, visitors will not catch sight of the pope. If you show up outside St. Peter's at noon on a Sunday, you can see Pope Benedict XVI give the *Angelus* blessing from his apartment window overlooking the piazza. Smaller **papal audiences** are held on Wednesday mornings in St. Peter's Square or the modern auditorium just to the south. Don't expect to have any meaningful one-on-one time with the pontiff, however—the gathering is slightly more intimate than a high school graduation ceremony. For tickets, contact the **Prefettura della Casa Pontifica** (☎ **06/698-83-017;** fax 06/698-85-863) several weeks in advance. (In a pinch, you can sometimes gain last-minute admission on Tues afternoon by inquiring with the Swiss Guard at the Portone di Bronzo—the big bronze door—located in the colonnade to the right of St. Peter's Basilica.) Throughout the year, there are always plenty of pope-led special services for Catholic holidays, beatifications, and such, for which pilgrims always turn out in aggressive droves. For the wretched masses who didn't wake up at 5am to gain a spot close to the action, Vatican TV broadcasts everything on Jumbotrons in front of St. Peter's.

Museums & Galleries

➔ **ACEA–Centrale Montemartini** ★★ OSTIENSE Major cool points for this unique museum, which looks like a scene out of some as-yet unmade movie about Venus and Mars getting it on in the boiler room. The blackish-blue, heavy metal innards—industrial pipes, primitive turbines, gigantic bolts, and defunct machines—of this decommissioned electricity plant make an unexpected but totally sexy backdrop to white marble statues of gods and goddesses, the leftovers from the Capitoline Museums' vast collection of ancient sculpture. The power station, which stopped generating electricity in the 1960s, has a wonderfully retro machine-age look to it, like depictions of "the future" in old movies—ominous-looking levers and cranks and control panels with mystifying buttons throughout—except that it's populated by an unlikely crew of toga-wearing (or buck-naked) transplants from 2,000 years ago. The juxtaposition of these luminous marble figures, who've unwittingly been catapulted ahead several millennia, out of their opulent ancient environs and into a cold room filled with imposing and unfamiliar machinery, is aesthetic genius. Because the Capitoline Museums' cache of sculpture is so immense, even the 400 or so "second-tier" works of art displayed here are masterpieces. Above the *Sala Caldaie* (Boiler Room), there's a nice cafe/bookshop where you can hang out, overlooking the century-old furnaces and ancient torsos of Apollo. *Via Ostiense 106, near Piazza del Gazometro.* ☎ *06/574-8030. www.centrale montemartini.org. Admission: 4.50€. Tues–Sun 9:30am–7pm. Metro: Piramide. Bus: 23 or 271.*

MTV **Best** ➔ **Capitoline Museums** ★★★ ANCIENT ROME Atop ancient Rome's citadel hill, the Campidoglio, the Michelangelo-designed halls of the Capitoline Museums are home to some of the most important sculptures in the world. In terms of sheer quantity, the collection is second only to the Vatican Museums, but in terms of personality, the Capitoline wins hands down. Start your visit in the Palazzo Nuovo (on the east side of the square). In the courtyard, you'll find the reclining statue of **Marforio,** believed to be a river god, since all water gods are represented lying down in classical statuary. Behind a protective glass wall to the right is the star piece of the entire museum, the nearly perfectly preserved bronze **equestrian statue of Marcus Aurelius** ★★★ (ca. A.D.180). Unfortunately, the glass prohibits a great view of the work, but if you compare it to the copy out in the middle of Piazza del Campidoglio, you'll see that the original is a stronger, more convincing of imperial *gravitas*. The only reason this magnificent bronze survives today is because someone in the medieval period mistakenly identified it as Constantine on horseback. Constantine was the emperor who legalized Christianity, so the Church actually went out of its way to protect and conserve the statue. When they finally realized who it was—the philosopher-emperor Marcus Aurelius (recognizable by his curly 2nd-century-A.D. hairdo, a far cry from Constantine's severe, helmet-head look)—they were past the point where melting down antiquities was acceptable.

Inside the Palazzo Nuovo, the **Dying Gaul** ★★ (Gaul = Frenchman) is one of the more celebrated marble sculptures in the collection. Wincing in pain from his mortal wounds, trying to prop his body up, the 1970s-moustached Gaul looks like a bad guy who got jacked by Starsky and Hutch and woke up in an alley somewhere. In the **Hall of Emperors** ★ (also in the Palazzo Nuovo), you'll meet with the unnervingly lifelike stares of several centuries' worth of imperial busts. In Roman art, portraiture tended to be realistic (as opposed to idealistic), so the faces are intensely communicative and personal—if a guy had a bulbous nose in real life, it was depicted as such in art; if he had big ears (as Claudius did), that was shown, too.

Throughout the halls of the Palazzo Nuovo, there are drunk satyrs and smirking fauns to keep you company, which is especially fun in winter, when the museums are deserted. Across the piazza, the Palazzo dei Conservatori houses the 5th-century- B.C. bronze **Capitoline She-Wolf** ★★, mascot of Rome, with babies Romulus and Remus suckling at her breasts, in Room 4. In the courtyard, you'll discover the photogenic fragments of the **colossal statue of Constantine** ★. The gigantic marble foot and pointing hand are the subject of many a Roman postcard. The rest of the Palazzo dei Conservatori is a *pinacoteca* (picture gallery), with the occasional ancient Roman, Renaissance, or baroque sculpture thrown in to keep it interesting. The *pinacoteca* has a number of fine works by Caravaggio (his strangely naked and youthful *John the Baptist*), Titian, Tintoretto, and Guido Reni. Do not leave the Capitoline Museums without going downstairs to the ponderous tufa corridors of the **tabularium** ★★. This was the ancient Roman archive hall (78 B.C.) and today it sits underneath Palazzo Senatorio (the bell-towered building on Piazza Campidoglio), modern-day city hall. The tabularium is in remarkably good condition, considering its age and all the weight it bears; nowadays it's used to connect the two wings of the museums and offers stupendous views over the Forum, immediately below. *Piazza del Campidoglio.* ☎ *06/671-02-071. www.museicapitolini.org. Admission: 7.80€. Tues–Sun 9am–7pm; public holidays 9am–1pm. Closed Jan 1, May 1, and Dec 25. Bus: 30, 40, 46, 62, 64, 70, 87, 170, or H.*

📺 Best → **Galleria Borghese** ★★★
VILLA BORGHESE   Immensely entertaining and mercifully manageable in size, the collection at this 17th-century garden estate is museum perfection. Ancient Roman **mosaics** ★★ in the entrance salon depict gory scenes between gladiators and wild animals (dripping guts is a recurrent theme). In Room 1, Canova's risque **Pauline Bonaparte** ★ (1805–08) lies, topless, on an inviting marble divan. Bernini's staggeringly skillful sculptures of **David** ★★, **Apollo and Daphne** ★★★, and **Rape of Persephone** ★★ (1621–24), in rooms 2 to 4, are so emotionally charged as to elicit sympathy, and so realistically rendered that their subjects seem to be breathing. In the Apollo and Daphne especially, which represents a maiden fleeing the amorous pursuits of Apollo the only way she knows how—by turning herself into a tree—the bark, roots, and leaves that attend her transformation are stunningly delicate, while the overall composition is deeply melancholy.

The paintings by Caravaggio in Room 8 range in tone from luscious (***Boy with a Basket of Fruit***, 1594) to disconcerting (***Sick Bacchus*** ★★, a self-portrait, 1593) to strident and grisly (***David and Goliath*** ★, 1610). Renaissance masterpieces like Raphael's *Deposition* (1507) and Titian's **Sacred and Profane Love** ★★ (1514) hang casually upstairs in the *pinacoteca,* as well a bit of 16th-century soft porn in Correggio's ***Danäe*** ★★ (1531). In the *Danäe,* Cupid peels back a bed sheet to reveal the shy maiden's porcelain flesh, while Jupiter, disguised as a "golden shower" overhead, peeps at Danäe's spreading legs. Steamy! The museum's strict reservations policy keeps crowds to a blessed minimum; be sure to book at least a few days in advance. *Villa Borghese, Piazzale Scipione Borghese 5, near Via Pinciana.* ☎ *06/32810. www.galleriaborghese.it. Admission: 12.50€ (reservation fee additional 2€); guided tour 5€€. Tues–Sun 9am–7pm. Closed public holidays. Reservations required; try to book 1 week in advance. Bus: 52, 53, 116, or 910 to Via Pinciana. Tram: 3 or 19 to Viale delle Belle Arti.*

→ **Museo della Civiltà Romana** ★★ EUR Few tourists make it down to the fascist-era suburb/office-park of EUR, but those who do are usually headed to the field-trip-favorite Museum of Roman Civilization, which has small-scale and full-scale models of the most famous ancient Roman buildings and monuments. The exhibits are dated and dusty but illuminating nonetheless, since they show a complete picture of structures, like the Theater of Marcellus, that are now only half intact in real life. The highlight of the museum is the truly gigantic (and phenomenally impressive) 1:250 scale **model of ancient Rome** ★★★ as it looked in the 4th century A.D. The model was made in the fascist period and takes up an entire, vast room with 10m-high (33-ft.) ceilings. You could spend hours inching along the catwalks above the model, peering at the hundreds of temples, baths,

gardens, palaces, and aqueducts. The miniature Circus Maximus alone is over 2m long (6¹/₂ ft.). *Piazza Giovanni Agnelli 10, off Via Cristoforo Colombo.* ☎ *06/592-60-41. Tues–Sat 9am–7pm; Sun 9am–1pm. Admission: 6.20€. Metro: EUR Palasport or EUR Fermi.*

→ **Museo Nazionale Romano** ★ TERMINI If you've got some time to kill before you need to catch a train, this bright and airy palazzo right across the street from Termini has an embarrassment of ancient riches, including Roman paintings, mosaics, statues, and inscriptions. Frescoes teeming with delightful animal and vegetable motifs, rescued from the bedrooms and dining rooms of Roman villas, are the highlight here, and totally unique among Rome's museums. The National Roman Museum's mind-boggling collection of Etruscan and Roman artifacts, including stone inscriptions, vase fragments, everyday tools, marble busts, frescoes, and mosaics, is so vast, it's housed in four separate buildings: Palazzo Massimo alle Terme (Largo di Villa Peretti 1; metro: Termini); Palazzo Altemps (Piazza San Apollinare 44; buses to Piazza Navona); Baths of Diocletian (Viale Enrico de Nicola 79; metro: Repubblica); and Crypta Balbi (Via delle Botteghe Oscure 31; buses to Largo Argentina). ☎ *06/399-67-700. Admission 6€. Tues–Sun 9am–7pm.*

→ **National Etruscan Museum at Villa Giulia** ★★ VILLA BORGHESE One of Rome's lovelier and more undervisited museums, Pope Julius III's gorgeous Mannerist villa houses priceless Etruscan artifacts, including intricate gold jewelry and a charming his-and-hers sarcophagus, from the civilization that ruled Italy before the Romans. Near the end of the itinerary that the museum has set for visitors to follow, look out for the cases of jewelry, where pins and necklaces are decorated with miniscule animals rendered in tiny granules of gold—that this level of intricate detail was possible

2,500 years ago, and that it still exists, is astonishing. *Piazzale di Villa Giulia 9, at Viale delle Belle Arti.* ☎ *06/322-6571. Admission 4€. Tues–Sat 9am–7pm; Sun 9am–1pm. Bus: 52, 490, or 495. Tram: 2, 3, or 19.*

Churches

Rome is a minefield of churches. They're freakin' everywhere. Duck into any of Rome's countless houses of God, and you're likely to stumble upon a painting by Caravaggio, a sculpture by Bernini, ancient mosaics, or best of all, a saint's decaying body part! All of Rome's churches are free to enter (though some charge you a few euros to visit a subterranean level), so take advantage of their cool interiors in summer.

→ **Crypt of the Capuchin Monks** ★★★
VENETO   Macabre yet oddly pleasing, this must-see church crypt is decorated with the dismantled skeletons of thousands of monks. Delicate ribs are arranged in frou-frou curlicues on the walls, while clunkier femurs are stacked like firewood on the floor. Each chapel is a bizarre diorama where propped-up monks, still in their desiccated skin and cassocks, strike cautionary poses. It's really quite creative—shoulder blades are angels' wings; inverted pelvises form the shape of hourglass, indicating our time is running out, etc. At the very end of the crypt, there's a Grim Reaper made of bones on the vault overhead, and an uplifting plaque that reads: "What you are, we used to be; what we are, you will be." *Attached to the church of Santa Maria della Concezione. Via Veneto 27, at Via San Nicola da Tolentino.* ☎ *06/488-27-48. 1€–2€ donation expected. Daily 7am–noon and 3:45–7:30pm; crypt Fri–Wed 9am–noon and 3–6pm. Metro: Barberini. Bus: 52, 53, 62, 80, 95, 116, 175, or 492.*

→ **Basilica San Clemente** ★★ ANCIENT ROME/SAN GIOVANNI   This "lasagna of churches" (so-called because of its many

layers, each deliciously interesting!) is the best place in Rome to understand the city's archaeological evolution. The ground-level chapels aren't particularly exciting (even though they're about 800 years old); the excavations (scavi) underneath the church are what's so fascinating about San Clemente. Descend 18m (59 ft.) through medieval and paleo-Christian layers to the lowest level, where adherents of the ancient cult of Mithras met and performed grisly rituals and sacrifices in the long, rectangular *mithraeum* (where the followers of the cult gathered). Adding to the ancient mystique, there's a haunting drip-drip-drip of an underground river that echoes throughout the subterranean corridors. *Via di San Giovanni in Laterano, at Piazzale San Clemente.* ☎ *06/ 704-51-018. Admission to church free; 3€ for excavations. Mon–Sat 9am–12:30pm and 3:30–6:30pm (until 6pm Oct–March); Sun 10am–12:30pm and 3:30–6:30pm. Metro: Colosseo. Bus: 85, 87, 117, or 571. Tram: 3.*

FREE → **San Giovanni in Laterano** ★
SAN GIOVANNI   The cathedral of Rome and mother church of the world is not St. Peter's in the Vatican, but this church dedicated to St. John. The spare, slightly grave interior is by Borromini (1646); the façade, with its chorus line of saints, dates from 1735. In a separate building across the piazza are the Scala Santa (holy stairs) and the Sancta Sanctorum ("holy of holies"), boasting rare 13th-century frescoes by Cimabue and relics of furniture allegedly from the Last Supper. Lateran Palace was the HQ of the Catholic Church until early 20th century (when the city/state of Vatican City was created in 1929). *Piazza di San Giovanni in Laterano 4.* ☎ *06/77-20-79-91. Free admission to church; 2€ for cloister. Daily 7am–7pm, until 6pm Oct–March. Metro: San Giovanni. Bus: 85, 87, 117, or 571. Tram: 3.*

FREE → **San Pietro in Vincoli** ★
ANCIENT ROME   Lots of tourists and art

history students are drawn to this church just above the Forum to see Michelangelo's **Moses** ★, which is part of the unfinished tomb of Pope Julius II, located here. The stern *Moses* is well worth seeing, but as Michelangelos go, the Sistine Chapel, the *Pietà* (in St. Peter's), and the *David* (in Florence) are all much more impressive. (Interesting factoid: In sculpture and painting, Moses is almost always depicted with horns; this is due to a misreading of a Latin translation of the Old Testament, in which Moses is described as having a "crown of light" *[corona]* on his head—someone read it as *corna* ["horns"], and the rest is art history.) The church also contains a glass reliquary case with two sets of shackles (hence the name of the church, "St. Peter in Chains"), which supposedly bound St. Peter when he was held captive in Jerusalem and when he was an inmate in the Mamertine Prison in Rome. According to legend, Pope Leo I was examining the two sets of chains one day in the 5th century A.D. when the chains miraculously welded themselves together. *Piazza di San Pietro in Vincoli 4A, off Via Cavour.* ☎ *06/488-28-65. Free admission. Daily 7am–12:30pm and 3:30–7pm (until 6pm Oct–March). Metro: Colosseo. Bus: 60, 75, 84, 85, 87, 117, 175, or 571.*

FREE → **Santa Cecilia** ★ TRASTEVERE This incredibly peaceful basilica—an 18th-century reworking of a medieval church—is dedicated to the patron saint of music, who was martyred here in the 3rd century A.D. Inside, altar mosaics dazzle, and fragments of Pietro Cavallini's wonderful 13th-century fresco of the *Last Judgment* can be seen at limited times. Cecilia was exhumed from her tomb in the crypt here in 1599, long enough for Stefano Maderno to sculpt the lovely (but disturbing—her throat is slashed) statue of the saint's still-uncorrupted body below the altar. The church is one of the most popular in Rome for weddings, as evidenced by

omnipresent grains of rice on the ground near the front door. *Piazza Santa Cecilia, off Via di Santa Cecilia.* ☎ *06/581-90-20. Free admission. Daily 7:30am–noon and 4–7pm. Bus: 23, 280, or 780. Tram: 8.*

FREE → **Santa Croce in Gerusalemme** ★★ SAN GIOVANNI/ESQUILINO It's a bit out of the way, but if you make the trip to this church ("Holy Cross in Jerusalem"), you'll be rewarded with some big-time relics which are supposed to be from the actual Passion of the Christ—three pieces of the True Cross, a nail, and two thorns from the Crown of Thorns are kept in a display case in a chapel to the left of the altar. Also be on the lookout for a finger, said to be the very one doubting St. Thomas stuck into Christ's wound. The relics aren't huge or very recognizable, but it's still pretty cool. (As you enter the super-holy reliquary in the back, you'll see a big piece of old-looking wood mounted on the gray marble wall—don't get too excited, this is a piece of the Good Thief's cross, not Christ's.) You can't take pictures in Santa Croce, but the sacristy gift shop has postcards of all the relics. *Piazza di Santa Croce in Gerusalemme 12.* ☎ *06/701-47-69. www.basilicasantacroce.it. Free admission. Daily 6am–12:30pm and 3:30–7pm. Metro: Vittorio. Bus: 649. Tram: 3.*

FREE → **Santa Maria della Vittoria** ★ QUIRINALE/TERMINI The poor sacristan who runs this church is always in a bad mood, and it's no wonder: No one comes to his church to pray. Instead, they come to be voyeurs of Gianlorenzo Bernini's super-risqué **Ecstasy of St. Teresa** ★★ (1647–52; in the Cornaro Chapel, to the left of the altar). The marble sculpture shows the mystical saint clutching her breast, parting her lips, and rolling her eyes back into her head in a moment of "spiritual rapture" that looks for all the world like another kind of climax. (Bernini was known for being a ladies' man, and this facial expression is proof that he was well versed in the body language of love!) From their "box seat" to the side, the animated Cornaro family members react to the ambiguously scandalous spectacle. For the record, St. Teresa recounted her religious ecstasy thus: "In (the angel's) hands I saw a great golden spear, and at the iron tip there appeared to be a point of fire. This he plunged into my heart several times so that it penetrated my entrails. When he pulled it out I felt that he took them with it, and left me utterly consumed by the great love of God. The pain was so severe that it made me utter several moans. The sweetness caused by this intense pain is so extreme that one can not possibly wish it to cease. . . ." To quote *When Harry Met Sally,* I'll have what she's having. *Via XX Settembre 17, at Largo Santa Susanna.* ☎ *06/482-61-90. Free admission. Daily 6:30am–noon and 4:30–6pm. Metro: Repubblica. Bus: 60, 62, or 492.*

FREE → **Santa Maria in Trastevere** ★★
TRASTEVERE   The first church in Rome dedicated to the Virgin Mary is spectacular inside and out, with a landmark Romanesque brick bell tower, colorful frescoes, mosaics, and loads of recycled ancient marbles. The basilica was built in the 4th century A.D. on the site of a *taberna meritoria,* a kind of VFW predecessor where ancient Roman veterans of foreign wars could come, drink, and regale each other with stories from the front lines of battle against Goths and Huns. Santa Maria in Trastevere is best visited just after Mass has let out (usually 6:15pm on weeknights), when the basilica is still fragrant with incense. The eponymous square in front of the church acts as a kind of common living room for the neighborhood—it seems that every resident of Trastevere crosses the wide expanse of cobblestones here at some point or another during the day. *Piazza Santa Maria in Trastevere.* ☎ *06/581-94-43. Free admission. Bus: 23, 271, 280, or 780. Tram: 8.*

FREE → **Santa Maria Maggiore** ★★
TERMINI/ESQUILINO   In this perfect example of the prototypical basilica, the main nave, flanked by two lower and narrower side aisles, terminates in a curved apse, which is decorated with dazzling polychrome and gold mosaics. Near the right side of the main altar, a modest marble slab marks the tomb of baroque superstar Gian Lorenzo Bernini; the epitaph, inlaid in bronze, is a pithy summary of his life: "He decorated the city." Santa Maria Maggiore is one of Rome's four patriarchal basilicas. *Piazza di Santa Maria Maggiore.* ☎ *06/48-31-95. Daily 7am–7pm (last admission 15 min. before closing). Free admission. Metro: Termini or Cavour. Bus: 70.*

FREE → **Santa Maria Sopra Minerva** ★★ PANTHEON   The only Gothic church in the city is a soothing contrast to the sometimes gaudy baroque interiors of many Roman churches. Blue, peaked vaults awash in a starry sky motif, the tombs of St. Catherine of Siena and Fra Angelico, and a bad Michelangelo. Pointy medieval arches—meant to emphasize heaven—create soaring vaults. To the right of the main altar is Michelangelo's underwhelming *Christ Carrying the Cross* (1514–20); the ridiculously prudish golden loincloth was added later. *Piazza della Minerva 42.* ☎ *06/679-39-26. Free admission. Daily 7am–noon and 4–7pm. Cloister Mon–Sat 8:30am–1pm and 4–7pm. Bus: 30, 40, 46, 62, 64, 70, 81, 87, 116, 492, or 571.*

FREE → **Santo Stefano Rotondo** ★★
SAN GIOVANNI/COLOSSEUM   Worth the trek to this rustic piazzetta on the Celio is this intensely atmospheric church. The cute old sacristan who will tell you everything there is to know about the church if you have 8 hours to spare. The whole place has a railway roundhouse feel to it, with the added plus of R-rated frescoes of the Greatest Hits of Christian martyrdoms. *Via di Santo Stefano Rotondo 7, at Via della Navicella.* ☎ *06/421-191. Free admission.*

What to Do When It's Raining in Rome

The typical Roman weather forecast includes abundant sunshine and blue skies, which is great, because Rome is all about wandering around and stopping at open-air sights. But believe it or not, Rome gets more annual rainfall than London. Certain months are rainy (March is often 31 straight days of drizzle), and on many a summer afternoon, the skies open up and pound the city with a clamorous thunderstorm. On wet days, it can suck to be a tourist, but it can also be a lot of fun. Heavy rain sends wimpier tourists running for cover in their hotels and tour buses, leaving normally thronged sights like the Trevi Fountain and Colosseum deserted. Just accept that you're going to get soaked (great stress relief, as long as it's not too cold), and you'll have Rome's greatest monuments to yourself. Except one: the Pantheon. When it rains, crowds rush to the 1,900 year-old temple for good reason—the 9m-wide (30-ft.) hole in the dome of the Pantheon is open to the sky, so it becomes a giant shower during a downpour. (In a light drizzle, the effect is not nearly as impressive; wait for a really big storm.) The Vatican is another good rainy day activity, although thousands of other tourists will have the same idea. Alternatively, hop on one of the more scenic public transportation lines, like bus 95, bus 175, or tram 3, and ride back and forth until the sun comes back out.

Tues–Sat 9am–1pm year-round; Nov–Mar Mon–Sat 2pm–4pm, Apr–Oct Mon–Sat 3:30–6pm. Bus: 81.

→ **Scala Santa and Sancta Sanctorum** ★ SAN GIOVANNI   Taken from Jerusalem in the 4th century, the Holy Stairs (Scala Santa) are climbed by good pilgrims on their knees. At the top, the "Holy of Holies" has a bench that is said to be from the Last Supper and Cimabue frescoes. *Piazza di San Giovanni in Laterano 14. ☎ 06/70-49-44-89. Free admission for Scala Santa; 3€ for Sancta Sanctorum. Daily 6:30–11:50am and 3:30–6:45pm. Metro: San Giovanni. Bus: 85, 87, or 571. Tram: 3.*

Playing Outside

Parks

Believe it or not, Rome has more trees and parkland per square kilometer than any other large city in Europe. The most central and most used park in the city is the **Villa Borghese** ★★ (www.villaborghese.it; metro: Spagna or Flaminio; bus: 52, 53, 116, 490, or 910; tram: 3 or 19), which extends over 80 hectares (198 acres) of groomed green hills in the northeast part of the *centro*. Villa Borghese has lawns with spots of sun or shade where you can hang out and read, picnic, make out, etc., and paved paths where you can go

for a nice jog. There's also a little lake where you can rent a rowboat, and kiosk throughout the park where you can rent inline skates and bikes. The view over the city from the Pincio terrace, on the western edge of the park, is one of the best in Rome. Clear across town, just west of the Gianicolo hill and Trastevere, the **Villa Doria Pamphilj** ★★ (bus: 44, 75, or 870) is the largest park in Rome, with vast regions that border on wilderness. In the more frequented parts of the park, there are jogging paths, soccer fields, a 17th-century villa, and a turtle pond. Villa Pamphilj is the park you should use if you're planning on doing a full Renaissance-style picnic spread with wine. Open containers aren't technically allowed in Villa Pamphilj (neither is lying out in a bathing suit), but the mounted cops who patrol the park won't hassle you as long as you're not bothering anyone. Back in the centro, the **Villa Celimontana** (south of the Colosseum; metro: Colosseo; bus: 60, 75, 81, or 175; tram: 3) is smaller but lovely, with paved paths, fragrant gardens, and pretty views.

Biking

If you're going to ride a bike around Rome, stick to the peaceful confines of the Villa Borghese, or only ride on Sundays, when traffic is light in the *centro*. Otherwise, biking in Rome can be very stressful. On the other hand, it can be really enjoyable if you have a guide to lead the way through the traffic. **Enjoy Rome** (Via Marghera 8/a; ☎ **06/445-1843;** www.enjoyrome.com) runs a 3¹/₂-hour **bike tour** several days per week from March to November. The tours take you to the Villa Borghese, Piazza Del Popolo, the Mausoleum of Augustus, the Spanish Steps, Piazza Venezia, the Mouth of Truth, the Circus Maximus, and the Colosseum. The tours cost 20€ for riders aged 26 and under; it's 25€ for people over 26. Tours are suspended during rainy weather; call the office for schedule details.

Boating

Rome's riverboat service, the **Battelli di Roma,** stops in the *centro storico* under Ponte Cestio, Ponte Sisto, and Ponte Sant' Angelo and travels north to the **Foro Italico** (which we highly recommend; see p. 175). The view is not always scenic (unless you consider half-submerged Vespas and nutrias "scenic"), but your feet will welcome the alternative means of locomotion. As the riverside vegetation thickens at the northern end of the run, toward the Foro Italico, you can almost picture Romulus and Remus floating down here in their basket 2,800 years ago. ☎ **06/693-80-264.** www.battellidiroma.it. Tickets 1€ (shuttle service); 10€–50€_ guided, wine-tasting, or dinner cruises).

ROME & LAZIO

Born to Run

If you're obsessed with running and don't mind inhaling all the toxic fumes that the vehicles of Rome emit, there are a number of places you can go for a jog:

➤ **Villa Borghese** This is the no-brainer choice. The park is filled with wide, paved paths that alternate between shade and sun. Piazza di Siena, in the southern part of Villa Borghese, is a tree-lined dirt track where tons of fashionable Romans love to work out.

➤ **Villa Pamphilj** This huge park above Trastevere is a good option for runners who like hilly terrain and mix of groomed and dirt trails. Just don't venture into the more heavily wooded areas, as that's where the pervs tend to hang out.

➤ **Circus Maximus** Make like an ancient chariot racer and gallop your little heart out under the blistering Roman sun. There's no shade here, and you'll have to watch out for broken bottles and dog poop, but the setting is gloriously historic. One lap is about 1 km (a little over half a mile). Just south of here, the shady green belt along Viale delle Terme di Caracalla draws a fair number of serious Roman runners.

Roma & Lazio Soccer Games

The Most Fun You Can Have on a Sunday in Italy

To experience Roman culture at its most fervent, don't go to Mass—go to a
MTV Best soccer game ★★★. Full of pageantry, dramatic tension, and raw
emotion, the home games of **AS Roma** (www.asromacalcio.it) and **SS Lazio**
(www.sslazio.it), the city's two Serie A (Italian premier league) teams, can be
far more spectacular than any fancy theater event, and certainly more interactive (when was the last time you got beaned in the head by a sandwich,
thrown by an irate fan, at *La Boheme*?) *Romanisti* far outnumber *laziali*, but
both fan bases pack the Stadio Olimpico, coloring the stands with the red and
yellow of Roma or the light blue and white of Lazio, every weekend from
September to June. If you go to a game, invest in a team scarf (sold at concession stands outside the stadium), and learn a few stadium choruses both
teams have a few easy ones set to the tune of "The Entertainer" and the
march from *Aida*. Alcohol is not a part of stadium culture, but pyrotechnics
are. To get mad props from the locals, stop by **Porta Portese** (see "Shopping," p. 202) before the game and pick up some colored smoke bombs
(fumogeni) or firecrackers *(petardi)* to set off outside the stadium. Before
games involving heated rivalries, such as the unbelievably intense Roma-Lazio
derby that takes place twice a year, expect tear gas; other than that, the stadium is safe. The cheapest section, the Curva (behind the goalposts), is where
all the hardcore fans go (the *romanisti* in the Curva Sud stand up during the
whole game); the Tribuna Tevere Laterale or Distinti sections are a good compromise if you want to see more of the game and not be bear-hugged by ran-
doms when the home team scores.

All games are played at the **Stadio Olimpico,** Foro Italico, Viale dello Stadio
Olimpico (☎ 06/323-73-33 ticket office; bus: 32, 271, or 280; tram: 2). Tickets
go on sale exactly 7 days before game time and can be purchased at the
Stadio Olimpico—on game day only, from the box office or *bagherini*
(scalpers); or at *tabacchi* stores displaying the "Lottomatica" logo. For Roma
games, you can buy tickets at the official **AS Roma store** at Via Colonna 360
(☎ 06/678-65-14). For Lazio games, tickets are available at **Lazio Point** on
Via Farini 34 (☎ 06/482-67-68). Tickets are 15€–90€ (no credit cards).

Shopping

The **Spanish Steps** area (Via Condotti and
the web of streets leading off Piazza di
Spagna) is where all the fancy, big-name label
stuff is—Gucci, Prada, *yadda yadda yadda*—
but chances are you didn't budget a 750€ pair
of boots into the ol' travel finances. The good
news is, you can also get some real shopping
done in Rome, but you do need to know
where to go. The tiny side streets off Campo
de' Fiori, including **Via dei Giubbonari** and
Via dei Baullari, have a high concentration

of independent boutiques for young and hip
urbanites, as well as a few hole-in-the-wall
places selling trendy belts and accessories
for 5€ or so.

Via del Governo Vecchio, to the west of
Piazza Navona, has more of the same,
although some shops there skew older, more
bohemian, and more expensive. Just south of
the Vatican, **Via Cola di Rienzo** is one of
the Romans' favorite all-purpose shopping
streets, with a wide array of chain boutiques

for both sexes and all price ranges. The classic retail street in Rome, **Via del Corso,** is a chaotic strip of young Romans on parade. All of Via del Corso is lined with shops, but the northern half, from Via del Tritone to Piazza del Popolo, is where most of the action is, with stores like Miss Sixty and tons of kids hanging out on their *motorini.* The scene on Via del Corso—especially on weekends—is worth experiencing at least once, but the boutiques there are often too crowded with idle browsers to get any really good shopping done.

Halfway down Via del Corso (opposite Piazza Colonna) is the **Galleria Colonna mall** (aka Galleria Alberto Sordi)—it's not very big, and the stores are nothing you couldn't find elsewhere in town, but its covered halls make it the only place in Rome where you can comfortably do retail damage during a downpour. Finally, as a last resort, you can also head to **Via Nazionale.** One of central Rome's grimier thoroughfares, Via Nazionale has most of the mass-market chain boutiques, plus some good cheap shoe stores, and an excellent dress shop, L.E.I., listed below.

Clothes, Shoes & Accessories

➜ **Energie** ★ Supplying trendy teens and 20-somethings with flashy sportswear, jeans, shoes, and bags with a surf-y, resort-y feel, this techno-blaring mainstay on the upper half of Via del Corso is where you need to shop—over and over—if you're young and hoping to fit in with Rome's cool kids. *Via del Corso 408–409.* ☎ *06/687-1258.*

➜ **Ethic** ★★ The boutiques in this local chain are full of vintage-inspired styles and materials that will give you a more "downtown" MaryKate Olsen–type of look while still being practical. Especially good for skirts, wash-and-wear dresses, and knits in chic, jewel-tone colors. *Piazza Benedetto Cairoli 11–12 (at the southern end of Via Giubbonari).* ☎ *06/6830-1063. Other locations at Via del Pantheon*

46–47. ☎ *06/6880-3167; Via del Corso 85,* ☎ *06/3600-2191; and Via Cola di Rienzo 301,* ☎ *06/3974-6045.*

➜ **Fuori Orario** ★★ Home of hot leather jackets (for men and women) at very fair prices. For sexy red leather motorcycle jackets, or funky turquoise leather blazers, or more basic styles in neutral colors, this miniscule corner boutique in the most charming, cobblestoned part of Trastevere can't be beat. *Via del Moro 29 (at Via della Pelliccia).* ☎ *06/581-7181.*

➜ **L.E.I.** ★ Whether you have a spring formal or a fall wedding coming up, L.E.I. has an amazing selection of dresses to choose from (labels include global names like D&G, as well as more under-the-radar, local designers) and a tireless staff that will keep bombarding your dressing room until you find the perfect frock. (If a hem needs to be shortened, or a bodice taken in, you'd be wise to have the alterations job done locally—Italian tailors are fast, inexpensive, and ridiculously talented.) They also sell accessories and shoes to help complete your head-to-toe party look. The goods at L.E.I. are high quality, so don't expect bargain-basement prices, but there's usually something for every price range. The newer location, right near Campo de' Fiori at Via Giubbonari 103 (☎ **06/687-5432**), can be hit-or-miss; the original outlet on ugly Via Nazionale tends to have the better stock. *Via Nazionale 88.* ☎ *06/482-1700. Bus: 40, 60, 64, 70, 170, or H.*

➜ **Martina Novelli** ★★ Chicks with a shoe habit should not miss this tiny shop on Piazza Risorgimento, just outside the Vatican City walls. (On payday in Rome, my friends and I used to make a beeline here.) Some seasons feature stronger collections than others, but when you see the hot and truly unique styles, priced at a fraction of what other designer-ish boutiques are asking, it's hard to walk away without making a purchase. Best of all, the cool, candid chicks who work here are unafraid to share their gut feelings about what looks best on you, so you're sure to end up with a pair you won't regret. *Piazza Risorgimento 38.* ☎ *06/3973-7247. Bus: 23, 81, 271, or 492. Tram: 19. Metro: Ottaviano.*

→ **Pinko** ★★ Ditch the Juicy Couture and upgrade to a more sophisticated and edgy urban look—think Avril Lavigne gets feminine—from this northern Italian women's label. Some of the clothes are definitely more runway than reality, but browse the upstairs racks and you'll find cool dresses, great pants and jackets, and an endless selection of sexy tops. Pinko isn't exactly cheap, but the manufacturing quality is right up there with Stella McCartney and other labels you can't afford. The sales staff, made up of young local men and women, can also be good sources for the Roman club scene, if that's what you're interested in. *Via dei Giubbonari 76–77.* ☎ *06/6830-9446. Bus: 30, 40, 46, 62, 64, 70, 87, 492, or 571. Tram: 8.*

→ **Posto Italiano** ★★ Amid all the narrow shop fronts on busy Via Giubbonari, this store is a must for any guys or girls looking for a cool pair of shoes at a great price (styles you won't find back home start at 69€). The selection is excellent for how tiny the space is—with comfy boots, sexy fuchsia stilettos, and leather sandals, there's not a dorky style in sight. The "Italian Place" is very popular with locals in-the-know, so you'll have to vie for the attention of the salespeople. *Via Giubbonari 37/a.* ☎ *06/686/9373. Bus: 30, 40, 46, 62, 64, 70, 87, 492, or 571. Tram: 8. There a newer branch at Viale Trastevere 111,* ☎ *06/5833-4820. Bus: 23, 280, 780, or H. Tram: 8.*

→ **Prototype** ★ Proof that the sexiness of Italian men can transcend the formal Armani/Versace/etc. gear they're usually associated with, this *hippissimo* (nah, that's not a real word, but it should be) unisex boutique off Campo de' Fiori has racks packed with cool and casual button-down shirts, cargo pants, graphic T-shirts, and a central

table displaying the best sneakers ever designed—Converse All-Stars—in a wide range of colors and prints. *Via Giubbonari 50 (off Campo de' Fiori).* ☎ *06/6830-0330. Bus: 30, 40, 46, 62, 64, 70, 87, 492, or 571. Tram: 8.*

→ **Sole** ★ Belts inspired by papal vestments, mixed-media trench coats, and other edgy stuff only Italian chicks know how to rock—the women's garments and accessories at this friendly little boutique off Campo de' Fiori have tons of attitude. The only downside is that prices are a tad steep—although, considering that Italy is about 1 year ahead of the U.S. when it comes to fashion, your purchase here could be a great cutting-edge investment. Whatever you do, don't let them talk you into buying that leather micromini skirt that deep down you know should only be worn by streetwalkers. *Via dei Baullari 21 (off Campo de' Fiori).* ☎ *06/6880-6987. Bus: 30, 40, 46, 62, 64, 70, 87, 492, or 571. Tram: 8.*

→ **Stefanel** ★★ For Italians, Stefanel functions more or less like Banana Republic does in the U.S.—it may not be the most exciting place to shop, but it's nevertheless their go-to chain store for women's and men's basics (and since this is Italy, these are basics with flair). I can never go shopping in Italy without buying at least something here, like wardrobe-building sweaters in solid colors (with more interesting cuts and knit details than their American counterparts); camisoles and tanks; and blazers and jackets that will give any outfit instant polish. There are dozens of locations in Rome and hundreds more throughout Italy. *Piazza Venezia 5.* ☎ *06/6992-5836. Other locations are at Via del Corso 122,* ☎ *06/6992-5783, and Via Cola di Rienzo 223,* ☎ *06/321-1403. www.stefanel.it.*

Department Stores

→ **COIN** ★★ Italy's biggest department-store chain, with two locations in Rome, has some great finds in the jewelry and accessories departments (e.g., well-priced knock-offs of the latest European runway looks), but stay away from the clothing floors, where merchandise tends to be overpriced and inexplicably frumpy. The makeup floor is also the place where you can stock up on your MAC lip glosses and Clinique cleansers. *Via Cola di Rienzo 173.* ☎ *06/708-0020. www.coin.it. Metro: Ottaviano. Branch at Piazzale Appio 7; metro: San Giovanni.*

➜ **La Rinascente** ★ Similar to COIN, for all intents and purposes, La Rinascente tends to do better on the scarves and hats front (good to know if you're doing souvenir-shopping for anyone who lives in a cool climate), and has a more familiar array of lingerie (i.e., not as much boudoir-ish padding and lace) on the underground level, in case you need to replenish your bras and underwear while on holiday in Rome. *Piazza Colonna (Via del Corso/Via del Tritone).* ☎ *06/679-7691. Bus: 62, 71, 85, 95, 116, 175, or 492. There's another store at Piazza Fiume (Via Salaria),* ☎ *06/ 884-1231, bus: 60, 63, or 630. www.rinascente.it.*

Books, Music & Media

Romans, and Italians in general, have surprisingly sophisticated musical tastes—you're bound to find plenty of great stuff and meet interesting people at the city's better record stores, where tourists almost never tread.

➜ **Disfunzioni Musicali** ★ In the left-wing university 'hood of San Lorenzo, "musical dysfunctions" is a place to pick up rare imports and cult recordings, and the dozens of flyers deposited here by various event promoters are a good way to get in on what's happening in the dance clubs and live venues. *Via degli Etruschi 4 (off Via Tiburtina.* ☎ *06/446-1984. www.disfu.com. Bus: 71 or 492. Tram: 3 or 19.*

➜ **La Feltrinelli** ★ Italy's largest bookstore chain has recently gone Borders-style, launching a series of integrated book and media stores, including the Roman flagship at Largo Argentina, which has a good, if small, selection of English-language books (most

paperback bestsellers and books on Roman history and tourism). For a much more comprehensive selection of English (and Spanish, French, and German) titles, check out the branch at Via V.E. Orlando, near Piazza della Repubblica. *Largo di Torre Argentina 11.* ☎ *06/6866-3001. www.lafeltrinelli.it. Bus: 30, 40, 46, 62, 64, 70, 87, 492, or 571. Tram: 8. Also Via V.E. Orlando 78–81,* ☎ *06/487-0171, metro: Repubblica, bus: 40, 64, 70, 170, 175, or 492.*

➜ **Pink Moon** ★★ An incredibly well-informed and friendly staff make it well worth the minor trek to this music store south of Trastevere. If you have a record player, there's a fantastic selection of 45s, covering music from the '40s to the '90s. *Via Pacinotti 3/c (off Viale Marconi).* ☎ *06/557-3868. www. pinkmoonrecords.com. Bus: 170 to Viale Marconi. Tram: 3 or 8 to Stazione Trastevere.*

➜ **Ricordi** Part of the Feltrinelli group, Ricordi is a mass-market record store with flashy video displays, CD bar-code scanning listening stations, and other megastore fare. Like similar stores in the U.S., displays are set up according to the best-selling CDs, so if there's a current Italian chart-topper you're looking for, you'll be able to find it easily here. Europeans love dance and pop compilations, and Ricordi will not let you down on that front. The Via del Corso location also has a box office that handles ticket sales for most of the big name music acts that come to Rome. The Termini location is open 365 days a year. *Via del Corso 506, near Piazza del Popolo.* ☎ *06/361-2370. At Forum Termini,* ☎ *06/ 8740-6113.*

Specialty

➜ **Ditta G. Poggi** ★★★ This old-school artists' supplies and vintage stationery shop makes for a fascinating (and mercifully quiet) detour off the tourist path between Piazza Venezia and the Pantheon. Inventory from the past 50 years that never sold out can still be found here, often at the original price.

Students can find all kinds of unique school supplies, like kitschy elementary school composition books from the 1960s that make cool travel journals. Aspiring artist-types can pick up sketchbooks and charcoals and try their hand at drawing the ruins of the Roman Forum. You could be the next Michelangelo, but you'll never know until you try! *Via del Gesù 74–75 (off Via Plebiscito).* ☎ *06/678-4477. www.poggi1825.it.*

Markets

→ **Porta Portese** ★★ Rome's famous weekly flea market isn't always the most rewarding shopping experience, but as a cultural experience, however, Porta Portese is very worthwhile. You will see vendors hawking rusty Vespa parts and plumbing components from the 1930s (and miraculously enough, people buying them). Most tourists who brave the crowds and sheer size of the market are looking to score amazing vintage shoes and clothes, and if you arrive early enough in the morning (as in 7am) and are willing to dig through bins of used clothing, you will come upon the occasional Gucci jacket or fabulous 1970s polyester shirt. Otherwise, most of the apparel is newer and unremarkable (though plentiful and cheap), or simply irrelevant to travelers. But if you're in the market for lawn furniture, there are definitely some deals to be had! One particularly authentic stretch of the market, on rustic Via Portuense, is open during the week, with a wonderful assortment of motorcycle helmets, plastic tables, and fireworks (handy if you're going to see a soccer game). *Piazza di Porta Portese, Via Portuense, Piazza Ippolito Nievo, Via Ettore Rolli, Trastevere. Full market: Sun 7am–2pm. Fireworks, auto parts, lawn furniture (Via Portuense): Mon–Sat 9am–2pm. Bus: 75, 780, or H. Tram: 3 or 8.*

→ **Via Sannio** ★ The stands on this street just south of the church of San Giovanni in Laterano (St. John Lateran) are great for picking up knock-offs of the latest trendy belts and accessories, as well as decent-quality leather jackets, and soccer team jerseys. Like a kinder, gentler, less varied version of Porta Portese. *Via Sannio, off Piazzale Appio. Mon–Sat 9am–1pm. Metro: San Giovanni. Bus: 85, 87, or 850.*

→ **Mercato di Testaccio** ★★ There are more "picturesque" markets in the city, but this food and dry goods bazaar, a covered mazelike space in the heart of the Testaccio neighborhood, is the real deal, and a colorful, convivial spectacle of Roman daily life. You walk in, and your nose is immediately treated to the perfume of ripe apples, fresh basil, and cured pork (among innumerable other culinary delights). All around you, local residents of this tight-knit community chatter with each other, as well as with the vendors they've been coming to for years, as they wheel their canvas carts from stall to stall, stocking up on all the vegetables, cheeses, and meats they'll need for the next few days. Butchers' cases are festooned with paraphernalia from the AS Roma soccer team (which has cultlike status in Testaccio), and all who enter can expect to be greeted with gusto, even if you're only a curious tourist. *Piazza Testaccio. Mon–Sat 7am–1pm. Metro: Piramide. Bus: 23, 75, 95, 170, or 280. Tram: 3.*

Road Trips: All Roads Lead from Rome . . .

Ever wondered where all those roads that lead to Rome lead *from?* Whether you're after some sun and surf at the beach or the fresh air and quiet charm of a hill town, the Lazio region offers a tantalizing array of rewarding escapes from the big city. Most of these destinations are pretty tourist-free, and all are within easy striking distance of central Rome, whether by train, bus, or rental car.

The outskirts of Rome are especially strong on cultural side trips that are totally doable in a day. The most classic of them all

Road Trips from Rome

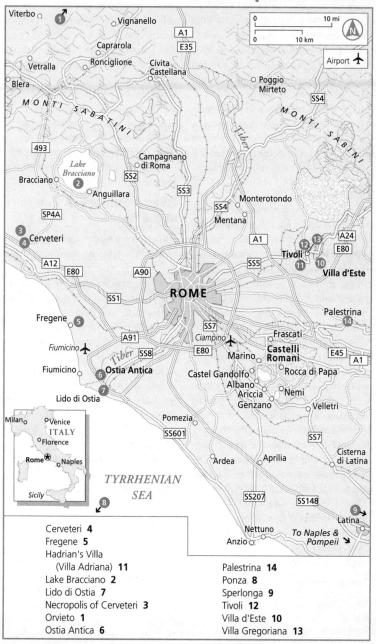

Viterbo ○
Vignanello ○
Caprarola ○
Vetralla ○
Ronciglione ○
Blera ○
Civita Castellana ○
Poggio Mirteto ○

A1
E35

0 ——————————— 10 mi
0 ——————————— 10 km

Airport ✈

M O N T I   S A B A T I N I

Tiber

SS4

M O N T I   S A B I N I

493

Lake Bracciano

Campagnano di Roma ○

Bracciano ○

SS2

SS3

Anguillara ○

Monterotondo ○

SS4

Mentana ○

SP4A

Cerveteri

A1

Tivoli

A24
E80

Villa d'Este

A12

E80

SS5

A90

SS1

ROME

Fregene

A91

SS7

Palestrina

Frascati ○

SS7

Ciampino ✈

E80

Castelli Romani

E45

A1

Fiumicino ✈

SS8

Marino ○

Fiumicino ○

Ostia Antica

Castel Gandolfo ○

Rocca di Papa ○

Lido di Ostia

Albano ○
Ariccia ○
Genzano ○

Nemi ○

Velletri ○

Pomezia ○

Milan ○

Venice ○

ITALY

○ Florence

Rome ✪ ○ Naples

Sicily

SS601

Ardea ○

Aprilia ○

Cisterna di Latina ○

TYRRHENIAN SEA

SS207

SS148

Latina

Nettuno ○

To Naples & Pompeii ↘

Anzio ○

Cerveteri **4**
Fregene **5**
Hadrian's Villa (Villa Adriana) **11**
Lake Bracciano **2**
Lido di Ostia **7**
Necropolis of Cerveteri **3**
Orvieto **1**
Ostia Antica **6**

Palestrina **14**
Ponza **8**
Sperlonga **9**
Tivoli **12**
Villa d'Este **10**
Villa Gregoriana **13**

is **Tivoli,** which has two very cool sites (which also happen to be on the UNESCO list of protected World Heritage Sites), the **Villa d'Este** and **Villa Adriana,** within 5km (3 miles) of each other. The trip to Tivoli takes the best part of 7 hours (which includes getting there, seeing both villas, and getting back). Even easier is the trip out to the fascinating ruins of **Ostia Antica,** ancient Rome's port town. I am also a huge fan of **Cerveteri,** a wildly exotic-feeling Etruscan "city of the dead," where you can climb all over and inside hundreds of 2,600-year-old tombs.

Tivoli

The steeply terraced gardens of the 16th century **Villa d'Este** ★★★ (☎ **0774/31-20-70**; Tues–Sun 8:30am to 1 hr. before sunset; 6.50€) are world famous for their astounding orgy of fountains, from gushing gargoyles to inviting grottoes with waterfalls. Five km (3 miles) down the hill from Villa d'Este and Tivoli proper are the vast and delightful remains of 📺 Best **Hadrian's Villa** ★★★ (☎ **0774/53-02-03**; daily 8:30am to 1 hr. before sunset; 6.20€), whose ingenious architecture and landscape design features are totally unique in the Roman world. Highlights of the 2nd century A.D. emperor's summer playground include the Canopus, a faux Egyptian canal with sunbathing marble crocodiles and an elegant arcade supported by caryatids, and the Maritime Theater, an elaborate island "living room" and circular lap pool once equipped with an artificial current.

To get to Tivoli, take a COTRAL bus to Tivoli/Villa Adriana from Ponte Mammolo metro (about 1 hr). Between the Villa d'Este (Tivoli *centro*) and Villa Adriana, take the local orange bus (about 15 min).

Ostia Antica

The extensive ruins at this once-booming port town offer a fascinating look at daily life in ancient Rome—especially interesting are the Corporations Square, with its great mosaics; apartment blocks; the Roman version of Starbucks; baths; and the perennial-favorite ancient latrine. (If you get an early start, you can even do Ostia Antica in half a day; in summer, consider combining your tour of the ruins with a trip to the beach at Ostia Lido; see below). The ruins are on Viale dei Romagnoli (☎ 06/5635-2830) and are open Tuesday through Sunday 8:30am to 1 hour before sunset. Admission is 4€. From Piramide metro/Porta San Paolo station, take the Ostia-Lido train to Ostia Antica (1€; about 30 min).

Ostia & Fregene: A Day at the Beach

Ostia Lido ★ is hardly a shimmering Mediterranean resort, but it's super easy to reach from the city center, and (locals claim), its dark sand expedites tanning. To get there, take the Ostia Lido train from Piramide metro/Porta San Paolo station to Ostia Centro, Stella Polare, or Cristoforo Colombo (about 40 min.; 1€); from any of these stops, it's a short walk to the water, which is chock-a-block with beach clubs (about 10€ per day), mostly frequented by families during the week. The **Kursaal** beach club (Ostia's most revered) also has a saltwater pool with a high dive, at Lungomare L. Catulo 38 (☎ 06/5647-0977).

For access to Ostia's free beaches, take a bus from Cristoforo Colombo to the Spiaggia Libera di Castelporziano (locally known as *i cancelli*), where there are pretty dunes but few facilities—just a couple of snack huts here and there. The *lungomare* (seaside drive) in Ostia is where almost all Roman dance clubs relocate from June to September, so if you can swing a ride out here on a summer night (there's no late-night public transportation), it's a great place to party.

About 20km (12 miles) up the coast, **Fregene** ★★ tends to be more popular with

Our Favorite Road Trips Less Traveled

About an hour's bus ride northwest of Rome is the fantastic Etruscan necropolis at **Cerveteri** ★★★ (Necropoli della Banditaccia; ☏ **06/994-00-01;** take a COTRAL bus from Lepanto metro)—a totally Indiana Jones–ish, junglelike environment where you can climb all over and explore the cavernous innards of hundreds of 2,500-year-old tumuli (giant mound-shaped burial chambers). Other easy day trips from Rome are **Lake Bracciano** ★ (COTRAL bus from Lepanto metro, about 45 min.), where you can visit a castle and go for a swim; **Orvieto** ★★ (train from Roma Termini, about 1 hr.)—perched high atop a spur of red tufa, this Umbrian town has picturesque medieval architecture and an exquisite *duomo* (see chapter on Umbria); and **Palestrina** ★, a sleepy (and very provincial) medieval town just southeast of Rome (take a COTRAL bus to Palestrina from Ponte Mammolo metro, about 1 hr.). There, you'll find the impressive Roman ruins of the 1st century B.C. hillside sanctuary of Fortuna Primigenia hovering above the mist, as well a fine archaeological museum with stunning views across the suburban plains toward Rome.

younger, more image-conscious Romans, but if you don't have a car, it's more of a pain to get here than to Ostia. Romans act as if Fregene is a million times more fabulous than Ostia (the town does have a sunnier, more resort-y feel to it), but it's not exactly a tropical paradise. Unfortunately, Fregene's high concentration of superbronzed poseurs means that there's a permanent film of coconut oil on the water's surface. There's also a continuous stream of low-flying jets overhead, on final approach to Fiumicino airport nearby.

Still, Fregene has an intangible, almost nostalgic "it" factor that makes it the darling of many a stylish Roman. Beaches are the widest and sandiest you'll find near Rome, and there are tons of great seafood restaurants. For amazing spaghetti *alle vongole* and fab people-watching, try beachfront **Il Mastino** ★★, Via Silvi Marina 19 (☏ **06/ 6656-0966**). Fregene's numerous private beach clubs are all about 10€ per day; otherwise, the beach at the center of town is a public beach where you can plop down your towel for free. To get to Fregene, take a COTRAL bus from Lepanto metro (at least 1 hr.), more on weekends.

Beautiful Beaches & Party Islands South of Rome

As a past resident of Rome, maybe I'm biased, but for me, beachtime in Italy is synonymous with Lazio's southern coastline—including the town of Sperlonga and the island of Ponza. Easily accessible by no-hassle train, bus, and/or boat from central Rome (the farthest, Ponza, is just under 3 hr. away), these are some of the best, least pretentious seaside destinations in Italy—and while they're inundated with Romans from July to August, they're totally under the radar of foreign tourism. The water's clean, the scenery's gorgeous, the vibe is chill, and the food's amazing. And that's not all: Having gone to these places at least once a week for five summers, I can't even remember a day when there was a cloud in the sky. Take me with you?

SPERLONGA

If you get an early start and want to make a full day of going to the beach, pretty **Sperlonga** ★★, with its whitewashed town and bougainvillea, really feels like an escape.

There are two main stretches of beach: The first, which runs along the modern part of town, is a straight stretch of sand with

ROME & LAZIO

more waves and tons of beach clubs; the second section of beach lies south of the Torre Truglia (an old sea tower), in the crescent-shaped bay of Sperlonga. Here, the water is quieter and the beach is wider. It's still beach club central, but it's less cramped-feeling.

For an amazing rustic lunch of local seafood (which you can eat in your bathing suit and bare feet), try **L'Angolo** ★★ (☎ **0771/548808**), right on the sand in the southern section of beach. If you get an early but not-too-early start from Rome, you can be on the sand by 11am; but even if you don't arrive until noon, you've still got a good 4 hours before you might want to start thinking about making the trek back to the city. If you can spare the time, however, a night in Sperlonga is a fantastic treat, as the town has gorgeous views over the bay at sunset and into the evening. The **Corallo Hotel** ★, Corso San Leone 3 (☎ **0771/548-060;** www.corallohotel.net), has doubles from 80€ to 180€.

No slouch in the sightseeing department, Sperlonga also offers a unique archaeological site in **Tiberius's Grotto** ★★ on Via Flacca (☎ **0771/54-80-28**), an ancient dining room built on an island inside a seaside cave (which you can paddle into with the rowboat they provide!). From Roma-Termini, take a Naples-bound *diretto* train to Fondi (1 hr 10 min; 5.60€), then catch the local bus to Sperlonga (10 min; 1€.)

PONZA

This telephone-shaped island, less than 3 hours from downtown Rome, is one of the best-kept secrets in the Mediterranean. But since I have a big mouth, I'm going to tell you about it.

First of all, it's drop-dead gorgeous, with dramatic lizardlike contours, volcanic coves that look like moonscapes, and a lot of fascinating history, from ancient Roman times to World War II. Ponza is the summertime refuge of choice for upper-middle-class

Romans—many of whom have houses or apartments here—and you'll find a very happening, down-to-earth scene of teenagers through 30-somethings partying and tanning here from June to September.

You'll definitely want to spend at least 1 night on Ponza; **Hotel Mari** is a rather characterless 1970s joint, but the location on the harbor couldn't be a more convenient place to crash (and to find your way back to, after a night of boozing). It's at Corso Carlo Pisacane 19 (☎ **0771/80101;** www.hotelmari.com). Doubles are 85€ to 180€. The hotel is closed November to February.

Getting there   Take a *diretto* train from Roma-Termini to Anzio (1 hr.; 2.90€). From there, Caremar fast ferries (www.caremar.it) depart for Ponza (1½ hr. crossing time; 19.20€) several times a day.

A Perfect Day on Ponza

Make the first stop of the day **Bar Tripoli,** just above the marina at Corso Carlo Pisacane 15 (☎ **0771/809862**), the de rigueur destination for your morning coffee.

Next, head down to the harbor and **rent a small motorboat** ★★★. The absolute most fun way to experience Ponza is to go zipping around the island, stopping to jump in the water whenever you need to cool down or feel like exploring a hard-to-reach cove. In the main port area, just west of the ferry dock, **DivaLuna** (☎ **0771/809906,** 339/2347608 (cell), or 339/3212619 (cell); www.divaluna.com) rents *gommoni* (Zodiac-style motorboats—no experience necessary) from 50€ for a half-day (usually all you'll need); most boats can accommodate four people comfortably, and all have some sort of sun shade.

If you're planning on making the highly recommended 13km (8-mile) journey northwest, across the open sea, to the uninhabited island of **Palmarola** ★★★, with its gorgeous protected coves, you should get a bigger boat with a slightly more powerful motor, otherwise the crossing can be choppy and seem interminable. Before you set out on your circumnavigation, stop at the **calzone kiosk** ★ (right on the harbor) and get a cheap picnic of cheesy, carb-y goodness to take with you. You can bring booze, but make sure you also bring plenty of water, and have a designated driver who can safely bring your ship into shore! (Okay, Mom . . .) Once you've made your trip around the island, ditch your boat back at the port, and board one of the **shuttle boats to Frontone** (4€ round-trip), Ponza's see-and-be-seen beach spot for *aperitivo,* which can only be reached by sea.

Sip a few mojitos in the terraced outdoor bar at **Sporting Club Spiaggia di Frontone** ★ (☎ **0771/80755**), or on the sand itself, alongside tanned and toned *O.C.* cast look-alikes. Head back to the port; shower, apply aloe, and chill at the hotel. Hit the port again at around 8pm for some shopping and strolling, and finally, eat an amazing seafood meal somewhere at 9 or 10pm.

BEACHES

Chiaia di Luna ★★★ The best beach on Ponza (and one of the best in Italy), and the only one easily accessible on foot from the port, is this bay shaped like a half-moon, whose broad, sandy shore is backed by a towering wall of amber-colored tufa, 100m high (328 ft.) and 200m long (656 ft.). Because of its position on the western side of the island, Chiaia di Luna doesn't get full sun until after noon. Protected by the enormous rock wall behind it, the water in the gorgeous bay stays calm all day. There are a few beach clubs here, but you can also just throw your towel down in the public stretches of sand. A number of snack huts are also set up on Chiaia di Luna, serving the oh-so satisfying mozzarella, tuna, tomato, and prosciutto sandwiches that are typical of the beaches near Rome.

ROME & LAZIO

Florence & Tuscany

There's something about the cradle of the Renaissance and capital of Tuscany that makes you want to stand up straighter as you traipse from sight to sight, or strike your best sophisticated-person pose as you idle on a street corner, trying to read your map. Italy's most refined big city, Florence has roots that go back several thousand years to Etruscan and Roman times, but it's the golden age of Firenze—the 14th and 15th centuries—that is the overriding theme, and preserved in incredibly sharp focus here today. From the medieval stage set of Piazza della Signoria to graceful Renaissance churches and squares to grids of narrow, noble streets lined with sandstone *palazzi*, walking around the historic center of Florence is like time-warping back to the fabulous 1400s—especially if you do it by night.

When darkness falls on Florence, the city takes on a stunning, mystical aura unlike anything you'll experience during the bustle of daytime. The monuments are floodlit, and the streets seem haunted by the ghosts of Florence's illustrious and sometimes violent past. It's not too hard to imagine a Renaissance prince walking by and tipping his hat to you on Via dei Calzaiuoli; the din of marble hoists and workmen on the construction site of the Duomo; or the satisfied roar of the masses every time someone was burned at the stake below Palazzo Vecchio.

Florence draws as many visitors as Rome, but its smaller size makes it much more manageable for the short-term visitor. However, its compact layout also means that Florence's most famous sights are heavily touristed all day long—a state of affairs that can feel like an oppressive Renaissance theme park. Indeed, modern-day Florentine authenticity can be hard to find on a hot day in July, but we'll tell you where to look. Though its greatest art and architecture might have been created half a millennium ago, Florence is far from over the hill. The Tuscan gregariousness of its residents gives the city plenty of Italian vitality and a large student population keeps the nightlife going strong, all year round. Everywhere you go in Florence, there's a mash-up of ambient noise: the beeping of scooters, the idle chatter seeping out of the ubiquitous gelato shops, the clinking of wine glasses in the open-air restaurants, the classical guitarist busking in Piazza della Repubblica. Accompanying the noise is an irresistible composition of hearty scents—coffee beans, stewing vegetables, roasting meat . . .

Once the temptation proves irresistible, dip into one of the many Tuscan osterias for which the city is so famous and satiate your taste buds with generous dishes of Florentine cuisine. If you're not comatose after indulging in decadent gnocchi and *bistecca alla fiorentina,* hit one of the dance clubs or pubs that have earned Florence its reputation as one of the best hangouts in Italy for young people.

A word to the wise: Summer in Florence is *hot* and can be trying—A/C isn't everywhere, and there's only so much gelato you can ingest to cool down. Simply reserving your tickets to the Uffizi and Accademia in advance will spare you a ton of unnecessary stress (and sunburn that you'd otherwise get waiting on line) and make your stay a lot more enjoyable. Finally, take a cue from the locals and make time for getting out of the city center. On a sweltering day, a trip to San Miniato al Monte or the hill town of Fiesole is guaranteed to recharge your batteries.

FLORENCE & TUSCANY

Florence

The Best of Florence

Best Way to See the Duomo

At night, when you're not looking for it. Instead of heading straight to Piazza del Duomo the moment you get into town, let it sneak up on you as you stroll the *centro:* When, down some narrow lane, the overgrown gingerbread house creeps into your peripheral vision, it will knock your socks off. See p. 257.

Best Hostel

Hostel Archi Rossi In fact, we think it's one of the best hostels in Italy. At first glance,

the graffitied walls give the impression that the hostel was once a squatters' haunt, but look more closely and you'll realize the inscriptions are notes left by previous guests. Have breakfast in the common room, and hang out after a day of touring to watch movies in English then there's the snack beer which offers cold beer at 3€ a bottle. Take your brew and enjoy it in the garden, it's an atmospheric spot where you can spend an evening socializing with fellow travelers, or just preload before hitting the bars. See p. 225.

Tuscany

Best Doable Hotel

Hotel Burchianti   Ahhh, relax! If it were not for the language barrier, I wouldn't hesitate to take this proud owner of Hotel Burchianti out to a movie and use her senior citizen discount for all it's worth. She treats all her guests like royalty, welcomes them with a priceless smile, and makes sure that you have enough caffeine in your system before you hit the town. It's only a matter of time before

this place, teeming with character and in a convenient part of town, becomes a tourist favorite. See p. 231.

Best Gelateria

Vivoli   They scoop out the gelato by the gallon here daily, and with good reason. Even though locals believe that the dense dessert was tastier in Vivoli's earlier days, the quality is still leaps and bounds better than most gelaterias in Florence. An afternoon spent in

Santa Croce is nowhere near complete without a visit to this institution. Prepare yourself for the most delicious brain freeze ever. See p. 240.

Best Museum on a 5€ Budget

Santa Croce   One of the few Florentine sites with an admission fee lower than 5€ is, of course, a church in the southeast part of the city; but it offers a collection of frescoes and sculptures by some of the greats, including Giotto and Donatello, that outshines many a museum. You'll also find a "Who's Who" of Florence buried within the grounds of Santa Croce—Michelangelo and Galileo's mortal remains are permanent residents of the gorgeous church. See p. 261.

Best Spot for Escaping the Tourist Rush

Piazza d'Azeglio   The park near the corner of Via della Colonna and Via L.C. Farini is a perfect place to kick back and watch a wide range of locals interact. There's always a handful of kids playing with a beat-up soccer ball, a few hippie 20-somethings trying to learn the nuances of juggling devil sticks, elderly couples relaxing on the park benches, and toddlers playing in the small playground on the edge of the park. It's a bit of a hike north of the center, so you won't run into many tour groups here, even if the Hotel Regency is on the north end of the park.

Best Dive Bar

Teatro Scribe   The tiny street of Via delle Seggiole is a little eerie, but that's what makes Teatrino so charming. Revelers flock to the grungy watering hole for cheap beer when everything else closes at 2 or 3am. See p. 243.

Best Bling Bar

Capocaccia   Sunglasses are a must here, not for the intense Tuscan sun, but to shade your eyes from the blinding glare from the ridiculous jewelry worn by the clientele. Don't worry about the sheer amount of Louis Vuitton or D&G, just strut around with a little attitude and you'll be fine. See p. 241.

Best Place to Get Embarrassingly Hammered

Red Garter   It's an American-themed speakeasy. 'Nuff said. See p. 243.

Getting There

BY AIR

There are no direct flights to Florence from the U.S. Nonstop flights from the States to Italy go to Rome or Milan. If your flight lands in Rome, the Leonardo Express train will take you from Fiumicino International Airport to the Roma Termini train station for 9.50€. From Rome's central station, trains leave almost every 30 minutes to Florence's Santa Maria Novella station (trip time 1½–2½ hr., depending on the class of train). If you fly into Milan's Malpensa airport, catch the **Malpensa Shuttle** bus (price 5€) into Milano Centrale train station; from there, trains for Florence-Santa Maria Novella station depart every 30 minutes or so (trip time is 3–4 hours, depending on the class of train).

If you fly into other European cities, such as London, Paris, Amsterdam—or even Rome or Milan—for that matter, you can catch a connecting flight into Florence's **Peretola-Amerigo Vespucci** domestic airport. When you arrive, for 1€, you can take bus 62 into the center of the city.

Another option is flying through Pisa's **Galileo Galilei** airport. Pisa is only an hour from Florence by train or bus. If you're flying out of Pisa, the Florence Air Terminal, at track 5 at Florence's Santa Maria Novella train station, offers a convenient setup where you can check your luggage and get your boarding pass then take the train to Pisa (the train can take 1–2 hr.; check the daily schedules).

BY TRAIN

If you're traveling to Florence from within Italy, rail is by far the most efficient, hassle-free option. As you roll toward the city, from the north or the south, you'll pass wonderful

From	Fast Train	Next Fastest Train
Rome	*ES* 1 hr 40 min, 30€	*IC* 2 hr 30 min, 22€
Venice	*ES* 2 hr 50 min, 27€	*IC + R* 3 hr 30 min, 20€
Milan	*ES* 2 hr 45 min, 29€	*IC* 3 hr 20 min, 22€
Bologna	*ES* 1 hr, 14€	*IC* 1 hr 10 min, 8€
Naples	*ES* 3 hr 40 min, 43€	*IC* 4 hr 50 min, 36€

little medieval hill towns and cypress-dotted farmland to put you in a Tuscan frame of mind. Florence is one of Italy's most train-friendly cities, since its position in the middle of the country means that almost all trains travel through the city's main station, **Firenze-Santa Maria Novella** (not to be confused with the secondary station, Firenze-Campo di Marte). Santa Maria Novella (or **S.M.N.**, as it's known to rail jockeys) is in the northwest part of the city center, and within walking distance of almost all hotels and sights. (It's also a fine example of fascist, or rationalist, 1930s architecture.) If you're heading into Florence by rail from other parts of Europe, you'll often have to connect to disembark from your international train and hop on a national (Trenitalia) train in Bologna, Milan, Turin, or Venice.

Keep in mind that it's not at all unusual for Italian trains (especially the regional lines) to run a few minutes to an hour behind schedule. The exception is the Eurostar, which almost always runs on time—Mussolini would have been proud. While trains that arrive and depart perfectly on schedule are also quite common, it's a good idea to build an extra hour or two into your schedule to accommodate such potential setbacks.

Some train times and second-class prices to Florence from other popular Italian cities (times and prices also valid vice versa) are listed above.

For more information about the national train system, see the Planning chapter, or consult Trenitalia's extremely handy, multi-lingual website, **www.trenitalia.com**.

BY CAR

Florence is a few kilometers east of the A1 *autostrada* that runs vertically through much of Italy, from Naples in the south to Milan in the north. The A11 connects Florence to Lucca and all points west, and the Raccordo Firenze-Siena highway links Florence with Siena, 40km (25 miles) to the south, while the SS67 plugs Florence into the party-hearty coast of Romagna, to the northeast. Once you're in the area, try to ditch the wheels in a long-term parking facility on the outskirts of town.

If your hotel doesn't have its own garage, someone on the staff will direct you to the nearest one or will arrange valet parking. Garage fees average 18€ to 25€ per day, depending on the size of your car. Most garages charge 1€ per hour.

The most centrally located garages are the **International Garage,** Via Palazzuolo 29 (☎ 055/282386); **Garage La Stazione,** 3A Via Alamanni (☎ 055/284768); **Autoparking SLL,** Via Fiesolana 19 (☎ 055/2477871); and **Garage Anglo-Americano,** Via dei Barbadori 5 (☎ 055/214418). If these are full, you can almost always find a space at the **Garage Porte Nuove,** Via delle Portenuove 21 (☎ 055/333355).

Driving into the center of Florence is a nightmare of epic proportions due to construction on the roads surrounding the old city. Parking is another issue entirely; expect to pay upwards of 15€/day for private lots in

Information for Rail Pass Users

European rail passes are good for second-class travel on Italian Intercity (**IC**) trains as well as the sluggish *regionale* (**R**) and *diretto* (**D**) trains, but if you want to travel on Italy's express service, the Eurostar (**ES**), you'll have to pay a supplement—consult the literature that comes with your pass for more details. Note also that all Eurostar tickets must be booked at least 24 hours in advance, which gets you an assigned seat. (See Eurailpass box, p. 48.)

the center, or risk getting your ride towed due to unintelligible parking signs. In the heart of old Florence, there are electronically controlled columns that keep nonauthorized traffic (i.e., you) from entering certain streets (only a special pass issued to residents will lower the columns), so if you come up to one of these barricades, your 15-point turn skills will be severely tested. Trying to find your way around with a car in Florence will invariably lead to a run-in with a traffic cop, which is actually a good thing. Just put on your best brain-dead tourist act and tell them you're looking for your hotel, and they'll send you on your merry way in no time.

As soon as you've unloaded your stuff at the hotel, ditch the wheels at **Piazza Libertà,** in the northern part of the city center. There, the **Parterre** parking lot offers a pretty good deal, charging 15€ for each 24-hour period. Another option, and more convenient if you're staying in the Oltrarno, is the **Porta Romana** lot (at the southwest end of the Boboli Gardens, entry from Piazza della Calza), which also charges 15€ for 24 hours. Whatever you do, get rid of that car and

have someone hide the keys from you until you're ready to leave Florence for good.

How about driving a car *outside* the city? Well, that's another matter entirely, and one which we heartily endorse. Tuscany is one of the most beautiful and congenial places in Italy for road tripping—the sun-blanketed hills, the cypress-lined country roads, the endless places to stop and eat . . . it really is as wonderful as those coffee-table books would have you believe. If you're traveling alone or with one other person, consider renting the popular Smart car, mainland Europe's smaller and more cartoonish analogue to the Mini Cooper (they have those here, too). Two-seater Smarts are tiny, fuel-efficient, and shockingly chic. **Happy Rent,** at Borgo Ognissanti 153/r, southwest of Santa Maria Novella station (☎ **055/239-9696;** www.happyrent.com), will rent you a Smart for 75€/day. Slightly more economical Fiat hatchbacks are available for 65€/day.

BY BUS

In the wider streets around Santa Maria Novella train station, you'll find the scattered stalls where Lazzi and SITA coach buses gather to pick up passengers, wipe their sweaty windshields, and bitch about their aching axles (I told you those cobblestones were a pain). Bus travel in Italy is generally slower (but no less expensive) than train travel, but sometimes it's your only option, especially if you're coming into Florence from a smaller Tuscan hill town that doesn't have a train station. For more info about the myriad destinations accessible by bus, check posted schedules in the offices at the **Lazzi station** (www.lazzi.it) near Piazza Adua, or at the **SITA depot** (www.sitabus.it) on Via Santa Caterina da Siena (directly southwest of S.M.N.).

Orientation

Florentines don't have specific names for the different parts of the city center—they generally just divide it into the area around the

Florence Neighborhoods

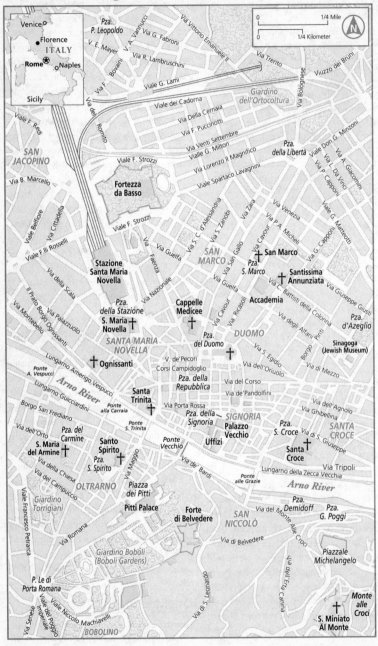

Duomo (north of the Arno), and the **Oltrarno** (south of the river). To help you understand what sort of scene you might encounter if you wander in various directions within the heart of the old city, we've broken down the lay of the land into the following arbitrary neighborhood distinctions, based around principal monuments, piazzas, or churches. The longest distance you might cover in any one stretch, from Santa Maria Novella train station in the west to Santa Croce in the east, for instance, is a leisurely 30-minute walk.

➜ **Santa Maria Novella** For better or worse, most visitors' first taste of Florence is the neighborhood around the train station, in the northwest part of the city center. The Santa Maria Novella area is hardly the Florence of the postcard racks, and it can get a little scummy with vagrants that ply Via Nazionale, making obscene comments at tourists. However, the area around Florence's train station is not nearly as seedy as the area around Rome's main station, Termini, and it's also much more convenient to the heart of town, since Florence is so much smaller than Rome. Some bright spots in the area include the church of Santa Maria Novella to the south, and its adjacent grassy piazza, a clean and relaxing spot to relax while you wait for a train. You'll have no trouble finding an economical place to sleep around here; there are a ton of hotels within a 1-block radius to satisfy any budget.

➜ **The Duomo** There is never a shortage of tour groups and other camera-toting pedestrians in the geographic center of Florence, about a 10-minute walk east of the train station. Busloads of visitors stream from the monumental cathedral, Santa Maria del Fiore, and its baptistery, on down to the Ponte Vecchio every day, and countless souvenir stores take advantage of this by bumping up prices on things such as film, maps, drinks, and other travelers' necessities. Naturally, you'll also find most of Florence's high-end hotels clustered around

the city's most famous landmark. Just to the southwest, Piazza della Repubblica is another large square—and not a particularly pretty one—with its fair share of cafes and buskers. For shoppers, the streets just south of the Duomo are packed with midrange stores of every kind.

➜ **Piazza della Signoria** A few blocks southeast of the Duomo, this enormous L-shaped square around the crenellated and clock-towered Palazzo Vecchio has long been the civic heart of Florence; it's also where the city's avalanche of art really begins. A marble statue of Neptune, atop his fountain, can be found in the northwest corner of Piazza della Signoria. There, he crooks his neck and watches the exit doors of the Uffizi gallery spit out busloads of tourists like exhaust fumes. When night falls, summer crowds around Piazza della Signoria are often treated to open-air concerts near the entrance of the Uffizi. During these free shows, moving about is nearly impossible—you're better off hanging around the gelaterias and restaurants on the fringes of the square. For the best views, try visiting after midnight. When the crowds thin out, the Uffizi, fountain of Neptune, and Palazzo Vecchio are illuminated by floodlights, and the expansive "square" becomes a truly memorable sight.

➜ **San Lorenzo** Between the train station and the Duomo, this neighborhood was the Medicis' old stomping ground, but today, it's most famous for its markets. Shopping here can be hectic but gratifying—the stalls of Mercato di San Lorenzo and Mercato Centrale are a raucous collection of leather vendors, Florentine stationery sellers, and produce hawkers. Watch your purse or wallet, as pickpockets love the cramped conditions and won't hesitate to snatch your euros. Sights worth checking out in this 'hood are the church of San Lorenzo and the attached Laurentian Library, an unusual architectural work by Michelangelo.

➜ **San Marco** In spite of the long queues outside the Galleria dell'Accademia to see Michelangelo's *David,* the largely residential area of San Marco north of the Duomo remains relatively quiet. Everything and everyone seems more laid back as they stroll through the cafe-lined Piazza San Marco. With the university a few blocks away, it's not surprising that you'll find Florence's more alternative stores and restaurants in San Marco. Also in the neighborhood is the magnificent porticoed Piazza Santissima Annunziata. There are a few hotels, but some are located too far north to be convenient for all the frequent walks you'll make down to the Duomo and Ponte Vecchio.

➜ **Santa Croce** The eastern end of the old city is home to funky boutiques and Florence's "Pantheon"—the church of Santa Croce is home to the tombs of many famous Italians, including Michelangelo. In the streets surrounding Piazza Santa Croce, you'll find workshops of leather artisans where leather hounds will find goods of impeccable quality and a selection far more varied than at the busy market stalls of San Lorenzo. Also in this vicinity is Vivoli (p. 240)—a visit to Florence is not complete until you sample its unparalleled gelato.

➜ **Piazza Santa Trinità** The glitziest of stores, including the world headquarters of Ferragamo, grace Piazza Santa Trinità, north of Ponte Santa Trinità, one bridge west of Ponte Vecchio. Compared to the its ever-popular cousin, Ponte Santa Trinità seems deserted, but it provides one of the best perches in all of Florence (see "Ponte Picnic: The Best View of Florence," p. 241) from which to admire the Arno and Ponte Vecchio. Florentines and travelers with bulging wallets can be seen preening up and down the high-end retail corridor of Via Tornabuoni, toting bags with the designer boutique names (Prada, Pucci, Cavalli, and Tod's) turned to face the street.

➜ **Oltrarno** The district "beyond the Arno" (on the southern side of the river) is the preferred hangout of Florence's more bohemian citizens. With the galleries of the Pitti Palace and the Boboli Gardens serving as the main attraction, the westernmost end is all that most tourists see of the Oltrarno. Cool lounges like Negroni and Zoe, east of Ponte Vecchio, keep Florence's south side throbbing after nightfall. You'll also find incredible inconspicuous hotels and restaurants hidden along streets like Borgo San Jacopo, home to the Cinghiale Bianco, a fantastic Tuscan osteria, and the luxurious Hotel Lungarno.

➜ **The Hills** Rising to the north and east of the city are the stately green hills of Florence. A few cultural attractions thrive in the distance, but the fresh air and vistas—back to the city center, where the Duomo looks like the *Titanic* amid a sea of rust-colored icebergs—are the real reasons people head for the higher ground. Florentines' preferred hilltop retreat is the town of **Fiesole,** a 25-minute ride on bus 7 from Piazza Santa Maria Novella. More centrally located, but still requiring a hike (or bus), Piazzale Michelangelo is a magnificent perch on the southeastern end of the Oltrarno.

Getting Around

WALKING

Stow away your flip-flops unless you want to wake up the next morning to a grapefruit-sized, pus-filled blister on each heel. While the city is best explored on foot, the cobblestoned roads can be quite uncomfortable if you plan on trekking in your Tevas. This is the place to break out your closed-toe, comfortable walking shoes, if you haven't already.

You might also want to stay on your toes when using the pedestrian walkways; as Florentine pet owners don't care much for picking up after their quadrupeds. The Smart cars and scooters that buzz randomly by are actually very pedestrian friendly. Somehow they avoid using their horns unless they are truly forced to (e.g., to avoid hitting a drunk tourist asleep in the middle of the road). Jaywalking is an art that locals have perfected; watch and learn from the masters while you're in town. Crossing main thoroughfares without worrying about oncoming traffic is something you might have always associated with a hand gesture or two and a "Watch it, buddy!", but Florentine motorists are surprisingly zen about letting pedestrians dart in front of them.

You can easily cover the entire breadth of the compact city in a matter of hours on foot. Everything revolves around Piazza del Duomo. If you get lost, try to locate the Duomo by peeking between side streets and alleys. More often than not, you'll be able to backtrack to the Duomo and reacquaint yourself with the layout of the streets radiating from the center. Of course, this being Italy, street names change every few blocks, and street numbers are even more confusing: They don't really follow any sort of ordinal sequence, and furthermore, they're divided into *rosso* ("red," commercial addresses) and *nero* ("black," residential addresses), which explains the "r" or "n" you'll see after street numbers.

In any case, Florence's diabolical street plan will probably have you crumpling up that city map and utilizing your newfound knowledge of Italian curses, such as the ever-useful *Ma che cazzo?!?* ("WTF?"). For finding your way to restaurants and bars, you'll definitely need a good, highly detailed map (available at most newsstands). Otherwise, locals are helpful and proficient enough in English and hand signals to help you on your way.

Besides the Duomo, Florence's other useful navigation tool when you're on foot is the river Arno. The bridges that connect the northern and southern halves of the city serve as handy markers for the main streets of Florence. Going north from Ponte Vecchio

will lead you to Via Calimala, Piazza della Repubblica, and the Duomo. Ponte Santa Trinità will bring you through the swanky Via de' Tornabuoni area, and Ponte alle Grazie leads tourists north to Santa Croce and south to Via de' Renai (where you can visit the chic nightspots Negroni and Zoe, p. 243.)

MOTOR SCOOTERS

An integral part of the Italian experience is the use of the motor scooter. Sure, it's underpowered; and it's considered dorky in some other parts of the world (less dorky here in the U.S. as the price of gas goes up); but in Italian cities, a *motorino* is not only cool—it's as essential a tool in the human existence as the opposable thumb. You'll find that every block in Florence has at least a dozen *motorini* parked along, or on top of, the sidewalk. With murderous gas prices and claustrophobic streets, it's no wonder Florentines prefer Vespas to Escalades. Maneuvering through the crowded and busy historic center on the back of your own 50cc bike can be a thrill, but until you've got a few miles in dense traffic under your belt, stick to the wider, less-congested thoroughfares on the outskirts of town. If you decide to brave the throngs of tourists, prepare to have a trigger finger on the horn and one foot ready to steady yourself on the ground. **Due Ruote,** a division of Happy Rent (Borgo Ognissanti 153/r, southwest of Santa Maria Novella station; ☎ **055/239-9696;** www.happyrent. com), has Piaggio Liberty 50cc (plenty of power, even for two riders) scooters for 40€/day, with discounted rates for longer-term rentals.

To rent a scooter, you must be 18 or over and must leave a passport, a driver's license, and the number of a valid credit card.

PUBLIC TRANSPORTATION

The only form of public transit in Florence is the **ATAF** bus, which you might never use, unless you go to the hills (for Piazzale Michelangelo, take bus 12 or 13; for Fiesole,

Quick Walking Tour of Florence

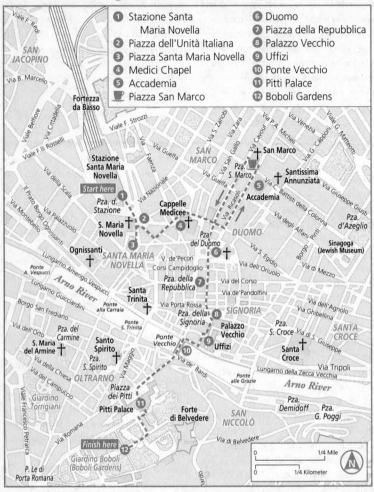

❶ Stazione Santa Maria Novella
❷ Piazza dell'Unità Italiana
❸ Piazza Santa Maria Novella
❹ Medici Chapel
❺ Accademia
🚌 Piazza San Marco
❻ Duomo
❼ Piazza della Repubblica
❽ Palazzo Vecchio
❾ Uffizi
❿ Ponte Vecchio
⓫ Pitti Palace
⓬ Boboli Gardens

take bus 7; both leave from Piazza Santa Maria Novella). Tickets good for an hour cost 1€ and can be purchased at any newsstand or *tabacchi* shop. If you plan on using the bus within a larger timeframe, you can obtain a ticket valid for 3 hours for 1.80€. A 24-hour ticket is also available for 4.80€. Don't forget to validate the ticket once you board the bus at one of the yellow time-stamping machines. If you get caught riding without a validated ticket, you're in for a heavy fine. If all the machines are broken, notify the bus driver. Smaller, electric buses can get you close to the *centro storico,* but are not necessary in the compact area. A bus map would be handy, but ATAF hasn't gotten around to printing one just yet. In the meantime, schematics and schedules of the various lines are online at **www.ataf.net**, or you can call their offices: ☎ **055/5650-2222.**

Quick Walking Tour of Florence

Worst-case scenario: While planning your European jaunt, you only managed to allocate a single day in Florence. Instead of complaining, I'll provide a little walking tour that shouldn't take more than an afternoon and will still give you a decent impression of the city.

It's logical to start in the place where most people arrive, Stazione Santa Maria Novella. Work your way south to Piazza dell'Unità Italiana and take a couple of minutes to grab a map from one of the newsstands. Piazza Santa Maria Novella is just to the southwest and is a great photo opportunity. Go back to Piazza dell'Unità Italiana and follow Via de' Panzani until you reach Via del Giglio, and then hang a left. Two blocks down is the Medici Chapel. Gawk at the Michelangelo pieces and then follow the northern wall of the church of San Lorenzo all the way to Via Ricasoli. Walk north until you see a line of reddened foreigners wrapped around the corner. The line leads to the Accademia and ends at the feet of the marble *David*.

You must be pretty hungry by now, so head over to Piazza San Marco, just a block north. Find a bench and enjoy a *panino* from one of the adjacent vendors. Now that you've refueled, find Via Cavour (it runs alongside the western edge of Piazza San Marco) and turn left. Within 10 minutes of strolling down the wide street, you'll reach the foot of the Duomo. Take pictures of the impossibly large cathedral, and after you've bought your souvenirs, mosey on down to the southwest corner (near the Battistero) and look for Via dei Calzaiuoli. Follow it south for about 6 blocks. While you dodge camera-toting tour groups, take a peek down the western side of Via del Corso for a glimpse of Piazza della Repubblica. The piazza is best visited after dinner when the buskers and vendors are in full swing. Come back here after your walking tour to relax and chill out. But first, more attractions are in order!

The end of Via dei Calzaiuoli is the beginning of Piazza della Signoria. Prepare to spend at least an hour here. The Palazzo Vecchio and the surrounding statues are great photo opportunities, but the Uffizi to the south will swallow most of your afternoon. Hit the major rooms (p. 254), apologize to Durer and Perugino as you fly by their paintings, and allocate 15 minutes to Michelangelo's and Botticelli's masterpieces. It's a disservice to the artists, but you'll make it up to them when you plan your next (longer) trip to Florence. Grab an espresso after you've sprinted through the halls, and get ready for the last leg of the tour.

Leave the Uffizi and find the Arno to the south. You'll spot Ponte Vecchio just to the west; follow Lungarno delle Grazie to the famed bridge (the street will change names, becoming Lungarno Acciaiuoli, as you near the Ponte Vecchio). Again, wade through the crowds, and cross the Arno. Be sure to do a little window-shopping in the jewelry stalls that line Ponte Vecchio. The beginning of Via Guicciardini curves to the west after Ponte Vecchio, leading you to the Pitti Palace. This is where the walking tour will leave your barking dogs. Spend the remainder of the afternoon scoping out more masterpieces of Renaissance art inside the Pitti, or feel free to give the culture-absorbing and crowd-tolerating parts of your brain—as well as your feet—a rest in the Boboli Gardens.

TAXIS

For the most part, you'll have no use for taxis, but if you're carrying heavy luggage and just want to get from the train station to your hotel in the Oltrarno without a hassle, taxis are handy indeed. The other situation in which you might want a cab is if you're going out to the any of the nightspots in the outskirts. There are **taxi stands** in front of the train station and in Piazza Santa Maria Novella, Piazza della Repubblica, Piazza del Duomo, Piazza Santa Croce, Piazza San Marco, and Piazza di Santa Trinità. You can also **call** for a cab at ☎ **055/4242,** 055/4390, and 055/4798. When the operator picks up, give the street address of your location as clearly as possible, and if there's a cab available, a recorded voice will tell you the *sigla* (medallion number) of the taxi they're sending. It's usually a city or river name, followed by a number (e.g., Arno 55). Most hotels will call a cab for you, but performing this task yourself will make you feel like the Italian language pro you are.

CYCLING

Bicycles are perfect if you're not ready to tackle the noisy, gas-powered scooter. Bikes can get you in the even narrower back alleys and are a much cheaper option. You can rent a two-wheeler from **Geordie Chopin,** located in several areas of Florence (in Santa Croce, Via Fiesolana 10/r, just north of Piazza G. Salvernini; ☎ **055/245-013**). Expect to pay around 2.50€ per hour, up to 12€ to 18€ per day, depending on the model. **Florence by Bike** (Via San Zanobi, 91/r, at Via delle Ruote; ☎ **055/488-992**) is another bike rental outfit, where city bikes go for 7.50€ for 5 hours, or 13€ a day. Bike theft isn't as prevalent as you'd think, but it does happen, so be sure to use the lock that rental agencies provide, and don't park it in some dark alley or park overnight. Also, make sure it's equipped with a bell; it'll make rolling through the crowded streets a lot

easier on the vocal chords. If they still don't get out of your way, be ready to belt out a hearty *muoviti*! ("move it!").

Florence Basics

TOURIST OFFICES

Stock up on your basic maps and brochures at the train station branch of **Florence's tourism board** (Piazza della Stazione 4; ☎ **055/212-245;** Mon–Sat 8:30am–7pm and Sun 8:30am–1:30pm). For even more information, head toward the Duomo. The **tourist office** on Via Cavour 1/r, just north of Via de' Gori (☎ **055/290-832;** www.firenzeturismo. it; Mon–Sat 8:30am–6:30pm and Sun 8:30am–1:30pm) has an even more comprehensive collection of brochures and maps. But instead of getting the stuff for free, you'll have to pay a nominal fee for their goods and services.

Youth information services Unfortunately, there's no physical office where visitors can chat up clerks behind a layer of Plexiglas. Give them a ring at ☎ **055/234-7329,** and for your first question, ask them why they haven't opened up an office.

RECOMMENDED WEBSITES

(Most of these homepages are in Italian; click on the British flag icon for the English version of the site.)

○ **www.firenzeturismo.it** Official site of the Florence tourism board has links to art-historical information, visitor services, a comprehensive hotel and restaurant-finding tool, and much more.

○ **www.firenze.net** Independent tourism portal with info on events, nightlife, and weather, plus accommodations booking service for Florence and Tuscany.

○ **www.comune.fi.it/inglese** Florence's municipal website, with event listings and basic city info here.

○ **www.ataf.net** The official site of Florence's public transit authority is the only

Culture 101: Fitting In in Florence

Language: For decades, the open-air Renaissance classroom that is Florence has hosted platoons of foreign students, so English is widely spoken in the historical center. In fact, Florence is perhaps the only place in Italy where you can walk into a bar, deliver your best *"una Coca-Cola, per favore,"* and they'll respond, in a perfect, bored-American accent, "Diet or regular?" The predominance of English in the city center can take the wind out of your sails if you're going for full immersion, but for those who don't speak a word of Italian and don't care to learn, you'll love this aspect of Florence.

All tourist-oriented establishments, like large museums, popular restaurants, and transportation offices, are also staffed by fluent English-speakers. Locals outside the international tourism world can, for the most part, comprehend basic English words, so any further explanation is usually accompanied by a charadelike performance. Showing patience will take you far, as with any other city. Once your frustration gets the best of you, you'll draw less favorable reactions from Florentines. Take a breath, smile, and if they can't help you, politely say *"Grazie"* ("Thank you") and try a shopkeeper or waiter in a nearby restaurant. Worst-case scenario: Look for any bookstore or souvenir store and refer to the Italian-English (or vice versa) vocabulary and phrase guides.

Dress: Summer brings out the *fashionistas.* Men aren't at all shy when it comes to experimenting with colors and can usually be found combining bold, contrasting colors in their dress. Dudes will don the clam diggers and linen shirts, but, like the women, accessories are the focal points. Be it a pair of outrageous sneaks or neon belts, outfits aren't complete without the extra exclamation point. More casual dress involves T-shirts with asymmetrical prints and designer jeans. Women are a little edgier, lately wearing military-influenced tank tops during the summer heat along with their trendy skirts. Of course, their accessory of choice comes in the form of the big-label and big-lensed sunglasses. Dolce & Gabbana is the popular label among the 20-somethings for both eyewear and clothes.

Drinking: While Florentines have seen far too many exchange students' away-from-home antics to be shocked by outrageous behavior anymore, it's never cool to be an obnoxious drunk in this refined and elegant city. Young Florentines definitely know how to party, but there are some ground rules: 1) No singing "Come On Eileen" on Ponte Vecchio at midnight. 2) No open containers unless you see other well-groomed locals doing it. 3) No bodyshots off *David*'s toe!

place to find detailed bus maps and schedules.

○ **www.trenitalia.com**   Find train timetables, prices, and other info on the official website for Italy's national train system.

○ **www.aeroporto.firenze.it**   Information about the Amerigo Vespucci Airport.

Timetables, airport concessions and restaurants, and even a little airport history is available on the site.

○ **www.firenzemusei.it**   Admission fees, hours of operation, reservation numbers, and other practical info about Florence's most important museums.

Florence Nuts & Bolts

ATMs Cash machines (called *bancomat* in Italy) are everywhere in this well-touristed town, but you probably won't need to carry around a ton of euros while you're in Florence, since credit and debit cards are accepted almost everywhere. A few things you will need cash for: to-go refreshments at the local cafe, monument admissions, drinks, and buses, if you choose to take them. As always, plan your cash withdrawals carefully: The exchange rate is favorable through foreign ATMs, since the banks trade in large volume, but you're hit with fees of more than $5 (depending on your bank) every time you take out money while abroad.

Cellphone providers/service centers If you can't bear to be without a phone, several stores rent cellphones to students, tourists, and anyone else who needs it short term. The best provider for cellphone rental is **Campus Telecom** (Via de' Conti 22/r, near San Lorenzo; ☎ **055/277-6469;** www.webpuccino.it; Mon–Sat 10am–10pm and Sun noon–9pm). They're popular among international students who are in Florence for a semester or longer, but visitors can also use their services (via Vodafone or Wind). Incoming calls from the U.S. and Canada won't cost you a cent (not the case for the person calling you, unfortunately) and if you dial a number in either country, you'll pay .27€ for each minute.

Embassies & Consulates If you're aching for the sight of the red, white, and blue (and had your fill of the Red Garter, see "Partying"), look no farther than the U.S. consulate at Lungarno Vespucci 38 (200m/656 ft. west of Ponte Vespucci). We hope you'll never need to seek help at the consulate, but if something happens to your passport, you can call for assistance at ☎ **055/266-951** or head to the actual building. It's open Monday to Friday from 9am to 12:30pm.

Emergencies In an emergency, call the *polizia* at ☎ **113;** for nonemergencies (like lost or stolen property), use ☎ 055/49771 or visit the main police station (*questura*) at Via Zara 2 (near San Lorenzo). You can also turn to Italy's Army police force, the **Carabinieri** (who wear red-striped trousers designed by Valentino), to report emergencies or other disturbances of the peace. Call the Carabinieri at ☎ **112** for emergencies only; for non-emergencies, ☎ 055/2061. Their station (*caserma*) is at Borgo Ognissanti 48 (west of Santa Maria Novella). If your pocket gets picked, turn to the multi-lingual **tourist aid police** (☎ **055/203-911**) at Via Pietrapiana 24/r (near Santa Croce). To report a fire, a gas leak, or a grandma stuck in an elevator, dial ☎ **115** for the *Vigili del Fuoco* (fire department).

For **medical emergencies,** call an ambulance at ☎ **118,** or visit the *pronto soccorso* (emergency room, where you will not be charged for treatment, regardless of your insurance status) at the **Ospedale Santa Maria Nuova,** Piazza Santa Maria Nuova 1 (just east of the Duomo), ☎ 055/27581. The **Polizia Municipale,** who handle dog bites and other petty crimes, are at ☎ 055/328-333, and the **Vigili Urbani,** who write parking tickets and tow cars and are the bane of every Italian driver's existence, are at ☎ 055/32831.

Internet/wireless hot spots **InternetTrain** (www.internettrain.it), with its 15 locations throughout town, is the best place to check your e-mail, online train schedules, or the status of your fantasy baseball team. Walk a few blocks in any direction on a main thoroughfare and chances are you'll run into an InternetTrain. Purchase an access card that keeps track of your minutes (it's valid in any of the locations); rates run about 3€ an hour. They also sell drinks and snacks, making it a great rest stop for sightseers. The location on Via de' Benci, just south of Santa Croce (Via de' Benci 36/r; ☎ 055/263-8555; Mon–Fri 9:30am–1am, Sat 10am–1am, Sun noon–1am), is one of the largest, with 30 PCs, and it's frequently full of students and/or young travelers. Aside from the bars and hostels, you'll run into a large crowd of English-speaking college students there on exchange programs or summer break. Other locations are at Borgo San Jacopo 30/r (just south of Ponte Vecchio); Via Zannoni 1/r 9 (near San Lorenzo); Piazza Stazione 14/38 (opposite the train station); and Via Porta Rossa 38/r (south of Piazza della Repubblica).

Laundromats   Yeah, that isn't the Arno that reeks of 3-day-old prosciutto . . . head to one of the branches of **Wash & Dry** to get your threads smelling a bit fresher. There are eight locations in Florence, two in the city center: Via del Sole 29/r (just south of Piazza Santa Maria Novella) and Via Ghibellina 143/r (near Santa Croce). Both are open daily from 8am to 10pm. 3.50€ will get you one load washed, another 3.50€ will get you 20 minutes in the dryer. *Caution:* Always be sure to check the temperature settings of washers and dryers: Hot is *very* hot, so unless you are looking to shrink your wardrobe so that it'll fit better in your backpack, choose a lower setting.

Most loads take 60 minutes to dry, so think carefully about how much you really need to wash, otherwise you might end up blowing the day's food budget on hot air. (If you're only doing undergarments and socks, the hotel sink and a travel bottle of Woolite is a time-honored cost-cutting technique. Washing larger garments in the room is frowned upon, and let's be honest, you'll never get those Citizens really clean by sloshing them around in the bathtub.) There's also an Internet point at each Wash & Dry, but don't count on checking your e-mail while you wash. More often than not, the computers are broken down or buried underneath a stack of detergent.

Luggage storage   Blindly searching for hotels with a 40-pound pack on your back can lead to an embarrassing faceplant on the cobblestones. Luckily, the *deposito bagagli* (luggage storage counter) at Santa Maria Novella train station will help lighten your load. Whatever you don't need to bring while you're out and about can be stowed for 12 hours at 3€ per piece; if you need to keep your stuff there longer, each successive 12-hour period will cost you 2€ per piece.

Postage & Shipping   Stamps *(francobolli)* are sold at all *tabacchi;* they ask you how many postcards you're sending and where, and you tell them—it's a simple transaction. Postage for postcards and letters to anywhere in Europe or the Mediterranean basin is 0.52€; for the rest of the world, it's 0.62€. Red post boxes are on the sides of buildings in Florence; drop your postcards in the *"tutte le altre destinazioni"* (all other destinations) slot, as opposed to the *"città"* slot. Some hotels also have a mail drop. When you start to accumulate too many souvenirs, or you realize that you're never going to wear those hiking boots you packed, the easiest thing to do is ship 'em home.

Florence's main **post office** is just off Piazza Mercato Nuovo at Via Pellicceria 3 (☎ **055/211-147**; www.poste.it/en). Open Monday through Friday from 8:15am to 7pm and Saturday 8:15am to 12:30pm, the post office sells nifty yellow boxes and any other packaging supplies you might need. There are a few forms to fill out for parcels going overseas, but for all the bad press Italian government agencies get, the national mail system is actually quite hassle-free nowadays, with an excellent delivery record.

If you have important documents to send or need to get souvenirs to relatives securely and quickly, and you don't want to chance it with Italian bureaucracy, go to **Mail Boxes Etc.,** and see what brown can do for you; ship your stuff via UPS from the MBE branches at Lungarno Guicciardini 11/r (☎ 055/212-002); Corso dei Tintori 39/r (☎ 055/246-6660); and Via della Scala 13/r (☎ 055/268-173).

Restrooms   When you're out and about in Florence and nature calls, you should have no qualms about stopping in the nearest bar/cafe or restaurant and politely asking if you can use their *bagno*. This is standard practice throughout Italy—unlike in the U.S., Italian bathrooms are *not* for customers only. Drinking and eating establishments are required by law to allow anyone to use their toilet, although strung-out and derelict types are often told, "Sorry, the bathroom is out of order." So, as long as you're polite and not brandishing hypodermic needles, you'll be pointed to the restroom, which is usually a not-very-clean stall and almost invariably *in fondo a destra* (in the back, to the right).

There are also public restrooms in the train station that charge a fee, but they're mostly used by folks who don't know to ask at restaurants, and by junkies who got turned away at all the bars and restaurants.

Safety   By and large, Florence is a safe city. The only crime prevalent in the city center is pickpocketing. Keep your belongings close while you shop in the tightly packed market zones and in Santa Maria Novella train station. As with other big cities, avoid dimly lit alleyways, the lowest part of the riverbanks, and unpopulated parks at night.

Telephones   There are public pay phones *(cabina)* at the train station, in major piazzas and bus terminals, and at certain coffee bars (look for the white-and-red phone sign out front or the sticker in the window). Italian pay phones take a prepaid plastic card, called a *scheda telefonica,* which is issued by Telecom Italia and which must be purchased at a *tabacchi* store. Cards are sold in denominations of 2.50€, 5€, and 10€; in order for them to work, you must break off the perforated tab on the corner of the card. (A common rookie mistake is failing to break off the tab and then, when the card doesn't work, getting all huffy with the person who sold you the "defective" card. Don't do that.)

Local calls (anything with a "055" prefix) are pretty cheap—maybe 0.20€ for a short call, as are calls to land lines in other Italian cities (0.50€ for a short call to book a hotel in your next city, for example). Be aware, however, that calls from Italian land lines to Italian cellphones (three-digit prefixes beginning with "3," such as that given you by Alessandro, the guy you met at Space Electronic last night) are horrendously expensive and will probably bleed your *scheda telefonica* dry in a matter of seconds.

Calls from Italian pay phones to overseas phone numbers aren't as pricey as you might think, especially after 7pm Italian time (late morning/early afternoon in North America), so as long as you can keep it somewhat brief, a call home shouldn't run you more than a few euros. If you're going to be chatting for a while, however, it does add up.

The best bet, if you need to call home frequently, are **international phone cards** (anywhere from 5€ to 20€, available at newsstands or *tabacchi*) issued by a number of private companies that often have more advantageous rates for calling abroad than those issued by the phone company. These private phone cards usually have a PIN code

FLORENCE & TUSCANY

that you reveal by scratching off a grey bar on the back, and a series of access numbers to call before you're connected with Mom and Dad. Keep in mind that you will still need a dial tone to use one of these cards, and to get a dial tone at a pay phone, you always need to insert a Telecom Italia *scheda telefonica*. Moral of the story? Use the phone at your hotel, where the dial tone is free, when you need to call home. If dialing direct from your hotel phone (that is, without any PIN codes or phone cards), always ask hotel staff upfront what their charges are. Some hotels make a sizeable profit off guest phone use; other more honest souls only charge you what the phone company charges them, with no markup whatsoever.

Sleeping

Florence has a ton of accommodations options for every budget and taste, but the city is also inundated almost year-round with tourists, trade-fair attendees, and gourmands, so it pays to book as far in advance as possible. Remember, you can always cancel reservations, penalty-free, within 48 hours of your planned arrival. Most of Florence's hotels are concentrated in the area north and just east of the train station, in Santa Maria Novella, and while the train station isn't the most romantic 'hood in town, it really is an easy walk from here to all the sights (which is *not* true of Rome and its train station). During high season, your chances of finding a decent (and decently priced) place go down dramatically as the day wears on, so if your train arrives in Florence at 5pm, you could be in for some frustration if you haven't booked ahead.

If you don't have any luck with any of the places listed here, you can call **Consorzio Firenze Albergo** (Florence Hotel Consortium) at ☎ **055/270-7278,** open Monday to Friday 9am to 1pm and 3 to 6pm. You can also do a search through its online database at **www. firenzealbergo.it**. There's also a hotel-reservations kiosk at the train station, staffed by young and usually friendly English speakers.

HOSTEL

📺 (Best) ➔ **Hostel Archi Rossi** ★★★
Probably the best hostel in Italy. If you ever wanted to experience the crackhouse lifestyle,

but without the dirty syringes littering the floor and junkies slumped in the corner, then look no farther than the Archi Rossi, 2 blocks from Santa Maria Novella station. At first glance, the graffitied walls give the impression that the hostel was once a squatters' haunt, but look more closely and you'll realize the inscriptions are notes left by previous guests. The rooms, which sleep from 4 to 10, coed or female-only, are extremely clean and spacious, with large closetlike lockers where you can throw your backpack or suitcase. Some rooms have private bathrooms, while others have shared shower and toilet off the main hallway. The hostel also has a common dining room where fried eggs and bacon are served most mornings, and where movies in English are shown most nights. After a long day of art-gawking, pony up 3€ at the reception snack bar for a sizeable bottle of cold beer and head for the interior garden—furnished with Italianate carved stone benches and tables, plaster casts of the Venus de Milo, and ample greenery, it's an atmospheric spot where you can spend an evening socializing with fellow travelers, or just preload before hitting the bars. If you get bored at the Archi Rossi, there's always the city of Florence outside. *Via Faenza 94/r (just north of Via Nazionale).* ☎ *055/290-804. www. hostelarchirossi.com. Single bed in large dorm (10-person, coed) 21€, medium dorm (8-person, female only) 22€, small dorm (6-person, coed or female only) 23€, small dorm (5-person, coed or female only) 24€, small dorm (4-person,*

Sleeping in Florence

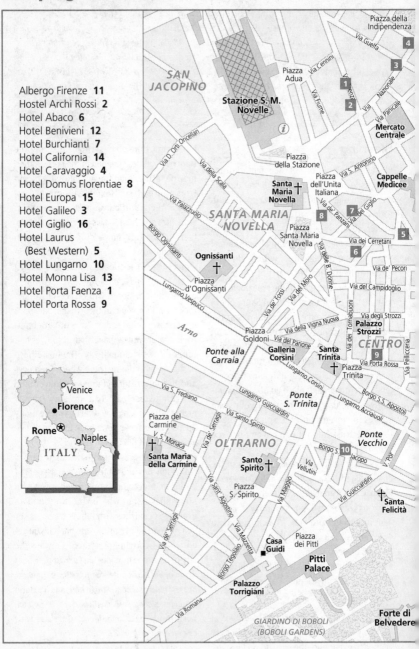

Albergo Firenze **11**
Hostel Archi Rossi **2**
Hotel Abaco **6**
Hotel Benivieni **12**
Hotel Burchianti **7**
Hotel California **14**
Hotel Caravaggio **4**
Hotel Domus Florentiae **8**
Hotel Europa **15**
Hotel Galileo **3**
Hotel Giglio **16**
Hotel Laurus
  (Best Western) **5**
Hotel Lungarno **10**
Hotel Monna Lisa **13**
Hotel Porta Faenza **1**
Hotel Porta Rossa **9**

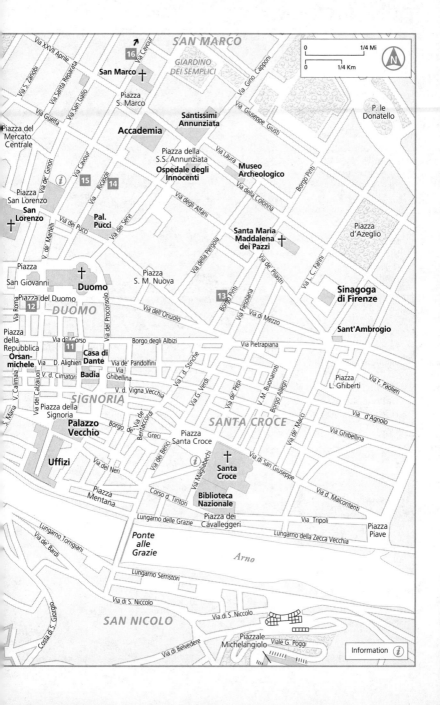

Eating in Florence

Accademia Restaurant **22**
Acqua al Due/
   La Via dell'Acqua **14**
Badiani **21**
Bottega del Gelato **6**
Caffetteria Piansa **20**
D'Antico Noé **17**
Festina Lente **23**
I Raddi **8**
Il Pizzaiuolo **18**
Il Vegetariano **24**
La Giostra **19**
La Maremma **12**
Le Mossacce **16**
Nella **5**
Nerbone **3**
Osteria de' Benci **11**
Osteria del
   Cinghiale Bianco **7**
Paoli **15**
Rivoire **25**
Salumeria Verdi **10**
Trattoria Antichi Cancelli **2**
Trattoria Enzo e Piero **1**
Trattoria La Casalinga **9**
Trattoria Sostanza **4**
Vivoli **13**

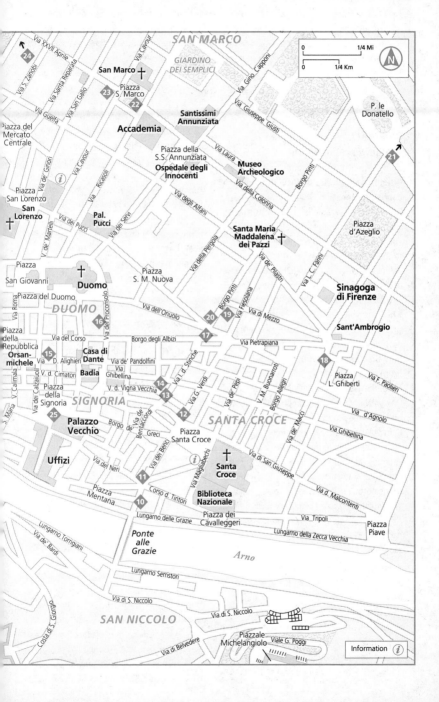

coed or female only) 25€; single room (shared bathroom) 30€; triple room (private bathroom) 75€. Amenities: Common room; open-air garden/terrace; free Internet point; laundry facilities; personal lockers; TV room. Reception open 6:30am–2am. Rooms closed 11am–2:30pm for cleaning (common rooms, Internet point, etc., are still open during that time).

CHEAP

→ **Albergo Firenze** This is a spotless though institutional-feeling government-rated two-star, offering little in the way of charm. Its location, halfway between the Duomo and Piazza della Signoria, is the real selling point. Whether or not you stay here, you will probably walk by the Albergo Firenze 10 times during the course of the day, which means that if you do stay here, you can stop off in your room to change shoes, deposit leather goods bought at San Lorenzo, etc., whenever you please. The Firenze also boasts 57 units—way more than other economical options in the heart of the historic center—so they'll often have availability when other properties are booked solid. All rooms have full baths with tubs; not all have shower stalls. One of our writers stayed here when she was on a student program and remembers decor being bland and staff being impersonal, but also remembers feeling quite smug about catching sight of the Duomo's candy stripes down the side streets immediately adjacent to the hotel. *Piazza Donati 4 (Via del Corso, off Via Calzaiuoli).* ☎ *055/214-203. www.albergofirenze.net. Single 65€–78€, double 75€–98€, triple 106€–132€. Rates include breakfast. In room: A/C, TV, hair dryer, safe.*

→ **Hotel Abaco** ★★ I can't say enough about Bruno, the owner of this place. One look at him, with his Hawaiian shirt and shiny bald head, and all who enter the Abaco feel at ease. Bruno will see to it that you have everything you'll need. He'll do laundry for a reasonable price, personally bring you to a luggage store if you need a replacement

rucksack (mine had broken, and he spent the best part of an afternoon helping me find the right store), and he'll impart his vast knowledge of the town, from the 1400s to the present day. Incredibly enough, this is only a government-rated one-star—well-laid-out rooms have old-world furnishings to match the Renaissance theme of the hotel, high wood-beamed ceilings, and gilded-edge sofas. Further adding to the charm of the property, each room is named after a famous Italian artist (Caravaggio, Michelangelo, Leonardo, etc.) and, quite adorably, contains prints and color schemes fitting with the respective artist. Guests in a few rooms avail of the common lavatory in the hallway, but most have full private facilities; all are equipped with a private shower. *Via dei Banchi 1 (at Via dei Cerretani).* ☎ *055/238-1919. www.abaco-hotel.it. Double with shower 72€–82€, with full bathroom 85€–95€; triple with shower 95€–105€, with complete bathroom 110€–125€; quad with complete bathroom 135€–155€. Rates include breakfast. Amenities: Internet point; laundry service. In room: A/C, TV.*

→ **Hotel California** ★ It's too easy a target, so I'll skip the obvious but tempting Eagles references. Hotel California offers quite a bit for its relatively low price tag. As with several other hotels in the center of Florence, many rooms have atmospheric little touches here and there—brick arches, frescoes, vaulted ceilings, partial views of the Duomo—that remind you that you're sleeping in the middle of the cradle of the Renaissance. Shower in the simple, spotless bathroom (a few rooms have Jacuzzi tubs), enjoy your buffet breakfast on the cozy terrace and then get a head start on the *David*-seeking hordes at the nearby Accademia. A stay here is as soothing as the warm smell of colitas—whatever that is—rising up through the air. *Via Ricasoli 30 (2 blocks north of the Duomo).* ☎ *055/ 282753. Fax 055/283499. www.californiaflorence.it. Single 60€–120€, double 75€–180€, triple 120€–243€, quad 145€–300€. Rates* include breakfast. In room: A/C, TV, some bathrooms w/Jacuzzi.

→ **Hotel Europa** Get through the dark, creepy entrance on the first floor and see if you can find someone at the front desk. I waited a good 20 minutes before I saw a single soul in the sparsely decorated reception, so you may want to bring a book when you check in. Otherwise, the rest of the hotel is quite cozy; some of the small, comfortable rooms even have spectacular views of the Duomo. The staff, when available, is friendly enough to warrant a return trip to this affordable inn. *Via Cavour 14 (just north of Via de' Gori).* ☎ *055/239-6715. www.webhoteleuropa.com. Standard: single 60€–100€, double 80€–140€, triple 120€–180€, quad 140€–210€; Superior/Suite (upgraded furniture and view): single 100€, double 140€, triple 170€, quad 210€. Rates include breakfast. Amenities: Internet point; laundry service. In room: A/C, TV, hair dryer, minibar, safe.*

→ **Hotel Porta Faenza** ★ The combination of newer technologies and 18th-century decor is a little awkward in this government-rated three-star a few blocks from the train station. The keycard slots, DO NOT DISTURB buttons at the door, and the talking elevator seem out of place in this otherwise charming and comfortable hotel. Decor is colorful and warm, and some rooms have restored wood-beam ceilings; all rooms have full private bath. The pleasant staff is extremely knowledgable and will even give you an abridged history of the building, which includes a noteworthy bit of archaeology near the Internet point—a medieval well: In the 13th century, the well provided water for the three surrounding buildings (two of which now make up Hotel Porta Faenza). *Via Faenza 77 (a few blocks north of Via Nazionale).* ☎ *055/217975. Fax 055/210101. www.hotelportafaenza.it. Single standard 60€–100€, double standard 80€–150€, triple standard 100€–160€, quad*

110€–170€. Rates include breakfast. In room: A/C, TV, hair dryer, Internet port, minibar, safe.*

DOABLE

MTV Best → **Hotel Burchianti** ★★★ If you're lucky, when you arrive at the door of Hotel Burchianti, you'll be greeted by the warm smile of Rela, the septuagenarian super-hostess. Rela maintains a gem of a hotel—one of Florence's best boutique properties—in an unassuming part of Via del Giglio. We recommend booking well in advance for a room at the Burchianti; such a classy, cozy and affordable place in the heart of Florence won't be secret much longer. Each room contains sumptuous Baroque frescoes and stuccoed reliefs that are still being uncovered by the management—the former tenants of the building inexplicably white-washed the gorgeous 17th-century wall decorations. Furnishings vary from room to room: Some beds are 19th-century four-posters, others have elaborate wrought-iron headboards; but everything looks inviting and is warmly lit. If it's available, try to book the spacious Degli Angeli suite, to the right and rear of the bar. The dreamlike scene painted on the ceiling above the bed will render the TV, or any other form of entertainment, useless. Security, for those concerned, is a non-issue—every guest needs to be buzzed in at the front gate, a painless process, even if you've had a few nightcaps out on the town. *Via del Giglio 8 (off Via Panzani).* ☎ *055/212796. www.hotelburchianti.com. Single 90€–120€, double 130€–170€, triple 160€–220€, suite 150€–230€, studio 170€–230€. In room: A/C, TV, hair dryer, minibar, safe.*

→ **Hotel Caravaggio** ★ Across the street from Piazza Indipendenza, this hotel offers its guests the luxury of having quiet green space right outside its doors. Thanks to recent restorations, guest rooms are immaculate and comfortable. Unfortunately, the renovations were also heavy-handed in places, leaving the hotel a bit too modern-feeling, even though a few wonderful antique touches, like iron stoves, have been preserved. Nevertheless, you'd be hard-pressed to find cleaner bathrooms in Italy. You could almost eat off the pristine, newly installed bathtubs. If one were so inclined, one could dump a couple gallons of milk and cereal in there and have an in-room breakfast. Silly rabbit, Trix are for exfoliating! *Piazza Indipendenza 5 (just north of Via Guelfa).* ☎ *055/496310. Fax 055/4628827. www.firenzewelcomehotels.com. Single 70€–140€, double 98€–220€, superior double 120€–240€, triple 140€–250€, quad 150€–300€. Amenities: Bar (open 24 hr.); Internet point. In room: A/C, TV, Internet ready, Jacuzzi (some rooms), minibar, safe.*

→ **Hotel Domus Florentiae** ★ As far as automatic doors go, the Domus has, quite possibly, the slowest sliding door I've ever seen. Once you finally get through the pregnant pause of the entryway, you'll be welcomed by an amicable staff and a bright, elegant reception. There are only 14 rooms, handsomely appointed with ochre- and rose-toned jacquard bedspreads and curtains, wide-plank wood floors, and pretty, understated light fixtures; each has a larger-than-average, clean bathroom. Despite its proximity to the street, the thick windows help ensure a quiet slumber. It's a definite upgrade from the Universo next door. Just bring a book (I hear *War and Peace* is a good read) to pass the time while you're waiting to get through the entrance. Prices vary wildly from low to high season, so if you're coming in peak periods, the Domus Florentiae moves into "Splurge" territory. *Via degli Avelli 2 (Piazza Santa Maria Novella).* ☎ *055/2654645. Fax 055/2776429. www.domusflorentiahotel.com. Single 85€–180€, standard double 95€–250€, superior double 105€–270€. In room: A/C, TV, hair dryer, safe.*

→ **Hotel Galileo** ★ The throw rugs on the tiled villa floor and the sturdy dark-wood furnishings give the accommodations here a bucolic quality that you'd normally expect to find in an agricultural hill town outside of Florence. The 31 rooms, decorated in a refined Tuscan style with warm colors and dark woods, have all the modern comforts you'll need, and the friendly staff will try to accommodate other requests you might have. *Via Nazionale 22/a (near Via Guelfa).* ☎ *055/496645. Fax 055/496447. www.galileohotel.it. Single 80€–90€, double (single use) 120€, double standard 130€–140€, double superior 150€–170€, triple 175€–190€ (comes with bottle of red wine). Buffet breakfast included. In room: A/C, TV, hair dryer, minibar, safe.*

→ **Hotel Giglio** ★ The only knock against Hotel Giglio, besides a name similar to a ghastly movie I was once subjected to on a flight from New York to Milan, is that it's about a 15-minute walk from the train station or the Duomo. On the plus side, it's close to the Accademia, and the streets surrounding it are especially quiet compared to centrally located hotels in Florence. If you don't mind walking the few extra blocks, Hotel Giglio is the perfect spot for a relaxing night's rest. Rooms are pristine and furnished nicely, with walls painted a rich buttercream hue, and bedding in muted green (according to the experts, the most conducive color for peaceful slumber). The experienced staff, handpicked by the ever-hospitable manager Marco (who also manages the restaurant Cinghiale Bianco, p. 237) from well-respected hotels in Italy, are veritable fountains of Firenze knowledge. Furthermore, breakfasts are generous, and there's a 24-hour bar. You can't ask for much more. *Via Cavour 85 (at Via Sant'Anna).* ☎ *055/486621. Fax 055/461163. www.hotelgiglio.fi.it. Single 80€–125€, double 90€–170€, triple 110€–195€, quad 130€–220€. Breakfast included. Bus 1, 11, 17, 7. In room: A/C, TV, Internet point, safe.*

→ **Hotel Porta Rossa** Frescoed ceilings seem to be the norm for hotels that want to add a little extra historical flair and possibly an extra star to their rating. It's no different at the Porta Rossa. It started out as an inn for foreign travelers in the 14th century and then became part of a merchant's property in the 16th century. While the reception and foyer (and billiard room!) give off quite an elegant, petite-grand-dame aura, the rooms are less chic. (On their website, which has no pictures of the actual accommodations, management is coy on the subject, saying "We hope that you will appreciate the surprise element involved when booking a room with us.") Which is not to say that the rooms are uncomfortable—the owners of the "Red Door" have kept much of the hotel's unique period furnishing and frescoes in the relaxing rooms. Watch out for that first step, though: In some rooms, beds sit upon diabolical, toe-destroying stepped platforms. *Via Porta Rossa 19 (just off Piazza Santa Trinità).* ☎ *055/287551. Fax 055/282179. www.hotelportarossa.com. Single 125€, double (single use) 166€, double (2 separate beds) 166€, triple 210€, quad 245€. Rates include breakfast. Amenities: Laundry service. In room: A/C, TV, minibar.*

SPLURGE

➜ **Hotel Benivieni** ★ For the past 4 years, Ines has been running this little-known, converted 15th-century manor with as much gusto as her demeanor would suggest. The moment you walk past the foyer, you forget that you're around the corner from the Duomo. The sunny, semiexotic, and spacious reception area feels more like Casablanca than Tuscany. Little touches in the already spotless rooms, like vaulted ceilings in the ground-floor rooms, add to the high-class aura of the inn. Bathrooms are borderline luxurious, but the price might be a bit excessive. Ultimately, the real luxury here, and what you're paying for, is being 50m (164 ft.) from the Duomo. *Via dell'Oche 5 (2 blocks south of the Duomo).* ☎ *055/238-2133. Fax 055/2398248. www.hotelbenivieni.it. Single 220€, double 220€. Rates include breakfast. Amenities: A/C; TV; garage; garden/terrace; Internet point; safe.*

➜ **Hotel Laurus (Best Western)** Drop by the frigid lobby at this government-rated four-star, perfectly placed between the Duomo and the train station, for a breather from the sizzling summer weather. Crash on the relaxing red sofas, grab a copy of *USA Today,* and pretend to wait for a guest. If you decide to pony up for a room, you'll find comfortable, if cookie-cutter, chain-hotel offerings. The small LCD TV screens are a nice touch, but everything else, from furniture to the lighting, is typical franchise fare: You might as well be in Albuquerque, as there's no Florentine influence anywhere within the rooms. On the upside, such familiar decor—and reliable *Amerrrican* air-conditioning—should guarantee you a super night's sleep, and the English-fluent staff are hospitable to a fault. *Via Cerretani 54/r (at Piazza Santa Maria Maggiore).* ☎ *055/2381752. Fax 055/268308. www.vivahotels.com. Single 150€, superior single (improved view) 160€, double 200€, superior double 215€. Rates include breakfast and are higher during high season. Amenities: Restaurant; bar; laundry service; luggage storage; tour desk; transportation rental desk. In room: A/C, satellite TV, hair dryer, DSL Internet connection, minibar, safe.*

➜ **Hotel Lungarno** ★★★ This is where wealthy travelers book a room to get away from wealthy tourists. The difference between the two is that the former know where to blow their cash, whereas the latter haphazardly reserve a room at a big international chain five-star next to the Duomo. The Lungarno, the flagship of the Ferragamo family's exclusive Lungarno Hotels group, is literally "along the Arno," tucked away in a chic part of the Oltrarno. There is no 6m (20–ft.) sign proclaiming its presence, nor is there a line of valets waiting to take your Benz. Instead, it sits quietly confident in its own luxurious splendor knowing that well-informed guests will make their way to Borgo San Jacopo. Some hotels love to highlight the small fresco on the ceiling or the two bricks from the original archway, but Hotel Lungarno scoffs at their attempt at tying historical features into the decor. They incorporate entire archways and vaulted ceilings throughout their cavernous rooms and throw in posh, contemporary furniture to balance the new and old perfectly. For those who can do without the castle-keep-ish stone walls and brick arches, there are classier and more modern rooms to satiate your desire to live like royalty. The location provides guests with unparalleled views of Ponte Vecchio and the Arno. Clean out your savings account, book a night here, and worry about how you'll eat for the next 2 weeks *after* you've spoiled yourself silly in the Lungarno. If it's still beyond your budget, you can always come and have a drink or meal at the hotel's splendid riverside **Borgo San Jacopo** restaurant. *Borgo San Jacopo 14 (between Ponte Vecchio and Ponte Santa Trinità).* ☎ *055/27261. Fax 055/268437. www.lungarnohotels.com. Single 220€, double (single use) 330€, double classic 350€, double superior 460€, double deluxe 520€, executive 570€, junior suite 720€–1,030€, presidential suite 1,380€– 2,500€. Amenities: A/C; satellite TV; fax and modem line available; conference rooms; bar; limo service; garage.*

➜ **Hotel Monna Lisa** ★★ The real *Mona Lisa* may be in Paris, but you'll get your fill of Leonardo's demure damsel (also known as *La Gioconda* in Italy) at this luxury hotel a few blocks behind (east of) the Duomo. Originally a 13th-century convent, it was converted into a hotel in 1956. Random bits of art (mostly of the *Mona Lisa*) are sprinkled throughout the enormous property, but the most noteworthy is the *Rape of the Sabines* statuette. This miniature, rough version was the model that earned the sculptor Giambologna the commission for the real, full-size marble statue now found in Piazza della Signoria. Another work worth checking out is the painting of the *Mona Lisa* in the common area near the courtyard. Yup, that's a *canna,* or marijuana

cigarette, in the madame's coy lips. Art aside, the hotel interior is decadent, with plush chairs, paintings gracing every wall, and high, wood-beamed ceilings. The lush courtyard is the perfect place to enjoy your breakfast when the weather is pleasant. You'll without a doubt be pampered in this joint. Pun definitely intended. *Borgo Pinti 27 (off Via dell'Oriuolo).* ☎ *055/2479751. Fax 055/2479755. www. monnalisa.it. Single classic (shower only) 110€–150€, superior 122€–180€; double (single-use) classic 140€–230€, superior 155€–250€; double classic 182€–290€, superior 207€–350€; triple 235€–415€; quad 270€–497€; junior suite 280€–500€; suite 410€–700€. Breakfast included. Amenities: A/C; TV; minibar; safe; parking; garden; Internet point; gym; solarium.*

Eating

Florentine cuisine takes full advantage of all the ingredients that thrive in the fields of Tuscany, and of the beasts that graze upon it. Menus are never without a good amount of olive oil, tomatoes, mushrooms, truffles, wild boar, and beef.

Once you've settled on a place to stuff your stomach, expect at least two or three courses to arrive at your table. Simple meals traditionally start off with an antipasto, or appetizer; the classic starter in Florence is *crostini,* toasted slices of country bread slathered with some kind of paté, usually chicken liver (try it, it's quite tasty). After that gets your taste buds going, they'll get you started on the primi, or first courses, which are usually some kind of *ribollita* (stewy soup of cabbage, beans, and bread), risotto (rice dish with creamy sauce), or a pasta dish. Save some room for the main Tuscan event: the secondi, or meat-based courses. Florence's own *bistecca alla fiorentina* (1-inch-thick beef steak on the bone—mmm!!—meant to be shared by two diners) is the envy of all Italy and well worth the splurge if you love red meat. If you don't, most restaurants also offer hefty slices of pork and chicken that will have you full and asking for the check in no time. If you're a vegetarian or vegan, take advantage of the many vegetable-based soups and pastas, and, since we're in Tuscany, beans, beans, and more beans!

As for *vino,* you are in Chianti country, so you should probably test Tuscany's most famous red at least once on its native turf. However, any restaurant's *vino della casa* (house red or white wine, brought out in $^1/_4$-, $^1/_2$-, or 1-liter carafes—however you wish) is also made locally and usually very drinkable, and it's always much cheaper than ordering bottles of "serious" wine. When the bill arrives, take a peek and see if the tip *(servizio)* has been included. If it hasn't, adding on an extra 5% to 10% is customary, depending on how attentive the wait staff has been. Even if the service was outstanding, a gratuity of 15% or more is extravagant in Italy.

CHEAP

➔ **Festina Lente** SNACK/SANDWICH This miniature diner in San Marco is another place to get a meal for less than 5€. Apart from the usual snack bar fare of premade sandwiches, you can score a slab of lasagna or a small dish of risotto for a measly 4€. It's a tiny place, so ask for your grub to go *(da portare via),* grab some napkins and a spork, and look for an empty bench in Piazza San Marco. *Via Cavour 52 (at Via de' Gori). Daily for lunch. Sandwiches 3€–4€; primi (lasagna or risotto) 4€.*

➔ **Il Vegetariano** ★ VEGETARIAN Florentine and Tuscan food are usually meat-heavy, so for greener alternatives, head for this casual spot, a 10-minute walk north of the Duomo. As if you couldn't deduce this from the name, Il Vegetariano is one of few real restaurants in Florence where all meals are 100% vegetarian. Menus vary from day to day, but you'll find variations on typical local dishes with ingredients like squash, olives,

sprouts, and bean curd replacing meat. Leave it to the health-food restaurant to have an alternative service system, too: first you order, then you pay, and then, when your food is ready, you pick up your plate from the server behind the counter. In any case, the results are extremely palatable, and the prices are reasonable, so if you have to indulge your travel partner's repeatedly voiced desire to try tofu boar, Il Vegetariano is your spot. *Via delle Ruote 30r (off Via Santa Reparata).* ☎ *055/475030. Primi 5€–6€; secondi 7.50€–8€. No credit cards. Tues–Fri 12:30–2:30pm, Tues–Sun 7:30pm–midnight. Closed 3 weeks in Aug and Dec 24–Jan 2.*

➔ **Le Mossacce** ★★ FLORENTINE Finding a restaurant that serves local cuisine that doesn't break the bank *and* is a block away from the Duomo is almost impossible. Luckily, I said "almost." Le Mossacce is a trattoria small in stature, big on ambience, and easy like Sunday morning on the wallet. Once you're seated, chipper waiters will take the time to explain all their dishes and specials of the day. You can be polite, pretending to be interested, and wait until they're finished, or you can just blurt out "*bistecca alla fiorentina*" the second they arrive. This steak is the king of Florentine cuisine and actually not that expensive once you realize the price is for *two* people. Most important of all, the gorgeous hunk of meat is grilled to perfection by masters who'd rather be flogged in Piazza della Signoria than serve you an overcooked steak. Although Le Mossacce is close to the Duomo, it's tucked away on Via del Proconsolo, a street rarely inundated with tourists. *Via del Proconsolo 55r (a block south of the Duomo).* ☎ *055/294361. Primi 4.20€–4.70€; secondi 4.70€–14€. Mon–Fri noon–2:30pm and 7–9:30pm.*

➔ **Nerbone** ★ FLORENTINE/TUSCAN Head to this outpost at the Mercato Centrale and enjoy their *panino con bollito,* a boiled beef sandwich that's dipped in meat juices

(Florentines call this *bagnato*). Writer Marchesa Bona Frescobaldi claims that this *bagnato* is "as much a symbol of Florence as is Michelangelo's *David*"—a bit of an exaggeration, but you get the point. The chefs proudly call their offerings "the food of the people," referring to such dishes as *trippa* (tripe) *alla fiorentina*. The tripe is cooked in tomato sauce with a sprinkling of Parmesan. *Ribollita* is a hearty, slow-cooked stew made with old bread and vegetables (it's far more delicious than it sounds). Also try their chickpea or garbanzo soup and their pasta with Tuscan sausages and beans. Opened in 1872, this simple side-street stall has only five tables, which are always full. Don't despair; join the locals at the bar. *Mercato Centrale (entrance on Via dell'Ariento; ground-floor stand no. 292).* ☎ *055/219949. Table reservations not accepted. Main courses 3.10€–8€. Cash only. Mon–Fri 7am–2pm; Sat 7am–5pm. Closed 1 week at Christmas and 2 weeks in Aug (dates vary).*

➜ **Salumeria Verdi** SNACK/SANDWICH Admission from the museums leaving you with fewer euros than you thought? Stroll by Via Giuseppe Verdi and check out Salumeria Verdi. They always have specials in the afternoon for *primi piatti* (usually variations on lasagna) that will only set you back 3.80€. The serving size is also pretty decent for the price. *Via Giuseppe Verdi 36 (3 blocks south of Santa Croce).* ☎ *055/244-517. Sandwiches/platters 7€–16€. Open Mon–Sat for lunch.*

DOABLE

➜ **Accademia Restaurant** ★ CREATIVE FLORENTINE Hailing from Brooklyn, Gianni Aldo's wife has certainly influenced the way the native Florentine runs his restaurant. Many of the dishes in Accademia Restaurant marry traditional Tuscan fare with a Williamsburg twist with great gastronomic success. If you opt out of their four-dish, four-wine prix-fixe menu (35€), you can pick and choose from their á la carte creations. While you munch on their warm, homemade bread,

order the Michelangelo salad. It comes teeming with pear, pecorino (you know it as *romano*, a hard, tangy cheese made from sheep's milk), pine nuts, honey, and arugula. Follow it up with their homemade pasta; we emphatically recommend the ricotta-and-spinach-stuffed ravioli in a truffle sauce. If you still have room, scarf down the *filetto di manzo al Brachetto bacche di ginepro*. If you think the name is a mouthful, wait until they plop the beef filet, marinated and cooked in Brachetto wine with juniper berries, in front of you. Glazed onions, who didn't make the cut to be part of the dish's name, also play an essential supporting role. Brooklyn's loss is Florence's gain! *Piazza San Marco 7/r.* ☎ *055/217343. Primi 7€, secondi 13€; lunch primi 6€, secondi 9€.*

➜ **Acqua al Due/La Via dell'Acqua** ★★ TUSCAN Show me someone who's studied in Florence in the past 10 years, and I'll show you someone who sings the praises of Acqua al Due. An institution favored by broke exchange-program types, this homey trat near Santa Croce is famous for its *assaggio di primi,* a sampling of five different types of pasta or risotto that'll only set you back 8€. If the thought of five rounds of pasta has your carb-conscious soul quaking in its boots, there's also the *assaggio di insalate* (salad sampler). If you care to venture into secondi territory, Acqua al Due offers carnivores the chance to sample tender and juicy beef strips drizzled in a variety of sauces (the balsamic vinegar–based glaze is a decadent and velvety treat you'll not soon forget). All in all, everything's pretty affordable, they're open late, and you're almost sure to find fellow young international folk with whom to strike up a conversation. Just be sure to make a reservation. La Via dell'Acqua, the new sister restaurant around the corner, is garnering praise for its comfier vibe. *Via della Vigna Vecchia 40/r (at Via dell'Acqua).* ☎ *055/284-170. www.acquaal2.it. Reservations required. Primi 7€–8€; secondi 8€–17€. Daily 7:30pm–1am.*

➜ **I Raddi** ★ TUSCAN   If you ever find yourself in the depths of the Oltrarno, craving Tuscan cuisine, you can find reasonably priced options in I Raddi. Owner Duccio prepares a menu of saliva-inducing dishes like the *tagliolini ardiglione,* made up of sausage and herbs, and *peposo alla fornacina con spinaci,* a plate of beef baked in wine and served with a side of spinach. It might be a little tough locating this tiny joint at the southern, dog-legging end of Via Ardiglione, but the substantial meals are well worth your perseverance. *Via Ardiglione 47r (off Via de' Serragli, about 500m/1,640 ft. south of Ponte alla Carraia).* ☎ *055/211-072. www.iraddi.it. Reservations recommended. Primi 7€; secondi 10€–15€. Mon–Sat noon–3pm and 7–11pm. Closed 10 days in Feb and a week in mid-August.*

➜ **La Maremma** ★ TUSCAN   La Maremma (named after Tuscany's "wild west" cowboy country) is the place in Santa Croce to grab tasty Tuscan eats. Luca prepares an amazing *quaglia al ripieno Vermentino;* the stuffed quail, doused in the subtle Vermentino wine sauce, is tender and bursting with flavor. Before you dive into the main course, though, start off with the traditional *crostini alla fiorentina:* toasted canapés with chicken-liver pâté. Throw in the '60s soul hits of Al Green and Aretha with the sharp red-and-black decor, and you're left with a relaxing and satisfying Florentine dining experience. *Via Verdi 16/r (1 block north of Santa Croce).* ☎ *055/244615. Fax 055/240972. www.ristorante lamaremma.it. Primi 6€–8€; secondi 10€–15€. Closed Wed.*

➜ **Nella** ★ FLORENTINE   Waking up in time for breakfast is incredibly hard to do in Florence. After a tiring day of sightseeing and a bacchanalian night of . . . well . . . bacchanalia, most mornings start around 11. Make up for it by indulging yourself at Nella, a small, homey trat between the Ponte Vecchio and Piazza Santa Trinità. Lunch, served from noon to 3pm, is pretty much a locals' scene. Ask the gruff but energetic owner, Federico

(who bears an odd resemblance to Emeril Lagasse), to serve you the *gnocchetti rosé* (mini potato-pasta dumplings in a creamy tomato sauce) in all its messy glory. Once you wipe the smile, and the sauce, off your face, dig in to the pepper-crusted pork loin. The tangy cuts and the accompanying potatoes might be a hair salty for some tastes, but it's still mouth-watering. As Federico has his roots deeply entrenched in music, many visiting artists and musicians stop by Nella for lunch or dinner and, in addition to the family-run aspect, a very tight relationship between Federico and the majority of his patrons is obvious. When you've finished your main course, finish off your meal with the outstanding *panna cotta.* A riff off of his grandmother's recipe, the gooey and rich hockey puck of cooked cream is dusted with a fine chocolate powder. Federico brags that it's the best in Florence, and I can't argue with him. *Bam! Via delle Terme 19/r (near Via Pelliceria).* ☎ *055/218925. Lunch primi 6€, secondi 11€; dinner primi 8€, secondi 10€–16€. Closed Sun.*

➜ **Osteria de' Benci** ★ TUSCAN   Frequented by plenty of in-the-know locals, this trattoria offers reliably tasty cuisine and great value in a lively setting. Beyond traditional Tuscan plates *(ribollita, trippa alla fiorentina),* you can also try more creative pastas, which change according to the season. One standout on the list of unusual primi is the "drunk spaghetti" *(spaghetti all'ubriacone),* which is boiled in red wine and then tossed with garlic and *peperoncino* (red pepper). Steak and beef fillet are also excellent here, but you might want to save your appetite and your euros for their fantastic desserts. *Via de' Benci 13/r (just south of Piazza Santa Croce).* ☎ *055/234-4923. Primi 8€; secondi 10€–20€. Closed Sun.*

➜ **Osteria del Cinghiale Bianco** ★ TUSCAN   When he's not tending his charming inn, the Hotel Giglio (p. 232), Marco can be found managing his father Massimo's restaurant on the southern side of the Arno. Once you cross Ponte Santa Trinità, duck down Borgo San Jacopo to the left, and then look for the wooden boar sign on your right. Marco and his first-rate staff will pluck you from the door and proceed to wait on you hand and foot. Don't even think about not ordering their *ribollita*: the fresh beans, lush spinach, and hearty potatoes will warm up your taste buds for the main event—the wild boar. Featured not only in the restaurant's namesake and in the random pieces of art within the dining area, the wild boar meat is, not surprisingly, the main ingredient in many of the dishes. Try the wild boar salami if you want a small sample before ordering your main course. For the less adventurous, tender and juicy beef sirloin strips are available (served rare). Not in the mood for meat? The ravioli with porcini mushrooms are bursting with woodsy flavor—they're in season in the fall. Finally, close it out with a shot of *digestivo*: Choose between an *amaro* (bitter, like Montenegro); *limoncello*, a sweet lemon elixir; or *grappa*, a colorless firewater made from the dregs of the wine-making process—not for the faint of stomach but much prized by those who've acquired the taste. *Borgo S. Jacopo 43/r (between Ponte Vecchio and Ponte Santa Trinità).* ☎ *055/215706. www.cinghiale bianco.it. Primi 5€–10€; secondi 9.50€–16€ Mon–Fri 6:30–11:30pm, Sat–Sun noon–3pm and 6:30–11:30pm.*

→ **Trattoria Antichi Cancelli** FLORENTINE Perhaps a testament to their brisk business, the waitstaff must have forgotten to remove the bright, multicolored streamer that lines the top of one of the walls. A remnant of a birthday celebration months ago or a sad attempt at lively decoration, it clashes clumsily with the farm motif and its scythes, pitchforks, mini-plows, and yokes. The food, luckily, fares much, much better. The *risotto dello chef* is served with Gorgonzola cheese, arugula, and red radicchio. The result is an interestingly textured risotto with a tangy

aftertaste. The veal *scaloppine al limone* with potatoes is a tad bland and watery, but for 8€, shake some salt and pepper over the sucker, and soak up the extra moisture with some bread. A small concession, I daresay, for the privilege of dining amidst scythes! *Via Faenza 73/R (a few blocks north of the train station).* ☎ *055/218927. Primi 6€; secondi 8€–10€. Tues–Sun noon–11pm.*

→ **Trattoria Enzo e Piero** ★★ TUSCAN Tourists who come to Florence in late summer are not only subjecting themselves to heatstroke, but missing out on this gem of a restaurant, which battens down its hatches and heads for the hills for the best part of August. For three generations, the seafood-laden menu has been filling the stomachs of locals and foreigners alike. A true family business (Massimo runs it, his son is the chef, and his daughter is a hostess), the traditions also translate to the menu: Fish is only served on Fridays and Saturdays. Plates like the *linguine argentario*, highlighted by cherry tomatoes, assorted seafood, garlic, and chile, give your palate a pleasant kick. Follow it up with *tagliata di manzo alla Massimo*, a plate of grilled boneless rib steak on a bed of greens, drizzled in a green-peppercorn sauce with rosemary. Still got room for dessert? Massimo's *nonna* concocted a cool, fluffy tiramisu recipe that'll cap off your meal with a smile-inducing decadence. *Via Faenza 105/r (a few blocks north of the train station).* ☎ *055/ 214901. Primi 6€; secondi 7€–14€. Open for lunch and dinner, closed Sun.*

→ **Trattoria La Casalinga** ★ FLORENTINE The meals at "The Housewives Trattoria" are made up of simple but tasty local dishes, and portions are Hungry-Man-sized—this is the place to go when you want to spend less than 10€ *and* fill your stomach to the point of protrusion. The *ribollita* starter stew is robust and satisfying, preparing diners for an even bigger portion of *bollito misto*, a hodgepodge of boiled meats in a salty sauce. It sounds crude—like something Shrek might throw together on a winter's night—but the flavors are potent and delicious, with no discernible trolls around. *Via Michelozzi 9/r (300m/984 ft. south of Ponte Santa Trinità, off Via Maggio).* ☎ *055/267-9243. Primi 3.50€–4€; secondi 5€–10€. Mon–Sat noon–2:30pm and 7–10pm.*

→ **Trattoria Sostanza** ★ FLORENTINE Dining at the extremely informal Trattoria "Substance" can feel a bit like eating in a high school cafeteria, given that the tables stretch almost the length of the room (which has also earned the restaurant its nickname, *Il Troia,* "the trough"). Waiters add to the casual, teen-angsty vibe by immediately engaging you with banter that borders on too much information. Once you've had a heart-to-heart with your server, order the *tortellini in brodo,* the traditional Emilian meat-stuffed pasta in broth. Save some room for your secondo, which should be the tasty *trippa alla fiorentina* (tripe with tomatoes). *Via Porcellana 25r (at Borgo Ognissanti).* ☎ *055/212-691. Reservations recommended. Primi 6.20€–7.30€; secondi 6.80€–18€. No credit cards. Mon–Fri noon–2:15pm and 7:30–9:45pm. Closed Aug.*

SPLURGE

→ **D'Antico Noé** ★★ TUSCAN The sandwich place next door gets much praise, but the tiny osteria of the same moniker deserves some recognition. At "Old Noah's Place," hidden in a somewhat dark alley, a balding beauty named Massimo creates dishes from the freshest ingredients available. I'm not talking grocery-fresh, but dude-comes-in-with-a-bushel-of-vegetables-and-Massimo-throws-them-straight-in-the-pot fresh. Watch him handpick enormous mushrooms on the side table and then trudge into the kitchen. The atmosphere by itself is worth the price and is perfect for a cozy, romantic dinner. With fewer than eight tables and some scattered stools, the setting makes you feel like you're Massimo's personal guest each time you walk in the door. He'll hoarsely suggest the simple but exquisite pasta with mushrooms, doused only in olive oil and garlic, to start. Those

with a huge appetite may then want to order a full steak, but Massimo also serves smaller *filetti* (entrecôte). Whichever you choose, he'll plop an impossibly tender and juicy slab of beef, accompanied by his favorite ingredient: mushrooms. Before you get your check, though, one last treat comes your way: In summer, cap off your delightful meal with an enormous slice of watermelon. *Volta di San Piero 6/r (just north of Piazza Santa Maria Maggiore).* ☎ *055/2340838. Primi 8€–10€; secondi 15€–20€. Mon–Sat noon–late.*

→ **La Giostra** ★ TUSCAN If you can afford it, try to have a meal at La Giostra. Although the owner is an Austrian prince of Hapsburg descent, he does have a Medici or two in his family tree. They start you off with a complimentary flute of *spumanti* before you plunge into the tasty *crostini misti* and exquisite primi. Among my favorites are *tortelloni alla Mugellana* (handmade potato-stuffed pasta in ragù), *gnocchetti alla Lord Reinolds* (potato dumplings in a sauce of stilton and Port), homemade *tagliatelle* with tiny wild asparagus spears, and ravioli stuffed with brie in a sauce with thinly sliced, lightly fried artichokes. For an encore, try the *nodino di vitella ai tartufi bianchi* (veal slathered in eggy white truffle sauce with fresh truffle grated on top) or the lighter *spianata alle erbe aromatiche di Maremma* (a huge platter of spiced beef pounded flat and piled with a salad of rosemary sprigs, sage, and other herbs). Don't leave without sampling the sinfully rich Viennese Sacher torte, made from an old Hapsburg family recipe. The dining room, with tons of vintage photographs framed on the walls and soft, warm lighting, is welcoming and lively. *Borgo Pinti 10/r (3 blocks east of the Duomo).* ☎ *055/241-341. www.ristorantelagiostra.com. Reservations recommended. Primi 10€–14€; secondi 14€–21€. Daily noon–2:30pm and 7pm–midnight.*

→ **Paoli** ★ TUSCAN Generally, you'll want to avoid restaurants near the Duomo because, as with hotels, the closer you are to the

Florentine centerpiece, the more you'll have to pay. Paoli supplies guests with food that almost warrants the higher price tag. Your stomach will thank you, and probably won't bother you for a long time, if you order their *entrecote di manzo arlecchino*. The "harlequin" beef is marinated in a cognac-cream sauce that will perk your taste buds the second the aroma escapes the kitchen. Paoli has one of the most *suggestivo* (oft-used Italian word for "evocative") settings in town, with tables under a 14th-century vaulted ceiling whose ribs and lunettes are covered with fading 18th-century frescoes. In mushroom season you can order *risotto ai funghi*. *Via dei Tavolini 12/r (off Via dei Cerchi).* ☎ *055/216-215. Reservations recommended. Primi 6€–12€; secondi 14€–18€. Wed–Mon noon–3pm and 7pm–midnight.*

PIZZERIA

→ **Il Pizzaiuolo** ★★ NEAPOLITAN/PIZZA Despite their considerable skill in the kitchen, Florentines just can't make a decent pizza. It takes a Neapolitan to do that, so business has been booming ever since Naples-born Carmine opened this pizzeria. Even with a reservation, you'll probably have to wait for a spot at a long, crowded, and noisy marble table. Save the pizza for a main dish; start instead with a Neapolitan first course like *fusilli c'a ricotta* (homemade pasta spirals in creamy tomato-and-ricotta sauce). Of the pizzas, you can't go wrong with a classic margherita (mozzarella, tomatoes, and fresh basil), or spice up your evening with a pizza *diavola*, topped with hot salami and olives. *Via de' Macci 113r (at the corner of Via Pietrapiana).* ☎ *055/241-171. Reservations required for dinner. Pizza 4.50€–10€; primi 6.50€–13€; secondi 7.50€–13€. Mon–Sat 12:30–3pm and 7:30pm–midnight. Closed Aug.*

CAFES

→ **Caffetteria Piansa** SANDWICHES An interesting mix of jazz and late '80s pop entertains the tired masses that drop by this bar/sandwich shop. There's not a whole lot food-wise to fill the stomach, but the assortment of *panini*, desserts, and aperitifs make Caffetteria Piansa a perfect place to re-energize and rest. Listen for the Charlie Parker/ Bangles mash-ups. *Borgo Pinti 18/r (3 blocks east of the Duomo).* ☎ *055/234-2362. Sandwiches 4€–6€. Open daily for lunch and dinner.*

→ **Rivoire** ★ Once full of history and now mainly full of tourists. Nonetheless, Rivoire has a chunk of prime real estate, with alfresco tables, on the medieval stage-set of Piazza della Signoria. Come here for the sublime setting, but don't expect an equally splendid social scene—Rivoire is always busy, but patrons tend to be of the older, cappuccino-and-check-please variety. *Piazza della Signoria/Via Vacchereccia 5/r.* ☎ *055/214-412. Mon–Sat 8am–10pm.*

📺 Best → **Vivoli** ★★★ GELATERIA My theory as to how the majority of Florentines aren't morbidly obese lies in the tiny pink plastic shovel at Vivoli. If customers were supplied with anything bigger than a dollhouse teaspoon, the dense frozen treat would be inhaled and their measurements would suddenly read like the jersey numbers of defensive linemen. God created gelato to be less fattening than ice cream, but it still does pack a caloric punch. But go ahead: Buy a 1.50€ cup, fill it up with your favorite flavors and a dollop of whipped cream, and work it off by climbing the dome of the Duomo . . . or just strolling north on Via Isola delle Stinche. While there are hundreds of gelato joints in Florence, none can touch the popularity and quality of Vivoli. *Via Isola delle Stinche 7/r (1 block west of Santa Croce),* ☎ *055/2392334. Tues–Sun 9am–1am. Closed Aug and Jan–Feb.*

Partying

Unlike other cities in Europe, the club scene in Florence isn't as crazy or beer-soaked as Berlin's or Amsterdam's, but it's still gobs of

Ponte Picnic: The Best View of Florence

If you have 20€ and a sense of adventure, you don't need to visit one of the overpriced, overrated restaurants to have a romantic dinner along the Arno. The best view of the Ponte Vecchio is not from the chi-chi restaurant at the Lungarno hotel, but from the oft-neglected **Ponte Santa Trinità.** If you've noticed the exterior features of the bridge, you'll already know about those triangular ledges jutting off the sides. What many might not know is that these platforms make for a romantic picnic dinner. Bring a bottle of chianti, several sandwiches, and a blanket to the bridge, and at your own risk, hop over the stone guardrail. Once you step onto the east ledge you'll find that there's plenty of room: Its widest point measures approximately 6m (20 ft.) across, and it extends out fairly far, too (4m/15 ft.).

Once you've set everything up, you'll be treated to what is, quite possibly, the best view in all of Florence. Since the sun sets to your back, the unobstructed Ponte Vecchio is swallowed up in an orange glow for 20 minutes, while the wake of the Arno shimmers underneath. Locals who already know about the perch might beat you there, so it's a good idea to get there at least 30 minutes before sunset. It should be said that hopping over the guardrail onto these ledges is technically illegal, but as long as you're seated a bit in from the edge, and not breaking chianti bottles over anyone's head, the cops won't bother you. If you do happen to catch that one pain-in-the-ass Carabiniere, pray that your sandwiches are up to snuff and try bribing him with your leftovers.

fun. Put on your sharpest duds and get your dancin' shoes on if you plan on meeting any locals. On any given weekend night, most of the 20-something crowd can be found inside one of the pulsating clubs. There are a handful of killer bars and pubs for the off night when you don't feel particularly energetic, but you'll be missing out—Florence is one foot-happy town.

To find the hot spots for the upcoming Saturday, you'll be wise to ask around the hipsterish stores on Via Nazionale. Store owners and staff are always happy to suggest various haunts to anyone strolling around their stores. While you check your e-mail in one of the Internet spots, check for flyers near the entrance. Almost every Internet point is full of flyers and ads for upcoming events. More often than not, these flyers will also give you free admission to whichever club it's advertising.

Drink prices in Italy are basically as follows (in all but the chichi-est places in Rome, Florence, Milan, Venice) generally run about as follows:

Glass of wine in enoteca (wine bar): from 2€, for a totally drinkable local wine that you may have never heard of, all the way up to 8€ for a particularly special vintage of Brunello or Barolo. Most people drink something in the 3-4€ range. Wine is by far the cheapest (and classiest, since quality is so high) way to get drunk in Italy.

Pint of beer (lager, ale, Guinness, whatever): 4€ during happy hour; 5€ after happy hour; this is the standard in all the big cities.

Cocktails/mixed drinks: 4-5€ in casual, laid-back bars; 7-10€ in trendier spots.

BARS/LOUNGES

MTV **Best** → **Capocaccia** ★★ Don your D&G shades, Zegna suit, and whatever

Gelato: Unmasked, Uncovered & Unfrozen

There's a reason why you'll never find a Ben and Jerry's in Italy: They know their concoctions are no competition for the creamy, rich goodness known as **gelato**. Gelato, very dense compared to ice cream, is actually less fattening since it's made with milk instead of the heavier, higher-calorie cream. Sorbet, more popular in the United States, is actually gelato without any dairy products (thus the similar texture). Florentines will tell you that their city is the gelato capital of Italy, and the institution that other gelaterias model themselves after is **Vivoli** ★ (p. 240). Some locals swear by **Badiani** (Viale dei Mille 20r), but the hike to the sports stadium might not be worth the trouble. The best *melomero* (my favorite melon flavor, mixing cantaloupe and watermelon) can be found in the **Bottega del Gelato** (Via Por Santa Maria 33r), not far from Ponte Vecchio. Look for the neon sign on the left as you're heading north from the bridge.

Ingesting the frozen treat is half the fun. The other half is the process of ordering. The protocol for obtaining a cup or cone starts off with paying at the cashier. Point to the size that you think you can handle, pay the clerk, and take your receipt. Act like a true Florentine and don't limit yourself to a single flavor; even the smallest of cups deserves a variety of tastes. Scan the glass display—ask for as many taster spoons as you'd like—and when you've decided, hand the receipt to the scooper and try to pronounce each flavor's name (or just point). The dollop of whipped cream *(panna)* on top is optional, but it's free, so why not go for it? In case you're wondering what some of the names mean, here are a few translations to get you started:

- **Stracciatella:** Chocolate chip and cream. (The chips are small, flecklike chips, not well-shaped drops.)
- **Bacio:** Chocolate hazelnut. A derivation of this, **variegato di Nutella,** features ribbons of the gooey topping in a cream gelato base.
- **Nocciola:** Hazelnut
- **Mirtillo:** Wild blueberry
- **Frutti di bosco:** Wild berries
- **Zuppa Inglese:** Italian sponge cake. Chunks of it are thrown into the smooth gelato for rare texture.
- **Fior di Latte:** What you might call vanilla for its plain color, but there's no vanilla extract. Just milk and sugar.

For a refreshing combination, give **agrumi** (citrus mix of lemon, lime, and orange) and **melone** (cantaloupe) a whirl. Craving something rich? Combine classic chocolate with **pistacchio** (must be gray-green; the neon green variety is just an ultrasweet version that hides the natural taste of the pistachio), and throw some Nutella in there for texture.

hairstyle Beckham is sporting (either David or Victoria) and saunter around Capocaccia. This zoo of locals is a venerable breeding ground where every month is mating season. The cream of Florence society come here to show off their Louis Vuitton feathers while occasionally enjoying the prime location on the Arno. Even if the chi-chi scene isn't your kind of thing, it's still a fun time. The *aperitivo* (happy hour) buffet is generous—and free, as long as you buy a drink—and the scenery at sunset is unbeatable. *Lungarno Corsini 12–14 (between Ponte Santa Trinità and Ponte alla Carraia).* ☎ *055/210751. www.capocaccia.com. Tues–Sun lunch noon–4pm and aperitivo/dinner 6pm–1am.*

→ **The Lounge** ★★ This swank new bar/restaurant, whose heavily designed interiors must have cost a small fortune, has quickly become a popular aperitivo and after-dinner drink spot with stylish 20- and 30-something Florentines. The restaurant, which serves sushi and small plates, as well as more elaborate, creative local cuisine, looks like what I imagine a Japanese hunting lodge would look like, with elongated silk divans, lacquered wood-backed chairs, and antlers mounted above the doorway. In the less formal lounge area, dining tables are casually interspersed with zebra-skin coffee tables and high-backed, white-leather armchairs. (Order some club soda with your red wine—lest ye get sloppy and spill your drink on the furniture!!) Later at night, quaffers take to the Pink Room, a strikingly minimalist space suffused in a sensual fuchsia glow, with comfy white-canvas banquettes, cushions, and cocktail tables galore, and space-age ottomans where you can rest your feet. On warm nights, The Lounge has a well-furnished terrace, with sleek outdoor furniture, facing the piazza. *Piazza Santa Maria Novella 9/10/r.* ☎ *055/264-5282. www.thelounge.it.*

→ **Moyo** ★ Two doors down from the raucous Red Garter sits the chic Moyo, demurely attracting the well dressed with its classy outdoor terrace and hip music. The champagne swiggers are mostly made up of late 20-somethings, and foreigners are few and far between. As long as you're reasonably dressed (jeans are okay if you're not wearing them with your old "co-ed naked lacrosse" shirt—trust me, it's not funny in America, and it sure as hell isn't funny in Florence), you'll have a grand ol' time. Nurse your mojito and scoff at the drunks stumbling out of the Red Garter (before joining them). *Via de' Benci 23/r (2 blocks south of Piazza Santa Croce).* ☎ *055/247-9738. Daily from lunch until late.*

→ **Negroni and Zoe** ★ Both are in the Oltrarno, close to the river, and both draw the same type of crowd; in fact, color scheme and address are the only things that set these two happening lounges apart. From *aperitivo* (happy hour) till 1am, you'll find a diverse mix of revelers populating the smallish interior, ranging from students to older locals. Try to find a seat in the street-side terrace and enjoy the calm tree-lined park across the way. Evenings can get busy, but the quiet area and the proximity to the river make for a relaxing, yet fun night of cocktail sipping. *Negroni: Via dei Renai 17 (between Ponte Vecchio and Ponte alle Grazie).* ☎ *055/243-647. www.negronibar.com. Daily. Zoe: Via dei Renai 13/r (between Ponte Vecchio and Ponte alle Grazie).* ☎ *055/243-111. Mon–Sat. No cover.*

📺 (Best) → **Red Garter** ★ Relive the glory days of your college career on Via de' Benci. Every Thursday, this divey bar draws a mostly American crowd, but Australians and Brits also partake in the beer pong tournament that starts at 10:30pm. Things can get rowdy pretty quickly and, as the sign near the entrance may suggest, management seems to have had problems in the past with the racket raised by patrons: *"Ai clienti che lasciano il locale chiediamo di rispettare la quiete del vicinato"* (roughly translated: Keep it down while you're leaving). *Via de' Benci 33/r (2 blocks south of Santa Croce). No cover.*

📺 (Best) → **Teatro Scribe** ★ Locals call this hole-in-the-wall near Santa Croce *teatrino,* and with good reason. With not a whole lot of room to kick back and drink their ridiculously cheap beer, this "little theater" fills up to SRO fast. It's one of the few places open past 3am where house or techno isn't being blasted into your tired ears. Early in the evening, it can be difficult to find the entrance. Once they open their doors on the

Partying in Florence

Capocaccia **7**
Central Park **5**
Crisco **18**
Fiddler's Elbow **4**
H2O2 **16**
Loonees **10**
Meccanò **6**
Moyo **14**
Negroni **13**
Red Garter **15**
Space Electronic **2**
Tabasco **11**
Teatro Scribe **17**
Tenax **1**
The Friends Pub **8**
The Lounge **3**
Yab Yum **9**
Zoe **12**

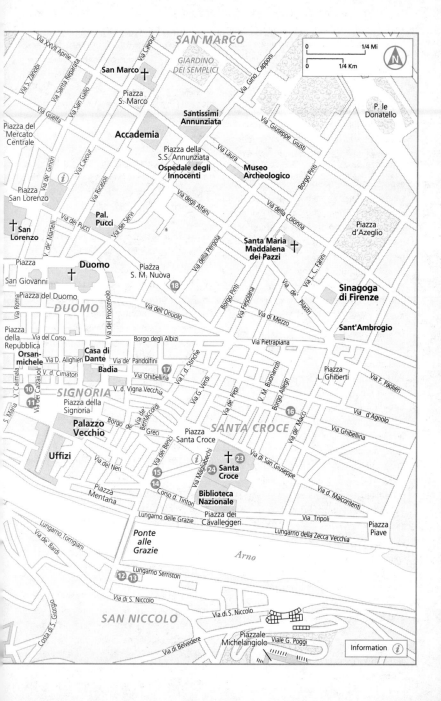

dark, borderline eerie street of Via delle Seggiole, just follow the crowd of young Florentines (or follow your ears to the music emanating from the bar's PA). *Via delle Seggiole 8/r (off Via Ghibellina).* ☎ *055/234-5594.*

PUBS

→ **Fiddler's Elbow** ★ Right on Piazza Santa Maria Novella, opposite the train station, this is probably Florence's most successful "Irish" pub, always packed with a lively crowd that's equal parts young Florentines, resident expats, and international students. Pints of Guinness, Harp, Strongbow cider, and others are 3.50€ until 9pm, 4.50€ after that. In warm weather, an improvised "beer garden" is set up on the piazza out front, and on some nights, there's a live Celtic band fiddling away—prompting many an ill-advised Michael Flatley *Lord of the Dance* impersonation—inside the pub. *Piazza Santa Maria Novella 7/r.* ☎ *055/215-056. Daily 5pm–2am.*

→ **The Friends Pub** ★ Looking for a simple place to chill and listen to good indie Britrock? Cross the Arno and look for The Friends Pub. The usual Harp, Kilkenny, and Guinness are on tap and bartender Alessandro has a mix of Oasis, Gorillaz, and the Zutons on constant rotation. Bartenders here are friendly and aren't shy about partying with patrons. Don't make the same mistake I did though: They *will* outdrink you if you dare challenge them. *Veni, vidi, vomiti . . .* I came, I saw, I puked. *Borgo San Jacopo 51r (just southeast of Ponte Santa Trinità).* ☎ *055/294930. Daily 11am–late.*

→ **Loonees** ★★ Every pint of beer in this immensely popular student joint, a few blocks south of Piazza della Repubblica, comes with a free shot. Need we say more? Inside, you'll find a fun-loving mix of locals and foreign college kids trying to hear each other over the live, or at least very loud, music that plays here every night. *Via Porta Rossa 16/r.* ☎ *055/238-1290. Tues–Sun. till late. Closed Aug.*

CLUBS

→ **Central Park** Drink a ton of water before venturing to Central Park, the favorite dance club of local rich kids. Working your way through the five dance floors, combined with the 2km (1¼-mile) walk west of Santa Maria Novella just to get here, you'll be burning calories left and right. With the surrounding sport complexes (velodrome, ippodrome [horse racing track], and tennis club) to the north and Central Park in the south Parco delle Cascine basically offers Florentines aerobic activities 24/7. Create your own triathlon of a 30km (19-mile) bike ride, a tennis match, and breakdance battles. *Via Fosso Macinante 2 (western outskirts—take a cab!).* ☎ *055/353-505. Cover 8€ (free for students before 12:30am). Tues–Sat 11pm–3am.*

→ **H202** Tired of hearing the same hip-hop, R&B, and drum'n'bass at the discos in Florence? H202, in addition to being a great place to check out concerts, walks the path less traveled and frequently pumps out funk, house, and Afro-beat. You'll still hear electronica once in a while (especially on the weekend), but selection is unique and more than danceable. Sundays feature live bands. On other days, head to the second floor, plop down on one of the comfy chairs, and enjoy some *Fela Kuti. Via Ghibellina 47/r (near Santa Croce).* ☎ *055/243239. Thurs–Tues 10pm–1am Oct–May.*

→ **Meccanò** Head nodders need not apply here. Everyone who fills the four dance floors of Meccanò knows how to use the beats for all they're worth. It's a tough decision between Central Park and Meccanò, given that they're 200m (656 ft.) away from each other. Most partygoers hit Central Park first, and when it closes its doors at a geriatric 3am, they finish off at Meccanò. Cover can get a little steep, but promoters from both Yab and Meccanò collaborate to dish out flyers that'll get you in for free. Otherwise, it'll set you back a cool 20€. So you'd best find one of those flyers from stores or Internet points around the city. *Viale degli Olmi 1 (western outskirts—take a cab).* ☎ *055/331271. Cover 20€, free with flyer or with international student card. Tues–Sat 11pm–late.*

→ **Space Electronic** ★ This club holds the dubious distinction of being the place where one of our writers heard her first Backstreet Boys song, "Everybody," back in 1997—it was love at first manufactured pop hook. We checked back in with "Lo Space" in late 2005 and we're happy to report that nothing has changed. Eight years later, Space Electronic is still going strong, guided by the singular mission of bringing international college students and horny Florentines together in one cheesy, but quite fun, multifloor dance party. Downstairs, there's an American-style bar with karaoke ("In da Club" was getting lots of play at the time this guide was researched); upstairs, a flying spaceship hovers over the laser-lit dance floor. If you're looking to score some cool points or are over 21, hit up Yab Yum instead, but if you just want to get sweaty singing songs everyone knows, and maybe get your freak on with a cute local student, Space Electronic's your joint. *Via Palazzuolo 37 (just south of Santa Maria Novella).* ☎ *055/293-082. www.spaceelectronic.net. Cover 10€–15€, free with flyer or student ID. Daily 10pm–late.*

→ **Yab Yum** ★ Known simply as "Yab" these days, this ritzy locale on Via Sassetti provides a convenient spot for swingers to work up a sweat. Arrive at 9:30, tackle one of the shiny nouveau-industrial booths, and sit down to a fine dinner with a group of friends before downing your cocktails. Mondays are the nights in the summer for "YabSmoove," where hip-hop rules the PA. You can dole out 20€ to get in, or better yet, search some of the Internet points in Florence to find a flyer that'll get you in for free. R&B, soul, and funk are featured on other nights if Smoove isn't quite your thing. All consumption charges at Yab are done via the DrinkCard you're handed on the way in—it's marked every time you

A Concert Venue

Tenax ★★ is the ultimate concert venue in Florence. Everyone from the noise-pop rockers Jesus and Mary Chain to electronica's Tricky to the indie queen Ani DiFranco has stopped by this bar/club/concert hall in the outskirts near the airport. Despite covers as high as 20€ on Saturdays, Tenax is always full of local youths dancing up a storm. Check out their site at www.tenax. org and, if you're aching for a good ol' fashioned "WTF?" click on "Philosophy" and then "Toilet Zone." Via Pratese 46 (Peretola, northeastern outskirts). ☎ 055/ 308160. Cover 10€–20€. Bus 29, 30. Tues–Sun 10pm–4am.

imbibe an alcoholic beverage, and you pay the cashier the cost of your drinks plus the cover charge on your way out of the club. Lose the card and pay the maximum amount. (As for the name, Yab stands for "you are beautiful," one of the most time-tested English pick-up lines in all of Italy—second only, perhaps, to "you are *so* beautiful." *Via Sassetti 5 (just northwest of Mercato Nuovo).* ☎ *347/7248847 (cellphone). www.yab.it. Thurs–Sat and Mon–Tues. Cover 8€–20€; free for international students, with 1-drink minimum.*

GAY & LESBIAN

ArciGay/Lesbica (aka *Azione Gay e Lesbica*), Italy's largest and oldest gay organization, has a center in Florence at Via Pisana 32r (☎ **055/220250;** www.azionegayelesbica.it). It's open for visits from Monday to Friday 6 to 8pm.

Tabasco, Piazza Santa Cecilia 3/r (☎ **055/ 213000**), is Florence's (and Italy's) oldest gay dance club, open daily 10:30pm to 3am, with a 10€ to 13€ cover. The crowd is mostly men in their 20s to 40s. Florence's leading gay bar, **Crisco,** Via San Egidio 43r (☎ **055/ 2480580**), is for men only, open Wednesday through Monday from 10:30pm to 3:30am and Friday and Saturday from 10:30pm to 5 or 6am. Cover is 9€ to 15€.

Sightseeing

They don't call Florence the world's greatest open-air art history classroom for nothing: There are a staggering number of museums, churches, and attractions in the Renaissance capital, so it might be smart to get your bearings and figure out your sightseeing plan of attack before you start hitting monuments and paying admission fees willy-nilly. Begin by visiting the tourist office, where helpful clerks will know exactly what events are taking place and which museums are closed for renovations or holidays. Otherwise, the staff at your hotel or hostel are often quite knowledgeable about opening hours, discounted tickets, and other insider tourist info. Keep in mind that Monday—as in the rest of Italy—is most museums' closing day (that goes for the Uffizi, the Accademia, and the Pitti), so if you're in Florence on a Monday, it'll give you a good excuse to do your laundry (or buy some new clean clothes) and catch up on e-mails and postcards.

MUSEUMS

➔ **Accademia** ★★ Definitely avoid coming here between noon and 3pm. Lines are not only around the block, but the location of the Accademia gives tourists no shelter from the afternoon sun—those who come here to gaze upon Michelangelo's *David* will leave not only with lifelong memories of the most famous statue in the world, but a nasty case of sunburn to boot. Once inside, however, you'll instantly forget about your flaking and scorched skin when you catch a glimpse of the *David*, with his slingshot coolly draped over his left shoulder and massive right hand holding on to a stone, just in case Goliath came back for another ass-whooping. When you're finished gawking at the naked biblical hero, take the time to inspect Michelangelo's *Prisoners*. These four unfinished torsos give

visitors an idea of how a Michelangelo sculpture came to life. The exposed six-pack abs demonstrate that Michelangelo dealt with extremities as just that, pieces emanating from a central, powerful point. (The *Prisoners* were to have decorated the tomb of Pope Julius II, at the church of St. Peter in Chains in Rome. Of the ambitious original tomb design, Michelangelo's *Moses* is the only monumental statue that was completed.) Also sprinkled around the museum are many works by Michelangelo's students—some are so skillful that they're often mistaken for products of the master chiseler himself. Fortunately, the museum's plaques will tell you who made whom. *Via Ricasoli 58–60 (2 blocks north of the Duomo).* ☎ *055/238-8609. www. sbas.firenze.it/accademia. Reserve tickets at* ☎ *055/294-883 or www.firenzemusei.it. Admission 6.50€. Tues–Sun 8:15am–6:50pm; last admission 30 min before close. Closed Christmas, Jan 1, May 1. Bus 1, 6, 7, 10, 11, 17, 25, 31, 32, 33, 67, 68, 70.*

➔ **Bargello** ★★ If the Uffizi and the Pitti have all of Florence's best paintings, the Museo Nazionale del Bargello has all the statues. In this imposing palazzo, once home to prisons and torture chambers, the hits just keep on coming; the most famous piece here is probably Michelangelo's *Drunk Bacchus* (1497), an uncannily realistic depiction of the god who keeps ordering shots after last call. Earlier works include a bronze *David* (1440) by Donatello—the first free-standing nude sculpture since antiquity, which must have influenced Michelangelo—and some bronze panels of the *Sacrifice of Isaac* by Ghiberti and Brunelleschi. In their bid to win the commission for the job of casting the bronze doors for Florence's baptistery, the two sculptors submitted these panels to the judges: Ghiberti won. Don't miss the Bargello's Giambologna masterpieces: in *Mercury* (1564), one of the Dutch artist's best works, the fleet-footed messenger god truly looks as if he could take off and fly away at any moment.

Finally, if you catch sight of a downward-gazing bronze bust that looks oddly familiar but you can't quite place it, it's probably Daniele da Volterra's portrait of Michelangelo; this depiction of the master is the most frequently reproduced image of him. *Via del Proconsolo 4 (2 blocks south of the Duomo).* ☎ *055/238-8606. www.sbas.firenze.it/bargello. Reservations* ☎ *055/294-883 or www.firenze musei.it. Admission 4€. Daily 8:15am–1:50pm. Closed 2nd and 4th Mon and 1st, 3rd, and 5th Sun of each month.*

→ **Museo Archeologico** ★ Florence's archaeological museum still manages to attract a handful of tourists even though the majority of visitors in town have eyes only for Michelangelo and Botticelli. It's their loss, for the Museo Archeologico houses a fascinating and not-too-overwhelming collection of Roman, Egyptian, and Etruscan artifacts—which will look positively exotic after all the Renaissance art you're bombarded with in the rest of Florence. One of the most interesting and important pieces here is the ferocious 5th-century B.C. Etruscan bronze *Chimera*, a mythical beast that's part snake, part lion, and part goat. You'll also score points with the ol' art history prof if you check out the 1st-century B.C. bronze *Arringatore* ("Orator"); it's an Etruscan statue, but the guy is wearing a Roman toga, which is indicative of cultural influences going back and forth between the Etruscans and the Romans at the time. *Via della Colonna 36 (a few blocks north of the Accademia).* ☎ *055/23-575. Admission 4€. Mon 2–7pm; Tues and Thurs 8:30am–7pm; Wed and Fri–Sun 8:30am–2pm.*

→ **Museo dell'Opera del Duomo (Duomo Works Museum)** ★ With fascinating wooden models of the original design for the Duomo, as well as some of the actual machinery that built the church, from the 13th to the 15th centuries, this is a must for aspiring engineers (and anyone else who habitually flips to the History Channel when nothing else is on TV). The rest of the museum is dedicated to preserving and showcasing masterpieces of art deemed too delicate or valuable to stay where they were originally intended—inside or on top of the Duomo itself. Among the museum's permanent works is one of Donatello's more morbidly fascinating sculptures, a late work in polychrome wood of *The Magdalene* (1453–55), emaciated and veritably dripping with penitence. Another important piece is Donatello's *Beardless Prophet,* with its drooping, aged face; and just in case you haven't had your fill of gloom, Brunelleschi's death mask is also on display. *Piazza del Duomo 9.* ☎ *055/230-2885. www.operaduomo.firenze.it. Admission 6€. Mon–Sat 9am–7:30pm; Sun 9am–2pm. Tickets sold until 30 min. before close. Bus: 6,11,14,17, or 23.*

→ **Palazzo Pitti** ★★ The main tourist draw in the Oltrarno, by far, is the Palazzo Pitti and the relaxing greenery of the Boboli Gardens (p. 262) immediately adjacent. Apparently, with hopes of getting on *MTV Cribs,* Cosimo de' Medici's wife decided to upgrade the former home of banker Luca Pitti, thus creating the palace, which is now an enormous museum complex housing the fabulous Medici collections of art, separated into the **Galleria Palatina,** the **Galleria d'Arte Moderna, Galleria del Costume (Costume Gallery), Appartamenti Reali (Royal Apartments), Museo degli Argenti (Silver Museum)** and the **Giardino Boboli.** Note that admission to the palace is free, but you'll have to pay to enter the most interesting galleries, and admission prices have been steadily rising. What most people are heading for when they make their way to the Pitti is the Galleria Palatina. The majority of the paintings here are from High Renaissance artists—like Raphael, Titian, Rubens, and the proto-baroque Caravaggio—skewing about 100 years later than the most famous works at the Uffizi, with more entertaining and light-hearted themes, for the most part. If, on the other hand, you have no interest in looking

Sightseeing in Florence

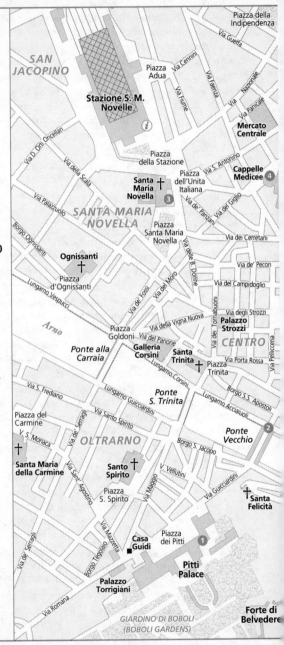

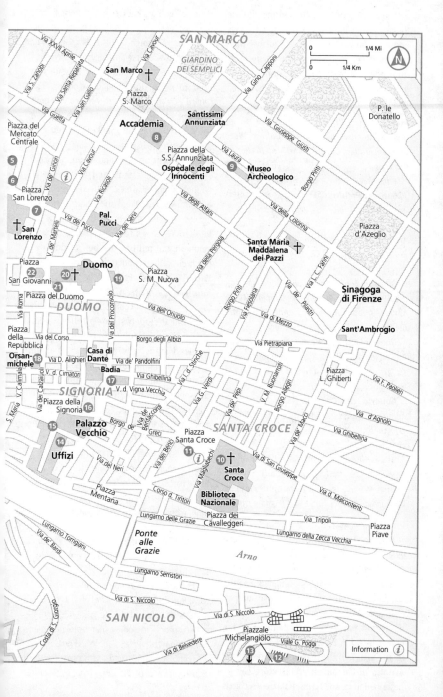

at one more 400-year-old painting, but are looking instead for a place to catch some rays and work on your tan, look no further than the large flagstoned space in front of the drive up to the palace. In summer, don't be surprised to find it littered with sunbathers atop their towels.

Piazza Pitti (Oltrarno). Inclusive ticket includes admission to Palatine Gallery, Silver Museum, Gallery of Modern Art, and the Boboli Gardens. Full price 10.50€, reduced price 5.25€ (18–25 EU residents or EU teachers).

Galleria Palatina ☎ 055/238-8614, reservations ☎ 055/294-883. www.firenzemusei.it. Admission 6.50€ (w/entrance to Royal Apartments), 1.55€ optional booking, 50% off 18- to 25-yr-olds from EU. After 4pm 8€. Tues–Sun 8:15am–6:50pm.

Giardino Boboli ☎ 055/265-1816. Admission 4€. Daily Nov–Feb 8:15am–4:30pm; March 8:15am–5:30pm; April–May and Oct 8:15am–6:30pm; June–Sept 8:15am–7:30pm.

Galleria d'Arte Moderna ☎ 055/238-8601. Admission 5€. Daily 8:15am–1:50pm. Closed 1st, 3rd, and 5th Mon, and 2nd and 4th Sun of each month.

Galleria del Costume ☎ 055/238-8713. Admission 5€. Daily 8:15am–1:50pm. Closed 1st, 3rd, and 5th Mon, and 2nd and 4th Sun of each month.

Museo degli Argenti ☎ 055/238-8709. Admission 4€. Daily Nov–Feb daily 8:15am–4:30pm; March 8:15am–5:30pm; April–May and Oct 8:15am–6:30pm; June–Sept 8:15am–7:30pm.

LANDMARKS

→ **Piazza della Signoria** ★★★ A sublime example of showstopping civic architecture, Piazza della Signoria is a jumble of imposing medieval government halls and monumental statuary and fountains clustered around an L-shaped, flagstoned public square. The dominant and most theatrical feature on the piazza, by far, is **Palazzo Vecchio** ★★, built in the 13th century based on a design by Arnolfo di Cambio. If architecture can be described in canine terms, Palazzo Vecchio is

a pit bull with its hackles up. With its façade of rough masonry, its teethlike crenellations, and its 92m-high (308-ft.) clocktower thrusting upward like an angrily craning neck, this is aggressive medieval fortress design bred to perfection. And no wonder: The "guard-dog" that is Palazzo Vecchio was built in a time of fierce feuding in Florence, when the Republic was busy making teacup-Chihuahua-sized Tuscan hill towns whimper under Florentine rule, and when, on occasion, Florence found itself on defensive haunches, under attack by even bigger dogs like Milanese dukes and their powerful armies. In times of external threat, the bell in Palazzo Vecchio's tower would be rung to summon the militia—the bell's odd, low-pitched wail earned it the nickname "La Vacca" (The Cow). Piazza della Signoria has long been the center of civic life in Florence: Parts of Palazzo Vecchio still function as city hall, and the open square itself has seen plenty of spectacular, and often violent, public demonstrations. In 1497, a monk named Girolamo Savonarola decided his fellow Florentines were too wealth- and culture-obsessed, so he lit a fire in Piazza della Signoria (the so-called "Bonfire of the Vanities") and threw all the books and valuables he could find into the flames. Respected contemporaries such as Botticelli did the same, and Savonarola became quite the hero . . . at least for a few months. By the next year, Savonarola had fallen out of favor with the mob, who burned him at the stake in 1498, on the exact spot in Piazza della Signoria (marked by a plaque in front of the fountain of Neptune) where they had cheered the Bonfire of the Vanities.

On the Loggia dei Lanzi (the arcaded platform on the southern side of the square), statues by some of the Renaissance's greatest sculptors—including Giambologna's marble *Rape of the Sabine Women* and Benvenuto Cellini's bad-ass bronze *Perseus with the Head of Medusa*—lend even more drama to the stage of Piazza della Signoria. Most of the other statues are copies of originals now housed in museums around town: the oft-photographed *David* of Piazza della Signoria is a facsimile of Michelangelo's 1504 original, now in the Accademia. Most of the interior of the Palazzo Vecchio is open to the public; the monumental chambers where the Signoria (city council) used to meet are decked out with grandmotherish bling—ridiculous amounts of fussy gold and over-the-top Renaissance frescoes. *Palazzo Vecchio: Piazza della Signoria.* ☎ *055/276-8465. www. comune.firenze.it. Mon—Wed and Sat—Sun 9am—7pm; Thurs 9am—2pm. Admission 6€.*

FREE → **Ponte Vecchio** ★★ The legend of the German commander with a soft spot for bridges is well documented. The gist of it goes like this: In World War II, to slow American troops and their push north, Axis commanders destroyed bridges over strategic rivers in Italy. All of Florence's bridges were reduced to rubble, except for Ponte Vecchio ("Old Bridge"). So entranced by the beauty and history of the bridge was the Nazi commander that he decided to destroy the buildings at each end of the bridge rather than topple the structure entirely. His cultural mercy left Florentines with their gorgeous landmark intact. Ponte Vecchio dates to the 13th century, when the shops and stalls built over the span were used by butchers and tanners, who used to soak animal hides in vats of urine as part of the leather-curing process. The Medici, who had to walk past the foul-smelling workshops every time they crossed the Arno (via the private walkway known as the Vasari Corridor, still preserved on the eastern edge of the bridge), were so disgusted by the perpetual stench on Ponte Vecchio that they kicked all the butchers and tanners out in 1593, freeing up real estate for more neutrally odored goldsmiths and silversmiths, who have been the bridge's sole tenants for 400 years. One goldsmith in particular, Benvenuto Cellini, is immortalized

by a bust in the center of the bridge. Be sure to walk over Ponte Vecchio at least once at night, when all the jewelry shops are shuttered with their ancient-looking wooden doors and locks. *Via Por Santa Maria/Via Guicciardini. Bus: B or D.*

CHURCHES

There are about a gazillion churches in Florence that you can visit; we've listed the most important ones (most of which charge an admission fee), but there are plenty of smaller churches that you can enter for free and see Renaissance masterpieces that have been hanging above the same altar for over 500 years.

→ **Battistero (Baptistery)** ★★ With green-and-white marble striping, Florence's octagonal baptistery looks like a pretty gift box, and it would be even more visually impressive if it weren't dwarfed by its gigantic neighbor across the square—the Duomo. In any case, the baptistery's bronze doors are the real reason the building is swarmed like a honeycomb from dawn to dusk by tourist bees. The famous **east doors** ★★★ (facing the Duomo) have 10 scenes from the Old Testament and were cast in bronze and gilded by Lorenzo Ghiberti from 1425 to 1452. Twenty-seven years to make a couple of doors? It makes you admire the vision and patience of Renaissance art patrons. Earlier in life, when he was 22, Ghiberti won a heated competition (against the likes of Donatello and Brunelleschi) to cast the baptistery's ★★ **north doors;** the 28 gilded scenes from the New Testament were executed from 1403 to 1424.

Before Ghiberti came along, the baptistery only had one set of doors: the relief panels on the **south doors** were made by sculptor Andrea Pisano from 1330 to 1336 and look like they came from The Home Depot by comparison. If you really want to understand what all the fuss is about Ghiberti's doors, come to the baptistery early in the morning on a clear day. Start on the south side and check

The Uffizi: one of the World's Great Museums

The Uffizi ★ ★ ★ is the granddaddy of museums in Florence, and has as much to offer when it's closed as when it's open. My favorite perch at night to finish my gelato or to enjoy Florence by moonlight is the courtyard of the Uffizi after 9pm. Surprisingly, there very few people milling around and the Carabinieri rarely pass by on their routine patrols. It's impossible to remain unmoved when you're sitting on the steps (on the Arno side of the Uffizi), gazing at the statues of Dante, Michelangelo, and other Renaissance legends uniformly lit by the spotlights along the base of each bust. Giotto's bell tower in the distance is an 85m-high (279-ft.) exclamation point for the whole experience. As for visiting the museum, give yourself at least a couple days to absorb the 40+ rooms within the gallery. Remember that much like the Accademia and the Duomo, lines to enter the museum can get downright ridiculous—if you haven't reserved your ticket in advance, you can wait more than an hour. Also, if you arrive at the Uffizi later in the day, you risk having the museum close on you (signs around the entrance state that after 5pm, entrance to the Uffizi is not guaranteed). While waiting in the queue, look around at the courtyard statues scowling at the caricaturists and sketchers duping tourists into buying their chicken-scratch drawings. Upon entering the gallery itself, note that many of the paintings constantly get shuffled around and rooms are routinely closed off (they're still renovating from a 1993 terrorist bombing), so be sure to pick up a map at the information desk. Originally built as an office complex for the Medici (*uffizi* is an archaic word for "offices"), the Uffizi's horseshoe layout is rather straightforward.

Most art museums house their masterpieces in two or three rooms, but the Uffizi draws no distinction between its works because, well, *every* work of art here is a masterpiece. As you walk the halls, however, you'll notice it: *There's something about Mary.* If all the depictions of the Madonna start to make your vision fuzzy, don't worry: you're not having a stroke—the immaculate conceiver was the most requested subject in the Renaissance (kind of like "I Will Survive" at weddings), and she still hangs in kaleidoscopic profusion on the walls of the Uffizi. Amid the sea of Marys, there are some more distinctive must-sees:

➤ **Michelangelo's *Holy Family*:** The moment you enter **room 25**, all eyes fix on this lushly colored and detailed *tondo* (round painting), one of Michelangelo's earliest works. The attention given to the characters' limbs, their meticulously painted muscles, and the beautifully rich hues are unfathomable to the novice viewer, and a wonderful comparison for those who have seen, or will be seeing, Michelangelo's later frescoes at the Sistine Chapel in Rome.

out Pisano's clunkers, then walk around to the left, past the door-less west wall, to the north wall and Ghiberti's first set of doors. The figures here are much more realistic— everyone has a charged facial expression, and everyone is actively involved in their

scenes, which (still confined to quadrifoil-diamond frames) are easier to read than Pisano's restrained, wooden-feeling Gothic panels. Now, walk around to the east doors (that's where all the crowds will be): When the morning sun hits the gilding on Ghiberti's

➤ Botticelli's *Birth of Venus* and *Primavera:* Sure, we've all seen posters of these willowy babes in college girls' dorm rooms, but I gotta say, they're a lot hotter in real life. In person, *Primavera* looks less like a 15th-century blacklight poster and more like a snapshot of stoned chicks doing their twirling dance at Lilith Fair, circa 1482. In *Venus,* who sways precariously to the port side of her trusty mollusk, we see the love goddess as an erotic tease who lazily, and only partially, covers the private parts of her porcelain flesh with ropes of auburn hair L'Oreal wishes it could claim. One look at these romantic canvases and you'll begin to understand why Renaissance Faire–goers do it—they're hoping to enter the blissed-out world of a Botticelli painting. Take time to admire their muses, free of mind-altering substances, in **room 10/14.**

➤ **Leonardo da Vinci's *Annunciation:*** Mary again. **Room 15** contains Leonardo da Vinci's depiction of the archangel Gabriel kneeling (and seeming to say "I'm not worthy") before the Virgin Mary—you've seen this on countless Christmas cards. Though some critics still don't believe that a young Leonardo painted this masterpiece, the consensus is that he completed it while an apprentice to Andrea del Verrocchio. In any case, the restraint in the figures' bodily position is intriguing, almost otherworldly (not unlike the unresolvable suspension in the *Mona Lisa*); and the background, with its motley arrangement of cypresses, pines, and a rock formation in the hazy distance, is pure Leonardo.

➤ **Caravaggio's *Medusa* and *Bacchus:*** Be sure to slow down once you reach the last corridor before the Uffizi's exit. Moved from the main galleries, Caravaggio's best works, from the 1590s, were placed in the first floor (named "The New Rooms.") *Medusa*'s strung-out expression is a little disturbing, but to be fair, she's just had her head severed from her body, and there are snakes growing where her hair should be. *Bacchus,* everyone's favorite slumping lush, offers a toast, pinky extended, to any who admire his come-hither pose and Carmen Miranda–style headpiece of grapes and leaves. In both works, Caravaggio employs his trademark waxy flesh effects and contrasting light and shade to achieve a high-keyed and engaging picture.

Piazzale degli Uffizi 6. ☎ *055/238-8651. www.polomuseale.firenze.it/english. Admission 8.50€. Tues–Sun 8:15am–6:50pm. For reservations* ☎ *055/ 294-883 (booking charge of 3€, but highly recommended in high season) or www.firenzemusei.it.*

most famous doors, the Old Testament panels go stunningly, cinematically ablaze. If you can take the time to look at each exquisitely rendered scene individually, you almost forget you're looking at 600-year-old art. Full of engaging background details, emotion and dynamism, the east doors look like still shots from some sweeping Biblical epic—where special effects have been cast in 1,000-degree furnaces and burnished by hand. Years after Ghiberti's death, Michelangelo was standing before these doors and someone asked his opinion. His response sums up Ghiberti's life accomplishment: "They are so beautiful that they would grace the entrance to Paradise." They've been called the Gates of Paradise ever since. Note that panels now mounted here are excellent copies; the originals are displayed in the Museo dell'Opera del Duomo. If you spend the 3€ it takes to get inside the baptistery, you'll find columns pilfered from ancient Roman buildings and a spectacle of mosaics above and below—it's nice, but all things considered, that 3€ might be better spent on a beer later in the afternoon. *Piazza San Giovanni.* ☎ *055/230-2885. www.operaduomo.firenze.it. Mon–Sat noon–6:30pm; Sun 8:30am–1:30pm. Admission 3€.*

→ **Cappelle Medicee (Medici Chapels)** ★★
Michelangelo-designed tombs for the Medici family in the **Sagrestia Nuova** (New Sacristy) are the big hoopla here; unfortunately, they should have been an even bigger hoopla, but Michelangelo never got to finish the tomb for Lorenzo de'Medici the Magnificent—for his tomb, the wise ruler of Florence, poet of note, and moneybags behind much of the Renaissance only got a dinky marble slab and inscription. Furthermore, he has to share the unfinished tomb with his brother, Giuliano, who was assassinated in the Duomo during the Pazzi Conspiracy. (They did, however, get a lovely statue of the Virgin Mary by Michelangelo.) The vaulted spaces of the new sacristy are done up in harmonious tones of white *intonaco* (plaster) and dark grey *pietra serena*. On the left wall is Michelangelo's tomb of Lorenzo, duke of Urbino (and Lorenzo the Magnificent's grandson). Below him, *Dawn* (female) and *Dusk* (male), a pair of Michelangelo's most famous sculptures (1524–31), languish over the elongated curves of the tomb. *Dawn* and *Dusk* mirror the similarly fashioned and equally important *Day* (male) and *Night* (female) across the way (1526–33), on the tomb of Giuliano, Duke of Nemours. The two male figures on the tombs, *Dusk* and *Day*, are typically Michelangelesque,

with exaggerated musculature that is simultaneously lumpy and sinewy. The two female figures, on the other hand, are startlingly ridiculous-looking. If artists learn from what they observe in real life, it's pretty clear in *Dawn* and *Night* that Michelangelo wasn't getting much action from the Florentine ladies. The sculptures' breasts have nothing natural or sensually plump about them—they're just sort of tacked on, like rounded pieces of fruit, to well-cut, and clearly male pectoral muscles. Their slightly sagging midriffs also bear the vestiges of male anatomy, like a guy whose abs start to show again after he loses a bunch of weight. Finally, *Night's* formidable thighs look as if they could give Lance Armstrong some trouble if both signed up for the Tour de France.

For a real 180-degree turn in artistic style, or lack thereof, check out the **Cappella dei Principi** (Chapel of the Princes). Begun in 1604, this mausoleum has the dubious distinction of being one of the world's most gloriously god-awful memorials, dedicated to the Medici grand dukes—the clan got more and more inbred as the years passed, and the Medici princes buried here were some of Florence's most dysfunctional and arrogant tyrants. The domed chapel is an exercise in bad taste, like a centrifuge in which cut marbles and semiprecious stones have been splattered onto the walls and ceiling with no regard for composition or chromatic unity. For more than a century, ducal funds were poured into further cluttering and gem-encrusting of the monstrosity, until the rarely conscious Giangastone de'Medici drank himself to death in 1737 without an heir—even so, the chapel decoration committee kept up their tasteless work for 200 more years: They were still finishing the floor in 1962! Off to the left and right of the altar are small treasuries full of gruesome holy relics in silver-bedecked cases. *Piazza Madonna degli Aldobrandini (behind San Lorenzo).* ☎ *055/238-8602. Admission 6€. Daily 8:15am–5pm.*

Dome Guys & Door Guys

Who's Who in Florentine Architecture

With all the culture you're trying to absorb in Florence, the names of architects and who built what can get confusing. Here's a cheat sheet for quick reference:

Arnolfo di Cambio, aka "Medieval Guy" (1245–1310): Gothic sculptor and architect; designed Palazzo Vecchio and drew the original plans for the Duomo.

Filippo Brunelleschi, aka "Dome Guy" (1377–1446): "Brew-nell-*esky*" was a very busy architect in 15th century Florence; most celebrated for engineering the vaulting of the dome on the Duomo; originally trained as a goldsmith/clock-maker; paranoid-genius type; hated Ghiberti; buried under the Duomo.

Lorenzo Ghiberti, aka "Door Guy" (1378–1455): "Ghee-*bear*-tee" cast the celebrated gilded bronze "Gates of Paradise" for the eastern entrance of the Baptistery, as well as the slightly less-famous northern doors; also worked on the Duomo, but Brunelleschi was better at it and a control freak, so Ghiberti backed off and stuck to bronze sculpture most of the time; buried in Santa Croce.

Michelangelo, aka "Renaissance Guy" (1475–1564): in Florence, the sculptor, painter, and architect is best known for the *David,* the *Holy Family* in the Uffizi, the Medici Chapels, and the Laurentian Library at San Lorenzo; buried in Santa Croce. He also dabbed at the ceiling of the Sistine Chapel in Rome.

Closed 1st, 3rd, and 5th Mon as well as 2nd and 4th Sun of each month.

→ **The Duomo (Santa Maria del Fiore)** ★★★ If at all possible, see the Duomo for the first time at night, and when you're not really looking for it. There are few sights in Italy as breathtaking as the accidental glimpses you catch of its moonlit white, green, and red marble walls, down a deserted alley, from a few blocks away. These visual snippets that hint at the Duomo's majestic bulk are far more magical and impressive than any straight-on shot of the cathedral in broad daylight. Built from 1296 to 1466 and funded by the powerful Wool Merchants' Guild, the church is crowned by an impossibly large, terra-cotta-tile-clad cupola (dome). The dome dominates the skyline of Florence in the same way Jupiter dominates the solar system—nothing even comes close to its size. More than just a grandiose monument, the cupola of the Duomo is an enduring marvel of engineering, whose ingenious construction methods were devised almost single-handedly by Filippo Brunelleschi. Unlike St. Peter's in the Vatican, which is all about the fabulously ornate interior, Florence's Duomo is all about the candy-striped and red-topped exterior. If you do want to go inside, however, there are a number of ways to do so. For 6€ for each, you can **climb the dome** ★★★ (463 steps) or Giotto's 14th-century **campanile** ★★ (bell tower, 414 steps) immediately adjacent. Both offer spectacular panorama of Florence's rooftops and the surrounding hills, but the dome ascent allows you an up-close-and-personal encounter with Brunelleschi's masonry techniques. When you emerge at the balcony, just below the lantern, the views down the steep walls of the dome will have your heart in your throat (in a good way).

For its part, the campanile affords climbers the special treat of looking back on the

Who *Were* These Medici, Anyway?

Florence's most powerful and influential family started out in the medical profession, hence their name: *medici* (pronounced *Meh*-dee-chee) means "doctors." The Medici coat of arms features three balls, which some eager art history students interpret as pharmaceutical pills, but they're actually just balls. A soldier under Charlemagne in the 9th century, Averardo de' Medici slew a Saxon giant that had three balls attached to his mace: whether *mace,* a shafted weapon, is code for something else, and Averardo's quarry really had three testicles, we'll probably never know. In any case, the three balls have been the symbol of the Medici ever since. By the 1300s, the Medici had risen to power in Florence thanks to their fortune made as pawnbrokers and bankers, with branches and ATMs throughout Europe. Cosimo il Vecchio ("the old," 1389–1464) and Lorenzo the Magnificent (1449–92) were by far the most admirable characters in the clan, endowing Florence with generous artistic and cultural patronage; Lorenzo even adopted the young Michelangelo so that he could carry out his apprenticeship as a guest in the Medici household. A few Medici princes became popes: Giovanni de' Medici, the son of Lorenzo, became Pope Leo X (1513–21). One of the fattest pontiffs on record, Leo X rode around Rome on a white elephant named Hanno and excommunicated Martin Luther in 1521 (which Luther ignored by burning the decree). Another Medici pope, Clement VII (1523–34), was forced to hide out in Rome's Castel Sant'Angelo for 6 months when Holy Roman Emperor Charles V sacked the Eternal City in 1527. He later died from eating the dreaded death cap mushroom, the most poisonous mushroom in the world. After ruling Florence for more than 400 years, the Medici clan finally died out for good in the 18th century.

Duomo's southern wall from a zoomed-in and elevated perspective. The stairways for both the dome and the campanile are narrow and steep, not for the claustrophobic or faint-hearted. The interior of the Duomo itself is free to enter but not nearly as impressive as the outside, although it is interesting to look up at the underside of the dome's inner shell. (In high season, however, lines to get into the Duomo can take over an hour. In that case, you have our permission to skip it.) If you go inside the cathedral, you'll find sparse frescoes and mosaics as well as some *Godfather*-style history: In one of the pews near the transept (where the short arm of the church's Latin-cross shape intersects the long arm, under the dome), a hit man hired by the wealthy Pazzi family stabbed and killed Giuliano de' Medici on Easter Sunday in 1478, in an attempt to

overthrow the city government (the so-called "Pazzi Conspiracy"). In the Santa Reparata excavations below the cathedral, you can also visit the tomb of Brunelleschi. (To see his death mask, you'll have to visit the Museo dell'Opera del Duomo, above.) *Piazza del Duomo.* ☎ *055/230-2885. www. operaduomo.firenze.it. Church: Mon–Wed and Fri 10am–5pm; Thurs 10am–3:30pm; 1st Sat of month 10am–3:30pm, other Sat 10am–4:45pm; Sun 1:30–4:30pm. Free admission to church and free tours every 40 min daily, 10:30am– noon and 3–4:20pm. Cupola: Mon–Fri 8:30am–6:20pm; Sat 8:30am–5pm (1st Sat of month to 3:20pm); 6€. Campanile: Daily 8:30am–6:50pm; 6€.*

FREE → **Orsanmichele** ★ The "Garden of St. Michael," a tall, blocky building halfway down Via dei Calzaiuoli, looks more like a

Gothic warehouse than a church—which is because the 14th century structure started out as a granary/grain market. After a miraculous image of the Madonna appeared on a column inside, however, the lower level was turned into a chapel. The city's merchant guilds commissioned such masters such as Ghiberti, Donatello, Verrocchio, and Giambologna to cast or carve sculptures of the guilds' patron saints to set in the street-level tabernacles around the exterior. Across Via dell'Arte della Lana from Orsanmichele's main entrance is the 1308 Palazzo dell'Arte della Lana (Palace of the Wool Guild). This Gothic palace was home to medieval Florence's most powerful body, the Wool Merchants' Guild, which employed about one-third of Florence in the 13th and 14th centuries. Up the stairs inside Palazzo dell'Arte della Lana, you can cross over the hanging walkway to the first floor (American second floor) of Orsanmichele. These are the old granary rooms, now housing a museum of the statues that once surrounded the exterior. A few are still undergoing restoration, but eight of the original sculptures are here, well labeled, including Donatello's marble *St. Mark* (1411–13); Ghiberti's bronze *St. John the Baptist* (1413–16), the first life-size bronze of the Renaissance; and Verrocchio's *Incredulity of St. Thomas* (1473–83). Actually getting into Orsanmichele is a game of Russian roulette—neither the museum nor the church pays much attention to their posted hours, which are largely dependent on the whims of fickle and limited staff. Still, it's worth a try. *Via dell'Arte della Lana 1 (at Via Calzaiuoli).* ☎ *055/284-944. Church open erratic hours (though never open during riposo). Museum daily 9–9:45am, 10–10:45am, 11–11:45am (plus Sat–Sun 1–1:45pm). Closed 1st and last Mon of month. Free admission.*

→ San Lorenzo and Laurentian Library

★★ It's surrounded by the loud stalls of the leather market, and its façade of rusticated masonry is unfinished: San Lorenzo hardly looks distinguished from the outside, but it's most likely the oldest church in Florence, founded in A.D. 393. San Lorenzo was the city's cathedral until the bishop's seat moved to Santa Reparata (later to become the Duomo) in the 7th century. More important, it was the Medici family's parish church, and as those famous bankers began to accumulate their vast fortune, they started a tradition of lavishing it on this church that lasted until the clan died out in the 18th century. (The Medici tombs, listed separately below, have a separate entrance around the back of the church and have different hours.) The first thing Giovanni di Bicci de' Medici, founder of the family fortune, did for the church was hire Brunelleschi to tune up the interior, rebuilding according to the architect's plans in 1426. The first great consolidator of Medici power, Cosimo il Vecchio, whose wise behind-the-scenes rule made him popular with the Florentines, died in 1464 and is buried in front of the high altar. The plaque marking the spot is simply inscribed PATER PATRIAE—"father of his homeland." On the wall of the left aisle is Bronzino's huge fresco of the *Martyrdom of St. Lawrence (Martirio di San Lorenzo)*—not a masterpiece in the annals of art history but a fun picture nonetheless. A flinty early Christian and treasurer of the Church, Lawrence was commanded by emperor Valerian to hand over the church's wealth, and when he appeared before the Roman officials with thousands of sick, poor, and crippled people and announced, "Here is all the church's treasure," the Romans were neither impressed nor amused and decided to martyr him on a gridiron over hot coals. Feisty to the end, at one point while Lawrence lay there roasting he called out to his tormentors through gritted teeth, "Turn me over, I'm done on this side." Bronzino's less sentimental vision of the story looks like a Broadway musical number (or a Britney Spears video)—a riot of barely clad figures strike improbable, well-choreographed muscle-flaunting poses, while

Recommended Reading: Brunelleschi's Dome

Before, during, or after your trip to the Duomo of Florence, pick up a copy of *Brunelleschi's Dome: How a Renaissance Genius Reinvented Architecture* (Penguin, 2001). The plans to build a dome with the size and proportions that you see today existed as early as 1366, and the Opera del Duomo, which oversaw the cathedral works, solemnly swore never to deviate from that design. The only problem was, no one had the faintest idea how to do it—at 350 feet in total height and 143 feet in diameter, Florence's dome would be, and still is, the largest masonry dome in the world. Optimistic that among the great minds in Florence at the time, there might be someone who could invent a way to engineer the enormous dome, the Wool Guild in charge of the Opera del Duomo held a contest in 1418, asking any qualified members of the public to step forward and present their plans. A 41-year-old clockmaker named Filippo Brunelleschi eventually won the commission, and even though he didn't design its appearance, the dome exists today thanks to Brunelleschi. Ross King's 167-page account of how the dome of the Duomo was built is a gripping read that really brings the sights, sounds, and smells of Renaissance Florence to life. Some chapters deal with conditions at the worksite (inside an unfinished cathedral, 60m/200+ ft. off the ground); others relate the mechanical details of Brunelleschi's ingenious solutions to the problems of lifting and placing millions of pounds of brick, marble, and sandstone. Throughout the book, there's plenty of juicy intrigue where Brunelleschi's volatile personality clashes with other prominent Renaissance figures. What's most compelling, however, is the scale of the project, and the fact that human beings—Brunelleschi foremost among them—made it happen, with no precedent to guarantee that it would work. So, grab a blanket and head to the Boboli Gardens; finish the book over a long afternoon, and then head back over to the Duomo to be even more impressed by the achievement of the dome and the context in which it was raised.

in the middle of the picture, St. Lawrence reclines atop his barbecue (oddly, in the same exact position as Michelangelo's *Adam* in the Sistine Chapel), gazing back at his persecutors as if to say, "Dude, cut it out."

Near this fresco is an entrance to the cloister and just inside it a stairwell to the right leading up to the **Biblioteca Laurenziana (Laurentian Library)** ★★, which can also be entered admission-free without going through (and paying for) the church (the separate entrance is just to the left of the church's main doors). Michelangelo designed this library in 1524 to house the Medici's manuscript collection, and it stands as one of the most brilliant works of Mannerist

architecture. The vestibule is a whacked-out riff on the Renaissance, all *pietra serena* (dark grey stone) and white plaster walls like a good Brunelleschi piece, but turned inside out. There are phony piers running into each other in the corners, pilaster strips that support nothing, and brackets that exist for no reason. On the whole, however, it manages to remain remarkably coherent. The Laurentian Library's real star feature, however, is Michelangelo's elegant, and totally original, *pietra serena* tripartite staircase: the central flight of stairs consists of broad, convex steps that seem to flow toward you like cooling lava, while the more rectilinear lateral stairs seem to possess the upward motion of an escalator. This actual library part, however—filled with intricately carved wood and handsomely illuminated manuscripts—was closed indefinitely in 1999 until "urgent maintenance" is completed. *Piazza San Lorenzo.* ☎ *055/216-634. Admission to church 2.50€, free to Laurentian Library. Church Mon–Sat 10am–5pm. Laurentian Library Mon–Sat 9am–1pm.*

FREE ➜ **San Miniato al Monte** ★★ Just 150m (492 ft.) south of Piazzale Michelangelo, on a promontory surrounded by cypress and olive groves, is this Romanesque church, whose gleaming façade of white Carrara and green Prato marble is visible from the lowlands of downtown Florence. One of the few ancient churches of Florence to survive the centuries virtually intact, San Miniato was built to honor the eponymous saint, an eastern Christian who settled in Florence and was martyred by decapitation in the 3rd century A.D. The legend goes that—in a feat that would horrify NBA referees—the decapitated Minias picked up his head, put it back on his shoulders, walked across the river, climbed up the hillside, and didn't lie down to die until he reached a cave at this spot. *Via del Monte alle Croci/Viale Galileo Galilei (behind Piazzale Michelangelo).* ☎ *055/234-2731. www.san-miniato-al-monte.com. Easter to early Oct daily 8am–7:30pm; winter Mon–Sat 8am–1pm and 2:30–6pm, Sun 8am–6pm. Free admission.*

MTV Best ➜ **Santa Croce** ★★★ Of the dozens of churches you can visit in Florence, Santa Croce, in all its Gothic glory, really shouldn't be missed. If you had the dough and the influence, you could buy a tomb plot here back in the day and reserve yourself a first-class ticket to the big *duomo* in the sky. The inventory of boldface name sepulchers here reads like an all-obituary *US Weekly* from Renaissance Florence. But tombs of the rich and famous are not the only attraction at Santa Croce: Its Gothic interior is wide and gaping, with huge pointed stone arches creating the aisles and an echoing nave trussed

with wood beams, in all giving the architecture a wonderful barnlike feel (an analogy the occasional fluttering pigeon only enforces).

On the right aisle is the first tomb of note, a mad contraption by Giorgio Vasari containing the bones of the most venerated of Renaissance masters, Michelangelo Buonarroti, who died of a fever in Rome in 1564 at the ripe old age of 89. He was originally buried in the Eternal City, in the church of the Santissimi Apostoli, but the Florentines managed to sneak him out so that they could bury him here in Santa Croce.

Another eternal tenant of Santa Croce is one of the victims of the Inquisition, Galileo Galilei, whose excommunication from the Catholic Church was lifted only in 1992, 350 years after his death. His 18th-century tomb, decorated appropriately with a heliocentric relief, lies near that of Lorenzo Ghiberti, the 15th-century sculptor who cast the famous bronze doors on the baptistery. Don't be fooled by Santa Croce's pompous monument to poet Dante Alighieri—it's only a cenotaph (empty tomb). A Florentine native, now regarded as the father of the Italian language, Dante died in 1321 in Ravenna after a long and bitter life in exile from his hometown (on trumped-up embezzlement charges), and Ravenna has never seen fit to return the bones to Florence, the city that would not readmit the poet when he was alive. Next comes a wall monument to Niccolò Machiavelli, the 16th-century Florentine statesman and author whose famous book *The Prince*, the ultimate how-to manual for a powerful Renaissance ruler, presents politics and human nature in a practical, but not necessarily ethical or moral, way. Beyond Machiavelli's cenotaph is a 19th-century funerary monument (with a real body this time): Here lie the remains of Gioacchino Rossini (1792-1868), composer of the *Barber of Seville* and the *William Tell Overture*. With all these tombs, plus Gaddi's stained-glass windows, Giotto's frescoed chapels, and Donatello's Crucifix, Santa Croce is one of the most art- and relic-packed churches in Italy. *Piazza Santa Croce.* ☎ *055/244-619. Mon–Sat 9:30am–5:30pm; Sun 1–5:30pm. Admission 4€.*

→ **Santa Maria Novella** ✶ So, your train to Venice is delayed for an hour? No worries, this just gives you time to pay a visit to the church that is the namesake for—and literally across the street from—Florence's main train station. Whether or not you need to kill time while that Intercity gets a new locomotive, Santa Maria Novella is worthy of a quick look. Of all Florence's major churches, this home of the Dominican order is the only one with an original façade that matches its era of greatest importance. The lower Romanesque half was started in the 14th century; in the 16th century, Leon Battista Alberti got out his protractor and finished the façade, adding a classically inspired Renaissance top that not only went seamlessly with the lower half but also created a Cartesian plane of perfect geometry. Inside, Giotto's recently restored *Crucifix* hangs in the center of the nave. Against the second pillar on the left of the nave is the pulpit from which Galileo was denounced for his heretical theory that Earth revolved around the Sun. Just past the pulpit, on the left wall, is Masaccio's *Trinità* (ca. 1428), the first painting in the world to use perfect linear mathematical perspective. Florentine citizens and artists flooded in to see the fresco when it was unveiled, many remarking in awe that the coffered ceiling seemed to punch a hole back into space, creating a chapel out of a flat wall. The transept is filled with spectacularly frescoed chapels. *Piazza Santa Maria Novella.* ☎ *055/282-187. Mon–Thurs and Sat 9:30am–5pm; Fri and Sun 1–5pm. Admission 2.70€.*

Playing Outside

Dodging Vespas and standing in those museum queues not providing the exercise you're looking for? Head to **Parco delle Cascine**—a former game reserve of the Medici, on the western outskirts of town—and you'll find tennis courts, wooded jogging paths and several pools. Tennis will set you back about 25€; for the same price, you can also hit around with a certified coach. To the west is the **Campo di Marte,** encircled by the Viale Manfredo Fanti. Plenty of soccer fields are available for foot-happy athletes, and you can catch locals here playing pickup games on the weekend. There's even a baseball diamond on the northeast corner if you can find enough people to field a team (okay, wishful thinking).

→ **Boboli Gardens** ✶✶ The less sports-inclined can wander through Florence's "green lung" par excellence, attached to the back of the Pitti Palace in the Oltrarno section south of the river. For a 4€ admission fee, the former property of Luca Pitti, a 15th-century Florentine banker, can become your own playground. While there aren't any hedge-mazes to recreate your own version of the final scene of *The Shining*, there are fountains, statues, grottoes, and secluded gardens perfect for spending a lazy Sunday afternoon. *Piazza Pitti 1.* ☎ *055/265-1816. Admission 4€. Daily 8:15am–1 hr. before sunset.*

→ **Fiesole** ✶✶ Smart Florentines escape the heat and crowds of the city center by heading for the hills. A one-time Etruscan stronghold, the hilltop village of Fiesole is just over 2 miles northeast of the Duomo. Catch bus 7 from Piazza Santa Maria Novella, and in under 30 minutes, you can be breathing fresh air, enjoying a meal on restaurant-lined **Piazza Mino** (Fiesole's panoramic main square), or tromping through the **Teatro Romano** archaeological park (Via Portigiani 1; ☎ **055/59477;** open daily 9am–sunset; closed Tues Nov–Mar) that spills down the hillside, including some fascinating ruins of a Roman theater and the well-preserved heating system of some Roman baths.

Go La Fiorentina!

The main sports stadium, **Stadio Comunale Artemio Franchi,** plays host to the local soccer team, **La Fiorentina.** Their season—in Italy's premier Serie A league—runs from September through May. Fiorentina fans are a lively but nonviolent bunch, so if you're in town when they've got a **home game** ★★, you're in for a wonderful cultural spectacle. For tickets, show up at the stadium box office 3 hours before game time (Via Manfredi Fanti 4; ☎ 055/262-5537), or check out www.acffiorentina.it. Good seats cost from 20€–45€; "tribune of honor" seats'll set you back 140€. Women get a 30% discount on all but the most expensive tickets. Hit the stands out front before the game and pick up some purple scarves to show your support.

FREE ➔ **Piazzale Michelangelo** ★ This panoramic piazza high above the Oltrarno is the requisite park-and-make-out spot for young Florentine studs who manage to snag themselves a foreign female fling. By day, it's also a de rigueur stop for tour buses. The balustraded terrace offers a sweeping vista of the entire city, spread out in the valley below and backed by the sensual green hills of Fiesole beyond. The monument to Michelangelo in the center of the piazza is made up of bronze replicas of *David* and his sculptures from the Medici chapels. Take bus 12 or 13 from Piazza Santa Maria Novella, or walk from the Oltrarno. (On foot, the most direct route here is from Ponte Vecchio, to Via de' Bardi, which changes names to Via San Niccolò, then turn right at Porta San Miniato onto Via del Monte alle Croci. Less direct and steeper, but with plenty of stunning views along the way, is Ponte Vecchio-Costa dei Magnoli-Via di Belvedere-Via del Monte alle Croci.)

Shopping

When you show up in Florence and realize that your khaki Ex-Officio pants with the zip-on legs ain't gonna cut it in this chic city, it doesn't take much time or money to get you outfitted *propah*—just head to the zoo of market stalls around San Lorenzo for fun and inexpensive, this-minute fashion accessories, T-shirts, jeans, and, of course, leather jackets (which are not the highest quality and can be a bit expensive). As for the other ubiquitous item in the outdoor markets—marbled, old-world Florentine stationery—just ask yourself this: How many letters to grandma are you really going to write? You might want to save that 10€ for a glass of wine or three. (Yeah, we're looking out for you.)

Florence is perhaps the best shopping city in Italy—its layout, which is far more compact than Rome's or Milan's, means that you can cover a lot of retail territory in a single shopping-dedicated afternoon, even if you're just wandering around. If you want to approach credit card debt in a more targeted fashion, head for these key zones: mass-market, and mostly affordable chain stores are in the area immediately **south of the Duomo** (Via Roma, Via Calzaiuoli, Via del Corso); designer boutiques are scattered a bit everywhere, but mainly concentrated on and around **Via Tornabuoni;** smaller, funkier boutiques are on **Via de' Neri** in Santa Croce; and artisans still practice and sell their old-world crafts in the **Oltrarno.**

BOOKS, MUSIC & MEDIA

➔ **Data** ★ You're trudging through the crowded streets of Florence on a sweltering summer day, carrying a 50-lb. backpack, hung over, and looking for your hotel (which, when you find it, you discover to be on the third floor of an elevatorless building). You're seized by an overwhelming desire to hear the Rolling Stones' "Beast of Burden." Make your way over to Data—the city's best resource for '60s and '70s rock, blues, and soul—and ask the clerk if he'll sell your pitiful soul a copy of *Some Girls*. *Via de' Neri 15/r (Santa Croce).* ☎ *055/287-592.*

➜ **La Feltrinelli** Italy's equivalent of Barnes & Noble has several locations in Florence. Though there are heaps of used bookstores in Florence to scour for books in English, if you're looking for a particular Pynchon, minus the dog-eared pages, Feltrinelli's your best bet. *Via Cavour 12–20.* ☎ *055/219-524. www.lafeltrinelli.it.*

➜ **Piccadilly Sound** ★ Head to San Marco if your CDs are getting tired and boring. The clerks' English may not be up to snuff, but throw out some names and he'll find it in no time. Most albums released before 2005 are reasonably priced (I found Zep's *Houses of the Holy* and Nick Drake's *Five Leaves Left* selling for 10€). New releases and recent albums can go as high as 20€. *Piazza San Marco 11.* ☎ *055/11-220.*

CLOTHES, SHOES & ACCESSORIES

Shopping hours in Florence are generally daily from 9:30am to noon or 1pm and 3 or 3:30pm to 7:30pm, though increasingly, many shops are staying open through the mid-afternoon *riposo,* especially the larger stores and those in the more touristed areas.

➜ **Bologna** ★★ Try as we might, we can never resist buying a pair of shoes or boots here when we're in town. Its location, on heavily touristed Piazza del Duomo, might make savvy shoppers think that they can dig deeper into Florence's backstreets and find better shoes, but this is not the case. Bologna does a brisk business, so if you want to try something on, you'll have to assert yourself to get a sales clerk's attention; once you do, they'll be your staunch, opinionated ally in choosing the best—hottest or most practical, let 'em know your needs—footwear to perfume your luggage with the aphrodisiac smell of Italian leather. With most pairs priced around 250€, Bologna's not cheap, but you're guaranteed several seasons' worth of "*where did you get those boots?!?!*" back home. *Piazza del Duomo 13/15/r.* ☎ *055/290-545.*

➜ **e-vision** ★ A couple doors down from Ultra, ladies can find more elegant options at e-vision. Dresses and tops feature a remarkably Italian flair with flowing lines and asymmetric patterns. Clerks don't understand English well but try to help you as best they can. Fortunately, they understand the universal language of "MasterCard" and "Visa." *Via Nazionale 154.* ☎ *055/496-300.*

➜ **G'Art** ★ This local men's label has racks full of obscure, arty T-shirts that'll make a significant dent in your stash of euros. Layer it with one of their cleanly designed blazers and you're ready to impress. Pieces here are pricey, but compared to other, more established names found on Via Tornabuoni, that 250€ blazer looks like a steal. *Via dei Pecori 15/17r.* ☎ *055/289-497. www.gart.it.*

➜ **Peluso** ★ Peluso is like Payless, only oozing style. Designed like a condensed warehouse, the store offers women slides, pumps, boots, and flip-flops that'll match any outfit or bag. (The selection is awfully sparse for dudes.) Local artisans design most of the shoes, but prices remain extremely reasonable. Some pairs can be had for as low at 14€, which probably means you won't be walking miles in them, but you'll at least have the memories when they're worn out. *Via del Corso 1/11r.* ☎ *055/268-283. Also Via del Corso 6/8r.* ☎ *055/282-235.*

➜ **Sieni Alessandra** Essentially a camping store, you can find backpacks, hiking boots, sleeping bags, and outdoor clothing for your stay in the camping areas in the hills or to replace some of your beaten up gear. There are two brands that you can purchase here: the Italian camping equipment company Ferrino and the American outdoor behemoth Columbia. *Via dell' Ariento 73/r.*

➜ **Ultra** ★ Via Nazionale has a small stretch of edgy boutiques where you can stock up on the latest styles. Ultra is one such shop. Old-school Nikes, Carhartt gear, tons of G-Star and footwear from Duffs give you an idea of the various stateside influences. Giovanni, the clerk, is always willing to help you find the right vintage T-shirt or pair of weathered jeans. If you're absolutely clueless about Florence's nightlife, ask Giovanni, who's well versed in the alternative world of Firenze. *Via Nazionale 118/r.* ☎ *055/216017. Daily 10am–1pm and 3:30–8pm. Another location is at Via XXVII Aprile 37/r,* ☎ *055/489-861.*

DEPARTMENT STORES

→ **COIN** ★★ Gotta love COIN—this department store might not offer the coolest shopping bags for flaunting your purchases around town, but Florentines are faithful to its consistently strong selection of fashion accessories (better quality than what you'll find at the open-air market stalls) and housewares (good souvenirs for Mom and Dad). When that trip to Miu Miu left you sticker-shocked, but you still want to buy something in this 'hood south of the Duomo, stroll on down to the open arms of *mamma* COIN, and get a trendy pair of socks for 4€. *Via dei Calzaiuoli 56/r.* ☎ *055/280-531. www.coin.it.*

→ **La Rinascente** Florence's other midrange department store beats COIN on just three counts: the cosmetics floor; the ingerie selection; and the rooftop cafe, which has splendid views over the Duomo, Palazzo Vecchio, and rosy rooftops. *Piazza della Repubblica 1.* ☎ *055/219-113.*

SPECIALTY

→ **Bartolucci** It's hard to miss Bartolucci in all its wooden glory in either of these streets and it's easy to be overwhelmed by the sheer amount of timber in this toy store. The Italian chain has two locations where you can get your niece or nephew a kitschy chunk of lumber. As for your 6-year-old pyromaniac cousin, he might enjoy a charming Florence snowglobe. *Via Condotta 12/r.* ☎ *055/211-773. www.bartolucci.com. Also at Borgo dei Greci 11/a-r,* ☎ *055/239-8596.*

→ **Old English Store** If you're aching for a cup of Earl Grey (the only reason I came to this place), Old English Store has everything . . . well, British. Bolts of tartan cloth (in case you forgot to buy some in Scotland), cans of authentic teas, and even chocolate and candies from the U.K. can be had here. It's also a fantastic place to just step out of the Florentine state of mind and inspect the tailored pants and ties. Once you had your fill of all things British, get out of there, grab a gelato, and enjoy Firenze! *Via Vecchietti 28/r.* ☎ *055/211-983.*

The Chianti Region: Enjoy the Wine & a Slower Pace

If there is a place in the world with more hilltop castles and vineyards packed together, I'd be amazed. Driving through Chianti is like taking a Disney ride through a medieval age where barons ruled vine-tangled fiefdoms unspoiled by billboards and strip malls. It's easy to take that ride back in time: Buy a map, rent a car, and drive the SS222 from Florence down to Siena, or vice versa. It's a relatively short drive, and if you don't get too caught up in the atmosphere (and the wine), it should only require 2 days.

We've divided the region in two: the **Florentine Chianti** which is (duh!) closer to Florence, and the **Sienese Chianti** (Siena has a section of its own a little later in this chapter).

Getting There & Getting Around the Chianti Region

BY CAR

Public transportation is practically nonexistent through this scenic series of valleys between Siena and Florence. The only way to

The Chianti Region

Florence

Bagno a Ripoli

San Piero a Ema

A1

Grassina

Ugolino

La Chiantigiana
SS222

Impruneta

S. Stefano a
Tizzano

A1

Castello di Tizzano

San Polo in Chianti

San Casciano
in Val di Pesa

Strada
in Chianti

Spedaluzzo

Castello di
Vicchiomaggio

Le Bolle

SS2

Castello di Verrazzano

Castello di
Uzzano

Dudda

Badia a
Passignano

San Cresci

Castello di
Querceto

Lucolena di Sotto

Tavernelle in
Val di Pesa

Montefioralle

Greve in
Chianti

Lucolena

Sambuca

Fontodi

Barberino
Val di Pesa

Rignana

Castello
Vignamaggio

Panzano
in Chianti

Lámole

San Donato
in Poggio

Piazza

Castello di
Volpaia

Monsanto

Badia a
Coltibuono

SS429

Pietrafitta

Villa

Castello de
la Panareto

Castellare
Winery

Radda
in Chianti

Villa Strozzi-Sonnino

Gaiole in
Chianti

← To San Gimignano

Castellina
in Chianti

Vertine

Barbischio

Poggibonsi

San Giusto

Meleto

Castagnoli

Fonterutoli

Castello di Ama

SS408

Colle di
Val d'Elsa

Lecchi

Castello
di Brolio

San Sano

Monteriggioni

Quercegrossa

Monti

SS484

SS2

SS222

Fattoria dei
Pagliaresi

Arno River

ITALY

Milan Venice

Florence Chianti
Region

Rome

Naples

Siena

Fattoria della
Aiola

🍇 **Vineyard**

ⓘ Information

0 ——— 2 Mi

0 ——— 2 Km

N

Chianti 101: What You Need to Know About the Wine

The Chianti is one of the world's definitive wine regions, in both history and spirit; these hills have been an enological center for several thousand years. In fact, one local grape, the *Canaiolo nero*—one of the varietals that traditionally goes into Chianti Classico—was known to the ancients as the "Etruscan grape." The name Chianti, probably derived from that of the local noble Etruscan family Clantes, has been used to describe the hills between Florence and Siena for centuries, but it wasn't until the mid–13th century that Florence created the Lega del Chianti to unite the region's three most important centers—Castellina, Radda, and Gaiole—which chose the black rooster as their symbol. By 1404 the red wine produced here was being called *chianti* as well, and in 1716 a grand ducal decree defined the boundaries of the Chianti and laid down general rules for its wine production, making it the world's first officially designated wine-producing area. In the 19th century, one vintner, the "Iron Baron" Ricasoli, experimented with varietals using the sangiovese grape as his base. Working off centuries of refinement, he eventually came up with the perfect balance of grapes that became the unofficial standard for all chianti.

Soon the title "chianti" was being taken in vain by hundreds of poor-quality, vino-producing hacks, both within the region and from areas far-flung, and the international reputation of the wine was besmirched. To fight against this, Greve and Castelnuovo Berardenga joined the original Lega cities and formed the *Consorzio del Gallo Nero* in 1924, reviving the old black rooster as their seal. The *consorzio* (still active—their members produce about 80% of the Chianti Classico bottled) pressed for laws regulating the quality of chianti wines and restricting the Chianti Classico name to their production zone.

When Italy devised its DOC and DOCG wine appellation laws in the 1960s, chianti was one of the first to be defined as DOCG *(denominazione di origine controllata e garantita)*, guaranteeing its quality as one of the top wines in the country. Today, of the 100 sq. km (39 sq. miles.) of vineyards in the hills between Florence and Siena, some 6,972 hectares (17,220 acres) are devoted to the grapes that will eventually become Chianti Classico and carry the seal of the black rooster.

explore the Chianti effectively is to drive. But you should know that many of the side roads off the major SS222 (aka the Chiantigiana) are unpaved, often steep, and sometimes heavily potholed.

Car-rental agencies in Florence include **Avis,** Borgo Ognissanti 128r (☎ 800/230-4898 in North America, or 055-213629 locally; www.avis.com); **Italy by Car,** Borgo Ognissanti 134r (☎ 055-287161); and **Hertz,** Via del Termine (☎ 800/654-3131 in North America, or 055-307370 locally; www.hertz.com).

BY BIKE

Biking through the Chianti can be one of Tuscany's most rewarding and scenic strenuous workouts. You can rent a bike in Greve (the unofficial capital of the area) at **Ramuzzi Marco**, Viale Falsettacci 6 (☎ **055/853-037;** turn right at tourist office; it's down on the left; the cost is 13€ to 16€ per day (scooters 16€–23€ per half-day or 26€–39€ per full day), though the daily price goes down the longer you keep it. The region's low mountains and stands of ancient forest are also excellent for hiking.

BY BUS

You can visit the major towns by bus, but be prepared to stay a while until the next ride comes along. **SITA** (☎ **055/214-721;** www. sita-on-line.it) from Florence services Strada (40 min. from Florence), Greve (65 min.), Panzano (75 min.), Radda or Castellina (95 min.), and Gaiole (2 hr.); it leaves at least hourly for stops up through Greve and Panzano and at least one to three times a day all the way through to Gaiole. About eight (Mon–Sat) **Tra-in** buses (☎ **0577/204-111;** www.comune. siena.it/train) from Siena hit Radda, Gaiole, and Castellina; and, you can get to Impruneta with a **CAP** bus (☎ **055/214-637;** www.cap autolinee.it) from Florence.

Florentine Chianti Basics

The unofficial capital of the area is **Greve** in Chianti, and its **tourist office** (☎ **055/ 854-6287;** fax 055/854-4149), is in a modern little shack on the right just as you arrive in Greve coming from the north; the staff makes an effort to provide some Chianti-wide info. From Easter to October, it's open Monday through Friday from 10am to 1pm and 3 to 7pm, Saturday from 10am to 1pm. In winter, it might keep shorter hours. You can also try **www.chianti.it/turismo**, a site with links to many hotels and restaurants in the area.

Sleeping in Florentine Chianti

Besides the choices below, the **Castello Vicchiomaggio** wine estate (☎ **055/854-079;** fax 055/853-911; www.vicchiomaggio.it), just north of Greve, offers seven basic self-catering apartments in a National Monument Renaissance castle. Each sleeps two to six and has a kitchenette, TV, hair dryer, iron, and safe. Most have a countryside view, and while there are no phones, there is a pool on a panoramic terrace. Prices start at 100€ per night for two people. During high season, they often require a 1-week minimum stay. March through November, **Castello di Verrazzano** (☎ **055/853-211;** www.verrazzano.com) also

rents seven double rooms, breakfast included, at 77€ for one person, 103€ for two people, and 129€ for three people. Two apartments with kitchenette are available; one, for two people, is 103€, while the apartment for four people is 129€. The apartments require a stay of at least 3 nights.

DOABLE

➔ **Hotel Giovanni da Verrazzano** The Verrazzano hotel/restaurant sits across from its namesake's statue on Greve's triangular central piazza. The rooms are on the smallish side, the furnishings functional but nice, with painted wrought-iron bed frames with firm mattresses, dark-wood furniture, terra-cotta floors, spotless bathrooms, and a handful of wood-beamed ceilings. Those on the front overlook the mismatched arcades of the piazza, while the back rooms have tiny terraces with late-morning sun, potted plants, and a view over lichen-spotted roof tiles to the Chianti hills. The four-sleeper in the attic is perfect for families, and the **restaurant** (www.ristoranteverrazzano.it) serves hearty portions of highly recommendable Tuscan fare in a laid-back trattoria atmosphere, with alfresco summer dining at tables on a terrace atop the arcades. *Piazza G. Matteotti 28, 50022 Greve in Chianti (FI).* ☎ *055/853-189. Fax 055/ 853-648. www.verrazzano.it. 10 units, 8 with bathroom (shower only). Double without bathroom 77€, with bathroom 99€; triple 133€; quad 158€. Half and full pension available. Breakfast 9€ included with triples and quads. Closed Jan 15–Feb 15.*

➔ **Villa Rosa di Boscorotondo** ★★ This villa offers wonderful countryside seclusion at modest prices—a rarity in the Chianti. Giancarlo and Sabina Avuri, who own Florence's Hotel Torre Guelfa, opened this huge pink villa as a roadside inn in 1998, retaining the original features and roominess while modernizing with an elegance that lends it an antique rustic air. The curtained beds on wrought-iron frames rest under gorgeous beamed ceilings, and rooms along the front open onto two huge terraces that drink in views of the small valley in which the villa nestles. There are a series of small drawing rooms, a pool with a view, and a path that leads through the vineyards all the way to San Leolino church outside Panzano. Famed butcher Dario Cecchini provides the meat for fixed-price dinners (25€ not including wine) on the terra-cotta terrace in summer. *Via San Leolino 59 (on the SS222 between Panzano and Radda), 50022 Loc. Panzano in Chianti (FI).* ☎ *055/852-577. Fax 055/856-0835. www.resort villarosa.com. 15 units. Double 70€–130€; triple 100€–140€. Rates include breakfast.*

SPLURGE

➜**Villa Vignamaggio** ★★ You can't actually stay in the room where Mona Lisa grew up, but you can certainly make do with suites, each with a tiny kitchenette and complimentary bottle of the estate's award-winning chianti. This is one of the most comfortable *agriturismi* on the market, offering hotel-style amenities such as daily maid service. The heavy wood-beam ceilings and the comfortable rustic furnishings mesh well with the contemporary designer lights, spanking-new bathrooms, and cast-iron bed frames; four suites even have Jacuzzi tubs and air-conditioning. You can stay in one of several suites in the villa, rent the small cottage next door, or shack out in a suite in one of the old stone peasant houses dotting the property on either side of the road. *Villa Vignamaggio (5km/3 miles southeast of Greve), Greve in Chianti.* ☎ *055/854-661. www.vignamaggio.com. Double 150€, apartment 210€. Turn off the SS222 just south of Greve onto the Lamole road, then follow the signs.*

Eating in Florentine Chianti
DOABLE

➜**Bottega del Moro** ★ TUSCAN Modern art and a view over the tiny Greve River are the backdrop at this pleasant trattoria in the center of Greve. After *bruschetta al pomodoro,*

dig into the light *maltagliati del Moro* (wide noodles with slivers of porcini and prosciutto in butter-and-sage sauce) or the richer *crespelle alla fiorentina* (pasta crepes stuffed with ricotta and spinach and served in a cheesy béchamel garnished with tomato purée). For an encore, try *coniglio al forno* (tender, meaty rabbit baked with spices and black olives). The local specialty is *zampone con puree* (stewed pigs' feet). Whatever you order, see if they're offering *pecorino con pere* as a *contorno* (side dish)—the creamy, firm, fresh sheep's cheese pairs excellently with the soft, sweet slices of ripe pear. *Piazza Trieste 14r (a tiny park on the east side of the main road near the south end of Greve).* ☎ *055/853-753. www.greve-in-chianti.com/ il-moro.htm. Reservations recommended. Primi 5€–7.50€; secondi 11€–15€. Thurs–Tues 12:15–2:15pm and 7:15–9:15pm. Closed 1st week of May and Nov.*

➜**La Cantinetta di Rignana** ★★ TUSCAN From Greve, follow the signs to Montefioralle, then toward Badia a Passignano until the signposted turnoff. A medieval ramble of stone houses at the end of a long dirt road hides La Cantinetta, one of the Chianti's most genuine countryside trattorie. You can have lunch on the glassed-in patio with a sweeping view of the vineyard, but I prefer ducking under the hanging bunches of sausages and pendulous prosciutto ham hocks to eat inside. Here a congregation of reproduction Madonna and Child icons on one wall stare down the small armada of hammered copper pots and lanterns across the way. The staff is given to warbling snatches of folk songs and opera as they prepare handmade pasta (ravioli, gnocchi, or tagliolini) with your pick of rich sauces—the thick, pasty *noci* nut sauce is excellent. Grilled meats top the main courses (*coniglio*, rabbit, is charred to perfection), or try the delicious *involtini di manzo* (beef slices rolled up with vegetables). The white-chocolate mousse is legendary. If the beautifully isolated setting appeals to you, the attached farm also offer seven basic country-style rooms from April to early November for 95€ for a double, including breakfast (minimum 3 nights; book at ☎ 055/852-065; www.rignana.it). *Loc. Rignana, Greve in Chianti.* ☎ *055/852-601. www.lacantinettadirignana.it. Reservations strongly recommended. Primi 6.50€–8€; secondi 8.50€–11€. Wed–Mon 12:30–2:15pm and 7:30–10:30pm. Closed Nov 30–Dec 22.*

SPLURGE

→ **La Cantinetta di Spedaluzzo** ★ ★
TUSCAN Atop a rise in the Chiantigiana, this countryside trattoria offers friendly service and excellent Tuscan dishes. The *crostini caldi al fornello* are do-it-yourself affairs—spread the pâté of your choice onto slabs of toasted peasant bread. The *ribollita* is especially tasty, with some meat for flavor, and comes with an enormous urn of olive oil to ladle over it. *Pipe al sugo ricco* are large maccheroni in a duly rich sauce of pork, mutton, beef, and strips of tomato. The stars of the secondi are the *involtini ai porcini* (veal rolls cooked in a sauce of concentrated porcini mushrooms), the *salsicce al tartufo* (a pair of salty sausages with white truffles chopped into the mix), and the huge *bistecca alla fiorentina.* Don't leave without ordering their homemade tiramisu for dessert, one of the best I've ever tasted. They've added a glassed-in veranda with a fireplace for three-seasons dining with a view. *Via Mugnana 93, Loc. Spedaluzzo (halfway between Strada and Greve on SS222).* ☎ *055/857-2000. Reservations required. Primi 8€–12€; secondi 7€–15€. Tues–Sun 12:30–2:30pm and 7:30–10:30pm. Closed for 3 weeks in late Feb/early Mar.*

Sightseeing in Florentine Chianti

ON THE ROAD TO GREVE

Cross Florence's eastern Ponte San Niccolò and follow the signs from Piazza Ferrucci on the other side toward Grassina and the SS222 Chiantigiana. South on the SS222 takes you through Strada in Chianti, and at the bend in the road called Le Bolle is a right turnoff for **Vicchiomaggio** (☎ **055/854-079;** fax 055/853-911; www.vicchiomaggio.it). This 10th-century Lombard fortress was modified in the 15th century and is today one of the best preserved of the typical Chianti castles.

Its estate, under British ownership, produces well-regarded wines, including Ripa delle More, a sangiovese/cabernet sauvignon whose 1997 vintage won "three glasses" from Gambero Rosso (the Italian oenological equivalent of two Michelin stars). You can taste for free at the roadside **Cantinetta San Jacopo** wine shop (on the SS222 right at the turnoff for the castle) daily from 9am to 12:30pm and 2:30 to 6:30pm (as late as 7:30pm in summer). Sadly, visits to the cellars, parts of which date to the 10th century, are now limited only to groups, though it's worth the short drive up here just to look at the castle exterior and for the countryside views. They do, however, offer cooking courses (anywhere from 1 or 2 hr. to several days).

A bit farther along on the right is the turnoff for **Castello di Verrazzano** (☎ **055/854-243** or 055/290-684; fax 055/854-241; www.verrazzano.com), the 12th-century seat of the Verrazzano family. Young Giovanni Verrazzano, born here in 1485, became restless with viticultural life and sailed out of the Chianti under the bridge named for him in New York Harbor (just kidding!).

The estate has been making wine at least since 1170, and you can sample it Monday through Friday from 8am to 6pm. Tours of the gardens and cellars run Monday through Friday starting at 11am (lasting until 3pm); book ahead at least a day in advance, a week or more in advance in high season (May and June especially). The cost is 10€ for a tour and tasting of three wines, and 32€ if you take the light lunch as well (you'll get a few more wines, too). On weekends, you can buy the wine at the small stand on SS222 (☎ 055/853-211).

IN GREVE

This oversized village is the center of the wine trade and the unofficial capital of Chianti. The statue in the center of the central Piazza Matteotti is of the intrepid explorer Giovanni Verrazzano (for whom the New York bridge is named), and the narrow end of the piazza spills into the tiny Piazzetta Santa Croce. Greve is the host of Chianti's annual September **wine fair,** and there are, naturally, dozens of wine shops in town. Some of the better ones are the **Bottega del Chianti Classico,** Via Cesare Battisti 2–4 (☎ 055/853-631; www.chianticlassicoshop.com), and the **Enoteca del Chianti Classico,** Piazzetta Santa Croce 8 (☎ 055/853-297). At Piazza Matteotti 69–71 is one of Italy's most famous butchers, **Macelleria Falorni** (☎ 055/854-363; www.falorni.it), established in 1700 and still a cornucopia of hanging prosciutti and hundreds of other cured meats, along with a decent wine selection.

IN PANZANO

The Chiantigiana next cuts through the town of Panzano; the tourist office is **InfoChianti,** Via Chiantigiana 6 (☎ 055/852-933; www.infochianti.com; Tues–Fri 10am–1pm and 3–7pm, Sat 10am–12:30pm and 3:30–7:30pm, Sun 10am–1pm). The town is known for its embroidery and for its "Poet Butcher" **Dario Cecchini,** Via XX Luglio 11 (☎ 055/852-020). Cecchini loves to entertain visitors with classical music and tastes of his products, while he recites the entirety of Dante's "Inferno" from memory. (Something of a local character, Dario has been featured on more than one TV program in Italy; he held a large, well-publicized mock funeral for the *bistecca fiorentina* on the day it was temporarily outlawed in 2001 during Europe's mad cow disease outbreaks.)

Sleeping in Sienese Chianti

Also see the Albergaccio (p. 272) for an inexpensive room connected with the restaurant.

CHEAP

➔ **Hotel Il Colombaio** ★ This modest, excellently priced hotel sits in a 16th-century stone house at the edge of Castellina (near the Etruscan tomb and a 5-min. walk into town for restaurants) and once housed shepherds who spent the night after selling their sheep at market. The good-size rooms with their sloping beam-and-tile ceilings, terracotta floors, and iron bed frames seem to belong to a well-to-do 19th-century farming family. Upstairs accommodations are lighter and airier than the ground-floor rooms (formerly stalls) and enjoy better views over the vineyards (a few overlook the road). Six of the rooms are in an annex across the road. The house's old kitchen has been converted into a comfy rustic reading room. You breakfast in winter under stone vaults and in summer on a terrace sharing its countryside vistas with the pool. *Via Chiantigiana 29, 53011 Castellina in Chianti.* ☎ *0577/740-444. Fax 0577/740-402.* *www.albergoilcolombaio.it.* *Double 87€–103€. Rates include continental breakfast.*

DOABLE

➔ **Borgo Argenina** ★★ From the flagstoned terrace of Elena Nappa's new hilltop B&B (she bought the whole medieval hamlet), you can see the farmhouse where Bertolucci filmed *Stealing Beauty* in 1996. Against remarkable odds (she'll regale you with the anecdotes), she has created a dreamy rural retreat. When you arrive, you'll likely find Elena upstairs next to a roaring fire in the kitchen, sewing. Elena's design talents (she was a fashion stylist in Milan) are amazing, and the guest rooms boast antique wrought-iron beds, deluxe mattresses, handmade quilts, hand-stitched lace curtains, and time-worn terra-cotta tiles. The bathrooms are made to look old-fashioned, though the plumbing is modern. There is a 3-night minimum stay. Be warned, when getting directions from Elena, that the place is not easy to find. *Loc. Argenina (near San Marcellino Monti), Gaiole in Chianti.* ☎ *0577/747-117. www .borgoargenina.it. Double 130€ double; suite for 3 people 180€. Rates include country breakfast. Ask for directions when reserving. Amenities: Laundry service; room service (breakfast). In room: Hair dryer, minibar.*

→ **Podere Terreno** ★★ Paris-born Silvie, who used to run a Florentine art gallery, and her Italian husband, Roberto, are your gracious hosts at their small 16th-century farmstead turned *agriturismo* topping a hillock between Radda and Volpaia. They and their son, Francesco, treat you like family—the last one to go to bed has to turn out the lights, the home-cooked dinner is served promptly at 7:30pm, and they'll scold you if you aren't being a good guest. With this quiet countryside retreat slowly growing in fame, the nightly extended family can get quite multinational. Most who sign up for just a night or two in the simple, comfortably rustic rooms with old peasant furnishings and firm beds on terra-cotta floors return the following year to stay for a week. Breakfast includes salami, excellent homemade marmalades and jams, and soft sheep cheese; and, the scrumptious dinner is accompanied by their own velvety chianti, consistently rated among the top 25 in the Classico region. *Strada per Volpaia (2km/1¼ miles north of Radda off the road to Volpaia), Radda in Chianti.* ☎ *0577/738-312. www.podereterreno.it. 95€ per person, including breakfast and obligatory dinner half pension.*

Eating in Sienese Chianti

DOABLE

→ **Albergaccio** ★ CREATIVE TUSCAN On the outskirts of Castellina, this place offers an excellent mix of fine cuisine and rustic timbered atmosphere with valley views. Francesco Cacciatori glides through the place serving a changing roster of dishes steeped in local traditions but enlivened by the creativity of chef Sonia Visman. Among the tasty combinations, I recommend the *bavette con timo e pecorino di fossa* (thin noodles with tomatoes, thyme, and specially aged pecorino cheese) and *gnocchi di ricotta con tartufo marzolo* (dollops of ricotta with shaved truffles and thyme leaves). The *rollé di maiale con cavolo nero* (pork involtini made with black cabbage, tomatoes, and wild fennel) and *piccione speziato con fichi caramelati al marsala* (stuffed pigeon with figs caramelized in Marsala wine) are fine secondi. They also rent five rooms across the street for 73€ per double, including breakfast (call ☎ **0577/ 741-166**). *Via Fiorentina 63, Castellina in Chianti (just outside the walls along the road toward San Donato).* ☎ *0577/741-042. www. albergacciocast.com. Reservations highly recommended. Primi 11€–13€; secondi 16€–19€; tasting menus 45€. Mon–Sat 12:30–2:15pm and 7:30–9:30pm. Closed last 2 weeks of Nov and 1st week of Dec.*

→ **Le Vigne** TUSCAN The aptly named Le Vigne is tucked between the rows of vines washing the slopes southeast of Radda. You can watch vintners working the vines as you sip your wine and sample such well-turned dishes as *pici all'aglione* (hand-rolled spaghetti with tomatoes, leeks, and a dab of pancetta), bready *ribollita*, boned duck stuffed with porchetta, and excellent *agnello alla griglia* (tender lamb chops grilled with aromatic herbs). Definitely order the homemade *patate fritte*, thinly sliced discs of potato fried in olive oil. *Podere Le Vigne (off the SS408 to Villa just east of Radda in Chianti).* ☎ *0577/738-640. Reservations recommended. Primi 5€–9.50€; secondi 8.50€–14€. Wed–Mon 12–2:30pm and 7:15–9:30pm (open daily in summer). Closed Nov 15–Mar 15.*

Sightseeing in Sienese Chianti

CASTELLINA

This is one of the more medieval-feeling hill towns of the region and a triumvirate member of the old Lega del Chianti. The closest thing to a **tourist office** is the Colline Verdi travel agency, Via della Rocca 12 (☎ **0577/740-620**). Castellina's medieval walls survive almost intact, and the central piazza is dominated by the imposing crenellated rocca fortress. You can taste a few drops of *vino* at La Castellina's enoteca and shipping point in the ground floor of the family palazzo at Via Ferruccio 26 (☎ 0577/740-454). The **Bottega del Vino,** Via della Rocca 13 (☎ **0577/741-110**; www.enobottega.it), is a good wine shop.

VINEYARDS

From Castellina, you can take a long but rewarding detour on the road to Poggibonsi into the Val d'Elsa to visit the **Monsanto vineyards** and medieval estate, which produces a 100% sangiovese chianti (traditionally, it is a mix with other grapes as well), and chardonnay. They started bottling that last one after discovering an Etruscan tomb on the property, which also inspired them to extend their vast cellars with a huge hall built using a low Etruscan-style arch. Down here and in the original 18th-century cellars are stored thousands of bottles from every year of production—many still for sale. They do tastings and direct sales Monday through Friday from 8:30am to 12:30pm and 1:30 to 6pm; reserve a tour of the cellars for 16€ per person at least a few days in advance.

Seven kilometers (4¹/₃ miles) north of Radda on a secondary road is **Castello di Volpait** (☎ 0577/738-066; www.volpaia.com), a first-rank wine estate with a medieval stone heart. The castle here was a Florentine holding buffeted by Sienese attacks and sieges from the 10th to 16th centuries. The still-impressive central keep is all that remains,

but it's surrounded by an evocative 13th-century *borgo* (village). You can tour the winery—installed in a series of buildings throughout the little village (with an eye to preserving its medieval visual charm, owner Giovannella Stanti Mascheroni is busily having the electrical wires and high-tech plumbing through which the wine flows buried seamlessly inside the stone walls)—for 11€ to 23€ per person (Sun–Fri) depending on the size of the group (cheaper for larger groups), and includes tasting of the wines and their fantastic olive oil. Call ahead, preferably a week in advance. The central tower has an enoteca (open Mon–Sat 10am–6pm; closed Feb) for drop-in tastings and direct sales of some of the wines that helped found the Chianti Consorzio in 1924, plus award-winning (and scrumptious) olive oils and the only farm-produced vinegars in the Chianti. They also rent apartments and two small villas and lease out a small hotel on a neighboring hill of the estate.

CASTELLO DI BROLIO

Follow the scenic road leading south out of Radda toward Siena, and past the town of Gaiole, the SS484 branches east toward Castelnuovo Berardenga and this famous castle. The Chianti as a region may date to the 1200s, but Chianti Classico as a wine was born here in the mid–19th century. The Brolio castle has been in the Ricasoli family since 1141, though its vineyards date from at least 1007; the current fortress was rebuilt in 1484. "Iron Baron" Bettino Ricasoli inherited it in 1829 at age 20 and, before he went off in 1848 to help found a unified Italy and become its second prime minister, spent his days here, teaching—really dictating—scientific farming methods to his peasants. He also whiled the time tinkering with grape varietals. By the mid–19th century, he'd arrived at a quaffable formula balancing sangiovese, canaiolo, trebbiano, and malvasia grapes that was used when Italy's wine-governing DOC and DOCG laws were written in the 1960s. You can visit the castle grounds, including the small chapel (Bettino rests in peace in the family crypt) and the gardens, and walk along the wall for a good view of the lower Chianti valleys.

Admission is 3€ In summer, the gardens are open daily 9am to noon and 3 to 6pm; in winter, from 9am to noon and 2 to 5pm (☎ 0577/749-066; www.ricasoli.it; pull the bell rope and wait).

San Gimignano: City in the Country

40km (25 miles) NW of Siena; 57km (35 miles) SW of Florence

If the sounds of hydraulic brakes and diesel engines interrupt your Tuscan idyll, it's thanks to towns like San Gimignano. Year-round, tour buses roll in to this classic Chianti day-trip spot, snap some photos of this gorgeous medieval town and its famous skinny towers, and then roll back out. By evening, the place is nearly deserted. It is an oddity, this hilltop mini-metropolis in the middle of the fields that once boasted some six dozen towers. Each was built by a wealthy family jockeying for power and position, leaving their little burg studded with miniature skyscrapers. Only about 14 true towers remain, though the stubs of the rest of them, long since toppled, remain scattered around the city. Still, especially after the tour buses exit down the windy road, San Gimignano retains its magical, medieval charm and is a perfect pit stop for those cruising the vineyards between Florence and Siena.

Getting There

BY CAR

If you have a **car,** leave Florence (1¹/₂ hr.) or Siena (1 hr., 10 min.) by the Firenze-Siena *autostrada* and drive to Poggibonsi, where you'll cut west along a secondary route (S324) to San Gimignano. There are parking lots outside the city walls. Parking costs average around 2€ per hour, and several are within walking distance. The lots that are a bit further from the town provide shuttle buses.

BY TRAIN

The **rail station** nearest to San Gimignano is at **Poggibonsi,** serviced by regular trains from Florence (4.70€) and Siena (2.20€). At Poggibonsi, buses depart from the front of

the rail station at frequent intervals, charging 1.60€ each way to the center of San Gimignano for the 25-minute ride. For information, call ☎ 0577/204246.

BY BUS

About 20 buses a day make the 25-minute run from the bus/train station at **Poggibonsi** to San Gimignano Monday through Saturday, but only nine buses run on Sunday. Obviously, that 8-mile stretch will be much more convenient by car.

Buses operated by **TRA-IN** (☎ 0577/204111) serve San Gimignano from Florence with a change at Poggibonsi (trip time: 85 min.); the one-way fare is 7€. TRA-IN also operates service from Siena, with a change at Poggibonsi (trip time: 50 min.); the one-way fare is 6.50€. In San Gimignano, buses stop at Piazzale Montemaggio, outside the Porta San Giovanni, the southern gate. You'll have to walk into the center because vehicles aren't allowed in most of the town's core.

Tourist Office

The **Associazione Pro Loco,** Piazza del Duomo 1 (☎ 0577/940008), is open daily November through February from 9am to 1pm and 2 to 6pm, and March to October 9am to 1pm and 3 to 7pm.

Sleeping

Hotels in this most popular hill town aren't cheap. Those watching their euros might want to stay in the more modern satellite community of **Santa Chiara,** just a few minutes' walk from Porta San Giovanni. Also, note the economic doubles available at Le Vecchie Mura (p. 276). You can check out pictures of all

San Gimignano

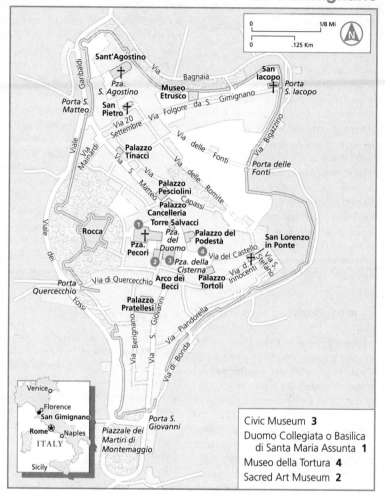

Civic Museum **3**
Duomo Collegiata o Basilica
 di Santa Maria Assunta **1**
Museo della Tortura **4**
Sacred Art Museum **2**

the hotels below (and others) at **www. sangimignano.com**.

DOABLE

→ **Hotel Bel Soggiorno** Owned and run by the Gigli family since 1886, the Bel Soggiorno rooms provide views of the countryside below (three share a panoramic terrace) or of the ultramedieval, if souvenir-ridden, main street in town. The modern, medium-size accommodations are mostly fitted with cheap, functional furniture and beds verging on the over-soft. Little of the original 13th-century structure shows through, and its general lack of antique charm makes it the least desirable of the hotels within the walls. But the friendly family management and highly recommended **restaurant,** serving Tuscan fare in a half-medieval, half-plate-glass panoramic environment, keep the Bel Soggiorno in the running. *Via San Giovanni 91 (near Porta San Giovanni).* ☎ *0577/940-375.*

www.hotelbelsoggiorno.it. Double 95€–120€. Includes breakfast.

→ **Hotel Leon Bianco** ★ Typical of a 500-year-old building turned hotel, the rooms here can't seem to agree on a style or decor scheme, but most retain some element from the 14th-century palazzo—a painted-wood-beamed ceiling here, an old stone wall in a bathroom there, or a brick barrel vault filling one room. Accommodations look out over the pretty well of the tower-lined piazza out front or across a garden next door and rooftops to a glimpse of the countryside. (A few, however, overlook the partially glassed-in courtyard of the lobby.) "Superior" rooms are merely larger and come with minibars. *Piazza della Cisterna 8.* ☎ *0577/941-294. www.leonbianco.com. Standard double 90€, with view 105€; superior double 130€. Includes breakfast.*

SPLURGE

→ **L'Antico Pozzo** ★★ L'Antico Pozzo is the choicest inn within the walls, a 15th-century palazzo converted to a hotel with careful attention to preserving the structural antiquity but still including mod cons (like Internet access). The subdued elegance and comfort offer the most medieval-feeling experience in this most medieval of cities. Over the building's colorful history it has hosted Dante, the Inquisition trials, a religious community, and an 18th-century salon. "Superior" doubles have 17th-century ceiling frescoes and the smaller "standard" rooms on the third floor have wood floors and a view of the Rocca and a few towers, while other rooms look over the street or the rear terrace (where breakfast is served in summer). *Via San Matteo 87 (near Porta San Matteo).* ☎ *0577/ 942-014. www.anticopozzo.com. Double 130€; superior double 150€. Rates include breakfast.*

Eating

CHEAP

→ **Le Vecchie Mura** TUSCAN/ITALIAN Even better than holing up in the cavernous 18th-century former stalls, with worn terra-cotta bricks cross-vaulting the ceiling, is booking a table on the wall-top panoramic terrace in summer. Inside, the bench-lined tables get crowded even in winter, as locals, tourists, and families show up for the simple home cooking at reasonable prices. The satisfying *ribollita* comes with sliced pungent red onion on the side, but the *tagliatelle al cinghiale* (noodles with wild boar) offers it serious competition. The house specialty is *cinghiale alla vernaccia* (chunks of tender wild boar marinated in vernaccia white wine and served with green sauce and black olives), or you can try *cervo in bianco* (venison in white-wine sauce). They also rent out two simple double rooms, with bathroom, for 49€. *Via Piandornella 15 (a twisty walk down the first right off Via San Giovanni as you walk up from Porta San Giovanni).* ☎ *0577/940-270. www.vecchiemura.it. Primi 6.50€–7.50€; secondi 8€–13€. Wed–Mon 6–10pm. Closed Dec–Feb.*

DOABLE

→ **La Mangiatoia** ★★ TUSCAN "The Eatin' Trough" is a quirky mix of largish but still cozy rooms with heavily stuccoed stone walls inset with backlit stained-glass cabinet doors. This place is fond of Latin quips and dramatic classical music, and the staff is friendly and helpful. The food's a mix too—stick to the more unusual dishes, intriguing and excellently prepared choices where the cook seems to try harder. The *gnocchi deliziose* (spinach gnocchi in a delicious Gorgonzola sauce) is good, as is the *tagliatelle dell'amore* (with prosciutto, cream, tomatoes, and a little hot spice). Afterward, try the *coniglio in salsa di carciofi* (rabbit with artichokes), but I'd choose the more adventurous *cervo in dolce et forte*, an old Sangimignanese recipe of venison cooked with pine nuts and a strong sauce of pinoli, raisins, vinegar, and chocolate—traditionally used to cut the gaminess of several-day-old venison. The desserts are excellent. *Via Mainardi 5 (near Porta San*

Matteo). ☎ *0577/941-528. Primi 8€–12€; secondi 12€–15€. Wed–Mon 12:30–2:30pm and 7:30–10pm. Closed early Nov 4–early Dec.*

➔**Osteria delle Catene** ★ TUSCAN This is an *osteria* true to its name, a small gathering place offering ultratraditional dishes to accompany its well-priced selection of local wines. The decor can only be described as minimalist medieval, with contemporary paintings and modern lighting in concert with an abbreviated barrel vault made of handcast bricks. A great appetizer to pair with your vernaccia is the *piatto misto di prosciutto* (with both pig and boar ham) along with *formaggi Toscani* (Tuscan cheeses). The *ribollita* adds a purée of cannellini beans to the usual mix, and the *penne al porro* (stubby pasta quills in cheesy cream sauce) and *pipe coi broccoli* (maccheroni with broccoli-based vegetable purée cut with onions) are eminent pasta choices. If you're still hungry, try the Tuscan standbys *salsicce con fagioli all'uccelletto* (grilled sausage with beans stewed with tomatoes) and *stracotto al chianti* (beef muscle cooked in chianti wine). *Via Mainardi 18 (near Porta San Matteo).* ☎ *0577/941-966. Primi 7€–9€; secondi 12€–14€; fixed-price menu without wine 17€. Thurs–Tues 12:30–2pm and 7:30–9:30pm. Closed occasionally Dec–Feb.*

SPLURGE

➔**Dorandó** ★★★ TUSCAN The Dorandó is an elegant place tucked away off Piazza Duomo, where the stone-walled rooms, alabaster platters, and knowledgeable waiters create a backdrop for San Gimignano's best dining. The menu doesn't just list dishes but describes each one's history in detail as the chef attempts to keep the oldest traditions of Sangimignanese cooking alive—many of the dishes purport to be medieval, some even Etruscan, in origin—while balancing nouvelle cuisine philosophy with hearty home-cookin' quality. Dishes vary with the season and market, though if the excellent *cibreo* (chicken

livers and giblets scented with ginger and lemon) makes it back onto the menu, by all means order it. The desserts are excellent, too. *Vicolo dell'Oro 2.* ☎ *0577/941-862. www.ristorantedorando.it. Primi 12€–15€; secondi 18€–21€; tasting menus 47€. Tues–Sun 12:30–2:30pm and 7:30–9:30pm. Closed mid-Jan to mid-Mar.*

Sightseeing

San Gimignano is sometimes called "the Manhattan of Tuscany" because it preserves 13 of its noble towers, giving it a "skyscraper" skyline. In the heyday of the Guelph and Ghibelline conflict, San Gimignano (aka *San Gimignano delle Belle Torri*/San Gimignano of the Beautiful Towers) had as many as 72 towers. Its fortresslike severity is softened by the subtlety of its harmonious squares, and many of its palaces and churches are enhanced by Renaissance frescoes because San Gimignano could afford to patronize major painters.

In the town center is the **Piazza della Cisterna,** so named because of the 13th-century cistern in its heart. Connected with the irregularly shaped square is its satellite, **Piazza del Duomo** ★★, whose medieval architecture of towers and palaces is almost unchanged. It's the most beautiful spot in town. On the square, the **Palazzo del Popolo** ★ was designed in the 13th century, and its **Torre Grossa,** built a few years later, is believed to have been the tallest "skyscraper" (about 53m/174 ft. high) in town.

You can buy a **cumulative ticket** that covers the Torre Grossa and its Museo Civico; little Pinacoteca painting **gallery** in the Palazzo Pubblico; the tiny **Museo Archeologico** detailing the region's Etruscan era and the adjacent **Spezeria Santa Fina** (a preserved Renaissance pharmacy); the new **Galleria d'Arte Moderna** modern art gallery; and the weird little **Museo Ornithologico,** a couple of glass cases with stuffed birds in the dimly lit confines of a tiny, deconsecrated church—basically all the museums in town *except* the Collegiata, the Museo d'Ate Sacra, and the privately run Torture Museum. The ticket costs 7.50€ adults and 5.50€ for ages 6 to 18.

→ **Collegiata** ★ The main church in town, once a cathedral, is not much from the outside, but the interior is smothered in 14th-century frescoes, making it one of Tuscany's most densely decorated churches. Off of the right aisle, the **Cappella di Santa Fina** is covered with frescoes by Florentine master Domenico Ghirlandaio, who decorated the tiny chapel's walls with some of his finest, airiest works. With the help of assistants, he frescoed two scenes summing up the life of Santa Fina, a local girl who, though never officially canonized, is one of San Gimignano's patron saints. Little Fina, who was very devout and wracked with guilt for having committed the sin of accepting an orange from a boy, fell down ill on a board one day and didn't move for 5 years. Eventually, St. Gregory appeared to her and announced her death, whereupon the board on which she lay miraculously produced flowers. When her corpse was carried solemnly to the church for a funeral, the city's towers burst forth with yellow pansies and angels flew up to ring the bells. The town still celebrates its child saint every year on March 12, when the pansies on San Gimignano's towers naturally bloom. *Piazza del Duomo.* ☎ *0577/940-316. Admission on cumulative ticket, or 3.50€. Mar 9:30am–5pm; Apr–Oct Sun–Fri 9:30am– 7:30pm, Sat 9:30am–5pm; Nov–Jan 26 Mon–Sat 9:30am–5pm, Sun 1–5pm. Closed Jan 27–Feb 28.*

→ **Torre Grossa** Climb this 14th-century tower for one of the best tower-top views of the cityscape and rolling countryside in all Tuscany. Before the step workout, though, check out the **civic painting gallery** on the palace's second floor. *Piazza del Duomo.* ☎ *0577/940-340 (ask for museo). Admission on cumulative ticket, or 5€. Daily Mar–Oct 9:30am–7:20pm, Nov–Feb 10am–5:50pm (until 1:30pm Dec 24–31).*

→ **The Torture Museum** Sort of like the popularity of wax museums in tourist locales, there seem to be a lot of these lately in Tuscany, but this is one of the first. Otherwise known as the Museum of Medieval Criminology and the Inquisition, it is found in the medieval **Torre del Diavolo (Devil's Tower)** and its iron maidens, racks—both the spiked and unspiked varieties—chastity belts, various bone-crunching manacles, breast-rippers, and other medieval party favors indeed have a suitably satanic flavor. *Via del Castello 1 (just off Piazza della Cisterna).* ☎ *0577/942-243. Admission 8€, 5.50€ students. Daily Mar 16–July 18 10am–7pm, July 19–Sept 17 10am–midnight, Sept 18–Nov 1 10am–8pm; Nov 2–Mar 15 Mon–Fri 10am–6pm, Sat–Sun 10am–7pm.*

SEEING MORE OF SAN GIMIGNANO & ITS ENVIRONS

The tourist office sponsors **guided walks** through the countryside April through October, 2 to 3 days a week (usually weekends), costing 10€ to 15€ per person. Because the country edges right up to San Gimignano's walls, you could also easily set out on your own to wander with a good map—the tourist office also sells a map and catalog marked with suggested hikes and walks, or you can pick up a regional map from any of the local souvenir stands.

Siena: It's a Horse Race!

34km (21 miles) S of Florence

Walking into Siena ★★ is like taking a trip back into the Dark Ages (without the bubonic plague). It doesn't have the same Renaissance flavor of Florence—marauding Florentine troops in the 13th century made sure of that. Siena's financiers and merchants were in direct competition with those in Florence, and so Florentine Guelphs found a great excuse to wipe them off the map when Siena turned Ghibelline in the 13th century.

The two cities duked it out for about 400 years, and what the Guelphs failed to destroy over that time, the Black Death more than mopped up in the 14th century. This once great textiles and banking city (Monte dei Paschi di Siena, still in existence, is considered the world's oldest bank) was decimated, and literally so: Not much more than ten percent of the original population was left.

What remains today is a serious-looking, brown-brick city of red tiles and Gothic art: a somber portrait that stands in stark contrast to the personality of the Sienese: fun loving, wine drinking, and full of sarcastic wit. It is a great place to stay for a while, if you have the time—one good excuse would be to enroll at the city's university for foreigners—and make some friends in a city that seems stuck in the Middle Ages. In order to relive the past in one short weekend, try to time your visit to coincide with the city's inimitable horse race, the Palio (see box). It is Siena boiled down to its core: colorful pageantry and flowing wine, bitter rivalries and underhanded dealings, and a deep respect for traditions that the Sienese refuse to forget.

The university (founded in 1240) is still a major force in the town, and the conversation you'll overhear between locals in the streets is the purest Italian dialect in the country. However, you might have to wait until evening because most residents retreat into the seclusion of their homes during the days full of tour buses. They emerge to reclaim the cafes and squares at night, when most visitors have gone.

Getting There

BY BUS

Reaching Siena by bus is often more convenient than by train. For one thing, Siena's train station is outside town. Furthermore, the buses to and from Florence are more frequent and usually faster. The bus company **Tra-in** runs express (19 daily; 75 min.) and slower buses (18 daily; 90 min.–2 hr.) from Florence's SITA station to Siena's Piazza San Domenico or Piazza Gramsci.

Siena is also connected with San Gimignano (hourly Mon–Sat; change in Poggibonsi; 55–65 min. not including layover), Perugia (two to four daily; 85 min.), and Rome's Tiburtina station (five to seven daily; 2 hr. 47 min.). Follow the signs to Siena's Tra-in bus ticket office, underneath Piazza Gramsci in the pedonale della Lizza (☎ **0577/204-246**

Okkio! Parking's *Expensive* in Siena

Siena **parking** (☎ 0577/22-871) is now coordinated, and all the lots charge 1.50€ per hour or 36€ per day, ranking it among the most expensive parking on the planet. Luckily, almost every hotel has a significant discount deal with the nearest lot. All are well signposted, with locations just inside city gates Porta Tufi (the huge and popular Il Campo lot, though is a 20-min. walk from the Campo!), Porta San Marco, and Porta Romana; under the Fortezza (another large lot) and around La Lizza park (the latter closed market Wed and soccer Sun); and at Piazza Amendola (just outside the northern gate Porta Camollia). Ask your hotel about parking when booking—many have deals with one of these lots to get you anywhere from 50% to 100% off. You can park for free a bit farther away around the unguarded back (northwest) side of the Fortezza all week long. There's also free parking outside the southeast end of town at Due Ponti (beyond Porta Pispini) and Coroncina (beyond Porta Romana); from both you can get a *pollicino* (minibus) into the center.

or 0577/204-225; www.trainspa.it), and there's another small office in the city's train station (☎ 0577/204-245).

BY TRAIN

Some 19 trains daily connect Siena with Florence (90 min.–2¹/₄ hr.) The train station (☎ 0577/280-115) is at Piazza Fratelli Roselli, about 3km (2 miles) north of town. Take the C minibus to Piazza Gramsci in Terza di Camollia or a taxi.

BY CAR

It's a gorgeous car ride from Florence, and lots of Tuscany-trippers prefer their own wheels for exploring all the hill towns and roadside attractions. There is an *autostrada* highway direct from Florence called the "Si-Fi" or you can take the more scenic routes, down the old Via Cassia SS2 or the Chiantigiana SS222 through the Chianti.

From Rome get off the A1 north at the Val di Chiana exit and follow the SS326 west for 50km (31 miles). From Pisa take the highway toward Flórence and exit onto the SS429 south at Empoli (100km/62 miles total).

Still, having your own ride won't get you any closer to the center of town. Trying to drive into the one-way and pedestrian-zoned center isn't worth the massive headache.

Siena Orientation

Siena is splayed out like a "Y" along three ridges with deep valleys in between, effectively dividing the city into thirds, called *terze*. The *terze* are each drawn out along three main streets following the spines of those ridges. The southern arm, Terza di San Martino, slopes gently down around Via Banchi di Sotto (and the various other names it picks up along the way). To the west is Terza di Città (home to the Duomo and Pinacoteca), centered on Via di Città. Terza di Camollia runs north around Via Banchi di Sopra. These three main streets meet at the north edge of Piazza del Campo, Siena's gorgeous scallop-shaped central square.

Getting Around

ON FOOT

Although it feels like a small Tuscan hill town, Siena truly is a city (albeit a small one), and its sites are widely spread. There is no efficient public transport system in the center, so it's up to your feet to cover the territory. There are plenty of steep ups and downs and no shortcuts from one *terza* to another without a serious workout.

BY BUS

The city does run minibuses, called *pollicini* (☎ 0577/204-246), which dip into the city center from 6am to 9pm. The B services the Terza di San Martino and out the Porta Pispini gate, as does bus 5 (there's also an N night bus on this route 9pm–1am). Confusingly, there are four A buses, differentiated by color. *A pink* goes around Terza di San Martino (and out the Porta Romana gate), as does bus no. 2; *A green* and *A yellow* cover Terza di Città (green from Porta Tufi to the Duomo, yellow from Porta San Marco to the Duomo); and *A red* takes care of the southerly part of Terza di Camollia (from Piazza della'Indipendenza out Porta Fontebranda).

BY TAXI

You can call for a radio taxi at ☎ 0577/49-222 (7am–9pm only); they also hang out at the train station and in town at Piazza Matteotti.

Siena's Tourist Office

The tourist office, where you can get a great free map, is at Piazza del Campo 56 (☎ 0577/280-551; fax 0577/270-676. From Mar 21 to Nov 11, it's open Monday through Friday from 8:30am to 1pm and 3 to 7pm, and Saturday from 8:30am to 1pm; winter hours are Monday through Saturday, 8:30am to 7:30pm.

Central Siena

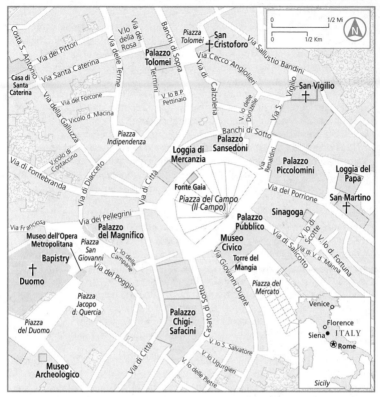

Recommended Websites

○ **www.terresiena.it** The provincial tourist board's website can help you find a hotel and keep you up to date on what's happening in and around the city.

○ **www.sitabus.it** Information and schedules for buses going to San Gimignano and the rest of Tuscany.

Sleeping

Siena is a haven for well-to-do tourists exploring Tuscany by car, and while the hotel siutation reflects that, you can still find reasonably priced accommodation. For help finding a room, stop by the **Siena Hotels Promotion** booth on Piazza San Domenico (☎ 0577/288-084; fax 0577/280-290; www.

hotelsiena.com), where for 1.50€ to 4€, depending on the category of hotel, they'll find you a room and reserve it. The booth is open Monday through Saturday from 9am to 7pm (until 8pm in summer). In the underground office of Parcheggio il Campo parking lot, Via Fontanella 4, is **Protur** (☎ 0577/45-900; fax 0577/283-145; www.protur.it), which will book you a room for free; it also runs guided tours of Siena and its province.

CHEAP

➔ **Hotel Cannon d'Oro** ★ It's just a few blocks up the shop-lined Via Banchi di Sopra (its name changes to Via Montanini) to this 15th-century palazzo. Most rooms are plain but large, though the decor is livened up in some with old-fashioned beveled mirrors in

Culture 101: It's All About the Palio

Twice a year, Siena packs the Piazza del Campo with dirt and runs a no-holds-barred bareback horse race around it—the inimitable Palio—the highlight of a full week of trial runs, feasts, parades, spectacles of skill, and solemn ceremonies. The tradition, in one form or another, goes back to at least 1310.

The Palio is a deadly serious competition, and while Siena doesn't mind if visitors show up (you may, in fact, find yourself adopted into the *contrada* of the first person you make friends with and invited to the communal feasts), but in the end visitors are peripheral. The Palio is for the Sienese.

To understand the Palio—really, to understand Siena—you must know something of the *contrada* system. In the 14th century there were about 42 *contrade,* neighborhood wards that helped provide militia support for Siena's defense. The number of wards was reduced until the current 17 were fixed in 1675. Each is named after an animal or object—*Drago* (Dragon), *Giraffa* (Giraffe), *Istrice* (Porcupine), *Onda* (Wave), *Torre* (Tower)—and each has its own headquarters, social club, museum, and church.

Each *contrada* has always been responsible for its own. You are born into the *contrada* of your parents, are baptized in your *contrada*'s open-air font, learn your *contrada*'s allies and enemies at an early age, go to church in your *contrada*'s oratory, almost invariably marry within your *contrada,* spend your free time hanging out in the *contrada* social club, and help elect or serve on your *contrada*'s governing body. Even your funeral is sponsored by the *contrada,* which mourns your passing as family. In a way, it's like a benevolent form of Hollywood's mythical Mafia—but no *contrada* tolerates unlawfulness, and as a result Siena has a shockingly low crime rate.

Ten *contrade* are chosen by lot each year to ride in the **July 2** Palio (established in 1659). The other seven, plus three of the July riders, run the even bigger Palio on **August 16** (which dates from 1310). Although both races are technically equal in importance, the August Palio gets the most attention, partly because it's older but mainly because it's a sort of rematch, the last chance to win for the year. Actually, chance really is what wins the Palio: Your opportunity to ride, the horse you're given, and the order you're lined up on the track are each chosen by separate lots; even your jockey is a wild card. He's always imported—traditionally a horseman from the Maremma, Tuscany's "Wild West" country, but many come from Sardegna and Sicily these days as well—and you'll never know how well he'll ride, whether the bribe one of your rival *contrade* may slip him will outweigh the wages you paid, or if he'll even make it to the race without being ambushed. If your jockey does turn on you, you'd better hope he's thrown quickly. The Palio, you see, is a true horse race—the horse is the one that wins (it's hoped no rivals have drugged it), whether there's a rider still on it or not. The jockey's main job is to hang onto the horse's bare back and thrash the other horses and their riders with the stiff ox-hide whip he's given for the purpose. The Palio may at this point seem pretty lawless, but there actually is one rule: No jockey can grab another horse's reins.

At the two 90-degree turns of the Campo, almost every year a rider or two—and occasionally an entire horse—goes flying out of the racetrack to land among the stands or slams up against the mattresses padding the palazzi walls.

The Palios really start on June 29 and August 13, when the lots are drawn to select the 10 lucky racers and the trial races begin. Over the next 2 days, morning and afternoon trial runs are held, and on the evening before each Palio, the *contrade* hold an all-night feast and party lasting more or less until the 7:45am Jockey's Mass in the Cappella della Piazza on the Campo. There's a final heat at 9am, then everybody dissolves to his or her separate *contrada* for last-minute preparations. The highlight is the 3pm (3:30pm in July). Blessing of the Horse in each *contrada*'s church—a little manure dropping at the altar is a sign of good luck—at which the priest ends with a resounding command to the horse: "Go forth, and return a winner!"

Unless invited by a *contrada,* you're probably not going to get into any of the packed churches for this, so your best strategy is to stick around the Campo all day. Because standing in the center of the Campo for the race is free (the grandstands require tickets; see below), you should ideally stake out a spot close to the start-finish line before 2pm. Just before 5pm, the pageantry begins, with processions led by a contingent from Montalcino in honor of it harboring the last members of the Sienese Republic in the 16th century. The *palio* banner is drawn about the piazza in the War Chariot (a wagon drawn by two snowy white oxen), and *contrada* youths in Renaissance costume juggle huge, colorful banners in the *sbandierata* flag-throwing display.

At 7:30pm (7pm in July) the horses start lining up between two ropes. Much care is taken to get the first nine in some indeterminate perfect order. After countless false starts and finagling, suddenly the tenth horse comes thundering up from behind, and as soon as he hits the first rope the second one is dropped and the race is on. Three laps and fewer than 90 seconds later, it's over.

If standing in the middle of the hot and crowded Campo doesn't attract you—and anyone with a small bladder might want to think twice, as there are no facilities and no one is allowed in or out from just before the procession until the race is over (about 3½ hr.)—you can try to buy a ticket for the grandstands or at a window of one of the buildings surrounding the piazza. These are controlled by the building owners and the shops in front of which the stands are set up and cost anywhere from 350€ for a single seat to 1,220€ for a window seating four people. They sell out up to 6 months before the race.

Palio Viaggi, Piazza Gramsci 7 (☎ 0577/280-828), can help you score a few, and the tourist office has all the contacts for individual shops and buildings if you want to negotiate directly for a seat. If you show up late and sans ticket, make your way up Via Giovanni Duprè to the Piazza del Mercato behind the Palazzo Pubblico; the police stationed there will often allow people into the Campo between the processions and the race itself. For fascinating pictures, factoids, and general history, check out **www.ilpalio.org.**

Siena Eating, Sleeping & Sightseeing

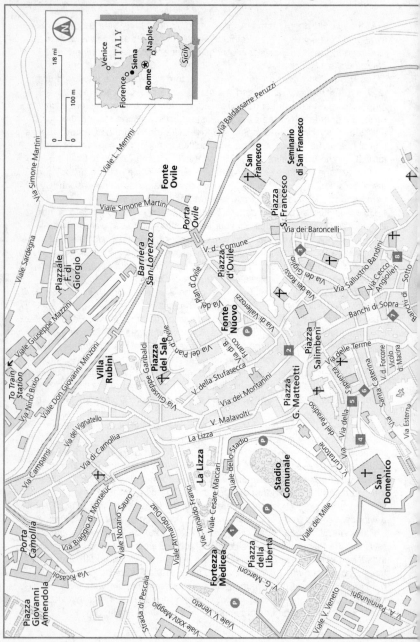

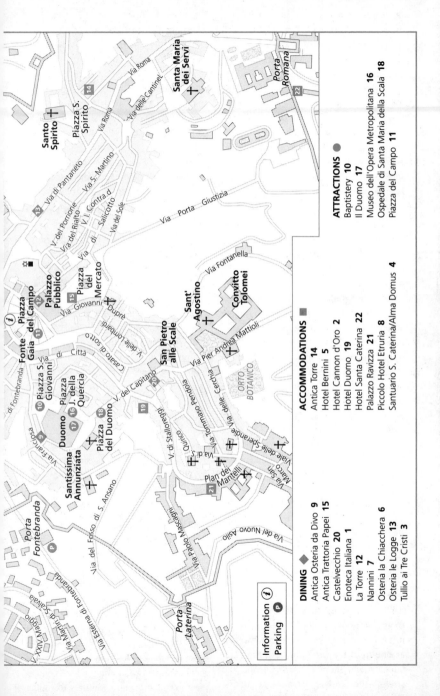

ATTRACTIONS ●
Baptistery **10**
Il Duomo **17**
Museo dell'Opera Metropolitana **16**
Ospedale di Santa Maria della Scala **18**
Piazza del Campo **11**

ACCOMMODATIONS ■
Antica Torre **14**
Hotel Bernini **5**
Hotel Cannon d'Oro **2**
Hotel Duomo **19**
Hotel Santa Caterina **22**
Palazzo Ravizza **21**
Piccolo Hotel Etruria **8**
Santuario S. Caterina/Alma Domus **4**

DINING ◆
Antica Osteria da Divo **9**
Antica Trattoria Papei **15**
Castelvecchio **20**
Enoteca Italiana **1**
La Torre **12**
Nannini **7**
Osteria la Chiacchera **6**
Osteria le Logge **13**
Tullio ai Tre Cristi **3**

Information ⓘ
Parking Ⓟ

the wardrobe doors or an antique chest of drawers. At less than 100€ per double, you'll be pleasantly surprised by the worn terra-cotta floors or medieval stonework walls. The bathrooms are very compact, with amusing anachronisms—they've installed heated towel racks but haven't yet been hit with the fuzzy towel revolution. *Via Montanini 28 (a few blocks north of Il Campo), 53100 Siena.* ☎ *0577/44-321. Fax 0577/280-868. www.cannondoro.it. Easter–Oct double 90€, triple 116€; Oct–Easter double 70€, triple 90€. Continental breakfast 6€. Parking 13€ in nearby garage. Bus: C.*

→ **Hotel Bernini** ★ Mauro and Nadia oversee a very amiable, homey set of clean and, for the price, comfortable rooms decorated with the odd antique. The firm beds rest on patterned tiling and are surrounded by whitewashed walls curving into the ceilings. (A few have painted wood beams.) Some accommodations are hung with printed curtains in the archways. A pair of rooms has a distant view of the Duomo's flank, and all are quiet, as the place sits atop St. Catherine's house-cum-convent. The bathrooms are all brand-new. If you ask, they'll let you go up on the terrace for views of the city and valley. This is a family environment, and on rainy days, Mauro breaks out his accordion to entertain guests. *Via della Sapienza 15 (near San Domenico), 53100 Siena.* ☎/fax 0577/289-047. www.albergobernini.com. *Double without bathroom 62€, with bathroom 82€; triple without bathroom 87€, with bathroom 107€. Sometimes rates are discounted up to 20% in slow periods. Breakfast 7€. No credit cards. Parking in public lots. Closed Dec 1–28. Bus: A (red), C, 2, or 10.*

→ **Piccolo Hotel Etruria** ★ This small family-run hotel can thumb its nose at the big corporate chains, as it offers equally comfortable modernity with twice the character at one-third the price. In both the main building and the *dipendenza* across the street, the rooms have tiled floors; brand-new, wood-toned built-in furnishings with stone-topped desks and end tables; and leather strap chairs. The bathrooms are immaculately new, and everything is kept spotless. This place gets a star for being as clean, comfortable, and central as you're ever going to find, especially at these prices. Book early. The only real drawback is the 12:30am curfew. *Via delle Donzelle 3 (off Via Banchi di Sotto), 53100 Siena.* ☎ *0577/288-088. Fax 0577/288-461. hetruria@tin.it. Double 75€, triple 99€. Continental breakfast 5€. Closed around Dec 10–27. Bus: A (red), B, or N.*

→ **Santuario S. Caterina/Alma Domus** Down below San Domenico church in an untouristy part of Siena, this simple, cheap hotel is run by the nuns of St. Catherine, so it's pretty tame, to say the least, but offers a kindly hospitality and meditative calm. Many of the midsize rooms have balconies with great views of the Duomo across the little valley. While you can receive calls only on your room phone (plans are afoot to make the phones fully operational in the near future), there are four pay phones. Guests share a common living room and a TV room—and a lamentable 11:30pm curfew. *Via Camporeggio 37 (the steep street down off Piazza San Domenico), 53100 Siena.* ☎ *0577/44-177. Fax 0577/47-601. Double 55€, triple 70€, quad 85€. Breakfast 6€. No credit cards. Bus: 1, 3, 6, 10, 18, 30, 31, 37, or 106.*

DOABLE

→ **Antica Torre** ★ The very friendly Patrizia Landolfo and her family run one of Siena's most simply elegant hotels, in a 16th-century tower house atop a brick-lined 600-year-old potter's workshop, which serves as a minuscule breakfast room. A travertine staircase leads to rooms that are on the cozy side of small, with marble flooring, iron filigree headboards, old writing desks, and gauzy curtains. The rooms on the street are a smidgen larger, but those in back are quieter. The best rooms are the two on the top levels with a view over the Sienese rooftops to rolling

FLORENCE & TUSCANY

green hills. The old tower is on a residential side street near the Porta Romana, a 10-minute stroll down Via Banchi di Sotto from the Campo. *Via di Fieravacchia 7, 53100 Siena.* ☎/*fax 0577/222-255. Double 90€–107€. Prices lower in slow periods. Breakfast 7€. Parking in streets around hotel or public lot nearby.*

➜ **Hotel Duomo** ★★ This hotel, located just south of its namesake, is housed in a 12th-century palazzo that once served as barracks for medieval troops, though the only reminders of this are the Renaissance central staircase and the ancient brickwork in the basement breakfast room. Most carpeted accommodations are of a modest size but not cramped, and the modern furnishings are as tasteful as functional gets, some with worn veneer units, others with newer wicker-and-wood pieces. The bathrooms are tiny, but the mattresses are good. If you want to secure one of the 12 "panoramic" rooms with a view of the Duomo, be sure to ask when booking. The friendly staff is polished and professional. *Via Stalloreggi 34–38 (halfway between the Duomo and Il Campo), 53100 Siena.* ☎ *0577/289-088. Fax 0577/43-043. www.hotelduomo.it. Double 130€, triple 171€, quad 186€. 20%–40% less in slow periods. Rates include buffet breakfast.*

SPLURGE

➜ **Hotel Santa Caterina** ★ You'll find some of the friendliest folks in Siena here. The rooms have tile floors (antique terracotta flooring in some), soft beds, and furniture made of old wood; and, many have a view down one of the most green, unspoiled valleys around Siena. (Most of the others have been filled with housing developments.) In summer you can have breakfast in the pretty little garden; there's a new glassed-in breakfast veranda for winter dining. *Via Enea Silvio Piccolomini 7 (just outside the Porta Romana), 53100 Siena.* ☎ *0577/221-105. Fax 0577/271-087. www.hscsiena.it. Double 144€, triple 195€. Rates include buffet breakfast. Bus: A (pink), N, or 2.*

➜ **Palazzo Ravizza** ★ The Santi-Ravizza family has run this hotel in a 17th-century Renaissance palazzo since the 1920s. It's a bit overpriced in the high season, when you have to take dinner here, but an excellent deal in winter. (Make sure to call ahead, as some years they close for a month to renovate.) The rooms tend to be large, with high ceilings—some gorgeously frescoed, a few with painted details around the wood beams. *Pian dei Mantellini 34 (near Piazza San Marco).* ☎ *0577/280-462. Fax 0577/221-597. www.palazzoravizza.it. High season (Mar 31–Nov 21 and Dec 26–Jan 6) require half pension: standard double 160€, superior double 180€, suite 220€–270€; low season without pension: standard double 130€, superior double 150€, suite 180€–230€. 10% discount for stays of more than 3 nights. Rates include breakfast.*

Eating

Sienese cuisine is perhaps the most typical of Tuscany, and is worth the trip to the city. It features more meat than most Italian dishes—the famous Chianina valley that provides the country with the Fiorentina steak is not far away—and the countryside fills Siena's kitchens with a menu full of wild game: pheasant *(faggiano)*, wild boar *(cinghiale)* and even the stray pigeon *(piccione)* are the most popular. For starters, try the local *pici* or small, hand-rolled pasta, covered with a meat or mushroom ragù.

Siena also sits squarely in the middle of three internationally known wine-producing areas: Chianti, of course, to the north, and Montalcino and Montepulciano to the south. Top that off with the two nearby whites, Orvieto and Vernaccia di San Gimignano, and you will never want for an outstanding bottle of reasonably priced wine.

There's no reason to look for beers and cocktails in Siena, and the Sienese won't go out of their way to provide it for you. Why would they? Indeed, you should see Siena, and Tuscany in general, as a chance to take a break from the late-night partying, mostly because you'll be hard-pressed to find it. I have tried many times and failed.

In Siena, nightlife revolves around cafes and wine bars. Below are the two most popular.

COFFEE BARS & WINE BARS

→**Enoteca Italiana** The 16th-century Fortezza Medicea has been turned into a public park. Its courtyard is an open-air theater, its ramparts are a place for a stroll and a view, and its vaults are filled with Italy's national wine museum. Seated at small tables in the tunnel-like brick halls or out on the terraces in summer, you can sample a choice selection of Tuscan and Italian wines by the glass or go all out on an entire bottle from their extensive *cantine* (more than 1,200 labels cool their heels here). It wouldn't be fair to say this is a truly representative collection, because not all vintners choose to take part, but it has been Italy's official state-mandated *museo del vino* since 1950. Out of Italy's some 4,000 wines, it preserves all the 266 kinds of DOC *(denominazione origine controllata),* each of the 17 DOCG *(denominazione origine controllata e garantita)* labels, and every last one of Italy's 128 IGT *(indicazione geografica tipica)* wines. *Fortezza Medicea.* ☎ *0577/288-497. www.enoteca-italiana.it. Free admission. Glass of wine 2€–5€; cold plate of typical regional foods 7.50€–12€. Mon noon–8pm; Tues–Sat noon–1am.*

→**Nannini** Be sure to try the *panforte* (made of honey, nuts, and fruit) along with your coffee here at Siena's top cafe. Here's a general price guide to how much a coffee and pastry will run you: Espresso standing up at bar: .75€–.90€; cappuccino standing up at bar: .90€–1.10€; pastry standing up at bar 1€–1.50€; prices double when you sit down at any bar; prices triple when you sit down at fancy places. *Via Banchi di Sopra 22–24.* ☎ *0577/41-591. Mon 6:30am–8:30pm; Tues–Sat 6:30am–midnight; Sun 8am–8:30pm.*

CHEAP

→**Antica Trattoria Papei** ★ SIENESE Although tourists now know to filter behind the Palazzo Pubblico to this large family-run trattoria, locals still hang on vigorously, returning for the simple but good Sienese fare. In summer, you can dine alfresco on the unsightly piazza with a view of the Terza di San Martino. If you're eating inside, head to the left of the door or upstairs for wood-ceilinged ambience—the modern room to the right is where they try to stick the tourists. The *pappardelle al sugo di cinghiale* (pasta ribbons in wild boar sauce) is a traditional dish, while the *pici alla cardinale* (chewy fat spaghetti in tomato sauce with hot peppers and chunks of pancetta) is a bit more original. Keep it spicy with *coniglio all'arrabbiata* (rabbit cooked in white wine, rosemary, and sage with garlic and a pinch of *peperoncino*), or try *anatra alla Tolomei* (duck stewed with tomatoes). *Piazza del Mercato 6 (behind the Palazzo Pubblico).* ☎ *0577/280-894. Reservations suggested. Primi 6.20€; secondi 6.50€–10€. Tues–Sun noon–3pm and 7–10:30pm.*

→**Osteria la Chiacchera** SIENESE CUCINA POVERA This is a tiny joint with worn wooden tables, terra-cotta floors, and barrel ends embedded everywhere. "The Chat" proudly serves humble Sienese *cucina povera* (poor man's grub). Couples come here to make eyes at each other and save money on the date (not only is it cheap, but there's no cover charge or service fee—tips are greatly appreciated). A choice first course is the *pici boscaiola* (long strands of fat, hand-rolled pasta in tomato-and-mushroom sauce), though the *penne arrabbiata* (in piquant tomato sauce) goes pretty quickly, too. Secondi are simple peasant dishes like *salsicce e fagioli* (grilled sausages with beans) and *stracotto* (beef and boiled potatoes in piquant tomato sauce). They also do a mean chocolate pie. *Costa di Sant'Antonio 4 (near San Domenico, off Via della Sapienza under the Hotel Bernini).* ☎ *0577/280-631. Reservations* recommended. *Primi 5€–7€; secondi 6€–8€. No credit cards. Daily noon–3pm and 7pm–midnight.*

→ **Tullio ai Tre Cristi** SIENESE   A staunchly traditional trattoria in the heart of Giraffe territory since 1830, Tullio has a distinct *taverna* feel. The two long dining rooms are ribbed with brick arches and hung with painted plaques representing the *contrade,* and the tables are lined up along creaky wall benches as if waiting to be set for a medieval feast. The *antipasto Tre Cristi* is a fanned-out assortment of large crostini and prosciutto rolls, and if *pici al porcino* (homemade fat spaghetti with porcini mushroom sauce) or *pappardelle alla lepre* (wide pasta ribbons in hare ragù) don't catch your fancy, try *penne alla carrettiera* (in a spicy hot garlic and peperoncino tomato sauce). For your second course, go for the *medaglione al burro verde* (veal medallion cooked in herbed butter) or the *cappelle di porcini* (grilled caps of porcini mushrooms—the traditional poor Tuscan's steak, and a flavorful dish that also happens to be vegetarian). *Vicolo di Provenzano 1 (follow the signs down Via Rossi off Via Banchi di Sopra).* ☎ *0577/280-608. Reservations recommended. Primi 5€–8€; secondi 7€–18€. Thurs–Tues 12:30–2:30pm and 7:30–10:30pm. Closed last 15 days Dec. Bus: A (red) or C.*

DOABLE

→ **Castelvecchio** ★★ CREATIVE TUSCAN/VEGETARIAN   This intimate and personable little restaurant has a devoted following of regulars who enjoy Simone Romi's skilled service and Mauro Lombardini's daily changing menu of creative Tuscan cuisine. There's at least one meatless dish nightly, and on vegetarian Wednesdays there's only one meat dish available. On my last visit I had an excellent risotto of zucchini, mint, and basil, a delicious lentil-and-turnip soup, *pennette* in tomato sauce sprinkled with crunchy cream, vegetable pie with a mashed-potato crust, and chicken with peppers and onions.

Via Castelvecchio 65 (off Via San Pietro). ☎ *0577/49-586. Reservations recommended. Primi 6€–7€; secondi 9€–11€; tasting menu without wine 25€ each for 2 people only. Apr–Sept 12:30–2:30pm and 7:30–9:30pm; Oct–Mar Wed–Mon 12:30–2:30pm and 7:30–9:30pm. Bus: A (green, yellow).*

→ **La Torre** TUSCAN   You can usually trust a place that doesn't hide its kitchen. La Torre's is in plain view, next to a dozen tightly packed tables under an undulating brick ceiling. It's a popular place, so reserve ahead or show up early. All the pasta is homemade (none more deliciously than the *pici* and the plump tortellini) and served with the sauce of your choice and a generous heap of Parmesan cheese on top. Afterward, try the *vitello arrosto* (slices of roast veal) or *piccione al forno* (oven-baked pigeon). *Via Salicotto 7–9 (9m/30 ft. off Il Campo to left of the Palazzo Pubblico).* ☎ *0577/287-548. Reservations recommended. Primi 6€–8€; secondi 9€–10€; menù turistico with wine 18€. Fri–Wed noon–3pm and 7–10pm. Closed Aug 17–Sept 1. Bus: A (pink), B, or N.*

SPLURGE

→ **Antica Osteria da Divo** ★★ CREATIVE SIENESE   This former trattoria has gone mid-scale and greatly improved its menu to offer excellent innovative dishes rooted in Sienese traditions in a sophisticated but warm atmosphere of soft jazz. It is a true find and a memorable experience; in the basement are actually Etruscan tombs carved from the tufa. *Pici al ragout di lepre* (thick hand-rolled pasta strands in hare ragù) and *gnocchetti di patate con erba cipollina e pecorino di fossa* (gnocchi with chives on a parmigiano pastry crust swimming in melted pecorino cheese) are palate-pleasing primi. For the main course, they ascribe to the growing school of Italian cooking wherein a side dish is included with each secondo (making a meal here less costly than the prices below would suggest). *Via Franciosa 25–29 (behind the left flank of*

Siena's Cumulative Tickets

Siena has several **reduced-price cumulative ticket** combos you can pick up at any of the participating museums or sites. One, valid for 2 days, covers civic museums—**Museo Civico, Santa Maria della Scala,** and the contemporary art gallery in the **Palazzo delle Papesse** on Via di Città (where admission is usually 4€–5€—for 9€ total.

There are also two combined tickets that are valid for 7 days and are seasonally based. From November to March 14, you can get a 13€ 7-day ticket that includes all the sites listed above on the 2-day ticket, and also gives you access to **Museo Dell' Opera Metropolitana, Baptistery,** and **Libreria Piccolomini.** From March 15 to October for 16€, the same ticket covers all seven sites listed above plus **S. Bernardino** and **Museo Diocesano.**

Additionally, some attractions sell their own cumulative tickets, as the one for admission to both the **Museo Civico** and **Torre del Mangia**—a savings of 1.50€ over separate admission tickets.

the Duomo). ☎ 0577/284-381. Reservations recommended. Primi 7€–10€; secondi with side dish 16€–22€. Daily noon–2:30pm and 7–10pm. Bus: A (green, yellow).

→ **Osteria le Logge** ★★★ SIENESE/ TUSCAN Le Logge is many a local's choice for a special night out, offering excellent cooking in a sedate, yet not sedated, atmosphere. The *taglierini al tartufo* has a light butter sauce that doesn't mask the delicate flavor of the black truffles. Heavier primi include *malfatti all'Osteria* (spinach-and-ricotta balls in a creamy tomato sauce) and *ravioli ripieni di pecorino e menta* (ravioli stuffed with sheep's-milk cheese and mint in a sauce flavored with port). The staff is friendly and accommodating. I once visited with a vegetarian, and our waitress quickly established his eating parameters (does he eat fish? cheese?), proceeded to mark everything on the menu he could order, and then had the kitchen concoct for him a suitable secondo of all the veggies they had on hand. Meatier palates can enjoy the *bistecche di vitello* (tender veal steaks) or delicate *carpaccio di pesce spada affumicato* (smoked swordfish sliced and pounded into thin disks). Via del Porrione 33 (just off the Campo). ☎ 0577/ 48-013. Reservations recommended. Primi 7€–10€; secondi 14€–18€; tasting menu 40€.

Mon–Sat noon–2:45pm and 7–10:30pm. Closed Jan 1–Feb 7. Bus: A (pink) B, or N.

Sightseeing

There's much to see here. Start in the heart of Siena, the shell-shaped **Piazza del Campo.** Pause to enjoy the **Fonte Gaia,** which locals sometimes call the Fountain of Joy because it was inaugurated to great jubilation throughout the city, with embellishments by Jacopo della Quercia (the present sculptured works are reproductions—the badly beaten-up original ones are in the town hall). You'll want to linger in one of the cafes along its edge.

→ **Piazza del Campo** ★★★ This grandiose square, known simply as *il Campo,* is shaped like a scallop shell and sits on the site of the former Roman forum, now surrounded by some of the most beautiful facades in Tuscany and lined with bars and cafes where you can enjoy the stunning view. It's also where Siena's harrowing horse race, the Palio, has been held every July and August for 400 years. The brickwork pavement is divided by white marble lines into nine sections representing the city's medieval ruling body, the Council of Nine. The Campo's tilt, fan shape, and structure are all a calibrated part of the city's ancient water system and underground canal network. At the top of the Campo is a poor 19th-century replica of Jacopo della Quercia's 14th-century masterpiece fountain, the Fonte Gaia, while the only surviving medieval buildings on the square are, at the top, the curving façade of the battlemented 13th-century Palazzo Sansedoni and at the fan's base, the city's focal point and town hall, the Palazzo Pubblico. This is the city's finest Gothic palace, and the Museo Civico inside is home to Siena's best artwork. The Cappella della Piazza, at the left end of the palazzo's base, was raised to give thanks that at least parts of the city had been spared from the Black Plague. Rising above it is the brick **Torre del Mangia,** the second-tallest tower in medieval Italy and named after a lazy bell ringer nicknamed *Mangiaguadagni,* or "profit eater." If you don't mind close quarters and are in decent shape, climb the 503 steps for a stunning view across the city and the rolling countryside beyond. *Piazza del Campo. Tower:* ☎ *0577/226230. Admission 5.50€. Nov 1– March 15 daily 10am–4pm and March 16–Oct 31 daily 10am–7pm.*

➜ **Il Duomo** ★ ★ The Duomo was built from around 1215 to 1263, while its façade was redesigned in 1265. But in 1339, having defeated Florence 80 years earlier, Siena was finally the big man on the Tuscan campus and so began its most ambitious project yet: to turn the already huge Duomo into the transept of a new cathedral, one that would dwarf St. Peter's in Rome and trumpet Siena's political power, spiritual devotion, and artistic prowess. The city started the new nave off the Duomo's right transept but completed only the fabric of the walls when the Black Death hit in 1348, decimating the population and halting building plans forever. The **half-finished walls** remain—a monument to Siena's ambition and one-time wealth.

You could wander inside the Duomo for hours, just staring at the **flooring,** a mosaic of 59 etched and inlaid marble panels (1372–1547). Some of the top artists working in Siena lent their talents, including Umbrian

master Pinturicchio, Domenico di Bartolo, Matteo di Giovanni, and especially Beccafumi, who designed 35 scenes (1517–47)—his original cartoons are in the Pinacoteca.

Pinturicchio is the star in the **Libreria Piccolomini** built in 1485 by Cardinal Francesco Piccolomini (later Pope Pius III— for all of 18 days before he died in office) to house the library of his famous uncle, Pope Pius II. The marble entrance was carved by Marrina in 1497, above which Pinturicchio was commissioned to paint a large fresco of the *Coronation of Pius III* (1504). In the center of the room is a Roman copy of the Greek Praxiteles' *Three Graces,* which Pinturicchio, Raphael, and Canova studied as a model. Pinturicchio and assistants covered the ceiling and walls with 10 giant frescoes (1507) displaying Pinturicchio's rich colors, delicate modeling, limpid light, and fascination with mathematically precise, but somewhat cold, architectural space. The frescoes celebrate the life of Aeneas Silvio Piccolomini, better known as the humanist Pope Pius II. The next-to-last scene on the left wall records the act Siena most remembers the pope for, canonizing local girl Catherine as a saint in 1461.

Beneath the church is the latest artistic discovery in Siena, in a room widely referred to as the **"crypt,"** although no bodies have been found buried here. More likely the subterranean room is an old entrance to the Romanesque church. What the 21st-century restoration workers scraped up was a cycle of frescoes painted between 1270 and 1275, shedding some light on the early development of the Sienese school.

The crypt has only been viewable since 2004, and scholars have yet to attribute the cycle to a particular artist. Some have speculated it may be the work of Duccio, though he would have been exceedingly young at the time. What is more or less certain is that the style and composition, such as the way Christ's feet are oddly crossed on the crucifix, have been mirrored, almost copied, in the paintings in the church above. Though chipped and still a little rough around the edges, the vibrant blue, gold, and burgundy colors have been impressively preserved thanks to the lack of light and humidity in this part of the church since the 1300s, when the room was entirely interred. *Piazza del Duomo.* ☎ *0577/283-048. www.operaduomo.it. Admission to church free, except when floor is uncovered Sept–Oct, then 5.50€; Libreria Piccolomini on cumulative ticket, or 1.50€ ($1.75). Daily Mar 15–Oct 9am–7:30pm, Nov–Mar 14 10am–1pm and 2:30–5pm. Admission to the crypt 6€ ($7.20). Daily Sept–May 9:30am–7pm, June–Aug 9:30am–8pm.*

→ Museo dell'Opera Metropolitana ★

In the walled-up right aisle of the Duomo's abortive new nave, Siena's Duomo museum contains all the works removed from the façade for conservation as well as disused altarpieces, including Duccio's masterpiece. It also offers one of the city's best views. The **ground floor** has the fascinating but weatherworn façade **statues by Giovanni Pisano** and his school (1284–96), and aluminous marble tondo of the *Madonna and Child* ★ carved in refined *schiacciato* relief. Most scholars now agree it's the work of Donatello. There are more statues out a side door, but that leads to the exit, so first head up the stairs.

Upstairs is the museum's, if not the city's, masterpiece, **Duccio's** *Maestà* ★★. It's impossible to overstate the importance of this double-sided altarpiece, now separated and displayed on opposite sides of the intimate room. Not only did it virtually found the Sienese school of painting, but it has been considered one of the most important late medieval paintings in all Europe since the day it was unveiled. When Duccio finished the work on June 9, 1311, it was reportedly carried in procession from the painter's workshop to the Duomo's altar by the clergy, government officials, and every last citizen

in Siena. The centuries have been unusually kind to it. Although eight of the predella panels are in foreign museums and one is lost (12 pinnacle angels suffered similar fates), it's otherwise remarkably intact and in great shape.

Also, almost overlooked here is Pietro Lorenzetti's incredible *Birth of the Virgin.* The perspective in the piece may be a bit off, but Lorenzetti broke traditions and artistic boundaries with his fabrics, his colors, and (most important) the architectural space he created. Instead of painting a triptych with a central main scene and two unrelated side panels of saints, as was the norm, Lorenzetti created a single continuous space by painting vaulted ceilings that seem to grow back from the pointed arches of the triptych's frame. Pietro never got a chance to develop these ideas; this is the last work he painted before succumbing to the plague.

If you take the stairs (past rooms of baroque canvases and church vestments) that lead up to the walkway atop the would-be façade of the "New Duomo," you get the best visualization of how the enlarged Duomo would have looked as well as sweeping **views** across the city's rooftops with the Torre del Mangia towering over the Palazzo Pubblico. *Piazza del Duomo 8.* ☎ *0577/42-390 or 0577/283-048. www.operaduomo.siena.it. Admission on cumulative ticket, or 5.50€. Daily Mar 15–Sept 9am–7:30pm, Oct 9am–6pm, Nov–Mar 14 9am–1pm.*

→ Baptistery ★

The Duomo's baptistery was built in the 14th century beneath the cathedral's choir and supports a Gothic façade left unfinished by Domenico di Agostino (1355). The upper walls and vaulted ceilings inside were **frescoed by Vecchietta** and his school in the late 1440s (look for the alligator) but "touched up" in the 19th century. What you're here to see, though, is the **baptismal font** ★ (1417–30). The frames are basically Gothic, but the gilded brass panels were cast by the foremost Sienese and

Florentine sculptors of the early Renaissance. Starting on the side facing the altar, Siena's master Jacopo della Quercia did the *Annunciation to Zacharias.* Giovanni di Turino did the next two, the *Birth of the Baptist* and the *Preaching of the Baptist.* The *Baptism of Christ* is by the author of the Baptistery doors in Florence, Lorenzo Ghiberti, who collaborated with Giuliano di Ser Andrea on the *Arrest of St. John.* The final panel is perhaps the greatest, Donatello's masterful early study of perspective and profound depth in the *Feast of Herod. Piazza San Giovanni (down the stairs around the back right flank of the Duomo).* ☎ *0577/283-048. www.opera duomo.it. Admission on cumulative ticket, or 2€. Daily Mar 15–Sept 9am–7:30pm, Oct 9am–6pm, Nov–Mar 14 10am–5pm.*

➜ **Ospedale di Santa Maria della Scala** ★ The first fresco you see, just after the ticket booth, is Domenico Beccafumi's luridly colored *Meeting at Porta Andrea* (after 1512). Off to the left, just past the bookshop, is the entrance to the **Sala del Pellegrinaio,** which held hospital beds until just a few years ago. The walls were frescoed in the 1440s with scenes from the history of the hospital and its good works (all labeled). Most are vivid masterpieces by Domenico di Bartolo, richly colored and full of amusing details. However, Vecchietta did the upwardly mobile orphans over the exit door; Jacopo della Quercia's less talented and little known brother, Priamo, did a cartoonish scene on the left wall; and a pair of mannerist hacks filled in the spaces at the room's end.

The collection in Siena's new modern **archaeology museum,** recently incorporated into the Santa Maria della Scala complex, is small, and while there's nothing of earth-shattering significance, there are some good pieces for a museum hardly anyone knows exists. Wander past fading frescoes to examine Etruscan bronzes, black *bucchero* vases, funerary urns in terra cotta and alabaster, and some Roman coins. *Piazza del Duomo 2.* ☎ *0577/49-153. www.santamaria. comune.siena.it. Admission on cumulative ticket, or 4.70€ with reservations, 5.20€ without reservations. Mar 15–Nov 5 Mon–Sat 10am–6:30pm; Nov 6–Mar 14 Mon–Sat 10:30am–4:30pm.*

Shopping

Although Siena's shopping scene can't compete with that in Florence, you'll still find a good selection of stores and boutiques. Most stores are generally open Monday through Saturday from 10am to about 7pm (though some take the midday *riposo*).

➜ **Antica Drogheria Manganelli** Siena's classiest stop for food. since 1879 makes its own *panforte* (one of the few left) and delicious soft *ricciarelli* almond cookies. It also carries the tops in Tuscan products, like vinegar from Castello di Volpaia and cured meats from Greve in Chianti's Falorni butchers. *Via di Città 71–73.* ☎ *0577/280-002.*

➜ **Cortecci** If you absolutely need to get some big-label shopping done right now, bring your credit cards for a date with Armani, Gucci, Versace, Burberry, Missoni—and some more affordable labels—to this place, which has been dressing the Sienese since the 1930s. *Via Banchi di Sopra 27.* ☎ *0577/280-096. www.corteccisiena.it. There's also a branch on Il Campo at 30–31;* ☎ *0577/280-984.*

➜ **La Terra di Siena** It looks like a bargain basement–type place with stacks of regional products like Sienese cookies and area wines, honeys, cheeses, and meats, but it carries quality merchandise (at great prices). *Via G. Duprè 32.* ☎ *0577/223-528.*

➜ **Tessuti a Mano** After all the brand-name nonsense around Italy, it's nice to see a little homemade stuff every once in a while. As the name of the store suggests, Fioretta Bacci weaves all her incredible scarves, shawls, and sweaters by hand. Her two giant looms take up most of the room. *Via San Pietro 7.* ☎ *0577/282-200.*

Arezzo: *La Vita e Bella*

85km (53 miles) SE of Florence

Arezzo, much to its residents' disbelief, is best-known among American tourists as the backdrop to Roberto Benigni's Oscar-winning film *Life Is Beautiful* (1999). They take photos of the house where a local man famously yells up to a window, "Maria, throw down the key!" Never mind that the poet and historian Petrarch was born here or that the city is covered in masterpieces by Piero della Francesca; ever since the Ghibellines in Arezzo were toppled by the Guelphs led by Florence, this once-powerful Tuscan town has been accustomed to humiliation as a second-class attraction.

This is good news for you, because it means fewer tour buses and virtually no lines (though it also means some mediocre hotels and an uninspiring restaurant scene). The best times to visit are the first Sunday of every month, when local antique dealers fill the streets with some outrageously cool items from God-knows-what century, and especially on the third Sunday in June and the first Sunday in September, when Arezzo puts on its own Palio of sorts. The medieval jousting tournament, the **Giostra del Saracino,** features armored horseback riders who gallop across the dirt-filled Piazza Grande, with their lances aimed at a dummy of a Saracen, or North African pirate. When the knights strike their lances on his shield, the Saracen swivels, and his other arm is carrying a whip. Hitting the shield's bull's-eye is only half the trick—the other is dodging the whip.

Getting There

BY TRAIN

Arezzo sits on the main line between Rome and Florence, so there are 22 trains per day leaving the capital for Arezzo; it takes about 2 hours for the fast Intercity or Eurostar trains,

and about 3 hours for the slow ones. Even better is to leave from Florence, with 45 trains per day, about 40 minutes for the quick ones and 90 minutes for the slow ones. The **train station** (☎ 0575/20-553) is at Piazza della Repubblica just southwest of the city walls, which is to say, downhill. Get ready to do some climbing to get to the major sites.

BY CAR

By car, the quickest route from Florence or Rome is the **A1** *autostrada.* You can **park,** usually not free, along Via Niccolò Aretino just inside the southwest corner of the walls and Via B. Alberti, behind the train station. There's free parking on Via Pietri and Vai XXV Aprile.

BY BUS

If you're coming from Siena, the best way is definitely by bus which takes about an hour and a half (SITA buses (☎ 0575/749-818; www.sita-on-line.it) and they also leave from in front of the train station.

Arezzo Basics

TOURIST OFFICE

The **APT information office** is at Piazza della Repubblica 28, just outside the train station (☎ 0575/377-678; www.apt.arezzo.it; Mon–Fri 9am–1pm and 3–7pm, Sun 9am–1pm). There's a provincial APT office at Piazza

Getting Around Arezzo

Once in town, the only transportation you will need is your own two feet. All of the sites and restaurants are literally within a few blocks' walk–the only catch is that those blocks are on a serious incline.

Arezzo

Piazza S. Domenico

Via S. Domenico

Casa di Vasari

Via XX Settembre

Via Sassoverde

Duomo

Via Ricasoli

Via dei Pileati

Viale Bruno Buozzi

Via Pellicceria

Piazza Grande

Piaggia di Murello

Via Cesalpino

S. Maria delle Pieve

Via S. Lorentino

Via Cavour

Via Garibaldi

Piazza S. Francesco

Via Cavour

Via Mazzini

Minerva

Via Fontanella

Via I Leone Leoni

Piazza di Badia

Badia

Basilica di San Francesco

Via della

Via Garibaldi

Via Porta Buia

Via Monaco

Via de Cenci

Via Pietro Aretino

Via Petrarca

Piazza Guido Monaco

Via della Madonna del Prato

Via Roma

Via Francesco Crispi

Anfiteatro Romano

Via Guido

Via della

Corso Italia

ITALY

Florence

Via Frà Guittone

Arezzo

Rome

Viale Piero della Francesca

Via Spinello Via Niccolò Aretino

Viale Michelangelo

ⓘ Information

0   25 Miles

0   25 Kilometers

Risorgimento 116 (☎ 0575/23-952 or 0575/23-523; fax 0575/28-042); go up Via Guido Monaco a block and turn right; call for hours. The website **www.cittadiarezzo.com** is also very helpful for planning a visit.

Sleeping

Hotels are few and far between in Arezzo, and those that exist mainly cater to businessmen passing through, which means they aren't cheap, and not very interesting. The best way to see Arezzo is on a day trip, and spend the night in Siena or Florence, or at a small B&B in the countryside. But if your plans require an overnight, here are a couple of suggestions:

DOABLE

→ **Hotel Continentale** In a 1950s building on the south edge of Piazza Guido Monaco, the Continentale offers uninspiring but comfortable modern rooms with built-in white lacquer furniture and floral-print curtains and upholstery. Try to get one away from the main street or piazza, both of which suffer from traffic noise. Rooms whose numbers end in "22" are larger and come with satin quilts, plush easy chairs, curtained archways, and nifty flip-top desks. A recent restoration has added air-conditioning to all the guest rooms. A new breakfast room was also part of the restoration, or you can take breakfast on a large panoramic terrace upstairs in summer.

Piazza Guido Monaco 7 (between the station and San Francesco). ☎ *0575/20-251. Fax 0575/350-485. www.hotelcontinentale.com. 73 units. Double 98€, triple 132€. Breakfast 8€. Parking 10€ in nearby garage.*

SPLURGE

➔**Cavaliere Palace Hotel** This is the nicest (but priciest) game in town. The functional furnishings and carpeted floors are pleasantly unassuming and comfy, and you can breakfast on a viewless terrace in summer. The hotel is tucked on a side street off the right of Piazza Guido Monaco, so it's generally quieter than the Continentale. *Via Madonna del Prato 83 (off Via Roma just east of Piazza G. Monaco), 52100 Arezzo.* ☎ *0575/26-836. Fax 0575/21-925. www.cavalierehotels.com. 27 units. Double 135€. Rates include breakfast. Parking 15€ in nearby garage.*

Eating

CHEAP

➔**Antica Osteria L'Agania** TUSCAN This small joint doesn't bother with a wine list; a staff member plunks down a bottle of the eminently quaffable house chianti, and you pay for what you drink. The locals pack into this long, wood-paneled room for unpretentious food like their grandmas used to make. They come especially for the thick rib-sticking *ribollita,* but you can also mix and match gnocchi, tagliatelle, and creamy polenta with the basic Tuscan sauces (the gnocchi and the ragù make a nice combo). The trattoria proudly offers the lovely "local dishes" foreign visitors rarely order, such as tripe and the very fatty *grifi e polenta* (chunks of veal stomach in polenta). You may find your taste buds more attuned to the *arista* (roast pork) or *polpette fritte con patate* (fried meatballs with roast potatoes). *Via Mazzini 10 (near San Francesco).* ☎ *0575/295-381. www.osteriagania.it. Reservations recommended. Primi 4€–7€; secondi 8€–10€.*

Tues–Sun noon–3pm and 7–10:30pm. Closed last 2 weeks of June.

DOABLE

➔**Buca di San Francesco** ★ ARETINE The Buca resides in the frescoed cellar of a 14th-century palazzo and has been run by the same family for over 70 years. Mario de Filippis likes to keep "the memory of old flavors" in his ancient dishes. Try the respectable *ribollita* or good *bringoli casalinghi con il sugo finto* (homemade spaghetti in chunky tomato sauce). If you're waffling over a secondo, order *la saporita di bonconte,* a plate piled with portions of all the restaurant's specialties—tripe, roasted sausages, baked rabbit, and others—a dish from the days when an army on the march had to make a communal stew out of what each man could muster (it comes with a commemorative plate). They'll keep pouring the *vin santo* until you run out of *cantucci* (biscotti) or fall off your chair, and they love sending you off with a bag of little goodies. *Via San Francesco 1 (next door to San Francesco).* ☎ *0575/23-271. www.bucadisanfrancesco.it. Reservations recommended. Primi 5€–10€; secondi 8.50€–11€. Wed–Mon noon–2:30pm; Wed–Sun 7–9:30pm. Closed 2 weeks in July.*

➔**Le Tastevin** INVENTIVE ARETINE Tastevin serves up Aretine dishes but plenty of innovative foods, too. The *risatoni a'le Tastevin* is a creamy version with truffles and asparagus, while the very good *penne alla Tastevin* comes in a cream sauce of puréed yellow peppers. Or, you can try a variety of fish dishes or a *bistecca di vitello al pepe verde* (beef cooked in its own juices with whole peppercorns). Be aware, however: If you're not a regular, service can verge on rude. *Via de' Cenci 9 (between Via Madonna del Prato and Corso Italia).* ☎ *0575/28-304. Reservations recommended. Primi 5€–7€; secondi 8€–11€. Tues–Sun 12:30–3pm and 7–10pm.*

The Wave Love Festival

If you're in Arezzo in the middle of July, don't miss the 6-day **Arezzo Wave Love Festival (www.arezzowave.com)**, as it's chock-full of punks, hippies, hipsters, yuppies, and more. Thousands gather in Arezzo for a cultural binge unlike that found in Florence. Ten locations in town host 13 different stages/performance areas:

➔ **Word Stage/Comicswave:** Workshops, spoken-word performances, and comedy acts take place in the Anfiteatro near Via Margaritone.

➔ **Psycho Stage/Wake Up Stage:** The Wave Festival's severely bipolar stage in the Colle del Pionta is a venue for chill, lesser-known acts in the morning, reserved for the early risers. But come afternoon, it morphs into a riotous platform for acts like the Mosquitos to warm up crowds waiting for the main stage to come alive at 7pm.

➔ **Teatrowave:** Head to Via Bicchieraia, where you can satisfy your thespian cravings. Mostly performed in Italian, up-and-coming playwrights put their work to the test on this stage.

➔ **Cabawave:** Near Teatrowave sits Cabawave. In the afternoon, the aptly named stage plays home to raucous cabaret acts from the area.

➔ **Cinewave:** The first 3 nights showcase indie films and workshops, again mostly local and Italian.

➔ **Classicwave/Socialwave:** Centrally located in the Piazza San Jacopo, Italian classical musicians treat locals to a beautifully set-up stage in the evening. Socialwave has two locations, one in a smaller soccer field near the Main Stage and the other near Piazza San Jacopo. Emphasis here is, you guessed it, on social causes. This is where you'll find speakers and politicos on their soapbox.

➔ **Giocawave:** Kiddies aren't forgotten about during the Wave Love Festival. Until 7pm, children can hang out and go nuts near the Main Stage area.

➔ **Main Stage:** The biggest acts come on stage at 7pm in the main soccer field in the southeastern corner of Arezzo. In recent years, Motorhead, The Kills, British Sea Power, and Soulwax were a few that performed on the main stage. I missed my favorite local band, lcd soundsystem, by 1 day last year, but all was well when Adam Freeland came to Elettrowave the next day.

➔ **Elettrowave:** Stock up on Red Bull for Elettrowave, the late-night event that takes place 2 out of the 6 days. It's way out in the Centro Affari e Convegni (Arezzo's conference venue), where convention center halls are sectioned off into the Main Room, Cabaret Electronique, and Different Beat. The latter is the most interesting with a specific country highlighted each day. In 2005, one day featured three acts from India, most notably Talvin Singh, and the other focused on Brazil.

Partying

Arezzo is a small town, but on weekends, it has become pretty lively in recent years. A bar to start out at is **Martini Point,** at 53 Comune di Badia Teldalda, ☎ **0575/714035.**

Sightseeing

Arezzo's main square, **Piazza Grande,** is charmingly off-kilter. Since 1200, it has listed alarmingly to one side, creating a slope crowned with a graceful loggia designed in 1573 by Giorgio Vasari. Perpendicular to where the shop-filled tunnel-like loggia runs out of the square sits the composite Palazzo della Fraternità dei Laici. The Gothic lower half (1377) has a detached Spinello Aretino fresco of the *Pietà* and a Bernardo Rossellino *Madonna della Misericordia* (1434) in bas-relief above the door. The upper loggia was built in 1460, and the clock bell tower added by Vasari in 1552.

This piazza is also the backdrop for most of the Arezzo scenes in Benigni's *Life Is Beautiful.* There is a plaque commemorating the film which you'll see as you walk uphill along the piazza, in the right-hand corner.

→ **San Francesco** ★★ One of the greatest fresco cycles by one of the greatest artists of the Renaissance covers the sanctuary of this 14th-century church. Piero della Francesca's *Legend of the True Cross* (1448–66) has drawn art-loving pilgrims from around the world for centuries. Piero's work features perfect perspective and hauntingly ethereal, woodenly posed figures that nonetheless convey untold depths of emotion. It fascinates art theorists just as his innovative narrative schemes and figurative style earned him the admiration of his contemporaries. The entire cycle was gorgeously restored from 1985 to 2000 to fix the extensive damage wreaked by 500 years of fires, earthquakes, Napoleonic troops, and creeping dampness in the plaster. You can see them from the ropes at the base of the altar steps, about 10m (33 ft.) away, but it is well worth booking a ticket to get up close. A new policy requires visitors to make reservations to view the fresco cycles. Twenty-five people are admitted every 30 minutes, and are required to leave at the end of the time slot. You're required pick up your tickets at least a half-hour before your entry time or

risk losing your space on the tour. *Piazza San Francesco.* ☎ *0575/20-630. Required reservation for Piero cycle tickets at 0575/24-001, 06-32-810, or www.pierodellafrancesca.it. Admission to church free; Piero cycle 5€ including the booking fee. Church daily 8:30am–noon and 2:30–6:30pm. Piero cycle by 30-min. guided tour only, leaving on the half-hour Mon–Fri 9am–6pm; Sat 9am–5:30pm (5:45pm in winter); Sun 1–5:30pm. Box office closes 1 hr. earlier.*

FREE → **Santa Maria della Pieve** ★ This 12th-century church is Lombard Romanesque architecture at its most beautiful, with a craggy, eroded **façade** ★ of stacked arcades in luminous beige stone. The spaces between the columns of the arcades get narrower at each level, which, along with the setting on a narrow street, only adds to the illusion of great height. The occasional carved column was mixed in; look for the human telamon in the top row. The fat 36m (118-ft.) bell tower "of the hundred holes" with its mullioned windows is a 1330 addition. If the restoration on the main doorway is finished, you can admire the medieval reliefs lining it. They depict the months of the year, including the two-faced pagan god Janus sitting in for the month of January (named after him).

The arches in the interior are just starting to get plucked to Gothic pointiness, and dozens of windows light the place. On the high altar above the raised crypt is a 1320 polyptych of the *Madonna and Child with Saints*—all wearing gorgeously worked fabrics—by Sienese master Pietro Lorenzetti. In the crypt, with its carved medieval capitals, is a 1326 reliquary bust by Aretine goldsmiths Peter and Paul; inside are the remains of Arezzo's patron saint, St. Donato, a local bishop martyred in the 5th century. *Corso Italia 7.* ☎ *0575/22-629. Free admission. Daily May–Sept 8am–7pm; Oct–Apr 8am–noon and 3–6pm.*

FREE → **Duomo** At the highest point in town, surrounded by the Parco il Prato with its 16th-century Medici fortress ruins, Arezzo's cathedral was slowly agglomerated between 1278 and 1510, though it took until 1859 to raise the neo-Gothic bell tower and until 1935 to finish the simple façade. Among the masterpieces inside, the greatest may be the stained-glass windows (1519–23) by the undisputed master of the form, the French immigrant Guillaume de Marcillat. This is one of the few complete cycles of his work in Italy that hasn't been destroyed—due to internecine wars, neglect, later building projects, flood, fire, World War II, etc.—and it includes the *Pentecost* rose window in the facade; the *Calling of St. Matthew*, the *Baptism of Christ*, the *Expulsion of Merchants from the Temple*, the *Adulteress*, and the *Raising of Lazarus* along the right wall; and *Saints Silvester and Lucy* in the chapel to the left of the apse. De Marcillat, who left France after becoming a Dominican friar (apparently to avoid murder charges), was no mean frescoist either, and painted the first three ceiling vaults of the nave. The large Cappella della Madonna del Conforto (Lady Chapel) in the left aisle near the church entrance preserves several della Robbia terra cottas, including an *Assumption,* a *Crucifixion,* and a pretty *Madonna and Child* by Andrea, plus a polychrome *Madonna and Child with Saints* attributed to Giovanni. In the small baptistery is a font bearing Donatello-school *schiacciato* relief panels—the *Baptism of Christ* scene may have been carved by Donatello himself. *Piazza del Duomo.* ☎ *0575/23-991. Free admission. Daily 7am–12:30pm and 3–6:30pm.*

FREE → **San Domenico** The interior of this 1275 church, fronted by a brick-lined piazza planted with lime trees, is very dark, but to the left and right of the altar are fuse boxes where you can switch on the lights. Lots of good 14th-century **fresco fragments** line the walls, and over the high altar is a painted *Crucifix* ★ by Cimabue, brilliantly restored and returned to this place of honor in early 2003.

On the entrance wall are frescoes of the *Crucifixion* and the *Life of St. Nicholas of Bari* by Parri di Spinello. On the right wall, under a Gothic canopy, Luca di Tommé painted a very young *Christ with the Doctors of the Church* in the Sienese style. The chapel to the right of the high altar contains a 14th-century stone *Madonna and Child* and a delicate fresco of the **Annunciation** by Spinello Aretino. More frescoes line the church's left wall, and the last one on your right as you leave is a 15th-century *St. Vincent Ferrer.* According to Giorgio Vasari, this is the only known work by his grandfather, Lazzaro Vasari. *Piazza San Domenico.* ☎ *0575/22-906. Free admission. Daily Nov 3–Mar 22 9am–6:30pm; Mar 23–Nov 2 9am–7pm.*

→ **Casa di Vasari (Vasari's House)** Giorgio Vasari bought this house in 1540 and decorated it with rather bland, semi-mannerist paintings with the help of his contemporaries and students. There are works by Il Poppi, Alessandro Allori, Santi di Tito, and, of course, Giorgio himself. The best of the Vasari pieces are a *Deposition* in the second room and a painting in the first room of **Virtue, Envy, and Fortune** duking it out on the ceiling. It features a nifty optical trick: The figure that appears to be on top changes as you view it from different perspectives. *Via XX Settembre 55.* ☎ *0575/409-040. Admission 4.90€, 2.90€ ages 18–25. Wed–Sat and Mon 9am–7pm; Sun 9am–1pm.*

→ **Museo Archeologico Mecenate** Relic lovers will adore the pottery fragments, terra cotta bowls, and artifacts stored in Arezzo's Archaeology Museum. For those not swayed by antique shards, there's a "recreation" of what an ancient room in Arezzo looked like. After seeing rooms filled with plush red furniture, potpourri, and rose petals, I was surprised to find that every home in ancient Arezzo was furnished by Ethan Allen. *Via Margaritone 10.* ☎ *0575/20-882. Admission 4€. Daily 8:30am–7:30pm, tickets sold until 7pm.*

Pisa: Holding Up the Tower

22km (14 miles) S of Lucca; 81km (50 miles) W of Florence

Pisa is the ultimate Tuscan day trip. Millions of people descend annually on The Leaning Tower and its neighboring architectural miracles on Campo dei Miracoli square. Few realize that it was once a major naval power (which is fair enough, since the sea no longer reaches all the way inland) or that the city has long had one of the nation's premier universities, or even that Galileo—who taught in Padua—was born here, though many are familiar with his antics of dropping large things from one of the city's better-known towers.

Getting There

BY TRAIN

There are more than 20 trains daily from Rome (3 hr.). From Florence, 40 daily trains make the trip (80–90 min.). Three to four trains an hour run from nearby Livorno (15 min.); and there are trains running approximately every hour from Siena (100–110 min.). Lucca zips 24 runs here every day (20–30 min.). On the Lucca line, day-trippers (and anyone staying in any of the hotels listed here except the Royal Victoria) should get off at the San Rossore station, just a few blocks west of Piazza del Duomo (Campo dei Miracoli) and its Leaning Tower. All other trains, and the Lucca one eventually, pull into Pisa Centrale station (☎ 050/41-385). From here,

bus no. 1, 3, or 11 will take you to Piazza del Duomo. (You can also walk to the Leaning Tower from Pisa Centrale—it's a flat, straightforward, and pleasant 20-minute stroll north, and across the Arno.)

BY CAR

For those in a car, the SS12 or S12r comes here from Lucca; the A12 comes down the coast from the north, and the SS1 runs north and south along the coast. Park just outside Porta Santa Maria, either along Via A. Pisano (metered; 1€ per hour 8am–8pm) or in the nearby lot at Via C. S. Cammeo 51 (same rates).

BY BUS

Lazzi (☎ 0583/584-876; www.lazzi.it), on Via d'Azeglio, runs hourly buses from Florence (2–2¹/₂ hr.), but you have to connect through Lucca (hourly runs; 20–30 min.).

BY AIR

Pisa also has an airport, named after Galileo Galilei (general info ☎ 050/500-707; www.pisa-airport.com), which is 3km (2 miles) south of Pisa. Many budget European carriers such as Ryanair and easyJet fly here. Trains zip you downtown to the train station in 5 minutes (1€), whereas a taxi ride to town will cost 4€ to 8€.

Pisa Basics

TOURIST OFFICE

The main tourist office is just outside Porta Santa Maria on the west end of Campo dei Miracoli at Via C. Cammeo 2 (☎ 050/560-464 or 050/830-253; www.pisa.turismo.toscana.it; daily May–Oct 9am–7:30pm, until 5:30pm Nov–Apr). A small office is to the left as you exit the train station (☎ 050/42-291). Either can hand out maps and pamphlets, but they're oddly uninformed on the city of Pisa. Considerably more knowledgeable "Custodians of the Duomo" usually hang around the Museo dell'Opera del Duomo desk.

Getting Around Pisa

Once in town, the city bus service, **CPT** (☎ 050/505-511 or 800/012-773 in Italy; www.cpt.pisa.it) is a good way to get around this medium-sized city. Buses nos. 1, 3, and 11 run most directly to Campo dei Miracoli from the main train station. You can also call a **taxi** at ☎ 050/541600.

Pisa

ITALY
○ Venice
Pisa ● ○ Florence
✱ Rome
Sicily

.2 Miles
.2 Kilometers

Ponte della Vittoria
Lungarno Bruno Buozzi
Via del Borghetto
Piazza Guerrazzi
Ponte della Fortezza
Via A. Ceci
Piazza G. Mazzini
Piazza della Repubblica
Via S. Andrea
Lungarno Mediceo
Arno
Via G.B. Bruno
Via G. Bruno
Lungarno Galileo Galilei
Via San Martino
Via P. Gori
Viale Bonaini
Via Benedetto Croce
S. FRANCESCO
Piazza S. Francesco
Piazza Martiri della Libertà
Via S. Lorenzo
V. Case Dipinte
Borgo Stretto
Piazza Garibaldi
Via G. Oberdan
Lungarno Pacinotti
Lungarno di Mezzo
Piazza XX Settembre
S. Sepolcro
Via del Carmine
Corso Italia
S. MARTINO
Piazza Vittorio Emanuele II
Staz. Centrale (Train Station)
Piazza S. Caterina
Via G. Carducci
Via L. Bianchi
Via Card. Pietro Maffi
Via dei Cavalieri
Piazza dei Cavalieri
Via S. Frediano
Piazza S. Frediano
Via D. Cavalca
Piazza D. Alighieri
Lungarno Gambacorti
Via Giuseppe Mazzini
Via Francesco Crispi
S. ANTONIO
Via Nino Bixio
Via Cesare Battisti
Via Card. Capponi
Via della Faggiola
Via Martiri
Via Cavallotti
del Mille
Santa Maria
Piazza F. Carrara
Piazza Solferino
Lungarno R. Simonelli
Via Mazzini
Via della Maddalena
Ponte Solferino
Lungarno Sonnino Sidney
P. S. Paolo Ripa d'Arno
Arno
Via Contessa Matilde
Duomo
Piazza del Duomo
Via Card. Arcivescovado
Piazza Arcivescovado
Via Galli-Tassi
ORTO BOTANICO
Via Roma
Via A. Volta
Piazza S. Manin
Piazza D. Manin
S. MARIA
Via Paolo Salvi
Via Risorgimento
Via Enrico Fermi
Via Voltturno
Via Nicola Pisano
Ponte della Cittadella
Via Bonanno Pisano
Piazza Andrea del Sarto
Stazione Pisa- S. Rossore
Viale delle Cascine

ACCOMMODATIONS ■
Albergo Gronchi **6**
Villa Kinzica **5**
Hotel Royal Victoria **9**

DINING ◆
Al Ristoro dei Vecchi Macelli **10**
Da Bruno **7**
Trattoria S. Omobono **8**

ATTRACTIONS ●
Baptistery **1**
Camposanto **2**
Piazza del Duomo **3**
The Leaning Tower **4**

A helpful **private tourism consortium** (supported by the state) shares office space with the Via C. Cammelo tourist office (☎ **050/830-253;** fax 050/830-243; www. pisae.it); among other services, it will book rooms for free.

To find out what's going on in town, pick up a copy of the free weekly *Indizi e Servizi* (at some newsstands and hotels).

Sleeping

Pisa is such a major day-trip site that few people stay here overnight, which helps keep hotel prices down, but also limits selection. The hotel desk in the main tourist office will book you a room at no charge. The low season for most hotels in Pisa is July through August.

CHEAP

➔ **Albergo Gronchi** This is a very plain, *very* decrepit, but very cheap hotel that stays full (and is in this book) both because of its location on the edge of Piazza del Duomo and for the fact that the rooms along the front have that ultimate Pisan hotel amenity: a view of the Leaning Tower (or at least the top half). The weak-springed beds and worn furniture of the fair-size rooms are redeemed by some frescoed ceilings on the first floor. Room 29 has a balcony with Leaning Tower views. No rooms have bathrooms. *Piazza Arcivescovado 1 (just off Piazza del Duomo).* ☎ *050/561-823. Double 35€. Small discounts for longer stays. No credit cards.*

DOABLE

➔ **Villa Kinzica** The carpeted medium-size rooms in this middle-range hotel have modern wood furniture and tasteful art prints on the walls. Around the corner from the Leaning Tower, the Kinzica's rooms are mostly arranged on the front and east sides, so you can open your window and have a camera-ready shot of the campanile. Half the rooms have air-conditioning. The bathrooms are modern but small, and the price is excellent for the location and comfort. *Piazza*

Arcivescovado 2 (just off Piazza del Duomo). ☎ *050/560-419. Fax 050/551-204. www.hotel villakinzica.it. 34 units. Double 108€, triple 124€. Rates include breakfast. Bus: 4.*

SPLURGE

➔ **Hotel Royal Victoria** ★ The Royal Victoria opened in 1839 as Pisa's first hotel, uniting several medieval towers and houses, and is Pisa's only inn of any real character. The rooms on the Arno tend to be larger, as do the quieter (and cooler) ones installed in the remains of a tower dating from the 980s. There are many frescoed ceilings, and one room is a triumph of *trompe l'oeil,* including fake curtains painted on the walls surrounding the bed. They have several rooms with common doors that can be turned into family suites for four (with two separate bathrooms). The new small, plant-filled terrace is a lovely place to take drinks or sun surrounded by roof tiles. *Lungarno Pacinotti 12 (near Ponte di Mezzo).* ☎ *050/940-111. www.royal victoria.it. Double with bathroom 128€, triple with bathroom 138€. Rates include breakfast.*

Eating

If you're not careful, you'll find some pretty uninspiring chow in Pisa, especially at the pizzerias near the Duomo. By venturing a little closer to the center of the city you'll find what the locals do: excellent seafood and other classic Pisan dishes.

CHEAP

➔ **Trattoria S. Omobono** ★ CASALINGA PISANA   Around a column surviving from the medieval church that once stood here, locals gather to enjoy authentic Pisan home cooking. You can get away with a full meal, including wine, for under 20€, opening with something like *brachette alla renaiola* (an antique Pisan dish consisting of large pasta squares in a purée of turnip greens and smoked fish) or *tagliatelle alla scarpara* (in a sausage ragù). The secondi are simple and straightforward: *baccalà alla livornese* (salt

Piazza del Duomo

If You Build It, They Will Pay to Come

On a grassy lawn wedged into the northwest corner of the city walls, medieval Pisans created one of the most beautiful squares in the world. Historically dubbed the Campo dei Miracoli (Field of Miracles), **Piazza del Duomo** ★★★ contains an array of elegant buildings oddly placed on the edge of town. When it was built between the 11th and 13th centuries, the square was against the city walls, surrounded by farmland. But this peripheral location also somehow plays a role in the piazza's uniqueness. A hidden part of its appeal, aside from the beauty of the buildings, is its spatial geometry. The piazza's medieval engineers knew what they were doing. If you take an aerial photo of the square and draw connect-the-dot lines between the centers, doors, and other focal points of the buildings and the spots where streets enter the piazza, you'll come up with all sorts of perfect triangles, tangential lines of mathematical grace, and other unfathomable hypotenuses. (Incidentally, only the tourist industry calls it Campo dei Miracoli. Pisans think that's just a bit too much and refer to it, as they always have, as Piazza del Duomo.)

Admission charges for the group of monuments and museums on the campo, excluding the Leaning Tower (which costs 17€ and must be booked in advance), are tied together in a similarly complicated way, but with less mathematical grace. The Cattedrale alone costs 2€. Any other single sight is 5€. Any two sights are 6€. The Cattedrale plus any two other sights is 8€. An 8.50€ ticket gets you into the Baptistery, Camposanto, Museo dell'Opera del Duomo, and Museo delle Sinopie, while a 10.50€ version throws in the Cattedrale as well. For more information and to book your tickets for the Leaning Tower, visit their collective website, **www.opapisa.it.**

cod with tomatoes) or *maiale arrosto* (thinly sliced roast pork), with which you can order fried polenta slices or ultra-Pisan *ceci* (garbanzo) beans. *Piazza S. Omobono 6 (the piazza next to the market square Piazza Vettovaglie).* ☎ *050/540-847. Reservations recommended. Primi 6€; secondi 8€. Mon–Sat 12:30–2:30pm and 7:30–10pm. Closed Aug 8–20. Bus: 1, 2, or 4.*

DOABLE

→ **Da Bruno** ★ CASALINGA PISANA The decor is typical, cluttered trattoria—paintings of the Duomo, pictures of the owner with famous people and of the local soccer team, copper pots—for this is a typical trattoria that has been dignified to *ristorante* status only through its years of deserved success. It specializes in tried-and-true Pisan dishes. The *prosciutto con crostini* antipasto is as good as it comes, to be followed by *pasta e ceci*

(pasta with garbanzo beans) or *zuppa pisana* (a very bready Pisan ribollita). Although you can order well-turned versions of *agnello arrosto* (roast lamb) or *coniglio al forno* (baked rabbit), the famous secondo here is a *Pisan baccalà con porri,* salt cod cooked with leeks and tomatoes. Try the tiramisu sundae, with chocolate chips and syrup on top. *Via Luigi Bianchi (outside Porta Lucca on the north end of town).* ☎ *050/560-818. www.pisaonline. it/trattoriadabruno. Reservations recommended. Primi 8€–10€; secondi 10€–15€. Wed–Sun noon–3pm and 7–10:30pm. Bus: 1 or 4.*

SPLURGE

→ **Al Ristoro dei Vecchi Macelli** ★ SEAFOOD/PISAN This is Pisa's finest restaurant, excelling at both fish and meat dishes but always local Tuscan at heart. It offers antipasto samplers either *di mare* (surf)

Sunken Archaeological Treasure

Back in Hiding, for Now

The old Medici Arsenale, Lungarno Simonelli, houses the finds of the remarkable ongoing excavation of the 10 ancient **Roman wooden ships** ★—spanning the 1st century B.C. to the Imperial Age, from riverboats to seafaring vessels—stumbled upon by workers expanding the San Rossore train station in 1998. After just 2 years open to the public, however, the museum closed its doors for restoration in January 2004, and won't open them again until at least 2007. This is truly disappointing, as it is one of the most interesting exhibits in Tuscany, and certainly more appealing to return visitors to Pisa than another jaunt up the tower.

Buried by silt in the 12th century (which has since moved the shoreline 8km/26 ft. west), these docks where the Arno met the sea were probably half marshy flatlands, half lagoon—much like modern-day Venice. Alas, this sort of harbor is prone to flash flooding during storms, a recurrent event that probably sank these ships at various times over the centuries.

Fortunately for us, their sudden demise also meant that much of their contents has survived, from holds filled with clay amphorae (whose seals have preserved shipments of olives, cherries, walnuts, and wine for 2,000 years) to sailors' quarters still kitted out with their belongings: leather sandals, sewing kits, even a wax writing board. In the half-decade since the discovery, maritime archaeologists had uncovered two more vessels, including what may be the only Roman warship ever recovered intact. The museum, **Museo Navi Antiche di Pisa** (☎ 050/21-441 or 055/321-5446; www.navipisa.it), when it reopens, will display the ships' contents (including a sailor's skeleton), and, when all the work is complete, will let you watch the arduous restoration of the vessels. It remains to be seen whether it will reopen with the same hours and prices as before: Tuesday through Sunday from 10am to 1pm and 2 to 6pm (until 9pm in summer); admission 3€.

or *di terra* (turf), and though the specialty primo is a *minestra fagioli rossi e frutti di mare* (a creamy purée of red beans with clams, cuttlefish, and mussels), they make their pasta in-house, so the *ravioli farciti di maiale* (pork ravioli in broccoli sauce) offers stiff competition for your palate. Sticking to land, you can follow your first course with the *coniglio disossato e farcito con salsa al tartufo* (slices of stuffed rabbit in cream-truffle sauce). The *spigola con salsa di cipolle e ostriche gratinate* (sea bass cooked with onions and oysters) makes a good fishy secondo. Via Volturno 49 (at the corner of Via N. Pisano). ☎ 050/20-424. Reservations strongly recommended. Primi 11€–13€; secondi 16€–18€; fixed-priced menus without

wine 42€–60€. Thurs–Tues 12:30–3pm and 7:30–10pm; Sun 8–10pm. Bus: 5.

Sightseeing

SIGHTS AROUND THE PIAZZA DEL DUOMO

→ **Baptistery** ★★ Italy's biggest baptistery (104m/341ft. in circumference) was begun in 1153. It may not look it, but if you include the statue on top, this building is actually taller than the Leaning Tower across the square. The interior is surprisingly plain but features the first of the great Pisano pulpits. Nicola Pisano was the founder of a great line of Gothic sculptors who liberated their art from the static iconography of medievalism and whose work would influence Ghiberti and

Donatello and so pave the road for the Renaissance. The pulpit Nicola carved for the baptistery (1255–60) is his masterpiece. The other main attraction of the baptistery is its renowned acoustics. When it's crowded in summer, you may have to bribe a guard to warble, but when there are fewer people (come early in the morning), lean over the ropes to get as near to center as possible and let fly a clear loud note, listening to it echo around the room as it fades. Even better, sing two notes a half-octave apart and listen for their echoing atonal mingling. When a choir sings here, you can hear it for miles. *Piazza del Duomo.* ☎ *050/560-547. www.opapisa.it. For admission fees, see box above. Daily Apr–Sept 8am–7:30pm; Mar and Oct 9am–5:30pm; Nov–Feb 9am–4:30pm. Bus: 1, 3, or 11.*

➔ **Camposanto** Begun in 1278 by Giovanni di Simone to house the shiploads of holy Golgotha dirt (the mount where Christ was crucified) brought back by an archbishop from the Crusades, the Camposanto has been burial ground for Pisan bigwigs ever since. Most funerary monuments are recycled Roman sarcophagi or neoclassical confections installed in the peacefully arcaded corridor encircling the patches of green in the center. *Piazza del Duomo.* ☎ *050/560-547. www.opapisa.it. Daily Apr–Sept 8am–7:30pm; Mar and Oct 9am–5:30pm; Nov–Feb 9am–4:30pm. Bus: 1, 3, or 11.*

➔ **The Leaning Tower** ★★★ (Campanile, or Torre Pendente) The fact is, most medieval towers still standing in Italy haven't been able to keep perpendicular over the centuries. But it's the Leaning Tower of Pisa that has captured the world's fascination and become international shorthand, along with spaghetti, for Italy itself. The tower's problem—and that of Pisan engineers who have been trying to overcome it for more than 800 years—is you can't stack that much heavy marble on top of a shifting subsoil foundation and keep it all straight. It was started in 1173—the date on the wall of 1174 owes to an old Pisan quirk of

starting the year with the date of the Virgin's conception—by Guglielmo and Bonanno Pisano (who also sculpted the Duomo's original bronze doors). They got as far as the third level in 1185 when they noticed the lean, at that point only about 3.8cm, but enough to worry them. Everyone was at a loss as to what to do, so work stopped for almost a century and wasn't resumed again until 1275 under the direction of Giovanni di Simone. He tried to correct the tilt by intentionally curving the structure back toward the perpendicular, giving the tower its slight banana shape.

The only major blip in the tower's long career as a world-famous Italian freak-show attraction came in 1590, when a hometown scientist named Galileo Galilei dropped some mismatched wooden balls off the leaning side to prove to an incredulous world his theory that gravity exerted the same force on two falling objects no matter what their relative weights.

For several decades, a series of complicated and delicate projects has been directed at stabilizing the subsoil. In 1989, more than a million people climbed the tower, but by 1990 the lean was at about 15 feet out of plumb and, by order of a mayor's office concerned for safety, the tower was closed to the public. At 3:25pm on January 7, 1990, with the tower's bells sounding a death knell, the doors were closed indefinitely. In 1992, steel cables were belted around the base to prevent shear forces from ripping apart the masonry. In 1993, even the bells and their dangerous vibrations were silenced, and the same year a series of lead weights was stacked on the high side to try to correct the list. In 1997, engineers took a chance on excavating around the base again—this time carefully removing more than 70 tons of soil from the foundation of the high side so the tower could gradually tip back. In December 2001, righted to its more stable lean of 1838 (when it was a mere 4m/13 ft. off its center), the tower reopened to the public. Now, however, the number of visitors is strictly controlled via compulsory 35- to 40-minute guided tours—and a massive admission charge. However, it's worth every penny. Visit **www.opapisa.it/boxoffice** to book tickets. It's wise to book *well* ahead; if you show up in Pisa without reservations in the height of the tourist season, you will not be able to get into the tower. The climb involves 294 steps around the tower's spiral staircase. Because of the lean, the steps do not uniformly lift you higher, and some actually go downhill, which means you may well be sick to your stomach when you finally get to the 55m-high (180 ft.) top. Dizziness and vertigo

are a real issue up there—when it becomes viscerally clear that you're 4m (13 ft.) off-kilter, you'll want to grab onto the handrails for stability. With that in mind, your Leaning Tower adventure could be tricky if you're hung over. *Piazza del Duomo.* ☎ *050/560-547. www.opapisa.it/boxoffice. Admission by reservation only. 17€ (15€ ticket plus 2€ advance sales fee). Show printed proof of receipt at the ticket offices of Opera della Primaziale Pisa 1 hr. prior to scheduled visit. Daily 8:30am–11pm mid-June to Aug; 8:30am–8:30pm mid-March to mid-May and Sept; 9am–7pm Oct; 9:30am–5 or 6pm Nov to mid-March. Bus: 1, 3, or 11.*

Lucca: Lots & Lots of Walls

72km (45 miles) W of Florence

Cycling around this walled city—the preferred mode of transportation in this town—you'll see why your friends who visited Tuscany came back raving about Lucca. It is arguably the most charming of the major cities in Tuscany, but don't expect too much bustle: Most folks who come here are couples interested in some peace and quiet and a romantic dinner. That said, the isolated city has also made pretty serious contributions to Italian history, most notably in the music category. The city had a "singing school" as early as A.D. 787, and gave the world a number of composers; most famous among them is Giacomo Puccini (1858–1924), whose *Tosca, Madame Butterfly, Turandot,* and *La Bohème* have become some of the world's favorite operas. Lucca boasts some pretty heavyweight ancient history as well. Its plains were inhabited more than 50,000 years ago, and as a Roman *municipium,* it was the site of the First Triumvirate between Julius Caesar, Pompey, and Crassus in 56 B.C.

Getting There

BY TRAIN

Lucca is on the Florence–Viareggio train line, with 21 trains daily passing through Florence

(trip time: 70–90 min.), Pistoia (50 min.), and Montecatini Terme (35 min.). The short hop from Pisa takes about 20 to 30 minutes (24 trains daily, 12 on Sun). The **station** (☎ **848/888-088**) is a short walk south of Porta San Pietro, or you can take the *navetta* (minibus) no. 16 into town.

BY CAR

Pisa is just around the corner on the SS12, and the speedy A11 *autostrada* connects Lucca with Florence.

BY BUS

There are hourly buses from Florence and Siena (**Lazzi;** ☎ **0583/584-876;** www.lazzi.it) to Lucca's Piazzale Verdi, each of which take about an hour.

Sleeping

There are only four hotels within the walls, so unless you book ahead you may have to make do with one of the fully amenitied bland modern joints near the train station. These include the **Rex,** Piazza Ricasoli 19 (☎ 0583/955-443; fax 0583/954-348; www.hotelrexlucca.com), where doubles run 100€, and the **Moderno,** Via V. Civitali 38 (☎ 0583/55-840; fax 0583/53-830; www.albergomoderno.com),

Lucca

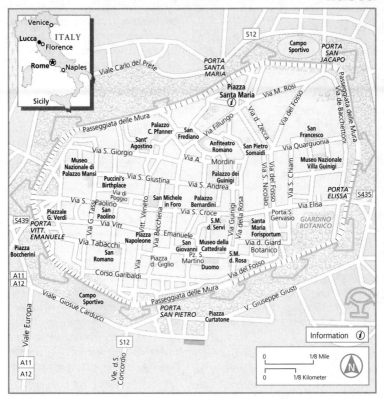

where doubles cost 65€. Inside the walls, there is the **Albergo Diana,** Via del Molinetto 11 (☎ 0583/492-202; fax 0583/467-795; www. albergodiana.com), which has nine passable plain doubles with bathroom, phone, and TV for around 52€ to 67€, and six nicer rooms in the *dependance* around the corner for 83€ to 114€, half a block from the Duomo. But the staff can turn from seemingly friendly to downright nasty at the drop of a hat. It is, however, the cheapest thing going within the walls.

HOSTEL

→ **Ostello S. Frediano** This youth hostel has 140 beds in 20 multibed rooms and 8 miniapartments sleeping six. The cost is 16€ per day for a bunk in a multibed room. Space

in the miniapartments is 39€ for two people, 58€ for three, 78€ for four. Lock-out is noon to 3:30pm; curfew is at midnight. *Via della Cavallerizza.* ☎ *0583/469-957. www.ostello lucca.it.*

DOABLE

→ **Hotel La Luna** This hotel is divided between two buildings on a dead-end street off Lucca's main shopping promenade and a few steps from the medieval houses following the curves of the Roman amphitheater. The rooms are mostly furnished in circa-1980s style, but a few lush 17th-century frescoes grace the second-floor rooms in the older half of the hotel—including no. 242, a quad. The bathrooms range from spacious to cramped, from tub plus box shower to a

Gettinç Around Lucca

A fleet of *navette* (electric minibuses) whiz dangerously down the narrow streets, but you can get around easily on foot. Or better, do as the locals do and take a **bike.** There are several places to rent them. Only one bicycle shop in town is open all day: **Antonio Poli,** Piazza Santa Maria 42 (☎ 0583/ 493-787; www.biciclettepoli.com; daily 8:30am–7:30pm; closed Sun mid-Nov to Feb and Mon mornings year-round). There you can rent a bike for 2.50€ for 1 hour or for 11€ for a full day; a mountain bike is 3.10€ per hour or 16€ for a full day. You can also try **Cicli Bizzarri** next door at Piazza S. Maria 32 (☎ 0583/ 496-031; www.ciclibizzarri.com; Mon–Sat 8:30am–1pm and 2:30– 7:30pm, and Sun Mar to mid-Sept). Bizzarri's rates are 11€ for 1 day; mountain bikes are 16€ per day.

curtainless wall nozzle, but all have fluffy towels. The accommodating owners keep the place very clean and well maintained. *Corte Compagni 12 (off Via Fillungo near the amphi theater).* ☎ *0583/493-634. www.hotellaluna. com. Double 110€, suite 175€. Breakfast 11€.*

→ **Piccolo Hotel Puccini** ★★ This tiny hotel boasts Lucca's best location: just off the central piazza of San Michele. Your neighbor is the ghost of Puccini, who grew up across the street. The prices are fantastic for the location and comfort. And Paolo and his staff are the friendliest hoteliers in town. They even offer bike rental. Most of the rooms are smallish, but they have been renovated with firm beds, compact bathrooms, floral-print wallpaper, carpeting, and reproduction opera playbills framed on the walls. From the 12 rooms along the front (this street sees little traffic), you can lean out and see a sliver of the fabulous San Michele façade half a block

away. The hotel doesn't allow smoking in any rooms, and is planning to install small fridges (empty, because Paolo doesn't want to have to overcharge for the contents as most hotels do). The Puccini fills quickly, so be sure to book ahead. *Via di Poggio 9 (just off Piazza San Michele).* ☎ *0583/55-421. www.hotelpuccini. com. Double 80€. Breakfast 3.50€.*

SPLURGE

→ **Hotel Ilaria** ★ The Ilaria is a classy deluxe hotel entered from a jasmine-scented courtyard. The modern rooms are fitted simply but stylishly with cherry veneer built-in units. The rooms with double-paned windows—you don't even need them on this quiet street— opening onto the little canal out front are nice, but even better views are over the gravelly tree-filled garden out back. Three of these rooms even open onto a shared terrace, and there's also a public terrace dotted with potted camellias and shaded by a giant sycamore. The same group owns three restaurants in town, including the Buca di Sant'Antonio, highly recommended below, and you can work out a pension deal. They've recently completed renovations to a nearby medieval church, creating six junior suites, one suite, and four wheelchair-accessible doubles. They've also jacked up their prices by over 25%, which is a shame. *Via del Fosso 25, 55100 Lucca.* ☎ *0583/469-200. Fax 0583/991-961. www.hotelilaria.com. Double 230€, triple 260€. Rates include breakfast.*

Eating

Lucca is famous for its extra-virgin olive oil, a light-green elixir with a fresh olive taste that's drizzled on just about every dish in these parts. The most typically Luccan dish is the creamy, filling *zuppa di farro,* a soup made with spelt, an emmer or barleylike wheaty grain cooked al dente. The Lucca area is also known for its asparagus, strawberries, and honey. Accompany any dish with Lucca's excellent and little-known DOC wines, Rosso delle Colline Lucchesi and Montecarlo.

CHEAP

→ **Da Guido** LUCCHESE/TUSCAN This place is great—a small locals' hangout, run by an extended family, not much more than an overgrown bar but offering one of the truest meals in town. If the TV in the corner is annoying, you can try sitting outside, although the buzzing of the mopeds past your table might be worse. Either way, the food will be fantastic. Start with the homemade *tortelli della casa* (meat ravioli in a ragù), *penne all'arrabbiata* (in a spicy hot tomato sauce), or *riso ai funghi* (rice with porcini mushrooms) before digging into the *coniglio arrosto* (roast rabbit). *Via Cesare Battisti 28 (near Piazza Sant'Agostino and San Frediano, west of the Roman amphitheater).* ☎ *0583/ 476-219. Primi 5€–7€; secondi 7€; menù turistico with wine 11€. Mon–Sat noon–2:30pm and 7:30–10pm. Closed 3–4 weeks in Aug.*

→ **Pizzeria da Felice** PIZZERIA If you just want to grab a slice and a Coke for 5€, this is the place. It serves up generous slices of real wood-oven pizza ,and you can also sample two Lucchese specialties: *cecina* (a flat bread made of ceci beans) and

Lucca Basics

The **tourist information office** is inside the east end of the city walls at Piazza Santa Maria 35 (☎ 0583/ 919-931; fax 0583/469-964; www. luccaturismo.it; summer daily 9am– 7pm; Nov–Mar daily 9am–1pm and 3–6pm). It provides an excellent free pocket map and good pamphlets on Lucca and the Garfagnana. The comune also has a small local info office on Piazzale Verdi (☎ 0583/ 442-944) that keeps similar hours. For events and theater, pick up the English-language monthly *Grapevine* for 1.50€ at most newsstands. Another good, private website for lots of Lucca info is **www.in-lucca.it**.

castagnaccio (a sort of chestnut flour pita, split with each half wrapped around sweetened fresh ricotta). *Via Buia 12.* ☎ *0583/ 494-986. Pizza slices/baked goods 1€–3€. Tues–Sat 9:30am–2pm and 4–8:30pm; Mon 11am–2pm and 4–8:30pm.*

DOABLE

→ **Da Giulio** ★ LUCCHESE/TUSCAN HOME COOKING This cavernous and very popular trattoria is short on antique charm but long on antique tradition. Don't let the modern decor put you off—the friendly service and genuine peasant cuisine are as trattoria as they come. The soups are superb, such as the *farro con fagioli* (spelt and beans) and the *farinata* (a creamy soup of polenta corn grain with beans and veggies), or you can try the *maccheroni tortellati* (large pasta squares in ricotta, tomatoes, and herbs). *Pollo al mattone* (chicken breast roasted under a heated brick) is the secondo most in demand, but *spezzatino con olive* (stewed beef with olives) runs just behind. They also have plenty of local specialties—tripe, horse tartare, and veal snout—to whet your appetite. The homemade tiramisu is heavenly. *Via Conce 45, Piazza San Donato (in the northwest corner of the walls).* ☎ *0583/55-948. Reservations recommended. Primi 5€–6€; secondi 7€–25€. Tues–Sat and 3rd Sun of month noon–3pm and 7–11:30pm. Closed 10 days in Aug and 10 days around Christmas.*

→ **Da Leo** ★ TUSCAN/LUCCHESE It isn't often a homespun trattoria dramatically improves its cooking while retaining its low prices and devoted following of local shopkeeps, groups of students, and solitary art professors sketching on the butcher paper place mats between bites. This place is now good enough to recommend for the best cheap meals in the center. There's usually an English menu floating around—the good-natured waiters are used to dealing with foreigners who've discovered one of the most authentic Lucchese dining spots in town, run by the amiable Buralli family. This isn't as much a bare-bones tavern as Guido's, not quite as polished an operation as the well-regarded Giulio's, but still as beloved by a devoted local following. Its location, two steps from the central Piazza San Michele, draws tourists who happen by, lured into the peach-colored rooms by the aroma of roasting meats and the scent of rosemary. The food isn't fancy, but they do traditional dishes well: *minestra di farro, spaghetti pancetta piselli* (with pancetta bacon and sweet peas), *arrosto di manzo con patate arrosto* (roast beef and potatoes), and the excellent *zuppa ai 5 ceriali* ("four-cereal" soup with emmer, red and green lentils, barley, a cousin to black-eyed peas, and cannellini beans). *Via Tegrimi 1 (just north of Piazza San Michele).* ☎ *0583/492-236. www.trattori adaleo.it. Reservations recommended. Primi 5€; secondi 9€–16€. No credit cards. Mon–Sat noon–2:30pm and 7:30–10:30pm.*

SPLURGE

➜ **La Buca di Sant'Antonio** ★★★ LUC-CHESE   Since before 1782, La Buca has been the premier gastronomic pit stop inside Lucca's walls. It's a maze of a place with copper pots and musical instruments hanging everywhere. It's attracted the likes of Puccini, Ezra Pound, and others who in times past just wanted to read the restaurant's secret stock of banned books. They like to keep it formal but friendly and pour you a glass of spumante before bringing out your *coppa Garfagnana con crostini della casa* (Lucchese salami with excellent fried crostini). The first course is a tossup between the *ravioli di ricotta alle zucchine* (fresh ricotta-stuffed ravioli in rich butter sauce, topped with julienned zucchini) and the *tortelli Lucchesi al sugo* (meat-filled ravioli in a scrumptious ragù). For a secondo, though, do try the house specialty *capretto nostrale al forno con patate alla salvia* (tender spit-roasted kid with roasted sage potatoes). This is one of

the few pricey Tuscan restaurants I return to year after year. *Via della Cervia 3 (a hidden alley just west of Piazza San Michele; follow the signs).* ☎ *0583/55-881. Reservations highly recommended. Primi 6€–7€; secondi 12€–13€. Tues–Sat 12:30–3pm and 7:30–10:30pm; Sun 12:30–3pm. Closed 1st week of Jan and 1st week of July.*

Shopping

The sunny, scenic hills around Lucca have been famous since the days of the Romans for their olive oil. You won't have to look far to find it—every supermarket, butcher shop, and delicatessen in Lucca sells a huge variety, in glass or metal containers. But if you want to travel into the surrounding hills to check out the production of this heart-healthy product, the best-known company selling its products on rustic Tuscan farms is **Maionchi,** Via Tofori 81, in the hamlet of Capannori (☎ **0583/978194**), 18km (11 miles) northeast of Lucca.

Take a stroll along the town's top shopping streets, **Via Fillungo** and **Via del Battistero.** The best gift/souvenir shops are **Insieme,** Via Vittorio Emanuele 70 (☎ **0583/ 419649**), and **Incontro,** Via Buia 9 (☎ **0583/ 491225**), which places a special emphasis on Lucca's rustically appealing porcelain, pottery, tiles, and crystal.

The best wine shop in town is the **Enoteca Vanni** ★, Piazza Salvatore 7 (☎ **0583-491902;** www.enotecavanni.com), with hundreds of bottles of local and Tuscan vintages.

One of Italy's top **antiques markets** is held the third Saturday and Sunday of every month in Piazza Antelminelli and the streets around the Duomo. The last 2 weeks of September also bring an **agricultural market** to Piazza San Michele, featuring Lucca's wines, honeys, and olive oils.

Sightseeing

Yes, Lucca has a nice cathedral and several other churches and museums, but when

Opera, Classical Music & Feast Days!

In Puccini's hometown, you'll find a devotion to opera, and in October and November his work is showcased at the **Teatro Comunale del Giglio**, Piazza di Giglio (☎ 0583-467521; fax 0583-490317). Sleepy Lucca comes to life during July and August at the time of the classical music festival, the **Estate Musicale Lucchese**. Venues spring up everywhere, and the tourist office keeps a list. The town also comes alive on July 12, when residents don medieval costumes and parade through the city, with the revelry continuing late into the night. More classical music performances fill the town in September during the **Settembre Lucchese Festival**, highlighted by Volto Santo feast day on September 13. The crucifix bearing the "face" of Christ (normally housed in a chapel in the Duomo) that tradition holds was carved by Nicodemus himself is hauled through town in a candlelit procession.

compared to others around Tuscany, they're not particularly important. Spend most of your time in Lucca taking in the sights from its walls, enjoying a nice meal and then maybe poking your head in a tower or a church before you leave. It's just *being* here that people enjoy most about Lucca.

THE WALLS

The walls ★★ are what make Lucca Lucca, and they comprise a city park more than 4km long (2¹/₂ miles) but only about 18m wide (16 ft.), filled with avenues of plane, chestnut, and ilex trees planted by Marie Louise Bourbon in the 19th century. The shady paved paths of Lucca's formidable bastions are busy year-round with couples walking hand in

hand, tables of old men playing unfathomable Italian card games, families strolling, children playing, and hundreds of people on bicycles, from tykes to octogenarians.

Rent a bike (see "Getting Around Lucca," above) and take a Sunday afternoon spin, peering across Lucca's rooftops and down into its palace gardens and narrow alleys, gazing toward the hazy mountains across the plain, and checking out the 11 bastions and 6 gates. The 1566 Porta San Pietro, the southerly and most important gate into town, still has a working portcullis, the original doors, and Lucca's republican motto, "Libertas," carved above the entrance. You can also visit a photo archive and some of the tunnels under the bastions daily from 10am to noon and 4 to 6pm. You must make an appointment in advance (8am–2pm) with CISCU, the **International Center for the Study of Urban Walls** (☎ 0583/496-257; www.ciscu.it), located in the gatehouse at no. 21 near the San Paolino bastion (south of Piazzale Verdi on the west end of town).

The defensive walls you see today—a complete kidney-shaped circuit built from 1544 to 1654—are Lucca's fourth and most impressive set and perhaps the best preserved in all Italy. About 12m high (39 ft.) and 30m wide (98 ft.) at their base, the ramparts bristled with 126 cannons until the Austrian overlords removed them. The walls were never put to the test against an enemy army, though it turned out they made excellent dikes—there's no doubt the walls saved the city in 1812 when a massive flood of the Serchio River inundated the valley. Elisa Bonaparte Baciocchi was governing Lucca at the time from her villa outside the walls, and when she tried to get into the city for safety, the people didn't want to open the gates for fear of the surging waters. Lest they let their princess—and, more important, the sister of Europe's emperor—drown, however, they hoisted her highness over the walls rather unceremoniously with the help of a crane.

→ **Cappella di Santa Zita & Palazzo Pfanner** The Chapel of St. Zita was built in the 17th century to preserve the glass-coffined body of the patron saint of ladies-in-waiting. As a serving girl in the 13th-century Fatinelli household, Zita was caught sneaking out bread in her apron to feed poor beggars on the street. Her suspicious master demanded to know what she was carrying, to which she answered, "Roses and flowers." She opened her apron and, with a little Divine Intervention, that's what the bread had become. Every April 26, the Lucchesi carpet the piazza outside with flowers to celebrate the miracle and bring out her shrunken body to kiss and caress. Up to the left of the high altar is a massive stone monolith, probably pilfered from the nearby Roman amphitheater. The Cappella Trenta, fourth in the left aisle, contains another Jacopo della Quercia masterpiece, an altar carved with the help of his assistant Giovanni da Imola (1422) as well as a pair of tombstones from the master's chisel. A long restoration was recently finished on Lucca's finest fresco cycle in the second chapel of the left aisle, painted by Amico Aspertini (1508–09). In the *Miracles of St. Frediano,* the Irish immigrant bishop saves Lucca from a flood in a realistic way—though he symbolically performs a miracle in the middle ground by raking a new path for the water to be diverted away from the city, naked-torsoed workmen take the prudent pragmatic step of building a dam as well.

Around the left side of the church and down Via Battisti, at Via degli Asili 33, is the 17th-century **Palazzo Pfanner** (☎ **0583/491-243**), whose 18th-century walled garden out back was featured in Jane Campion's 1996 film *Portrait of a Lady.* In 1999, the palace reopened to visitors, housing a costume collection and offers a peek inside those fabulous gardens. Admission is 2.50€ each to visit the gardens or the palazzo (in other words, 5€ for both). It's open March 1 to November 15 daily from 10am to 6pm. If you tool around the city's ramparts you can look down into the gardens for free. Piazza San Frediano. ☎ **0583/493-627.** April to mid-Nov Mon–Sat 7:30am–noon and 3–5pm; Sun 10:30am–5pm.

FREE → **Piazza Anfiteatro** ★ Near the north end of Via Fillungo, a series of houses was built during the Middle Ages into the remains of a 1st- or 2nd-century A.D. Roman amphitheater, which had been used for centuries as a quarry for raw materials to raise the city's churches and palaces. The outline of the stadium was still visible in the 1930s when Duke Ludovico asked local architect Lorenzo Nottolini to rearrange the space and bring out the ancient form better. Nottolini pulled down the few structures that had been built inside the oval, restructured the ground floors of each building, and inserted four tunneled entranceways, but he retained the jumbled medieval look the differing heights of the tower stumps and houses give the place. Nothing other than the occasional market and kids playing soccer interrupts the oval space ringed with lazy cafes and a few shops. *Piazza Anfiteatro. No phone. Daily 24 hr.*

→ **Torre Guinigi** Only one of the two towers sprouting from the top of the 14th-century palace home of Lucca's iron-fisted ruling family still stands, but it certainly grabs your attention. Historians tell us that many of Lucca's towers once had little gardens like this on top—the city was civilized even in its defenses—but that doesn't diminish the delight at your first glance at this stack of bricks 44m high (144 ft.) with a tiny forest of seven holm oaks overflowing the summit. For a closer look, climb the tower (230 steps) for a spectacular view of Lucca's skyline with the snow-capped Apuan Alps and the Garfagnana mountains in the distance. Up here, you can also see the oval imprint the Roman amphitheater left on the medieval buildings of Piazza Anfiteatro (see below). *Via Sant'Andrea, at Via Chiave d'Oro.* ☎ *0583/48-524 or 0583/491-205. Admission 3.50€ adults (a cumulative* ticket with the other tower, Torre dell Ore, is also offered). Daily Mar–May 9am–7:30pm,

June–Sept 15 9am–midnight, Sept 16–Oct 9:30am–8pm, Nov–Feb 9:30am–5:30pm.

Elba: Island of Exile & Good Times

12km (7¹/₂ miles) off the coast at Piombino; 179km (111 miles) SW of Florence

Elba is a great spot to take a break from church surfing, catch some rays, and take a dip in some of the Mediterranean's bluest waters. And if you're a little tired of behaving yourself in quiet Tuscan towns, Elba might be your best bet for some well-deserved misbehaving.

This is the working-man's island resort, visited mainly by middle-class Italian families and German tourists, who together fill just about every available inch of hotel and camping space in August and September. What Elba lacks in glamour, it makes up for in variety. It's Italy's third-largest island, but it's much, much smaller than Sicily or Sardinia. So while it has a tall mountainous interior speckled with ancient mining villages, the sea is never far away. Coastal fishing and port towns in soft pastels are interspersed with modest sandy beaches.

Of course, it does have some history too, most famously the ghost of Napoléon Bonaparte. When the would-be emperor of Europe was first defeated, he was exiled to Elba to rule as the island's governor. Beginning May 3, 1814, the Corsican general busied himself with revamping the island's economy, infrastructure, and mining system—perhaps out of nation-building habit or merely to keep himself and his 500-man personal guard occupied. Napoléon managed to be a good boy until February 26, 1815, at which point the conquering itch grew too strong and he sailed ashore to begin the famous Hundred Days that ended in his crushing defeat at the Battle of Waterloo. The island is proud to have had, no matter how briefly, a resident of such considerable note, and preserves his two villas and various other mementos of the Napoleonic era.

Getting There

BY FERRY

The easiest way to get to the island is by **ferry** from Portoferraio, Elba's capital, from the coastal town of Piombino. Piombino, in the southern, flattish part of Tuscany known as the Maremma, lies about 50 miles south of Livorno on the old Roman road, the Aurelia, nowadays known as the SS1 highway. Unfortunately, there is no train service into the Maremma, and bus service is scarce. Like Chianti, this region is almost exclusively reached by car. Those without a car should consider reaching Elba from Livorno. The ferry company Toremar runs boats to Elba's other ports (Cavo, Rio Marina, and Porto Azzurro) as well as a longer-haul ferry from Livorno to Elba once daily (plus an extra Sat run) from May 24 to September 14 that calls on Capraia (and sometimes also Gorgonza) along the way. Toremar in Livorno is at the Porto Mediceo (☎ **0586/896-113**).

In general, throughout the high season, it's best to reserve, especially if you're taking a car over.

There are two major ferry companies, **Toremar** (☎ **199/123-1990**, or 565/31-100 in Piombino, 0565/918-080 in Portoferraio; www.toremar.it) and **Moby Lines,** also known as NAV.AR.MA (☎ **0565/225-211** or 0565/221-212 in Piombino, 0565/914-133 in Portoferraio; www.mobylines.it). Both run regular ferries (*traghetto* or *nave*) that take about an hour. Toremar also offers slightly faster (40 min.) but almost twice as expensive hydrofoils *(aliscafo)* on which you can't take a car. Toremar has the most ferry runs daily, especially off season, with hourly runs April through August and six to eight daily in winter. Year-round, there are three or four hydrofoils daily to Cavo, on Elba's northeast

Elba

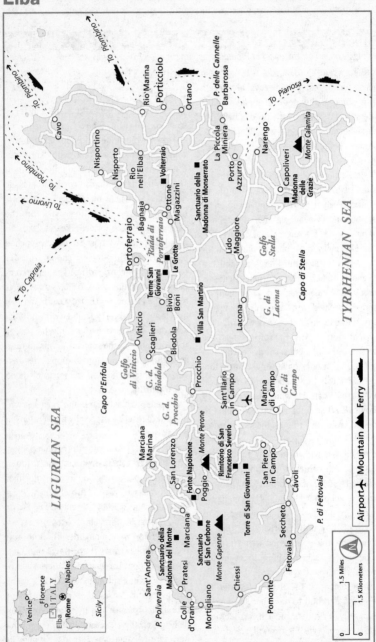

Rio Marina
Porticciolo
Ortano
P. delle Cannelle
Barbarossa

To Pianosa →

Cavo

To Piombino

Nisportino

Narengo

Monte Calamita

Nisporto

La Piccola
Miniera

To Piombino

Rio
nell'Elba

Capoliveri

To Livorno ←

Bagnaia

Volterraio

Porto
Azzurro

Madonna
delle
Grazie

Portoferraio

Ottone
Magazzini

Sanctuario della
Madonna di Monserrato

Rada di
Portoferraio

Le Grotte

LIGURIAN SEA

To Capraia ←

Terme San
Giovanni

Lido
Maggiore

Golfo
Stella

Bivio
Boni

Villa San Martino

TYRRHENIAN SEA

Capo d'Enfola

Viticcio

Golfo
di Viticcio

G. d.
Biodola

Scaglieri

Biodola

Procchio

Sant'Ilario
in Campo

Lacona

Capo di Stella

G. di
Lacona

G. d.
Procchio

Marina
di Campo

G. di
Campo

Marciana
Marina

San Lorenzo

Monte Perone

Fonte Napoleone

Poggio

Rimitorio di San
Francesco Severio

San Piero
in Campo

Cávoli

Airport ✈ Mountain ▲ Ferry ⬛

Sant'Andrea

Pratesi

Sanctuario della
Madonna del Monte

Marciana

Sanctuario
di San Cerbone

Monte Capenne

Torre di San Giovanni

Seccheto

P. di Fetovaia

Colle
d'Orano

Mortigliano

Chiessi

Fetovaia

Pomonte

ITALY

Venice

Florence

Elba

Rome

Naples

Sicily

P. Polveraia

1.5 Miles

1.5 Kilometers

0

0

N

coast, plus three to four direct to Portoferraio in summer only. You can compare both companies' schedules quickly and easily at **www.traghetti.com**.

You'll find uncrowded ticket offices on the right side of the road as you approach Piombino, more crowded offices just before the port on the right, and packed offices at the port itself (all well sign-posted). One-way ferry tickets are about 5.50€ to 7.50€ per passenger including tax (the price depends on the period). Cars with one person in them cost 27€.

Hydrofoils cost between 7€ and 10€ per passenger to Portoferraio or about 5.50€ to Cavo. You can park at a number of garages and lots at the Piombino docks for 8€ to 12€ per day.

Toremar's office in Portoferraio is at Calata Italia 23; Moby Lines' Portoferraio office is at Via Ninci 1.

Getting Around

BY CAR

Drivers will have no problem, as the island's road system is quite good. If you want to rent a car on Elba, contact **Hertz,** Viale Elba 4 (☎ 0565/917-148; www.hertz.com); **Maggiore,** Calata Italia 8 (☎ 0565/930-222 or 0565/903-212; www.maggiore.it); or **Happy Rent,** Viale Elba 5 (☎ 0565/914-665; www.renthappy.it).

BY SCOOTER/BICYCLE

To rent a scooter or bike—not a bad way to tool around—try these places in Portoferraio: **BW's Racing,** Via Manganaro 15 (☎ 0565/930-491; www.bwsrent.com) or **Two Wheels Network,** Viale Elba 32 (☎ 0565/914-666). Rates vary widely depending on season, but expect scooters to run 38€–49€ per day and bikes and mountain bikes starting at 8€.

BY BUS

Elba is also blessed with an excellent bus network run by **ATL** (☎ **0565/914-392**). Buses leave Portoferraio from the main terminal at Viale Elba 20 in the new town (turn right out of the tourist office, then right again at the main street), serving just about every town on the island. (If you know the name of a beach between villages where you want to be let off, tell the driver.) You can store your bags at the bus station for 1.30€ per bag per day. It's open daily in summer from 8am to 8pm and winter from 7:40am to 1:20pm and 4 to 6:05pm.

Elba Basics

TOURIST OFFICES & USEFUL WEBSITES

Elba's main tourist office is in Portoferraio's new town at the ferry dock, Calata Italia 26, up the stairs (☎ **0565/914-671;** fax 0565/916-350; www.arcipelago.turismo.toscana.it; Mon–Sat 8am–2pm and 3–6pm; in summer also sometimes Sun 8am–2pm).

Two websites are loaded with info and pictures (and paid for by local businesses, so take it all with a grain of salt): **www.elbacom.it,** mostly in Italian but with spiffy music; and **www.elbatuttanatura.com,** put up by an Elban hotel devoted to enjoying the natural wonders of the island (with a downloadable newsletter in English).

For help in the hotel hunt, head to the **Associazione Albergatori Isola d'Elba,** Calata Italia 20 (☎ **800/903-532** toll-free in Italy or 0565/914-754; fax 0565/917-865; www.albergatorielbani.it; Mon–Fri 9am–1pm and 3–7pm, Sat 9:30am–12:30pm). Though it isn't an official body, its network does include most hotels on the island, and it'll be happy to give you a catalog and price list.

Elba Orientation

Elba is 17 miles across and 11 miles wide, with Portoferraio on its northern shore. It is the major city and where you will likely spend most of your time. Along the eastern shore are Elba's other port towns—Cavo, Rio Marina and Porto Azzurro. The old Spanish capital of Porto Azzurro, has a 1603 fortress built so well they're still using it as a prison. Today, the fortified Spanish port is one of the island's major resort cities, but you can catch a whiff of the past in the shop fronts and bustle of the old quarter around Via d'Alarcon. From Porto Azzurro, you can see the fortified Capo Focardo across the bay, with the nice resort beach of Narengo leading up to it.

South of Porto Azzurro lies eastern Elba's most picturesque town, the ancient mountainside village of Capoliveri. It's full of twisty old streets, a large terracelike main Piazza Matteotti, and cavernlike bars like the **Enoteca Elba,** on the piazza's edge (☎ **0565/ 968-707**), where you can quaff Elba's wines by the glass until 2 or 3am. In fact, the town is known for its nightlife, as well as for its traditional Thursday market.

On western Elba, Marciana, the island's oldest settlement, is the most attractive and the central base for exploring western Elba. It's a picturesque and very steep little town made of minuscule tree-shaded piazze and winding stepped-stone streets stacked atop one another.

Sleeping

Seasons on the island have seemingly infinite gradations. The highest season is August, when the island is packed with vacationing Italians and you'll find the highest prices and most hotels booked months in advance (and at most places at least half-board required). The second most crowded and expensive seasons are Easter and Christmas, again often with one meal obligatory. Then come various midseasons in June, July, late spring, and early fall. The lowest season is winter, when most places are closed but those that stay open often offer discounts on rack rates. Most of the accommodation on the island is in Portoferraio, where you'll find the best offers for short-term stays.

CHEAP

In a word, **camping.** Bring a tent, sleeping bag, mosquito repellent, and the works.

Campers will discover plenty of options at the tourist office. Ask for a catalog of campgrounds, because sacking out on most beaches is frowned on, and you'll often get shooed away.

DOABLE

→ **Ape Elbana** One of the island's oldest inns, the "Elban Bee" is very simple but sits on the main square in Portoferraio's old town—best for those who didn't come exclusively for a beach vacation. The basic furniture is a bit worn, but the beds are firm, the tile floors clean, and the price as good as you're going to find, especially off season. Twelve of the rooms even have air-conditioning. Some look over the main piazza, while others spread their vista across the rooftops. *Salita Cosimo de' Medici 2, Portoferraio (in the center of the old town, on Piazza della Repubblica).* ☎ *0565/914-245. apelbana@elba2000.it. Double low season 60€–70€, high season 80€–90€, Aug 1–31 with half pension 125€. Rates include breakfast.*

→ **Bellavista** ★ This is a secluded, semi-isolated oasis a 20-minute drive beyond Marciana, set above one of Elba's trendier, quieter villages. The family-run Bellavista is aptly named: Its position at the isthmus of a short peninsula gives most of the accommodations a "beautiful view" of the sea in three directions, and on clear days you can see the whole of the Tuscan coast, Gorgona, Capraia, and Corsica from many windows and the shared terrace. Most rooms still sport uninspired furnishings (though they were replacing those at press time) and cool tile flooring, but they have just finished restructuring the lower floor with new bathrooms and furniture, along with tiny terraces that overlook the owners' modest vineyards and gardens to the infant chestnut grove and wooded Sant'Andrea spur and blue sea beyond. Trails lead into these woods, down to the little Sant' Andrea beach in one direction, or to secluded shoals in the other. Only two rooms are without views. *Sant'Andrea, 57030 Marciana.*

☎ 0565/908-015. Fax 0565/908-079. www. hotel-bellavista.it. Low season double 60€–74€, high season 86€–up. Half pension (10€–24€ depending on the season) available. Small discounts for longer stays. Rates include breakfast.

→ **Villa Ombrosa** On the north shore behind Portoferraio, off Le Ghaie beach, the Ombrosa is one of the best all-around places in Portoferraio. The furnishings and bathrooms vary from room to room, and while a few rooms push the small side of medium, most have plenty of space—they even have some rooms with a connecting door you can turn into a two-room suite. Try to get a sea-view room, most of which come with a balcony (a 4€–13€ supplement). Rates include a beach umbrella and lounge chairs. Half- and full-board options are available. Via A. de Gasperi 3, Portoferraio. ☎ 0565/914-363. www.villaombrosa.it. Double low season 69€–99€, shoulder season 80€–138€, high season 129€–139€ with half pension. Rates include breakfast.

→ **Villa Ottone** ★★ This genteel hotel's showpiece is a gorgeous 19th-century villa overlooking the bay, with basic furnishings but frescoed ceilings (in most rooms) and fantastic views from the front rooms. But the 1970s main building is also fine, renovated several years ago to add wicker units to rooms on the lower floors and 19th-century-style furnishings and Jacuzzi shower/bathtub combos to the nicer (and pricier) third-floor accommodations. All enjoy small terraces with at least a lateral sea view. Sit in the frescoed bar at the Villa's porch above the private beach and watch the sun set over Portoferraio across the waters. The hotel requires a minimum stay of 3 days and half pension, and rates are highly variable depending on the season, the view, and whether you can control the air-conditioning in your own room or whether, as in the original villa, it's centralized and hence not all that chilling. Loc. Ottone (about 15–20 min.

around the bay from Portoferraio). ☎ 0565/933-042. Fax 0565/933-257. www.villaottone.com. May 7–May 28 and Sept 10–Oct 15 double 174€–252€, suite 280€–380€; May 28–Jun 18 and Aug 27–Sept 10 double 206€–320€, suite 320€–440€; Jun 18–July 30 and Aug 20–Aug 27 double 250€–332€, suite 360€–510€; July 30–Aug 20 double 320€–460€, suite 400€–610€. All rates include half pension. Free parking. Closed Oct–Apr.

Eating

CHEAP

→ **Pane e Pomodoro** ITALIAN A great pit stop for a quick focaccia sandwich or a simple *tavola calda* dish such as lasagne. There's also a simple bar with a small glassed-in veranda off the side should you want to sit. Panini go for about 2€, main dishes and pizza for 4.50€ to 7€. Via Cavalieri di Vittorio Veneto, Portoferraio (between the town gate and main square). Open daily for lunch. ☎ 0565/917-121.

DOABLE

→ **Emanuele** ★★ ELBAN/SEAFOOD Behind a beach-bum bar façade hides what most Italian gastronomic critics agree is the best dining on Elba. Snuggled into the beach at the Enfola headland, friendly family-run Emanuele excels at marrying the catch of the day and pick of the crustaceans with fresh pastas and seasonal vegetables. Reserve ahead for one of a few tables on the pocket-size courtyard out back, strewn with gravel and shaded by pine trees and umbrellas just feet from the waves lapping at the pebble beach. The *garganelli branzino e verdure* (sea bass scented with rosemary and tossed with zucchini, carrots, oil, and a bit of peperoncino) is outstanding, as is the simple *tagliolini bottarga e carciofi* (thin pasta strands twirled with grated tuna roe and artichoke hearts). For a secondo, have them grill or oven-roast the sea bream, grouper, or perch pulled in by local fishermen that morning, or try the island specialty *totani alla diavola* (small cuttlefish cooked up with oil and hot peppers). Save room for the *torta di mele* (warm caramelized apple torte drizzled with sweetened cream). *Loc. Enfola (15 min. west of Portoferraio along coast).* ☎ *0565/939-003. Reservations highly recommended. Primi 7€–12€; secondi 9.50€–18€; fixed-price menu without wine 25€. Daily noon–3:30pm and 7:30–11pm. Closed mid-Oct to Easter and Wed until June 15.*

➜ **La Barca** ELBAN "The Boat" is one of Portoferraio's best restaurants. It sees its fair share of tourism but remains a place locals return to for well-prepared fish dishes and a friendly atmosphere. You can dine alfresco under an awning on the quiet street out front or inside surrounded by island art and with a fresh tulip on your table. The *gnocchi all'Elbana* is a good preparation of the potato dumpling pasta with a mix of tomato sauce and pesto, while the *spaghetti alla bottarga* is more traditional—thin spaghetti in butter with dried tuna eggs grated over it. For a secondo, try the catch of the day baked in the oven (the *spigola*, or sea bass, is good) or the *stoccafisso con patate* (dried cod cooked with potatoes, onions, and parsley). *Via Guerrazzi 60–62, Portoferraio (in the old city, a block up from the dock on the landward arm of the "U").* ☎ *0565/918-036. Reservations strongly recommended. Primi 7.50€–13€; secondi 8€–16€. Thurs–Tues 12:30–2pm and 7:30–10pm (June to mid-Sept, dinner is served daily). Closed mid-Jan to mid-Feb.*

Partying

Okay, maybe it's not the Greek isles, but Elba has its share of summer nightlife spread all over the island with plenty of chances to break a sweat, or chill with other tanned bodies after midnight. Finding a cold beer in the evening won't be a problem—there are about a dozen pubs in each major town that pretty much rock all afternoon in the summertime, but hitting the disco will take just a little homework. There are a handful of them on the island, though each a bit out of town.

➜ **Club 64** Elba's first real club was founded in 1964, hence the name, and has kept up with the times (as have some of the '60s-generation hipsters behind the bar). The music is as cutting edge as you would expect for a place with as much experience as this—with three rooms, you can choose between mellow funk, more progressive house, or go all out for hard-nosed techno in the "Groove Room." The location in the shady greenery of the hills offers a mercifully cool breeze. *In Capannone, about halfway between Portoferraio and Marciana, just above the beaches of Biodola and Scaglieri.* ☎ *0565/969-988. www.club64.net. Fri–Sun nights.*

➜ **Il Convio** Club 64's home on the sand, Il Convio is the place to come for a no-holds-barred après-beach party: bikinis, fruity cocktails, and fresh, loud tunes. When it's packed—and on summer weekends it almost always is—the party spreads from in front of the turntables all the way down to, and into, the water. Il Convio is just outside Marina di Campo, on the southern side of the island, where the sand is best and the water bright blue. *Cavoli beach, Campo nell'Elba.* ☎ *0565/987-150. www.ilconvio.com. Open high season (mid–May to mid–Sept) daily 5pm–2am.*

➜ **Sugar Reef** For great live music and a night out a la Key West (i.e., if you forgot your Prada shades and all you brought to wear was a Hawaiian shirt) you'll feel right at home at Sugar Reef. The crowd is laid back and the music (varying from jazz to Latin to rock) is good, and you top it all off with a view of the sea from the terrace. *Capoliveri.* ☎ *338/9179026. www.sugar-reef.com. Daily 11pm.*

Playing Outside
BEACHES

The further south you go in Tuscany, the better and sandier the beaches, and Elba is no exception. There are dozens of different sorts of sands and levels of peace and quiet.

Napoleon Slept Here . . . & Here . . .

In Portoferraio's upper reaches is the house where Napoléon lived in exile for 9 months: The **Villa dei Mulini** (☎ 0565/915-846) doesn't excite much, but you do get to wander through the emperor's apartments and see the books he kept in his study. March through October, it's open Monday through Saturday from 9am to 7pm and Sunday from 9am to 1pm (it sometimes keeps longer hours in summer). Admission is 3€, though the 5€ cumulative ticket also gets you into Napoléon's summer villa just outside Portoferraio (see below); you have 3 days to use the other half of the ticket. There's a rocky little beach, Le Viste, signposted down the backside of the sheer cliff behind the villa. On your way back down toward the docks, stop off at the **Chiesa della Misericordia** (☎ 0565/914-009) or **Santissimo Sacramento** (no phone)—both have copies of Napoléon's death mask.

South of Portoferraio, the road divides at Bivio Boni to head east and west. A short trip west (right) then off the main road, following the signs, will lead you to the entrance to the **Villa San Martino** (☎ 0565/914-688), the more interesting of the two villas Napoléon left on the island. The pretentious neoclassical façade wasn't the ex-emperor's idea—his step-nephew had it constructed years after his death to honor him with its giant *N*s all over. Head to the left to be escorted up a path to Napoléon's more modest cottage—for the former ruler of half the known world, he had surprisingly simple tastes. The only extravagance is the Egyptian Room, celebrating his most successful campaign with *trompe l'oeil* desert scenes glimpsed between hieroglyphic-painted walls and columns. It keeps the same hours as the Villa dei Mulini (above).

The tourist office can provide you with information on the best sort of beach to fit your desires—loud and busy? Isolated and pristine?—but in general, it is safe to say that the southern coast has the best sand and better chances of finding something isolated. In Portoferraio itself, cut through the edge of the new town to the north shore, past Le Ghiaie, Portoferraio's only real (but not great) beach. Farther beyond are better beaches at **Acquaviva, Sanzone,** and **Viticcio.** Barely connected to the rest of the island out here is the large green hump of **Capo d'Enfola,** closed to cars and a lovely place to take an easy hike. You'll also find a small beach at Magazzini, and a bit farther along is the turnoff for a dirt road detour to the 14th-century Santo Stefano, a pretty little Pisan Romanesque church perched on a small olive-planted hilltop. The main road leads north to the fine beaches at Ottone and Bagnaia.

FLORENCE & TUSCANY

Umbria

When the stresses of Italian tourism reach their boiling point, retreat to the hills of Umbria. An easy detour from Rome or Florence, this landlocked and verdant region is a great place to take a load off and enjoy a few days of deep breaths and fresh air. For all its rolling topography, olive groves, and medieval charm, Umbria is often billed by tourism promoters as "the next Tuscany," but we like Umbria just the way it is—grayer and greener than Tuscany, with a less privileged (and less touristed), heartier soul. But don't expect Umbria to be all peace and quiet: The regional capital, Perugia, is one of Europe's greatest college towns and the absolute best place in Italy to party while you study the language.

The other principal destinations in the region—Gubbio, Orvieto, Spoleto, and Terni—are picturesque and congenial medieval cities, each with strong traditions and independent spirits. Most of Umbria lies within an hour or two of Rome or Florence, but some Umbri have never been to the big city. Some have never seen the sea.

Umbria is the kind of region where wild boar run across the roads on the outskirts of town, only to be shot by locals who then make their own prosciutto out of the unlucky swine. If you're here in the summer, you might be lucky enough to stumble upon some crazy Umbria festival (sagra) where they're dressed up in period costumes and impaling effigies of pirates on horseback (and feasting on wine and wild mushrooms).

With roots that go back as far as Etruscan times, Umbria has plenty of ruins, art, and history to keep culture vultures busy—though it's not nearly as well endowed with Renaissance Madonna-and-Child paintings as Tuscany (not necessarily a bad thing).

At the end of this chapter, you'll find a non-Umbrian entry, the splendid and happening university town of Urbino, which is in the Marche region, just north of Gubbio. There aren't enough easily accessible, young, and fun places in Le Marche, so we didn't do a whole chapter on it, and since Urbino is just 30km (19 miles) from the Umbrian border, we stuck in it here. But don't be fooled by its proximity: Once you lay eyes on monumental, marble-clad, ducal Urbino (the "ideal Renaissance city"), you'll know you're a world away from the boar-chasing, mushroom-picking earthiness of Umbria.

Perugia: Ancient & International (and a Great Place to Party!)

164km (102 miles) SE of Florence; 176km (109 miles) N of Rome

In Perugia, you can hear groups of young Swedish women chatting in their native tongue and then ordering a panino with prosciutto in accentless Italian. You can observe an Asian man reading the local newspaper, and next to him, a student from Calabria telling a joke to another friend from his hometown. Perugia is a wonderful little world where cultures and countries collide and coexist in an enchanting city whose roots go back to Etruscan times.

Centrally located in Italy's boot-shaped peninsula, Perugia is home to the **Università per Strainieri di Perugia** (University for Foreigners, see box on p. 338) and the **Università degli Studi di Perugia** (Perugia University), thereby bringing together students from throughout Italy and from across the world. It is also one hell of a steep city—one of the popular local sayings is *c'è sempre una salita* ("there is always a climb"). Perugia is a walking city where you rarely feel plagued by congested streets of *motorini* and menacing Fiats, so your legs will get a workout, but your eyes will always get a beautiful surprise. Perugia's streets dive in and out of old buildings, arches, and high walkways, often providing sublime views of the Umbrian countryside that stretches out like a big green blanket

below. *Le scalette* ("the steps") of the central *Duomo* provide a perfect people-watching perch, and also a view straight down Corso Vannucci, the city's principal street.

Perugia is at its most crowded and liveliest in July, when the world-renowned 10-day **Umbria Jazz Festival** (p. 339) descends on the city.

Fortunately for fun seekers, even when the jazz circus leaves town, Perugia stays true to form as a college town and provides year-round entertainment for its residents. Nestled within the twisting alleyways and side streets are kitschy pubs and intimate dance clubs. Weather permitting, there's always beer being tossed around and ingested in Piazza IV Novembre. The center of it all, Fontana Maggiore, becomes an atmospheric and cheap outdoor bar, perfect for meeting locals, warming up your evening, or getting trashed (see "Partying"). I use the word "locals" extremely loosely, however: The presence of such a diverse student population turns the faces of those milling about Corso Vannucci into a wonderful cultural mix that you can't find in other, more bucolic towns in Umbria. Places like Musica, Musica, a record store with an industrial transformation of an ancient fountain, and the divey

Rock Castle Café take the historic elements of the city and gives it a swift kick in its medieval pants.

The overall result of these stores, bars, universities, and festivals is a beautifully bohemian community that has made Perugia into not only Umbria's municipal capital, but its social and cultural capital as well. In layman's terms, hanging out and partying here is a frickin' fun time.

The Best of Perugia

Best Pub

Buskers A great happy hour with *aperitivo*, dart tourneys on Wednesday, live music, and a kitchen make this watering hole one of the liveliest in town. See p. 334.

Best Cheap Meal

La Botte The Pizza Botte (6.50€), baked in a wood-fired oven with a slew of vegetable and meat toppings, will keep your stomach *and* your wallet fat.

Best Place to Take a Breather

Piazza Italia Grab a panino across the street from the piazza on Via Baglioni 7 and find a spot on one of the park benches in this surprisingly peaceful square. Better yet, plop down on the large steps below the monument and do a little people-watching. While you're there, give half of your sandwich to the emaciated gryphon atop the Palazzo della Provincia. Apparently the mystical beast's all-gnome, no-carb diet does nothing for his muscle mass.

Best Place to Bust a Move

It might be the only place within the city walls to really let loose, but **Domus Deliri** still gives clubs outside of Perugia a run for their money. The music here is usually cheesy and/or dated, but that's what makes it so much fun—students and tourists alike party hearty until 6am. See p. 335.

Best Peroni Perch

Piazza IV Novembre Crack open your liter bottle, get the friendly folks at nearby Mania to pour it in a plastic cup, and relax on *le scalette*. This outdoor watering hole is what keeps Perugia's heart pumping and its liver teetering on the verge of cirrhosis.

Best Bar

No question about it: **Rock Castle Café** can't disappoint. Fantastic music is constantly churned out of the PA, and there's a cheap happy hour, chill clientele, cheap beer, friendly bartenders, and, uh, cheap beer. See how many pints of Beck's you can fit in during the 5€ Power Hour. See p. 335.

Best Umbrian Eating Experience

Restaurant Altromondo Gaze at the ancient ceilings and equestrian ribbons as you sample the divine recipes of *nonna* Anna Maria. The *torello perugino* and the *grigliata altromondo* will floor your taste buds, and her grandmotherly hospitality will make it impossible for you *not* to hug her. Just don't creep up on her when you do it—she's over 70 years old. See p. 332.

Getting There

BY TRAIN

By far the best option for getting to Perugia is by train. Florence and Rome are the natural choices for hopping onto a train to the Umbrian capital. It's about 2 hours from either city with an Intercity (IC) train, over 3 hours with a Diretto (D) train. There are roughly a dozen trains daily between Florence and Perugia, and almost 20 between Rome and Perugia. *Word to the wise:* Fight the urge to get off at the Perugia-Università stop when coming in from the north. I know you're excited to see what the brouhaha is all about, but you'll be dropped off quite a distance from the city. If you're coming from Florence, wait until you get to the Perugia stop; it's the one immediately following Perugia-Università stop.

A one-way ticket from Rome costs 10€ to 24€. Most trains from Florence connect in Terontola, although there are eight daily direct trains as well. A one-way fare is 7.90€. For information and schedules, call ☎ 892021. The train station is away from the main historic center of town, at Piazza Vittorio Veneto. Bus nos. 6, 7, 9, or 15 run to Piazza Italia, which is as close as you can get to the center.

BY BUS

Buses are also a viable, if slightly uncomfortable (during the summer months especially), option. From Florence, it should take you a little over 2 hours and about 2¹/₂ from Rome. Buses for Perugia also depart from the Umbrian towns of Assisi, Todi, Spoleto, and Gubbio, and the Tuscan town of Chiusi (on the main train line between Rome and Florence; Chiusi is also the connecting point for buses and trains to Siena). Keep in mind that there are a lot fewer buses than trains for Perugia. SITA only sends one bus daily from Florence and five from Rome. Reservations are a must.

BY CAR

Driving your own car into Perugia is another story. While the scenery along the main highways of Tuscany and Umbria is some of the most breathtaking in Italy, having a car in Perugia can be a bit of a pain. Parking is damned near impossible in the city center,

and driving on the cobblestoned roads can slow to a crawl when pedestrians wander about. If you're determined to fuel your road-rage desires, Perugia can be reached from Rome and points south by taking the A1 (autostrada) north and then switching to the SS204 (strada statale, or state highway) near Orte. Drive a little farther and then get on the SS3bis north. If approaching Perugia from the north, take the A1 south and then get on the SS75bis heading east. From either direction, just keep following the white centro signs with the nifty bulls-eye graphic, and you'll eventually reach your target, the medieval-looking part of town.

Once you're there, you'll need to park your car somewhere; look for the blue P signs, indicating municipal parking lots, which are all connected by public escalators to the citadel-like heart of town. On the south side of the city, near the train station, the underground lot at Piazza Partigiani (take the escalator up to Piazza Italia) is probably the most convenient option. Two other pay lots are under the Mercato Coperto (elevator up to Piazza Matteotti) and at Pellini (escalator up to Via dei Priori). Below Pellini is a free lot at Piazza della Cupa, connected by escalator to Pellini.

OKKIO! DRIVING Around Umbria

Watch Out for the Wild Boar!

If you want to tour the innumerable quiet and beautiful medieval hill outside of Perugia, in the pretty countryside of Umbria, you'll need a car. Rental agencies like **Maggiore** (the Italian partner of National and Alamo), Avis, and Hertz all have offices at Perugia's train station. Driving in rural Umbria is quite a pleasure, as the distances are fairly short, everything is well signed, and you'll enjoy the freedom of stopping wherever you want along the way to eat at rustic taverns and jolt up at out-of-the-way coffee bars where you'll likely run into colorful locals. Just don't try to drive at night, as almost nothing is lit, even on major roads. Novice drivers in Umbria run the risk of broadsiding a herd of wild boar, and the dark expanses of countryside can get scarily bleak. (If you do take out a boar, throw it in the trunk and let it age for about a year. Boar prosciutto is quite a country delicacy.)

UMBRIA

Getting Around & Orientation

ON FOOT

Once in town, you'll most likely only need two bus tickets for your entire stay in Perugia (unless you visit the Perugina chocolate factory): one ticket to get you from the train station to Piazza Italia, and another for the return trip. (If you utilize Perugia's sneaky public escalators, which whisk you up through the ruins of the ancient town to the daylight of the high city center, you won't even need the bus at all.) Otherwise, you'll be working those sneakers for all they're worth. Mopeds and Smart cars also whiz by on the streets, but Perugia is a town best suited for strollers and wanderers.

Enclosing almost all of the high, historical *centro* of Perugia, the thousand-year-old city walls are most prominent in the south end of the city. You can simulate the effects of a StairMaster workout by making the steep climb to the citadel from outside the walls, or you can take the long, public escalators (night owls beware, they're only open until 1:45am) tucked inside the medieval wall. Exploring the entire area within the walls shouldn't take a brisk walker more than 3 hours (which accounts for getting somewhat lost and having to backtrack), and while the altitude change won't have your ears popping, you can certainly feel proud of your efforts when you look down to admire the formidable walls from 100m (328 ft.) above on Corso Vannucci.

The streets of Perugia's *centro* are surprisingly easy to navigate, and it takes only a couple of glances of the map to get a hang of the town layout. There are three main arteries within the city walls that run roughly north-south: **Corso Vannucci** (Perugia's main drag), **Via Baglioni** and **Corso Cavour.** If you ever get lost, find one of these arteries (just go east-west and you're bound to hit one of the three). Once

you're on one of them, it's as easy as going uphill to reach the city center and going downhill to reach the train station (in the south) or the Perugina chocolate factory (to the north).

Outside the city walls, Perugia's postcard-perfect medieval looks give way to more modern (read: uglier) architecture and lower-cost housing. The university buildings lie mostly in the area to the north of (and downhill from) Perugia's *centro storico*.

BY BUS

Buses are cheap and, unless you have quads of steel and/or are extremely masochistic, are the best option, beside the public escalators, for going up the rather steep ascent from the train station to the town proper. (Taxis are another alternative, but one from the train station to Piazza Italia will cost you anywhere from 8€ to 10€. Be warned, too, that taxi rates get inflated on Sun and holidays with special supplements.)

Buses 6, 7, 9, 11, 13D, 13S, and 15 shuttle between the train station and Piazza Italia. Buses with a number of 15 or lower are run by **APM** and are very frequent. Buses 80 and higher are a different story. They're run by **ACAP** and are quite scarce, running at most seven buses a day. You can buy tickets at the train station or in any newsstand for .80€. If you decide to pay once you're on the bus, tickets can be bought for 1.50€. There are also options for 10 (7.20€) and 20 (14€) rides as well as monthly (35€), 3-month (78€), and annual (255€) passes, but the discounts aren't really worth it unless you plan on spending more than 3 weeks. Oh, and a word of caution: It seems awfully tempting to just hop on the bus without buying a ticket, but if you do get caught, you'll be slapped with a fine of 32€. Trust me, that can of Fanta you planned on buying with the saved .80€ just won't taste as good.

Culture 101: Enjoying Your Drink in Public

There's no better feeling after a long hot day of sightseeing than plopping down on *le scalette,* cracking open a bottle of Peroni, and admiring the revelers at the Piazza IV Novembre, but you might want to think again before twisting off that bottle cap. While drinking alcohol is not only allowed but encouraged in this public square, you'd be smart to pour that beer into a cup before you enjoy it in the piazza. Bring your drink to one of the nearby establishments (see **Mania,** p. 335.) and they'll transfer its contents to a plastic cup. Drinking from the bottle is frowned upon and technically not allowed anywhere on *le scalette* or Piazza IV Novembre. We're guessing the combination of broken bottles and open-toed shoes led officials to prohibiting the glass containers.

BY MOTOR SCOOTER

If your legs have turned to jelly from one too many ascents of Perugia's Himalayan slopes, or you just want to motor around the fringes of the city, rent a scooter. Smaller towns like Perugia make for great scooter driver's ed: you can work on your skills here before attempting the crazy traffic of Rome. **Noleggio Scooter** (Via Pinturicchio 76/Via della Volpe 5; ☎ **075/572-0710;** www.scootyrent.com) rents out the ubiquitous Italian vehicle at incredibly reasonable rates. You can hop on for an hour (2€), a day (15€), 4 days (50€) or a month (240€).

Perugia Basics

Grab your free city map and get any information you need at the **city tourism office** at Piazza IV Novembre 3 (☎ **075/573-6458;** www.umbria-turismo.it). It's just behind the stairs on the right of the Palazzo dei Priori. Hours are Monday through Saturday 8:30am to 1:30pm and 3:30 to 6:30 pm, and Sundays 9am to 1pm. The **APT** (tourism office for the province of Umbria) is at Via Mazzini 6 (☎ **075/572-8937**). At either location, you can pick up a copy of *Viva Perugia* (1€), a monthly publication with information about special events, concerts, and exhibitions going on in town.

The youth information service office, **InformaGiovani,** has all the info you young 'uns need, if you can get up in time for their limited opening hours. There are plenty of brochures to take away (and further clutter your backpack), or you can just scan the bulletin boards for other relevant info. InformaGiovani is at Via Idalia 1 (☎ **075/572-0646**) and is open Monday through Friday 10am to 1:30pm, and with additional hours Monday through Wednesday from 3:30 to 5pm.

Recommended Websites

- ◐ **www.perugiaonline.com** Find a hotel, figure out how to get to the city, and see what events are going on in Piazza IV Novembre on this site. Super-informative.

- ◐ **www.english.umbria2000.it** Official site of the Umbrian regional tourism board. Very cleanly designed and packed with practical and cultural info about the region.

- ◐ **www.en.umbriaonline.com** Tons of info about surrounding cities and towns, perfect for scoping out possible side trip destinations.

- ◐ **www.eurochocolate.com** and **www. umbriajazz.com** Serotonin and saxophones . . . need we say more? These are the official sites for the two best festivals Perugia has to offer.

Perugia Nuts & Bolts

ATMs   The stores and restaurants in Perugia can quickly empty your wallet, purse or fanny pack, but you can easily refill it at one of the street-side ATMs on Corso Vannucci. The most convenient, and possibly safest, location is on Piazza Italia. Before you walk up Corso Vannucci, look to your left and you'll see an outdoor ATM adjacent to the cafe. Now, with your new stash of euros, ditch that horrific fanny pack and get a normal container for your cash. You'll get the most favorable exchange rate by getting money from the ATM (as opposed to exchanging U.S. dollars in cash at some archaic currency exchange kiosk), but it's better to withdraw large denominations infrequently, as opposed to 50€ here and there, as you'll be charged a fee of at least 5€ for each withdrawal.

Crisis Lines
   Psychiatric Service ☎ 075/5412732
   SOS Asthma ☎ 337/237-993
   Battered Women's Helpline ☎ 075/5045596
   Drug Help Line (9am–8pm) ☎ 800/016600 or 840/002244
   Alcoholics Anonymous Association of Perugia ☎ 075/35624

Emergencies   If your stuff gets stolen, or if you just like men in uniform, give the fuzz a buzz: ☎ 112 for the Carabinieri and ☎ 113 for the police. The main precinct (questura) of the polizia in Perugia is in Piazza dei Partigiani (☎ 075/572-3232). This is also where you'd come if you were planning to stay awhile and needed an Italian stay permit (permesso di soggiorno). If you're in need of medical attention, you can call an ambulance at ☎ 118 or reach a doctor at ☎ 075/34024. The vigili del fuoco (firemen—mmm, sexy) answer to ☎ 115 (good to know if there's a fire and/or you need a date), and if you want to battle that parking ticket, you can call the vigili urbani (the traffic cops) at ☎ 075/506-751.

Internet Points   Weirdly enough for a town with so many students, most Internet spots in Perugia are sketchy little places that have three or four computers that rarely work. The best place to check your e-mail is at "ಐ," Via Cartolari 14 (☎ 075/572-1650; atcommunications2000@yahoo.it). It's open from Monday to Friday 10am to 11pm and Saturday and Sunday 3 to 11pm, and there are about 20 terminals, so finding an available computer won't be a problem.

Laundromats   There are several dry cleaning places in the northern stretch of Corso Cavour, but self-serve coin-operated laundromats are tougher to find. The best deal in the city center is **Lavanderia Yuki** (Corso Garibaldi 76). Give Fabrizio 6€ and 2 hours, and he'll wash, dry, and fold your load. It's open Monday through Friday 10am to 1pm and 3:30 to 7:30pm.

Post Offices   Need to ship that 10-kilogram Baci chocolate that you got suckered into buying after drinking too many beers on le scalette? No worries, Piazza Matteotti is home to the main post office, open Monday through Saturday 8am to 6:30pm.

Restrooms   If you fail to convince a waiter at a random bar or restaurant that your bladder is in a critical state, fear not. There are a few public toilets sprinkled, pun intended, around Perugia. There's one near Corso Vannucci 27 (look for the sign in the alley). Another one is perfectly placed in Palazzo dei Priori, on Piazza IV Novembre, which, if you've been paying attention to this chapter so far, you should know is Perugia's most popular beer-guzzling spot. Here, the loo is tucked away in an alley called Via della Gabbia. Go in for a pit stop, and then head back out to the piazza for more booze.

Safety   The streets of Perugia are surprisingly safe. That's not to say that there are absolutely no pickpockets or muggers, but the alleyways and side streets are usually harmless. As in the rest of Italy, do keep an eye out for gypsies; in Perugia, they generally hang out by the train station or among the crowds strolling Corso Vannucci. Drugs are certainly present in the city—a given for any university town—but steer clear of dealers, and you'll be fine.

Telephoning Tips   If you're calling a local number from within the city, you'll still have to dial Perugia's city code, **075,** first. For international calls, students here purchase the **Edicard** from the Pavone Theater (Corso Vannucci) and swear it gives the best bang for the buck. To get a dial tone at any pay phone, you'll first need to insert a regular Italian phone card, issued by Telecom Italia, which can be purchased from *tabacchi* stores in denominations from 2.50€ to 10€. Break off the corner tab before inserting the card into the pay phone. Local calls (to 075 numbers) probably won't run you more than .20€, and calls to land lines throughout the rest of Italy (055 for Florence, 06 for Rome, etc.) stay pretty cheap, too. But if you're calling a cellphone (all mobile numbers in Italy, regardless of where they're based, start in 333, 335, 338, 339, 340, 347, 348, 380, etc.), beware: The charges from pay phones and other land lines to mobile phones are outrageous (often higher than calling the U.S.!), so keep the conversation short. Finally, before you start dialing away from your hotel room to chat with your friends back home, be sure to check with the reception staff about how much it'll cost you. Some hotels charge guests an exorbitant premium for phone use; other more honest souls just ask you to pay whatever the phone company charges them.

Sleeping

Considering the relatively small area that Perugia covers, there are a surprising number of hotels to choose from. Naturally, the main avenue of Corso Vannucci is littered with at least a dozen options in the first half kilometer. Scoring a cheap bed, however, is a different story. There are three hostels that claim to be in the city limits of Perugia, but only one is actually deep in the center of the town (The Youth Center of Perugia). The other two are a 20-minute bus ride from the city walls. If all the hotels are reciting their "Sorry, we are full" line, the tourist office near Palazzo dei Priori, in Piazza IV Novembre, will help you find short-term accommodations.

HOSTEL

➔ **The Youth Center of Perugia** Location is the best feature of this hostel. The other two hostels in Perugia are quite a hike from the city center, but they have slightly better accommodations than this hostel. The bathrooms at the Youth Center are relatively new and clean, but the plastic sanitary platforms can be a bit slippery and dangerous. Rooms are simple and linen is provided (for 1.50€), but the metal bunk beds seem to double as seismic sensors, quaking and trembling at even the slightest touch. With the hostel's location right behind Piazza IV Novembre and high volume of locals who party there, sleep will be hard to come by, especially for those with rooms overlooking Via Bontempi. The hostel has a midnight curfew, but night staff opens the doors for 5 minutes on the hour until 3am to let in stragglers. There's also a kitchen, TV room, reading room, and Internet access (you'll need to buy a phone card outside of the hostel to use it) but you'll probably spend most of your time on the terrace. There, you'll be treated with an amazing view of Perugia, and you'll also be able to meet fellow travelers. The terrace closes at midnight, but by then you'll be on your way to the piazza with your newfound drinking partner anyway. *Tip:* When checking into the hostel, be sure to arrive a little bit before 4pm. The doors will be shut, but it pays to wait on the steps outside, because everyone else who's checking in that day will likely arrive at 4pm on the dot. You'll be glad you came early when you walk up to the reception area and realize that only one poor soul is manning the desk, painfully slowly at that. With only three people in front of me at check-in time one summer day, it took me an hour to get settled in. *Via Bontempi 13.* ☎ *075/5722880. Fax 075/573-9449. www. ostello.perugia.it. Single bed (room of 4 or more) 13€. Linen 1.50€. Shared bathrooms. Amenities: Midnight curfew; Internet access; kitchen; security lockers; TV room. Check-in 4–11:30pm; check-out 7:30–9:30am. Closed Dec 15–Jan 15.*

CHEAP

→ **Hotel Rosalba** ★ If you're looking for some quality rest and a homey environment, go south from the city and you'll find a quaint 18th-century villa sitting just outside of the city walls. Rooms are bright and immaculate with the combination of white floors and walls and dark woods. Adriana, the lovely octogenarian owner, is ridiculously hospitable and is always there to welcome you with a warm smile after a long day of exploring the city. Also noteworthy is the fact that this inexpensive family run hotel provides air-conditioning in each room, a

rarity in cheap hotels in Umbria. *Via del Circo 7 (south of Piazza Partigiani).* ☎ *075/ 572-8285. www.hotelrosalba.com. Single 45€, double 65€. In room: A/C, TV.*

→ **Hotel Sigma** In the southeast corner of Perugia, Paolo and Carla run a small, pleasant hotel of 23 rooms. The outmoded decor does little to detract from its coziness, and the quiet environment ensures quality rest. Most rooms are truly no-frills, but for a few more euros, you can secure a "plus" room. These slightly improved accommodations include a safe, refrigerator, air-conditioning, and a much better view of the countryside. Some rooms are Internet-ready, with Ethernet ports where you can plug in your laptop. *Via del Grillo 9 (off Corso Cavour).* ☎ *075/ 572-4180. Single 48€, double (single use) 54€, double plus (single use) 60€, double 60€, double plus 70€, triple 85€. Breakfast 6.50€ per person. In room: TV, Internet access. "Plus" rooms: A/C, TV, minibar, safe.*

→ **Hotel Umbria** Getting to Hotel Umbria can be a little off-putting at first, as the sign on Corso Vannucci is quite misleading. Just follow our directions: Head down the alleyway, hop over the garbage behind the restaurant, go down the stairs, and then turn left. Once you finally reach it, Hotel Umbria's cute little entrance is a welcome sight, especially at night when the aforementioned alleyway can get a little scary. The accommodations themselves are pleasant, if simple. The bathrooms are clean, and the beds are comfy for the price. Since it's a little off of the main streets, the area is relatively quiet, and you're guaranteed a decent night's sleep. *Via Boncambi 37 (just east of Piazza Danti).* ☎ *075/5721203. Fax 075/5737952. www.hotel- umbria.com. Single 45€, double 67€, quad 85€. Check website for special promotions/ rates. Rates include breakfast.*

DOABLE

→ **Hotel Fortuna** Hotel Fortuna is tucked in one of the cooler side streets of Perugia and

Perugia Sleeping & Sightseeing

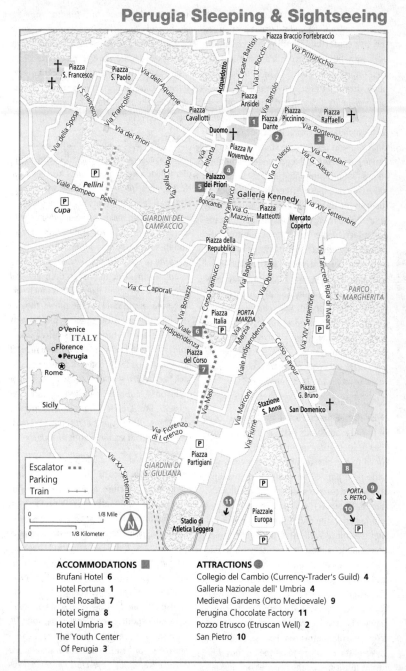

ACCOMMODATIONS ■
Brufani Hotel **6**
Hotel Fortuna **1**
Hotel Rosalba **7**
Hotel Sigma **8**
Hotel Umbria **5**
The Youth Center
  Of Perugia **3**

ATTRACTIONS ●
Collegio del Cambio (Currency-Trader's Guild) **4**
Galleria Nazionale dell' Umbria **4**
Medieval Gardens (Orto Medioevale) **9**
Perugina Chocolate Factory **11**
Pozzo Etrusco (Etruscan Well) **2**
San Pietro **10**

houses 51 simple, yet attractive, rooms. The hotel is only a few hundred yards away from the city center but is still relatively quiet, even with the common room awkwardly situated on the third floor. It's hard to imagine hotel guests getting rowdy in the late hours since, given its location and price, Hotel Fortuna plays host mostly to patrons of the *Matlock*-watching age group. If you're hurting for cash and you really have your heart set on staying at Fortuna, they provide "economy" rooms that offer the same amenities, but in a more cramped space. Either way, get psyched for a sweet round of bingo-beer-pong with your senior friends. Or, you could just take advantage of the free Internet point. Over Easter, long weekends, Umbria Jazz Festival, New Year's Eve and New Year's Day, the Eurochocolate Festival, and All Saints' Day (Nov 1), there's a minimum stay of 3 nights, with higher rates charged. *Via Bonazzi 19 (at Via Larga).* ☎ *075/572-2845. Fax 075/573-5040. www.umbriahotels.com. Single 58€–86€, double (single use) 67€–96€, double 75€–124€. Economy rooms available; call for rates. In room: A/C, TV, minibar, safe.*

SPLURGE

→ **Brufani Palace Hotel** ★★ Grab a couple of friends, pool your cash, and try to score the cheapest room in this joint. Then hop on down to the basement and have your own little pool party. The vaulted ceilings also shelter a separate sauna, but it really isn't necessary since it's already extremely hot and humid in the pool room. Oh, did I mention the ruins? Well, what pool party would be complete without its own set of Etruscan ruins? An ancient well adjacent to the pool and treadmills is in full view, although it is protected by a considerable layer of Plexiglas. Hotel Brufani has pretty much everything to content even the most fickle of folks, from marble bathroom floors, to-die-for views of the countryside off the balcony, luxurious furniture . . . the list goes on, perhaps

justifying the price tag. *Piazza Italia 12.* ☎ *075/573-2541. Fax 075/572-0210. www.brufanipalace.com. Single 215€, double (single use) 275€, double 320€, junior suite 440€, suite 750€, royal suite 850€. Breakfast 23€. Amenities: Restaurant; exercise room (2 treadmills); indoor pool; private parking; sauna. In room: A/C, TV/VCR, minibar, safe.*

Eating

Umbrian cuisine relies on local, earthy ingredients like porcini mushrooms, truffles from Norcia, and *cinghiale* (wild boar, which actually run free in the streets in Umbria's smaller villages), which make for hearty dishes with fantastically rich flavor and texture. Traditional, several-course meals can run you upwards of 15€, but the servings are never disappointing. Due in part to their general hospitality, Perugians like to fill as much surface area as possible on the plates they're serving. Those with smaller budgets or appetites are in luck—this is, after all, a student town, and there is no shortage of affordable and lively eateries where you can kick back with a slice of pizza and watch "The Simpsons," dubbed in Italian, on the big-screen TV. Lunch hours are typically 12:30–3pm; dinner starts at 7:30pm, and most restaurants will seat you until 10:30pm.

COFFEE BARS

→ **Caffè Morlacchi** The Etruscan ruins, medieval architecture, and international student vibe are all feathers in Perugia's cap, sure, but one of its greatest treasures is Caffè Morlacchi, home to one of the best cappuccinos in all of Italy. Pay attention, because that's a statement we don't make lightly. In addition to offering up heavenly coffee, Morlacchi is a popular student hangout with a hip atmosphere and friendly vibe, so if you study in Perugia and frequent Morlacchi, don't be surprised if you return to the city and are recognized by one of the cafe's owners. *Piazza Morlacchi 8.* ☎ *075/572-1760. Espresso, cappuccino, .75€–1.50€. Daily 7am–10pm.*

Mad Kitchen Skillz

Just a few kilometers out of Perugia proper, in the village of Casaglia, the **Scuola di Arte Culinaria Cordon Bleu Perugia (Cordon Bleu Cooking School of Perugia)** can be a fun way to while away a few midday hours while getting up close and personal with the hearty culinary traditions of Umbria. English-speaking instructors offer 3-hour tourist-oriented classes called "Lunch in Umbria," "World-Famous Italian Dishes," "Fresh Pasta," and "Bread and Pasta." You'll get schooled in the importance of ingredient selection and kitchen skills and have an awesome feast while you're at it. Classes Wed–Sat, 10am–1pm. 75€ per class includes instruction and materials. Via dei Lillà 3, ☎ 075/592-5012 or 333/981-3695 (for English). www.cordonbleuperugia.com

CHEAP

MTV Best ➔ **La Botte** ★ UMBRIAN/PIZZA If your stomach is getting the best of you while you wait for the nearby hostel to open, grab a meal here. The smells from the kitchen are a simple, yet effective, marketing campaign, snatching hungry folks off Via Bontempi. While many locals frequent La Botte ("the barrel") for lunch, tourists are often drawn to the *menù turistico* and its extremely easy-to-digest 10€ price tag. The prix fixe meal includes a primo *piatto* (pasta or risotto), secondo (meat or fish) and *contorno* (salad or vegetable dish). There are also a ton of pizzas to choose from, and while their cheese-filled tortellini are certainly tempting, we recommend you go for the filling and satisfying Pizza Botte (6.50€) instead. While you're there, check out the bathrooms—a wacky cartoon sequence tells you how to use the "automatic" toilet seat. *Via Volte della Pace 31 (near Via Bontempi).* ☎ *075/572-2679. Primi 6€; secondi 6€–7€. Open daily for lunch and dinner.*

➔ **Mediterranea Pizzeria** PIZZA Yes, I know it's another pizzeria, but this one needed to be mentioned. Manager Gregorio can be found here flirting with the waitresses or playing with the dog, but he'll always find time to convince you to try their *pizza mediterranea.* The select herbs are extremely refreshing and the size of the pie will leave most quite satisfied. For those who must be super-sized, there's the *pizza Vesuvio.* As massive as its namesake volcano, the Vesuvio is a behemoth stacked with a variety of greens and meats, and, depending on how fresh out of the oven it is, a smoking crater! Beware, this formidable pie has an equally formidable price of 12€, unheard of for pizza in Italy, so you might want to split it with a friend. The pizzeria's streetside terrace is a pleasant place to enjoy your meal or to watch Gregorio try his luck with seducing female pedestrians—the Golden Retriever, of course, is a great foil for his amorous pursuits. *Via G. Marconi 11 (off Corso Cavour).* ☎ *075/572-4021. Pizzas 3.70€–6€. Wed–Mon for lunch and dinner.*

➔ **Pizzeria Pompei** PIZZA The perfect place to have a relaxing, casual dinner after an afternoon stroll in the Medieval Gardens. Since it's just outside the city walls, it's no surprise that the clientele is made up of mostly locals. As far as your appetite is concerned, Pizzeria Pompei has some awesome calzones for a paltry 4.50€. If you skipped lunch and need a little extra, there are larger ones available for 8€. *Borgo XX Giugno 14 (at Via S. Anna).* ☎ *075/572-7931. Pizzas 4€ and up; primi 5€; secondi 6€–7€. Tues–Sun 7pm–1am.*

DOABLE

➔ **Énoné** TUSCAN/UMBRIAN For 10€, you can experience "Drunch," a dinner and cocktail

UMBRIA

with a DJ spinning while you eat. The venue for your hybrid meal is Énoné, an ambitious mixed-breed restaurant/wine bar/club in the southeast part of the city. The inset shelves, trendy furniture, and dim lighting give off a classy ambience, but winers and diners here keep the vibe casual, rarely dressing up in anything beyond jeans, printed T-shirts, and a key accessory or two. Musicians usually accompany your dinner, but the genre of music varies, so you might want to call and find out what music they're playing before you sit down to your risotto only to find the DJ blaring techno samples of party whistles. *Corso Cavour 61 (at Via Giulia).* ☎ *075/5721950. Primi 6€–8€; secondi 10€–15€; menu degustazione (4-course tasting menu) 26€. Wed–Sun for dinner (until 1am).*

→ **Ragni Restaurant** UMBRIAN The reception area of Ragni, with its chic furnishings and dark lighting, gives off a pretentious vibe, but all notions of snobbiness are forgotten once you're seated in the main dining area. There, the relative age of the restaurant is fully recognized. At the time of this review, Ragni was in its infancy—barely 2 months old. The interior, aside from the swanky entrance, looks a bit like a refurbished hotel breakfast room, but the staff and owner try mightily, and succeed at times, to give the place a high-class feel. Dishes are presented in a professional and attractive manner, and they definitely do not disappoint with regard to taste and serving size. The spunky, pierced waitress there is helpful, but in her limited grasp of the English language she informed me that one of the dishes I was eating was made out of "Bambi." After quietly sobbing at the thought of the cute Disney fawn being butchered, I soon realized that ribes (currant) jam was a perfect complement to the slightly salty flavor of one of my favorite childhood characters. *Via Baldeschi 8/A (near Piazza Ansidei).* ☎ *075/572 3395. Primi 8.50€; secondi 13€; menu degustazione 25€; menu tipico (4-course traditional Perugian meal)* 20€. *Added service charge of 2.50€. Mon–Sat for dinner; also Sun during Umbria Jazz Festival.*

MTV Best → **Restaurant Altromondo** ★★ TRADITIONAL UMBRIAN Anna Maria knows her Umbrian cuisine. For 38 years, she's provided Perugia with exquisite traditional dishes and indefatigable hospitality. Altromondo is a converted monastery that combines the ancient vaulted ceilings with the modern flair of track lighting, fake exposed pipe, and a glass enclosed foyer. With a snazzy interior and menu to salivate over, you'll be treated to an intimate and gratifying dinner. Their dishes are characteristic *cucina umbra,* loaded with truffles and porcini mushrooms. You'd be absolutely foolish to miss out on the *penne alla norcina* or the *grigliata Altromondo* (mixed grilled meats) with its succulent veal. Many of their dishes utilize ingredients that are grown on the Altromondo farm, giving them a fresh and distinct flavor that tastes *un'altromondo* ("another world") away from mass-produced fare. A definite must for those wanting a proper Perugian meal. *Via C. Caporali 11 (at Via Bonazzi).* ☎ *075/572-6157. Primi 6.20€; secondi 8.30€–13€. Mon–Sat for dinner.*

Partying

The capital city of Umbria truly comes alive at night. Corso Vannucci, the main thoroughfare, lights up like a medieval tarmac with hundreds of people fueling up on Peroni in Piazza IV Novembre, at the north end of the runway. Rather than taking off at Corso Vannucci's southern terminus of Piazza Italia, revelers seem to stay in a constant holding pattern around **Piazza IV Novembre** ★★★. There, students, locals and tourists alike take part in one of the most elegant keg parties Italy has ever seen. Most of the younger folk gather at the steps of the Palazzo dei Priori, while the 30- and 40-somethings tend to relax in the street-side cafes.

Perugia Partying & Eating

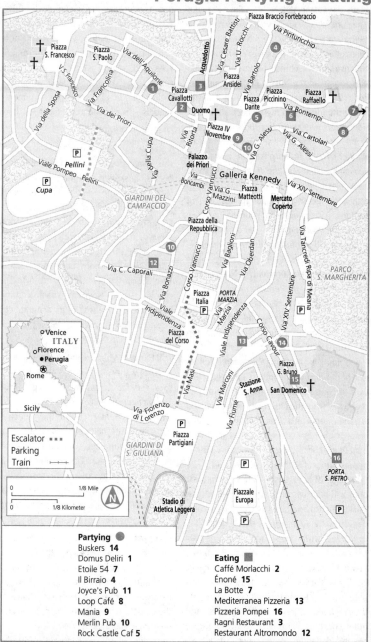

Partying ●
Buskers **14**
Domus Deliri **1**
Etoile 54 **7**
Il Birraio **4**
Joyce's Pub **11**
Loop Café **8**
Mania **9**
Merlin Pub **10**
Rock Castle Caf **5**

Eating ■
Caffé Morlacchi **2**
Énoné **15**
La Botte **7**
Mediterranea Pizzeria **13**
Pizzeria Pompei **16**
Ragni Restaurant **3**
Restaurant Altromondo **12**

The center of attention throughout all this mirth and merriment is the Fontana Maggiore, which can be your bladder's worst nightmare after a few liters of Italy's finest. Thankfully, many of the cafes nearby will let you use their facilities (if they don't, see "Restrooms" in the Nuts & Bolts section earlier in this chapter). If the piazza gets a little too hectic for you, Perugia's back alleys and side streets are the perfect spots for couples, and those with an awful sense of direction, to wander. You'll be surprised at how many pubs and restaurants are tucked in the most unexpected places. During the jazz festival, rather than getting a map for venues and jam stations, try exploring by yourself. Let your ears guide you, and when you do find a jam station, it will be both gratifying and relaxing.

If the outdoors isn't your thing, pubs might be the best alternative. Most of the indoor boozing in Perugia takes place in pubs, as clubs and regular American-style "bars" aren't as widespread in the city center. If you're looking for some hip-hop or R&B clubs, Omar at Ruff Stuff (see "Shopping") is the venerable source for all things hip-hop happening in the area. He'll even organize a small carpool to clubs farther away from the city center if the demand is high enough. (His "environmentally responsible" service seems to have the fringe benefit of earning him a few extra female phone numbers at the end of the night.)

Outside of Rock Castle Cafe's deals, most pubs will pour you a cold pint for 3€ or less. During the Umbria Jazz Festival, a beer company usually sponsors the event and lines the streets with outdoor taps. A cup of beer here will generally cost jazz fans 4€. Glasses of wine can come even cheaper, starting at 2€ if you take your *vino* standing up at a bar, perhaps double that if you choose to sit down. Bloody Marys, vodka lemons, and other cocktails will run you anywhere from 5€–8€, depending on how posh the watering hole is.

If you're worried about what to wear more than how much you'll spend, don't. Only the swankiest places (of which Perugia has perhaps three) will require you to wear a decent pair of slacks and shoes. Otherwise, anything goes, and comfort is key, especially on the cobblestone streets. So, don't worry about feeling out of place with your runners or sandals—it's all good in the medieval 'hood.

PUBS & BARS

MTV Best ➔ **Buskers** ★★ Who knew that this place used to be a feeding area for horses? Buskers is now the stomping ground for patrons who want to enjoy great live music while they down their favorite pints. If your stomach needs something substantial other than Guinness, there's a kitchen (sadly, no trough) to satisfy your raging appetite. Add a kick-ass happy hour (6:30–8:30pm, with the all-important free-with-drink-purchase buffet of *aperitivo* snacks) and you have one of liveliest pubs around. *Corso Cavour 46/Via Guerriera 37.* ☎ *075/572-9202. www.buskers.it. Daily 5pm–2am.*

➔ **Il Birraio** When the librarians at Biblioteca Augusta want to get wasted, they don't have to go very far. Across the street sits Il Birraio. They actually produce their beer in the golden vats near the entrance, and they're actually quite tasty. The main seating area and its windowed surroundings make for an enjoyable beer-tasting session. On certain days, Il Birraio plays host to various live music acts. Be on the lookout for flyers or posters for shows. *Via delle Prome 18 (off Piazza Danti).* ☎ *075/572-3920. Tue–Sun 5pm–1am.*

➔ **Joyce's Pub** One of the more popular pubs in Perugia, Joyce's has the usual offerings of Harp, Kilkenny, and Guinness on tap. The multiple rooms on various levels are great for sheer coziness, but the seat of choice is on the outdoor back terrace. There, between the buildings, you'll get a great view of the surrounding hills. *Via Bonazzi 15 (off Corso Cavour).* ☎ *075/573-6800. Daily 5pm–2am.*

➜ **Mania** ★★ Okay, so this really isn't a bar and it doesn't even have any seats, but it's the place that feeds the masses in the Piazza IV Novembre. Pronounced "Mahn-ee-ah," this place is a snack/candy store that sells cold drinks during the day. At night, it doles out various beers on the cheap and even provides a service to people who don't buy their alcohol there: The kind souls at Mania will transfer your liquid gold into plastic cups for you since drinking from bottles is technically not allowed on the steps *(le scalette)*. The genial owner of Mania has also become somewhat of a local legend. He's nicknamed "Celentano" because of his uncanny resemblance and aspirations to be like the Italian singer of the same name (Adriano Celentano is like an Italian Neil Diamond with a political agenda . . . sort of . . . only quirkier, ganglier, and somehow sexier). Once in a while, he'll come out and try to play the part by flirting with patrons. *Piazza IV Novembre 40.* ☎ *075/ 572-6939. Daily 11:30am–late.*

➜ **Merlin Pub** For a pub that gives off the authentic feeling of an Irish pub, it's surprising that the staff here have a hard time understanding English. Instead, use the international language of pointing (using your index finger, otherwise you'll get a truckload of sass) to pick out your pint. The brick arches leading up to the entrance of the pub are notable, but everything else here is standard. If all the other pubs are packed, this is a good place to fall back to. On the plus side, there's a kitchen that churns out some decent snacks if you're battling a case of the munchies. *Via del Forno 19 (off Via Fani).* ☎ *075/5722708. Daily 5pm–2am.*

📺 (Best) ➜ **Rock Castle Café** After the steps in Piazza IV Novembre, this is our favorite place to down a brew. Rock Castle might be considered a pub, but it also feels like the closest thing to a dive bar in Perugia. There are dartboards, multiple taps of Irish and English ales, happy hour deals that your wallet will appreciate, and music on the PA that's actually worth listening to (rock, ska, punk, hip-hop, electronica). Come here on Thursdays for their Power Hour, and for an unbeatable 5€ you'll be the proud owner of four pints of beer (between 9 and 10pm). Rock Castle isn't on any main street or road, but getting there is painless. Follow Corso Vannucci up to Piazza IV Novembre and veer to the right. Just before Piazza Danti, there will be a small alleyway on the right with a sign for the Pozzo Etrusco. Head down the dark passage and Rock Castle Café will be at the end, right next to the Etruscan Well. ☎ *075/ 572-2315. www.rockcastle.biz. Daily 5pm–2am.*

CLUBS & LOUNGES

📺 (Best) ➜ **Domus Deliri** Even though most of the dance clubs are outside of the city walls, "the house of delirium" is a fun and convenient spot (and the only spot in the city center) to hear semi-danceable music. Tunes here are hit or miss and are heavy on the obsolete hits of the '90s, but it doesn't detract locals from filling up the floor. You can join in on the party, too, provided you can find the place—it's a little tricky: Step 1: Head to Piazza Morlacchi and spot the cafe on the left. Step 2: Once there, go straight and at the second left, you'll find Domus on the right-hand side. Step 3: Go in and start flailing your limbs to some Ace of Base until the wee hours of dawn. *Via del Naspo 3 (near Piazza Morlacchi). Tue–Sun 11pm–6am.*

➜ **Etoile 54** Domus might be the most popular dance spot in Perugia's old town center, but the honor of swankiest club in the outskirts goes to Etoile 54, a *discoteca* occupying a 19th-century villa complex a few kilometers outside of town. Cinquantaquattro has chic sofas, sexy Art Deco paneling, slick lighting, and tasty cocktails that will impress even hardened New York and London nightlife veterans. The club, which is open only Thursday and Saturday, sees a steady flow of students who want to dress up, as well as other trendy locals and wannabes. You definitely need wheels to reach this place, and we're assuming you don't have a car. Not to worry, a shuttle bus leaves the Università per gli Stranieri at 11pm and return shuttles leave the club between 3 and 4am. *Via Madonna del Piano 109.* ☎ *075/38710. www.etoile54.com. Thu and Sat 10pm–4am.*

➔ **Loop Café** This is the place to go when you're looking for a laid-back night. The dark, lounge-y atmosphere is perfect for the jazz acts or the kooky beat poets that perform on its tiny stage. While you sip your cocktail and listen to someone play some standards, you can admire some of the artwork (if you strain your eyes in the dark) from the old couches and ratty chairs that clutter the rest of the space. *Via della Viola 19 (at Via del Balcone).* ☎ *328/613-7300 (Davide, the manager's cellphone). Daily 8pm–2am.*

Sightseeing

➔ **Collegio del Cambio (Currency-Traders' Guild)** I used to work at a currency exchange office at JFK airport, and the only piece of art in my booth was a crudely drawn crayon depiction of me strangling a customer. Back in the old days, currency exchange folks in Perugia had a bit more importance, so they hired Perugia's Pietro Vannucci (Perugino) to brighten up their offices. Perugino left his impression on many places in Perugia, but the Exchange Guild received one of his more imposing pieces. There he frescoed one room with various Christian themes and one of his students frescoed the other. While the frescoes are remarkable, there isn't much else to justify the 3.10€ admission. If you're pressed for time in Perugia and only have time for one museum, skip this two-room attraction and instead devote your time to the Galleria Nazionale. *Corso Vannucci 25.* ☎ *075/572-8599. Admission 2.60€. Mar 1–Oct 31 and Dec 20–Jan 6 Mon–Sat 9am–12:30pm and 2:30–5:30pm, Sun 9am–1pm; Nov 1–Dec 19 and Jan 7–Feb 28 Tues–Sat 8am–2pm, Sun 9am–12:30pm.*

➔ **Galleria Nazionale dell'Umbria** ★★ If you're itchin' to check out Umbrian art, mosey on over to the Galleria Nazionale. It holds the best collection of paintings and sculptures created by famed Umbrian Renaissance masters such as Perugino (born Pietro Vannucci), Piero della Francesca, and Pinturicchio. The latter's *Polyptych of Sant'Antonio* (Room 11) is not to be missed, as the use of unique perspectives and techniques not normally used by his peers make it hard to believe it was created as far back as the 1400s. My favorite piece is near the end of the gallery visit, in Room 22. Here you'll find the *Flagellazione* by Francesco di Giorgio Martini. This 15th-century bronze relief sculpture reveals the technique, also used by Donatello, of bringing figures to the foreground while adding vividness to the perspective. The soft light above the relief panel also enhances the pleading figure and its desperation. The best time to visit the gallery is on the weekend, just as it opens, when there are no swarms of schoolchildren to kick out of your way. On an early Saturday or Sunday morning here, you'll be eerily but pleasantly surprised to find that you're the only person in a room at any one time, which means you'll have plenty of time to get up-close-and-personal with the many (and we mean many) faces of the Madonna and Child. *Corso Vannucci 19.* ☎ *075/574-1247. www.galleria nazionaleumbria.it. Admission 6.50€, 3.25€ EU citizens 18–25 years, free for students in architecture, cultural heritage, archaeology, or art history (must show enrollment certificate or equivalent). Daily 8:30am–7:30pm. Closed first Mon of each month, Jan 1, and Dec 25.*

FREE ➔ **Medieval Gardens (Orto Medioevale)** The signs for this place can't help but conjure an image of some kind of cross between a Medieval Times restaurant and Busch Gardens Old Country, but Perugia's *Orto Medioevale,* luckily, does not involve gorging yourself on mutton and then boarding a roller coaster with 5G turns. Instead, the gardens here offer an amazing view of the surrounding countryside as well as labeled trees and flowerbeds to help you brush up on your Latin botanical nomenclature. Bring your significant other here for a stroll and you're all but guaranteed some romantic brownie points. As tempting as the fountains look when you're parched on a hot summer day, a sign warns the thirsty: *"Acqua non potabile."* Fine, but whatever that stoned-looking gardener in the corner is mixing with his MiracleGro cocktail, we want some of *that. Borgo XX Giugno (head through San Pietro and follow the signs for the Università degli Studi di Perugia).* ☎ *075/585-6432. Mon–Fri 8am–5pm. Free admission.*

FREE ➜ **Perugina Chocolate Factory** ★ The home of Perugia's famous chocolate confection, the hazelnutty *Bacio Perugina,* isn't right in town, but it's close enough. You'll have to use public transportation from Piazza Italia to get your sugar rush (and, uh, all those beneficial antioxidants that chocolate contains). After half an hour of jolting around on bus no. 7, your palate will be bombarded with that sweet, serotonin-producing confection. Tours are available by appointment, but if it's just chocolate you want, Perugina has a store in the city center (Corso Vannucci 101) for all (and we mean *all*) your chocolate needs. *Strada Pievaiola (San Sisto).* ☎ *075/527-6796. Free admission. Mon–Fri 9am–1pm and 2–5:30pm.*

➜ **Pozzo Etrusco (Etruscan Well)** For a rather expensive respite from the blistering heat, you might consider forking over the 2.50€ it costs for a bit of culture *and* a cool break from the Italian sun. However, this attraction sounds more adventurous than it really is—we were disappointed when the Etruscan Well turned out not to be a portal to a *Goonies*-ish fantasy world, just an oversized, 2,300 year-old Brita hewn in soft, volcanic tufa rock. Do watch your step as you tour this relic of ancient plumbing: even though the water should be sitting inside the well, the steps around the well and the bridge

over the well itself are drenched and can be awfully slippery. Admission is reduced to 2€ if you're part of a group, so call up Chunk, Sloth, and the Fratelli brothers, and make it a party. Your Pozzo Etrusco ticket also gets you into San Severo, where you can see Raphael's first fresco, a depiction of the Holy Trinity (1505–08), and into the Sant'Angelo Tower. *Piazza Danti 18.* ☎ *075/573 3669. Admission 2.50€, 2€ for groups of 15 or more. Apr–Oct Wed–Mon 10am–1:30pm and 2:30–6:30pm; Nov–Mar Wed–Mon 10am–1:30pm and 2:30–5pm. Closed Jan 1 and Dec 25.*

FREE ➜ **San Pietro** ★ This basilica in the southeastern part of Perugia contains some of the most amazing frescoes, by such Renaissance artists as Giorgio Vasari, Perugino, and Guido Reni, in Umbria. Ten frescoes, five on each side, flank the main aisle of the elegant 10th-century basilica. Admire them from one of the pews that seem to be as old as the basilica itself, but also notice the arches and columns below the fresco panels. Each arch is elaborately detailed and well worth an extra look. Before you head out to the adjacent Medieval Gardens, ask the man tending to the basilica to turn on the lights (a donation of .50€ is standard), and you'll be able to see the interior in all its glory. While you're at it, also pay a visit to the sacristy on the right. There you'll see five Perugino paintings that were once stolen from the basilica. *Borgo XX Giugno (near the southern end).* ☎ *075/ 34770. Free admission. Daily 8am–noon and 4pm–sunset.*

Shopping

Throwing money around in Perugia is a cinch. Corso Vannucci contains most of the big-name stores, and vendors of all kinds of goods are more than happy to take your euros on this cosmopolitan street. Smaller independent stores can be found on Corso Vannucci's side streets, as well as Corso Cavour and Via Baglioni. Most stores are open Monday to Saturday from 9:30am to 7:30 or

MTV ✪ Get Fluent In Italian, Pronto

Here's the scenario: You fell in love with a local while on vacation in Italy, and the only words you know in Italian, "ciao," "pizza," and "mafia," it turns out, do not form the basis for good communication in a relationship. If you need to kick your Italian skills into high gear in a hurry, the absolute best place in all of Italy to learn and perfect the language is Perugia's **Università per Stranieri di Perugia** (University for Foreigners, **www.unistrapg.it**). One-month intensive courses cost 400€ and are astonishingly effective—people who study here for even 30 days end up way more fluent than those who've taken classes in college for a year. For students with more time, there are also semester-long courses (starting at 750€) which cover Italian art and culture in addition to grammar and vocab. Most professors don't even speak English, thereby providing true immersion, but don't worry, chances are that some of your classmates, who may hail from Sweden, France, or Japan, will speak English, which is a huge bonus when you want to hit the pub and relax in your native tongue after a long day of class.

Perugia is an international college town in an Etruscan/medieval town's clothing—whether you're a native speaker, or only know how to say *"prego,"* you'll find your way around and meet others who are trying to do the same. In addition, the Italian students who go to the regular university in Perugia (some study in the same building, Palazzo Galienga, that houses the Università per Stranieri) are very open to meeting and socializing with "foreign" students, and welcome the opportunity to exchange language lessons. Though the university does provide resources for finding rooms and apartment shares, it's a good idea to arrive in Perugia a week or two before classes start to look for housing.

8pm, closing for a few hours between 1–4pm for *la pausa* (midday break). Sunday, as in most of the rest of Italy, is a retail holiday, with most shops closed all day, or open only very limited hours, to indulge your impulses.

➜ **Brandy Melville** With a name like this, you might think you're walking into a pub in a whaling town, full of peg legs and wistful waitresses, but no . . . Brandy Melville is one of Italy's newer, preppy little clothing chains, and it pretty much channels Abercrombie & Fitch, pandering to the young and uninspired. Clothes here are well made, though, and most of them have a slightly unique touch that reminds buyers that it's not *exactly* like the overpriced American chain. Naturally, clerks here are of the attractive sort, and each possesses a vapid Prozac-like perma-grin. *Via Bonazzi 10.* ☎ *075/573-6261. www.brandy melville.com.*

➜ **Enoteca di Perugia** ★ Find the perfect complement to your romantic picnic on the lawn of San Francesco in this wine cellar. In addition to *vino* from Perugia, Assisi, and Orvieto, you can also find some quality rums here, and budding chefs can obtain superior truffles, the Umbrian delicacy, to add a kick to their polenta. A sitting area is available for wine tasting. *Via Ulisse Rocchi 18.* ☎ *075/572-4824.*

➜ **Filosofi Bookshop** If, somehow, this guide isn't fulfilling your literary needs (and we can't imagine why it wouldn't), Filosofi has the best selection of books to make that train ride to Rome go by a lot faster. The choice of English paperbacks is a little thin, but it's your best bet in Perugia. You'll have to walk a little more than usual to reach this place, just outside the city walls. *Via dei Filosofi 20 (near Piazzale Europa).* ☎ *075/30473. http://libreriabookshop.com.*

➔**4th Dimension** Did someone say shades? If your eyes feel rather naked and out of place among the throngs of shielded *occhi* on Corso Vannucci, you don't have to go very far from the city center to find help. Walk about 50m (164 ft.) southeast from Piazza IV Novembre and enter 4th Dimension. Sunglasses are part of the standard Italian uniform, summer and winter, day and night, and you'll find some from D&G, Ray-Ban, Diesel, and other brands here. I'm still trying to figure out the name, though. If the 4th dimension is time, shouldn't they have opened up a watch store? Alright, enough of that nerdiness. *Southeast corner of Piazza IV Novembre.*

➔**Musica, Musica** ★ Perugia's place to get some aural pleasure. No, this isn't the red-light district (get your mind out of the gutter!),

it's Musica, Musica. Selection here is awfully wide, and there's even a mini-museum of collectibles in the back corner. There you'll find newspaper clippings from old *Rolling Stone* magazines, vintage 45s, concert tickets from the '60s and '70s, and other memorabilia. Even the decor is worth a look in this place. The vaulted ceilings and converted fountain (now covered in fake vines and what looks to be a diamond-plated cross) hint at the building's origin as a Perugian noble's stable and, combined with the rock posters and art, give the store an oddly appealing Medieval-hippie vibe. I, like, challenge you to a joust, dude. *Via Oberdan 51.* ☎ *075/20923.*

➔**Ruff Stuff** Ride your tricked-out Escalade to Corso Cavour to get decked out in the ghetto fabulous store of Ruff Stuff. With the

Umbria Jazz Festival

The exploits of drunken, drugged-out groupies in the rock world have been well documented . . . maybe too well. We could wax repulsive about sexed-out, lipstick-smeared fans of '80's arena rock, but that would get old faster than a Tommy Lee drum solo. Instead, we'll focus on the followers of the classier genre of jazz, who believe it or not, know how to kick back and throw one hell of a bitchin' block party. To witness this first-hand, head to Corso Vannucci in Perugia in the middle of July for the MTV (Best) **Umbria Jazz Festival.** For 10 days, the main artery of the hill town morphs into continuous jam session with a kilometer-long stretch of beer taps, quenching the student population's cravings and reviving the college-damaged livers of middle-aged masses. Throw in a few outdoor stages and some jam stations for some tunes, and you have at your disposal some of the greatest days you'll ever experience in Italy.

   Umbria Jazz is a sprawling affair that encompasses the whole city. Concerts by respected artists are held in the various theaters and venues, free performances are given on stages in the different piazzas, and then there are the "jam stations." These randomly placed "stations" can be found in the back alleys of Perugia. Those who stumble upon them are treated to impromptu sessions where musicians from the festival (easily identified by the large laminated IDs draped around their neck and/or by the skunky stench from a session of a different kind) gather. Made up of guitars, scatting singers, some form of brass instrument and whatever item the percussionist can find (sometimes a wine bottle, other times a simple plastic chair), the sessions can go on late into the night. Once in a while, a random musician will pop out of nowhere and belt out a trombone solo that'll floor the crowd. Apparently, the July festival is the only place you can lug around a trombone in hopes of being socially accepted by strangers.

Festivus for the Rest of Us

More Parties in Perugia!

Okay, so the Umbria Jazz Festival is the mother of all festivals in Perugia, but there are a ton of other worthwhile festivals that occur in the city. Here are a few:

→ The **Eurochocolate Festival,** held every October, is where chocolate makers come to wheel and deal with chocolate buyers and give tourists an extra opportunity to fill their suitcases with bricks of the brown aphrodisiac. Unfortunately, as this is mostly a trade-show type event, there aren't a whole lot of free samples or gifts for the sweet-toothed man on the street, but at the end of the festival, there's a chocolate-carving contest along Corso Vannucci, and the shavings and chiseled-away chunks left over when the sculptures are finished are all up for grabs. www.eurochocolate.com.

→ The **Puppet Festival** in September is chock-full of workshops, performances, and conventions for puppeteers and puppet lovers. Speaking of puppet *lovers,* they'd make a killing with ticket sales if they held a forum about how the raunchy and radical puppet flick *Team America* revolutionized puppet cinema with its refreshing innovation of puppet love scenes. But I doubt that'll happen. Email: info@tieffeu.com

→ **Umbria Jazz Winter** is the neglected younger brother of the much cooler and older summertime Umbria Jazz Festival. In January, while the latter is in the basement of his parents' home, smoking up and eating Cheetos, the former comes to life. A small number of jazz artists and a sizeable contingent from the Berklee School of Music give Perugia a teaser for the real deal in July. www.umbriajazz.com.

→ Pulp aficionados take solace! During the **Umbria Book Fair,** Perugia becomes inundated with parchment and paper cuts. This isn't the same book fair that we had as 8-year-old kids in elementary school, where reps from Scholastic gave out free posters of kittens in the gym in the name of promoting literacy. Instead, publishers from around Umbria hold book signings, workshops, and readings for several days in November.

exception of gold caps for your pearly whites and oversized diamond-encrusted medallions, you'll find every complement to finish pimpin' out your outfit. Omar runs a small boutique on Corso Cavour where you'll be able to grab the latest couture from Ecko, Enyce, Rocawear, Fubu, and Dickies. He's also the one to see for hip-hop festivities in and around Perugia. If the demand is high enough, he'll even organize a carpool to his favorite reggae haunt, 2 Lune (Tuoro Sul Trasimeno, on Lake Trasimeno, 30km/19 miles from Perugia). Hopefully, by the time this guide hits shelves he'll have also opened up

Perugia's first specialized music store, called 7 Inch, near the San Domenico church. The store will focus on, you guessed it: hip-hop and R&B. Needless to say, Omar is *the* man. *Corso Cavour 116.* ☎ *075/5723394.*

→ **Underground** Looking to ditch the duds to impress the ladies on the dance floor at Domus? Men can find some snazzy threads here that'll satisfy you to your metrosexual heart's content. Women can find equally stylish clothing in the Via Oberdan location. Local labels like D-Squared and more familiar names, such as Von Dutch and Dolce & Gabbana, fill the racks of Underground. If you can't decide on the perfect party suit, Marco and the other clerks will jump through hoops to help you find exactly what you're looking for. Now if only you could get some shades to match your tunic and pastel linen pants. . . . *Men's store (Underground Uomo): Via Baglioni 52. ☎ 075/5723993. Women's store (Underground Donna): Via Oberdan 17. ☎ 075/5723174.*

Gubbio: Where You Can Be Certifiably Nuts

40km (25 miles) NE of Perugia, 92km (57 miles) SE of Arezzo, 55km (34 miles) N of Assisi

This is far and away the silliest-sounding place in Italy (as an encore, the residents are called *Eugubiani*) but in fact it is a no-nonsense town, a city of distilled medieval fundamentals. Sharp-edged fortresslike buildings of light stone line long roads that are stacked up the base of the monumental tree-covered pyramid of a mountain.

It was a modestly prosperous city during Roman times—it still boasts a Roman theater—but the fact that the Via Flaminia skipped it helped keep Gubbio out of the limelight and free from complete absorption into the empire. In effect, Iguvium (as it was called in antiquity) managed to remain an autonomous city of the Umbri while many of its Etruscan neighbors were subjected and turned into Roman towns.

Though it was a worthy opponent for bellicose Perugia down the road, Gubbio never neglected its spiritual side. It welcomed St. Francis, and later his monastic cult, and became particularly beholden to the saintly Assisian after one visit. Francis, on hearing of the problem the Eugubians were having with a voracious wolf, went out into the woods and had a serious tête-à-tête with the offending lupine. Francis returned to town with the giant black wolf trotting at his heels and, in front of the townsfolk, made a pact with the wolf that it would no longer attack the local sheep and men if the town would feed it regularly; the deal was sealed with a paw-shake.

If it's starting to sound like Gubbio is almost as odd as its name, well, you ain't seen nothing yet. The town's shops sell certificates proving that you are certifiably nuts if you run circles around one of its fountains, and few other towns in Italy can hold a candle to its collection of torture instruments and medieval warfare paraphernalia.

Getting There

The closest **train** station is at Fossato di Vico (☎ 075/919-230), 19km (12 miles) away on the Rome–Ancona line. Ten trains run daily from Rome (2¼ hr.), and nine daily from Spoleto (40–60 min.). Nine daily **buses** (six on Sun) connect the train station with Gubbio (30 min.)

The bus transport company **ASP** (☎ 075/922-0918) has 11 buses Monday through Saturday (four on Sun) from Perugia's Piazza Partigiani (1 hr. 10 min.). ASP also runs a daily 8:10am bus from Assisi's Piazza Matteotti to Gubbio (50 min.). If you're coming from the north, you'll probably have to change in Umbertide, from which there are three daily ASP runs to Gubbio (45 min.). From Florence, take the daily 5pm **SULGA** bus (☎ 075/500-9641; www.sulga.it) to Perugia, where in 40 to 70 minutes (no connection on Sun) there's an ASP connection to Gubbio. The total traveling time is 3 hours. Monday through Saturday, there's a 4pm SULGA bus from Rome's Tiburtina station (3 hr. 20 min.). Buses to and from Gubbio arrive at and leave from Piazza 40 Martiri. Tickets are available at the newsstand on the piazza.

By **car,** the SS298 leads north from Perugia through rugged scenery. The most convenient parking lot (pay) is off Piazza 40 Martiri. There's also free parking off Via del Teatro Romano on the south edge of town and at the base station for the *funivia* (p. 347), outside the east walls.

Gubbio

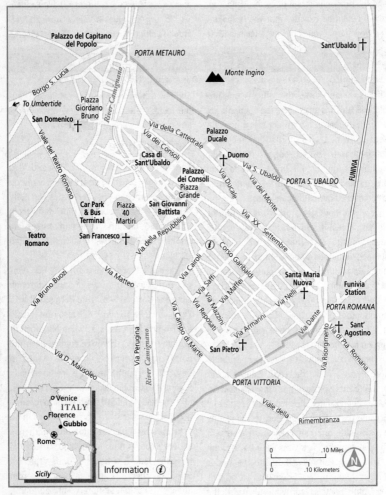

Palazzo del Capitano del Popolo

Sant'Ubaldo †

PORTA METAURO

Borgo S. Lucia

River Camignano

Monte Ingino ▲

← To Umbertide

Piazza Giordano Bruno

San Domenico †

Via della Cattedrale

Via dei Consoli

Palazzo Ducale

Casa di Sant'Ubaldo

Duomo †

Via S. Ubaldo

PORTA S. UBALDO

FUNIVIA

Viale del Teatro Romano

Palazzo dei Consoli

Piazza Grande

Via Ducale

Via del Monte

Car Park & Bus Terminal

Piazza 40 Martiri

San Giovanni Battista

Via XX Settembre

Teatro Romano

San Francesco †

Via della Repubblica

ℹ

Corso Garibaldi

Santa Maria Nuova †

Funivia Station

Via Bruno Buozi

Via Matteo

Via Cairoli

Via Saffi

Via Mazzini

Via Maffei

Via Nelli

Via Armanni

Via Dante

PORTA ROMANA

Sant' Agostino †

Via di Pta. Romana

Via D. Mausoleo

Via Perugina

Via Campo di Marte

River Camignano

Via Reposati

San Pietro †

Via Risorgimento

PORTA VITTORIA

Viale della Rimembranza

Venice
ITALY
Florence
● Gubbio
Rome ☀
Sicily

Information ℹ

0   .10 Miles
0   .10 Kilometers
N

Gubbio Basics

The **tourist office** is at Piazza Oderisi 6, a wide spot on Corso Garibaldi (☎ 075/922-0693 or ☎ 075/922-0790; fax 075/927-3409; www.umbria2000.it, www.global-umbria2oo.it, or www.comune.gubbio.pg.it). It's open Monday through Friday from 8:30am to 1:45pm and 3:30 to 6:30pm, Saturday from 9am to 1pm and 3:30 to 6:30pm, and Sunday from 9:30am to 12:30pm and 3:30 to 6:30pm;

October through March, afternoon hours are 3 to 6pm. The website **www.easygubbio.it** also has lots of good info, for example, on festivals, and Gubbio is a festival sort of town.

Sleeping

CHEAP

➔ **The Hotel Gattapone** A solid, centrally located, affordable choice. All the rooms have private bathrooms, and many have balconies.

All the rooms have private bathroom and balconies, and you'll also find air-conditioning (not always a given in a hotel of this class). The hotel also offers packages for biking, hiking, wellness, and wine/gourmet. *Via Ansidei 6.* ☎ *075/927-2489. Fax 075/927-2417. www.mencarelligroup.com. Double 83€–99€. Amenities: Bar; coffee room; rooms for those w/limited mobility. In room: A/C, TV, minibar.*

DOABLE

→ **Hotel Bosone Palace** ★ The Bosone was built for the Raffaelli family in the 14th century and counted Dante among its first guests. (He stayed here after getting booted out of Florence on trumped-up embezzlement charges.) Splurge and book one of the Renaissance suites, with ceilings stuccoed and gorgeously frescoed in the 17th century, even though the furnishings are imitation era pieces. (Try for no. 212, which has the larger bathroom and frescoes in both rooms.) Even if you opt for the standard doubles, you aren't sacrificing. The spacious carpeted or wood-floored rooms are decorated with a studied simplicity the Brunelleschian Renaissance would've appreciated. The breakfast room sports 18th-century grotesques and stuccoes. *Via XX Settembre 22 (near Piazza Grande), 06024 Gubbio (PG).* ☎ *075/922-0688. Fax 075/922-0552. www.mencarelligroup.com. 30 units. Double 103€, 4-person junior suite 145€. Rates include breakfast.*

SPLURGE

→ **Hotel Relais Ducale** ★★ You can't get more central than Gubbio's (and the Mencarelli family's) newest hotel. In 1998, the former medieval and Renaissance guest quarters of Duke Montefeltro's palace returned to their original purpose—with all the modern amenities added. The largish rooms are outfitted with antiques, and the bathrooms with heated towel racks and Jacuzzis (in some). The mansard rooms with their sloping ceilings are a bit cheaper, but the rooms on the upper floors of the Foresteria have a panorama over the jumble of rooftops and Piazza Grande to the stitched-together fields of the green valley beyond. But even Foresteria rooms on the first and second floors are memorable—a pair inhabits long barrel-vaulted rooms of rough ancient stone. The Caffè Ducale attached to the hotel opens directly onto the center of Piazza Grande, and on summer mornings guests can breakfast on the square. You can even take summer dinners by candlelight on a small hanging garden—or opt for a half-pension deal at the Taverna del Lupo (p. 344). *Via Galeotti 19/Viale Ducale 2 (can also enter from the cafe in the center of Piazza Grande), Gubbio.* ☎ *075/922-0157. Fax 075/922-0159. www.mencarelligroup.com. Double 130€–190€; junior suite 199€–230€. Rates include breakfast. Parking free in public lots nearby. Amenities: Restaurant (w/outdoor dining on the main town square); bar; laundry service; nonsmoking rooms; room service (24-hr.); rooms for those w/limited mobility. In room: A/C, TV, dataport, hair dryer, minibar, safe.*

Eating

CHEAP

→ **Taverna del Buchetto** UMBRIAN This is a crowded local joint, with rough-hewn low wood-beamed ceilings and stuccoed walls. It fills the 13th-century granary where guards from the neighboring Porta Romana gatehouse once stored the tolls paid in the only currency peasant merchants could muster: grain and chickens. The food today is less basic but remains simple peasant fare: *crespelle al buchetto* (a thick sheet of pasta wrapped up with ricotta and spinach and baked with tomatoes and mozzarella) or vegetable minestrone. They also make wood-oven pizzas. Though there's a sizable official list of secondi, the staff would much rather bring you local grilled meats like *agnello alla scottadito* (mutton thrown on the grill with rosemary sprigs and olive oil) and *fegatino di maiale* (grilled pork livers). The desserts are

Candle Racing in Gubbio

The biggest annual bash in Gubbio, the pagan **Corso dei Ceri** on May 15, is one of Italy's top traditional festivals. At 10:30am, a dense crowd packs into Piazza Grande to watch the solemn and inscrutable ceremonies atop the steps of the Palazzo dei Consoli. They involve the mayor, the bishop, three teams of burly young men in colorful silk shirts, and the keys to the city. Suddenly the teams go inside the palace and come charging out with three giant wooden battering ram–like objects called *ceri*, or "candles"—possibly after Ceres, the goddess of the harvest, in whose honor this race may once have been run.

With the 5m-long (16-ft.) candles lined up against the panoramic edge of the square, the teams slip into one end of each a pair of perpendicular poles and attach small statues of St. George, St. Anthony, or the city's patron St. Ubaldo to the other end of each candle. Then each team captain climbs up the poles of his candle and is handed a giant painted ceramic vase full of water. At 11:30am, men hanging directly onto the bell tower's largest bell use their body weight to start it swinging and ringing—the signal to raise the candles. The three captains give a shout, and as their teams leverage the *ceri* (candles) upright, the captains heave the water-filled jugs as far as they can into the crowd. The mass of people parts briefly to let the vases fall and shatter, then descends on the shards in a mad frenzy to acquire a piece—it signifies good crops and good luck for the next year. The candles, now upright, each topped by a saint, and shouldered by the teams, are run three times around the piazza, and then taken off on a long prescribed route through the city streets.

At 2pm, the teams leave the candles on Via Savelli della Posta and return to the Palazzo dei Consoli, where they sit down to an enormous seafood banquet in the medieval hall. At 4:30pm, there's a solemn religious procession of the relics of St. Ubaldo and the *ceri* as they're carried to Via Dante. At 6pm, the real race begins. The teams grab their candles and make another frenetic run through town. With candles swaying and people cheering, they race again around Piazza Grande and then hightail it up to the gate to the mountain road. After a brief pause, the teams pick up their candles and, perhaps the most stupefying part of the whole day, begin running like the devil straight up the mountainside. It's more than 300m (984 ft.) of vertical elevation along a switchbacked road, but they reach the finish line at the mountainside basilica of Sant'Ubaldo in under 6 minutes. The first one inside the front doors tries to shut them before the losers get there. But, and this is the best part, the whole race is fixed. St. Ubaldo always wins. The real contest is to see how many times the runners let their candle fall; those that touch ground the fewest times are the real winners of the day.

homemade, and the hearty laughter of the young owner Fabrizio and his cronies competes with the TV to add noise to the general convivial chaos. *Via Dante 30 (at Porta Romana).* ☎ *075/927-7034. Reservations recommended. Pizza 3.50€–9€; primi 7€–9€; set-price menus without wine 14€–18€.* *Tues–Sun noon–3pm and 7–11pm. Closed 2 weeks in Feb.*

SPLURGE

➜ **Taverna del Lupo** ★ ITALIAN/UMBRIAN
Each of the five tunnels of vaulted stonework that make up this 30-year-old Eugubian

culinary landmark feels like a little medieval trattoria. This is where Rodolfo Mencarelli launched in 1968 what has become a small Umbrian hospitality empire—it includes the hotels Bosone, Relais Ducale, and Gattapone. Begin with the *delizie tipiche Umbre,* "typical Umbrian delicacies" that may include a *rosa di arista* (a cold salad of roast pork topped with thinly sliced pears and pecorino cheese). The *frittatina gentile con lamelle di tartufo* (cheese omelet under a shower of white truffle flakes) is excellent, as is the *sfogliatina del Lupo con tartufo* (a light lasagna made with cheese, bits of ham and mushrooms, tiny cubes of tomato, and white truffle shavings). To stay with the precious white mushroom, you can order as a secondo the *scaloppina affogato di tartufo* (a tender veal scallop "drowning" in truffles) or the simple and juicy *agnellino* (charcoal-grilled Umbrian lamb). The ever-changing desserts are inventive and delectable. *Via Ansidei 21 (on the corner of Via Repubblica, a few blocks uphill from Piazza 40 Martiri). 075/927-4368. Reservations strongly recommended. Primi and secondi 7€–18€; tasting menus without wine 18€–46€. Tues–Sun 12:15–3pm and 7pm–midnight.*

Sightseeing

→ **Duomo** On your way up Via Ducale toward the cathedral, peek through the grate over the basement storeroom of the Palazzo dei Canonici, where sits a rather large 15th-century wine barrel, boggling the mind with its 19,760-liter capacity. The interior of the 13th-century cathedral is striking for its "wagon vaulting," a receding series of pointed arches defining the graceful bulk and space of the single central nave. Most of the art on the nave altars is by local talent, including multiple works by Virgilio Nucci, Benedetto Nucci, Sinibaldo Ibi, and Antonio Gherardi. In the fourth niche on the right is a Pietà by Dono Doni, who also painted the Way to Calvary in the seventh niche. In between the

two, the fifth chapel on the right is a florid baroque contraption (1644–72). The fine stained glass in the presbytery is a 1913 opus, and don't miss the Nativity in the left aisle's sixth niche, a work by a follower of Pinturicchio (perhaps Eusebio di San Giorgio).

The restored Palazzo dei Canonici next door now contains a small **Museo Diocesano,** with paintings by Sassoferrato and Il Pomarancio; admission to the museum costs 4.50€ for adults. *Via Ducale and Via della Cattedrale.* ☎ *075/922-0904. www.museogubbio.it. Daily 10am–1pm and 3–7pm.*

→ **Museo Civico e Pinacoteca Comunale (Palazzo dei Consoli and Museum)** On Gubbio's main square, Piazza Grande, is the 14th-century Palazzo dei Consoli, whose off-center 91m (298-ft.) bell tower dominates Gubbio from afar. Inside the vast and poorly lit barrel vault of the main hall, used for public assemblies of the medieval commune, is the town's archaeological museum, with the largest collection of Roman materials in Umbria. There are dozens of broken statues, stretches of cornice, and other architectural fragments, inscriptions, sarcophagi, and amphorae, all leaning against the walls as if someone just set them down temporarily—it's been this way for decades. At the base of the staircase are a few rooms with small found objects like coins and metal implements and, in a back room, the seven Eugubian Tables. These bronze tablets preserve the most extensive example of the Umbrian language. (The Umbri apparently had no alphabet of their own, so they used first Etruscan and later Latin characters and adapted them to spell Umbrian words phonetically.) The tablets were inscribed from 200 to 70 B.C. and tell a bit about Gubbio's ancient territory and enemies but mainly detail the finer points of religious divination—they're priestly textbooks to help find the will of the gods through animal sacrifice and watching the flight patterns of birds. These are the single most detailed set of religious

You, Too, Can Be Certifiably Crazy!

Via dei Consoli runs downhill out of the west end of Piazza Grande past medieval palazzi to Largo del Bargello and its Gothic Palazzo del Bargello (1302), the city's first medieval town hall. At the tiny square's center is the **Fontana dei Pazzi** (Fountain of the Crazies): You can become a certified Eugubian lunatic if you run around the fountain three times—sticklers will also need to draft three locals to splash water on them as they run. You may pick up your *patente da matto* ("certificate of madness") from any of the surrounding shops. Speaking of odd habits, in the palaces along these streets you'll notice many bricked-up openings that look caught between being a door and being a window. Usually near the main entrance but a few feet above ground, these are known as *porte della morte* ("doors of the dead"). Tradition holds they were used strictly to convey corpses on their final journey out of the house. Whether this was indeed one of the purposes of these doorways—which show up across northern Umbria and nearby Tuscan towns such as Cortona, as well as in the south of France—is unknown. But the fact that behind them is usually a narrow stair leading directly up to the first floor (American second floor) suggests the doors more likely served in times of defense, when the main portal was blocked off.

instructions and explanations that survive from any antique culture and are of incalculable value for the insights they offer into the religious and social life of the ancient world. A local farmer turned up the tablets while he was plowing his fields in 1444, and the city convinced him to sell them for 2 years' worth of grazing rights. *Piazza Grande.* ☎ *075/927-4298. Admission 5€, 2.50€ ages 7–25. Daily Apr–Sept 10am–1pm and 3–6pm, Oct–Mar 10am–1pm and 2–5pm.*

→ **Palazzo del Capitano del Popolo** This 13th-century palazzo was restored by its occupant, who has assembled a collection of medieval torture instruments but uses them as a draw for visitors so he can show off his homemade charts. These, he claims, prove the sky quadrants drawn by the ancient Umbri soothsayers and codified in the Eugubian Tables (housed in the Palazzo dei Consoli) were focused on this spot. Stop by only if you're interested in rusty chastity belts, back-breaking racks, and other torture devices. *Via Capitano del Popolo at Via Gabrielli.* ☎ *075/922-0224. Admission 3€. Daily 10am–8pm.*

→ **Porta Romana** The 13th-century Porta Romana is the only survivor of the six identical defensive towers that guarded Gubbio's entrances. Its private owners are serious history buffs who have restored the gate tower and set up an eclectic, but worthy, museum inside. The museum's most valuable installation is a collection of more than 250 majolica pieces spanning local production from 1500 to 1950. In the central display case are two Maestro Giorgio plates signed and dated 1530, another one attributed to him, and eight pieces by his son and workshop. (The city itself owns only one of Maestro Giorgio's works.)

The old guard tower above is equipped with lances, crossbows, axes, and a 19th-century suit of armor. The owners are inordinately proud of their chastity belt collection, and preserve an odd crossbowlike sling with which nobles once stoned birds. The gaping hole in the floor was defensive, used to pour boiling water down on attackers—hot oil, Hollywood siege scenes notwithstanding, was much too expensive to waste in this manner. *Porta Romana (Via Dante 24).* ☎ *075/922-1199. www.museoportaromana. supereva.it. Admission 2.60€ adults. Daily 9am–1pm and 3:30–7:30pm (until 8pm in summer).*

FREE → **San Francesco** One of the earliest churches built in honor of St. Francis, this bulky structure with three Gothic apses and an octagonal bell tower was raised in the mid–13th century. Inside, all three apses were painted with high-quality frescoes by the Eugubian school. (There's a free light switch behind the speaker next to the confessional on the left aisle to illuminate the chapels.) The chapel to the right of the main apse was frescoed in the 14th century on two levels with the Life of St. Francis in the upper half and a gaggle of saints in the lower. A cloister behind the apse (enter around the back at Piazza 40 Martiri no. 4) preserves a 14th-century crucifixion fresco and pieces of a 3rd-century A.D. Roman floor mosaic that still show some color. Across Piazza 40 Martiri, named after the 40 citizens who were shot by Nazis in 1944 for aiding the partisan movement, is the squared-off, second-story brick arcade of the **Loggia dei Tiratori.** Built in 1603 as a space where local textile workers could dye wool and stretch it to dry, the loggia is the best surviving example of these structures, which were once widespread throughout the peninsula. *Piazza 40 Martiri. No phone. Free admission. Daily 7:30am–noon and 4–7pm.*

FREE → **Teatro Romano** South of the city walls toward the west end of town, in an overgrown grassy park where Eugubians walk their dogs, the remains of a large Roman theater sprout weeds. Although mined during the Middle Ages for its limestone blocks, the theater's cavea has been restored, and several arches that once ringed the back remain. Normally closed to visitors, the theater is used in summer for classical music performances under the stars, with the illuminated buildings of medieval Gubbio as a backdrop. On the gravel of the parking lot between the theater and the main road, old men gather to play bocce ball in the late afternoon. *Off Via del Teatro Romano.*

Playing Outside

EXPLORING THE MOUNTAINS AROUND GUBBIO

→ **Bottaccione Gorge** Out the Porta Metauro, the road toward Scheggia winds above the Camignano stream in the Bottaccione Gorge between mounts Ingino on the right and Foce on the left, a steep and rocky landscape spotted with ilex trees. The 390m (1,279 ft.) of folded geologic strata here recorded a 50-million-year slice of time, including the evidence that led to the popular theory that a huge asteroid impact caused the extinction of the dinosaurs. (American scientists found radioactive minerals, uncommon on Earth but not in asteroids, in the geological layer here corresponding to 65 million B.C.)

On Mount Foce, off a path reached by backtracking down Via del Fosso from Porta Metauro, are the remains of prehistoric Cyclopean walls and the 13th-century Hermitage of Sant'Ambrogio, with some frescoes inside and a 14th-century aqueduct nearby.

→ **Monte Ingino** Outside Porta Romana, a left up Via San Gerolamo leads to the base of the *funivia,* a ski-lift contraption that dangles you in a little blue cage as you ride up the side of Mount Ingino (see below for hours and cost; you can also walk up steep Via San Ubaldo from behind the Duomo, a vertical elevation of 300m/984 ft.). It lets you off just below the Basilica di Sant'Ubaldo. The current structure is a 16th-century incarnation over whose high altar the withered corpse of the local patron saint, Ubaldo, is preserved in a glass casket. Stored in the aisle are the three giant wooden *ceri* used during the annual Corso dei Ceri (see "Festivals & Markets," earlier in this section).

You can take a path leading from the sanctuary farther up the mountainside to the traces of the 12th-century *Rocca* (fortress), sitting on the pinnacle of the 900m (2,950-ft.) mountain. The virtually unspoiled, wide Saonda Valley lies beyond Gubbio, but even more spectacular is the **panorama** ★★ that opens up east across the surprisingly wild Apennine Mountains and the snowy peaks of Monte Cucco National Park at the Marches' border in the distance. A few trails run off here if you want to do some backwoods exploring.

The *funivia* (☎ 075/927-3881) lift runs daily, but with excruciatingly complicated hours: November through February from 10am to 1:15pm and 2:30 to 5pm; March from 10am to 1:15pm and 2:30 to 5:30pm (Sun 9:30am–1:15pm and 2:30–6pm); April through May from 10am to 1:15pm and 2:30 to 6:30pm (Sun 9:30am–1:15pm and 2:30–7pm); June from 8:30am to 1:15pm and 2:30 to 7pm (Sun 9am–7:30pm); July through August from 8:30am to 7:30pm (to 8pm Sun); September from 9:30am to 7pm (Sun 9am–7:30pm); and October from 10am to 1:15pm and 2:30 to 5:30pm. Round-trip tickets are 5€; one-way tickets are 4€.

Shopping

Gubbio's fame as a ceramics center had its beginnings in the 14th century. In the 1500s, the industry rose to the height of its fame. Sometime during this period, Mastro Giorgio pioneered a particularly intense iridescent ruby red that awed his competitors. Today, pottery workshops are found all over town, with beautiful flowery plates lining the walls of shop doorways. You can't miss them.

Two of the best outlets are in the town center: **Ceramica Rampini** ★, at Via Leonardo da Vinci 94 (☎ 075/9272963), where you can visit the workshop, and the Rampini store, at Via dei Consoli 52 (☎ 075/9274408). Its largest competitor, **La Mastro Giorgio** ★, Piazza della Signoria 3 (☎ 075/9271574), opens its factory at Via Tifernate 10 (☎ 075/9273616), about 1km (²/₃ mile) from the center, to visitors who phone in advance.

Gubbio is also known for its replicas of medieval crossbows (*balestre*), which are prized as children's toys and macho decorative ornaments by aficionados of such things. If you feel like you can get it back on the plane home, head for **Medioevo,** Ponte d'Assi (☎ 075/9272596). Your souvenir will cost from 13€ for a cheap version to as much as 75€ for something much more substantial.

Spoleto & the Mother of All Festivals

48km (30 miles) SE of Assisi, 209km (130 miles) S of Florence, 64km (40 miles) SE of Perugia

This Umbrian town, pleasant and interesting as it is, would not be in this book or on any other major itinerary if not for the world-renowned festival here every summer. Dreamed up in 1958 by the Italian-American composer Gian Carlo Menotti, the Spoleto Festival brings heavy-duty culture to Spoleto in the form of music, dance, and theater showcased by premier Italian and international performers. The celebration of modern works, both conservative and experimental, draws thousands of visitors annually.

Although it often seems to revolve around it, Spoleto doesn't begin and end with the festival. A forgotten small city in the 1950s when Menotti chose it as the festival site, Spoleto started out as a Bronze Age Umbri settlement. And as a Roman town in the 3rd century B.C., it repulsed the fierce invader Hannibal. Strategically situated on the ancient Via Flaminia from Rome to the late imperial capital of Ravenna, Spoleto became the stronghold of many powers during the Dark Ages. The Lombards made it the capital of their empire in the 8th century A.D., and the duke they installed here governed all Umbria and much of the rest of central Italy. At the turn of the 12th century, Spoleto fell into papal hands, and its twilight began.

In the 12th century, Spoleto was the birthplace of Alberto Sotio, the earliest known Umbrian painter, and Lo Spagna, a pupil of Perugino. But the city's main nonmusical treasures are Roman and medieval. Though nothing other than the Duomo, containing Filippo Lippi's last fresco cycle, and the graceful Ponte delle Torri really stands out, the town as a whole makes for an interesting afternoon.

Getting There

Spoleto is a main station on the Rome-Ancona line, and all 16 daily **trains** from Rome stop here (about 1½ hr.). From Perugia, take one of the 20 daily trains to Foligno (25 min.) to transfer to this line for the final 20-minute leg. The one-way fare from Rome to Spoleto is 7€ to 12€. The fastest train takes about 90 minutes; those requiring connections can take 2½ hours. Trains also run several times a day between Perugia and Spoleto; the ride lasts about an hour and costs 3.50€ to 8.20€ each way. The **rail station** in Spoleto (☎ 892021)

is at Piazza Polvani, just outside the historic heart. Notice the gigantic statue in front by Philadelphia-born artist Alexander Calder. SSIT bus no. A, B, C, or D will take you from the station into Piazza della Libertà in the town center, for 1€. Buy your ticket for the Circolare at the bar, perhaps along with an espresso, in the rail station.

If you're coming by **car,** Spoleto is *over* the SS3 (the road tunnels under the city), the old Roman Via Flaminia running north from Rome and connecting in Foligno with the SS75 from Perugia. Parking in the old town is free only along Via Don Bonilli next to the soccer stadium and off Viale dei Cappuccini. (Turn left off the SS3 onto Viale G. Matteotti, then left again.) There's also a parking lot off Piazza della Vittoria on the north end of lower Spoleto.

Spoleto's bus company, **SIT** (☎ **0743/ 212-211;** www.sitbus.com), runs buses into Piazza della Vittoria (connected to Piazza Garibaldi) from Perugia (two afternoon runs, weekdays only; 1 hr.) and Rome (an early morning and midafternoon run to Terni, where you can switch to many Spoleto-bound coaches; 2½ hr. total). If you can reach Foligno by other means, there are lots of buses from there.

UMBRIA

The Spoleto Festival

Spoleto's be-all and end-all annual event bridges the end of June and early July. 📺 Best The Spoleto Festival ★★★ (www.spoletofestival.it) is 3 weeks of world-class drama, music, and dance held in evocative spaces like an open-air restored Roman theater and the pretty piazza fronting the Duomo. The festival's cultural beacon keeps the arts alive here for part of the rest of the year. A secondary "Spoletoestate" season of music, art, and theater runs from just after the festival ends through September. (Contact the tourist office for info.) The "A. Belli" opera and experimental musical theater season runs from late August to October (☎ 0743/221-645; fax 0743/222-930; www.tls-belli.it). May and June are full of organ concerts in local churches, and the theater season runs November through March. (Call the Communal Cultural Office at ☎ 0743/218-202 for details.)

Spoleto Basics

The large **information center** at Piazza della Libertà 7 (☎ **0743/220-773** for hotels and such, ☎ 0743/238-920 for sightseeing and events; fax 0743/46-241; www.umbria2000.it) hands out scads of info and an excellent, if oversized, map. It's open daily from 10am to 1pm and 2 to 7pm.

Sleeping

CHEAP

➔ **Hotel Aurora** The Aurora is on a quiet courtyard just off Corso Mazzini where it exits Piazza Libertà, with amenities and a level of comfort surprisingly high for its government two-star rating and low prices. The modern rooms have been refitted with faux 19th-century cherry-veneer furniture, new beds, and rich, quasi-Renaissance-style fabrics on the cloth headboards, coverlets, and window curtains. The worn carpet is currently being replaced with hardwood flooring. A few rooms have balconies. The hotel is allied with the Apollinare underneath, a restaurant famed for its fine Umbrian cuisine (add 16€ per person for half-board option and 26€ for full-board plan). *Via Apollinare 3 (near Piazza Libertà). ☎ 0743/220-315. Fax 0743/221-885. www.hotelauroraspoleto.it. Double 52€–80€. Rates include breakfast.*

➔ **Hotel Charleston** ★ Many of the rooms in this friendly hotel nestled in a medieval district next to the new modern art museum are quite large and have a 1970s artist's loft feel, with good use of available space and mismatched but tasteful furnishings—though the new owners are replacing most with antique-style pieces. Rough-hewn chestnut-beamed ceilings mirror the wood-plank floors (some are carpeted), and the walls are hung with modern art prints and original works. The firm beds are spread with Black Watch plaid coverlets. If you're feeling particularly hedonistic, you can cough up 10€ for a trip to the basement sauna, or just cozy up on a

cushy sofa before the wintertime fire crackling between the TV and sitting lounges. The room TVs come with VCRs, and the front desk always has a movie or two in English. They also organize all sorts of specialized tours (cooking classes, horseback rides, truffle hunts, and so on). *Piazza Collicola 10 (near San Domenico). ☎ 0743/220-052. Fax 0743/221-244. www.hotelcharleston.it. Double 59€–121€, triple 93€–143€. Rates include breakfast. Parking 10€. Amenities: Bar; dry cleaning; laundry service; nonsmoking rooms; room service (24-hr.); sauna. In room: A/C, hair dryer, minibar.*

DOABLE

➔ **Nuovo Hotel Clitunno** ★ Little is left from the time when this 19th-century palazzo was a firehouse. But the Tomassoni family's welcome augments the comfort and warmth of the public area's fireplace, beamed ceilings, and gold-plastered walls. To accommodate disparate tastes, some guest rooms were left in "standard" style, with stylish contemporary furnishings in warm pastel colors, while 10 were refitted in 2001 as *"camere in stile,"* or "old-style rooms." Request one and you'll get parquet or terra-cotta floors, antique iron beds and sconces, armoires, and rough-hewn ceiling beams. All have new bathrooms but only 15 of the standard-style rooms offer a handsome view over the Vale Spoletino. The friendly Tomassoni brothers, Francesco and Filippo, really put themselves out for guests. *Piazza Sordini 6 (just west of Piazza della Libertà), 06049 Spoleto (PG). ☎ 0743/223-340. Fax*

Spoleto

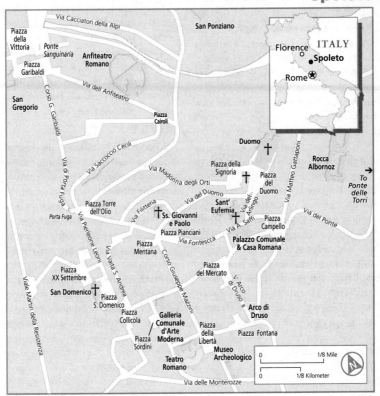

Via Cacciatori della Alpi

Piazza della Vittoria

Ponte Sanguinaria

Piazza Garibaldi

Anfiteatro Romano

San Ponziano

ITALY

Florence ○

● Spoleto

Rome ✕

Via dell'Anfiteatro

San Gregorio

Corso G. Garibaldi

Piazza Cairoli

Via Saccoccio Cecili

Via di Porta Fuga

Duomo ✝

Rocca Albornoz

Via Matteo Gattaponi

→ To Ponte delle Torri

Piazza della Signoria ✝

Via Madonna degli Orti

Via del Duomo

Piazza del Duomo

Piazza Torre dell'Olio

Porta Fuga

Via Pierleone Leoni

Via Filitteria

✝ Ss. Giovanni e Paolo

Sant' Eufemia

Via del Ponte

Piazza Pianciani

Via A. Saffi

Piazza Campello

Piazza Mentana

Via Fontescca

Palazzo Comunale & Casa Romana

Via Valta S. Andrea

Corso Giuseppe Mazzini

Piazza del Mercato

Piazza XX Settembre

Viale Martiri della Resistenza

San Domenico ✝

Piazza S. Domenico

V. Arco di Druso

Arco di Druso

Piazza Collicola

Galleria Comunale d'Arte Moderna

Piazza della Libertà

Piazza Fontana

Piazza Sordini

Museo Archeologico

Teatro Romano

Via delle Monterozze

0   1/8 Mile
0   1/8 Kilometer

0743/222-663. *www.hotelclitunno.com.* 45 units. *Standard double 84€–134€; in style double 94€–140€. Rates include buffet breakfast. Free parking. Closed Feb.*

SPLURGE

→ **Hotel Gattapone** ★★ Spoleto's most stratospheric hotel is a clutch of 17th-century buildings clinging to the cliff behind the *Rocca*—isolated and surrounded by nature but still only a 3-minute stroll from the Duomo. It was formerly an artist's home, and its interiors were remodeled to maximize views of the valley and the remarkable 14th-century arched bridge nearby. Most of the wood-floored accommodations have plenty of elbowroom, and while the styling dates from the hotel's birth in the 1960s, it has aged well. The

superior rooms have large picture windows, big bathrooms with tubs, and often a dais separating the beds from the sofa-and-desk living area. The standard rooms aren't as large or well appointed but are still worthwhile. The small terrace off the conference room overlooks the full splendor of the bridge, and terraced gardens off the other end of the buildings, where the view, alas, is marred by a highway, are in the works. *Via del Ponte (near the fortress at the top of town).* ☎ *0743/223-447. Fax 0743/223-448. www.hotelgattapone.it. Standard double 140€–170€, superior double 170€–230€. Breakfast included. Free parking. Amenities: Laundry service; lounge; non-smoking rooms; room service (breakfast only). In room: A/C, TV, hair dryer, minibar, safe.*

Eating

CHEAP

➜**Enoteca Provinciale** UMBRIAN This wine store cum osteria replaces the livestock stalls of a medieval tower with a handful of wooden tables and a radio locked on the Italian pop station. Some regulars drop by just for a sandwich; others swill the day away with dozens of Umbrian wines. *Strengozzi* is handmade spaghetti served *alla Spoletina* (with spicy-hot tomato sauce), *al tartufo*, or in a game-based *ragù*. The standout soup is *zuppa di farro* (with crushed baby grains enlivened by veggies and meat). The secondi suit all appetites: simple panini, delicately flavored *frittata al tartufo* (an omelet for the indulgent in all of us), and daily specials like wild boar cooked in Sagrantino red wine and truffled *agnello* (mutton). Order your wine by the glass so that you can sample a cross section of the best Umbria has to offer, and finish with the local bitter liqueur *amaro di tartufo*. *Via Aurelio Saffi 7.* ☎ *0743/220-484. Primi 5€–10€; secondi 6€–13€; wine 1€–6€ per glass; menù turistico with wine 15€. Wed–Mon 11am–3pm and 7–11pm (until midnight in summer).*

➜**Trattoria del Festival** ★ UMBRIAN The cavernous pair of vaulted brick rooms here are large enough to host the festival hordes yet still leave room for die-hard locals who come for the best fixed-priced menus in town. The two more "expensive" of these are the ones to order, because they let you sample a pair of primi (chef's surprise, but one sure to involve truffles) and include all the incidentals save wine. Start with a foot-long *bruschetta al pomodoro* with a couple of cream-stuffed veal rolls before sinking your fork into the *tagliatelle tartufate* (a particularly successful use of the elusive black mushroom) or the *penne all'erbe* (in a hot-and-spicy tomato sauce laden with chopped herbs). The secondi also tend to be very simple but good. If you don't care for the excellent *frittura al tartufo* (mixed meat fry with truffles), try the *salsicce alla brace* (grilled sausage) or the *pollo arrosto* (roasted chicken). *Via Brignone 8.* ☎ *0743/220-993. www.trattoriadelfestival.com. Reservations recommended. Pizza 3.60€–4.40€; primi 4.65€–8€; secondi 7€–9€; fixed-price menus without wine 12€–22€. Sat–Thurs 11am–4pm and 6pm–midnight. Closed Feb.*

DOABLE

➜**Il Panciolle** ★ UMBRIAN The flagstone terrace out back is scattered with tables in summer, lorded over by a spreading pine, and affords a panorama of rooftops that spills into the valley below. Inside the stone walls, under wood ceilings, you can hear the meat of your secondo sizzling over the large open fire. This former cheap trattoria has lately put its waiters in suits and nearly doubled its prices, but the cooking remains excellent. The *strangozzi alla montanara* is topped with minced veggies and a hint of *peperoncini*, and the *spaghetti al rancetto* is served in a marjoram-scented tomato sauce with *guanciale* (pork cheek, like bacon). Put the open fire to good use for your secondo and order *carne alla brace* (grilled meat)—the *spiedino misto* gets you a sampler of sausage, steak, lamb, and beef filet flavored with bay leaves. Vegetarians might enjoy a grill of the smoke-cured cheese *scamorza*. *Via del Duomo 3–5.* ☎ *0743/ 45-598. www.ristoranteilpanciollespoleto.com. Reservations recommended. Primi 6.50€–14€; secondi 6.50€–17€. Thurs–Tues 12:30–2:30pm and 7:45–10:45pm. Closed Aug 1–12.*

SPLURGE

➜**Il Tartufo** ★★ UMBRIAN Get your appetite and credit card ready for a night at Spoleto's oldest restaurant in the company of Umbria's quasi-divine fungal tuber. The chefs work all seasons of truffle: the coveted white in autumn and early winter and the black *pregiato* the rest of the year. The small dining room is an intimate arrangement of reddish veneer paneling and tables accessorized with pink roses. As Mozart wafts over your table, you can inaugurate the evening with a *terrina di polenta* (slices of truffle-flake polenta in sauce covered with large shavings of truffle). *Strangozzi al tartufo* is the classic truffled pasta primo, or take a tartufo break with the sᴜ ᴺg-flavored *orecchiette alla polpa di olive* (tiny handmade pasta shapes served in a sauce of Gorgonzola and crushed olives). The *petto di faraona* is a guinea hen breast stuffed with a mix of potato and truffles. The simplest dish is often exquisite—for example, the veal *scaloppa al tartufo*. *Piazza Garibaldi 24.* ☎ *0743/40-236. Reservations required. Primi 7.50€–15€; secondi 13€–26€; set-price regional menu without wine 19€; set-price traditional menu without wine 30€–35€. Tues–Sat 12:30–3pm and 7–10:30pm; Sun 12:30–3pm. Closed last 2 weeks in July.*

Sightseeing

The Duomo and the Ponte delle Torri are Spoleto's only real attention-grabbers, so if you're pressed for time, skip the lower town (most of which was rebuilt after extensive bombing during World War II) and head straight up to Piazza della Libertà to see the highlights of upper Spoleto.

➔ **Casa Romana** This 1st-century A.D. patrician house supposedly belonged to Vespasia Polla, the mother of the Emperor Vespasian. The intricate monochromatic patterns in the mosaic floors are well preserved, and you can also see the marble well-cap and the bases of a few carved columns supporting the display cases of smaller excavated materials. *Corner of Via Visiale and Piazza Municipio.* ☎ *0743/224656. Tues–Sun (daily in summer) 10am–8pm. Admission 2.07€.*

FREE ➔ **Duomo** ★★ The most beautiful main square in town is Piazza del Duomo, with the cathedral backed by the *Rocca*-crowned green hills behind it. It makes a fitting stage for the Spoleto Festival finale and, on a more daily basis, a fine soccer field for local children. A 3rd-century A.D. Roman sarcophagus serves as a public fountain at the base of the stairs, and the small octagonal-roofed Santa Maria della Manna d'Oro is to the left. But the main attraction here, and in Spoleto altogether, is the unique facade of the 12th-century cathedral with a 1207 mosaic by Solsternus surrounded by eight rose windows. The bell tower was pieced together using stone looted from Roman temples, and the porch is a 1492 addition.

The cathedral was built to replace a church razed by Frederick Barbarossa in 1155, when the emperor destroyed Spoleto for refusing to pay him tribute. The Duomo's interior retains its original pavement, but the rest was baroqued in the 17th century for Pope Urban VII, who's commemorated with a Gian Lorenzo Bernini bust high above the central door inside. The first chapel on the right has a not-quite-finished fresco (1497) by a 17-year-old Pinturicchio lit by a light box, which also illuminates the early-16th-century frescoes adorning the chapel next door. The right transept is home to a Madonna and Child with Saints (1599) by baroque master Annibale Carracci as well as the empty tomb of Filippo Lippi, designed by his son, Filippino, at the request of Lorenzo de' Medici. According to Giorgio Vasari, Lorenzo couldn't convince the Spoleteans, who "lacked any great marks of distinction and especially the adornment of eminent men," to give the body back to Florence when the irascible painter died just before completing his fresco cycle here. Though technically a monk, Filippo was quite the womanizer, and when he died, rumors ran wild that he'd been poisoned by the enraged family of a local girl whose honor he had compromised. Filippo's bones mysteriously disappeared a few centuries later, and some say they were removed and scattered by her still-indignant descendants.

As you leave the Duomo, you'll pass the entrance to the **Cappella delle Reliquie (Reliquary Chapel)** on the left aisle, restored in 1993. They include 16th-century

UMBRIA

intarsia wood cupboards, a 14th-century painted wooden Madonna and Child, and a letter written and signed by St. Francis. (Assisi has the only other bona fide signature.) *Piazza del Duomo.* ☎ *0743/44-307. Cathedral: Daily 8am–12:30pm and 3–5:30pm (until 7pm Mar–Oct).*

FREE → **Ponte delle Torri** ★★ Walk along the right flank of the fortress, Via del Ponte, and once you're around the bend, take in the stunning view of this magnificent bridge which looks for all the world like an incredibly well-preserved Roman aqueduct. Nine tall pylons and graceful, narrow arches span the sheer walls of the valley behind Spoleto, a gorge swimming in the dense green of an ilex forest. The 80m-high (262-ft.), 228m-long (748-ft.) bridge was most likely raised by Eugubian architect Gattapone in the 13th century, though the two most central piers contain traces of older masonry, supporting the long-held theory that the bridge was built on an ancient Roman aqueduct. The span received the hard-won praise of Goethe in 1786 (apparently because he thought the whole shebang was Roman) and is named after the 13th-century towers that are crumbling at its opposite end. If you hit it at the right time of the morning, when the sun is climbing toward its daily apex and casting 45-degree rays of light over the gorge, the Ponte delle Torri cuts the sun's rays in half—a fantastic sight to see. The top rays shoot into the valley, illuminating it quite magically, and while the lower rays are blocked by the bridge, keeping the rest of the valley dark green. *Via del Ponte.*

→ **Rocca Albornoziana** Up Via Safi from the Duomo is this well-preserved fortress built from 1359 to 1362 by Gubbio's master architect, Gattapone, for the pope's watchdog, Cardinal Albornoz, who governed this leg of the Papal States. Various popes later holed up here when visiting Spoleto. It rests atop the site of the oldest prehistoric settlement in Spoleto and was used as a prison until 1982—celebrity inmates included members of the Red Brigades terrorist organization and Mehmet Ali Agca, who tried to assassinate Pope John Paul II in 1981. It's now open to the public as a museum and space for exhibitions and performances. *Piazza Campello.* ☎ *0743/43-707 or 0743/223-055. Admission 4.65€. Mar 15–June 10 and Sept 16–Oct Mon–Fri 10am–1pm and 3–7pm, Sat–Sun 10am–7pm; June 11–Sept 15 daily 10am–8pm; Nov–Mar 14 Mon–Fri 2:30–5pm, Sat–Sun 10am–5pm.*

→ **Teatro Romano** At the edge of Piazza della Libertà, Via Apollinare leads down to the entrance to the 1st-century A.D. Roman theater. The theater was partly destroyed and buried over the ages and all but forgotten before 1891, when local archaeologist Giuseppe Sordini began excavating. Extensively restored in the 1950s, it now serves as the most evocative stage for performances during the Spoleto Festival. It retains some of the original spectators' benches as well as a remarkably intact vaulted passageway under the cavea behind the seats. *Via S. Agata.* ☎ *0743/223-277. Admission (includes Archaeological Museum) 2€. Daily 8:30am–7:30pm.*

Todi: A Taste of the Middle Ages

43km (27 miles) W of Spoleto; 40km (25 miles) S of Perugia; 203km (126 miles) S of Florence

If you had to inflict the word "quaint" on any Italian town, Todi ★ would be a front-runner. It's one of the most picturesque hill towns, a warren of narrow medieval streets twisting and plunging off at every angle, with many alleys whose graceful sets of shallow stairs flow down the center. It's a cobble of mottled grays accented with brick, all surrounding a picture-perfect central square celebrated as one of the finest medieval spaces on the peninsula.

Seemingly frozen in the Middle Ages, aside from its almost Swiss cleanliness and pristine condition, Todi actually has much deeper roots. It claims a 2nd-century A.D. martyr to prove it was Christianized early; while only a few bits of the 42 B.C. Roman Tuder survive, traces of the Etruscan border town Tutare are scarcer still. Even the Etruscans were relative newcomers, having conquered the city from an Umbri tribe that probably had displaced the Iron Age squatters who occupied the site in 2700 B.C.

Todi doesn't harbor much great art, with the exception of one jewel of High Renaissance architecture; the wine and cuisine aren't particularly outstanding; and its long heritage is more in the history books than in plain view. People come here mainly just to look; to drink in the vistas from the town's terraces and the medieval character of its alleyways; to nap, picnic, and play in the public gardens; and then move on.

Todi's once-upon-a-time atmosphere hasn't gone unnoticed. It sees its share of film crews, and has gotten press in America as one of the world's eminently livable cities. Property speculators and Italian businessmen have taken advantage of its relative proximity to Rome to buy medieval palazzi, set up housekeeping, and commute to the city. But notwithstanding the disproportionate number of Alfas, Mercedes, and even Range Rovers purring down the constricted medieval streets, Todi remains a showcase hill town, and a refreshing break from a culture-heavy Italian tour.

The best time to visit is in the morning, when churches are open and you can get a good photograph of Santa Maria della Consolazione with the sun at your back.

Getting There

Todi is on the private **FCU train** line (**www.fcu.it**), not the state-run FS rail routes. There are about a dozen trains daily from Perugia's FCU stations (45 min.). From Spoleto, take the train to Terni (22 daily) and transfer to the FCU line (14 per day; about 1 hr. total travel time). There are about eight runs daily from Rome to Terni that meet up with an FCU train (about 2 hr. total). At Todi, get off at Ponte Rio (not Ponte Naia) station (☎ **075/894-2092** or 075/882-092), where a bus will be waiting to take you the 5km (3 miles) up to town. If you're staying at Villa Luisa, tell the driver and he'll let you off at the first stop.

There are two **bus** terminals in town. From Piazza della Consolazione, there are four to eight runs daily to and from Perugia (40–60 min.); and one early morning run to and early afternoon run from Orvieto (2 hr.). From Piazza Jacopone, a bus runs daily to and from Rome center and Fiumicino airport (2–2¹/₂ hr.), and there's a Friday-only midday tourist run to and from Orvieto (2 hr.).

If you're **driving,** Todi is off Umbria's central highway, the E45, which branches off the A1 *autostrada* heading north from Rome at Orte and continues past Todi to Perugia. The SS79bis makes its winding way between Todi and Orvieto, but the less scenic SS448 is quicker. You can park free in lots just south of the Porta Romana and along the west side of town either below Porta Amerina or behind Santa Maria della Consolazione. Pay parking in the town's center is available in front of the Nicchioni.

Todi Basics

The central **tourist office** is under the arches of the Palazzo del Popolo (☎ **075/894-2526**). It's open Monday through Saturday 9:30am to 1pm and 3:30 to 7pm, Sunday 10am to 1pm and 3:30 to 7pm (in winter it closes at 6pm, and is not open Sun afternoons). The hilltop town is very walkable—wear comfortable shoes for the steep inclines and descents—and you can see most of the art the town has to offer in a couple of hours. It is a good pit stop for some exercise on the drive between Orvieto and Perugia or Assisi, but there are few hotels or restaurants to catch your attention.

UMBRIA

Sleeping

There is one hotel within Todi's walls, and it's a Splurge (but it's nice and it's new).

Not far from town, another nice (but splurgy) place to stay is **Tenuta di Canonica,** Località La Canonica 75–76 (☎ **075/ 8947545**), 5km (3 miles) northwest of Todi. Here Maria and Daniele Fano have converted a brick farmhouse and former medieval tower into a dining room with exposed stone walls, brick floors, and high ceilings. Their dining room is only for guests of their 11 attractively furnished bedrooms, costing 130€ to 170€ double or 180€ to 230€ junior suite, including breakfast. There is also an outdoor pool.

→ **Fonte Cesia** ★ In 1994, the first hotel in Todi's historic center opened its doors on a successful melding of modern architectural glass and wood elements with a 13th-century palazzo. The public spaces are particularly evocative, with lots of low brick vaulting in the bar, breakfast and dining rooms, and reading and TV lounges. In summer, breakfast is served in a nook of the huge palm-shaded terrace that sits atop the hotel's 17th-century namesake fountain. The standard rooms are carpeted and wallpapered in textured creams, and have command-center headboards, pleasantly unassuming dark-wood furniture, and matching fabrics on the chairs, bedspreads, and curtains. Each of the suites has a small balcony or terrace and is unique—and worth the splurge, especially when the high-season cost of a double brings the prices close to that of a suite. The "Novecento" has 19th-century antiques, the "Jacopone" Wassily chairs and a claw-foot tub, and the "Venturini" a canopy bed. *Via Lorenzo Leonj 3 (off Piazza S. Jacopo).* ☎ *075/894-3737. Fax 075/894-4677. www.fontecesia.it. Double 140€–164€, suite 192€–208€. Rates include breakfast. 33€ supplement per person for half pension, 49€ supplement per person for full pension. Free parking.*

Eating

There is not much choice in the restaurant department, either. There is little to write home about except the Umbria ("Doable"), which is highly regarded.

→ **Umbria** ★ UMBRIAN Not only does the Umbria have some of the best food in Todi, it also has one of the best views—call ahead in warm weather to reserve a table on the vine-shaded outdoor terrace. In winter you can warm yourself by the huge fireplace and dine in the 15th-century interior under wood-beamed ceilings and wagon-wheel chandeliers. The spaghetti *alla boscaiola* is so scrumptious you almost needn't bother considering the *polenta con funghi e tartufo nero* (truffle shavings and bits of their poorer fungal relatives atop creamy polenta). Enjoy a steak grilled over the open fire, or try the popular *fritto di mozzarella, olive, e carciofi* (fried mozzarella mixed with olives and artichokes) or the tender *anatra stufata con lenticchie* (duck cooked, but not covered, with tomatoes and spices served with a side of tiny lentils). *Via S. Bonaventura 13 (through arch between the Palazzi del Popolo and Capitano).* ☎ *075/ 894-2737. Reservations strongly recommended. Primi 5€–11€; secondi 8€–13€. Wed–Mon 12:30–2:30pm and 7:30–10:30pm.*

Sightseeing

FREE → **Piazza del Popolo** ★ This is not only the center of Todi but also the center of an ideal, a balance of secular and religious buildings in transitional Romanesque-Gothic style that epitomizes the late medieval concept of a self-governing *comune.* On the south end of the piazza squats the brick-crenellated marble bulk of the **Palazzo dei Priori,** started in 1293 and finished in 1339 with the crowning touch of a bronze eagle, Todi's civic symbol. Some lunching Umbri (or Etruscans, depending on which version of the legend you choose) supposedly founded the town

A MoΛk & HIS Christmas Carols

Jacopone (1230–1306) started out in grand Franciscan style, living a fun, sometimes debauched, materialistic life in Todi. But when his young wife died, he had a spiritual crisis. He started going about on all fours like a dog, eating filthy food, and acting like such a nut that the Franciscans didn't at first accept his ecstasies as religious. For quite a while they refused to let him don their robes. He is chiefly remembered for telling off, in verse form, Dante's old nemesis, the reprehensible Pope Boniface VIII (the written jibes got him 5 years in a Roman dungeon). He also wrote late-medieval poetry set to music that became, for all intents and purposes, the world's first Christmas carols.

after an eagle nicked the picnic blanket out from under them and then dropped it on this hill. (Historically, though, the eagle as city symbol makes its first appearance in 1267.)

FREE → **San Fortunato** ★ Across the Piazza del Popolo, go around the right side of Palazzo dei Priori, and a right at Piazza Jacopone will take you to Todi's second major sight. This massive Franciscan shrine of was begun in 1291, but finishing touches dragged on to 1459. Rumor has it that the Tuderti, basking in medieval wealth, commissioned Lorenzo Maitani for a sculpture on the façade that would top even his own masterpiece on nearby Orvieto's Duomo. Jealous Orvietan authorities, not to be outdone by rival Todi, decided the most expedient way to prevent this was simply to have the artist killed. Cross the gardens to see the central doorway carvings, testament to the greatness the rest of the façade could have had. It's a late-Gothic tangle of religious, symbolic, and just plain naked figures clambering around vines or standing somberly under teensy carved Gothic canopies.

FREE → **Temple of Santa Maria della Consolazione** To the right of the San Fortunato's façade, a little path leads up to the town's public park, bordered by a low rambling wall and featuring a large round tower stump—all that remains of Todi's 14th-century *Rocca*. At the other end of this park starts the winding path that wends down to Todi's High Renaissance masterpiece, the Temple of Santa Maria della Consolazione. Like its cousins in Prato and Montepulciano, this 90-year effort of Renaissance architectural theory, begun in 1508, is a mathematically construed take on a classical temple, a domed structure on a Greek-cross plan. It reposes in quiet, serious massiveness on a small, grassy plot. Although huge, it carries its mass compactly, with all lines curving inward and the domes and rounded transept apses keeping the structure cubically centered. The interior, however, is nothing special.

UMBRIA

Orvieto: Tunneling into Umbria

86km (53 miles) SW of Perugia; 152km (94 miles) S of Florence; 45km (27 miles) W of Todi; 87km (54 miles) W of Spoleto

If you're driving up toward Orvieto, the first thing that strikes you is how the city seems to grow right out of the narrow spur of reddish-brown volcanic rock on which it sits. The Tiber and Paglia rivers washed away everything around this little outcropping, and the

buildings were made from blocks of the same *tufa,* giving the impression the city emerged by itself from the rock.

It cries out to those passing through from Rome to Florence, hinting at its treasures: a breathtaking cathedral, a world-renowned wine, and little hidden tunnels burrowed into the monolith. Make sure to save time for an afternoon here you won't soon forget.

Getting There & Getting Around

Fourteen **trains** on the main Rome–Florence line stop at Orvieto daily. It is at roughly the halfway point (slightly closer to Rome), taking about an hour and a half in either direction. You arrive at the station in the modern town, below the rock, from which you should immediately take the adjacent cable car to the top. It only takes a few minutes and costs .90€ for a combination cable car/bus ticket: The "A" bus heads to Piazza del Duomo and the "B" bus to central Piazza della Repubblica via Piazza XXIX Marzo (it then doubles back to the Duomo).

If you're coming by **car:** from Todi, the SS448 is the fastest route, but the twisty SS79bis is more scenic; from Perugia, shoot down the SS3bis through Deruta to Todi and branch off from there. The SS71 runs here from just east of Chiusi in southern Tuscany, and the A1 *autostrada* between Florence and Rome has an exit at the valley town Orvieto Scalo.

The most convenient free **parking** is in Orvieto Scalo outside the train station at the top of the funicular run on Piazza Cahen (with both free and pay spaces); and, if you can find room, the free lot off Via Roma.

It simply does not make sense to take the bus to Orvieto, since there's only about one per day from Rome, and none from most other cities.

Sleeping

The hotel situation in Orvieto is pretty grim. Most inns are of a consistently bland modern motel style, and the price doesn't come close to justifying the accommodations. Like other small Tuscan cities, you should consider them more of a day trip and spend the night in a bigger city. But if you find yourself in need of a room in Orvieto, check out the following:

Orvieto Tourist Office/Websites

The tourist office is opposite the Duomo at Piazza Duomo 24 (☎ 0763/341-772). It's open Monday to Friday from 8:15am to 1:50pm and 4 to 7pm, Saturday from 10am to 1pm and 3:30 to 7pm, and Sunday from 10am to noon and 4 to 6pm. Also visit **www.comune.orvieto.tr.it, www.umbria2000.it,** or **www.orvienet.it.**

CHEAP

➜ **Hotel Virgilio** This place has 13 very basic modern rooms with some of the ugliest lamps around, but it's the only cheapie in town and it's smack on Piazza Duomo. *Piazza Duomo 5–6.* ☎ *0763/341-882. www.hotelvirgilio.com. Double 50€–85€.*

DOABLE

➜ **Hotel Duomo** ★ This place used to be a cheap place to crash until it was overhauled in the late 1990s, but the new Hotel Duomo still offers an excellent price for the location, with far more comfort and amenities. A few rooms overlook the cathedral's striped flank. There's a small garden out front for alfresco breakfasts in summer. *Vicolo di Maurizio 7 (near the Duomo).* ☎ *0763/341-887 or 0763/393-849. www.orvietohotelduomo.com. Double 85€–105€. Includes breakfast. In room: A/C, TV, hair dryer, minibar, modem access.*

➜ **Palazzo Piccolomini** ★★ Converted in 1997 from a 16th-century palazzo, the family-run Piccolomini is the best hotel in town. It retains some palatial grandeur in echoey salons and the remnants of decorative frescoes, but the rooms tend toward the elegantly simple, with missionary-style wood furnishings, compact bathrooms, and modernized comforts (some suites have plush touches like heated towel racks and canopied beds). The

Orvieto

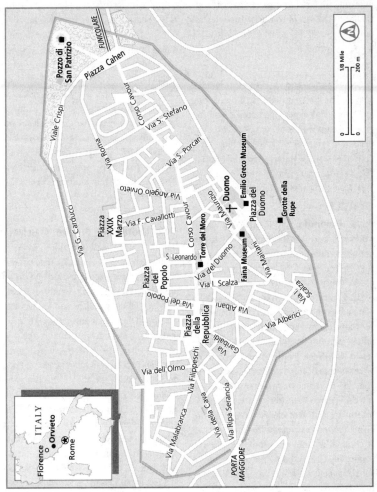

basement breakfast room is carved out of living tufa, and in late 1999 the owners of Le Grotte del Funaro opened a restaurant, **La Taverna de' Mercanti,** affiliated with the hotel underneath. *Piazza Ranieri 36 (2 blocks down from Piazza della Repubblica).* ☎ *0763/ 341-743. www.hotelpiccolomini.it. Double 116€–138€, triple 142€–175€. Breakfast 11€. Amenities: Restaurant; bar; laundry service; nonsmoking rooms; room service (24-hr.); rooms* *for those w/limited mobility; wine cellar. In room: A/C, TV, dataport, hair dryer, minibar, safe.*

Eating

Orvieto is a great place to grab a bite to eat, though actually, every single time I've come I've had the excellent "Etruscan" rabbit (yes, I am a cruel and primitive man) and of course a generous helping of the local white wine. The unofficial pasta of Orvieto is *umbrichelli,* simple flour-and-water spaghetti rolled out unevenly by hand and somewhat chewy—similar to the *pici* of southern Tuscany, but not as thick. No matter what you order, it's hard to go wrong here.

CHEAP

➔**San Francisco** A budget traveler's heaven: The 450 seats actually fill up during lunch in summer, perhaps because you can get a full meal with wine for 12€ to 20€. The restaurant serves pizzas in the evening. *Via B. Cerretti 10 (off Via Maitani near the Duomo).* ☎ *0763/343-302. Daily noon–3pm and 7–10:30pm (in winter, it closes Sun evenings).*

DOABLE

➔**La Palomba** ORVIETANA A giant wooden Pinocchio marks the entrance to this unpretentious place, where sticking to the *"La Casa Consiglia"* ("the house suggests") part of the menu will guarantee a memorable meal of good home cooking. After putting away a plate of warm *crostini misti*, try one of the specialty homemade *umbrichelli* dishes, either *tartufati* (in light butter-and-truffle sauce with fresh truffle grated on top) or *all'arrabbiata* (if it isn't *piccante* enough for you, add peperoncini-spiked olive oil). You can cool your mouth afterward with a simple omelet stuffed with cheeses or order the divine *filetto alla cardinale* (beef filet cooked in cardinal-colored red wine). *Via Cipriano Manente 16 (1st left under the arch at Piazza della Repubblica).* ☎ *0763/343-395. Reservations recommended. Primi 4.70€–7.50€; secondi 6€–10€. Thurs–Tues 12:30–2:15pm and 7:30–10pm. Closed 20 days in July and/or Aug.*

➔**Tipica Trattoria Etrusca** ★ ORVIETANA Squirreled away under a 15th-century palace, this trattoria was a workers' lunch hangout early in the 20th century. The vaulted ceilings are divided by magnificent tufa arches with a massive column at the center and modern art on the walls. Start with *umbrichelli dell'Orvietana* (in a spicy hot tomato sauce mixed with *pancetta*) or the

homemade gnocchi. The *coniglio all'Etrusca* (rabbit in a green sauce of herbs and spices) is the house special secondo, but don't rule out the *abbachio allo scottadito* (lamb so piping hot it'll "burn your fingers"). Desserts tend toward antique Orvietan sweets, including fresh ricotta dusted with sugar, cinnamon, and a sweet berry sauce. Ask to see the wine cellars, carved from the living tufa beneath. *Via Lorenzo Maitani 10 (1 block from the Duomo). 0763/344-016. Reservations recommended. Primi 4.50€–14€; secondi 6€–16€; fixed-price menu without wine 20€. Tues–Sun noon–3pm and 7:45–10pm. Closed Jan 7–Feb 7.*

SPLURGE

➔**Le Grotte del Funaro** ★ UMBRIAN Dating from at least the 1100s, when the eponymous *funaro* (rope maker) had his workshop here, these grottoes carved into the tufa are filled with delectable smells of Umbrian cooking that draw Italians and tourists alike. (In fact, all this restaurant is missing is an animatronic rope-maker scene in the back corner, where the *funaro* and his crew of Umbrian Paul Bunyan types heave tufa boulders up through the shaft.) The *bruschette miste Umbre* give their Tuscan *crostini* cousins a run for the money, but save room for the *ombrichelli del Funaro* (in a heavy sauce of tomatoes, sausage, artichokes, and mushrooms). For a sampling platter of the best grilled meats, order the *grigliata mista* (suckling pig, lamb, sausage, and yellow peppers) or a fish dish. The wine cellar offers just about every Orvieto Classico, including a good selection of half bottles. After 10pm, the restaurant transforms into a piano bar; if you're here for lunch, retire outside to digest with the aid of the spectacular view from the terracelike piazza. *Via Ripa Serancia 41 (at the west end of town near Porta Maggiore; well signposted). 0763/343-276. www.ristoranti-orvieto.it. Reservations recommended. Primi 9€–15€; secondi 10€–13€; fish tasting menu without wine 32€*

Orvieto's "Cumulative Ticket"

The useful *Carta Unica* cumulative ticket for 13€ adults and 11€ students and those over 60 gets you into the Duomo's Cappella San Brizio, the Musei Archeologici Faina e Civico, the Torre del Moro, and the Orvieto Underground tour—plus either one funicular plus one bus ride *or* 5 hours in the ex–Campo della Fiera parking lot. It's available at the tourist office, the sights listed below, and the cable car depots.

(minimum 2 people). Tues–Sun noon–3pm and 7pm–midnight. Closed 1 week in July.

Sightseeing

→ **Crocifisso del Tufo** This 4th-century B.C. necropolis of houselike stone tombs lies about halfway around the north edge of town off Viale Crispi. Some tombs you can still see Etruscan script, written from right to left, on the door lintels, but the funerary urns and other relics found inside have long since been carted off to museums. *Viale Crispi.* ☎ *0763/343-611. www.archeopg.arti.beniculturali.it. Admission 2€. Apr–Sept Mon–Sat 9am–7pm; Oct–Mar Mon–Sat 8:30am–5:30pm (June–Sept until 11pm Sat). Bus: 1.*

→ **Duomo** ★★★ Orvieto's most striking sight is, without a doubt, the façade of its Duomo. The overall effect—with the sun glinting off the gold of mediocre 17th- to 19th-century mosaics in the pointed arches and intricate Gothic stone detailing everywhere—has led some to call it a precious (or gaudy) gem and others to dub it the world's largest triptych. It is, to say the least, spectacular.

The Duomo, started in 1290, owes much of its glory to the Sienese artist Lorenzo Maitani. Maitani not only shored up the unsteady structure with his patented buttresses but also left a Gothic stamp on the building, especially the façade. Here he executed, with the help of his son, Vitale, and Niccolò and Meo Nuti, the excellent carved marble relief panels in the lower part. The scenes on the left are stories from Genesis; God fishes around inside Adam's rib cage with an "I know I left an Eve in here somewhere" look on His face.

The far right panels are a Last Judgment preamble for the Signorelli frescoes inside. The most striking is the lower-right panel, a jumble of the wailing faces of the damned and the leering grins of the demonic tormentors dragging them to eternal torture. The anguish and despair are intense, possibly because the damned didn't realize Hell would contain quite so many snakes.

Inside, to the right of the high altar is the recently restored Cappella di San Brizio, containing one of the Renaissance's greatest fresco cycles . Fra' Angelico started the job in 1447 but finished only two of the vault triangles, then the city's council brought in pinch-hitter Pinturicchio in 1490, but the Perugian painter inexplicably cut out after just 5 days. It wasn't until 1499 that Cortonan Luca Signorelli strode into town, with the council hailing him Italy's most famous painter and practically throwing at him the contract to finish the paintings. After completing the ceiling vaults to Fra' Angelico's designs, Signorelli went into hyperdrive with his own style on the walls. By 1504, the Duomo had some of the most intense studies ever seen of the naked human body, plus a horrifically realistic and fascinating rendition of the *Last Judgment*. Michelangelo, master of the male nude, who was most impressed, made many sketches of the figures, and found a prime inspiration for his own *Last Judgment* in the Sistine Chapel.

The first fresco on the left wall is *The Preaching of the Antichrist*. The Devil-prompted Antichrist discourses in the center, Christians are martyred left and right, soldiers scurry about a huge temple in the background, and the Antichrist and his followers get their angelic comeuppance on the left. The prominent whore in the foreground reaching back to accept money for her services is a bit of painterly revenge—it's a portrait of a girlfriend who had recently dumped Signorelli. In the arch to the left of the altar, angel musicians summon the lucky ones in the *Calling of the Chosen,* and then, on the right, there's how the other half dies: *The Entrance to Hell.* This fresco sets you up for the last and most famous scene: the writhing, twisting, sickly colored mass of bodies, demons, and horror of *The Damned in Hell.* Signorelli didn't pull any punches here. Tightly sinewed parti-colored demons attack and torture the damned while a few of their comrades, menaced by heavily armed angels in full plate mail, toss humans down from the sky. One winged devil is making off with a familiar blonde on his back—the jilted artist's ex-mistress again. *Piazza del Duomo.* ☎ *0763/341-167. Admission to Cappella San Brizio (☎ 0763/342-477) by cumulative ticket or 3€ adults. Tickets available at tourist office across the piazza. Daily 7:30am–12:45pm and 2:30–7:15pm (closing 5:15pm Nov–Feb and 6:15pm Mar and Oct). Cappella San Brizio opens 10am but is closed Sun morning.*

➔ **Grotte della Rupe (Etruscan Orvieto Underground)** This tour leads groups down into Etruscan caves and tries to explain the network of tunnels honeycombing the tufa subsoil. The visit can be overly explanatory, but you do get to see an underground medieval olive press, probably recycled from an Etruscan structure, perhaps a temple. You can also peer down a few claustrophobically narrow Etruscan-era wells, wander around a subterranean quarry for *pozzolana* (a volcanic stone powdered to make cement mix) in use as late as the 19th century, and tour a series of Etruscan pigeon coops (no, seriously) carved

out of the cliffside tufa. *Piazza Duomo 24 (tourist info office). ☎ 0763/344-891. www. orvietounderground.it. Admission (by guided tour only) by cumulative ticket, or 5.50€ adults, 4.50€ Pozzo della Cava ticket holders, 3.50€ students and seniors. Tours daily at 11am, 12:15pm, 4pm, and 5:15pm (other times can be arranged). Closed Feb.*

➔ **Pozzo di San Patrizio (St. Patrick's Well)** ★ Orvieto's main military problem throughout history has been a lack of water. Clement hired Antonio Sangallo the Younger to dig a new well that would ensure an abundant supply in case the pope should have to ride out another siege. Sangallo set about sinking a shaft into the tufa at the lowest end of town. His design was unique: He equipped the well with a pair of wide spiral staircases, lit by 72 internal windows, forming a double helix so that mule-drawn carts could descend on one ramp and come back up the other without colliding. The shaft was nicknamed St. Patrick's Well when some knucklehead suggested that it vaguely resembled the cave into which the Irish saint was wont to withdraw and pray. What you get for descending the 248 steps is a close-up view of that elusive water, a good echo, and the sheer pleasure of climbing another 248 steps to get out. *Viale San Gallo (near the funicular stop on Piazza Cahen). ☎ 0763/343-768. Admission 3.50€ adults; cumulative ticket with Museo Emilio Greco 4.50€. Daily Mar–Sept 9:30am–7pm, Oct–Feb 10am–6pm.*

➔ **Torre del Moro** In the 19th century this served as a main water tank for the city's new aqueduct system, then became the bell-ringing communal timekeeper when a mechanical clock was installed in 1876. You can clamber up for a sweeping view of the city and, on clear days, the countryside as far as mounts Cetona and Amiata. *At the intersection of Via Duomo and Corso Cavour. ☎ 0763/344-567. Admission by cumulative ticket, or 2.60€ adults. Daily Nov–Feb*

Tunneling through the Tufa

Throughout the centuries, residents of Orvieto dug into the rock in search of water. The practice was started by the Etruscans, and continued by the Romans, the people of the Middle Ages (who also used some defunct wells as rubbish dumps), and even Renaissance Pope Clement VII.

Through the ages, the man-made cavern system has also been used for wine and oil production and storage, artisan workshops, escape tunnels for nobility, and quarries for tufa building blocks and the *pozzolano* dust to cement them with. The official position seems to relegate this peculiar mole-like tendency to the past, dating the last tunneling and the closing of the last *pozzolano* mine to the late 19th century. But what everyone appears to ignore are the elevator shafts the city sank through the cliff in 1996 to connect the new parking lots with Orvieto proper—the Orvietani are still tunneling.

Besides the *comune*-run Grotte della Rupe caverns, many shops and other private buildings sit atop underground excavations—scholars suspect the military base covering a fifth of the city (and closed to visitors) hides some of the finest. Perhaps the best accessible ones are under an *enoteca,* the **Pozzo della Cava,** Via della Cava 28 (☎ 0763/342-373; www.pozzodellacava.it), whose personable owner used to invite his customers to poke around his Etruscan tunneled basement gratis. Then the town decided to excavate, discovered an important historic well, set it up as an official tourist sight, and started charging admission. (Sometimes, when no one's looking, the amused shopkeeper still lets you scurry down for free.) The excavations consist of six caves containing, among other things, a few medieval refuse shafts and a kiln from 1300, an Etruscan cistern, and, of course, a well almost 4.5m (15 ft.) in diameter and more than 30m (98 ft.) deep, first used by the Etruscans and later enlarged by Pope Clement VII. It's open in the summer Tuesday through Sunday from 8am to 8pm. Admission is 1.70€ adults and 1.20€ for students, seniors, and holders of tickets to Grotte delle Rupe, Pozzo Patrizio, or the funicular.

10:30am–1pm and 2:30–5pm, Mar–Apr and Sept–Oct 10am–7pm, May–Aug 10am–8pm.

Shopping

Orvieto's local white wine, **Orvieto Classico,** is made from grapes that thrive in the local chalky soil and are sometimes fermented in caves around the countryside. You'll be able to buy glasses of the fruity wine ("liquid gold") at any tavern in town, but if you want to haul a bottle or two back to your own digs, try the town's best wine shop, **Foresi,** Piazza del Duomo 2 (☎ 0763/341611).

You can also find lace and carved wooden objects here. For lace, go to **Duranti,** Via del Duomo 13–15 (☎ 0763/344606), which

carries tablecloths, handkerchiefs, and frilly curtains. You'll also find imported European scents and locally distilled perfumes. You'll find a wide selection of hand-carved wooden items at **Michelangeli,** Via Gualverio Michelangeli 3 (☎ 0763/342660), where you can find everything from full-scale furniture to an ornate cup and bowl.

Antonia Carraro, Corso Cavour 101 (☎ 0763-342870), is a fabulous place to stock up for a picnic or just to buy locally made breads, olive oils, cheeses, salamis, wines, and biscotti.

Orvieto is also known for its pottery, which is best seen on Saturday mornings at the **pottery market** on Piazza del Popolo.

Urbino: Renaissance City & College Town

101km (63 miles) NE of Perugia, 107km (66 miles) NE of Arezzo

Like many other places on UNESCO's list of World Heritage sites, Urbino seems like it was lifted out of an illustrated book of fairy tales and pasted on a hill in the middle of nowhere. It is coined the "ideal Renaissance city" for a number of reasons: the impeccable architecture of its Ducal Palace and the quaint medieval burg that surrounds it; because the legendary painter Raphael was born here; and mostly because it contains one of the world's oldest universities, founded in 1564.

These days, the University of Urbino is no longer a rare center of enlightenment—in fact, it is one of many solid middle-tier schools in Italy and it happens to attract young city-dwelling students looking to get away from urban life. What is extraordinary, on the other hand, is its draw for foreigners. For some 50 years it has offered a summer course in Italian language and culture and the *"non-parlo-italianos"* have arrived in flocks. Several American colleges, such as the University of Tennessee and the College of William and Mary, offer programs in Urbino in conjunction with the university or other local classrooms. (See "Studying in Urbino," p. 365.)

While the average study-abroad type flies straight to Florence or Rome to bask in an artistic paradise with thousands of other tourists, those who study in Urbino get a more genuine university experience. First of all, it actually feels like a college town: The school's 20,000 students easily outnumber the resident population of 15,000, and the makeup of the local pubs certainly reflects it.

Yes, the green mountains and valleys of Le Marche are isolated by Italian standards, but the inimitable mosaics of Ravenna are not too far away, and the art of eastern Tuscany and northern Umbria are a day trip at the most. Those who come here for the summer consider themselves pretty lucky to be just 30 minutes from the Adriatic beaches and the madness that unfolds in Rimini every August.

Urbino itself is enough to hold your attention. Protected by its walls, the ancient city is perched high on a ridge. Its original shape, similar to a ship's bow, was designed by the Romans and remained virtually unchanged in the Middle Ages. In the 15th century it began to flower under the Dukes of Montefeltro, who commissioned such painters as Raphael, Piero della Francesca, and Paolo Uccello and the poet Torquato Tasso, and put Urbino on the cultural map.

Getting There

It is not easy to get to Urbino via public transportation from any major city. It has no nearby train station. The most direct way is to take a **train** from Bologna to Pesaro—all of the trains calling at Pesaro are of the slow variety—which requires about 2 hours along the Adriatic coast (closer to 3 hours if you have to change in Rimini), and from Pesaro, **buses** operated by SOGET (☎ **0722/2233**) run to Urbino, taking 55 minutes and costing 2.05€ one-way. You can purchase tickets aboard.

The best way is by car. Because of winding mountain roads, drivers often choose to approach Urbino from Pesaro by heading south along A14 to Fano. Once here, cut southwest along E78 until you reach the signposts leading north into Urbino's center.

Sleeping

CHEAP

➜ **San Giovanni** In the heart of the old city, this hotel offers the best value in town in its

Urbino Tourist Office

Across from Palazzo Ducale, the Tourist Office at Via Puccinotti 35 (☎ 00722-2613) is open Monday and Saturday 9am to 1pm, Tuesday to Friday 9am to 1pm and 3 to 6pm.

Studying in Urbino

A lot of American universities offer a semester aboard in Urbino; longer and shorter stays abound as well. Websites for just a few of the established programs at major universities are listed below:

- University of South Carolina:
  www.cas.sc.edu/dllc/Italian/Urbino/info2001.html
- Rutgers: www.rci.rutgers.edu/~italian/studyabroad.html
- SUNY–New Paltz: www.newpaltz.edu/studyabroad/prog_fasp_urbino.html
- University of Central Florida:
  www.cas.ucf.edu/forlang/urbino/frames.php?URL=studyabroad.html
- ISEP/University of Urbino:
  www.planetedu.com/listings/esl/3938/x/verbose/degree

simply furnished, well maintained, and comfortable bedrooms. Many of them open onto panoramic views of Urbino itself, especially rooms 26 to 30. The hotel is installed in a restored medieval building, with a low-cost pizzeria and restaurant on the ground floor. Most of the bedrooms are fairly spacious, although the bathrooms are small with showers. There are no phones in the rooms, however. To reach it from the landmark Piazza della Repubblica, head to town on Via Mazzino, turning right where it's signposted. *Via Barocci 13.* ☎ *0722/2827. Double without bathroom 35€, with bathroom 38€–55€. No credit cards. Closed in July and Christmas week.*

SPLURGE

→ **San Domenico** ★★ One of the prestige addresses in Le Marche, this first-class *albergo* lies adjacent to the Church of San Domenico, with which it shares a wall. In fact, from the fourth floor of the hotel you can look through a window down into the church. A 4-minute walk from the main square of town, the hotel is the most convenient in Urbino, lying across from the Ducal Palace. The hotel is imbued with comfort, elegance, and taste, having been carved from a 15th-century convent between the cathedral and the university. Bedrooms are large and furnished with thoughtful extras for your comfort, including armchairs equipped for shiatsu massage. There is also a

fitness center in the building. *Piazza Rinascimento 3.* ☎ *0722/2626. Fax 0722/2727. www.viphotels.it. Double 110€–286€, suite 213€–379€. Parking 5€–8€.*

Eating

DOABLE

→ **Nene** ITALIAN This rustic country cottage serving good food lies on a hillside 2km (1¼ miles) west of the center. You get traditional dishes well prepared and served by a hospitable team in a welcoming environment. All of the dishes are prepared with products that change with the season. Frozen foods don't go over big with the patrons of this restaurant, who flock here to feast on such homemade fare as gnocchi with gorgonzola and pistachios or else grilled polenta. From ravioli to pappardelle, the homemade pastas are the best in the area. Filet of beef and various poultry dishes are prepared with a certain flair, as is the array of freshly made desserts offered daily. *Via Crocicchia.* ☎ *0722/2996. Reservations recommended. Main courses 6€–18€. Tues–Sun 12:30–2:30pm and 7:30–10:30pm.*

SPLURGE

→ **Vecchia Urbino** ★ ITALIAN The town's finest dining room lies in the center of the ancient Lavagine quarter, reached along narrow lanes. Even though in the town's urban center, it is like a rustic yet elegant

UMBRIA

country inn. Its cuisine is closely linked to the surrounding agricultural district known for its first-rate regional products, among the finest in all of Italy. The restaurant, which opened in 1985, is a family-run concern and enjoys a devoted local clientele with educated palates. The staff is the most welcoming and professional in town. Gabriele and Eugenia Monti use organic ingredients when possible, and you'll delight in their offerings of fresh game, black and white truffles, savory cheese, and extra-virgin olive oils used in the salads, pasta, and meat dishes. Freshwater fish is shipped in from the seaside town of Fano. Their lasagna, using a hand-rolled pasta, is among the best we've tasted, the sauce using chicken giblets, pork, veal, and other meats blended with a white sauce made in a *bain-marie*. Rabbit is marinated in white wine and stuffed with a mixture of lard and fresh rosemary. Those faint of heart might want to skip the charcoal-grilled lamb's head, a favorite of local gourmands. *Via dei Vasari 3/5.* ☎ *0722/4447. Reservations required. Main courses 8.50€–26€. Wed–Mon noon–3pm and 7–11pm.*

Sightseeing

Locals are not modest—but are somewhat accurate—in hailing Urbino as "the ideal Renaissance city." In a secluded mountain setting, it basks in its former glory but is not as culturally isolated today as it might have been. The hub of the town is the animated triangle of **Piazza della Repubblica,** lying in a dip between the twin humps of a hill. Its Università di Urbino is one of the oldest in the world, founded in 1564. Its student population and never-ending stream of art-conscious international travelers lend the town a cosmopolitan air.

Urbino was home to two celebrated native sons. Raffaello Sanzio (1483–1520), more popularly known as Raphael, came from here, as did Donato Bramante (1444–1514). Bramante

introduced the early Renaissance style to Milan and the High Renaissance style to Rome, where his most famous design was St. Peter's Basilica.

This mellow old artistic city was once surrounded by walls, the outlines of which can still be traced. Many old palaces are more or less still standing as they did in the days when Urbino was plagued with Gothic wars. These bastions of history have earned Urbino the honor of being on the UNESCO list of World Heritage Sites.

→ **Casa Natale di Raffaello** Raphael lived here until he turned 14. It is a house from the 15th century that belonged to the future artist's father, Giovanni Sanzio, and it is filled with mementos and period furnishings, including coins, books, and portraits. In the room where the painter was born, a fresco by the young artist, *Madonna and Child,* has been preserved. Some art critics attribute this painting to Raphael's father. *Via Raffaello 57.* ☎ *0722/320105. Admission 3€. Mar–Oct Mon–Sat 9am–1pm and 3–7pm, Sun 10am–1pm; Nov–Feb Mon–Sat 9am–2pm, Sun 10am–1pm.*

→ **Oratorio di San Giovanni Battista** You won't find too many medieval paintings that were created by the blood of a freshly killed lamb, but that is indeed the claim to fame of the frescoes by the Salimbene brothers, depicting the life of Saint John the Baptist, found in the older (14th century) of the two adjacent churches here. *Via Barocci.* ☎ *347-6711-181. Admission 2€. Mon–Sat 10am–12:30pm and 3–5:30pm; Sun 10am–12:30pm.*

→ **Palazzo Ducale** ★★ **and Galleria Nazionale delle Marche** ★ The greatest palace ever built in Le Marche has just about everything you could ask for in an Italian art museum, including a painting by Raphael, works attributed to Botticelli, and an art-theft mystery story to boot.

After checking out the inner courtyard with its delicate lines and the ground floor rooms, head up a grand staircase to the apartments above. Here you'll find some of the greatest art of the Renaissance, rivaled only by Florence. Uccello painted the *Profanation of the Host* in 1465, a work that frequently appears in art history books. The great Piero della Francesca left behind *Madonna of Senigallia* and *Flagellation of Christ.* The *Ideal City,* a masterpiece of perspectivist wizardry, is often attributed to him. But the most important painting in the collection is Raphael's *The Mute One.* It is the portrait of a "gentlewoman," her face, like *Mona Lisa*'s smile, usually called enigmatic by art historians. Finished in 1507, the picture now rests in a Plexiglas cage, having been stolen in 1975, one of the country's most sensational art thefts. However, it was found in good condition 2 years later and returned to Urbino. The best for last: The ducal study is decorated with stunning inlays often attributed to Botticelli. They are mounted on panels depicting well-known men. *Piazza Duca Federico 107.* ☎ *0722/ 322625. Admission 4€ adults, 2€ ages 18–25. Mon 8:30am–2pm; Tues–Sun 8:30am–7:15pm.*

UMBRIA

Bologna & Emilia-Romagna

Without question, Emilia-Romagna is the best undiscovered region of Italy. Why more people, young and old, don't come here is a bit of a mystery. Flat as a pancake, and more famous for its world-renowned gourmet items than anything else, it doesn't have the natural beauty of Tuscany or the Bay of Naples, nor the ruins of Rome, nor the canals of Venice, but what Emilia-Romagna *does* offer are the essential ingredients to enjoying the good life in Italy—food, fashion, fun, and above all, friendliness—without the hassle and crowds of the more well-known destinations.

Some call Emilia-Romagna the "bread basket of Italy" for being the home of lasagna, eggplant parmigiana, and spaghetti Bolognese, but this is not a region of country bumpkins—the towns here are quite wealthy and surprisingly sophisticated, with tons of young people curious to meet foreign visitors. Despite their obvious prosperity, there is a certain down-to-earth quality to the people here, Emiliani and Romagnoli, that must come from having such a strong tradition of cultivating comfort food. In the interest of full disclosure, we should tell you that Emilia-Romagna is not the sunniest region in Italy. But the fog that often hangs over Emilia-Romagna only highlights the human warmth you'll encounter. Instead of being warmed by the sun, you're warmed by the cozy *centro storico* and fun-loving people of each town. At night, when the mist descends on the handsome cityscapes of Emilia-Romagna, you feel a bit like Sherlock Holmes, staking out your next carafe of Sangiovese or plate of pumpkin ravioli.

Train hopping between the region's constellation of manageable cities—like Bologna, Ravenna, Ferrara, and Parma, each of which offers delicious local culinary specialties, hip bars, and trendy shops—can get downright addictive. Bologna, the regional capital, is one of the coolest cities in Europe, home to the oldest university in the world, and astonishingly undervisited—and maybe it's better that way, but we want to spread the gospel and highly recommend you check it out. Almost-seaside Ravenna is celebrated the world over for its mosaics, and when you're finished gaping at the dazzling artwork, you'll drool over the local flatbread, the *piadina romagnola*. Ferrara and Parma are slower-paced and elegant, with even less penetration by tourists despite being totally picturesque and genteel. Finally, no summer trip to Emilia-Romagna is complete without a few days on the Riviera Romagnola. The sporty and sandy beach towns of Rimini, Riccione, and Milano Marittima, on the Adriatic coast south of Ravenna, throw the best nonstop parties anywhere on the Italian peninsula.

Bologna: Ancient City, Young at Heart

52km (32 miles) S of Ferrara, 151km (94 miles) SW of Venice, 378km (234 miles) N of Rome

To be old and still be considered cool by throngs of young 'uns is no simple feat. Johnny Cash pulled it off. The '68 Mustang definitely pulled it off. Mick Jagger . . . well, not so much. With several impressive millennia on them, however, the city of **Bologna** ★★★ has all three beat and, thanks in part to the world's oldest university located in the heart of the city, it also has 400,000 groupies/inhabitants. Walk along the miles of the city's trademark porticoes and you'll quickly realize that Bologna is really a 22-year-old in a 700-year-old's body. Its noticeably edgier and more alternative flavor is a stark contrast to the glamorous aura of Milan to the west and the classical grace of Florence to the south.

Rome has the Colosseum and the Vatican, Florence has its Duomo and the Uffizi, and Venice has its canals. Bologna has, well, no sights you've ever heard of—which is one of the reasons it's often overlooked by vacationers on the Italian circuit. But if you want to take a break from tourist hordes and spend a day or two hanging out, eating,

partying, and shopping in an elegant, energetic, and manageable medieval college town, Bologna can't be beat.

Bologna is much more world-renowned for its food than its photo ops, though there are plenty of those, too, in the handsome heart of the old city. But Bologna didn't earn its nickname of *La Grassa* ("the fat") by accident. Carbs are king in this town. Emilia-Romagna takes great pride in being the region that brought you tagliatelle, tortellini, and *lasagne* (the Italian spelling of the scrumptious pasta dish). To top it all off, *everything* in Bologna, it seems, is served with ample sides of local cured hams and cheeses. Not to worry, though: A climb to the top of Bologna's Torre Asinelli is a quick and satisfying way to write off one of your meals.

One of the first things you'll notice when you step out of the train station and onto Via dell'Indipendenza is that Bologna actually feels like a full-fledged city. Unlike Florence's cramped, cobblestoned roads, the wide, blacktopped streets that lead to Piazza Maggiore, the center of old Bologna, host a

Emilia-Romagna

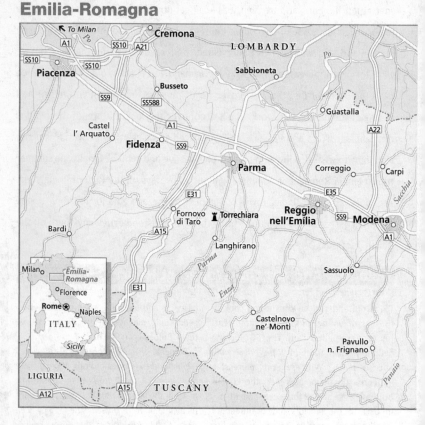

patchwork of cold, post-war concrete-and-steel buildings and centuries-old porticoes that, in addition to sheltering pedestrians from the sun, help visitors envision a Bologna in its glory days as a commercial and intellectual center some 600 years ago. The closer you get to Piazza Maggiore (home to Bologna's grandest buildings and default gathering place), the less chronologically confusing the architecture gets. The 13th-century structures in the heart of town create a medieval cityscape daubed with every shade of red, orange, and tan imaginable. Bologna's layout is a perfect combination of modern pragmatism and historic character that few cities in the world, let alone Italy, can match. Year after year, domestic surveys consistently rank Bologna as Italy's most livable city.

The next refreshing thing you'll find in Bologna is that the social makeup of the locals is just as varied as the urban environment. The streets overflow with a motley assortment of personalities. Punky students with neon mohawks and piercings galore smile as they clink by, only to be followed by a group of yelping teenage girls clad in expensive Dolce & Gabbana dresses. All the while, in a nearby gelateria, a gray-haired 70-year-old retiree—pants hiked up to his armpits, exposing a saucy six inches of ankle and varicose veins—chats with a totally polite, budding hip-hop mogul decked out in Ecko tracksuit and full bling. Simply spend 2

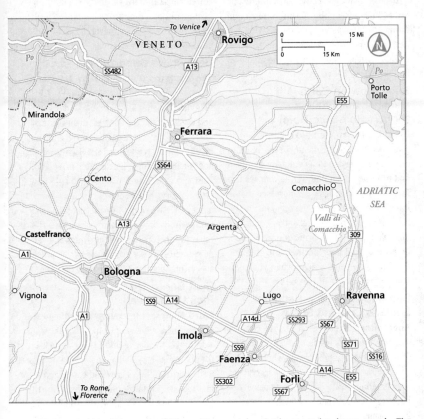

minutes watching the parade of life on Via dell'Indipendenza, and you'll get a good sense of the cultural quirkiness that pervades every square inch of the city.

Instead of offering a perfectly quaint, storybook provinciality (such as you find in more touristed parts of Tuscany or Umbria), Bologna spikes its medieval charm with cosmopolitan vitality. It's such a handsome and lively town, you may well find yourselves asking, as we do every time we visit the city, "Why don't more tourists come here?" What Bologna lacks in famous individual postcard sights, it certainly makes up for in gourmet offerings and impeccable Italian style—but one of the best things about Bologna is that it's still somewhat unknown to the outside world.

John Grisham set his latest novel, *The Broker*, in Bologna, and once the inevitable movie adaptation is made, everyone will see just what a captivating place the world's oldest college town is and will probably start to travel here in greater numbers. So, get here before the secret's out.

The Best of Bologna
Best Outdoor Resting Spot
Piazza Maggiore   Surrounded by Palazzo Re Enzo, Palazzo del Podestà, the Basilica of San Petronio, and Palazzo d'Accursio, Bologna's main square has imposing sights to behold in every direction. You'd think there'd be hordes of tour groups and visitors—but remember, most tourists overlook Bologna

altogether, leaving the city's most interesting attractions and public spaces comfortably crowd-free. On many nights, there's a fog that descends over the city and creates an especially bewitching aura around the medieval buildings here. See p. 390.

Best "How on Earth Is It Cheaper than 200€ a Night?" Romantic Hotel

Hotel Porta San Mamolo   Better book a room here before it gets any better or more expensive. Every room is uniquely designed and furnished beautifully. Little touches like the ceramic room signs, beds dressed in fine linen, first-rate china in the breakfast room, and plenty of plants make the Porta San Mamolo a perfect romantic getaway. You'll manage to fool your partner into thinking that you blew 300€ a night when you actually spent a fraction of that. See p. 381.

Best Place to Tape Hannibal Lecter's Cooking Show

Anatomical Theater   The 17th-century *Teatro Anatomico,* inside the historic Archiginnasio university building, is where Bolognese med students used to pick apart corpses on a luminous white marble slab back in the day. Outfitted in ornately carved maple wood and teeming with body parts in the artwork, the theater is an intensely atmospheric, totally unique sight. See p. 395

Most Saliva-Inducing Street

Via Pescherie Vecchie   Like a Whole Foods Market under 13th-century wooden porticoes, the heart of Bologna's outdoor food market is ripe with mouthwatering sights and scents, from the earthy goodness of prosciutto and Parmigiano-Reggiano emanating from corner delis, to the stands of plump garlic and fresh herbs, to the iced crates of glistening whole swordfish.

Best Place to Observe Bolognese Beautiful People in their Natural Habitat

The lounges and bars on **Via Clavature and Via de' Musei** (see box, p. 386), or at the posh coffee bar, **Zanarini** (p. 383). When all the posing and preening there gets to be a bit much, make a break for the more casual pubs and bars around Via Zamboni.

Best Photo Opportunity

The cross streets east of Piazza Maggiore There are five streets (Via Rizzoli, Via Castiglione, Via Santo Stefano, Strada Maggiore, and Via Zamboni) that intersect in an area just east of the historic center, and right in the middle of it all are the Due Torri (Two Towers) and the Basilica of S. Bartolomeo e Gaetano. This area is drenched in suggestive 13th- and 14th-century architecture: ancient brick arches, massive wood-beam porticos, and the wonderfully off-kilter pair of towers. The taller tower, Torre Asinelli, provides an even more impressive perch at its apex, from which spectacular photos of Bologna can be taken.

Best Bar to Try to Pick Up a Local

Corto Maltese   If seducing the Bolognese women/men with your slinky moves isn't working on the dance floor, try your luck at the pool table. Mojo failing you in nine-ball as well? Corto Maltese's crowded bar is a great last resort. Capitalize on the general mirth and strike up a conversation with some drunk eye candy. If *that* still doesn't work, it's safe to say you're going home solo. See p. 389

Best Club to Whip Out Your Worst Moves

Link Club   For the simple reason that they've got an enormous floor and the DJ tends to play techno on slow nights. You could have a massive seizure and still look good if there's techno blaring through the speakers. Link really gets going when international DJs (or even respected local ones) come into town.

Best Alterna-Shop to Get Trendy Threads

Combo (for Guys); Free Shop (for Gals) Combo (p. 397) has all the labels to keep you in the loop with the university crowd. If the clothes there don't pique your interest, the clerks surely will. They're very easy on the eyes and flirting with them might make you accidentally buy something. I guess that's how I ended up with five maroon tracksuits. Ladies will love the couture in Free Shop (p. 398). Instead of trendy labels, they have amazing, lower-profile designers to fill their racks. Dresses and jackets here are bold, integrating sass, smarts, and sophistication. Your bank account might be a little sore after shopping here, but at least you'll look damned good.

Best Restaurateur/Owner

Alberto   Owner of Bar Alberto & Giovanna, a small bar not far from the lovely Porta San Mamolo area, Alberto had me at "hello" (or, once he started flapping his wings to do a chicken impression). Whether or not it was meant to entertain, it showed that Alberto loves his store and his customers. Take a seat and shoot the breeze with him for an hour or two. See p. 383.

Best Off-Beat Museum

Museo Tattile di Pittura Antica e Moderna   Let your fingers have a little fun in this "tactile museum," where some of the most renowned masterpieces of classic and modern painting are rendered in three dimensions for the sight-impaired (and anyone else interested in feeling up a Botticelli babe). And, it's free! See p. 394.

Getting There

BY AIR

Bologna's **Guglielmo Marconi International Airport** (☎ **051/6479615**) only serves flights from within Europe. The runways were extended in 2004 to accommodate larger aircraft, but most flights outside of Europe will still touch down in either Milan or in Rome. If you are flying into Guglielmo Marconi, the Aerobus (one-way ticket 4.50€) leaves the airport every 20 minutes for the air terminal at the rail station. With any luck, flights from farther-flung cities will also start

touching down at Bologna's Marconi airport, situated a mere 6km ($3^3/_4$ miles) northeast of the city.

BY TRAIN

As with most travel in Italy, rail is still the best way to reach Bologna. Because of its geographic location in the middle of the Italian peninsula, Bologna's **Stazione Centrale** (Piazza Medaglie d'Oro 2; ☎ **892021**) is one of the busiest in the country and can be reached from many points in Europe. Munich, Frankfurt, and Paris are some of the major hubs it's connected with via overnight train. A mind-boggling number of tourists only travel *through* the station to reach other parts of Italy, seeing nothing of Bologna beyond the blue BOLOGNA C.LE station signs, as they hang out and wait for their connecting trains.

Trains arrive hourly from Rome (trip time: $3^1/_2$ hr.). A one-way fare costs 42€. From Milan, trip time is $1^1/_2$ hours, costing 25€ one-way. Bus nos. A, 25, and 30 run between the station and the historic core of Bologna, Piazza Maggiore.

BY CAR

Driving is also a pretty stress-free way to reach Bologna (second, perhaps, to taking the train). The Italian *autostrada* (highway) is remarkably user-friendly, with abundant, crystal-clear signage and few traffic snarls. Unless you go for a drive in the scenic *colli bolognesi* (hills west of the city), however, you'll find that the countryside around Bologna, as in the rest of Emilia-Romagna, is mind-numbingly flat.

If you are driving from Rome, Florence, or any point from the south, the A1 highway will take you within a few kilometers of Bologna. Drivers from Milan can also use the A1 southbound to get them to the same area. From places like Venice, Padova, and Ferrara to the northeast, you can shoot down the A13. Finally, beach bums spending the weekend in Ravenna or resort towns like Rimini and

Riccione on the east (Adriatic) coast can depend on the A14 highway to get back in time for class on Monday. (For routes and tolls on the *autostrada*, check out www.autostrade.it.) Traffic signs guiding you from the highway off ramps into the heart of town are easy to follow, even if you know only three words in Italian. Just keep looking for the white CENTRO signs with the bull's-eye graphic, and you can't go wrong. Eventually you'll get to the tangle of roads that make up the city's *centro storico*.

Thanks to the wider, asphalt-paved streets like Via dell' Indipendenza, driving is actually a breeze in Bologna. Parking is another issue. Call your hotel to inquire about parking options; the few inns that do offer parking spaces in their garages tend to be reasonably priced, anywhere from 10€–18€ for a 24-hour period. Otherwise, just follow the blue P signs to a private or municipal parking lot or garage. Your best bet is the parking lot near Piazza VIII Agosto (between the train station and Piazza Maggiore), which charges a reasonable 12€ for 24 hrs. Leave your car on the street only at your own risk: Break-ins are all too common in Italy, and unless you have a Ph.D. in Italian street-parking rules, you'll probably find a *multa* (parking citation) slapped under your windshield wiper within 10 minutes of turning off the engine and locking the vehicle.

BY BUS

We've mentioned this repeatedly, but buses are usually the last resort for any traveler in Italy (with the exception, perhaps, of Sicily). Rarely on time and almost always uncomfortable, the buses can cost almost as much as taking the train and can sometimes be more expensive than flying (especially for longer distances). If flights are booked solid and you missed the one available train to your obscure destination, then check out the schedules posted in the Autostazione di Bologna located in Piazza XX Settembre 6, at the northernmost part of Via Indipendenza.

Bologna Orientation

Bologna's city center, shaped like an irregular pentagon, is wonderfully compact and easy to navigate. Most major streets and roads radiate from **Piazza Maggiore,** while the busier *viali* circumscribe the area, creating the city's strange five-sided wagon wheel shape. The northeast quadrant is where the university buildings and student population are concentrated, where it's noticeably livelier and chock-full of pubs for post-class drinking. The northwest, especially near Piazza dei Martiri, is where you'll find less-than-savory folk hanging around the fountain and discount stores. Head south, towards Piazza Maggiore, and the scene changes dramatically; the architecture and atmosphere become much more aesthetically pleasing. The few tourists who do decide to visit Bologna usually concentrate on exploring everything south of and around Piazza Maggiore. Besides the big museums and attractions, you'll also find more luxurious shopping in the south. The area is a great deal quieter than other parts of town, perfect for a relaxing post-dinner stroll. If you venture even farther south and a bit to the east, you'll stumble upon the Giardini Margherita public park, just outside the old city walls. (See "Playing Outside," later in the Bologna section of this chapter.)

Getting Around
BY PUBLIC TRANSPORTATION

Cheap transportation comes in the form of the ATC's dark red **buses** (www.atc.bo.it). Tickets are 1€ for 60 minutes of travel, or 3€ for a day pass, and can be purchased at *tabacchi* shops, newsstands, and from self-service ticket machines at bus stops and aboard some buses. A **citypass**—a booklet of eight tickets, each valid for 1 hour—costs 6.50€. Once you board, you must have your ticket validated or you'll be fined up to 150€.

The clean, upholstered vehicles run right on schedule, but Bologna's bus system is not

Driving Tips

The northern part of the city center and the surrounding fringes are the best places to utilize your wheels, should you decide to rent a car or moped. If you decide to ride around the Piazza Maggiore area, stick to the main streets like Via Rizzoli, Via Castiglione, and Via Farini. Even if they get busy and clogged, it's less stressful than trying to navigate the narrower side streets that are usually one-ways and dead-ends. In nice weather, consider renting a scooter and heading for the hills (the *colli bolognesi*) south and west of the city. The pleasure of navigating this rolling countryside on a Vespa is what inspired "50 Special," a hit single by one of Italy's biggest pop stars, 26-year-old hottie and Bologna native Cesare Cremonini.

Speedy (Via Alberelli 1/a; ☎ 051/401317, 338/4178286, or 338/4404440; daily 8am–10pm) rents 50cc scooters for 30€ per day, and higher-powered *scooteroni* for 50€ per day. Take bus 13 from Piazza Maggiore.

For four-wheeled vehicle rentals, **Maggiore** (the Italian partner of National and Alamo) has good rates and an office a few blocks south of the train station (Via Cairoli 4; ☎ 051/252525; Mon–Fri 8am–12:30pm and 2–7pm, Sat 9am–1pm). **Avis** also has an office opposite the station at Viale Pietramellara 27/d (☎ 051/255024; Mon–Fri 8am–noon and 2:30–6:30pm), and **Hertz** is right around the corner at Via Amendola 16 (☎ 051/254830; Mon–Fri 8am–8pm, Sat 8am–1pm).

without its frustrations. I spent an hour waiting for a particular bus, only to find out that the stop I was waiting at was technically "closed" since it was cordoned off with yellow tape. Thinking that the benches were just being fixed, I waited ages for the bus to arrive and when it did, the driver signaled that the stop was not functional (through a mix of shoulder shrugs and hand waves) and denied me passage.

The bus map can be just as aggravating. More of a schematic, the posted graphic of the bus lines looks like colorful spaghetti, marking only the starting point and terminus of each line. You're better off trying to decipher the bus stop signs themselves. The bus numbers and their respective schedules are displayed on the street-side signs and are much more helpful than any of the bus drivers or maps. Having said all that, since everything in Bologna is within walking distance anyway, you'll probably only need to utilize public transportation to get from the train station to your hotel and vice versa.

BY BICYCLE

Explore the city on a two-wheeler by renting from **Due Ruote** (Via S. Stefano 14; ☎ 051/233-337; www.dueruotebologna.it) for a weekend (15€) or a day (10€). Bicycles aren't as common on the roads as in Florence, Ferrara, or Padova, but they're the perfect form of transportation for broke college students who can't afford to gas up a Fiat or even a Vespa at Italy's horrendous fuel prices. Rather than weave through pedestrians and cars on Via Indipendenza, bring your wheels to the public gardens. The paths make for a much more relaxing ride than any pedestrian-filled piazza.

ON FOOT

First things first: The center of Bologna is rather tiny, and wheels are not a necessity. In fact, it's more of a pain to roll around bumper-to-bumper traffic than to traipse on your own two feet around the sheltered arcades that line Bologna's key streets. That's not to say that playing pedestrian for the day is without its pitfalls. Be sure to buy a detailed city map at a *tabacchi* shop or at the train station. The glossy and colorful free map published by the Associazione Provinciale Albergatori Bologna (Hoteliers' Association of Bologna) is good, with major attractions bulleted, but not all hotels have it, and it does omit some of the smaller side streets that are essential for finding your way to that secluded restaurant on the west side. Once you start studying the city plan, you'll realize that whoever initially drew the layout of the city must have been the Jackson Pollock of the Middle Ages. Streets spastically change directions, creating a mazelike network of doglegging roads which locals navigate with ease.

Unlike Rome and Florence, drivers in Bologna are not accustomed to braking for ditzy tourists who've decided to stop in the middle of a busy road to take a picture of something that looks quaint. When crossing any streets that are open to automobile traffic, pedestrians will have to watch out for Smart cars and buses that whip around blind corners, seemingly hell-bent on committing vehicular manslaughter.

Another annoyance (er, charming quirk) is the fact that roads, even the major arteries, change names every couple of blocks. You'll certainly run into this when you hit the center and walk along the boulevards that run east-west above and below Piazza Maggiore. Via Rizzoli turns into Strada Maggiore past the Due Torri, and if you head west, it morphs into Via Ugo Bassi. Parallel to Via Rizzoli, go west on Via Farini and watch the signs turn into Via de' Carbonesi, then to Via Barberia and then finally Via Sant'Isala, all in a matter of a few kilometers.

Wandering the city is another thing altogether. If you couldn't care less about getting to the archaeology museum at the stroke of noon, then Bologna is a fantastic city to get lost in. Luckily, the busy thoroughfares that surround the city limits prevent you from straying too far. Most visitors then

Culture 101: That's Bologna!

So many things are attributed to the presence of the University of Bologna, but it's unavoidable. The locals here, for the most part, understand and speak English rather fluently. If they're under 40, it's pretty much guaranteed. This cosmopolitan influence also translates to the way the locals dress. You'll find more American clothing labels here than in Venice or Florence. Rebellious students want to stand out from the local fashions (which, trendy as they are, can be pretty conformist), and the most effective way to do this is to dress differently. Wear whatever you feel like wearing and you'll blend in with the rest of the independent-minded crowd.

backtrack to the centrally located Piazza Maggiore as a reference point. From there, Via dell'Indipendenza leads north to the train station, Via Zamboni brings you northeast to the university region, and Via Santo Stefano and Via Castiglione go to the public gardens in the south.

Tourist Offices

General information for tourists is available over the phone at ☎ 051/246-541. If you'd rather browse the brochures in person or chat with someone face to face, then head to one of three tourist offices. There's one in the train station on Piazza Medaglie d'Oro 2 (Mon–Sat 8am–8pm). There's another in the airport that's also open Monday to Saturday 8am to8pm and Sunday 9am to 3pm. Otherwise, the main tourist office is placed in the always-busy Piazza Maggiore 1 (daily 9am–8pm). Another option in Piazza Maggiore (Palazzo del Podestà) is the **Centro Servizi per i Turisti** (☎ 051/6487607; www.cst.bo.it; Mon–Sat 10am–2pm and

3pm–7pm, Sun 10am–2pm). It's run by the hoteliers' and tour operators' associations of Bologna and can help you find accommodations and arrange guided tours. They also publish an excellent free map.

Youth information offices, **Informagiovani,** are at Piazza Maggiore 6 (inside Palazzo d'Accursio; ☎ 051/204539) and are open Monday through Wednesday and Friday 10am to 6pm, and Thursday 2 to 6pm.

Bologna **Nuts & Bolts**

Crisis centers   La Casa Delle Donne Per Non Subire Violenza is the Women's Rape Crisis/Domestic Violence Center, and you can reach it at ☎ 051/333-173 or at their offices on Via dell'Oro 3 (Mon–Fri 9am–6pm). Another organization you can go to for crises of a different nature is the Italian Red Cross (Croce Rossa Italiana; Via del Cane 9; ☎ 051/581-858; www.cribo.it/cribo).

Emergencies   Call ☎ 113 for the Bologna police. The firemen answer to ☎ 115, while an ambulance can be summoned by calling ☎ 118. For general emergencies, call ☎ 112. Looking for Jenny? ☎ 867-5309. One-hit wonders from the '80s can solve *any* emergency.

Internet/Wireless Hot Spots   To check your e-mail, update your blog, peruse train schedules, or just kill some time on the Net, stop by Via de' Giudei and look for **Net.Arena** in the historic center. There are only six computers, but it's air-conditioned and quiet (Via de' Guidei 3/d; ☎ 051/220-850; Mon–Fri 10am–9:30pm, Sat 1–7:30pm). You're charged .50€ for each 10-minute interval. If all of the computers there are taken, head to **HappyNet** (Via Oberdan 17/b; ☎ 051/199-84179; Mon–Fri 9am–11pm and Sat–Sun 10am–11pm.) You'll need to learn how to operate the vending machine to get your "ticket" (1.20€ for 30 min.), but the clerk there'll be happy to help out. There are more than 20 computers here and it's open until 11pm, when you'll find only the die-hard video gamers battling virtual opponents and loneliness.

If you're going to be in town for a while, consider getting a library card at the Sala Borsa (p. 392). You'll need to prove your temporary residence in Bologna (e.g., a school certificate), but once you've joined, the library offers free Internet access for its members. Nonmembers can pay 2.50€ per hour to log on at the Sala Borsa.

Laundromats   Chances are, unlike the local vagrants, you'll want to wash your threads somewhere other than the fountains in one of the piazzas. The best place to freshen up your clothes is at **Lava & Lava** (Via d'Irnerio 35/b). It's open every day from 7am to midnight and it's mostly filled with students zoning out and watching the spin cycle. Washing a load costs 3€ and using the dryer for the same load will cost the same.

Post office   If you bought one too many souvenirs, send some home and lighten your load. The sluggish (and oft unreliable) Poste Italiane's main office can be found on Piazza Minghetti 1 (☎ 051/230-699; Mon–Fri 8am–6pm, Sat 8am–noon).

Restrooms   Public restrooms are pretty much nonexistent in Bologna. Restaurant owners, bartenders, and a few store owners, luckily, will let you use their facilities without giving you attitude or making you buy anything from their establishment. Politely ask the waiter or clerk and they'll point you to the john.

BOLOGNA & EMILIA-ROMAGNA

Safety Despite the number of vagrants and derelicts in certain sections of Bologna (especially around the train station), crime isn't much of an issue. Pickpockets, as usual, tend to choose their targets in cramped tourist attractions, so use common sense: Keep your belongings close and be alert. Bologna has the dubious distinction of being the site of the worst domestic terrorist act in Italian history, the so-called Strage di Bologna: on August 2, 1980, Italian right-wing extremists set off a massive bomb in the train station, killing 87 and injuring 177. Thankfully, it was an isolated act, and the city hasn't seen anything remotely terrorist-related since then.

Sleeping

Bologna has plenty of accommodations for all budgets; as with any larger Italian city, most hotels are concentrated near the train station, and whatever economical options there are in the heart of the old town tend to get booked quickly in peak periods. We always recommend that you fork over a little extra cash for a bed in the *centro,* if you can afford it, but this isn't quite as critical in Bologna. The train station area may not be beautiful, but it isn't such a horrible alternative, as it's only a short bus ride (or 20-min. walk) to the medieval ambience in and around Piazza Maggiore.

HOSTELS

→ **Centro Turistico di Bologna** Of the three hostels in Bologna, two are actual youth hostels, and all are located a few kilometers northeast of the city center. The best of the lot, the Centro Turistico di Bologna, has a slight identity crisis. It advertises itself as a hostel, but it's really a camping hotel that rents out spaces for tents and RV as well as cheap bungalows to those who didn't bring their North Face or Winnebago. Private units are available, or you can shack up in a shared bungalow with one, two, or three other campers. "Chalets" (i.e., trailer homes) are also available for single travelers and couples. Getting to the campground involves a 20-minute bus ride from the city center, making location this hostel's worst feature. (To make matters worse, there's only one bus an hour connecting the camping ground to

the city center—on the hour from the camping ground to the city, from 9am–9pm, at 40 min. after the hour from the city center to the campground, from 8:40am–10:40pm. There's another bus that runs later and more frequently, but it drops you off on the other side of the enormous field adjacent to the camp.) Location issues aside, the parklike accommodations are not bad. With the exception of the faulty A/C (prepare to sleep naked in summer, for the sweltering heat permeates even in the dark), there are plenty of pluses, including laundry facilities, a swimming pool, and a cozy little bodega/cafe for guests, who are mostly young and European (e.g., hot Dutch chicks on road trip). If you've ever wondered what happened to the old bassist of the Queens of the Stone Age, he apparently got offered a job here as a bartender/waiter; the friendly dude behind the counter is a scary clone of Nick Oliveri, goatee and all. *Via Romita 12/4a (northeast of city center).* ☎ *051/325-016. www.hotelcamping.com. Bungalow and chalet rates (private): Single 55€–88€, double 68€–78€, triple 85€–110€, quad 95€–130€. Camp area: 5€–7€, with RV 8€–12€. Shared bungalow (4 person): 24€–35€ per person.*

CHEAP

→ **Hotel Centrale** ★ Just a few minutes' walk west of the action at Piazza Maggiore, the affordable and quiet Hotel Centrale is a good bet for budget-conscious travelers who'd rather stay near the heart of things than in the grittier train station area. With

Bologna Sleeping & Eating

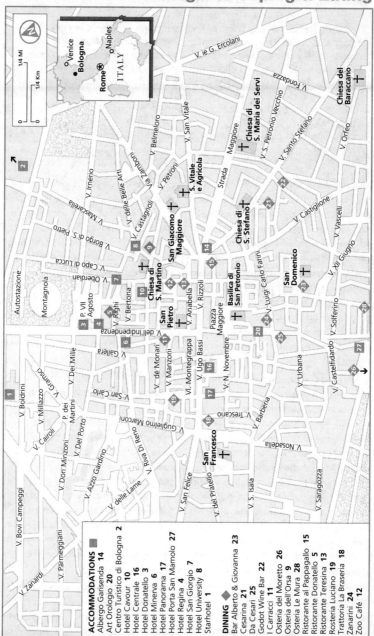

ACCOMMODATIONS ■

Albergo Garisenda **14**
Art Orologio **20**
Centro Turistico di Bologna **2**
Hotel Cavour **10**
Hotel Centrale **16**
Hotel Donatello **3**
Hotel Minerva **6**
Hotel Panorama **17**
Hotel Porta San Mamolo **27**
Hotel Regina **4**
Hotel San Giorgio **7**
Hotel University **8**
Starhotel **1**

DINING ◆

Bar Alberto & Giovanna **23**
Cesarina **21**
Da Cesari **25**
Godot Wine Bar **22**
I Carracci **11**
Osteria del Moretto **26**
Osteria dell'Orsa **9**
Osteria Le Mura **28**
Ristorante al Pappagallo **15**
Ristorante Donatello **5**
Ristorante Teresina **13**
Rosteria Luciano **19**
Trattoria La Braseria **18**
Zanarini **24**
Zoo Café **12**

OKKIO! Conventional Wisdom

One thing can derail your plans of finding a place to sleep: the Fiera di Bologna. Bologna's convention center is the busiest in Italy, hosting auto shows, toy fairs, tanning bed expos . . . you name it. When one of these shows comes to town, you might be hard-pressed to find a bed at any price.

If you're having trouble finding vacancies, try calling the **Centro Servizi per i Turisti** (☎ 051/6487607; www.cst.bo.it; Mon–Sat 10am–2pm and 3–7pm, Sun 10am–2pm). It's run by the hoteliers' association of Bologna and can be quite a miracle worker when the city is invaded by conventioneers. (You can also monitor the Fiera calendar at www.bolognafiere.it to avoid the problem dates altogether.)

rich-colored fabrics to warm the decor, rooms in this inn, which occupies a few floors of a patrician palazzo, are much more elegant, and just more "furnished," than what you find at most other government-rated two-stars, though not all have private bath. Staff is pleasant but lethargic, so don't expect them to bend over backwards with restaurant suggestions and other tourist tips. *Via della Zecca 2 (at Via Ugo Bassi),* ☎ *051/225114. Single 50€–70€, double 78–96€. Amenities: Bar. In room: TV, telephone. Some rooms have shared bath.*

➔ **Albergo Garisenda** For penny pinchers who demand picturesque, the Garisenda can't be beat. Accommodations are no-frills, but this government-rated one-star is a stone's throw from the Due Torri (if you can throw a stone 20m/66 ft.) and market streets around Via Pescherie Vecchie, and only a hop, skip, and jump from the bar-and-lounge-rich "social market" around Piazza della Mercanzia and Via Clavature. Book well in advance, as there are only seven rooms, and with a location as desirable as this, they fill up fast. *Galleria del Leone 1/Via Rizzoli 9 (off Piazza della Mercanzia).* ☎ *051/224369. garisenda@infinito.it. Single 60€, double 85€–110€.*

➔ **Hotel Minerva** The gaunt man with the greasy T-shirt, apparently the owner, proclaimed that the upcoming renovations will improve his government-rated one-star

establishment greatly. Hopefully a bunch of changes will take place by the time this guide goes to print, but so far the only thing he specifically mentioned was separating the bathrooms from the bedrooms. Currently, the showers are in a corner of the bedroom with only the curtains separating it from the rest of the quarters. The toilet, as well, is in plain sight when you retire for the night in your bed. The rest of the hotel is awfully dark, even in the bright Bologna afternoon. The Minerva is the place you call when everything else is booked. *Via de' Monari 3 (at Via dell'Indipendenza).* ☎ *051/239-652. Double 90€.*

➔ **Hotel Panorama** With basic but comfy rooms and a friendly reception, Panorama is a good budget choice, conveniently located in a somewhat gritty, 19th-century palazzo 100m (328 ft.) west of Piazza Maggiore. All rooms have shared bath down the hall, and some rooms have views of the green hill country to the south and west of the city, hence the name of the hotel. *Via Livraghi 1 (at Via Ugo Bassi).* ☎ *051/221802. www.hotel panoramabologna.it. Single 55€, double 70€, triple 85€, quad 95€, quintuple 105€. In room: TV.*

➔ **Hotel San Giorgio** Summer can get agonizingly hot in Bologna. Many budget hotels offer electric fans since they can't afford air-conditioning. The government-rated two-star San Giorgio goes so far as to close an entire floor due to the torrid temperatures—the fifth floor is closed in the summer months because it sits unshielded by surrounding buildings and gets uncomfortably warm. And if the fifth floor is closed off because of the heat, you'd probably be wise to steer clear of the fourth floor, since it's probably scorching there as well. Accommodations, with sparse furnishings and hospital-like TVs in most rooms, reflect the price of this inexpensive hotel, making it the perfect place for tourists who spend most of their days out and about. Some rooms are wired, with PCs and high-speed connections, but there are only a handful of them available. *Via delle Moline 17 (just east of Via Oberdan).* ☎ *051/248-659. www.sangiorgiohotel.it. Single 50€–100€, double 80€–100€. Rates include buffet breakfast. Amenities: Bar. In room: TV.*

DOABLE

→**Hotel Cavour** Waste not, want not. Vacancy is never an issue when a hotel really doesn't care. In the government-rated three-star Hotel Cavour, wide hallways give an apartment-like feel, and rooms are unusually spacious (some even have fireplaces). Management does not do a whole lot to fill the voids. The potential is endless, though, when you see the quaint courtyard (most entrances of the 48 rooms overlook it). It's still a decent option for those on a budget or for groups looking to play a game of shuffleboard in their rooms. *Via Goito 4 (at Via dell'Indipendenza).* ☎ *051/228-111. Single 65€–165€, double 90€–200€. Rates include breakfast. In room: A/C, TV, minibar, safe.*

→**Hotel Donatello** Aside from the Big Three on Viale Pietramellara, Hotel Donatello is the next closest hotel (at least on Via dell'Indipendenza) to the train station. The sparse reception is a bland omen for guests and could very well double for a dentist's waiting room. Guestrooms in this three-star aren't much better, although they are clean and acceptable accommodations. There are better deals in the area, but if all are fully booked, Donatello is a suitable back-up. *Via dell'Indipendenza 65 (at Via dei Mille),* ☎ *051/248-174, fax 051/244-776, www.hoteldonatello.com. Rates: Single 60€–110€, double 80€–190€, triple 105€–215€. Amenities: 24-hr. bar. In room: A/C, TV, minibar.*

MTV **Best** →**Hotel Porta San Mamolo** ★★ In another lifetime, hotelier Roberto Condello must have been Michael Jackson's personal surgeon. His hotel, the Porta San Mamolo, is a much comelier patient, and keeps getting a face-lift, a tummy tuck, or just a collagen injection, even if it doesn't really need it. Fortunately, all the additions and changes keep making the Porta San Mamolo a cozier, more luxurious place to stay. An elevator in the adjacent building is being installed, as well as balconies for rooms in the recently acquired property. Guest rooms are all uniquely laid out around a courtyard, a result of the hotel gradually assimilating surrounding buildings into its grounds over time. Any structurally sound historical aspects from the original building have been preserved, and Roberto takes pride in showing off the distinctive characteristics of each room. Curtains and sheets cut from expensive fabrics and simple yet elegant furniture keeps with the 18th-century theme. Breakfast is served in an enclosed glass terrace in the middle of the courtyard and it starts your day with an elegant, filling meal. Try not to drop the china, though; it's crafted by Churchill, and a broken plate will set you back 18€. The owner also recognizes the inexpensive merits of greenery, while many other hotels seem to overlook this simple touch. Plants are plentiful and add to the homey and comfortable vibe that saturates every square yard. Add to that an incredibly helpful front desk staff, and you'll find yourself wondering how this place is still so affordable. With changes underway, this government-rated three-star may soon be upgraded to a four-star: Check before you book! *Vicolo del Falcone 6/8 (at Via Miramonte).* ☎ *051/583-056.*

www.hotel-portasanmamolo.it. Single 85€–181€, double (single use) 95€–210€, double 110€–290€, suite 155€–300€. Rates include buffet breakfast. In room: TV, Internet ports.

→ **Hotel University** ★ Despite its proximity to a couple of bars, the government-rated three-star Hotel University's decor might be the loudest thing on the block. There are 21 rooms, some of which are themed with zebra-print sheets and safari-like pillows that might turn off some. Others are a little classier, draped in royal-like patterns and colors. Surprisingly, the whole animal thing works with the black-and-white scheme of the rooms, as well as the modern motif of the rest of the hotel. The rooms are comfortable, and you're guaranteed a great night's sleep. Via Mentana 7 (just north of Via Marsala). ☎ 051/229-713. www.hotel-university.com. Double 80€–180€. Rates include breakfast. Amenities: Bar; Internet point. In room: A/C, TV, hair dryer, minibar, safe.

SPLURGE

→ **Art Orologio** ★★ Everything in Art Orologio oozes an aged decadence, and it's expected from a hotel whose name and logo both relate to clocks. Guests start their day off in the semi-palatial breakfast room with its elaborate chandelier. Not a bad setting to down your toast and coffee. As for the rest of the hotel, the paint, carpet, and furniture are all dressed in the deepest and richest of hues—you'd be hard pressed to find the faintest hint of pastel in the hotel. You can't help but feel like royalty when you admire the fantastic dark woods that the doors are cut from and that accent the rooms and hallways. Deluxe rooms get additional perks, one of which is a decent view of Piazza Maggiore. Hotel Art Orologio sits just half a block away from the piazza, in a lovely square, and if you're lucky, the accordion busker will be hanging around the park benches and the charming storefronts just outside the hotel to complete the picture-perfect scene. Via de'

Pignattari 11 (just west of Piazza Maggiore). ☎ 051/745-7335. www.bolognaarthotels.it. Single 120€–300€, double (single use) 130€–320€, double 170€–320€, suite 270€–468€. Rates include buffet breakfast. Amenities: Free use of bicycles; Internet point. In room: A/C, TV, safe.

→ **Hotel Regina** ★ The Hotel Regina sits near the crusty Hotel Cristallo, but it's miles away in comfort. (If someone suggests the Cristallo, show them the back of your hand and curl your thumb, index, ring and pinkie finger.) The receptionist at the Regina may come off as a little cold, but the accommodations fare much better. Rooms mirror the theme of the decadent reception area, sans marble, and set up guests for a comfortable night's slumber. Via dell'Indipendenza 51 (at Via de' Falegnami). ☎ 051/248-878. Single 170€, double 200€. Discount if booked online. Rates include buffet breakfast. Amenities: Bar; dry cleaning; laundry service; lounge; non-smoking rooms; room service (breakfast only). In room: A/C, TV, dataport, hair dryer, minibar.

→ **Starhotel** ★★ Close to the train station, the government-rated four-star Starhotel panders to young business folk as well as trendy, well-to-do vacationers. The sharp, bold black uniforms with orange accents are indicative of Starhotel's character: simple with a dash of attitude. Rooms are modern and plush but cleanly designed, no frills and extravagance. The smallest room they offer is technically a double, and it has every vital amenity for any executive: a full desk, Internet capability, and a minibar. Viale Pietramellara 51 (across from train station). ☎ 051/246-178. www.starhotels.com. Superior single 150€–235€, deluxe single 170€–300€, executive single 190€–310€; deluxe double 170€–300€, executive double 190€–310€; junior suite 210€–335€. Amenities: Restaurant; bar; fitness room; free Internet/office point; laundry/dry cleaning; safe deposit boxes. In room: A/C, TV, hair dryer, wireless Internet, minibar.

Eating

While the university and its students give Bologna the reputation of being a young, alternative city as well as being Italy's intellectual center, the kitchens and restaurants also make it the culinary capital of northern Italy. Bologna is best known for the delicious, saliva-inducing cold pork sausage: mortadella. Another famous foodstuff, spaghetti Bolognese, is derived from the local *tagliatelle al ragù* (pale yellow, egg-based pasta ribbons in a sauce of ground veal and pork and tomato), which is leaps and bounds better than the bastardized version of the same name found in North American restaurant chains. No matter how long you plan on staying, you can guarantee that your brain and belly will be filled to capacity by the time you leave. Unfortunately, the only downside to eating in Bologna is that it's a bit more expensive than in other Italian cities, so you might want to consider grabbing a sandwich for lunch somewhere—all *alimentari* (grocery/delis) will make them for you, and save your money for that special meal, whether it's a cheaper-than-dinner lunch at a fancy place, or a blowout dinner that's your special treat.

COFFEE BARS & LIGHT FARE

As a general range, if you have your espresso standing up at bar, expect to pay around .75€–.90€; cappuccino standing up at bar: .90€–1.10€; if you have a pastry standing up at bar as well, add on another 1€–1.50€; prices double when you sit down at any bar; prices triple when you sit down at fancy places.

MTV Best → **Bar Alberto & Giovanna** ★ A walk through the affluent area of Via Farini can work up a mean appetite. Fortunately, there's a place to grab a snack without paying exorbitant prices. Skip the uptight cafes and ritzy bars and look for Vicolo Barbazzi 1. Alberto, the owner, is a kind, bespectacled man who'll explain each of his sandwiches to

you in Italian. If your knowledge of the language doesn't extend past *ciao* and *grazie* it doesn't matter. Alberto uses hand motions and impersonations to explain what is what. Make sure you're paying attention when he gets to the chicken cutlet: his clucking chicken impression, complete with flapping wings and strut, is worth the price of the sandwich alone. If the bar is empty, he'll sit down next to you and talk about how he'll one day be the proud owner of the red Ferrari Maranello parked on the street outside. He might have to augment his act with a couple more animal impressions to fund those wheels. *Vicolo Barbazzi 1 (just southeast of Piazza Cavour). Mon–Fri 7am–7pm. No credit cards.*

MTV Best → **Zanarini** ★ Dashing politicos and professor-types mix with the rest of Bologna's *bella gente* at this snazzy coffee bar and *pasticceria* on the pedestrianized Piazza Galvani. If your aim is simply to get some caffeine in your bloodstream, you can take a cappuccino standing up at the gorgeously restored bar inside; but to fully partake of the Zanarini scene, don some red chinos and a rakish hairdo, grab a table outside, and strike your best languorous-intelligentsia pose. *Piazza Galvani 1 (at Via Farini).* ☎ *051/275-0041. Daily 7am–10pm.*

→ **Zoo Café** Zoo Café is popular among students for two things: lunch and post-class binge drinking. Stop by the neon orange oasis for one of their tasty sandwiches and a Coke. Hopefully that picture on the wall of the man wearing an elephant bikini won't ruin your appetite. *Via Oberdan 19/C (at Via San Simone).* ☎ *346/024-5599 (cellphone). Daily 7am–7pm.*

CHEAP

→ **Osteria dell'Orsa** Students and locals love coming to this haunt for a casual sit-down lunch. Also open for dinner, it's more popular during midday. Wooden benches and tables make up the furniture inside, and while there is a small outdoor sitting area across the way, stick to the interior of dell'Orsa;

bums like to use the area around the restaurant entrance as their urinal. Subway smell aside, their panini are filling and don't fall short in the taste department. *Via Mentana 1/F (at Via Marsala).* ☎ *051/231-576. www. osteriadellorsa.com. Daily noon–1am. Primi 5.50€–7€, panini 4.50€, salads 6.50€.*

→ **Osteria del Moretto** ★ Farther south of the historic district, you'll find posh bars and restaurants that match the high-class stores in the area. Keep walking south, just outside the walls past the Porta San Mamolo area, and you'll find a more down-to-earth dining option in Osteria del Moretto. Half bar, half restaurant, it's the perfect place to unwind after a long day, when you don't feel like dressing up for dinner. The trattoria offers a variety of plates, but their version of the ultra-typical *tagliatelle al ragù* (aka spaghetti Bolognese) is a satisfying one. Grab a couple of drinks, sit down to a comfortable meal, and then enjoy the rustic Porta San Mamolo neighborhood. *Via di San Mamolo 5 (just south of Piazza di Porta San Mamolo).* ☎ *051/580-284. Primi 5€–6€; secondi 8€–14€. Daily for dinner and drinks until 3am.*

→ **Cesarina** The open-air dining area of Cesarina is unbeatable in the summer. Luckily, the food isn't half bad, either. Trot over to Piazza Santo Stefano and give their lasagna a whirl. Layered with ham and fontina cheese, it's rich, creamy, and tangy. With kick-ass comfort food like that, it's no wonder the restaurant's been around for 70 years. *Via Santo Stefano 19/b (west side of Piazza Santo Stefano).* ☎ *051/232-037. Tues–Sun for lunch and dinner. Primi 6€–8€; secondi 9€–14€.*

DOABLE

→ **Da Cesari** ★ BOLOGNESE   Don't leave Bologna without trying the *tortellini* from Da Cesari. Bursting with ricotta and spinach, they'll leave you smiling for at least an hour after you've left the restaurant. (Or maybe that was the Sangiovese?) Other dishes

include traditional Bolognese meats like veal, as well as the less common rabbit, and the Cesari family prepares each plate with amazing care. *Via de' Carbonesi 8 (at Via Massimo D'Azeglio).* ☎ *051/237-710. Mon–Sat for lunch and dinner. Closed 1st week of Jan. Reservations recommended. Primi 8€–10€; secondi 12€–16€.*

→ **Osteria Le Mura** ★★ BOLOGNESE Whether it's intentional or not, the dark red-and-brown color scheme in this dimly lit trattoria evokes the hues of its best product—meat—done to pink-middled perfection. In the quiet Porta San Mamolo area a 5-minute walk south of Piazza Maggiore, Osteria Le Mura sees a clientele of mostly locals (and guests from the Hotel Porta San Mamolo, across the street), who get fired up for the cheesy but fun karaoke band that takes to small corner stage on weekends. The creative *crostini* are highly recommended for appetizers, and the rich desserts are to die for. (Too many Italian desserts are dry, but here, we are happy to report, butter is used generously.) In the middle, choose from a variety of pastas and a whole host of grilled meats and fish, all paired with excellent, inexpensive wine. Vegetarians can round out their meals with side dishes or steamed or roasted vegetables. *Vicolo del Falcone 13/A (off Via Paglietta).* ☎ *051/331772. Primi 8€–10€; secondi 12€–15€. Tues–Sun for dinner.*

→ **Ristorante Donatello** EMILIA-ROMAGNA Named after the grandfather of the current manager, Donatello is a celebrity magnet. (Or, at least that's what the wall of fame seems to impress on diners.) Italian heroes Andrea Bocelli, soccer star Roberto Baggio, and French movie star Gerard Depardieu have all, at one time or another, dined at this Tuscan restaurant, and their mugs are permanently captured among the hundred or so photos on the walls. Stare at the 1920s furniture and high ceilings, but order their *cotoletta Donatello,* and your attention will be taken hostage by the glorious breaded veal cutlet with prosciutto di Parma, Parmigiano-Reggiano cheese, and mushrooms. *Via A. Righi 8 (off Via dell'Indipendenza).* ☎ *051/235438. Primi 8€–10€; secondi 11€–16€. Sun–Fri for lunch and dinner. Closed Aug.*

➜ **Ristorante Teresina** BOLOGNESE If you have the option, try to score the outdoor seats of Ristorante Teresina. Wedged in an alleyway, you'd think it wouldn't be the most romantic of settings. You couldn't be more wrong. In the evening, the surrounding buildings act as a buffer to the noisy thoroughfares of Via Oberdan and nearby Via Rizzoli. Noise will be the last thing on your mind when it comes time to order. They offer two menus: one meat, one fish (sorry, vegetarians). Give the yummy *fettucine con alici fresche e olive* (with fresh anchovies and olives) a whirl, even if you think you don't like anchovies; the slippery, salty, but-not-too-fishy pasta won't disappoint. *Via Oberdan 4 (just north of Via Rizzoli).* ☎ *051/228-985. Primi 9€–10€; secondi 9€–18€. Mon–Sat for lunch and dinner.*

➜ **Rosteria Luciano** ★ BOLOGNESE After you've drooled on the street-side window, watching the cooks spin around and churn out dish after dish, mosey on in and find a seat in Rosteria Luciano. Without looking at the menu, order yourself the *scaloppe cotoletta alla Bolognese.* Before American Southerners concocted the "turducken," Bologna had its twist on layered meat; the *scaloppe cotoletta* is a baked dish of veal slathered with ham and parmigiano cheese. Even if you're not a fan of veal, this plate is hard to pass up once it's put in front of you in all its aromatic, steaming glory. *Via Nazario Sauro 19 (at Via San Giorgio).* ☎ *051/ 231-249. Thurs–Tues for lunch and dinner. Primi 6€–9€; secondi 11€–28€. Reservations recommended.*

➜ **Trattoria La Braseria** BOLOGNESE With the walls covered with signed soccer jerseys and the smell of deep-fried goodness coming out of the kitchen, it's hard to believe that Trattoria La Braseria is not some kind of sports bar. Yet, try as you might, you will not find one TV in the place. Wine racks in the rear and a solid menu remind guests that while it's a casual setting, you can sit down and enjoy a traditional Bolognese meal. If the aromas are too enticing and you want some oily goodness, settle for the *pollo fritto con zucchine,* a tasty take on deep-fried chicken with zucchini. *Via Testoni 2 (at Via Ugo Bassi).* ☎ *051/222-839. Primi 10€–13€; secondi 16€–20€. Cover/service 3€. Mon–Sat for lunch and dinner.*

SPLURGE

➜ **Godot Wine Bar** ★★ EMILIA-ROMAGNA While Godot takes pride in its extensive wine selection, the name "wine bar" is an unfortunate misnomer that takes too much attention away from the marvelous menu that the owner, Piero, has crafted. As with many restaurants in Italy, the choice seats are street side in the chill, soothing night air. Via Cartoleria tends to get dark with the lack of streetlamps, but the candlelit tables create an amazing ambiance for your meal, and the grub will knock your taste buds on the cobblestoned floor. For starters, try the sea bass with capers, drizzled with olive oil on a dollop of tomato purée. Served cold, it's remarkably tasty and refreshing and doesn't overwhelm you with flavor. To accompany the dish o' fish, Piero will suggest the Murgo, a mildly fruity white wine from Mt. Etna. If sea bass isn't your thing, try the tuna with mint pesto. Half raw, half grilled, and topped with pine nuts, the tuna is texturally wonderful and highly recommended. This time, Piero'll hook you up with a pinot grigio from the Sud Tirol. The main dish you shouldn't miss is the veal chop with ground zucchini. Some might find it slightly greasy, but the veal is actually very tender, with an excellent consistency. This is where the wine really complements the dish; ask for the Olmatello (Sangiovese di Romagna, in particular "La Berta" 2001). It cuts through

Sippin' in Style, *Alla Bolognese*

If you've had your fill of drinking Guinness in Italian "Irish" pubs, head for the [MTV] [Best] design-led watering holes and tapas-style eateries on **Via Clavature and Via de' Musei**, just southeast of Piazza Maggiore. Many a Bolognese night on the town never leaves the confines of these two tiny streets, where you'll find some of the city's hottest young hangouts, all conveniently located within a 1-minute walk of each other.

Al Calice WINE BAR   With casual, chest-height tables strategically placed along both sides of the delightful medieval Via Clavature, this lively and unpretentious joint, whose name means "at the chalice," has been snagging passersby for local wines by the glass (from 4€) and generous *taglieri* (wooden cutting boards of regional cheeses, cured meats, and olives, from 9€) since 1939. Al Calice also offers a wine-tasting menu, paired with more pork and cheese, and *tigelle,* a special Bolognese biscuit. The menu also offers oysters, caviar, and Cristal, but Al Calice still feels more like a traditional, hunk-of-mortadella/glass-of-Sangiovese kind of place. *Via Clavature 13/a (at Via Drapperie).* ☎ *051/264506. www.barilcalice.it. Mon–Sat 9am–2am.*

Café le Palais LOUNGE   If, by some miracle of plate tectonics, Venice ever collided with France, and then both slammed into the Indian subcontinent, the local bar in the resulting new geographical location might look like the interior of Café le Palais, perhaps Bologna's most stylish place for a drink. As if furnished with finds from a caravan of bathroom-tile liquidators, the front room has an Eastern, almost Moorish look, a hall features a mosaic of small convex mirrors, and the shabby-chic rear salons have worn and comfortable French chairs upholstered in velvet. But the choicest spots at Café le Palais are "outside," under the vaults of the fully porticoed Via de' Musei; here you'll find substantial leather armchairs and table lamps that give the covered street the feel of a plush living room. Down-to-earth clientele skews a bit older and artier than at the other bars in the vicinity—feel free to show up in your best maudlin ensemble of beret, baggy sweater, and absent gaze, and wax nostalgic about Paris in the '30s, all over a glass of Pernod. *Via de' Musei 4 (at Via Clavature).* ☎ *051/648-6963. www.cafelepalais.com. Tues–Sun 8:30am–2am.*

Nu Lounge Bar WINE BAR   Climbing the wide stairs to Nu Lounge Bar is like approaching the Supreme Court of Bolognese wannabes. Without a

the meat like a Ginsu knife. Don't miss a chance to dine here; Piero is a fantastic host and his culinary choices are unmatched (maybe only by his wine expertise). I'm just waiting for Godot . . . to change the wine bar moniker. *Via Cartoleria 12 (off Via Castiglione).* ☎ *051/226-315. Set 3-course menus ranging from 30€–40€. Closed Aug.*

➜ **I Carracci** ★ ITALIAN/INTERNATIONAL
If someone offers to take you out to dinner and you want to milk him/her for all he/she is

worth, then suggest I Carracci. The grub here is heavy on the stomach as well as the wallet. Management probably needs the extra cash to maintain the intricate frescoes that date all the way back to the 1700s. The *tortellini in brodo* (in broth) is more exciting than the traditional name would suggest. The thick broth and soft pasta dumplings (filled with meat or cheese) are extremely filling, and the taste builds the further you get into the meal. If you're craving something meatier, try the doubt, this is where Ben Stiller would come to get into character if he ever had to do a movie about Italian fashion victims. Populated by impossibly trendy clones (who, like Derek Zoolander, are at least all very good-looking and friendly), "Nu" is self-styled "fashion-chic bar," with a lacquered black-and-glass interior and cocktails with names like "Nu Flava." The whole thing is just this side of ridiculous, but it's also fun, and if you want to understand the meaning of the word *fichetto* (young, Italian, and aspirationally cool), you've gotta check it out. Dress code is casual during the daytime here, but if you're coming after 7pm, you'd better look the part: Wear ye black or wear ye denim, so help you God, just tuck your jeans into your boots! As "fashion-chic" as Nu Lounge tries to be, it's frequented by plenty of normal people, too. (We saw a 15-year-old Napoleon Dynamite lookalike guzzling wine with his parents here one night.) Drink options include wines by the glass (posted on the blackboard behind the bar, from 4€), and a rambling menu of cocktails (most are 8€). Especially warming in winter is the Grasshopper, a rich and minty concoction made with crème de menthe, crème de cacao, and milk. There are a few seats indoors, and plenty more on the porticoed patio, where all the smokers hang out, but table service costs more. You can also eat at Nu Lounge, as long as your appetite will be sated by exotic nibbles (foie gras with *crostini*, curried chicken with rice, tuna tartare) and precious desserts (tarts, tortes, and puddings). *Via de' Musei 6 (at Via Clavature).* ☎ *051/222532. www.nu-lounge.com. Tues–Sun 10am–2am.*

Rosa Rosé WINE BAR/LOUNGE Just down the street from Al Calice, Rosa Rosé is an indoor/outdoor spot done up in a mod black-and-white motif. The chic interior is surprisingly cozy and inviting, given its color scheme, but the alfresco scene, ironically, has a colder feel. Most of the canvas chairs and tables are set up in such a way that you have to face your own tablemates—the horror!—when the whole point of being at a place like this is watching other people go by. There's really nowhere to stand up and drink here, so stop by or call ahead to make a reservation for one of the more sociable tables. Rosa Rosé is also one of Bologna's top caterers, so the food menu is full of tasty, tidy morsels and nouvelle cuisine entrees. *Via Clavature 8/b (between Via Drapperie and Via Castiglione).* ☎ *051/225071. www.rosarose.it. Mon–Sat 10am–2am.*

wild boar. The northern Italian specialty is prepared perfectly here, and the slightly stringy meat explodes with flavor. Reservations are a must. *Via dell'Indipendenza 8 (at Via Altabella).* ☎ *051/225-445. Daily for lunch and dinner. Primi 10€–14€; secondi 15€–28€.*

→**Ristorante al Pappagallo** ★★★ BOLO-GNESE The Gothic look of the area around Piazza della Mercanzia and the entrance of Pappagallo are a little misleading about what you get inside the restaurant. Look past the iron chandelier, and you'll find the main seating area is a brighter, more contemporary setting, which might disappoint some who were hoping for more of a 13th-century dungeon vibe. Get over your decor delusions, and you'll find that the food takes most of the spotlight anyway. Locals and tourists alike swear that the best eats in Bologna come from "The Parrot." If hunger has gotten the best of you, the waiter will suggest the enormous *costola di vitello alla bolognese.* It feeds two, but it could easily feed three or four. This veal chop dish is one of their more popular dishes, and with good reason: The almost-cloyingly tender veal explodes in your mouth, with Parmigiano-Reggiano cheese highlighting the already tangy meat. *Piazza della Mercanzia 3.* ☎ *051/231-200. Secondi, 10€–20€. Mon–Sat for lunch and dinner.*

Partying

Bologna's student population influences many aspects of everyday life, though it's nowhere near the effect it has on the nightlife. You won't find a more tolerant city in Europe this side of Amsterdam, and you'll find a jaw-dropping amount of variety in bars, clubs, and lounges. The liberal way of life translates to how the young carry themselves in the dark recesses of the pubs or in the glittery dance floor of the discotecas. They move, drink, and talk seemingly without a care in the world. Luckily, it's contagious and when you've downed a couple drinks, you feel like one of them. Perhaps it's the instantaneous fraternity or just the carefree way they carry themselves, but it makes Bologna perhaps the greatest party city in Italy. Pick up a copy of *Zero51* (for the city's area code, 051) in your hotel lobby, hostel reception, tourist office, or various stores to find out what events and concerts are happening in a given night.

Drink prices in Italy are basically as follows (in all but the chichi-est places in Rome, Florence, Milan, Venice):

Glass of wine in enoteca (wine bar): from 2€, for a totally drinkable local wine that you may have never heard of, all the way up to 8€ for a particularly special vintage of Brunello or Barolo. Most people drink something in the 3–4€ range. Wine is by far the cheapest (and classiest, since quality is so high) way to get drunk in Italy.

Pint of beer (lager, ale, Guinness, whatever): 4€ during happy hour; 5€ after happy hour; this is the standard in all the big cities; could be a little cheaper in more remote places.

Another Fun Bar

The great thing about **La Linea** ★ is that it's open for the most part of the day. It's smack-dab in the middle of Piazza Maggiore (slightly to the northeast of it) and many locals and tourists grab their first cocktail of the day here. The parlor-like interior, at least during the day, is usually empty since everyone likes to fill the outdoor area under the enclosed alley/walkway. At night, though, there's nary an empty seat anywhere, and La Linea is chock-full of a great mix of students and foreigners. Along with some chill, quality music, La Linea is a fantastic lounge where you can kick back and admire the antiquity of the surrounding buildings. *Piazza Re Enzo 1/11 (off Piazza Maggiore).* ☎ **051/296-5134.**

Cocktails/mixed drinks: 4–5€ in casual, laid-back bars; 7–10€ in trendier spots.

Most clubs are open from 10pm until 2 or 3am; most don't really get going until 11pm or midnight. Music clubs get going a bit earlier, as live acts usually go on at 10 or 10:30pm.

PUBS

➜ **Birreria Amadeus** This Italian pub boasts a selection of over 100 different beers. Try as you might, you won't be able to sample all of them in a week, especially with beers like Ceasurus pumping out of one of their taps. This horribly strong ale checks in at 12% alcohol by volume. To sop up the excess alcohol, plenty of sandwiches, burgers, or pizzas are also on offer. *Via G. Dagnini 1 (at Via A. Murri).* ☎ *051/623-4011. Daily 5pm–2am.*

➜ **Celtic Druid** ★ If you want to avoid all the other cookie-cutter pubs in Bologna, pay a visit to this rowdy water hole. The barkeeps are a fun, English-speaking bunch, and they'll provide some entertainment while they pour you that perfect pint. Happy hour takes place daily from 7 to 8:30pm. If you find yourself in town during some holiday, there's no place more festive than the Celtic Druid. The staff dresses up, the inside is redecorated, and the music is always spot-on. *Via Caduti di Cefalonia 5/c (at Via Rizzoli).* ☎ *051/224-212. www.celticdruid.com. Daily 5pm–2am.*

→**English Empire** Pubs usually don't house palm trees, but the kids at English Empire don't really seem to care. Students love hitting this pub after class or just for a quick brew on the weekends. The palm trees and the open doors keep the interior cool and calm, perfect for a pint in the Bologna heat. Food is served here as well, but with hot dogs and hamburgers as the stars of the menu (and "English" in the name of the establishment), you're better off sampling your *cucina bolognese* elsewhere. You'll also find a pool table in the back (not a full-sized snooker table, unfortunately) and an old smoking room that's been rendered useless with the smoking ban recently passed in Italy. *Via Zamboni 24/A (at Largo Respighi).* ☎ *051/227245. Mon–Fri 9am–3am; Sat–Sun 5pm–3am.*

CLUBS & LIVE MUSIC VENUES

→**Chet Baker** The perfect place for a swanky, laid-back evening. All the jazz club standards are present: dark lighting (alas, no indoor-smoking law = no smoky haze), candlelit round tables around the small stage, and the usual clientele of cool cats. There's a restaurant and dining area, but the action happens when the Italian jazz acts hop on stage in the concert room. Bring a date, sport a skinny tie loosened just so, order some brandy, and be cool, ya dig? *Via Polese 7/a (at Via Riva di Reno).* ☎ *051/223-795. www.chetbaker.it.*

MTV **Best** →**Corto Maltese** ★ The divey club draws an edgier crowd, but there's music for every aural palate, ranging from '70s and '80s rock to dance to funk to R&B. If music isn't your thing, there's a pool table in the

back as well as a lounge area to kick back. Chalk up a cue and shark some locals, or hit the dance floor and mesmerize 'em with your interpretational dance to the Scorpions' "Rock You Like a Hurricane." Happy hour in Corto Maltese strikes long after the sun goes down, at a reasonably late 9–10pm, recently changed from a more orthodox 7–9pm. Next door is the Drink Factory, a bartender school that churns out future booze slingers for places like Corto Maltese. *Via del Borgo S. Pietro 9/2a (at Via delle Moline).* ☎ *051/229746. www.cortomaltesediscobar.com. Daily 7pm–4am.*

→**Kinki** Hugely energetic and bubbly, Kinki seems a little out of place in the city center, so close to the historic heart of Bologna. The very gay friendly *discoteca*, open until 5am and sometimes later, is the place to be when all other pubs and clubs have closed their doors. From the moment the DJ starts spinning until the wee hours of dawn, Kinki and the revelers keep the floor shaking and the neighbors awake. The Torre Garisenda most probably owes its precarious tilt to the seismic beats from Kinki. *Via Zamboni 1 (just past the two towers).* ☎ *347/512-1985 (cellphone). www.kinkidisco.com. Tues, Fri–Sat 11pm–5am.*

MTV **Best** →**Link** This concrete blob somehow draws the biggest names in electronica. Locals used to be able to walk to the club when it was a 10-minute walk north of the train station. Nowadays it's situated a couple of kilometers from the city limits, but bus shuttles from the train station are usually offered during busy nights, or when a big DJ is in town. On concertsnights, admission is usually free to this frighteningly popular dance club. (Consult *Zero51* or check the site for events and cover charge). The enormous first floor is dedicated to the movers and shakers, while the bars on the second floor is where they fuel up on Campari. *Via Fantoni 21 (northeast outskirts of city).* ☎ *051/633-2312. Wed–Sat. Cover charge varies.*

A Fabulous Gay Bar

Cassero (Via Don Minzoni 18; ☎ 051/6494416) is Bologna's most popular gay bar, with a noisy, discolike atmosphere and floor shows. The biggest attraction is the setting—the club occupies one of Bologna's medieval gates, the top of which serves as a roof garden and open-air dance floor in good weather. Cassero is also the Bologna headquarters of Arcigay and Arcilesbiche, a gay and lesbian center organizing cultural meetings and entertainment. Thursday is set aside for women, on Friday theatrical performances of interest to the gay and lesbian community take place, and on Sunday disco fever takes over (events vary widely and are scheduled at different times).

➔ **Vicolo Bolognetti** Vicolo, as it's better known to locals, is another half concert-venue, half dance-club. On rare occasions, dance performances, theater productions, and DJ sets also take place in the confines of the venue. On nights without live acts, you'll hear tunes that range from tango to rock to world beat. There's usually no cover, but if there's a special event or if it's tango night, expect to shell out a small amount (8€–10€) to get in. *Vicolo Bolognetti 2 (off Via Begatto).* ☎ *349/259-5803 (cellphone). Closed Monday.*

➔ **Zoom** A mix of gay and straight clientele, Zoom is best visited during the "park nights." This themed evening converts the interior of the club into an artificial green space, complete with Astroturf and faux-starlight. *Via Mascarella 6o/a (at Via Irnerio).* ☎ *051/241-963.*

Sightseeing

Walking around Bologna is not like running a gauntlet of tourist must-sees (with all due respect to the Museum of Upholstery), but what the city does offer is a remarkably handsome and well-kept, earth-toned tableau with some imposing medieval palaces, towers, and churches, and of course, porticoes, porticoes, and more porticoes. A gift of 13th-century Bologna's Golden Age, when the urban population hit an all-time high, the city's trademark porticoes were built above the sidewalks to create housing for students and other low-rent tenants. Some of Bologna's grander porticoes have elaborately frescoed vaults and thick red drapes, whose heavy swags can barely contain them, making the arcades look like tired eyes longing to close.

The majority of Bologna's most interesting sights are in a pretty compact area, so don't worry about following the map too carefully—if you're wandering aimlessly around Piazza Maggiore, you're bound to hit pretty much everything on this list.

PUBLIC MONUMENTS

MTV Best FREE ➔ **Piazza Maggiore**
★★ Sand-colored cobblestones lend a monumental expansiveness to Bologna's main square, which is surrounded by the dramatic facades of Palazzo Re Enzo and the adjacent Palazzo del Podestà, the basilica of San Petronio (see churches below), and Palazzo d'Accursio with its 13th-century belltower. A rather gorgeous portico, known to local pedestrians as the Pavaglione—complete with heavy red drapes between the arcades to shield shops from harsh afternoon light—lines the eastern edge of Piazza Maggiore. The small streets leading east from the square take you to the most characteristic parts of medieval Bologna, including the food market around Via Pescherie Vecchie and the popular bars and lounges around Via Clavature. The northwestern patch of the public space is properly called **Piazza Nettuno,** with its namesake fountain (see below) and the **Sala Borsa library** and war memorials.

FREE ➔ **Fontana del Nettuno** ★★
There's a story behind this once-scandalous fountain, now considered by some to be the

Bologna Partying & Sightseeing

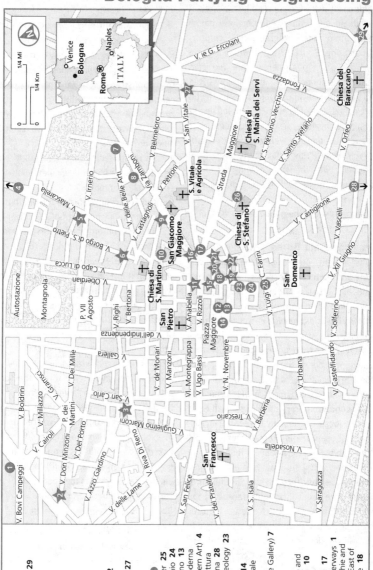

symbol of Bologna. Apparently, conservative Church fathers were appalled by the original scandalous sculpture's "proportions" below the torso and ordered the sculptor, Giambologna, to bring Neptune's male member down to less heroic scale. The artist grudgingly cooperated, but he still was able to sneak in a clever use of perspective. If you view the statue of Neptune and his left arm at just the right angle, the extended index finger doubles as a rather well-endowed, uh, 11th finger. People now relax at the base of the fountain, with the water rushing out of the four sirens' busts, while the less fortunate try to cleanse themselves in the smaller corner fountains when the police aren't watching. Piazza Nettuno.

FREE → **Sala Borsa** ★ It's not really a tourist "sight," per se, but as the heart of culture and multimedia in modern-day Bologna, the Sala Borsa is well worth a visit. What is it, you ask? Well, it's one of Italy's great archaeological hybrids, which has, in past incarnations, been a Roman basilica, a fortress, stables, a pharmaceutical garden, a stock exchange (hence the name, *Sala Borsa*), a boxing ring, and a basketball court. Today, it's a bookstore and library with Internet cafe (only open to library members), with cafes on the loggia overlooking the central atrium, and 2,000-year-old Roman ruins visible through the Plexiglas panels that make up the floor. Many students and other young Bolognese pass through the Sala Borsa at least once a day. The main façade of the building, facing Piazza Nettuno, features moving memorials to Bolognese who died in World War II—in battle, during bombardment of the city, or in the Nazi concentration camps. Another plaque bears the names and often agonizingly young ages of the 87 people who died in the terrorist bombing of the Bologna train station (Strage di Bologna) in 1980. *Piazza Nettuno 3 (west side of square).* ☎ *051/204400. www.bibliotecasalaborsa.it.*

Mon 2:30–9:30pm; Tues–Fri 9am–9:30pm; Sat 9am–7pm. Admission free.

→ **Torre Asinelli and Torre Garisenda** ★★ Towers, the ultimate phallic symbol, used to be all over Bologna. Throughout the Middle Ages, noble families built hundreds of towers to demonstrate their wealth and power, earning the Bologna the nickname of *La Turrita* ("the tower'd"). Most of the city's towers have been castrated or otherwise chopped down, but two prominent ones, Torre Asinelli and Torre Garisenda, remain standing, side by side, as icons of a virile medieval Bologna. To switch metaphors, the smaller Torre Garisenda is comparable to the diminutive Nicole Richie, measuring only 49m (161 ft.) and, like its counterpart in the first season of "The Simple Life," listing dangerously off-kilter. In its early years, part of the tower was amputated in fear of total collapse. Torre Asinelli, is an imposing 102m (335 ft.) tall, and anyone can enter the monument. The Asinelli tower also tilts slightly, but not to the extent of its companion. For a great workout, you can climb the narrow, dizzying steps to the top, where you get a great sense of Bologna's wagon-wheel layout. The top of the Torre Asinelli puts you so far above the rest of the buildings that the city below looks like a satellite image of red rooftops. If you're thinking of exploring the smaller Garisenda tower next door, don't bother—it's off-limits. (If you try going in, like I did, you'll look foolish pulling the iron ring on the door, to no avail.) *Piazza di Porta Ravegnana (eastern end of Via Rizzoli). Daily 9am–6pm. Admission 3€.*

HISTORIC NEIGHBORHOODS

→ **The Jewish Ghetto and Jewish Museum** Just north of the two towers, between Via Oberdan and Via Zamboni, was the area of the old ghetto, where Bolognese Jews were required to live from the late 14th century to the late 16th century, when a Church edict forced all Jews out of the city and into the ghetto of nearby Ferrara. The appropriately named Via dell'Inferno ("Street of Hell") was the main artery of the ghetto, where residents made a living off of preparing tripe, and the narrow streets and alleys here (Via Purgatorio, Via Limbo, Via Canonica, Vicolo S. Giobbe, Vicolo Mandria, Via del Carro) still give some sense of what life would have been like in the gated ward (which was surrounded, not accidentally, by six churches). During the day, Jews could leave the enclosure by way of the gates (now removed) at Via dei Giudei and Via Oberdan, but at sundown, the gates were closed and Jews were not allowed out in the city. A plaque at Via dell'Inferno 16 marks the spot where the 15th-century synagogue used to be. A small museum in the vicinity, the **Museo Ebraico (Jewish Museum),** has some display chronicling the history of the Jews in Bologna, from medieval times through the 20th century. *Museum: Via Valdonica 1/5 (just north of Via Zamboni).* ☎ *051/2911280. www. museoebraicobo.it. Admission 4€; 2€ students under 26 with valid ID. Sun–Thurs 10am–6pm; Fri 10am–4pm. Closed Jewish holidays.*

🅼🆅 Best → **Via Pescherie Vecchie and Market Streets East of Piazza Maggiore** ★★ It's not the longest of streets, but east of the porticoes of Piazza Maggiore lies the picturesque Via Pescherie Vecchie ("Old Fishmongers' Street"). For a stretch of 200m (656 ft.), the narrow path is bursting with outdoor produce stands, cheese vendors, and butcher stalls, every Monday to Saturday, 8am to 2pm or so. Briny notes of fresh *branzino* mix with the ripe juiciness of tomatoes and pungent porkiness of prosciutto to create an olfactory opus that'll have you drooling in no time. Hang out and watch the crowds of real Bolognese angle to get in on some custom-cut swordfish steaks or plump *anguilla* (eel) at the fishmongers' stands. The scene looks like something straight out of the 16th century, except that shoppers are wearing Gucci instead of goofy pantaloons,

and overflows into nearby Via Drapperie and Via Ranocchi ("Frogs Street"—we don't want to think too much about what foodstuffs they used to sell there). *Via Pescherie Vecchie.*

CHURCHES

FREE → **Basilica San Petronio** ★★ An Italian-Gothic behemoth begun in the late 14th century, San Petronio is one of the largest churches in the world, measuring 133m long, 60m wide, and 48m high (436 x 197 x 157 ft.). Unfortunately, its gargantuan façade, which marks the southern side of Piazza Maggiore, was never finished. The fancy marble decorations that mimic architectural orders halt abruptly about a third of the way up, exposing the rest of the façade for what it is— a plain old brick wall. Inside the basilica, soaring Gothic cross vaults fly over the central nave and smaller side aisles. Unpainted and unstuccoed, the vaults have a simplicity of form that calls to mind taut nautical riggings, making San Petronio feel like the hull of a formidable sailing ship. The best time to admire the interior of the basilica is in the late afternoon or early evening, when the rays of light from the setting sun come in through the windows and cast a searing illumination over the chapels on the left. One of the chapels in particular, the Cappella di San Petronio, stands out in this natural spotlight with the smallest details made visible on its

Neither *duomo* nor *cattedrale* . . .

While San Petronio is Bologna's largest and most visible church, it is neither *duomo* nor "cathedral." By virtue of Catholic semantics, there can be only one *cattedrale* ("seat" of the bishop) or *metropolitana* ("mother of the city") per diocese; the cathedral of the diocese of Bologna is the church of San Pietro, a few blocks north of San Petronio.

gold and black iron gates and gilded candles. Be sure, too, to stop by the Bolognini Chapel (fourth on the left), where the 15th-century frescoes representing heaven and hell are hauntingly beautiful. *Piazza Maggiore.* ☎ *051/ 225-442. Daily 7:30am–1pm and 2–6:30pm (until 6pm from Oct–Mar). Free admission.*

FREE → **Santo Stefano** ★ In this unique and atmospheric church complex, open doorways lead to unexpected new chambers that have been grafted onto the sanctuary over time. There are actually seven separate churches here, and even if you're walking catatonic, you're bound to stumble into at least four of them, or out into the pretty cloister. The adorable elderly priest in the gift shop will do a priceless sales pitch, about a third of which is in English, for anything you pick up and express an interest in. The piazza outside the church, with the stunning, draped-and-porticoed **Piazza di Pilatus** is one of the most photogenic in Bologna. *Via Santo Stefano 24 (Piazza Santo Stefano).* ☎ *051/223256. Daily 8am–noon, 3–6pm. Free admission.*

MUSEUMS

→ **Museum of Archaeology** ★ If you don't have time to check out all the exhibits here, at least make a quick run through the hall of Greek and Roman busts. The subtle modeling of portrait heads' exquisitely detailed mugs is best admired in bright daylight. The rest of the museum contains impressive collections of mostly funerary art from Egypt and Italy. Fortunately for you, unfortunate for the curators, the museum is crowd-free. For the most part, you can examine the Egyptian tombs in complete silence and solitude. And really, it's the only way to fully enjoy 4,000-year-old sarcophagi. *Via dell'Archiginnasio 2 (just south of Piazza Maggiore).* ☎ *051/233-849. Admission 4€. Tues–Sat 9am–6:30pm; Sun 10am–6:30pm.*

→ **Galleria d'Arte Moderna (Gallery of Modern Art)** Go ahead and admit it, after a week in Italy, classical sculptures and 15th-century triptychs tend to become a blur. Let your senses switch gears in the Galleria d'Arte Moderna of Bologna, just northeast of the city center. Collections in the "GAM" are from the 19th to 21st centuries and heavy on Italian artists you've never heard of, but there are also works by bigger-name artists like J.M.W. Turner and Man Ray, and photographers like Edward Weston. Check the website for current exhibitions. *Piazza Costituzione 3 (at Via Stalingrado).* ☎ *051/502-859. www.galleria dartemoderna.bo.it. Admission 4€. Tues– Sun 10am–6pm. Closed May 1.*

☆ Best FREE → **Museo Tattile di Pittura Antica e Moderna** It's probably safe to say that this museum is the only place where feeling up the Mona Lisa is not only acceptable, but encouraged. At Bologna's Tactile Museum of Classical and Modern Painting, masterpieces of Italian painting have been rendered as three-dimensional sculptures, so that the blind can fondle the famed clamshell, for instance, in Botticelli's *Birth of Venus,* and enjoy the world's most celebrated works of art through touch instead of sight. Even if you're in possession of all your senses, the exhibitions here are definitely worth a visit. Because of the museum's limited opening hours, booking in advance is recommended. *Via Castiglione 71 (at Via Arienti).* ☎ *051/332-090. www.cavazza.it/arte/ edmnv/comunic.en.htm. Fri 9am–6pm; Sat 9am–1:30pm. Free admission.*

→ **Palazzo Poggi** As the seat of the University of Bologna, the Poggi Palace has many functions, including being home to dozens of exhibit halls, mostly relating to the sciences, a bit disjointed but appealingly Frankenstein's lab in their look and layout. When they're open, the anatomy museum and natural history museum are worth checking out for their campy and/or graphic displays. (Palazzo Poggi might also be your only chance to visit a museum of domestic animal anatomy.) Scan the website for upcoming

Your Dead Body's a Wonderland!

Knowing that the **Archiginnasio** is the oldest building of the oldest university in the world is exciting in itself. The tingle factor shoots way up, however, when you find out it's also home to the world's first [MTV Best] **Anatomical Theater** ★★—cue the high-pitched Gothic choral music—a gloriously chilling space where early Bolognese medical students performed their *practica* on open cadavers, and where you can all too easily picture Hannibal Lecter doing food prep, harvesting organs to sauté with fava beans and drink with a nice Chianti. (Cue the sibilant lip-sucking noise.) At first glance, the 17th-century "theater," with its ornate maple decorations, resembles a baptistery, but instead of finding a baptismal font at the sunken center of the room, there's a balustraded, coffin-shaped enclosure; inside it is a table on which rests the marble dissection slab, whose baroque divots and curves give it the shape of human torso. When the theater was in use, students and other morbidly curious types could stand and observe the anatomical experiments from risers along either side of the slab, today polished clean of blood stains. At the open end of the theater is the so-called "reader's chair" (*cattedra del lettore,* sitting just above the *cattedra del dimostratore,* or "demonstrator's chair"): the higher chair is flanked by the *Spellati* (literally, the "de-skinned"), two sinewy, flayed human figures sculpted in bronze in the 18th century. Above the chair, a seated female figure represents the goddess *Anatomia.* At her side, a winged *putto* flies up to offer the deity a femur, pledging his worship of the cult of body parts.

Mythological figures with medical attributes are all over the theater; look for them in the coffered ceiling and wall panels. Heavily bombed by the Allies in 1944, the Archiginnasio complex was completely rebuilt the following year using most of the original materials. Teatro Anatomico, Archiginnasio, Piazza Galvani 1 (southern end of Via dell'Archiginnasio). ☎ **051/276-811.** www.archiginnasio.it. Mon–Fri 9am–6:45pm; Sat 9am–1:45pm. Free admission.

exhibitions and double-check opening hours—they tend to change quite often, especially in summer, when museum staff wisely opt to hightail it out of the sweltering city and go to the beach or the mountains. *Via Zamboni 33 (near Largo A. Trombetti).* ☎ *051/209-9398. www.unibo.it/musei/palazzopoggi. Check website for updated opening hours.*

→ **Pinacoteca Nazionale di Bologna (National Picture Gallery)** ★ Don't miss a chance to check out some of the treasures stored in the Pinacoteca Nazionale di Bologna. The collection spans the 13th to the 18th centuries and includes the standard Italian smattering of medieval triptychs and Renaissance portraits, with works by such A-listers as Giotto, Titian, and Raphael. Renovations have modernized the interior, so you can walk the airy halls without that museum-mold odor to weigh you down. The airiness does not always carry over to the artwork on the walls: one of the gallery's most moving canvases is Guido Reni's *Slaughter of the Innocents* (1611), in which distraught women look skyward as one of Herod's soldiers holds a dagger poised to come down on babies already unconscious on the ground. Also intense is Guercino's *St. Sebastian Cured by St. Irene* (1619), in which Irene sponge-bathes a dazed-looking Sebastian while an attendant attempts to remove the arrows that have impaled Sebastian's limbs. Get that man some morphine. *Via delle Belle Arti 56 (at Via G. B. de Rolandis).* ☎ *051/420-9411. www.pinacoteca bologna.it. Tues–Sun 9am–7pm. Closed holidays. Admission 4€. Bus: 36, 37.*

TWO SPECIAL TOURS

FREE **→ Ducati Museum and Factory**
A few kilometers south of the city center, satisfy your need for speed by checking out the greatest modern motorcycle's museum/factory. Admission here is free, although you have to pay for the nominal bus fare to get there, and gear-nuts will get a kick out of the displays and machinery. There are guided tours twice daily, once at 11am and another at 4pm. On Saturdays, tours are available all day long. In any case, booking a tour in advance is a must. *Via Ducati 3, Borgo Panigale, Bologna.* ☎ *051/641-3111 (to book tours,* ☎ *051/ 641-3343, or infotour@ducati.com). www. ducati.com. Free admission. Mon–Fri with tours at 11am and 4pm. Sat nonstop tours 9:30am–1pm. From Piazza Maggiore, take bus 13 (1€, about 40min.) to Borgo Panigale; ask for the Ducati stop.*

→ Underground Waterways Who doesn't love an underground archaeological tour that involves water? It's so Disney. Well, in Bologna, the cultural association Amici delle Acque ("Friends of the Waters") runs walking tours of the city's eerily fantastic underground waterways. There are no animatronic Dutch maidens singing "It's a Small World" along the route, but you'll get a fascinating look at the extensive network of subterranean aqueducts, cisterns, and canals that have served Bologna since antiquity. *Viale Pietramellara 11.* ☎ *051/522401. Admission varies from 6€–12€ depending on tour. Call for schedule.*

Playing Outside

The only true playground in Bologna is the **Giardini Margherita,** on the southeastern edge of the city center (Viale Gozzadini; Apr–Sept daily 6am–midnight, Oct–March daily 7am–6pm). Kick back on the edges of the small lake (which, with its cement banks, looks like a low-budget zoo habitat for otters) and take a break from the khaki-colored urban sprawl. You can go for a jog and enjoy the wooded areas during the day, but once the sun sets, head over to the "chalet." It's a snack bar by day, but later in the evening, loud beats and mobs of locals turn it into a fabulous nightclub.

Another popular spot for locals to relax lies in the northeast of the city. There, the University of Bologna maintains the gorgeous **botanical gardens** (Via Irnerio 42; ☎ **051/351-299;** Mon–Fri 8am–3pm, Sat 8am–1pm, closed holidays). It's a sprawling 2,000 hectares (5,000 acres) and contains just as many species of plants and trees. Aside from being a green space to escape the city commotion, the gardens also are home to three greenhouses and an area where various habitats are recreated.

If you want to witness a frenetic *calcio* match, the local **soccer** team, *il Bologna*, plays its league games on Sundays (and sometimes during the week) in the Stadio Renato Dall'Ara, west of the city. Soccer season runs from late August through late May or early June. Tickets are surprisingly cheap and can be purchased from the stadium box office (Via A. Costa 174; ☎ **051/611-1125**).

Shopping

Milan and Florence have cornered the market in glitzy labels and extravagant couture. Bologna, due in part to the large population of Italians under the age of 30, has taken its influences from both cities and added its own edgier, more alternative take on some classic styles. Spray-painted T-shirts have replaced linen shirts, fauxhawks have replaced the Euromullet, and old-school Vans hug the feet instead of Ferragamo. Don't fret if you can't live without Mr. Vuitton, just head to the area south of Piazza Maggiore. Via Farini is a well-off area highlighted by a ritzy mall and the stores of Dolce & Gabbana, Roberto Cavalli, Giorgio Armani, Hermes, and, not too far off, Gucci. Needless to say, Via Farini is where you'll find a slightly older crowd doing their window-shopping. Another popular shopping area is at the **Generali** area, near Via Rizzoli and Via Calzolerie. Here you'll find some small boutiques and **COIN,** one of Italy's more popular department stores, always great for socks, scarves, gloves, and other fun, affordable accessories.

All the basics should be in the general area surrounding Via dell'Indipendenza. There, you'll find pharmacies, a grocery, and other conveniences that you'd find in your own neighborhood. A word about pharmacies, though: true *farmacie*—those marked with neon green crosses—sell prescription drugs, over-the-counter medications, tampons, and some make-up, but not the full gamut of toiletries you're used to finding at American drugstores. If you're looking for a simple bar of soap, bottle of shampoo, or laundry detergent, look for a *profumeria* like **DM** (Via dei Mille 10/a; ☎ 051/421-1254). **Coop** (Via Montebello 2/a; Mon–Fri 8am–8pm, Sat 8am–7:30pm) is one of Italy's national supermarket chains. If you'd rather cook your own meal or are on a tight budget, Coop will have everything at your culinary disposal, with a deli counter, packaged foods, and wine.

Guys, if you're looking to treat yourself to a nice, old-fashioned straight-edge shave, head to **Le Marchi** (Piazza Cavour 5D). This old-school barber, with dark wooden mirrors, will make you feel at ease while they slather on warm shaving cream and take swipes with a straight blade. And I haven't forgotten about you gals—there's a salon that'll give you preferential treatment and a kick-ass set of locks at **Toni and Guy** (Via Oberdan 11; ☎ 051/275-0038; www.toniandguy.it). You can get spiffy for a night out at

Kinki. You'll pay around 25€ for a blow out, and 40€ and up for a snazzy Italian 'do.

Store hours are another thing. Don't get the wrong idea and think that storeowners enjoy short workdays, closing at 3pm. Like many other cities, Bologna's citizens take a midday *riposo,* closing shop for a couple of hours in the late afternoon. Take this time to cool off your credit cards, find a spot to relax in a nearby piazza, and enjoy the sights. Once you've garnered enough strength to spend another wad of euros, the stores should be open again. If you find yourself wandering the porticos of Bologna in August, you'll find that most of the city shuts down for a month before the undergrads return to swarm the streets. While many stores are still open, they sometimes take a slightly longer *riposo* in the August afternoons. Some even take incredibly long *riposi,* closing for the entire month of August.

CLOTHING & ACCESSORIES

→**Aloha** Tried to ollie Neptune's arm in Piazza Maggiore and tore your favorite Emerica shirt? Aloha on Via del Borgo San Pietro should have a suitable replacement for you. The local skate store has racks full of Quiksilver, Emerica, DC, and Split as well as boards, trucks, and other skateboard accessories. When the winter rolls around, snowboarding gear replaces the trucks and wheels. *Via del Borgo San Pietro 26/A (off Via delle Moline).* ☎ 051/240-217. www.alohabologna.com.

MTV Best →**Combo** ★ This boutique in the north of Bologna is one of the better places to sift through racks of jeans and T-shirts. The clerks are cute and the music is never disappointing. The few times I stopped by, Massive Attack's "Mezzanine" was getting heavy rotation every time (extra brownie points from me). Selection isn't huge, but the few labels they do have are quality names. My favorite, Obey, can be found here as well as Stussy, Ecko, and Paul Frank. Come here for blazers, denim, T-shirts, or track jackets.

BOLOGNA & EMILIA-ROMAGNA

Piazza VIII Agosto 5 (off Via Indipendenza/Via Irnerio). ☎ *051/421-1642. www.combo.it.*

→ **Ethic** J. Crew's sassier twin sister apparently fled to Bologna to escape the wretched confines of American style. Women can find similar clothing at Ethic with an obvious Italian flair. Dresses are colorful and find the perfect balance between flowy and form-fitting, a difficult thing to do for summer fashion. As a result, most of the outfits here are tailored for the slimmer figures common in Italy. *Via Indipendenza 61/a (at Via San Giuseppe).* ☎ *051/245-004. www.ethic.it.*

MTV Best → **Free Shop** ★ The best local shop for younger women in Bologna lies in Free Shop. Mannequins here sport funky dresses, asymmetrical skirts, and uniquely patterned blazers. Each design oozes attitude, all the while combining classy forms and colors with careful subtlety. Guys, if you could trade in your Y-chromosome for an X, this is the first store where you'd max out your credit card. *Strada Maggiore 7/E (just east of Piazza Porta Ravegnana). Mon–Sat 9:30am–12:30pm and 4–7:30pm.*

→ **Scout** Sometimes it's a little too easy to make comparisons to American stores, but the moment you enter Scout, you'll immediately think you've entered Urban Outfitters. A small section of kitschy toys and a much larger selection of denim and T-shirts, you can't help but see the similarity. The only place in town to grab a Jesus bobblehead and a pair of jeans. *Via A. Righi 10 (near Via Venturini).* ☎ *051/235-749. www.scout.it. Mon–Sat 9:30am–7:30pm.*

MUSIC, BOOKS & MEDIA

→ **Gospel Music Caffe** Finally, a music store with a little originality! Gospel Music Caffe combines the social benefits of a sit-down cafe with listening stations for cultural cultivation. Unfortunately, you won't find a huge variety of CDs here, but they do sell some vinyl, if that's any consolation. Otherwise, it's perfect for grabbing a panino and

the latest attempt at a record by U2. *Via d'Irnerio 10A (at Via Borgo S. Pietro).* ☎ *051/254-020. Mon–Sat 9:30am–7:30pm.*

→ **Modo Infoshop** Even if you're not looking for a used book or CD here, Modo's a great place to kick back with a friend. The seating area in the back, along with two Internet points, makes it more of a lounge than anything else. During the school year, students grab their used textbooks here and chill with classmates. Don't leave without checking out some of the awesome T-shirts designed by the same university kids. *Via Mascarella 24/b (off Via delle Belle Arti).* ☎ *051/587-1012. www.modoinfoshop.com. Tues–Sat 10am–8pm; Mon 10am–early afternoon.*

→ **Nannucci** If there's a CD to be found in Bologna, it'll be found here. Selection runs the entire gamut here, from jazz to world beat to indie rock to easy listening, even. The good: Thirteen different Talking Heads albums and Velvet Underground getting massive airplay on the speakers. The bad: Out of 10 different Stevie Wonder CDs, no *Songs in the Key of Life*. I'd like to think someone bought five copies of it before I came in. The ugly: Some CDs are out of alphabetical order. Yeah, that's the only thing I can think of . . . this place has everything else covered. *Via Oberdan 7 (north of Via Rizzoli).* ☎ *051/237-337. Mon–Sat 9am–7:30pm.*

→ **Rockhouse** Buying vinyl overseas probably isn't the smartest thing to do. Records are big and bulky and can be a pain to ship. The one exception is if you find a rare record at Rockhouse. Claudio Menegatti is the owner of the music store and a self-proclaimed vinyl nut. You'll find many collectibles here from the collection he's been building since '65. Open for less than a year, it's already garnered a cult following with the usual regulars coming in, donning headphones, and spinning old jazz LPs. Even if you're not going to buy anything, come in, listen to some Wilson Pickett, and chill with Claudio. *Via Portanova 2/D (at Via C. Battisti). Mon–Sat 10am–7pm.*

My Bologna Has a First Name

A quick way to piss off a local is to pronounce the city name like the famous sandwich meat. For a quick background on how this town got its moniker, class is now in session: Bologna rose to prominence in the 5th century B.C. as a successful Etruscan city, then called *Felsina,* with many trade links to other parts of Europe. Soon after, an attack by the Galli Boi resulted in 200 years of Celt rule. (By all accounts, the Galli Boi were a fairly crude lot, but they did introduce pork farming to this region, and we shall certainly thank them for that.) From this period, the name of the city changed from Felsina to *Bononia,* derived from the Celt word for "city": *boi* or *bona.* The city remained Bononia when the Romans took over (187 B.C.), and since then, it's morphed into the more familiar *Bologna* and has also garnered multiple nicknames by Italians.

➜ *Bologna la dotta:* **Bologna the Learned,** from its reputation as being a kick-ass speller and the only home-schooled city in Italy. Then again, it could also be that it's the intellectual capital of Italy, home to the oldest university in the world.

➜ *Bologna la grassa:* **Bologna the Fat,** due to the fact that the renowned local cuisine is heavy on meat, dairy, and carbs. In other words, if it packs a caloric wallop, it's probably on the menu in Bologna.

➜ *Bologna la rossa:* **Bologna the Red,** for two possible reasons. First, the panorama of Bologna's skyline is mottled with red brick and marble structures. Second, the political tendencies of the city lean towards the left. The intellectual culture and the forward-thinking university breed liberal-minded scholars and a more tolerant environment in Bologna. Despite the recent election of a right-wing mayor, the city is still a socialist and communist hub.

➜ *Bologna la turrita:* **Bologna the Tower'd.** During Bologna's heyday, the city was teeming with towers, a product of proud families and individuals trying to outdo each other. Fast-forward to today and you'll find that most of those towers have either toppled or been taken down. The Due Torri, or "two towers" of Garisenda and Asinelli, still stand, delightfully atilt, at the crossroads of Strada Maggiore, Via Zamboni, and Via Rizzoli.

➜ **Basket City.** While the rest of Italy lives, breathes, and eats soccer, Bologna stands alone as a hoops town. The two basketball teams of **Fortitudo** (www.fortitudo.it) and **Virtus** (www.virtus.it) pull the city into a rim-rockin' frenzy. Their rivalry can get as intense as Red Sox/Yankees, Tarheels/Blue Devils or Mary-Kate/Ashley.

And, for the record, the sandwich meat known as "baloney" in North America did originate here, but it's called *mortadella.* Delis will make up panini with slices of it, but mortadella is usually served in cube form, as a *stuzzichino* ("toothpick snack") along with cheese and olives.

FOOD, WINE & LOCAL CRAFTS

➜ **Celebes** Armando Baravelli creates some fantastic pieces of ethnic art and sells his work from this tiny store. While the influences aren't Bolognese (mostly Indian, Moroccan, Indonesian, and Balinese), it's a cool place to check out the unique creations of a local artist. *Via San Simone 1/2 (at Via Oberdan).* ☎ 051/275-0225. *Mon–Sat 10am–2:30pm; Mon–Wed and Fri–Sat 4–7:30pm.*

➔ **Godot Wine Store** Piero, the owner of the Godot Wine Bar, truly knows his wine. You can come here and grab the first red that catches your eye, but do him and any other wine aficionado a favor and ask for some help. Don't worry, his English is spot-on and he'd rather send you off with the correct Sangiovese than sell you some random, unnecessarily expensive wine. Piero's staff is also just as capable and very helpful. *Via Santo Stefano 12/b (Piazza Santo Stefano).* ☎ *051/ 226-315. www.godotwine.it.*

Ravenna: Miles of Tiles

74km (46 miles) E of Bologna, 145km (90 miles) S of Venice, 130km (81 miles) NE of Florence

There's bling, and then there are the mosaics of Ravenna.

Of all the small Italian cities you could pick for a detour off the tourist track, Ravenna ★★★ shines for its stunning, world-famous mosaics, which illuminate the interior of many a plain brick-walled building like Byzantine Lite-Brites. Gorgeously colorful and absolutely delightful, the 5th- to 7th-century mosaics—which are under the UNESCO World Heritage protectorate—are a feast for eyes that are tired of trying to appreciate paintings of the Madonna and Child in dusty museums elsewhere in Italy.

And then, there's Ravenna itself. Maybe you've never heard of Ravenna, but this compact and elegant town a few kilometers inland from the Adriatic Sea was once the capital of the Roman Empire (albeit during the bitter end, from A.D. 402–476, when the Western Empire decisively fell), and it still comports itself with the dignity that befits a place with such a feather in its cap. The narrow medieval thoroughfares that make up the heart of Ravenna's *centro storico* are filled with cozy cafes, lively taverns, and shops selling cutting-edge fashion. Ravenna is an amazingly chic town, and because it's so manageable for pedestrians, it's one of the best cities for tourists who want to outfit themselves in the latest Italian looks at humane prices.

The people of Ravenna and its region, Romagna, are known for being a fun-loving and earthy lot who look you in the eye, who speak frankly and directly, and it's true—we've always found the locals here to be an authentic, welcoming bunch. If they don't win you over, their kitchens definitely will. *Cucina romagnola* is strong on comfort food, so whether you prefer the catch of the day from the Adriatic, or stuffed pheasant with porcini mushrooms, or *piadina,* the godfather of all flatbreads, you'll find plenty of eats to fill your belly and generous glasses of Sangiovese to warm your soul.

Give yourself 2 nights here if you can, but if time is tight, 1 full day in Ravenna can be quite satisfying—you'll just leave wanting more.

The Best of Ravenna

Best Local Foodstuff

Piadina   Made with flour, water, salt, and pork lard and cooked on a hot terra-cotta plate, Romagna's trademark flatbread is simple, but it's nearly impossible to find anyone who does it justice outside this region. Taste a real *piadina,* such as that at Ravenna's **Ca' de' Vén** (p. 407), and you'll be a lifelong devotee to this humble creation that looks like a pancake and tastes like the best home-style biscuit you've ever had, only better, since it's made with the essence of bacon.

Most Stunning Mosaics

San Vitale   We love all of Ravenna's mosaics, but if we have to play favorites, the prize must go to the **Basilica of San Vitale** (p. 410), one of the most memorable sights in Italy. The mosaics here are superbly over-the-top, splendid in the most literal sense of the word, lighting up the interior of the octagonal Byzantine church with an orgy of color and pictorial narratives.

Best "Medieval Mess Hall" Dining Experience

Ca' de' Vén   We can't say enough about this Ravenna institution, which looks a bit like the cafeteria at Hogwarts, and where Sangiovese-slinging waitresses serve up the best *piadina* in town. Be sure to eat at least one meal here. See p. 407.

Best Aperitivo Spot

Osteria Cappello   On the ground floor of the Albergo Cappello hotel, belly up to the bar, where there are dozens of wonderfully unfamiliar wines to sample by the glass or bottle, and an eye-popping free smorgasbord of prosciutto, *salame*, hard cheeses, olives, stuffed phyllo rolls, even fried cubes of dough, all in an inviting, home-at-your-noble-palazzo-for-the-holidays atmosphere. See p. 409.

Best Place to Crash

Albergo Cappello   In a great location, you can easily stop in and out all day long, staying in one of the unique rooms in a 16th-century palazzo. Unbelievably helpful reception staff make this a lovely home base while you're in Ravenna—and it isn't even a splurge. See p. 406.

Getting There

BY TRAIN

Rail is the easiest way for most to reach Ravenna. Frequent trains connect Ravenna with Bologna (about 30 min. away), which is one of the busiest rail hubs in Italy, so getting here by train is a cinch from almost anywhere in the country. With frequent service Ravenna can easily be visited on a day trip; one-way fare is 5€. There's also frequent service from Ferrara, which connects to Venice; one-way fare from Ferrara is 4.30€. The train station is a 10-minute walk from the center at Piazza Fernini (☎ 892021). For more info, check out handy **www.trenitalia.com**.

BY CAR

Getting to Ravenna by car is pretty easy; the city lies off a spur of the A14 *autostrada*, which runs southeast from Bologna to Rimini, Ancona, and Pescara on the Adriatic coast. Once you're off the highway, you'll need to follow a confounding number of white *CENTRO* signs that seem to be leading you around in circles. Just keep following them, even though you feel like the butt of some kind of practical joke, and you'll eventually reach the nefarious tangle of streets, many of which are pedestrian-only, that make up the *centro storico*.

Unless you have a very detailed map (and a tranquilizer gun with which to calm your nerves), don't even try to drive straight to your hotel. Ditch the Fiat in one of the public parking lots, remove any valuables, and leave the car there until it's time to head back out of town. Parking fees and hours during which payment is required are confusing and dynamic—check with your hotel or ask at the *tabacchi* store, where parking vouchers can be purchased.

Ravenna Orientation

Ravenna's size and the way its attractions are spread out make it very pedestrian-friendly. Most people's point of arrival is the train station, which lies on the east side of Ravenna's roughly pentagonal *centro storico* (also called the *città d'arte* by some locals). From the train station, it's about a 20-minute walk across the heart of the old city to Ravenna's number-one attraction, the mosaic-filled Basilica of San Vitale and Mausoleum of Galla Placidia, which is about as far west as most visitors are likely to travel. **Piazza del Popolo** lies in the exact center of town (10 min. south of San Vitale, 10 min. west of the train station); this public square and its neighboring streets are where you'll find the city's most atmospheric medieval and Renaissance architecture. The picturesque streets between Piazza del Popolo and San Vitale have plenty of charming eateries; also in this area, Via Cavour is the city's principal shopping thoroughfare. South of Piazza del Popolo is the so-called Zona Dantesca (Dante Zone), for the presence of Dante's tomb and the Museo Dantesco. About halfway between Piazza del Popolo and the train station is Via di Roma, a broad avenue running north-south, home to plenty of mass-market shops and Sant'Apollinare Nuovo, one of Ravenna's most popular mosaic churches. In the northeast corner of town is the Rocca Brancaleone, a medieval fortress and citadel surrounded by a green archaeological park. Another church with celebrated mosaics, Sant'Apollinare in Classe, is in Classe (of all places!), about 5km (3 miles) south of town and accessible by bus from the piazza in front of the train station.

Getting Around

Ravenna's historical center is so small that you'll be doing most of your exploring **on foot**, but the city's **bus** system is an efficient way to get around if you need to reach destinations just outside the city center, like Sant' Apollinare in Classe, Mirabilandia, or the beaches nearby. Ravenna's buses are operated by the **Azienda Trasporti e Mobilità (ATM),** Piazzale Farini (☎ **0544/689900;** www.atm.ra.it).

Like most city dwellers of Emilia-Romagna, Ravennati are all about **bicycling**—you'll see locals slicing expertly in and out of pedestrian traffic in the car-free zones of the *centro storico,* and you might be tempted to join them. Having a bike might be a bit of a liability, though, if you just want to wander, since you'll have to keep hopping off, parking, and locking. If, on the other hand, you're trying to hit all the mosaic sights in 1 day, a bike can be quite useful. Those determined to hit the cobblestones on two wheels can rent bikes from **Cooperativa San Vitale,** Piazza Farini, in front of the train station (☎ **0544/37031).** Rates range from about 1€ for an hour, to 7.75€ per day, and 25€ a

OKKIO! The Mildly Disorienting Free Tourist Map

The tourism board of Ravenna publishes an excellent map of the city, which is given out free at all hotels and tourist offices. (You'll probably end up with several copies, so thorough is the distribution of this thing.) *One word of caution:* As attractive and handy as this map is, it can be disorienting since the compass is rotated 1/4 turn—east is at the top of the map, north is to the left, and so on. So, if you're walking from the train station to San Vitale in the afternoon, you're heading west and toward the sun, but on the map, it looks like you're going south. (People who normally have a good sense of direction, like me, can get seriously confused by this.)

week. Some hotels also provide bikes for guests free of charge.

If you're hauling luggage and need a lift from the train station to your hotel, there's a taxi stand at Piazza Farini (in front of the station). However, most hotels are a flat and fairly easy walk from the station. Otherwise, unless you're stuck at Mirabilandia during a train workers' strike, we can't imagine why you would need a taxi in Ravenna—but just in case: **Radio Taxi** answers its phones daily between 7am–8pm (☎ **0544/33888).**

Ravenna Basics

The main **tourist office** is a few blocks north of San Vitale at Via Salara 8 (☎ **0544/35755;** www.turismo.ra.it; daily 9am–7pm), with a smaller branch at Piazza del Popolo 1 (☎ **0544/482111).** There's also another tourist office outside the church of

Ravenna

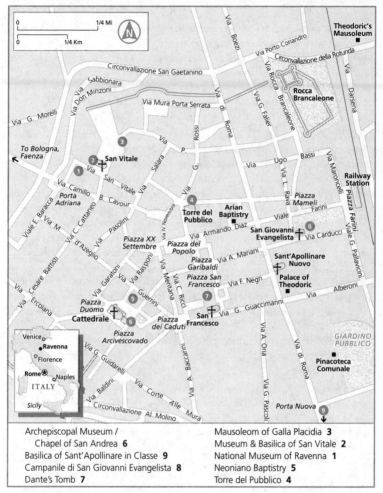

Archepiscopal Museum /
  Chapel of San Andrea **6**
Basilica of Sant'Apollinare in Classe **9**
Campanile di San Giovanni Evangelista **8**
Dante's Tomb **7**

Mausoleom of Galla Placidia **3**
Museum & Basilica of San Vitale **2**
National Museum of Ravenna **1**
Neoniano Baptistry **5**
Torre del Pubblico **4**

Sant'Apollinare in Classe, a few kilometers outside the city center, at Via Romea Sud 226 (☎ 0544/473661).

Recommended Websites

◌ **www.turismo.ra.it** Your one-stop shop for all the practical information a tourist in Ravenna might need, with a comprehensive list of hotels, museum and monument hours, and events. The site is clean and well designed, but the English version is a bit spotty, with whole paragraphs left untranslated.

◌ **www.ravennamosaici.it** Designed and maintained by the Catholic organization that oversees most of Ravenna's famous mosaics, the site is a bit out there, but there is some decent art-historical commentary about the major works, albeit with a heavy theological bent.

Ravenna Nuts & Bolts

ATMs Cash machines (called *bancomat* in Italy) are everywhere in this well-to-do town, but you probably won't need to carry around a ton of euros while you're in Ravenna, since credit and debit cards are accepted almost everywhere. A few things you will need cash for: cappuccino at the local bar (as well as all those glasses of wine at *aperitivo* time), monument admissions, and buses, if you choose to take them. As always, plan your cash withdrawals carefully: The exchange rate is favorable through foreign ATMs, since the banks trade in large volume, but you're hit with fees of more than $5 (depending on your bank) every time you take out money while abroad.

Emergencies In an emergency, call the *polizia* at ☎ 113; for nonemergencies (like lost or stolen property), use ☎ 0544/299111 or visit the main police station *(questura)* at Via Berlinguer 10. You can also turn to Italy's Army police force, the **Carabinieri** (who wear red-striped trousers designed by Valentino), to report emergencies or other disturbances of the peace. Call the Carabinieri at ☎ 112 for emergencies only; for nonemergencies, ☎ 0544/270000. Their station *(caserma)* is at Viale Pertini 11 (southwest side of town). To report a fire, a gas leak, or a grandma stuck in an elevator, dial ☎ 115 or ☎ 0544/281511 for the *vigili del fuoco* **(fire department),** based at Viale Randi 25 (southwest side of town).

For medical emergencies, call an ambulance at ☎ 118, or visit the *pronto soccorso* (emergency room, where you will not be charged for treatment, regardless of your insurance status) at **Ospedale Santa Maria delle Croci,** Via Missiroli 10 on the far west side of town (☎ 0544/285111).

The *polizia municipale,* who handle dog bites and parking tickets and are the bane of every Italian driver's existence, are at Piazza Mameli 8, just west of the train station (☎ 0544/482999).

Laundromats If you want to mix with the stylish denizens of Ravenna, it might be a good idea to hit the town with clean laundry. The local branch of the Italian franchise **Onda Blu** is at Via Ravegnana 155/Y (near Via M. Pasi, on the south side of the city center; take bus 3 or 33). It's open daily 8am–10pm. Washing machines cost 3.50€ per load (30 min); dryers cost 3.50€ for each 20 min. (A full load should take 60 min. to dry.) *Caution:* Be sure to check the temperature settings of washers and dryers; hot is *very* hot, so unless you are looking to shrink your wardrobe so that it'll fit better in your backpack, choose a lower setting. If you're only doing undergarments and socks, the hotel sink and a travel bottle of Woolite is a viable and time-honored cost-cutting technique.

Luggage Storage Hauling around Tuscan ceramics or other cumbersome souvenirs acquired en route? That's what *deposito bagaglio* (luggage deposit) at the train station is for, baby! You'll be charged 6€ per piece for a 24-hour period, so be sure to consolidate smaller bags into one parcel. *One caveat:* Train station luggage storage is normally a safe service, with very few problems reported, but because your goods are attended by human beings in a large room, mixed in with other people's stuff, "mistakes" are inevitable from time to time.

Postage & Shipping   Postage stamps *(francobolli)* are sold at all *tabacchi;* they'll ask you how many postcards you're sending and where—it's as simple as that. Postage for postcards and letters to anywhere in Europe or the Mediterranean basin is 0.52€; for the rest of the world, it's 0.62€. Red post boxes are on the sides of buildings in Ravenna; drop your postcards in the "*tutte le altre destinazioni*" (all other destinations) slot, as opposed to the "*città*" slot. When you start to accumulate too many souvenirs, or you realize that you're never going to wear those hiking boots you packed, the easiest thing to do is ship 'em home. The central Poste Italiane office of Ravenna is just southeast of Piazza del Popolo at Piazza Garibaldi 1, ☎ 0544/243306. Open Mon–Fri from 8am–6:30pm, and Sat from 8am–12:30pm, the post office sells nifty yellow boxes and any other packaging supplies you might need. There are a few forms to fill out for parcels going overseas, but for all the bad press Italian government agencies get, the national mail system is actually quite hassle-free nowadays, with an excellent delivery record. For more information on postal services, visit the English version of the Poste Italiane's official website at www.poste.it/en.

Restrooms   When you're out and about and nature calls, you should have no qualms about stopping in the nearest bar/cafe or restaurant and politely asking the management if you can use their *bagno.* This is standard practice throughout Italy—unlike in the U.S., Italian bathrooms are *not* for customers only. Drinking and eating establishments are required by law to allow anyone to use their toilet, although strung-out and derelict types are often told, "Sorry, the bathroom is out of order." So, as long as you're polite and not brandishing hypodermic needles, you'll be pointed to the restroom, which is usually a not-very-clean stall and almost invariably *in fondo a destra* (in the back, to the right).

Telephones   There are public pay phones *(cabina)* at the train station, in major piazzas and bus terminals, and at certain coffee bars (look for the white-and-red phone sign out front or the sticker in the window). Italian pay phones take a prepaid plastic card, called a *scheda telefonica,* which is issued by Telecom Italia and which must be purchased at a *tabacchi* store. Cards are sold in denominations of 2.50€, 5€, and 10€; in order for them to work, you must break off the perforated tab on the corner of the card.

Local calls (anything with a "0544" prefix) are pretty cheap—maybe 0.20€ for a short call, as are calls to land lines in other Italian cities (0.50€ for a short call to book a hotel in your next city, for example). Be aware, however, that calls from Italian land lines to Italian cellphones (three-digit prefixes beginning with "3,") are horrendously expensive and will probably bleed your *scheda telefonica* dry in a matter of seconds.

Sleeping

Ravenna may not be overflowing with hotel options, but what there is is clean, pleasant, and fairly well-priced. A room in the heart of the *centro storico* will spoil you with convenience, but since Ravenna is so small, and everything's walkable anyway, it's not the end of the world if all you can find or afford is a bed near the train station.

HOSTEL

➜**Ostello Galletti Abbiosi** ★ Leave it to elegant Ravenna to have a "hostel" that could easily pass for a three-star hotel. Centrally located in a former noble family's palace across from the mosaic-filled church of Sant'Apollinare Nuovo, the Ostello Galletti Abbiosi might be priced higher than your average HI, but your extra euros get you huge, spare, and airy rooms with vaulted and frescoed ceilings, as well as lush plants and teal furniture to keep the place from looking like a hospital ward. The hostel has an Internet station and provides free bikes for guests' use, and there's A/C, TV, telephone, minibar, and a private bath with shower and hair dryer in each room. And, if you feel like praying, there's even a private chapel on-site, which the late Conte Galletti Abbiosi insisted on having on the premises. See what we mean? This is not your average hostel. *Via di Roma 140 (off Via Carducci).* ☎ *0544/31313. www.galletti.ra.it. Single 50€–55€, double 80€–90€, triple 85€–100€, quad 100€–120€.*

CHEAP

→ **Locanda del Melarancio** ★★ Housed in a rustic three-story building on a characteristic corner of the *centro storico*, the "Sweet Orange Inn" makes an endearing effort to revive the ancient Italian institution of the *locanda*, a multitasking, homey place where you can sleep, eat, and drink. What this *locanda* seems to excel at, however, is drink: The pub on the ground floor is a hugely popular hangout for stylish Ravennate teens and 20-somethings. On the first floor, there's a restaurant, and on the top floor, there are six basic guest rooms with shared bath. If the spartan decor doesn't make you feel warm and fuzzy, the antiquated philosophy of the place will, and the price is right for such a prime location. See the "Eating" and "Partying" sections for Locanda del Melarancio restaurant and pub listings. *Via Mentana 33 (at Via Gessi).* ☎ *0544/215258. www.locanda delmelarancio.it. Single 35€, double 50€, triple 65€. All rooms have shared bath.*

→ **Hotel Minerva** ★ If the Melarancio (see above) is booked, your next best affordable hotel option is Hotel Minerva, in a modern building near the train station, a 10-minute walk from the *centro storico*. Outside the station, hang a right on the first street and you'll be at the Minerva's doorstep, which makes this hotel a godsend if you're toting heavy luggage. The 18 rooms are immaculate, with a few cozy touches like plaid bedspreads, but for the most part, this is the same bland modular decor you'll see in budget hotels all over Italy. Even though the hotel pretty much backs up on the railyard, Ravenna's train station doesn't see much nighttime traffic, so don't worry about thundering locomotives keeping you up at night. *Viale Maroncelli 1 (off Piazza Farini).* ☎ *0544/213-711. www.minerva-hotel.com. Single 53€, double 90€, triple 110€, quad 120€. Breakfast included. In room: A/C, TV, hair dryer.*

DOABLE

MTV Best → **Albergo Cappello** ★★★
One night in the noble Palazzo Minzoni, in the heart of Ravenna's *centro storico*, and you'll want to move in permanently. *Cappello* means hat, and in this case, it's a gentleman's bowler. Expect retro style and understated class from this inn, which is run not as a formal hotel but as an elegant guest house, with minimal, discreet staff. What staff there is couldn't be lovelier—whether Susanna or Giulia are manning the reception desk, you're guaranteed a warm welcome, a strategic map markup, and tons of great insider info about Ravenna to help you get the most out of your stay. Guest rooms are luxuriously spacious, with coffered and frescoed high ceilings. The boothlike bathrooms (some rooms actually have two) have dark-wood paneling which, combined with the fluffy white terry towels, give them a sexy, Orient Express feel. (We loved the bathrooms so much, we preferred to drink our pre-going-out glass of *prosecco* on the chair in the shower room instead of the vast bedroom outside.) In any other Italian city, this hotel would be firmly planted in the "Splurge" category; but since it's in off-the-beaten-track Ravenna, the Cappello remains delightfully doable pricewise, even for the suites. On the ground floor of the property, you'll find the house wine bar and restaurant, **Osteria Cappello** (p. 409), which

has one of the best *aperitivo* buffets we've seen in Italy, and outstanding local specialties at lunch and dinner. See the "Eating" and "Partying" sections for Osteria Cappello restaurant and bar listings. *Via IV Novembre 41 (at Piazza A. Costa).* ☎ *0544/219813. www.albergocappello.it. Double 110€, suite 130–180€. Breakfast included. In room: A/C, TV, hair dryer, minibar, handicapped accessible.*

→ **Centrale Byron** Nicely appointed, with somewhat dated, imitation Art Deco interiors, this government-rated three-star hotel is right in the heart of things, just off Piazza del Popolo, with decent-sized standard rooms and smaller economy rooms (which aren't as cramped as you'd think). If you're looking for a *centro storico* hotel with a few amenities, and the Albergo Cappello is full, the Centrale Byron is a good bet. *Via IV Novembre 14 (just north of Piazza del Popolo).* ☎ *0544/212225. www.hotelbyron.com. Economy: single 50€–55€, double 80€–90€; standard: single 58€–65€, double 95€–110€, triple 100€–130€, quad 120€–150€. Breakfast included. In room: A/C, TV, hair dryer, minibar.*

Eating

You will not go hungry in Ravenna. Food in this region is of the filling and hearty variety, heavy on cheese, pork, starch, and wild game, paired with a healthy dose of delicious *vino romagnolo* like Sangiovese, or the lesser-known white, Pagadebit.

Plenty of bars in Ravenna offer a sumptuous predinner *aperitivo,* a lively happy hour where you pay only for whatever you drink, alcoholic or not, and have access to a complimentary buffet of finger foods. *Aperitivo* eats are so generous in this part of Italy that they often replace dinner, which is fine, since you'll save money and probably meet more people, but if you do this every night, you'll miss out on the delicious local cuisine that restaurants offer. Whatever you do, make sure you stop by Ca' de' Vén (see below) for a *piadina.* This unbelievably tasty flatbread

is the kind of transcendental travel experience that you will almost certainly write home about.

COFFEE BARS

In general, these are the prices you should expect to pay at cafes and coffee bars: for an espresso, standing up at bar: .75€–.90€; cappuccino standing up at bar: .90€–1.10€; pastry standing up at bar 1€–1.50€; the prices will double when you sit down at any bar; and they triple when you sit down at fancy places.

→ **Caffè Corte Cavour** In a chic little courtyard off Via Cavour, this cafe is a great place to sit and write postcards or read up on mosaics before hitting San Vitale and Galla Placidia, just a few blocks away. It's also strategically located in Ravenna's prime retail zone, so when all that shoe trying leaves your energy sapped, you can stop in here and refuel with a shot of espresso. *Via Cavour 51 (inside the courtyard between Via Salara and Via Cattaneo).* ☎ *0544/30154.*

→ **Costacafe** Croissants at hotel breakfast buffets have a way of tasting like petrified wood more often than not, so for something soft, sweet, and warm, and a more authentic Italian cappuccino, head for Costacafe, one of Ravenna's nicer coffee and snack bars. A delicious array of sandwiches can also be had here—good to know when you're trying to save some euros by not going out to a restaurant for every meal. *Piazza A. Costa 5 (at Via IV Novembre).* ☎ *0544/212812. Daily 6am–11pm.*

CHEAP

📺 Best → **Ca' de' Vén** ★★★ If you're only in town for one meal, this is the only address you need to know. Brightly colored flags with medieval heraldry flap in the wind outside this Ravenna institution, whose dining room just oozes antiquity, with vaulted brick-and-timber construction and big, dark-wood communal tables. The menu lists other dishes, like hearty pastas and game, but stick with the *piadina romagnola*—it's what they do best here, and what keeps this place in the "Cheap" category. Almost pancake-ish in appearance, though not as sweet, Ca' de' Vén's *piadina* is made with pork lard and grilled on a terra-cotta plate. You can order your *piadine* stuffed with ham and cheese, but they're equally divine without any toppings at all, fresh from the oven and plopped down in a basket on your table. Ca' de' Vén, which means "house of wine" in dialect, does not ignore its namesake, stocking hundreds of labels of Italian whites and reds, mostly regional varietals. We recommend having them bring you a bottle or three of Sangiovese, Romagna's satisfying old standby. Middle-aged waitresses are raspy-voiced, no-nonsense, warm, and personable, a refreshing reminder in this handsome town that the people of Romagna come from rugged stock. Stop by in the early evening to make a reservation, and make sure they don't stick you at the long table running down the middle of the room; the table's massive width means that all the members of your party sit side-by-side, not across from each other, and the overhead light is *waaay* too bright for the tavern-y atmosphere. *Via Corrado Ricci 24 (between Via Gordini and Piazza San Francesco).* ☎ *0544/30163. Piadina 4€–7€; other dishes 10€ and up. Tues–Sun for lunch and dinner.*

DOABLE

→**Ristorante La Gardèla** EMILIA-ROMAGNA/SEAFOOD The menu won't bowl you over with its originality—you can choose from a bit of everything, including stuffed pastas, meat, and fish—but the quality is high, making this more than just a tourist trap on the heavily trod route between the train station and San Vitale. *Via Ponte Marino 3 (at Vicolo Gabbiani).* ☎ *0544/217147. Primi 10€–12€; secondi 12€–20€. Fri–Wed for lunch and dinner.*

→**Locanda del Melarancio** EMILIA-ROMAGNA ★ Upstairs from the pub and downstairs from the inn of the same name, the restaurant part of the Locanda del Melarancio offers traditional *cucina romagnola* in a long, cozy, pink-tinged dining room. If you decide to dine here, plan to take it easy at the *aperitivo* buffet before dinner. This restaurant's fare is on the heavy side—a bit like Thanksgiving dinner, all year round—with hors d'oeuvres like pumpkin gratin with shaved *lardo,* and entrees that frequently make use of unusual fowl, such as stuffed pigeon with chestnuts, figs, and mushrooms (although there was talk of blacklisting wild poultry dishes, due to the bird flu scare, as we were researching this guide). Lighter eaters can find plenty of agreeable options on the lengthy menu, but if you cringe at the idea of cheese and pork making an appearance in pretty much every dish, better give the Melarancio (and indeed, this whole region of Italy) a wide berth! *Via Mentana 33 (at Via Gessi).* ☎ *0544/215258. www.locandadel melarancio.it. Primi 8€–12€; secondi 12€–18€.*

→**Oste Bacco** ★ The country-farmhouse dining room makes for a lively and welcoming atmosphere for local specialties hailing from both surf and turf. The chef makes the most of seasonal and freshest available ingredients, so let yourself be guided by the waiter (or neighboring tables in the know), who might suggest a delicious in-season vegetable or pasta made with a freshly caught fish you've never heard of. As "Bacchus" is your "host," expect a generous flow of top-quality *vino romagnolo* to accompany your meal. *Via Salara 20 (off Via S. Vitale),* ☎ *0544/35363. Primi 8€–12€; secondi 12€–18€. Wed–Mon for lunch and dinner.*

→**Osteria Cappello** EMILIA-ROMAGNA ★★ At first, we dismissed this as just some fledgling hotel restaurant that probably wasn't worth our valuable meal time, but boy, were we wrong. (And we should have known better, considering how good the *aperitivo* spread is here before dinner.) When we finally decided to sit down and eat at the

Cappello, we found the food to be some of the best we've tasted in Emilia-Romagna. Enormous, perfectly dressed salads don't pander to dainty dieters; these huge bowls of gorgeous greens become a nest for hearty toss-ins like bacon and Gorgonzola. On the pasta menu, we're still dreaming about (and drooling over) that plate of homemade tagliolini with fresh *funghi porcini* and Parmigiano-Reggiano. *Via IV Novembre 41 (at Piazza A. Costa).* ☎ *0544/219876. www.albergo cappello.it. Primi 8€–12€; secondi 12€–18€.*

➜ **Rustichello** EMILIA-ROMAGNA ★   Mix with a crowd of mostly locals at this lively trattoria just west of San Vitale, outside the old city walls. Rustichello is especially great if you're too tired to make any decisions about what to eat, because the opinionated owner prefers to decide for you. There's no printed menu, so if you have any dietary objections (e.g., you don't eat veal or rabbit), tell him *no vitello* or *no coniglio.* Whatever you're served, it will probably be delicious: antipasti with cold cuts, cheeses, and *piadina,* primi of stuffed pasta, and secondi of succulent roast meat, spiced oh-so-perfectly, will all give you something to talk about on the walk from here back to your hotel. *Via Maggiore 21/23 (at Circonvallazione S. Gaetanino).* ☎ *0544/36043. Primi 8€–10€; secondi 10€–16€. Mon–Fri for dinner.*

Partying

Ravennati are the first to admit they lack a full-fledged nightlife, but there's still plenty of hanging out and drinking to be done in the lively *centro storico.* For starters, you can get your buzz on at one of Ravenna's myriad *aperitivo* joints, which give you really good, free food along with your reasonably priced glasses of wine. Make some friends at the bar, and this can be a very fun way to pass several hours. In warm weather, you can always enjoy cocktails (or more wine) on the alfresco cafe tables of Piazza del Popolo, and year-round, a few key pubs and bars (like Locanda

del Melarancio and Fellini, below) are always packed with mirth and young scenesters. If that's not enough for you, get out of town—literally. Everyone here knows that the best clubs are in **Milano Marittima,** a beach resort enclave a 15-minute drive from Ravenna (p. 413).

🅼🆅 **Best** ➜ **Osteria Cappello** ★★ *APERITIVO*   During happy hour, buy a glass of wine (from 3€) at the cozy, dark-wood paneled bar at the Albergo Cappello, and let the feeding frenzy begin. The bar counter is piled high and low with platter after platter of complimentary *aperitivo* snacks, including savory hors d'oeuvres, cheeses and meats, even cubes of sugar-sprinkled fried dough (it's uncanny, eating donut holes never felt so classy). The bar is crowded and lively with 20- and 30-somethings until 8pm or so, when the room empties out and everyone heads to dinner—although after partaking of this tantalizing spread, you might not have much of an appetite left. *Via IV Novembre 41 (at Piazza A. Costa).* ☎ *0544/219876. www.albergo cappello.it.*

➜ **Fellini** *APERITIVO/AFTER-DINNER HANG-OUT*   On the northwest side of the parking lot of Piazza Kennedy, the imposing, fascist-era Casa del Mutilato di Guerra ("house of the war-mutilated") is home to Ravenna's most swinging bar/lounge. It's an absurd but rather fabulous location (which is true of most of Italy's fascist architecture that has been requalified for nocturnal entertainment) where local *fichetti* (hipsters and wannabes) are drawn like moths to a flame. Expect a buzzing scene and lots of mojito-sipping from *aperitivo* time (7–9pm) until 1am, at which hour patrons go home or migrate to one of the discos in the seaside town of Milano Marittima, about 15km (9$^1/_3$ miles) away. *Piazza Kennedy 15.* ☎ *0544/215741. www.felliniscalino5.it.*

➜ **Locanda del Melarancio** *APERITIVO/ PUB*   It's mating season year-round for the young Ravennati behind the plate-glass windows at the corner of Via Mentana and Via Gessi, a busy and narrow pedestrian thoroughfare in the heart of the *centro storico*. Perfectly primped teens and 20-somethings hang out at the pub room of the Locanda del Melarancio, drinking beer or Coke and flirting like crazy from the *aperitivo* hour till after midnight. *Via Mentana 33 (at Via Gessi).* ☎ *0544/215258. www.locandadelmelarancio.it.*

Sightseeing

No matter where you've been or what art you've seen, I guarantee you have never seen anything like the mosaics in Ravenna ★★★. There are plenty of images we can conjure to describe them—a glitter factory after an explosion is one example—but until you see the mosaics for yourself, you can't imagine how impressive they are. Created between the 5th and 7th centuries A.D. to adorn the insides of the city's churches, baptisteries, and mausolea, the mosaics today remain in an unbelievably perfect state of preservation. With so much vivid color (you'll be struck by how much green and blue is used, in addition to every other color in the rainbow, and gold) and subtle and entertaining pictorial details, the mosaics are a welcome contrast from the paintings and sculptures of Italian art that, important as they are, frankly start to look repetitive after a while.

If you have time for nothing else, be sure you see San Vitale, but the "Big Four" for mosaics are **San Vitale,** the **Mausoleum of Galla Placidia, Sant'Apollinare Nuovo,** and **Sant'Apollinare in Classe,** which is a short bus ride outside the city center. The 5th-century Neonian Baptistery (next to the Duomo) and the 6th-century Arian Baptistery (just west of the train station) also have fine, brightly colored mosaics. Do yourself a huge favor and pick up a guidebook at one of the main sights' gift shops; whether you read up on the mosaics before or after you see them

in person, it makes everything that much more interesting.

THE MAGNIFICENT MOSAICS

📺 **Best** → **Basilica di San Vitale** ★★★ Entering San Vitale is like cracking open a geode. On the exterior, the church is plain brick, but once you step inside, you are treated to a visual orgy that builds with the basilica's elegant barrel-vaulted ambulatory and climaxes with a truly stunning explosion of sparkling color in the 6th-century mosaics that cover every nook, cranny, and curve of the apse. To get the most out of your visit here, we suggest you purchase a guidebook in the church's gift shop.

There are all kinds of wonderful details to be discovered on San Vitale's bejeweled walls—you just need to stand in the presbytery (the "hall" area leading to the apse itself) and let your mouth gape open for a while as you take it all in. We love the adorable vignette of Moses affectionately petting the underside of a sheep's muzzle (lower part of the right wall of the presbytery), and the perplexed and perplexing face of St. Andrew, along the underside of the arch that marks the entrance to the presbytery. On the left wall of the presbytery, look for the panel showing scenes in the life of Abraham: at the right, Abraham, standing next to Sarah, offers a pygmy-sized "calf" to three people sitting at a dining table; on the left side, a sword-wielding Abraham is about to chop off Isaac's head when God (symbolized by a hand from out of the heavens) stops him in the nick of time. (The adorable little ram watching the scene from below will be sacrificed instead.) San Vitale's most famous mosaic panels are in the apse, where a scene depicting the emperor Justinian and his attendants faces a congruent scene, depicting his wife, the empress Theodora, and her posse, on the opposite wall. Chances are you know nothing about Justinian and Theodora, but as soon as you see their entourages and enigmatic facial expressions, you can just tell there was plenty of juicy gossip behind the scenes. *Via di San Vitale. www.ravennamosaici.it. Daily Apr–Sept 9am–7pm, Mar and Oct 9am–5:30pm, Nov–Feb 9:30am–5pm. Admission 7.50€ adults, 6.50€ for students. Ticket also good for Galla Placidia (recommended), Sant'Apollinare Nuovo (recommended), Battistero Neoniano, and Museo Arcivescovile.*

→ **Mausoleum of Galla Placidia** ★ This petite, cross-shaped sepulcher next door to San Vitale is home to Ravenna's oldest wall mosaics, but not to the actual tomb of Galla Placidia (she was buried in St. Peter's in the Vatican). A sometime queen of the Goths, sometime Roman empress, Galla Placidia had the mausoleum built in the early 5th century A.D. The mosaics are full of lovely animal and vegetable motifs, from thirsty deer seeking a drink of water on a side lunette to glossy fruit growing on a trained vine under an arch. The barrel vaults are covered with mosaics of rich blue, dotted with starbursts and flower blossoms that look like a wintry snowflake scene. *Via di San Vitale. Visitor center:* ☎ *0544/541611. www.ravennamosaici.it. Daily Apr–Sept 9am–7pm, Mar and Oct 9am–5:30pm, Nov–Feb 9:30am–5pm. Admission 7.50€ adults, 6.50€ students. Ticket also good for San Vitale (recommended), Sant'Apollinare Nuovo (recommended), Battistero Neoniano, and Museo Arcivescovile.*

→ **Basilica di Sant'Apollinare Nuovo** ★★ Some of our favorite mosaics in this church are on the left wall, near the front door. At the very top of the left wall, above the windows, if you squint really hard, you can see a rad mosaic of Christ healing the paralytic of Bethesda: the newly mobile guy walks off, toting his invalid's cot on his back, and looks back as if to say something to Christ, whose face and gesture seem to say, "Talk to the hand! You've been enough trouble for one day!" Lower down on this wall, look for the mosaic depicting the port city of Classe, headquarters of the Roman

fleet since the days of Julius Caesar. This scene is a simple composition, with zero use of perspective, but you can make out the water, with a few ships stacked vertically in the harbor, the city walls, and above, the amphitheater and aqueduct of Classe. The main strips of mosaics in the church, above the arcades, are impressive but repetitive—processions of virgins, saints, and prophets in white robes stand with their heads cocked solemnly toward Jesus at the front of the line. On the right wall near the apse, check out the sweet leopard-print stirrup pants on the Three Kings, carrying their pots of frankincense and myrrh. *Via Roma.* ☎ *0544/219518. www.ravennamosaici.it. Daily 10am–5pm. Admission 7.50€ adults, 6.50€ students. Ticket also good for San Vitale (recommended), Galla Placidia (recommended), Battistero Neoniano, and Museo Arcivescovile.*

→ **Basilica di Sant'Apollinare in Classe** ★ It's well worth the short trip beyond the city walls to see this mosaic-rich basilica, which used to be right on the Adriatic (the seashore has since receded a few kilometers away). The church's namesake saint, Apollinare, stars as the orating figure in the apse, whose semidome is resplendent with green and gold and a blue sky with 99 stars. As with so many of the mosaics in Ravenna, the delight is in the details: knee-high lambs with cute little cloven hooves gather in the grass around St. Apollinare, and spunky, spindly little flowers crop up out of random rocks. Next to the window on the left, find the panel showing Constantine IV receiving the book of *Privilegia*, surrounded by a bunch of haggard-faced guys who look like they just got back from doing time at Folsom. Honestly, what's the deal with those dark circles under their eyes? Nearby is the archaeological site *(zona archeologica)* of the harbor of Classe, former headquarters of the Roman fleet that was established by Julius Caesar. *Via Romea Sud, Classe.* ☎ *0544/473569. Mon–Sat 8:30am–7:30pm; Sun 1–7:30pm. Admission 2€, or 6.50€*

includes Museo Nazionale and Mausoleum of Theodoric. Bus 4 from Piazza Farini (train station) to Sant'Apollinare in Classe. Zona Archeologica di Classe: Via Marabina 5. ☎ *0544/67705.*

OTHER SIGHTS

FREE ➔ **Dante's Tomb and Museo Dantesco** ★ When the Black Guelphs took over Florence in a violent coup in 1301, Florentine native, poet extraordinaire, and White Guelph party member Dante Alighieri was condemned to perpetual exile. He eventually settled in Ravenna in 1318, where he began writing the *Divine Comedy* (that's the famous trifecta of *Inferno, Purgatory,* and *Paradiso* for you literarily-challenged). Dante died in Ravenna just 3 years later, on September 14, 1321, at the age of 56. His remains are still here, inside a 15th-century marble sarcophagus, in front of which a votive lamp of Tuscan olive oil burns in his memory. The epitaph on his tomb contains a dig at Florence; it reads PARVI FLORENTIA MATER AMORIS, which basically amounts to calling Florence an absentee mother. Florence, of course, would go on to seriously regret having kicked out the greatest poet of medieval Europe and father of the Italian language. Dante's *cenotaph* (empty tomb) is in Florence at Santa Croce. *Via Dante Alighieri 9 (off Via Gordini and Via C. Ricci).* ☎ *0544/30252. Daily 9am–7pm. Free admission.*

Playing Outside

FREE ➔ **Giardini Pubblici** Ravenna's main public park is not the lush, expansive landscape that so many Italian cities enjoy, but if you just want to take your panino somewhere for a casual alfresco meal on a nice day, there are benches, lawns, trees, and a fountain here. *Viale S. Baldini (due south of the train station and Piazza Farini).*

➔ **Mirabilandia and Mirabilandia Beach** Billed as Italy's "state-of-the-art" amusement park, Mirabilandia ("Marvel Land") is like Six Flags on Xanax. It does boast two decent roller coasters (one wooden, one

suspended, with loops and ancient-Mayan-city themed landscape), some log flumes, and a rad "Possessed Saucepans" ride (*Pentole Stregate*) where you spin around in gigantic cauldrons. Most of the attractions, however, are "family-oriented"—i.e., rides putter along at agonizingly slow speeds while adults pretend that it's fun. The adjacent park, Mirabilandia Beach, has water slides and a wave pool and lots of sand. (For water slides, however, we prefer Aquafan in Rimini, which has a toilet-flush simulation ride; p. 430.) Two of the "marvels" of Mirabilandia are that you can bring dogs (though not on the rides), and there's a chapel where Mass is celebrated on Sundays. The park is a fun way to take a break from art-gawking (it can also be a hilarious cultural lesson in Italian family dynamics), and an easy side trip from Ravenna. *Parco della Standiana, SS 16, km 162, Mirabilandia–Ravenna.* ☎ *0544/561111. www.mirabilandia. com. Early April to early Sept daily 10am–6pm; July–Aug, and 1st weekend of Sept daily 10am–11pm; mid-Sept to early Oct Sat–Sun 10am–6pm. By bus: Bus 176 (1€) leaves Ravenna's Piazza Caduti every 90 min and takes 20 min to reach Mirabilandia. By train: take a Rimini-bound regionale train (there's 1 per hour) to Lido di Classe-Lido di Savio (10 min, 1.45€), and then take the free Mirabilandia shuttle from the train station to the park entrance.*

Shopping

For those who've been traveling around Italy, who've been disappointed or overwhelmed by retail opportunities in Rome or Milan, and who are just waiting for their dream Italian shopping spree to take wing, get ready for lift-off in Ravenna. This well-dressed town is chock-full of hip and trendy, well-priced independent boutiques and friendly branches of the major Italian chains like Benetton and Stefanel. Just walk the key streets in the zone around Via Cavour, Via IV Novembre, Via Cattaneo, and Via d'Azeglio, and you're sure to find plenty of irresistible storefronts to suit your needs, but some of our favorites are listed below.

For the more artistically inclined, the gift shops on Via San Vitale carry mosaic-inspired merchandise—kid-friendly make-your-own-mosaic kits, picture frames, etc.

Shopping hours in Ravenna are generally Mon-Sat 10am to 8pm. Some smaller boutiques still take the midday *riposo*, closing from 1–3pm or 2–4pm; larger chain stores are open continuously throughout the day. Unfortunately, you can't shop on Sunday, except for at the souvenir/tchotchke shops near San Vitale; all other retail establishments are closed.

APPAREL

→ **Maria Cristina** This men's and women's fashion emporium off the lovely Corte Cavour can outfit you from your newsboy cap down to your knee-high boots. There are some big-label, expensive items here, but there are also plenty of affordable and trendy wardrobe-building pieces, including a wall full of jeans from hot, under-the-radar European designers. *Via Cavour 36, 46, and 51/e (between Via Salara and Via Cattaneo).*

→ **Trendy** We're actually not sure if this place is called 3 Trendy, Tre Trendy, or just Trendy, but who cares? Local chicks swarm this women's boutique for fabulous fashions at a fraction of the price you'd normally pay for clothes and accessories this chic and

well-made. On a recent visit, we made off with unique and sassy trenchcoat–style knit cardigans for 60€ each. *Via IV Novembre 22 (at Piazza A. Costa).* ☎ 0544/33109.

LEATHER

→ **Punto Pelle** The uninspired name, "Leather Point," might lead you to believe this is one of Italy's ubiquitous, conservative "hand-crafted" leather outlets; but no, the goods here are modern and edgy, like mailbags in washed elastic leather, distressed and grommeted suede belts, and sexy classics like black nappa motorcycle jackets. The surprisingly low price tags are pretty cool, too. *Via Cavour 68 (between Via Salara and Via Cattaneo).* ☎ 0544/32275.

SHOES & ACCESSORIES

→ **Cinti** This Italian chain makes its own of-the-moment shoes at impulse-friendly prices . . . it's just too bad they're not more comfortable. (Choose a style with a not-too-high heel, or a rounded toe, and you should be fine.) Embellished, sharp-looking women's shoes are priced in the 60€–90€ range (fantastic, huh?), and boots (from rugged motorcycle styles to vixenish tall-shaft stilettos) are a mere 100€–140€. Guys, there's something here for you, too; most men's styles are under 80€, including some great-looking hybrid sneaker-shoes. Cinti also sells a small selection of trendy belts, outerwear, and handbags. *Piazza A. Costa 1/2 (at Via IV Novembre).* ☎ 0544/218097.

Milano Marittima: A Road Trip to the Beach

102km (63 miles) SE of Bologna.

"Maritime Milan" is the most chic of the Romagna beach towns, just 15km (9¹/₃ miles) from Ravenna and easily reached by train or bus. Pronounced "Milano Mar–*eet*-tee-ma," this tiny resort village has a pretty harbor and, as is typical for this part of the Adriatic coast, dense umbrella pinewoods just behind the beaches. Which is why everything in the vicinity is called *pineta* (pinewood) this or

pini (pines) that. If you're looking to relive spring breaks past with a crowd of really good-looking, fun-loving Italians who perhaps should have outgrown this years ago, you've come to the right place. Milano Marittima and the rest of the Riviera Romagnola is all about tanning, sand sports, outrageous beach parties, and glam clubs. When you need to recover and do something more sedate, there's also a golf club and a thermal spa.

Getting There

From Ravenna, take one of the hourly Rimini-bound *regionale* trains to Cervia-Milano Marittima station (2€; about 20 min). A slower bus (no. 176) leaves Ravenna's Piazza Caduti for Milano Marittima every 90 min or so; the ticket costs 1€ and trip time is about 40 min.

Recommended Websites

○ **www.comunecervia.it** The official site for the city of Cervia, of which Milano Marittima is technically part. Useful information and links to hotels, restaurants, transportation, and events.

○ **www.chrhotelreservation.it** This local accommodations resource is useful if you're only planning to spend a night or two and you're having trouble with hotels that won't budge on their 3-night-minimum rule.

○ **www.milanomarittima.it** An independent site with lots of paid placements, but it'll give you a good sense of the sort of scene and characters you can expect to encounter in the resort town.

Milano Marittima Orientation

Milano Marittima is a small community, little more than a square kilometer in area, where everything is within walking distance. (The pedestrian-friendliness, however, doesn't stop vacationers from parading their BMWs and Ferraris around the circular avenue of Viale Romagna.) The Rotonda Primo Maggio traffic circle is the hub from which the rest of town radiates. About 200m north of here, the *pineta* begins, with boutique and restaurant-filled Viale Matteotti at its inland edge. Roman-numeraled *traverse* (crossroads) lead east from Viale Matteotti through the pinewood toward the beach. On the shore itself, you'll find row upon row upon row of

beach clubs—some connected to hotels, some not—where you'll be charged about 16€ per day for the use of a beach chair, umbrella, showers, and changing rooms.

Sleeping

There are about eight gajillion hotels in Milano Marittima (give or take one or two), so unless you're coming in the middle of August, you shouldn't have a problem finding vacancy. Obviously, you pay a bit more to be on the beach, but isn't being able to shuffle out the door and onto the sand after breakfast worth the extra 10€ a day? Note that prices at many properties are per *person*, not per room, and many inns have a 3-night-minimum stay policy, although some are willing to bend the rules in off-peak periods like May, June, and late September. In general, hotels are open from April to the end of September, and for a week or two around Christmas and New Year's Eve. All the hotels listed below fall into the "Cheap" category.

➔ **City Beach Resort** This beachfront property on the 15th *traversa* has its own private cabanas and color-coordinated beach furniture (of course!). All rooms in the high-rise structure have balconies and sea views. *XV Traversa 13.* ☎ *0544/995289. www.citybeach resort.com. 50€–85€ per person (highest prices are in Aug). 3-night minimum. Breakfast included.*

➔ **Koko** In this new hotel a bit inland from the action at Rotonda Primo Maggio, lights are kept low so as not to upset heads that might be recovering from the previous night's overindulgences. Likewise, there are a steam bath and sauna designated for "purification" after an evening's festivities. Catering also to those who need a room for their own purposes for just a few hours, Koko also rents "fast rooms" at 50€ for 5 hours. *Viale Nullo Baldini.* ☎ *0544/939001. www.kokohotel.com. Single 40€–85€, double 40€–100€.*

➔ **Hotel Miami Beach** This government-rated four-star with Art Nouveau decor is connected to the Papeete Beach club (see below), which is one of the most paparazzi'd establishments on the Riviera Romagnola. Hotel Miami beach is definitely one of the more upscale choices right on the water in Milano Marittima. While it isn't exactly the pinnacle of luxury, its rooms have plush furnishings that will make you think twice about throwing an in-room rager. For your hedonistic pursuits, look no further than the Papeete Beach Club, a raucous outdoor party that takes place on the sand directly opposite the hotel every night in summer. Papeete Beach club is one of the most paparazzi'd establishment because it's where all the tanned and toned hotties go, where you might spot soccer players, TV showgirls, or the latest reality TV "star" basking in his or her 15 minutes of fame. *III Traversa 31.* ☎ *0544/991628. www.hotelmiamibeach.com. Single 80€–135€, double 120€–180€. Breakfast included.*

→ **Hotel Garnì Napoleon** Also affiliated with the Papeete Beach club, the government-rated one-star Napoleon is 1 block from the beach, and even more affordable than the Hotel Miami Beach. *III Traversa 16.* ☎ *0544/991108 or 0544/991514. Single or double 55€–85€. Breakfast 8€.*

Partying

If you're too tired from sunbathing and traveling to hit the clubs (they get going quite late here), at least partake of the *aperitivo* scene (5:30pm–8ish), which is often more fun and much cheaper anyway. Be aware that Italians dress for the *aperitivo* as if they've just come off the beach, in their bikinis and sarongs and flip-flops, but they've actually gone back to their hotels, showered, and reapplied hair gel, so that they can hit the meat market of the *aperitivo* looking oh-so-carefree and *just right*. (So, you might want to consider freshening up yourself rather than showing up at happy hour in your Coppertone-stained tank top and sweaty swim trunks.)

Later on, brace yourself for pricey cover charges and cocktails (think covers of 10€–20€ and drinks from 5€–10€, with the occasional free shot thrown in) at one of Milano Marittima's fabulous *discoteche*. Otherwise, you might find that it's just as enjoyable to hit the beach with some refreshments and enjoy the moonlight over the pines.

→ **Papeete Beach** ★ This is one of the wilder *aperitivo* spots on the beach of Milano Marittima, where loud music blares from 6pm on and Veuve Clicquot spray-downs are not uncommon. Clientele is oiled, tanned, chiseled, and waxed—depending on your tastes, some of the men might be *too* oiled and waxed. As is de rigueur on the Italian seaside, girls show up wearing pseudo-beachy outfits, but with uncannily perfect hair and make-up. Papeete Beach is a past winner of *GQ Italy's* "Best Beach Club" award, thanks in no small part to the hot chicks tending bar here. *III Traversa 281.* ☎ *0544/991108 or 0544/991208. www.papeetebeach.com.*

→ **Pineta Glam Club** ★★ To the celebrity-magazine-reading public in Italy, "la Pineta" is synonymous with swank, transgressive nightlife—professional soccer players and their TV game-show dancer girlfriends are always photographed here, and if Lindsay Lohan ever visited the Romagnola Coast, no doubt she'd make an appearance at the Pineta, too. Simply put, you just can't come to Milano Marittima and *not* go to this club. And, try as we might to ridicule it, Pineta is stylish as hell. Sexy and sleek decor is full of minimalist leather banquettes and blingy crystal fixtures (with a vintage chandelier or two to counterbalance the modernism), edgy-looking toilets (only in Italy would so much attention be paid to urinal aesthetics), and potted cacti galore. But the club's best flora comes in the form of live pine trees whose mature trunks have been incorporated into the permanent structure. Clientele, who are mostly in their 20s and 30s, aren't always as sophisticated as the furnishings, but everyone is here to have a good time. Pineta's DJs are among the most sought-after in Italy, and usually spin an unpretentious, party-sustaining mix of house music and more familiar dance hits. *Viale Romagna 66.* ☎ *0544/994728. www.pinetadisco.com.*

➔ **Villa Papeete** Sister to the waterfront Papeete Beach, this is a nightclub that takes itself quite seriously, selling tacky branded merchandise (e.g., chokers with PAPEETE spelled out in rhinestones) to create some kind of lifestyle image. Nevertheless, the club rivals Pineta with its high number of young and beautiful national celebrity and reality-show cast-off appearances. *Via Argine Destro 15.* ☎ *0544/992033 or 333/9330350 (cellphone). www.villapapeete.com.*

Rimini & Riccione: Partying on Italy's Adriatic Beaches

Rimini is 116km (72 miles) SE of Bologna; Riccione is 125km (77 miles) SE of Bologna.

Every weekend in the summer, Florentines, Bolognese, and anyone else who needs a break from their tourist-infested or over-heated hometowns gets the hell out of Dodge and heads for refuge at the seaside playgrounds of the **Riviera Romagnola.** From chic Milano Marittima down the Adriatic coast to the party hot spots of Rimini and Riccione and beyond, orderly grids of beach umbrellas and lounge chairs—so densely packed and so color-coordinated that they're visible from space—receive platoons of sun seekers and revelers from June through August.

Raging in Rimini and Riccione is a time-honored tradition Italians and other Europeans, but the northeastern coast of Italy, Venice aside, is mostly unknown to Americans. Granted, the landscape here is no Amalfi Coast, but ubiquitous pinewoods, wide and sandy beaches, and the general prosperity that characterizes so much of northern Italy, keep the Riviera Romagnola very attractive in its own way. Furthermore, you'll find a much less inhibited and younger crowd here than in other more well-known, and more expensive, Italian beach resorts.

Between Rimini and Riccione, the former draws the lion's share of the visitors in the summer. More petite Riccione is a boutique-like version of Rimini, with some of the region's most famed nightclubs in its hills overlooking the sea. Rimini's waterfront, at first glance, is like gazing back into '80s TV, with a *Miami Vice* vibe (sans the neon), with buildings and people dressed in every shade of pastel. Many beachfront hotels and Art Deco cafes seem to be replicas of the *Golden Girls* set. Luckily the muscle-heads and beach bunnies that traipse up and down Viale Amerigo Vespucci are easier on the eyes than Bea Arthur in a one-piece. Once the summer approaches, sidewalks become a runway for itty-bitty swimsuits that show off every curve and bulge. And that's just the men—the women's bikinis aren't bad, either.

If the 30km (19 miles) of beaches between Rimini and Riccione aren't enough, there are a bevy of other attractions to keep holiday-makers happy: some 458 bars, 22 clubs, 18 cinemas, 2 amusement parks, and a dolphinarium near a pear tree! With so much to do, and so many outdoor activities, the Riviera Romagnola has the reputation of being one of the fittest regions around. The beaches aren't just for kicking back and getting that perfect tan. The empty spaces between the grids of beach chairs and umbrellas are filled with athletic folk playing beach tennis or flailing their legs in "foot volley" (a combination of soccer and volleyball that requires crazy skills). Picking sand out of hard-to-reach places might not appeal to some, so there are plenty of other options inland for anyone looking for some athletic activity (see "Playing Outside," later in this section). Legendary filmmaker Federico Fellini was born and raised in Rimini, and cinema buffs can visit the museum here dedicated to his life and *oeuvre*.

Anyone under 40 will find that the Riviera Romagnola is an asylum where everyone, whether for a week or a weekend, can get away with acting like a 20-year-old. If you *are* a 20-year-old, then just act like yourself. You'll have lots of company. Athletic and beach activities aside, the nightlife in Rimini and Riccione is as loud as it gets in Europe. The whole city seems to be immersed in a maelstrom of alcohol, neon, and music once the sun sets. The tawdry clubs digest revelers, then regurgitate them back on to the beach the next morning for a day of Frisbee, sunbathing, and swimming, and many hotels rent no-questions-asked "fast rooms" for 5-hour stints during daylight hours. It's a vicious and beautiful Bacchanalian cycle that fun-loving Italians can't wait to return to every summer.

The Best of Rimini & Riccione

Best Place to Crash for under 20€

Hostel Jammin', Rimini A kick-ass staff, great location and guests, free bicycle rentals, and reasonably comfortable beds. Try to score a bed near the street-side window: during the summer you'll fall asleep to the cool, relaxing coastal breeze. Just make sure good weather is in the forecast—I left my window open during a typhoonlike storm and awoke to a frigid, damp coastal torrent. See p. 423.

Best Club to Find a Glass Pyramid, Banana Trees & Whales

Cocoricò, Riccione No, they didn't move the Louvre to Riccione and convert it into a cabaret. As cool as that would be, the kitschy Cocoricò is where you want to spend your last night in Emilia-Romagna. The nonsensical environment will leave you with a lasting

impression while the bars will give you an even longer hangover. See p. 427.

Best Cheap Eats

Il Baretto della Buona Piadina, Rimini The *piadina* flatbread sandwich is Romagna's equivalent to the late-night sub in the States. If you want a substantial snack, or if you don't have a lot to spend, the stuffed *piadina* is perfect for the frugal diner. They're usually filled with a variety of meats, cold cuts, cheeses, and vegetables. Il Baretto is the institution where locals flock for the best *piadina* on the coast. For a measly 8€, you can decide for yourself. See p. 425.

Best Beach Activity

Foot volley is way too hard, Ultimate Frisbee on sand can get tiring, and sunbathing, well . . . sitting half-naked in the baking sun is only fun for so long. That leaves the exciting sport of **kitesurfing** at beach centers #28 and #86. Instructors will help anyone unfamiliar with the difficult sport, and after a few classes, you may even catch a few waves. Once you do, the only difficult part about kitesurfing will be trying to wipe off the grin when you do catch that first wave. See p. 430.

Best Bar to Bring Your Water Wings & Get Drunk

Rock Island, Rimini Rock Island is on a tiny jetty in *marina centro* and the line to the discobar can sometimes reach the mainland. It's extremely popular, and with good reason: Speakers near the bar pump out unabashed rock that goes as far back as the early '70s and the dance floor inside is perfect for flirting with the young Riminese. Water surrounds the bar on three sides, and there's no lifeguard on duty, so try to resist the temptation to go overboard after a few tequila shots. See p. 426.

Best Proof That We're *Not* the Most Intelligent Species

Delfinario (Dolphinarium), Rimini Compared to these mammals, Flipper is a B-list actor who will probably show up on next

BOLOGNA & EMILIA-ROMAGNA

Rimini

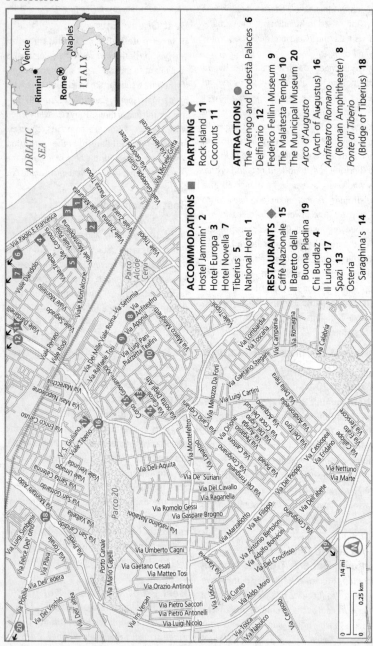

PARTYING ⭐
Rock Island **11**
Coconuts **11**

ATTRACTIONS ●
The Arengo and Podestà Palaces **6**
Delfinario **12**
Federico Fellini Museum **9**
The Malatesta Temple **10**
The Municipal Museum **20**
Arco d'Augusto
  (Arch of Augustus) **16**
Anfiteatro Romano
  (Roman Amphitheater) **8**
Ponte di Tiberio
  (Bridge of Tiberius) **18**

ACCOMMODATIONS ■
Hostel Jammin' **2**
Hotel Europa **3**
Hotel Novella **7**
Tiberius **5**
National Hotel **1**

RESTAURANTS ◆
Caffè Nazionale **15**
Il Baretto della
  Buona Piadina **19**
Chi Burdlaz **4**
Il Lurido **17**
Spazi **13**
Osteria
  Saraghina's **14**

Riccione

season's *Surreal Life*. The choreographed cetaceans in the Dolphinarium are ridiculously well trained and entertaining. They put together fantastic shows that make little children giggle, parents gasp in awe, and stoned college students crave a tuna sandwich. See p. 428.

Getting Around/Getting into Town

BY AIR

Rimini's **Federico Fellini-Miramare Airport** is small but modern, with a steady flow of flights from Rome, Munich, Naples, and a few other major European cities. If you're coming from Rome, a cheap flight from **AirAlps (www.airalps.at/index_en.htm)** might be your best option; four flights leave daily (only two Sat–Sun) from Roma-Fiumicino (Leonardo da Vinci Airport) to Rimini. Fellini International is actually in the Republic of San Marino, but to get to your flight, take bus no. 9 from Rimini's train station. The bus leaves every 30 minutes and it's much cheaper than a taxi (a bus ticket costs 1€, while a taxi is around 16€.)

BY TRAIN

A brand-new, connection-free Eurostar train links Rome with Rimini and Riccione. There are two departures per day, and trip time is about 4¹/₂ hrs. Otherwise, as Rimini and Riccione lie off Italy's main train corridors, you'll probably have to connect in Bologna (1 hr. away) or Ravenna (30 min. away) to a Rimini or Riccione train. Rimini's train station is just between the city and *marina centro*. If your hotel is somewhere along the water, you might want to hop a local bus or hail a cab.

Everything looks walkable on the map, but the only way to reach the beach is to walk underneath one of the underpasses along the tracks. Unfortunately, these are a 10-minute walk in either direction. It's an annoying detour that'll be even more bothersome if you have a lot of luggage.

Riccione's *stazione* is also near the beach but on the wrong side of the tracks, so you have to traipse up or down the tracks for a few blocks to reach the crossings that take you east toward the sea.

BY CAR

The A14 *autostrada* runs alongside both Rimini and Riccione, so driving is a painless affair. Unless you're already south of the two cities and on the coast, you'll have to go through Bologna to merge onto the A14. Take the A1 from Florence or Milan or the A13 from Padova to reach Bologna. From there, head south on the A14. Traffic can get a little congested, especially on Fridays and Sundays when the weekenders are coming and going, so try to pick off-hours hours when you head out.

Driving Tips

Driving down the coast can be a wonderfully satisfying experience, and Rimini is the perfect place to drive to or from. The cheapest deal from **Europcar,** Via Ravegnani 18 (☎ 0541-54746; Mon–Fri 8:30am–12:30pm and 2:30–7pm, Sat 8:30am–2:30pm), is just over 100€ a day for a compact Fiat (extra charges Sat). It may not be the top-down cruiser you were looking for, but with the money you save, you can stick your head out the window for the same effect.

Roads in Rimini and Riccione are not particularly complicated, so it's tough to get lost, especially with the Adriatic available as a visual compass. Parking along the beach can get tricky, as well as expensive, but drive farther inland and you'll find a number of parking lots where you can leave your car for a nominal fee (most of the times though, parking in these lots is free).

Orientation

Rimini and Riccione are 15 minutes apart and connected by the handy bus no. 11. (See "By Public Transportation," below.)

➔ **Rimini** While the city is divided into several sections, you need only concern yourself with the two major neighborhoods: **downtown** and **marina centro.** Downtown, aka *centro storico,* is surrounded by remnants of the city walls that once stood tall along the shore. (Throughout Italy, the shoreline has receded about 5km/3 miles in the last few millenia.) *Marina centro* is the Italian equivalent of Miami's South Beach, complete with Viale Amerigo Vespucci as its Ocean Drive. Hotels are a dime a dozen in both areas, so don't worry if you haven't booked a room (pickings are a little slim during the Paganello Ultimate Tournament and other festivals, but hotels downtown will most likely have vacancy during the beach events).

➔ **Riccione** One part hill town, two parts beach resort: Shake and serve on ice. Rimini's younger sister still draws a great number of visitors, but most partiers and club-goers head to the hills for the nightlife. The farther up the hill you go, the more impressive the view and the more devastating the cover charge. A good rule of thumb: The more Adriatic you see, the more euros you'll end up shelling out. This applies not only to clubs, but to restaurants, hotels, and shopping.

BY PUBLIC TRANSPORTATION

The cheap and efficient **TRAM** bus system of Rimini is a great option for shuttling between the city and *marina centro.* Tickets are 1€ and are usable for 90 minutes. Validate them the moment you board the bus or, if you're unlucky, an official will pop out of nowhere and tag you with a substantial fine. Any newsstand, bar, or *tabacchi* shop will sell you a ticket.

The best way to travel between Riccione and Rimini is on bus no. 11. The line starts in *marina centro* of Rimini and ends right in Riccione. If you're drunk and/or disoriented, the simplicity of the line makes it easier for you not to miss your stop. Get on and off in Rimini on Viale Amerigo Vespucci or Viale D'Annunzio in Riccione.

BY BICYCLE

The fitness capital of Italy is perfect for riding a bike. The busy beachside drives *(lungomare)* of both Rimini and Riccione are a cinch to navigate, and many of the small streets within the city center of Rimini only accommodate bicycles and pedestrians. **Manuelli Luciano,** Lungomare Tintori 53/P (☎ **0541/380558**) rents bicycles at a reasonable rate in Rimini, while **Tekno Bike Store,** Via Nazionale Adriatica 55 (☎ **0541/607773;** www.teknobikestore.it) serves cyclists in Riccione. Tekno gives customers an option by offering both mountain bikes (12€) and racing bicycles (14€–20€).

ON FOOT

Walking between Rimini's downtown and *marina centro* can be a hike for some,

BOLOGNA & EMILIA-ROMAGNA

RIMINI IS POSITIVELY FELLINIESQUE!

La Dolce Vita, Fellini's epic film of a young journalist consumed by his desire for some association with fame, is set in 1960s Rome, but the highlife of sex and raunchy parties almost mirrors that of modern-day Rimini. Check out the flick and then visit Fellini's home and museum. If you're itching for something edgier, rent *8½* (the title refers to the number of movies Fellini had made at that time—eight films and one half feature called *Luci del Varietà*). You'll see La Saraghina in all her wacked-out glory.

especially if you're lugging a 40-pound back-pack; otherwise it's doable. The walk between the two goes through the tree-lined Viale Principe Amedeo. The surrounding area is quiet and residential, so you don't have to worry about running into unsavory drifters or bums. In fact, the majority of the city is well kept, and there are few conspicuous vagrants on the streets. Riccione is quite similar, with the exception of the overlooking hill. Everything else is set up in a pseudo-grid system. While a map is helpful for both towns, once you're familiar with the main avenues, you'll rarely need to stray far from them.

Rimini & Riccione Basics

The second you arrive in Rimini, head straight to the **tourist office** and grab a couple of maps and brochures. When arriving by train, exit the station and face Piazzale C. Battisti, where the tourist office is directly to your left. If they can't help you there, head to Piazzale Fellini for the main tourist office, Piazzale Fellini 3 (☎ 0541/56902; Mon–Sat 8:30am–7pm, Sun and bank holidays 9:30am–12:30pm and 3:30–6:30pm).

Recommended Websites

○ **www.turismo.provincia.rimini.it/eng** Rimini's Tourism Council website is chock-full of useful information about museums, restaurants, hotels, and transportation. Great first site to visit if you're curious about Rimini, as well as Riccione.

○ **www.riminiairport.com** Get all your arrival and departure info from the Federico Fellini International Airport's site. It also provides information on getting to and from Rimini to the airport.

○ **www.tram.rimini.it/Proxy/home agenzia/home.html** The TRAM Public Transportation site is great for checking out online maps, prices, and times. It also has details on parking lots and their rates.

○ **www.comune.rimini.it/include/index.htm** Rimini's official municipal site lists all events and happenings in the city. Unfortunately, it's all in Italian and there's no English translation, but you can get a good idea of what's going on by looking at the pictures and knowing even a few words of Italian.

RIMINI & RICCIONE **Nuts & Bolts**

Emergencies Let's hope you never have to use these digits:

First Aid or Ambulance ☎ 118

Local hospital ☎ 0541/705111

Carabinieri (military police) ☎ 112

Polizia ☎ 113 or ☎ 0541/22666

Fire Department ☎ 115

Coast Guard ☎ 0541/50121

Internet/Wireless Hot Spots Conveniently located next to what is, I imagine, Rimini's only sex store, email@beach is a great spot to kick back, relax, and see if eBay had a better deal on your trembling sex toy. There are six computers in the air-conditioned, showroomlike space. Track lighting, bright wooden floors, and white slinky chairs make for an enjoyable hour of e-mailing and cooling off. It's at Viale Amerigo Vespucci 29c (☎ 0541/709387; www.emailbeach.it). Rates are 1.50€ for 15 minutes, 2.50€ for 30 minutes, 3.50€ for an hour, or 10€ all day.

Laundromats I'm sure the 8 square inches of cloth that most beach-goers wear isn't a whole lot to wash, but there's got to be a coin-operated machine somewhere in Rimini, right? Well, no. Since the town's only laundomat closed, your only option beyond the hotel sink is a *tintoria* (full-service laundry and dry cleaner) if you want to get your threads smelling fresh.

Post Offices   Send your tasteless postcards of scantily clad beach bums to destinations where they're not considered porn from Rimini's main post office, not far from the Arco d'Augusto, Piazzale Giulio Cesare 2 (☎ 0541/634280). It's open from Monday to Saturday 8am–6:30pm.

Restrooms   Public bathrooms and showers pop up every hundred meters or so as a service to the sandy patrons. Listen to the ocean breeze and make your own waves in the porcelain.

Sleeping

Anyone looking for a place to crash in Rimini/Riccione will have three options: beachside, *centro storico,* and the area between. Beachside might cost you a sunburnt arm and a leg, but you'll have the Adriatic at your doorstep and you can be as lazy as you want in the all-inclusive resorts that line the coast. If you actually want some shuteye, the hotels in *centro storico* will give you a better shot at peaceful slumber. It's a bus ride away from the beaches, but you'll find a much quieter atmosphere at night within the old city walls of Rimini town. Finally, the area between the water and the *centro storico* is where you'll find the best deals. It's definitely worth the extra 100 yards from the beach since you'll be saving a ton of cash *and* you're within walking distance of either the water or the city center.

If the properties below are full, check with the tourist office or browse their website, **www.turismo.provincia.rimini.it/eng**, under the "hospitality" link—they keep an excellent database of available rooms for all budgets.

HOSTEL

MTV Best → **Hostel   Jammin'**   ★★
Rimini–Marina centro   Life is always a beach in Hostel Jammin'. Despite the somewhat cheesy name, it's an appropriate one for the laid-back atmosphere. On arrival, the

staff greets you with a smile a mile wide and quickly gets you checked in. A few years ago, the hostel was a small hotel; it was only recently converted into a budget-friendly option for young travelers. Most guests are younger Europeans on vacation, and you'll notice that Hostel Jammin' draws a good number of gorgeous 20-somethings. Try striking up a conversation with them in the bar/common area. It's usually open until midnight or 1am and you'll always find a few people gathered on the outside patio strummin' a guitar or playing cards while downing cheap booze (3€ for a large bottle). As for the rooms, they manage to squeeze in an inordinate number of beds, but you'll still manage to get a good night's sleep. A decent breakfast, complete with fruit, eggs, various cereals, yogurt, juices, and coffee, is also included in the nightly rate. Hostel Jammin' also offers free use of bicycles (20€ deposit required, refunded on return), and they have a spot on the beach where they supply you with towels and other necessities. *Note:* The security lockers near the reception are a little tricky. I almost lost all my important documents when I realized that the lockers require a 1€ coin *each* time you open the locker. *Viale Derna 22.* ☎ *0541/390800. www.hosteljammin. com. Bed in shared room (6–8 people) with private bathroom 18€, with common bathroom 14€. Amenities: Bar, free beach services, free use of bicycles, Internet point, laundry room.*

CHEAP

➜**Hotel Europa** ★ *Rimini–Marina centro*
It'll be tough to find a cheaper night's stay this close to the beach. On the north side of Viale Amerigo Vespucci, this government-rated three-star Hotel Europa gives visitors on a budget a chance to be a few hundred meters from the water. Guests are given decent accommodations with late '70s/early '80s decor. Along with the inexpensive rates, the hotel offers a couple of plans that can make it easier on the wallet for particular groups (check website for exact benefits of each plan). If you decide to give Hotel Europa a whirl, be aware that the minimum stay is 3 nights. *Viale Amerigo Vespucci 83.* ☎ *0541–390862. www.hoteleuropa.rn.it. Single 35€–55€, double 65€–100€, triple 82€–125€, quadruple 93€–142€. Amenities: Lounger and umbrella rental. In room: AC, TV, fridge (upon request, 7€), hair dryer, safe.*

➜**Hotel Novella** ★ *Rimini–Marina centro*
Hotel Novella is a little farther away from the beach (a block and a half) but it's perfect if you're looking for a quieter spot. Tucked in a cozy corner of Viale Dandolo, this government-rated three-star is surrounded by trees and buildings that shelter it from the noisy Viale Amerigo Vespucci. The people behind the desk are particularly pleasant and attentive. *Viale Dandolo 1.* ☎ *0541/24724. novella@inhotel.it. Single 30€–59€. In room: A/C, TV.*

DOABLE

➜**Tiberius** *Rimini–Marina centro*   By Riminese standards, the government-rated three-star Tiberius is fairly modern. It's in the *Marina centro* part of Rimini and is in close proximity to the beach. Here, rooms feel more like digs in a contemporary hotel and the furnishings are a bit more up-to-date (as opposed to the '70s- and '80s-style furnishings that are de rigueur in many of Rimini's hotels). Gone are the chrome tube chairs and tables, replaced by classic wooden desks and side tables. The change in environment is a

welcome one, disorienting as it may be. The staff is delicious and the American-style buffet is amazingly friendly. Did I mention it was disorienting? *Viale Cormons 6.* ☎ *0541/54226. www.hoteltiberius.it. Single 46€–73€, single superior 51€–78€. In room: A/C, TV, minibar, safe.*

SPLURGE

➜**National Hotel** ★ *Rimini*   Of the few hotels actually on the beach, the government-rated four-star, mod-looking National is one of the older and pricier choices. Wade through the jungle of golf trophies in the lobby and book one of the larger executive rooms if you can afford it, but be warned that decor, while comfortable, is dated and all over the stylistic map. (Which brings us, once again, to the Florida analogy. . . .) The Meridien, the neighboring hotel, provides direct competition for affluent clientele and the National tries to hold its own by offering tons of amenities. There's a streetside pool, Jacuzzi, restaurant, bar, tanning salon, weight room, and massage tables. Kiddies can hang in the little children's club in the basement, but I'd probably go there just to whoop 5-year-olds in a game of foosball. *Viale Amerigo Vespucci 42.* ☎ *0541/390940. www.national hotel.it. Single: 82€–114€; double: 122€–182€; suite: 346€–546€. Buffet breakfast included. Amenities: Restaurant, bar, pool, solarium, spa. In room: A/C, TV, hair dryer, Internet access, minibar, safe.*

➜**Grand Hotel Des Bains** ★★ *Riccione*
The grande dame of Riccione's beachfront zone, the Grand Hotel des Bains is a great place to step back in time and pretend you're a captain of industry living the good life on the Riviera Romagnola. Set in an elegant Art Nouveau palazzo with wrought-iron gates and entrance courtyard with fountains and palm trees, the hotel has fabulously well-maintained, luxurious common areas and attentive staff. In keeping with the swanky, early-20th-century seaside theme, guest

rooms are done up in streamlined 1920s furnishings in soft colors. (Executive suites kick it up a notch with bolder colors, chintz, and gilt mirrors.) The property also features two swimming pools—one indoor, heated year-round and one outdoor—two restaurants, and a piano bar clad in acres of swirling ivory-colored marble. *Viale Gramsci 56.* ☎ *0541/ 601650. www.grandhoteldesbains.com. Single 100€–180€, double 180€–300€. Amenities: Fitness center, Internet point, pool, salon, sauna, solarium. In room: A/C, TV, hair dryer, minibar, safe.*

Eating

It's no surprise that fish and crustaceans reign supreme in the coastal towns of Rimini and Riccione. These creatures find their way into the Tuscan-influenced dishes in many of the restaurants and eateries, keeping the active locals well fed and happy. One local favorite is the *piadina* (see **Il Baretto della Buona Piadina,** below). The flatbread specialty won't drain you of your euros, and its homey flavor will coax a smile from your famished body.

CAFE/SNACK

→ **Caffè Nazionale** *Rimini*   As good as they are, *piadine* can get old quickly if you're eating them 24/7. If your budget is still in the red, there's plan B: panino and Coke. Many bars offer cheap panino meals, but Caffè Nazionale has the advantage of being smack in the center of Rimini's *centro storico.* Order a panino and Coke for 5€, sit down in the diner-like booths, and watch some local news on the TV. When you're reenergized, head 'round the corner and do some sightseeing in Piazza Cavour or Piazza Tre Martiri. *Corso D'Augusto 201.* ☎ *0541/26523. Mon–Sat 7am–8pm.*

CHEAP

📺 Best → **Il Baretto della Buona Piadina** ★★ *Rimini*   A few nights—check that, a *single* night—of clubbing and drinking in Rimini will do a number on your bank

account. You can spend much of your cash paying the ludicrous covers and use whatever's left for a *piadina,* the legendary local snack in Emilia-Romagna. The flatbread delights are somewhat like pita sandwiches, but are much tastier (they're made with pork fat—mmmm—pork fat. . . !) and more filling. The bread is made of flour, lard, and salt and filled with all sorts of ingredients (anything from prosciutto to various cheeses and vegetables). Il Baretto, north of the city center on Via Covignano, wins the hearts and stomachs of locals and visitors year in and year out. It's where you'll want to go if you're aching for a cheap, high-quality meal. *Via Covignano 245.* ☎ *0541/753274. Daily 11am–1am. Piadina 8€–10€.*

DOABLE

→ **Chi Burdlaz** SEAFOOD/ITALIAN *Rimini* This trendy open-air oasis on Viale Amerigo Vespucci churns out loud R&B on its speakers and mouthwatering seafood on its plates. Grab a chair near the faux tree breaking through the ceiling, and after you've ordered the crawfish cooked in brandy, test your Italian and try to translate the cursive writing plastered on the ceiling. Another dish you must sample is the succulent calamari with potatoes and rosemary. If seafood isn't your thing, the separate pizza menu offers some tasty alternatives. Wash it all down with a bottle of *vino* from their decent selection of local, Tuscan, and Umbrian wines, and you're set for a night on the town. *Viale Vespucci 63.* ☎ *0541/709900. www.chiburdlaz.com. Daily for lunch, dinner, and late-night eats (until 3am in summer). Primi 8€–9€; secondi 13€–16€.*

→ **Il Lurido** ★★ SEAFOOD *Rimini*   I admit that I throw around "don't miss" and "must visit," a fair amount, but I really *do* mean it here. Il Lurido is the restaurant that locals and visitors alike agree is the best place to sate your hunger. Seafood is meticulously prepared and cooked to perfection (mere mortals can try and resist their mussels, but they always fail). Whether it's fish, crustacean, or cephalopod (that's octopi and squid . . . turn on that Discovery Channel, will ya?!), there's something for every seafood lover. *Piazzetta Ortaggi 7.* ☎ *0541/24834. Tues–Sun for lunch and dinner. Primi 9€–12€; secondi 14€–18€.*

➜**Spazi** ITALIAN/SNACKS *Rimini* Sun-drenched Piazza Cavour is surrounded by impressive architecture as well as a few eateries from which to admire it. Spazi, possibly the most laid back, is the preferred spot, offering salads, sandwiches, and cocktails. In the middle of the day, order *tagliolini gamberi e zucchini,* with succulent shrimp and zucchini, and enjoy the porticoes of the Arengo and Podestà palaces from the patio. *Piazza Cavour 5.* ☎ *0541/23439. Primi 7€–12€; secondi 7€–13€.*

SPLURGE

➜**Osteria Saraghina's** ★★ SEAFOOD/ITALIAN *Rimini* Saraghina's dishes are as traditional as they get in Rimini. The fish-heavy menu includes a fried seafood platter that has a variety of deep-fried fish and squid. After a day of Frisbee, volleyball, and basketball on the beach, diners feel a lot less guilty ingesting the crispy, sinfully good seafood. As for the restaurant's name, "La Saraghina" was a slightly scary and crazed character in Fellini's flick *8½* who sensually danced the rumba in certain dreamlike sequences. The character had her roots in Fellini's younger days in Rimini, where he and his friends would watch a prostitute try and lure fishermen, garnering her the nickname "The Sardine Lady" or "La Saraghina." Needless to say, you'll find several tasty dishes containing the small fish on the menu. *Via Poletti 32.* ☎ *0541/783794. Primi 10€–14€; secondi 12€–18€.*

➜**Terrazza Ceccarini** SEAFOOD *Riccione* ★★ The selection in Terrazza Ceccarini may be limited, but it makes choosing between their incredible dishes a little easier. Their salads, squid, and seabass are all top-notch, with the latter being the most satisfying. The white fish meat is awesomely tender and flakes off the fork with ease. *Viale Ceccarini 101.* ☎ *0541/693468. Tues–Sun noon–2pm and 7–10:30pm. Primi 8€–14€; secondi 18€–24€.*

Partying

The beach activities are mostly there for visitors to while their time away before hitting the *aperitivo* scene, and then more bars and dance clubs. Rimini is a nightlife hot spot first and foremost. Partiers tend to split their time between the killer clubs of Riccione and the easygoing watering holes of Rimini. No matter which town you end up in, you'll find something to your liver's and libido's liking.

Expect cover charges to run around 10€–20€, and drinks to range from about 5€–10€, with the occasional free shots you might expect from party beach town. The hierarchy of priciness is always wine (cheapest), beer, mixed drinks (most expensive).

BARS

MTV Best ➜**Rock Island** ★★ *Rimini* You couldn't pick a better name for this joint. It sits on a barge just off the beach, and patrons are treated to good old-fashioned rock-'n'-roll tunes until 4am. Stay outside with the spunkier crowd downing reasonably priced suds in the open air, enjoying the surrounding ocean view, or head inside and hit the dance floor. A cold bath will help you sober up after a few too many beers, but make sure it's within the confines of your hotel and not in the crashing surf a few yards from Rock Island. *Piazzale Boscovich/Molo di Levante.* ☎ *0541/50178. www.vcs.it/rockisland. Daily 7pm–4am.*

CLUBS

➜**Coconuts** *Rimini* Whip out those salsa moves and sip a mojito in Coconuts, one of Rimini's hottest dance clubs. If your Latin mojo is a little lacking, worry not, they offer

Three Outfits a Day Keep the Fashion Police Away!

For those of you not versed in the ways of Italian beach or island holidays, you should know that Italian *signorinas* wear *three* outfits a day when they vacation on the seaside. **Outfit #1:** bathing suit, sarong or dress, and flip-flops, for the beach. **Outfit #2:** different bathing suit, different sarong, and different flip-flops, for the *aperitivo* hour. **Outfit #3:** "going out" clothes for dinner and clubs. As ridiculous as it sounds, the pseudo-just-off-the-beach Outfit #2 is de rigueur, so you might as well join 'em. Head back to your hotel for a shower and freshening up before you hit happy hour, or risk a fine from the *polizia fashionista!*

a regular dance floor with house/R&B as well as a Latin-flavored dance area. It also houses the best collection of gorgeous patrons, so while you take a break between tango numbers, you can rest your eyes on beautifully dressed Riminese. *Lungomare Tintori 5.* ☎ *0541/52352. Daily from early evening until 4am.*

🎵 Best ➔ **Cocoricò** ✶✶ *Riccione* By name alone, you might confuse Cocoricò with Coconuts, but that's where the similarities end. In fact, you can't confuse Cocoricò with any other place in the world. (But just in case you were wondering, "confusion is sex," according to one of the signs above one of the bars.) If that adage holds true, the interior decorators of the club must be a very kinky bunch. Some would call it überkitschy, but I call it "alien avant-garde." Name a random object and chances are you'll find it inside this Riccione discotheque. Whales and pyramids coexist beside the club-goers while

the music arrogantly straddles the line between edgy and trashy. *Viale Chieti 44.* ☎ *0541/605183. www.cocorico.it. Cover about 20€.*

➔ **Pascia** *Riccione* With a nightlife comparable to Rimini's, Riccione draws many night owls to its offbeat clubs and bars. Pascia is a perfect buffer between Rimini's techno-blasting discobars and Riccione's more unusual haunts. Revelers are amazingly approachable and even recluses will find themselves having a great time. Music runs the gamut from house to hip-hop, and your wallet won't suffer too badly from the drink prices. *Via Sardegna 1.* ☎ *0541/604207. Thurs–Sun 10pm–4am.*

➔ **Peter Pan** *Riccione* My unfortunate roommates at the hostel got suckered into paying Peter Pan's ridiculous cover. The poor Dutch guys were promised by promoters a free beer (which came in a tiny cup) and a T-shirt (an ultracheesy XXL polyester blend shirt with "Peter Pan" emblazoned in gaudy, bold print) for 21€. Absurd cover aside, the club itself isn't that bad. It's mighty popular with locals, and the P.A. mostly blasts Euro-trance. Picking up anyone here is close to impossible with so many non-English speakers, but if your Italian and cheekbones are flawless it could be worth a try. *Viale Abruzzi 147.* ☎ *0541/641335. Thurs–Sat 10pm–5am.*

Sightseeing

Despite the party-hearty reputation Rimini has earned, there are plenty of attractions for anyone keen on learning a little bit while they work on their tans. The ancient Roman city **Ariminum** that once stood here, left some potent reminders of its presence, including the ist-century A.D. **Arch of Augustus,** an amphitheater, and the **Ponte di Tiberio** bridge (p. 428). As Rimini is where Italians go to get away from their art-packed

Roman Rimini

Arco d'Augusto (Arch of Augustus) ★ It's slightly older than Keith Richards, but the Arch of Augustus has the same pockmarked and damaged surface as the aging guitarist. The looming gate was erected in 27 B.C. to give Caesar Octavianus Augustus mad props for restoring the Via Flaminia, which enters Rimini (ancient Ariminum) via this arch. All roads lead to Rome, and if you head south on the Flaminia, you'll eventually end up in the Eternal City after about 325 km (202 miles). Despite its age and condition, you can still make out plenty of details on the arch: the engraved attic (that's the top, for laymen) is still legible, and the reliefs (sculpted panels) of Roman gods on the structure are still clear enough for you to distinguish Minerva from Neptune. *Via XX Settembre (just north of Viale Tripoli).*

Anfiteatro Romano (Roman Amphitheater) The few ruins left of the elliptical structure are a far cry from the grand and imposing Colosseum in Rome, but the amphitheater (literally, "double theater," for its fully round shape) located in the southeastern corner of Rimini was an impressive, 15,000-spectator arena for gladiator and wild-animal fights from the 2nd to the 5th centuries A.D. The coastline used to be just meters away, so the amphitheater was the first thing that greeted ships that came in to port. *Ahh,* nothing like sailing back from the Dacian Wars and watching some more organized slaughter! Set in a grassy area amid shady pines, the site makes for some relaxing amateur archaeologizing. *Via Vezia (just east of Viale Roma).*

Ponte di Tiberio (Bridge of Tiberius) ★★ Call 'em tech geeks if you want, but the Romans kicked ass at transportation engineering. Rimini's Ponte di Tiberio, a five-arched bridge over the Marecchia river (called Ariminus in antiquity), is living proof of their prowess with a protractor and a pile of rocks. The perfectly preserved bridge was begun by Augustus in A.D. 14 and finished in A.D. 21 by his successor, Tiberius, hence the name. *Viale XXIII Settembre 1943.*

cities, you'll find that museums and historical sites are never packed.

This might be a plus for anyone looking to take in a little culture, but don't kid yourselves: The beaches, bars, and clubs are the real reason why throngs of visitors flood the streets of Rimini year-round.

➔ **The Arengo and Podestà Palaces** *Rimini* The former was a place where the "People's Council" would make decisions on municipal matters. Legend has it that debtors were forced to sit three times on a rock slab, the **Lapis Magnum** (the "great stone"), which is no longer there. Each time they made contact with this stone, the guilty had to proclaim: *"Cedo bonis!"* My elementary knowledge of Latin translates the phrase into: "I promise

to pay you back." Next door to the Arengo (to the north) is the slightly younger Podestà Palace. Rather than doling out fistfuls of justice, the Podestà served as a government building and then became a residence for important Riminese. Both buildings have seen several restorations and the Podestà now regularly holds exhibitions. *Piazza Cavour. Hours/admission vary depending on exhibit. Check when you get there.*

MTV **Best** ➔ **Delfinario** ★★ *Rimini* The ear-splitting clicking, squealing, and splashing coming from Piazzale del Porto isn't Fran Drescher giggling and playing Marco Polo. It's one of the few "dolphinaria" in Europe. It's mostly a family attraction, but it's relaxing at the dolphin shows and strolling through

Culture 101: Rimini & Riccione Beach Behavior

Before you skip down Viale Amerigo Vespucci with your floaties, you might want to know a few things about the sandy playground. Aside from the regular public spaces, hotels and hostels usually have their own little slivers of sand (clearly marked by signs with oversized numbers) that are reserved for their guests. In addition, they'll also provide plenty of amenities like towel service or umbrella rental. Make sure you chat up the concierge or front desk staff as you head out, or you might miss out on some hotel/hostel perks. You can also contact the **Rimini Beach Attendants' Cooperative** (☎ 0541/381548) for info about renting loungers, umbrellas, etc.

Once you're beachside, you'll realize that this ain't exactly your grandma's beach. Here you'll find Internet points sprinkled every 500m (1,640 ft.) as well as libraries that supply sunbathers with some reading material while they bake. If those Umberto Eco paperbacks seem a bit intense, no worries: There are also plenty of newsstands selling trashy celebrity magazines (*Novella 2000, Eva Tremila,* and *Vippissime* are the best in terms of guess-whose-cellulite-this-is? photojournalism).

As widespread as topless bathing is in the rest of Italy and the Mediterranean, the sporty babes on the beach of Rimini and Riccione tend to keep both pieces of their bikinis on at all times. Keep your swimsuits PG-13 and you'll steer clear of the beach officials' ire. Meanwhile, guys wear anything from baggy board shorts to—you guessed it—Speedos. So, for those male readers who've ever wondered what it would be like to go out in front of thousands of people in a glorified nylon fig leaf, rest assured: What happens on the Riviera Romagnola *stays* on the Riviera Romagnola.

the piranha displays is a great way to work off last night's monster hangover. Just fight the temptation to do a body shot off the dolphin's blowhole. *Piazzale del Porto.* ☎ *0541/50298. www.delfinariorimini.it/indexen.html. Apr showtimes 4:30pm (Mon–Fri), 4 and 5:30pm (Sat–Sun); May showtimes 4:45 and 6pm; June showtimes 4:45, 6, and 9:30pm; July and Aug showtimes 4:45, 6, 9:30, and 10:30pm; Sept showtimes 4:45.6, and 9:30pm; Oct showtimes 4:30pm (Sat–Sun only). Admission 10€.*

FREE ➔ **Federico Fellini Museum** *Rimini* Rimini's celluloid hero is immortalized on Via Clementini with a museum containing information all about the man. For those who don't have his work on their Netflix queue, Fellini was the Oscar-winning director and screenwriter for classics such as

La Dolce Vita, Amarcord, and *8 ¹/₂.* He was born in Rimini and spent a great deal of time shuttling between his hometown and Rome, where he passed away in 1993. If you're staying in Rimini for more than a day, you really don't have any excuses for not paying homage to one of film's greatest visionaries. It's 3 blocks from the rail station and if the admission were any cheaper, they'd be paying you to go. *Via Clementini 2.* ☎ *0541/50303. www.federicofellini.it. Tues–Fri 4–7pm, Sat 10am–noon, Sun 10am–noon and 4–7pm. Free admission; call ahead for a guided tour.*

➔**The Malatesta Temple** *Rimini* Designed by Leon Battista Alberti, adorned with panels by Giotto, and topped with a fresco by the legendary Piero della Francesca, the Malatesta Temple started out as a memorial tomb for Sigismondo Pandolfo Malatesta (sometimes called "the wolf of Rimini") a feudal prince who was a fierce warrior as well as a patron of the arts. Completed long after his death, it now stands as Rimini's most important landmark. It has recently been restored to its initial splendor and the mesmerizing marble is back to its original and brilliant colors. It's an active church. *Via IV Novembre 35.* ☎ *0541/51130. Daily, 8.30am-7.30pm, closed during Mass.*

→ **The Municipal Museum** *Rimini* Rimini doesn't have as many museums as other cities in Italy, but its Municipal Museum makes up for it by combining historical exhibits with paintings and sculptures from the 14th to 20th centuries. On the first two floors you'll find the Pinacoteca (picture gallery), where the walls feature masterpieces by famous locals like Cagnacci, Bellini, and Cantarini. Well, okay, famous maybe to just the Riminese and art history buffs, but it's still worth your euros. *Via L. Tonini 1.* ☎ *0541/21482. Sept 16–June 15 Tues–Sat 8:30am–12:30pm and 5–7pm, Sun 4–7pm; June 16–Sept 15 Tues–Sat 10am–12:30pm and 4:30–7:30pm (Tues July–Aug extended hours from 9–11pm), Sun 4:30–7:30pm. Admission 4€.*

Playing Outside

With the exception of winter, the Riminese and Riccionese spend their days far from the confines of any walls. Scads of activities are at the disposal of visitors and locals. The most obvious playground are the miles of beaches along the Adriatic. A bird's-eye view of the sandy stretches reveals thousands of beach chairs, umbrellas, and bronzed sunbathers. Every few kilometers, other amenities are offered to the beach bums, including basketball courts, gyms, and volleyball/foot volley courts.

During the Easter season, discs swarm through the air during the **Paganello Ultimate Frisbee International Tournament** (www.paganello.com). Thousands flock to the sand and crowd the beaches with hundreds of matches. Disc chuckers from afar travel to Rimini and partake in the festivities. Events aren't limited to just matches and exhibitions; there are also concerts, firework displays, and beach barbecues.

If you're not feeling particularly Hasselhoffy, the beaches aren't the only places to get your blood flowing and sweat dripping. Every conceivable summer sport can be played in the several gyms in Rimini and Riccione. Tennis, soccer, golf, go-karting (yeah, some consider it a sport), and, of course, dancing can all be done, played, driven, or learned in the various facilities. Hit the links at the **Rimini Golf Club,** Via Tenuta Amalia 109 (☎ **0541/678122**) or call the **City Council's Sports Department** (☎ **0541/704451**) for information about the facilities you're looking for.

Thrill seekers aren't forgotten about either. On the beach, look for beach centers #28 and #86 for some kite-surfing. If you're a kite-surfing novice ⓜ Ⓑest, instructors on center #86 will provide newbies with tips and in-depth instruction (for info ☎ **0541/384513**). Farther inland, amusement parks in both towns draw every age group to their rides and attractions.

Riccione is home to one Europe's biggest waterparks, **Aquafan** ★, dizzyingly outfitted with waterslides, pools, and flumes for all ages. Ever wondered what it feels like to be flushed down the toilet? Admit it, it might be fun. That's why the Speedriul usually has a sizeable queue for folks waiting to be shot down a tube and onto this funnel-like sink. After splashing in circles a few times, gravity will pull you into the hole in the middle and a final tube will spit you out like a bad batch of chowder. It's located at Via Ascoli Piceno 6 (☎ **0541/606454**; www.aquafan.it) and is open daily from June 4 to September 11 10am to 6:30pm; full-day admission is 20€, afternoon admission 13€ (after 3pm).

When the sun goes down, there are outdoor screens where you can catch a flick while inhaling the ocean air. Six **cinemas on the beach** come to life in the evening. Drive-ins may be a thing of the past, but who needs cars when you have a beach chair, a margarita, and a nice summer breeze? (For movie info call ☎ **0541/51331**.)

Finally, if you want to stay away from buildings during your entire stay in Rimini and Riccione, you can sleep under the stars in Riccione. There are extensive camping options towards the south if you feel like roughing it.

Pitch a tent or sing "Kumbaya" around a *falò* (bonfire) at **Camping Riccione** (www.campingriccione.com), **Camping Fontanelle** (www.campingfontanelle.com), or **Camping Adria** (www.campingadria.com). All are near the intersection of Via San Gallo and Via Torino. Rates are from 3€ to 8€ per person.

Parma: Mmm . . . More Than Cheese

97km (60 miles) NW of Bologna, 121km (75 miles) SE of Milan

Mmm, Parma. . . . The city that gave the world Parmigiano-Reggiano and prosciutto di Parma won't be the most exciting stop on your tour, but you'll enjoy eating, shopping, and strolling in one of northern Italy's more congenial towns. Parma is a great detour off the Florence–Milan corridor. In this slower-paced town of about 175,000 residents, you can walk everywhere (on impeccably maintained stone-slab streets), the monuments can be covered in a matter of hours, the shops are super-stylish, and no matter which way you turn, there are delis and wine bars eager to fill you up with the local cheese, prosciutto, *salame*, and Lambrusco wine. From September to June, international students on the Erasmus exchange program fill the elegant streets of Parma with a palpable energy and flood the bars along Strada Farini, on the south side of town, every night. For a well-earned break from traffic and culture, head for the vast gardens of the Parco Ducale (on the west side of the *Torrente,* Parma's lethargic river) where you can also jog off the extra pounds you gained from all that pork and dairy.

Getting There

BY AIR

The nearest major international airports are Malpensa and Linate airports in Milan, about an hour and a half by train or car from Parma.

BY TRAIN

Parma is served by the Milan-Bologna rail line, with 30 trains a day arriving from Milan (trip time: 1 1/2 hr.); the one-way fare starts at 7€. From Bologna, 47 trains per day arrive in Parma (1 hr.); the one-way fare is around 4.70€. There are nine connections a day from Florence (2 hr.); the one-way fare begins at 17€. Note that Intercity (IC) and Diretto (D) trains stop in Parma, but not Eurostar (ES) trains. Check out train times, prices, and connections info at the very handy www.trenitalia.com.

BOLOGNA & EMILIA-ROMAGNA

Parma on Foot, Bus & Taxi

Parma is small and flat enough that you can walk everywhere. **Buses** in Parma are run by TEP (www.tep.pr.it), and bus tickets cost 1€ for 90 minutes. If you need a cab, you can call **Radiotaxi** at ☎ 0521/252-562.

OKKIO! Strada or Via?

The Italian words for "street," *strada* and *via,* are used interchangeably in Parma. So, if you're looking for Via Garibaldi on the map and can't find it, try Strada Garibaldi.

Parma Tourist Office

The main **tourist office** is located at Via Melloni 1/a (☎ 0521/218-889; www.turismo.comune.parma.it; Mon–Tues and Thurs–Sat 9am–7pm, Wed 9am–1pm and 3–7pm, Sun 9am–1pm).

BY CAR

Parma lies just off the A1 *autostrada,* which runs between Milan and Bologna, and to Rome and Naples. Follow the highway exit signs to Parma *centro.* The *centro storico* of Parma is full of one-way streets and dead-ends. Ditch the car in one of the public parking lots (like the large underground structure on Viale Toschi), remove any valuables, and leave it while you're in town.

Parking fees and hours during which payment is required are confusing and dynamic—check with your hotel or ask at the *tabacchi* store, where you can buy parking vouchers.

Getting Around

PARMA ORIENTATION

Central Parma is circumscribed by broad, tree-lined boulevards, but the heart of the old city—the part that most tourists are concerned with—is a much smaller area, about

Official Website

For all your Parma needs, head for the official website of the Parma tourist board—www.turismo.comune.parma.it—is there anything it can't do?? Pretty much everything you could possibly want to know about Parma is available on this wonderfully comprehensive, multilingual site.

4km (2¹/₂ miles) from north to south, and 2km (1¹/₄ miles) from east to west. The train station lies at the very northern tip of this area. The "river," **Torrente Parma,** runs north-south along the western side of town, and Parma's main park, the **Parco Ducale,** lies just south of the train station, on the west side of the river (in the zone known as *Oltretorrente*). **Piazza Garibaldi** is the main square, sitting where main east-west arteries Strada Mazzini and Strada della Repubblica meet. Strada Farini is the principal street running south of Piazza Garibaldi, and where most of the cool cafes and bars are. North of Piazza Garibaldi is where most of the hotels and sights are located, including the cathedral (Duomo), the Palazzo della Pilotta, and the Teatro Regio.

Parma Nuts & Bolts

ATMs   Banks and cash machines (called *bancomat* in Italy) are all over the streets of the *centro.* You probably won't need to carry around a ton of euros while you're in Parma, since credit and debit cards are accepted almost everywhere. You will need cash for cappuccino at the local bar, as well as all those glasses of wine at *aperitivo* time. As always, plan your cash withdrawals carefully; the exchange rate is favorable through foreign ATMs, since the banks trade in large volume, but you're hit with fees of more than $5 (depending on your bank) every time you take out money while abroad.

Bike Rental   Adjacent to the Toschi public parking structure, **Parma Punto Bici,** Viale Toschi 2 (☎ 0521/281-979; www.parmapuntobici.it) is the best deal in town, with regular pedal-bikes starting at 3€ for 5 hours, and only 5€ for 10 hours. They also have cool electric bikes available for 0.90€ per hour. Parma Punto Bici is open Monday to Saturday 9:30am to 1pm and 3:30 to 7pm, and Sunday 10:30am to 1pm and 3:30 to 7:30pm.

Otherwise, **Parma City Bike,** Viale Mentana 8/a (☎ 0521/235-639), will rent you a no-frills bicycle for 5€ for a half-day or 8€ for a full day. They're open Monday to Friday from 8:30am to 1:30pm and 3:30 to 7:30pm. On Saturdays, they're open from 8:30am to 1:30pm.

Emergencies   In an emergency, call the *polizia* at ☎ 113; for nonemergencies, use ☎ 0521/238-888 or visit the main police station *(questura)* at Borgo della Posta 14. You can also turn to Italy's Army police force, the **Carabinieri** (who wear red-striped trousers designed by Valentino), to report emergencies or other disturbances of the peace, ☎ 112. In Parma, the Carabinieri are at Via Fonderie 10 (☎ 0521/281-323). To report a fire, gas leak, or a cat stuck in a tree, dial ☎ 115, for the *vigili del fuoco* (fire department).

For medical emergencies, call an ambulance at ☎ 118, or visit the *pronto soccorso* (emergency room, where you will not be charged for treatment, regardless of your insurance status) at **Ospedale Maggiore,** Via Gramsci 14 (☎ 0521/703084).

Internet   The Youth Services office, **Informagiovani,** Via Melloni 1/b (☎ 0521/218749) has four Internet stations which may be used for up to an hour each day; it's a good idea to stop by or call ahead to reserve your slot (Mon–Tues and Fri–Sat 9am–1pm and 3–7pm; Wed 9am–1pm; Thurs 9am–7pm). **TSI Informatica Cyberpoint,** Via d'Azeglio 72/d (☎ 0521/504-148) has 10 Internet terminals and is open Mon to Sat from 9am to 8pm, charging 6€ per hour.

Postage & Shipping   Postage stamps *(francobolli)* are sold at all *tabacchi;* they'll ask you how many postcards you're sending and where—it's as simple as that. Postage for postcards and letters to anywhere in Europe or the Mediterranean basin is 0.52€; for the rest of the world, it's 0.62€. Red post boxes are on the sides of buildings; drop your postcards in the "tutte le altre destinazioni" (all other destinations) slot, as opposed to the "città" slot. When you start to accumulate too many souvenirs, or you realize that you're never going to wear those hiking boots you packed, the easiest thing to do is ship 'em home. The central Poste Italiane office of Parma is at Via Pisacane 1 (off Strada Garibaldi; ☎ 0521/222-414; Mon–Fri 8am–6:30pm, Sat 8am–12:30pm). The post office sells nifty yellow boxes and any other packaging supplies you might need. There are a few forms to fill out for parcels going overseas, but for all the bad press Italian government agencies get, the national mail system is actually quite hassle-free nowadays, with an excellent delivery record. For more information on postal services, visit the English version of the Poste Italiane's official website at www.poste.it/en.

Restrooms   When you're out and about in Parma and nature calls, you should have no qualms about stopping in the nearest bar/cafe and politely asking the management if you can use their *bagno.* This is standard practice throughout Italy—unlike in the U.S., Italian bathrooms are *not* for customers only. Drinking and eating establishments are required by law to allow anyone to use their toilet, so as long as you're polite, you'll be pointed to the restroom.

Telephones   There are public pay phones *(cabina)* at the train station, in major piazzas and bus terminals, and at certain coffee bars (look for the white and red phone sign out front or the sticker in the window). Italian pay phones take a prepaid plastic card, called a *scheda telefonica,* which is issued by Telecom Italia and which must be

BOLOGNA & EMILIA-ROMAGNA

purchased at a *tabacchi* store. Cards are sold in denominations of 2.50€, 5€, and 10€; in order for them to work, you must break off the perforated tab on the corner of the card. (A common rookie mistake is failing to break off the tab and then, when the card doesn't work, getting all huffy with the person who sold you the "defective" card—we don't want you to be a rookie.) Local calls (anything with a "0521" prefix) are pretty cheap—maybe 0.20€ for a short call, as are calls to land lines in other Italian cities (0.50€ for a short call to book a hotel in your next city, for example).

Be aware, however, that calls from Italian land lines to Italian cellphones (three-digit prefixes beginning with "3") are horrendously expensive and will probably bleed your *scheda telefonica* dry in a matter of seconds. Calls from Italian pay phones to overseas phone numbers aren't as pricey as you might think, especially after 7pm Italian time, so as long as you can keep it somewhat brief, a call home shouldn't run you more than a few euros. If you're going to be chatting for a while, however, it does add up. The best bet, if you need to call home frequently, are international phone cards (anywhere from 5€ to 20€, available at newsstands or *tabacchi*) issued by a number of private companies that often have more advantageous rates for calling abroad. These private phone cards usually have a PIN code that you reveal by scratching off a grey bar on the back, and a series of access numbers to call before you're connected with Mom and Dad. Keep in mind that you will still need a dial tone to use one of these cards, and to get a dial tone at a pay phone, you always need to insert a Telecom Italia *scheda telefonica*. Moral of the story? Use the phone at your hotel, where the dial tone is free, when you need to call home. If dialing direct from your hotel phone (that is, without any PIN codes or phone cards), always ask hotel staff up front what their charges are. Some hotels make a sizeable profit off of guest phone use; other more honest souls only charge you what the phone company charges them, with no mark-up whatsoever.

Sleeping

Understandably enough, Parma rests on its culinary laurels and neglects the accommodations side of things; hotels here tend to suck. Even so, they fill up faster than you'd think for such an overlooked tourist destination, so be sure to call at least a few days in advance. If you get stuck, the people at the Tourist Office (see above) can usually make a few calls on your behalf and find vacancies at B&Bs or small room-rental outfits when the other budget accommodations are booked.

CHEAP

→ **Hotel Moderno** About as spartan as you can get without actually traveling back in time 2,500 years to southern Greece. Nevertheless, for its location near the station and cute, grandfatherly guy at the reception, this is a great place to crash for budget travelers in Parma. You pull into the station, dump your stuff here, and then you're free to walk around the *centro storico*. About half the rooms have private bath; those without bath share shower and toilet down the hall. *Via A. Cecchi 4.* ☎ *0521/772-647. Single 50€–65€, double 70€–80€, triple 8€–100€, suite 130€.*

DOABLE

→ **Hotel Button** ★ The Button is a local favorite, one of the best bargains in the town center, just off Piazza Garibaldi. This is a family-owned and -run hotel, and you're made to feel welcome. The guest rooms are simply but comfortably furnished and generally spacious, although the decor is dull. The bathrooms are a bit cramped but tidy containing shower stalls. There's room service but no restaurant, and the bar never closes.

Strada San Vitale Borgo Salina 7 (off Piazza Garibaldi). ☎ *0521/208039. 40 units (shower only). 113€ double, 138€ triple. Rates include continental breakfast. Free parking. Closed July 18–Aug 17. Bus: 8. Amenities: Cafe; dry cleaning; laundry service; room service (24-hr.). In room: A/C, TV, dataport, hair dryer.*

Splurge

→ **Hotel Verdi** ★★ Facing the Ducal Gardens, this Art Nouveau hotel preserves the elegance of the early 20th century while meeting the needs of today's visitors. The guest rooms feature parquet floors, briarwood furnishings, and fine linens. The marble-lined bathrooms offer luxurious soaps, thick towels, and body oils. The adjacent Santa Croce restaurant offers a refined yet cordial atmosphere resplendent with period art, furnishings, and lighting in which to savor traditional cuisine and fine Italian wines. In summer, a brick courtyard, alive with greenery, allows you to dine outdoors. The garage at the rear of the hotel is guarded. During the day, you can walk through the Ducal Gardens (Parco Ducale), landscaped by the French architect Petitot and decorated with statues by another Frenchman, Boudard. With its splashing fountains, wide expanses of greenery, and gravel paths, the gardens make a great place to relax. Admission is free. *Via Pasini 18;* ☎ *0521/293539. www.hotel verdi.it. 20 units (shower only). Double 150€–190€, triple 180€–220€. Free parking. Amenities: Bar; dry cleaning; laundry service; room service (24-hr.). In room: A/C, TV, dataport, hair dryer, minibar, safe.*

Eating

With all due respect to the Baptistery and Archaeological Museum, you don't come to Parma to sightsee. You come to eat. Count on Parmigiano-Reggiano cheese with everything and generous helpings of cured pork—from prosciutto to unusual local *salames*—wherever you go. The typical *primo piatto* (pasta or soup dish) in Parma is *cappelletti in brodo,*

small ravioli stuffed with veal, cheese, and nutmeg, served in chicken or veal broth—a rainy or sick day favorite. While Parma is celebrated for its prosciutto, it's considered pretty ordinary here. On special occasions, locals eat *culatello,* which is made from the uppermost muscular part of the hind leg (not the whole thigh, as in prosciutto). Culatello costs twice as much as prosciutto, and I gotta say, you can taste the difference. The wine you'll be drinking a lot of in Parma is the local, ruby-red, robust Lambrusco, which goes beautifully with all that pork and cheese. Before setting off to dinner, stop for an *aperitivo* at one of the cafes on Piazza Garibaldi, Parma's handsome main square. All drink orders come with a generous plate of mini-sandwiches and other antipasti that'll keep you going for a while.

SNACKS

→ **Salumeria Verdi** ★★ DELI This handsome, old-world deli is a shrine to all of Parma's gourmet products, with all the Italian cheese, hams, and salamis imaginable. It's a great place to stock up for a picnic lunch, and the *culatello* sandwich on a *rosetta* roll may be the best 4€ you'll spend on food in Italy. If you have any cheese freaks at home in need of souvenirs, they also sell covered bowls in the shape of Parmigiano-Reggiano wheels, perfect for storing the grated cheese in the refrigerator. *Via Garibaldi 69/a,* ☎ *0521/ 208-100. Mon–Sat 8am–1pm and 3:30–7pm.*

→ **Tapas Pub** ★ SNACKS A favorite lunch spot of local students, this Spanish-style snack bar in the Oltretorrente district is also a pizzeria and an Internet cafe, and at night, you can get sangria and beer and watch Italian and international soccer games alongside plenty of friendly young people. *Via d'Azeglio 67/b.* ☎ *0521/285-688. Daily until 2am. Snacks from 2€.*

CHEAP

→ **Pizzeria La Duchessa** ★ PIZZA The most popular pizzeria in Parma is right on the

Hog Heaven: What It Takes to Become Prosciutto

Piglets whose hind legs are destined to become prosciutto (Parma ham) must be at least 9 months old and weigh at least 150kg. For a pig thigh, making it to actual prosciutto status is a bit like pledging a fraternity. The workers rub salt in your exposed flesh, leave you to dry for months on end, smear fat on you, let you sit some more, and then poke you with a sharpened piece of horse bone to make sure you don't smell bad. If you make it through pledge period, which lasts about a year, you're branded for life with the five-pointed "Parma" star that marks you as an elite member of the Prosciutto di Parma brotherhood. And what do you get for your patience and loyalty? A couple hundred bucks, most of which goes to The Man (the prosciutto factory), and a life sentence in the deli counter, where a machine slices you into paper-thin sheets. (Whole prosciutto thighs retail for about $350 in the U.S., about half that much in Italy.) But at the end of the road, it will all have been worth it, because the fatty, salty goodness of you, a Parma prosciutto thigh, brings happiness to all who eat it.

Most prosciutto consumers have never heard of it, but Langhirano (about 5km/3 miles south of Parma *centro*), is the town where all Prosciutto di Parma is made. Langhirano lies in what is known as the *zona tipica,* an atmospherically and topographically unique pocket of rolling hills between the Enza river and the Torrente Stirone. Accept no imitations: Due to its particular air, the *zona tipica* is the only place in the world where it's possible to achieve the special, slightly sweet flavor of Prosciutto di Parma. It all starts to the west of Parma, in the Tyrrhenian Sea, where marine breezes travel inland, passing over pinewoods, acquiring a slight pine aroma as they go. The winds then brush against the mountains, losing the saltiness of the sea air, and roll farther eastward, adding the perfume of chestnut trees to their particular bouquet, until they reach, at long last, the *zona tipica* and Langhirano. Langhirano's 189 prosciutto factories make about 10 million *prosciutti* a year, about 8 million of which are distributed in Italy and 2 million are exported. For more hamtastic facts check out the website of the Consorzio Prosciutto di Parma, www. prosciuttodiparma.com.

Tour a Prosciutto Factory

One *prosciuttificio* (prosciutto factory) in Langhirano is set up to receive visitors (reservations are required). **Salumificio La Perla** (no relation to the lingerie maker) offers two visitors' programs: Program 1: Visit the prosciutto factory, watch the curing process in action, then sample the house prosciutto (3€ per person). Program 2: Visit the prosciutto factory, watch the curing process in action, and then sample the house prosciutto, other various regional cold cuts, Parmigiano-Reggiano cheese, bread, wine, and homemade dessert (13€ per person). During your visit, you'll be required to wear a white lab coat and, of course, the obligatory food-prep *cuffia* (canvas cap) to keep your stray hairs from spoiling the whole process. To reserve a visit, call or e-mail a few days in advance. *Località Quinzano di Sotto 3, Langhirano.* ☎ *0521/853572. www.salumificiolaperla.it.*

main square, open late and almost always crowded, especially if you want an outdoor table, but the pizzas are fabulous, especially when washed down with a carafe of Lambrusco. *Piazza Garibaldi 1.* ☎ *0521/235962. Tues–Sun 7:30pm–midnight. Pizzas from 6€.*

DOABLE

→ **Gallo d'Oro** ★★ PARMIGIANA The sister restaurant to Corrieri (below), this is one of our favorite trattorias. It has an unpretentious decor with flea-market items such as antique cinema posters and old-fashioned toys. Downstairs is a bodega where locals pile in to taste the wine of the region, especially Lambrusco, which seems to go with anything served in Parma. Start with the *salumi misti,* a variety of locally cured hams. All the pasta dishes are homemade, including *tortelli ripieni* (pasta stuffed with cottage cheese and fresh spinach). For a main course, we recommend the roasted lamb stuffed with bread, cheese, and eggs. A Parma classic is the chicken breast rolled with a prosciutto and parmigiano and offered in a white-wine sauce. *Borgo della Salina 3.* ☎ *0521/208846. Reservations recommended. Main courses 6.50€–14€. Mon–Sat noon–2:30pm and 7:30–11pm.*

→ **Trattoria Corrieri** ★★ PARMIGIANA I've got four words for you: *filetto all'aceto balsamico.* When I lived in Rome, I was known to hop on a 5-hour train to Parma just to taste the amazing beef fillet with balsamic vinegar sauce at Corrieri. To start your meal, order the *culatello* (a finer version of prosciutto) platter—the helpings are unbelievably generous. Adding to the warm and homey vibe, wheels of Parmigiano-Reggiano and prosciutti hang from the ceiling, and tables are dressed in red-and-white-checked tablecloths. Old newspaper clippings and awards in dark-wood frames clutter the walls, which were probably once white but have turned yellow from the pork fat aroma that hangs in the air at all times in Parma, as well as

cigarette smoke from the pre-2005 days when smoking was allowed in Italian restaurants. The cramped rooms closer to the entrance are actually favorable to the too brightly lit larger dining room that occupies the corner of the building. *Via Conservatorio 1 (2 blocks south of Strada Mazzini).* ☎ *0521/234-4426. www.trattoriacorrieri.it. Primi from 7€; secondi from 12€. Mon–Sat noon–2:30pm and 7:30–10:30pm.*

SPLURGE

→ **Parizzi** ★★★ PARMIGIANA/ITALIAN In the historic center of town, the building that houses Parizzi dates from 1551, when it first opened as an inn; the current restaurant was opened in 1958 by the father of the present owner. Seated under the skylit patio, you'll enjoy rich cuisine that's among the best in this region of Italy. After you're shown to a table in one of the good-size rooms, a cart filled with antipasti is wheeled before you, containing shellfish, stuffed vegetables, and marinated salmon. Then you might be tempted by *culatello,* cured ham made from sliced haunch of wild boar; a pasta served with a sauce of herbs and Parmigiano-Reggiano; a parmigiano soufflé with white truffles; or roasted guinea fowl with Fonseca wine. *Strada della Repubblica 71.* ☎ *0521/ 285952. Reservations required. Main courses 12€–18€. Tues–Sun noon–2:30pm and 7:30–10:30pm. Closed 3 weeks in Aug.*

Partying

It's safe to say your craziest nights in Italy won't be in Parma, but you can still hit up the local scene and find plenty of buzz. Strada Farini (aka Via Farini), which runs south from Piazza Garibaldi, is the target zone where most young people head for *aperitivo* and after-dinner drinks. As in much of Italy, Monday nights are pretty dead.

In general, here's about what you'll pay for a drink in a bar or pub: **Glass of wine in enoteca (wine bar):** from 2€, for a totally drinkable local wine that you may have never heard of, all the way up to 8€ for a particularly special vintage of Brunello or Barolo. Most people drink something in the 3–4€ range. Wine is by far the cheapest (and classiest, since quality is so high) way to get drunk in Italy.

Pint of beer (lager, ale, Guinness, whatever): 4€ during happy hour; 5€ after happy hour: this is the standard in all the big cities; could be a little cheaper in more remote places.

Cocktails/mixed drinks: 4–5€ in casual, laid-back bars; 7–10€ in trendier spots.

→ **Enoteca Fontana** ★★ Parma's best-loved wine bar is a huge scene at *aperitivo* time (happy hour, from 7–9:30pm or so), when Parmigiani of all ages crowd in for glasses of the local Lambrusco and sandwiches of Parmigiano-Reggiano and prosciutto (of course!). *Strada Farini 24A.* ☎ *0521/286037. Tues–Sun until 10pm.*

→ **Le Malve** ★ Another of the more popular joints on Via Farini, Le Malve has outdoor tables, a dimly lit interior bar, and loud music. It's especially busy on Friday and Saturday nights, when the crowd of young Parmigiani and resident students spills out onto the street. *Strada Farini 12/b.* ☎ *0521/234-051. Mon–Sat until 1am.*

→ **Tonic** ★ On a side street near Via Farini, this place has an easy-going, energetic vibe. Cocktails and beer, as opposed to wine, are the drinks of choice, and theme nights are frequently organized. On Sundays, there's very happening *aperitivo* from 6:30 to 10:30pm. *Via Nazario Sauro 5 (off Strada Farini).* ☎ *0521/286-066. Tues–Thurs and Sun until 1am; Fri–Sat until 3am.*

DISCOTECAS

A bit removed from the *centro,* and not necessarily worth the trek unless you can score a free ride with someone, **Dadaumpa,** Via Emilio Lepido 48 (☎ **0521/483813**), is a stylish dance club frequented by 20- and 30-somethings. Also out of town, **Lotus**

(formerly known as Astrolabio), Via Zarotto 86A (☎ **335/781-5672** cell), is the preferred *discoteca* of the under-25 set.

Sightseeing

→ **Abbey of St. John (San Giovanni Evangelista)** ★ Behind the Duomo is this church of unusual interest. After admiring the baroque front, pass into the interior to see yet another cupola by Correggio. From 1520 to 1524, the High Renaissance master depicted the Vision of San Giovanni. Vasari, author of *Lives of the Artists* and a contemporary of Correggio, liked it so much that he became completely carried away in his praise, suggesting the "impossibility" of an artist conjuring up such a divine work and marveling that it could actually have been painted "with human hands." Correggio also painted a St. John with pen in hand, in the transept (over the door to the left of the main altar). Il Parmigianino, the second Parmesan master, did some frescoes in the chapel at the left of the entrance. You can visit the abbey, the school, the cloister, and a pharmacist's shop, where monks made potions for some 6 centuries, a practice that lasted until the closing years of the 19th century. Mortars and jars, some as old as the Middle Ages, line the shelves. *Piazzale San Giovanni 1.* ☎ *0521/235311. Free admission to church and cloisters; 2€ for the pharmacist's shop. Daily 8am–noon and 3–6pm; pharmacist's shop Tues–Sun 8:30am–1:30pm.*

→ **Baptistry (Battistero)** ★★ Among the greatest Romanesque buildings in northern Italy, Parma's tall, octagonal, pink-marble baptistery (1196–1270) was the work of Benedetto Antelami. The edifice is ringed by four levels of recessed terraces, which, if it weren't for the girly color of the marble, would give off a more austere, prison-watch-tower vibe. The interior walls of the baptistery are divided by 16 structural ribs, and the cupola is richly frescoed with biblical scenes that have the overall look of an American

Gothic quilt. But it's Antelami's wonderful allegorical sculptures of the months and zodiac signs, in the niches along the inner walls, that are the most interesting works of art here. *Piazza del Duomo 7.* ☎ *0521/235886. Admission 4€. Daily 9am–12:30pm and 3–6:30pm.*

FREE ➔ **Duomo/Cattedrale** ★ Built in the Romanesque style in the 11th century, with 13th-century Lombard lions guarding its main porch, the dusty pink Duomo stands side by side with a *campanile* constructed in the Gothic-Romanesque style and completed in 1294. The façade of the cathedral is highlighted by three open-air loggias. Inside, two darkly elegant aisles flank the central nave. The octagonal cupola was frescoed by a master of light and color, Correggio (1494–1534), one of Italy's greatest painters of the High Renaissance. His fresco, *Assumption of the Virgin* (1522–34), is an art history class chestnut—when the professor wants to make a point about Renaissance artists foreshadowing the baroque, expect slides of Correggio's work in the Parma cathedral. In the transept to the right of the main altar is a Romanesque bas-relief, *The Deposition from the Cross,* by Benedetto Antelami, each face bathed in tragedy. Made in 1178, the bas-relief is the best-known work of the 12th-century artist, who was the most important sculptor of the Romanesque in northern Italy (and author of the sculptures on the baptistery, across the piazza). *Piazza del Duomo.* ☎ *0521/ 235886. Free admission. Daily 9am–12:30pm and 3–7pm.*

➔ **National Gallery (Galleria Nazionale)** and **National Archaeological Museum (Museo Archeologico Nazionale)** ★★ Palazzo della Pilotta was built by the Farnese family in Parma's heyday as a duchy in the 16th century. The palace was not used as a residence but as the headquarters for court and state services (stables, hay store, arms room, theater, and barracks). Badly damaged by bombs in World War II, Palazzo della

Pilotta has been restored and turned into a museum complex. The National Gallery offers a limited but well-chosen selection of the works of Parma artists from the late 15th to 19th centuries, notably paintings by Correggio and Parmigianino. In one room is an unfinished head of a young woman attributed to Leonardo da Vinci. Correggio's *Madonna della Scala* (of the stairs), the remains of a fresco, is also displayed. But his masterpiece is *St. Jerome with the Madonna and Child.* Imbued with delicacy, it represents age, youth, and love—a gentle ode to tenderness. In the next room is Correggio's *Madonna della Scodella* (with a bowl), with its agonized faces. You'll also see Correggio's *Coronation,* a golden fresco that's a work of great beauty, and his less successful *Annunciation.* One of Parmigianino's best-known paintings is *St. Catherine's Marriage,* with its rippling movement and subdued colors. You can also view St. Paul's Chamber (Camera di San Paolo), which Correggio frescoed with mythological scenes, including one of Diana. The chamber faces onto Via Macedonio Melloni.

On the same floor as the National Gallery is the **Farnese Theater** (Teatro Farnese), a virtual jewel box, evocative of Palladio's theater at Vicenza. Built in 1618, the structure was bombed in 1944 and has been restored. Admission to the theater is included in the admission to the gallery; however, if you want to visit only the theater, it costs 2€. Also in the palazzo is the **National Archaeological Museum.** It houses Egyptian sarcophagi; Etruscan vases; Roman and Greek-inspired torsos; Bronze-Age relics; and its best-known exhibit, the Tabula Alimentaria, a bronze-engraved tablet dating from the reign of Trajan and excavated at Velleia in Piacenza. The grassy areas around the Palazzo della Pilotta are suitable for chilling out and picnicking, although the Parco Ducale, across the river, is much prettier. *In the Palazzo della Pilotta, Piazzale della Pilotta*

BOLOGNA & EMILIA-ROMAGNA

15. ☎ 0521/233309 (National Gallery) or ☎ 0521/233718 (Archaeological Museum). National Gallery: admission 6€; Tues–Sun 8:30am–1:30pm. Archaeological Museum admission 2€; Tues–Fri 8:30am–2pm, Sat–Sun 8:30am–7:30pm.

Playing Outside

While Parma is not nearly as bike-dependent as Ferrara, a **bicycle** is still a great way to get around, especially if you only have a day to get a feel for the city. Old-school bikes and efficient electric bikes can be rented for mere pocket change at **Parma Punto Bici,** located near the Viale Toschi parking structure, on the east bank of the Torrente Parma (for full details, see "Parma Nuts & Bolts," above).

FREE ➔ **Parco Ducale** ★★ With its splashing fountains, wide expanses of greenery, and gravel paths, the sprawling gardens across the river from the Palazzo della Pilotta make a great place to relax and picnic. If you haven't brought your own grub, there's a cafe in the park that serves sandwiches, drinks, and gelato. If the Parco Ducale looks a bit, well, *French* to you, it's because the park was landscaped by the French architect and Parma hero Petitot and decorated with statues by another Frenchman, Boudard. In

Parma Calcio (Soccer)!

From August to May, you can catch a big-time Italian soccer game at **Stadio Tardini/FC Parma** ★★. Pick up some yellow-and-blue paraphernalia outside the stadium to blend in with locals. The liveliest (and cheapest) seats are in the Curva section. Tickets are sold at the stadium box office, and range in price from 20€ to 120€. Viale Partigiani d'Italia 1 (east of the city center, about 20 min. on foot). ☎ 0521/505-111. www.fcparma.it. Bus: 9.

OKKIO! Never on a Thursday

Like many towns in Emilia-Romagna, the whole city of Parma tends to shut down on Thursday afternoons. That means that small businesses and most shops will be closed from 1 or 2pm on Thursday and won't open again until Friday morning at 9 or 10am. Restaurants and bars, thankfully, do not observe the Thursday afternoon "holiday."

the 18th century, cult members used to gather at Petitot's Temple of Arcadia for role-playing games in which they pretended they were frolicking in the groves of Arcadia, the mythological forest of the gods. *Strada delle Fonderie. Take Ponte G. Verdi across the Torrente Parma from Palazzo della Pilotta. Daily 7am–6pm in winter, 6am–midnight in summer. Free admission.*

Shopping

In addition to being one of Italy's prime food zones, the region of Emilia-Romagna is also one of Italy's prime shopping zones. The towns here are wealthy, with a high concentration of stylish men and women who need to outfit themselves in the hippest threads at all times. Parma is no exception, and in the streets north and south of Piazza Garibaldi, you'll find tons of trendy boutiques eager to sell you to-die-for shoes, dresses, jackets, and sweaters.

Parma's most famous food product—parmigiano (Parmesan) cheese, the best being Parmigiano-Reggiano—is world-famous. Virtually every corner market sells thick wedges of the stuff, but if you're looking to buy your cheese in a special setting, head for the **Salumería Garibaldi,** Via Garibaldi 42 (☎ 0521/235606). You might also take a walk through the city's **food market** at Piazza Ghiaia, near the Palazzo della Pilota; it's open Monday through Saturday from 8am to 1pm and 3 to 7pm.

Enoteca Fontana, Via Farina 24A (☎ 0521/286037), sells bottles from virtually every vineyard in the region, and the staff is extremely knowledgeable.

Ferrara: A Neat Little Package of *La Dolce Vita*

52km (32 miles) N of Bologna, 100km (62 miles) SW of Venice

Sometimes when you're traveling in Italy, you're so busy trying to see and do everything every day and partying every night that you forget to slow down and live *la dolce vita* like the locals do. When your brain and body just need a break, catch the next train to Ferrara.

Halfway between Venice and Bologna, Ferrara ★★ may just be Italy's greatest neat-little-package city. It has a fairy-tale castle with a moat and drawbridge, broad and shady bike paths that follow the old walls around the city, a bustling *centro* with cozy streets, trendy shops and cafes, and awesome local cuisine that's big on comfort food—pumpkin ravioli being the specialty. Ferrara is wealthy, well-groomed, and sophisticated, with a strong university population

This Is How We Roll: Biking It in Ferrara

Make no mistake about it: bikes are an entire lifestyle in Ferrara. Not motorcycles, not Vespas, not high-tech Lance Armstrong numbers, but old-school, gearless, basket-on-the-front *bicycles*. Most hotels in Ferrara provide bikes for guests free of charge. Bike riders wield so much power on the streets of Ferrara that even buses and cargo vans know better than to challenge them, even on the busier main thoroughfares. In the narrow streets of the *centro*, aggro old men without concern for pedestrians' life or limb tear down the cobblestones like Miss Gulch in *The Wizard of Oz*. If you're gonna bike it in Ferrara (and you absolutely should), be ready to bust out those old arm signals you learned when you were a kid, because you'll annoy drivers and fellow bikers if you don't indicate your upcoming turns. If you start to get the hang of urban riding and want pesky pedestrians to get out of your way, tap lightly on your bell.

The one ride that's a must in Ferrara goes north from the Castello Estense, down beautiful (but bumpy) **Corso Ercole d'Este** ★★★ to the **tree-lined bike path** ★★★ that hugs the city walls. You can ride all the way around the city, or stop when you've made it halfway around, and then head back into the *centro*. When you're ready to shop, bar-hop, or wander the thoroughfares immediately surrounding the Duomo and the Castello Estense, ditch the bike—the constant hopping off, parking, and locking will seriously cramp your strolling style. Always lock your bike (even the hotel loaner jalopies), as theft is all too common.

If your hotel doesn't provide a bike, you can rent one from super-friendly Gigo and Paola at **Estense Bici** near the *duomo*, Via Voltapaletto 11/a (☎ 349/173-7116; www.estensebici.tk); **Pirani e Bagni,** at the train station, Piazzale Stazione 2 (☎ 0532/772190); **Romanelli Primo,** Via di Luna 10 (☎ 0532/206017); or **Itinerando,** Piazzale Kennedy 6/8 (☎ 0532/202003; www.itinerando.it). Day rentals will set you back 8€–10€.

Ferrara's Official Website

The official website for tourism in Ferrara and its province is **www. ferraraterraeacqua.it,** and it has great links to recommended itineraries, info on the major sights, and a database for hotels and restaurants.

that keeps the town filled with modern energy despite its medieval roots. You can also turn down your hearing aid here; bicycles, not motor scooters, are how you get around in Ferrara. What's more, Ferrara is the town that gave us Bruno Tonioli, the Italian judge from *Dancing With the Stars.* Don't think of Ferrara as a major destination—just think of it as detox when you've OD'ed on being a tourist.

Getting There

BY TRAIN

Getting to Ferrara by train is a breeze from anywhere in central or northern Italy. Ferrara lies on the major train line that runs between Bologna and Padua, on the way to Venice. Frequent trains connect Ferrara with Bologna (about 30 min. away, to the south) and Padua (Padova, 30 min. away, to the north). Venice is about an hour north of Ferrara by rail; Florence is about 2 hours south, and Rome is about 4 hours south. Check out train times, prices, and connections info at **www.trenitalia.com.**

BY CAR

Getting to Ferrara by car is pretty easy, as the city lies right off the A# *autostrada* that runs between Bologna and Padova. Once you're off the highway, just keep following the white *CENTRO* signs and anything that points to Castello Estense, which is at the dead center of old Ferrara. We suggest you not drive at all in Ferrara. Park in a public parking lot, and leave the car until you leave town. Parking fees and hours during which payment is

required are confusing and dynamic—check with your hotel or ask at the *tabacchi* store, where parking vouchers can be purchased.

Orientation/Getting Around

Ferrara is shaped more or less like a pentagon whose southeast side has sprung a leak. The moated and turreted **Castello Estense** is the city's biggest monument and its geographical center. The heart of the *centro* (where most shops and restaurants and the *duomo* are located) lies just south of castle. One of the loveliest streets in Italy, **Corso Ercole d'Este,** runs north from the Castello Estense area to the arbored bike paths that run along the old city walls. The train station is about 1.5km (1 miles) west of the Castello Estense. Ferrara as a whole is best explored by bike, but when you're exploring the nucleus of historic buildings and side streets around the Castello Estense and *duomo,* it makes more sense to walk.

The only trip you probably won't make on foot or by bike is from the train station to the heart of the old city, and vice versa. If you're hauling luggage and need a lift from the train station to your hotel, there's a taxi stand in front of the station. Otherwise, **ACFT** city-run buses 1, 2, 3C, 4C, 9, and 21 connect the train station with the Castello Estense area, which lies within a few minutes' walk of most hotels. Bus tickets cost 1€ each way. For more info about ACFT, Ferrara's public transportation system, check out www.acft.it. For a cab, you can call **Radiotaxi** at ☎ **0532/ 900-900.**

Ferrara Basics

The main **tourist office** is at the Castello Estense (☎ **0532/299-303;** infotur@provincia. fe.it; Mon–Sat 9am–1pm and 2–6pm, Sun 9:30am–1pm and 2–5:30pm). There's another branch at Piazza Municipale 11 (☎ **0532/ 419-474;** Mon–Sat 9:30am–1:30pm and 2:30–5:30pm, Sun 9:30am 12:30pm, closed Sun in Jan, Feb, July, Aug, Nov, and Dec).

Ferrara Nuts & Bolts

ATMs   Ferrara has long been a moneyed town, and you don't have to look far to find cash machines (called *bancomat* in Italy) around the streets of the *centro*. You probably won't need to carry around a ton of euros while you're in Ferrara, since credit and debit cards are accepted almost everywhere. You will need cash for cappuccino at the local bar, as well as all those glasses of wine at *aperitivo* time. As always, plan your cash withdrawals carefully: the exchange rate is favorable through foreign ATMs, since the banks trade in large volume, but you're hit with fees of more than $5 (depending on your bank) every time you take out money while abroad.

Emergencies   In an emergency, call the ***polizia*** at ☎ 113; for nonemergencies (e.g., your bike gets stolen), use ☎ 0532/294-311 or visit the main police station (*questura*) at Corso Ercole d'Este 26. You can also turn to Italy's Army police force, the **Carabinieri** (who wear red-striped trousers designed by Valentino), to report emergencies or other disturbances of the peace, ☎ 112. To report a fire dial ☎ 115, for the ***vigili del fuoco*** (**fire department**).

For medical emergencies, call an ambulance at ☎ 118, or visit the *pronto soccorso* (emergency room) at **Ospedale Sant'Anna** (Via Rampari di San Rocco 15; ☎ 0532/236-903 or 0532/236-224; www.ospfe.it).

Internet   Along the north side of the *duomo*, **Ferrara Internet Point,** Via Adelardi 17 (☎ 0532/191-0876) is open Monday through Friday 11am to 11pm, and Saturday 11am to 7pm.

Luggage Storage   Hauling around Tuscan ceramics or other cumbersome souvenirs acquired en route? That's what *deposito bagaglio* (luggage deposit) at the train station is for, baby! You'll be charged 6€ per piece for a 24-hour period, so be sure to consolidate smaller bags into one parcel.

Postage & Shipping   Postage stamps (*francobolli*) are sold at all *tabacchi;* they'll ask you how many postcards you're sending and where—it's as simple as that. Postage for postcards and letters to anywhere in Europe or the Mediterranean basin is 0.52€; for the rest of the world, it's 0.62€. Red post boxes are on the sides of buildings; drop your postcards in the *"tutte le altre destinazioni"* (all other destinations) slot, as opposed to the *"città"* slot. When you start to accumulate too many souvenirs, or you realize that you're never going to wear those hiking boots you packed, the easiest thing to do is ship 'em home. The central Poste Italiane office of Ferrara is at Viale Cavour 27 (☎ 0532/297-336; Mon–Fri 8am–6:30pm, Sat 8am–12:30pm). The post office sells nifty yellow boxes and any other packaging supplies you might need. There are a few forms to fill out for parcels going overseas, but for all the bad press Italian government agencies get, the national mail system is actually quite hassle-free nowadays, with an excellent delivery record. For more information on postal services, visit the English version of the Poste Italiane's official website at www.poste.it/en.

Restrooms   When you're out and about in Ferrara and nature calls, you should have no qualms about stopping in the nearest bar/cafe and politely asking the management if you can use their *bagno*. This is standard practice throughout Italy—unlike in the U.S., Italian bathrooms are *not* for customers only. Drinking and eating establishments are required by law to allow anyone to use their toilet, so as long as you're polite, you'll be pointed to the restroom.

Telephones　There are public pay phones *(cabina)* at the train station, in major piazzas and bus terminals, and at certain coffee bars (look for the white-and-red phone sign out front or the sticker in the window). Italian pay phones take a prepaid plastic card, called a *scheda telefonica*, which is issued by Telecom Italia and which must be purchased at a *tabacchi* store. Cards are sold in denominations of 2.50€, 5€, and 10€; in order for them to work, you must break off the perforated tab on the corner of the card. (A common rookie mistake is failing to break off the tab and then, when the card doesn't work, getting all huffy with the person who sold you the "defective" card—we don't want you to be a rookie.) Local calls (anything with a "0532" prefix) are pretty cheap—maybe 0.20€ for a short call—as are calls to land lines in other Italian cities (0.50€ for a short call to book a hotel in your next city, for example). Be aware, however, that calls from Italian land lines to Italian cellphones (three-digit prefixes beginning with "3") are horrendously expensive and will probably bleed your *scheda telefonica* dry in a matter of seconds. Calls from Italian pay phones to overseas phone numbers aren't as pricey as you might think, especially after 7pm Italian time, so as long as you can keep it somewhat brief, a call home shouldn't run you more than a few euros. If you're going to be chatting for a while, however, it does add up. The best bet, if you need to call home frequently, are international phone cards (anywhere from 5€ to 20€, available at newsstands or *tabacchi*) issued by a number of private companies that often have more advantageous rates for calling abroad. These private phone cards usually have a PIN code that you reveal by scratching off a gray bar on the back, and a series of access numbers to call before you're connected with Mom and Dad. Keep in mind that you will still need a dial tone to use one of these cards, and to get a dial tone at a pay phone, you always need to insert a Telecom Italia *scheda telefonica*. Moral of the story? Use the phone at your hotel, where the dial tone is free, when you need to call home. If dialing direct from your hotel phone (that is, without any PIN codes or phone cards), always ask hotel staff upfront what their charges are. Some hotels make a sizeable profit off of guest phone use; other more honest souls only charge you what the phone company charges them, with no markup whatsoever.

Sleeping

Ferrara is a pretty congenial place to bed down for the night. There are plenty of cozy, atmospheric, budget-friendly places within a few minutes' walk of the Castello Estense. If you can shell out a few more euros, upgrade to one of the government-rated three- or four-star hotels, which will give your tired backpacking soul some sanity-restoring comforts and amenities for a fraction of the price you'll find for similar accommodations in Italy's bigger, more touristed cities.

CHEAP

→ **La Lupa**　As basic as it gets, "The Wolf" only has nine rooms, most of which are tiny and do not have private bath. But the value for location (a 5-min. walk from the *duomo* and Castello Estense) is great. *Vicolo della Lupa 8.* ☎ *0532/760-0070. Single 35€–40€, double 40€. In room: TV.*

→ **San Paolo** ★　Style is not the San Paolo's strong suit—this government two-star looks as if it's been decorated by a young bachelor who's just discovered the wonders of Ikea. However, rooms are pretty darn big for how cheap they are, and the hotel's location puts you within steps of Via delle Volte (Ferrara's coziest street, covered by dozens of medieval brick arches) and within 5 minutes of the cathedral and the Castello Estense. All rooms have full bath, and you can avail of the San Paolo's fleet of bikes for an extra charge of 8€ per day. *Via Baluardi 9 (off Piazza Travaglio).* ☎ *0532/762-040. www.hotel sanpaolo.it. Double from 83€. Amenities: Bike rental. In room: A/C in most rooms, TV.*

➔ **Santo Stefano** Rooms at this friendly inn, a bit south and west of the cathedral and castle, are far from luxurious, but they're warmed by rose-hued fabrics and light woods. The building is a 20th-century structure, meaning a bit low on charm, but all rooms have such modern conveniences as full private bath, A/C, minibar, TV, and phone. *Via Boccacanale Santo Stefano 21 (south of Piazza Saint Étienne).* ☎ *0532/206-924. www. hotelsantostefanoferrara.com. Single 47€, double 72€, triple 80€. Rate includes breakfast. Amenities: Free use of bikes. In room: TV.*

DOABLE

➔ **Corte Estense** ★ Straight outta the swingin' 1600s, this government-rated three-star, conveniently located a few blocks south of the cathedral, has plenty of atmosphere. Most rooms have a cozy, minstrel's-lodge feel, with slanting, wood-beam ceilings and homey antique furniture; a few rooms are small and bland, done up in 10 shades of off-white. All rooms have full private bath. The hotel also boasts a truly lovely interior courtyard where you can sit and have a drink or write a postcard—with storybook brick walls, shuttered windows, a garden well, and well-placed lighting, it looks like something from the set of *The Bold and the Beautiful: Ferrara. Via Correggiari 4A (2 blocks south of Piazza della Cattedrale).* ☎ *0532/242-168. www. corteestense.it. Double 110€–150€, including breakfast. In room: A/C, TV, Internet (in-room broadband cable), minibar.*

➔ **Europa** ★ Ferrara's most venerable hotel is far from fancy, but if you stay here, you'll be able to tell your friends back home that you slept on the same property where Mussolini once lodged. Other illustrious past guests include Giuseppe Verdi and the Savoy monarchs. Ranging widely in terms of comfort and character, some rooms have coffered and frescoed ceilings and priceless Ferrarese terra-cotta floor tiles (laid out in a traditional tone-on-tone checkerboard pattern); some singles are cramped and charmless *Death of a Salesman*–type accommodations. Staff at the Europa can be aloof, but they'll at least give you a key and point you to the shed where the hotel's fleet of battered but perfectly serviceable old-school bicycles are kept; borrow a bike (free of charge) and go for a spin past the castle (a block away) and down villa and garden-lined Corso Ercole d'Este to the broad bike paths that follow the medieval walls around the city. There's also a public terminal for Internet (extra charge) in the lobby. *Corso Giovecca 49 (at Via Palestro).* ☎ *0532/205-456. www.hoteleuropaferrara. com. Double 90€–115€, triple 115€–140€, quadruple 140€–165€, frescoed suite 115€– 145€. Breakfast included. In room: A/C, TV, hair dryer, minibar, handicapped accessible.*

SPLURGE

➔ **Ripagrande Hotel** ★ Occupying the 15th-century Palazzo Beccari-Freguglia (about 5 min. south of the cathedral), the Ripagrande is outfitted with ancient columns, arches, marbles, and tapestries. The conversion of the property into a hotel is not as fabulous as it could be, perhaps—room decor is all over the place—but it's hard to find a government-rated four-star at this price anywhere in Italy, much less in the *centro storico* of one of the country's wealthiest towns. In some of the superior rooms, beds are in a separate, lower-ceilinged nook; and parlor-style living areas have round wooden table and chairs where you can imagine the Este dukes might have had their buddies over for a late-night round of Texas Hold 'em. Junior suites (which constitute 20 of the hotel's 40 units) are an even funkier arrangement, with sleeping lofts and antique writing desks. Bathrooms are narrow but fairly luxurious, with plenty of warm-toned marble, bathtubs, and plants. If you have a choice of rooms, definitely ask the reception staff if you can see the multiple options, as each unit has a wildly varying personality. *Via Ripagrande 21 (off Via del Turco).* ☎ *0532/762-250. www. ripagrandehotel.it. Double 155€–175€, junior suite 160€–205€. Amenities: Free use of bikes. In room: A/C, TV, minibar.*

Eating

You really can't go too wrong, food-wise, in Ferrara. It isn't touristy enough to be ridden with bad-quality tourist traps, so as long as you like to eat hearty, you'll do fine. On a typical Ferrarese menu, you'll find plenty of meat and cheese antipasti, stuffed pastas, and more meat and cheese. *Cappellacci di zucca alla Ferrarese* are ravioli stuffed with pumpkin and served with a meat-and-tomato sauce; you can also get your *cappellacci* with sage and butter (which I happen to prefer, since it allows the full flavor of the pumpkin to come through), but know that this preparation is more associated with nearby Mantua. Another belly-bulging Ferrarese treat is *salama da sugo,* a local pork salami that is boiled for 5 hours and served hot, surrounded by a generous ring of mashed potatoes.

COFFEE BARS

→ **Caffè Europa** ★ At this elegant and lively 1930s-era coffee bar, the baristi—from journeymen in their teens to 60-something lifers—are a white-shirted and black-aproned crew who take immense pride in their craft, pulling espresso and frothing milk with the kind of focus and flair that only Italians seem to possess. Forgo your hotel's breakfast buffet and come here instead to perk up, Ferrarese-style, on perfectly prepared

cappuccino and freshly baked pastries. There are no tables, so do as the locals do: Stake a claim somewhere along the bar and down your coffee standing up. *Espresso/cappuccino .75€–1.10€; pastries .90€–2€. Corso Giovecca 51/53 (at Via Palestro).* ☎ *0532/ 207-408. Daily 6am–10pm.*

CHEAP

→ **Al Brindisi** FERRARESE ★★ When I'm in Ferrara, I never miss a meal at this cozy little spot along the north wall of the cathedral. Billing itself as the oldest *enoteca* in Italy, "Cheers" has an energetic, down-to-earth vibe, with a small bar area, a few wooden booths, and a milling crowd that spills beyond the stools and tables of the enclosed patio area and onto the cobblestoned street. If you're smart, you'll let your drink and food choices be guided by the guys who run the place. Their wine selections are too dizzying for a novice to navigate—let them choose a flight of glasses to pair with your meal, or just a good all-around bottle to go with everything, and you won't be disappointed. On the comprehensive and budget-friendly food menu, you'll find an extensive list of cheeses (a particular point of pride for the *enoteca*), plus Emilian staples like *cappellini in brodo* (meat-stuffed pasta in broth), *cappellacci di zucca,* and *salamina da sugo.* There are also a bunch of cold plates, from hearty salads to plates of traditional Italian-Jewish cold cuts. *Via degli Adelardi 11 (along the north wall of the cathedral).* ☎ *0532/209-142. www.al brindisi.com. All dishes 5€–8€. Daily for lunch and dinner.*

DOABLE

→ **La Romantica** FERRARESE ★★ One of Ferrara's most delightful dining experiences is in what used to be the stables of a 17th-century merchant's house. In a bright, fashionable decor, the well-trained chefs dazzle your palate with one taste sensation after another. Here is a chance to dine on several rare regional recipes, including *cappellacci di* zucca (pumpkin-stuffed ravioli in red sauce, given added flavor by walnuts and Parmesan cheese). Another excellent pasta dish is garganelli with asparagus, or you can partake of the intriguing salami-like local sausage, *salama da sugo,* which is boiled to perfection and served with creamy mashed potatoes. Their *tagliolini neri con veraci e zucchine* (thick spaghetti, made black by squid ink, served with clams and zucchini) is the best shellfish pasta Ferrara can offer. *Via Ripagrande 36. ☎ 0532/765-975. www.trattoriala romantica.com. Primi 10€–13€; secondi 10€–15€. Thurs–Tues for lunch and dinner.*

→ **L'Oca Giuliva** MODERN ITALIAN ★★ When discriminating Ferrarese palates need a break from traditional local cuisine, they go to L'Oca Giuliva to sample the latest gourmet creations from chef Gianni Tarroni. Lucky for you, this stylish trat with modern art on the walls also keeps it real on one side of the menu, offering impeccable versions of those Ferrara classics *cappellacci di zucca* and *salama da sugo.* You can order antipasti, primi, and secondi a la carte, but the restaurant's five-course tasting menus are a great option for curious and hungry types; the "traditional" Ferrarese menu is 35€ per person; while the chef's more innovative menu is 45€ a head. Ferrara is food country, so don't stress about what to order, because everything here is delicious. And with glasses of wine starting at just 2.50€, you can also keep to your budget while having an amazing meal. If you decide to eat here, it's a good idea to make a reservation and put on your nicer clothes—it's not fancy, but it is a chicer setting than your average homey trattoria. *Via Boccacanale di Santo Stefano 38. ☎ 0532/ 207-628. Primi from 7€, secondi from 10€. Tasting menus 35–40€. Wed–Sun lunch, Tues–Sun dinner.*

PARTYING

→ **Fusion Bar** ★★ APERITIVO This sleek and stylish bar, frequented by students and hipster Ferrarese in their 20s, has one of the best *aperitivo* buffets we've ever seen in Italy. Buy into the happy hour antipasti free-for-all with a glass of Bosco Eliceo (a typical local red, from 2.50€) or whatever else you feel like drinking. Several huge wheels of Parmigiano-Reggiano sit on the bar, with heavy cheese-picks provided to help you quarry away wedges of Italy's king of cheeses. Then, you can help yourself to platter after platter of prosciutto and other local cured meats and salamis and fat green olives. The crowd, which tends to hang out along the buffet, perching their wine glasses next to the trays of free gourmet food, is stylish and friendly and 100% tourist-free, so this is a great place to come if you want to meet some cool young locals. *Via delle Scienze 8/a. ☎ 0532/201-473. www.fusion-bar.it. Tues–Sat 8:30am–2am; Sun 6:30pm–2am; closed Mon.*

Sightseeing

Why do we love Ferrara so much? Because, unlike so many Italian cities, it does not bombard us with sights we feel obligated to see! The Castello Estense is fun to explore, but if you don't have the time, euros, or energy to go monument traipsing, you can see it well enough from outside.

→ **Castello Estense** ★ A castle with a moat and drawbridge, right in the middle of an illustrious Renaissance city? There must be some good blood-and-guts stories here, right? Well, truth be told, this picturesque centerpiece of Ferrara doesn't look like it has seen a whole lot of heavy artillery. The walls show no sign of ever being hit by flaming arrows or catapult shots. In the moat, disturbingly large fish (no sharks or crocodiles, alas) swim peacefully, feeding off crumbs that pedestrians toss into the murky water. In 1385, the people of Ferrara, frustrated by famine and poverty, began to revolt against the Este family, who had ruled Ferrara since time immemorial. Feeling the heat, Niccolò II d'Este decided it was time to build a castle to fend off the troublesome little people. After the initial hostility died down, the castle became less a fortress than a residence for the Este family. Over the centuries, particularly egregious enemies of the Este dukes were imprisoned in the medieval cells below the moat. Today, visitors can explore multiple levels of the castle, from the dungeons to the tower (which costs 1€ extra and involves climbing 122 steps). *Largo Castello/Viale Cavour/Corso Ercole d'Este/Corso Martiri della Libertà.* ☎ *0532/299233. www.castello estense.it. Tues–Sun 9:30am–4:45pm (last entry to the tower 4pm). Admission 6€.*

→ **Palazzo dei Diamanti/Pinacoteca Nazionale** After the Castello Estense, this is Ferrara's next most-hyped attraction. It's called the "Palace of Diamonds" for the pyramid-shaped pink and white stones that project along the building's two exposed exterior walls. It's not as beautiful as it sounds, but the Palazzo dei Diamanti is worth a visit—if you're dying for some more culture—because it houses the Pinacoteca Nazionale (National Picture Gallery) of Ferrara. The permanent collection features works from the 13th to 18th centuries, by Ferrarese painters you've probably never heard of; the temporary exhibitions that the Palazzo dei Diamanti hosts are usually much more interesting. If you want to take a pass on the art gawking for once, you have our full permission; you can just go for a bike ride down Corso Ercole d'Este, hop off for a quick look at the outside of the Palazzo dei Diamanti, and then keep riding. *Corso Ercole d'Este 21.* ☎ *0532/205-844. www.pinacotecaferrara.it. Tues–Wed and Fri–Sat 9am–2pm; Thurs 9am–7pm; Sun 9am–1pm. Admission 4€.*

Playing Outside

Ferrara, as eight million tourist-office brochures loudly trumpet, is the *città delle biciclette!* They might be stating the obvious, but it's true: Bikes are everywhere here. For a

OKKIO! Never on a Thursday

Like many towns in Emilia-Romagna, the whole city of Ferrara tends to shut down on Thursday afternoons. That means that small businesses and most shops will be closed from 1 or 2pm Thursday and won't open again until Friday morning at 9 or 10am. Restaurants and bars, thankfully, do not observe the Thursday afternoon "holiday."

fantastic half-day excursion, stop in at any deli *(alimentari)* in town, have them make up a sandwich for you, and then take your bike to the broad, tree-lined paths that follow the polygonal fortification walls around the city, and stop for a picnic when you get hungry. Peace and quiet, fresh air, and finally, some rest for the bottoms of your tired feet! For more about biking in Ferrara, see sidebar "This Is How We Roll: Biking It in Ferrara," on p. 441.

Shopping

In addition to being one of Italy's prime food zones, the region of Emilia-Romagna is also one of Italy's prime shopping zones. The towns here are wealthy, with a high concentration of stylish men and women who need to outfit themselves in the hippest threads at all times. Ferrara is no exception, and in the streets around and to the south of the cathedral, you'll find tons of trendy boutiques eager to sell you to-die-for shoes, dresses, jackets, and sweaters. The open-air markets (Mon–Sat 9am–1pm) near the cathedral can hook you up with knock-off bags and belts for about 15€.

Enoteca Al Brindisi, Via Adelardi 11 (☎ *0532/209142*), stockpiles the fruits of the Ferrarese harvest in historically evocative settings.

Venice & the Veneto

S^{*tep 1:*} Build a city on top of wood pilings in the middle of a lagoon.

Step 2: Paint the buildings bright colors and embellish their façades with storybook details like ogee arches and wheel tracery.

Step 3: Make the canals so narrow and bendy that only a preposterously long and skinny vessel, a gondola, can navigate them.

Step 4: From this bizarre "urban" setting, conquer half the Mediterranean seaboard.

Whatever the Italians were on when they thought up Venice, we want some of that.

You know, of course, that Venice is a magical, canal-filled city whose 1,500-year existence seems to defy logic. So, we're going to cut to the fine print and tell you up front the things you need to know to make the most of your (too short) visit to this extraordinary place.

The average backpacker's first foray into Venice goes something like this: Arrive in the morning on some sort of night train from the south of France or Vienna, walk around, too disoriented, hot, and unshowered to enjoy anything; follow the tourist crowds to Piazza San Marco; dodge pigeons; eat at McDonald's; make the obligatory "wow, look at all the canals" remark; get back on the train. It's dizzying, unsatisfying, and all too common—you can do better, and we're here to show you how.

You need to spend the night—not to partake of any wild nightlife (there is none in Venice) but because cruise-ship day-trippers maraud the city until 5 or 6pm every day. When they scurry back aboard their 2,400-passenger behemoths, Venice exhales and is infinitely more enjoyable for those who've stayed behind. Even if you only have 12 hours to devote to Venice, make them the night shift.

Next, accept right off the bat that you will pay through the nose for *everything* in Venice—from food and drink to accommodation, there's a premium on everything—just make it a part of your budget, and it won't stress you out. I don't care if you eat bread and water for dinner, but you do need to splurge on three things: **a Bellini at Harry's; a drink of any kind on Piazza San Marco;** and—I cannot stress enough how wonderful this is—a **late-night gondola ride.** (We're sensitive to money concerns, but in Venice, these are the areas where you go big, or go home having missed the point.)

The thing about Venice is that it's so otherworldly, it attracts everyone, young and old, inexperienced and sophisticated. Everyone can have a great time, but the young, especially, should not come to Venice expecting a traditional party scene. Make no mistake—Venetians are serious wine drinkers, and you can be, too, but what nightlife there is tends to stay mellow and end early. Not that the city is catatonic after dark, but Venice is the leg on your whirlwind Italian tour where you get your good night's sleep. (If you've brought a significant other, however, don't count on too much sleep—the romance of the canals will have you walking around and making out all night.)

Venice is a charmer, all right: There's a mystical quality that touches everything here, including tired and sweaty backpackers who don't have the time or money to do it "right." So, even if the gondola ride and the violin concerto on Piazza San Marco elude you, that last *vaporetto* run of the night, past the moonlit palazzi of the Grand Canal, strains of diesel engine humming in the background, isn't such a bad substitute.

In addition to this loveliest of cities, we've included several destinations in the Veneto that can be done as daytrips or overnights, from Romeo and Juliet's **Verona** to the university town of **Padua,** the architectural treasures of **Vicenza,** and the market town of **Treviso.**

Venice

The Best of Venice

Best Way to Spend Your Evening

Skip the full, sit-down dinner (unless you've got money to burn). Instead, hit up the **lounges and bars** in Campo Santa Margherita (in Dorsoduro) or Campo San Giacometto (in San Polo off the Rialto Bridge) for drinks and small plates. At around 11pm, head for the docks at Piazza San Marco and find one of the few gondoliers who hasn't gone home for the night. With the money you saved on not having a real dinner, the price of a **nighttime gondola ride** is a bit less outrageous. Late at night, Venice belongs to you: There is no traffic on the canals, and gondoliers will usually let the passably sober try their hand at *voga veneziana* (Venetian-style rowing) on the Grand Canal. Totally unforgettable, and so freakin' romantic that same-sex heterosexual traveling companions may well want to make out with each other. See p. 466.

Best Hangout

Piazza San Marco may be tourist central, but the hordes come here for a reason: The view of the Basilica di San Marco, with the exotic Palazzo Ducale shimmering in the sunlight in the background, is overwhelmingly beautiful. (By this logic, the pigeons of the world must be real aesthetes, since they all seem to live in this square.) For an entirely different atmosphere, come here early in the morning or around dusk, when the grand piazza is eerily quiet and wonderfully peaceful—even the pigeons seem to have taken a breather. See p. 483.

Best Low-Key but Glamorous Escape

It's 5pm, you're in Piazza San Marco, or in front of the Palazzo Ducale on Riva degli Schiavoni, and *ugh, there are so many tourists around!* The only solution is to duck into **Harry's Bar** ★★. True, you'll be surrounded by more tourists, but the bar is cozy (with no windows, no canal views—which is why it's an escape) and utterly unpretentious. Do put on your cleanest clothes before visiting, however. At Harry's, the drink *de rigueur* is the Bellini—a blend of white peach nectar and sparkling *prosecco* wine that was apparently invented here—at 14€, it may be the most expensive cocktail you'll ever throw back, but believe us, it will probably be the most delicious as well, so make it last! See p. 499.

Best Place to Veg Out and Rest Your Feet

Board the water bus 1 or 82, grab an outside seat on the prow, and go for a **round-trip *vaporetto* ride on the Grand Canal** ★★★. The mesmerizing motion picture that will play out before your eyes—Venetian-Gothic palazzi, candy-striped boat-docking pylons, police boats and garbage scows, flotillas of singing gondoliers—is sure to stick with you for a lifetime. If you have any Vivaldi on your iPod, even better. At any Grand Canal vaporetto stop, board a boat traveling toward the train station *(ferrovia);* hop off and travel back down the canal's inverted S-curve; and finish up with the monumental views as the Grand Canal opens up into the *bacino* (basin) of San Marco. See p. 454.

Best Cafes for People-Watching

The best cafes in the city are those that line **Piazza San Marco,** and they are worth the splurge for the experience alone: from here, you have a front row seat of the action in the square, and the view of its stunning surroundings. For a fabulous, romantic (and for now, insider) canal-side setting, **Naranzaria** ★★ (p. 500) and **Bancogiro** ★★ (p. 499) on Campo San Giacometto (north of the Rialto Bridge in San Polo) can't be beat.

Getting There

BY AIR

Venice's **Aeroporto Marco Polo** (☎ 041/2606111; www.veniceairport.it) is in Mestre, the mainland section of the town. In the

OKKIO! Getting Lost in Venice

It's a given. With street names that are spelled one way on a map and another way in person, street numbers that follow no conventional order, and alleys that wind around and around only to stop at dead ends, pretty much everyone finds themselves lost at some point. Here are a few tips to help you find your way:

→ First, invest in a good **map**. Buy one from a tourist stand, about 2.50€.

→ Next, if you're looking to find a specific address such as a restaurant or hotel, figure out what **district,** or *sestiere,* it's located in. Keep in mind that 1) addresses are usually given as a number and district—there *are* "street" names in Venice, but for some reason, they usually don't appear in any official printed addresses—and 2) address numbers repeat in each district.

→ Use the **signs!** If you do find yourself lost in a labyrinth of alleys, look up for the quasi-handmade signs pointing in the direction of such major landmarks as Piazza San Marco, the Rialto Bridge, the Accademia, and the Ferrovia (train station). These signs work wonders in getting you untangled.

→ Most importantly, if you find yourself lost, **don't panic!** Venice is safe, and getting hopelessly disoriented here is part of the fun. In a worst-case scenario, don't think about that movie *Comfort of Strangers* (1990), where Rupert Everett and Natasha Richardson get lost in Venice and meet Christopher Walken, who takes them home to his crippled wife Helen Mirren in a crumbling old palazzo! Remember that whatever direction you walk in, you will eventually hit water, as well as a vaporetto stop.

arrivals area, you'll find ATMs, currency exchange, and a tourist information center that also books accommodation.

The cheapest, but least exciting, way to get into town is by taking the orange **city bus,** which costs 1€ and takes about 30 minutes, or the blue **shuttle bus** (www.atvo.it) which costs 2€ but only takes 20 minutes. These buses drop passengers off at Piazzale Roma, from which it's usually a vaporetto ride to your hotel. To arrive in style from the airport, take a **water bus** (marked Alilaguna ACTV/Cooperativa San Marco; www.alilaguna. it) to either Fondamenta Nuove (on the north end of Cannaregio) or Piazza San Marco; the 45-minute ride costs 10€. Tickets for the shuttle buses and water buses can be bought in the arrivals hall of the airport.

BY TRAIN

Venice has two train stations, so be sure to get off at **Venezia-Santa Lucia** (Venice proper) and not Venezia-Mestre, which serves the ugly industrial mainland of greater Venice. A few Venice-bound trains will actually end at Mestre instead of going one more stop to Santa Lucia—in that case, take one of the frequent shuttle trains—it's only a 10-minute ride between Mestre and Santa Lucia. The ticket office is open 6am to 9pm. In the train station, you'll also find a tourist office, currency exchange, luggage storage, and several restaurants.

On exiting Santa Lucia train station, you'll find the Grand Canal in front of you, a sight that makes for a heart-stopping first impression. You'll find the docks for a number of vaporetto lines (the city's public ferries or water buses) to your left and right. Head to the booths to your left, near the bridge, to catch either of the two lines plying the Canal Grande: the no. 82 express, which stops only at the train station, S. Marcuola, Rialto Bridge, S. Tomà, S. Samuele, and Accademia before hitting San Marco (26 min. total); and the mis-named no. 1 *accelerato,* which is actually the local, making 14 stops between the station and San Marco (a 31-min. trip). Both leave every 10 minutes or so, but every other no. 82 stops short at Rialto, meaning you'll have to disembark and hop on the next no. 1 or 82 that comes along to continue to San Marco.

BY BUS

ACTV buses (www.actv.it) arrive in and depart from Venice at Piazzale Roma, serving such Veneto cities such as Treviso and Padua. If you're heading to one of those places next, and you want to see what it's like to bus it in Italy (it's not that exciting), you can purchase tickets at the office in the square. For information and schedules, contact the ACTV office at Piazzale Roma (☎ 041/272211).

BY CAR

The only wheels you'll see in Venice are those attached to luggage. Venice is a city of canals and narrow alleys. No cars are allowed—even the police and ambulance services use boats. Arriving in Venice by car is problematic and expensive—and downright exasperating if it's high season and the parking facilities are full (they often are). You can drive across the Ponte della Libertà from Mestre to Venice, but you can go no farther than Piazzale Roma at the Venice end, where many garages eagerly await your euro. Do some research before choosing a garage—the rates vary widely, from 19€ per day for an average-size car at the communal **ASM garage** (☎ 041/272-7301; www.asmvenezia.it) to 26€ per day at private outfits like **Garage San Marco** (☎ 041/523-2213; www.garagesanmarco.it), both in Piazzale Roma. If you have reservations at a hotel, check before arriving: Most of them offer discount coupons for some of the parking facilities; just ask the hotel in which garage you need to park and pay for parking upon leaving the garage.

Vaporetto line nos. 1 and 82, described under "By Train," above, both stop at Piazzale Roma before continuing down the Canal Grande to the train station and, eventually, Piazza San Marco.

Getting Around

Two words: 1) Walk. 2) Vaporetto. (Romantic as they are, gondolas are ridiculously expensive and should never be used as a practical means of transportation from point A to point B.)

ON FOOT

Venice is small enough that you can walk wherever you need to go—that is, if you're able to find it (see "Getting Lost in Venice," above). You'll navigate many twisting streets whose names change constantly and don't appear on any map, and streets that may very well simply end in a blind alley or spill abruptly into a canal. You'll also cross dozens of footbridges. You'll find yourself drifting inexplicably north when you could've sworn you were walking due south. Treat getting bewilderingly lost in Venice as part of the fun, and budget more time than you'd ever think necessary to get wherever you're going.

As a city full of water, Venice serves modes of transportation that float first and foremost: You might be surprised at how few

OKKIO! Don't Go the Wrong Way on the 82

The no. 82 goes in two directions from the train station: left down the Canal Grande toward San Marco—which is the (relatively) fast and scenic way—and right, which also eventually gets you to San Marco (at the San Zaccaria stop) but takes more than twice as long because it goes the long way around Dorsoduro, *not* along the Grand Canal, and serves mainly commuters. Make sure the no. 82 you get on is headed to "San Marco."

bridges there are for pedestrians to cross the canals. The Grand Canal itself only has three bridges: the Ponte degli Scalzi in front of the train station, the shop-lined Ponte di Rialto in the center of the city, and the wooden Ponte Accademia in the south, not far from Piazza San Marco. This makes getting to the other side of the main waterway a bit of a problem, right? Fear not: *Traghetti* are gondola-style "ferries" that shuttle people across the Grand Canal where there are no bridges around. Look for them under signs that say CALLE DEL TRAGHETTO. The .50€ fare is payable to the gondolier when you step aboard. To make the crossing like a true Venetian, do it standing up—although this is perhaps not advisable in choppy traffic on the Grand Canal, or if you've just had a few too many *spritz* at the local bar.

Whether or not you really *need* to take a *traghetto*, it's fun; for the experience, try the Santa Sofia crossing that connects the Ca' d'Oro (Cannaregio) and the Pescheria fish market (San Polo), opposite each other on the Grand Canal just north of the Rialto Bridge—the gondoliers expertly dodge water traffic at this point of the canal where it's the busiest and most heart-stopping.

VAPORETTO

When your feet start to blister and your quads start to burn from climbing countless canal bridges, get to know your new best friend, the vaporetto ★. They may not be as graceful as gondolas, but the sputtering hum of these clunky boats is a welcome sound when you've spent a long day walking. Vaporetto stops are easy to spot—they're modern glass-and-steel shelters with yellow signs. Not only are they a convenient way to move up or down the Grand Canal, vaporetti offer some gloriously cinematic views as they snake their way down the reverse S-curve of Venice's "main street." The ticketing system (see below) is confusing, but unless you're only staying in Venice for a few hours, the **10.50€/24-hour Grand Canal ticket** is the one you'll want, since it permits unlimited trips on the Grand Canal. If you're staying for more than 2 days, it's worth forking over the 22€ for the 72-hour Grand Canal ticket. Though most people don't pay it (and don't end up in jail), there is a 3.50€ charge for luggage.

Comprehensive maps of the vaporetto system are available at the tourist office and at vaporetto stops. In general though, the boats will either run through the city along the Grand Canal, or around the perimeter of the city. The only vaporetti most visitors need are the 1 and 82, which ply the Grand Canal every 15 minutes from 7am to midnight (every hour midnight–7am).

If you decide to make the trek out to the islands of Murano, Burano, or Torcello, a number of vaporetti make the trip from Fondamenta Nuove, on the north side of Castello. Only the no. 12 vaporetto goes all the way to Burano and Torcello. To cross the lagoon to the beaches of the Lido, hop on the vaporetti 1, 6, 52, or 82 from the San Zaccaria–Danieli stop (near Piazza San Marco).

Ticket prices are as follows: 24-hour ticket including Grand Canal, 10.50€; return ticket with one Grand Canal trip, 7€; Grand Canal single trip, 5€; single fare no Grand Canal, 3.50€; return ticket with no Grand Canal, 6€; 72-hour pass including Grand Canal, 22€. The luggage charge for all trips is 3.50€. (You'll also see a much lower price bracket posted on the vaporetto ticket info boards, but this reduced rate is only available for full-time residents of Venice—and no, you can't pretend to be one.) For more information on public transportation in Venice: **www.actv.it**.

USING STREET MAPS & SIGNAGE

The free map offered by the tourist office and most hotels has good intentions, but it doesn't even show—much less name or index—all the *calli* (streets) and pathways of Venice. For that, pick up a more detailed map (ask for a *pianta della città*) at news kiosks (especially those at the train station and around San Marco) or most bookstores.

Venice *Vaporetto* System

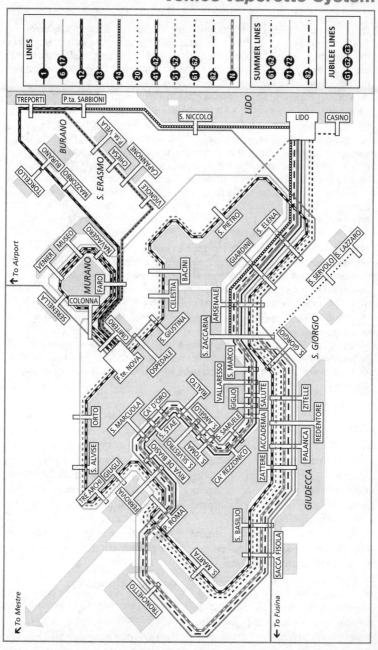

What If I Fall into a Canal?

Does it happen? Yes, but not as often as you might think, given that there are 150 canals in the city, and often no balustrades between the water's edge and the pedestrian areas. Chalk it up to the fact that, unlike Dublin or Amsterdam, Venice is not a city where you ever really get that wasted. Unless you bust out the *Macarena* on your gondola ride, chances are you'll stay on terra firma during your stay here. During *acqua alta* (tidal high water) however, all the canals overflow into the city for a few hours until the tide goes back down, and a little splish-splash contact with nasty canal water is inevitable.

Are there any adverse health effects? Well, yeah. Considering the fact that sewage, cigarette butts, and other sundry hazmats inevitably find their way into the city's waterways, the canals of Venice are only slightly cleaner than New Orleans after Hurricane Katrina, and certainly dirtier than New York's East River (there are probably fewer dead bodies, though). Should you take an accidental dip, grab some Dial and head straight for a decontamination shower back at the hotel. And throw away the clothes—canal stink is one memory of Venice you can do without.

How deep are the canals? It's romantic to think of Venice as magically existing on top of some bottomless sea, but in reality, the canals aren't very deep. The Grand Canal is 3m (10 ft.) deep at its shallowest, 5m (16 ft.) deep at its deepest. Other canals can be as shallow as knee-height. So, if you can't swim, you're better off falling into a side canal (just be careful not to hit your head).

But it's hot out. Unless you're planning an underwater heist (a la the safe-stealing scene in *The Italian Job*), we don't recommend you treat any of Venice's canals as a place to swim. Even the dogs of Venice know better than to jump in. (And if you're here in summer, when the canal sludge is at its most rank, or in winter, when low tide exposes a visual of what lies beneath, you'll know why.)

The best (and most expensive) is the highly detailed **Touring Club Italiano map,** available in a variety of forms (folding or spiral-bound) and scales. Almost as good, and easier to carry, is the simple and cheap **1:6500 folding map** put out by **Storti Edizioni** (its cover is white-edged with pink, which fades to blue at the bottom).

Still, Venice's confusing layout confounds even the best maps and navigators—even after repeat visits. You're often better off stopping every couple of blocks and asking a local to point you in the right direction (always know the name of the *campo*/square or major site closest to the address you're looking for, and ask about that).

As you wander, look for the ubiquitous yellow signs (well, *usually* yellow) whose destinations and arrows direct you toward five major landmarks: **Ferrovia** (the train station), **Piazzale Roma, Rialto** (the main bridge), **San Marco,** and the **Accademia** (also useful as the only other Grand Canal bridge below the train station).

Whatever you do, don't let the disorientation frustrate you—it's just part of the magic of Venice.

Venice Orientation

Venice is comprised of over 100 small islands, divided into six districts, or *sestiere:*

Cannaregio In the northern part of the city, it's probably the least scenic and most

Venice Neighborhoods

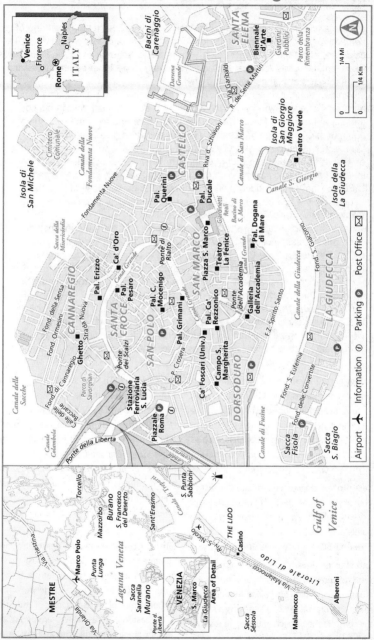

Figuring Out *Casas, Calles & Canales*

If, after a few days in Rome and Florence, you were just getting the hang of correlating your map to the reality of your new surroundings, you can put aside any short-term success upon your arrival in Venezia. Even the Italians (non-Venetian ones) look befuddled when trying to decipher street names and signs (given that you can ever find any).

Venice's colorful thousand-year history as a once-powerful maritime republic has everything to do with its local dialect, which absorbed nuances and vocabulary from far-flung outposts in the East and from the flourishing communities of foreign merchants who, for centuries, lived and traded in Venice. A linguist could gleefully spend a lifetime trying to make some sense of it all. It's been a successful one, though. From Venetian dialect we've inherited such words as *gondola* (naturally), *ciao, ghetto, lido,* and *arsenal.*

But for the Venice-bound traveler just trying to make sense of Venetian addresses, the following should give you the basics. (And don't even try to follow a conversation between two *gondolieri!*)

ca' The abbreviated use of the word *casa* is used for the noble *palazzi,* once private residences and now museums, lining the Grand Canal: Ca' d'Oro, Ca' Pesaro, and Ca' Rezzonico. There is only one palazzo, and it is the Palazzo Ducale, the former doge's residence. However, as time went on, some great houses gradually began to be called *palazzi,* so today you'll also encounter the Palazzo Grassi or the Palazzo Labia.

Calle Taken from the Spanish (though pronounced as if Italian, i.e., *ca*-lay), this is the most commonplace word for street, known as *via* or *strada* elsewhere in Italy. There are numerous variations. *Ruga,* from the French word *rue,* once meant a *calle* flanked with stores, a designation no longer valid. A *ramo*

grungy part of Venice, but also the most convenient place to base yourself: from the train station, head down busy Lista di Spagna to find cheap accommodation and food, services geared toward budget travelers such as laundry and Internet facilities, and a decent nightlife scene.

Castello The largest district, in the east of Venice, this is primarily a residential and working district, and is also home to pricey hotels and restaurants, many lined up along Riva degli Schiavoni, a popular promenade.

San Marco This is the core of Venice, and tourists know it: There is a constant crowd along its shop-filled alleys and in its restaurants and piazzas. Piazza San Marco sits in the south of the district, and around it you'll find designer boutiques, ritzy restaurants, and pricey accommodations.

Dorsoduro To the south and east of San Marco, this quiet, sunny section of town is filled with museums and small hotels. It is becoming more of an artsy, trendy area to live, especially among the university population. Consequently, the neighborhood's Campo San Margherita is a buzzing place at night. The Zattere, a 16th-century quay, is also a popular place for a stroll, offering up stellar views of the lagoon and its islands.

Santa Croce Between Dorsoduro and Cannaregio, this is probably the least-visited district, which makes it a quiet place for a stroll if you're looking to experience Venice without a mob of tourists in front of you. Stick to the eastern side, as the western part of the district is mainly industrial and not at all interesting.

(literally "branch") is the offshoot of a street, and is often used interchangeably with *calle*. *Salizzada* once meant a paved street, implying that all other, less important *calles* were once just dirt-packed alleyways. A *stretto* is a narrow passageway.

campo   Elsewhere in Italy it's *piazza*. In Venice the only *piazza* is the Piazza San Marco (and its two bordering *piazzette*); all other squares are *campi* or the diminutive, *campielli*. Translated as "field" or "meadow," these were once small, unpaved grazing spots for the odd chicken or cow. Almost every one of Venice's *campi* carries the name of the church that dominates it (or once did) and most have wells, no longer used, in the center.

canale   There are three wide, principal canals: the Canal Grande (affectionately called "il Canalazzo," the Canal), the Canale della Giudecca, and the Canale di Cannaregio. Each of the other 160-odd smaller canals is called a *rio*.

fondamenta   Referring to the foundations of the houses lining a canal, this is a walkway along the side of a *rio* (small canal). Promenades along the Grand Canal near the Piazza San Marco and the Rialto are called *riva* as in the Riva del Vin or Riva del Carbon, where cargo such as wine and coal were once unloaded.

piscina   A filled-in basin, now acting as a *campo* or piazza.

ramo   Literally "branch," a small side street.

rio terà   A small canal that's been filled in with earth. Literally, "buried canal."

salizzada   The word originally meant "paved," so any street you see prefaced with *salizzada* was one of the first streets in Venice to be paved.

sottoportego   An alley that ducks under a building.

San Polo   The smallest of Venice's districts, sitting between San Croce and San Marco, this is the commercial heart of the city, with its produce markets and store-lined Rialto Bridge. Here, you'll also find moderately priced hotels and restaurants, as well as the new crop of cool wine bars off Campo San Giacometto.

Venice Basics

TOURIST OFFICES

In general, tourist offices function mainly as hotel and tour booking venues, with very little general information available. On the positive side, however, there are various branches scattered throughout the city:

- The **airport branch:** in the arrivals hall. Open daily 9:30am to 7:30pm
- **Train station** branch: open daily 8am to 6:30pm
- **Piazzale Roma** branch: open daily 9:30am to 3:30pm
- **San Marco** branch: open daily 9am to 3:30pm

Contact information for all branches is ☎ 041/5298711 (www.turismovenezia.it;).

The tourist office's **LEO Bussola** brochure is useful for museum hours and events, but their map only helps you find vaporetto lines and stops (it's well worth buying a street map at a news kiosk; see "Getting Around," earlier in this chapter). More useful is the info-packed monthly *Un Ospite di Venezia* (www.unospitedivenezia.it); most hotels have a handful of copies. Also keep an eye out for the ubiquitous posters around town with exhibit and concert schedules. The classical concerts held mostly in churches are touristy but fun and are advertised by an army of

Okkio! Getting Your Feet Wet in Venice

During the notorious tidal *acqua alta* (high water) floods, sirens sound to alert Venice that the lagoon is about to backwash into the city, leaving up to 1.5m to 2m (5 or 6 ft.) of water in the lowest-lying streets (Piazza San Marco, as the lowest point in the city, goes first). These floods can start as early as late September or October, usually taking place November to March. As many as 50 a year have been recorded since they first started in the late 1700s. It's not as apocalyptic as it sounds—the city is well-equipped for *acqua alta* and there are dozens of temporary footbridges set up around town, and some hotels provide disposable, construction-orange *acqua alta* waders. Otherwise, wet feet are a given. The waters usually recede after just a few hours and are often virtually gone by noon. The complex system of hydraulic dams being constructed out in the lagoon to cut off these high tides (the controversial Moses project, whose progress ebbs and flows depending on who is in government) won't be operational until perhaps the end of this decade.

costumed touts handing out leaflets on highly trafficked streets.

Recommended Websites

○ **www.veniceworld.com**: Venice World: Provides general information on things to see and do in Venice, as well as a directory of websites related to travel in Venice.

○ **www.doge.it**: Venezia Net: Provides information on culture, events, and tourist resources. There's an excellent map, and lots of information on events in the city.

Venice Nuts & Bolts

Currency   Money can be changed at the train station (though with a hefty commission charge), and at various banks and exchange centers throughout the city. ATMs are everywhere.

Emergencies   If you fall into a canal and have a phone handy (or in any other serious emergency), call ☎ 112 for the Carabinieri, ☎ 113 for the police, ☎ 118 for an ambulance, and ☎ 115 for the fire department. The Campo Santi Giovanni e Paolo hospital is in Castello in Campo Santi Giovanni e Paolo (☎ 041/5294516).

Internet   The cheapest Internet cafes are in Cannaregio:

Casanova: 15min: 2.50€ (1.50€ with student discount), 30min: 4€ (2.50€ with student discount), 60min: 7€ (4€ with student discount). Lista di Spagna 158A, Cannaregio. ☎ 041/2750199. Open late (attached to disco).

VeNice: 15min: 2.50€, 30min: 4.50€, 60min: 8€. They offer a student discount, but only for local students. Fax, webcam, and CD-burning services. Lista di Spagna 149, Cannaregio. ☎ 041/2758217. Open 9am to 11pm.

Planet Internet: 15min: 3€, 30min: 5€, 60min: 8€. Student discount 50%. Printing and fax services also available. Rio Terà San Leonardo 1519, Cannaregio. ☎ 041/5244188. Open 9am to midnight.

Laundromats **Speedy Wash:** wash from 5€, dry 3€ for 15min, detergent 1€. Rio Terà San Leonardo 1520, Cannaregio. Open 8am to 10pm.

Luggage Storage Luggage storage is available in the train station; as of now, the lockers on platform 1 have yet to be converted to accept euros, and so are not in use. Instead, use the left luggage service on platform 14. Open 6am to midnight. 3.80€ for the first 5 hours, .60€ per hour after that. Maximum 5 days.

Post Office The main post office is near the Rialto Bridge on Salizzada Fondaco dei Tedeschi 5554, San Marco. ☎ 041/2717111. Open Monday to Saturday 8:15am to 6pm.

Restrooms There are clean public toilets all over the city, charging 1€.

Safety Venice is generally a safe city. As always though, guard your valuables and watch out for pickpockets in crowded areas like Piazza San Marco, and on busy vaporetto lines, like the 1 and the 82.

Telephone Tips Public phones will accept either coins or phone cards. Buy local and international phone cards at *tabacchi* shops. (For complete instructions on how to make a payphone or cellphone call from Italy, see box on p. 46)

Tipping In most tourist-oriented restaurants, a service charge is usually included in the bill. Feel free to add a little extra (5%–10%) for deserving service, if not already included in the bill.

Sleeping

Though Venice is chock-full of hotels, finding accommodation any time of the year can be a problem—to avoid roaming the streets in search of any empty bed, book a place to stay as far in advance as possible; a month or two in advance is not unreasonable. If you do arrive without a reservation, seek out the A.V.A. (The Venetian Hoteliers Association) which helps with finding accommodation, although it may not be as cheap as you'd like (☎ **800/843006** toll-free within Italy or ☎ 041/522-2264 from abroad; www.venice info.it). There are offices in the airport, the train station, and at Piazzale Roma. Simply state your budget, and they'll do their best to confirm a hotel while you wait.

We've listed the *sestiere* of each accommodation after its name, so you can get an idea of where it is located.

HOSTELS

→ **Ostello di Venezia (HI)** GIUDECCA Inconveniently located on Giudecca Island, with the sterile environment typical of HIs,

this hostel nonetheless provides a clean, cheap option if you're just looking for a place to lay your head and don't mind commuting to and from Venice proper (which can be a costly affair if you weren't already planning on buying a 24-hr. vaporetto ticket). The hostel offers a quiet garden and TV room for relaxing at the end of the day, and a restaurant with mediocre food. *Fondamenta delle Zitelle 86.* ☎ *041/5238211. www.ostellionline. org. Dorms 18.50€, breakfast included. HI membership required. Vaporetto: Zitelle.*

→ **Ostello Santa Fosca** ★★ CANNAREGIO Venice's best hostel option, especially if you're looking for ambience. Near the Rialto Bridge, the hostel is a garden oasis providing sanctuary from the city's heat and crowds. Rooms are spacious and clean and shared bathrooms are numerous. Try to score a room on the top floor; the others are a bit dark and dingy. The hostel offers Internet access and a kitchen (in summer only). *Cannaregio 2372 (off Campo Santa Fosca).* ☎ *041/715733. www.santafosca.it. Dorm bed 19€, single 22€, double 44€. Rolling Venice and student*

Sleeping & Eating in Venice

ACCOMMODATIONS ◼
Albergo ai do Mori **41**
Albergo San Samuele **17**
Albergo Santa Lucia **2**
Domus Civica **8**
Gerotto Calderan **4**
Hotel Adua **3**
Hotel Ai Due Fanali **7**
Hotel Al Piave **37**
Hotel Ala **13**
Hotel American-Dinesen **26**
Hotel Belvedere **48**
Hotel Bernardi-Semenzato **28**
Hotel Colombina **40**
Hotel Da Bruno **35**
Hotel Do Pozzi **45**
Hotel Dolomiti **1**
Hotel Falier **12**
Hotel Galleria **22**
Hotel Messner **49**
Hotel San Cassiano
  Ca'Favretto **6**
Hotel San Geremia **4**
Hotel Tivoli **14**
Locanda Fiorita **18**
Ostello di Venezia (HI) **50**
Ostello Santa Fosca **5**
Pensione Accademia **24**
Pensione La Calcina **27**
Violino d'Oro **46**

DINING ◆
A La Valigia **15**
A Le Do Spade **31**
Accademia Foscarini
  Snack Bar **23**
Ai Tre Spiedi **30**
Bancogiro **32**
Bar Accademia **21**
Bistrot de Venise **36**
Brek **4**
Caffè Florian **44**
Campo Santa Margherita **16**
Cantina do Mori **10**
Harry's Bar **47**
Mercato Rialto **34**
Naranzaria **25**
Osteria alla Botte **15**
Osteria alle Botteghe **19**
Osteria Enoteca Ai Artisti **20**
Osteria Vivaldi **11**
Pizzeria ae Oche **9**
Pizzeria/Trattoria al
  Vecio Canton **38**
Rosticceria San Bartomoleo **33**
Rosticceria Teatro Goldoni **39**
Trattoria alla Rivetta **42**
Trattoria da Gianni **29**
Trattoria da Remigio **43**

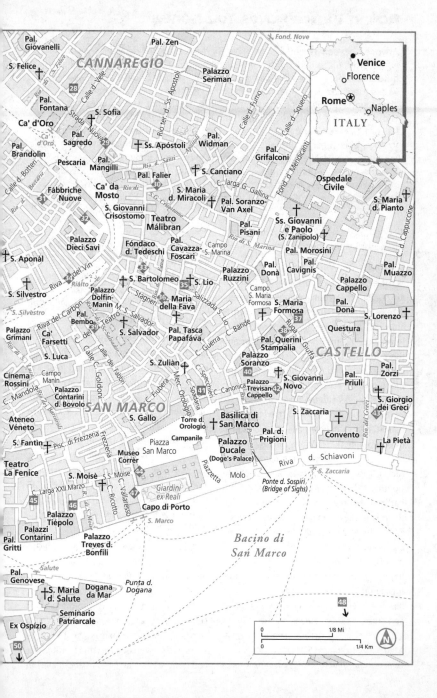

Rolling Venice Saves You Money

Anyone between 16 and 29 is eligible for the terrific **Rolling Venice pass,** which gives discounts in museums, restaurants, stores, language courses, hotels, and bars across the city (it comes with a thick booklet listing everywhere it entitles you to get discounts). It's valid for 1 year and costs 2.60€. Year-round, you can pick one up at the **Informagiovani Assessorato alla Gioventù,** Corte Contarina 1529, off the Frezzeria west of St. Mark's Square (☎ **041/274-7645** or 041/274-7650), which is open Monday to Friday 9:30am to 1pm, plus Tuesday and Thursday 3 to 5pm. July to September you can stop by the special Rolling Venice office set up in the train station daily 8am to 8pm; in winter you can get the pass at the Transalpino travel agency just outside the station's front doors and to the right, at the top of the steps, open Monday to Friday 8:30am to 12:30pm and 3 to 7pm, and Saturday 8:30am to 12:30pm.

discount. Vaporetto: San Marcuola (or a 10-min. walk from the train station).

CHEAP

➜ **Albergo ai do Mori** ★★ SAN MARCO
Antonella, the young hands-on owner/manager, creates an efficient yet comfortable ambience here. The more accessible lower-floor rooms (there's no elevator and the hotel begins on the second floor) are slightly larger and offer rooftop views, but the top-floor rooms boast views of San Marco's cupolas and the Torre dell'Orologio, whose two bronze Moors ring the bells every hour (the large double-paned windows help to ensure quiet). You'll also find tiled bathrooms (with hair dryers and heated towel racks), TVs, firm mattresses, and air-conditioning. Nearly every room has a private bathroom, and a 2001 renovation revealed the rest of the wood beams on the ceilings. The walls were painted bright colors and comfy new furnishings were added. Room nos. 4 (a small double) and 5 (a triple) share a bathroom and a small hallway and can be turned into a suite. Additionally, Antonella has now opened a four-room annex nearby. *San Marco 658 (on Calle Larga San Marco), 30124 Venezia. ☎ 041/520-4817 or 041/528-9293. Fax 041/520-5328. www.hotelaidomori. com. 15 units. Double 50€–135€, suite (up to 5*

people) 180€–220€. Ask about lower off-season rates. Vaporetto: San Marco (exit Piazza San Marco beneath Torre dell'Orologio; turn right at Max Mara store and hotel is on left, just before McDonald's). Amenities: Bar; concierge; nonsmoking rooms. In room: A/C, TV, hair dryer, safe.

➜ **Albergo San Samuele** ★★ SAN MARCO
This friendly guesthouse is a steal considering the central location near Piazza San Marco. Room decor is an attempt at elegance—with floral wallpaper and satin bedspreads—and most units have views of the street below. And there's only 10 of them, so be sure to book *way* in advance any time of year. *Salizzada San Samuele 3358, San Marco. ☎ 041/5228045. www.albergosan samuele.it. Single with shared bath 26€–46€; double with shared bath 36€–75€, with private bath 46€–105€; triple 60€–135€. Breakfast 4.50€. Vaporetto: San Samuele.*

➜ **Albergo Santa Lucia** CANNAREGIO
Bordered by roses, oleander, and ivy, the flagstone patio/terrace of this contemporary building is a lovely place to enjoy breakfast, with coffee and tea brought to the table in sterling silver pots. The kindly owner, Emilia Gonzato, her son Gianangelo, and his wife, Alessandra, oversee everything with pride, and it shows: The large rooms are simple but

bright and clean, with modular furnishings and a print or pastel to brighten things up. *Cannaregio 358 (on Calle della Misericordia), 30121 Venezia.* ☎ *041/715-180. Fax 041/710-610. www.hotelslucia.com. 18 units, 12 with bathroom. Double without bathroom 50€, with bathroom 110€. Extra person 20€. Rates include continental breakfast. Generally closed Dec 20–Feb 10. Vaporetto: Ferrovia (exit the train station, turn left onto Lista di Spagna, and take the 2nd left onto Calle della Misericordia). Amenities: Concierge; room service (breakfast); tour desk. In room: Hair dryer (ask at desk).*

→ **Domus Civica** ★ SAN POLO   This so-called "hostel" has not a single dorm bed, but offers cheap private rooms instead. Geared toward a student population, rooms are basic but clean and bright. This is, however, not the best place to stay if you plan on partaking in any nighttime debauchery: Even though it's conveniently located near bar-lined Campo Santa Margherita, there is a 12:30am curfew. *Campiello Chiovere Frari 3082, San Polo.* ☎ *041/721103. www.domuscivica.com. Single 28.50€, double 52€, triple 78€.*

Discount with Rolling Venice card, ISIC, or university ID. Vaporetto: San Tomà. Amenities: Free Internet access, TV room.

→ **Gerotto Calderan** ★ CANNAREGIO   Through the big brass doors (you'll need to buzz to get in) you'll find an efficient hotel with friendly service, facing busy Campo San Geremia. Rooms are a bit small and you'll have to lug your baggage up several flights of stairs but the clean rooms, especially those with views of the square, are worth the effort. For a cheap option, the hotel often offers dorm-style accommodation, which is essentially a bed in a five-bed room, and may involve sleeping extremely close to fellow travelers. There's a credit card or deposit required for reservation, as well as a 12:30am curfew and a lockout from 10am–2pm. *Campo San Geremia 283, Cannaregio.* ☎ *041/715562. www.casagerottocalderan.com. Dorm-style accommodation 25€, single 41€–55€, double 60€–98€, triple 84€–108€. Vaporetto: Ferrovia. Amenities: Internet access.*

→ **Hotel Adua** ★ CANNAREGIO   A charming hotel housed in a 17th-century building. Rooms are nothing special, but are at least clean and

VENICE & THE VENETO

Another Money-Saving Pass

The **VeniceCard** (www.venicecard.it) is a good investment if you plan on visiting several museums and taking frequent rides on the vaporetti. The **orange** VeniceCard entitles you to unlimited travel on the vaporetto system, free entry at Venice's civic museums (including Palazzo Ducale, Museo Correr, Ca' Rezzonico, the Glass Museum on Murano, and the Lace Museum on Burano, and others), free use of the public toilets (otherwise 1€ each time you have to pee), and discounts at many restaurants. The cheaper **blue** VeniceCard gets you free travel on the vaporetti, use of the toilets, and some restaurant discounts (but not free entry to the museums). The cards are divided into two age brackets, Junior (up to age 29) and Senior (30 and over), and come in 1-day, 3-day, and 7-day validities.

1-day orange card: 21.50€ junior; 28.50€ senior. 1-day blue card: 14.50€ junior; 16.50€ senior.

3-day orange card: 43.50€ junior; 52.50€ senior. 3-day blue card: 29€ junior; 32.50€ senior.

7-day orange card: 65€ junior; 74.50€ senior. 7-day blue card: 45.50€ junior; 49.50€ senior.

We Heart Gondolas!

So what if a 50-minute ride costs more than several days' meals? Riding a
[MTV Best] gondola ★★★ is one of the most magical, memorable experiences
you'll have in all of Europe. We are the first to call out any overrated tourist
attractions, but when it comes to the gondola, I guarantee you that any
guidebook or so-called Venice expert who dismisses it as overrated has
never tried it. Yes, it's touristy, and no, you'll never see Venetians riding
around in them, but a ride in a 12m (39-ft.) sleek black gondola is truly as
romantic as it looks—especially if you go at night.

There are major gondola *stazi* near all the Grand Canal bridges and off
Piazza San Marco, as well as some smaller moorings on side canals. Look for
the SERVIZIO GONDOLE signs and the telltale striped shirts (yes, they all wear
them). The straw hats come out in summer. While the prices are all the same
from gondolier to gondolier, it doesn't hurt to do some tire—er, gunwale—
kicking: The older gondoliers tend to be the charmers, the romantic real
Venetians who will serenade you (and any passing women) with lilting gondola
chanteys. (The younger guys tend to be too cool to bust out the chanteys.) On
the other hand, the younger gondoliers are the ones who work the later shift
and are therefore your best bet if you want to pilot a gondola on the Grand
Canal at midnight. (*Note:* There is no guarantee that a gondolier will let you
drive his 35,000€ craft, but if you play your cards right, it could happen.)

Know Before You Go:

→ *When to gondola:* If I can give you one piece of advice about Venice, it's
this: Do not waste your precious euros on a broad-daylight gondola ride.
As you walk around the city from 10am to 5pm, you'll see why. During the
day, the most picturesque canals (in the *sestiere* of San Marco) are a
log-jam of gondolas, each filled with six middle-aged day-trippers. The
gondoliers look annoyed because it takes them 10 minutes to go 20 feet;
the tourists are annoyed for the same reason, because 10 minutes is 20%
of their gondola time! (In that case, it does seem like a rip-off.) A good time
to board your gondola is late afternoon, just before sundown, when the
light does its magic on the canal reflections, and most of the day-tripper
crush has cleared out of the city. Even better, go for your gondola ride late-
night (which in Venice means somewhere between 10pm and midnight at
the absolute latest). By then, most of the gondoliers have already gone
home, but you can usually find a few stragglers at the gondola moorings

comfortable and have A/C, TV, and phone.
Those facing the street are a bit noisy, but offer
great views of the action on budget-traveler-
central Lista di Spagna down below. *Lista di
Spagna 233A, Cannaregio.* ☎ *041/716184. www.
aduahotel.com. Single with shared bath 70€,
with private bath 100€; double with shared
bath 80€, with private bath 120€. Breakfast
included. Vaporetto: Ferrovia (5-min. walk from
the train station).*

→ **Hotel   Bernardi-Semenzato**   ★★
CANNAREGIO   The exterior of this weather-
worn palazzo belies its charming interior,
which offers exposed hand-hewn ceiling
beams, air-conditioned rooms outfitted with
antique-style headboard/spread sets, and
bathrooms modernized and brightly retiled.
The enthusiastic young English-speaking
owners, Maria Teresa and Leonardo Pepoli,
offer government-rated three-star style at

(stazi) off Piazza San Marco and a little farther south, at Campo San Moisè. (The late-night gondoliers are the younger, laid-back ones who are more likely to tolerate your tipsy state and maybe even let you try your hand at the oar on the Grand Canal—try *that* during the day!!)

➤ *Where to gondola:* The most magical canals and romantic canal-side buildings are in San Marco; you're bound to cruise down a lot of them if you board your gondola from the *stazi* in front of Piazza San Marco, Campo San Moisè, or the Rialto Bridge. Try to minimize your gondola time on the Grand Canal; its choppy waters are better suited to larger craft like vaporetti. However, the Grand Canal is the one place where gondoliers sometimes let you drive—late at night, its wide-open waters mean that you can flail around, drop the oar, etc., and not run the risk of crashing into a wall and ending up a splintery wreck.

➤ *Bring booze:* Yes, it's allowed, and even encouraged—but do the classy Venetian thing and get a bottle of *prosecco* (a sparkling white wine) as opposed to a flask of Jagermeister. Stop off at a local cafe or grocery store before your ride to buy a chilled bottle, and be sure to grab at least some plastic cups. (If you can find some, bring real glasses.) Bottoms up: You only have 50 minutes.

➤ *How much?* Though it's often quoted in print at differing official rates, expect to pay 62€ for up to 50 minutes (77€ between 8pm and 8am), with up to six passengers, and 31€ for another 25 minutes (39€ at night). Any gondolier will always quote much higher rates when negotiating a fare with tourists, but as long as there are other gondoliers around willing to take your euros, he can be bargained down to somewhere near the "official" rate. Late at night, when he's the last gondolier around, good luck paying less than 100€ for 50 minutes. *Note:* Gondoliers do not take Visa, Amex, or MasterCard; it's cash only, and at these ridiculously inflated prices, there is definitely no need to leave a tip.

And what of the serenading gondolier immortalized in film? The ensembles of accordion player and tenor you'll see accompanying the flotillas of middle-aged tourists during the day are frankly god-awful; for that experience, the Venetian Hotel in Las Vegas is a much better deal.

All Venetian gondolas are regulated by the **Ente Gondola** (☎ 041/528-5075; www.gondolavenezia.it), so call if you have any questions or complaints.

one-star rates (prices get even better off season). Upstairs rooms enjoy higher ceilings and more light. The *dépendance* (annex) 3 blocks away offers the chance to feel as if you've rented an aristocratic apartment, with parquet floors and Murano chandeliers—room no. 5 is on a corner with a beamed ceiling and fireplace, no. 6 (a family-perfect two-room suite) looks out on the confluence of two canals, and no. 2 overlooks the lovely

garden of a palazzo next door. The Pepoli family recently opened yet another annex nearby consisting of just four rooms, all done in a Venetian style, including one large family suite (two guest rooms, one of which can sleep four, sharing a common bathroom). *Cannaregio 4366 (on Calle de l'Oca), 30121 Venezia.* ☎ *041/522-7257. Fax 041/522-2424. www.hotelbernardi.com. Hotel: 18 units, 11 with bathroom. Main annex: 7 units. New annex: 4*

where You wanna Be

Since Venice is small, and everything's a relatively short walk or vaporetto ride away, it doesn't matter much where you stay (as long as you're not on the island of Giudecca, which is inconvenient, or Mestre, which is inconvenient *and* ugly). **San Marco** is many visitors' top choice for accommodations, but it's the busiest and most heavily trodden *sestiere*—you'll be in the heart of the action, but you might find yourself wishing you could escape it. For budget accommodations, your best bet is **Cannaregio,** where there are a ton of decently priced hotels within a 10-minute walk of the train station. For convenience to San Marco and atmosphere, I am partial to **Dorsoduro.**

units. For Frommer's/MTV Italy readers: 60€ double without bathroom, 90€ with bathroom; 82€ triple without bathroom, 98€ with bathroom; 90€ quad without bathroom, 108€ with bathroom. Rates include continental breakfast. 10% less off season. Vaporetto: Ca' d'Oro (walk straight ahead to Strada Nova, turn right toward Campo SS. Apostoli, and look for Cannaregio 4309, a stationery/toy store on your left; turn left on Calle Duca, then take 1st right onto Calle de l'Oca). Amenities: Concierge; room service (limited); tour desk. In room: A/C, TV, dataport, hair dryer, safe.

→ **Hotel Da Bruno** ★★ CASTELLO   Run by the Sartore family for three generations, the hotel is centrally located, close to the Rialto Bridge on a busy shopping street. Rooms have A/C, TV, and phone, and are furnished in a traditional Venetian style with elegant mahogany furniture and lush curtains and drapes. The cozy bar off the lobby is a good place to unwind at the end of the day. Salizzada San Lio 5726A, Castello 5726A. ☎ 041/5230452. www.hoteldabruno.com. Single 60€–160€, double

80€–215€, triple 120€–260€. Breakfast included. Vaporetto: Rialto.

→ **Hotel Dolomiti** ★ CANNAREGIO   For those who prefer to stay near the train station, this is an old-fashioned, reliable choice. Because it has large, clean but ordinary rooms spread over four floors (no elevator), your chances of finding availability are better here, one of the larger places I suggest. It's been in the Basardelli family for generations—the current head manager, Graziella, was even born in a second-floor room—and they and their efficient polyglot staff supply dining suggestions, umbrellas when necessary, and big smiles after a long day's sightseeing. Rooms without bathrooms always come with sinks. The Basardellis are slowly renovating the guest rooms; those that don't have air-conditioning now will soon. Cannaregio 72–74 (on Calle Priuli ai Cavalletti), 30121 Venezia. ☎ 041/715-113 or 041/719-983. Fax 041/716-635. www.hoteldolomiti-ve.it. 32 units, 22 with bathroom. Double without bathroom 60€–90€, with bathroom 80€–140€; triple without bathroom 84€–111€, with bathroom 120€–180€. Extra bed 20€. Inquire about low-season discounts. Rates include continental breakfast. Closed Nov 15–Jan 31. Vaporetto: Ferrovia (exit train station, turn left onto Lista di Spagna, and take 1st left onto Calle Priuli). Amenities: Bar; concierge; tour desk. In room: A/C (newest rooms), hair dryer (newest rooms).

→ **Hotel Do Pozzi** ★ SAN MARCO   Duck off bustling Calle Larga just 150m (492 ft.) from St. Mark's Square and you'll find a hidden little *campiello* whose namesake "two wells" flank the round tables where hotel guests take breakfast in warm weather. The quietest rooms overlook this tiny square from flower-fringed windows. All guest rooms have a tidy, modern style with embroidered fabrics, a few 18th-century Venetian-style pieces, Murano chandeliers, wood floors, and glass mirrors on the closet doors to make the cozy quarters seem roomier. Nos. 20 and 40 get slivers of

Grand Canal views down a short street; no. 47 opens onto the noisy shopping of Calle Larga, but it comes with frescoed ceilings and a small sitting room. Rooms in the seven-room annex **Dependance Favaro** around the corner are largely the same. Guests can receive a 10% discount off meals at the hotel restaurant **Da Raffaele.** *San Marco 2373 (off Calle Larga/Via XXII Marzo), 30124 Venezia.* ☎ *041/520-7855. Fax 041/522-9413. www.hotel dopozzi.it. 30 units, plus 6 in Dependance Favaro. Double 92€–230€. Extra bed 40€–50€. Vaporetto: Santa Maria del Giglio (walk straight up from vaporetto stop into Campo Santa Maria Zobenigo, turn right out of the campo and cross the bridge, doglegging slight left and right again onto broad Calle Larga; take the 1st right down a narrow alley to the hotel). Amenities: Restaurant; concierge; dry cleaning (same-day); laundry service; non-smoking rooms; room service (breakfast and bar); tour desk. In room: A/C, TV, hair dryer, minibar.*

→ **Hotel Falier** ★ DORSODURO   The Falier is particularly worth booking when half-price low-season rates apply. It is a reliable good value at this price range, with standard-size rooms (and modern bathrooms) attractively decorated with white lace curtains and flow-ered bedspreads; some even have wood-beamed ceilings. The old-world lobby has potted ferns, Doric columns, and triangled, marble floors. Detractors may feel the need to be closer to Piazza San Marco, when in truth the Falier is much closer to the real Venice. It is situated in a lively area lined with stores and bars between the large Campo Santa Margherita, one of the city's most char-acter-filled piazzas, and the much visited Frari Church. *Dorsoduro 130 (Salizzada San Pantalon), 30135 Venezia.* ☎ *041/710-882 or 041/711-005. Fax 041/520-6554. www.hotel falier.com. 19 units. Double 80€–190€. Rates discounted 50% during low season. Rates include continental breakfast. Vaporetto: Fer-rovia. If you've packed lightly, the walk from*

the train station is easy, easier yet from the Piazzale Roma. From the train station, cross the Scalzi Bridge, turn right along the Grand Canal for 45m (148 ft.), then left toward the Tolentini Church. Continue along the Salizzada San Pantalon in the general direction of Campo Santa Margherita. Amenities: Concierge; tour desk. In room: A/C, TV, hair dryer, safe.

→ **Hotel Galleria** ★★ DORSODURO   If you've always dreamed of flinging open your hotel window to find the Grand Canal in front of you, choose this 17th-century palazzo. But reserve way in advance—these are the cheapest rooms on the canal and the most charming at these rates, thanks to owners Luciano Benedetti and Stefano Franceschini. They overhauled the hotel in 2004, keeping a sumptuous, 18th-century look in public spaces and giving a cozier look to the new bedrooms. Six guest rooms overlook the canal; others have partial views that include the Ponte Accademia over an open-air bar/cafe (which can be annoying to anyone hoping to sleep before the bar closes). Breakfast, with oven-fresh bread, is served in your room. *Dorsoduro 878A (at foot of Accademia Bridge), 30123 Venezia.* ☎ *041/523-2489. Fax 041/520-4172. www.hotelgalleria.it. 10 units, 6 with bathroom. Double without bathroom 110€, with bathroom 120€–155€. Rates include con-tinental breakfast. Vaporetto: Accademia (with Accademia Bridge behind you, hotel is just to your left, next to Totem Il Canale gallery). Amenities: Concierge; room service (limited); tour desk. In room: Hair dryer.*

→ **Hotel San Geremia** ★★ CANNAREGIO If this gem of a government-rated two-star hotel had an elevator and was in San Marco, it would cost twice as much and still be worth it. Consider yourself lucky to get one of the tastefully renovated rooms—ideally one of the seven overlooking the *campo* (better yet, one of three top-floor rooms with small ter-races). The rooms have blond-wood paneling with built-in headboards and closets or whitewashed walls with deep-green or burnished rattan headboards and matching chairs. The small bathrooms offer hair dryers and heated towel racks, and rooms without bathrooms were recently renovated. Everything is overseen by an English-speaking staff and the owner/manager Claudio, who'll give you helpful tips and free passes to the winter Casino. *Cannaregio 290A (on Campo San Geremia), 30121 Venezia.* ☎ *041/716-245. Fax 041/524-2342. 20 units, 14 with bathroom. For Frommer's readers: Double without bathroom 77€, with bathroom 114€. Ask about rates/availability for singles, triples, and quads and off-season rates (about 20% cheaper). Rates include continental breakfast. Vaporetto: Ferrovia (exit the train station, turn left onto Lista di Spagna, continue to Campo San Geremia). Amenities: Concierge; room service (breakfast); tour desk. In room: TV, hair dryer, safe.*

→ **Hotel Tivoli** ★★ DORSODURO Located in the northern part of Dorsoduro, close to the Grand Canal. Rooms are a bit dark but nonetheless attractively furnished with dark wooden bed frames and armoires. There's also a charming communal garden area perfect for kicking back at the end of the day. All rooms have TV, phone, and heating (though no A/C). *Ca' Foscari 3838, Dorsoduro.* ☎ *041/5242460. www.hoteltivoli.it. Low season: single from 50€, double from 70€; high season: single from 80€, double from 130€. Breakfast included. Vaporetto: San Tomà.*

DOABLE

→ **Hotel Ai Due Fanali** ★★ SANTA CROCE Ai Due Fanali's 16th-century altar-turned-reception-desk is your first clue that this is the hotel of choice for lovers of aesthetics with impeccable taste and restricted budgets. The hotel is located on a quiet square in the residential Santa Croce area, a 10-minute walk across the Grand Canal from the train station but a good 20-minute stroll from the Rialto Bridge. Signora Marina Stea and her daughter Stefania have beautifully restored a part of the 14th-century *scuola* of the Church of San Simeon Grando with their innate *buon gusto*, which is evident wall to wall, from the lobby furnished with period pieces to the third-floor breakfast terrace with a glimpse of the Grand Canal. Guest rooms boast headboards painted by local artisans, high-quality bed linens, chrome and gold bathroom fixtures, and good, fluffy towels. Prices drop considerably from November 8 through March 30 with the exception of Christmas week and Carnevale. Ask about the four equally classy waterfront apartments with a view (and kitchenette) near Vivaldi's Church (La Pietà) east of Piazza San Marco, sleeping four to five people at similar rates per person. *Santa Croce 946 (Campo San Simeone Profeta), 30125 Venezia.* ☎ *041/718-490. Fax 041/718-344. www.aiduefanali.com. 17 units. Double 95€–210€, triple 119€–262€, apt 185€–380€. Rates include breakfast. Closed most of Jan. Vaporetto: a 10-min. walk from the train station or get off at the Riva di Biasio stop. Amenities: Bar; concierge; dry cleaning; laundry service; room service (limited). In room: A/C, TV, dataport, hair dryer, minibar, safe.*

→ **Hotel Al Piave** ★★ CASTELLO The Puppin family's tasteful hotel is a steal: This level of attention coupled with the sophisticated *buon gusto* in decor and spirit is rare in this price category. You'll find orthopedic mattresses under ribbon candy–print or floral spreads, immaculate white-lace curtains, stained-glass windows, new bathrooms, and even (in a few rooms) tiny terraces. The family suites—with two bedrooms, minibars, and shared bathrooms—are particularly good deals, as are the small but stylishly rustic apartments with kitchenettes and washing machines (in the two smaller ones). A savvy international crowd has discovered this classy spot, so even with renovations that have expanded the hotel's size, you'll need to reserve far in advance. *Castello 4838–40 (on Ruga Giuffa), 30122 Venezia.*

☎ 041/528-5174. Fax 041/523-8512. www.hotel alpiave.com. 13 units. Double 100€–210€, triple 150€–230€, suite for 3 160€–240€, suite for 4 200€–265€, suite for 5 220€–300€. Often heavy discounts off season. Rates include continental breakfast. Closed Jan 7 to Carnevale. Vaporetto: San Zaccaria (walk straight ahead on Calle delle Rasse to small Campo SS. Filippo e Giacomo, take right on Calle San Provolo, and cross over canal to Campo San Provolo; take a left, cross 1st small footbridge, and follow zigzagging street that becomes Ruga Giuffa). Amenities: Concierge; tour desk. In room: A/C, TV, fridge (family suite), hair dryer, minibar, safe.

→ **Hotel American-Dinesen** ★★★ DOR-SODURO   I'll take the American over the astronomically expensive Cipriani, the Gritti, or the Danieli any day. For its friendliness, style, and location—on the lovely San Vio canal, which meets the Grand Canal only 100m (328 ft.) away—this place is a dream. With Oriental carpets, plush armchairs, marble flooring, and polished woods, the lobby feels like a real lobby, not just an after-thought with a makeshift reception desk (as is the case in too many moderate Italian hotels). Staff is ever bright and hospitable, and there's always a charming member or two of the Sutera family, who manages the hotel, on hand to greet guests. Of the hotel's 30 rooms, the best choices are the larger corner rooms and the nine rooms overlooking the canal; some even have small terraces where you can stand, turn to the right, and watch the passing traffic on the Grand Canal. Every room is outfitted with traditional Venetian-style furnishings that usually include hand-painted furniture and Murano glass chandeliers. Bathrooms are small but immaculate, and outfitted with all the comforts and amenities you'll need. If it's late spring, don't miss a drink on the second-floor terrace beneath a wisteria arbor dripping with plump violet blossoms. This hotel enjoys great word-of-mouth among Venice habitués, so book early. Dorsoduro 628 (on Fondamenta Bragadin), 30123 Venezia. ☎ 041/520-4733. Fax 041/520-4048. www.hotelamerican.com. 30 units. Double 130€–250€, with canal view 180€–300€. Extra person 60€. Rates include buffet breakfast. Vaporetto: Accademia (veer left around the Galleria dell'Accademia museum, taking the 1st left turn and walk straight ahead until you cross the 1st small footbridge. Turn right to follow the Fonda-menta Bragadin that runs alongside the Rio di San Vio canal. The hotel is on your left). Amenities: Bar; car-rental desk; concierge; Internet point; laundry service; nonsmoking rooms; room service (limited); tour desk. In room: A/C, TV, dataport, hair dryer, minibar, safe.

→ **Hotel Messner** ★ DORSODURO   Hotel Messner is one of the best choices in the Guggenheim area at budget-embracing rates. The Messner is a two-part hotel: In the Casa Principale (Main House) are the handsome beamed-ceiling lobby and public rooms of a 14th-century palazzo and modernized guest rooms with comfortable modular furnishings and Murano chandeliers (three overlook pic-turesque Rio della Fornace). The 15th-century dépendance (annex) 18m (60 ft.) away doesn't show quite as much close attention to detail in the decor, but is perfectly nice. In summer you can take breakfast in a small garden. In 2002 the owners opened another set of units, a six-room annex just 27m (90 ft.) away. Ask about the annex when booking. Dorsoduro 216–217 (on Fondamenta Ca' Balà), 30123 Venezia. ☎ 041/522-7443. Fax 041/522-7266. www.hotelmessner.it. Main House, 13 units; Annex, 20 units. Main House: double 145€, triple 165€, quad 190€; Annex: double 115€; triple 145€. Ask about discounts such as Aug special: 4 nights for the price of 3. Rates include continental breakfast. Closed Dec 1–27. Vaporetto: Salute (follow small canal immediately to right of La Salute; turn right onto 3rd bridge and walk straight until seeing white awning just before reaching Rio della Fornace). Amenities: Restaurant; bar; concierge; nonsmoking rooms; room service

(24-hr.). *In room: A/C (main house), TV (main house), dataport (main house), hair dryer, safe.*

↟Hotel San Cassiano Ca'Favretto ★★
SANTA CROCE Call this place a doable/splurge, with two stars for its location and views. About half the rooms here look across the Grand Canal to the gorgeous Ca' d'Oro (accounting for the highest rates), and tend to be larger than the others, most of which open onto a side canal. Built into a 16th-century palace, the hotel is steeped in dusty old-world elegance, with Murano chandeliers (but no elevator). The rooms are outfitted in modest, dark-wood 1970s-style faux antiques. The breakfast room is done in 18th-century-style pastels and stuccoes—get down to breakfast early to snag one of the two tiny tables on the wide balcony overlooking the Grand Canal. There's also a wood-beamed bar and TV lounge with a canal-view window and a few small tables on the private boat launch where you can sip an *aperitivo* in the evening, gaze at the Ca d'Oro, and just generally make other tourists on the passing vaporetti intensely jealous because they're booked elsewhere. *Santa Croce 2232 (Calle della Rosa), 30135 Venezia.* ☎ *041/524-1768. Fax 041/721-033. www.sancassiano.it. 35 units. Double 70€–360€, triple 91€–423€. Rates include breakfast. Vaporetto: San Stae (turn left to cross in front of the church, take the bridge over the side canal and turn right; then turn left, cross another canal and turn right, then left again; cross yet another canal and turn right, then immediately left and then left again toward the Grand Canal and the hotel). Amenities: Bar; car-rental desk; concierge; dry cleaning; laundry service; massage (in-room); nonsmoking rooms; room service (limited); tour desk. In room: A/C, TV, dataport, hair dryer, minibar, safe.*

↟Locanda Fiorita ★★ SAN MARCO The owners have created a pretty little hotel in this Venetian red palazzo, parts of which date from the 1400s. Its overall style is 18th-century Venetian. The wisteria vine partially covering the façade is at its glorious best in May or June, but the Fiorita is excellent year-round, as much for its simply furnished rooms boasting new bathrooms (now with hair dryers) as for its location on a *campiello* off the grand Campo Santo Stefano. Room nos. 1 and 10 have little terraces beneath the wisteria pergola and overlook the *campiello:* They can't be guaranteed on reserving, so ask when you arrive. Each of the two rooms without bathrooms has its own private facilities down the hall. Just a few meters away is **Ca' Morosini** (☎ **041/241-3800;** fax 041/522-8043; www.camorosini.com), the Fiorita's three-star annex. There you'll find more rooms with views of the *campo. San Marco 3457a (on Campiello Novo), 30124 Venezia.* ☎ *041/523-4754. Fax 041/522-8043. www.locandafiorita.com. 16 units. Double 145€, 110€ without bathroom. Rates include continental breakfast. Vaporetto: S. Angelo (walk to the tall brick building, then turn right around its side; cross a small bridge and turn left down Calle del Pestrin; a bit farther down on your left is a small square 3 stairs above street level; hotel is against the back of it). Amenities: Concierge; nonsmoking rooms; room service (limited); tour desk. In room: A/C, TV, dataport, hair dryer, minibar (annex only), safe (annex only).*

↟Pensione Accademia ★★ DORSO-DURO This pensione is beloved by Venice regulars. You'll have to reserve far in advance to get any room here, let alone one overlooking the breakfast garden, which is snuggled into the confluence of two canals. The 17th-century villa is fitted with period antiques in first-floor "superior" rooms, and the atmosphere is decidedly old-fashioned and elegant (Katharine Hepburn's character lived here in the 1955 classic *Summertime*). Formerly called the Villa Maravege (Villa of Wonders), it was built as a patrician villa in the 1600s and used as the Russian consulate until the 1930s. Its outdoor landscaping (the

Venetian rarities of a flowering patio on the small Rio San Trovaso that spills into the Grand Canal and the grassy formal rose garden behind) and interior details (original pavement, wood-beamed and decoratively painted ceilings) still create the impression of being a privileged guest in an aristocratic Venetian home from another era. *Dorsoduro 1058 (Fondamenta Bollani, west of the Accademia Bridge), 30123 Venezia.* ☎ *041/521-0188 or 041/523-7846. Fax 041/523-9152. www. pensioneaccademia.it. 27 units. Double 130€–185€, superior double 170€–235€. Off-season discounts available. Vaporetto: Accademia (step off the vaporetto and turn right down Calle Gambara, which doglegs 1st left and then right; it becomes Calle Corfu, which ends at a side canal; walk left for a few feet to cross over the bridge, then head to the right back up toward the Grand Canal and the hotel). Amenities: Bar; concierge; dry cleaning; laundry service; massage; room service (limited); tour desk. In room: A/C, TV, dataport, hair dryer, minibar, safe.*

→ **Pensione La Calcina** ★ DORSODURO British author John Ruskin holed up here in 1876 when penning *The Stones of Venice* (you can request his room, no. 2, but good luck getting it), and this hotel on the sunny Zattere in the southern Dorsoduro has remained a quasi-sacred preference for writers, artists, and assorted bohemians. You can imagine their horror when a recent overhaul was announced. Luckily, it was executed quite sensitively, with the third-generation owners even refusing to add TVs. What *is* different are the rates, which have been creeping up. Half the unfussy but luminous rooms overlook the Giudecca Canal in the direction of Palladio's 16th-century Redentore. The outdoor floating terrace and the rooftop terrace are glorious places to begin or end the day. The three suites and two apartments were added in 2002. *Dorsoduro 780 (on Zattere al Gesuati), 30123 Venezia.* ☎ *041/520-6466. Fax*

041/522-7045. www.lacalcina.com. 28 units. Double with bathroom but without canal view 99€–148€, with bathroom and canal view 130€–186€; suite or apt 187€–239€. Rates include buffet breakfast. Vaporetto: Zattere (follow le Zattere east; hotel is on water before 1st bridge). Amenities: Restaurant; concierge; laundry service; room service (24-hr.). In room: A/C, hair dryer, safe.

→ **Violino d'Oro** ★★ SAN MARCO This small boutique hotel at a tiny *campiello* with a marble fountainhead on the main shopping drag from San Marco to the Accademia may be new, but the style is ever-popular 18th-century Venetian. The rooms, bathed in rich colors, are compact but graced with nice touches such as gold decoration on the marble-top desks, modest stuccoes and Murano chandeliers on the ceilings, very firm beds, and heated towel racks in the bathrooms. Six rooms even overlook Rio San Moisè canal. The low-season rates are incredible, and even high-season rates are (for Venice) decent for this level of comfort and style. The entire hotel is nonsmoking. *San Marco 2091 (Via XXII Marzo), 30124 Venezia.* ☎ *041/277-0841. Fax 041/277-1001. www.violino doro.com. 26 units. Double 60€–300€. Extra bed 50€. Ask about lower rates during low season. Rates include buffet breakfast. Vaporetto: San Marco–Vallaresso (walk straight up Calle di Ca'Vallaresso, left on Salita San Moisè; cross the wide footbridge and the hotel is just across the little campiello on the left). Amenities: Bar; concierge; dry cleaning; laundry service; nonsmoking rooms (whole hotel); room service (24-hr.). In room: A/C, TV, dataport, hair dryer, minibar.*

SPLURGE

Venice can be one of the most expensive cities in Europe. For hotels, there's "splurge" as in "this will be the most expensive thing I do on my trip," and there's "splurge" as in "It's a good thing I have a large trust fund!" Our splurges are directed more to the former, but if you happen to have a couple thousand (euros or dollars) a night, we direct you to the "Very Expensive" section of the Venice chapter in *Frommer's Italy,* and check out such imposing specimens as the Gritti Palace and the Cipriani.

➔ **Hotel Ala** ★ SAN MARCO This government-rated three-star hotel is in the heart of Venice, only a few minutes walk from Piazza San Marco, yet it seems far removed from the hysteria that predominates on that square. Devotees of Venice return year after year to Ala's comfortable precincts, which—while not spectacular—are tasteful and well maintained. For nearly 2 decades, the hotel has been owned by the Salmaso family. The much-restored property dates back to the early 18th century, and, in fact, appears in a work painted by Canaletto. The decor of the bedrooms is a marriage of modern functionality with lacquered Venetian baroque style. Some of the units have a Jacuzzi, and a beautiful and spacious suite has been installed in the attic. Tarnowska's **American Bar** is named for the Russian countess Maria Tarnowska (one of her lovers was murdered inside the building in the 1800s). *Campo S. Maria del Giglio, 30124 Venezia.* ☎ *041/5208-333. Fax 041/5206-390. www.hotelala.it. 85 units. Double 120€–340€, triple 150€–310€, junior suite 340€. Rates include buffet breakfast. Vaporetto: Giglio. Amenities: Piano bar; cigar corner; dry cleaning/laundry service; nonsmoking rooms; tea room; roof terrace. In room: TV, minibar.*

➔ **Hotel Colombina** ★ SAN MARCO A 5-minute walk from Piazza San Marco is a hard-to-find hotel that's a bit of a Venetian secret. After extensive renovation, this hotel is a little gem, offering luxurious and spacious bedrooms. The tasseled draperies and reproduction Venetian antiques give it some glamour. All is calm and tranquil inside, but the location is in a maze of narrowing alleys and international hordes going who knows where. A lovely buffet breakfast is set out every morning. The more expensive rooms are like suites—hence the very high price tag. *Calle del Remedio, Castello 4416, 30122 Venezia.* ☎ *041/2770525. Fax 041/2776044. www.hotel colombina.com. 32 units. Double 180€–420€, suite 295€–800€. Rates include buffet breakfast. Vaporetto: San Marco. Amenities: Coffee bar; dry cleaning; laundry service; non-smoking rooms; room service (24-hr.); rooms for those w/limited mobility. In room: A/C, TV, dataport, hair dryer, minibar, safe.*

Eating

Venetian cuisine, though not without its delicacies—including such fish specialties as *saor:* whole sardines marinated in vinegar— is hardly the stuff Italian food legend is made of; let's be frank, you came to Venice for the canals, not the weird seafood. If you do choose to eat at Venetian restaurants, you

Kickin' It Lido-Style

The Lido—you know, where those pictures of Nicole Kidman during the Venice Film Festival are taken— offers an entirely different Venice experience. The city is relatively close, but you're really here to stay at an Italian beach resort and day-trip into the city for sightseeing. Although there are a few lower-end, moderately priced hotels here, they are entirely beside the point of the Lido and its jet-set reputation. If you are looking for a more reasonable option—and one that's open year-round—check out the modern **Hotel Belvedere,** Piazzale Santa Maria Elisabetta 4 (☎ **041/526-0115;** fax 041/526-1486; www. belvedere-venezia.com). It's across from the vaporetto stop, has been in the same family for nearly 150 years, and sports a good restaurant and a free beach cabana. It charges 44€ to 229€ per double.

Dining on a Budget in Venice

Pizza is the fuel of Naples and *bruschetta* and *crostini* (small, open-face sandwiches) the rustic soul food of Florence. In Venice it's *tramezzini*—small, triangular white-bread half sandwiches filled with everything from thinly sliced meats and tuna salad to cheeses and vegetables; and *cicchetti* (tapaslike finger foods such as calamari rings, speared fried olives, potato croquettes, or grilled polenta squares), traditionally washed down with a small glass of wine, or *ombra* ("some shade from the sun"). Venice offers countless neighborhood bars called *bacari* and cafes where you can stand or sit with a *tramezzino*, a selection of *cicchetti,* a panino (sandwich on a roll), or a *toast* (grilled ham and cheese sandwich). All of the above will cost approximately 1€ to 3€ if you stand at the bar, as much as double when seated. Bar food is displayed on the countertop or in glass counters and usually sells out by late afternoon, so you can't always rely on it for a light dinner, though light lunches are a delight. A concentration of popular, well-stocked bars can be found along the Mercerie shopping strip that connects Piazza San Marco with the Rialto Bridge, the always lively Campo San Luca (look for Bar Torino, Bar Black Jack, or the character-filled Leon Bianco wine bar), and Campo Santa Margherita. Avoid the tired-looking pizza (revitalized only marginally by microwaves) you'll find in most bars; informal sit-down neighborhood pizzerias everywhere offer savory and far fresher renditions for less, plus your drink and cover charge—the perfect lunch or light dinner.

can often eat very well, although you will usually pay a hefty price for doing so—you can either suck it up and deal with it, or you can forgo traditional sit-down meals and grab some *cicchetti* (finger foods) from the local *bacaro* (wine/snack bar) instead. Restaurants near tourist attractions often offer a special tourist menu, which is usually overpriced and so should be avoided. Most restaurants also tack on a cover charge and service charge, though cheaper eateries draw in customers by advertising no cover or service charge. Venice also has some of the best gelato in all of Italy, one indulgence in this city that you *can* afford.

As with the "Sleeping" section, we've included the neighborhood of each restaurant/cafe.

CHEAP

→ **Accademia Foscarini Snack Bar** ★ ITALIAN/DORSODURO A cheap canal-side option, located more centrally on the Grand Canal next to the Accademia Bridge. After a tiring exploration of the Accademia, stop in to re-energize; definitely go for the pizza. Try to get a seat right by the water for maximum scenery and gondola viewing. Toast, panini, and other snacks run from 2.50€–6€, pizza 7€–10€. Includes cover and 10% service charge. *Dorsoduro 878C.* ☎ *041/5227281. Daily 7am–9pm. Vaporetto: Accademia.*

→ **A La Valigia** ★ ITALIAN/SAN MARCO A huge, multiroom establishment with a hearty atmosphere, the place is usually packed with both locals and tourists who fill the place with their chatter and laughter. And the food ain't bad either, especially at this price, with pasta from 7€, pizza 5€–7€. *San Marco 4697 (1 block over from Le Bistro de Venise).* ☎ *041/5212526. Open daily for lunch and dinner. Vaporetto: Rialto.*

→ **Brek** ★★ ITALIAN CAFETERIA/ CANNAREGIO Good old Brek, a chain of cafeteria-style restaurants serving up hearty—and cheap—pastas and salads. The Venice branch serves mainly the hungry masses of people waiting for their train or budget travelers who lodge on Lista di Spagna. Pick up items in the cafeteria, grab a flask of cheap wine, and check out with the cashier before sitting down. Dishes start from 3€ and go up, but not a lot. The bar in the front serves up coffee drinks and pastries. *Lista di Spagna 124A, Cannaregio.* ☎ *041/ 2440158. www.brek.com. Daily 8:30am–11pm.*

→ **Cantina do Mori** ★★★ WINE BAR & SANDWICHES/SAN POLO Since 1462 this has been the local watering hole of choice in the market area; legend even pegs Casanova as a habitué. *Tramezzini* are the fuel of Venice— sample them here, where you're guaranteed fresh combinations of thinly sliced meats, tuna, cheeses, and vegetables, along with tapaslike *cicchetti.* They're traditionally washed down with an *ombra.* Venetians stop to snack and socialize before and after meals, but if you don't mind standing (there are no tables) for a light lunch, this is one of the best of the old-time *bacari* left. And now that it serves a limited number of first courses like *melanzane alla parmigiana* (eggplant Parmesan) and *fondi di carciofi saltati* (lightly fried artichoke hearts), my obligatory stop here is more fulfilling than ever. Sandwiches and *cicchetti* bar food run about 1€–2€ per serving. *San Polo 429 (entrances on Calle Galiazza and Calle Do Mori).* ☎ *041/522-5401. Mon–Sat 8:30am–9:30pm. Vaporetto: Rialto*

(cross Rialto Bridge to San Polo side, walk to end of market stalls, turn left, then immediately right, and look for small wooden cantina sign on left).

→ **Osteria alla Botte** ★ *CICCHETTI*/SAN MARCO It's a grease-fest, but far preferable to McDonald's. They offer awesome fried calamari. The hot guys in red t-shirts working the bar will choose a wine for you: they're all good, and all cheap. It's a hard place to find, in a portico maze east of Rialto Bridge, but you should make the effort. A crowd of students and young locals spills out into secluded alleyway, and perch their glasses on nearby building ledges. There's a good selection of hand-cut cheese and meats, as well as pasta dishes, and the wine list has over 100 selections. *Campo San Bartolomio. San Marco 5482.* ☎ *041/520-0279. www.osteria allabotte.it. Vaporetto: Rialto.Primi 5€; secondi 7€–10€.*

→ **Osteria alle Botteghe** PIZZA & ITALIAN/ SAN MARCO Casual, easy on the palate, easy on the wallet, and even easy to find (if you've made it to Campo Santo Stefano), this is a great choice for pizza, a light snack, or an elaborate meal. You can have stand-up *cicchetti* and fresh sandwiches at the bar or window-side counter, while more serious diners head to the tables in back to enjoy the dozen pizzas, pastas, or *tavola calda,* a glass counter—enclosed buffet of prepared dishes

Hot Spots! The Bars of Campo San Giacometto

On the San Polo side of the Grand Canal, right where it bends west above the Rialto Bridge, a number of very hip (and for now, very Venetian) wine bars have opened in Campo San Giacometto (or Giacometo, depending on whose spelling you go with), in the medieval buildings that once belonged to Venice's fruits and herbs market. **Naranzaria** and **Bancogiro** (see "Partying," later in this chapter) are more popular for drinks, but both serve food (antipasti and other light fare) and have convivial indoor bar areas as well as cozy upstairs seating. Best of all are the chic outdoor tables, set up on broad, otherwise empty swathes of esplanade that face the Grand Canal. So much unused space right on the Grand Canal, all for your enjoyment . . . does it get any better than this?

like eggplant *parmigiana*, lasagna, and fresh-cooked vegetables in season, reheated when you order. *San Marco 3454 (on Calle delle Botteghe, off Campo Santo Stefano).* ☎ *041/ 522-8181. Primi 4.15€; secondi 7€–8€; menù turistico 8.80€. Mon–Sat 11am–4pm and 7–10pm. Vaporetto: Accademia or Sant'Angelo (find your way to Campo Santo Stefano by following stream of people or asking; take narrow Calle delle Botteghe at Gelateria Paolin [in northwest corner] across from Santo Stefano).*

➜ Osteria Enoteca Ai Artisti ★ LIGHT ITALIAN/DORSODURO

This little restaurant proves that it is in fact affordable to dine at an outdoor table right alongside a canal, if you can manage to snag one of the few tables. Otherwise, grab something to go from the bar inside and munch away while walking along the water. Don't let the name of the canal—Rio della Toletta (and not, as some mistakenly read, Toilette) dissuade you. *1169A Dorsoduro (on the street from Campo San Barnaba to the Accademia, just after crossing the 1st bridge). Toast 2.20€–2.50€; panini 3.50€; pizza 6€–7€. Cover charge 1.50€. Daily 7:30am–9pm.*

➜ Pizzeria ae Oche ★★ PIZZERIA & ITALIAN/SANTA CROCE

Whenever I just want to hole up with a pizza in a relaxed setting, I head for the Baskin-Robbins of Venice's pizzerias, an American-style tavern restaurant of wood beams and booths decorated with classic 1950s Coca-Cola signs and the like. Italians are zealously unapologetic about tucking into a good-size pizza and a pint of beer (with more than 20 served); the walk to and from this slightly peripherally located hangout (with outside eating during warm weather) allays thoughts of calorie counts. Count 'em: 85 varieties of imaginative pizza fill the menu, including a dozen of the tomato-sauce-free "white" variety *(pizza bianca)*. The clientele is a mixed bag of young and old, students and not, Venetians and visitors. *Santa Croce 1552 (on Calle del Tintor south of Campo San Giacomo dell'Orio).* ☎ *041/52-41-161. Reservations recommended for weekends. Pizza 4.30€–7.40€; primi 5.20€–6.30€; secondi 5.80€–7.50€. Tues–Sun noon–midnight (daily in summer). Vaporetto: equidistant from Rio San Biasio and San Stae. You can walk here in 10 min. from the nearby train station; otherwise, from the vaporetto station find your way to the Campo San Giacomo dell'Orio and exit the campo south on to the well-trammeled Calle del Tintor.*

➜ Pizzeria/Trattoria al Vecio Canton PIZZA & ITALIAN/CASTELLO

Good pizza is hard to find in Venice, and I mean that in the literal sense. Tucked away in a northeast corner behind Piazza San Marco on a well-trafficked route connecting it with Campo Santa Maria Formosa, the Canton's wood-paneled taverna-like atmosphere and great pizzas are worth the time you'll spend looking for the place. There is a full trattoria menu as well, with a number of pasta and side dishes *(contorni)* of vegetables providing a palatable alternative. *Castello 4738a (at the corner of Ruga Giuffa).* ☎ *041/528-5176. www.alvecio canton.com. Reservations not accepted. Primi and pizza 6€–9€; secondi 11€–18€. Wed 7–10:30pm; Thurs–Mon noon–2:30pm and 7–10:30pm. Vaporetto: San Zaccaria (from the Riva degli Schiavoni waterfront, walk straight ahead to Campo SS. Filippo e Giacomo, then turn right and continue east to the small Campo San Provolo; take a left heading north on the Salizzada San Provolo, cross the 1st footbridge, and you'll find the pizzeria on the 1st corner on the left).*

➜ Rosticceria San Bartomoleo ★★ FAST VENETIAN/SAN MARCO

For a quick cheap bite to eat when you're on the go, this cafeteria-style restaurant is the place to be, judging by the crowd at mealtime. For super-cheap snacks, pick and choose from the various *cicchetti* (Venetian-style tapas) at the counter; they're all tasty. For a heartier meal, venture up to the formal dining area upstairs

A Couple of (Expensive) Classics

There are some places in Venice that will cost an arm and a leg for anything off the menu, yet are worth it for the experience alone even if only for a drink or snack—one which you may regret skipping out on.

When the crush of tourists at Piazza San Marco gets to be too much, duck around the corner to Calle Vallaresso like the fabulous Venice regular you are and take a load off at **Harry's Bar,** the grandfather of all Cipriani bars and restaurants throughout the world. For its legendary status—Hemingway drank here, and it's the bar that invented the white-peach-nectar-and-prosecco Bellini—Harry's may not impress you at first glance. The straight-outta-the-1930s room is tiny and dark, with no canal views, and half of the patrons are shorts-wearing tourists. However, having a Bellini at Harry's is nevertheless a memorable experience—as much for its amazing taste as for its 14€ (ow!) price tag. They say there's only peach nectar and sparkling wine in there, but the delightful buzz it gives leads me to believe they're also adding some other mystery spirit to the mix. If you can, grab a stool at the bar: from there, you can monitor the swish of the door for possible famous-people sightings, and you can also watch how many Bellinis are poured during the course of your visit, do the math, and realize what a cash cow this place is. Calle Vallaresso 1323, San Marco. ☎ 041/5285777. www.cipriani.com. Daily 10:30am–11pm, later in the summer.

One of the most touristy, yet most pleasant, experiences in Venice is having a drink in one of the cafes in Piazza San Marco. Come during the day to rest your feet and watch the flock of tourists swarming the square, or stop in at night after dinner for an elegant end to the day. The best of the cafes here is **Caffè Florian** ★★, where waiters dressed in white tuxedos serve expensive drinks to the beat of a live orchestra. The food here is nothing special, especially considering the price, so be sure to fill your belly elsewhere. Still, no one will rush you, and if the sun is warm and the orchestras are playing, we can think of no more beautiful public open-air salon in the world. Piazza San Marco 56–59. ☎ 041/5205641. Coffee and tea from 5€, cocktails from 11€, snacks and light lunch (served 12–2:30pm) 8€–19.50€.

and order a pasta dish. *Calle della Bissa, San Marco 5424A.* ☎ *041/5223569. Cicchetti .90€–1.30€ each, pasta dishes from 5.90€. Tues–Sun 9am–9:30pm; also Mon 9am–4pm from Easter to Nov 14. V. Vaporetto: Rialto (with bridge at your back on San Marco side of canal, walk straight ahead to Campo San Bartolomeo; take underpass slightly to your left marked sottoportego della bissa; you'll come across the rosticceria at 1st corner on your right; look for gislon [its old name] above entrance).*

→ **Rosticceria Teatro Goldoni** ITALIAN & INTERNATIONAL/SAN MARCO   Bright and modern (though it has been here for over 50

years), this showcase of Venetian-style fast food tries to be everything: bar, cafe, *rosticceria,* and *tavola calda* (hot-foods deli) on the ground floor and pizzeria upstairs. A variety of sandwiches and pastries beckons from a downstairs display counter, and another offers prepared foods (eggplant *parmigiana,* roast chicken, *pasta e fagioli,* lasagna) that'll be reheated when ordered; there are also a dozen pasta choices. A number of combination salads are a welcome concession to the American set and are freshest and most varied for lunch. This won't be your most memorable meal in Venice, but you won't walk away hungry or broke. *San Marco 4747 (at the corner of Calle dei Fabbri).* ☎ *041/522-2446. Pizza and primi 6€–15€; secondi 8€–20€; menù turistico 14€. Daily 9am–9:30pm. Vaporetto: Rialto (walk from San Marco side of bridge to Campo San Bartolomeo and exit it to your right in direction of Campo San Luca).*

DOABLE

➔ **Ai Tre Spiedi** ★★★ VENETIAN/ CANNAREGIO Venetians bring their visiting friends here to make a *bella figura* (good impression) without breaking the bank, then swear them to secrecy. Rarely will you find as pleasant a setting and appetizing a meal as in this small, casually elegant trattoria with reasonably priced fresh-fish dining—and plenty to keep meat eaters happy as well. The *spaghetti O.P.A.* (with parsley, peperoncino, garlic, and olive oil) is excellent, and the *spaghetti al pesto* is the best this side of Liguria. Follow it up with the traditional *bisato in umido con polenta* (braised eel). This is one of the most reasonable choices in town for an authentic Venetian dinner of fresh fish; careful ordering needn't mean much of a splurge either—though inexplicably, prices have risen dramatically in the past couple years. *Cannaregio 5906 (on Salizzada San Cazian).* ☎ *041/520-8035. Reservations not accepted. Primi 4.50€–12€; secondi 9.50€–18€; menù turistico 15€–20€. Tues–Sat noon–3pm; Tues–Sun 7–10pm. Vaporetto: Rialto (on San Marco side of bridge, walk straight ahead to Campo San Bartolomeo and take a left, passing post office, Coin department store, and San Crisostomo; cross 1st bridge after church, turn right at toy store onto Salizzada San Cazian). Closed July 20–Aug 10.*

➔ **A Le Do Spade** ★★ WINE BAR & VENETIAN/SAN POLO Since 1415, workers, fishmongers, and shoppers from the nearby Mercato della Pescheria have flocked to this wine bar. There's bonhomie galore here among the locals for their daily *ombra*—a large number of excellent Veneto and Friuli wines are available by the glass. A counter is filled with *cicchetti* (potato croquettes, fried calamari, polenta squares, cheeses) and a special *picante* panino whose secret mix of superhot spices will sear your taste buds. Unlike at most *bacari,* this quintessentially Venetian cantina has added a number of tables and introduced a sit-down menu, (above), which is a better choice for stand-up bar food. *San Polo 860 (on Sottoportego do Spade).* ☎ *041/521-0574. www.dospade venezia.it. Primi 6€–10€; secondi 7€–10€; menù fisso (fixed menu) 13€–18€. Mon–Wed and Fri–Sat 11:30am–3pm and 6–11:30pm; Thurs 9am–3pm. Vaporetto: Rialto or San Silvestro (at San Polo side of Rialto Bridge, walk away from bridge and through open-air market until you see covered fish market on your right; take a left and then take 2nd right onto Sottoportego do Spade). Closed Jan 7–20.*

➔ **Osteria Vivaldi** ★★ VENETIAN/SAN POLO Rumored to be where composer Vivaldi once actually lived, the building now houses a cozy restaurant resembling a rural wine bar. For a special treat, try the grilled lobster, a steal at only 17€. *San Polo 1257.* ☎ *041/5238185. Pasta dishes 6€–12€; fish entrees 9€–17€; meat entrees 9€–15€. Cover charge 1.50€. Daily 10:30am–2:30pm and 5:30–10:30pm. Vaporetto: Rialto.*

➔ **Trattoria alla Rivetta** ★★ SEAFOOD & VENETIAN/CASTELLO Lively and frequented by gondoliers (always a clue of quality dining for the right price), merchants, and visitors drawn to its bonhomie and bustling popularity, this is one of the safer bets for genuine Venetian cuisine and company in the touristy San Marco area, a 10-minute walk east of the piazza. All sorts of fish—the specialty—decorate the window of this brightly lit place. Another good indicator: There's usually a short wait, even in the off season. *Castello 4625 (on Salizzada San*

Provolo). ☎ *041/528-7302. Primi 6€–10€; secondi 10€–15€. Tues–Sun noon–2:30pm and 7–10pm. Vaporetto: San Zaccaria (with your back to water and facing Hotel Savoia e Jolanda, walk straight ahead to Campo SS. Filippo e Giacomo; trattoria is tucked away next to a bridge off the right side of campo).*

→**Trattoria da Giani** ★ VENETIAN/CANNAREGIO   One of the more affordable restaurants along busy Lista di Spagna, with a cozy terrace and friendly service. A good place to sample traditional Venetian cuisine, such as *saor* (sardines marinated in vinegar), served here with a dollop of polenta, as well as seafood dishes, which may be disappointing if you've previously splurged on high-quality food in the city. *Cannaregio 4377. Seafood appetizers around 6€; primi around 8€; seafood secondi 11€–16€. Vaporetto: Ferrovia.*

→**Trattoria da Remigio** ★★ ITALIAN & VENETIAN/CASTELLO   Famous for its straightforward renditions of Adriatic classics, Remigio is the kind of place where you can order simple *gnocchi alla pescatora* (homemade gnocchi in tomato-based seafood sauce) or *frittura mista* (a cornucopia of seafood fried in clean oil for a flavorful but light secondo) and know that it will be memorable. It bucks current Venetian trends by continuing to offer exquisite food and excellent service at reasonable prices. The English-speaking headwaiter, Pino, will talk you through the day's perfectly prepared fish dishes (John Dory, sole, monkfish, cuttlefish). You'll even find a dozen meat choices. Dine in one of two pleasant but smallish rooms. Remigio's is well known though not as easy to find; just ask a local for directions. *Castello 3416 (on Calle Bosello near Scuola San Giorgio dei Greci).* ☎ *041/523-0089. Reservations required. Primi 3.50€–8€; secondi 8€–20€. Wed–Mon 1–3pm; Wed–Sun 7–11pm. Vaporetto: San Zaccaria (follow Riva degli Schiavoni east until you come to white Chiesa della Pietà; turn left onto Calle della Pietà, which jags left into Calle Bosello).*

SPLURGE

→**Bistrot de Venise** VENETIAN/SAN MARCO   An upscale restaurant with traditional Italian atmosphere, often housing exhibitions from local artists in the dining room. This is a good place to come for a sampling of traditional Venetian cuisine; the restaurant offers set menus that are pricey but well-coordinated with a good sampling of the city's best cuisine. *Calle dei Fabbri 4685, San Marco.* ☎ *041/5234740. www.bistrot devenise.com. Primi around 10€; secondi 15€–17€; classic Venetian sample menu 38€ including antipasti, soup, seafood entree, dessert; historic Venetian menu 55€ including seafood antipasti, pasta, fish or lamb entree, dessert. Daily noon–11pm. Vaporetto: Rialto.*

CAFES/SNACKS

For a true Venetian experience, take a coffee break in a cafe in one of the city's piazzas or campos—try **Piazza San Marco** for the ultimate experience (see above), **Campo Santa Margherita** for something affordable (see listings under "Partying" for ideas), or the stylish, Art-Deco **Bar Accademia** (immediately east of the Accademia bridge, on the Dorsoduro side), to mix with gondoliers on break.

PICNICKING

You don't have to eat in a fancy restaurant to have a good time in Venice. Prepare a picnic, and while you eat alfresco, you can observe the life of the city's few open piazzas or the aquatic parade on its main thoroughfare, the Grand Canal. And you can still indulge in a late dinner *alla Veneziana.* Plus, doing your own shopping for food can be an interesting experience—the city has very few supermarkets as we know them, and small *alimentari* (food shops) in the highly visited neighborhoods (where few Venetians live) are scarce.

The Best Picnic Spots

Alas, to stay behind and picnic in Venice means you won't have much in the way of green space (it's not worth the boat ride to the Giardini Pubblici past the Arsenale, Venice's only green park). An enjoyable alternative is to find some of the larger piazzas or *campi* that have park benches, and in some cases even a tree or two to shade them, such as Campo San Giacomo dell'Orio (in the quiet *sestiere* of Santa Croce). The two most central are **Campo Santa Margherita** (*sestiere* of Dorsoduro) and **Campo San Polo** (*sestiere* of San Polo). For a picnic with a view, scout out the **Punta della Dogana area (Customs House)** ★★ near La Salute Church for a prime viewing site at the mouth of the Grand Canal. It's located directly across from the Piazza San Marco and the Palazzo Ducale—pull up on a piece of the embankment here and watch the flutter of water activity against a canvaslike backdrop deserving of the Accademia Museum. In this same area, the small **Campo San Vio** near the Guggenheim is directly on the Grand Canal (not many *campi* are) and even boasts a bench or two.

If you want to create a real Venice picnic, you'll have to take the no. 12 boat out to the near-deserted island of **Torcello,** with a hamper full of bread, cheese, and wine, and reenact the romantic scene between Katharine Hepburn and Rossano Brazzi from the 1950s film *Summertime.*

But perhaps the best picnic site of all is in a **patch of sun on the marble steps** leading down to the water of the Grand Canal, at the foot of the Rialto Bridge on the San Polo side. There is no better ringside seat for the Canalazzo's passing parade.

MARKETS: ALL THE PICNIC FIXINGS

Mercato Rialto

Venice's principal open-air market is a sight to see, even for nonshoppers. It has two parts, beginning with the produce section, whose many stalls, alternating with that of souvenir vendors, unfold north on the San Polo side of the Rialto Bridge (behind these stalls are a few permanent food stores that sell delicious cheese, cold cuts, and bread selections). The vendors are here Monday to Saturday 7am to 1pm, with a number who stay on in the afternoon.

At the market's farthest point, you'll find the covered **fresh-fish market,** with its carnival atmosphere, picturesquely located on the Grand Canal opposite the magnificent Ca' d'Oro and still redolent of the days when it was one of the Mediterranean's great fish markets. The area is filled with a number of small *bacari* bars frequented by market vendors and shoppers where you can join in and ask for your morning's first glass of prosecco with a *cicchetto* pick-me-up. The fish merchants take Monday off (which explains why so many restaurants are closed on Mon; those that are open are selling Saturday's goods—beware!) and work mornings only.

Campo Santa Margherita

On this spacious *campo,* Tuesday through Saturday from 8:30am to 1 or 2pm, a number of open-air stalls set up shop, selling fresh fruit and vegetables. You should have no trouble filling out your picnic spread with the fixings available at the various shops lining the sides of the *campo,* including an exceptional *panetteria* (bakery), Rizzo Pane, at no. 2772, a fine *salumeria* (deli) at no. 2844, and a good shop for wine, sweets, and other picnic accessories next door. There's even a conventional supermarket, Merlini, just off the *campo* in the direction of the quasi-adjacent *campo* San Barnabà at no. 3019. This is also the area where you'll find Venice's heavily photographed **floating market** operating from a boat moored just off San Barnabà at the Ponte dei Pugni. This market is open daily from 8am to 1pm and 3:30 to 7:30pm, except Wednesday afternoon and Sunday. You're almost better off just buying a few freshly prepared sandwiches (panini when made with rolls, *tramezzini* when made with white bread).

Shopping

Hands down the best place to shop in Venice, especially if you can't afford the swank boutiques around Piazza San Marco, is the **Rialto Market.** And even if you're not looking for anything in particular, window shopping here—if you can deal with the crowds—is a fun way to spend an afternoon. Tiny stores cover the length of the Rialto Bridge, and then continue along the streets leading from the bridge all the way through Campo San Polo and up to the train station. Here, you will find glassware, masks, jewelry, shoes, fresh produce, and the usual tourist kitsch (e.g., random T-shirts of kittens wearing gondolier get-ups). Stores usually open around 10am, and the bridge becomes utterly crowded by mid-afternoon with window-shopping tourists, and then quiets down again in the early evening as shops close.

Day Trips: Islands in the Lagoon

When you've managed to see everything of interest in Venice and your feet and senses need a break, the outer-lagoon destinations of Murano, Burano, and Torcello make for some pleasant island-hopping and a deserved change of pace (all are easily reached by vaporetto). While Murano and Burano are best known for their craft industries (glass and lace), Torcello's peaceful meadows are utter heaven after Venice's crowds.

MURANO

Known for its glass-blowing industry, this is where many of those pretty glass products you see in the Rialto Market come from. Most people come here to visit the factories and watch the glass blowers in action—they're at their best in the late morning once they've gotten warmed up, but they're pretty amazing to watch any time of the day. If you're interested in purchasing glassware, you can do so from the factory showrooms, but definitely do some bargaining. And if that's not enough

glass for you, visit the **Museo del Vetro di Murano,** a museum dedicated to the history and production of glass. Fondamentana Giustinian 8. ☎ **041/739586.** Admission 4€. Apr–Oct 10am–5pm, Nov–March 10am–4pm. Closed Wed. To get to the island, take vaporetti 5, 13, 41, 42, DM, or LN from Fondamenta Nuove.

BURANO

If Murano is the island of glass, Burano is the island of lace, and has been famed for its products for centuries. At the **Scuola di Merletti di Burano** (The Lace School of Burano), you can watch students at work, and then pick up some lace products (to counterbalance those leather items you bought in Florence) from the showroom. San Martino Destra 183. ☎ **041/730034.** Admission 4€. Nov–March 10am–4pm, Apr–Oct 10am–5pm. Closed Tues. To get here, take vaporetto LN from Fondamenta Nuove.

TORCELLO

Wandering through Torcello's grassy meadows and over its ancient stone bridges, you can truly forget about the hustle and bustle of the city across the water. This is definitely the place to go for a relaxing afternoon, as things here seem to move at a pace in tune with its medieval-like setting. Besides doing a whole lot of strolling, while on the island visit the **Cattedrale di Torcello**, a 7th-century church housing Byzantine mosaics portraying Madonna with her child adjacent to nightmarish scenes of hell. Admission 6€. March–Oct 10:30am–5:30pm, Nov–Feb 10:30am–5pm. To get here, take vaporetto LN from Fondamenta Nuove or vaporetto T from Burano.

Sightseeing

Venice has enough historic and artistic treasures to keep visitors busy for weeks. In all likelihood, however, you'll only be here for a day and a half, which is just enough time to squeeze in the main attractions. A visit to

A Very, Very Short History of Venice

Venice was officially founded in 412 when refugees fled the wrath of Attila the Hun, and then the Lombards moved in a century later. By the end of the 10th century, Venice had risen as a commercial superpower ruling the trade routes along the coast. Things went great until the 14th century, when the republic was devastated by the plague, which reduced its population by 50%. Then, in the Renaissance, Venice found herself involved in many military entanglements with such powers as Genoa and Spain, which ended in defeat at the hands of Napoleon in 1797. Meanwhile, as its trade routes were taken over by rising European powers such as England and Portugal, Venice lost its wealth and sheen and began a steady descent into decay. The only thing that kept the city, which joined Italy in 1866, from utter decline was its popularity as a tourist destination. Today, Venice clearly relies heavily on tourism to keep it afloat, judging by the crowds that swarm the city and its attractions.

Piazza San Marco is a must—you could easily spend a day exploring its historic buildings and hours soaking up the atmosphere in the square. The city's best museums are close together in Dorsoduro, offering up artwork that's old and new and all excellent. Be sure to make time to amble through the city's winding alleyways away from the tourist crowds, and don't be afraid to get lost (see "Getting Lost in Venice" earlier in this chapter for tips on finding your way). Don't leave the city without a cruise or three along the Grand Canal from an outside seat on a vaporetto.

HANGING OUT

→ **Campo Santa Margherita** ★★ Aaahh, without a gondola or canal in sight, this elongated rectangle is one of the last vestiges of unpretentious, authentic daily life in old Venice. During the day, it's a mix of dapper elderly local men in felt hats and wool vests shooing pigeons and shooting the breeze with the news agent, and a younger set of Venetian and international students and artists who hang out at the myriad hip cafes on the square. At night, this is where most of the alcohol is consumed in Venice, so if you're looking for a lively, fun-loving atmosphere (albeit one that's not as picturesque as the more watery parts of the city) come to Campo Santa Margherita.

→ **Eastern tip of Dorsoduro and Le Zattere** ★★ When you want to escape the crowds, grab a gelato, and go for a stroll, head across the Grand Canal from San Marco and make your way to the eastern tip of Dorsoduro, the "frontier" of old Venice. The esplanades in front of **La Salute** church and the triangular **Dogana da Mar** (old customs house), which sits at the pointy extremity of Dorsoduro, provide breathtaking (and sometimes blustery) vistas over the lagoon and some of the more memorable moments you can have in Venice, especially at sunset. Along the southern side of Dorsoduro, the **Zattere** promenades offer the famous **Gelateria Da Nico** (Fondamenta Zattere, Dorsoduro 922; ☎ **041/522-5293**) and views across the Giudecca Canal to—you guessed it—the island of Giudecca. The Zattere are an especially exciting place to be when Death-Star-sized cruise ships pull down the canal, threatening to steamroll any gondolas in sight. (Thousands of "stormtrooper" passengers aboard the ships lay siege to Piazza San Marco and the Rialto Bridge during the day.)

MTV **Best** → **Piazza San Marco** ★★★ The classiest and usually most congenial place to hang out in Venice is undoubtedly Piazza San Marco. You could spend hours just sitting on the steps, watching all the action in

Sightseeing in Venice

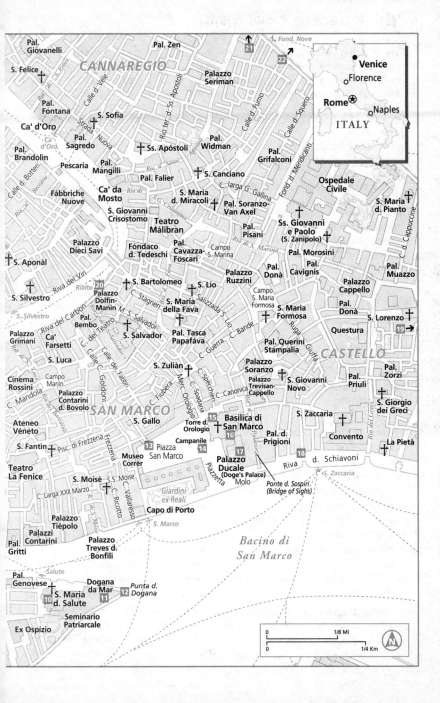

Pal. Giovanelli

CANNAREGIO

S. Felice

Pal. Zen

Palazzo Seriman

21

22

Fond. Nove

Venice
Florence
Rome
Naples
ITALY

Pal. Fontana

S. Sofia

Ca' d'Oro

Pal. Sagredo

Pal. Brandolin

Pescaria

Pal. Mangilli

Ss. Apóstoli

Pal. Widman

Pal. Grifalconi

Ospedale Civile

Ca' da Mosto

Pal. Falier

S. Canciano

C. larga G. Gallina

S. Maria d. Pianto

Fábbriche Nuove

S. Giovanni Crisostomo

S. Maria d. Miracoli

Pal. Soranzo-Van Axel

Ss. Giovanni e Paolo (S. Zanipolo)

Palazzo Dieci Savi

Teatro Málibran

Pal. Pisani

Fóndaco d. Tedeschi

Pal. Cavazza-Foscari

Campo S. Marina

S. Aponàl

Riva del Vin

Palazzo Ruzzini

Pal. Donà

Pal. Cavignis

Pal. Morosini

Pal. Muazzo

S. Silvestro

Rialto

20

S. Bartolomeo

S. Lio

Campo S. Maria Formosa

Palazzo Cappello

S. Silvestro

Palazzo Dolfin-Manin

Salizzada S. Lio

S. Maria Formosa

Pal. Donà

Pal. Bembo

S. Maria della Fava

Ruga Giuffa

S. Lorenzo

19

Palazzo Grimani

Ca' Farsetti

S. Salvador

Pal. Tasca Papafáva

Questura

CASTELLO

S. Luca

Pal. Querini Stampalia

Cínema Rossini

Campo Manin

S. Zuliàn

Palazzo Soranzo

Pal. Priuli

Pal. Zorzi

Palazzo Contarini d. Bovolo

SAN MARCO

Palazzo Trevisan-Cappello

S. Giovanni Novo

S. Giorgio dei Greci

Ateneo Véneto

S. Gallo

Torre d. Orologio

15

Basilica di San Marco

S. Zaccaria

Convento

La Pietà

S. Fantin

16

Campanile

14

Pal. d. Prigioni

13

Piazza San Marco

17

18

Teatro La Fenice

Museo Corrèr

Palazzo Ducale (Doge's Palace)

Riva d. Schiavoni

S. Moisè

Pizzetta

Molo

Ponte d. Sospíri (Bridge of Sighs)

S. Zaccaria

C. Larga XXII Marzo

Giardini ex Reali

Capo di Porto

Bacino di San Marco

Palazzo Tiépolo

Palazzi Contarini

S. Marco

Palazzo Treves d. Bonfili

Pal. Gritti

Salute

Pal. Genovese

S. Maria d. Salute

10

Dogana da Mar

11

12

Punta d. Dogana

Seminario Patriarcale

Ex Ospizio

0   1/8 Mi
0   1/4 Km

The Incredible Sinking City

The fact that Venice is sinking is nothing new: Scientists have noted the strange phenomenon for hundreds of years, caused by the fact that Venice is built on marshy ground, which sinks in the same way a sponge does when you apply pressure. The problem is the rate at which Venice is sinking. Venice typically sinks at a rate of about 7cm a century—not a very worrisome amount—but scientists now say that the city has sunk 24 cm in the past 100 years alone.

Anyone who has visited Venice during high tide has witnessed the consequence of this sinking: enormous flooding that is doing serious damage to the city's famous landmarks. Take St Mark's Basilica: due to its sinking foundation, the building now leans slightly to the left. Numerous projects have been suggested to fix the problem, such as the **Moses Project** (Progetto Mosè; www.progettomose.com/eng/home.html), a dam project aptly named after the famous biblical character. The idea is to build gates at points where seawater enters the lagoon so that when water levels rise, the gates can be shut and prevent water from flooding the city. Environmentalists, however, argue against this project as the closed gates will prevent water from moving out of the city as well, causing a backlog of water pollution, and harming the fish and plant life in the water. A controversial new plan has recently been proposed. This plan aims to solve the flooding problem by not only preventing Venice from sinking further, but actually seeks to raise the city. The 93-million euro project involves digging enormous holes under the city and then pumping them with water. This extra water will expand the layer of sand lying underneath the city and will push the city higher up, at a rate of around 3 cm a year. It still remains to be seen how the city will deal with these problems, but the fact remains that if it doesn't do something soon, Venice may very well end up underwater.

the square. Amidst the hordes of tourists that cram into the piazza, flocks of pigeons feed on breadcrumbs and dodge playful children. The piazza is flanked by the most popular tourist attractions in the city—most tourists spend virtually their entire visit here.

Sip on an overpriced coffee at one of the historic cafes lining the piazza, or simply sit on the steps and listen to the live orchestra music for free. The truly sadistic can buy a pack of birdseed for 1€ and get swarmed by overfed birds.

→ **Riva degli Schiavoni** ★ Known for being the toniest waterfront promenade in Venice, the "Bank of Slaves" stretches north from Piazza San Marco into the *sestiere* of Castello. Here, the Grand Canal ceases to exist, having

already spilled into the *bacino di San Marco*, so the spectacular views from here take in the monumental structures on the islands of San Giorgio Maggiore and Giudecca, across the water in the middle of the lagoon. Riva degli Schiavoni is also a great vantage point for observing the circus that attends the arrival of the monstrous cruise ships that drop anchor in the lagoon on a daily basis. Thousands of day-trippers stream in from the floating apartment buildings on shuttle boats and proceed to flood St. Mark's Square and the Rialto Bridge until it's time for them to set sail again in the late afternoon. Otherwise, Riva degli Schiavoni is the place where older tourists—or those with enough cash to afford the luxury hotels on this strip—shuffle along, past kitschy souvenir stands, congratulating themselves on how fabulous they are.

HISTORIC BUILDINGS AND MONUMENTS

In and around Piazza San Marco:

The most important, and most popular, historic buildings are all conveniently located in or around Venice's monumental main square:

➜ **Basilica di San Marco (St. Mark's Basilica)** ★★★ Stepping into Piazza San Marco, you are automatically struck by the beauty of the basilica; on a hot, hazy day it shimmers like a mirage and is utterly surreal. Legend has it that the basilica was built in the 9th century after the body of St. Mark, patron saint of Venice, was smuggled out of Alexandria in a pork barrel and secretly brought to Venice. The interior of the church is stuffed with ornate mosaics depicting the life of St. Mark and scenes from the Old Testament, as well as various treasures looted when Venice took part in the medieval Crusades. Off the main nave are the baptistry, the treasury, and the presbytery, which holds St. Mark's sarcophagus on an altar. Behind the altar is the Pala d'Oro, an altar screen encrusted with a dizzying amount of jewels. Upstairs, you'll find the Marciano Museum, whose main attraction is the Triumphal Quadriga: a 4th-century quartet of bronze horses snatched up by crusaders in Constantinople. Also upstairs, step out onto the Loggia dei Cavalli, a balcony offering a bird's-eye view of the piazza below. Free guided tours are given at 11am Tuesday and Wednesday (highly recommended). *San Marco, Piazza San Marco.* ☎ *041/522-5697. Basilica, free admission; Museo Marciano (St. Mark's Museum, also called La Galleria, includes Loggia dei Cavalli), 1.50€; Tesoro (Treasury), 2€; Baptistry, 1.50€. Basilica, Tesoro, and Pala d'Oro: summer Mon–Sat 9:45am–5pm; Sun 2–5pm (winter hours usually shorter by an hour). Museo Marciano: summer daily 9:45am–5pm (winter*

hours usually shorter by an hour). Baptistry: 9:45am–5pm. Vaporetto: San Marco (Vallaresso or Giardinetti).

➜ **Torre dell'Orologio (Clock Tower)** Only 20 years after it was supposed to be finished, (in time for the 500-year anniversary of its 1496 construction)—the clock tower *finally* reopened to the public on May 27, 2006. The famous tower stands on the north side of Piazza San Marco, next to and towering above the Procuratie Vecchie (the ancient administration buildings for the republic). For now, the tower is shrouded in scaffolding and vinyl sheeting that's screen-printed with images of the Empire State Building, Big Ben, the Eiffel Tower, or the Leaning Tower of Pisa—part of the restoration firm's homage to the great towers of the world. Visits of the open construction site must be arranged in advance and are geared mostly to those with a keen interest in technical restoration details. The tower's actual clock mechanism is original from the Renaissance and still keeps perfect time (although it recently received a cleaning by luxury timepiece maker Piaget). The two bronze figures, known as "Moors" because of the dark color of the bronze, pivot to strike the hour. The base of the tower has always been a favorite *punto di incontro* ("meet me at the tower") for Venetians, and is the entranceway to the ancient Mercerie (from the word for merchandise), the principal souklike retail street of both high-end boutiques and trinket shops that zigzags its way to the Rialto Bridge. *San Marco, Piazza San Marco. At press time, it was possible to request a guided tour of the clock tower via the website, but information about opening hours and admission fee (if any) was not available. www.torreorologio.it. Vaporetto: San Marco (Vallaresso or Giardinetti).*

➜ **Campanile (Bell Tower)** ★★ What may seem like a simple tower, no different from so many others in the country, is actually a structure with quite the notorious history. The

Piazza San Marco

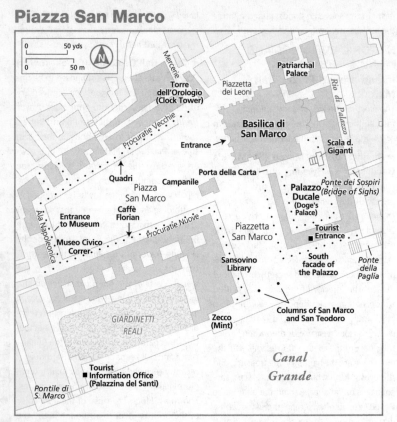

campanile was first built in the 10th century (and modified in the 16th century) as a military watchtower, and its bells were originally used to signal various events, such as the start and end of the work day, the summoning of senators to the Doge's Palace, and to announce the execution of prisoners who were kept hanging from the tower in cages before having their heads chopped off. In 1902, Venetians received a huge shock when the bell tower gracefully crumbled into the piazza below, miraculously killing no one (although one unlucky *gatto* was flattened in the debacle—meow). Ten years later, in 1912, the tower had been rebuilt (using many of the original materials), a replica of its former self with one new addition—an elevator. (Venice's

bell tower also inspired the design of the 1914 *campanile* on the UC Berkeley campus.) In more recent history, in 1997, near the 200th anniversary of the downfall of the Republic of Venice, a group of Venetian separatists stormed the tower and from its top declared that the piazza had been liberated. Police soon arrived on the scene and, after scaling the tower, arrested the fanatics. Today, the bells of the tower are rung just for the amusement of the tourists who line up to ride the elevator to the top for the stellar views of the square and the lagoon beyond. *Piazza San Marco.* ☎ *041/5224064. Admission 6€, audioguides 3€ or 2€ with Rolling Venice card. Daily 9:30am–4pm (until 8pm July–Sept). Vaporetto: San Marco (Vallaresso or Giardinetti).*

➔ **Palazzo Ducale (Doge's Palace)** ★★★
Looking more like a Turkish palace than the former residence of the Venetian Doges, or mayors, the stunning palazzo shimmers like a mirage in the *piazzetta* right next to St. Mark's Basilica and gives you a good idea of the sumptuousness of Venice's glory days. The "Doge house" was originally built in the 13th century and then rebuilt in the 16th century after most of it was destroyed in a fire; this was perhaps a blessing as when it was reconstructed, the great Venetian painters of the time were invited to contribute artwork. Today, the palace is essentially a museum housing this art collection. Upstairs, check out the works by Veronese and Tintoretto. Then, venture downstairs into the old apartments of the Doges for a glimpse into the life of these city rulers, and stop into the Grand Council chamber for a view of Tintoretto's massive *Paradise*. The notorious Council of Ten used to operate in this room, where they would sentence criminals to horrendous forms of punishments. The nearby Ponte dei Sospiri, or **Bridge of Sighs** ★, connects the palace with the old prison blocks, and is aptly named for the reaction of the prisoners as they crossed the bridge to meet their sad fate. See box below, "Who Let the Doges Out?" for info on the highly recommended guided tours of the palace. *Piazzetta San Marco.* ☎ *041-2715911. Admission 11€; students, Rolling Venice cardholders 5.50€. Admission also buys entry into the Museo Correr, the Museo Archeologico Nazionale, and the Monumental Rooms of the Biblioteca Nazionale Marciana. Audioguides 5€. Nov 1–March 31 9am–5pm (ticket office 7am–4pm); Apr 1–Oct 31 9am–7pm (ticket office 7am–6pm).*

A HISTORIC AREA

➔ **Ghetto Nuovo (The Jewish Ghetto)** ★★ The original European *ghetto* (the term is derived from the Venetian word for foundry) was founded in 1516 by the city not because of any ill will towards Jewish Venetians but as a way to get the Roman Catholic Church leaders off their backs, who at this point in history were expelling Jews from a good part of Western Europe. At its heyday, persecuted Jews from all over Europe flocked here, creating a multicultural community whose diversity is still evident today:

VENICE & THE VENETO

who Let the Doges Out?

For an insider look at and tons of fascinating anecdotes about the Doge's Palace, I cannot recommend the **"Itinerari Segreti" (Secret Itineraries)** ★★★ guided tours highly enough. The tours offer an unparalleled look into the world of Venetian politics over the centuries and are the only way to access the otherwise restricted quarters and hidden passageways of this enormous palace, such as the **doges' private chambers** and the **torture chambers** where prisoners were interrogated. The story of ladies' man extraordinaire Giacomo **Casanova's imprisonment** in, and famous **escape** from, the palace's prisons is the tour highlight (though a few of the less-inspired guides harp on this aspect a bit too much). I strongly recommend you **reserve in advance,** by phone if possible—tours are often sold out at least a few days ahead, especially from spring through fall—or in person at the ticket desk. Guided tours that promise to take visitors into "the most secret and fascinating rooms in the Palace" run daily at 9:55am, 10:45am, and 11:35am. Book at the museum information desk, by calling ☎ **041/520-9070,** or online (at least 24 hr. in advance) at www.teleart.org/itinerarisegreti. The Secret Itinerary tour costs 12.50€, or 7€ for students, EU citizens over 65, and Rolling Venice cardholders.

the ghetto contains five synagogues: the German Synagogue, the Spanish Synagogue, the Italian Synagogue, the Levantine (aka Turkish) Synagogue, and the Canton Synagogue. When Napoleon brought down the Venetian Republic in the early 19th century, the ghetto was dismantled and the city's Jews merged with the mainstream population. Today, only about 30 of Venice's 500 Jews still live in the ghetto, but the lively atmosphere still remains. The center of the action is around Campo del Ghetto Nuovo, flanked by the German, Levantine, and Spanish synagogues, as well as the Museo della Comunità Ebraica (Museum of the Jewish Community), housing various historical artifacts from the ghetto. Walk through the square, and its radiating alleyways with Jewish shops, kosher eats, and Holocaust memorials, and you'll wonder if you're in Italy or Israel. For those with a serious interest, the museum offers in-depth walking tours of the ghetto. The ghetto is best avoided on Saturdays, the Jewish Sabbath, when everything is closed and there is not a soul in sight. *Museum: Campo di Ghetto Nuovo 2902B.* ☎ *041/715359. 10€. Sun–Fri 10am–7pm June–Sept; 10am–4:30pm Oct–May. Walking tours depart hourly from the museum at 10:30am Sun–Fri.*

MUSEUMS/GALLERIES

➜ **Accademia** ★★★ Venice's most famous and crowded gallery, this is *the* place to come to view spectacular Venetian art. Even if you have little interest in 13th-century paintings depicting Christ in various poses of near death, of which there are too many here, the paintings in this museum are still worth a visit, simply for their opulence and amazing state of preservation. The collection follows a chronological order, beginning with those done in the 13th century, and ending with 18th-century works. The majority of the paintings are religious-themed; besides Christ, other featured stars include Madonna, Madonna and *Bambino*, and various angels

and saints. Giorgione's *Tempest* is the most famous painting in the gallery (in room 5), but to the average eye, there is really nothing too impressive about this painting. Others that do stand out, and are worth a glance, include Giovanni Bellini's series of Madonna and Bambini paintings, Lorenzo Lotto's gloomy *Portrait of a Young Man,* Paolo Veronese's *Feast In the House of Levi* (check out the handy info sheet for the controversial story behind this painting), and both Bellini and Carpaccio's versions of the *Miracle of the True Cross*—which take place at the San Lorenzo and Rialto bridges, respectively—for great depictions of 14th- and 15th-century daily life in Venice. *Campo della Carità, Dorsoduro.* ☎ *041/5222247. Admission 6.50€. Tues–Sun 8:15am–7:15pm; Mon 8:15am–2pm. Tours Fri 11am–1pm, Sat 3:30–5pm, Sun 10am–noon and 3:30–5pm;.call ahead to reserve.*

➜ **Peggy Guggenheim Collection** ★★ About as different as you can get from the Accademia, and perhaps a bit of a shock to the senses if you go from one to the other, this gallery houses the collection of well-known art curator Peggy Guggenheim, of the same Guggenheims behind the Guggenheim museums in New York, Bilbao, Berlin, and Las Vegas. The building—Palazzo Venier dei Leoni—is not only the former residence of the curator; in fact, it also houses Peggy Guggenheim herself—or at least her final resting place, in a corner of the sculpture garden next to a tree donated by Yoko Ono! The gallery itself contains various modern works, from cubists Picasso and Gris, to Italian futurists Balla and Boccioni, to surrealists like Giorgio De Chirico and Salvador Dali, as well as Peggy's ex-husband Max Ernst. Jackson Pollock is also well represented here—but don't look too long at his intense paintings or you'll hurt your eyes. Works by Miró, Kandinsky, Chagall, and the wonderful Pegeen Vail (Peggy's daughter) are also on display. When you're finished strolling through the gallery, have a seat at its canal-side entrance and watch the traffic go by. *Palazzo Venier dei Leoni, Dorsoduro.* ☎ *041/2405411. www.guggenheim-venice.it. Admission 10€, students 5€. Wed–Mon 10am–6pm.*

➜ **Scuola Grande di San Rocco (Confraternity of St. Roch)** ★★★ This museum is a dazzling monument to the work of 16th-century Venetian painter Tintoretto—it holds the largest collection of his work anywhere. The series of the more than 50 dark and dramatic works took the artist more than 20 years to complete, making this the richest of the many confraternity guilds or *scuole* that once flourished in Venice.

Jacopo Robusti (1518–94), called Tintoretto because his father was a dyer *(tintore)*, was a devout, unworldly man who only traveled once beyond Venice. Having never really left the dream world that was his hometown, Tintoretto filled his epic canvasses with phantasmagoric light and intense, mystical spirituality.

The downstairs room is fine, but you won't really be blown away until you walk upstairs and feast your eyes on the truly wow-inducing Sala dell'Albergo, where the most notable of the enormous, powerful canvases is the moving *La Crocefissione (The Crucifixion)*. In the center of the gilt ceiling of the great hall, also upstairs, is *Il Serpente di Bronzo (The Bronze Snake)*. Among the eight huge, sweeping paintings downstairs, each depicting a scene from the New Testament, *La Strage degli Innocenti (The Slaughter of the Innocents)* is the most noteworthy, so full of dramatic urgency and energy that the figures seem almost to tumble out of the frame. As you enter the room, it's on the opposite wall at the far end of the room.

There's a useful guide to the paintings posted inside on the wall just before the entrance to the museum. In the upstairs and downstairs halls, there are large mirrors that you can walk around with and angle up for better viewing of the ceiling paintings. There are a few Tiepolos among the paintings, as well as a solitary work by Titian. Note that the enormous works (recording Venice being saved from yet another plague) on or near the staircase are not by Tintoretto. *San Polo 3058 (on Campo San Rocco adjacent to Campo dei Frari).* ☎ *041/523-4864. www.scuola grandesanrocco.it. Admission 5.50€, 4€ students. Daily 9am–5:30pm (winter hours usually shorter by about an hour). Vaporetto: San Tomà (walk straight ahead on Calle del Traghetto and turn right and immediately left across Campo San Tomà; walk as straight ahead as you can, on Ramo Mandoler, Calle Larga Prima, and Salizzada San Rocco, which leads into campo of the same name—look for crimson sign behind Frari Church).*

➜ **Museo Storico Navale and Arsenale (Naval History Museum and the Arsenal)** ★★ The Naval History Museum's most fascinating exhibit is its collection of model ships. It was once common practice for vessels to be built not from blueprints, but from the precise scale models that you see here. The prize of the collection is a model of the legendary *Bucintoro,* the lavish ceremonial barge of the doges. Another section of the museum contains an array of historic vessels. Walk along the canal as it branches off from the museum to the Ships' Pavilion, where the historic vessels are displayed.

To reach the arsenal from the museum, walk up the Arsenale Canal and cross the wooden bridge to the Campo dell'Arsenale, where you will soon reach the land gate of the Arsenale, not open to the public. Occupying one-fifth of the city's total acreage, the arsenal was once the very source of the republic's maritime power. It is now used as a military zone and is as closed as Fort Knox to the curious. The marble-columned Renaissance gate with the republic's winged lion above is flanked by four ancient lions, booty brought at various times from Greece and points farther east. It was founded in 1104, and at the height of Venice's power in the 15th century, it employed 16,000 workers who turned out merchant and wartime galley after galley on an early version of massive assembly lines at speeds and in volume unknown until modern times. *Castello 2148 (Campo San Biasio).* ☎ *041/520-0276. Admission 3€. Tues–Sun 9:30am–12:30pm; Tues–Sat 3:30–6:30pm. Vaporetto: Arsenale.*

→ **Ca' Rezzonico (Museo del '700 Veneziano; Museum of 18th-Century Venice)** ★★ This museum, in a handsome palazzo on the Grand Canal, reopened after a complete restoration in late 2001. It offers an intriguing look into what living in a grand Venetian home was like in the final years of the Venetian Republic.

Begun by Baldassare Longhena, 17th-century architect of La Salute Church, the Rezzonico home is a sumptuous backdrop for this collection of period paintings (most important, works by Venetian artists Tiepolo and Guardi, and a special room dedicated to the dozens of works by Longhi), furniture, tapestries, and artifacts. This museum is one of the best windows into the sometimes frivolous life of Venice of 200 years ago, as seen through the tastes and fashions of the wealthy Rezzonico family of merchants—the lavishly frescoed ballroom alone will evoke the lifestyle of the idle Venetian rich. The English poet Robert Browning, after the death of his wife Elizabeth Barrett Browning, made this his last home; he died here in 1889. *Dorsoduro (on the Grand Canal on Fondamenta Rezzonico).* ☎ *041/241-0100 or 041/520-4036. Admission 6.50€, 4.50€ students. Wed–Mon 10am–6pm. Vaporetto: Ca' Rezzonico (walk straight ahead to Campo San Barnabà, turn right at the piazza and go over 1 bridge, then take an immediate right for the museum entrance).*

A Canal and a Bridge

🅫🆅 Best → **Canal Grande (Grand Canal)** ★★★ A leisurely cruise along the

3.2km-long (2-mile) "Canalazzo," from Piazza San Marco to the Ferrovia (train station), or the reverse, is an absolutely spellbinding moving picture that just doesn't seem real—and one of life's great experiences. Hop on the no. 1 vaporetto in the late afternoon (try to get one of the coveted outdoor seats in the prow), when the weather-worn colors of the former homes of Venice's merchant elite are warmed by the soft light and reflected in the canal's rippling waters, and the busy traffic of delivery boats, vaporetti, and gondolas that fills the city's main thoroughfare has eased somewhat. The sheer number and opulence of the 200-odd palazzi, churches, and imposing republican buildings dating from the 14th to the 18th centuries is enough to make any boat-going visitor's head swim. Many of the largest are now converted into imposing international banks, government or university buildings, art galleries, and dignified consulates. They unfold along this singular ribbon of water that loops through the city like an inverted S, crossed by only three bridges (the Rialto spans it at midpoint) and dividing the city into three *sestieri* neighborhoods to the left, three to the right. Some of the waterfront palazzi have been converted into condominiums whose lower water-lapped floors are now deserted, but the higher floors are still the coveted domain of the city's titled families; others have become the summertime homes of privileged expatriates. The two most popular stations are Piazzale Roma/Ferrovia (train station); and at Piazza San Marco. Vaporetto: 1; 82. See "Getting Around," earlier in this chapter, for vaporetto ticket prices.

→ **Rialto Bridge (Ponte di Rialto)** ★★ One of the great icons of Venice, this elegant marble arch over the Grand Canal is lined with overpriced boutiques and is teeming with tourists. Until the 19th century, it was the only bridge across the Grand Canal, originally built as a pontoon bridge at the canal's narrowest point. Wooden versions of the bridge followed; the 1444 one was the first to include shops, interrupted by a drawbridge in the center. In 1592 this graceful stone span was finished to the designs of Antonio da Ponte, who beat out Sansovino, Palladio, and Michelangelo with his plans that called for a single, vast, 28m-wide (25-ft.) arch in the center to allow trading ships to pass. The name "Rialto," which—like other Italian place names such as "Capri"—has come to be synonymous with glamour, is derived from *rivus altus* ("high bank"). Flotillas of singing gondoliers are common in the waters around the Rialto Bridge, making for a great (and very self-aware) photo-op. *Ponte di Rialto. San Polo and San Marco. Vaporetto: Rialto.*

A Church, a Square and a Customs House

→ **Santa Maria della Salute (Church of the Virgin Mary of Good Health)** ★ ★ It's not as hyped, but with its bulbous dome and fanciful styling, "La Salute" is as recognizable a feature in the Venetian skyline as the basilica of San Marco. This crown jewel of 17th-century baroque architecture proudly reigns over the commercially and aesthetically important eastern tip of Dorsoduro, across from the Piazza San Marco, where the Grand Canal empties into the lagoon. The first stone was laid in 1631 after the Senate decided to honor the "Virgin Mary of Good Health" for delivering Venice from a plague (and after the completion of the neighboring Chiesa di San Giorgio). Along with the Piazza San Marco, city elders were looking to create an ensemble of awe-inspiring structures to impress those arriving in Venice for the first time—I'd say they succeeded. They accepted the revolutionary plans of a young, relatively unknown architect, Baldassare Longhena (who would go on to design, among other projects, the Ca' Rezzonico). He dedicated the next 50 years of his life to overseeing its progress (he would die 1 year after its inauguration but 5 years before its completion).

The only great baroque monument built in Italy outside of Rome, the octagonal Salute is recognized for its exuberant exterior of volutes, scrolls, and more than 125 statues and rather sober interior, though one highlighted by a small gallery of important works in the sacristy. (You have to pay to enter the sacristy; the entrance is through a small door to the left of the main altar.) A number of ceiling paintings and portraits of the Evangelists and church doctors are all by Titian. On the right wall is Tintoretto's *Marriage at Cana*, often considered one of his best. *Dorsoduro (on Campo della Salute). ☎ 041/522-5558. Church, free admission; sacristy, 1.50€. Daily 9am–noon and 3–5:30pm. Vaporetto: Salute.*

FREE → **Squero di San Trovaso** ★ ★ One of the most interesting (and photographed) sights you'll see in Venice is this small *squero* (boatyard), which first opened in the 17th century. Just north of the Zattere (the wide, sunny walkway that runs alongside the Giudecca Canal in Dorsoduro), the boatyard lies next to the Church of San Trovaso on the narrow Rio San Trovaso (not far from the Accademia Bridge). It is surrounded by Tyrolian-looking wooden structures (a true rarity in this city of stone built on water) that are home to the multigenerational owners and original workshops for traditional Venetian boats (see "Pimp My Gondola!" below). Aware that they have become a tourist site themselves, the gondola makers don't mind if you watch them at work from across the narrow Rio di San Trovaso, but don't try to invite yourself in. It's the perfect midway photo op after a visit to the Accademia galleries and a trip to the well-known gelateria, Da Nico (Zattere 922), whose chocolate *gianduiotto* is not to be missed. *Dorsoduro 1097 (on the Rio San Trovaso, southwest of the Accademia Gallery). No phone. Free admission.*

→ **Dogana da Mar (Customs House)** ★ ★ An amazing spot from which to take in the full glory of Venice, the eastern tip of

Pimp My Gondola!

Putting together one of the sleek black boats is a fascinatingly exact science that is still done in the revered traditional manner at boatyards such as the **Squero di San Trovaso** (see above). The boats have been painted black since a 16th-century sumptuary law—one of many passed by the local legislators as excess and extravagance spiraled out of control. Whether regarding boats or baubles, laws were passed to restrict the gaudy outlandishness that, at the time, was commonly used to outdo the Joneses.

Propelled by the strength of a single *gondoliere,* these boats, unique to Venice, have no modern equipment. They move with no great speed but with unrivaled grace—when you see them slip around the tight corners of the city's inner canals, it's hard not to be awestruck. The right side of the gondola is lower because the *gondoliere* always stands in the back of the boat on the left. Although the San Trovaso *squero,* or boatyard, is the city's oldest and one of only three remaining (the other two are immeasurably more difficult to find), its predominant focus is on maintenance and repair. They will occasionally build a new gondola (which takes some 40–45 working days), carefully crafting it from the seven types of wood—mahogany, cherry, fir, walnut, oak, elm, and lime—necessary to give the shallow and asymmetrical boat its various characteristics. After all the pieces are put together, the paint job, the *ferro* (the iron symbol of the city affixed to the bow), and the wooden crotch that secures the oar are commissioned out to various local artisans. A fully tricked-out gondola (with the opulent cushions and metallic accoutrements) can cost as much as 35,000€.

Although some 10,000 of these elegant boats floated on the canals of Venice in the 16th century, today there are only 350. But the job of *gondoliere* remains a coveted profession, passed down from father to son over the centuries.

Dorsoduro is covered by the triangular customs house that once controlled all boats entering the Grand Canal. You don't actually go inside the Dogana da Mar. It's just a landmark from which you face the bacino and take in this glorious view. It's topped by a statue of Fortune holding aloft a golden ball. Now it makes for remarkable, sweeping views across the *bacino* of San Marco, from the last leg of the Grand Canal past Piazzetta San Marco and the Doge's Palace, over the nearby isle of San Giorgio Maggiore, La Giudecca, and out into the lagoon itself. *Fondamenta Dogana alla Salute. Vaporetto: Salute*

GARDENS AND PARKS

FREE ➔ **Giardini Reali** ★ In a city with a serious lack of green space (unless, of course, you count the algae-infested sections of canal

water), this tiny patch of solitude behind bustling Piazza San Marco is a blessing. Yes, it's small and dirty and over-crowded, but if you can manage to snag a seat of one of the shady benches, you'll appreciate this little oasis that provides an often-needed respite from the heat and tourist crowds. Before settling in, purchase an ice cream or cold beverage from one of the vendors at the park gates and then give your feet a deserving rest. *Vaporetto: San Marco (Vallaresso or Giardinetti).*

FREE ➔ **San Michele** ★★ Proving that Venetians have a knack for flair in virtually everything they do, this island-cum-cemetery is the final resting place for Venetians, and makes for a quiet escape from the city. When Napoleon brought his army to town, he ordered Venetians to haul their dead across the lagoon instead of burying them in the city. The tradition continues today, and 200 years of funerals has resulted in a severe shortage of space. The city has come up with some pretty gory solutions: The dead are allowed to rest peacefully for 12 years—just enough time to decompose. The remains of those with wealthy relatives are then sealed in a metal box and put in storage, while the less fortunate are merely tossed in the nearby boneyard. The majority of the island is devoted to the Catholic deceased, and it's also the prettiest park of the cemetery with well-groomed walkways and cultivated gardens. The other sections are worthy of a visit as well: seek out the grave of Greek Orthodox composer Igor Stravinsky and Protestant poet Ezra Pound. To get here, take vaporetto 41 or 42 heading toward Murano.

OTHER FESTIVALS AND FEAST DAYS

- **The Feast Day of San Marco:** celebrating the patron saint of Venice (April 25).
- **Biennale d'Arte:** A showcase of international modern art, with dance performances, theater, film, and art exhibitions fills the pavilions of the public gardens at the east end of Castello and in the Arsenale from late May to October every odd-numbered year. Many great modern artists have been discovered at this world-famous show. In the past, awards have gone to Jackson Pollock, Henri Matisse, Alexander Calder, and Federico Fellini, among others. Tickets (10€) can be reserved online or by calling ☎ **199-199-100** in Italy. www.labiennale.org.
- **Voga Longa:** An annual rowing race open to the public, where participants race to Burano and back, and crowds on the shore cheer in support (mid-May).
- **The Festa del Redentore:** Stupendous fireworks mark the celebration of the end of the plague that hit Venice in 1576 (3rd

weekend in July). The festival is centered around the Palladio-designed Chiesa del Redentore (Church of the Redeemer) on the island of Giudecca: a bridge of boats across the Giudecca Canal links the church with the banks of Le Zattere in Dorsoduro, and hundreds of boats of all shapes and sizes fill the lagoon. It's one big floating *festa* until night descends and an awesome half-hour *spettacolo* of fireworks fills the sky.

- **Venice International Film Festival:** Screenings of Italian and international films in various venues throughout the city. A few Hollywood big-names make an appearance on the Lido each year. (late Aug–early Sept)
- **The Regata Storica:** Venice's version of the Rose Parade, during which various boats decorated to the nines file in procession along the Grand Canal (first Sun in Sept).

Playing Outside

Although cliché, taking a **canal ride** ★★★ is a must in Venice. And it does not have to leave your wallet empty either! The cheapest way to ride along the Canal Grande is on the no. 1 or 82 vaporetto (see "Getting Around," earlier in this chapter, for prices), which takes about an hour to wind all the way down the canal. On the way, ignore the crowd and noise of the motor, and voila, you have an affordable canal ride. For a really beautiful ride, take the N vaporetto late at night, when the majority of the crowds have gone to bed and Venice is lit up—simply stunning. For a gondola trip see the box "We Heart Gondolas!," earlier. You can also go for a super el-cheapo gondola ride of sorts by taking one of the *traghetti* shuttle service (.50€, 2 min.) across the Grand Canal (see "Getting Around").

LIDO BEACHES

Once a retreat enjoyed only by the upper strata, the Lido is a resort island to the south

The Big Festival: *Carnevale a Venezia*

Carnevale ★★ is the ultimate shindig in Venice, with 2 weeks of pre-Lent debauchery (usually in Feb), including masked balls (with tickets costing upward of 500€!), concerts, and fireworks. No matter how you partake, a mask—if not a full-fledged costume—is mandatory. See **www.turismovenezia.it/eng**.

Venetians once more are taking to the open piazzas and streets for the pre-Lenten holiday. The festival traditionally was the unbridled celebration that preceded Lent, the period of penitence and abstinence prior to Easter, and its name is derived from the Latin *carnem levare,* meaning "to take meat away."

Today Carnevale lasts no more than 5 to 10 days and culminates in the Friday to Tuesday before Ash Wednesday. In the 18th-century heyday of Carnevale in La Serenissima Republic, well-heeled revelers came from all over Europe to take part in festivities that began months prior to Lent and crescendoed until their raucous culmination at midnight on Shrove Tuesday. As the Venetian economy declined, and its colonies and trading posts fell to other powers, the Republic of Venice in its swan song turned to fantasy and escapism. The faster its decline, the longer, and more licentious, became its anything-goes merrymaking. Masks became ubiquitous, affording anonymity and the pardoning of a thousand sins. Masks permitted the fishmonger to attend the ball and dance with the baroness, the properly married to carry on as if they were not. The doges condemned it and the popes denounced it, but nothing could dampen the Venetian Carnevale spirit until Napoléon arrived in 1797 and put an end to the festivities.

Resuscitated in 1980 by local tourism powers to fill the slower winter months when tourism comes to a screeching halt, Carnevale is calmer nowadays, though just barely. The born-again festival got off to a shaky start, met at first with indifference and skepticism, but in the years since has grown in popularity and been embraced by the locals. In the 1980s Carnevale attracted an onslaught of what was seemingly the entire student population of Europe, backpacking young people who slept in the piazzas and train station. Politicians and city officials adopted a middle-of-the-road policy that helped

of Venice, and is usually overrun with tourists, particularly those with a lot of money. It's not the most gorgeous stretch of beach in Italy, and the polluted waters don't make for the most pristine swimming environment, but the sandy beaches do make for a nice place to soak up some Italian rays. Even if you only come for a few hours, the Lido is a nice break from the museums and monuments of Venice proper—they're not going anywhere. While the Lido has gotten a bit more democratic since its days as a *beau-monde* refuge, you should definitely pack a lunch to avoid the still-absurd prices at the

island's restaurants. The nicest beach area is, of course, the privately owned stretch in front of the ritzy hotels; although it's technically reserved for guests, you probably won't be hassled if you inconspicuously set up camp here. Otherwise, try the free but dirtier public bathing beach at the end of Lungomare Gabriele d'Annunzio, at the eastern end of the island. To get to the Lido, take vaporetto 1, 52, or 82.

Partying

In general, Venice does not have much of a booming nightlife, and what there is usually establish Carnevale's image as neither a backpacker's free-for-all outdoor party nor a continuation of the exclusive private balls in the Grand Canal palazzi available to a very few.

Carnevale has returned to its dazzling best, a harlequin patchwork of musical and cultural events, many of them free, that appeal to all ages, tastes, nationalities, and budgets. At any given moment, musical events are staged in any of the city's dozens of piazzas—from reggae and zydeco to jazz to baroque and chamber music. Special art exhibits are mounted at museums and galleries. The recent involvement of international corporate commercial sponsors has met with a mixed reception, although it seems to be the direction of the future.

Carnevale is not for those who dislike crowds. Indeed, the crowds are what it's all about. All of Venice becomes a stage, and all its men and women players. Whether you spend months creating an extravagant costume, or grab one from the countless stands set up about the town, Carnevale is about giving in to the spontaneity of magic and surprise around every corner, the mystery behind every mask. Masks and costumes are everywhere, though you won't see anyone dressed up as generic 1970s vintage store grab-bags. Emphasis is on the historical, for Venice's Carnevale is the chance to relive the glory days of the 1700s when Venetian life was at its most extravagant. The places to be seen in costume (only appropriate costumes need apply) are the historical cafes lining the Piazza San Marco, the **Florian** being the unquestioned command post. Don't expect to be seated in full view at a window seat unless your costume is straight off the stage of the local opera house.

The city is the quintessential set, the perfect venue; Hollywood could not create a more evocative location. This is a celebration about history, art, theater, and drama, as one would expect to find in Italy, the land that gave us the Renaissance and Zeffirelli—and Venice, an ancient and wealthy republic that gave us Casanova and Vivaldi. Venice and Carnevale were made for each other.

VENICE & THE VENETO

ends early. Most people usually have a drink at a campo cafe, and then walk around for a bit, soaking up the dreamy atmo before heading to bed. The best places for this are Piazza San Marco (see below), the *campi* on either side of the Rialto Bridge, and for a slightly more boisterous, international-budget-traveler scene, Cannaregio's Lista di Spagna. Of course, the best way to cap off a night in Venice is to get a bottle of prosecco and go for a late-night gondola ride (see box: "We Heart Gondolas!," p. 466).

Those looking for a party can check out the following bars and clubs, mostly located around Campo Santa Margherita (lively and unpretentious) in Dorsoduro, and Lista di Spagna (backpacker-oriented, but borderline tacky) in Cannaregio. You can also ask any of the younger staff at your hotel—they'll be able to tell you where the current hot hangouts are ("hot" being a relative term in serene Venice).

Finally, just because Venice is not a city of velvet ropes and bouncers does not mean it's acceptable to wear flip-flops and shorts out on the town at night. The look you're going for is casual but chic, which means your cleanest and least wrinkled pair of jeans or other pants, and a "real shirt" of some sort (i.e., not a graphic T-shirt). Ladies, if you've brought a skirt or dress, now would be a good time to bust it out. (But keep the shoes flat—most people look ridiculous trying to walk around Venice in heels.)

There's not a general rule of thumb for what days/nights these bars and clubs are open. In Venice, there's no one set closing day, since their "work week" is not like most cities, it revolves around tourism and the esoteric Venetian people who still live in Venice.

And here's a very general guide to what you'll be paying for a drink on your wanderings:

Glass of wine in enoteca (wine bar): from 2€, for a totally drinkable local wine that you may have never heard of, all the way up to 8€ for a particularly special vintage of Brunello or Barolo. Most people drink something in the 3-4€ range. Wine is by far the cheapest (and classiest, since quality is so high) way to get drunk in Italy.

Pint of beer (lager, ale, Guinness, whatever): 4€ during happy hour; 5€ after happy hour.

Cocktails/mixed drinks: 4-5€ in casual, laid-back bars; 7-10€ (or a bit more) in trendier spots.

AROUND PIAZZA SAN MARCO

For tourists and locals alike, Venetian nightlife mainly centers around the many cafe/bars in one of the world's most remarkable piazzas: Piazza San Marco; even Napoléon called it the

Finding Out What's On

Check out the free magazine *A Guest in Venice* for festival, concert, and nightlife listings, or take a look online at **www.unospitedivenezia.it**. While bars are busy from early evening onward, Venice's clubs don't really get going until around midnight.

most beautiful drawing room of the world. It is also the most expensive and touristed place to linger over a Campari or cappuccino, but a splurge that should not be dismissed too readily.

The nostalgic 18th-century **Caffè Florian** ★★ (San Marco 56A–59A; ☎ **041/520-5641**) on the south side of the piazza, is the most famous (closed Wed in winter) and most theatrical inside; have a Bellini at the back bar for half what you'd pay at an indoor table; alfresco seating is even more expensive when the band plays on, but it's worth every cent for the million-dollar scenario. It's said that when Casanova escaped from the prisons in the Doge's Palace, he stopped here for a coffee before fleeing Venice.

On the opposite side of the square at San Marco 133–134 is the old-world **Caffè Lavena** (☎ **041/522-4070;** closed Tues in winter) and at no. 120 is **Caffè Quadri** ★ (☎ **041/522-2105;** www.quadrivenice.com; closed Mon in winter), the first to introduce coffee to Venice, with a restaurant upstairs that sports Piazza San Marco views. At all spots, a cappuccino, tea, or Coca-Cola at a table will set you back about 5€. But no one will rush you, and if the sun is warm and the orchestras are playing, I can think of no more beautiful public open-air salon in the world.

➜ **Bacaro Jazz** ★ It's a mix of recorded jazz (played a bit too loud), rough plank walls, industrial-steel tables, and a corrugated aluminum ceiling at this happening cocktail bar. The happy hour specials (BOGO Heineken for 7€, cocktails from 8€) make this a good place to stop for a post-sightseeing or predinner drink, or a late-night snack: the kitchen serves up pasta, seafood, and snacks till closing. (Not to be confused with the pricey and pretentious Bacaro Lounge, which should be avoided.) *San Marco 5546. www. bacarojazz.com.* ☎ *041/5285249. Thurs–Tues 4pm–2am. Happy hour 4–7pm. Vaporetto: Rialto. On the street due north of Campo San Bartolomeo, just before the first bridge.*

Spritzville!

Everyone knows about the Bellini, but for many Venetians (and especially younger ones), the cocktail of choice is the *spritz*, a refreshing combo of white wine, Aperol (an orange bitter that's slightly sweet), or Campari (a red bitter that's *very* bitter), and a splash of soda. You'll see this sparkler all over the city from 6pm on through to the wee hours—to order one, ask for *uno spritz, per favore,* and then notice how fabulous its orangey-red color looks against the greenish-blue canals.

MTV Best → Bancogiro ★★ At this cool, modern osteria, set in the arcades of the old fruit and herb market west of the Rialto Bridge, you'll find *cicchetti, spritz, ombre,* and boozy locals eating plates of who-knows-what at the bar. You can have a full, creative Venetian meal in the vaulted upstairs room, or a drink and snack at the tables set up behind the bar outside, on a broad (and remarkably underused) stretch of *fondamenta* right on the Grand Canal. *Campo San Giacometto. San Polo 122.* ☎ *041/523-2061. Tue–Sat until midnight or later; Sun for lunch only. Vaporetto: Rialto.*

→ **Centrale Lounge** ★ This sleek and sexy bar in the heart of San Marco has its own private boat dock, for those who are arriving by gondola or water taxi. For the rest of us, there's a pedestrian entrance on Piscina Frezzeria. Every night, a DJ spins a mix of chill-out, house, and lounge music. The crowd is a young and good-looking mix of locals and out-of-towners. Some of the bartenders are clearly hoping to be discovered by visiting talent agents and will act snobby toward non-Hollywood types. The best nights here are Thursdays—from 7pm on, there's a free buffet, a friendly vibe, and jazz and Latin tunes. *Piscina Frezzeria. San Marco 1659/b.* ☎ *041/296-0664. www.centrale-lounge.com. Wed–Mon 6:30pm–2am. Vaporetto: Vallaresso.*

→ **Devil's Forest** ★★ As popular with tourists as it is with real Venetians, this Italian version of the classic Irish pub, in an alley off Campo San Bartolomeo, has such quintessential features as Irish brew on tap (pints from 4.50€), football (all right, soccer) on the big screen, and even an authentic red phone booth. Backgammon and chess boards are also available for patrons, making this a great place to kick back and warm up if you're in Venice during the biting cold of winter. *Calle Stagneri 5185, San Marco.* ☎ *041/5200623. www.devilsforest.com. Daily 8am–12:30am. Vaporetto: Rialto.*

→ **Duchamp** ★★ Rumored to be named after a controversial French Dada artist, this casual bar across the campo from Orange Bar caters to a more bohemian crowd, though the city's trendsetters have also deemed this place as cool. The place is especially popular at the start and end of the night. *Dorsoduro 3019 (in Campo Santa Margherita).* ☎ *041/5286255. Daily 10am–2am. Vaporetto: Ca' Rezzonico.*

MTV Best → Harry's Bar In 1932, famed restaurateur and hotelier Giuseppe Cipriani opened this now-legendary watering hole near the Vallaresso vaporetto stop. Named for his son Arrigo (Italian for Harry), it has been a preferred, if overpriced, retreat for everyone from Hemingway—when he didn't want a Bloody Mary, he mixed his own drink: 15 parts gin, 1 part vermouth—to Woody Allen. Regulars prefer the close and elegant front room to the upstairs dining room (decent cooking, and they invented *carpaccio,* a dish of thinly sliced raw beef now served throughout Italy). Harry's is most famous for inventing the Bellini, a mix of champagne and peach juice. Prices—for both drinks and the fancy cuisine—are rather extravagant, with the house Bellini priced at 14€. *Calle Vallaresso. San Marco 1323;* ☎ *041/528-5777. Vaporetto: Vallaresso.*

➜ **Hotel Monaco** ★★ When it comes to setting, the Hotel Monaco beats Harry's Bar hands-down. The splendid waterfront restaurant here has some of the prizest real estate in Venice, with postcard views of La Salute church across the Grand Canal, and San Giorgio Maggiore across the lagoon. Eating here is outrageously expensive, but you can come before the dinner hour (between 6 and 7pm) for an *aperitivo,* or after dinner (10pm) for a nightcap. If you're unsure, just ask the friendly guys in the lobby if it's a good time to stop in for a drink. Expect a crowd of older luxury-hotel types, although this spot is also popular with the younger international jet set. *Calle Vallaresso. San Marco 1332.* ☎ *041/520-0211. monaco.hotelinvenice.com. Pastas from 20€; secondi from 25€; drinks 10€–15€. Open daily for lunch and dinner. Vaporetto: Vallaresso.*

MTV Best ➜ **Naranzaria** ★★ We challenge you to find a more fabulous, unpretentious spot for a few cocktails than this wine bar with 50 exclusive-feeling seats on the wide-open Erbaria esplanade, facing the Grand Canal just north of the Rialto Bridge. The 16th-century building here used to be the citrus market of Venice (*naranza* means orange in Venetian), where scurvy-prone sailors would come to fuel up on vitamin C after long stints on the high seas. Nowadays, a friendly, young, and hip crowd comes here to fuel up on sushi and sashimi (prepared by Japanese chef Akira) and light fare from northern Italy. The kitchen's only open until 11pm, but you can drink *ombre* of fantastic wines from the Veneto and Friuli regions, *spritz,* or after-dinner *digestivi* until 1 or 2am most nights—all the while taking in an unbelievably uncluttered Grand Canal view. *Campo San Giacometto. San Polo 130.* ☎ *041/724-1035. www.naranzaria.it. Tue–Sun 10am until midnight (or later, depending on the night). Vaporetto: Rialto.*

➜ **Orange Bar** ★★ It doesn't take a genius to figure out where they got the name for this hip restaurant and champagne lounge on Campo Santa Margherita: Everything is orange! Grab a drink at the curvy bar in the main room and plant yourself by the window, or on one of the orange patio chairs in front. Upstairs, a roof terrace offers a great view of the masses in the lively *campo* below. For a quieter setting, take a seat on the terrace in the back. With a name like this, there's only one drink imaginable: an orange, Aperol-based *spritz.* *Dorsoduro 3054A (in Campo San Margherita). www.orangebar.it.* ☎ *041/5234740. Daily 7am–2am. Vaporetto: Ca' Rezzonico.*

➜ **Senso Unico** ★ A favorite of American students (and the young-to-old real Venetians who are fascinated by them), this cozy British-style pub, just 2 minutes from the Guggenheim and the Accademia, is a relaxed and friendly place to have a glass or pint of something after gawking at the art in the nearby museums. *San Vio, Calle della Chiesa. Dorsoduro 684. No phone. Open Wed–Mon 10am–1am. Vaporetto: Accademia.*

➜ **Torino@Notte** ★ When you're wandering around after dinner in the *sestiere* of San Marco, join the party that spills well out from the plate-glass windows of this bar in Campo San Luca. Torino at Night has brought this square to life after dark with live jazz many nights, unusual beer from Lapland, and good panini. *San Marco 459 (Campo San Luca).* ☎ *041/522-3914. Tues–Sat 7pm–2am. Vaporetto: Rialto.*

NIGHTCLUBS

➜ **Casanova** ★ Techno beats pound in this moderately popular club, frequented by both locals and tourists, which doubles as an Internet cafe during the day. And no need to worry about appropriate attire here: in the darkness, and the borderline-tacky environs of Lista di Spagna, nobody will notice that stain on your shirt or the dirt on your jeans. *Lista di Spagna, Cannaregio 158A.* ☎ *041/2750199. Fri 13€ cover includes 1 drink; Sat 10€ cover. Daily 10pm–4am. Vaporetto: Ferrovia.*

Verona, Where We Lay Our Scene . . .

114km (71 miles) W of Venice, 80km (50 miles) W of Padua, 61km (38 miles) W of Vicenza

Ahh, fair Verona! This elegant and exceedingly well-kept city is a must-see on the northern Italian tourism circuit, for three very good reasons: opera, wine, and romantic tragedy. The annual opera season, with performances held in a 2,000-year-old Roman amphitheater in the middle of the city, draws huge crowds and is a magical experience even if you're not a fan of the opera. Verona also produces some delicious wines—some of Italy's best, in fact—which in restaurants are often cheaper than water, and even the cheapest of the cheap still tastes fabulous. But most people know Verona as the setting for Shakespeare's most well-known tale, *Romeo and Juliet,* the irresistible romance of which draws busloads of day-tripping tourists to the city daily. Whether the fabled couple actually lived in fair Verona (if they existed at all) remains a philological problem on a par with "Is there a God?"—but the city has cashed in on the myth anyway by contriving plenty of photogenic, admission-charging sites related to the star-cross'd lovers. (Of course, spoilsports will always point out the fact that "Juliet's balcony" was added to "Juliet's House" in the 1920s.) Check your cynicism at the train station, and don't be such a stickler for historical accuracy, and you'll get caught up in the heart-rending story of the legendary lovebirds, too.

Today, with its cobblestoned streets and well-preserved piazzas, prosperous Verona looks very much as it would have in its 13th- and 14th-century heyday, when the town was governed by the Della Scala (or Scaligeri) family (whose emblem—a ladder—can still be seen on buildings and monuments all over town). But Verona's history goes even deeper than its striking medieval and Renaissance buildings: Roman Verona is very much in evidence today, from a street plan that dates to the reign of Augustus, to its imposing ancient fortification gates, to the splendid Arena. When sipping a glass of wine on a terrace in Piazza Brà after an opera show at the Arena, you can almost imagine Romeo calling up to Juliet's balcony nearby—that is the magic of Verona.

Getting There

BY AIR

Verona's **Aeroporto Valerio Catullo** (www.aeroportoverona.it) lies 16km (10 miles) from the city center. Flights connect Verona with major Italian destinations, as well as European cities such as London, Vienna, Barcelona, and Amsterdam. To get to the city from the airport, catch the **shuttle bus** that runs to the city's train station (20 min).

OKKIO! Verona Is Not for the Broken-Hearted

If you're recovering from heartbreak, Verona's pervasive atmosphere of romance can be a tough pill to swallow. The constant crowds at the attractions related to *Romeo and Juliet,* the lovey-dovey couples strolling hand in hand through impossibly quaint alleyways, and the walls covered in amorous graffiti all attest to the fact that true love, and real-life Romeos and Juliets, might actually exist. It's enough to make the bitterly broken-up vomit; but then again, with suggestions of love all around Verona, conditions are near-perfect for a little midvacation fling. Just watch out for those vials and daggers . . . and if your sweetie kills herself, make sure she's *really* dead before you off yourself! *Right,* Romeo?

Veronese Wines 101

Verona and its surrounding region are well known for their delectable wines. For those who know little more about wine other than the fact that it's red or white, made from grapes, and fun to drink, here's a run-down of the most popular wines produced in the region, all worthy of a sampling.

➡ **Valpolicella:** a dry, dark-red wine with a spicy berry flavor. Good to drink with meat dishes and strong cheeses.

➡ **Bardolino:** from the eponymous region, a red wine with a fruity aroma and raspberry taste. Good to drink with meat and fish.

➡ **Amarone:** a coveted red wine that literally takes years to produce; it's aged for 3 years in oak barrels and then another year in the bottle, giving it a strong smell and powerful, spicy taste. Good to drink with red meat.

➡ **Soave:** made from grapes grown in the Soave region, this white wine has a floral aroma and a slightly almondy aftertaste. Good to drink with appetizers, soups and salads, as well as seafood, poultry, and pasta.

➡ **Bianco di Custoza:** a white wine with a fruity aroma of apple and apricot. Good to drink as an aperitif, or with seafood or soup.

—*adapted from The Live Literature Association's City Center Map*

BY TRAIN

Verona is a principal stop on the northern Italy's main east-west train line. Verona's main train station is **Porta Nuova,** at Piazza XXV Aprile in the southern part of the city. It's about a 20-minute walk to the center of town, straight up Corso Porta Nuova, or you can catch bus 72 or 73 from the piazza outside the train station. The ticket office is open daily 6am to 9pm. The railway information office open 7am to 9pm. Left luggage is open 7am to 11pm, and it's 3.80€ for the first 5 hours, .60€ per hour for the next 6 hours, .20€ per hour after that.

BY BUS

The **APT** bus station is in front of the train station in Piazza XXV Aprile (☎ **045/ 887-1111**). Buses run frequently to other destinations in the Veneto region, such as Venice, Padua, and Vicenza, though it's *much* easier to travel by train.

Getting Around

ON FOOT

Verona is small enough to be easily managed on foot. Just 1km (²/₃ mile) north of the train station, Piazza Brà, with the famous Arena (Roman amphitheater) in the middle, is the hub of action in the *città antica* (ancient city). From Piazza Brà, the rest of the tongue-shaped old city protrudes north, surrounded on three sides by the Fiume Adige (Adige river). Shop-lined Via Mazzini is the main artery running north-south in the old city, from which you can access all the major sites. Past the *città antica,* cross any of the bridges over the Adige to reach the quieter sections of town, where you'll find such attractions such as the Teatro Romano and Archaeological Museum (to the northeast), the Giardino Giusti (east), and the youth hostel. If, like most visitors to Verona, you're only in town for a day, stick to the old city, as the modern developments outside the 16th-century fortification walls are fairly charmless.

BY BUS

If you're carrying a heavy load, or are just plain lazy, yellow city buses are run by Verona's **ATM** (Azienda Mobilità e Trasporti, Via F. Torbido 1; ☎ 045/887-1111; www.atm.it). Tickets cost 1€ (1.20€ if you buy them from the driver)—pretty

Verona

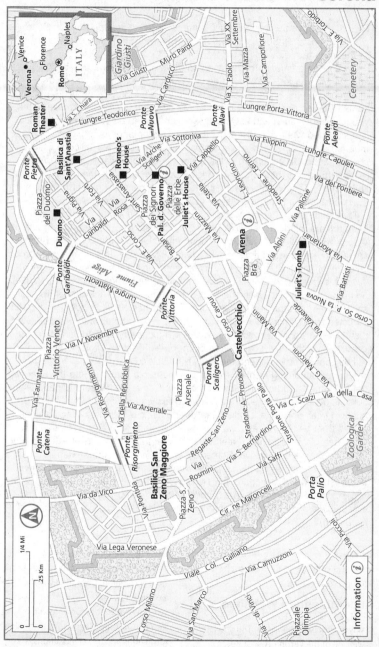

Romeo and Juliet For Dummies

For those whose freshman English curriculum didn't include R&J (or those who didn't actually bother to read it), here's a basic rundown of the story, with all the important details:

Once upon a time, in the Italian town of Verona, two families—the Capulets and the Montagues—had hated each other for as long as each could remember. On the night the Capulets throw a huge party, a certain Montague named Romeo decides to crash it. At the party, he catches a glimpse of the young Juliet Capulet and is instantly smitten. Juliet falls for Romeo, too, and is devastated when she discovers that he's a Montague and that their love is thus forbidden. She goes out to lament her sorrows on her balcony when who should happen to be lurking in the bushes below but dear Romeo himself. ("But soft! What light through yonder window breaks? It is the east, and Juliet is the sun!") The two share a poignant moment, confessing their love for each other, and after a night of passion, they are secretly married the next day.

That same day, after the wedding, Romeo's two buddies Benvolio and Mercutio are minding their own business while strolling through the streets of Verona when Juliet's cousin Tybalt confronts them and starts a fight. Romeo arrives on the scene in time to see Tybalt kill Mercutio. In a fit of rage, Romeo takes revenge by killing Tybalt. As punishment, he is banished from Verona.

Juliet is crushed when she hears the news about her new husband, and things go from bad to worse when she finds out that her father—unaware of his new son-in-law—has arranged for her to marry a guy named Paris. Juliet meets with a trusted friend, Friar Lawrence, and together they come up with a complicated plan: Juliet will drink a special potion that will fool everyone into thinking she's dead. ("Alack the day!") Once she's been "buried" in the Capulet tomb, Romeo will be sent to revive her and the two will be able to live happily ever after.

All goes according to plan, except for one tragic glitch: Before the Friar can get to Romeo and let him know of the plan, Romeo hears from a friend that Juliet is dead. Overcome by grief, Romeo rushes to Juliet's tomb, swallows his own (real) poison, and falls dead beside his love. Minutes later, Juliet wakes from her fake death and is shocked to find Romeo dead beside her. With the plan foiled, and no reason left to live, Juliet kills herself—this time, for real: she throws herself over Romeo's body, driving his "happy dagger" through her heart. And thus ends the woeful tale of the most famous lovers in the Western world, Juliet and her Romeo.

(We should also note that the publisher of the guide you are now reading also publishes both the "For Dummies" series and the classic "Cliff'sNotes." Hint, hint!)

much every route leads to Piazza Brà, and many also continue to the main train station, Stazione Porta Nuova.

Recommended Websites

○ **www.tourism.verona.it**. The official website of the Verona Tourist Board, and a great source of information on attractions and events in Verona, and practical information such as transportation, accommodation, and even the weather.

○ **www.verona.com**. Download the *Verona Guide* here, with information on attractions and accommodations. There is also a handy events calendar.

Sleeping

While Verona has many hotels and guest-houses for a city its size, accommodation can often be hard to find, due to the numerous trade fairs that descend on the city in the summer, so it's a good idea to reserve ahead. If you arrive without a place to stay, **C.A.V. (Cooperativa Albergatori Veronesi)** runs an accommodations booking service (Via Patuzzi 5; ☎ **045/8009844;** www.cav.vr.it).

That said, Verona does have a variety of places to lay your head, suiting all budgets. While those around Piazza Brà are the nicest, they also tend to be the most expensive, although a few bargains can found, especially if you plan ahead and book early. Cheap-sleep options abound along Corso Porta Nuova, though some are a bit seedy.

CHEAP

➜ **Hotel Arena** Nothing extraordinary here—rooms are small and bare, but this is nonetheless a viable option if you're on a budget and want a private room. It's near the train station, so this hotel is also a good option if you're arriving at night or have an early departure. *Stradone Porta Palio 2 (at Vicolo Cieco Porta Palio).* ☎ *045/8032440. www.albergoarena.it. Single 42€ with shared bath, 50€ with private bath; double 65€ with shared bath, 75€ with private bath.*

➜ **Ostello della Giovane** ★ Unless you've packed your *Mrs. Doubtfire* costume in your luggage, guys are out of luck at Verona's other hostel option—this charming little place just outside the city center is women-only. There's a pretty garden courtyard, but for an all-female facility, bathrooms are lacking in quantity, and there is a strict 11pm curfew (and they *will* lock you out if you are late). *Via Pigna 7 (off Via Garibaldi near the Teatro Romano).* ☎ *045/596880. www.casadellagiovane.com. Dorm 13€, double 28€, triple 66€–69€.*

➜ **Ostello della Gioventù Villa Francescati (HI)** No surprises here if you've ever stayed in a Hostelling International hostel before: This is a large soul-less place about 2km (1¼ mile) northeast of Piazza Brà, across the Adige river, with little to offer besides a place to store your belongings and lay your head. The massive hostel is a bit better than other HIs, however, as it's housed in a pretty converted 16th-century villa with a nice garden, which provides at least a bit of atmosphere. The hostel also offers laundry facilities, a restaurant, common room, and parking. *Salita Fontana del Ferro 15 (east of Via Redentore).* ☎ *045/590360. Dorm 15€, private room 17.50€ per person. Breakfast included. HI membership required. Bus 73.*

DOABLE

➜ **Hotel Aurora** ★ They could use some more decor to add a little life to the place, but the location, right on Verona's monumental market square, is compensation enough, with an upstairs terrace perfect for watching the bustle in the piazza below. Recently renovated rooms all have TV, A/C, and phone. *Piazza della Erbe 2.* ☎ *045/594717.*

So, Why Is It Called Piazza Brà?

We see you snickering—and, truth be told, we wondered about this ourselves. In some unreleased early version of the Shakespearean play, did Juliet once strip down to her corsetry in Verona's main square and profess her love for Romeo before a shocked populace? No—the name has far more boring origins. *Brà* comes from the German *breit,* which means "open space." (For the record, the Italian word for "bra"—as in, underwire, strapless, padded, etc.—is *reggiseno;* and Italians would probably crack a smile, too, if they came across a "Reggiseno Square" while on vacation abroad.)

Verona Tourist Office

The main office of the Verona Tourist Board is on Via Degli Alpini 9, across from the Arena in Piazza Brà (☎ 045/8003638; www.tourism. verona.it). It's open Monday through Saturday 9am to 7pm, Sunday 9am to 3pm. There is also a smaller branch office located in the train station (☎ 045/8000861; Tues–Sat 8am–7:30pm, Sun–Mon 10am–4pm).

www.hotelaurora.biz. Single 56€–68€ with shared bath, 90€–116€ with private bath; double 90€–130€ with private bath. Breakfast included.

➜ **Hotel Torcolo** ★★ Just off of Piazza Brà, this hotel is half the price of others in the area but worth twice as much; friendly staff and cozy rooms make this place feel like home. Spotless rooms, most with views of the action in the street below, come with A/C, TV, and minibar. The hotel also has a small terrace out front, where breakfast is served in summer. Vicolo Listone 3 (at Via Carlo Cattaneo). ☎ 045/8007512. www.hotel torcolo.it. Single 50€–92€, double 70€–112€. Breakfast included in summer, otherwise 7€–12€.

SPLURGE

➜ **Hotel Giulietta e Romeo** ★★ You don't need to buy into the Romeo and Juliet hype to stay here, although it is a fitting place for hopeless romantics who want the complete Veronese experience. Recently renovated rooms are a bit dark but cozy and clean and have TV, A/C, phone, and minibar. The hotel also has a bar, TV lounge, Internet access, and parking for guests. Vicolo Tre Marchetti 3 (near Piazza Brà). ☎ 045/8003554. www. giuliettaeromeo.com. Single 70€–120€, double 115€–210€, triple 130€–230€. Breakfast included.

Eating

Unless you're a hard-core carnivore, you'll probably walk away from Verona with fonder memories of its wine and romance than its food. Rather intimidating local specialties include stewed horsemeat (pastissada de caval) and tripe (animal stomach), all slathered with cren, a kind of Veronese horse-radish sauce. Of course, most people don't want to eat Seabiscuit or the innards of a petting zoo, so you can always stick to the ubiquitous pizza and pasta (topped with more mainstream meats and veggies), or fish from Lake Garda, washed down with enough vino to make any dish taste divine.

CHEAP

One of the best ways to eat in Verona is also the most affordable: Grab a panino or pizza from one of the stalls in Piazza della Erbe, and either munch away while shopping in the market, or join the crowd on the stairs of the bank across the street. Pizza (sold by weight) and panini are 2€ to 4.50€, available at lunch only.

➜ **Brek** ★★ ITALIAN CAFETERIA Good old Brek, a chain of cafeteria-style restaurants serving up hearty—and cheap—pastas and salads. The food must be good, as it's always packed, and usually with locals. Pick up items in the cafeteria, grab a flask of inexpensive wine, and settle up with the cashier before sitting down. This outlet has a large terrace out front, making you wonder why people pay twice the price to eat virtually the same thing next door. Piazza Brà 20. ☎ 045/ 8004561. www.brek.com. Dishes from around 3.50€. Daily 8am–10pm.

➜ **Zac Café** ★ PIZZA/ITALIAN Probably the most affordable of the more formal restaurants lined up along the piazza, where you can dine with the Arena as a backdrop. The restaurant resembles an American idea of what an Italian restaurant should look like, with checkered tablecloths and cheesy music, and offers a large selection of pizzas, as well as pasta and sandwiches. Prices drop quite a bit if you eat inside—but then you miss out on the atmosphere and scenery outside. *Piazza Brà 22.* ☎ *045/8036370. Pizza slices from 2.40€; whole pizzas 4.80€–8.10€ inside or 5.50€–8.80€ on the terrace; pasta from 5€ inside or 5.70€ on the terrace; sandwiches 2.50€–3.60€ inside or 2.70€–3.90€ on the terrace. Cover charge 1€ inside or 1.50€ on the terrace. Tue–Sun 11:45am–2:30pm and 6pm–2am.*

DOABLE

→ **Caffè al Teatro** ★ Down the street from Piazza Brà, on the way to the Castelvecchio, this hip corner cafe serves snacks and light meals, making it a great place to while away an afternoon resting your feet and catching up on postcard-writing while sipping a cappuccino. *Via Roma 10 (off Via Manin). No phone. Snacks 1.80€–3.50€; pasta 4.90€–5.70€; panini 4.10€–4.70€. Mon–Sat 7am–11pm.*

→ **Cantore** ★★ PIZZERIA If you find yourself with a hankering for some good pizza in Verona, this is the place to come: Their selection is huge and inviting. Located in a quiet alley off busy Via Mazzini, the restaurant has ample indoor seating as well as a canopied terrace that will make you feel as though you're dining in the backyard of a villa in a vineyard. *Via Cantore 2 (off Via Mazzini).* ☎ *045/8031830. Primi from 7€; secondi 8.50€–17€; pizza 4.30€–7.20€. Cover 1.50€. Daily noon–3pm and 6–11pm (Sept–May closed Mon).*

SPLURGE

→ **Bottega del Vino** ★★ ITALIAN/WINE BAR Join the crowds of locals at this long-running restaurant, where skillfully prepared cuisine includes simple but intensely flavorful pasta dishes, but where the real star of the show (as indicated by the name) is wine.

This *bottega* ("shop") has a legendary selection (over 80,000 bottles!) of wine, including about 50 by-the-glass choices at the bar; don't be shy about asking for help in seleeting a wine—that's what the staff here works and lives for. *Vicolo Scudi di Francia 3 (just north of Via 4 Spade, off Vicolo Scala).* ☎ *045/8004535. Primi 7.50€–8.50€, secondi 9€–33€. Wine by the glass from 2€. Cover charge 4€. Tues–Sun 10:30am–3pm and 6pm–midnight.*

→ **Osteria Giulietta e Romeo** ★★ VERONESE Just north of Piazza dei Signori, this is a romantic spot, as the name suggests, and perfect if you're going for the whole Shakespearean theme. This is also the place to come if you find Verona's local delicacies appealing: Ingredients such as horsemeat, veal *(vitello),* and tripe *(trippa)* dominate the menu, though those with less-adventurous taste buds will also find a satisfying selection of "safer" dishes to choose from. *Corso Sant'Anastasia 27 (at Vicolo 2 Mori).* ☎ *045/8009177. Fixed price menus including primi and secondi 13€–20€. Tues–Sat noon–3:30pm and 5:30pm–midnight; Mon 3:30pm–midnight.*

CAFES

→ **Caffè Barbarani** ★★ Of the several cafes in Piazza della Erbe, this one is in the center, considerably cheaper than its neighbors, and a perfect place to people-watch and soak up the atmosphere while enjoying coffee, beer or wine, or a light meal. *Piazza delle Erbe 14.* ☎ *045/8030021. Coffee from 1.80€; sandwiches from 4€; pasta from 6€.*

→ **M27** ★★ The only cafe on trendy Via Mazzini, with something for all moods and occasions: Choose between the funky bar on the main floor, the cozy terrace with couches and Internet access upstairs, or the garden terrace in the back. *Via Mazzini 27 (between Via Adua and Via 4 Spade).* ☎ *329/2341978 (cellphone). Coffee from 1.80€; cocktails from 3€; pizza 3.50€–7. Tue–Sun 9am–2am.*

Partying

Verona does not have much nightlife; the highlight is really the opera during the summer. Most clubs are located on the outskirts of the city, making them difficult to access without a car, and often not worth the hassle. People generally take it easy at night, strolling around Piazza Brà and stopping for a sample of local wine and the numerous wine bars in the city.

The grande dame of local cafe society is the **Antico Caffè Dante** in the beautiful Piazza dei Signori (☎ **045-594259**). Inside Verona's oldest cafe, the setting is formal and meals are pricey; so you might want to snag an outdoor table instead, where you can soak in the million-dollar view of one of Verona's loveliest ancient squares.

Wine-lovers will be in their element when they discover the 80,000-bottle selection at **Bottega del Vino,** Vicolo Scudo di Francia 3 (off Via Mazzini; ☎ **045-8004535**). This bottega opened in 1890, and the old-timers who spend hours in animated conversation seem to have been here ever since. The atmosphere is reason enough to come by, and five dozen wines are available by the glass. Regulars, journalists, and local merchants often fill the few wooden tables at mealtimes, ordering simple and affordable but excellent dishes, such as homemade risottos.

Put on your dancing shoes and head for **Disco Berfis Club,** Via Lussemburgo 1 (☎ **045-508024**), or **Bar/Disco Tribu,** Via Calderara 17 (☎ **045-566470**), where the rhythms echo what's being broadcast in New York and Milan.

Gays and lesbians can call **Circolo Pink,** Via Scriminari 7 (☎ **045-8012854**), to get details on gay cultural activities, parties, or newly opened bars. You can call the hot line Tuesday and Thursday 9 to 11pm and Saturday 4 to 6pm. It is closed in August.

Sightseeing

Most people are drawn to Verona by its Shakespearean claim to fame—whether you buy the whole *Romeo and Juliet* thing or not, the related sites are still worth visiting: you can step out onto Juliet's "balcony," rub the breast of her statue below for good luck, and pay your respects to the unfortunate couple at Juliet's so-called tomb. Beyond the star-cross'd lovers, Verona is also home to an incredibly well-preserved open-air Roman amphitheater, with its hugely popular opera season in the summer, and a Roman theater where theatrical performances are still held. Throughout the old city, dog-legging alleyways radiate from beautiful piazzas, begging to be discovered.

HISTORIC BUILDINGS

➔ **Arena di Verona** ★★ Built in the 1st century A.D., this centerpiece of Verona was initially used to host gladiatorial fights, jousts, dances, and even the circus when it came to town. Since the 18th century, it has functioned mainly as a theatrical venue. In 1913, to commemorate the birthday of the legendary composer Giuseppe Verdi, an annual opera season was created which still runs today (see details under festivals and events). Even if opera is not your style, it's worth sitting through a performance for the atmosphere alone; sitting under the Verona stars, doing what others have done here for thousands of years, is sublime no matter what your musical tastes. During the day, the Arena is open to visitors (for a fee). There's not much offered in the way of exhibits or information, just some machines that will spit out prerecorded blurbs on the history of the Arena if you pump them full of change. Rather, the attraction here is the empty arena itself: climb to the highest row for a bird's-eye view of the action in Piazza Brà below. *Piazza Brà.* ☎ *045/8003204. Entry during the day 4€, students 3€. Tues–Sun 8:30am–7:15pm; Mon 1:30–7:15pm.*

➔ **Casa di Giulietta (Juliet's House)** ★
By now, you should all know the story: Boy meets girl, boy romances girl from below her

balcony, boy's family feuds with girl's family, boy and girl would rather die than be apart so end up committing suicide. As Veronese legend has it, this is where Juliet lived when she met Romeo; here is the very balcony (circa 1928) from which Romeo and Juliet professed their love! Shining like a beacon in the courtyard, the right breast of the bronze statue of Juliet is supposed to bring good luck to anyone who rubs it, which explains its discoloration, and the lineup of tourists waiting for their turn. The courtyard is often packed with tour groups, so it's best to go first thing in the morning or at the end of the day. You can venture inside the villa beyond the gift shop, though you'll have to pay for the privilege. Inside, you'll find some uninteresting furniture and ceramic pieces from the period, but the real reward for the price of admission is the privilege of stepping out onto Juliet's balcony and delivering your best high-school caliber "O Romeo, Romeo, wherefore art thou, Romeo?" Although signs all over warn of steep fines for writing on the courtyard walls (the gift shop even supplies special notebooks for writing messages and professions of love), the walls still continue to be covered with graffiti proclaiming eternal devotion, and the security guard merely slaps the hands of those he catches—a small price to pay for declaring your love. *Via Cappello 23 (at Via Stella).* ☎ *045/803-4303. Free entrance to courtyard, where you can view the Juliet statue and the exterior of the balcony. Villa: 4€, students 3€. Combination ticket with Tomba di Giulietta: 5€, students 4€. Tues–Sun 9am–7pm, Mon 1:30–7:30pm.*

➜ **Castelvecchio** ★ This "Old Castle" was built during the second half of 14th century by the Della Scala family, who ruled Verona at the time. From then, it was used mainly for military purposes until it was destroyed during WWII. It has since been restored and converted to a museum. Admire the castle's exterior from the courtyard for free, or else pay the entrance fee for the museum housing the Civic Fine Arts Collection, with such treasures as local Veronese works from the 14th to the 18th centuries—the most famous of which is Francesco Caroto's remarkable *Youth with a Portrait of a Puppet.* Showing the clear influence of Leonardo da Vinci, the puppet in the drawing looks like a childish copy of famous *Vitruvian Man.* The museum also houses a sculpture gallery with eerily lifelike 14th-century statues and the sarcophagus of saints Bacchus and Sergius, who were deemed heretics and put to death in the 12th century. *Corso Castelvecchio 2 (near Via Roma).* ☎ *045/594734. www.comune.verona. it/Castelvecchio/cvsito. Admission 4€, students 3€. Free 1st Sun of the month. Tues–Sat 8:30am–7:30pm; Sun 1:30–7:30pm. Last ticket sales 15 min. before closing.*

➜ **La Casa di Romeo (Romeo's House)** It's not open to the public as a monument per se, but what the Veronese will half-heartedly tell you was the model for Shakespeare's Montague household is now the Osteria del Duca restaurant. *Via Arche Scaligeri 2.* ☎ *045/594474.*

➜ **La Tomba di Giulietta (Juliet's Tomb)** ★ Supposedly the site where first Juliet, and then Romeo, professed their choice to die rather than live apart, and where both then proceeded to kill themselves. In order to view the tomb, you are required to visit the adjacent museum first—indeed, pushy museum workers will ensure that you do not skip any part of it. The upper floor contains rescued statues and frescoes from old villas, while downstairs you can view newly restored Veronese artwork. The tomb itself is in a little room underground, and looks more like a stone bath than the heroine's final resting place . . . suffice it to say that a little imagination and romanticism are required here. Outside, a peaceful but neglected garden houses crumbling statues of Romeo and Juliet. *Via del Pontiere 5 (at Vicolo San Domenico).*

Verona's Classic Churches

Verona has some beautifully preserved churches—enough to keep you busy for at least a whole day. The largest, and most worthy of a visit, is the **Basilica di Sant'Anastasia** ★★ built between the 13th and 15th centuries (it was never fully completed) and known for its exemplary Gothic architecture. The 12th century **Duomo** ★ sits on the site of an ancient Roman church, remains of which can still be seen. The church also contains artwork by Titian and other local artists, as well as the 14th-century tomb of St. Agatha. The impressive Romanesque **Basilica San Zeno** ★, named for Verona's patron saint, was completed in the 12th-century and is best known for its massive bronze doors, said to be the first bronze castings since Roman times, and decorated with scenes from the Old and New Testament and from the life of San Zeno. The rosette-shaped window on the facade is known as the *Ruota della Fortuna* ("Wheel of Fortune"). Inside, you're bombarded with frescoes galore, though it's Mantegna's 15th-century triptych, *Madonna and Child Enthroned with Saints,* that draws the most attention; you'll see it behind the altar. Finally, **Basilica San Fermo** ★, an 11th-century church of Roman-Gothic design, sits on the site where saints Fermo and Rustico were tortured to death in the 6th-century; their remains lie inside the church.

The Verona Church Association administers entrance into Verona's churches. Regular admission is 2.50€ per church. However, if you are interested in visiting several churches, it pays to purchase a cumulative ticket, which allows entry into all five churches: adults 5€, students 4€. Contact information for all churches is ☎ 045/592813 (www.chieseverona.it). Ticket sales end 15 minutes before closing. No entry during services.

Sant'Anastasia (Piazza Sant'Anastasia, north end of Corso Sant'Anastasia): Monday through Saturday 9am to 6pm, Sunday 1 to 5pm.

San Zeno (Piazza San Zeno, near Via Pontida, on the south side of the old city): Monday through Saturday 8:30am to 6pm, Sunday 1 to 6pm.

San Fermo (Stradone San Fermo, at Ponte delle Navi): Monday through Saturday 10am to 6pm, Sunday 1 to 6pm.

Duomo (Piazza Duomo, northwest corner of the old city): Monday through Saturday 10am to 5:30pm, Sunday 1:30–5:30pm.

☎ 045/8000361. Admission: 3€, students 2€. Combo ticket with Casa di Giulietta: 5€, students 4€. Free 1st Sun of the month. Tues–Sun 8:30am–7:30pm; Mon 1:30–7:30pm. Last ticket sales at 6:45pm.

→ **Teatro Romano and Museo Archeologico** ★★ While this Roman theater is utterly unimpressive in size if you've just come from the Arena, its lesser state of preservation and the surrounding ruins (around the back of the theater) give it an air of authenticity that its more famous counterpart lacks. Come during the day for great views of the city center across the river from the top row of the theater, or at night in the summer for one of the frequent plays or concerts. The museum is housed in the remains of a 15th-century monastery, up a steep flight of stairs behind the top of the theater. Guide sheets in multiple languages, in each room, provide ample information about the various statues and relics housed here. There is also a reconstructed model of the theater and monastery in a room off of the courtyard.

Regaste Redentore (from the old city, cross Ponte Pietra and walk east). ☎ *045/8000360. Admission 3€, students 2€. Includes admission to both the theater (not during performances though) and the museum. Free 1st Sun of the month. Mon 1:30–7:30pm; Tues–Sun 8:30am–7:30pm. Ticket sales end 15 min. before closing.*

PIAZZAS AND GARDENS

➜ **Giardino Giusti** ★★ It's even farther away from the center than the Teatro Romano, but once you arrive you'll realize it was worth the effort, as well as the exorbitant entrance fee. Originally designed in the 15th century as the backyard of Agostino Giusti, a powerful knight who also served as a squire of the Grand Duchy of Tuscany, the garden contains fountains, statues, and staircases that intermingle with terraces and perfectly manicured hedges—there's even a hedge labyrinth. For stunning views of the city's rooftops, follow the cypress-lined path up the hill and climb the tower. The garden is incredibly quiet, despite the roaring traffic outside, providing a serene retreat from the city. *Via Giardino Giusti (cross Ponte Nuovo and walk east).* ☎ *045/8034029. Admission 5€. Daily 9am–8pm in the summer and 9am–7pm in the winter.*

FREE ➜ **Piazza delle Erbe** ★★ Once a produce and spice market (hence the name, "herbs square"), today the piazza is home to a mushroomlike colony of white-umbrellaed stalls selling mostly tourist kitsch, including some particularly ghastly ROMEO AND JULIET UNIVERSITY OF LOVE T-shirts. The market atmosphere still persists today, as crowds of both locals and tourists mingle among the wares and then soak it all up over an espresso from one of the cafes lining the piazza. In the afternoons, tour groups pack in to photograph the stunning buildings (some with their gorgeous original frescoes fading on upper floors), and to pose on the platform where, once upon a time, criminals were pounded with produce by angry mobs. Don't leave Piazza delle Erbe without walking underneath the curved **whale bone** hanging below the Arco della Costa ("arch of the rib"); according to Veronese legend, this primitive polygraph will fall on top of the first person to pass under it who has never told a lie. After more than 300 years in place, the bone has yet to fall. *Between Corto Porta Borsari and via Mazzino.*

➜ **Piazza dei Signori** ★ Just about everything in this wonderfully evocative medieval piazza (besides the 19th-century statue of Dante) was under construction at the time this guide was researched. By publication time, however, the renovations should be complete, and visitors will once again be able to appreciate how much effort it takes to keep this place looking so old, yet so pristine. Dante is honored in the piazza because he spent time in Verona after being exiled from his native Florence, and before dying in Ravenna. The **Torre dei Lamberti,** a 12th-century tower, offers great panoramic views of Verona to those who manage to climb to its 85m (279-ft.) top (3€ to get to the top by elevator, 2€ to climb it on your own two feet). Also in the square are the 13th-century residence of the Della Scala family, once powerful rulers of the city; the Palazzo della Ragione, a 12th-century Gothic palace; and the Loggia del Consiglio (Portico of the Counsel), located behind the Dante statue. Nearby the Arche Scaligere, in front of the church of Santa Maria Antica, are the intricate marble sepulchres and wrought-iron fence of the Della Scala princes' open-air mausoleum, including the tombs of Cangrande ("Big Dog"), Cansignorio ("Dog Lord"), and Mastino II ("Mastiff the Second"). *Between Corso Sant'Anastasia and Via Della Costa.*

Verona Festivals, Events & Entertainment

○ **Verona Opera Festival** ★★★: The annual opera season, with performances held in the spectacular, open-air Arena di

Verona (p. 508), runs June to August, with full-scale productions of *Aïda, Carmen,* and *Madame Butterfly* last summer (2006). A detailed schedule is available at the tourist office or on the website. Depending on the location of the seat, tickets run anywhere from 14€–142€. Box office: Via Dietro Anfiteatro 6B; call center: ☎ 045/8005151; www.arena.it

◌ **Shakespeare Festival** ★: The main highlights of this festival, running June to August at the Teatro Romano, are the Italian versions of Shakespeare's classic plays. Other performances include jazz concerts and ballet shows. Check with the tourist office for a detailed schedule.

Shopping

For souvenirs, visit the jumble of stands in Piazza della Erbe (see listing, above). Elegant Veronese outfit themselves at the swanky shops and designer boutiques that line Via Mazzini and Corso Borsari—good places for window-shopping for those of us who can't justify spending 300€ on a pair of shoes.

You'll find a concentration of vendors selling antiques or old bric-a-brac in the streets around **Sant'Anastasia,** or head to **Piazza delle Erbe** for a more or less constant roster of merchants in flea market–style kiosks selling dusty, and often junkier, collectibles of yesteryear, along with herbs, fruits, and vegetables.

Padua (Padova): St. Anthony and the University

42km (26 miles) W of Venice, 81km (50 miles) E of Verona, 32km (20 miles) E of Vicenza

When Venice's crowds and—in summer—smelly canals become overwhelming, a mere 30-minute train ride will magically transport you to Padua, which may lack some of the beauty of its neighbor, but is nonetheless a cool, peaceful haven with enough of its own parks, sights, and piazzas to warrant at least a day's exploration. If you do visit Padua, you'll often find yourself surrounded by religious pilgrims, who flock to the **Basilica di Sant'Antonio** in droves from all over the world.

Padua is also a well-established university town; the University of Padua was founded in 1222, students in the past have included the likes of Dante, Galileo, and Donatello. This leads to an interesting mix of people, as pilgrims and ancient-looking monks and nuns mix with crowds of students hanging out in between classes. You're likely to go all day without hearing any English here: most of the locals who actually do speak the language will often reply in Italian. Padua is also home to the **Scrovegni Chapel,** known by some as the "Sistine Chapel of the North,"

which has celebrated frescoes by Giotto. Although certainly not as exciting as the other big Veneto towns, Padua most definitely has her charm, even for the non-religious.

Getting There

BY TRAIN

The **train** is best if you're coming from Venice, Milan, or Bologna. Trains depart for and arrive from Venice once every 30 minutes (trip time: 30 min.), costing 7.50€ one-way. For information and schedules, call ☎ **892021** in Italy. Padua's main rail terminus is at **Piazza Stazione,** north of the historic core and outside the 16th-century walls. A bus will connect you to the center.

Left luggage, next to the tourist information office, costs 3.87€ (exactly!) for 24 hours, daily 6am–9:30pm.

BY BUS

Buses from Venice arrive every 30 minutes (trip time: 45 min.), costing 3.10€ one-way. There are also connections from Vicenza

Padua

Information ⓘ

Via Toti
Via A. da Bassano
Via P. Sarpi
ARCELLA
Stazione F.S. ⓘ
Via Jacopo d'Avanzo
Via Monta
Porta Trento
Via Citolo da Perugia
Piazzale Stazione
Carlo Goldoni
Fiere di Padova
Via Nicolò Tommaseo
Via Pescarotto
Via P. Bronzetti
Porta Savonarola
Via Fusinato
Via Reggio di Bogio
Via di Sole
Via S. Giovanni Da Verdara
Piazza de Gasperi
Corso Garibaldi
Via Giotto
Via Trieste
Viale Colombo
Via Voltumo
Via Orsini
Piazza Petrarca
Piazza Eremitani
Chapel of the Scrovegni
Via L. Loredan
Porta Portello
Riviera A. Mussato
Via S. Fermo
Piazza Insurrezione
Piazza Garibaldi
Via Porciglia
Via F. Marzolo
Corso Milano
Via S. Lucia
Chiesa di Santa Sofia
Piazzetta Nievo
Via Belzoni
Chiesa di San Nicolò
Via Morgagni
Via Fallopio
Chiesa di San Massimo
Via S. Prosdocimo
Riviera
Via Vescovado
Piazza Duomo
Via Roma
Piazza Antenore
Via Cesare Battisti
Via Gabelli
CENTRO
Porta San Giovanni
Chiesa di San Tomaso
Paleocapa
V. Brondolo
Riv Tito Livio
Via del Santo
Via San Francesco
Parco Treves
Via Cernaia
Piazza Castello
V. Rogati
Via Umberto I
Via Rudena
Basilica di Sant'Antonio
Porta Pontecorvo
Porta Saracinesca
Porta
V. Torresino
V. Dimesse
Piazza del Santo
Via Cavalletto
Prato della Valle
Via Santa Maria in Vanzo
Via Cavazzana
Via 58 Fanteria
Via Goito
Via S. Pio X
Corso Vittorio Emanuele
Via Carducci
Via Sanmicheli
Via Marghera
Piazzale S. Croce
Porta S. Croce
Via G. Bruno

0 ___ 1/4 Mi
0 ___ 1/4 Km

Padua ● Venice
○ Florence
Rome ✪
○ Naples
ITALY

every 30 minutes (trip time: 30 min.) at 3.10€ one-way. Padua's bus station is at Via Trieste 42 (☎ **049-8206844**), near Piazza Boschetti (buses depart from Piazza Boschetti), 5 minutes from the rail station.

Getting Around

It's about a 20-minute walk from the train station to the heart of the city, but it's a pleasant stroll down Padua's main street, Corso del Popolo (which changes into Corso Garibaldi, Via Cavour, Via Roma, and then Via Umberto) if your baggage isn't too heavy. Once in the center, everything is within walking distance, and handy signs around town point towards all the main sights. If you'd prefer to take the bus, the major hub is in front of the train station, with buses running along Padua's main artery as well as to the major attractions. You can pick up a route map and buy tickets from the tourist office.

TOURIST OFFICES

The IAT Information Office is in the train station, offering very little paper material in English but a good free map, and the helpful staff are happy to answer questions (☎ **049/ 8752077**). It's open Monday through Saturday 9:15am to 7pm and Sunday 9am to noon. The Galleria Pedrocchi branch, near Piazza Cavour, is open Monday to Saturday 9:30am to 12:30pm and 3 to 7pm (☎ 049/8767927).

Culture 101: The Life of Saint Anthony

What does it take to have the most popular namesake in the country, and one of the most-visited churches in the world built in your honor? Saint Anthony was born in the early 13th century in Portugal, and was involved in military conquests until he found a higher calling and, after enrolling at the local monastery, went to Morocco for missionary work. On his return, a vicious typhoon swept his boat away, eventually casting it on the shores of Italy. Anthony found his way to Assisi where he became the spiritual son of Saint Francis, and a great preacher of the faith. After spending a great portion of his life in Padua, he died in the 1230s after performing such miracles as bringing dead infants back to life and even getting fish to listen to his preaching, and was pronounced a saint a mere 10 years after his death. Twenty years after that, the basilica in Padua was built for him. Anthony is best known to Catholics as the patron saint of lost objects, so pilgrims flock to his tomb to ask for the return of lost things—though if you've lost your passport, you should probably also visit the embassy. Pilgrims and other relic hunters also come to view his tongue and jawbone—still intact after nearly 700 years, and a sure sign of his amazing ability to spread the word of God.

Sleeping

When Venice and Verona are packed solid, Padua is a good place to spend the night—the other Veneto towns are a short train ride away, making the commute manageable. Near the train station, there are numerous accommodation options on Corso Garibaldi, though these tend to be a bit run down, and the area gets seedy at night. A far better option, especially for those who actually plan to spend some quality time in Padua, are the affordable and much nicer hotels centrally located near the basilica.

CHEAP

→ **Casa del Pellegrino** ★ A definite no-frills place, but a great bargain if you don't mind furniture and decor that's probably older than you, and the location near the basilica can't be beat. Rooms have TV and A/C, and the hotel has a restaurant, bar and lounge, and parking. *Via Cesarotti 21 (near Piazza del Santo).* ☎ *049/8239711. www. casadelpellegrino.com. Single from 39€ without bath, 53€ with bath; double from 50€*

without bath, 64€ with bath. Breakfast 6€. Closed for a few weeks in December.

→ **Ostello Citta di Padova (HI)** ★ Popular with Italian students, this is the only hostel in town, and is definitely a real bargain, although you'll have to put up with the sterile environment and strict rules typical of HIs. Rooms are large and clean, although bathrooms get a little crusty towards the end of the day. The hostel is in a quiet area close to the city center, and has Internet access, laundry, and a common room. *Via Aleardi 30 (take Via Rogati off of Via Roma, and then turn left on Via Aleardi).* ☎ *049/8752219. pdyhti@tin.it. 8-bed dorms 15€. Breakfast included. HI membership technically required, but they often don't bother to check.*

DOABLE

→ **Hotel Al Santo** ★ You'll find nothing fancy in this cute little place close to the basilica, just basic but nicely sized rooms. The hotel's restaurant provides decent grub at affordable prices. *Via del Santo 147.* ☎ *049/ 8752131. www.alsanto.it. Single 55€–65€, double 80€–100€. Breakfast included.*

➔ **Hotel Corso** ★ Close to the train station, this hotel is one of the better options among the budget hotels in this area, although it's getting to be a bit past its prime (don't be fooled by the posh lobby). Rooms could use some renovations, but are comfortable, with TV and A/C, and offer great views of the Giardino dell'Arena across the street, and the staff are friendly. *Corso del Popolo 2.* ☎ *049/8750822. htlcrs@virgilio.it. Single from 78€, double from 103€. Breakfast included.*

➔ **Hotel Sant Antonio** ★★ A friendly, family-run place in a quiet area in the western section of town. The rooms here are on the small side, but immaculately clean. The doubles, with upstairs annex, are a steal—managers swear there's no extra charge for all the extra room. All rooms have phone, TV and A/C. *Via San Fermo 118 (off Via Matteotti).* ☎ *049/8751393. www.hotelsantantonio.it. Single 40€ with shared bathroom, 46€ with*

OKKIO! Get a Room . . . (Not!)

Italians are famous the world over for their affectionate behavior; here, even guys will kiss each other on the cheek when they meet on the street. And anyone who has spent time in the country knows that Italians are not at all shy about public displays of affection. But this is taken to the extreme here. Maybe it's because Padua is a university town, and therefore extra hip and laid-back, or maybe there's something in the Padua water that increases libido; children playing and adults strolling in Prato Della Valle have to pick their way through amorous couples getting hot and heavy on the grass. Locals seem to accept this make-out fest without batting an eye, so try not to gawk yourself as you may spoil the mood.

private bathroom; double with private bathroom 89€. Breakfast 7€.

SPLURGE

➔ **Hotel Majestic Toscanelli** ★★ A beautifully decorated government-rated four-star hotel with a gardenlike atmosphere. Rooms are in the process of being renovated, increasing the beauty of this hotel, and once complete they will be stunning; furnished with classy mahogany furniture and satiny fabrics, you'll never want to leave. The hotel has wireless Internet, parking, dinner restaurant, and bar. *Via dell'Arco 2 (off Via Marsala, off Via Roma).* ☎ *049/663244. www.toscanelli.com. Single 95€–115€, double 153€–172€, suite 205€–215€. Breakfast included.*

Eating

For fresh foodstuffs, visit the produce markets in Piazza delle Erbe and Piazza della Frutta. Here, you will view what are undoubtedly the largest mushrooms and plumpest grapes you'll ever see. The lane between the two markets has fresh meats and seafood.

CAFES

➔ **Bottega del Caffè** ★ Next door to Panificio alla Rosa, and right on Piazza dei Signori, you can have a drink inside, or pull up to the take-out window and throw down an espresso; locals stop by on bicycles for a quick caffeine fix without even dismounting. *Piazza dei Signori 25. Specialty coffees 1€–2€. Mon–Sat 7am–7:30pm.*

➔ **Caffe Pedrocchi** ★★ This place is a hot spot in the heart of Padua; impossible to miss, this huge cafe that dominates Piazza Cavour. Initially opened in 1831, and remodeled after being badly damaged during WWII, it has historically been a popular gathering place for intellectuals and political groups; you can just imagine Galileo discussing his latest finds at a table in the corner when he studied at the university here. Today, the Pedrocchi is popular with tourists and swank *padovani.*

Padua's Official Website

··

The official website of the tourist office is **www.turismopadova.it**, and offers information on attractions, accommodation, and events as well as general information on the city.

The cafe looks super-fancy and even intimidating from outside, but staff are friendly and drinks are only moderately expensive—and even cheaper if you stand at the bar. *Via VIII Febbraio 15 (in Piazza Cavour).* ☎ *049/8781231. www.caffepedrocchi.it. Daily 9:30am–12:30pm and 3:30–8pm. Bar open 9am–9pm, until midnight on weekends.*

→ **Panificio alla Rosa** ★★ A small bakery offering delicious takeout goodies near Piazza dei Signori, where the staff dress in charming uniforms straight out of a fairy tale. *Via Dante 6.* ☎ *049/8751991. www.panificionline.it. Baked goods from 1€. Thurs–Tues 7:45am–1pm and 5–8pm. Cash only.*

CHEAP

→ **Alexander Bar** ★★ PANINI   One lone table sits out front, but plenty others fill cozy corners in the back. Popular with foreign students, this is a good place for a meal or a drink at night, offering up cheap panini and beer. *Via San Francesco 38.* ☎ *049/652884. Panini from 3€; coffee and beer from 2.50€. Mon–Fri 10am–2am; Sat–Sun noon–2am.*

→ **Brek** ★★ ITALIAN CAFETERIA   Good old Brek, a chain of cafeteria-style restaurants serving up hearty—and cheap—pastas and salads. The food must be good, as it's always packed, and usually with locals. Pick up items in the cafeteria, grab a flask of cheap wine, and check out with the cashier before sitting down at a table. *Piazza Cavour 20.* ☎ *049/8753788. www.brek.com. Primi 3€–6€; secondi 3.50€–8€. Daily 11:30am–3pm and 6–10pm.*

→ **Café Des Artes** ★ ITALIAN   One of several joints along Via del Santo, especially popular with the student crowd at lunch time who rush through for a cheap and tasty bite between classes. *Via del Santo 64. Paninis 2.40€–3€; lunch specials, such as pizza, beer and coffee for 4€. Daily 7am–1am.*

DOABLE

→ **La Corte dei Leoni** ★★ PADUAN   The menu is small, but quality is what counts here. Dine on nouveau Paduan cuisine on the outdoor terrace, or sample a glass of wine from the overwhelmingly large selection in the cellar. *Via Pietro d'Abano 1.* ☎ *049/8750083. Primi 7.50€–10€; secondi 14€–20€. Tues–Sun 12:30–2:30pm and Tues–Sat 6:30pm–12:30am.*

→ **Pizzeria Al Borgo** ★★ PIZZA   This popular restaurant next to the basilica offers a huge selection of pizzas—it's almost more fun to randomly choose from the Italian-language menu rather than trying to decipher what's what. Take in the view from the terrace or have a seat in the cozy restaurant while watching your pizza being assembled and put into the oven in the open kitchen behind the bar. *Via Luca Beludi 56 (next to the basilica).* ☎ *049/8758857. Margherita pizza 3.70€, other varieties up to 8.50€. 2€ cover charge. Mon–Fri 11am–midnight; Sat–Sun 11am–1pm and 3pm–midnight.*

Partying

Padua is eerily quiet in the evening, considering that it is after all a university town. Any action that does actually occur is in **Piazza delle Erbe,** where groups of students hang out and socialize in the evening before maybe heading out to a bar later on. This is a good place to head at the start of the night to find out where the latest hot spots are.

The oldest wine bar in town is **Enoteca da Severino,** Via del Santo 44 (☎ **049-650697**). **La Corte dei Leoni,** Via Pietro d'Abano 1 (☎ **049-8750083**), is more of a restaurant, but it offers live music on weekends.

BARS & CLUBS

→ **Extra Extra** ★ Padua's busiest club, although it's a bit of a trek to get here—you'll have to take a taxi or make friends with a local car owner. Locals dressed in flashy attire pack the dance floor and dance the night away to pounding techno beats. Don't even bother showing up before midnight unless you want the entire dance floor to yourself. *Via Ciamician 145. Daily 11pm–4am.*

→ **Fishmarket** ★ Market is the right word for this bar, where a mainly student crowd comes to pick up a different kind of fresh catch of the day. There is often live music here, and good drink specials; Wednesdays are usually packed when the bar offers two-for-for drink specials. *Via Fra Paolo Sarpi 37.* ☎ *348/514-0628 (cellphone). www.fish market.it.*

→ **Highlander Scottish Pub** ★ This Italian version of the Scottish pub is a popular place where British music blares and good beer flows behind the bar. *Via San Martino Solferino 69.* ☎ *049/659977. Daily 11am–2am.*

Sightseeing

EXPLORING PADUA

The main attraction for the pilgrims who flock to Padua is the Basilica di Sant'Antonio and its secondary attractions. Even if you're not here for religious salvation, the architecture and artistry of the basilica are enough reason to visit. The other big draw, and more of an artistic than religious attraction, is the Cappella degli Scrovegni (Scrovegni Chapel). The Archeological Museum and Art Museum are worthy of a visit, as is Palazzo Zuckerman. While in Padua, allow for some time to stroll along Via Roma—through its various name changes—to soak up the student environment, and relax among the Roman statues in Prato della Valle. You can spend a full day exploring the town, or take 2 days for a slower-paced visit and more hanging-out time.

FREE → **Basilica di Sant'Antonio** ★★★ Drawing millions of pilgrims and curious tourists every year, this building dominates the Paduan skyline. It was built in the 13th century to honor Padua's patron saint, St. Anthony (see sidebar above). Although it's full of architecture and art worthy of admiration, most flock to the Basilica for contact with St. Anthony's physical remains: There is a constant lineup of those waiting to caress his tomb or view his still-intact **tongue and jawbone.** While in the basilica, watch the entertaining **Mostra,** a retro-style presentation on the life of the saint (with free souvenirs handed out to those who make it to the end), and consider visiting the Museum of Popular Devotion, which houses various objects symbolizing the intense devotion for Saint Anthony. The courtyards of the basilica also have some fine statues and gardens. *Piazza del Santo. Information office:* ☎ *049/8789722. www.basilicadelsanto.org. Basilica: daily 6:20am–7pm in the winter and 7:45pm in the summer. Mostra (allow 30 min.): daily 9am–12:30pm and 2:30–6pm. Museum: 9am–1pm and 2:30–6:30pm. Free admission.*

→ **Cappella degli Scrovegni** ★★ Positioned as the Sistine Chapel of northern Italy, the chapel was built by Enrico Scrovegni in the 14th century as a means of redeeming his father's soul. Huge crowds flock here to gaze in awe at Giotto's brilliant blue-tinged

The PadovaCard Saves Time, Money

The **PadovaCard** is a worthy investment if you plan on seeing the cultural sights here. At a mere 14€, only a few euros more than admission to the Cappella degli Scrovegni, it's valid for 48 hours *and* includes admission to the major sights as well as free public transit.

floor-to-ceiling frescoes depicting the lives of Jesus and the Virgin Mary, and the various vices and virtues (in the Last Judgment scene, above the entrance, look for Scrovegni offering the chapel to Mary). The chapel has undergone extensive restorations by the city, and in order to further protect the frescoes, there are strict rules for entering: Visitors must buy a ticket for a particular 30-minute time slot which involves hanging around in the waiting room for 15 minutes. Next, you have to pass through a high-tech quarantine area that stabilizes humidity and air purity—to protect the frescoes, and to keep the chapel from catching the bird flu. Once inside the chapel, you can admire Giotto's frescoes for 15 minutes before being herded out for the next group. To learn more about Giotto and his work, visit the adjacent multimedia room. *Piazza Eremitani 8, off Corso Garibaldi.* ☎ *049/8204513. www.cappella degliscrovegni.it. Admission 12€, students 5€ (includes entrance to the Musei Civico). Daily 9am–7pm. Free March 25. While reservations are technically required at least 72 hrs in advance, you can often just show up at the ticket office and see if any tickets are available. To reserve: call the reservation line at* ☎ *049/201-0020, or reserve online. Arrive at the ticket office at least 10 min before your time slot.*

FREE ➜ **Giardino dell'Arena** ★ The gardens surrounding the Cappella degli Scrovegni make for a pleasant break from the busy city road outside, and a nice place to rest after

visiting the chapel. *Piazza Eremitani 8. Feb–Nov daily 8am–5:45pm, March–Oct 8am–6:45pm, Apr–Sept 8am–7:15pm, July–Aug 8am–8:45pm.*

➜ **Musei Civico** Padua's city museum actually encompasses three museums. The **Archeological Museum** ★ is on the ground floor of the same complex as the Cappella degli Scrovegni. Statues, sculptures, mosaics, and other various Roman relics from as far back as the 8th century B.C. are housed here, as well as some interesting Egyptian and Greek artifacts. Upstairs, the **Art Museum** ★ contains over 3,000 Veneto paintings from the 14th to 19th centuries, including works by such greats as Giotto, Bellini, and Titian. Across the street, **Palazzo Zuckerman** ★ is a well-preserved example of one of the new city bourgeois buildings constructed a century ago. Enrico Zuckerman, a wealthy button factory manager, commissioned Milanese architect Filippo Arsio to build his dream home. Admire it from the outside, and then visit the two museums inside: the applied and decorative arts museum on the first floor, with various objects used by Paduans since the Middle Ages such as glass, ceramics, jewelry, and furniture—which highlights why furniture produced in the area was in such great demand in the past. The costume collection is interesting, though the coin collection is not. *Piazza Eremitani 8* ☎ *049/8204551. www.padovanet.it/museicivici. Admission 12€ including entrance to Cappella degli Scrovegni, or 10€ for the museums only;*

Hop on the Citysightseeing Bus

If you're short on time, are tired of walking around, and prefer a more structured visit, **Citysightseeing** operates a hop-on hop-off tour bus from May to October which stops at all major sights and piazzas. When you see something that catches your interest, get off the bus and take a look around and then catch the next bus that comes along, usually around 30 minutes later. Pick up the bus at any of the principal attractions, such as the basilica, Piazza delle Erbe, or Prato della Valle. ☎ **049/7629793.** www.padova.city-sightseeing.it. 24-hour tickets cost 13€; buy them on board.

students 5€ including admission to Cappella degli Scrovegni. Tues–Sun 9am–7pm.

→ **Palazzo della Ragione** ★★ This huge building marks the historical center of Padua, and is today still in the middle of the action, surrounded by the city's bustling markets. The most striking thing about the building is its sheer size. Built in the early 13th century, it initially housed stores and workshops on the ground floor and city offices on the top floor, until it was converted to the city law courts in the 14th century. Upon entering the building, let your eyes adjust to the dim lighting and then admire the unique frescoes that depict the astrological cycles rather than the typical religious fare. In the west end is a large 15th-century wooden horse donated to the city nearly 200 years ago. In the northeast corner sits the so-called Stone of Shame: in the Middle Ages, debtors were made to sit on the stone in their underwear before being banished from the city. *Via VIII Febbraio.* ☎ *049/8205006. Admission 8€, students 4€. Feb–Oct Tues–Sun 9am–7pm; Nov–Jan Tues–Sun 9am–6pm.*

FREE → **Prato Della Valle** ★★ What was once a large Roman theater is today one of Europe's largest piazzas, located at the convergence of Via Umberto I, Via Cavalletto and Via Cavazzana. On the outer edge, pedestrians, joggers, and dog walkers make their rounds. Inside, a moat is rimmed with statues of famous Paduans of the past, and several bridges cross over to the inner grassy knoll with a fountain in the center. Here, students study, make out, and nap between classes under the shade of inviting trees. In the summer, festivals and carnivals are often held here.

Padua Festivals, Events & Entertainment

On June 13, Pilgrims flock the city to mark the anniversary of the death of **St. Anthony.** And from October through April, you can enjoy Teatro **Verdi**'s classical music season (www.teatroverdipd.it).

Shopping

Because its economy doesn't rely on tourism, you'll find a wide roster of upscale goods and luxury items, and less emphasis on souvenirs and handcrafts here. To windowshop on the good life *alla Padovese,* trek through the neighborhood around the landmark **Piazza Insurrezione,** especially the **Galleria Borghese,** a conglomeration of shops off Via San Fermo.

Droves of shoppers head to the **Prato delle Valle** on the third Sunday of every month, when more than 200 antiques and collectibles vendors set up shop for the day. The square, one of the largest in all Europe, also hosts a smaller **weekly market** on Saturday. Shoes from nearby Brenta factories are the prevalent product, but the range of goods offered remains eclectic.

If you found the designer shops of Venice too pricey, you'll encounter the same merchandise by walking along **Via San Fermo,** where you'll find Prada, Armani, Gucci, Hermès, Max Mara, and the like.

VENICE & THE VENETO

Treviso: Trip to a Market Town

25km (16 miles) N of Venice, 50km (31 miles) NE of Padua

It's hard to believe that Treviso was severely damaged during WWII. The well-to-do city—the capital of the Veneto—has the calm pace of a place that has not changed much over the past few centuries. The only signs of change are the various WWII monuments and memorials in Piazza dei Trecento. Otherwise, the city has been beautifully restored and still very much resembles the quaint market town it has been since medieval times.

Treviso is also the world headquarters of United Colors of Benetton, and you'll find of effortlessly chic locals around town that attest to this fashionable heritage. It's also the birthplace of tiramisu, that delectable dessert!

Getting There

BY TRAIN

Treviso is about a 30-minute **train** ride from Venice, on the Venice-Udine train line. The train station sits to the south of the town in Piazzale Duca d'Aosta. The ticket office is open daily from 6am to 9pm. Left luggage is held for 3€ for first 12 hours, 2€ for additional 12-hour periods. The station is open Mon through Friday 7am to 8pm, and Saturday, Sunday, and holidays 8:30am to 6pm. Photo identification required.

BY BUS

The station at Lungosile Mattei 21 gets **buses** on the La Marca bus line (☎ **0422-577311**) from Bassano del Grappa nine times daily, a trip of 1 hour costing 4€ one-way. From Padua, buses arrive every 30 minutes; the trip takes 1 hour, 10 minutes, and costs 4.50€ one-way. The ACTV line (☎ **0422-541281**) runs two buses an hour from Venice, a 30-minute trip for 3€. The ACTV office in Treviso is at Lungo Sile Mattei Antonio 29.

BY CAR

Take A11 from Venice through Mestre for 10km (6¹/₄ miles); head northeast on A4 for 5km (3 miles), and then take Route S13 for 16km (10 miles) north to Treviso.

Getting Around

Treviso is small enough to navigate by foot. From the train station, at the southern edge of the city center, follow Via Roma north over the river and through various name changes to Piazza dei Signori, the center of town—in all, about a 10-minute walk.

Treviso Tourist Office

The APT tourist office is in Piazza Monte di Pietà 8, behind Piazza dei Signori (☎ 0422/547632; www.provincia.treviso.it; Sun–Mon 9am–12:30pm, Tues–Sat 9am–noon and 3–6pm).

Sleeping

Treviso doesn't have a whole lot to offer in the way of accommodation, as most visitors only come for the day (there's not much to see or do at night here). If you're looking for a peaceful night in one of Italy's wealthiest towns, try one of these places, all located within the city walls:

CHEAP

➜ **Albergo Campeol** ★★ A family hotel centrally located close to Piazza dei Signori, with bright rooms that have TV and phone, and excellent views of the town in some. The elegant lobby is decorated with cheery murals painted on the walls. *Piazza Ancilotto 4. ☎ 0422/56601. www.albergocampeol.it. Single 52€, double 83€, triple 98€. Breakfast 5€.*

➜ **Tre Santi Hotel** If you're looking for a cheap place to stay and don't mind being a bit out of town, check out this little hotel. Rooms are basic (what you'd expect from a budget hotel?) but clean. *Via Postumia 25. ☎ 0422/55109. Single 43€, double 60€.*

DOABLE

➜ **Hotel Carlton** ★★ A four-star establishment just north of the train station, with gorgeous modern rooms that have phone, A/C, TV, and a bathtub if you're lucky, all at a great price. The hotel has Internet access, laundry service, bar, and restaurant with garden terrace. Parking is available. *Largo Porta Altinia 15, off Via Roma. ☎ 0422/411620. www.hotel carlton.it. Mon–Thurs single 95€, double 130€; Fri–Sun single 70€, double 100€. Breakfast included.*

Eating

CHEAP

➜ **Biffi** ★ CAFE   Cafe life rules in Treviso, and this is the nicest of the three cafes lining Piazza del Signori: It has the largest covered seating area, which is a blessing in the summer heat, and a cozy tavern-style dining area inside, all with views of the action in the busy piazza. Perfect for cheap snacks and light meals in a casual environment. *Piazza dei Signori 28.* ☎ *0422/540784. www.biffitv.it. Coffee from .80€; panini 2€–3€.*

➜ **Brek** ★★ ITALIAN SELF-SERVICE   Good old Brek, a chain of cafeteria-style restaurants serving up hearty and cheap pastas and salads. The food must be good, as it's always packed, and usually with locals. Pick up items in the cafeteria, grab a flask of cheap wine, and check out with the cashier before sitting down. This location, near the train station, has a pretty garden terrace overlooking the main street. *Corsa del Popolo 25 (at Viale Cardona).* ☎ *0422/59012. Daily 11:30am–3pm and 6:30–10pm.*

➜ **Leccolandia** ★★ GELATO   A great place to stop for a cool treat at the end of Via Calmaggiore, across the street from the Duomo. Pick your flavor and enjoy it from the steps of the Duomo. *One scoop .80€, 2 scoops 1.50€. Mon 11am–11:30pm; Wed–Sun 10am–11:30pm.*

DOABLE

➜ **Da Pino** ★★ ITALIAN   Hearty dishes in the center of the action in Treviso . . . what more could you ask for? Of the restaurants in Piazza dei Signori, Da Pino is the best option for a full meal, with a huge selection of pizzas, as well as filling meat dishes like veal steak and wiener schnitzel. *Piazza dei Signori 23.* ☎ *0422/56426. www.dapino.it. Pizza 5.50€–9€; primi 6€–10€; secondi 10€–16€. Cover charge 2€; 10% service charge added to bill. Daily 12pm–2:30pm and 7pm–1am.*

Sightseeing

EXPLORING TREVISO

Treviso is worth a visit not because of any special sights in particular, but because of the atmosphere: Everything here happens at a pace that is slow enough to entice any busybody to relax, yet lively and pretty enough to keep visitors and residents from utter boredom. Spend a few hours, or an entire day, watching locals gather around Piazza dei Signori, and window shop along Via Calmaggiore, the main shopping street—but beware of the hefty price tags in the fancy stores . Be sure to investigate the quiet cobblestone alleyways running off Calmaggiore that will transport you back in time hundreds of years. Throughout town, the river Sile and its charming network of **canals**★★ are crossed by pedestrian bridges and shaded by venerable elm trees and elegant palazzi that line their banks. Outside Treviso's old city walls there is very little of interest—the area is mainly residential—and not as rewarding to explore.

FREE ➜ **Duomo** ★   Although it was built only in the 1830s, it looks much older, with its marble staircase and Romanesque pillars. Inside, you'll find 14th-century frescoes by the altar and crypt, including Titian's

Something Fishy in Treviso

For a picturesque slice of old Treviso, check out the **fish market** on the islets in the Cagnan canal (every morning Mon–Sat). In any other Italian city, this would probably be some kind of commercially exploited tourist attraction, but since Treviso is pretty much ignored by mass tourism, the market is a truly authentic place to see multiple generations of fishmongers make their living.

A Day Trip: The Wine Roads from Treviso

The rolling foothills of the Dolomites around Treviso are known for their fine wines. If you have a car, take a drive along the two highways known as the **Strade dei Vini del Piave** in honor of the nearby Piave River. Both begin at the medieval town of **Conegliano,** where the tourist office is at XX Settembre 61 (☎ 0438-21230), open from Tuesday to Friday 9am to 12:30pm and 3 to 6pm, and Saturday and Sunday from 9am to 12:30pm and 2:30 to 6pm.

You won't find route numbers associated with either of these wine roads, and each is badly signposted en route, beginning in central Conegliano. The less interesting is the **Strada del Vino Rosso (Red Wine Road),** running through 40km (25 miles) of humid flatlands southeast of Conegliano. Significant points en route include the scenic hamlets of Oderzo, Motta, and Ponte di Piave.

Much more scenic and evocative is the **Strada del Vino Bianco (White Wine Road),** or, more specifically, the **Strada del Prosecco,** meandering through the foothills of the Dolomites for about 39km (24 miles) northwest of Conegliano, ending at Valdobbiadene. It passes through regions famous for their sparkling *prosecco,* a quality white meant to be drunk young, with the characteristic taste and smell of ripe apples, wisteria, and acacia honey. The most charming of the hamlets you'll encounter (blink an eye and you'll miss them) are San Pietro di Feletto, Follina, and Pieve di Soligno. Each is awash with family-run cantinas, kiosks, and roadside stands, all selling the fermented fruits of the local harvest and offering platters of prosciutto, local cheese, and crusty bread.

The best hotel for establishing a base here is in Conegliano. The **Canon d'Oro,** Via XX Settembre 131, 31015 Conegliano (☎ 0438-34246), occupies a 15th-century building near the rail station and charges from 105€ for a double or 140€ for a suite.

If you're looking for a bite to eat in Conegliano, try our favorite restaurant, **Tre Panoce,** Via Vecchia Trevigiano 50 (☎ 0438-60071). Occupying a 16th-century stone building, it charges around 26€ for full meals that include a celebration of whatever is in season (wine not included). Your pasta could be flavored with radicchio, fresh mushrooms, wild herbs, or local cheese. Tre Panoce is in the hills above Conegliano, half a mile from the town center. It's open from Tuesday to Saturday noon to 2:30pm and 8 to 10pm (closed Aug). The most formal restaurant in town is **Al Salisà,** Via XX Settembre 2 (☎ 0438-24288), in a stone building with 12th-century foundations. The excellent menu includes roasted veal with wild herbs, sea bass with seasonal vegetables and basil-flavored white-wine sauce, and fettuccine with wild duck. Expect to spend 25€ and up for a meal. It's open from Thursday to Tuesday noon to 3pm and 7:30 to 11pm.

Annunciation. Piazza del Duomo. Daily 7:30am–noon and 3:30–7pm. Sun and holidays 7:30am–1pm and 3:30–8pm. Modest dress required. No entrance during mass.

➔ **Museo Civico** ★ Treviso's city museum contains two sections: The first is devoted to ancient artifacts such as bronze relics and Roman ruins, neither of which are very exciting. Rather, spend time in the museum's painting collection, which houses works by such Veneto greats as Bellini and Titian, as well as other Italian painters. *Borgo Cavour*

24. ☎ 0422/658422. Admission 3€. Tues–Sat 9am–12:30pm and 2:30–5pm, Sun and holidays 9am–noon.

FREE → **Piazza dei Signori** ★★ The center of town, and the default meeting place for all Trevigiani. The main attractions here are the large cafes that line the piazza, perfect for resting your feet and enjoying a beverage while you watch all the action. On the east side of the piazza lies Palazzo dei Trecento, filled with WWII monuments and memorials. Climb up the stairs for a good view of the area.

Shopping

Treviso is incredibly fashionable considering its small size. A stroll down Via Calmaggiore, with all the major designers well represented, highlights the affluence of Treviso's citizens, who all seem to be able to afford to shop here. The area around Piazza Borsa has even more stores that are best appreciated from the window if you don't want to fall into ridiculous credit card debt.

Treviso Festivals, Events & Entertainment

On or around August 15, there's the Feast of the Assumption, with street theatre, dance, music competitions, and other celebrations. And Treviso has a **monthly antiques fair** on Borgo Cavour on the fourth Sunday of every month (except July).

The cherries grown in the surrounding area ripen in June. At that time, you can buy them at all local markets, especially the **open-air market** on Tuesday and Saturday morning sprawling across Via Pescheria. Otherwise, one of the best selections is found at **Pam** supermarket, Piazza Borsa 18 (☎ **0422-583913**).

Vicenza: Oh, Those Villas!

32km (20 miles) W of Padua, 74km (46 miles) W of Venice, 51km (32 miles) E of Verona

Vicenza's local pride is based on two claims to fame: money and architecture. The town has one of the highest incomes in the country and in fact has long been a center of wealth, and there are tons of gorgeous **villas** ★★★ in the surroundings attesting to this. Otherwise, a walk through the center, where the wealthy citizens stroll among fashionable boutiques, also highlights their prosperity. Second, Vicenza is synonymous with 16th-century architect Andrea di Pietro della Gondola, better known simply as Palladio, who moved to Vicenza as a youth and made his artistic dreams a reality in Vicenza's various piazzas. In Vicenza, if the architecture is not Palladio's, then it is most likely the work of one of his students.

Getting There

Most visitors arrive from Venice via **train** (trip time: 1 hr.), costing 9€ one-way. Trains also

arrive frequently from Padua (trip time: 25 min.), charging 4.45€ one-way. For information and schedules, call ☎ 892021 in Italy. Vicenza's rail station is at Piazza Stazione (Campo Marzio), at the southern edge of Viale Roma.

The ticket office is open daily 6am to 8:30pm. Luggage storage is available from 9am to 1pm and 3 to 7pm for 3.87€ per 24 hours. Vicenza is also accessible by **bus** from the major Veneto towns. The bus station is just to the left of the train station.

Getting Around

The train and bus stations lie to the south of the center; to get to the heart of the town, walk up Viale Roma, across from the train station, and turn right onto Corso Palladio when you reach the end of the street at Giardini

Palladio: The Man Behind Vicenza's Most Famous Cribs

Everything in and around Vicenza screams Palladio, the name of its most famous resident, and if you can toss around some basic knowledge of this architectural juggernaut while in town, you'll have locals eating out of your hand.

Hailed as one of the greatest architects in the world, Andrea di Pietro della Gondola was born in 1508 in Padua. As a teenager, he worked as a stone-cutter's apprentice before running away and landing up in Vicenza, where he resumed the stonecutting life. But fate was to have a different plan in mind for him, and destiny came in the form of an elderly scholar, Gian Giorgio Trissino, who hired the young man to help him renovate his villa. Trissino, who dubbed Andrea as Palladio, served as a mentor by introducing him not only to the principles of classical architecture, but also to the wealthy patrons in the area. A year later, Palladio began construction on his first villa, and a decade later found himself the most sought-after architect in the Veneto, receiving commissions for various villas in the area as well as several religious buildings in Venice. Inspired by the **strong, symmetrical, colonnaded façades** of **Roman temples,** Palladio's architecture is typically **square or cruciform in shape,** with subsidiary buildings connected to the main villa by **classical colonnaded porticoes.** Palladio also managed to find time to publish several architecture books; his most famous, *I Quattro Libri dell'Architettura (The Four Books of Architecture),* was published in 1570 and is still in circulation today. Palladio died a proud old man in 1580, ensuring that his ideas lived on in the work of his students.

Salvi (Salvi Gardens). Vicenza is small enough to easily access everything by foot.

Tourist Office

The tourist office is at Piazza Matteotti 12, at the end of Corso Palladio, next to the Teatro Olimpico (☎ **044/320854;** www.vicenzae. org). It's open daily 9am to 1pm and 2 to 6pm. There is a branch office at Piazza dei Signori 8, open daily 9am to 2pm and 2:30 to 6pm.

Sleeping

HOSTEL

➔ **Ostello Olimpico Vicenza (HI)** ★ As sterile and devoid of atmosphere as any other HI, but unlike the others that are usually a trek to get to, this hostel is actually centrally located near the Museo Civico. This is the only hostel in town, and so your best bet for budget accommodation. Rooms are large, bright, and clean. The hostel has a TV room. *Via Giuriolo 9.* ☎ *044/4540222. Dorm 15.50€. HI membership required.*

CHEAP

➔ **Hotel Due Mori** ★ One of the oldest hotels in town, this family-run establishment is in an 18th-century building behind Piazza dei Signori. Rooms are basic but elegantly furnished with antique furniture. *Contrà Do Rode 24/26.* ☎ *044/4321886. www.hoteldue mori.com. Single with private bathroom 45€; double 52€ with shared bathroom, 77€ with private bathroom. Breakfast 5€.*

Doable

➔ **Hotel Castello** ★★ A swanky hotel with amenities that would usually come with a much higher price tag, such as a piano bar, sauna, gym, reading and TV room, and parking. Rooms are a bit dark but decently sized and have TV, phone, minibar, and A/C. *Contrà Piazza del Castello 24.* ☎ *044/4323585. www.hotelcastelloitaly.com. Single 90€, double 120€, triple 150€, four-bed suite 175€. Breakfast included.*

➔ **Hotel Giardini** ★ Clean, modern rooms in a centrally located hotel, with TV, A/C, minibar, and phone. The hotel has a bar, reading and TV room, and parking. *Via Giuriolo 10.* ☎ *044/ 4326458. www.hotelgiardini.com. Single 83€, double 114€, triple 119€. Breakfast included.*

SPLURGE

➔ **Hotel Campo Marzio** ★★ Stylish rooms are exquisitely decorated, each with a slightly different theme, and have TV, phone, A/C, and minibar. Recently renovated superior versions are worth the extra few euros for the Jacuzzi tub. The hotel has a restaurant, bar, and parking. *Viale Roma 21.* ☎ *044/ 4545700. www.hotelcampomarzio.com. Single 90€–155€, 99€–165€ for superior; double 134€–225€, 144€–238€ for superior. Breakfast included.*

Eating

CHEAP

➔ **Pizzeria Vesuvio** ★★ PIZZA A charming little place down a quiet alley off of Corso Palladio, with a large selection of pizzas and *bruschetta. On the first alley on the left from Musei Civici (#204). Pizza 3.50€–6€; panini 2.60€–3€; bruschetta 3.50€–4.70€. Daily noon–3pm and 6pm–midnight.*

➔ **Righetti** ★ ITALIAN A self-service trattoria offering up cheap, but tasty, eats.

Vicenza's Official Website

The official website of the Vicenza tourist office is **www.vicenzae.org,** with information on accommodation and restaurants, the town's sights, and events and festivals.

Choose from a changing variety of dishes, and enjoy your meal in the rustic, cozy dining room. *Piazza Duomo 3–4.* ☎ *0444/543135. Primi around 3€; entrees from 4€. Mon–Fri noon–2:30pm and 7–10pm. Cash only.*

DOABLE

➔ **Antica Casa della Malvasia** ★★ VICENZIAN This restaurant dominates an entire side street, with a large restaurant on one side and an upscale terrace on the other. There is also a casual bar, and live music at night. The menu changes daily. A huge selection of wines, so a good place to stop in for a drink. *Contrà delle Morette 5 (off Corso Palladio).* ☎ *0444/543704. Primi 4.70€; entrees 7.50€–12€.*

➔ **Nirvana Caffe** ★ CASUAL ITALIAN Centrally located next to the entrance to the Teatro Olimpico, with affordable, healthy vegetarian dishes in a casual environment— exactly what you'd expect from a place with such a new-age-y name. *Piazza Matteotti 8.* ☎ *0444/543111. Panini and bruschetta around 3.10€; salads 3.80€–7€; pasta dishes around 6€. Daily 8am–2am.*

Partying

➔ **Il Borsa** ★ A funky bar off of Piazza Signori. Stop in for a coffee during the day, or a drink at night. *On the middle alley leading off Piazza Signori. Coffee from 1€, beer from 2.50€, snacks 1.50€–4.80€; breakfast served 6€. Daily 9am–2am.*

Festivals & Events

In Vicenza you can enjoy music presented in settings of architectural splendor. The outdoor **Teatro Olimpico** (see review below), Piazza Matteotti (☎ **0444-222800**), hosts cultural events from April to late September. For information about the programs being presented, call the theater. Look for a changing program of classic Greek tragedy (*Oedipus Rex* is an enduring favorite), Shakespearean plays (sometimes translated into

Italian), chamber music concerts, and dance recitals. You can pick up schedules and buy tickets at the gate daily from 11am to 7pm. Tickets are 15€ to 50€, although in rare instances some nosebleed seats go for 7.50€.

Then there is a series of concerts scheduled in June, the **Concerti in Villa.** Every year, it includes chamber music performed in or near villas (often privately owned) in the city's outskirts. Look for orchestras set up on loggias or under formal pediments, and audiences sitting on chairs in gardens or inside. Note that these depend on the whims of both local musicians and villa owners. Contact the tourist office (p. 524) for details.

Sightseeing

Vicenza can easily be explored in a day. Its most attractive sights include the Teatro Olimpico and the various piazzas designed by Palladio and his students, especially Piazze delle Erbe and Piazza dei Signori. Not far from the town, several villas are open to the public.

FREE ➔ **Giardini Salvi** ★ A pretty urban garden, at the intersection of Viale Roma and Corso Palladio. Roman statues dot the gravel paths, and benches under huge trees make for a shady resting spot. *Daily 7:30am–10pm.*

➔ **Museo Civico** ★ The building which houses this art museum is itself a work of art! Palazzo Chiericati is a 16th-century villa designed, like everything else here, by Palladio. The museum's collection of religious-themed paintings holds nothing impressive, but its collection of works depicting Greek gods and nymphs frolicking in mythical times provide a welcome secular break. When on the ground floor, be sure to look up; the artwork on the ceiling is perhaps the most impressive. Information sheets are provided in each room. *Piazza Matteotti. ☎ 044/4222800. Admission 7€, students 4€. Includes admission to the Teatro Olimpico. Tues–Sun 9am–5pm.*

FREE ➔ **Piazza dei Signori** ★ This is the center of town, and has been for centuries. The most important building here is the **Basilica Palladiana,** which was originally a Gothic-style Assembly Hall before being revamped by Palladio in the 1540s; his work here earned him his first taste of fame. Palladio's restorations remain intact, except for the roof which was destroyed in WWII and has since been rebuilt. The **Torre di Piazza** is a 12th-century clock tower that was part of the original basilica and retains its Gothic architecture. Finally, the **Loggia del Capitano,** with its marble pillars and arches, was begun by Palladio in the 16th century but was never fully completed. *Basilica: Mon–Sat 9:30am–noon and 2–7pm, Sun 9:30am–12:30pm and 2–7pm. Free admission.*

➔ **Teatro Olimpico** ★★ Even if you aren't able to catch one of the frequent performances here, you should at least take a peek inside this 16th-century theater which some consider to be Palladio's greatest work. Beautiful marble statues grace the upper tier of the Greek-inspired *cavea,* which has 14 semicircular rows of seats. The entire theater, though indoor, is designed to resemble an outdoor theater: a faux sky covers the ceiling and the walls are decorated with townscapes. Palladio's amazing *scenae frons* (permanent backdrop to the stage) was purpose-built for the ancient Greek tragedy *Oedipus Rex* by Sophocles, which was performed in 1585 at the Teatro Olimpico's inauguration. *Piazza Matteotti. ☎ 044/4222800. www.olimpico. vicenza.it. Admission 7€, students 4€. Includes admission to the Museo Civico. Tues–Sun 9am–5pm. Check with tourist office for a schedule of performances.*

VICENZA'S VILLAS

When wealthy Venetian merchants began moving to the mainland in the 15th century, rulers in the Vicenza region were worried about losing power to these new inhabitants, and so decreed that the Venetian "immigrants" build innocent villas rather than threatening palaces. The Venetians complied, and today have left a stunning legacy in the region. Most villas are quite a trek away from Vicenza, but there are two that are easily reached either by bus or long walk.

→ **Villa Rotonda** ★★ Probably the most visited of Vicenza's villas, the Rotonda (also known as Villa Capra Valmarana) was designed and initially constructed by Palladio in 1550, and then finished by one of his students. Admire it from the outside, or visit the elaborately decorated interior. ☎ *044/321793. Admission 5€ for the exterior and 10€ for the interior. Grounds open March–Nov Tues–Sun 10am–noon and 3–5pm. Entrance inside the villa is on Wed only. Bus 8.*

→ **Villa Valamarana** ★★ Upon arrival here, you may wonder if the effort to get here was worth it, and if you stick to exploring the grounds only, with its residence, guesthouse, and stables, this opinion might stick. But take a look inside and you will be much impressed by its furnishings and decor, especially the well-preserved frescoes. ☎ *044/321803. www. villavalmarana.net. Admission 6€. Tues–Sun 10am–noon and 3–5pm, Mar–Oct. By appointment rest of the year. Bus 8 or walk about 10 min. from Villa Rotonda.*

Milan & the Lakes

People who tell you that Milan is one of the ugliest cities in Italy and isn't worth a visit are on the one hand right, and on the other hand, couldn't be more wrong. There are uglier cities in Italy (Pescara and Livorno are tied for the most hideous) but, no, it's not exactly Venice either. And as far as world-famous art and architecture, Milan is certainly not Florence or Rome. But it does happen to be the third-largest city in the country, and in many respects, it's the most important.

Just the sheer number of media, fashion, and finance firms based here should give you a clue that *something* is going on. Milan is one of the top places to work in Italy and certainly the best place to party. Forget pounding Peronis on some sad, marble fountain and watching small-town kids gawk back at you—this is where Madonna comes to get into the groove, and she has some 40-plus years of nightlife under her bustier.

Milan's nightclubs are the liveliest in Italy and the shopping is possibly the best in the world. The *aperitivo,* or happy hour, is unbeatable anywhere else, the two soccer teams (A.C. Milan and Inter) are regular winners (next only to Torino's Juventus in the standings) and, yes, there is at least some art to check out. Leonardo Da Vinci's *Last Supper* is a must-see on any trip to Europe. Nearby Bergamo is also busting with precious paintings and palaces.

Meanwhile, the design scene in Milan—think contemporary art meets chairs and can openers—will change your whole outlook about kitchenware.

For those who came to see Old Europe, and snap photos of the same, tired monuments, you might give this place a skip, or at least after a shot of the Duomo and La Scala. For those who want to see the future, and have a blast in a cosmopolitan, European city, you have come to the right place.

By the way, there is some natural beauty here, too. Just 40 minutes to the north, the mountains and shores of Lake Como have absolutely floored everyone who has ever seen them, from Pliny to Stendhal to D.H. Lawrence, right down to my mother.

Milan (Milano)

572km (335 miles) NW of Rome; 142km (88 miles) N of Genoa; 257km (160 miles) W of Venice

The Best of Milan

Best Pub

Bar Magenta Especially during the *aperitivo* hour, college students and yuppies disguised as such spill out of this ancient bar into the outdoor seating and nearby alleyways. Soak up that superfluous pint with Magenta's legendary sandwiches crafted by old men and an even older, hand-cranked meat slicer. See p. 546

Best Cheap Meal

Luini Panzerotti Everyone knows pizza is always the cheapest way to go, and pizzerias are absolutely everywhere in Milan. So how about a new variation on the theme? The *panzerotto* is the stuffed-dough snack that inspired Hot Pockets. And this place is a classic for them. Three euros will get you a quick, filling lunch. See p. 541.

Best Model-Watching

Louisiana Bistro You won't need to speak much Italian in this former brothel owned by a New Mexico native. In fact, to chat up that welterweight blonde in the cowboy hat, you'd be better off busting out some Czech or Lithuanian. Male models are also easily spotted—they're the ones who look like they just walked out of an aftershave commercial but are swigging from flasks hidden under their jackets. (Male models are paid significantly less than their fairer-sex colleagues). See p. 547.

Best Club

This fashion-frenzied metropolis is swimming in dance floors and turntables, and the granddaddy of them all is the **Hollywood.** Other spots may have a more interesting clientele and fresher sounds these days, but nobody tops this Corso Como mainstay for eye-candy potential. See p. 547.

Best Budget Shopping

Let's face it, unless you've got Daddy's plastic in your purse, you won't be buying much in the "golden triangle" around Via Manzoni. A better bet is to scour the shops around **Via Torino.** Funky, lower-priced gems are hiding there amid some otherwise cheesy gear. **Corso Buenos Aires,** on the opposite side of the Duomo, is a mecca for the budget-minded but well-dressed middle class.

Best Milanese Eating Experience

La Trattoria Milanese is, ironically, a rare bird in Milan. While the menu offers fine dining, the cozy atmosphere, closely packed tables and reasonable prices give you that warm, fuzzy feeling that's hard to find in an otherwise standoffish city. See p. 542.

Getting There

BY AIR

Milan is the most easily reached city in Italy. There are two international airports, **Linate** and **Malpensa,** and another not far away, in Bergamo.

If you're flying to Milan directly from North America—for example, on Delta, American, United, Alitalia, or Continental—you will end up at Malpensa, the farther of the two airports from the town center. The **Malpensa Express** train (9€, one-way) connects the main terminal (Terminal 1) with Cadorna Station, not far from the Duomo. It runs every half-hour and the trip takes about 40 minutes. Or, there are buses that are just as frequent, and cheaper (5.50€), but the trip is at least 20 minutes longer and even then you run the risk of hitting hella traffic in the city's northern suburbs. Taxis are a luxury at 75€ or so, and the only time you should consider it is if you're running late for your flight and it's not anywhere near rush hour. For information on Malpensa and Linate, try **www.sea-aeroportimilano.it**.

It's much easier to get to the city center from **Linate** airport, but you'll likely only have that choice if you're flying from elsewhere in Europe, as it handles only Alitalia and other European carriers. Downtown buses leave from right in front of the terminal every 10 minutes and require a regular bus ticket, which costs 1€. For a taxi to downtown, expect to shell out about 20€. Finally, there is **Bergamo's Orio al Serio** airport, which handles traffic from mostly charters and European budget airlines such as Ryanair and easyJet. You can take one of the hourly buses from the terminal to Milan's Garibaldi station for 6.70€. That's usually the best bet, although another option is to take a bus to Bergamo's train station (1€ and 10 min. away) and from there a train into Milan (3€–4€ depending on the arrival station in Milan, which is about an hour away.) Information is at **www.orioaeroporto.it**.

BY TRAIN

The main rail station for arrivals is Mussolini's mammoth **Stazione Centrale,** Piazza Duca d'Aosta (☎ 892021), where you'll find the National Railways information office open daily 7am to 9pm.

More than 100 trains pull in and out of its central station every day, including high-speed trains going to Naples, Venice, and Turin. Hundreds more rumble in and out of its outlying stations. Most people who are in Milan, it is safe to say, got here by train. There are Eurostar trains leaving for points east and south just about every hour, and in between are several Intercity trains, and the slower regional ones. Eurostars are faster and more expensive than the Intercity trains, and you should always book a seat 24 hours ahead, especially on Rome-bound routes on Fridays and Sundays.

In general, you can save some money by taking an Intercity train instead of a Eurostar if you have a little time to spare. For example, Venice is 21€ ($2^3/_4$ hr. away) on the Eurostar, versus 19€ (3 hr.) on the Intercity. Rome is 47€ ($4^1/_2$ hr.) on the Eurostar, and 41€ (6 hr.) on the Intercity. The price difference to Florence is the most dramatic: 29€ ($2^3/_4$ hr.) on the Eurostar, and only 18€ (3 hr. and 40 min.) on the Intercity.

In terms of difference between the two trains, Eurostar is a modern train with bright interiors and clean upholstery. The Intercity is definitely more shopworn, with seating compartments that carry a faint reek of cigarettes and old food. No-smoking cars in the Eurostar really are smoke-free, whereas this rule isn't always strictly respected on the Intercity. Also, A/C in the Eurostar always works, while A/C in the Intercity *usually* works (otherwise, open windows do the trick). The food quality is the same in both lines: there are decent (but never great) snacks in the café car, and there's a full-service restaurant car (serving lunch and dinner only at set meal times) on most trains—Eurostar and Intercity—that travel for more than 4 hours or so. One final advantage to traveling on Eurostar trains is that they're not affected by national train strikes, which happen about once per month in Italy. As for the Intercity, only trains with a final

By Bus? Not Likely . . .

After living in Milan 4 years, I can say with confidence that I've never heard of anyone arriving here by bus (except from a few obscure suburbs late at night.) Apparently there are long-haul buses that pull in and out of Garibaldi Station, but in just about every case you can get where you're going by train for about the same price and in much less time. The one occasion when tourists and locals do use long-haul buses is on a weekend ski trip to the Alps. Those charters depart from in front of the Castello Sforzesco, and trips can be arranged through a travel agent.

destination outside Italy (e.g. Munich, Paris, Vienna) are immune to the strikes.

BY CAR

Milan sits at the crossroads of the nation's major highways, not that you should take that into consideration when planning your trip. Moving around by car is almost never a good idea here. Unlike in Tuscany, in Lombardy, you can get anywhere worth going by train, and finding parking in Milan is no less unpleasant as it is in midtown Manhattan. If you're driving to Milan, A4 is the principal east-west route for Milan, with A8 coming in from the northwest, A1 from the southeast, and A7 from the southwest. A22 is another major north-south artery, running just east of Lake Garda. But once you arrive, put your car in a garage and keep it there. Don't even try to drive around the crowded, confusing main tourist areas of Milan.

Getting Around

SUBWAY, BUSES & TRAMS

Milan has three **subway** lines: MM1, MM2, and MM3, colored red, green, and yellow, respectively.

The **red line** runs from Sesto San Giovanni in the north, runs along shopping haven Corso Buenos Aires to Porta Venezia and on to the Duomo, then continues past the Castello Sforzesco (Cairoli) to Cadorna station and soon splits into two lines—one route runs to the tradefair grounds (Amendola-Fiera) and San Siro soccer stadium (QT8); the other goes through a well-to-do residential area near the Teatro Nazionale.

The **green line** runs from just south of the Navigli neighborhood (Porta Genova) and runs through Brera (Lanza and Moscova), passes under the Corso Como nightlife district (Garibaldi), crosses the red line at Piazzale Loreto, and then continues on to the industrial northeastern corner and into the suburbs.

The **yellow line** starts near the Rogoredo train station (which I have never had the displeasure of visiting in 4 years of traveling around Italy from Milan), moves north through Porta Romana, crosses the red line at the Duomo, cruises through the city's most expensive shopping and real estate at the Montenapoleone and Turati stops, meets the green line at the Stazione Centrale, and finishes up in the seldom-seen northern side of town.

There are dozens of **tram** and **bus** lines, each important in their own way, but the most important ones to remember are the 29 and the 30, which curve around the city's inner ring road, from the Repubblica metro stop all the way around to the Navigli, and the 3 and the 14, which run from the Duomo south along Via Torino and also end up near the Navigli. Those are key tram lines because they bring you to places which are a far walk from the subway, whereas the other neighborhoods are fairly well connected.

MILAN & THE LAKES

Milan Public Transit Info

To find information and schedules for Milan's forms of public transport, call ☎ 800/808180, or visit **www.atm-mi.it** (click the link in the upper-right-hand corner for the English version).

Subways, buses, and trams require the same tickets: 1€ for a single ride, good for 75 minutes. Other options include a 24-hour pass (3€), a 2-day pass (5.50€), a weekly pass (16.75€ for the first one, 9€ for a renewal), and a monthly pass (37.75€, 30€ for a renewal.) for a monthly pass. Weekly and monthly passes are most useful for people who go to work on a daily basis. For those who prefer to take it one day at a time, a better option might be the carnet of 10 tickets (9.20€).

Trams are far and away the best way to ride. The old light fixtures, rumbling wheels, and ancient wooden benches are so cool, in fact, that the City of San Francisco has been buying up Milan's old trams and running them along the tracks of Market Street and the Embarcadero. Gradually, however, Milan is amassing a fleet of newer trams, all of which are quieter and air-conditioned but a little shorter on charm.

The honor system of ticketing (you will only need to present it if an official climbs aboard the bus or tram and checks) is so tempting that you may decide to try your luck. Be warned that you are risking a 100€ fine and significant public shame.

Once you stamp your ticket, it is valid for 75 minutes. Don't throw it away upon leaving the metro, since there's a good chance you'll want to use it right afterward to hop a bus or tram. Unfortunately the system doesn't work in reverse: You have to stamp a fresh ticket every time you get on the subway.

TAXIS

Finding a taxi is fairly easy in Milan, as long as there isn't a subway strike or a heavy bout of rain. Look for the white cars with thin red stripes: If the taxi light is lit, you're in business. Cab meters start at 3.10€, and add a nighttime surcharge of 3.10€ and a Sunday surcharge of 1.55€. Expect to shell out up to 15€ for a typical ride across town. Tips are slightly smaller than in the U.S.; as a rule of thumb, round up to the nearest euro and add one. If you're broke, don't feel bad about pocketing all the change instead. Two taxi numbers to call (speaking in Italian, of course) are ☎ 02/4040 and ☎ 02/8585.

ON FOOT

During one subway strike, when all the cabs were taken, I was faced with the option of walking from one end of Milan to the other to get to work. It took about an hour and 15 minutes, and that was literally walking across the entire city. Milan is not a huge place. Subway stops, for the most part, will get you within 15 minutes of where you need to go. Just remember to wear comfortable shoes, because cobblestones, rough patches in the sidewalk, and tram tracks can make the going a little rough at times.

Milan Orientation

Milan is set up as a classic medieval city, with a cathedral and a fortress (the Castello Sforzesco) at its epicenter, and concentric rings around it that once hosted defensive walls. Each of the gates in the walls, in turn, were named after the city or region toward which that road led. So you have **Porta Venezia** in the northeast, **Porta Romana** in the south, and **Porta Genova** and **Porta Ticinese** (toward the Ticino River) in the southwest. Everything inside these gates can roughly be termed the *centro storico.* The ring roads that connect them are the most useful in the city, and any long-distance cab ride will certainly involve the so-called *circonvallazione.*

Different neighborhoods around those gates have developed different identities over the years, though maybe not quite as noticeably in, say, Rome or Venice.

For orientation purposes, it's best to think of the city as a clock. Directly north of the Duomo, between 11 o'clock and 12:30, is the **Brera** neighborhood. It was once known for illicit activities at night, but was taken over by a bohemian crowd in the 1960s. Like any artistic neighborhood on the rise, it became gentrified soon thereafter and now has not only art galleries, but a large concentration of bars, clubs, and restaurants that make up the heart of the city's nightlife. North of Brera is **Corso Como,** which, again, is known mostly for its nightlife, and north of that is an up-and-coming neighborhood known as the **Isola,** as it is virtually isolated from the rest of the city by Stazione Garibaldi.

Clockwise from Brera, at about 1 o'clock, is **Montenapoleone**—far and away the most expensive neighborhood in Milan, playing host to the top clothing stores and the homes of those who own them. Nearby, around the Turati metro, is a posh business district playing home to, among others, the U.S. Consulate and the soccer team A.C. Milan. Further out is the central train station and the mostly immigrant-dominated neighborhoods that surround it.

Just to the east of the Duomo, at almost 3 o'clock, spreading out toward Porta Venezia and Piazza Cinque Giornate, is an upper-middle-class residential neighborhood that really won't grab your attention, except for the nearby Public Gardens. But leading northeast from Porta Venezia is **Corso Buenos Aires,** a convenient place to shop for affordable clothing and goods.

Four o'clock and five o'clock, well, tourists can pretty much ignore that area and move straight down to **Porta Romana.** This is a little out of the way for most tourists, so the restaurants and clubs around here are mostly populated with locals.

In the wedge between six and eight o'clock is one of the most fun and interesting parts of the city. It begins at the bottom end of **Via Torino**—where you'll find the skateboard set around San Lorenzo and the yuppie bars around Sant Ambrogio (another stronghold of the wealthy Milanese)—and extends down to the **Navigli,** the loudest neighborhood at night, with pubs and a lot of action on the street.

The rest of the western edge of the city would be largely forgettable were it not for the *Last Supper,* the tradefair, and San Siro on the northwestern corner. Approaching 10 o'clock is Cadorna station, the Castello Sforzesco, and the western edge of Brera.

Milan Basics

TOURIST OFFICE

Facing the Duomo, the **tourist office** is just to your right in a boxy, Soviet-looking building on the same square (Via Marconi 1; ☎ **02/7252 4301;** www.milanoinfotourist.com). It's open 9am to 1pm and 2 to 6pm. There are a number of free brochures to pick up, as well as *Hello Milano,* which has a great listing of local events. Expect to stand in a brief line to speak with someone.

RECOMMENDED WEBSITES

- **www.hellomilano.it** This site can answer almost any question you have—in English—about hotels, nightlife, events, and tourist sights, and is a good online resource for maps of the city.
- **www.easymilano.it** This is the online version of Milan's expat community magazine, most useful for classified ads for long-term and short-term apartment rentals. The magazine, which you can download from the site, is also a good place to learn about other English-language events and opportunities around the city.
- **www.mymi.it** Certainly the hippest online venue for news on local dining, clubbing, art shows, fitness centers, etc., but it's in Italian only.

○ **www.anteospaziocinema.it** Feel like a movie? Click on the "Sound & Motion" tab on this site for a downloadable list of English-language films playing in Milan.

○ **www.cosmit.it** Official site of the Salone del Mobile, Milan's design trade show, one of the city's top international events.

○ **www.inter.it** and **www.acmilan.com** Check out Milan's two top soccer teams online for info about games at their legendary San Siro stadium.

Milan **Nuts & Bolts**

ATMs Everywhere. Just look for the BANCOMAT signs. Note that ATMs in Milan can remind you of old-school Christmas-tree lights: One goes out and they all go out, due to connection failures that usually last a few hours. Many *bancomats* still go offline at midnight, which was meant to minimize damage from wallet theft, but more importantly it protects you from yourself. Stock up before you go out at night at keep a close eye on the outflow.

Crisis Lines

→ **Drug Help Line** (Daily 9am–8pm) ☎ **800/016600** or ☎ 840/002244

→ **Rape Help Line** (Mon–Thurs. 10am–1pm and 2:30–6pm) ☎ **02/5501 5519**

Emergencies For immediate help, call the Carabinieri at ☎ **112,** or else the police at ☎ **113.** (There is also an English-speaking staff at ☎ 02/863 701). To report theft or other crimes, go in person to the *questura,* or police headquarters, at Via Fatebenefratelli 11 (between Brera and the Public Gardens; metro:Turati) or at any other police precinct or Carabinieri barracks around the city. To report and replace a lost or stolen passport, this will be your first stop before you apply for a new one at the consulate. The U.S. Consulate is located right outside the Turati metro. For traffic accidents, parking tickets, and minor problems, you will deal instead with the municipal police (or *vigili;* ☎ 02/77 271) whom you will find patrolling major intersections or else writing up tickets in their green-and-white cars.

For **medical emergencies,** call the *pronto soccorso,* or ambulance, at ☎ **118.** If you can make to the hospital on your own, the most central of all is Ospedale Fatebenefratelli (Corso Porta Nuova 23; ☎ 02/63 631; metro: Turati) in the Brera area, or else Ospedale Maggiore (Via Francesco Sforza 28; ☎ 02/55 031; metro: Missori. Some people on staff speak English.) For nonemergencies, English-speaking patients might find it more helpful to visit the American International Medical Center (Via Mercalli 11; ☎ 02/5831 9808; metro: Missori).

Internet Cafes There are several sleek and flashy Internet spots around Milan run by big corporations such as Mondadori and Telecom Italia, but for the best deal, look for the international telephone centers run by, and catering to, immigrants. There is at least one in every neighborhood. There are fewer terminals but you will pay about half the price a larger place charges. Below are a few of the more popular, bigger venues. Prices range from 4€–6€ per hour.

→ **Grazianet,** Piazza Duca d'Aosta 14 (next to central train station), ☎ 02/6700 543. About 70 spots.

→ **Mondadori Multicenter,** Via Marghera 28 (near the Duomo), ☎ 02/48047311. About 20 spots.

→ **Internet Enjoy,** Alzaia Naviglio Pavese 2 (on the Naviglio Pavese canal), ☎ 02/835 7225. About a dozen spots.

→ **Phone@point,** Via Vigevano 20 (near *The Last Supper*), ☎ 02/58307274. About 20 spots.

Laundromats   A convenient spot to have your clothes washed is **Minola,** south of the Duomo at Via San Vito 5 (follow Via Torino from the Piazza del Duomo for about 5 blocks where it intersects with Via San Vito), ☎ 02/5811-1271, metro: Missori. The staff will do your laundry (wash and dry) for 10€ per 5kg and dry cleaning for 12€ per 5kg. It's open Monday to Friday from 8am to 6pm and Saturday from 8am to noon.

Luggage Storage   Here for just the day? Drop off your heavy gear at the **Stazione Centrale.** The luggage room is open daily from 5am to 4am; the fee is 2.60€ per piece of baggage for each 12-hour period. Note that luggage storage rooms in Italian train stations are sometimes closed in Italy when terrorist threats are perceived as high, so don't count on this option.

Post Offices   There's no such thing as a quick stop at the post office. Getting there late morning midweek may help your chances of avoiding the rush. There are dozens of offices spread out around the city, but the **main branch** is just outside the Cordusio metro: Via Cordusio 4 (☎ 02/7248 2126). It's open Monday to Saturday 8am to 7pm.

Restrooms   Doubtlessly, the best place to answer nature's call is in a bar. To make a *bella figura*, order a cup of coffee and then look for the head, which also gives you better odds that the restroom isn't "out of order." Amazing how toilet technology is so shaky that half the restrooms are always closed in Italy for repairs! Like "broken" credit card machines, "out-of-order" toilets can quickly fix themselves with some hard questions.

Safety   Milan—and Italy in general—is a pretty safe place as far as violent crime is concerned. Even pickpockets are rarer here than in Rome. That said, it is never a good idea for a woman to walk through a park alone late at night. Parco Sempione is particularly dubious, as it is rife with seedy characters. The central train station and the adjacent neighborhood around the Caiazzo metro are also not the best places to take a leisurely late-night stroll. On the whole, though, don't be squeamish about moving around late at night in Milan.

Telephoning Tips   If you're calling a local number from within the city, you'll still have to dial Milan's city code, 02, first. For international calls, pick up an international calling card from the bar, or else head to one of the immigrant-run phone centers. To get a dial tone at any pay phone, you'll first need to insert a regular Italian phone card, which can be purchased from *tabacchi* stores in denominations starting at 5 euros. Break off the corner tab before inserting the card into the payphone. Local calls (to 02 numbers) probably won't run you more than .20€; if you're calling a cellphone (numbers starting in 333, 335, 338, 339, 340, 347, 348, 380, etc.), the charges from pay phones are outrageous.

MILAN & THE LAKES

Sleeping & Eating in Milan

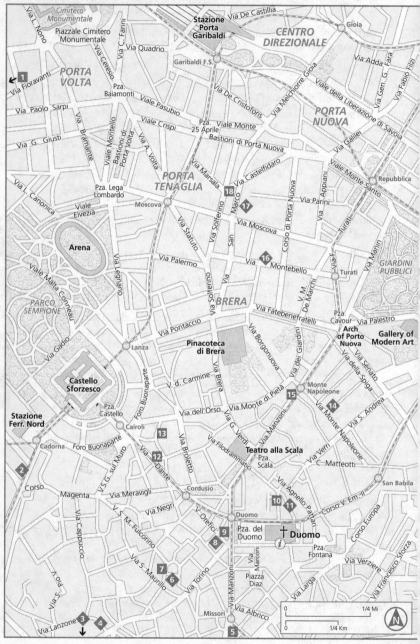

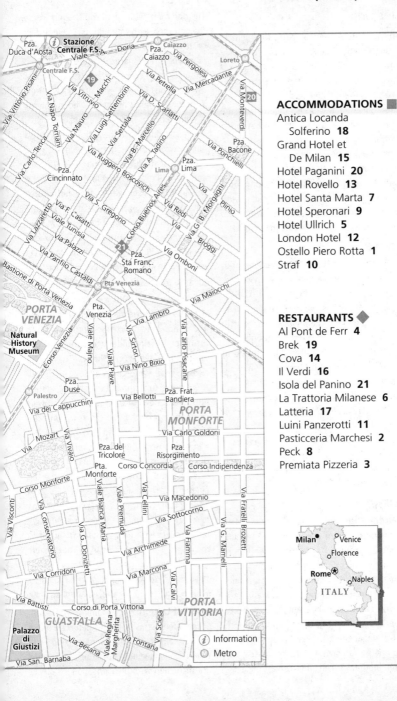

ACCOMMODATIONS ■

Antica Locanda
  Solferino **18**
Grand Hotel et
  De Milan **15**
Hotel Paganini **20**
Hotel Rovello **13**
Hotel Santa Marta **7**
Hotel Speronari **9**
Hotel Ullrich **5**
London Hotel **12**
Ostello Piero Rotta **1**
Straf **10**

RESTAURANTS ◆

Al Pont de Ferr **4**
Brek **19**
Cova **14**
Il Verdi **16**
Isola del Panino **21**
La Trattoria Milanese **6**
Latteria **17**
Luini Panzerotti **11**
Pasticceria Marchesi **2**
Peck **8**
Premiata Pizzeria **3**

ⓘ Information
◯ Metro

Sleeping

You need to budget to spend the night in Milan. *Nothing* is cheap. Hotels start at a rock-bottom price of 60€ per double and rocket upwards from there. But there are a few reasonable options, listed below.

In a pinch, you can also inquire with the **hotel booking kiosk** in the Stazione Centrale (main train station)—they act as a clearinghouse for unsold rooms in cheerless government-rated three-stars near the train station. It won't be the most romantic room in town, but you can get a double with private bath, minibar, slippers, and *cuffia doccia* (shower cap) for about 70€ a night.

HOSTEL

→ **Ostello Piero Rotta** Milan has one youth hostel and it is nowhere near the city center. It is out by the stadium, in the San Siro neighborhood, and unless you've come specifically to see a game and then leave, there's little reason to stay here. There's no doubt that this is the cheapest option, but with dorm beds with shared bathrooms at 19€ a head, you and a friend might want to pitch in a few extra euros for a cheap double downtown. *Via Salmoiraghi 1.* ☎ *02/3926 7095. Fax: 02 33000191. www.ostellionline.org/ostello. php?idostello=208. Single bed plus breakfast 19.50€. Closed Dec 23–Jan 13. Metro: QT8. Bus: 90, 91, 68. Amenities: Internet access; laundry; TV room.*

CHEAP

→ **Hotel Paganini** Occupying an old house off the north end of Corso Buenos Aires, the stomping grounds for some rather lonely looking women on the street corners after 9pm, the Paganini appears to be a dismal option as you are buzzed in and walk up to the front desk. Still, the management goes to great lengths to keep this a clean, no-nonsense budget hotel: The guest rooms are large and bright, with high ceilings, solid beds, and banal modular furnishings of varying ages.

The one room with a bathroom is just inside the entrance, with wood floors, a ceiling decorated with molded stuccoes, and plenty of elbowroom. The shared facilities are modern enough and kept spanking clean by the owners (one of whom lived in Brooklyn, New York for a number of years), who are happy to point their guests to restaurants and sights. The best rooms are in the rear, overlooking a huge private garden. There is much to be said for this location: The station is only a 10-minute walk way down Via Pergolsi, and if shopping is on your agenda, the nearby Corso Buenos Aires is one of the city's bargain fashion meccas. *Via Paganini 6, 20131 Milano.* ☎ *02/204-7443. 8 units, 1 with bathroom. Double 65€. Parking in garage across street 12€, free on street. Metro: Loreto. Tram/Bus: 33, 55, 55/, 56, 56/, 90, 91, or 93. Amenities: Concierge. In room: Hair dryer.*

→ **Hotel Speronari** ★ This is a real find, a budget hotel in a deluxe location, tucked into a tiny pedestrian side street between Via Torino and Via Mazzini. The staff is earnest, and the rooms are basic but done well: cool tile floors, functional furnishings, ceiling fans, brand-new cot springs, and fuzzy towels in the bathrooms. Even those without full bathroom have a sink and bidet, and all save a few of those without bathrooms have TVs. Rooms on the third and fourth floors are brighter, and those on the courtyard a tad quieter than rooms facing the street. *Via Speronari 4, 20123 Milano.* ☎ *02/8646-1125. Fax 02/7200-3178. hotelsperonari@inwind.it. 33 units, 17 with bathroom. Double without bathroom 73€, with bathroom 93€–104€; triple without bathroom 98€, with bathroom 140€; quad with bathroom 155€. Metro: Duomo or Missori. Tram: 1, 2, 3, 4, 12, 14, 15, 19, 20, 24, or 27.*

→ **Hotel Ullrich** ★ A 10-minute walk south of the Duomo, this attractive pensione offers a lot of comfort in addition to its good location. The management is friendly, and rooms are furnished with pleasant modern pieces and decent beds. Each has a tiny washroom with sink and bidet but no toilet; large, spanking-clean bathrooms are in the hallway. Rooms on the street side open to small balconies, but are noisier than those overlooking the *cortile* (courtyard). One of the bathrooms is equipped with a washing machine, and guests can do a load for 10€. The Ullrich books up quickly, so be sure to call ahead. *Corso Italia 6, 21023 Milano.* ☎ *02/8645-0156 or 02/804-535. 7 units, none with bathroom. Double 70€–75€, triple 90€–100€. Metro: Duomo. Tram: 15, 24, 65, or 94.*

DOABLE

→ **Antica Locanda Solferino** ★★★ If this charming old hotel in the arty Brera neighborhood hadn't been discovered long ago by members of the fashion world and film stars (this was Marcello Mastroianni's preferred Milan hostelry), you would consider it a find. The rooms have more character than they do modern comforts, but, to the loyal guests, the eclectic smattering of country antiques and Art Nouveau pieces more than compensate for the absence of minibars. Nor do the repeat customers seem to mind that some of the bathrooms are miniscule (though modern), or that there is no lobby or breakfast room (coffee and rolls are delivered to your room). So be it—this is a delightful place to stay in one of Milan's most enticing neighborhoods, and reception manager Gerardo Vitolo is very friendly. New Jacuzzi baths and air-conditioning in some rooms only add to the experience. The rooms on the tiny courtyard are quieter, but those on the street have plant-filled balconies (the best is no. 10 on the corner, if you don't mind a tub rather than a shower). The management also has started renting two apartments in the neighborhood, each with a living room, bedroom, and a Jacuzzi, with the decorations straight out of the 1960s. *Via Castelfidardo 2, 20121 Milano.* ☎ *02/657-0129 or 02/659-2706. Fax 02/657-1361. www.anticalocandasolferino.it. 11 units.*

Double 130€–200€; apt 170€–220€. 40€ extra bed. Rates include breakfast served in room. Parking 20€–25€ in nearby garage. Closed 2–3 weeks in mid-Aug. Metro: Moscova or Repubblica. Tram/Bus: 11, 29, 30, 33, 41, 43, or 94.

→ **Hotel Rovello** The Rovello is on a quiet street between the Duomo and the Castello. The unusually large guest rooms occupy the first and second floors of a centuries-old building and incorporate many of the original architectural details, including exposed timbers and beamed ceilings. Handsome contemporary Italian furnishings are set off by gleaming hardwood floors, the tall casement windows are covered with attractive fabrics, and walls are painted in soothing green and gold tones. The orthopedic mattresses are covered with thick quilts for a homey feel. Many of the rooms have dressing areas in addition to the large new bathrooms. A breakfast of rolls and coffee is served in a sunny room off the lobby. *Via Rovello 18, 20121 Milano.* ☎ *02/8646-4654. Fax 02/7202-3656. www.hotel-rovello.it. 10 units. Double 100€–186€. Metro: Cordusio. Tram/Bus: 1, 2, 3, 4, 12, 14, 18, 19, 20, 24, or 27.*

→ **Hotel Santa Marta** The narrow Via Santa Marta is my favorite street, a slice of old Milan, cobblestoned and lined with charming old buildings, one of which houses the Santa Marta. It's also across the street from one of the city's best-value restaurants (the Milanese), and a short walk from the Duomo and other sights. Recent modernizations have preserved the old-fashioned ambience while adding such modern comforts as air-conditioning. The tile-floored guest rooms are comfortable and decorated with a matter-of-fact fashion sense, some cramped, others quite large. *Via Santa Marta 4, 20123 Milano.* ☎ *02/804-567 or 02/804-621. Fax 02/8645-2661. Double 160€–186€; triple 190€–257€. Continental breakfast included. Parking in nearby garage 15€. Closed 15 days in Aug. Metro: Cordusio or Duomo. Tram: 1, 2, 3, 4, 12, 14, 15, 19, 20, 24, or 27.*

➜ **London Hotel** ★ The London sticks to its old-fashioned ways. The big fireplace and cozy green-velvet furniture in the lobby say a lot about the comfort level and friendly atmosphere that bring many guests back time after time. Just beyond the lobby, there's a bar where beverages are available almost around the clock; guests can purchase cappuccino or a continental breakfast in the morning. Upstairs, the rooms look like they haven't been redecorated in a number of decades, but they're roomy and bright, and the heavy old furnishings lend a charm very much in keeping with the ambience of the hotel. Rooms on the first floor tend to be the largest, and they get smaller as you go up. Guests receive a 10% discount at the trattoria next door, the Opera Prima. *Via Rovello 3, 20121 Milano.* ☎ *02/7202-0166. Fax 02/8057-037. www.hotellondonmilano.com. 29 units. Double 100€–150€. Continental breakfast 8€. Parking 25€ in nearby garage. Closed Aug and Christmas. Metro: Cordusio. Tram/Bus: 1, 2, 3, 4, 12, 14, 18, 19, 20, 24, or 27. Amenities: Bar; concierge; same-day dry cleaning; laundry service; room service (limited). In room: A/C, TV, dataport, hair dryer.*

SPLURGE

➜ **Grand Hotel et De Milan** ★★ Okay, this one's a bit of a reach. But if you're going to talk the fashion talk on Via Manzoni, you might as well walk the walk—especially if you've got a credit card and it's the beginning of the billing period and the end of the vacation. Perhaps Milan's most intimate luxury hotel, the Grand Hotel et De Milan balances family management with refined service. It's perfectly positioned between La Scala (3 blocks away) and the shopping of Via Montenapoleone just up and across the street. The bathrooms are done in marble and the beds king-size in rooms with heavy curtains, chipped stone floors, elegant upholstered furnishings, and muted skylight domes. Deluxe rooms are larger than classic rooms,

and have genuine antiques. *Via Manzoni 29, 20121 Milano.* ☎ *02/723-141. Fax 02/8646-0861. www.grandhoteletdemilan.it. Classic double 448€, deluxe double 520€, jr. suite 605€, suite 840€–1,025€. Breakfast 35€. Amenities: 2 restaurants, bar; exercise room open 24-hr.; bike rental; room service; in-room massage. In room: A/C, TV w/pay movies, dataport, minibar, hair dryer, safe. Metro: Montenapoleone.*

➜ **Straf** ★★ Hidden behind a 2-century-old façade, this hotel is close to La Scala and the deluxe shopping street, Via Montenapoleone. The landmark Duomo lies outside your door. Its burnished brass and black stone create a minimalist aura for the jet set who check in, making it one of the hottest hotel addresses in town. Stylish and comfortable, bedrooms are elegant. The special rooms are five units equipped for chromotherapy and aromatherapy, with Japanese auto massage chaise longue. Even the less grand accommodations will still make you feel fashionable. The architect, Vincenzo De Cotiis, used scratched mirrors, burnished brass, iron, and black stone among other materials, to create an aura. It's original and impressive—not just another "modern concept" place. *San Raffaele 3.* ☎ *02/805-081. www.straf.it. Double 257€–325€ (15% discount often available for Internet bookings). Amenities: Restaurant; bar; business services; car rental; dry cleaning; fitness room; laundry service; massage; nonsmoking rooms; room service (24-hr.); rooms for those w/limited mobility. In room: A/C, TV, dataport, hair dryer, minibar, safe. Metro: Duomo.*

Eating

The Milanese are that rare breed of Italian who appreciate a quick meal. Lunch is generally a sandwich or salad on the run. Dinner, on the other hand, is time to relax. The area is famous for its veal cutlet (*cotoletta milanese*), its filling *cassouela* stew, and of course, *risotto milanese*. One other peculiarity of Milanese restaurants, besides their strangely efficient service, is that very few of them offer outdoor seating. Expect a cozy indoor atmosphere, sometimes with a funky modern decor. Oh, and it's not going to be cheap . . . that is, unless you can forego a real "meal." The generous buffet spreads offered at *aperitivo* hour—usually a mix of carbs, cheeses, and cured meats—provide plenty of calories, and they're free as long as you buy something to drink.

CAFES

There are hundreds of coffee bars around Milan, and all serve a stand-up cup of espresso, but for something more Audrey Hepburn-esque, try out one of these refined pastry shops. In terms of what you'll pay, for espresso standing up at bar: .75€–.90€; cappuccino standing up at bar: .90€–1.10€; pastry standing up at bar 1€–1.50€; remember the prices double when you sit down at any bar; and the prices triple when you sit down at fancy places.

Pasticceria Marchesi, Via Santa Maria alla Porta 13 (☎ **02/862-770;** Metro: Cardusio), is a distinguished pastry shop with an adjoining wood-paneled tearoom. Since it's only steps from Santa Maria delle Grazie, you can enjoy the old-world ambience and a cup of excellent coffee (or one of the many teas and herbal infusions) as you dash off postcards of the *Last Supper.* Of course, you'll want to accompany your beverage with one of the elegant pastries, perhaps a slice of the *panettone* (cake laden with raisins and candied citron) that's a hallmark of Milan. No one prepares it better than they do at Marchesi. It's open Tuesday to Sunday 8am to 8pm.

Cova, Via Montenapoleone 8 (☎ **02/ 600-0578;** Metro: Montenapoleone), smack in the Golden Triangle, is in its third century of refined surroundings near the similarly atmospheric Museo Poldi-Pezzoli. Women will feel at home if they're wearing heels and carrying a shopping bag from one of the local

stores. It's open Tuesday to Sunday 8am to 8pm.

CHEAP

➔ **Brek** CAFETERIA No, it's not Milanese. Yes, it's a chain cafeteria. But if you want to eat cheaply and well, this is the place. Pastas and risotto are made fresh; pork, veal, and chicken are roasted to order; and the large selection of cheeses would put many a formal restaurant to shame. Excellent wines and many kinds of beer are also available. Behind-the-counter service is friendly and helpful. *Via Lepetit 20.* ☎ *02/670-5149. www.brek.it. Primi and pizza 3€–6€; secondi 3.50€–7€. Mon–Sat 11:30am–3pm and 6:30–10:30pm. Metro: Stazione Centrale.*

📺 Best ➔ **Luini Panzerotti** SNACKS A Milan mainstay since 1948, it's so good they've even opened a branch in London. At this stand-up counter near the Galleria, you'll have to elbow your way through a throng of well-dressed patrons to purchase the house specialty: *panzerotto,* a pocket of pizza crust stuffed with all sorts of ingredients, including the basic cheese-and-tomato. You'll also find many different kinds of panini here. *Via S. Radegonda 16.* ☎ *02/8646-1917. www.luini.it. Panzerotto 2.50€. Cash only. Mon 10am–3pm; Tues–Sat 10am–8pm. Closed Aug. Metro: Duomo.*

➔ **Isola del Panino** SANDWICHES This cafelike sandwich shop, in the midst of the bustle of the Corso Buenos Aires discount shops, sells some 50 different kinds of panini. You needn't feel you are foregoing an Italian experience in enjoying one of these sandwiches. In Milan, a panino is a very popular snack or lunch choice and is usually served warm; bread is stuffed with seafood, cheese, salami, vegetables, whatever, then grilled. *Via Felice Casati 2.* ☎ *02/2951-4925. Sandwiches from 3€. Cash only. Tues–Sun 8am–midnight. Metro: Lima.*

➔ **Peck** ★ DELI Milan's most famous food emporium offers a wonderful selection of roast veal, risottos, porchetta, salads, aspics, cheeses, pastries, and other fare from its exquisite larder in this natty snack bar around the corner from its shop. If you choose to eat here, you will do so at a stand-up bar where, especially around lunchtime, it can be hard to find elbowroom. This shouldn't discourage you, though, because the pleasure of having access to such a cornucopia of delicacies at a reasonable price will be a gourmand's vision of paradise. *Via Spadari 9.* ☎ *02/802-3161. www.peck.it. Primi 3.50€–8€; secondi 9€–13€. Mon–Sat 7:30am–9pm. Closed Jan 1–10 and July 1–20. Metro: Duomo.*

➔ **Premiata Pizzeria** PIZZA/PAN-ITALIAN The most popular pizzeria in the Navigli stays packed from early dinnertime until the bar-hopping crowd stops by for late-night munchies. The restaurant rambles back forever, exposed copper pipes tracing across the ceilings of rooms wrapped around shaded outdoor terraces set with long, raucous tables. Seating is communal and service hurried, but the wood-oven pizzas are excellent. If you're hungrier, there's a long menu of pastas and meat courses, while lighter appetites can enjoy a selection of salads or platters of cheese or *salumi* built for two. *Via Alzaia Naviglio Grande 2.* ☎ *02/8940-0648. Pizzas 4.50€–12€. Wed–Mon noon–2:30pm; daily 7:30–11:30pm.*

DOABLE

➔ **Al Pont de Ferr** ★ PAN-ITALIAN This is one of the more culinarily respectable of the dozens of restaurants around the Navigli, with tables set out on the flagstones overlooking the canal (regulars know to bring tiny cans of bug spray to battle the mosquitoes in summer). The *paste e fagioli* is livened up with bits of sausage, and the ricotta-stuffed ravioli inventively sauced with a pesto of *rucola* (arugula) and veggies. For a second course you can try the *tocchetti di coniglio* (oven-roasted rabbit with potatoes), *porchetta* (pork stuffed with spices), or the vegetable

cous-cous alla Trapanesi—or just sack the whole idea of a secondo and order up a *tavolozza* selection of excellent cheeses. There's a surprisingly good selection of half bottles of wine, but most full bottles start at 15€ and go senselessly higher. *Ripa di Porta Ticinese 55 (on the Naviglio Grande).* ☎ *02/ 8940-6277. Primi 6€–11€; secondi 14€–19€. Mon–Sat 12:30–2:30pm and 8pm–1am. Tram: 3, 15, 29, 30, or 59.*

➔ **Il Verdi** ★ PASTA/VEGETARIAN This trendy but cozy restaurant has earned the distinction of spawning the city's first yuppie scene in the '90s, initially drawn to its healthy, vegetarian cuisine. Some things have changed since then: The menu is still healthy and the clientele relatively young, but now there is something for all tastes. The most popular dish seems to have remained the risotto with pears drizzled with balsamic vinegar, though the salads are perhaps the best in the city, especially those with crabmeat and avocados. The wine selection is also very good. *Piazza Mirabello 5.* ☎ *02/ 659-0979. Primi 10€–14€; salads from 9€. Mon–Sat 12:30–2:15pm and 7:30pm–midnight. Metro: Turati.*

Best ➔ **La Trattoria Milanese** ★★ MILANESE Don't be fooled by the boring, touristy-sounding name. Tucked into a narrow lane in one of the oldest sections of Milan, just west of the Duomo, this is a Milanese institution. In the three-beamed dining room, local families and other patrons share the long, crowded tables. The *risotto alla Milanese* with saffron and beef marrow, not surprisingly, is excellent, as is a minestrone that's served hot in the winter and at room temperature in the summer. The *cotolette alla Milanese,* breaded and fried in butter, is all the better here because only the choicest veal chops are used and it's served with the bone in, and the *osso buco* is cooked to perfection. If you want to try their twin specialties without pigging out, the dish listed as *risotto e osso buco* buys you a half portion each of their *risotto alla Milanese* and the *osso buco* for just 18€. Polenta with rich Gorgonzola cheese is one of the few nonmeat second courses. *Via Santa Marta 11. ☎ 02/ 8645-1991. Reservations required. Primi 7€–10€; secondi 6€–18€; menù turistico 30€ without wine. Wed–Mon noon–3pm and 7pm–1am. Metro: Cardusio.*

➔ **Latteria** The main business here at one time was dispensing milk and eggs to a press of neighborhood shoppers, but now the emphasis is on serving the La Brera neighborhood delicious, homemade fare in a room decorated with paintings and photographs of roses. The minestrone and other vegetable soups are delicious, as are the many variations of risotto, including some otherwise hard-to-find variations such as *riso al salto* and a delicious dish of leftover *risotto alla Milanese* that is fried with butter. The menu changes daily, and the friendly staff, including owners Arturo and Maria, won't mind explaining the different dishes. The place is tiny, and doesn't take bookings, so if you want to get one of the popular tables, arrive when it opens or wait until 8:30pm or later when a few will free up as the early-dining tourist clientele clears out and the locals take over. *Via San Marco 24. ☎ 02/ 659-7653. Reservations not accepted (and it fills up fast). Primi 9€–10€; secondi 7€–13€. No credit cards. Mon–Fri 12:30–2:30pm and 7:30–10pm. Metro: Moscova.*

Partying

If any place in Italy knows how to rage, it is Milan, though this may not be hardcore partying as you know it. In a city obsessed with keeping up appearances, the temptation to down that extra shot—or any shot, really—and start stripping and grinding on a bar counter is met with pause and due discipline. In general, Italians frown on drunkenness. The Milanese are no different.

What sets Milan apart from other Italian cities is that there is actually a cocktail culture at all. These are the people who invented the *aperitivo,* the 6 o'clock martini or *negroni* that paves the way for dinner. It is a tradition to be celebrated. Well-dressed locals, fresh from the office, savor a half-priced happy hour cocktail or two and help themselves to the free buffet.

Free? Yes. And good. Well, it depends where you go. All you need to do is pass by a bar at 6pm and take a look in the window. Invariably, the spread will include some sort of cold pasta dish, rice salad, possibly some *frittate,* or omelets, and a selection of cold cuts. Every bar tries to outdo the other to bring in the *aperitivo* crowd, so every year the buffets get better. It is no secret that the city's student population counts this as dinner. Not fine dining, but then, not bad for free.

After dinner, the next decision is where to go out at night. There are bars and clubs spread out over the city, but the five areas with the most action are Corso Como, Porta Romana, Porta Ticinese, the Navigli canal neighborhood, and most famously, Brera.

In general, Corso Como draws the fashion crowd, Porta Ticinese the design crowd, Porta Romana is more local-oriented, while Brera and the Navigli are the bread-and-butter of Milan partying. If you don't feel like getting dressed up and just want to put back a few beers at long wooden tables, go to the Navigli.

PUBS AND BARS

Drink prices at Milan's trendier bars and clubs—such as 10 Corso Como—are the highest in Italy. Fashionistas and financiers can afford a long night of 12€ cocktails; the rest of us, not so much. The good news is that there are also plenty of places (frequented by normal, unpretentious locals) where drinks can be had for much cheaper (and they're probably more potent, too). The Navigli, the canal-side district southwest of

Partying & Sightseeing in Milan

Culture Vulture: Opera & Theater

The most complete list of cultural events appears in the large Milan newspaper, the left-wing *La Repubblica.* Try for a Thursday edition, which usually has the most complete listings.

The world's most famous opera house is **La Scala** ★★★, Piazza della Scala (metro: Duomo). La Scala is fully restored, with a technologically advanced stage and a splendid auditorium. Critics have raved about the new acoustics. There are now three moveable stages and 200 added seats. Tickets are hard to come by and should be arranged as far in advance as possible. Costing from 10€ to 170€, tickets can be purchased at **Biglietteria Centrale,** in the Galleria Vittorio Emanuele, Piazza della Scala corner (☎ 02/720003744; daily noon–6pm; metro: Duomo). For more information, search out www.teatroallascala.org.

Other operas are staged at the modern 2,500-seat, newly constructed auditorium, **Teatro degli Arcimboldi,** Zona Bicocca, Viale dell'Innovazione (☎ 899/500022), on the northern outskirts of Milan. It lies alongside a university campus and dreary housing developments. Since the new opera house is difficult to reach by public transportation, the theater operates shuttle buses departing from the Piazza Duomo between 6:45 and 7pm on the nights of performances. Otherwise, you have to take the metro to the Zara stop and from there take a tram (no. 7) to the auditorium. Tickets cost 20€ to 155€. The opera house is closed in midsummer (late July and all of Aug). The new season begins every year on December 7, although the program for the upcoming season is announced the previous September.

Conservatorio, Via del Conservatorio 12 (☎ 02/7621101; metro: San Babila), in the San Babila neighborhood, features the finest in classical music. Year-round, a cultured Milanese audience enjoys high-quality programs of widely varied classical concerts. Tickets cost 15€ to 35€.

Piccolo Teatro, Via Rivoli 2, near Via Dante (☎ 02/72333222; metro: Cordusio), hosts a wide variety of Italian-language performances. Its director, Giorgio Strehler, is acclaimed as one of the most avant-garde and talented in the world. The theater lies between the Duomo and the Castle of the Sforzas. It's sometimes hard to obtain seats. It's closed in August. Tickets cost 20€ to 70€.

the Duomo, is especially recommended for drinkers on a budget: it's packed with pubs and bars geared towards Milan's strapped-for-cash student population. Finally, when in Milan, remember the *aperitivo!* Virtually every bar in the city offers a free buffet of snacks and munchies at happy hour. Stop in for a drink at 7pm and stuff your face for a few hours—tons of young Milanese forgo expensive "real restaurants" and make the *aperitivo* spread their dinner every night.

MTV Best ➔ **Bar Magenta** Locals have begun calling this place the Picadilly of Milan, either for its publike atmosphere or the fact that it is a favorite among the English-speaking community. Despite the pints of Guinness and American-style cocktails, this is definitely not an "expat bar." It is a Milanese legend, and the first stop for any scarf-wearing *tifoso* headed toward San Siro for a soccer game. With expert meat slicers and an endless supply of *cotolette milanese* on hand, the Magenta also gets my vote for best late-night sandwich in town. Expect Motown, rock, and R&B classics on the speakers. *Via Carducci 13.* ☎ *02/805 3808. Tues–Sun 8am–3am; Mon 5pm–3am.*

→ **Last Blast** One of dozens of beer-happy pubs to choose from on the Naviglio Pavese canal, the Last Blast is unique because it has good, live music. The tables are usually packed in front of singer/guitarist Roberto Santoro, who every night covers the gamut from U2 to Patti Smith to Italy's answer to Bob Dylan, Fabrizio de Andre. *Via Acanio Sforza 15.* ☎ *02/5810 5685. Tues–Sun 5pm–2am.*

→ **Le Biciclette** Like 10 Corso Como, this isn't the sort of place where you'd want to turn up wearing your backpack, but then it isn't suffocatingly *fashionista,* either. The crowd is culture vulture meets yuppie. Black is a popular color for those who come here to sip a cocktail, check out the latest art on show, and dip into one of the city's better *aperitivo* buffets. *Corner of Via Torti and Corso Genova.* ☎ *02/5810 43259. Mon–Sat 6pm–2am; Sun 12:30–4pm and 6pm–2am.*

MTV **Best** → **Louisiana Bistro** MTV Generation, welcome home. A former Brera-bordello-turned-party-central brings in models in casual wear with its videos on the tube, great tunes on the turn tables, and all the burgers and fries you can eat. There's nothing Italian about the place at all (the owner is from New Mexico), but that seems to be what the clientele likes best. The Louisiana is also one of the only places in town to catch the Super Bowl on the big screen. *Via Fiori Chiari 17.* ☎ *02/8646 5315. Tues–Sat noon–3pm and 6pm–2am; Sun 11:30am–3:30pm and 6pm–2am.*

→ **10 Corso Como** If *expensivo* were an Italian word, it might be the first to come to mind to describe this precious gem on the outdoor catwalk that is Corso Como. It's also undeniably one of the coolest bars in town, encompassing not only a cocktail lounge and outdoor cafe, but also a design boutique, art gallery, and record store. See and be seen with the big names in Italian fashion, if you've got the threads and the cash. *Corso Como 10.* ☎ *02/2901 3581. Daily 11am–3pm and 6pm–2am.*

→ **Victoria Café** This is classic Milan: Liberty style decor, a killer cocktail, friendly bartenders, and a swarming *aperitivo* hour packed with people who work for a living. If you're in the Duomo area and looking for a good place for a drink before venturing further afield for the night, this is the place. *Via Clerici 1.* ☎ *02/8053598. Mon–Fri 7:30am–2am; Sat–Sun 5pm–2am.*

CLUBS AND LOUNGES

→ **Casablanca Café** If you get through the door (face control is tough to pass) get to the back room immediately, in the Moroccan-style tent .Pretty much commercial stuff here, nothing too cutting edge, but a chill night out for the late 20s/30-something set. *Corso Como 14.* ☎ *02/6269 0186. Tues–Sun 6:30pm–3am. Closed Aug. Admission 10€–15€ (includes a drink).*

→ **De Sade** You never know what you're going to turn up at this spot. Music varies from night to night, and so does the clientele. If you're up for some adventure, this is the place. *Via Piazzi 4.* ☎ *02/688 8898. Thurs–Sun 9:30pm–3am. Closed June–Aug. Admission 16€–20€ (includes a drink).*

MTV **Best** → **Hollywood** Hollywood is like Disneyland: touristy, childish, but something that even the stars never outgrow. The celebs usually show up on Sunday night, Friday is student night, and Wednesday seems to draw the largest crowd: "pervert" night. It's sort of hard to, well, put a finger on what exactly that means, but it is definitely a sexy night not to be missed. *Corso Como 15.* ☎ *02/659 8996. Tues–Sun 10:30pm–4am. Admission 15€–20€ (includes a drink).*

→ **Old Fashion Café** The Old Fashion is tucked away inside Parco Sempione and is a nice hideaway from the too-cool-for-school fashionista crowd. This is how the rest of the city lives—in fact, it's so down to earth you may even hear a little Neil Diamond. Wednesday nights, when foreigners get in for free (bring some ID) while Mondays and Saturdays are slightly more upscale. Sunday brunch is also pretty good. *Viale E Alemagna 6. ☎ 02/8056 231. Metro: Cadorna. Tram: 1 or 27. Wed–Sat 8:30pm–4am. Brunch noon–4pm Sun. Admission 8€–20€, depending on the night.*

LIVE MUSIC

The **Ca'Bianca Club,** Via Lodovico il Moro 117 (☎ **02/89125777;** metro: Bisceglie), offers live music and dancing on Wednesday night, from folk music to cabaret to Dixieland jazz. This is a private club, but no one at the door will prevent nonmembers from entering. The show, whatever it might be, begins at 10:30pm (closed Sun and in Aug). Cover is 16€ for the show and the first drink, or 45€ to 80€ for dinner.

At **Le Scimmie,** Via Ascanio Sforza 49 (☎ **02-89402874;** bus: 59), bands play everything from funk to blues to creative jazz. They also serve food. Doors open nightly around 8pm, and music is presented 10pm to around 3am.

Rolling Stone, Corso XXII Marzo 32 (☎ **02-733172;** tram: 4 or 20), features headbanging rock bands. It's open every night, usually 10:30pm to 4am, but things don't get going until at least midnight. The club is closed in August. Cover ranges from 10€ to 30€.

GAY & LESBIAN CLUBS

Nuova Idea International ★★, Via de Castillia 30 (☎ **02/69007859;** metro: Garibaldi), is the largest, oldest, and most fun gay disco in Italy, very much tied to Milan's urban bustle. It prides itself on mimicking the large all-gay discos of northern Europe, and it draws young and not-so-young men. There

is a large video screen and occasional live entertainment. It is open Tuesday and Sunday 9:30pm to 1:30am, Thursday and Friday 10:30pm to 3am, and Saturday 10pm to 4am. Cover is 8€ on Tuesday and Thursday, 11€ on Friday, 18€ on Saturday, and 10€ on Sunday.

Straights flock to **After Line,** Via Sammartini 25 (☎ **02/6692130;** metro: Stazione Centrale), but the club enjoys even more popularity among Milan's gay community. Many nights are devoted to themes. Strong drinks and recorded music fill the night air, and the place is very cruisy. It's open nightly 9pm to 3am.

Sightseeing

FREE → **Castello Sforzesco** Though it's been clumsily restored many times, most recently at the end of the 19th century, this fortresslike castle continues to evoke Milan's two most powerful medieval and Renaissance families, the Visconti and the Sforza. The Visconti built the castle in the 14th century and the Sforza, who married into the Visconti clan and eclipsed them in power, reconstructed it in 1450. The most influential residents were Ludovico il Moro and Beatrice d'Este (he of the Sforza and she of the famous Este family of Ferrara). After ill-advisedly calling the French into Italy at the end of the 15th century, Ludovico died in the dungeons of a château in the Loire valley—but not before the couple made the Castello and Milan one of Italy's great centers of the Renaissance. It was they who commissioned the works by Bramante and Leonardo da Vinci, and these splendors can be viewed on a stroll through the miles of salons that surround the Castello's enormous courtyard. The salons house a series of small museums known collectively as the Civici Musei Castello Sforzesco, which include prehistoric finds from Lombardy, and the last work of 89-year-old Michelangelo, his unfinished *Rondanini Pietà. Piazza Castello. ☎ 02/6208-3940. Free admission. Tues–Sun 9:30am–5:30pm. Metro: Cairoli, Cadorna, or Lanza.*

→ Duomo This is the fourth-largest church in the world with 135 marble spires, a stunning triangular facade, and 3,400-some statues which you can see up close and personal by climbing the stairs to the roof—one of the must-do's on your Milan checklist. It's also a great place to overlook the city and even the Alps on a clear day. You are joined high above Milan by the spire-top gold statue of *Madonnina* (the little Madonna), the city's beloved protectress. Don't expect anything too ornate on the inside, although it is a great place to come for some peace and quiet. The poet Shelley used to sit and read Dante here amid monuments that include a gruesomely graphic statue of *St. Bartholomew Flayed* ★ and the tombs of Giacomo de Medici, two Visconti, and many cardinals and archbishops. *Piazza del Duomo.* ☎ *02/860-358 or 02/8646-3456. Duomo: Free admission; daily 6:50am–7pm. Roof: Admission 3.50€, 5€ with elevator; daily 7am–7pm. Crypt: Admission 1.55€; daily 9am–noon and 2:30–6pm. Museum: Admission 6€; combination ticket for museum and elevator to roof 7€; Tues–Sun 9:30am–12:30pm and 3–6pm. Metro: Duomo.*

FREE →Galleria Vittorio Emanuele II Milan's late-19th-century version of a mall is this wonderful steel-and-glass-covered, cross-shaped arcade. The elegant Galleria is the prototype of the enclosed shopping malls that were to become the hallmark of 20th-century consumerism. It's safe to say that none of the imitators have come close to matching the Galleria for style and flair. The designer of this urban marvel, Giuseppe Mengoni, didn't live to see the Milanese embrace his creation: He tripped and fell from a girder a few days before the Galleria opened in 1878. Bad luck. Apparently, he never stuck his heel into the crotch of the bull painted on the Galleria's floor and spun around, as this supposedly will bring the spinner good karma. *Just off Piazza del Duomo and Piazza della Scala. While the stores keep regular business hours, the Galleria itself is open 24/7. Metro: Duomo.*

→ Santa Maria delle Grazie/*The Last Supper* ★★ Those who have read Dan Brown's *The Da Vinci Code* should come and check this out for themselves. (Don't want to give away the ending, but one of the clues is hidden in this fresco, painted by Leonardo between 1495 and 1497.) As famous as the painting (called *Cenacolo* or "little supper" in Italian) is today, it was a sorry state for a long time. The church was a Dominican convent when the fresco was commissioned, the monks cooked their meals behind the now-famous wall, and the artwork had to be touched up over and over again. To make matters worse, Allied bombing during World War II tore off the room's roof, leaving the fresco exposed to the elements for 3 years. In short, the *Last Supper* is a mere shadow of the work the artist intended it to be, but the work, which captures the moment when Christ told his Apostles that one of them would betray him, remains amazingly powerful and emotional nonetheless. Only 25 people are allowed to view the fresco at one time, and they must pass through a series of devices that remove pollutants from clothing. Accordingly, lines are long and tickets usually sold out days in advance. I'm serious: If you don't book ahead, you'll likely be turned away at the door, even in the dead of winter when you'd expect the place to be empty. *Piazza Santa Maria delle Grazie.* ☎ *02/8942-1146. Admission 6.50€ plus a booking fee of 1€. Tues–Sun 8am–7:30pm (may close at 1:45pm in winter). Metro: Cadorna or Conciliazione.*

Shopping

People don't come to Milan to sightsee. They come to shop. The internationally renowned "Golden Triangle" of Via Manzoni, Via Montenapoleone and Via della Spiga is the place for those looking to pick up the top names . . . at top prices. There can be no real substitute for the swanky bags and sexy shoes displayed in those vaunted windows, but life must go on, and indeed it does in the rest of the city.

The best time for the savvy shopper to visit Milan is for the **January sales,** when *saldi* (sale) signs appear in the windows. Sales usually begin in mid-January and, in some cases, extend all the way through February. Prices in some emporiums are cut by as much as 50% (but don't count on it). Of course, items offered for sale are most often last season's merchandise, but you can get some good buys. **Corso Buenos Aires** has some more sensible yet unique options sandwiched between the big retailers like Benetton, Zara, and Stefanel. The same is true around the **Duomo** and **San Babila,** which also houses names like Guess, Diesel, H&M, and the Italian department store where Giorgio Armani started off his career as a store window designer, **La Rinascente** (Piazza del Duomo; ☎ **02/88521;** metro: Duomo), which bills itself as Italy's largest fashion department store. In addition to clothing, the basement carries a wide variety of giftware, including handwork from all regions of Italy. There's a ground-floor information desk, and on the seventh floor are a bank, a travel agency, a hairdresser, an Estée Lauder Skincare Center, a coffee bar, and the Brunch and Bistro restaurants.

For a funkier take-home get-up, check out the pink boas and flame-embroidered jeans on **Via Torino.** Even further south from the Duomo, **Viale Papiniano** hosts a clothing market every Saturday, where you can dig through the piles of socks and underwear to get to some low-priced (as in: "they fell off a truck") gear by names like Versace and Dolce & Gabbana.

Moreover, Milan is the capital of design, as in kitchenware, lighting, and furniture. Art buffs will go gaga in Milan's hip, home-gadget boutiques that make Ikea look like an antique fair. The stores are found all over the city, but especially in the neighborhoods Porta Romana, Porta Ticinese, and Brera.

The Porta Ticinese area has probably the coolest stores, with stuff you can afford and aren't likely to find in the States. Most of the stores listed below are found in that neighborhood, which is just south of the Duomo at the end of Via Torino.

➜ **55DSL** This Diesel break-off, catering to skaters and snowboarders and those who party with them, has a great flagship in the Ticinese neighborhood with a minibar, a garden, and hip tunes. *Corso di Porta Ticinese 60.* ☎ *02/832 00500.*

➜ **Frip** This is what the Italians like to call "streetstyle": just the usual things you wear every day but that requires a distinctive genre in Milanese parlance. Then there are some more funky, exotic elements from brands like Kim Jones, Anne Sophie Black, and Pleasure Principle. *Corso di Porta Ticinese 16.* ☎ *02/832 1360.*

➜ **Muji** One of the de rigueur stops on Via Torino, this Japanese outfitter has a distinctly East-meets-Milan feel after the space was redesigned in 2005 by architect Chiara Aliverti. Pick up some Asian pajamas and a pack of super-chic stationery, or just admire the eclectic yet subtle collection. *Via Torino 51.* ☎ *02/809441.*

Playing Outside

Milan's two *calcio* (soccer) teams, **Inter** (www.inter.it) and **AC Milan** (www.acmilan.com), share a stadium in the San Siro neighborhood, known officially as Stadio Giuseppe Meazza, but usually referred to simply as San Siro. The stadium itself is worth a visit, as it was rebuilt for the 1990 World Cup and is a beautiful example of Milanese architecture. Of course, what you *really* want to see is a game. In the past few years, and really since their inception, Inter and Milan have battled it out at the top of the standings and, as you can imagine, there is no love lost between the two. (In fact,

Top Designer Fashions on the cheap

If you're not in the income bracket to shop at Prada or outfit yourself in Armani, you *can* purchase designer "seconds," rip-offs that look amazingly like the real thing, or last season's fashions—all at heavily discounted prices.

The wares of designer hot shots are best showcased at **Il Salvagente,** Via Bronzetti 16 (☎ 02/76110328), a legendary shop where you'll find people fighting each other for slashed prices on Alberta Ferretti, Marni, Armani, Prada, and others. At sales times (usually from early Jan into early Feb and once more in late June and July), prices are often cut by an astonishing 30% to 70%. Of course, you must shop wisely, as returns are forbidden. This outlet is the most famous designer discounter in all Italy. Forget the drab ambience, and even expect some clothing to have been worn on the runways (now *that's* a talking point . . .). Not all garments are in A-1 condition. Metro: San Babila.

Another outlet, **Biffi,** Corso Genova 6 (☎ 02/8311601), is one of Milan's oldest and most trend-setting boutiques, with discounts galore. Pick up a stylish scarf or a fur hat, as the fashion range is cutting edge and avant-garde. The labels of new designers are included along with Fendi and Romeo Gigli, plus a tempting selection of accessories. This old-world shop has been run by generations of the Biffi clan. An eclectic range of clothing from such designers as Eley Kishimoto to Jean-Paul Gaultier hangs from the racks. Marni ready-to-wear is displayed in its own mini-boutique, and there's also a branch for men just across the street. Metro: San Ambrogio.

A final outlet for designer discounts is **D Magazine Outlet,** Via Monte-napoleone 26 (☎ 02/76006027), on the main and very expensive shopping street of Milan. But it offers plenty of discounts from the names such as Fendi and Armani, along with other continental big names. We recently visited the shop with a Milanese fashion-conscious woman who admits to being a "Moschino faddie." She found several worthy purchases from Milan's "bad boy" of fashion, much of the merchandise conveying his wild and wacky sense of fashion, especially his parodies of Chanel designs. Designer names from Japan, England, and other countries are also for sale. Metro: Montenapoleone.

Inter—officially, Internazionale of Milan—was formed by a group of rebels from AC Milan in the early 1900s, when the league decided to ban international players. "Inter" then based itself temporarily in Switzerland.) They play each other twice a year in the regular season, and those tickets for the "derby" are particularly hard to find. The same is true when either plays Juventus of Turin, the other northern powerhouse. For other games, it should be enough to go the day before the Sunday game (though sometimes games are on Saturday) to one of the two official ticket sellers. Prices start at about 15€ for the cheap seats:

◌ For AC Milan home games, go to **Milan Point,** Via San Gottardo 2 (entrance in piazza XXIV Maggio; ☎ 02/8942 2711). Metro: Porta Genova or tram 29. Open 10am to 7:30pm Monday through Saturday. No credit cards.

◌ For Inter home games, go to **Ticket One** inside the Spazio Oberdan complex, Viale Vittorio Veneto 2 (☎ 02/2953 6577; www.ticketone.it). Metro: Porta Venezia. Open 10am to 10pm Tuesday to Sunday. No credit cards (Amex, MasterCard, and Visa are, however, accepted online).

The hardcore fans sit in their respective end zones (*curve* in soccer parlance) and these are raucous, sometimes dangerous places to be. Flying tomatoes and oranges turn into beer bottles, and on one occasion, a full-sized Vespa scooter was tossed from the second ring. (Ouch!) It's much better to find something close to midfield if you can afford it, or else up in the cheaper nosebleeds seats in the third ring. (*terzo anello*).

PICNIC POSSIBILITIES

Milan has two major parks: **Parco Sempione** and the **Giardini Pubblici**, or Public Gardens. The Gardens (metro: Palestro) are often filled on the weekend strollers, pony rides, and puppet shows. It is a beautiful park and an excellent place for a picnic, if slightly crowded. Parco Sempione (metro: Cordusio or Cadorna), on the other hand, is much larger and not quite as charismatic, but there's more space to toss a Frisbee.

If you really require some empty real estate, for example, for an uninterrupted, full-side soccer game, head out of the downtown toward **Parco Forlanini,** next to the Linate airport. There's not much in the way of amenities, but if you're looking for expanses of green on a hot, summer day, you'll find it here.

Bergamo: A Relaxing Day Trip from Milan

47km (29 miles) NE of Milan

Bergamo is a Lombard hill town that makes an ideal day trip from Milan, because it's so close and won't overwhelm you with too many sights.

Trains arrive from Milan once every hour, depositing passengers in the center of the Lower Town at Piazza Marconi. The trip takes an hour and costs 5€. The **bus station** in Bergamo is across from the train station. Buses arrive from Milan once every 30 minutes and cost 4.50€ one-way.

Most of the interesting sights are clustered around the two main squares in the Upper City, and once you've had a typical Bergamasco lunch, all that's left to do is take in the stunning view.

There is little reason to spend the night. Hotels here are nice but expensive, and there's not much to hold your attention after hours, since most young Bergamaschi head to Milan's clubs anyway (usually staying through the night and catching an early morning train back home).

Afterward, if you've already done Milan, move on to Lake Como by taking a quick train via Milan to **Como** (at the southern end of the Ramo di Como, the lake's western branch) or directly to **Lecco** (at the southern end of the Ramo di Lecco, the lake's eastern branch).

Bergamo Basics

The **Città Bassa tourist office,** Viale Vittorio Emanuele 20 (☎ 035/210-204; www. apt.bergamo.it), is 9 long blocks straight out from the train station; it's open Monday to Friday 9am to 12:30pm and 2 to 5:30pm. The **Città Alta office,** Vicolo Aquila Nera 2 (☎ 035/232-730; fax 035/242-994), is just off Piazza Vecchia, open daily the same hours.

Eating

Traditional Bergamasco cuisine involves a lot of polenta, cheese, sausage, and mushrooms and, of course, the local Franciacorta wines. Save some room in your schedule for lunch at one of the following restaurants, which are going to be much cheaper and miles more authentic than most of what you found in Milan.

➜ **Antica Hosteria del Vino Buono** NORTHERN ITALIAN   At this cozy trattoria tucked into smallish rooms in a corner house on Piazza Mercato delle Scarpe at the top of the funicular station, an enthusiastic young staff takes food and wine seriously. It's a

Lombardy & the Lake District

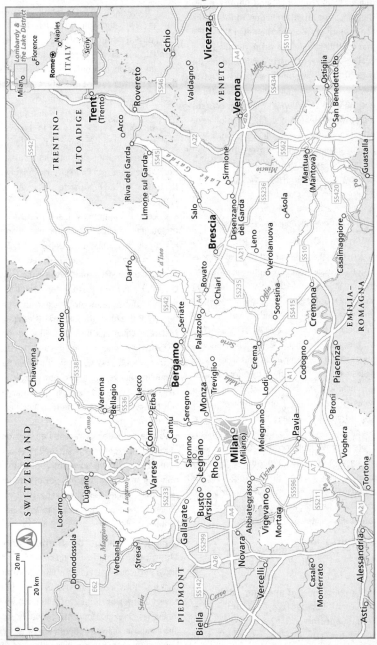

pleasure to dine in the handsome surroundings of brick, tile work, and photos of old Bergamo. For an introduction to food from the region, try one of the several tasting menus. Polenta figures prominently and is served *alla bergamasca* (with wild mushrooms) and sometimes with olive paste folded into it—you can even sample three with the *tris di polenta*. The main courses lean toward meat. A dish like roast quail or rabbit should be accompanied by a Valcalepio Rosso, a medium-strength red from local vineyards (avoid the house red, a harsh cabernet). *Via Donizetti 25.* ☎ *035/247-993. Reservations recommended. Primi 6€–8€ ($7–$9); secondi 8€–11€; menù turistico 13€. Tues–Sun noon–2:30pm and 7–10:30pm.*

→ **Vineria Cozzi** NORTHERN ITALIAN Cozzi isn't just a wine bar but a Bergamo institution. Its cane chairs are well worn with use by Bergamaschi and visitors who can't resist stopping in for a glass of wine while walking down Via Colleoni. Hundreds of bottles from throughout Italy line the walls and are served by the glass (from 1.55€). Sandwiches are always available, as are several kinds of cheese, but the changing daily offerings usually include several pasta dishes and polenta with rich cheese folded into it, perhaps a torta stuffed with fresh vegetables and a main course or two—if the duck breast stuffed with cabbage is available, order it. *Via Colleoni 22.* ☎ *035/238-836. www.vineriacozzi.it. Sandwiches from 4€; primi 8€–10€; secondi 8€–11€. Daily 11am–2am. Closed Wed in winter and Fri in summer. Also closed 10 days in Jan and 12 days in Aug.*

Partying

Via Gombito in the Città Alta is lined with *birrerie* (pubs) and other places to drink. Try the ever-popular **Papageno Pub,** Via Colleoni 1B (☎ **035/236-624**). In the Città Bassa, **Capolinea,** Via Giacomo Quarenghi 29 (☎ **035/320-981**), has an active bar up front, always packed with a young crowd.

Sightseeing

You will arrive in the **Città Bassa,** or Lower City, and that's about all you need to do there. Head directly up the cable car to the **Città Alta (Upper City).** To reach the cable car from the station, take bus no. 1 or 1A and make the free transfer to the **Funicolare Bergamo Alta,** connecting the Upper and Lower cities and running every 7 minutes from 6:30am to 12:30am. You can make the walk to the funicular easily in about 15 minutes by following Viale Papa Giovanni XXIII and its continuations Viale Roma and Viale Vittorio Emanuele II straight through town to the cable car station.

Once in the upper city, make your way to the summit and its two adjoining squares, Piazza Vecchia and Piazza del Duomo. The French writer Maurice Stendhal went so far as to call this heart of old Bergamo the "most beautiful place on earth." Here you'll see traces of the Venetian presence in the 12th-century **Palazzo della Ragione (Courts of Justice),** which has been embellished with a graceful ground-floor arcade and the Lion of San Mark's, symbol of the Venetian Republic, above a 16th-century balcony reached by a covered staircase. The interiors will remain closed over the next few years for renovations.

Piazza del Duomo, reached through one of the archways of the Palazzo della Ragione, is filled with an overpowering collection of religious structures that include the Duomo and the much more enticing Cappella Colleoni, the Baptistery, and the Basilica di Santa Maria Maggiore.

FREE → **Basilica di Santa Maria Maggiore** ★ Behind the plain marble façade and a portico whose columns rise out of the backs of lions lies an overly baroque gilt-covered interior hung with Renaissance tapestries. Gaetano Donizetti, the wildly popular composer of frothy operas, who was born in Bergamo in 1797 and returned here to die in 1848, is entombed in a marble sarcophagus that's as excessive as the rest of the church's decor. The finest works are the choir stalls, with rich wood inlays depicting landscapes and biblical scenes; they're the creation of Lorenzo Lotto, the Venetian who worked in Bergamo in the early 16th century and whose work you'll encounter at the Accademia and elsewhere around the city. The stalls are usually kept under cloth to protect the sensitive hardwoods from light and pollutants, but they're unveiled for Lent. The octagonal Baptistery in the piazza outside the church was originally inside but removed, reconstructed, and much embellished in the 19th century. *Piazza del Duomo.* ☎ *035/223-327. Free admission. May–Sept Mon–Sat 9am–noon and 3–6pm, Sun 8–10:30am and 3–6pm; Oct–Apr Mon–Sat 9am–noon and 3–4:30pm, Sun 8–10:30am and 3–4:30pm.*

FREE → **Cappella Colleoni** ★★ Bartolomeo Colleoni was a Bergamasco who fought for Venice to maintain the Venetian stronghold on the city. In return for his labors, the much-honored soldier was given Bergamo to rule for the republic. If you've already visited Venice, you may have seen Signore Colleoni astride the Verrocchio equestrian bronze in Campo Santi Giovanni e Paolo. Here, the pink-and-white marble exterior, laced with finely sculpted columns and loggias, is airy and almost whimsical. Inside, the soldier and his favorite daughter, Medea, lie beneath a ceiling frescoed by Tiepolo and surrounded by reliefs and statuary; here, Colleoni appears on horseback again atop his marble tomb. *Piazza del Duomo.* ☎ *035/210-061. Free admission. Apr–Oct daily 9:30am–12:30pm and 2–6pm; Nov–Mar Tues–Sun 9:30am–12:30pm and 2–4:30pm.*

Lake Como: Soak Up the Beauty

50km (31 miles) N of Milan

The hype is true and the cameras don't lie: **Lake Como** ★★★ is drop-dead gorgeous. Imposing mountains—the foothills of the Alps—cascade down to the lakeshore, where palm trees flourish on waterfront promenades. It's a geographic juxtaposition as improbable as it is stunning. All along the lake—but especially on the western shore of the Como branch—there are private villas so precious and dreamy that they seem to come out of a model train set.

During the filming of *Ocean's Eleven,* George Clooney was so bewitched by the lake that he bought a villa in Laglio (a tiny, unassuming village north of Como), where he makes several trips throughout the year. What Lake Como lacks, however, is that warm vibe typical of so much of Italy. Its piazzas don't buzz with activity, people tend to keep to themselves, and everything is so well groomed as to come off feeling more Alpine than Mediterranean—which of course

makes sense, given that it is a mountain lake, after all, not the seacoast!

High season on the lake runs from June to September, when all the seaside villages are booked to capacity, and boats filled with holiday-makers zip up and down the lake, hoping to catch sight of George Clooney out for a pleasure cruise. The vast lake, whose three slender basins meet in **Bellagio,** is almost melancholy the rest of the year, but the jaw-dropping beauty is always there. Bellagio is lovely but it's an older demographic—i.e., you won't be partying much—and most hotels are expensive. For a more affordable Lake Como experience, the towns on the western shore, from **Tremezzo** to **Menaggio,** have some budget-friendly hotels, but the view ain't as good as it is from Bellagio. At the base of the lake's western branch (the *ramo di Como*), the city of **Como** is also a good base.

Lake Como

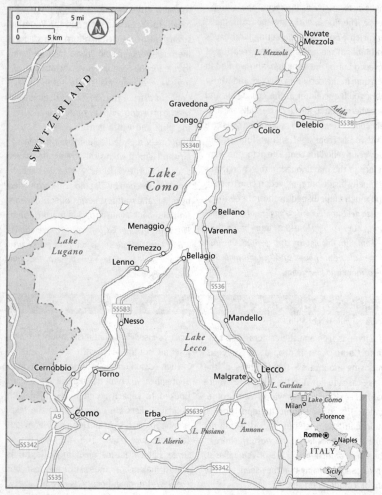

Getting There & Getting Around

BY TRAIN

Trains arrive daily at Como from Milan every hour. The trip takes 40 minutes, and a one-way fare is 5.85€. The main station, **Stazione San Giovanni,** Piazzale San Gottardo (☎ 892021), is at the end of Viale Gallio, a 15-minute walk from the center (Piazza Cavour).

BY BUS

Bus service connecting the major towns along the lake is offered by **SPT,** Piazza Matteotti (☎ 031/2769911). A one-way fare from Como to Bellagio is 2.60€, bus no. 30 to Bellagio. Travel time depends on the traffic.

BY BOAT

Once at the foot of the lake, the best way to get around is by boat, but keep in mind that the last boats usually leave in the evening.

One-way transit from Como to Colico at the northern end of the lake takes 4 hours by ferry and 90 minutes by hydrofoil, and includes stops at each of the towns en route. Transit each way costs 8€ to 12€, depending on which boat you take. One-way transit between Como and Bellagio takes 2 hours by ferry and 45 minutes by hydrofoil, and costs 6.20€ to 9.20€ per person. There's no service from Como between October and Easter.

From Como, boats stop first at Bellagio: by ferry 2 hours; by hydrofoil 35 to 45 minutes. They continue on to Menaggio: by ferry another 15 minutes; by hydrofoil, another 5 minutes. About half the boats then stop in Varenna as well (plus there are about two dozen short-haul ferries each from Bellagio and Menaggio to Varenna): by ferry another 10 minutes; by hydrofoil, another 5 minutes. You can also get day passes good for just the central lake or for the whole lake.

Many of the ferries carry cars for an additional fee. Schedules vary with the season, but from Easter through September a ferry or hydrofoil makes the trip from Como to Bellagio and other towns along the lake at least hourly. For more information, contact **Navigazione Lago di Como** (☎ **800/ 551-801** or 031/579-211; www.navigazione laghi.it); the office is in Como on Lungo Lario Trieste.

Bellagio

Nestled amid cypress groves and verdant gardens, its earth-toned old buildings climbing from the lakefront promenade along stepped cobbled lanes, Bellagio ★★ is often called one of the most beautiful towns in Italy. Be that as it may, Bellagio, as with much of the Comasco region, doesn't even feel like it's *in* Italy. The streets are quiet, everything's clean, people keep more to themselves—it reminds you of Switzerland. Nonetheless, the town's position, at the nexus of the three branches of the lake, provides tremendous **views** ★★★ across the *centro lago*, where

Bellagio Tourist Office

The Bellagio tourist office is at Piazza della Chiesa 14 (☎/fax **031/950-204;** www.bellagiolake como.com). Its hours are Monday and Wednesday to Saturday 9am to noon and 3 to 6pm, Tuesday and Sunday 10:30am to 12:30pm and 3:30 to 5:30pm.

formidable Alpine foothills slope down to the water. Bellagio also makes a good base for exploring the lake, since all kinds of ferries and hydrofoils stop at its boat terminals throughout the day. Because it's more expensive than other lakeside towns, Bellagio also tends to be filled with an older set of vacationers (i.e., your parents, and their British and German counterparts)—if you're looking for a younger scene, check out Menaggio (listed below).

One of the best ways to spend a summer evening in Bellagio is at one of the **concerts** held in the Chiesa di Cappuccini on the grounds of the Rockefeller Foundation between June and July. Also, Bellagio's **outdoor market** fills the waterfront every third Wednesday of the month.

SLEEPING
Cheap/Doable
➜ **Giardinetto** The best lodging deal is at this little hotel at the top of town, reached from the lakefront by Bellagio's narrow stepped streets. A snug lobby, with a big fireplace, opens to a gravelly grapevine-covered terrace, where you're welcome to bring your own food for an alfresco meal. Most of the rooms also overlook the terrace (a flight and a half with no elevator). Most are quite large and bright, with big windows (those on the upper floors provide nice views from balconies over the town and lake beyond, especially nos. 18–20) and furnishings like solid old armoires and, in the better rooms,

box-spring-and-mattress beds rather than Italy's usual cots. Some are on the airshaft, however, or come with no window whatsoever. The place is basic, but comfortable enough. *Piazza della Chiesa, 22021 Bellagio.* ☎ *031/950-168. 13 units, 11 with bathroom. Double without bathroom 45€, with bathroom 52€. Breakfast 6€. No credit cards. Closed Nov–Apr. In room: Hair dryer.*

➔ **Hotel Bellagio** ★ A few steps up from the main lakefront promenade and parking lot, this is a basic choice with antiseptic floor tiles and white walls in the halls, but rooms are attractive and spacious, and those facing west offer million-dollar views over the lake to the mountains. Brushing your teeth in the morning, looking out the window to that view . . . I tell ya, that's how to start your day! There's also a rooftop solarium and gym. *Salita Grandi 6.* ☎ *031/950-424. www.hotel bellagio.it. Double 80€–150€. Closed Nov–Mar. In room: A/C, TV, hair dryer.*

PLAYING OUTSIDE

One of Bellagio's famed gardens surrounds the **Villa Melzi** (☎ *031/951-281*), built by Francesco Melzi, a friend of Napoléon and an official of his Italian Republic. The villa was later the retreat of pianist Franz Liszt and is now the home of a wealthy Lombardian family; they allow the public to stroll through their acres of manicured lawns and fountains and visit a pavilion where a collection of Egyptian sculpture is on display. It's open March 18 through October daily 9am to 6:30pm; admission is 5€ .

Bellagio's other famous gardens are those of the **Villa Serbelloni,** occupying land once owned by Pliny the Younger and now in the hands of the Rockefeller Foundation. You can visit the gardens on twice-daily guided tours (reserve ahead), about 1½ hours long, in Italian and English (tours require 6 people minimum, 20 people maximum). From April to October, tours are Tuesday to Sunday at 11am and 4pm and cost 6.50€. For more information and to

book a spot on the tour, call ☎ **031/951-555.** You meet at the little tower on the back side of Piazza della Chiesa, a steep block-and-a-half up from the port.

You'll probably want to spend a lot of your time sunbathing and enjoying that lakeside scenery. If you're staying in Bellagio, most of the lakefront hotels have their own swimming **beaches.** Otherwise, you can walk 10 minutes north of the town center to swim in the lake at the free public facilities at **La Punta.**

An Adventure Outfitter

The Bellagio region has a great outfitter who can book you some light adventurous exploration for decent prices. The **Cavalcalario Club** (Loc. Gallasco 1, Bellagio (☎ **031/984-814;** cellphone 339/538-138; www.bellagio-mountains.it), runs mountain bike treks, horseback rides through panoramic mountain passes, kayak excursions around the lake, canyoning (a combination of hiking, swimming, rappelling, and, well, jumping up and down a river gorge), and tandem paragliding, lasting anywhere from an hour or 2 to 3 days, starting around 35€.

EATING

Cheap

➔ **La Grotta** ★ ITALIAN/PIZZERIA Tucked away on a stepped street just off lakefront Piazza Manzini, this cozy, informal restaurant consists of a series of vaulted-ceilinged dining rooms. The service is extremely friendly, and the wide-ranging menu includes many pasta and meat dishes. Most of the regulars, though, come for the fish specials, including lake trout. *Salita Cernaia 14.* ☎ *031/951-152. Primi 4.65€–6€; secondi 4.65€–13€; pizza 4.65€–10€. Tues–Sun noon–2:30pm and 7pm–1am (daily July–Sept).*

Doable/Splurge

➔ **Al Veluu** ★ LOMBARD/INTERNATIONAL Al Veluu, 1.6km (1 mile) north of Bellagio in nearby Tremezzo, is an excellent regional restaurant with plenty of relaxed charm and personalized attention. The terrace tables offer a panoramic sweep of the lake, and the rustic dining room with its fireplace and big windows is a welcome refuge in inclement weather. Most of the produce comes freshly picked from the garden; even the butter is homemade, and the best cheeses come from a local farmer. The menu is based on the flavorful cuisine of northern Italy: Examples are *missoltini* (dried fish from the lake, marinated, and grilled with olive oil and vinegar), *penne al Veluu* (with spicy tomato sauce), *risotto al Veluu* (with champagne sauce and fresh green peppers), and an unusual lamb pâté. *Via Rogaro 11, Rogaro di Tremezzo.* ☎ *0344/40510. Reservations recommended. Main courses 12€–20€. Wed–Mon noon–2pm and 7:30–10pm. Closed Nov–Mar 15.*

Varenna

You can spend some quality time climbing up and down the steep steps that substitute for streets in the charming village of **Varenna** ★ (on the eastern shore of the lake, about 20 min. by ferry from Bellagio) that until not too long ago was an active fishing village.

In season, ferries make the 20-minute run between Bellagio and Varenna about every half-hour. There's a tiny **tourist office** at Piazza S. Giorgio/Via 4 Novembre (☎ **0341/ 830-367**), open Tuesday to Sunday 10am to 12:30pm and Tuesday to Saturday 3 to 6pm.

EATING

➔ **Vecchia Varenna** ★★ LOMBARD/ SEAFOOD If you're traveling with your sweetie, don't miss the opportunity for a dinner at this romantic restaurant at the water's edge in Varenna's oldest section. Dining is in a beautiful stone-floored room with white stone walls or on a terrace on the water. The kitchen makes the most of local herbs and vegetables and, of course, the bounty of the lake—for starters, *quadrucci* (pasta pockets) are stuffed with trout, and

one of the best of the many risottos combines wild mushrooms and *lavarello* (a white fish from the lake). Grilled lake trout stuffed with mountain herbs is a sublime main course, though many other kinds of lake fish are also available. *Via Scoscesa 10.* ☎ *031/ 830-793. Reservations required. Primi 11€; secondi 15€. Tues–Sun 12:30–2pm and 7:30–10pm. Closed Jan.*

SIGHTSEEING

The main attractions in the area are actually outside Varenna.

The hilltop ruins of the **Castello di Vezio** (☎ **0341/831-000**) are about a 20-minute walk above the town on a gradually ascending path. The main reason for a visit is to enjoy the stunning views of the lake, its shoreline villages, and the backdrop of mountains at the northern end. May to June the castle is open daily 10am to 6pm, July to September 11am to 8pm; admission is 1€.

The gardens of the **Villa Monastero** (☎ **0341/830-129**) are more easily accessible, at the southern edge of town along Via 4 Novembre, and you can reach them by following the series of lakeside promenades through the Old Town from the ferry landing. This villa and the terraced gardens that rise up from the lakeshore were once a not-so-spartan monastery—until it was dissolved in the late 17th century when the nuns in residence began bearing living proof that they were on too-friendly terms with the priests across the way. If you find it hard to tear yourself from the bowers of citrus trees and rhododendrons clinging to terraces, you'll find equally enchanting surroundings in the adjoining gardens of the **Villa Cipressi** (☎ **0341/830-113**).

Both gardens are open daily March to October: Villa Monastero 10am to 7pm and Villa Cipressi 9am to 7pm. Admission is 2€ for one garden, 3.50€ to visit both. Call ☎ **0341/830-113** for more details.

Menaggio

The lively resort town of **Menaggio** ★ ★ hugs the western shore of the lake, across from Bellagio on its peninsula and Varenna on the distant shore. The real draw here, are the hills. Hikers should stop in at the **tourist office** on Piazza Garibaldi 8 (☎/fax **0344/ 32-924;** www.menaggio.com), open Monday to Saturday 9am to noon and 3 to 6pm (July–Aug also Sun 7:30am–6:30pm). The very helpful staff distributes a booklet, *Hiking in the Area around Menaggio,* with descriptions of more than a dozen walks, accompanied by maps and instructions on what buses to take to trail heads. The town's bus stop is at Piazza Garibaldi (on Sun, on Via Mazzini); tickets are sold at Bar Centrale or the newsstand on Via Calvi at the piazza.

SLEEPING

→ **Ostello La Primula** This excellent youth hostel is easily accessible from Bellagio and other towns on the Centro Lago by boat, and is frequented about evenly by frugal adults and backpacking students, all of whom congregate in the evening for a few beers and maybe some guitar playing on the balcony overlooking the lake. The dorms are relatively cozy, with no more than six beds per room. Most of the rooms have a view of the lake, too—nos. 3, 4, and 5 on the first floor even share a balcony. *One drawback:* no luggage lockers. It's run by a couple of ex-social workers, and they serve an 8.50€ dinner that's so good it even attracts locals (you're expected to set your own table on the terrace, retrieve each course as it's called, and wash your own dishes).

You can explore the surrounding countryside on one of the bikes that are available or get onto the lake in one of the kayaks (rental of either for a full day is 11€). Internet access is 3.50€ per 15 minutes; laundry is 3.50€ per load. The hostel offers special programs, such

as 1-week cooking courses and an organized weeklong hike through the area. Curfew is 11:30pm. *Via IV Novembre 86 (on the south edge of town), 22017 Menaggio (CO). ☎/fax 0344/ 32-356. www.menaggiohostel.com. 35 beds. 14€ per person in dorm; 14€ per person in family suites (sleep 4–6 people) with private bathroom. Breakfast included. No credit cards. Mar 15 to 1st weekend in Nov; office daily 8–10am and 5–11:30pm. Amenities: Restaurant; bar; bike rental; washer/dryer; watersports equipment rental. In room: No phone.*

SIGHTSEEING

The major nearby attraction is about 2.5km (1¹⁄₂ miles) south of town: The **Villa Carlotta** ★ (☎ **0344/40-405;** www.villa carlotta.it) is the most famous villa on the lake and is filled with romantic paintings and statues by Canova and his imitators. Mostly, though, you should see the gardens, with azaleas, orchids, banana trees, cacti, palms, and forests of ferns spreading in all directions. You can take the no. C10 bus from Menaggio or walk along the lake (a 30–45 min. walk). The nearest ferry landing is at Cadenabbia, just north of the gardens, though ferries to Menaggio are more frequent. The villa and gardens are open daily in the months of March and October from 9 to 11:30am and 2 to 4:30pm, and April through September from 9am to 6pm. Admission is 6.50€, 3.25€ for students.

PLAYING OUTSIDE
Watersports

The lido, at the north end of town, has an excellent beach, as well as a pool, and is open late June to mid-September daily 9am to 7pm. For information on waterskiing and other activities, contact **Centro Lago Service,** in the Grand Hotel Victoria along the lakeside Via Castelli (☎ **0344/320-03**). Also ask at the hostel (see above) about boat and bike rentals, which are available to nonguests during slow periods.

Villa Balbianello & Its Fascinating Final Resident

Villa Balbianello is the most brilliant gem on the lake, and it's open to the public. Built on the end of fingerlike promontory that sticks out into the western side of the lake, the 18th-century villa has lush terraced gardens and a preposterously gorgeous setting, with 270-degree views of mountains and water. The last resident of the villa was Guido Monzoni, supermarket-chain heir, world explorer, and apparent OCD-sufferer, who died in 1988 and bequeathed the property to the Italian Environmental Fund. All the rooms have been kept exactly as they were when he died, so you can see his fully stocked liquor cabinet, the room where he studied his maps when planning his next Arctic expedition, and in another room, the gear he wore on the expeditions. The Monzoni element is a totally unexpected highlight of what you go in thinking is going to be just another "historical homes" tour—just make sure your guide tells you all the juicy anecdotes. You can normally only get there by outrageously expensive water taxi (arranged by your hotel), but on Tuesdays, Saturdays, and Sundays, they open up the pedestrian path from the town of Lenno, 800m (a half-mile) away. To reach Lenno, take a bus from Tremezzo. Villa Balbianello, Via Comoedia, Lenno. ☎ 0344/56110. www. fondoambiente.it/english/Properties/Balbianell. March–Oct Tues and Thurs–Sun 10am–6pm. Garden 5€; garden and villa (Monzoni tour) 11€.

Como

Como ★ is the largest city on the lake, and a good hopping-off point to more interesting points north. The **regional tourist office** dispenses a wealth of information on hotels, restaurants, and campgrounds around the lake from its offices at Piazza Cavour 17 (☎ **031/269-712** or 031/264-215; www.lake como.org). It's open daily 9am to 1pm and 2 to 5pm (sometimes closed Sun in winter). There is also a **city tourist office** in a little trailer that has moved around a bit since it opened in 2000, but stays near Piazza del Duomo, and seems to have settled on a spot along Via Maestri Comacini around the right side of the cathedral (☎ **031/337-1063**). It's open Monday to Friday 10am to 12:30pm and 2:30 to 6pm, Saturday and Sunday 10am to 6pm.

SLEEPING

Doable/Splurge

→ **Terminus** ★★ Such a fine hotel and such a dull, unattractive name. This is no run-of-the-mill railway station hotel but a turn-of-the-20th-century Liberty era building, Como's most prestigious address. From its "command" position overlooking Lake Como, the hotel has been completely refurbished, and its public rooms evoke the style of the villa of some long-ago Lombard nobleman. Rooms come in a variety of sizes, ranging from rather small singles to spacious suites, and even a romantic room in the tower, idyllic for a honeymoon. Some of the luxurious accommodations offer terraces opening onto lakeside views. Each comes with a first-rate bathroom with tub or shower. The taste level is high, with sofas upholstered in elegant silk fabrics, bright floral patterns, and highly polished wood surfaces, often walnut or cherry. The garden terrace is a mecca in summer, and the cuisine is among the finest in the Lombard tradition. *Lungo Lario Trieste 14. 22100 Como. ☎ 031/329111. Fax 031/302550. www.albergoterminus.com. 40 units. Double 130€–211€, suite 280€–486€. Rates include continental breakfast. Parking*

18€. Amenities: Restaurant; bar; dry cleaning; gym; laundry service; nonsmoking rooms; room service (breakfast only); rooms for those w/limited mobility; sauna. In room: A/C, TV, dataport, hair dryer, minibar, safe.

EATING
Cheap
➜ **Ristorante Sociale** LOMBARD   Here you'll find simple dishes at low prices. This trattoria tucked under an arcade next to the Duomo's right flank is where Comaschi go after a play or concert at Como's Teatro Sociale (the walls are plastered with unsung heroes of the northern Italian stage and the yellowing posters of plays in which they appeared). It's where the local soccer team celebrates victories, where the equivalent of the ladies' auxiliary meets to have long, voluble conversations while enjoying one of the best-priced fixed menus on the lake. The fixed menus give you your choice of four primi (first courses), four secondi (second courses), side dish, and water or wine (though they usually give you both at no extra charge). Just steer clear of the fish—it's frozen . . . rather scandalous for a place located just 2 blocks from the fishing boats bobbing in the lake harbor. They also rent rooms. *Via Maestri Comacini 8.* ☎ *031/264-042. Primi 4€–8€; secondi 7€–14€; fixed-price menu 16€ with wine. Tues–Sun noon–2pm and 7:30–10:30pm.*

Doable/Splurge
➜ **La Colombetta** ★★ SEAFOOD/ITALIAN In the historic center, this restaurant—one of the resort's finest—is installed in an old church that dates from the early 14th century. There is a main high-ceilinged dining room plus two smaller dining areas installed in what were former chapels of a medieval church. In addition, there are two lounges upstairs—one for smokers, one for nonsmokers. Many old favorites appear on the menu along with several innovative dishes. Sardinia is also represented on the menu by both wines and cuisine. For a truly tantalizing

pasta, opt for the black tagliolini with mullet roe. It's not everyone's cuppa, but for the serious foodie a remarkable treat. You can also order sea bass cooked in a salt crust to preserve its aroma and juices. Well worth ordering is the fresh turbot with artichokes and asparagus or porcini mushrooms. One fish, called "gilthead," is cooked in Vernaccia, a wine imported from Sardinia. The dish is well crafted, and, in the words of our dining companion, "contains a bit of soul." *Via Diaz 40.* ☎ *031/262703. Reservations recommended. Main courses 12€–35€. Mon–Sat 12:30–2:30pm and 7:30–11pm; also Sun Mar–July 12:30–2:30pm and 7:30–11pm. Closed Dec 23–Jan 2.*

SIGHTSEEING
Part Gothic and part Renaissance, the **Duomo,** Piazza del Duomo, in the center of town just off the lake (☎ **031/265-244**), is festooned with some pretty wild masonry and sculpture. Statues of two of the town's famous native sons, Pliny the Elder and Pliny the Younger, flank the main entrance. Inside, beneath an 18th-century dome by Juvarra— the architect who designed much of Turin—is a lavish interior hung with mostly 16th-century paintings and tapestries, with lots of helpful leaflets in English to explain the major works of art. It's open daily 7:30am to noon and 3 to 7pm.

Como's main street, **Corso Vittorio Emanuele II,** cuts through the medieval quarter, where wood-beamed houses line narrow streets. Just 2 blocks south of the Duomo, the five-sided 12th-century **San Fedele** stands above a charming square of the same name; parts of the church, including the altar, date from the 6th century. It's open daily 8am to noon and 3:30 to 7pm. To see Como's most alluring church, though, it's necessary to venture into the dull outlying neighborhood southwest of the center where, just off Viale Roosevelt, you'll come to the five-aisle heavily frescoed **Basilica of**

Como's Lido

The best swimming in town is at the **Lido Villa Olmo,** Via Percernobbio 2 (☎ 031-570968), a pool adjoining a sandy stretch of beach for sunbathing (May 20–Sept 15). Admission is 6€, and it's open daily 9am to 6pm.

Sant'Abbondio (☎ 031/338-8111), a Romanesque masterpiece from the 11th century with great 14th-century frescoes (bring coins so you can illuminate them). It's open daily 8am to 6pm (unless a wedding, which is popular here, is on).

Lakeside life revolves around Piazza Cavour and the adjoining Giardini Pubblici, where the circular **Tempio Voltano** (☎ 031/574-705) houses memorabilia on the life and experiments of native son and electricity pioneer Alessandro Volta; its hours are Tuesday to Sunday 10am to noon and 3 to 6pm (2–4pm Oct–Mar); admission is 1.50€. For a quick retreat and some stunning views, take the funicular (☎ 031/303-608) for a 7-minute ride up to the top of Brunate, the forested hill above the town (it leaves from the Lungo Lario Trieste every 15 min. or so, in summer every half-hour).

SHOPPING

Because this lakeside city has such a thriving silk industry, there's great shopping for scarves, blouses, lingerie, and neckties. Before you buy, you might be interested in knowing more about the history and techniques of the silk industry; if that's the case, head for the **Museo Didattico della Seta,** Via Castelnuovo 1 (☎ 031/303180; Tuesday to Friday 9am to noon and 3 to 6pm; bus: 7). Maintained by a local trade school, it displays antique weaving machines and memorabilia going back to the Renaissance concerning the world's most elegant fabric. The relatively expensive admission is 8€.

Not all the silk factories will sell retail to individuals, but the best of those that do include **Martinetti,** Via Torriani 41 (☎ 031/269053).

Liguria & the Italian Riviera

Tucked into the northwest corner of Italy between Tuscany and the French border, Liguria is most well known for its pebbly beaches, terraced hillsides, port cities, and fishing villages stretched along the long arc of the Ligurian coast, which has drawn international jetsetters for over 200 years. In the past, the region was a favorite haunt of Ernest Hemingway and Ezra Pound; today it's a hip hot spot with celebs such as Michael Jordan and Naomi Campbell, who sail in on private yachts from around the Mediterranean.

The capital of Liguria, **Genoa,** was the birthplace of Christopher Columbus, and while the city is infamous for its squalid port and seedy side streets, it is also home to some of the country's finest *palazzi.* To the southeast, along the stretch of coast known as the Riviera di Levante, you'll find the trendy port towns of **Santa Margherita, Portofino,** and **Rapallo.** Farther down the coast lies the **Cinque Terre,** which is where you might want to head if you're all cultured out. The Cinque Terre and the Riviera Ligure are the one tourist-saturated part of Italy that won't bombard you with art and history, so if you're looking for pretty scenery and need to rest your brain for a while . . . head for the seaside villages.

The Cinque Terre is in fact, one of Italy's hottest tourist spots. It consists of five fishing villages strung along the coast. A hike along the forested, vineyard-clad trail that connects the towns is a must for any traveler to Liguria. And while you're in the area, sample the regional specialties, some of which have become famous throughout the world: Liguria is where pesto sauce and focaccia bread were invented; lesser-known *farinata,* a salty bread made from chick peas, makes for great budget snacking.

Liguria & the Italian Riviera

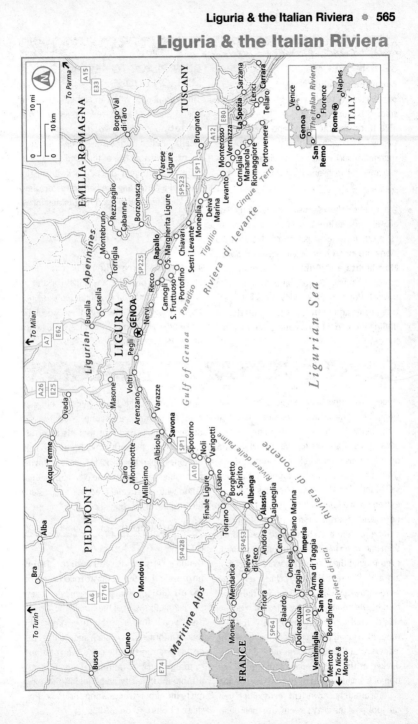

The Best of Genoa & Liguria

BEST MUSEUM

Aquarium of Genoa. Sure, the entrance fee of 13€ is likely to blow your budget, but the splurge is worth it: Here, you'll not only be able to escape the grime and seediness of Genoa for a couple of hours, but you'll be surrounded by such creatures as sharks, penguins, stingrays, jellyfish, and fish galore. See p. 573.

BEST BEACHES

While sandy shores along the Ligurian coast are a dime a dozen, by far the prettiest, cleanest, and often least-crowded stretch lies along **the stretch of coast between Santa Margherita and Portofino.** As you walk out of town from Santa Margherita heading towards Portofino, the sandy spots keep getting better and better; it's just a matter of finding the perfect patch and claiming it for the day.

BEST PLACE TO FEEL LIKE A MILLION BUCKS

The only people who can actually afford to spend more than a few hours in ritzy **Portofino** are Hollywood jet-setters and wealthy Italian businessmen. For the rest of us, experience a slice of the good life by sipping a ridiculously priced cocktail on the patio of a cafe along the harbor in Portofino and keep your eyes open for famous faces. See p. 580.

BEST WAY TO BURN OFF ALL THAT GELATO

The **Cinque Terre hike** is not just utterly stunning but provides a serious workout as well. By the time you've completed the Monterosso-Vernazza and Vernazza-Corniglia stretches, you'll have definitely earned a double-scooped gelato. See p. 586.

Genoa: A City with a Certain Charm

142km (88 miles) SW of Milan; 501km (311 miles) NW of Rome

Once a wealthy, bustling port city, today Genoa is not the cleanest nor most attractive Italian city, but there're still plenty of reasons to visit—pesto sauce, the aquarium, and an illustrious maritime history among them. Once upon a time, Christopher Columbus sailed the ocean blue from Genoa's port, and extremely wealthy Italians set up residence here and poured money into elaborate palazzi. Genoa has changed so much since then that when it hosted the 2001 G-8 summit, even though the city streets were cleared of any and all potentially shady characters (who were thrown into local prisons for the duration of the summit), and an iron barricade was erected to seal off the old city, the city was still deemed too dangerous for the world leaders, and the summit was moved to ships docked at the port! Today, with the exception of a small section of the old city, Genoa is unfortunately, downright seedy. But if you can look past the dirty streets with their neon

kitsch and grunge that seems to cling to everything and everyone who passes through, you'll find that there is a certain charm to the city, with its well-preserved old buildings, sparkling seaside, houses clinging to hillsides overlooking the city, and a population whose charisma breathes a refreshing life into the often squalid city.

Getting There

BY AIR

Genoa's airport is **Aeroporto Internazionale di Genova Cristoforo Colombo** (☎ 010/60151; www.airport.genova.it), several kilometers west of the city. In the arrivals area, you'll find a post office, bank, and tourist information booth. A shuttle bus connects the airport to the city's train stations, running every 30 minutes from 6:15am–11:20pm into the city and 5:30am to 10:30pm out to the airport from Stazione Brignole. Purchase tickets (3€) on the bus.

Genoa from Above

The best way to discover some beauty in Genoa is to view if from high above. From here, the dodgy characters, dirty streets, and neon signs are invisible, and the medieval rooftops and open waters dominate. Here are some of the best places to catch a glimpse of this side of the city:

→ For a view of Genoa's port, go for a ride on the cranelike lift known as **Il Bigo,** next to the aquarium. Maps along the walls of Il Bigo's cabin point out what's what. From here, a good 40m (131 ft.) above the ground, the entire port is visible, from docked cruise ships to industrial plants, as well as the rooftops of the city and the hills to the north. For information, see the listing for Acquario di Genova, p. 573.

→ Though locals ride the *funicolare* (funicular railway) for purely practical reasons, the slanted railway also provides travelers with panoramic views of the city. For the best views, try the one departing from Piazza del Portello, on the north side of the street between the tunnels. It's open daily 6:40am–midnight.

→ Another way to take advantage of the public transportation is to ride **bus 40,** which follows the windy streets up the hill behind Piazza della Nunziata. Get off on Via Costanzi, where the youth hostel has a huge terrace that you can sneak onto for a bird's-eye view of the city. Catch the bus either from Stazione Brignole, or from Piazza della Nunziata.

BY TRAIN

There are two main train stations in Genoa: **Stazione Principe** (aka Genova P.P.) in the north and **Stazione Brignole** (aka Genova B.R.) in the east. If you get off at the wrong station, frequent bus and train connections can easily transport you to the other station. Trains connect Genoa to major Italian cities such as Rome and Milan, and there is frequent service to Pisa, with stops along the Ligurian Riviera and the Cinque Terre on the way. In Stazione Principe, the ticket office is open daily 5:45am to 7:30pm for domestic reservations and 6am to 7:40pm for international reservations. The information office is open 7am to 9pm. In Stazione Brignole, the ticket office is open daily 6am to 10pm for domestic reservations, and 6:30am to 8pm for international reservations. Left luggage is available in both stations, open 7am to 11pm and charging 3.80€ for the first 5 hours, .60€ per hour after that up to 12 hours, and then .20€ per hour after that.

BY BUS

Buses connecting Genoa to other parts of Liguria, Italy, and Europe arrive and depart from the main bus station at Stazione Principe. For information and tickets, visit **PESCI** at Piazza della Vittoria 94r (☎ **010/564936**).

Getting Around & Orientation

Genoa lies in the northern corner of the Ligurian Sea, and so has a huge stretch of coastline. Unfortunately, with the exception of a small section, known as **Porto Antico,** the waterfront area is for the most part seedy and best avoided. The city's two train stations lie in the northern and eastern corners of the city, respectively. From Stazione Principe, take Via Balbi through Piazza della Nunziata to the Centro Storico (Old Genoa) and palazzo-lined Via Garibaldi. From Stazione Brignole, follow either Via San Vicenzo or Via Fiume to Via XX Settembre, the city's main shopping street. Piazza Ferrari

OKKIO! Watch Where You Walk in Genoa

Not to sound like a nagging parent, but in Genoa it is important to watch your back. While quiet back alleys may look like an appealing place to wander, they should be avoided, especially after dark and in the midafternoons and weekends when shops are closed and muggers prey on lone walkers. We inadvertently walked down a quaint side street during the lunch hour and received dirty looks from several scantily clad ladies hanging out in building doorways. Certain areas of the city, often filled with heroin addicts and prostitutes, should be avoided at all times: the area around **Via della Maddalena** and **Via Sottoripa,** as well as **Via di Prè** in its entirety. Always be extra vigilant when walking alone, keep your wallet safely hidden, and try not to flash expensive objects.

sits in the city center, and connects XX Settembre with Via Garibaldi (via Via XXV Aprile). Behind the city center, roads weave their way up the mainly residential hillsides.

BY BUS

Genoa has an excellent and extremely useful **bus** system: If at anytime you find yourself lost in the city, simply hop on one of the frequent buses running to and from both train stations. Purchase tickets at newsstands and ticket booths, and be sure to validate them on the bus. Tickets that allow for 90 minutes of travel cost 1€. Day passes can also be purchased for 3€. For more information on public transportation, visit **www.amt. genova.it**.

BY TAXI

Taxis are available at several stands in the city. To call a cab, dial ☎ **010/5966.** Taxis are especially handy if you're out late at night and looking for a safe way to get home.

ON FOOT

Since a good part of the old city is accessible only by foot, this is a good way to explore Genoa. Get a good map, and when looking for specific addresses, keep in mind that street numbers may occur twice, in different colors: Those in red are for commercial addresses, and those in black are for offices or residences.

Tourist Offices

The main **APT Tourist Office** is at Via Roma 11 (☎ **010/576791;** www.apt.genova.it), open daily 9:30am to 1pm and 2:30 to 6pm. Branch offices are located in Stazione Principe (☎ 010/2530671; open daily 9:30am–1pm and 2:30–6pm) and at the airport (☎ 010/6015247; open Mon–Sat 9:30am–1:30pm and 2:30–5:30pm, Sun 10am–1:30pm and 2:30–5pm.)

Sleeping

Genoa offers a variety of accommodation for all budgets, from a Hostelling International hostel to gorgeous guesthouses in converted palazzi. Be sure to avoid establishments in the Centro Storico and near the port, unless recommended below: You probably don't want to mix with the other hotel-seeking clientele there—they tend to rent their rooms by the hour.

HOSTEL

➜ **Ostello Per La Gioventù (HI)** ★ As with many other HIs, this place is big, far from the city center, and utterly soulless. And as an added bonus, the hostel is affiliated with a daycare center, so during the day there's no escape from the sound of screaming kids. In compensation, the views from the hostel can't be beat: It sits clinging to the cliffs above the city and has a huge terrace with great views of the sun setting over Genoa. The

Genoa

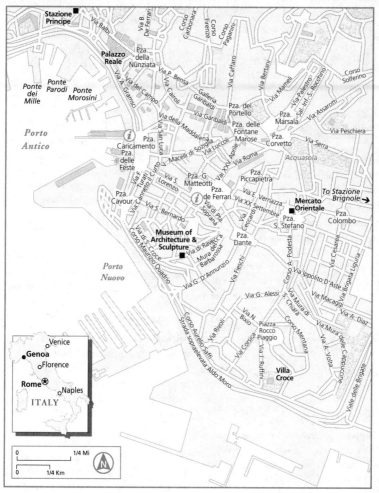

Stazione
Principe

Palazzo
Reale

Via Balbi

Via B.
De Ferrari

Corso
Gaboharia

Corso
Firenze

Corso
Paganini

Via
della
Nunziata

Via P. Bensa

Via del Campo

Via Caffaro

Via Bertani

Via Mameli

Via Palestro

Sal. Inf. S. Rocchino

Corso
Solferino

Ponte
dei
Mille

Ponte
Parodi

Ponte
Morosini

Via A. Gramsci

Via Carroli

Galleria
Garibaldi

Via Garibaldi

Pza. del
Portello

Pza.
Marsala

Via Assarotti

Via Peschiera

Porto
Antico

Via della Maddalena

Via San Luca

Pza.
Caricamento

Pza.
delle
Feste

V. Macelli di Soziglia

Via Luccoli

Pza. delle
Fontane
Marose

Pza.
Corvetto

Via Serra

Acquasola

Via XXV Aprile

Via Roma

Via F. Turati

Via Lanzerotto il Curto

Via S.
Lorenzo

Pza. G.
Matteotti

Pza.
Piccapietra

Pza.
Cavour

Via S. Bernardo

Pza.
de Ferrari

Via di Pta.
Soprana

Via E. Vernazza

Via XX Settembre

Mercato
Orientale

To Stazione
Brignole

Pza. di
Colombo

Via di S. Croce

Corso Maurizio Quadrio

Museum of
Architecture &
Sculpture

Via di Ravecca

Mura di
Barbarossa

Pza.
Dante

Via Ceccardi

Pza.
S. Stefano

Corso A. Podestà

Via Cesarea

Via Brigata Liguria

Porto
Nuovo

Via G. D'Annunzio

Via Fieschi

Corso A. Ippolito D'Aste

Via Mura di S. Chiara

Via Macaggi

Via A. Diaz

Via G. Alessi

Via N.
Bixio

Piazza
Rocco
Piaggio

Corso Aurelio Saffi

Strada sopraelevata Aldo Moro

Via Rivoli

Via Corsica

Via J. Ruffini

Corso Mentana

Via A. Volta

Villa
Croce

Viale delle Brigate

Via Mura delle Cappuccine

Venice

Genoa

Florence

Rome

Naples

ITALY

0   1/4 Mi
0   1/4 Km

---

hostel also has a TV room, Internet access, and a so-called bar that is essentially a cafeteria serving up mediocre but cheap meals. But as it is the only hostel in town, it makes for a good budget option. *Via Constanzi 120.* ☎ *010/2422457. www.geocities.com/hostelge. Dorm bed 15€; double room with shared bath 36€; 3-, 4-, and 5-bed family rooms, some with private bath, 16€ per person. Breakfast included. HI membership required. To get here: Take bus #40 from Stazione Brignole or Piazza* della Nunziata, a 30–40 min. ride, and ask the bus driver to let you off at the Ostello.

CHEAP

➜ **Albergo Caffaro** A no-frills establishment on the top floor of a converted palazzo offering eight basic rooms (there's not much here besides the bed) that nonetheless are cozy and feel more like a bedroom than a hotel room. *Via Caffaro 3 (off Piazza Portello).* ☎ *010/2472362. www.albergocaffaro.it. Single*

Recommended Website

The official website of the Genoa tourist board is www.apt.genova.it, with information on attractions, accommodation, and restaurants. This website is also a good place to look for upcoming events and local news.

35€ with shared bathroom, 45€ with private bathroom; double 50€ with shared bathroom, 60€ with private bathroom; triple 65€ with shared bathroom, 80€ with private bathroom.

→ **Albergo Carola** ★ Conveniently located near Stazione Brignole, the rooms here are basic but comfortable, and the owners have made an attempt to spruce things up with some decor—definitely request one with a garden view—and the bathrooms are clean. At the end of the day, the private garden is a quiet oasis perfect for re-energizing. *Via Gropallo 4/12 (near Piazza Brignole; ring the buzzer to enter).* ☎ 010/8391340. albergo carola@virgilio.it. Single 28€ with shared bathroom, 35€ with private bathroom; double 46€ with shared bath, 56€ with private bath.

DOABLE

→ **Agnello d'Oro** ★★ A family-run establishment housed in a 16th-century convent near Stazione Principe. Relax on the terrace, with views of the Centro Storico, after a long day of sightseeing. The rooms are nothing fancy, a bit sparse and even gloomy, but nonetheless clean—typical of what you'd expect in a convent. The hotel has a bar and offers parking. The rooms all have TV and phone. *Vico Monachette 6 (off Via Balbi).* ☎ 010/2462084. www.hotelagnellodorro.it. Low season single 65€, double 85€; high season single 100€, double 115€. Breakfast included.

→ **Hotel Cairoli** Family-run and centrally located in the Centro Storico, rooms are small

and a bit dingy, but bright and are surprisingly quiet despite the traffic outside. All have TV, phone, and minibar. The hotel also has a quiet terrace, and a bar off the lobby. To deter hookers who might be surfing the Internet for rooms to rent by the hour, the website is keen to state that room rates are for "overnight stop only." *Via Cairoli 14.* ☎ 010/2461454. www.hotelcairoligenova.com. Single 52€–77€, double 73€–88€. Breakfast 8€.

→ **Hotel Cristofo Colombo** ★★ The owners of this centrally located hotel could get away with charging a lot more for their rooms, which are gorgeously decorated with mahogany furniture, richly colored drapes, and chandelier lighting. And the view from the hotel's rooftop terrace is unbeatable. You'll even find a piano in the lobby. Guests receive a discount in nearby Caffè Barbarossa, a cozy cafe and pub. *Via Porta Soprana 59R (off Piazza Matteotti).* ☎ 010/2513643. www.hotelcolombo.it. Single 55€–80€, double 80€–95€, triple 100€–120€.

SPLURGE

→ **Best Western Hotel Metropoli** ★★ These are not the bland rooms you'd expect from a Best Western; recently renovated, and centrally located near Piazza Ducale, rooms here are gorgeously furnished with mahogany furniture and warm-toned colors. The sitting room in the lobby is ultrachic; lounging here in your dirty jeans may draw looks of dismay from fellow guests. *Vico dei Migliorini 8 (off Piazza delle Fontane Marose).* ☎ 010/2468888. www.bestwestern.it/metropoli_ge. Single 87€–142€, double 100€–180€. Breakfast included. Amenities: Bar; Internet access. In room: A/C, TV, minibar.

→ **Bristol Palace** ★★ This hotel is on the main shopping street, close to the Centro Storico, in a 19th-century palazzo. Staying here is like being a guest in a real opulent palazzo, albeit one updated with modern facilities: Chandelier-lit hallways lead to spacious rooms that are furnished with antiques—and carpeted, a rarity in European hotels. Many of the rooms have Jacuzzi tubs. *Via XX Settembre 35 (at Via Ceccardi).* ☎ *010/ 592541. www.hotelbristolpalace.com. Single 130€–269€, double 150€–370€, junior suite 450€–600€. Breakfast included. Amenities: Restaurant; bar; parking. In room: A/C, TV, radio.*

Eating

You haven't tried good pesto until you've had Genoese pesto: a flavorful pasta sauce made from pine nuts and basil, usually served over pasta though the Genoese often use it as an all-purpose condiment, the same way that we use ketchup or mayonnaise. Focaccia, a thick oily bread topped with various ingredients such as cheese or vegetables, is available at small stands and shops all over the city, and at 1€–2€ for a huge slab, it makes for a great cheap meal. For those who enjoy salty foods, sample some *farinata* as a snack; it's a thin bread made from chickpeas and flour and often loaded with salt.

CHEAP

➔**Kilt** ✭ GENOESE This no-frills self-service eatery near the aquarium probably won't be your most memorable dining experience, but provides hearty Genoese fare at an unbeatable price, ideal if you're hungry and short on cash. Dine on the daily menu amongst the city's blue-collar workers and prove wrong anyone who says experiencing authentic Genoa has to come with a large price tag. Too bad it's only open for lunch! *Piazza San Matteo.* ☎ *010/2513801. Full-meal special, including primi, secondi, and drink, from 8.50€. Daily noon–2:30pm.*

➔**Threagio** ✭✭ ITALIAN A popular bistro occupying most of quiet Piazza delle Erbe, with a huge terrace outside and small funky bar area inside. Offers up typical Italian dishes, as well as an extensive wine and cocktail list, making it a great nightspot. Stop in for a meal, an afternoon coffee break, or a cocktail after dinner. *Piazza delle Erbe 15r.* ☎ *010/2465793. Primi around 4.50€; secondi*

6€–8€; panini 2.50€–3€; coffee from .80€. Daily 11am–midnight.*

DOABLE

➔**Ristorante al Rustichello** ✭✭ SEAFOOD One of several popular places that line trendy Via San Vicenzo, this one is particularly worth seeking out for its seafood specialties and romantic atmosphere; it's named for the 13th-century romance writer from Pisa who was a close friend of Marco Polo. Dishes here are quite affordable, considering the upscale atmosphere. *Via San Vicenzo 59r (near Via Galata).* ☎ *010/588556. Primi 5€–7€; secondi 10€–15€. Daily noon– 2:30pm and 6:30–11:30pm.*

➔**Trattoria da Maria** ✭✭ ITALIAN A deservedly popular spot: The restaurant itself may seem like nothing special at first, but if you seek it out in this quiet alley, you'll find a cozy little place filled with locals dining on tasty and affordable dishes which change daily, served up by friendly staff who make time to stop and chat with regulars. *Via Testadoro 14r (look for the neon sign on Via XX Aprile).* ☎ *010/581080. Primi 6€–20€; secondi 8€–25€. Tues–Fri and Sun noon–2:30pm and 7–10pm; Mon noon–2:30pm.*

SPLURGE

➔**I Tre Merli** ✭✭ SEAFOOD/WINE BAR An upscale restaurant and wine bar. For something special, dine in class on sumptuous seafood dishes—try the swordfish rolls stuffed with ricotta and artichokes (16€). The restaurant also has an incredibly lengthy wine list, and staff are happy to make suggestions to overwhelmed amateurs, making it a good place to stop in for a snack and glass (or two) of wine. For New Yorkers who are familiar with the I Tre Merli in Soho, this is the same management. *Vico della Maddalena 26r (off Via Garibaldi).* ☎ *010/2474095. www. itremerli.it. Foccaccia and farinata from 7€; primi 11€–16€; secondi 16€–20€. Mon–Fri 12:30–3pm and 7:30pm–midnight; Sat 7:30pm– 1am.*

CAFES & WINE BARS

➜ **Blu di Ravecca** ★★ This small cafe and wine bar up the street from Museo Sant'Agostino offers up a quiet place during the day to catch up on journal writing or re-energize after a long day of sightseeing. Things pick up at night when they turn up the music and a trendy crowd stops in for pre- or post-dinner drinks. *Via Ravecca 65r (at Via Boccadoro).* ☎ *010/2511147. Panini 3€–3.80€; salad 4.50€–6€. 7pm–midnight Mon–Thurs, 7pm–2am Fri–Sat, closed Sun.*

➜ **Caffe degli Specchi** ★ A busy mirrored cafe on a (safe) alleyway near Piazza Matteotti, frequented by Genoa's business elite—you may find yourself the only one without a tie and briefcase here, especially during the morning espresso rush, and in the early evenings when the clientele mingle and wind down with a glass of wine. *Salita Pollaiuoli 43r (off Piazza Matteotti).* ☎ *010/2468193. Coffee from 1€; wine around 3.50€ per glass. Daily 8am–8:30pm.*

Partying

Genoa's student population makes for a lively party scene, especially on the weekends. People usually hang out in the piazzas, such as Piazza delle Erbe or Piazza Vittoria, or in cafes around Via San Vicenzo until around 11pm, when the bar and club scene picks up, and then they party hard until around 2 or 3am. Genoa's clubs are poorly located on the city outskirts, so you'll have to catch a taxi to get out there, but if you hit them on a good night, it'll be worth the effort. The area around the harbor is unsafe and should be avoided at all times, though especially late at night.

NIGHTCLUBS

The most popular gay spot is **La Cage**, Via Sampierdarena 167R (☎ **010-6454555**), attracting mainly males 21 to 40. There's a 5€ cover, and it's open Tuesday to Sunday 10pm to 3am.

One Wine, One Cocktail, One Beer...

Drink prices in Italy are basically as follows (in all but the chichi-est places in Rome, Florence, Milan, Venice):

Glass of wine in enoteca (wine bar): from 2€, for a totally drinkable local wine that you may have never heard of, all the way up to 8€ for a particularly special vintage of Brunello or Barolo. Most people drink something in the 3€-4€ range. Wine is by far the cheapest (and classiest, since quality is so high) way to get drunk in Italy.

Pint of beer (lager, ale, Guinness, whatever): 4€ during happy hour; 5€ after happy hour—this is the standard in all the big cities; could be a little cheaper in more remote places.

Cocktails/mixed drinks: 4€-5€ in casual, laid-back bars; 7€-10€ in trendier spots. Some obnoxious places in Milan charge more like 12€ for a simple gin and tonic.

➜ **DLF** ★ If you can manage to find your way to this club—housed in what used to be a cinema, with funky decor such as bright blue walls and velvet red couches—you'll find yourself surrounded by a crowd mixed with girls who look like supermodels, greasy guys intent on hitting on the supermodel look-alikes, and a whole lot of fashionable Italians trying to outdo one another in coolness. International DJs often spin here on weekends, and live shows are also occasionally held here. *Via Degola 9.* ☎ *010/593650. Thurs–Sat 10pm–3am.*

➜ **Eccentrica** ★★ This club seems to have something for all tastes, attracting a diverse crowd: several rooms pumping out different styles of music—including the main room with a huge dance floor and a large screen playing videos and cartoons—and a small room with sofas filled with couples who should seriously consider getting a room. *Via Porta d'Archi 9. Fri–Sat 10am–3am.*

BARS & LOUNGES

→**Caffè Latino** ★ Most people hang out in the middle of Piazza delle Erbe, but if you'd prefer an actual seat on the sidelines of the action, and don't mind paying for the privilege, this is one of several bars that line the piazza. Also good for late night eats, the Latino serves up delicious sandwiches until late. *Piazza delle Erbe 20r.* ☎ *010/2757549. Daily 6pm–2am.*

→**Le Corbusier** ★★ A coffeehouse and bar that draws in a bit of a pretentious crowd of local artists and actors. If you understand Italian, you'll have a hard time hiding your smile when eavesdropping on the incredibly self-important conversation of those around you. Luckily, the students who also frequent this place keep things down-to-earth. Sit by the window and watch the world go by outside, or admire the pieces in the frequent art and photo exhibitions that line the walls. *Piazza San Donato 36/38r.* ☎ *010/2468652. Daily 9am–2am; closed Sun in summer.*

→**Moretti** ★★ A cavernous bar that still manages to get incredibly packed, especially on a Friday night, with students who crowd around the bar's large wooden tables and drink away everything they've learned during the week. One of the only places in the city where you can show up in jeans and a T-shirt and not get the evil eye. *Piazza San Bernardo 75r.* ☎ *010/243777. 7pm–2am Tues–Sun.*

Sightseeing

In its heyday, Genoa was home to many wealthy merchants, who all deemed it necessary to build extravagant homes to flaunt their wealth. Today, Genoa's main attraction is its impressive lineup of beautifully preserved *palazzi*—visit their interiors, or simply walk

by the outsides of the old palaces for a poignant contrast between Genoa's historical prosperity and its present squalor. For something a little different, visit the city aquarium; the entrance fee is ridiculously high but it's money well spent—the place is full of exotic sea creatures in informative displays.

An excellent source of information on the city's numerous museums and galleries is the Museums and Culture in Genoa website: **www.museigenova.it**. If you plan on visiting several of these museums, the **Card Musei di Genoa** is a good investment; it allows free entry into 20 museums, including the city's palazzo, and entitles bearers to a discount at the aquarium. You can purchase the regular 48-hour card (16€), or the enhanced 48-hour card including public transport (a bargain at 20€). If you'd like more time, or plan on being back in Genoa in the near future, go for the annual card (adults 35€, students 20€).

MUSEUMS

MTV Best →**Acquario di Genova (Aquarium of Genoa)** ★★ Down at the port, this massive building houses Europe's largest aquarium. The admission is pricey, but well worth it. Here, view jellyfish, seals, sharks, alligators, dolphins, penguins, stingrays, and fish galore. The aquarium has exhibits on different marine habitats in the world, from the Red Sea to Antarctica, with a special exhibit on the biodiversity of Madagascar. There are also several opportunities to interact with the critters housed here: Help feed the sharks, pet nonstinging rays, and walk through a hummingbird-filled forest. Allow plenty of time to gaze in wonder at the marvelous creatures on display here, at least an hour but preferably two. *Ponte Spinola.* ☎ *010/2345666. www.acquariodigenova.it. Admission 13€. Mar–June and Sept–Oct Mon–Wed 9am–6pm, Thurs 9am–10pm, Fri–Sun and holidays 9am–8:30pm; July–Aug* daily 9am–11pm; Jan–Feb and Nov–Dec Mon–Thurs 9:30am–7:30pm, Fri–Sun and holidays 9:30am–8:30pm. Last entry 90 min. before closing.

➔ **Museo di Sant'Agostino (Sant' Agostino Museum)** ✴ From the outside, it's an 8th-century convent next to a 13th-century Gothic church; from the inside it's a museum mainly devoted to Genoese sculpture. Inside the church, medieval frescoes serve as a background to temporary exhibits featuring medieval Genoese art treasures—be sure to stop for a glimpse of Giovanni Pisano's 14th-century panels, created as a monument to Margherita of Brabant, the wife of a 14th-century German emperor, who died while in Genoa. For a breath of fresh air, and a moment of quiet solitude, wander amongst the sculptures scattered in the church's gardens, featuring the usual Romanesque pieces found in any Italian museum, as well as some more interesting wood and ivory pieces. *Piazza Sarzanno 35r.* ☎ *010/2511263. www. museosantagostino.it Admission 4€, free Sun if you can pass as a local. Tues–Fri 9am–7pm; Sat–Sun 10am–7pm.*

PALAZZO TOUR

Genoa's old city teems with stunning historical *palazzi*, or palaces, built by wealthy merchants around the 16th and 17th centuries. Walking down palazzo-lined **Via Garibaldi** can make you forget about the surrounding rundown city. For a quick tour of the palazzi, admire the stunning façades of the building by starting on **Via Balbi** and walking along Via Garibaldi to **Piazza delle Fontane Marose.** For a more in-depth tour, most of the palazzo are open to the public. If you do stop to take a peek inside, you'll find mostly unimpressive art collections but lavishly decorated rooms where you can get a sense of how the Genoese elite once lived.

➔ **Palazzo Bianco** The most overrated of Genoa's palazzos—being the White Palace, as expected, the interior is starkly designed all in drab white. It was built in the 16th century for the Grimaldi family, a centerpiece of the Genoese aristocracy who were forced to sell their home nearly 200 years later to cover their enormous debt; the building was bequeathed to the Genoa City Council soon after. Artwork from the 14th to the 17th centuries is found on the first and third floor; the extensive collection includes pieces by Italian masters as well as Flemish, Dutch, French, and Spanish artists. By far the most popular piece is Caravaggio's haunting *Ecce Homo,* found in Room 10 of the first floor. After browsing through these, take the elevator from the courtyard on the first floor to the second floor, which holds the building's most interesting exhibit: a survey of 19th-century Genoese style, with authentic jewelry, clothing, and accessories from the period. *Via Garibaldi 11.* ☎ *010/5572057. www. museopalazzobianco.it. Admission with cumulative ticket including Palazzo Rosso and Palazzo Tursi for 7€; purchase at the bookstore attached to Palazzo Tursi. Tues–Sat 9am–7pm; Sun 10am–7pm.*

➔ **Palazzo Ducale** ✴ This palazzo is best admired from a seat on the fountain in Piazza Matteotti, where you can take in its brightly colored exterior while receiving a refreshing sprinkle from the fountain. The palazzo was originally built in 1291 to house the city government, which was moved to Palazzo Tursi in the mid–19th century. At one point, the Ducale was also the residence of Genoa's Doge, or mayor. Today, the building contains administrative offices, as well as a small commercial space on the ground floor. If you care to venture inside, visit the museum upstairs, which has constantly-changing exhibits of modern art. *Piazza Matteotti 9.* ☎ *010/ 5574000. www.palazzoducale.genova.it. Admission varies based on exhibits. Museum Tues–Sun 9am–9pm.*

➔ **Palazzo Nicolosio Lomellino** ✴ Built by Nicolosio Lomellino in 1563, this small palazzo has since passed through various wealthy Genoese families. Be sure to check out the interior courtyard, which is dominated by the gorgeous nymphaeum fountain. While it's only open to individuals the first Saturday of every month, group tours occur throughout the week. If you're not there on a first Saturday, you might want to call and see if it's possible for you to join a group tour. The tour covers the fabulous frescoes done by Bernardo Strozzi on the first floor. In addition, the palazzo also features changing exhibitions of modern art (in the summer of 2006, it was "The Landmarks of New York"). *Via Garibaldi 7. ☎ 010/5957060. www.palazzolomellino.org. Admission 4.50€. Reservation required for guided tour. Open the first Sat of every month 10am–6pm.*

➔ **Palazzo Reale** ★★ The name of this palazzo translates into English as the Royal Palace, but you won't find any Genoese kings here. Rather, it gets its name from the Royal House of Savoy, who moved into the palace in the 19th century (it was originally built in the 17th century). This palace is the most impressive in size as it dominates nearly an entire block of Via Balbi. Inside, you'll find an impressive abundance of frescoes, as well as artwork by Veronese, Tintoretto, and Genoese big shots such as Piola and Grechetto, among others. Some rooms are still furnished with original 17th-century pieces, highlighting the luxurious life that was once lived here. *Via Balbi 10. ☎ 010/2710236. www.palazzorealegenova.it. Admission 4€ adults, 2€ ages 18-25, free for those under 18 or over 65. Or pay 6.50€ for a cumulative with Palazzo Spinola; free for those under 18 or over 65. Tues–Wed 9am–1:30pm; Thurs–Sun 9am–7pm.*

➔ **Palazzo Rosso** ★★ Built by the Brignole-Sale family in the 1670s, the Red Palace oozes wealth with its opulent red and gold decor. The building was initially owned by two brothers who each inhabited a separate floor; when the older one died, the younger one took over the entire building and began commissioning frescoes and importing artwork, a tradition which continued with future owners. The first floor holds the family's collection of decent 15th- and 16th-century Italian art—nothing too exciting. On the second floor, most of the mediocre 17th- and 18th-century art should be bypassed, but take a moment to appreciate the family portraits done by Flemish artist van Dyck—a status symbol of the time—and to admire the beautiful ceiling frescoes. Here, you'll find the highlight of the Palazzo tour: On this floor, several rooms are furnished with original period pieces, though sparsely, to allow visitors to get an idea of what the palazzo looked like when it was actually inhabited. Oh, what utter opulence! *Via Garibaldi 18. ☎ 010/2476351. www.museopalazzorosso.it. Admission with cumulative ticket including Palazzo Bianco and Palazzo Tursi for 7€; purchase at the bookstore attached to Palazzo Tursi. Tues–Sat 9am–7pm; Sun 10am–7pm.*

➔ **Palazzo Tursi** ★ This palace was built from 1565 to 1579 for Niccolò Grimaldi, an important Genoese aristocrat, and then acquired by the Duke of Tursi, and went on to house a Jesuit college, and eventually became Genoa's town hall in 1848. You can enter the building for free but will need to pay to enter the museum upstairs, in which you'll find, amongst other things, the first historical document mentioning Genoa (from 117 B.C.), and master musician Niccolò Paganini's old violin. You can also enter the museum from Palazzo Bianco. *Via Garibaldi 9. Admission to museum with cumulative ticket including Palazzo Rosso and Palazzo Bianco for 7€; purchase at the bookstore attached to Palazzo Tursi. Mon–Fri 8am–noon and 1–4pm.*

Sightseeing

➔ **Porto Antico** Genoa has managed to clean up one section of its dodgy waterfront, creating a safe, though somewhat sterile, piazza-like tourist area perfect for relaxing on a sunny day, especially after spending hours in the dark interior of the aquarium, also located here. Take in a bird's-eye view of the city with a ride on **Il Bigo** (a cranelike lift), stroll along the water with a gelato, or hang out in Molo Vecchio, the building in the middle that houses a movie theater, a video-game arcade, and several upscale restaurants—a good place to while away a rainy afternoon. For more information on Il Bigo, go to www.acquariodigenova.it/chi_bigo.asp. *Admission 3€. Discount with aquarium ticket stub. Jan–Feb Tues–Sun 10am–5pm; Mar–May and Sept–Dec Tues–Sun 10am–5pm; June–Aug Tues–Sun 10am–11pm, Mon 2–8pm.*

➜ **Centro Storico** ★ Around the 14th century, Genoa was in its heyday as one of the busiest port cities on the continent, which generated a huge amount of wealth for the local merchants. A walk through the Centro Storico, or the old city, highlights this incredible wealth: palaces that still remain impressive today fill winding cobblestone alleyways. Walking through this section of town will really give you a feel for life in the former glory days of Genoa. *A word of warning though:* Busy Via Garibaldi is a safe spot here, but the quiet alleyways in the area should be avoided when walking alone, when stores are closed, and at night.

HISTORIC BUILDINGS

➜ **Christopher Columbus's House** ★ Before he set sail for the Americas, Christopher Columbus supposedly dreamed of a round earth in this very house. It's said that his father lived here at some point, though whether Christopher himself ever actually lived here with him is a matter of some debate. All that remains is the marble-columned outer frame of the house, which sits in a small garden amidst the traffic and pedestrian bustle of Piazza Dante.

Shopping

Genoa doesn't have a whole lot to offer as far as shopping goes. If you're looking to pick up some reasonably priced clothing, follow the local crowds who flock to the shops along Via XX Settembre, Genoa's best shopping street. Here, brand-name stores sit amidst neon signs and fast-food joints.

For something "special," check out the selection at **Betty Page,** Via Ravecca 5r (☎ **039-010261023**), a bright-pink boutique specializing in retro-style used clothing with extra flair pieces from the 1950s to present, all screaming "glamour" with their sequin, feather, and lace trimming. Sure, you'll probably only wear it once before wondering what you were thinking, but at these prices you can afford to be decadent. It's open Tuesday to Saturday 10am to 12:30pm and 3:30 to 7:30pm.

Mercato Orientale ★, the sprawling food market, might not be as exotic as it was back in its heyday of the 17th century, but it is still one of Europe's greatest and most colorful markets. It's also full of great photo opportunities: You can capture not only the bounty of the Ligurian countryside, including olives, fresh herbs, and citrus fruits, but every known sea creature that's edible (many looking like they are not for the faint of heart!). The market stands at the edge of the historic core of Genoa and Stazione Brignole on Via XX Settembre, close to Via Consolazione. We like to go early in the morning when it opens Monday through Saturday at 7am, although it is bustling and active until noon.

After you visit the market you can wander the streets just north of here, including **Via Colombo** and **Via San Vincenzo,** which are filled with shops that evoke the late Middle Ages. Each one is devoted to a different delight, from the finest of olive oils, canned pestos, and a series of bakeries and pasticcerias.

Most of Genova shops at a large mall, **Centro Commerciale Fiumara,** Via Fiumara, Genova Sampierdarena (www.fiumara.net), 10 minutes from the center. It boasts more than 110 stores, 20 restaurants, and a multi-screen cinema.

Culture Vulture

Theater & the Performing Arts in Genoa

In the performing arts, the outstanding venue is the national theater, **Teatro di Genova** ☆, in residence in Teatro Carlo Felice, Passo Eugenio Montale 4 (☎ 010/53811). With an international season, the theater presents Europe's leading playwrights, directors, and actors, as well as operas. Tickets are available at Galleria, Cardinale Siri 6 (☎ 010-589329), open Tuesday through Saturday from 11am to 6pm and Sunday from 10am to 3:30pm.

Another venue for concerts, dance events, and other shows is **Teatro della Corte**, Piazza Borgo Pila 42 (☎ 010-5342200). Its ticket office is open Monday from 10am to 5pm, Tuesday from 8am to 9pm, Wednesday through Friday from 10am to 9pm, Saturday from 10am to 12:30pm and 3 to 9pm, and Sunday from 3 to 6pm.

Festivals/Events Calendar

○ **Trofeo Fantozzi:** A bike race for the cyclically challenged; here, it's not so much one's speed in the race that counts as one's overall score, with time allotted for romantic encounters along the route, and extra points awarded for having a favorable personality. A big party. May. **www.trofeofantozzi.it**.

○ **The Regatta Storica:** An annual sailing race with participants representing the coastal towns of Genova, Amalfi, Pisa, and Venice. The winner gets the privilege of hosting the next year's race, so it's not guaranteed to be held in Genoa. June.

○ **The Forte Sperone Theatre Festival:** Held in the Tosse theater in the fortified city of Forte Sperone, which sits atop Genoa's historic city wall, performances range from Shakespeare to local productions. July.

○ **Antique Market:** Piazzale Kennedy bursts with true gems—and appraisers on hand to verify their worth—as well as every kind of knickknack imaginable; this must be when the Genoese display their attics' contents in an attempt to liquidate and make a few bucks. Third week of September.

Santa Margherita Ligure: A Nice Beach Town

31km (19 miles) E of Genoa

Most people don't see more of Santa Margherita than the railway station; conveniently located between Rapallo and Portofino, on the east-facing coast of the Portofino peninsula, it makes for a popular transit point along the Ligurian coast. The town itself deserves a visit, however—not just because its beaches beat all others in the area in both quantity and quality, but because the Santa Margherita retains more of an authentic feel than Rapallo and Portofino due to the relatively low number of tourists who actually do stop here. Still, for such a small town, it's surprisingly bustling. Spend an afternoon exploring Santa Margherita's winding streets and waterfront area, lined with shops and restaurants, or simply lazing on the beach along the town's huge stretch of coastline.

Getting There

TRAIN

Santa Margherita sits on the Genoa–La Spezia and Genoa–Pisa train lines, and is easily accessible from Genoa, La Spezia, and the Cinque Terre. The train station is in Piazza

OKKIO! Sometimes You can't Get There from Here . . .

Santa Margherita lies on a busy train line, with trains between both Genoa and La Spezia, and Genoa and Pisa passing the town. However, if you plan on stopping here, be aware that while most trains stop here, others pass by without stopping—before boarding any train, ask at the train station ticket office to be sure. If you do end up on a train that bypasses Santa Margherita, get off at the next town—either Rapallo or Camogli, depending on which direction you're heading—and either backtrack on another train, or take the local bus over (see instructions below for Rapallo; for Camogli, ask in the train station).

Nobili, at the northern point of the town. The ticket office is open daily 6am–7pm. Three **trains** per hour arrive from Genoa daily from midnight to 10:20pm, costing 2.20€ one-way. For more information, call ☎ **892021** toll-free in Italy.

BUS

Buses run frequently between Portofino and Santa Margherita Ligure daily, costing 1€ one-way. You can also catch a bus in Rapallo to Santa Margherita for .80€; during the day one leaves every 20 to 25 minutes. For information, call ☎ **0185/288834.** Purchase tickets from the machine by the bus stop or from any *tabacchi* store.

FERRY

Tigullio Ferries (☎ **0185/284670;** www. traghettiportofino.it) makes frequent trips between Santa Margherita and Portofino (4.50€), Rapallo (3€), and San Fruttuoso (8€).

Ferries depart from the pier at Piazza Martiri della Liberta.

Getting Around

Santa Margherita is easily manageable on foot. From the train station, follow the winding road down to the waterfront. To get to the bus stop, make a right on Corso Andrea Doria, which runs along the water.

Tourist Office

The **APT** Tourist Office, Via XXV Aprile 2B (☎ **0185/287485;** www.apttigullio.liguria. it), is open Monday through Saturday 9:30am–12:30pm and 2:30–5:30pm.

Sleeping

If you're exploring the Riviera Levante, Santa Margherita is a great place to stay, as accommodation is considerably cheaper here than in neighboring Rapallo and Portofino—especially if you don't mind staying in town, away from the water. Keep in mind though, that this is still the Italian Riviera, and so "cheaper" does not necessarily mean "cheap."

CHEAP

➜ **Hotel Annabella** ★★ Run by the friendly Annabella, this hotel is an old apartment that has been converted into a cozy guesthouse, with simple but comfortable rooms. There are no private bathrooms, but the shared bathrooms are clean and plentiful. *Via Costasecca 10.* ☎ *0185/286531. tuamail@hotel annabella.com. Single 40€–45€, double 60€–75€, triple from 95€, quad from 115€.*

➜ **Hotel Europa** ★ A family-run hotel located a few minutes' walk from the waterfront. Rooms are large and quiet, but the decor may hurt your eyes upon first view, with wood paneling, blue satin sofas, and flowery bedspreads, but just remember that it'll all be invisible in the dark. Rooms have TV and phone, and some also have a balcony. The hotel has a restaurant, parking, and peaceful garden. *Via Trento 5.* ☎ *0185/287187.*

www.hoteleuropa-sml.it. Single 45€–65€, double 65€–110€. Breakfast included.

DOABLE

→ **Hotel Fasce** ★★ Friendly owners are happy to dispense free advice to guests, and offer such perks as free use of bicycles and special offers like free accommodation on your birthday and a complimentary dinner for those who stay several nights. Rooms are clean and bright and though are a bit stark and lacking in atmosphere; the quiet garden and rooftop solarium with views of the town below make up for this. Via Luigi Bozzo 3. ☎ 0185/286435. www.hotelfasce.it. Single 90€, double 100€, triple 129€, quad 150€. Breakfast included. In room: A/C, TV, minibar.

→ **Nuova Riviera** ★★ Located in a lovely little Art Nouveau (early 20th-century) villa a few hundred meters into town from the port, this family-run inn has a very accommodating staff who have been in the business for over 30 years. Rooms are large and airy and either have a balcony or big bay windows with views of the surrounding garden, whose palm trees are a refreshing reminder that you are indeed on vacation. The hotel also runs a nearby annex, offering up a few rooms with shared bath. Via Belvedere 10/2 (off Piazza Mazzini). ☎ 0185/287403. www.nuovariviera.com. Single 74€–89€, double 78€–100€. Breakfast included. Annex rooms: single 50€–64€, double 60€–74€. Breakfast not included.

Eating

For a sneak preview of your dinner, walk through the seafood market on Lungomare Marconi (daily 8am–12:30pm). Both Piazza Vittorio Veneto and Piazza Martiri della Libertà are lined with cafes that offer cool drinks and snacks. For a heartier meal, try these restaurants.

CHEAP

→ **Trattoria Da Pezzi** ★★ GENOESE A small, casual restaurant that's often packed with locals who flock here for cheap tasty

Regional Website

The official website for the Tigullio region, which includes Santa Margherita, is **www.apttigullio. liguria.it.** It offers information on transportation, accommodation, sights, and restaurants, and events in the town.

meals. There is no menu here; rather, customers are invited to select their meals from the daily specials on display at the front of the restaurant. Via Cavour 21. ☎ 0185/285303. Primi 3€–6.40€; secondi 3€–8€. Sun–Fri 11:30am–2:15pm and 6–9:15pm.

DOABLE

→ **Trattoria Baicin** ★★ ITALIAN A quiet, family-run restaurant where the cheerful owners cook, serve, and greet guests at the door. Food doesn't get any fresher than this: The pasta is made from scratch every day, and the seafood is purchased daily at the market nearby. Try the mouth-watering trofie alla genovese, gnocchi-ish pasta with vegetables and pesto (6€). Via Algeria 9. ☎ 0185/ 286763. Primi 4€–7.50€; secondi 9€–17€. 1.50€ cover charge. Tues–Sun noon–3pm and 7–11:30pm.

Sightseeing

Santa Margherita is a great place to come to relax for a day or two; its best attraction is its beautiful sandy **beaches** ★★. Grab a spot at one of the popular spots along the harbor, or walk down the road toward Portofino for less-populated and more scenic beaches. When not sunbathing and cooling off in the water, most people spend their time walking along the palm-tree-lined **promenade** ★ between Piazza Vittorio Veneto and Piazza Martiri della Libertà, or sipping a drink in one of the many cafes that line these piazzas. For something less hedonistic, visit the **Basilica di Santa Margherita** ★, noted for its opulent crystal chandeliers (Piazza

Caprera; ☎ **0185/286555**; daily 8am–noon and 3–7pm).

To explore Santa Margherita from underwater, stop in at one of the many dive centers in town. Try **DW&S Scuba Service,** which rents snorkeling and diving equipment, leads guided scuba and snorkel trips (from 25€), offers diving courses, and even has its own stretch of private beach (Via J. Ruffini 2A; ☎ **0185/282578;** www.dws-scubaservice.com).

Partying

After dinner, most people take a walk along the waterfront or have a glass of wine in a seaside cafe. Santa Margherita's nightlife centers around **Piazza Martiri della Libertà,** where in the summertime a young crowd hangs out in the square and its surrounding bars. Try **Sabot** ★, Piazza Martiri della Libertà 32 (☎ **0185/280747**), one of the most popular places in the piazza, with a live DJ on the weekends and delicious sangria on hand. It's open Wednesday through Monday 10am to 4am.

Looking for a completely unpretentious place to shoot some pool? Head for the **Old Inn Bar,** Piazza Mazzini 40 (☎ **0185/286041**), where you can play pool, drink bottled beers, and generally hang out with a crowd of young locals.

Portofino: A Day Trip to the Lifestyles of the Rich & Famous

35km (22 miles) SE of Genoa, 171km (106 miles) S of Milan

Why do people come here? The town consists of a small harbor surrounded by unaffordable restaurants housed in buildings that probably were nice about 50 years ago but today seem ready to crumble into the bay, and a short pedestrian street with even more unaffordable restaurants and designer fashion boutiques. To younger travelers, Portofino will seem past its prime, but due to its continuing popularity with the rich and famous, there is much hype surrounding the town. If your curiosity is strong enough to draw you here, or if you're looking for some majestic panoramas, visit Portofino as a day trip, walk around the town, and then take a scenic walk for beautiful views of the coast.

Getting There

BY TRAIN

There is no train station in Portofino: the nearest stations are in Santa Margherita or Rapallo, which are easily reached along the Genoa–La Spezia and Genoa–Pisa lines (check at the train station, as some trains do not stop at Santa Margherita). From there,

you'll need to catch a bus or ferry to Portofino.

BY BUS

Buses connect Portofino to Santa Margherita and Rapallo (1€). Catch the bus to Portofino Mare from Piazza Veneto in Santa Margherita, or from Piazza delle Nazioni in Rapallo, both of which are located in front of their respective train stations. Buses in Portofino arrive and depart from the stop across from the pharmacy in Piazza della Libertà, at the top of Via Roma. Purchase tickets from the machine next to the bus stop or from the *tabacchi* across the street, and be sure to validate it once on board.

BY FERRY

Tigullio Ferries (☎ **0185/284670;** www.traghettiportofino.it) makes frequent trips between Portofino and Rapallo via Santa Margherita. One-way tickets from Rapallo cost 6€, from Santa Margherita 3€.

Getting Around

Portofino is small, and so easily explored on foot. Via Roma is the main street in Portofino,

A Scenic Walk in Portofino

Portofino can easily be explored in a few hours. Take a stroll along the harbor and shop-lined Via Roma, and walk up the peninsula for spectacular views of the Mediterranean below.

To take in Portofino's best attraction—its gorgeous natural scenery—complete all or part of the following walk, which winds up at the peninsula next to the harbor.

1. Follow the signs off Piazza Martiri dell'Olivetta to **San Giorgio Church** ✶ (free entrance), which served as an observation post during the Roman era. The church is pretty, but nothing compared to the view, with the gulf to the east and the open sea to the west.

2. Continue up the path to **Castello Brown** ✶ (☎ 018/5267101; admission 4€; open 10am–7pm daily), which was built in the 16th century as a post to watch over the gulf. Inside the castle, once-stately rooms are now bare save for a few scattered paintings and carvings. Those in the Upper Gallery occasionally house cultural and art exhibitions. Off the Lower Gallery, the other Riviera towns are visible along the coast from the Belvedere Terrace.

3. Finally, continue along the path (if you still have the energy!) to the **Faro Lighthouse** ✶ at the top of the peninsula for the best views of all.

and runs from Piazza Martiri dell'Olivetta by the small harbor, where ferries land and depart, to Piazza della Libertà, where you'll find the bus stop.

Tourist Office

The **APT Tourist Office** is at Via Roma 35 (☎ **0185/269024;** www.apttigullio.liguria. it). It's open daily 10:30am to 1:30pm and 2 to 7:30pm.

Recommended Websites

○ **www.portofinoevents.com** A good source for information on what's going on in town.

○ **www.apttigullio.liguria.it** The official website for the Tigullio region, which includes Portofino, providing information on transportation, accommodation, sights, and restaurants, and in the town.

Sleeping

Unless you have serious cash, you're better off spending the night in Santa Margherita or Rapallo, or even in Genoa, and just visiting

Portofino for the day. The following are the cheapest of the few accommodation options available in town, although their price range puts them in the "splurge" category.

SPLURGE

→**Hotel Eden** ✶ One block off the harbor on a narrow side street, in a quiet garden setting away from the crowds. Rooms are small but elegantly furnished and have TV, phone, and A/C. The hotel has a bar, restaurant, and small peaceful garden where meals are served in the summer. *Vico Dritto 18.* ☎ *0185/ 269091. www.hoteledenportofino.com. Double 140€–270€. Breakfast included.*

→**Piccolo Hotel** ✶✶ Located a bit out of the way from the center of town, this government-rated four-star resort hotel in a converted villa is quiet and relaxing. Lounge on leather couches in the modern lobby, have a drink in the swank hotel bar, or soak up some rays on the private pebble beach in front. Rooms are nothing special and certainly not the main draw here; the regular rooms are downright ugly and the suites are tiny, though

A Visit to San Fruttuoso Abbey

Around the peninsula from Portofino (to the west) lies the **Parco di Portofino**, also known as the Portofino Promontory, a lush green area with well-marked hiking trails. One of the most popular hikes in the area is to the San Fruttuoso Abbey (about 2 hr. from Portofino; get a map from the tourist office in Portofino before setting out).

Alternately, **Tigullio Ferries** (☎ 0185/284670, www.traghettiportofino.it) runs boats several times a day to San Fruttuoso from Portofino (6.50€), Rapallo (8.50€), or Santa Margherita (8€). Built in the 10th century, the abbey was originally home to a community of Benedictine monks. When the abbey became defunct, local fishermen and pirates moved in, only to be kicked out when the Doria princes came to town and took over. The abbey itself, consisting of an old church and Benedictine monastery, is pretty, but nothing too exciting; the most interesting features are the white marble and grey stone tombs of the Doria family, housed in the chamber off of the lower cloister. Also worth checking out is the museum inside, documenting the history of the abbey, with original artifacts used by the monks. What is most striking, however, is the setting: San Fruttuoso sits right on the shore of the bay, with dense forest looming behind it. For the best views, climb up the Doria Tower, located on the road between the abbey and San Fruttuoso village. There is a large pebble beach in front of the abbey, perfect for cooling off and hanging out after the hike. Pack a lunch though, as the few restaurants along the harbor in the village are pricey and of mediocre quality. ☎ *0185/774480. www.fondoambiente.it. Admission 4€. Daily June–Sept 10am–6pm; Mar– May and Oct Tues–Sun 10am–4pm; Dec–Feb 10am–4pm on holidays only. Last entry 30 min. before closing.*

some have a balcony with great views of the bay. *Via Duca degli Abruzzi 31.* ☎ *0185/269015. piccolo@domina.it. Single 130€–220€, double 160€–260€. Rates include buffet breakfast. Public parking 19€. Amenities: Bar; dry cleaning; laundry service. In room: A/C, TV, hair dryer, Internet port, minibar, safe.*

Eating

Like everything else in the town, eating in Portofino is expensive. It is possible to find an affordable meal if you don't mind having it on the go. While the Portofino experience may just not seem complete without dining at one of the restaurants lining the harbor, a meal here will leave your wallet shockingly light; we suggest that if you want the experience, just stop in for a drink.

CHEAP

➔ **Canale Panificio Pasticerria** ★★ BAKERY   This is the cheapest place to eat in town, which explains its popularity; the line at the counter often stretches out the door at lunchtime. This small bakery serves up tasty minipizzas, focaccia, and *farinata*), as well as pastries for dessert. *Via Roma 30. Pizzas, farinata, and focaccia 1€–2€. Take-out only. Cash only. Mon–Fri 8am–7pm, Sat 8am–1pm. Closed Sun.*

DOABLE/SPLURGE

➔ **Delfino** ★★   If you happen to be in Portofino celebrating a special occasion, or feel like treating yourself to a ridiculously overpriced meal, this is the place to do it. A favorite of visiting celebrities—Michael Jordan and Naomi Campbell have been spotted here—the restaurant was founded in 1889 by Captain Crovari, who decorated the dining room with treasures he collected during his trips around the world. Dine on the terrace facing the harbor and its piazza, a beautiful setting at night when the lights of Rapallo twinkle in the distance. *Piazza Martiri Dell'olivetta 41.* ☎ *0185/269081. Reservations recommended Sat. Main courses 13€–30€. Apr–Oct daily noon–3pm and 7–11pm.*

→ **La Gritta** ★ A small bar along the harbor, this is a top choice for a coffee or cocktail; enjoy your drink while watching the harbor traffic from their pier-side barge. Staff are friendly and don't make you feel like a pauper if you can't afford the food here. *Calata Marconi 12.* ☎ *0185/269126. Light meals from 8€; drinks from 4€. Daily noon–1am.*

Rapallo: A Classic on the Riviera Levante

27km (17 miles) SE of Genoa, 161km (100 miles) S of Milan

The hype along the Riviera Levante is all about Portofino, but we think it's Rapallo that deserves the attention, because it has not become a Hollywood-infested tourist mecca like its neighbor, and it has managed to retain a small-town charm despite the fact that it's been a hot spot with tourists since the 19th century. Sitting at the crease where the Portofino peninsula meets the mainland stretch of the Ligurian coast, Rapallo's large harbor is more scenic, the restaurants along the seafront promenade are actually affordable, and the beaches are clean and inviting. Accommodation here is also reasonably priced, making it a good base for a stay along the coast.

Getting There

BY TRAIN

Rapallo sits on the Genoa–La Spezia train line, as well as the Genoa–Pisa line, with frequent trains every day, making it easily accessible from Genoa, La Spezia, and the Cinque Terre. The train station is on Via Bolzano, in front of Piazza Molfino, and a short walk from the waterfront. The ticket office is open daily 6am to 8pm. Three trains from Genoa stop here each hour from midnight to 10:20pm, costing 2.20€ one-way. A train also links Rapallo with Santa Margherita every 30 minutes, costing 1€ one-way. For more information, dial ☎ **892021** toll-free in Italy.

BY BUS

Frequent buses connect Rapallo with Santa Margherita (1€). In Rapallo, buses depart from Piazza delle Nazioni, in front of Piazza Molfino by the train station. Purchase tickets at a nearby *tabacchi*.

BY FERRY

Tigullio Ferries (☎ **0185/284670;** www.traghettiportofino.it) makes frequent trips between Portofino and Rapallo via Santa Margherita. One-way tickets to Portofino cost 6€, to Santa Margherita 3€. In August, there is also a daily ferry to Genoa (11.50€). Ferries depart from the pier in the middle of the harbor area.

Getting Around

Rapallo is small enough to be easily navigated on foot. From the train station or bus stop, follow Corso Italia to Piazza Cavour, and then keep heading straight down another few blocks where you will emerge from the busy town center and onto the stunning harbor.

Tourist Office

The **APT Tourist Office** is along the waterfront at Lungomare Vittorio Veneto 7 (☎ **0185/230346;** www.apttigullio.liguria.it; Mon–Sat 9:30am–noon and 3–7:30pm, Sun and holidays 9:30am–12:30pm and 4:30–7:30pm). Here you can pick up maps and accommodation information for Rapallo, as well as the other Riviera towns.

Sleeping

For a town this small and relatively undiscovered, Rapallo has a considerable number of accommodation options, many of them quite affordable, although even if you're prepared to shell out the big bucks, you won't find anything too luxurious. If you're going to splurge on accommodation, stay at one of the fancy places in Santa Margherita, or go all out and stay in Portofino. But if you don't mind spending a couple of nights in a basic no-frills hotel room, then Rapallo makes for a good overnight base for exploring the region.

CHEAP

➔ **Albergo La Piazzetta** Close to Piazza Cavour, the center of town, and a couple of blocks up from the waterfront, the Piazzetta is on the top floor of a building facing the piazza. Rooms are a bit noisy and consist of little more than a bed and desk, but are large, clean, and come with TV, phone, and A/C. *Galleria Montallegro 22/20.* ☎ *0185/53620. www.albergolapiazzetta.it. Single with shared bathroom 34€; double with shared bath-room 64€, with private bathroom 70€. Breakfast 3€.*

➔ **Hotel San Desiderio** A 5-minute walk west from the train station or Piazza Cavour, the San Desiderio is a bit out of the way (by Rapallo terms). Rooms are small and basic, with absurdly narrow bathrooms, and although they've been recently renovated, the furniture is in serious need of an upgrade. All rooms come with TV, phone, A/C, and small fridge. The hotel also has a bar and outdoor terrace. *Via San Desiderio 4 (off Via della Libertà).* ☎ *0185/66717. www.hotelsandesiderio. com. Single 35€–45€ with shared bathroom, 37€–50€ with private bathroom; double 40€–60€ with shared bathroom, 50€–80€ with private bathroom.*

➔ **Hotel Mignon Posta** ★ In a quiet area in the western part of town, spacious rooms are small and bright with homey touches such as vases of dried flowers and loveseats, and all have phone and TV. The hotel's restaurant offers tasty Italian fare and outdoor dining on the terrace in the summer. *Via Monsignor Boccoleri 12.* ☎ *0185/230230. www.riviera dellevante.it/mignonposta. Single 30€–39€, double 57€–72€.*

➔ **La Vela** ★ Run by a friendly family, the hotel is close to the waterfront with a quiet garden in back—a luxury at this price. Rooms are nothing fancy but are large and comfortable, though the shared bathrooms are sparse and have seen better days. All rooms have phone and TV, and a few have balconies overlooking the garden. The hotel has a restaurant and bar. *Via Milite Ignoto 21 (off the waterfront by Antico Castello).* ☎ *0185/50551. www.eliteristorante.it. Single with shared bath from 21€, with private bath from 25€; double with shared bath from 51€, with private bath from 56€.*

DOABLE

➔ **Astoria Hotel** ★★ A government-rated four-star establishment run by the Ciana Family, who have been in the hospitality business for over 130 years, and located 1 block up from the waterfront. Rooms are bright and simply furnished and come with TV, A/C, phone, radio, and minibar. The elegant lobby and bar have comfy leather couches. The hotel also has a small private garden. *Via Gramsci 4 (off Via Libertà).* ☎ *0185/273533. www.hotelastoriarapallo.it. Single 80€–120€, double 120€–170€, triple 150€–200€. Breakfast included.*

➔ **Hotel Miro** ★★ One of the best-located hotels in Rapallo, in the center of the harbor, right on the waterfront promenade. The lobby is opulently decorated with Oriental carpets, mirrored walls, and velvet sofas. Rooms are each uniquely furnished (some with canopies over the bed), are all very elegantly appointed, with TV, A/C, phone, and minibar. *Lungomare V. Veneto 32.* ☎ *0185/234100. www.hotelmiro.net. Double (single use) 67€–110€, double 77€–130€, triple 110€–150€. Breakfast included.*

Eating

CHEAP

➜ **La Rambla Café** ★ CAFE   One of the many cafes that line the waterfront promenade, this is a casual, unpretentious recommendation serving up light meals, ice cream, and drinks. Have a seat on the large terrace and dream of the day when you too will own one of the luxurious yachts anchored in the harbor. *Lungomare Vittorio Veneto. Sandwiches and snacks from 4€; coffee from 1.50€. Thurs–Tues 8am–8pm.*

➜ **Pizzeria Forno a Legna** ★★ PIZZERIA Just off the store-lined Via Giuseppe Mazzini, a block from the harbor, this spot serves up delicious cheap pizza—slices for snacks, or entire pies for a filling meal—that you can take to go and eat on the waterfront. *Vico Fortunio Liceti 7. Pizzas 2.50€–3.50€, slices around 1.50€. Tues–Sun 8:30am–12:30pm and 3–7:30pm.*

DOABLE

➜ **Ristorante Elite** ★★ SEAFOOD A block up from the water in La Vela Hotel, this restaurant has all the quality of those on the waterfront, but without the pretentious atmosphere and high prices. Locals come here for the dishes of local fresh seafood such as smoked swordfish, lobster, and other grilled fish. Carnivores or anyone else who's OD'd on fish can avail of meat entrees such as veal or beef filet. *Via Milite Ignoto 19.* ☎ *0185/50551. www.eliteristorante.it. Primi 4€–9€; secondi 8€–21€. Daily noon–2:30pm and 7:30–10pm. Closed Mon in the winter.*

Sightseeing

Rapallo's greatest attraction is its **waterfront** ★★. Here, restaurants and hotels line the crescent-shaped harbor, and locals and tourists alike stroll the long, palm tree–lined promenade. Facing the water, the **Antico Castello** marks the start of the harbor to the right—you can sunbathe on the boulders

Madonna! What a Festival!

From July 1 to July 3 each year, you can take part in Rapallo's **Madonna di Montallegro** celebration: an annual festival celebrating the statue of the Madonna that supposedly flew into the Santuario di Montallegro one miraculous day. The statue is paraded through the streets among throngs of devotees, and this is followed by a massive fireworks display by the water.

around the castle, but the castle itself is only open for special exhibitions. To the left, the requisite-in-Liguria **monument to Christopher Columbus** portrays the explorer pointing towards the New World. Farther down, sunbathers laze on sandy **beaches,** and yachts and sailboats fill the docks. For something a little more active, numerous scuba diving centers in town run chartered trips to spots along the Portofino Promontory. Try **Abyss Diving,** Via Vespucci 2 (☎ 338/151724; www.abyssdiving.it).

In town, the action centers around **Piazza Cavour** and its stores and cafes. From the piazza, shops line busy Via Giuseppe Mazzini.

For an aerial view of Rapallo and the Ligurian coast, take the *funivia* (cable car; 7€ for a round-trip ticket) from the eastern end of town up to the **Santuario di Montallegro** ★ (☎ 0185/239000; free admission). The 16th-century "Happy Mountain Sanctuary" has some well-preserved frescoes but otherwise is of little interest—the main draw is the stunning view. For an even greater view, continue walking uphill to the summit of Monte Rosa, where the panorama takes in the bowl of green hills—studded with villas that someday you will own, just as soon as you win the lottery—that slopes down to the water.

Cinque Terre: Five Breathtaking Towns

Monterosso: 8km (5 miles) E of Genoa

What once used to be five quaint villages devoted to fishing and the production of some of Italy's finest wine is now a tourist haven, although the **Cinque Terre** ★★★ ("five lands," pronounced *Cheen-quay Tehr-reh*) are still very much a place where time has stood still: Car-less cobblestone streets are lined with colorful narrow houses decorated with window plants and fresh laundry. Most visitors come here for the popular, breathtakingly scenic hike along the coast, leading through the five villages: **Monterosso, Vernazza, Corniglia, Manarola,** and **Riomaggiore.** Other travelers pack the coast's fine beaches on the weekends.

Missing out on either would be a shame. The Cinque Terre can be done as a hectic day trip from Genoa, but to fully appreciate and enjoy the region—the first man-made area to be declared a national park—try to spend at least 2 days here, allowing for time to explore the villages and relax your tired muscles on the beach.

Getting There

The towns of the Cinque Terre lie along the coast between the Ligurian towns of Levanto and La Spezia. Hourly **trains** run from Genoa to La Spezia, a trip of 1¹/₂ hours, where you must backtrack by rail to any of the five towns that you want to visit. From La Spezia there are regular trains to the little towns of Cinque Terre. Once at Cinque Terre, local trains at the rates of one every 2 to 3 hours go between the five towns. Be careful, however, as some stop only in Monterosso and Riomaggiore.

A local train runs about once an hour between Levanto and La Spezia, stopping in all five towns in between. There is also frequent service between La Spezia and both Florence and Rome, and several daily trains from Milan also stop here.

If you have a **car** and are coming from Genoa, take A12 and exit at Monterosso, the only town of the five that you can actually approach by car. A gigantic parking lot accommodates visitors, who then travel between the towns by rail, boat, or foot.

The **Navigazione Golfo dei Poeti** (ferry) plies the waters between Monterosso and Manarola or Riomaggiore eight times daily from April to October. For information and schedules, call ☎ 0187/732987. A one-way ferry ticket from Monterosso to Manarola costs 3€.

SUGGESTED ITINERARIES

If you only come for the day, plan on it being a long and hard one. The hike between all of

OKKIO! Beware of Slow-Moving Tourists

Forget about any image you may conjured in your head of a solitary hike through the Cinque Terre hills, where you are finally able to escape the hordes of Italy's summer tourists. Unless you hit the trails at the crack of dawn, you'll most likely find that ubiquitous, sometimes geriatric American tour group ahead and behind you, filing along at a snail's pace. For some reason, these tourists (who aren't handicapped) feel that they simply would not be able to complete the hike without their trusty ski poles in hand, and so in attempting to pass these groups you run the risk of being poked and prodded (ouch!). When the group stops for everyone to take a picture of the local man selling grapes on the side of the trail, take the opportunity to zoom past them, and hope that you can have at least 5 minutes of alone time on the trail before beginning the process again with the next tour group.

The Cinque Terre

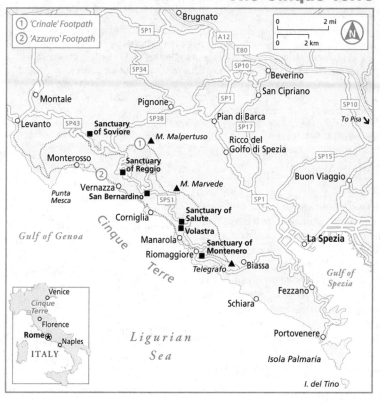

the towns takes a total average of 5 hours, longer if you actually stop in the towns, and you should. If you have 2 days, spend the first doing the actual hike, and the second exploring the towns, either by ferry or train. If you have 3 days, spend the third resting those tired muscles on one of the beautiful beaches in the Cinque Terre. The Cinque Terre also serve as a good base for exploring the towns in the Riviera, as they are connected by frequent train service.

The Cinque Terre card

In order to access the Cinque Terre trails, you need to buy a **Cinque Terre Card.** There are two kinds available: the first buys you access to the trails for 3€. The second includes trail access as well as unlimited train service on the line between Levanto and La Spezia (which encompasses all five towns) at the following prices: 1 day, 5.40€; 3 days, 13.50€; 7 days, 20.60€. The cards are available at checkpoints along the trail, as well as at park information offices at the train station in each town. Be prepared to show your validated card at the checkpoints along the trail.

OKKIO! A Train of Misinformation

Just because the train station information officer is sitting at a desk behind a glass window and wearing a uniform does not necessarily mean that he has any idea what he is talking about. The information and ticket booth workers at the Monterosso train station are notorious for giving out incorrect information: They tell you to take trains that do not exist, guarantee that trains stop in certain towns when they actually do not, and so on. Rather, check with the helpful staff at the tourist information office at the entrance of the train station—these friendly folks have a much better idea of what the deal is with the trains.

Getting Around

ON FOOT

This is really the best way to experience the Cinque Terre to the fullest. The trails between the towns are well marked and maintained, although they can become muddy and slippery on rainy days. The hardest trails are the two at the top end—between Monterosso and Vernazza, and between Vernazza and Corniglia—while the final, low-end trail, between Manarola and Riomaggiore, is actually an easy stone walkway. So, choose which end to start at based on whether you'd like to do the hard part first or last. If you tire of walking at any point, you can catch a train or ferry at the next town.

BY TRAIN

There is frequent train service between all five towns on the Levanto–La Spezia line. Pick up a schedule at the information office in the train station. If you purchase the more expensive Cinque Terre Card option, unlimited train access is included. For those with rail passes, these are valid on the trains and so the trail-only (3€) Cinque Terre Card is the better option.

BY FERRY

Golfo dei Poeti (☎ 0187/818440; www.navigazionegolfodeipoeti.it) runs a ferry service between all five towns. Boats run around once an hour, more or less frequently depending on the time of year. Price also varies depending on where you want to go; a ticket to stop at all five towns will cost 11.50€, or 5€ to stop only at the next town. Ticket booths and information are available at the harbor of each town.

Tigullio Ferries (☎ 0185/284670; www.traghettiportofino.it) runs day trips on two lines between Santa Margherita and Rapallo and the Cinque Terre from 15€ between July and September: Line 4 departs in the afternoon on Mondays and Fridays, and stops for an hour in Vernazza before returning to Rapallo and Santa Margherita. Line 5 departs in the morning on Wednesdays and Saturdays, and stops in either Riomaggiore or Vernazza for an hour and a half, and in Monterosso for 3½ hours, before returning to Rapallo and Santa Margherita.

Tourist Offices

There are Cinque Terre park offices in the train station at each town, providing information on the park and selling Cinque Terre Cards. However, they will not be able to provide information on accommodation.

The **tourist information office** in La Spezia at Via Mazzini 45, beside the port (☎ 0187/770900) also covers the Cinque Terre. Here, they can provide you with information on accommodation. There is also a branch office outside the train station.

Recommended Websites

○ **www.parconazionale5terre.it** The official website of the Cinque Terre

chiesa dei cappuccini: Views & a Van Dyck

Visit this 15th-century church for great views of the town below, and to gaze upon the region's most famous work of art: Flemish master Anthony Van Dyck's *Crucifixion*. It's on Salita Padri Cappuccini (look for signs off of the main street along the harbor before the tunnel). Admission is free, and it's open daily 9am to noon and 4 to 7pm.

National Park provides a ton of information for those interested in the environmental principles of the park, as well as practical information such as accommodation listings, trail conditions, and train and ferry schedules.

⊙ **www.cinqueterrenet.com** A comprehensive website, with information on hotels, restaurants, shopping, and transportation in the Cinque Terre, as well as helpful overviews of each of the towns.

Monterosso

The biggest and most populated of the five towns, Monterosso is also the most built-up and least quaint, although it definitely has its charm. The town has the largest selection of hotels and restaurants, and arguably the best beaches in the Cinque Terre. Sitting at the top of the Cinque Terre trail, it makes a good base if you plan on getting an early start on the trail.

EXPLORING MONTEROSSO

The train station sits in the center of town on Lungomare di Fegina. From here, turn right for the New Town, which is really more of a parking lot than anything else. Most of the upscale hotels are located here, as well as some restaurants and focaccerias. For the Old Town, turn left out of the train station, and take the shortcut through the tunnel, which leads to Piazza Garibaldi. From the piazza, Via Roma and Via Emanuele head through the town, and are filled with restaurants and souvenir shops; the alleyways are home to affordable accommodation options.

To reach the Cinque Terre trail, follow Lungomare di Fegina through to the old town, and then continue in the same direction up the hill and past the Il Castello bar.

SLEEPING

Rooms in private homes are available in town: look for the numerous signs around town and be sure to check out the rooms before agreeing to anything or handing over any money. Rooms usually go from around 30€–50€ per person. Otherwise, the hotels can get a bit pricey.

Cheap

➔**Hotel Souvenir** Best avoided if you can find cheap accommodation elsewhere or don't mind spending a bit extra for a decent place to stay, this hotel is nonetheless one of the most affordable options in town and therefore usually booked way in advance. The staff speak very little English, and you'll probably have to put up a fight to get a room even if you have a confirmed reservation. Rooms are tiny but clean, as are the shared bathrooms, which are nonetheless few and far between. *Via Gioberti 24 (off Via Roma).* ☎ *0187/817595. hotel_souvenir@yahoo.com. Double (single use) with shared bathroom 40€; double with shared bathroom 50€, with private bathroom 80€; triple with shared bathroom 75€, with private bathroom 105€.*

Doable

➔**Albergo Margherita** ★ A small hotel in the old town with friendly, helpful owners. The rooms are tiny and quite unattractive, with tacky wood paneling on the walls and

Hitting the Beaches

Monterosso is home to the Cinque Terre's only sandy **beaches** ★. The best, and most popular, stretch of sand is in front of the train station. There is another decent beach in front of Piazza Garibaldi, although it's a bit dirtier and sits next to the ferry traffic.

even tackier furniture, but they are nonetheless clean and cheaper than most other hotel rooms in town. *Via Roma 72 (at Via Gioberti).* ☎ *0187/808002. Double 60€–80€.*

➔ **Hotel Amici** ★ Located on a quiet street in the old town, rooms at this hotel are basic but comfortable, all with TV, A/C, and phone, and many with great views of the town and sea from the balcony, or else of the hotel's garden. Staff are very friendly and full of helpful advice about the Cinque Terre. *Via Buranco 36 (off Via Roma).* ☎ *0187/817544. www.hotelamici.it. Single 63€–78€, double 106€–136€. Breakfast included.*

Splurge

➔ **Hotel La Colonnina** ★ A family-owned hotel in the old town in a quiet garden setting. Bright rooms have TV, A/C, and phone, and a few have a balcony as well. The hotel has a solarium and rooftop terrace for relaxing at the end of the day. *Via Zuecca 6 (off Piazza Garibaldi).* ☎ *0187/817439. www. lacolonninacinqueterre.it. Double (single use) 70€, double from 95€, triple 130€, quad 160€. Breakfast included.*

EATING

Monterosso has a plethora of restaurants, the largest selection of all the Cinque Terre towns. For a cheap meal or snack, grab some focaccia or a mini pizza; otherwise dine on seafood and fresh pasta in one of the old town's restaurants.

Cheap

➔ **Focacceria Il Frantoio** ★★ BAKERY It's a tiny unremarkable local bakery from the outside, but don't pass this place by. Step inside for *farinata*, pizza and deliciously mouth-watering focaccia gobbled up by Monterosso's locals. *Via Gioberti 1 (off Via Roma).* ☎ *0187/818333. Farinata, focaccia, and pizza from 1€. Fri–Wed 9am–2pm and 4–8pm. Cash only.*

➔ **Ristorante Al Carugio** ★★ LIGURIAN SEAFOOD Wonderfully friendly staff make time to socialize with customers while busily serving up delicious seafood dishes—if you manage to catch the eye of a cute waiter, you may find yourself the lucky recipient of a free after-dinner liqueur. The restaurant has a small terrace in front and a cozy interior. Everything on the menu is delicious: try the delectable *cozze ripiene* (mussels stuffed with a mixture of bread crumbs, vegetables, Parmigiano-Reggiano cheese, and ham, for 10€). *Via San Pietro 9 (off Via Roma).* ☎ *0187/ 817367. www.ristorantealcarugio.com. Primi 5.50€–10.50€; secondi 8€–14€. Daily noon–2:30pm and 6–10:30pm.*

➔ **Ristorante La Cambusa** ★ SEAFOOD/ PIZZA Dine on the tiny outdoor terrace or the cozy wooden interior, with a crowd of both locals and tourists. The service might be a bit slow and unfriendly, but the delicious eats make up for it. Their seafood salad, with small samples of various marine friends, is delicious and worth the 8€. Their large pizzas rival those of Naples' in taste and quality. *Via Roma 6.* ☎ *0187/817546. Primi 4€–7.10€; secondi around 15€; pizza 4€–7.50€. Daily 11:30am–3pm and 6:30–11pm.*

PARTYING

Though Monterosso is the biggest of the Cinque Terre towns, it is somewhat lacking in nighttime debauchery—maybe everyone is just utterly beat from a day of hiking. Most people stroll along Via Roma and Via

Emanuele in the evening, perhaps stopping for a glass of local wine. There are two places in town that provide a place to drink and hang out at night:

→ **FAST** This place is eerily quiet during the day and even in the evening, but things pick up a bit at the bar around 11pm—too bad it closes shortly after. They also serve cheap panini throughout the day, for a light meal or late night snack. *Via Roma 13.* ☎ *0187/817164. Panini from 4€; beer from 3€. Daily 8am–midnight.*

→ **Il Castello** ★★ Up the hill from the old town at the head of the trail, Il Castello has ample outdoor seating, including a large terrace overlooking the sea. Il Castello serves up beer, cocktails, and snacks to a young crowd of backpackers and foreign students. Internet access is also available here (1€ for 15 min). *Via Lungo Ferrovia 70 (up the hill from Piazza Garibaldi).* ☎ *0187/818330. Snacks from 3.50€; beer from 2.50€. Daily noon–2am.*

Vernazza

Vernazza ★★ is hands-down the most picturesque of the Cinque Terre towns, which also means that it draws the largest crowds of tourists. The descent into Vernazza from the trail is breathtaking; observe the town from the ridge above before descending through the winding back alleys into town—this trail offers the most scenic approach into town of all the hikes. In the center of town sits a small crescent harbor, its neighboring piazza lined with restaurants, and its small pebble beach filled with sunbathers who swim amongst the fishing boats in the water.

The town centers around restaurant-lined Piazza Marconi, in front of the cove that serves as the harbor. The main street in Vernazza is Via Visconti, which runs from the train station to the harbor. On either side, you can explore the residential areas filled with narrow, and often steep, alleyways. To find the Cinque Terre trail, look for signs in the alleyway by the *farmacia* (pharmacy) on

From Monterosso to Vernazza

The hike between Monterosso and Vernazza takes around 90 minutes. The steps on either end are killer, but the middle leg is quite moderate. This is the most scenic of the hikes, taking you through the Ligurian jungle and past private vineyards. Ancient-looking locals greet tired hikers with refreshing grapes for sale.

Via Visconti—one side leads to Monterosso, the other up to Corniglia.

SLEEPING

Vernazza has a few hotel options, as well as many rooms for rent in private homes (look for the signs around town), both at affordable prices.

Cheap/Doable

→ **Albergo Barbara** ★★ The rooms may be in need of an upgrade—furniture and tile work seem to be older than most of the guests—but this still remains a deservedly popular place to stay, as the location (in the main square), the view from most of the rooms (of the harbor and the open sea beyond), and the friendly Swiss-Italian couple who run the place are all compensation enough. *Piazza Marconi 30.* ☎ *0187/ 812398. www.albergobarbara.it. Double 45€–80€.*

→ **Franca Maria Rooms** ★ One of many private rental agencies in town, Franca Maria offers one- or two-bedroom places (many with views of the town) with clean but small bathrooms,. If booking in advance, check out the room selection on their website and request your favorite. *Piazza Marconi 30.* ☎ *0187/812002. www.francamaria.com. Apr–Oct double 75€–90€, quad 125€–145€; Nov–Mar double 50€–70€, quad 80€–100€.*

Vermazza Beach

Vernazza has a small pebble beach in the harbor, though many choose to lie out on the adjacent boulders. A small swimming area is cornered off; otherwise you'll be competing with fishing boats for a spot in the water.

→ **Hotel Gianni Franzi** ⋆ You can rent a room in one of two buildings at this hotel, run by the owners of the restaurant of the same name: either in a restored historic home in the town center, or by the sea with breathtaking views of the sea and coast. Rooms are tiny but uniquely decorated with wooden ceilings, black-and-red-checkered floors, and funky artwork on the walls. *Piazza Marconi 1.* ☎ *0187/821003. www.giannifranzi.it. Single with shared bath 45€; double with shared bath 60€, with shared bath and small balcony 65€, with private bath 77€; triple with private bath 100€. Closed mid-Jan to mid-Mar.*

EATING

Vernazza has several restaurants lining Piazza Marconi, by the harbor, but you'll pay for the privilege of dining on the water. For cheaper eats, try the small take-out shops and casual restaurants along Via Visconti.

Cheap

→ **Pizza da Ercole** ⋆⋆ PIZZERIA Nothing satisfies hunger after a long hike like a pizza pie, and they serve them up cheap and tasty at this take-out pizzeria. Choose from a variety of slices or a large selection of pizzas that are large enough to share, and take your picnic to the harbor. *Via Visconti 34. Slices 2.50€–3€; whole pizzas 5€–7€. Wed–Mon noon–8:30pm.*

Doable

→ **Gambero Rosso** ⋆⋆ SEAFOOD Yes, you will be surrounded by tables and tables of other tourists soaking up the gorgeous scenery along the waterfront, but at this restaurant you're guaranteed quality food along with the view from the terrace. The "Red Shrimp" offers local seafood specialties such as fresh anchovies and stuffed mussels. For a well-deserved feast after a day of hiking, splurge on one of their set menus consisting of antipasti, primi, secondi, and dessert. *Piazza Marconi 7.* ☎ *0187/812265. Primi 8€–10€; secondi 12€–24€; set menus 38€–50€. Daily 12:30–3pm and 7–10:30pm.*

Corniglia

The quietest and least impressive of the Cinque Terre towns—it's nothing more than a few narrow residential alleyways—Corniglia does have one major selling point: the stellar views of the open sea from its hilltop location. However, this location also means that you'll have to descend a lengthy set of stairs to get to the train station, ferry pier, and the trail to Manarola.

The trail from Vernazza enters Corniglia from a paved road filled with parked cars. Once in town, Via Fieschi runs through town and turns into Via della Stazione near the train station. To get to the station, the next leg of the trail, and the beach, look for the sign on Via della Stazione, and then head

Spectacular View from a Fortress

Castello Doria ⋆, an 11th-century fortress, looks down on Vernazza from atop the town's seaside peninsula. The castle itself is not all that impressive and is mostly in ruins, but the view of the town and the sea from this height is spectacular, and worth the pain of climbing up here. Admission is 1€; it's open daily 10:30am to 7pm. Look for the signs off of Via Visconti, near the harbor, and follow the stair-laden alleyway up.

Vernazza to Corniglia

The hike between Vernazza and Corniglia takes about 1½ hours. The trail is killer on the knees; it begins with a steep climb that seems to go on forever, and when the ascent finally does end, it begins a sharp descent almost right away, with a heavenly respite at the end when the trail traverses through a flat shady grove. Around midpoint, you can scramble down the hill to the secluded nude beach (look for the sign on the trail), although females will be rudely gawked at by the predominantly male crowd.

down—and down, and down—the stairs. Once on flat ground, turn left for the train station and trail, or turn right for the beach.

BEACHES

Corniglia's Guvano Beach is a busy pebbly stretch along the water, but is perhaps not worth the money and effort it takes to get here; after descending the steps from the train station and turning right, you'll have to walk about 15 minutes through a dark, damp, and very sketchy tunnel, only to be required to fork over a ridiculous fee of 5€ to be allowed out the other end leading to the beach.

SLEEPING

Private rentals are definitely the way to go in Corniglia. Signs are posted all over town, or try the following suggestion:

➜ **La Posada Rentals** ★★ Offering spacious, airy, and clean rooms as well as fully loaded apartments with kitchen, laundry, living room, and terrace. If booking in advance, check out their website and choose your favorite room. *Via Fieschi 212.* ☎ *0187/812384 or 0187/821174; www.cinqueterre-laposada.com. Doubles w/shared bath 55€–60€; doubles w/bath 70€; triples w/bath 10€; apartment for 2 people 80€; apartment for 3 people 90€; apartment for 4 people 130€–140€.*

Cheap

➜ **Albergo Da Cecio** ★★ A family-run inn on the road heading into Corniglia from Vernazza. The rooms are large and sunny, and nicely furnished with mahogany pieces. Most

also have views of the sea. You'll be reluctant to leave this place, with a rooftop deck perfect for sunbathing, as well as a main-floor terrace adjacent to the inn's restaurant. The owners also offer a few rooms to rent in town. *Via Serra 11.* ☎ *0187/812043. Double 60€–70€. Breakfast 5€.*

EATING
Cheap

➜ **La Gata Flora** ★ PIZZERIA   One of several pizzerias in Corniglia offering up tasty pizza slices to ravenous hikers, as well as snacks to take on the road. *Via Fieschi 109.* ☎ *0187/821218. Slices from 2€, whole pizzas 3.50€–6€; farinata and focaccia from 1€. Daily 9:30am–4pm and 6–8:30pm.*

Doable

➜ **Ristorante Da Cecio** ★★ LIGURIAN Attached to the hotel of the same name (see above), dine on simple but fresh and tasty pasta dishes, while gazing out to the sea from the restaurant's terrace. *Via Serra 11.* ☎ *0187/812043. Primi 7€–10€; secondi 8€–15€. Thurs–Tues noon–3pm and 7–11pm. Closed Nov.*

What a View!

For a stunning **view** ★★ of the Cinque Terre coast to your right, and the open sea in front of you, follow Via Fieschi through to its western end, where it opens up onto Belvedere Santa Maria, a large cliffside terrace.

LIGURIA & THE ITALIAN RIVIERA

Corniglia to Manarola

The hike between Corniglia and Manarola takes about an hour. This leg of the hike is both less strenuous and less scenic than the previous sections, although there are stunning views of the open sea at several points along the trail.

Manarola

With houses that seem to be built on top of each other on the cliffsides, Manarola is postcard-perfect. The town has a definite rural charm to it, as locals still make their living here from the traditional enterprises of fishing and wine-making. Manarola is also the most lively of the Cinque Terre towns, most likely due to the fact that it houses the only hostel in the Cinque Terre, drawing in the young backpacker crowd.

From Corniglia, the Cinque Terre trail descends into Manarola from above, offering gorgeous views of the town below. Via Discovolo is the main road in town, running from the southern end of town, past the train station tunnel to Piazza Capellini, and then changing to Via Birolli before heading to the harbor. To get to the train station and the next leg of the trail, walk through the tunnel by Piazza Capellini.

Manarola doesn't have a whole lot to offer in the way of actual beaches. Rather, you can take a dip in one of two swimming coves in town, and then lie out on the surrounding boulders afterward.

SLEEPING

Manarola's hostel is perhaps the best budget accommodation option in the Cinque Terre. The town also offers several more pricey hotels, as well as private rentals—see the signs around town or inquire at Il Porticciolo restaurant (Via Birolli 93).

Hostel

→ **Ostello Cinque Terre** ★★ A lively place with large six-bed dorm rooms as well as four- to six-bed family rooms with their own private bathroom. Most have views of the sea, and all are clean and bright. Amenities include a sociable patio, Internet access, laundry facilities, a TV room, and restaurant. The hostel also rents kayaks, bikes, and snorkeling equipment. *Via B. Riccobaldi 21 (turn right upon exiting train station tunnel).* ☎ *0187/920215. www.hostel5terre.com. In high season (Mar 26–Sept 30) dorm bed 22€, 4-bed room 88€, 6-bed room 132€; in low season (Oct 1–Mar 25) dorm 17€, 4-bed room 68€, 6-bed room 102€. Breakfast 3.50€. Closed mid-Dec to early Mar.*

Cheap

→ **Albergo Ca' D'Andrean** ★ Five good-sized rooms, all with A/C and TV, and many with a terrace and stunning views of either the sea or the hills behind the town. At the end of the day, relax in front of the hotel's fireplace, in the garden, or at the bar. *Via Discovolo 101.* ☎ *0187/920040. www.cadandrean. it. Single 60€–65€, double 75€–88€, triple 95€–119€. Breakfast (which you can eat in the garden) 6€.*

EATING

Manarola offers some of the best seafood eateries along the Cinque Terre coast—Italians from neighboring towns even venture here for dinner—so, although most eating options won't be dirt cheap, they will most definitely be delicious and satisfying.

Cheap/Doable

→ **Aristide** ★★ SEAFOOD Dine on the restaurant's terrace, with a mix of tourists and locals, and watch the crowd stroll down Manarola's main drag. Seafood entrees such as crayfish and scampi are sure to delight any empty belly; for a sampling of the local sea critters, try the *frittura di mare* (fried

Manarola to Riomaggiore

The stretch between Manarola and Riomaggiore isn't so much a hike as it is a gentle walk. Here, the Cinque Terre trail transforms into the smooth, flat, stone pathway of the 🆃🆅 Best **Via dell'Amore** ("Road of Love"). The walk takes about 20 minutes along a lane filled with professions of love—including both official plaques naming loved ones and graffiti—covering the rocks along the way. The view here is gorgeous, with views of the sea the entire length. This is an utterly romantic spot at sunset, when the path is filled with strolling lovebirds.

seafood). *Via Discovolo 290.* ☎ *0187/920000. Primi 4€–7€; secondi 7€–15€. Tues–Sun noon–2:30pm and 7–10pm.*

➜ **Marina Piccola** ★★ SEAFOOD In the scenic piazza in front of Manarola's harbor, dine on succulent seafood dishes such as swordfish and octopus. *Via Lo Scalo 16.* ☎ *0187/920923. www.hotelmarinapiccola. com. Primi 4€–7.80€; secondi 8€–15€. Wed–Mon noon–2:30pm and 7–11pm.*

PARTYING

Manarola has the most to offer among the Cinque Terre towns in terms of a party scene, but don't expect anything too crazy: This is, after all, still a sleepy fishing village. There are often outdoor disco parties open to the public in the summer—look for posters advertising them around town. By far the most happening place in town is **La Cantina dello Zio Bramante** ★, a wine bar offering up live music most nights where guests are encouraged to join in, and the owners often do as well (Via Birolli 110; ☎ **0187/920442**).

Riomaggiore

The last (or first, depending on which way you're coming) of the Cinque Terre towns, Riomaggiore is unique in that things here look a bit newer, yet it still feels like an isolated village; newer-looking buildings surround the harbor, where fishermen continue in their traditional ways.

Via dell'Amore descends into the train station area. From here, turn right and walk through the tunnel to get to the town. Via Cristoforo Colombo, the main drag, leads up from the train station exit. For the harbor, walk down the stairs to the right of the tunnel exit, and follow Via Colombo to the water.

While there are ample swimming spots, Riomaggiore doesn't have a whole lot to offer in terms of actual beaches. People swim in the tiny harbor and then lounge on the surrounding boulders. Alternately, you can take the path to the left of the harbor, which leads to a small, quiet pebble beach.

SLEEPING

Riomaggiore offers a plethora of private rental agencies, many with offices along Via Colombo, as well as a couple more expensive hotel options.

Doable

➜ **Locanda Ca' dei Duxi** ★ In a 15th-century building that used to be owned by a wine-making family; today, the old wine cellar is used as the breakfast room. Rooms are basic but large and bright with new wooden furniture. All come with TV, A/C, and minibar, and a few have a terrace. The hotel also offers private rooms and apartments (with kitchenette, TV, and terrace) for rent. *Via Colombo 36/Via Pecunia 19.* ☎ *0187/920036. www.duxi. it. Double 60€–90€. Breakfast included.*

Splurge

➜ **5Terre Afitti** This outfit arranges private rentals in several buildings around town. Rooms are for the most part hit or miss, so be

Dive (or Kayak) into Riomaggiore

Coopsub Diving Center offers dive trips and equipment rental for certified divers, as well as lessons for those without certification. If you'd rather stay above the water, you can also rent kayaks and canoes here. Via San Giacomo. ☎ **0187/920011.** www.5terrediving.com. Kayak rentals: 5€/hr. for a single boat, 10€/hr. for a double boat.

sure to check the place out before agreeing to anything. *Via Colombo 174.* ☎ *0187/920331. www.immobiliare5terre.com. Single from 25€, double from 50€, triple from 75€.*

→ **Hotel Villa Argentina** ★★ About a 5-minute walk from the center of town, the hotel offers large rooms, most with balconies with views of the town and the sea. Their quiet terrace is a wonderful place to relax. They also rent private apartments for up to six people; inquire at the hotel for details. *Via De Gasperi 37.* ☎ *0187/920213. www.hotel villargentina.com. Single 77€–105€, double 94€–139€.*

EATING

Cheap

→ **Veciumuin Pizzeria** ★ PIZZERIA It's one of several pizzerias along Via Colombo offering cheap eats, but seek this one out for its large terrace perfect for watching the tourist crowd stroll along the main drag. *Via Colombo 83.* ☎ *0187/920487. Pizza 5€–8€, panini 3.50€–4€, focaccia 3€–7€. Cover charge 1€. Tues–Sun 10am–2:30pm and 6:30–11pm.*

Doable

→ **Trattoria La Lanterna** ★★ SEAFOOD There are two reasons to dole out the cash for a meal at La Lanterna: the great terrace offering views of the harbor where you can watch the fishing boats come in during the evening, and the tasty pasta seafood dishes, such as gnocchi with *frutti di mare* and spaghetti with mussels. *Via San Giacomo 46.* ☎ *0187/920589. Primi 6€–8€; secondi 7€–22€. Daily 11am–midnight.*

Naples & Campania

The sun-kissed Mediterranean coastline that stretches from Naples to Sorrento and south to Amalfi is one of the most stimulating, soul-stirring places on earth. With its southern boisterousness, over-the-top natural beauty, and fresh gastronomic bounty, Campania in many ways epitomizes the cherished notion of Italy as romance novel. On Ischia and the Amalfi Coast, waves lap at pink stucco buildings while fishing boats bob gently in the harbor. In Naples and Sorrento, people shout at each other across the street as they hang clothes on laundry lines outside their third-floor windows. Throughout the region, sexy women and swarthy men aren't shy about getting in your business, and we like it.

Mother Nature was on fire when she created the Bay of Naples and the Amalfi Coast. Wherever you go in Campania, there are lemon trees and bougainvillea and other untended, lush vegetation flourishing on dramatic cliffs that plunge to the sea. The formidable volcanic cone of Mt. Vesuvius, which could theoretically blow at any minute, is an inescapable presence in Campania, one which visitors see as ominous, but locals just see as a fact of life. The entire region is such a colorful canvas—the blue of the sea, the yellow-orange of the sun and omnipresent citrus fruits, the green of prolific plants and trees, the violet of flower blossoms, the red of tomatoes, the rust-to-black contours of Vesuvius—even artists couldn't pick a more vivid palette with which to paint life. And don't forget the food: There's reason why Campania is one of the few Italian regions with an obesity problem! This is the land that gave the world pizza, after all, and it's also home to *mozzarella di bufala campana DOP* (which Neapolitan kids eat in football-sized blobs every day), and some of the plumpest, naturally grown fruits and vegetables you'll ever come across. Add to that all the glistening swordfish, clams, calamari, and crustaceans that are hauled in from the Bay of Naples daily, and you are guaranteed to have some of your most memorable Italian meals in Campania.

Scared by what you've heard about Naples? Get over it. Naples is a mess of traffic and poverty—that's a fact. But there are also plenty of moments when it's the most stunning and delightful city you'll ever set foot in. (Like, when you're slurping up some melted mozzarella off a slice of pizza and watching the sun set over the green cliffs of Cape Posillipo.)

Pompeii, the most famous archaeological site in the world, fully lives up to its hype. The vast Roman city, frozen in time by the eruption of Vesuvius in A.D. 79, is a vivid, eerily modern-seeming portal to ancient civilization. When you need a break from urban chaos or ruin traipsing, the islands of Capri and Ischia are two of the most unforgettable treasures in the entire Mediterranean, and only a short hydrofoil ride away from Naples or Sorrento.

However, Campania is not a completely blissful summer fling—far from it. It doesn't take long to realize that the region has an unpleasant side, which you'll encounter on the dirtier streets of Naples, or when you ride the Circumvesuviana train past the blight of impoverished coastal suburbs like Torre Annunziata. As a tourist, you can avert your eyes, but to get some perspective on what life is like for a lot of people here, you should take some of the darker realities in with the good. The real Campania is grittiness mixed with overwhelming splendor. Wash it all down with a few glasses of Lacryma Christi ("Tears of Christ," a local wine made from grapes grown on the slopes of Vesuvius) and a few slices of fresh peach, whose color—as if by divine design—perfectly matches the amber glow of that gorgeous sunset over the water.

The Best of Campania

Best Food

Campania is the only place in the world where you can get real, fresh, honest-to-goodness *mozzarella di bufala campana DOP.* Toss it in a salad with tomatoes, or melt it on top of a pizza. Whatever you do, eat up.

Best Way to Travel Back in Time

Stepping through the gates of **Pompeii** is like entering a time machine that shoots you back about 2,000 years. The once-prosperous ancient Roman town was buried

O Sole Mio's Ukrainian Roots

The most famous Italian folk song ("My Sun") was written by a Neapolitan, Edoardo Capua, in the late 19th century. (And covered by Elvis Presley, who sang it as "It's Now or Never" in 1960.) Contrary to what you might imagine, the song was inspired not by the splendid sunset in the composer's hometown, over the Bay of Naples, but instead by a magnificent sunrise he witnessed over the Black Sea while in Odessa, Ukraine.

when Mt. Vesuvius erupted in 79 A.D. and is eerily well preserved today. Spend at least a day wandering down the stone streets, peeking into houses and storefronts where, with just a little imagination, you can easily envision what life was like before the eruption. See p. 618.

Best Museum

Like an ancient Roman garage sale (except that nothing's for sale), the halls of the **Museo Archeologico Nazionale** in Naples are where all the best stuff from the excavations at Pompeii ended up. Browse stupendous mosaics, emotionally charged marble sculptures, and everyday kitchen utensils, and be sure to reserve a guided visit to the Gabinetto Segreto, where they stashed all the ancient porn (figurines, frescoes, and phalluses galore) they uncovered at Pompeii. See p. 613.

Best Excursion

On Capri, the 2-hour **full-island boat tour** (11.50€) with Gruppo Motoscafisti is an exhilarating way to see the most beautiful island in the Mediterranean Sea. En route, the clumsy rowboat detour into the spectacular **Blue Grotto** is an absolute must that'll have you grinning from ear to ear. (So don't make the mortal mistake of skipping it just because it's supertouristy and costs an extra 8.50€.) See p. 656.

Naples: Loud, Wild, Energetic

219km (136 miles) SE of Rome

Naples and its citizens really do drum to a different beat—a crazy one. Neapolitans are loud and sassy, with uncannily boundless energy, and create an incredible electricity in the city that you will not likely find anywhere else. Many people who tour Italy skip Naples, as it has earned itself a bad rap as far as safety and beauty go. This bad rap persists inside Italy, too: when you tell Italians that you plan on going to Napoli, they will ask you why on earth you'd want to spend your time in that *posto del terzo mondo* ("third-world place"). Certain areas are still a bit sketchy—you do need to watch out for broad-daylight pickpockets and purse-snatchers—with plenty of dilapidated buildings downtown, and the industrial end of the harbor is a major eyesore, but Naples is not the Camorra (mob)-plagued dump some would have you believe.

On the wide, smiling coast of the Bay of Naples, with the broad, charcoal-y contours of Mt. Vesuvius looming to the southeast, Napoli has the most spectacular natural setting of any city in Italy. Furthermore, the city's wonderful seaside castles, lovely Art Nouveau palaces and gardens, and hilly vistas more than make up for the run-down urban areas you see. Once you get used to the maniacal pace (and take a few safety precautions), you will realize that those who skip Naples are missing out not only on an illustrious historical setting—Neapolis ("new city") was founded by the Greeks in 470 B.C. on the site of an older village called

How to Survive Neapolitan Traffic

Rumor has it that in Naples a driver's license is earned not by passing a test but by simply forking over some cash, which may explain why most drivers are unfamiliar with the rules of the road: Traffic lights are regarded as stop signs if regarded at all, lane markers are mere suggestions, and scooter drivers are given free range. Worse yet, many a Neapolitan driver will barrel down one-way tram lanes, flooring the accelerator and muttering something about the Santa Madonna if there happens to be a tram (traveling on its rightful tracks) coming toward him. This seems like utter chaos at first, but as long as everyone drives like a raving lunatic, some sort of order is maintained.

Unless you've had a lot of experience driving in such a manner, never *ever* get behind the wheel in Naples; even getting in a vehicle with a local driver can be a harrowing experience, leaving many crouched in the back with their hands over their eyes. You will, however, inevitably be confronted with this traffic nightmare when attempting to cross the street. Stepping off the curb at first will seem like a death wish, but it is quite simple if you follow one basic rule: just go. Don't go stepping into the middle of the freeway or in front of speeding vehicles, but generally cars and scooters will swerve around you when you cross their path, albeit at the last second just as your life is beginning to flash before your eyes. If in doubt, watch a local and then follow suit. (*Nota bene:* The same system works in Rome, too.)

Parthenope—but an absolutely delightful cultural experience: Neapolitans are boisterous, florid, and in your face, and they will be a big part of your time here. So, once again, take a deep breath: If you let yourself adapt to her crazy ways, Naples is sure to please.

The Best of Naples

Best View

It's nothing more than a wealthy neighborhood overlooking the city in a quiet area of town, but from the green cliffs of **Posillipo,** you can take in all the action of the bustling city below, and even make out Vesuvius and Capri in the distance. For the ultimate view, make the trek early in the morning and watch the sun rise over Naples. See p. 616.

Most Hospitable Place to Stay

Hostel of the Sun is a clean, comfortable hostel with a very sociable atmosphere, providing all the amenities in a superb location, but what truly makes this place a cut above the rest is its incredible staff, who absolutely love

their city and go out of their way to get guests to fall in love with Naples, too. See p. 604.

Best Pizza

Neapolitans love to brag that, in a country known for its pizza, this city serves the best—and those who try it agree! For the best of the best in a fun environment, stop in for dinner at **Brandi,** where pizza has been served up for over 200 years to such distinguished guests as Queen Margherita (for whom the margherita pizza is named) and Luciano Pavarotti. See p. 608.

Getting There

BY AIR

Naples' airport is **Aeroporto Capodichino,** Via Umberto Maddalena (☎ **081/7896259**), 6km (3³/₄ miles) north of the city, but a 30-minute ride through traffic-congested streets. To get into the city, take the **Alibus** (3€), which runs about every half-hour and stops at Napoli Centrale—Piazza Garibaldi train station (the stop is in front of

McDonald's; turn right when exiting the station) and in Piazza Municipio, near the port of Molo Beverello. If you prefer to splurge on a taxi, make sure the driver gives you the flat airport-to-city rate and does not use the meter.

BY TRAIN

Naples' train station is **Napoli Centrale** (sometimes abbreviated as NA C.LE), in **Piazza Garibaldi** (www.napolipiazzagaribaldi.it). Trenitalia (FS) trains connect Naples to other Italian cities such as Rome, Florence, Milan, and Venice. **Circumvesuviana** trains are regional subwaylike trains connecting Naples with Campania destinations such as Sorrento and Pompeii, and depart from the lower level of the train station. Rail passes are not valid on Circumvesuviana trains. Although the city center is close by, the area around the train station is pretty seedy, so you might not want to hang around, especially at night. Luckily, Piazza Garibaldi has plenty of buses and taxis to whisk you away from the squalor. Inside the station itself, there are travel agents where you can book your ferry and hydrofoil tickets to Capri and Ischia, to spare you the potential hassle of having to do so at the hectic ticket offices at the port. **365 Travel Agency**

is at ☎ **081/267-125** and open from 8am to 9pm daily. **Wasteels** is at ☎ **081/201-071** and is open daily 7am to 9pm.

BY BUS

SITA buses (connecting Naples to regional destinations such as Pompeii and Sorrento) depart from Piazza Garibaldi, in front of the train station. Alternately, if you're staying near the harbor or transferring from the ferry, you can also catch the bus from the SITA station by the port: the bus terminal is in the big red building at the end of the long parking lot next to the port.

BY FERRY

The main port of Naples is called **Molo Beverello.** Several ferry companies operate here, running ferries and hydrofoils to Sorrento, Capri, Ischia, and the Amalfi Coast (See section below, "Getting Around the Amalfi Coast & Islands by Water," which begins on p. 630). To get to the port, take any bus to Piazza Municipio and then walk down to the waterfront. The city's secondary port is called **Mergellina,** a few kilometers up the coast in a much nicer neighborhood. From Mergellina, there are hydrofoils to Capri and Ischia.

OKKIO! Street-Smart Shopping

Naples has some incredible bargains at the stalls and stands along the side streets of Via Toledo. However, when shopping here, there are three important rules to remember. First, bargain, and bargain hard. Second, never ever buy electronics off the street, no matter how good the deal seems or how desperately you think you need it—travelers have reported rushing home to open their new toy, only to find an empty box! And even if you are supplied with the item you purchased, you'll be lucky if you can get it to function properly. Don't waste your money. Third, when shopping here, realize that whatever you buy, be it sunglasses or a new T-shirt, it will be of dubious quality: Those sunglasses will break on the ferry to Capri, and that T-shirt will dye the rest of your clothes a terrifying shade of pink in the wash. Moral of the story: When shopping on the streets of Naples, if something seems too good to be true, be wise and realize that it most definitely is, and keep walking.

Getting Around

BY BUS (AUTOBUS)

Local orange **ANM** buses are often slow and crowded, although special circular lines (marked with an R) can be handy as they service most tourist sites and all intersect at Piazza Municipio, near the port. Other useful lines are the C16 (Mergellina–Vomero), C21 (Mergellina to Posillipo), C25 (Piazza Amedeo–Piazza Municipio), C27 (Piazza Amedeo–Via Manzoni–Posillipo), and 140 (Castel dell'Ovo–Mergellina-Posillipo). The night buses are notoriously unreliable and unsafe, and so should be avoided—if you're traveling more than a few blocks at night, and especially if you're alone, it's best to be safe and take a taxi. Purchase bus tickets (1€) from *tabacchi*, newsstands, and transport information booths. For more information, call the ANM information line at ☎ **800/639-525** (www.anm.it).

BY METRO (METROPOLITANA)

Naples' **subway** system is a good way to travel for longer distances on the outskirts of the Centro Storico and further inland—the metro has very few stops near the waterfront. From the train station, you can catch Metropolitana Linea 2 from platform 4, on the lower level. Elsewhere in Naples, Metropolitana stations are marked with a red M. Useful stops for tourists include Piazza Cavour (for the northern half of the Centro Storico), Montesanto (for the southern part of the Centro Storico and shopping on Via Toledo and the market of Via Pignasecca), Piazza Amedeo (for Chiaia), and Mergellina (for the hydrofoil port). The same tickets that are used on the bus are also used on the Metropolitana; purchase them at *tabacchi*, newsstands, and transport information booths.

BY FUNICULAR (FUNICOLARE)

These three super-slanted railways connect the lower parts of Naples to the Vomero district above, offering great views of the city along the way. The **Funicolare di Chiaia** departs from just east of Piazza Amedeo to Vomero (south of Piazza Vanvitelli and adjacent to the Villa Floridiana park). The **Funicolare Centrale** is a much longer line leading from the southern end of Via Toledo up to the Vomero (southeast of Piazza Vanvitelli). Finally, the **Funicolare di Montesanto,** farther north, is closed for restoration at press time. Use regular bus tickets (1€), which can be purchased at *tabacchi*, newsstands, and transport information booths.

BY TAXI

Neapolitan taxi drivers are well known for ripping off tourists, so insist on the driver using the meter (except for airport service, when they must abide by a set rate). There are taxi stations near major transport hubs and attractions, or you can call one of the following radio taxi dispatchers: **Taxivagando** (☎ 800/403-040); La Cometa (☎ 081/551-3422), or **La Sibilla** ☎ (081/551-0964).

ON FOOT

Although Naples as a whole is quite spread out—along the waterfront and up the hills—its main attractions are close to each other and easy to get to on foot, making walking a viable possibility during most of your stay. Walking at a leisurely pace from the Museo Archeologico in the north to Piazza Plebiscito, on the waterfront to the south, for example, won't take you more than 30 minutes, though it can end up being much longer if you stop to haggle with vendors along Via Toledo on your way down!

Naples Orientation

Naples is a large city; to help you figure out what's where, here's a rundown of the city by neighborhood and nearest landmarks. (Every guidebook has its own version of how to divvy up the Naples for tourists; for our arbitrary designations here, we've chosen the major landmarks that you'll likely come to know, and be able to orient yourself by, during your stay.) Another key to staying oriented in the city is to keep in mind that, while the Mediterranean seacoast is more or less north-south in most of Italy, Naples's shoreline actually faces south, due to its position on the crescent-shaped bay of Naples, which runs from Cape Misenum in the west to the Sorrentine peninsula in the east.

→ **Stazione Centrale** The area around the train station, especially the part to the east, has an abundance of budget accommodations, ethnic restaurants, and street vendors hawking everything from sunglasses to fresh produce. Unfortunately this is also the area that has given Naples its bad rap for seediness and sketchiness; it's dirty, smelly, unsafe, and full of folks you'd hate to meet in a dark alley.

→ **The Waterfront** Unfortunately, Naples has yet to take full advantage of its huge stretch of coastal land—the seaside area that runs adjacent to the center of town is essentially an industrial area and parking lot, with the port, Molo Beverello, at the eastern end, near the Castello Nuovo. If you venture a little farther (slightly southwest) down the coast, however, you'll find the sunny area of Mergellina, which has a bit more life and atmosphere to it, although it's constantly packed by cruise groups. There are numerous restaurants by the water, serving up delicious fresh seafood.

→ **Centro Storico** Called Spaccanapoli by the locals, this is the historical heart of the city. Wander through its maze of streets and you'll discover cheap restaurants and tiny shops, as well as churches and monuments, political buildings, and the university.

→ **Plebiscito** Stretching inland from the enormous rounded colonnade of Piazza Plebiscito, this neighborhood encompasses two sections: Straight ahead from the piazza, you'll find the posh shopping street Via Toledo and its adjacent shopping mall

Galleria Umberto I—probably the most ornately decorated shopping mall you'll ever find. To the west is the Quartieri Spagnoli ("Spanish Quarters"), a warren of narrow streets where you'll find cramped street-level apartments, restaurants, more shops, and vendors hawking virtually anything you can imagine.

→ **The Vomero and Posillipo** Just to the west of the city center, these are residential areas that sit high above the rest of Naples. The air is fresher and the views are splendid. Vomero is the livelier of the two—its centerpiece, cafe-filled Piazza Vanvitelli, is a popular evening hangout for young locals. The real stunner, however, is Posillipo: sitting on the verdant, fingerlike cliffs that bend toward the sea, dotted with gorgeous private villas, this is Naples at its snobbiest (and understandably so). Still, don't expect too much excitement here beyond the parks and views.

Tourist Offices

The main **EPT Tourist Office** is at Piazza dei Martiri 58 (☎ **081/4107211**; www.inaples.it). It's open Monday through Friday 9am to 2pm with a telephone information line available 8:30am to 3:30pm. There is also a branch office in Stazione Centrale (☎ 081/268779) that is open Monday to Saturday 8:30am to 8pm and Sunday 8am to 2pm.

There is also a helpful **OTC** tourist office in Palazzo Reale, next to the entrance to the Galleria Umberto I shopping mall (☎ **081/252571**). It is open daily 9am to 3pm.

Whichever tourist office you visit, be sure to pick up a free map and the indispensable tourist publication, *Qui Napoli,* which gives detailed information on the month's events, as well as a good rundown of the city's attractions, restaurants, and accommodations.

Recommended Websites

⊙ **www.inaples.it** The official website of the tourist office, with information on attractions, accommodation, transport,

Tu vuo' fa' o' napulitano?

So, you learned some Italian in school? Too bad—it's not going to help you much in Naples. While most Neapolitans understand "proper Italian," there are many who don't, and no one speaks it unless forced to communicate with an outsider (even then, it's a laborious process). Instead, the cacophony you hear shouted across the markets, between drivers, and at the coffee bars, is not *italiano* but *napoletano*. Except for a few simple, frequently mimicked phrases, the strong Naples dialect is as baffling to a Roman or a Florentine as another language. Furthermore, the Neapolitan accent has a bewildering sound. It is at once hard-edged and lilting, with a throatiness that makes the speaker sound as if he is oxygen-deprived. Practice some of the phrases below, and trust me, if you manage to use even one of these on a local, you'll score huge points. Pay particular attention to the pronunciation, and remember, if you're not gasping for air at the end of the sentence, you're not doing it right:

Neapolitan	Pronunciation	English
N'aggio capit'	n'adzho ca-*peet*	I don't understand (in Italian, *non ho capito*)
Site napulitano?	*see*-tay napulitanuh?	Are you Neapolitan?
Scusate	shcu-*saht*-uh	Excuse me
Mi dispiace	mi dish-*pyahsh*-uh	I'm sorry
A ro' sta'?	arrosh-*tah*?	Where is it? (in Italian, *dove sta?*)

etc. You can also get the online version of the *Qui Napoli* magazine.

○ **www.naplesnews.com** Get the Naples daily news in English here.

○ **www.napoli.com** *Around Napoli* website, providing information on sights and attractions as well as the history and culture of the city.

Sleeping

One good thing about the reluctance of tourists to visit Naples is that you can usually find a place to stay without a problem. Naples has some excellent hostels. There are also numerous budget hotels in the area near the train station (which is rather seedy).

If the places below are booked, try the **Promhotel** booth at the train station (☎ **081/266-908;** Mon–Sat 9:30am–1pm and 3:30–7pm, Sun 9:30am–1pm), or with the **365 travel agency** (in the train station; ☎ **081/267-125;** daily 8am–9pm).

HOSTELS

📺 Best → **Hostel of the Sun** ★★★
WATERFRONT/PORT Hands down the best budget accommodation in Naples, and perhaps in all Campania. Helpful, bubbly staff go out of their way to ensure that guests have a great time and make an effort to get to know everyone who stays there. There's a friendly, sociable atmosphere. Rooms are decently sized and bathrooms are clean. You have access to a kitchen, laundry, and Internet, and there's a lounge area with TV and DVD collection. *Via Melisurgo 15, 7th floor (off Via Depretis).* ☎ *081/420-6393. www.hostel napoli.com. High season dorm 20€; single 45€; double 55€, or 70€ with private bath; triple 80€, or 90€ with private bath; quad 90€, or 100€ with private bath. Low season dorm 18€; single 40€; double 50€, or 60€ with private bath; triple 70€, or 80€ with private bath; quad 80€, or 90€ with private bath. Breakfast included. Bus: R2.*

Naples

PARTYING ⭐
Enoteca
  Belledonne **23**
Kinky **14**
La Mela **23**
Lazzarella **16**
S'move Light Bar **23**
Velvet **15**

RESTAURANTS ◆
Attanasio **7**
Brandi **25**
Chalet Ciro **34**
Da Michele **11**
Di Matteo **9**
Dolcezze Siciliane **30**
Don Salvatore **34**
Gay-Odin **23**
Hosteria Toledo **20**
Piazza d'Arte **13**
Scaturchio **12**
Trattoria da
  Nennella **19**
Trianon da Ciro **10**
Umberto **23**

ATTRACTIONS ●
Castel dell'Ovo **33**
Castel Sant'Elmo and Certosa-
  Museo di San Martino **18**
Castello Nuovo **27**
Catacombs of San Gennaro **2**
Duomo **8**
Museo Archeologico Nazionale
  (National Archeology Museum) **3**
Museo e Gallerie di Capodimonte
  (Capodimonte Museum
  and Galleries) **1**
Palazzo Reale **26**
Parco della Floridiana **22**

ACCOMMODATIONS ■
6 Small Rooms **17**
Bella Capri **29**
Chiaia Hotel **24**
Grand Hotel Vesuvio **32**
Hostel of the Sun **28**
Hotel Garden Napoli **5**
Hotel Ginevra **4**
Hotel Il Convento **21**
Hotel Rex **31**
Hotel Zara **6**

➔ **Bella Capri** ★★ WATERFRONT/PORT
Across the street from the Hostel of the Sun, guests are often sent here when the other is full, and although it lacks the atmosphere of its neighbor, the staff are just as friendly and helpful. Here, you'll find brand-new dorms, with TV, A/C, and a bathroom in each room. There's also Internet access, a kitchen, and a laundry. In addition to the dorms, there are also private rooms available. *Via Melisurgo 4 (off Via Depretis).* ☎ *081/5529494. www.bella capri.it. Dorm 20€–22€; single with shared bath 45€–50€, with private bath 57€–69€; double with shared bath 50€–60€, with private bath 66€–80€; triple with shared bath 66€–84€, with private bath 80€–100€; quad with shared bath 80€–96€, with private bath 90€–110€. Breakfast included. Bus: R2.*

➔ **Ostello Mergellina (HI)** MERGELLINA
Somewhat inconveniently located in Mergellina, in the western end of the city by the waterfront, and of the sterile, homogenous environment typical of many Hostelling International properties, this place nonetheless provides a clean, cheap option when the other hostels are full (but definitely try them first). There's Internet access, a TV room, laundry, restaurant, and a pleasant terrace to sit on and mingle. *Via Salita della Grotta a Piedigrotta 23 (off Via Piedigrotta).* ☎ *081/7612346. www.hihostels.com. Dorm 14€, double 34€. HI membership required. Metro: Mergellina Station.*

➔ **6 Small Rooms** ★★ VIA TOLEDO/CENTRO
STORICO A sociable place run by a friendly Australian, with kitchen, TV, and large video collection. Rooms are small (hence the name) but bright and clean and some come with a small terrace. *Via Diodato Lioy 18 (near Piazza Carità).* ☎ *081/7901378. www.at6smallrooms. com. Dorm 18€, double 50€, triple 75€, quad 100€. Breakfast included. No reservations until night before. From train station, take the metro on platform 4 to Piazza Cavour, then change to line 1 and go to Piazza Dante; walk 5 minutes.*

CHEAP

➔ **Hotel Zara** ★ PIAZZA GARIBALDI/
STAZIONE CENTRALE In a nonsketchy area near the train station, this is a good budget option if you're arriving late or leaving early. Rooms are pretty bare and some are cramped, but all are clean and recently renovated. The hotel has a TV room, library, Internet access, and bar and the two young owners love to dole out advice to guests. *Via Firenze 81 (at Via Torino).* ☎ *081/287125. www.hotelzara.it. Single with shared bath 40€–45€, double with private bath 55€–65€, triple with private bath 75€–90€. Bus/metro: Piazza Garibaldi (main train station).*

➔ **Hotel Ginevra** PIAZZA GARIBALDI/
STAZIONE CENTRALE Another budget option close to the train station, this family-run hotel has a shabby lobby and rooms that are nothing special, but what do you expect at this price? At least they're clean, as are the bathrooms, and cheerful due to brightly colored decor. All rooms have phone and TV, and so-called superior rooms have A/C and fridge (though otherwise they're exactly the same). The hotel also offers Internet access. *Via Genova 116 (at Corso Novara).* ☎ *081/283210. www.hotelginevra.it. Single 30€ with shared bathroom, 55€ with private bathroom; double 55€ with shared bathroom, 65€–80€ with private bathroom; triple 75€ with shared bathroom, 85€–100€ with private bathroom; quad 100€ with private bathroom. Breakfast 5€. Bus/metro: Piazza Garibaldi (main train station).*

DOABLE

➔ **Hotel Garden Napoli** ★ PIAZZA
GARIBALDI/STAZIONE CENTRALE A nicer option near the train station—if you can ignore the traffic congestion and seediness of nearby Piazza Garibaldi. Rooms are large and airy, with TV, phone, and terrace in some, although there isn't much to look out on. The hotel has Internet access and parking. *Corso Garibaldi 92 (off Piazza Garibaldi).*

☎ *081/284826. www.hotelgardenapoli.it. Single 65€–122€, double 83€–148€, triple 100€–192€. Breakfast included. Bus/metro: Piazza Garibaldi (main train station).*

➜ **Hotel Il Convento** ★★ QUARTIERI SPAGNOLI/CENTRO STORICO   You can stay in the heart of the action in the Spanish Quarter, in a 17th-century palazzo. The owners say the hotel has been restored to resemble its original form, but it actually looks more like an 18th-century cottage inside, with small, cozy alcoves and dark wooden furniture. Rooms are nicely furnished with comfortable beds and welcoming decor. And although they are a bit cramped, rooms are also clean and bright, and have A/C, phone, radio, minibar, and TV. Most bathrooms also have bathtubs. The hotel also has a bar and parlor. *Via Speranzella 137A (near Piazza Carità).* ☎ *081/403977. www. hotelilconvento.it. Single 68€–145€, double 83€–180€, junior suite 115€–230€. Breakfast included. Discounts in Jan–Feb and July–Aug. Bus: R1, R3, or R4.*

➜ **Hotel Rex** WATERFRONT/SANTA LUCIA   A popular hotel with an older cost-conscious crowd (to them, this place is in fact "budget"), it's nicely located in a quiet area a half block from the waterfront. The hotel itself is lavishly decorated with brass mirrors, lush carpets, and old paintings, but the rooms are very basic, especially considering their price, and the bathrooms could use a good scrubbing. All rooms have TV, phone, and A/C. *Via Palepoli 12 (at Via N. Sauro).* ☎ *081/7649389. www. hotel-rex.it. Double (single use) 85€–105€, double 100€–125€. Breakfast included. Bus: R3. Tram: 1.*

SPLURGE

➜ **Grand Hotel Vesuvio** ★★ WATER-FRONT   From Grace Kelly and Humphrey Bogart to Bill Clinton and Ricky Martin, all the greats stay here when they come to Naples. Rooms have all the luxurious furnishings and amenities you'd expect from a grand

dame in a historic European city (and all the warm and attentive service you'd expect from the Neapolitans), but unless you can snag one of the water-facing rooms, with a superfab terrace where you can sip champagne while watching the sun set over the bay, you might as well take your euros elsewhere. The view is what makes the Vesuvio worth the splurge. Check the website for special discounted room rates—they're not exactly bargain-basement, but they're often at least 20% lower than rack rates. *Via Partenope 45.* ☎ *081/764-0044. www. vesuvio.it. Double 230€–336€ (Web rate); rack rates from 420€. Breakfast included. In room: A/C, satellite TV with pay-per-view shows, Internet connection, laundry service, minibar, room service. Bus: C25 or 140.*

➜ **Chiaia Hotel** ★★ PLEBISCITO   Stay in the heart of the action on happening Via Chiaia, around the corner from Piazza Plebiscito; look for the banner hanging above the entrance and buzz to enter the gates. Housed in a beautifully restored palazzo, rooms may be small but are bright and spotless, with heavenly comfortable beds, and A/C, TV, minibar, phone, and a Jacuzzi tub if you're lucky. Staff are a bit weary of those who don't exude richness, but can be helpful if questioned for advice. *Via Chiaia 216 (near Piazza Plebiscito).* ☎ *081/415555. www.hotel chiaia.it. Single from 95€, double from 150€. Breakfast included. Bus: R2 or R3.*

Eating

Naples is where pizza was invented, and it's still the best place in the world to eat it. Locals fiercely defend this culinary reputation, and it is a deserved one; even the cheap slices from the takeout stands are outstanding, though they are nothing compared to what you'll get in some of the restaurants that have been producing pizza pies for decades, if not centuries. If you tire of pizza, never fear. Being a coastal city, Naples also serves up delicious seafood, as well as delectable classic pasta dishes that are heavy on the tomatoes, garlic, and olive oil.

PIZZA

MTV Best → **Brandi** ★★ Serving up piping hot pies since 1780, Brandi's is a more upscale place to sample some of the best pizza in Naples. It's even rumored that the Margherita pizza (the kind with mozzarella and tomatoes) was invented here; as the story goes, in 1889 Brandi's "Pietro the Pizzamaker" was invited to the Royal Palace to prepare pizzas for the royal family. Even though Queen Margherita sampled many varieties with a complicated combination of toppings, her favorite in the end was the simple mozzarella and tomato, and the rest is pizza history. Sample this historic pizza, or go for one of the specialty pizzas named after celebrities who have dined here: The Don Luciano is named for opera singer Luciano Pavarotti, who is said to be the only customer yet to single-handedly finish this entire 20-topping monster. Brandi's seafood and pasta dishes are just as delicious as their pizzas—the seafood salad here is full of delicacies from the sea and large enough for a meal. Dine on the tiny terrace out front or in the cozy upstairs dining room. The entire place fills up minutes after opening, so a reservation is a good idea. *Salita S. Anna di Palazzo 1 (off Via Chiaia).* ☎ *081/416928. Primi 5.30€–9.50€; secondi 6.50€–12€, pizza 3.70€–26€. Daily 12:30–3pm and 7:30pm–midnight. Bus: C25 or R2.*

→ **Di Matteo** ★★ CENTRO STORICO Walking along Via dei Tribunali, it's very easy to mistake this little place for just another takeout joint if you even happen to notice it at all. Squeeze in past the busy cooks, ignoring the ashes dangling precariously close to the food from the cigarettes in their mouths, and head upstairs to the casual dining area where you'll be in for a real treat. The atmosphere may be lacking, but the pizzas are cheap, huge, and delicious—this is the best place to fill your belly on a tight budget. *Via dei Tribunali 94 (at Vico Gigante).*

☎ *081/ 455262. Pizzas 3€–5€. Mon–Sat 9am–midnight. Metro: Piazza Dante. Bus: R1 or R2.*

→ **Da Michele** ★★ CENTRO STORICO One of Neapolitans' favorite pizzerias, this super-authentic joint in Spaccanapoli only has two choices on its menu: pizza Margherita (with mozzarella, tomatoes, and a few basil leaves) and pizza marinara (without mozzarella). It's not exploding with flavor, but it's incredibly fresh and satisfying. To wash it all down, choose from water, Coke, Fanta, or beer. *Via Sersale 1.* ☎ *081/553-9204. Mon–Sat for lunch and dinner June–Aug; daily for lunch and dinner Sept–May. Closed 2 weeks in Aug. Pizzas from 3€. Bus: R2.*

→ **Trianon da Ciro** ★ CENTRO STORICO Across the street from Da Michele, Trianon is where locals come when the lines are too long at Da Michele, or when they feel like having something other than tomato sauce and mozzarella on their pie. *Via Pietro Colletta 46.* ☎ *081/553-9426. Daily for lunch and dinner. Pizzas from 4€. Bus: R2.*

CHEAP

→ **Trattoria da Nennella** ★★★ NEAPOLITAN/PLEBISCITO If you're looking for an authentic dining experience, you won't find a better place than this little restaurant in the Spanish Quarter. A wonderful family-run establishment where you can experience Neapolitans at their best: Customers shout

---

Best Pizza in Naples?

Try the **stands near the train station** ★★★. If you don't mind navigating the seedy, trash-strewn alleys around the train station, you'll find what is regarded by most true Neapolitans as the best pizza in the city. Greasy, drippy, piping hot slices are available to go for about 1.50€. Just keep an eye on your wallet as you scarf it down!

orders to busy waiters who then pass food from the busy kitchen over the heads of other customers. Other diners include working-class locals as well as big men in suits and dark glasses. Come with an appetite, as the daily menu includes two hefty courses: from the paper menu, choose one primi dish, one secondi dish, and one side dish. There's often a lineup, no matter what time you arrive; give your name at the door to be added to the waiting list. *Vico Lungo Teatro Nuovo 103 (off Via Toledo).* ☎ *081/14338. Daily menu including primi, secondi, and side dish 7€. Daily 11am–3pm and 7–11pm. Bus: C25 or R2.*

DOABLE

➜ **Hosteria Toledo** ★ NEAPOLITAN/PLEBISCITO The alleys of the Spanish Quarter are filled with little restaurants serving up satisfying local specialties; this is one of the best for quality, atmosphere, and price. This cozy restaurant offers a variety of local dishes, but the seafood entrees are the best: for a culinary adventure, try the cuttlefish or octopus. *Vico Giardinetto 78A (off Via Toledo).* ☎ *081/421257. Primi 5€–9.50€; secondi 6.50€–14€. Daily 7:30pm–midnight. Bus: C25 or R2.*

➜ **Umberto** ★ SEAFOOD/CHIAIA In Chiaia, Umberto is a family-run trattoria that has been serving up seafood and pasta dishes in a peaceful gardenlike setting for 90 years. Try the gloriously flavorful *tubettoni treddeta* (named after the owners' grandfather, who had three fingers—*tre dita*): pasta tossed with baby octopus, clams, and cherry tomatoes (9.50€). They also bake a mean pizza here. *Via Alabardieri 30 (near Piazza dei Martiri).* ☎ *081/418555. www.umberto.it. Salads 5.50€–8.50€; primi 5.50€–9.50€; secondi (both meat and fish) 5€–14€; pizza 3.20€–8.50€. Daily noon–4pm and 7pm–midnight. Bus: C25.*

SPLURGE

➜ **Don Salvatore** ★ SEAFOOD/WATERFRONT One of the few places in Naples where you can actually dine beside the sea, although you'll have to make the trek out to Mergellina to do so. At this busy place, packed with locals on the weekend, you can dine in a converted boat shed on some truly fine seafood, including pastas, calamari, and fish right out of the bay. *Via Mergellina 5.* ☎ *081/681817. Primi 6€–10€; secondi 10€–21€. Thurs–Tues noon–4pm and 7:30pm–midnight. Bus: C24 or R3.*

COFFEE, PASTRY & GELATO SHOPS

When it comes to a strong culinary tradition, Naples doesn't stop at pizza and seafood—oh, no. The city is also home to some pastry and gelato shops that are so kick-ass, locals will make pilgrimages across town, just to satisfy their sweet tooth. And since these treats only cost a few euros apiece, you should, too. (Stupid low-carb diets!) And for the caffeine-sensitive, you should know that Neapolitan coffee is known for its palpitation-inducing strength—every year, a few old timers keel over from having taken too many espresso shots during the day. (So, best not to have one late in the day if you want to get to sleep.) **Caffè Gambrinus,** the most well-known cafe/tearoom in Naples, is gorgeous but frequented by a stuffy, older set. Instead, just follow a local to a down-to-earth neighborhood bar.

➜ **Attanasio** ★★★ PASTRIES/STAZIONE CENTRALE If the area around the train station has one redeeming quality, it's this outstanding little pastry shop, where they make the best *sfogliatelle* on Earth. (*Sfogliatelle* are the Neapolitan version of *millefeuille*—triangles of layered puff pastry, filled with delicious ricotta.) In fact, when I used to live in Rome and was frequently traveling to Naples, my Roman acquaintances would place orders with me to pick up *sfogliatelle* at Attanasio. But they're best fresh out of the oven. *Vico Ferrovia 2/3.* ☎ *081/285-675. Tues–Sun 9am–8pm. Closed July. Bus/metro: Piazza Garibaldi (main train station).*

→**Chalet Ciro** ★★ GELATO/WATERFRONT
This hugely popular (and delightfully retro)
spot is immersed in tropical greenery along
the marina drive/parking lot of Mergellina
harbor. Stop in at Ciro's indoor/outdoor
counter for a cone or cup of gelato (regarded
by many as the best in Naples), a refreshing
macedonia (fresh mixed fruit cup), or a jolt of
espresso before or after your hydrofoil to
Capri or Ischia—or any time at all. To-go
orders start at 2€, but you'll pay double for
the privilege of eating your treat at the
outside tables. *Via Francesco Carracciolo,
Mergellina.* ☎ *081/669-928. www.chalet
ciro.it. Thurs–Tues 7am–2am. Metro: Mergellina. Bus: C24 or R3.*

→**Dolcezze Siciliane** ★★ PASTRIES/
SANTA CHIARA   If you're jonesing for some
Sicilian sweets, but Palermo is not in your
travel plans, no worries. The cakes and pastries here arrive fresh, daily, from Sicily—the
cannoli, especially, are outta control. *Piazzale Immacolotella Vecchia.* ☎ *081/552-1990.
Tues–Sat 7:30am–7pm; Sun 7:30am–2pm.
Closed part of July and Aug. Bus: C25 or R3.*

→**Gay-Odin** ★★ CHOCOLATES   Despite its
name, this is not a bar for homosexual Norse
gods but a tiny chocolate shop offering
up handmade desserts in several locations.
For the ultimate treat, try the Mt. Vesuvius:
a chocolate version of the famous volcano,
filled with creamy chocolate ganache.
Via V. Colonna 15B. ☎ *081/418282. Also Via
Toledo 214 (*☎ *081/400063). www.gay-odin.it.
Mon–Sat 9:30am–1:30pm and 4:30–8pm; Sun
noon–2pm.*

→**Piazza d'Arte** ★ COFFEE/SANTA CHIARA
On spruced-up Piazza Dante, this sleek bar has
become something of a hot hangout for those
who prefer the modern Milanese aesthetic to
traditional Neapolitan. Caffe espresso and cappuccino are the main event here, but they also
serve beer, wine, soft drinks, and snacks. *Piazza
Dante.* ☎ *081/564-5076. Daily 7:30am–
midnight. Coffee: .75€–1.10€; Metro: Dante.*

→**Scaturchio** ★★ PASTRIES/CENTRO
STORICO   This picture-perfect, old-guard
pastry shop, right in the heart of Spaccanapoli, is a city institution. You'll get better
sfogliatelle at Attanasio, but Scaturchio's
babà al rhum (traditional Neapolitan eggy
cake, soaked in rum) is a transcendent experience. Their *zeppole* (fritters dusted with
sugar and cinnamon) aren't bad, either.
Piazza San Domenico Maggiore 19. ☎ *081/551-
6944. www.scaturchio.it. Metro: Museo or
Piazza Cavour. Bus: R2.*

Partying

Despite the vibrant energy of the city's inhabitants, Naples is unexpectedly serene at
night; perhaps that's just what happens after
a heavy dinner of pizza and pasta. In the
summer, what action there is takes place outside; take a walk along the waterfront or
down Via Toledo, and then head to one of the
piazzas in the city center where you can either
pay high prices to sit in one of the bars lining
the piazza, or follow the local example and
spend a few euros on a beer from a street
vendor and chill in the piazza. The most popular piazzas, especially with a young crowd,
are **Piazza Santa Maria La Nova** (north of
the port at Piazza Municipio) and **Piazza San
Domenico** and **Piazza Bellini** in the Centro
Storico. For something a little more exciting,
and in cooler weather, Naples is home to
numerous bars and posh clubs. Here, style is
key, as is enough cash to pay exorbitant cover
charges . . . drinks and cocktails can head
toward and above the 10€ mark at the fancier
places, with cover charges ranging from 15€
and up.

BARS & PUBS

→**Enoteca Belledonne** ★★ CHIAIA   A
bit inland from Chiaia's pretty greenbelt, this
is a hot and unpretentious spot for an *aperitivo* (from about 7:30–9pm), with budget-
friendly wines by the glass. Belly up to the
bar with the after-work crowd of tanned (and

surprisingly friendly) Neapolitan yuppies who look like they've come straight from a Nautica photo shoot. *Vico Belledonne a Chiaia 18 (off Via Ferrigni).* ☎ *081/403-162. Daily 6pm–midnight. Closed Aug. Bus: C25 or R3.*

➡ **Kinky** ★★ CENTRO STORICO   A cafe in the early evening and laid-back bar at night, Kinky is popular with young trendsetters. If you've had a long day, spend a mellow night relaxing here. Also good place to stop by for a last drink at the end of a crazy night, as it's open late. *Via Cisterna dell'Olio 21 (off Via D. Capitelli, near Piazza Gesù Nuovo).* ☎ *081/5521571. Daily 5pm–4am. Bus: R1 or R4.*

➡ **Lazzarella** ★ CENTRO STORICO   A small trendy bar with high stools and stainless steel decor, this place is quiet enough to have a deep conversation over coffee or to hit on a local over cocktails. Also a great place to satisfy late-night munchies, as they serve up the usual Italian snacks as well as hot dogs and hamburgers. *Calata Trinità 7/8 (off Piazza Gesù Nuovo).* ☎ *081/551005. Daily 8pm–4am. Bus: R1 or R4.*

NIGHTCLUBS

➡ **La Mela** ★ CHIAIA   One of Naples' most exclusive clubs—don't even bother trying to get in unless you're dressed to kill, and even then you'll probably have to fight the crowd and suck up to the bouncers. Inside, you'll find the city's beautiful people, all trying to outdo each other in style and moves on the dance floor as they groove to live DJ beats. *Via dei Mille 40 (off Via Nisco).* ☎ *081/410270. Thurs–Sun midnight–4am. Bus: C25 or R3.*

➡ **S'move Light Bar** ★★ CHIAIA   Perfect for shaking off that pizza you just scarfed down at dinner, crowded and friendly S'move is the best place to bust a move in the Chiaia district. It's done up in a vaguely Moroccan theme and spread out over three floors with interconnecting lounge, dance floor, and bar areas. The ground floor gets the most traffic, while the downstairs level is mellower, with more cushy chairs to crash in. Upstairs, the

Where the Boys Are

Most gay nightlife in Naples is centered in Posillipo, where you'll find **Tongue**, Via Alessandro Manzoni 207 (☎ **081/7690800**). It has a mixed crowd, a large part of whom are gay, dancing to techno music. It is open only on weekends 9pm to 3am and charges a cover of 15€.

loft-style attic is frequented by young VIPs. If you're visiting Naples in summer, too bad; S'move is closed in July and August. *Vico dei Sospiri 10A (off Via Ferrigni).* ☎ *081/764-5813. www.smove-lab.net. Daily 8pm–4am. Closed July and Aug. Bus: C25 or R3.*

➡ **Velvet** ★★ CENTRO STORICO   One of the only clubs where you'll be let in the door in jeans and a T-shirt, this small, casual spot was a popular underground club in the 1980s and today cranks out the electronica. Live shows are also occasionally held here. *Via Cisterna dell'Olio 11 (off Via Domenico Capitelli, near Piazza Gesù Nuovo).* ☎ *339/6700234 (cellphone). www.velvetnapoli.it. Daily 10pm–2am. Bus: R1 or R4.*

Sightseeing

EXPLORING NAPLES

Amidst the mess that is Naples, there are some strikingly beautiful attractions, such as the city's two ancient castles, as well as the stunning domed shopping mall Galleria Umberto I. There are also some excellent museums, most notably Capodimonte and the National Archaeological Museum. While the city has yet to fully develop its waterfront area (there are surprisingly few places to dine on the water) and really has no decent beaches, it is still possible to find pockets of quiet beauty where the scenery can be admired. The area near the train station is quite seedy and seems to have seen no development at all in the campaign to clean up the city. But at the same time, the area makes for

Campania Artecard: Museums & Bus Fare!

If you plan on visiting a plethora of museums and historic sites in Naples and the surrounding region, these tourist cards give you a lot of bang for your buck, especially for those under 26 years of age. There are three types of cards:

→ The **Napoli and Campi Flegrei card** will buy 3 days of local transportation (including unlimited rides on public transportation, a trip on the Alibus airport shuttle, and a return trip on the MM1 line of the Metro del Mare ferry), free admission to two sites, and half-price admission to the rest (and free admission to all sites for those under 26). Adults 13€, age 18–25 8€.

→ The **3-Day All-Site + Transport card** is the best deal for most travelers, giving you free admission to a wider range of sites, including Pompeii, and transport on the regional Unicocampania network of city buses and metros, the Circumvesuviana train (for Pompeii and Sorrento) and even local buses on the islands of Capri and Ischia. Adults 25€, age 18–25 18€.

→ Finally, the **7–day All-Site card** includes free admission to all sites for a week, but unlike the 3-day card, Unicocampania transportation is *not* covered. Adults 28€, age 18–25 21€.

All Artecards also include discounts on things such as audio guides, theater tickets, parking, and additional attractions. Purchase the card at the airport, train station, port, participating museums, or online at **www.campaniartecard.it**.

some interesting exploration through markets and vendor-lined streets—just make sure not to flash any valuables and bring a friend, preferably a large one. Allow yourself at least a couple of days in the city, as that's how long it will take to begin to appreciate its craziness (and not just feel overwhelmed by it).

Festivals/Events Calendar

◐ **Maggio dei Monumenti ("May of Monuments"):** An annual festival highlighting Naples' rich cultural heritage, with numerous performances, shows, sporting events, and fairs taking place on the weekends, and free entry into many of the city's museums and monuments, which often hold special exhibitions. www.portanapoli.com/Eng. Apr–May.

◐ **San Gennaro Festival:** The annual celebration of the patron saint of Naples and his miraculous vials of blood, which are said to liquefy on this day every year; crowds of Neapolitans wait for the vials to

be revealed by the presiding cardinal, and breathe a collective sigh of relief when their contents are revealed in liquid form—if the blood fails to liquefy, it's a sign of imminent catastrophe. Sept 19.

◐ **Pizzafest:** A festival dedicated to—what else—pizza! The best pizzerias in the city and around Campania converge for this festival, serving up their best products, and competing for awards such as best pizza chef and best pizza. Performances and music also celebrate this beloved pie. **www.pizzafest.info**. Mid-Sept.

HANGING OUT

FREE → **The Centro Storico (Spaccanapoli)** ★★ Spend an afternoon wandering through the streets of Naples' historic district. If you've visited other historical districts in Italian cities, you'll appreciate this one: Here, instead of hordes of tourists, the streets are actually filled with locals. The streets are also stocked full of important, historic old churches and monuments. The main arteries of the district are the east-west running Via dei Tribunali and Via San Biagio dei Librai, which are bisected by Via Duomo—from here, wander through the tiny side streets that branch off and wind through the district. When you get hungry, stop in at Scaturchio (see "Eating," above) for delicious Neapolitan pastries like *babà al rhum* and *zeppole.*

FREE → **Along the Waterfront** ★★ Naples' coastline certainly could use some redevelopment in places, but there's still plenty to see and do along the stretch that runs from Castel Nuovo in the east to Chiaia and Mergellina in the west. Piazza Plebiscito is an impressive, colonnaded, and pedestrianized square where Neapolitans gather for political demonstrations and concerts. Just southwest of here are the remains of a volcanic crater, Monte Echia. Descend Monte Echia to the south, and you'll find Castel dell'Ovo jutting out into the sea. This is also where Naples' ritzy waterside hotels begin, along Via Partenope. Further west is the Riviera di Chiaia, with its pretty green belt in the Villa Comunale, Art Deco palazzi, and waterfront snack bars.

MUSEUMS & ART GALLERIES

MTV (Best) → **Museo Archeologico Nazionale** ★★★ CENTRO STORICO If you have time for only one museum in Naples, this is the one to see. Touted as the oldest and most important archaeological museum in Europe, it contains wonderful finds from Pompeii and Herculaneum, the ancient Roman towns that were remarkably preserved when Mt. Vesuvius exploded in the 1st century A.D. and covered everything in a thick deposit of ash, pumice, and volcanic mud. If you plan on visiting those sites, the collection here is not to be missed, and essential in providing a complete picture of just how sophisticated life was at the height of Roman civilization. On the first floor, you'll find

paintings ★, **household instruments and tools** ★★, and religious objects from Pompeii, as well as **gladiators' weapons and armor** ★★ found at the amphitheater. On the mezzanine, there are some outstanding **mosaics** ★★ recovered from Pompeii, including the impressive *Alexander Fighting the Persians* mosaic, from the House of the Faun. Also on the mezzanine, adjacent to the mosaic rooms, is the **Gabinetto Segreto** ★★ ("Secret Cabinet of Obscene Objects"), with some highly erotic objects and artworks, also found at Pompeii. (The Gabinetto Segreto can only be visited with a guided tour, normally offered every hour—call or inquire at the ticket booth when you arrive.) The ground floor is home to a mind-boggling collection of Greek and Roman sculpture, including the powerful *Farnese Hercules* ★★★ (3rd century B.C.), whose downcast gaze and hulking, fatigued figure is one of the finest examples of emotive, Hellenistic sculpture in the world. Also here, the 3rd-century B.C. *Farnese Bull* ★★★ is an enormous marble group—the largest single sculpture that has survived from antiquity—depicting the punishment of Dirce. The bare-chested central figure, Dirce, was tied to an enraged bull by two brothers (on either side of the sculpture) when, in the throes of Dionysiac possession (i.e., she was drunk), Dirce tried to do the same to their mother, Antiope. Both Farnese sculptures were found in the Baths of Caracalla, in Rome, in the 16th century. The museum's collection goes on and on with priceless Mediterranean antiquities, including finds from Magna Graecia and Egypt. *Piazza Museo 19 (off Via Pessina).* ☎ *081/440166. www.archeona.arti. beniculturali.it. Admission 6.50€, 18–25 years 3.75€. Wed–Mon 9am–7:30pm. Metro: Cavour or Museo. Bus: 47, CS, or E1.*

→ **Museo e Gallerie di Capodimonte** ★★ CAPODIMONTE/NORTH OF CITY CENTER This massive museum, housed in an 18th-century palace originally constructed as a royal hunting residence, is the most important art gallery in Naples, and home to the impressive Farnese collection of painting, on the first floor. Assembled from all the major schools of Italian and European painting, the collection includes pieces by such big names as Botticelli, Giovani, Bellini, and Caravaggio. Also on the first floor are the royal apartments, with furnishings and decorations from the 18th to 19th centuries. These rooms are beautifully decorated with wealth befitting royalty; you can imagine the parties that were held in the huge ballroom. The second floor houses a collection of 13th–18th century Neapolitan art that was rescued from various monasteries facing persecution in the 19th century. On this level, you'll also find contemporary art. To fully appreciate all of the masterpieces in Capodimonte, give yourself at least a couple of hours. Most of the signage is in Italian, but look for the helpful English information sheets in each room. *Via Miano 2 (off Corso Amedeo di Savoia).* ☎ *081/7499111. Thurs–Tues 8:30am–7:30pm. Admission 7.50€, EU citizens 18–24 years old: 3.75€. Audioguide 4€. Bus: R4.*

➔ **Catacombs of San Gennaro** ★ CAPODIMONTE/NORTH OF CITY CENTER Pay homage to the remains of San Gennaro, patron saint of Naples, whose bones were transferred to this underground cemetery in the 5th century. Well-preserved frescoes line the walls near his tomb. The subterranean alleys of Naples are also interesting to explore, though not for the claustrophobic. To explore the catacombs and alleys, you must enter on a guided tour, offered several times in the first half of the day. *Via Capodimonte 13.* ☎ *081/741101. Tues–Sun 9am, 10am, 11am, and noon. Admission 5€. Bus: R4.*

HISTORIC BUILDINGS

➔ **Castel dell'Ovo** ★ WATERFRONT/ROYAL NAPLES Built on the waterfront on Megaris Island, the "Castle of the Egg" gets its name from the legend of the enchanted egg supposedly buried beneath the building which protects the small island from calamities; skeptics say the name actually just refers to the island's egglike shape. Whatever its origins, this castle has had a full history; it was initially built as a residence for Roman philosopher Lucullus, then used as a monastery in the 7th century, converted to a fort in the 12th century, and then into a royal residence soon after, when Roger the Norman conquered Naples. In the 18th and 19th centuries, the building resumed its military functions, and was later used as a site for industrial operations. The castle fell into disuse soon after, and restorations began about 30 years ago. While the interior of the castle is only open during special exhibits, it's worth a visit even just to walk along the exterior edge for the gorgeous views of the bay—from here, you can see Vesuvius and the Amalfi Coast on a clear day. Outside the castle walls, restaurants and cafes fill cobblestone streets. *Borgo Marinari (off Via Partenope).* ☎ *081/2400055. Admission varies depending on exhibition. Mon–Sat 8:30am–7pm; Sun 8:30am–2pm. Bus: C24, C25, C28, or R3. Tram: 1.*

➔ **Castello Nuovo** ★★ WATERFRONT/PORT Naples' 13th-century "new castle" (also known as the Maschio Angioino, or Angevin Stronghold) is more interesting than the older, more picturesque Castel dell'Ovo. Inside, you can visit the dungeons where the Anjou monarchs kept their prisoners; according to tradition, the Fossa del Coccodrillo is where prisoners were eaten alive by crocodiles lurking in the ditch (now covered with a grate). There are also bones galore—in the glass-covered tombs of the Angevin barons, and in the glass-covered cemetery lying underneath the interior courtyard. From the castle's upper ramparts, there are, once again, gorgeous views of the city and bay. *Piazza Municipio.* ☎ *081/420-1241. Mon–Sat 9am–7pm; Apr–May also Sun 9am–2pm. Admission 5€. Bus: R2 or R3. Tram: 1.*

➔ **Palazzo Reale** ★★ WATERFRONT/ROYAL NAPLES A huge palace dominating the area adjacent to Piazza Plebiscito, it was built in the late 16th century for the expected visit of the new King Philip III who never ended up making it to Naples. It was later taken up by the Bourbons, descendants of the Spanish royal family. Facing Piazza Plebiscito, statues of former Neapolitan rulers line the exterior wall of the palace. Enter the complex around the corner on Via Chiaia, where you can wander the exterior grounds for free; here, you'll find piazzettas with fountains and statues, and a small garden whose shade and quietness provides a welcome respite from the bustling city outside. If you purchase a ticket, you'll be allowed into the interior. The royal apartments contain original furnishings, as well as numerous works of art from the period. The Court Theater is of interest for its papier-mâché statues, most of which are originals. And be sure to visit the rooftop garden with beautiful fountains and flowerbeds. In the interior of the palace, you'll also find the colossal library originally created by the Bourbons, and today housing over one million books. *Piazza del Plebiscito 1.* ☎ *081/400547. Admission: 4€; EU students: 2€. Thurs–Tues 9am–7pm. Bus: R2 or R3.*

→ Castel Sant'Elmo and Certosa-Museo di San Martino ★★ VOMERO Naples is full of fine vistas and great views; but **Castel Sant'Elmo,** perched high on the hill, ups the ante and offers visitors a truly breathtaking **panorama** ★★★. Take the elevator to the roof, where the six-pointed-star-shaped battlements offer stunning 360-degree views of the city, Vesuvius, and all that gorgeous water in the bay. Built in 1329 during the reign of Roberto of Anjou, and later enlarged when it became a fortress, Castel Sant'Elmo occasionally hosts temporary exhibitions during which you can take a walk through the dark halls of the castle. Next door, you'll find the **Certosa** (charterhouse) and **Museo Nazionale di San Martino,** housed in a 14th-century monastery and

displaying historical artifacts such as carriages and ship replicas, and historic documents, as well as a large collection of *presepi* (crèches, or nativity scene dioramas). *Castle: Via Tito Angelini 20.* ☎ *081/5784030. Admission 2€. Thurs–Tues 8:30am–6:30pm. Museum: Largo San Martino 5.* ☎ *081/5781769. Admission 6€. Tues–Sat 8:30am–7:30pm and Sun 9am–7:30pm. Take the Funiculare Centrale from Via Toledo (near Galleria Umberto I) to the top, then head right when you exit.*

FREE **→ Duomo** CENTRO STORICO Dedicated to the Madonna Assunta, construction began on Naples' Duomo in the 13th century, and was finished in the 14th century, although with renovations and additions to the Gothic façade, they were still hammering away in the early 20th century. (The church bell, damaged in an earthquake nearly 700 years ago, still sits injured in the bell tower, however.) Inside, treasures and artwork have piled on since the 14th century; check out Francesco Ierace's relief paintings of the life of San Gennaro above the portal, and Luca Giordano's 17th-century paintings on parts of the ceiling. The **Chapel of San Gennaro** houses the vials of the saint's blood that are said to miraculously liquefy three times a year: in May, December, and during the San Gennaro Festival in September. Offering a cool, quiet respite from the city, the church is worth a visit even if it's just to take a few minutes' break when the chaos of Naples becomes overwhelming. *Via del Duomo 147 (at Via Tribunali).* ☎ *081/449097. www.duomodinapoli.it. Free admission. Daily 8am–12:30pm and 4:30–7pm, holidays 8am–1:30pm and 5–7pm. Bus: C25 or R2.*

GARDENS & PARKS

FREE **→ Camaldoli Park** ★ VOMERO One of the better reasons to visit the residential district of Vomero, this park sits on a hill at the highest point in Naples, offering sweeping views of the chaotic city below, the bay, and even as far as Sorrento on a clear day. Originally a 16th-century hermitage of Camaldolian monks, all that remains of this heritage is the small Church of the Savior Saints. Spend an afternoon relaxing in the cool woods of the park, or walking along its rocky expanse. If you're lucky, you may spot some of the critters living in the park, such as lizards, bats, turtledoves, and quails. *Via Sant'Ignazio di Loyola. Daily 7am to 1 hr. before sunset. Funicolare: Piazza Piedigrotta.*

FREE ➔ **Parco della Floridiana** ★ VOMERO   Also in Vomero, and much easier to reach than the Camaldoli, this is local residents' favorite spot to stroll along green paths, or take the kids to the playground, which makes for some fun observing of Neapolitan family life. Since you're in hilly Vomero, there are good views over the bay from the southern edge of the park. *Via Cimarosa 77. ☎ 081/578-1776. Daily 8:30am to 1 hr. before sunset. Bus: E4 or V1. Funicolare: Chiaia or Centrale.*

MTV **Best** **FREE** ➔ **Posillipo** ★★ If you have some time to spare, this gorgeous, posh neighborhood offers the best views in Naples. From Posillipo's terracelike piazza, on a hill overlooking the city, you can take in sweeping panoramas of the entire city all in one glance; the splendid setting really does make the trek up here worth the effort.

Farther west is the **Grotta di Seiano (Discesa la Gaiola),** an 800m-long (2,624-ft.) ancient Roman tunnel that leads to the ancient Roman Villa Pausilypon, with arches cut away in the rock to allow views of the Trentaremi ("Thirty Oars") Bay, a small inlet where Roman ships once moored. *Grotto: ☎ 081/795-2003 for guided tours, offered Mon–Sat 9:30, 10:30, and 11:30am; free admission. To get to Posillipo: take bus 140 to Capo Posillipo, or take bus R3 to the end of the route at Via Mergellina, and then take the funiculare up to Via Manzoni. To get to the Grotta di Seiano and Villa Pausilypon, take bus 140 to Capo Posillipo, then F9.*

POZZUOLI: A FUNKY DAY TRIP TO SOPHIA LOREN'S BIRTHPLACE ★★

When we say funky, we really do mean funky. Pozzuoli is one of several towns to the west of Naples known as the *Campi Flegrei* (the Phlegraean ["fiery" or "burning"] Fields), famous for, among other things, its sulphurous stink. (Naples' proudest Hollywood export, Sophia Loren, was also born and raised here, although nowadays she downplays this suburban heritage.) Pozzuoli was founded in the 6th century B.C. by political exiles from the Greek island of Samos, fell under Roman rule in the 4th century B.C., and later became a fishing village and tourist spot popular for its thermal springs. Today, the town still has smoldering volcanic craters and well-preserved Roman ruins. Several decades ago, when the land started undulating due to volcanic forces, residents abandoned the town, only to move back a few years later to reconstruct everything, which explains why so many buildings look brand new; those that have yet to be restored display the scars of the catastrophe. To get here, take the metro line 2 to the very end. The tourist office is on Via Campi Flegrei 3 (☎ **081/5265068;** www.infocampiflegrei.it).

➔ **Solfatara** ★★ A short walk from the center of town is the otherworldly, rather cool Solfatara volcanic park. Unlike other volcano visits, no climbing is involved here; just follow your nose down the wooded paths from the park entrance to the stench of rotten eggs, and you'll emerge into the bizarre and barren, yellowish-white moonscape that is the Solfatara crater. On the paths that run the perimeter of the crater, there are hissing fissures, **vapor-spitting fumaroles,** and underground rumblings that remind you this isn't a dormant volcano (it hasn't erupted in over 800 years, however). In the center is the famed **bubbling mud pit;** this and other dangerous areas of the park are barricaded by fences and iron grates, and marked with yellow, Li'l Rascals-style OFF-LIMITS signs, but in typical Italian fashion, safety measures aren't all that strict. If you're dead-set on disfiguring yourself, you'll find plenty of **unguarded steam vents** where you can scald yourself with **sulfuric acid** that gurgles just beneath the ground. The crater sits in the midst of a eucalyptus-filled park, a lovely area for an afternoon picnic—lovely, aside from that omnipresent sulfur smell. *Via Solfatara 161.* ☎ *081/5262341. www.solfatara.it. Admission 5.50€. Daily 8:30am–7pm.*

→ **Anfiteatro Flavio (Flavian Amphitheater)** ★★ Pozzuoli's amphitheater—the third largest in Italy, after Rome's Colosseum and the amphitheater in Santa Maria Capua Vetere—was built in the 1st century A.D. under Nero's supervision and sat over 40,000 guests in its heyday. The main events here were contests between gladiators and fights between men and wild beasts that were kept in cages underneath the arena and then raised up with special trapdoors and pulleys. Later, in the 4th century, Christian martyrs were thrown to the beasts and then "saved" at the last minute, only to be beheaded instead. You can take a walk through the labyrinth of corridors leading through this underground area, admire the marble columns and statues that still stand, or take a seat in the amphitheater and let yourself drift off into an ancient reverie, imagining all the blood and gore that was spilled here. *Via Nicola Terracciano 75.* ☎ *081/5266007. Admission 4€, valid for 2 days and including admission to several other sites in the area. Wed–Mon 9am to 1 hr. before sunset.*

FREE → **Macellum** This strange pit in the center of town containing decaying marble columns was a bustling city market in the 1st and 2nd centuries, serving the busy port of Puteoli (Pozzuoli's Roman name). It is also known as the Tempio di Serapide because, when a statue of the Egyptian god Serapis was found in the market area, some thought that the ruins were those of an ancient temple. They have since been proved wrong. Though there's not too much to see here, you can take a walk through the area for free. Clamshells and other skeletons of small sea life are lodged in the stones of the ruins, indicating that the Macellum was submerged for a long time under seawater.

Playing Outside

BEACHES (NOT)

Don't come to Naples expecting stretches of sand. There is one word to describe the beaches here: disappointing. While the city has miles of coastline, there are no actual beaches. As testimony to this lack of development of what could be a prime stretch of waterfront, the old steelworks at Bagnoli, west of Mergellina, was closed down decades ago and has yet to be dismantled! That being said, when it gets hot, locals are content to grab a boulder on the rocky shore, and spend the day swimming in the water and lazing about near the seaside. It ain't exactly Mediterranean luxury, but it'll cool you down. Try the area to the west of Castel dell'Ovo or the shoreline in Mergellina.

Shopping

Bargains galore exist in Naples; this is the best place to pick up designer knock-offs from street vendors. Watch out for those looking to cheat tourists, bargain hard, and don't expect quality. And never, ever purchase electronic items off the street (see "Street-Smart Shopping," p. 601). For ultimate bargain shopping, stroll amongst the vendors lined along Via Toledo, and in the alleys of the Spanish Quarter.

For high-end shopping, **Via Toledo** is the main shopping street in Naples, and is a fun place to walk, window-shop, and observe the masses of locals doing the same. A stop in **Galleria Umberto I** ★ is a must: Even if you can't afford a single item in any of these

Wine Tasting in Campania

The wines produced in the harsh, hot landscapes of Campania seem stronger, rougher, and, in many cases, more powerful than those grown in gentler climes. Among the most famous are the **Lacrymae Christi** (Tears of Christ), a white that grows in the volcanic soil near Naples, Herculaneum, and Pompeii; **Taurasi,** a potent red; and **Greco di Tufo,** a pungent white laden with the odors of apricots and apples. One of the most frequently visited vineyards is **Mastroberardino,** 75–81 Via Manfredi, Atripalda, 83042 Avellino (☎ 0825-614111), which is reached by taking the A16 east from Naples. If you'd like to spend a day outside the city, driving through the countryside and doing a little wine tasting, call to make an appointment.

stores, you have to check out this incredible shopping mall, featuring a beautiful domed ceiling and gorgeous marble architecture—Mall of America, eat your heart out!

Finally, a shopping experience not to be missed if you really want to see Naples at its most traditional is the stretch of market stalls along **Via Pignasecca** ★★ (just west of Via Toledo and north of Piazza Carità). Here, you'll find a bazaar where fishmongers, perfume sellers, kitchenware boutiques, *salame* vendors, and lingerie shops draw the community daily, creating wonderful local color. (Most shops and vendors are only open 8am–1pm.)

Pompeii: What Happened When Vesuvius Went Off

24km (15 miles) S of Naples

On the morning of August 24, 79 A.D., Mt. Vesuvius blew its top big time. So powerful was the pyroclastic eruption that a column of ash and gas spewed as high as 33km (20 miles) above the crater. When it came back down, the shower of pumice darkened the midday sky and a cloud of volcanic gas descended on the prosperous Roman town of 📺 Best **Pompeii** ★★★, sealing the entire town and its 20,000 inhabitants in over 7m (23 ft.) of ash. Even deadlier, a burning cloud of hot volcanic gas surged through the city and asphyxiated, in a matter of minutes, anyone who had taken shelter and survived the ash fall. As cataclysmic as this was for the region below Vesuvius (destruction spread over 300 sq. km/117 sq. miles around the Bay of Naples), life went on elsewhere in the empire. Despite its former wealth, Pompeii was forgotten for over 1,500 years—until workers building a canal in the area stumbled across the ruins. What they found, of course, was only the tip

of the iceberg: full-scale excavations began in 1860 and are still ongoing.

Today, Pompeii is an incredible witness to both Roman life at the start of the first millennium, as well as the destructive havoc that a volcanic explosion can cause. Pompeii is on par with such archaeological sites as Cambodia's Angkor Wat and China's Great Wall. The city is astonishingly intact, and you can spend several wide-eyed hours wandering through streets, houses, baths, theaters, government buildings, and market areas that look and feel much as they would have 1,900 years ago. The amazing thing is that, with a few keys to understanding the ruins, you can totally picture yourself living here; in a Twilight Zone kind of way, it feels eerily familiar.

Aside from a few mosaics preserved *in situ* in Pompeii, all other artifacts found during the course of excavations at the site are kept in the Museo Archeologico in Naples (p. 613).

There, the inventory of frescoes, sculptures, and fascinating, modern-looking everyday objects is not to be missed if you're looking to get a complete picture of Pompeiian life. Pompeii is an easy day trip from Naples or Sorrento, but be sure to give yourself at least 3 hours in Pompeii, and even more if you can spare it. Just make sure to bring a hat and water, as there isn't much shade, and it gets mighty hot here from May to September.

Getting There

Note that the modern Italian spelling of the town is "Pompei," so all transportation signage, to the ruins or the modern town, will leave off the final "I."

BY TRAIN

From Naples, take a Sorrento-bound **Circumvesuviana** train (1.80€, no rail passes) and get off at the stop called Pompei Scavi–Villa dei Misteri. (The Salerno-bound train makes a stop at "Pompei," but this station serves the modern town and is quite some distance from the actual ruins. From the Pompei Scavi train station, turn right and walk down the hill (about 200m/656 ft.) to the Porta Marina entrance gate of the ruins.

BY BUS

SITA **buses** run to Pompeii from Naples (2.30€). They're supposed to run every 30 minutes, but are notoriously unreliable. Catch the bus from outside Stazione Centrale in Naples, or at the SITA bus station by the Molo Beverello port—it's in the red building at the end of the giant parking lot. Ask the driver for the Pompeii stop, as it's unmarked. From the bus stop, cross the street and walk up the street (in the same direction as the bus is heading) for a minute or two to reach the entrance gate.

Getting Around

Pompeii is divided into two sections: a modern town and the old town—the *scavi,* or excavations. There's not much of interest in modern Pompeii except for the FS train station and a few mediocre shops and restaurants. Spend your time in the old town.

Tourist Office

The main **tourist office** is in modern Pompeii at Via Sacra 1 (☎ 081/8507255; www.pompeiturismo.it; Mon–Fri 8am–8:30pm, Sat 8am–2pm). A more convenient branch office is near the ruins in Piazza Porta Marina Inferiore. There is also a small information booth at the Porta Marina entrance to the ruins.

Recommended Websites

○ **www.pompeiturismo.it**   The official website of the Pompeii tourist office, with practical information on the ruins and the town.

○ **www.pompeiisites.org**   Provides detailed information on the history of Pompeii, the excavation process, and the site today, as well as events in the area.

Eating

Your best bet is to pack a lunch and have a picnic among the ruins: if you leave the ruins for lunch you won't be allowed to re-enter, and the sole restaurant on the premises is a mediocre, overpriced, cafeteria-type deal (but you can get a beer there).

If you do need to eat in Pompeii, there are several cafes and restaurants outside Porta Marina and on Via Plinio serving up tasty, moderately priced pizza and panini, pasta, and fried calamari. Best of all are the street carts that set up shop where all the tour buses pick up and drop off their loads; here, you can get a huge to-go cup of the most refreshing citrus juice you'll ever have in your life, made from a blend of oranges and humongous, sweet local lemons.

OKKIO! Lots of Crowds at Pompeii

Pompeii sells more admission tickets than any other archaeological site or museum in Italy, so yeah, you should expect crowds. If you're wandering the ruins by yourself, you'll often find yourself stuck behind a large and slow tour group that seems to be oblivious to the fact that there are other people at the site who may not appreciate being blocked from entering or exiting buildings, or having to listen to the loud commentary of their guides. Most tour groups arrive at Pompeii at around 10 or 11am, and from then on there's no escape—you'll overtake one group only to be stuck in the midst of another. The best solution for independent travelers is to deal with an early morning wake-up, and get yourself to Pompeii as close to the 8:30am opening time as possible. (In summer, that's also the best way to beat the heat.) However, if you don't feel like attacking the site alone, and you want to get a better understanding of the context of the ruins, you can join one of these groups, which are formed ad hoc at the entrance of the site for about 8€–10€ per person (in addition to the entrance fee), depending on group size. Pompeii's official tour guides are overseen by an incredibly strict government agency, so they're very well informed and very good at putting things in perspective for foreign visitors with no background in the antiquities.

Why You're Here: The Ruins

There are several entrance gates to the Pompeii ruins, all leading to the Porta Marina ticket booth and bookshop area. There is free luggage storage here, as well as free clean toilets. Definitely pick up a map and guidebook at the information booth; the map gives good suggestions of itineraries based on how much time you have (although they actually only take about half the indicated time), and the guidebook gives insightful information on the various buildings and regions of the town.

For those with a strong interest in Pompeii, you may wish to pick up an **audioguide** or join a tour group—guides mingle among the crowd at the admissions area looking to form groups, for about 8€–10€ per person, in addition to the 10€ entrance fee. In the summer, it's also possible to do Pompeii at night, when the tour groups have gone home and soft lights illuminate the town. The ticket office can be reached at ☎ 081/8575347 or infopompei@tin.it. Admission is 10€, EU citizens age 18–34 5€. Audioguides 6.50€. The site is open April through October 8:30am to 7:30pm (last entrance at 6pm); from May 15 to October 11, night hours are Sunday through Tuesday 8:30 to 11:30pm (last entrance 10:30pm). Pompeii also opens its gates November through March 8:30am to 5pm (last entrance at 3:30pm).

EXPLORING ANCIENT POMPEII

The streets of Pompeii are lined with numerous **temples** dedicated to various gods and goddesses, **private residences** with original frescoes and mosaics, **public bathhouses,** and even **brothels.**

In some buildings, such as the **Stabian Baths** and the **Forum Granary,** you'll find what appear to be stone sculptures of people frozen in strange positions (crawling, prone, doubled over) with looks of terror on their faces. These are plaster casts of victims of the wrath of Vesuvius. Their bodies were caught in the flow of volcanic mud and ash fall when the volcano exploded; as time passed, their bodies decomposed and left hollow spaces in the hardened rock. Later, archaeologists and anthropologists poured

Pompeii

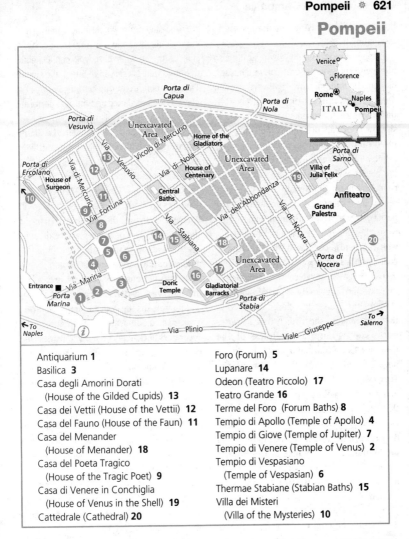

plaster into these empty volumes and reproduced the exact shape and position of Pompeiian residents—and even their pets—when they died over 1,900 years ago.

The Forum, a large pillar-lined square, served as the center of town. Temples, market stalls, and political offices surround the large promenade area. The best preserved bathing complexes in Pompeii are the **Forum Baths** and the **Stabian Baths,** where

the *apodyteria* (changing rooms) have well-preserved cubbies where patrons could store their togas. The vaulted ceilings of the bath chambers are lined with exquisite, fluted channels whereby condensation would gather and drain neatly down the walls of the room, instead of dripping over bathers' heads. (The restricted spaces of the baths are always packed with tour groups, so push your way in and try to catch what the tour guide is saying—it's usually pretty fascinating.)

Pompeii was a wealthy town, so it's also filled with ruins of elaborate private houses, hidden behind narrow hallways, called *fauces,* that connect them to the street. Past the *fauces,* each house had an atrium with a shallow pool, called an *impluvium,* that captured rainwater through a square opening, called a *compluvium,* in the roof. Leading off the atrium were frescoed and mosaic-filled rooms where household guests were received for meetings and banquets; farther back, or on a second floor in some cases, were the family's bedrooms, or *cubicula,* which were also decorated with ornate frescoes. All houses had some kind of back garden, or peristyle, with a central yard open to the sky surrounded by a shaded portico. Many of the houses are closed for restoration, but among the usually open houses worth seeking out are the **House of the Dancing Faun (Casa del Fauno),** with its huge peristyle garden; the **House of the Tragic Poet (Casa del Poeta Tragico),** home to the famous *Cave Canem* ("Beware of Dog") mosaic in the *fauces;* the **House of the Silver Wedding (Casa delle Nozze d'Argento);** the **House of Menander (Casa del Menander);** the **House of the Golden Cupids (Casa degli Amorini Dorati);** and the **House of the Vettii,** with its preserved kitchen area and porno wall frescoes.

Speaking of porno, you won't want to miss the popular **Lupanare,** or brothel. In this tiny two-story inn, Pompeii's "ladies of the night" entertained the gents on hard stone beds in oppressively small cells. Such tight quarters could hardly have been mood-setting, but to make up for it, well-preserved frescoes above each doorway advertised the brothel's bill of fare, illustrating in vivid detail all the various positions and sex acts the prostitutes offered. All that's missing is the "XXX" neon sign outside.

For some more wholesome family-style entertainment, head for the southeastern side of the town, where you can clamber over two well-preserved theaters: the **Great Theater,** built in the 2nd century B.C., hosted plays as well as dance and musical performances for audiences of up to 5,000 people. The smaller, and aptly named, **Small Theater** was built around 80 B.C. and held musical and poetry performances and probably had a roof; its Latin name, Theatrum Tectum, means "Covered Theater." The acoustics in both theaters are still great. Between them sits the **Quadriporticus of the Theaters,** an open area where theatergoers could stretch their legs during intermission or find shelter in case of rain.

Way in the outskirts of town, and so far that most visitors don't bother making the 20-minute trek, sits the Pompeii **Amphitheater,** a massive 20,000-seater built around 70 B.C. Spectators flocked here mainly to witness the gladiator battles between brave souls representing Pompeii and neighboring towns, but also for the popular *venatio* event, that is fights between specially trained *bestiarii* (animal fighters) and wild beasts from Asia and Africa. The amphitheater is equipped with two gates leading to the arena's center: one for participants to enter with pomp and flair, and one through which they were carried out at the end of the battle. It's not nearly as big as Rome's Colosseum, but the ruins are a lot more hands-on—you can climb on everything and even go "backstage" to the underground structures where the animals and gladiators were kept.

At Pompeii's multitudinous gift shops and souvenir stands, you'll see a lot of postcards of ritualistic figures on a deep red and black background; these are frescoes from the **Villa of the Mysteries,** which is technically part of the Pompeii site but separated from the main ruins by a 10-minute walk north of the Porta Marina gate. This villa was dedicated to

Herculaneum & Oplontis

"Hey, We Got Buried, Too!"

Pompeii gets all the hype, and justifiably so, but it wasn't the only site to be destroyed by Mt. Vesuvius in 79 A.D. and subsequently rediscovered. The next largest town, ancient **Herculaneum** ★★ (called **Ercolano** by Italians today), was pummeled by a violent surge of volcanic mud after the eruption, which meant that structural damage was more widespread than in Pompeii, whose buildings were covered by a more gentle rain of ash and pumice. Ercolano lies on the Circumvesuviana line between Naples and Pompei-Scavi (take a Naples-bound train from Sorrento or Pompei, or a Sorrento-bound train from Naples). The site is plenty impressive, and if there were no Pompeii, Ercolano would be packed with tour groups. Highlights of the site are its lovely mosaic nymphaeums (fountains), some wooden fixtures, and usual lack of crowds. Other than that, its offerings are similar to what you'll find at Pompeii, but over a smaller area—which is why some visitors find it more manageable, especially in the height of summer. *Corso Resina, Ercolano.* ☎ *081/857-5347. www.pompeiisites.org. Admission 10E; 18E ticket good for 3 days at 5 sites: Pompeii, Herculaneum, Oplontis, Boscoreale, and Stabiae. Nov–Mar 8:30am–5pm; Apr–Oct 8:30am–7:30pm (entrance until 90 min. before closing). Closed Jan 1, May 1, Dec 25. Circumvesuviana to Ercolano.*

   Oplontis ★, a short walk from the Torre Annunziata Circumvesuviana station (also on the Naples-Sorrento line), is famous for the Villa of Poppaea, a 1st century B.C. seaside estate that eventually belonged to Poppaea Sabina, Nero's second wife. (The sea is now several kilometers away; Oplontis today is surrounded by the ugly town of Torre Annunziata.) Kept cool by the shade of lemon groves (and the fact that most of it's below modern street level), Oplontis is a blessedly relaxing and deserted site, where you can walk, undisturbed, through room after frescoed room, explore colonnaded chambers, emerge into lush garden areas, and have a great time imagining the former wealth here, even if you don't fully understand what you're seeing. *Via Sepolcri, Torre Annunziata.* ☎ *081/862-1755. www.pompeiisites.org. Admission 5€; 18€ ticket good for 3 days at 5 sites: Pompeii, Herculaneum, Oplontis, Boscoreale, and Stabiae. Nov–Mar 8:30am–5pm; Apr–Oct 8:30am–7:30pm (entrance until 90 min. before closing). Closed Jan 1, May 1, Dec 25. Circumvesuviana to Torre Annunziata.*

Dionysus, or Bacchus, the god of wine, and the frescoes depict the "mysteries" of Bacchic worship—initiation to the cult involved the sacrifice of a young maiden's virginity to the god. She is first shown afraid, then in despair, then in pain, and finally in physical rapture. This seems like a bit of an off-color subject to have on the walls of your country house, but the Romans were into some kinky stuff. In any case, the frescoes are lush and saturated and well worth the hike out here.

   Another site worth visiting, outside of the actual ruins themselves, is the **Virtual Pompeii** exhibit ★ (Via Plinio 105; ☎ 081/5783593; www.virtualpompeii.it). Here, you can get a glimpse of what Pompeii looked like before that fateful day when Vesuvius destroyed it. The exhibit shows films using digital 3D technology that allow you to (virtually) stroll through Pompeii before the eruption, and then experience the catastrophe yourself. You'll need to book in advance, though; give them a call or book through the website. Admission is 7€ for one film or 12€ for two films. It's open daily 11:30am to 5pm.

Mt. Vesuvius

The only active volcano on mainland Europe, **MTV Best** **Vesuvio** ★★ is the mammoth volcano that buried Pompeii and the surrounding towns in lava and ash nearly 2,000 years ago. Since then, it has erupted 28 times—its last eruption was in 1944, and scientists monitoring the seismic activity of the region say it's overdue for its next big bang. With that in mind, if you're craving a bit of a hike, we recommend the ascent to the crater of this charcoal-colored giant that dominates the skyline of much of Campania. In the past, it was actually possible to climb *into* the volcano's crater, but today, the heat and steam emanating from the center make this impossible, so visitors must make do with peering inside from the rim of the crater, which is still plenty exhilarating!

GETTING THERE

Vesuvius is easily visited as a day trip from Naples, or in combination with a day trip to Pompeii or Herculaneum (in which case it's best to visit the volcano first, as buses stop running from Vesuvius at around 5:30pm).

From Naples, there are two ways to approach Vesuvius: first, you can take the **Circumvesuviana** train from Stazione Centrale in Naples heading toward Sorrento (1.80€, no rail passes) and get off at Ercolano Scavi. From here, take a **Trasporti Vesuviani** bus from outside the train station (3.80€ round-trip).

Or, you can take the bus or train to Pompeii (see the "Getting There" section in Pompeii for details), and from there catch a **Vesuviana Mobilità** bus from Piazza Porta Marina (8.60€ round-trip).

Either way, the hour-long bus ride to Vesuvius passes through villas, vineyards, and the occasional field of wildflowers, eventually dropping you 1,000m (3,280 ft.) up the volcano. From here, you'll have to walk about 20 minutes up to the crater, where you'll need to pay a somewhat exorbitant 6.50€ fee for the privilege of being there. On a clear day, with views over the bay of Naples that are breathtaking—if not downright vertiginous—the crunch of volcanic stone under your sneakers, and the quietly ominous steaming of the crater itself, it's absolutely worth it.

Sorrento: On a Clear Day . . .

50km (31 miles) S of Naples

Overrun with tourists, expensive, and kitschy, Sorrento ★★ is nonetheless worthy of at least a stop for the day if just for its utter beauty; the town sits perched up on the cliff ledges of the peninsula that marks the southern tip of the Bay of Naples. On a clear day (which is typical of the region), you can see Naples, Vesuvius, and Capri from here. The town acts as a convenient transit point between Naples and the Amalfi Coast and seems to attract mainly geriatric tour groups and jet-setting yuppies. But, with its stunning views and cute old city, Sorrento offers enough to entice anyone to at least stop for the day, if not a night as well.

Getting There

BY TRAIN

Circumvesuviana trains run frequently between Naples and Sorrento (about 1 hr., 3.20€), stopping at Pompeii in between (30 min., 1.80€). Rail passes are not valid on these trains. The train station sits just to the south of Corso Italia, to the east of the town center. Purchase tickets at the train station office.

BY BUS

SITA buses (☎ **199/730749**) connect Sorrento with Amalfi (2.40€) via Positano

Sorrento

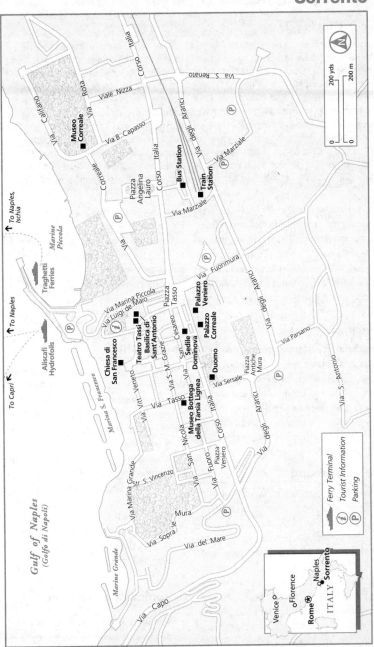

OKKIO! Watch Out for Scams in Sorrento

If something in Sorrento seems to be too convenient, if by a stroke of luck you just happen to be offered exactly what you need, beware that things are quite likely to be too good to be true. Take the recent taxi scam that has developed in the city: When crowds of tourists gather around taxi stands that are notoriously devoid of actual taxis, suddenly a guardian angel appears and in an authoritative and efficient manner arranges for a minivan to come pick everyone up and drop everyone off at their respective destinations. Thinking that the communal transport will be a bargain compared to a taxi ride, everyone happily piles into the minivan when it arrives shortly after, and then receives a total shock when the driver demands ridiculous fare from every passenger. During one such scam, taxi passengers had to pay 20€ each—when the minivan is full, that turns into a hefty profit for these miscreants.

(1.30€), leaving nearly every hour from just below the train station. Purchase tickets from the corner store at the train station entrance or at any *tabacchi* in town. Especially during the busy summer season, it's a good idea to arrive early and join the line up at the bus stop so that you're sure to secure a seat on the bus.

BY FERRY

Ferries run from **Marina Piccola,** down the steps and toward the water from Piazza Tasso. In the summer, there are frequent connections to Capri (from 5.80€) and Naples (from 4.50€), and Amalfi (7€), as well as daily connections to Ischia (15€) and Positano (7€). For more information about ferry and hydrofoil travel in the region, see p. 630.

Getting Around

Sorrento is small enough to navigate on foot. From the train and bus station, walk down the stairs and head down the street straight ahead to Corso Italia, the main street. From there, turn left and walk to Piazza Tasso, and then either continue on Corso Italia, or turn right on any of the side streets from there to get to the old city. From the port at Marina Piccola, walk towards the town and then up the stairs to Piazza Tasso. (The stairs from Marina Piccola to Piazza Tasso, and vice

versa, are not feasible if you have luggage; instead, take the bus.)

Public **buses** are the orange (as opposed to the blue or green SITA inter-regional buses), and cost 1€ for a 60-minute ticket. Line B runs between Piazza Tasso and Marina Piccola. Line D runs between Piazza Tasso and Marina Grande (the larger port where cruise ships and fishing boats dock).

Tourist Office

The **AAS Tourist Information Office** is at Lungomare de Maio 35 (☎ **081/8074033;** www.sorrentotourism.com; Mon–Sat 8:45am–6:15pm, closed holidays). To get here, head through Piazza Sant'Antonino to Via Luigi de Maio and enter into the compound on the right. As well as a poor-quality map, the tourist office has copies of the indispensable transportation schedule, which lists departure times for the Circumvesuviana train between Sorrento and Naples, the SITA bus schedule between Sorrento and the Amalfi Coast, and a list of ferry departures between Sorrento and Capri, Naples, Ischia, Positano, and Amalfi.

Recommended Websites

○ **www.sorrentoinfo.com**   The online Sorrento Information Guide provides a directory of hotels and restaurants, as well as general information on the city and its attractions, and valuable reviews of all these by other visitors.

○ **www.sorrentotourism.com** The official website of the Sorrento Tourist Office, with information on transport, accommodations, restaurants, and sites, as well as a handy map section.

Sleeping

Sorrento has some incredible accommodation options: Imagine waking up in a Mediterranean-style suite and stepping out onto your balcony to admire the view of the bay and the town below. If you can afford the splurge, check out the fancy hotels lined along Via del Capo. For those with more realistic budgets, there are more moderately priced places to stay, though finding budget accommodation can be difficult during peak season as the options are few and so tend to get grabbed quickly.

HOSTEL

→ **La Sirene** ★ This is the sole hostel in Sorrento, and by far the most affordable place to stay. Conveniently located on a noisy street near the train station, rooms with up to 10 dorm beds are bright with clean bathrooms, and some also have balconies, although there's not much to look out at. The hostel also runs a cozy cafe and bar next door, with a 10% discount for hostel guests. Other perks include Internet access and a TV room. *Via degli Aranci 160.* ☎ *081/072925. www.hostel.it. Dorm 16€–20€, double 50€ with bunk bed or 60€ with double bed. Breakfast included.*

CHEAP

→ **Hotel Linda** A no-frills budget hotel where you definitely get what you pay for. Rooms are cheap and those on the first of the hotel's two floors are clean and comfortable, but those on the upper floor are dingy and disappointing. Some have a balcony, though the view is only of the building's courtyard. The family who owns the hotel speaks little

English. *Via degli Aranci 125 (near the train station).* ☎ *081/8782916. Single from 35€, double from 65€.*

DOABLE

→ **Hotel Savoia** ★ At the Savoia, which is down the street from Piazza Tasso, the friendly staff offer up recently renovated, spotless rooms with phone, TV, and A/C, and some with balcony as well. At the end of the day, have a drink in the hotel bar or watch TV in the Mediterranean-style lobby. *Via Fuorimura 48 (near Via degli Aranci).* ☎ *081/ 8782511. www.savoia-hotel.com. Single 75€, double 100€, triple 120€. Breakfast included. 10% discount with cash payment.*

→ **Hotel Sorrento City** ★★ One of several hotels on busy Corso Italia, this is one of the few here that won't break the bank. Rooms are tiny but pretty, with tiled floors, silky bedspreads, and lush curtains. Some also have balconies large enough to sit on. Rooms also have TV, phone, and A/C. *Corso Italia 221 (near Via degli Aranci).* ☎ *081/8772210. www.italyby. com/hotelcity/index.html. Double 115€, triple 140€, quad 165€. Breakfast included.*

SPLURGE

→ **Hotel Bristol** ★★★ This is luxury! Nestled into a cliffside with unbelievable views of the bay and city below, this hotel offers up anything and everything you could ever need: two restaurants (one offering rooftop dining), a bar, pool, garden, gym, sauna, disco, and several lounges with comfy couches for relaxing and enjoying the views. For ultimate luxury, splurge on the junior suite: Huge rooms come with terrace and outdoor Jacuzzi. All rooms have A/C, TV, minibar, and phone, and most have a sea view. *Via Capo 10.* ☎ *081/8784522. www.acampora.it. Single 80€–180€, double 130€–280€, junior suite 220€–380€. Breakfast included.*

→ **La Tonnarella** ★★ One of several gorgeous hotels perched high up on Via Capo, this one is perhaps the closest to "doable."

Rooms are gorgeous, decorated in Mediterranean style, most with balconies overlooking the bay. Pictures of old Sorrento hang in the hallways. For utter opulence, and an amazing deal, suites are fitted with Jacuzzi, computer with Internet, flat-screen TV, terrace with outdoor bed, and incredible views. The hotel also has a small private beach, reached by elevator. *Via Capo 31.* ☎ *081/8781153. www. latonnarella.it. Double 130€–165€, suite 220€–270€. Breakfast included. Ask about discounts if you're staying for more than 2 nights.*

Eating

Sorrento has no shortage of restaurants, but being a touristy town, most are geared toward this crowd—which explains the plethora of establishments designed to imitate the British pub. Sorrento's Italian restaurants offer up the usual fare of pasta, pizza, and panini. For the best authentic seafood and great views, head to Marina Grande.

CHEAP

→ **Blu Water Rosticceria** ★ CAFE   One of the most affordable places for a light lunch or snack in the old town, with a large terrace area perfect for watching the crowds stroll by. This place also serves what could quite possibly be the largest mug of beer you will ever encounter. *Via Giuliani 35/37 (off of Corso Italia). Panini 4.50€; pizza slices from 3€. Monster beers 8€. Daily 11am–1am.*

DOABLE

→ **Ristorante e Pizzeria Giardiniello** ★★ ITALIAN   This charming little trattoria in the old town, in a gardenlike setting on a small alleyway, serves up seafood and traditional Sorrentine fare such as *gnocchi alla Sorrentina*, with mozzarella, tomato sauce, basil, and parmesan (5€). *Via Accademia 7 (near Via Giuliani).* ☎ *081/8784616. Primi 4.50€–7€; secondi 5.50€–13€; pizza 3.50€–6€. Daily 11am–2am.*

→ **Taverna dell'800** ★ PUB   An old-school British pub in old-school Sorrento, but probably one of the only places in Italy where you'll be able to satisfy a craving for fish and chips. They also serve up a mean burger here. The pub is a busy place in the evenings, particularly with British tourists. *Via Accademia 29 (at Via Tasso).* ☎ *081/8785970. Snacks (burgers, fries, etc) from 3€; fish entrees 6€–14€; meat entrees 6€–15€; pizza 4€–6€. Daily noon–3pm and 6pm–2am.*

→ **Bagni Sanna Restaurant and Snack Bar** ★★ SEAFOOD   The best of the restaurants that line Marina Grande's shore. Walk down the wooden pier to the casual, airy restaurant where diners graze on fresh seafood dishes and then retire to the end of the pier, where sun beds and a swimming area are provided for customers. What more could you ask for? As this is probably the best place in the city to swim, it's worth the price of a snack to be able to use the bathing facilities. *Marina Grande. Primi 6€–9€; secondi 6€–10€. Daily 11:30am–midnight.*

SPLURGE

→ **Fauno** ★ BISTRO CAFE   Sorrento doesn't get more touristy than this massive restaurant dominating an entire side of Piazza Tasso, but tourists flock here for good reason: From the huge terrace you can safely and comfortably watch the chaotic traffic and crowds flow through the piazza. *Piazza Tasso.* ☎ *081/8781021. Primi 10€–12€; secondi 12€–14€; pizza 8€–12€; sandwiches 7€–10€. Daily 7am–11pm.*

Partying

Sorrento's nightlife centers around Piazza Tasso and Corso Italia, where crowds come to stroll and people-watch in the evenings. For those looking to nurse a pint while watching sports, Sorrento offers several British pubs where you can do so, although you'll find nary an Italian in sight. Both locals and tourists of various ages fill the clubs in the city, partying until the early hours of the morning.

You'll spend 3 or 4€ for a glass of wine in the more laid-back places, 4 or 5€ for a beer, and 4 or 5€ for a cocktail; prices go up the trendier the spot.

➔ **Chaplin's Pub/The English Inn** ★ Sorrento's obsession with the English pub is evident at these two spots across the street from each other. Both are about as British as they come, with a brass bar spanning the length of the pub, Guinness flowing on tap, and crowds absorbed in the calcio (translation: "soccer") match. Chaplin's attracts an older crowd of football fans, while those at the larger English Inn seem to prefer conversation and a bit of dancing. *Chaplin's Pub: Corso Italia (18).* ☎ *081/8072551. The English Inn: Corso Italia 56.* ☎ *081/8074357. Both daily 11am–late.*

➔ **Fauno Bar** Sprawling across an entire side of Piazza Tasso, tourists flock here for the atmosphere and views. Even if you're not up for the pricey dinner served here (see listing above), Fauno is worthy of a stop for a drink on its massive terrace. Fauno also turns up the beats on the dance floor, and it's a riot watching aging yuppies attempt to get their groove on. Skip the touristy musical show offered in the adjacent theater in the evening. *Piazza Tasso.* ☎ *081/8781021. www.faunonotte.it. Bar and club open 7pm–2am.*

➔ **Matilda Club** ★★ A gigantic place down the stairs behind Piazza Tasso (look for the signs), with six floors offering anything and everything you could want in a club: a restaurant, pub, Internet cafe, disco, and comfy room for chilling out. Karaoke takes place 9pm to midnight, after which the music begins to pound and crowds pack the dance floor of the disco. *Piazza Tasso.* ☎ *081/8773236. Daily 7pm–3am.*

Sightseeing

Sorrento is a yuppie tourist's paradise, with swanky shopping boulevards and a charming and easily accessible old town, as well as a slew of fancy hotels with immaculate views of the bay.

HANGING OUT

The center of the action in Sorrento is **Piazza Tasso,** a busy square jam-packed with restaurants, traffic, and tourists. **Corso Italia,** the main street, runs through the piazza, and is full of swanky shops and pedestrian shoppers, making it a nice place for a stroll. From here, continue on to **Via Capo,** home to the fancy hotels and great views of the bay and its coastline. To escape the chaos, wander through Sorrento's old town.

Unfortunately, Sorrento is seriously lacking in beaches—the few that are here are privately owned by the upscale hotels. Your best bet for swimming is off a pier at Marina Grande (see below). Just don't go skinny-dipping; we did this one late night, several years back, and the locals called the Carabinieri on us. Not our proudest moment as American students, to be sure.

THE OLD TOWN

Running in between Corso Italia and the waterfront, Sorrento's **old town** ★ is a maze

The Best View in Town

Step onto the terrace of Piazza della Vittoria. From here, you get an unobstructed **view** ★★★ of the city of Sorrento to your left, the gorgeous bay extending out in front of you, and on a clear day Naples and Vesuvius in the distance. If you can get yourself out of bed early enough, the sunrise from here is spectacular.

of cobblestone streets that provide a welcome relief from the overwhelming traffic of Corso Italia, but not from the hordes of tourist groups that run rampant in the city. The most happening streets of the old town are Via Sant'Antonino and Via Giuliani, filled with restaurants and souvenir shops. In between, you'll find quieter alleyways with historic buildings, shops catering to locals, and a few restaurants. For a bit of culture, step in the ornate Church of Sant'Antonino, a 17th-century building dedicated to the patron saint of Sorrento; it's on Piazza Sant'Antonino and does not charge admission.

MARINA GRANDE ★★

A short but pleasant walk from the center of town, this small fishing village is a quiet oasis in Sorrento and much less touristy than the old town. Fishing boats line the beach, and nets hang to dry along the harbor. This is one of the only places around here where you can actually lay on a beach chair and take a dip in the sea, although you'll have to do so from the pier, as there is no actual beach. This is the best place in town to come for a seafood meal; several restaurants line the waterfront. To get here, follow Via Marina Grande from Piazza della Vittoria and then head down the steps to enter the village. Alternately, you can take the Line D bus from Piazza Tasso.

Getting Around the Amalfi Coast & Islands by Water

Unlike anywhere else in Italy (except Venice!), this is the part of the country where taking a ferry or hydrofoil is sometimes the most efficient (or only) way to get where you're going. Before we head into the rest of the chapter, which covers the Amalfi Coast and the islands of Ischia and Capri, we've taken the time to break down your transportation options between these destinations.

Between hydrofoils (*aliscafi*), high-speed ferries (*navi veloci*), and slow ferries (*traghetti*), there are dozens of daily crossings between mainland Italy (the ports of Naples and Sorrento) and Capri and Ischia, as well and up and down the Amalfi Coast.

Advance booking isn't necessary, which makes a last-minute decision to visit the islands easy from a transportation standpoint. Capri is closer to Sorrento (14km/8²⁄₃ miles), but Naples (30km/19 miles from Capri) is often a better jumping-off point since it's easier to reach from other parts of Italy. Ischia is a bit closer to Naples (34 km/21 miles), but it makes sense to sail to Ischia from Sorrento (96km/59 miles away) if you're already based in the south. A few boats connect the islands of Capri and Ischia.

The Major Ferry Operators

Call or visit the websites for up-to-date timetables, fares, and general information.

- ○ **Alilauro:** ☎ 081/991888, www.alilauro.it
- ○ **Caremar:** ☎ 199-123-199 (toll-free), www.caremar.it
- ○ **Medmar:** ☎ 081/333-4111, www.medmar group.it
- ○ **NLG (Navigazione Libera del Golfo):** ☎ 081/552-0763, www.navlib.it
- ○ **SNAV:** ☎ 081/428-5555, www.snav.it

Italian Hydrofoils & Ferries 101

Unless you can score an invite to one of the private megayachts that ply the waters of the Mediterranean, island hopping in Italy is done via two kinds of vessels: hydrofoils and traditional ferries. Hydrofoils are smaller, sleeker, more expensive, and often twice as fast as ferries, but they're less romantic, since you're confined to the boat's cabin, where train-style upholstered seats usually smell like a wet bathing suit, and windows fog up or are sprayed on as you jet across the sea, so you can't even really watch the scenery go by. (Don't be fooled—hydrofoils are not hovercraft; since you're cooped up in the cabin the whole time, you don't really get a sense of how fast you're going, or the fact that you're skimming over the water, so it's hardly a thrill ride.) Which is not to say that the ferry—the alternative to hydrofoils—is the *Queen Mary 2,* but at least you can walk out on the deck, get high on the fumes from the diesel engines, rock out to your iPod, feel the Mediterranean sea spray on your face, and watch the landscape come into focus as you near the port. So, if you're not in too much of a rush, we recommend the ferry. In bad weather or rough seas, hydrofoils cannot sail, so your only option in foul weather is the ferry. Both hydrofoils and ferries are equipped with some kind of snack bar, serving some basic premade sandwiches, packaged ice cream, and *caffè.*

FROM NAPLES TO CAPRI & ISCHIA

Naples has two ports, Mergellina and Molo Beverello, where passenger boats depart for Capri and Ischia. If you're going to Capri and coming from somewhere north of Naples, we recommend taking a Naples-bound Intercity (IC) train that stops at **Napoli-Mergellina** station; from there, it's an easy, 10-minute walk (through glorious Neapolitan art-nouveau architecture) to **Mergellina,** a small, hassle-free marina, where faster hydrofoils depart for Capri and Ischia four or five times per day. SNAV's service to Capri is 13€ each way per passenger; crossing time is 45 minutes. Alilauro's service to Ischia is 12.50€; crossing time is 45 min.

It's not nearly as civilized as Mergellina, but many more Capri- and Ischia-bound boats depart from **Molo Beverello,** Naples' larger and busier commercial port. To get there, take any Naples-bound train to **Napoli Centrale-Stazione Garibaldi,** and then it's a 10-minute cab ride to Beverello—a cab should run you 10€ or so, so make sure

they're not ripping you off. You can also get from the station to the port by taking the tram or bus 1 from the station to **Piazza Municipio,** but keep in mind this is more time-consuming and a bit of a hassle if you have luggage.

From Beverello, you can catch hydrofoils (operated by SNAV, www.snav.it, and NLG Linea Jet, www.navlib.it) and ferries (operated by Caremar, www.caremar.it, and Medmar, www.medmargroup.it) galore for Capri and Ischia, as well as the tiny fishing island of Procida. For Capri, SNAV hydrofoils cost 13€ each way; NLG hydrofoils are slightly cheaper at 12€; crossing time for both is 45 minutes. SNAV's hydrofoils to Ischia (12€) stop in Procida along the way, taking a total of 45 minutes to reach Ischia Porto. Caremar's "fast ferries" to Capri are 10.50€ per person, with a crossing time of 50 minutes; Caremar's regular ferries take a leisurely 1 hour, 25 minutes to reach Capri, but they're a bargain at 5.60€ per person, plus you chill out on the outside decks and wave to passing fishing boats. For Ischia, Caremar's fast ferry takes 45 minutes and costs 12€, while the regular ferries take 1 hour, 15 minutes and cost 6€. Medmar's ferry costs 8.50€ and takes 50 minutes.

Tip: When traveling from Beverello, always allow extra time before your boat's scheduled departure. With cruise liners, tankers, and fishing boats all docking here, it can be a bit chaotic trying to find the Capri-bound vessels.

FROM SORRENTO TO CAPRI & ISCHIA

Sorrento makes a good base for day-tripping around the Bay of Naples region (to Pompeii, Mt. Vesuvius, the Amalfi Coast, etc.). The Big Kahuna at Sorrento's **Marina Piccola** is Alilauro (also known as Consorzio LMP; www.alilauro.it), operating 20 daily hydrofoils to Capri (11.50€ per person; 15-min. crossing time) as well as five daily ferries

(8.50€; 20-min. crossing time) to Capri. **Caremar** (www.caremar.it) has a smaller presence in Sorrento, with only four ferries to Capri (5.80€; 20-min. crossing time). Alilauro also runs hydrofoils from Sorrento to Ischia (15.50€; 45-min. crossing time).

Tip: Sorrento's Marina Piccola is at the base of Sorrento's dramatic cliffs, a precipitous drop below the center of town. It's a good 10-minute bus or cab ride (and 30-minute, steep walk—unrealistic if you have luggage) from the town's Circumvesuviana (local train) station to the harbor, so be sure to allow extra time.

BETWEEN CAPRI & ISCHIA

If you're island hopping, **Alilauro** (www.alilauro.it) has one hydrofoil per day from Ischia to Capri, and vice versa (12.20€; 50-min. crossing time).

FROM THE AMALFI COAST TO CAPRI

Alilauro (www.alilauro.it) operates five hydrofoils (14€; 30-min. crossing time) and three ferries (11.50€; 45-min. crossing time) per day from Amalfi, and three hydrofoils (15.50€; 25-min. crossing time) and two ferries (12.50€; 40-min. crossing time) per day from Positano. *Note:* Boats from the Amalfi Coast, unlike those from other ports, must be booked at least 24 hours in advance.

For more specific information about getting around the Amalfi Coast via ferry, see the next section.

The Amalfi Coast

56km (35 miles) SE of Naples, 16km (10 miles) E of Sorrento, 266km (165 miles) SE of Rome

The Best of the Amalfi Coast

Best Splurge Accommodation

It started out as a 13th-century convent—supposedly founded by St. Francis Assisi himself—but today, guests at the **Luna Hotel** in Amalfi (p. 637) come to be pampered, not to meditate in pious solitude. Mediterranean-style rooms have great views of the coast, and hotel amenities include restaurants, a bar, solarium, and private beach. It's no wonder that celebrities often call this place home when they're in town.

Best Eats

You'll feel like a million bucks dining at **Osteria da Luisella Enoteca** in Atrani (p. 637), but it won't even come close to costing you that much! Friendly staff serve up succulent dishes made from locally produced ingredients. Dine on local seafood specialties (everything here is delicious!) on the terrace while watching the action in Atrani's central piazza.

Best Town

It might not be right on the water, but **Ravello,** perched like an eagle above the rest of the coastal towns, gets our vote for all-around fabulousness. Once you see the view over the sea from the terraces at Villa Cimbrone, we think you'll agree. See p. 639.

Positano

Founded by Pestan refugees who fled the plains of Poseidonia in the face of invading Saracens in the 10th century, Positano ★★ has since gone through several metamorphoses, from a quiet fishing village in the 1950s to the haunt of Western bohemians—Steinbeck and Kerouac sought solitude here. Today, it's the trendiest town on the Amalfi Coast, stocked full of boutiques and fancy hotels. It's easy to see why so many have been drawn to the town: It sits perched, seemingly precariously, on the cliffs, with roads and buildings climbing higher and higher from the waterfront, and has several decent beach and hiking options. Positano is a nice place to explore for the day, and also makes a good base for exploring the rest of the Amalfi Coast.

The Amalfi Coast

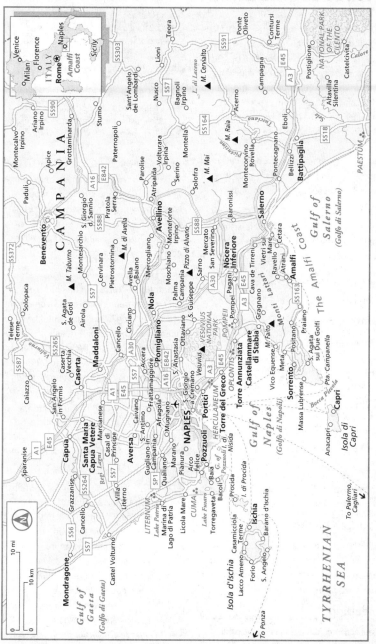

Getting There

BY BUS

SITA buses running between Sorrento and Amalfi stop in Positano (1.30€). There are two stops at the top of the town: one by Chiesa Nuova, and one at the top of Via dei Mulini. The drive between Positano and Amalfi takes much longer than expected, as the extremely talented bus drivers are required to maneuver the huge buses through tiny streets and around honking cars and scooters, just missing vehicles and pedestrians, and almost falling off the edge of the cliff—it's best not to look. Buses are often crowded.

BY FERRY

It's by far the more scenic, and less stressful option than the bus, and worth the extra cost. In the summer, there is regular ferry service between Positano and Amalfi (from 6€), Capri (from 12€), Sorrento (from 6€), and Naples (from 9€).

Getting Around

Positano's orange internal **buses** connect the top of the town to the waterfront down below (1€). Walking down into town is enjoyable but walking back up can be painful, as there is little flat ground in Positano; since the town is built on the cliff face, everything is either up or down. If you are staying in Positano and carrying a heavy load, you may want to plan your transportation needs based on the location of your accommodation, as carrying a heavy pack up from the harbor to the hostel, for example, is a nightmare!

Tourist Offices

The main **tourist office** is on Via del Saraceno 4 (☎ 089/875067; www.positanonline.it). There are also tourist information kiosks set up around town.

Sleeping

Most accommodations in Positano come with prices as steep as the topography. The very few exceptions are listed here, so be sure to

Official Website

The official website of Positano is **www.positanonline.it,** which boasts that it provides information on "all that is useful to know in occasion of your visit to Positano" such as listings for hotels and restaurants, and transportation schedules. The design of the site could use a serious update, however.

call ahead if you're traveling in high season. When you have some more money, come back to Positano and stay at the superluxurious honeymooner hotels **San Pietro** (www.ilsanpietro.it) or **Le Sirenuse** (www.sirenuse.it), where doubles start at well over 200€ in the off season.

HOSTEL

➜ **Ostello Brikette** ★ A bit of a hike (literally) from the center of Positano, convenient if you're arriving by bus but painful if you're coming from the harbor. Friendly staff offer clean dorm rooms and basic private rooms, some with a terrace overlooking the town and sea. The hostel also has a few apartments for rent in town (inquire here if interested, from 110€). *Via Marconi 358.* ☎ *089/875857. www.brikette.com. Dorm 22€, double 75€. Get off the bus at Bar Internazionale then walk back up the hill about 150m (492 ft.). Open late Mar–Nov.*

CHEAP

➜ **Pensione Maria Luisa** ★★ Located in a quiet area near Fornillo beach, this small place has a gorgeous terrace and garden with great views of the sea. Rooms are small and a bit gloomy, though some have huge terraces with breathtaking views—definitely worth the extra few euros. *Via Fornillo 42.* ☎ *089/875023. www.pensionemarialuisa.com. Double without terrace 65€–70€, with terrace 70€–80€. Get off the SITA bus at the Chiesa Nuova stop, take the local bus Grotta Fornillo, and walk 2 min. up the small street to the right.*

DOABLE

➜**Hotel Pupetto** ★ Nicely located just up the stairs from Fornillo beach, rooms are large and airy, though lacking in character. Guests have access to the hotel's stretch of beach out front. Rooms have phone, TV, A/C, and balcony with views of the sea. *Via Fornillo 37.* ☎ *089/875087. www.hotelpupetto.it. Single 80€–90€, double 130€–160€. Breakfast included.*

Eating

CHEAP

➜**La Zagara** ★★ CAFE Don't just stand at the window and drool over the delectable goodies, go in and try one; after climbing through Positano, you deserve it. The cafe also has panini and pizza for a light meal or snack, and live piano music in the evenings. Posted prices are for taking your food and drink standing up; if you decide to sit on the patio in back, you'll pay a bit more. *Via dei Mulini10/12.* ☎ *089/875964. Pastries from .80€, mini pizzas 2€, panini 3.50€. Daily 8am–midnight.*

DOABLE

➜**La Marinella** ★★ ITALIAN/SEAFOOD A casual beachside eatery that sits at the head of Spaggia dei Fornillo, perched above the sands and offering scenic views to enhance your dining experience, especially at sunset. Friendly staff serve up heaping portions of fresh seafood. *Via Positanesi d'America. Primi 7€–11€; secondi 6€–12€. Daily 11am– midnight.*

SPLURGE

➜**O'Guarracino** ★ SEAFOOD If you're looking to wine and dine a certain special someone, impress him or her by bringing them to this spot on the pathway between Positano's two beaches. Guarracino is a quiet, cozy restaurant with gorgeous views of the sea and delicious eats; try the house specialty, the *zuppa Guarracino,* a tomato soup stuffed full of seafood (18€). *Via Positanesi*

d'America, ☎ *081/982527 Primi 8€–16€; secondi 9€–23€; pizza 7.50€–13€. Daily 11am–3pm and 7–11pm.*

Partying

If you opt to spend the night, the town has one of the liveliest partying scenes along the coast. After dinner, most people stroll along Via dei Mulini and nearby streets, or enjoy a glass of wine on a terrace. Later on, there are two good places to party.

➜**Conwinum** ★★ In a converted cave where artists used to gather to exchange art and ideas, this is an Internet cafe and art gallery by day, wine bar and disco by night. Of the night spots in Positano, this is the casual option, popular with both locals and backpackers. Football (soccer) games are shown in season, and there is also live music most weekends (check for posters around town), and a disco on Saturday nights. *Via Rampa Teglia 12 (look for signs off of Via dei Mulini).* ☎ *089/812076. www.positano. conwinum.it. No cover. Drinks 6€–8€. Daily 8:30am–2am.*

➜**Music on the Rocks** ★ A swanky piano bar and disco popular with an older crowd who may look down their noses at you if you show up in jeans and a T-shirt. Crystal blue lighting lights up the huge dance floor, where groovers shake their booty to the DJ's tunes, surrounded by white pillars and arches with views of the beach outside. *Spaggia Grande Via Grotto del Incanto 51.* ☎ *089/875874. www.musicontherocks.it. Cover 10€–25€. Drinks 8 €–10€. Closed Oct–Easter.*

Sightseeing

HANGING OUT

Most people come to Positano to stroll through its winding streets. **Via dei Mulini** is the main street, and is packed with small— though expensive—boutiques, as well as art galleries featuring artwork you wish you could carry home, and stores selling jewelry, pottery, and the ever-present *limoncello,* a strong local lemon liqueur. For affordable shopping, head for the covered area of the street up from the Church of Santa Maria Assunta. For spectacular views, walk along Via Cristoforo Colombo, off of Via dei Mulini, or along Via Positanesi d'America, to the left of the harbor.

Playing Outside
BEACHES

There are two main beaches in Positano. Spaggia Grande is right next to the ferry port, and is a pretty sandy beach that gets quite crowded during peak times. Rent a chair or head for the small free section at the end. Spaggia del Fornillo is much quieter but is all privately owned, so you'll have to pay for a chair for the privilege of sunning here. Reach the beach by heading left and up the stairs from the ferry port. Along the way, there is a small sandy cove where you can lie out for free.

Amalfi: A Tiny Gem

61km (38 miles) SE of Naples, 18km (11 miles) E of Positano, 272km (169 miles) SE of Rome

Amalfi ★★ is great for several reasons: It's small enough that you can see everything and still have time for the beach; it's unpretentious and affordable; it has managed to retain its charm despite being a tourist magnet; and it's just so darn picturesque. Arriving in town by ferry, guests are greeted by views of the beach and the Duomo rising in the heart of the city. Amalfi also makes a good base for exploring other, more expensive, towns along the Amalfi Coast.

Getting There
BY FERRY

This is definitely the most stylish, although not always practical, way to arrive. Ferries run from Sorrento (from 7€), Positano (from 6€), and Naples (10€). Buy tickets from the booths along the pier.

Official Website

The official website of the Amalfi tourist office is **www.amalfitourist office.it,** providing information on hotels, restaurants, and sites in the regions as well as a searchable events calendar and general information on such topics as the town's history and a culinary survey.

BY BUS

SITA runs buses between Sorrento and Amalfi (about 2 hr., 2.40€), stopping in Positano along the way. The bus can be a bit of a nightmare as the road between Positano and Amalfi is windy and narrow, and so getting between the two towns takes forever and is a test of anyone's nerves. Buses arrive in Piazza Flavio Gioia, in front of the harbor. To get here from Naples, take the Circumvesuviana train to Sorrento (no rail passes), and then catch the SITA bus from there. Buy bus tickets at the *tabacchi* across the street from the piazza.

Getting Around

From Piazza Flavio Gioia, head straight up away from the water and through the archway, which will take you into Piazza Duomo. Via Lorenzo d'Amalfi runs straight up from there.

Tourist Offices

Amalfi's **AAST Tourist Office** is at Corso delle Repubbliche Marinara 27 (☎ **089/ 871107**). It's open Monday through Saturday 8:30am to 1:30pm and 3 to 5pm, although sometimes they decide to close early for apparently no reason.

Sleeping

CHEAP

➜ **A' Scalinatella** ★★ While Amalfi itself is lacking in dorm beds, nearby Atrani is home to this popular hostel. Dorm beds are provided in clean, bright rooms, and private rooms are available in several other buildings around town. The hostel has a kitchen, Internet access, and laundry, and organizes day trips for its guests. *Piazza Umberto I 6.* ☎ *089/871492. www.hostelscalinatella.com. Dorm 18€–21€; double 45€–60€ with shared bath, 50€–83€ with private bath. See directions below for getting to Atrani; once there, walk through the arch behind the beach and look for signs just beyond the piazza.*

DOABLE

➜ **Hotel Lidomare** ★ In a quiet small piazza just up from Piazza Duomo and run by friendly staff, this hotel is worthy of your euros only if you can wrangle one of the rooms with a terrace overlooking the sea; these are large, bright, and have Jacuzzi shower or tub. Cheaper rooms are a bit worn down and mildewy. *Via Piccolomini 9 (look for signs in top left corner of Piazza Duomo and walk up the stairs).* ☎ *089/871332. www.lidomare.it. Single 50€–55€, double 99€–120€. Breakfast included. In room: A/C, TV, minibar.*

➜ **Hotel La Ninfa** ★★ Offering everything you could ever want from a hotel, La Ninfa has large, brightly decorated rooms with A/C, TV, and computer hookups. It's worth the extra splurge for a room with a view; in these, even the view from the bathroom window is stunning. Spend the afternoon at the hotel's private beach, and at the end of the day relax in the hotel's garden or curl up in front of the lobby fireplace. *Via Pantaleone Comite.* ☎ *089/9831127. www.hotellaninfa.it. Double 80€–130€, 110€–160€ with view.*

SPLURGE

MTV Best ➜ **Luna Hotel** ★★★ One of the best hotels in town is housed in a 13th-century convent supposedly founded by St. Francis of Assisi. The Luna has attracted numerous celebrities in the past, including Humphrey Bogart and Ingrid Bergman. Airy, cleanly elegant Mediterranean-style rooms have large bathrooms and great views. The hotel has two restaurants, bar, courtyard terrace (the old cloister), solarium, private beach, and pool overlooking the sea. It's actually surprising this place doesn't cost more than it does. *Via Pantaleone Comite 33 (on the road leading to Atrani).* ☎ *089/871333. www.lunahotel.it. Double (single use) 160€, double 180€–220€, suite 310€–540€.*

Eating

DOABLE

➜ **Il Tari** ★★ ITALIAN/SEAFOOD There's no terrace here, but plenty of large windows for watching the evening crowd stroll by. The seafood pizza here is especially tasty (8.50€). *Via P. Capuano 9.* ☎ *089/871832. Primi 6.50€–13€; secondi 6€–20€; pizza 4€–8.50€. 1.50€ cover charge. Wed–Mon 11:30am–3pm and 7–10:30pm.*

➜ **Silverman** ★ SEAFOOD One of several restaurants that line Amalfi's beach, this one is the best value, has the most appetizing menu, and makes for a pretty romantic spot if you're looking to impress someone. *Primi 7€–12€; fish entrees 9€–20€; meat entrees 8€–10€; pizza 4.50€–7.50€.*

SPLURGE

MTV Best ➜ **Osteria da Luisella Enoteca** ★★ AMALFITAN/SEAFOOD Here you'll find upscale dining at affordable prices, with friendly, professional staff. The vegetables, fish, cheese, and olive oil are all locally produced. Try the mouth-watering house specialties: braised tuna with soy sauce (12€) and sea bass with green pepper (14€). *Piazza Umberto (Atrani).* ☎ *089/871087. www.osteria daluisella.it. Primi 8€–12€; secondi 10€–18€. Cover charge 2€. Thurs–Tues noon–3pm and 7–11pm.*

Hiding from the Crowds in Atrani

If you love Amalfi but can't deal with the hordes of others around who share your sentiments, **Atrani** ★ may provide an ideal respite. Follow Amalfi's waterfront street, with the water on your right, around the bend and either through the tunnel where you'll risk colliding with oncoming traffic, or through the restaurant next to the tunnel (the owners don't mind). Here, you'll find a welcoming stretch of sandy beach where you can either rent a chair or lie on the sand for free, and a cute piazza with several restaurants and even a couple of happening bars. Atrani is also home to a youth hostel, something lacking in Amalfi. But best of all, a visit here will allow you to escape the ferry loads of tourists and get a real feel for the Amalfi Coast.

Partying

Amalfi doesn't have a whole lot going on in the evenings. Most people stroll along Via Lorenzo d'Amalfi or hang out in Piazza Duomo. For a more lively scene, head over to Atrani, where a backpacker crowd fills the bars in Piazza Umberto. Try **Bar Directo** ★, Piazza Umberto I 1 (☎ **089/874231**), with a huge terrace occupying a large section of the piazza, or **La Risacca** ★, Piazza Umberto I 2 (☎ **089/871087**), its more lively neighbor.

Exploring Amalfi

HANGING OUT

Amalfi is very small and easily explored in a few hours, leaving the rest of the day for lounging on the beach. Cafe-lined Piazza Duomo is the center of the action, with tourists milling about the stairs of the Duomo and the fountain in the center. From here, Via Lorenzo d'Amalfi is the main street in town, filled with restaurants and souvenir shops. Narrow alleyways leading off of this street allow you to explore a quieter side of Amalfi, and often lead up to piazzettas with stunning views over the town and sea.

FREE ➜ **The Duomo** ★ Dedicated to St. Andrew the Apostle, this 10th-century Duomo dominates Amalfi from its position high above the center of town. Beautiful mosaics adorn the façade, and its bronze doors were crafted in Constantinople and then donated to the church in the 11th century by an Amalfitan noble. Next door, the 13th-century Cloister of Paradise houses ancient sarcophagi, including that of St. Andrew himself (minus his face, which was donated to a cathedral in Greece), sculptures, and ornate mosaics. *Piazza del Duomo.* ☎ *089/871059. Daily 9am–9pm (closes earlier in winter).*

➜ **Museo della Carta (Paper Mill Museum)** Once upon a time, it is said, Amalfi introduced paper to the rest of Italy, and was a paper production mecca; today, the ruins of numerous paper mills above the town testify to this. The museum, appropriately housed in an old paper mill, outlines the history of paper production and displays antique presses and old manuscripts. *Via delle Cartiere 23.* ☎ *089/8304561. www.museodellacarta.it. Admission 3.40€. Daily 10am–6:30pm.*

Playing Outside

HIKING

Hiking opportunities around Amalfi abound. Take the **Path of the Gods** ★★ to Positano (4 hr.), trek between Atrani and Ravello (2 hr.), or head inland to Pogerola. Get detailed instructions and maps from the tourist office.

BEACHES

Amalfi's main beach is of a decent size, but it is pebbly and dominated by rental chairs. There's a small free section at the end. It's

Heading Inland to Ravello

Who says you have to be on the water to be the most impressive town on the Amalfi Coast? Set back from the sea, 6km (3¾ miles) from Amalfi and over 335m high (110 ft.) in the hills, ☝ Best Ravello ★★★ is the bald eagle, the peregrine falcon, the white-winged dove of the Amalfi Coast. It's favored by an older, quieter set (as well as some famous writers, like Gore Vidal, who've purchased villas here), but it's so spectacular that everyone who visits the Amalfi Coast should come here for a half-day side trip. To get to Ravello, take a bus from Amalfi's Piazza Flavio Gioia; buses run about every hour, and fare is 1.20€ one-way—a small price to pay when you see what it takes to get a multiple-axle vehicle up the hair-pinned road to Ravello!

In town, the first major attraction you'll see from the bus stop is the **Villa Rufolo** ★, Piazza Duomo (☎ 089/857-657; daily 9am–6pm, until midnight Apr–Sept; admission 4€), with its Moorish-inspired architecture and terraced gardens offering sneak-peek views of the coastline below. A 10-minute hike from Villa Rufolo, up the narrow and stepped (but not particularly steep) Via Santa Chiara, is the **Villa Cimbrone** ★★, Via Santa Chiara 26 (☎ 089/857459; daily 9am–sunset; admission 3€)—absolutely not to be missed if you're going to make the trek up to Ravello. The villa's buildings, which the attendant will be keen to usher you toward, are fine and all, but the real star here is the **panoramic garden terrace** ★★★. From the white marble parapet, punctuated by evocatively "ruined" busts of Greek and Roman sculpture, the view over the coast, through the mist that so often hangs in the air here, is quite simply one of the most stunning vistas we've ever seen.

After you've worked up an appetite on the walk to and from Villa Cimbrone, retreat to **Cumpa' Cosimo** for lunch. Locals and celebs alike pack its tables for the best home cooking in town, including fried fish platters from the sea below, and vegetable and meat dishes in keeping with Ravello's more inland, hillside position. It's at Via Roma 44–46 (☎ **089/857156**) and is open daily for lunch and dinner.

NAPLES & CAMPANIA

worth the walk to Atrani for a quieter, nicer beach; to get there, walk along the street that follows the waterfront with the water on your right, around the bend and either through the tunnel and risk oncoming traffic, or cut through the restaurant next to the tunnel (they don't mind).

BOAT TRIPS TO THE EMERALD GROTTO

Five kilometers (3 miles) west of Amalfi is the millennia-old **Emerald Grotto (Grotta di Smeraldo)** ★★. This cavern, known for its light effects, is a chamber of stalactites and stalagmites, some underwater. You can visit daily 9am to 4pm, provided that the seas are calm enough not to bash boats to pieces as they try to land. The SITA bus (traveling toward Amalfi) departs from Piazza Flavio Gioia in Positano at 1-hour intervals throughout the day. En route to Sorrento, it stops at the Emerald Grotto. From the coastal road, you descend via an elevator and then take a boat ride traversing this eerie world for 5€. However, the best way to go is by boat all the way from Amalfi's docks; it costs 10€ round-trip.

Ischia: Life's a Beach

34km (21 miles) W of Naples

A short hop on the hydrofoil from Naples, Ischia (*Ees*-kee-ya) ★★★ has become the new *it* vacation destination for continental Europe's yuppie crowd. Most common among the tourist crowd are middle-aged Germans, who come here to subject themselves to various age-defying treatments involving Ischia's thermal waters—and then bake themselves under the hot Mediterranean sun. But if you can manage to break away from busy Ischia Porto, the main town, to one of the other settlements on the island, you'll discover a more laid-back, and breathtakingly beautiful island with friendly people, great beaches (much better than Capri's), and enough hiking to satisfy any fitness buff's craving. Give Ischia Porto a try, and then escape the dirty looks of the Prada-clad moneybags for Forio, Sant'Angelo, and the other towns along the coast. While Ischia is forever compared with Capri, its more striking—and more cliché—sister to the south, Ischia stands on its own as a wonderful, low-key getaway.

The Best of Ischia

Best Beach

While Ischia Porto's beaches erode so quickly that it's hard to tell if they'll be around next season, those who dare to venture beyond the island's main city to **Chiaia beach in Forio** are rewarded with a gorgeous stretch of sand in front of the harbor, where locals in skimpy suits frolic in the water and fill up on snacks from beachside restaurants.

Best Place to Party and Relax at the Same Time

Run by the friendly staff at the Ring Hostel, the **Hot Springs Party** (p. 644) is a great deal: For 10€, they feed guests all the wine you can drink, and then shuttle everyone down to the Sorgeto hot springs where you can bathe in thermal hot pools or refreshing sea water under the stars.

Ischia Orientation

The island is known for its sandy beaches, health spas (which utilize hot springs for hydromassage and mud baths), and vineyards producing the red and white Monte Epomeo, the red and white Ischia, and the white Biancolella. The largest community is at **Ischia Porto** on the eastern coast, a circular town seated in the crater of the extinct Monte Epomeo, which functions as the island's main port of call. The most lively town is **Forio** on the western coast, with its many bars along tree-lined streets. The other major communities are **Lacco Ameno** and **Casamicciola Terme,** on the north shore, and **Serrara Fontana** and **Barano d'Ischia,** inland and to the south.

Getting Around

Ischia's bus company **SEPSA** (☎ 081/991808; www.sepsa.it) runs a convenient transport system between the island's towns. There are three main lines: **CS** runs clockwise

Ischia's Magical Waters?

According to local folklore, Ischia's thermal waters are the tears of Typhoeus, a rebel Titan who was imprisoned by Zeus in the depths of the island. Whether the purported healing properties of the waters are due to this mythological origin or simply to complicated volcanic and chemical processes, Ischitani swear by their magical water, and most visitors to the island come specifically for this. All over Ischia, there are little rabbit holes in the ground where poor, long-suffering Typhoeus belches out his hot air.

Ischia

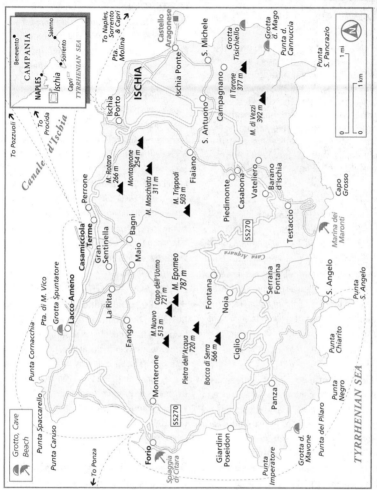

Around the island, **CD** runs counterclockwise, and the **no. 1** runs between Ischia Porto and Sant'Angelo. Purchase a 90-minute ticket (1.20€) or 24-hour ticket (4€) from ticket booths or *tabacchi,* and be sure to validate it once on board.

Ischia's towns are small enough to be easily navigated on foot, though overpriced taxis (with a minimum fare of 10€) offer transport within and between towns.

Sleeping

ISCHIA PORTO

Cheap

➜**Locanda Sul Mare** ★ Conveniently located near the port, rooms are small but clean, and funky art—such as mixed media works composed of old shoes—livens the place up. Some rooms have views of the bay. *Via Iasolino 94 (look for signs near port).* ☎ 081/981470. *Single 25€, double 50€.*

Tourist Office & Website

Ischia's tourist office, Industriali del turismo dell'isola d'Ischia, is in Ischia Porto at Via Alfredo De Luca 153 (☎ 081/3334820; daily 9am–1pm and 4–6pm. The official website is www.ischiaonline.it/tourism, providing a searchable accommodation database, interactive map, events listings, and general information about the island of Ischia.

Doable

→ **Hotel Villa Hermosa** Nobody here appears to speak English, but staff are nonetheless friendly and willing to patiently attempt communication. Rooms are simple but elegant. The hotel also has a decent restaurant, as well as a solarium and garden. *Via Osservatorio 4 (walk up main street from port and at the big intersection look for signs).* ☎ *081/992078. Single 50€, double 100€. Breakfast included.*

Splurge

→ **Hotel Il Moresco** ★★ A definite splurge, but we need to pamper ourselves once in awhile. This is where Hollywood starlets lay their heads when on Ischia—Jude Law, Gwyneth Paltrow, and Matt Damon all stayed here while filming *The Talented Mr. Ripley* on the island. The hotel has three pools heated by thermal waters, beauty and wellness centers, fitness room, private beach, piano bar, pool bar, and elegant restaurant. All rooms, done up in a Mediterranean-deco style, come with a terrace. It's a quiet garden setting. *Via Emanuele Gianturco 16.* ☎ *081/981355. www.ilmoresco.it. Single from 175€ in low season, 215€ in high season; double from 250€ in low season, 310€ in high season; suites from 440€ in low season, 480€ in high season. Includes half board. In room: A/C, TV, minibar, safe.*

FORIO

Hostel/Cheap

→ **Ring Hostel** ★★ One of three properties in Forio run by the friendly 20-something Colella brothers. In the evening, they will shuttle guests to their restaurant where you can eat Mamma's delicious home-cooking, and drink Papà's wine. Clean and bright dorm rooms each have their own kitchen and bathroom, and a new common room and rooftop terrace are in the works. Graffiti-covered walls testify to the good service here. *Via Gaetano Morgera 66.* ☎ *081/987546. www.ringhostel.com. Dorm bed 15€–25€, single 30€–45€, double 46€–60€, triple 66€–87€, quad 84€–92€. Walk up main street until road comes to a sharp curve by a shop called Bollicine, and take the small alleyway which winds back and forth through quiet residential areas; the hostel is in the second square, the green doors on the left right as you enter.*

→ **Ostello Il Gabbiano (HI)** As typical of Hostelling International properties, Il Gabbiano is a large building with sterile environment inconveniently located south of Forio. That being said, it is also by far the cheapest place to stay on the island, even if you factor in the bus fare, and provides great amenities such as a pool and garden. The beach is also close by. *S.S. Forio-Panza 162.* ☎ *081/909422. Dorm 13€. Breakfast included.*

Cheap

→ **Hotel Poggio Del Sole** ★★ Another of the Colella brothers' properties, offering basic rooms with TV, A/C, and clean bathroom, and many with balconies with great views of the harbor. Mamma Tina runs the restaurant downstairs (see listing, below), and the small swimming pool is open in the summer. When you arrive, give them a call and they'll come pick you up. *Via Baiola 193.* ☎ *081/987756. www.hotelpoggiodelsole.it. Single 32€–52€, double 64€–104€. Breakfast 3€.*

Eating

Dine on traditional Ischian cuisine such as seafood dishes and rabbit in Ischia Porto's restaurants—check out the side streets off of Corso Vittoria Colonna for less touristy restaurants. For the cheapest eats, hit the beach in Forio.

ISCHIA PORTO
Cheap

➜**Bar Diana** ★ ITALIAN/ISCHIAN   Yes, it is usually filled with German tourists, but this is also probably the most affordable place to eat on Ischia Porto's main street. The owner, a dead-ringer for Luigi of Super Mario Brothers fame, likes to explain each item on the menu to diners in order to help them choose. *Corso Vittoria Colonna 178/180.* ☎ *081/991024. Bruschetta 4.50€; pizza around 5€; also salads, daily specials, cocktails. Daily 7am–1am.*

Doable

➜**Sirena** ★★ SEAFOOD/ISCHIAN   A small trattoria on Corso Vittoria Colonna, popular with both locals and tourists who come to sample traditional Ischian cuisine in a cozy environment. If you have no qualms about eating a cute bunny, try the Ischian rabbit, raised traditionally in burrows underground. *Corso Vittoria Colonna 9.* ☎ *081/991190 Primi 4.50€–9.50€; secondi 6€–15€; pizza 3.10€– 6€. Daily 11am–3pm and 6–11pm.*

➜**Restaurant Mastu Peppe o Fraulese** ★ ITALIAN/SEAFOOD   Unlike other resort towns along the Italian coast, Ischia Porto has very few dining options along the harbor. This is probably the best, pleasantly situated in a quiet area off the main road, offering up tasty pasta and seafood dishes in a casual environment. *Via Iasolino 14.* ☎ *081/981912. Primi 4.50€–9€; secondi (mainly seafood dishes) 8€–17€. Open daily for lunch and dinner Apr–Oct; Tues–Sun for lunch and dinner Nov–Mar.*

FORIO
Doable

➜**La Ruota** ★★ SEAFOOD/ITALIAN   For the best food in town, head to one of the restaurants along Chiaia beach, and this one provides the best value of them all, with affordable but delicious seafood and pasta dishes served in a casual environment. Have a seat on the large terrace on the beach. *Via Spirito Santo, Chiaia Beach. Primi 5€–8€; secondi 5€–11€. Daily 11am–3pm and 7–10:30pm.*

➜**La Romantica** ★ SEAFOOD   Set in an atmospheric old building across the street from the harbor, this is a more upscale option in Forio (though not expensive), and true to its name. Soak up the romance and dine on delicious seafood; if you've had your fill of fish, the beef and veal entrees are sure to satisfy any carnivorous cravings. *Via Marina 46.* ☎ *081/997345. Primi 6.50€–14€; secondi 6.50€–13€. Daily noon–3pm and 7pm– midnight.*

➜**Poggio del Sole** ★★ ISCHIAN HOME COOKING   A family-run establishment (run by the Colella family that owns the prime accommodation venues in town), where Mamma Tina cooks up savory dishes such as rabbit with basil and tomatoes, and chicken cooked in a sand oven on the beach. The restaurant is dead at lunch, but lively in the evening when Papà's delicious homemade wine flows in abundance—an unlimited supply is included with the meal. It's an out-of-the-way location, but if you call the restaurant, they'll come pick you up. *Via Baiola 193.* ☎ *081/987756. Entrees 5€–25€. Daily menu, including pasta, entree, vegetables, and dessert, 15€. Daily noon–2am.*

Partying

Nightlife centers around Ischia Porto. Most people stroll down Corso Vittoria Colonna in the evening after dinner, window-shopping in the stores that stay open late due to the extra-long afternoon siesta. Both Ischia Porto and Forio have a few spots where both locals and tourists indulge in alcohol-imbibed pleasures, though on an off night (i.e., during the week and in the winter) these places are deserted. The cost of drinks is comparable to the mainland.

PORTO ISCHIA

→ **Friends Lounge** An Internet cafe by day, and bar and disco by night. This new spot is dead during the week—even the Internet terminals are deserted—but the place picks up late on the weekends, when young locals crowd around the bar amidst flashy lights. *Corso Vittoria Colonna 123.* ☎ *081/981589. Daily 9am–1pm and 4pm–3am.*

→ **New Valentino** ★ Ischia's most established, and most popular, disco. Open only on the weekends (there wouldn't be much of a point in opening during the week), this is definitely the place to be, if you can stand being surrounded by groping couples on the dance floor. For something a bit tamer, stop in at the Ecstasy piano bar next door. *Corso Vittoria Colonna 97.* ☎ *081/992653. Fri–Sun 11pm–5am.*

FORIO

→ **Atlantic** Forio's most happening night spot, although that isn't saying much. This usually quiet spot is a good place to stop in for a drink or two at night, but while it is also billed as a disco, the dance floor is usually deserted—although on random nights you can get lucky when the place suddenly becomes packed. Via Marina (look for signs past the harbor). *Daily 8pm–2am May–Sept.*

📺 Best → **Hot Springs Party** ★★ For something a little different that's both fun and relaxing, the Ring Hostel and its associated hotel often have hot springs party nights: For 10€ you get an hour of unlimited drinking at the hotel's restaurant and transport south to Sorgeto hot springs—utter heaven at night when the water is lit solely

by moonlight. The natural pools of steaming water buttress the sea, so you can easily cool off in the Mediterranean when things get too steamy in the hot water. For information, contact the Ring Hostel (☎ **081/987546;** www.ringhostel.com).

Sightseeing

EXPLORING ISCHIA PORTO

Most who visit here are German, wealthy, in search of immortality or at least the appearance of it. The harbor doesn't have much to it besides a few restaurants and travel agencies. Corso Vittoria Colonna is a nice place to stroll and window-shop trendy boutiques and vendors selling cheap knockoffs, and there is an abundance of street-side cafes from which you can watch the tourists stroll by. To reach Ischia Porto's beach, walk 1 block down any of the side streets off of Corso Vittoria Colonna.

→ **The Aragonese Castle of Ischia** ★★ Perched upon an island linked to the mainland by a stone bridge, this ancient castle was initially constructed as a fort by the Greeks in the 5th century B.C., and then later overtaken by a string of other conquerors ranging from the Romans, to the Normans to the Arabs. In the 14th century, when Mt. Trippodi erupted, and soon after when pirate raids became a frequent affair, the locals sought refuge in the castle's walls, and eventually a town developed. When the king of Naples took control of the castle in the 19th century, he converted it into a prison. In 1912, the castle was auctioned off and is now privately owned, though the new owners graciously let visitors in for an inflated fee. The castle grounds are vast, and even though only a small section is open to the public, you can easily spend a couple of hours here. Be sure to visit the Casa del Sole, housing an excellent modern painting exhibition, and the Nun's Cemetery, where dead bodies used to be put on benches where their body fluids were drained as they decomposed, while

Ischia's Eroding Beaches

The main beach in Ischia Porto is disappearing at an alarming rate as its sands get washed away into the sea. This has been a problem around the entire island, causing concern for those in the travel industry who rely on these beaches to draw tourists. Along the southern edge of Ischia, the situation has been remedied by digging up sand from the floor of the sea and replacing it on the beach, essentially creating a new beach—although proponents insist that they are just returning the sand to its rightful place. There are plans to implement a similar program on Ischia Porto's beach, though whether tourists will settle for these man-made beaches, and whether this dredging of the sea will cause future eco-geological problems, remains to be seen.

fellow nuns watched as a meditation on the uselessness of the body. For something a little less morbid, walk along the Path of the Sun, which gives access to enchanting views of the sea, as do numerous terraces around the castle. *Ischia Ponte.* ☎ *081/991959. Admission 10€. Daily 9:30am until sunset. From Ischia Porto take bus 7 or walk down Corso Vittoria Colonna about 20 min. to the very end.*

EXPLORING FORIO

On the west coast of Ischia, Forio is a small town with a wonderfully laid-back vibe, lacking the pretentiousness of Ischia Porto. With that in mind, Forio is a great place to base your stay on Ischia, or spend a relaxing day in. Buses and ferries drop off passengers on the main street that runs along the waterfront. From here, walk up the street next to the Captain Morgan booth to reach the old town and its labyrinth of winding alleys. Forio is home to possibly the nicest stretch of public beach on the island: Chiaia Beach ★, next to the harbor, is a long stretch of clean sandy beach lined with casual restaurants.

EXPLORING THE REST OF ISCHIA

Ischia's other major towns—Casamicciola, Lacco Ameno, Serra Fontana, Sant'Angelo, and Barano—are all easily accessible by public transport, and good places to spend a few hours hanging out in, although most don't provide more attractions than a quaint atmosphere and nice views.

Taking a Bus Tour

A great way to see Ischia in a reasonable amount of time is to take advantage of the efficient public transport system: the CS and CD buses run around the circumference of the island about every 30 minutes and stop in all major towns. Buy a 24-hour ticket, and then hop off the bus whenever you see something appealing, and hop back on the next bus. Heading counterclockwise, the section of the island from Ischia Porto to Sant'Angelo is the most interesting, as the towns along this stretch are the most lively and the views from the bus are stunning. From Sant'Angelo, you can either take the CS bus back the way you came, or continue around the island, cutting inland through rugged terrain—a beautiful ride, though it'll take over an hour to reach Ischia Porto.

➔ **La Mortella** ★★ When British composer William Walton lived on Ischia, he designed a garden to provide solitude and inspiration while he worked. Today, the gorgeous garden, with over 800 varieties of plants, and numerous fountains and sculptures, is open to the public and makes for a relaxing retreat. For those with a keen interest in the garden's creator, the attached museum houses photographs of Walton and his friends. And on the weekends, Campania's best student musicians are invited to the garden, where they give afternoon concerts. *Via Francesco Calise 39 (in between Forio and Lacco Ameno; ask the* *bus driver for the stop).* ☎ *089/986220. www.lamortella.it. Admission 10€. Concert tickets 15€. Apr–Nov Tues, Thurs, Sat–Sun 9am–7pm.*

TAKING THE WATERS

You don't have to spend a fortune staying in one of the posh hotels on Ischia in order to enjoy the island's thermal spas. **Poseidon** ✭, located south of Forio (☎ **081/908711;** www.giardiniposeidon.it), is pampering heaven! Take a local bus or taxi there. Entry includes access to 22 thermal pools of varying temperatures, the sauna and garden, and to a large stretch of beach where you'll be provided with a complimentary chair and umbrella, and also includes a hydro massage. And if this isn't enough, various healing treatments using thermal waters (such as steam inhalation and ear cleansing) are also available. Full-day admission is 28€, half-day admission (after 1pm) 22€. Daily 9am to 7pm.

Capri: Jewel of the Mediterranean

5km (3 miles) off the tip of the Sorrentine peninsula

If your idea of an island getaway is that tropical cliché of palm trees and endless sandy beaches—the sort of scene depicted on Capri Sun foil juice packs—well, the first thing to know is that the real **Capri** ✭✭✭, Italy's jewel of the Mediterranean, is not that kind of island. Capri, like most of Italy's celebrated islands, is a drama queen with strong features, proud bearing, and classical training. Maybe you've seen it in pictures, but Capri's lush beauty—lemon trees, bougainvillea, and umbrella pines flourishing on hillsides, limestone cliffs plunging thousands of feet down to the sea—will absolutely floor you once you see it in person. In a country with no shortage of splendid sights and settings, Capri is still thrilling, even by Italian standards.

The name Capri has humble origins—it's the plural of *capra,* or goat—but it has long stood for old-world glamour and Mediterranean chic. While some who vacation here are stuffy and snobby (or just German and obnoxious, depending on the season), limiting their experience of the island to the Louis Vuitton boutique on Via Camerelle, Capri also has a ton of zero-attitude, egalitarian, really fun things to do for the young and the poor, from ducking into the legendary Blue Grotto, to climbing over ruins of ancient Roman villas, to taking in the island's ubiquitous spectacular vistas over cocktails at sunset.

Capri is beautiful year-round, but for some, it's just too damn crowded in the high season, when the heat and hordes of day-trippers make it harder to enjoy the island's many delights (but when Capri's nightlife is at its peak). Come in the mild shoulder-season months (late Apr, May, early June, late Sept, or Oct, when it's often warm enough still for swimming), and stay for a night or two, and you'll have a less expensive, more comfortable, and probably more enjoyable experience. Finally, do us all a favor and learn how to pronounce the name: It's *Cah-*pree, not Ca-*pree.*

The Best Of Capri

Most Overpriced Yet Totally Worthwhile Tourist Attraction

The Blue Grotto Sure, it's obvious and touristy, but for the cringe-inducing price of 17€ (or 20€, if you do the full island tour), you get an adventure that involves climbing in and out of bobbing boats, singing sailors, and, of course, the gorgeous natural spectacle of pilot-light-colored water inside the cave itself. Bottom line? If you come to Capri and skip the Blue Grotto, you'll be missing out on one of the most fun and memorable things you can do on a trip to Italy. See p. 656.

Best Place to People-Watch

Just around the corner from the funicular's upper station, the **Piazzetta (Piazza**

Capri

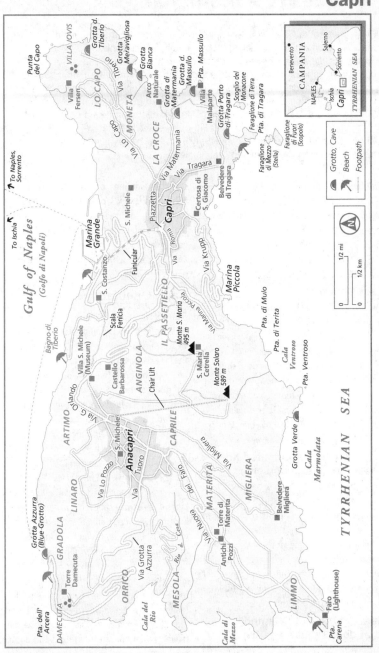

Gulf of Naples
(Golfo di Napoli)

To Naples, Sorrento

To Ischia

TYRRHENIAN SEA

CAMPANIA

Benevento
Salerno
Sorrento
NAPLES
Ischia
Capri
TYRRHENIAN SEA

Grotto, Cave
Beach
Footpath

1/2 mi
1/2 km

Punta del Capo
Villa Fersen
VILLA JOVIS
Grotta d. Tiberio
Grotta Meravigliosa
Grotta Bianca
Arco Naturale
Grotta di Matermania
Grotta d. Massullo
Pta. Massullo
Villa Malaparte
Scoglio del Monacone
Grotta Porto di Tragara
Faraglione di Terra
Pta. di Tragara
Faraglione di Mezzo (Stella)
Faraglione di Fuori (Scopolo)

LO CAPO
Via Tiberio
Via Lo Capo
Via Moneta
MONETA
LA CROCE
Via Matermania
Via Tragara
Belvedere di Tragara
Certosa di S. Giacomo
Via Giacomo
Piazzetta
S. Michele
Capri
Via Roma

Marina Grande
Funicular
S. Costanzo
Scala Fenicia
Bagno di Tiberio
Villa S. Michele (Museum)
Castello Barbarossa
IL PASSETIELLO
ANGINOLA
ARTIMO
Via G. Orlando
Via Marina Piccola
Monte S. Maria 495 m
S. Maria Cetrella
Monte Solaro 589 m
Chair Lift
Via Krupp
Marina Piccola
Pta. di Mulo
Pta. di Terita
Cala Ventroso
Pta. Ventroso

CAPRILE
LINARO
Via Lo Pozzo
S. Michele
Anacapri
Via Tuoro
Via Migliera
MATERITA
MIGLIERA
Belvedere Migliera
Grotta Verde
Cala Marmolata

GRADOLA
Grotta Azzurra (Blue Grotto)
Torre Damecuta
Pta. dell' Arcera
DAMECUTA
Via Grotta Azzurra
ORRICO
Cala del Rio
MESOLA
Rio d. Cesa
Via Nuova del Faro
Torre di Materita
Antichi Pozzi
Cala di Mezzo
LIMMO
Faro (Lighthouse)
Pta. Carena

TYRRHENIAN SEA

OKKIO! Beware Of Day-Trippers

Pretty and petite Capri is an eternally popular target for mass-tourism marauders on whirlwind package tours of Italy. These sunburned, sweaty, mostly middle-aged, sometimes drunk day-trippers besiege the narrow streets of Capri town in high season from about 11am until about 4pm, so if you're smart, you'll choose these hours of the day to hike up to Villa Jovis, visit the Blue Grotto (which is least crowded after 3pm), or go for a swim down at Marina Piccola. By late afternoon, it's safe to walk the streets around the Piazzetta again. By that time, the day-trippers—and their loot of gimmicky *limoncello* bottles and tacky, captain-style "Capri" hats—have all been corralled back on to their ferries to the mainland.

Umberto I) is tiny and not overtly glamorous, but it's a sieve, trapping all who stay on the island for at least one drink (and usually more) at some point during the day or night. If the Piazzetta's too mainstream for you—as it is for some überhip jetsetters—try the bar at the swank **Hotel Quisisana** (p. 652).

Best Cheap Meal

The one you make yourself! Never underestimate the power of DIY food when you're in a region (like Campania) where the local ingredients are so freakin' good. Hit up one of the *alimentari* (deli/grocer's) in the side streets northeast of the Piazzetta, have them make up a fresh tomato and mozzarella sandwich, and grab some beer or wine (just don't forget the opener). Enjoy your 5€ picnic on the beach or your hotel's terrace.

Best Way to Get Oriented (that doesn't require much energy)

For 11.50€ (a truly paltry sum on Capri), take a 2-hour **boat trip around the island** with Gruppo Motoscafisti Capri (p. 657). Low to the waterline, their old-school wooden launches offer thrilling views of Capri's dramatic coastline. Alternatively, head for Anacapri and ride the chairlift to the top of Monte Solaro, the island's highest lookout point, at 589m (1,932 ft.) above sea level.

Best Way to Get Oriented (that does require energy)

Our favorite hikes—to Villa Jovis, the Arco Naturale, and Grotto of Matermania—are just the right amount of strenuous; and the breathtaking views, combining dramatic rock formations and the sea, are so distracting that you won't even realize you're getting a great workout. Furthermore, the distances are short enough that you can do several during the course of your stay.

Capri Orientation

Capri is shaped more or less like an Oscar night dress, 7km (4⅓ miles) long from east to west, and barely 3km (2 miles) wide at its thickest section (the "hem" of the gown) from north to south. The eastern end of the island is the bust of the gown, where you'll find Capri town (160m/525 ft. above sea level), the famed Piazzetta, and most of the hotels, restaurants, shopping, and action in general. Pretty much everything on the eastern end of the island can and must be explored on foot. The "interior" of Capri town is a mostly level, residential warren of narrow, bougainvillea-filled lanes where local children leave their trikes and smudge-faced dollbabies parked against whitewashed walls. If you feel like working off those three gelatos you had yesterday, there are several really cool hikes you can take from Capri town, which range in difficulty from mellow to strenuous. Not feeling so energetic? Not to worry—Emperor Augustus nicknamed the island "Apragopolis" (roughly, "city of sitting around and doing nothing"); you can also loaf around, eat and drink, and simply enjoy the scenery, comforted by the fact that you are doing as one very famous Roman did.

The longer, western end of the island is considered by most to be the "real" Capri. It's quieter, more agricultural, and home to the sleepy, higher-altitude village of Anacapri (299m/981 ft. above sea level), Monte Solaro, and the Blue Grotto.

Getting Around

BY FUNICULAR

Once you've disembarked from your ferry or hydrofoil at Marina Grande, your next transportation experience on Capri is the funicular railway, which connects the port with the center of Capri town. *Note:* If you're not traveling with too many heavy bags, just bring your luggage aboard; otherwise, you'll have to take a taxi (about 10€) from the port to the town above. Funicular tickets are 1.30€ for one-way; 2.10€ for 60 minutes (one funicular ride plus one bus ride with transfer); and 6.70€ for 1 day (limit of two funicular rides, plus unlimited bus rides). Tickets for Capri's funicular and buses are plasticized "souvenir" cards, which require a deposit of 1€. Most visitors forget (or choose not) to turn them in at the end of their stay to reclaim the deposit, so the town of Capri makes an extra 1€ in taxes off almost everyone who sets foot here.

BY BUS

Capri's fleet of orange **buses** is handy when you need to travel between Capri town and Anacapri, to the beach at Marina Piccola, or if you're heading to the Blue Grotto by the overland route and not by boat. The bus also links Marina Grande with Capri town, but the funicular is a much faster and cooler way to climb the hill. The bus terminus of Capri town is located at Piazza Ungheria, just north of the funicular station and the Piazzetta. *Note:* Buses are packed in high season, so be prepared to push weaker and older people out of the way. Buses to and from Capri town are run by **SIPPIC** (☎ 081/837-0420); **Staiano**

Didn't I See You in Us Weekly?

And just so everyone in Capri has the chance to feel like they belong in the tabloids, even if they didn't sail in on P. Diddy's yacht from St. Tropez, there are "paparazzi" who circulate through the island's restaurants and nightspots and take your picture. They'll give you their card (to Foto Flash, Foto Blu, etc.), so when you're sober and exercising good judgment the next day, you can go to their shop and opt to purchase (for about 5€) your nanosecond of fame. Particularly photogenic nonfamous subjects might even end up on the photo shop's wall of fame, next to the likes of Mariah Carey and overly tanned Italian politicians and their arm candy.

(☎ 081/837-2422) operates the bus routes out of Anacapri for a fee of 1.30€ one-way, 2.10€ for 60 minutes (two rides or transfers), and 6.70€ for 1 day of unlimited bus rides (but only two funicular rides).

BY TAXI

Capri's signature taxis are convertible four-door, seven-seater sedans (some are Dolce-Vita-ish '50s cabriolets), which look totally gargantuan after all the shrunken Fiats and Smart cars you will have grown accustomed to seeing in Italy. Most budget travelers never use the taxis of Capri, as the fares run a steep 10€ for even short trips. After a long day of hiking up and down the island's rugged terrain, however, that taxi stand at the beach of Marina Piccola starts to look mighty tempting. All hotels and restaurants should call taxis for you, but if you want to call one yourself, do so by dialing the **Cooperativa Taxi di Capri (Co.Ta.Ca.)** at ☎ 081/837-6657.

Recommended Website

The official site of the AACST (Capri tourist office) **www.capritourism. com** is packed with all the practical information you could possibly need about everything from accommodations to outdoor activities.

ON FOOT

The narrow lanes of Capri town can only be navigated on foot (and by golf-carty vehicles that hotels use to lug guests' suitcases up from the port). A few hundred meters from the Piazzetta, where the whitewashed houses of Capri town give way to lemon and olive groves, paths lead to some of the island's most spectacular (and nonstrenuous) hikes. The easiest beach access, if you're walking, is at Marina Piccola, down the hairpin path of Via Krupp, which starts below the Certosa. (Via Krupp is technically closed due to rock slide dangers, but you can just sneak past the gate—you'll see all locals doing this.) The road from Capri town to Anacapri (4km/2¹/₂ miles away) is a narrow cliff-hugger, riddled with crosses and memorials—better not to do this one on foot. If you're feeling really hardcore, you can go down to Marina Grande and then hike up the ancient Scala Fenicia stairs to the edge of Anacapri. In Anacapri town itself, everything's fairly level and easy to reach on foot.

TOURIST OFFICE

There are three branches of Azienda Autonoma Cura Soggiorno e Turismo (AACST) Isola di Capri tourist office. In Capri town, there's an office on the Piazzetta (☎ 081/ 837-0686); in Marina Grande, they're along the port near the funicular station (☎ 081/ 837-0634). In Anacapri, the office is at Via G. Orlandi 59.

Sleeping

Most guidebooks shepherd budget-oriented travelers to the sleepy hamlet of Anacapri, instead of Capri town. We beg to differ: While Anacapri certainly has more budget options (and we do love the Villa Eva, see below), it's an older-demographic scene with little in the way of nightlife. (So, if you're partying in Capri town and have to get to your Anacapri hotel late at night, you'll have to fork over at least 20€ in cab fare.) Whatever you do, try not to stay in the overdeveloped port area of Marina Grande (where the ferries and hydrofoils arrive).

In Capri town proper, Via Roma and Via Marina Piccola (the roads leading down toward the beach on the south side of the island) are home to a number of Capri's more affordable government-rated one- and two-stars, but it's about a 15-minute uphill hike from here to the center of things. If you can splurge on lodging, panoramic Via Tragara (on the high eastern border of Capri town) is home to a whole slew of boutiquey government-rated three- and four-stars (only one, the Punta Tragara, is listed here), many with intimate, chalet-style accommodations and lovely swimming pools overlooking the bay at Marina Piccola.

CHEAP

➜ **Da Giorgio** ★ CAPRI   About 100m (328 ft.) down the road to the west of the Funicolare station is the government-rated one-star Da Giorgio, yet another testament to the civilized nature of the Caprese people: Even budget hotels on this island are tasteful and well kept. Rooms are bright and contemporary, with furniture painted the color of sea foam; a few rooms have small terraces with chair and table overlooking the Bay of Naples—a fine touch indeed in this price range. Its only slightly out-of-the-way location, away from the most picturesque part of Capri town, is the only strike against it. *Via*

Roma 34. ☎ *081/837-5777.* *www.dagiorgio capri.com. Double 85€–120€.*

➡ **Guarracino** CAPRI   In the quiet, green "Due Golfi" part of island, a 5-minute walk from the Piazzetta and a 10-minute walk to the beaches at Marina Piccola, this red stucco government-rated one-star is a cheerful option for budget travelers. There are no amenities beyond basic TV, telephone, and private bath in room, and air-conditioning, but it's welcoming, bright, and family-run, and most rooms have small balconies with potted geraniums. *Via Mulo 13.* ☎ *081/ 837-7140. www.albergoguarracino.sitonline.it. Double 100€–115€.*

➡ **Hotel La Tosca** ★★ CAPRI   For price, comfort, and location, this is the best deal on the island. In the heart of Capri town, on a narrow lane just a 5-minute walk from the Piazzetta, La Tosca is as classy as government-rated one-stars get in Italy. Rooms are simple, but cool (with A/C), relaxing, and immaculate; the lobby boasts a comfy library/lounge; and best of all, the communal terrace (where breakfast is served, and where you can bring your own food and drink any time of day you please) has wonderful views over whitewashed rooftops to the Faraglioni. Owner/manager Ettore, a soft-spoken, 50-ish gentleman, jaunts off on the hydrofoil many days for business affairs in Naples, but he's always helpful in suggesting scenic walks or arranging island boat tours for hotel guests. Needless to say, with rates as low as these, La Tosca fills up quickly, so be sure to book well ahead, especially from June to September. *Via Birago 5.* ☎ *081/837-0989. www.latosca hotel.com. Double 63€–125€. Breakfast included.*

➡ **Quattro Stagioni** CAPRI   A bit of a hike (but not a terrible one) from the action of Capri town, this simple inn on the way to Marina Piccola offers little in the way of charm, but the price is hard to beat on the island, rooms are clean and have air-conditioning, and there's a decent view from the terrace, where breakfast (included in the rates) is served. *Via Marina Piccola 1/a.* ☎ *081/837-0041. www.hotel4stagionicapri. com. Double 70€–130€.*

➡ **Stella Maris** CAPRI   The dowdiest of Capri's economical accommodations options, the "Star of the Sea" nonetheless boasts an enviable location, within a few blocks of the panoramic terrace of the funicular station and the Piazzetta. (The noisy bus terminal is also nearby, however.) Rooms are uninteresting but clean and fairly spacious and equipped with A/C, but note that the hotel will charge you an extra 10€ per day to use it. *Via Roma 27.* ☎ *081/837-0452. Double 70€– 110€.*

➡ **Villa Eva** ★★ ANACAPRI   Our token Anacapri entry, this is a fabulous place to stay if you'd like a little more room and a few more comforts, and you don't mind being a cab or bus ride away from the buzz of Capri town. With its lush garden setting and spacious, cottage-y rooms—and oh, did we mention the lovely swimming pool with poolside bar?— Villa Eva will make you think you've died and gone to budget-traveler heaven. With five- to eight-person apartments that start at 35€ per person, it's one of Capri's most affordable places to crash, and it doesn't even skimp on style or service-oriented staff. *Via la Fabbrica 8, Anacapri.* ☎ *081/837-1549. www.villaeva. com. Apts (no kitchen, but private bath). 5– 8 people: 35€–45€ per person; double 90€– 100€; triples 110€–140€; quads 140€–180€.*

DOABLE

➡ **Villa Krupp** ★★ CAPRI   This longtime favorite was the villa where early 20th-century Russian revolutionaries Gorky and Lenin stayed when on Capri. Surrounded by shady trees, it offers panoramic views of the sea and the Gardens of Augustus from its terraces. At this family-run place, the front parlor is all glass with views of the seaside and semitropical plants set near Hong Kong chairs, intermixed with painted Venetian-style pieces. Rooms are comfortable and vary in size, with spacious bathrooms. *Via Matteotti 12.* ☎ *081/837-0362. Double 110€–140€. In room: A/C.*

SPLURGE

➔ **Grand Hotel Quisisana** ★★ CAPRI Known to island habitues as simply the Quisi (pronounced "queasy"), this has long been Capri's go-to property for jetsetters (as evidenced by the 50 or so international flags flying on poles across the main façade). Its garden setting in Capri town, near the Piazzetta, is not the most dramatic on the island, but luxurious nonetheless. The Quisisana is accustomed to pleasing celebrities and other high-maintenance guests, so you'll find outstanding service and elegantly appointed rooms, with majolica floor tiles and charming terraces overlooking the hotel pool and grounds. Even if you can't shell out the serious ducats it takes to stay here, you can always avail of the swingin' scene—from early evening to the wee hours—at the **Bar Quisi** (p. 654). The **Quisi Spa,** also open to nonguests, offers all-important beauty treatments like pretanning body scrubs (one for tanned, and one for sensitive skin). Along with the spa, there is a pool, a gym, and tennis courts. All the rooms are air-conditioned, of course. *Via Camerelle 2.* ☎ *081/837-0788. www.quisi.com. Double 300€–610€.*

➔ **Hotel Punta Tragara** ★★ CAPRI This stylishly wavy pink palazzo, designed by Le Corbusier in the 1930s, sits on some of the most-prized real estate on Capri, at the jaw-dropping dead-end of Via Tragara, overlooking the Marina Piccola to the north. As is the case with other high-end properties on the island, rooms are not sumptuous—rich fabrics don't do well in marine air for very long—but are airy (and air-conditioned), comfortable, and bright, with many boasting

magnificent views over the sea through arched windows of rose-colored stucco. Of the hotel's two panoramic pools, one has a whirlpool, and both are filled with sea water. The hotel is a 15-minute walk from the Piazzetta, but if you're with a lover, the Punta Tragara is a divine place to end your stroll. *Via Tragara 57.* ☎ *081/837-0844. www.hotel tragara.com. Double 232€–370€. Rates include buffet breakfast. Amenities: Pool, gym, luggage service from port 6.80€/ piece.*

Eating

In Capri, as in the rest of Campania, get ready to indulge in plenty of tomatoes and mozzarella—this is the home of the Caprese salad, after all—and some of the most amazing seafood you'll have in your life. However, the island is also fraught with plenty of tourist traps serving up mediocre food, so try to steer clear of places where there are no locals dining. Eating all meals out can get pricey, and it's also a bit inconvenient, since you're likely to be out and about during lunch. Grab a sandwich with fresh prosciutto and mozzarella from any of the small delis in town. Note that a lot of Capri's restaurants have curtailed hours in the low and shoulder seasons (Apr–May and Sept–Oct), and many close down for the winter entirely.

CAFES

➔ **Bar Funicolare** CAPRI Stop by this cafe next to the funicular station, around the corner from the Piazzetta, to have your morning cappuccino and *cornetto* (croissant-like pastry) with the likes of Capri's harbor-master and other swarthy, marina-bound locals. Coffee and a pastry will set you back about 3€ or thereabouts if you take them standing up at the bar. *Piazza Diaz.* ☎ *081/ 837-0363.*

CHEAP

➔ **Da Giorgio** ★★ CAPRESE/CAPRI In the hotel of the same name, this is a favorite for island habitués who love its reasonable, traditional fare—linguine with *frutti di mare*, *pappardelle* with shrimp, and all kinds of grilled fish. The panoramic dining room overlooks the Bay of Naples, where all the seafood is caught daily. Everything at the restaurant is served on hand-painted DA GIORGIO ceramic plates. *Via Roma 34.* ☎ *081/837-5777. www. dagiorgiocapri.com. Primi 8€–12€; secondi 10€–15€. Daily for lunch and dinner Apr–Oct. Limited hours off-season.*

➡ **Il Solitario** ★ CAPRESE/ANACAPRI A delightful little eatery in quiet Anacapri, "The Hermit" is another insiders' favorite that will feed you dependable local fare (like ravioli Caprese, with ricotta and mozzarella, topped with tomato sauce) for far less than comparable restaurants in Capri town. Come for lunch before or after a trip to Monte Solaro, and enjoy the shade of the peaceful back garden. *Via G. Orlandi 96.* ☎ *081/837-1382. Primi 7€–9€; secondi 9€–12€. Daily for lunch and dinner Apr–Oct. Limited hours off-season.*

DOABLE

➡ **Da Gemma** ★ CAPRESE & SEAFOOD/ CAPRI Entered via a covered alleyway west of the Piazzetta, Gemma's is a Capri old-timer, with one of the unfussiest, most varied menus on the island. Still, this is Capri, so it's not exactly dirt cheap, but pizzas (Naples-style, with fluffier dough and real *mozzarella di bufala*) are an affordable way to go gourmet, and seafood pastas, made with freshly caught fish and *frutti di mare* from the Bay of Naples (which one side of the dining room overlooks), can be had without breaking the bank. Women can expect to be hit on by flirty waiters, and the room's every surface is covered in old photographs of famous clients past. *Via Madre Serafina 6.* ☎ *081/837-0461. Pizzas 8€–12€; primi 10€–15€; secondi 12€– 18€. Tues–Sun for lunch and dinner; daily in Aug. Closed Jan–Feb.*

➡ **Le Grottelle** ★★ CAPRESE/CAPRI It's a good 20-minute hike to get here, but the incredible location is worth it. On a steep slope near the Arco Naturale, half of the restaurant is perched on a terrace overlooking the plunging hillside and sea below, and the other half is built into a limestone cavern inside the hill itself. The standard array of ravioli and grilled fish is solid but not especially inventive, but local specialties like rabbit, which otherwise seem strange on Capri, seem to suit the rustic, alpine-refuge setting just fine. Since it's a considerable walk here from town, so you might want to call and make a reservation before you embark on the hike. If you do have to wait for a table, no big deal: The view will keep you plenty occupied. *Via Arco Naturale.* ☎ *081/837-5719. Primi 10€–15€; secondi 12€–18€. Daily for lunch and dinner July–Aug; Fri–Wed for lunch and dinner May–June and Sept; Fri–Wed for lunch only Apr and Oct.*

SPLURGE

➡ **Da Paolino** ★★ UPSCALE CAPRISE/ MARINA GRANDE If you love *limoncello* like we do, you must make a pilgrimage to what many call the best restaurant on the island. In case you hadn't figured out that lemons figure prominently in local cuisine, Paolino's decor will drive the point home. Waiters wear vests embellished with lemons; there are lemons on the plates; and best of all, you dine in a lemon grove halfway between Marina Grande and Capri town. The cuisine itself is upscale Caprese, with fine local pasta and seafood dishes. *Via Palazzo a Mare 11.* ☎ *081/837-6102. Primi 12€–15€; secondi 15€–25€. Daily for dinner June–Aug; for lunch and dinner Thurs–Tues Apr–May and Sept–Oct.*

➡ **Villa Verde** ★★ ITALIAN/CAPRI With a cozy indoor dining area and a lovely, enclosed garden patio, this fashionable trattoria down an alley near Taverna Anema e Core has awesome homemade pasta with seafood as well as other local specialties. Villa Verde can even stay in the "doable" category if you eschew the more elaborate lobster recipes and stick to pizza. *Vico Sella Orta 6.* ☎ *081/837-7024. www.villaverde.com. Primi 12€–20€; secondi 18€–30€. Daily for lunch and dinner Apr–Oct, Tues–Sun Nov–Mar.*

Partying

If you come to Capri in the peak summer months, you'll find plenty to do on the island at night. From casual wine bars to seaside dance floors, modern discotheques to raucous live-music taverns, there's something for everyone's taste and budget. Come to the island in the less-crowded months, and you'll find half those venues either closed for the season or depressingly deserted. When all else fails, head for the Piazzetta. No matter the time of year, you can always pull up a chair at one of the intimate cafe tables here, sip some *prosecco* before dinner or some *limoncello* after, and be in the company of plenty of others, from celebrities to marina hands, engaging in that time-honored southern Italian tradition: scoping each other out.

Drinks are a bit more expensive than on the mainland; add a euro or two to the average prices you'd pay back on the continent.

BARS

→ **Bar Tiberio** ★ CAPRI   Of the four cafes on the Piazzetta, this is generally the youngest and friendliest, offering a bit more than the others in the way of bar snacks. If you can't snag a table here, don't stress—angle for a front-row spot at Gran Caffe, Bar Caso, or Piccolo Bar, all within 15 feet of each other. *Piazza Umberto I.* ☎ *081/8370268. Thurs–Tues 6am–2am (sometimes to 4am).*

→ **Hotel La Palma** ★ CAPRI   The bar at this government-rated four-star hotel on the chi-chi shopping street of Via Vittorio Emanuele is recommended as an *aperitivo* spot. La Palma has a more subdued atmosphere than the Quisi (below), but its roof-garden setting, amid thick, imported tropical vegetation, is a sultry spot once you've found

your island honey for the night. There's also a restaurant here, the Relais La Palma, which does excellent, if pricey, Mediterranean fare. *Via Vittorio Emanuele 39.* ☎ *081/837-0133. www.lapalma-capri.com. Open daily.*

→ **Pulalli** ★ CAPRI   Inside the clock tower next to the Piazzetta, Pulalli was once an inn that accommodated new arrivals from the port below; it has since been transformed into a smart little wine bar that also serves small plates from early evening through the wee hours. There's a laid-back vibe and the view of the white lights strung loosely over the Piazzetta is rather magical. *Piazza Umberto I.* ☎ *081/837-4108. Small plates 5€– 10€; drinks 6€–8€. Open 8pm–2am Wed– Mon.*

MTV Best → **Bar Quisi** ★★ CAPRI   On the terrace of the Grand Hotel Quisisana, this elegant bar attracts a swinging scene of younger-generation jetsetters who've decided the Piazzetta has become, well, *too* popular. Nevertheless, the Quisi itself is quite well attended, especially during the *aperitivo* hour—from 6 to 9pm, come here to nibble on the free happy hour buffet and clink glasses with Ferrari scions and their entourages. Hey, you never know who you're gonna run into on Capri. *Via Camerelle 2.* ☎ *081/837-0788. www.quisi.it. No cover. Open daily until at least 2am.*

DISCOS & CLUBS

→ **Anema e Core** ★★ CAPRI   Sooner or later, all the jet-setters end up at Capri's most venerable nightlife institution, where entertainment is provided not by slick DJs spinning house music, and partying isn't done under low lights. Taverna Anema e Core is a folksy theater-in-the-round where Guido Lembo, local minstrel and "undisputed ruler of Capri," is "capable of transforming inhibited politicians into caterwauling crooners," and "known to have convinced the most prudish to abandon themselves in exotic dances," according to his own PR. Indeed, with his bouncy, addictive Neapolitan and Caprese melodies, Guido really does manage to get everyone in the room singing and dancing until the dawn's early light. As the club's brochure dictates, "enter the kingdom of Guido and relinquish all restraint"—safe in the knowledge that Giorgio Armani, Jay-Z, and Beyonce have all done it before you. Of course, how much fun you have depends a bit on the crowd in attendance that night (it can often be an older, B-list set), but toss back a few cocktails and hey, Bruno Tonioli from *Dancing With the Stars* starts to look more and more attractive across the room. *Via Sella Orta 39/e.* ☎ *081/837-6461. www.anemaecore. com. Daily May–Sept; Sat–Sun only in Apr and Oct. Cover 20€–25€.*

➜ **Number Two** ★ CAPRI One of the few discotheques proper on the island, this is where you go when you actually feel like dressing up and having a bona fide organized night out (which, on Capri, isn't often, but maybe that's just me). However, it's usually pretty crowded with foreigners and visiting Italians, thanks in large part to the fact that the club lets it be known that Naomi Campbell is a regular here when she's on Capri. *Via Camerelle 1.* ☎ *081/837-7078. Cover 10€–20€. Daily 10pm–4am Apr–Oct.*

➜ **O Guarracino** ★ CAPRI This rustic underground joint actually used to be an olive press, and there must be some oil left over in the place, because the men here sure have a lot of grease in their hair. Still, it's an animated watering hole with a mixed crowd where you can knock back a beer or five while live Neapolitan music is played. It's not as wild 'n' crazy as Anema e Core, and it's also not as expensive to get in—there's no cover. *Via Castello 7.*

Sightseeing

Most of the sights worth seeing in Capri are natural attractions—scenic hikes, boat trips, and beaches—which are listed in the "Playing Outside" section, below. But Capri wouldn't

be Italian if it didn't have its requisite number cultural heritage sites, too. There's a rather impressive archaeological site with ruins of an imperial Roman villa, a Carthusian monastery, even an adorably hokey "Capri in Miniature" attraction.

➜ **Capri in Miniatura** ★ ANACAPRI This pottery and limestone scale model of Capri certainly isn't the most spectacular thing you'll see on the island, but hey, we're fans of anything in miniature—and it does give you a good overview of how things are laid out. Sculpted and modeled entirely by the hands of artist Sergio Rubino, the endearing (and well-maintained) 18x9m (59- x 30-ft.) version of Capri sits in a huge tub of blue water, which is surrounded by viewing decks and glass-fronted dioramas with historical scenes of local life and folk traditions. Look out for the (highly imaginative) reconstruction of Emperor Tiberius's Villa Jovis; the harrowing events of October 1808, when Napoleonic troops scaled the western slope of the island and captured Capri; grape-gathering and stomping for the wine harvest; and an enthralling *mise en scene* of tourists bobbing in and out of the Blue Grotto. On the model of the island itself, which is represented with its modern-day appearance and structures, there's some dwarf vegetation (e.g., weeds as tall as the Certosa). *Via G. Orlandi 105.* ☎ *081/837-1169. www.capri-miniatura.com. Admission 3€.*

FREE ➜ **Certosa di San Giacomo** ★ CAPRI With its stuccoed arches and vaults half-collapsed in ruins, Capri's 14th-century Charterhouse of St. James has a gutted look that is somewhat reminiscent of the Texas Alamo. The building complex, on the southern slopes of Capri town, started out as a monastery for the Carthusian brotherhood of monks, who were forever quarrelling with the Capresi over grazing and hunting rights on the island. When, in the 17th century, a plague broke out among the islanders, the monks stayed disease-free by quarantining themselves within the walls of the Certosa, instead of helping the sick of Capri town. In true Neapolitan fashion, the incensed towns-people dumped the infected corpses of their plague victims over the walls and into the cloisters. The Certosa was also sacked and torched by pirates in 1553. By 1808, when Napoleon had subjected Capri to French rule, the Certosa became a prison. Today, it's a museum, school, and altogether pleasant place, with some fabulous views—what else is new, this is Capri—from its towers. *Viale Certosa.* ☎ *081/837-6218. Tues–Sun 9am–2pm. Admission free.*

➜ **Villa Jovis** ★★ CAPRI One of the bigger freak shows ever to assume the imperial throne, Tiberius ruled Rome from A.D.14 to 37 and in that time built no fewer than 12 villas on Capri, one dedicated to each of the gods. Of the original dozen, only three remain in any recognizable state, and Villa Jovis (dedicated to Jove, or Jupiter) was the most sump-tuous in its day, and today, the best preserved—which is not to say it's perfectly intact. You'll need to use your imagination to picture the bygone lavishness of the place; most of the villa's masonry and brick walls are reduced to rubble, and whatever marbles were recovered from the site are now in museums or private collections, but you can still make out a number of interesting struc-tures, including the rain-gathering cisterns that guaranteed a fresh and constant water supply to the emperor's palace in the sky. Still, the most impressive thing about the Villa Jovis is its lonely position on the high eastern end of the island, where, just beyond the archaeological site, grey limestone cliffs plunge 354m (1,161 ft.) down to the sea. (According to legend, it was from here, the Salto di Tiberio, that the fickle emperor used to toss disobedient subjects to their deaths.) Climb to the small chapel at the top of the ruins for some seriously breathtaking views over the sea to the tawny cliffs of Sorrento, 5km (3 miles) away. (If you suffer from

vertigo, you might want to skip this last step.) *Via Tiberio (only accessible by a 45-min. walk from the Piazzetta, up a steady but not stren-uous inclining path).* ☎ *081/837-0634. www.capriweb.com/Capri/VillaJovis. Daily 9am to 1hr before sunset. Admission 2€.*

Playing Outside

VISITING THE BLUE GROTTO (GROTTA AZZURRA)

Capri's most famous natural wonder—a sea cave whose water glows an otherwordly, incandescent blue due to unique refraction of the sun's rays—is hardly off the beaten path; everyone who lands on Capri should visit the grotto, and indeed most do. Getting there, however, is a minor odyssey, so there are a few things you should know before embarking. First, acquaint yourself with the grotto's convoluted system of admission fees. You have to pay to get to the cove area out-side the grotto, which is either 8.50€ for the Blue Grotto—only shuttle service from Marina Grande, or 11.50€ for the full-island circum-navigation trip (which we highly recom-mend); *then* you have to pay another 4.50€ per person to the guy in the dinghy who will row you and a few other passengers into the grotto itself; and finally, you have to pay a 4€ "monument" fee which ostensibly goes to the Capri heritage department and is used for the "upkeep" of the Blue Grotto. Whatever. In any case, that's what you have to pay (and you will get cute little ticket stubs for each component), so stop acting like you're being ripped off and just have fun, because it's totally worth it.

Next, be aware that getting to the Blue Grotto also requires agility. Once you've arrived at the rowboat staging—area outside the grotto entrance, you have to clamber awkwardly from your motorboat, over the open sea, to the dinghy, almost surely sus-taining bruises and maybe even flashing your fellow passengers in the process. When you and your rowboat-mates are about to enter the grotto, your captain will abruptly ask you to lie all the way down (more likely, he'll just manhandle you into position with a few meaningful grunts). This is necessary so that when he yanks you, via overhead chain, through the 1m-tall (3ft.) hole that is the entrance to the grotto, nobody gets decapitated. Once inside, you'll be treated not only to the truly magical quality of the silvery-blue light reflecting off the sea bottom, but to a chorus of pirate songs as the *Capresi* boatmen, in voices soft to booming, harmonious to off-key, join in for a memorable seafaring serenade.

The Grotto is at its least crowded after 3pm, but even during peak hours, it can be fun watching all the action as the rowboat guys jockey for passengers, bumping up against each other and shouting at each other in colorful dialect.

Swimming into the Blue Grotto is really only feasible after the boat traffic has called it a day (5pm or so), but it's a hairy endeavor that only experienced swimmers should attempt. Swells of any size tend to slap against the rock wall where the grotto entrance is located, so if you're not careful you could get seriously clocked in the head, and there's no lifeguard on duty.

BOAT TOUR AROUND THE ISLAND

Best If the trip to the Blue Grotto seems like a rip-off, the lovely 2-hour boat trips around Capri, offered by **Gruppo Motoscafisti Capri,** are an incredible bargain at 11.50€ per person. (When you get to the Blue Grotto, you still have to pay another 8.50€.) Cruise in a snappy and stylish traditional wooden launch while your handsome, charming old salt of a captain expertly navigates Capri's rugged coast and dramatic rock formations, guiding you in and out of tiny grottoes, and regales you with tales of how Roman Emperor Tiberius used to throw his prisoners off a cliff on the northeast corner of the island. The boats accommodate about 25 people, and even when they're full (July–Aug), everyone has a good view. The tours leave from Marina Grande (☎ **081/837-7714** or 081/837-5646; www.motoscafisticapri.com).

RIDING MONTE SOLARO CHAIRLIFT

It makes some sketchy squeaks and groans, but what the hell, this single chairlift in Anacapri takes you on a 12-minute ride from Anacapri town, over villagers' backyards and lemon groves, with views over the western end of the island to the sea, up to Capri's highest point, 589m-high (1,932-ft.) Monte Solaro. If you're feeling frisky, you can take the chairlift up and walk back down the hill (about 1 hr), or vice versa. Via Caposcuro 10. ☎ **081/837-1428.** Mar–Oct daily 9:30am to 1hr before sunset; Nov–Feb daily 10:30am–3pm. One-way 4.50€; round-trip 6€.

BEACHES

What passes for a "beach" in Capri is a rocky, bumpy, and above all, dinky stretch of terrain that meets the sea. Try as you might, you will not find any traditional expanses of sand on the island. (And once you've looked around at Capri's jagged and steep coastline, this state of affairs will hardly surprise you.) Many bathers (especially those more interested in sunning that swimming) opt for the luxury and stunning views of their hotel pools, but for those who want a good ol' fashioned dip in the Med, there is some glorious swimming to be done in the crystalline, deep emerald waters off Capri's shoals (see below)—and what's more, you won't have to dump the sand out of your bathing suit at the end of the day! If you're planning a longer outing, bring a sandwich from an *alimentari* in town; otherwise you're stuck with the pricey, often mediocre food at beach club restaurants.

WHERE TO SWIM

→ **Marina Piccola** ★ CAPRI   This is the no-brainer swimming destination for most who visit Capri. There are a few "beach clubs" (with restaurants and a few other facilities) here, but you can also just plop your towel down in the pebbly, free access zone around the rock outcropping known as the Scoglio delle Sirene ("Mermaids' Reef"). Swim out about 15m (50 ft.) for seemingly bottomless green-blue sea—you'll be so giddy at the color and clarity of the water you'll want to do a few somersaults, but when you come up for air, be sure to take in the gorgeous view back toward Capri's southern coast and the Faraglioni. *Bus to Marina Piccola, or 20-min walk down Via Krupp (technically closed, but those in the know just hop over the barricades).*

→ **La Fontelina** ★ CAPRI   This "beach" is hardly more than a few flattish rocks near the water, but you can go for a swim here with the Faraglioni (the huge rocks off Capri's south coast) towering overhead. Just watch out for passing motorboat traffic. *Località Faraglioni. Beach club* ☎ *081/837-0845. Steep 15-min walk from the end of Via Tragara, or access by motorboat from Marina Grande (10€ round-trip).*

→ **Bagni Nettuno** ★ ANACAPRI   One of the nicer, full-service bathing clubs on the island, it's also the only place from which it's possible to swim into the Blue Grotto. Note that swimming into the grotto, while permitted after 5pm when the tourist boats have all left, is a bit hairy, even in calm seas. See full listing for the Blue Grotto (p. 656) for advice. *Località Grotta Azzurra.* ☎ *081/837-1362. www.nettuno-capri.com. Bus from Capri or Anacapri to Grotta Azzurra.*

→ **Bagni Tiberio** MARINA GRANDE   Set below the remains of one of Emperor Tiberius's Capri villas (he had 12 total), this is one of few bathing establishments on the north side of the island, which gets shady quite early. In front of the beach, a steady traffic of motorboats shuttling between Marina Grande and the Blue Grotto means that the water is not as still and crystalline here as on other parts of the island. *Via Palazzo a Mare 41.* ☎ *081/837-0703. Bus to Bagni Tiberio or access by motorboat from Marina Grande (7€–8.50€ round-trip).*

Shopping

You'll find a microcosm of the international fashion world on Via Camerelle and Via Vittorio Emanuele—from Gucci to Pucci, the big designer names are all here.

Capri is also home to a number of homegrown specialties that make great souvenirs. For deluxe perfumes made right on the island, head for **Carthusia** (Viale Parco Augusto 2; ☎ **081/837-0368;** www.carthusia. com). Design your own sandals and have them hand-made on the spot at **Canfora** (Via Camerelle; ☎ **081/837-0487;** www.canfora. com). Feed your addiction for lemony after-dinner drinks at **Limoncello di Capri** (Via Listrieri 25/a; ☎ **081/837-3059;** www. limoncello.com). All the shops stay open late—the better to trap inebriated tourists who've had too much *limoncello* on the Piazzetta. **G4,** a fabulous shoe store on Via Vittorio Emanuele is an excellent place to bring your credit cards and impaired judgment.

Sicily

For a few years now, I've been predicting to friends, family, and random acquaintances that Sicily is the Next Big Thing in Italian tourism. Well, Sicily hasn't catapulted to the forefront of travelers' minds *yet*, but it should—it's significantly cheaper than the rest of Italy, it has fascinating cities with turbulent history, some of Italy's most drop-dead gorgeous ruins and architecture, amazing seafood and vegetables (the tomatoes are in a completely different league here), hundreds of miles of beaches, and some bad-ass volcanoes. Its size and layout are wonderfully manageable, with handy bus and train connections and well-marked highways, if you want to rent a car. Parts of Sicily are even farther south than the northern tip of Africa, and you can sense the geographical distance from the rest of Italy—the light is more intense; the land, while very green in places, has a rawer quality than the mainland. It can remind you of California, the American Deep South, or the Middle East.

Sicily's distance from the mainland is not only geographical but chronological. Many parts of the island are very much the 50-years-behind-the-times *Godfather* country that tourists expect when they visit Italy. Sicily is alluring, and days here are filled with food, laughter, and long espresso breaks. Because it has modernized a lot more slowly than the rest of the country, and because many of its cities are dingy and impoverished, Sicily is often considered the red-headed stepchild of Italy. The truth is, Sicily is the golden child, a place where people still respect the land and the sea and never tire of good village gossip. From Taormina (a popular spot with a breathtaking Greek theater), to Palermo (best described as a fishing village *and* big city in one) to the Valley of the Temples in Agrigento (where you can time-travel back to the 5th century B.C.) to the Aeolian Islands (north of Messina), Sicily is replete with contradictions, and yet somehow consistent. It is rugged and elegant, rustic and serene, a true diamond in the rough.

In Sicily, you must be prepared for memorable human encounters, like the train conductor named Salvatore who strikes up a conversation with you on a ride to one of the coastal small towns—chances are, he grew up in one of them and will give you the inside scoop. Most Sicilians you'll meet are just like they're depicted in the movies, old-fashioned, hot-blooded, and magnetically engaging—men are charming and chauvinistic, and women are radiant, often voluptuous, with a fair amount of drama in their veins. The other thing to keep in mind is that a huge number of Italian immigrants in the world came from Sicily: that means that almost every Sicilian has a relative (even if it's a distant one) in the U.S., Canada, or Australia, which will give visitors from those countries something to talk about, even if the only words you mutually understand are "pizza" and "Brooklyn." However, even if you understand Italian, you will spend your entire time trying to figure out what language the locals are speaking—Sicilian dialects are bewildering.

As for *la Cosa Nostra,* the Mafia does exist in Sicily, it's true, but it's completely invisible to tourists—just knowing that it's there, however, will give your time here that extra thrill. (A favorite game we like to play in the piazzas of Sicily is spot-the-mob-boss.) And if you want to visit the alleged home of the Godfather (a real one or Francis Ford Coppola's), you can indulge in a visit to Corleone. Yes, the town really exists; it's near Palermo, and the bus drops you off in Piazza Vittime della Mafia (Piazza of the Victims of the Mafia).

The Best of Sicily

Most Transporting Experience

Soak up the eerily present aura of the ancient Greeks in the **Valley of the Temples, Agrigento.** The evocative amber-toned skeletons of these six temples, situated along a dramatic rocky ridge, dotted with olive and almond trees, are among the most memorable archaeological ruins in the world. See p. 682.

Most Fabulous Way to Get Culture

In the summer, evening opera and theater performances under the stars at the **Greco-Roman Amphitheater in Taormina** are a

Sicily

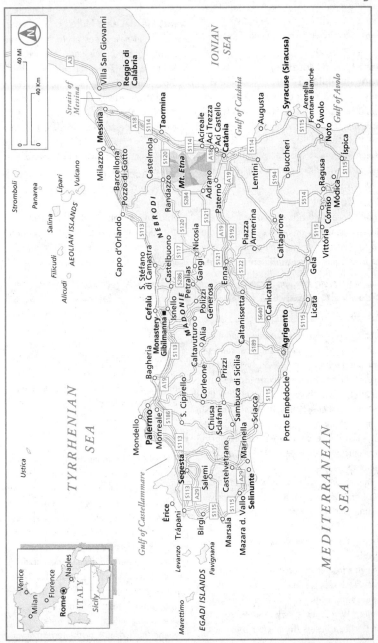

Reggio di Calábria

Villa San Giovanni

A3

40 Mi

40 Km

Straits of Messina

Messina

Milazzo

Barcellona

Pozzo di Gotto

Castelmola

Taormina

S113

A18

S114

Acireale

Aci Trezza

Aci Castello

Catánia

A18

S114

Augusta

Gulf of Catania

Syracusa (Siracusa)

Arenella

Fontane Bianche

Ávola

Noto

Ispica

Gulf of Avola

S115

Stromboli

Panarea

Lipari

Salina

Vulcano

AEOLIAN ISLANDS

Filicudi

Alicudi

Capo d'Orlando

S. Stéfano di Camastra

Castelbuono

S113

S120

Randazzo

Mt. Etna

S284

S114

Adrano

Paternò

A19

Nicosia

Gangi

Petralias

S286

NEBRODI

S117

S120

S121

Lentini

Buccheri

S194

Ragusa

Módica

Vittória

Cómiso

S115

S514

S115

TYRRHENIAN SEA

Ustica

Mondello

Palermo

Monreale

Bagheria

Cefalù

Monastery

Gibilmanna

Isnello

MADONIE

Polizzi Generosa

Alia

Caltavuturo

S. Cipirello

Corleone

Prizzi

Enna

Piazza Armerina

Caltagirone

Gela

Licata

Agrigento

S115

S122

S121

S640

Caltanissetta

Canicatti

S189

S113

A19

S186

Segesta

Mondello

Gulf of Castellammare

Érice

Trápani

Birgi

Marsala

Levanzo

Maretimo

Favignana

EGADI ISLANDS

Salemi

Castelvetrano

Mazara d. Vallo

Marinella

Selinunte

Chiusa Sclafani

Sambuca di Sicilia

Sciacca

Porto Empédocle

S113

A29

S115

S115

S115

MEDITERRANEAN SEA

Venice

Milan

Florence

Rome

Naples

ITALY

Sicily

divine way to say you did something grown-up and sophisticated on vacation (while also giving you a chance to scope out your cute fellow vacationers, who are doing the same thing). See p. 701

Best Island Getaway-from-the-Island

Only Italians, and now you, know about **Panarea,** but there are few places in Italy more fun, fabulous, and down-to-earth than this tiny Aeolian island. Rent a boat and explore gorgeous inlets, eat amazing seafood, and party with hip young people under the stars. See p. 704.

Best Dessert

I don't care if you think you've had "real Sicilian cannoli" anywhere else in the world. You ain't seen nothing until you try the fresh-squeezed **cannoli** here in the land where pastry tubes filled with ricotta were invented.

Most Hard-Core Hike

Badasses can make the ascent to the crater of **Mt. Etna** for top-of-the-world, outrageously breathtaking views over the sea and the rest of Sicily, but before you set out, be sure to find out the latest volcano advisory from the park headquarters. Etna is the mythological home of Hephaestus, the Greek god of fire, and when he gets pissed and starts spitting and rumbling, it's serious business. See p. 702.

Best Place for a Halloween Party

The super-freaky **Crypt of the Capuchin Monks in Palermo** contains thousands of dead bodies still dressed in their Sunday best, suspended from hooks on the walls. Yep, this is actually a tourist attraction. See p. 675.

Getting to & Getting Around Sicily

By Air

Flights into Palermo or Catania from mainland Italy are far and away the most convenient and the fastest links to Sicily. Palermo's airport, **Punta Raisi/Falcone-Borsellino Airport**, is the island's largest, with the greatest number of flights. It's 31km (19 miles) west of Palermo on the A29 highway. Catania's **Fontanarossa Airport** is worth considering if you'll be sticking to eastern half of the island.

There are tons of bus companies that take you from the terminal at Catania airport to destinations all over Sicily, including Taormina, Siracusa, and the port of Milazzo (for ferries and hydrofoils to the Aeolian Islands.

Flights from Rome or Milan to Palermo or Catania take approximately 1 hour, and there are several flights a day with different companies. **Wind Jet (www.volawindjet.it)** offers cheap tickets (from 100€ round-trip) but has lousy service, and the flights are almost always delayed. For a few euros more (from 110€ round-trip), **Air One (www.flyairone.it)** is a more dependable choice. You can also get to Sicily on the good old green-and-red tail fins of **Alitalia (www.alitalia.com)**, which has the most extensive network of airports served, but flights tend to cost a bit more (from about 150€ round-trip).

By Train

If you're dead set on milking that Eurailpass for all it's worth, you can get to Sicily by train, but it's *slooooooow*. (To cross the Straits of Messina, there's a ferry with train tracks that shuttles trains back and forth between terra firma!) The Rome-Palermo leg takes 11 hours, with seven trains arriving per day. If you have opted for the rail haul from Rome and don't have a Eurailpass, you'll pay 56€ for a one-way ticket. (At this point, flying is beginning to look more and more attractive. . . .) If you're coming to Sicily from Naples, we recommend the hydrofoil or the ferry. You can also go by train from Naples. The trip clocks in at about 9 hours.

By Car

Three *autostrade* (superhighways) link Palermo with the rest of Sicily. The most used route is A19 from Catania or A20 from Messina. From the west, A29 comes in from Mazara del Vallo. In addition, two main highways link Palermo: SS113 from Trapani in the west or Messina in the east, and SS121 from Catania and Enna in the east. Palermo is cut off from mainland Sicily. To reach it by car, you'll have to cross the Straits of Messina by ferries operated by FS, the state railway authority.

Once the ferry has landed at Messina, you still must face a drive of 233km (144 miles) to Palermo. If you're planning to drive from Naples or Rome, as many do, prepare yourself for a long ride: it's 721km (447 miles) south from Naples or 934km (579 miles) south from Rome.

By Sea

This is our favorite way to reach Palermo from mainland Italy. In Naples, the fastest and most convenient service over to Palermo is provided by **SNAV** (☎ **081/4285555**), which operates ferries to Palermo. The trip takes 10^1/$_2$ hours and costs 30€ to 69€ per person. A rival ferry is operated by **Tirrenia Lines** (☎ 199/123-199), which takes 10^1/$_2$ hours and costs 38€ to 74€. Schedules vary depending on the weather, so always call on the day of your departure even if you've confirmed your reservation the day before.

Getting Around the Island

Whether you choose to go by bus or by train, Sicily's cities, ports, and smaller towns are well connected by hassle-free public transportation. If you're on a Eurailpass, you'll probably opt for the train, but we have found the bus (air-conditioned, modern coaches) to be a more comfortable option for the

Safety in Sicily

Sicily is attracting greater numbers of foreigners, mainly from Europe, especially England and Germany. Many Americans continue to skip it, often because of their fear of the Mafia. However, the Mafia doesn't concern itself with tourists. It does exist (Sicily even made a cameo guest appearance on *The Sopranos*), but its hold seems to have lessened over the years. If you take the usual safety precautions (keep alert and don't flash jewelry), you'll be fine.

relatively short intercity jaunts. They're also cheaper than individual train tickets, if you don't have a Eurailpass. The longest distance you might cover in one haul on Sicily is 6 hours (from Catania to Trapani, say), but you'll probably break it up into shorter hops, staying overnight in the towns you encounter as you make your way around the island. As an example, a train or bus ride between Palermo and Catania takes about 3^1/$_2$ hours (about 12€ for the bus, 18€ for the train), and there are frequent departures. For rail information for Sicily or Italy in general, call ☎ **892021**. For buses in Sicily, a number of companies operate: **AST** (www.azienda sicilianatrasporti.it), **Interbus** (www.inter bus.it), **SAIS** (www.saisautolinee.it), **Segesta** (www.segesta.it), and **Cuffaro** (www. cuffaro.info).

Renting a car can also be a great way to get around. The distances are manageable, the roads and highways are mostly well maintained, and once you're out of the cities, traffic isn't as crazy as you might think.

There's nothing like straying from your trip itinerary to drive up to a random hill town, where you might stumble upon the most amazing *rigatoni alla norma* of your life! You'll pay a toll to use the *autostrada*, but the SS (*strade statali*) are free. Gas, as throughout Italy, is expensive. All the major rental companies have offices at Palermo and Catania airports, as well as locations in the more popular tourist destinations.

Palermo

721km (447 miles) S of Naples, 934km (579 miles) S of Rome

Part big city, part old-fashioned fishing village, Palermo ★★ is full of contradictions. It is wonderful, fascinating, and beautiful, and run-down, dirty, and chaotic at the same time. Being a tourist in Palermo takes a lot of energy. Not only are there tons of monuments and sights, but the city itself seems to want to eat you alive.

If by the end of the day you are not killed by the traffic or by the smog, you will certainly be exhausted by all the impressions you've gathered during the day. Whole neighborhoods remain bombed out from World War II, yet Palermo boasts some of the greatest sights and museums in Sicily. Unemployment, poverty, traffic, crime, and crowding are rampant, and city services just don't run as they should. But amid the decay, you'll find gloriously stuccoed oratories, glittering 12th-century mosaics, art museums, baroque palaces, and busy fish markets bursting with life and color. As you arrive in Palermo, you start spotting blond, blue-eyed *bambini* all over the place. Don't be surprised. If fair-haired children don't fit your concept of what a Sicilian should look like, remember that the Normans landed here in 1060 and launched a campaign to wrest control of the island from the Arabs. Today you can see elements of both cultures, notably in Palermo's architecture—a unique style, Norman-Arabic.

One of the reasons why Palermo is so interesting is that the city is never still. When you visit some cities, like Venice, Rome, and Paris, whatever you have been reading about the place before your trip will be confirmed once you get there. With Palermo, it's different; the city changes continuously, maybe not always for the better,

but it's definitely in motion. You might go there today, you could have been there 5 years ago, and maybe you will return in 2 years—it will never be the same. Every day the urban structure is tweaked and morphed, and the city's identity with it. This makes Palermo a city to return to, time and time again.

The Best of Palermo

Best Cultural Experience

The souk-like street market of **Vucciria** bombards you with smells, sounds, and sights you have probably never encountered before in your life! See p. 679.

Best Dining Bet

When the entrails used in so much Palermitan street food start to turn your stomach, head to **Antica Focacceria San Francesco** for some more recognizable, and totally delicious, dishes. If you had your heart set on fried spleen, they have that, too. See p. 673.

Best Place to Inhale Kind Bud

Seek asylum from the city chaos at the **cloisters of San Giovanni degli Eremiti** (p. 677) and the **garden of Santa Maria dello Spasimo** (p. 678), where the smell of jasmine and orange flowers will make you high.

Best Lunch on a Hot Day

Pistachio ice cream in a brioche (sweet bread bun).

Getting There

BY AIR

Flying from anywhere in mainland Italy (Rome, Milan, or Naples) to Palermo takes approximately 1 hour, and there are several flights a day with different companies. From the airport (Punta Raisi/Falcone-Borsellino) to Palermo is 30 km (19 miles) and getting into

Culture 101: A Palermo History Primer

Palermo was founded by the Phoenicians, then taken over by the Greeks, followed by the Romans and the Byzantines. During the 9th century A.D., the Muslims invaded Sicily and dominated for 2 centuries. During the Muslim regime the economy of Sicily grew stronger and Palermo was ahead in urban development compared to other European cities. Today, not one Muslim building remains, which is strange considering the importance and dimensions of the city during that period.

In the 11th century, the Normans conquered Sicily. They did not expel the Muslims—on the contrary, Muslim architects, craftsmen, and administrators were involved in many affairs. Most likely, the destruction of the Muslim buildings in Palermo occurred in the 16th century, when Sicily was under the Catholic reign of Spain. Since the Normans used Islamic knowledge and skills for their own interests, many signs of the Muslim culture can still be seen in the monuments of the Norman age: the Norman Palace, the Cathedral, San Giovanni degli Eremiti, the church of San Cataldo, the Zisa, and the Cuba.

town is very easy—you can go by train or by bus.

The train leaves every 40 minutes, takes 45 minutes, and costs 5€ (www.trenitalia.com). The **Prestia & Comande** bus (5€) leaves every 30 minutes and takes 50 min (if you don't get stuck in traffic) to reach central Palermo (making stops at Viale della Libertà, Politeama, Piazza Giulio Cesare and the central train station). As you approach the city, your surroundings may make you a bit nervous. First of all, you will pass thousands of flimsy-looking shanties by the seaside. These are in fact the "country houses" of people who live in the city. Closer to the city, where the rougher suburbs are, you will start to wonder if you want to get off the bus. The 15-story buildings, with their typically horrid 1960s architecture, surround you for miles and miles until, all of a sudden, the suburbs turn into the old and fascinating *centro* that more closely resembles your expectations of Palermo.

It's also possible to rent a **car** at the airport (all the major firms are represented) and drive into Palermo. Allow 30 to 45 minutes—longer, if traffic is bad—to get to the center of town from the airport.

BY TRAIN, BUS, OR CAR

For information about traveling by **train** to Palermo, see "Getting to & Getting Around Sicily," at the beginning of the chapter. The bus stations in Palermo along Via Balsamo are adjacent to the rail station. The trip from Rome costs 38€, but most bus fares on the island are inexpensive. For example, the cost from Trapani is 6.20€; from Agrigento, 7.20€; from Catania, 12€; and from Messina, 13€. After you arrive by **car** from mainland Italy at Messina, head west on A20, which becomes Route 113, then A20 again, and finally A19 before its final approach to Palermo.

BY BOAT

If you are not in too much of a hurry, it's fun to take the **ferry** from Naples to Palermo (about 10 hr). The boats are clean and comfortable, and if you take a boat that leaves in the evening you will wake up to a beautiful sunrise along the northern coast of Sicily. The ticket prices vary from low-high season and whether you want a seat on deck or a sleeping cabin, but expect to pay at least 30€ per passenger for steerage (a seat on deck), and from 65€ per passenger for a bed in a "first-class" sleeping compartment. The main

SICILY

OKKIO! Safety Concerns in Palermo

Two words: Stay alert. Palermo is home to some of the most skilled pickpockets around. Don't flaunt expensive jewelry, cameras, or wads of bills. Women who carry handbags are especially vulnerable to purse snatchers on Vespas. It's best to park your car in a garage rather than on the street; wherever you leave it, don't leave valuables inside. Police squads operate mobile centers throughout the town to help combat street crime.

boat companies are **Tirrenia** (☎ 091/602IIII; www.tirrenia.it) and **SNAV** (☎ 091/6317900 or 081/4285555; www.snav.it).

Getting Around Palermo

The easiest way to orient yourself in Palermo is to think of the city as a cross with **Via Vittorio Emanuele** as the vertical line and **Via Maqueda** as the horizontal line; the two lines meet at the Quattro Canti. So, in the top left part of the this "cross" you will find the part of the city called **Ballaró**, the top right part of the cross is the **Capo**, the lower right part (under the Capo) is the **Vucciria**, and beside it lies the **Kalsa**.

The walking distance from one point to another in Palermo's old town is never far—about 30 minutes tops. Sometimes it might feel like a hundred miles, especially if you are here in the summer when the sun is burning and the smog is thicker than ever. Always carry a bottle of water. When you visit a church, take time to cool off in the cloister or garden—they are heavenly oases in this often oppressive city.

If you're up for a bit of an adventure, you can also try taking the bus or the metro. The buses run from 4am–11:30pm and the metro from 6am–8:30pm. Tickets cost 1.50€ and

can be bought at the *tabacchi* store. Remember to validate the tickets in the orange and yellow time-stamping machines on the bus or in the metro station. For information, call **AMAT**, Via Borrelli 16 (☎ 091/6902690).

A tourist bus called *Giro Città* begins and ends its circuit at the Teatro Politeama. It stops at many monuments, including the Duomo and the Royal Palace. Departures are at 9am daily; tickets are sold on board, and there are no advance reservations. The cost is 11€ per person. For more information call ☎ 091/6902690.

There are **taxi** stands on almost all big piazzas: Piazza Castelnuovo (Politeama), Piazza Guilio Cesare (train station), Piazza Verdi (Teatro Massimo), and Piazza Indipendenza (Norman Palace). You can call a taxi at ☎ 091/225455.

Palermo Basics

There are a couple of tourist information points in the city, and the hotels often have maps and the basic city brochure. And by all means, do not be afraid of asking people for help! Sicilians are very helpful and will do their best—even if they do not speak a word of English—to help you find your way. But be careful to ask only one person at a time: The more Sicilians involved, the higher the risk you'll never find the place you're looking for!

For "professional" help, the main tourist information points are on Piazza Castelnuovo 34 (☎ 091/583847; Mon–Fri 8:30am–2pm and 3–6pm), and by the main train station on Piazza Giulio Cesare (Mon–Fri 8:30am–2pm and 3–6pm.) There's another tourist info office at the **Palermo airport** (☎ 091/591698).

Recommended Websites

◯ **www.aapit.pa.it** Before leaving for your vacation, you can send for tourist information about Palermo on this site.

Palermo

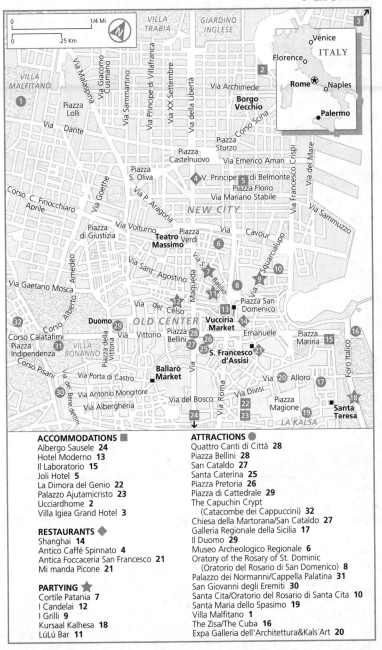

You can also read about events and culture, and find accommodation and lots of other practical information.

○ **www.bestofsicily.com** All kinds of information about Sicily.

ATMs *Bancomat* are found everywhere on Via Roma and Via Maqueda. If you want to buy stuff at the street markets, bring cash. Otherwise, most of the restaurants and stores take credit cards. If you need to go to the bank or the post office, most of the **banks** are found on Via Roma towards the Politeama.

Emergencies In an emergency, call the *polizia* at ☎ 113; for nonemergencies, use ☎ 091/210111 or visit the main police station (*questura*) on Piazza Vittoria 8 (Via Vittorio Emanuele). You can also turn to Italy's Army police force, the **Carabinieri** (who wear red-striped trousers designed by Valentino), to report a horse's head in your bed after having gone home with a virgin *siciliana*. Call the Carabinieri at ☎ 112 for emergencies only (for nonemergencies, ☎ 091/588333). Their station (*caserma*) is at Via Vittorio Emanuele 475. To report a fire, a gas leak, or a drunken Dane stuck in one of the magnolias in the Garibaldi garden, dial ☎ 115 or ☎ 091/6622160, for the *vigili del fuoco* (fire department), based at Via Scarlatti Alessandro 16 (Piazza Giuseppe Verdi).

For medical emergencies (if you feel a strange pain in your stomach after having eaten the *stigghiola* or the *milza*), call an ambulance at ☎ 118, or visit the *pronto soccorso* (emergency room, where you will not be charged for treatment, regardless of your insurance status) at **Ospedale Cervello,** Via Trabucco, 180, ☎ 091/6802111.

The *polizia municipale*, who handle dog bites and parking tickets and are the bane of every Italian driver's existence (except in Sicily, since they are all corrupt), are at Via Dogali 29 (Viale Leonardo da Vinci; ☎ 091/6954111).

Internet Points Internet spots are few and far between in Palermo, and most of them are quite expensive (at least 5€/hour): **Internet Café,** Via Candelai (☎ 091/327151; Tues–Sun 7pm–late **Aboriginal Internet Café,** Via Spinuzza 51 (☎ 091/6622229; daily 11am–11pm; **Palazzo Ziino,** Via Dante 53 (☎ 091/5407621; Tues–Sun 9am–7pm); **Villa Trabia,** Via Salinas 3 (library in the garden of Villa Trabia, Viale della Libertà; free Internet access for 1hr. with reservation; ☎ 091/ 7405943; daily 9am–2pm and 3–7pm).

Post Office The main **post office** is on Via Roma 320 (☎ 091/7535193). You cannot miss it—it is a massive building from the Fascist period. Opening hours are Monday to Saturday 8am to 6pm. If you only need stamps you can buy them at the *tabaccerie*, but why miss out an experience at an Italian post office? (We are being sarcastic.)

A BRIEF HISTORY OF *LA COSA NOSTRA*

In Sicily, they don't call it the Mafia (from the Arabic *mu'afah,* or "protection"). They call it *Cosa Nostra,* literally "our thing," but, more accurately, "this thing we have." Its origins are debated, but the world's most famed criminal organization seemed to grow out of the convergence of local agricultural overseers working for absentee Bourbon landowners—hired thugs, from the peasant workers' point of view.

Members of the Sicilian Mafia (or "Men of Honor," as they like to be called) traditionally operated as a network of regional bosses who controlled individual towns by setting up puppet regimes of thoroughly corrupt officials. It was a sort of devil's bargain with the national Christian Democrat party, which controlled Italy's government from World War II until 1993 and, despite its law-and-order rhetoric, tacitly left *Cosa Nostra* alone as long as the bosses got out the party vote.

The *Cosa Nostra* trafficked in illegal goods, of course, but until the 1960s and 1970s, its income was derived mainly from low-level protection rackets, funneling state money into its own pockets, and ensuring that public contracts were granted to fellow *mafiosi* (all reasons why Sicily has experienced grotesque unchecked industrialization and modern growth at the expense of its heritage and the good of its communities). But the younger generation of Mafia underbosses got into the highly lucrative heroin and cocaine trades in the 1970s, transforming the Sicilian Mafia into a world player on the international drug trafficking circuit—and raking in the dough. This ignited a clandestine Mafia war that, throughout the late 1970s and 1980s, generated headlines of bloody Mafia hits. The new generation was wiping out the old and turning the balance of power in their favor.

This situation gave rise to the first Mafia turncoats, disgruntled ex-bosses and rank-and-file stoolies who told their stories, first to police prefect Gen. Alberto Dalla Chiesa (assassinated 1982) and later to crusading magistrates Giovanni Falcone (slaughtered May 23, 1992) and Paolo Borsellino (murdered July 19, 1992), who staged the "maxitrials" of *mafiosi* that sent hundreds to jail. The magistrates' 1992 murders, especially, garnered public attention to the dishonorable methods that defined the new Mafia and, perhaps for the first time, began to stir true shame. (Palermo's Punta Raisi airport was redubbed Falcone-Borsellino in honor of the two fallen *mafioso*-catchers.)

On a broad and culturally important scale, it is these young *mafiosi*, without a moral center or check on their powers, who have driven many Sicilians to at least secretly break the unwritten code of *omertà*, which translates as "homage" but means "silence," when faced with harboring or even tolerating a "man of honor." The Mafia still exists in Palermo, the small towns south of it, and the provincial capitals of Catania, Trapani, and Agrigento. Throughout the rest of Sicily, its power has been slipping. Construction schemes and protection money were one thing; the heroin trade is another game entirely, and the Mafia is swiftly outliving its usefulness and its welcome.

Even in Palermo, the grip of *Cosa Nostra* is loosening. In the closing days of 2000, the city hosted a United Nations conference on combating organized crime. Palermo's mayor, Leoluca Orlando, proclaimed that his fragile city is "battling a great evil" and paid homage at the conference to those who died fighting the Mafia. As local officials have worked to fight the *mafiosi* and their corruption and stifling of Sicilian society, their efforts have been hailed as a Palermo renaissance.

Today civic groups and schools are conducting programs to help people, especially young Sicilians, to aid in loosening the stronghold of the *Cosa Nostra.* We never thought we'd see it in Sicily, but the **Museo Civico di Palazzo Provenzano,** Via Orfanotrofio 7, Centro di Cultura Polivalente (☎ **091/8464907**), operates in the village of Corleone, outside Palermo. (The village is a 1-hr. bus ride from Palermo on Gallo transport. For information on this bus service call ☎ **091/6171141,** with a one-way ticket costing 4.20€.) Corleone, of course, is a name familiar to all *Godfather* fans. It was depicted as the home of Salvatore Rina, the "boss of all bosses." Rina lived here for nearly a quarter of a century, as Italy's most wanted man. Much of the museum's exhibits consist of photographs documenting Mafia atrocities. Admission is free, and the museum is open Tuesday to Sunday 9am to 1pm and 3:30 to 6:30pm.

Palermo Neighborhoods

→ **Quattro Canti**   Palermo isn't the easiest place to get your bearings in, and since it is changing quickly there is no one fixed *centro.* Try to find a map as soon as you can (hotels often have free maps, if not, ask at the tourist office), but to understand the layout of the city there is one very helpful key: start off at Quattro Canti, where the city's two major thoroughfares Via Maqueda and Corso Vittorio Emanuele cross each other. This crossing was built in the 1600s and was inspired by the baroque Piazza Quattro Fontane in Rome. Each corner has three levels of decoration: the inferior level has four sculptures representing the four seasons, surrounded by Doric columns. The second level has four statues of Spanish monarchs in between Ionic columns, and the third level represents the four saints that protect the four quarters of the city divided by the crossing, flanked by Corinthian columns.

→ **The Kalsa**   Beneath the dirty façades of Palermo, the city is more romantic and glamorous than one can imagine. There are sumptuous palaces, churches with gold mosaics, and romantic gardens. **La Kalsa** (from the Arabic *Al Halisah,* meaning "the elect," "the pure," since this was the fortress and seaside residence of the emirs during the Muslim occupation) is the oldest and most interesting part of the city. (It's bounded by the port and Via Garibaldi and Via Paternostro to the east and west, and by Corso Vittorio Emanuele and Via Lincoln to the north and south; one of its main thoroughfares is **Via Butero.**) Much of the Arabs' work was destroyed when the Spanish viceroys took over, adding their own architectural interpretations; even worse, the Kalsa was pummeled during the

Allied air raid on May 9, 1943, and much of the zone is still in ruins. Just walking through the Kalsa, however, a casual observer can see that things are happening and that some of the dilapidated houses are being beautifully restored. Even though many people living in the Kalsa share their homes with ruins, hens, dogs, and poverty, this is the part of the city where you can experience the real Palermo. Beauty and ugliness go hand in hand, and that is what makes the Kalsa so authentic.

At the center of the Kalsa is **Piazza Marina,** one of the most romantic squares in Palermo. It's called "Marina" because the port of La Cala was here, but it silted up in the 1100s. In the middle of the piazza, the Garibaldi garden (1863) has enormous *ficus magnolide* trees (like gigantic magnolias) and a sultry look that reminds you of the American Deep South. Prestigious buildings from the Renaissance and baroque periods surround the piazza.

One of the most interesting buildings is **Palazzo Chiaromonte,** today part of the university, but during 1601 it served as the tribunal of execution; where the Garibaldi garden is today was the execution yard where convicts' heads were chopped off. One of the neighborhood's most dramatic churches (though not necessarily the oldest) is the fancifully baroque **Santa Teresa,** Piazza della Kalsa (☎ 091/6171658). This church is open only for services, although you can admire it from the outside. If it should happen to be open at the time of your visit, you can see an interior designed by Giacomo Amato (1643–1732). He is known for introducing Roman high baroque to Palermo, of which Santa Teresa is the most classic example. If it's open, you can visit the luminous interior to see impressive stuccoes of Giuseppe and Procopio Serpotta.

Another of the old town's most intriguing antique churches lies only a 5-minute walk northwest of Santa Teresa: the 13th-century **San Francesco d'Assisi** (☎ 091/6162819).

To reach it, begin at the Quattro Canti di Città and walk eastward along **Corso Vittorio Emanuele.** Cross over bustling Via Roma, and then turn right onto Via Paternostro until you reach the church on Piazza San Francesco d'Assisi. Visit the church, if for no other reason than to see its magnificent Cappella Mastrotonio, carved in 1468. Don't count on the church being open, however.

From Piazza San Francesco d'Assisi, follow Via Merlo to the **Palazzo Mirto** ★★, Via Merlo 2 (☎ **091/6164751**), to see how nobility lived in the days when this was an upmarket neighborhood. The palace, a splendid example of a princely residence of the early 20th century, contains its original 18th- and 19th-century furnishings. It's open Monday to Saturday 9am to 7pm, and Sunday 9am to 1pm. Admission is free.

➜ **Via Maqueda up to Viale della Libertà** The main historical street in Palermo is **Via Maqueda** ★, which starts at Teatro Massimo and ends at the train station. The traffic on this street never ends. And during the afternoons the narrow sidewalks are packed with people. There are eight zillion small shops along this street, most of them sell the same stuff, but it is worth taking a look because you can always find a leather handbag or shoes for a pretty low price! Crossing Via Maqueda is Via dei Candelai, once filled with small shops where they made candles. Today there is nothing much to see during daytime, but it fills up at night. Continuing on Via Maqueda, and walking past the Teatro Massimo★, you will soon arrive at the Politeama Theater★. These two theaters were built at the end of the 19th century, and both are excellent examples of Art Nouveau architecture. When it was built, Teatro Massimo was the biggest theater in Europe, hence its name. Walking up Via Maqueda, before reaching the Politeama Theater, you will come to **Via Principe di Belmonte,** one of the very few pedestrianized streets in Palermo. This "living room" of the city becomes overcrowded by well-dressed Palermitani on Saturday and Sunday afternoons.

The most glamorous part of Palermo would be the area around **Viale della Libertà** ★, which feels like a Parisian boulevard with residential buildings in Art Nouveau style and gardens along the sidewalks. If you are not interested in designer shops, there is not very much to see on this street besides the pretty buildings. You can go for a stroll down Viale della Libertà to the parks of Giardino Inglese or Villa Trabia, perfect spots to bring a picnic and take a break.

Sleeping

In August, when beach vacationers have to crash in Palermo before their morning flights back to the mainland, try to book your rooms at least a few days in advance.

CHEAP

➜ **Albergo Sausele** ★ This family-run inn stands out amid the depressing rail-station-area hotels. It boasts high ceilings, globe lamps, strikingly clean floors, modern art, and new wooden modular furnishings. The staff is hospitable, as is the resident St. Bernard named Eva. Rooms on the street can be noisy, so light sleepers should request one overlooking the peaceful courtyard. Rooms with shower-only bathrooms are certainly small and modest but are a pleasant choice. What makes this place special are the handcrafted and antique artifacts from around the world, collected by Giacomo Sausele in his travels. *Via Vincenzo Errante 12, 90127 Palermo. ☎ 091/6161308. www.hotelsausele. it. Double 90€, triple 123€. Rates include breakfast.*

➜ **Hotel Moderno** ★ One of the city's best cost-conscious overnight options lies on the third and fourth floors of a stately looking building that's among the grandest in its busy and highly congested neighborhood. Don't expect the same kind of grandeur inside that you'll see on the building's neoclassical exterior: You'll take a cramped elevator to the third-floor reception area, then proceed to your clean but very simple bedroom, which will be on either the building's third floor or the fourth. Each has a tiled bathroom with shower, lots of artwork, and not a great deal of direct sunlight. If you make a reservation here, be sure to reconfirm and double-reconfirm (especially if you're arriving in the evening), as hotel staff has a way of "losing" late arrivals' reservations and selling the room to the nearest warm body. *Via Roma 276 (at corner of Via Napoli), 90133 Palermo.* ☎ *091/588683. Double 75€.*

➜**Il Laboratorio** ★★ A B&B and restaurant hidden in a 17th-century seaside building. There is only one room, so you have to make reservations *well* in advance. But it is absolutely worth it—you have a view over the sea, the place is crazily decorated with antique ceramics, and it's cheap! One couple came here to spend a weekend but ended up staying for 3 weeks. The restaurant is open for dinner Thursday through Saturday and serves a fixed menu of traditional Sicilian food from 35€ per person. *Via Butera 1 (Via Alloro, towards the sea).* ☎ *091/327651. Double room 90€*

DOABLE

➜**Joli Hotel** ★★ A little hotel for couples, away from the heavy traffic but still only a few steps from culture and shopping. The building has been recently restored in a picturesque and romantic way, with frescoes on the ceiling and elegant furniture throughout the property. There is a large terrace with a wonderful view over Piazza Ignazio, where you can have your morning cappuccino or your afternoon tea. *Via Michele Amari 11 (Piazza Ignazio Florio).* ☎ *091/6111766. www.hoteljoli.com. Double 90€.*

➜**La Dimora del Genio** ★★ Most of the hotels and B&Bs are found in other parts of the city; this is one of the few that's in the most interesting part of Palermo, the Kalsa. Set in a building from the 15th century, the "Genius's Pad" is a palacelike apartment with only four rooms (all with private bathrooms). *Via Garibaldi 58 (not far from the station).* ☎ *347/6587664 (cellphone). www.ladimoradelgenio.it. No credit cards. Double from 110€*

SPLURGE

➜**Palazzo Ajutamicristo** ★★★ An extraordinary B&B (its name means "help me Christ") with only two small bedrooms in a stunning, endearingly romantic 15th-century palazzo. The building is a famous heritage site, where some scenes of *Il Gattopardo* (with Burt Lancaster and Alain Delon) were shot. Guests are free to wander in the loggia and on the magnificent garden terrace. If you are not a royal or your parents are not very important political figures, however, it might be difficult to get one of the rooms. (But as Paris Hilton says—if you are not born into a rich or important family, lie about who you are.) *Via Garibaldi 23 (not far from Stazione Centrale).* ☎ *091/6161894. www.palazzo-ajutamicristo.com. Price on request.*

➜**Ucciardhome** ★★ This is a small, exclusive, and super-chic hotel where you will find yourself in the company of businessmen and fashionista Milanese couples. Staying at this hotel will mean abandoning your picturesque image of Sicily and finding yourself in a place more typical of London or New York. All rooms are large with big windows, terraces, or balconies. The bathrooms are decorated with mosaics and the rooms with designer furniture. *Via Enrico Albanese 34 (close to the Giardino Inglese).* ☎ *091/348-426. www.hotelucciardhome.com. Double room from 150€.*

➜**Villa Igiea Grand Hotel** ★★★ The Villa Igiea was built in the early 1900s as one of Sicily's aristocratic estates, and today it's a fabulous place to pull Daddy's credit card out. Set in gardens on the sea, the hotel is lovely if you're going to spend time sunning and relaxing. But if you're looking for a base for seeing the city, town is a 15-minute taxi ride away. The structure resembles a medieval Sicilian fortress, with crenellated battlements and watchtowers. A circular temple, buttressed with modern scaffolding, still stands in the garden. Everywhere are clusters of antiques. The guest rooms vary from sumptuous suites with terraces to smaller, less glamorous rooms, many a bit worn and faded. The bathrooms have aging but still functional plumbing. The hotel is reached by passing through an industrial area north of Palermo. *Salita Belmonte 43, Acquasanta, 90142 Palermo.* ☎ *091/6312111. www.cormorano.net/sgas/villaigiea. Double 163€–424€, suite 421€–584€. Rates include breakfast.*

Eating

If you are feeling brave, you should try the typical food cooked and sold on the street, especially in the food markets. The star of this kind of street food is the *stigghiola,* which is a lovely compote of intestines of lamb and veal, chopped and fried together. Then there is *pane con milza,* that is, chopped spleen of lamb served in a bread roll with cheese on top. *Sfincione* is a typical Palermitan pizza with tomatoes, anchovies, onion, and grated cheese. If you are vegetarian or just disgusted, you can try *pane e panelle,* chickpea fritter sandwiches, and *cazzilli* or *quaglie,* cardoon, artichokes, or cauliflower deep-fried in batter. Other Sicilian snacks are the *arancini,* deep-fried rice balls with mozzarella or meat inside. The best *arancini* in town are at the Antico Caffè Spinnato.

CHEAP

➜ **Shanghai** ★★ This little, very ugly restaurant lies in the middle of the Vuccria market. It is not a Chinese restaurant, as the name suggests. As the owner explains, the restaurant has been given its Oriental name because of the view from here. Sitting on the terrace during the day, watching the market life play out before you, you feel like you're in the Far East. Don't let the unattractive entrance throw you off; once inside, you will be served great food for a very low price! At night, the piazza is filled with pot-smoking Palmeritan youth waiting for you to come out and join them. *Vicolo Mezzani 34 (Vucciria).* ☎ *091/589702.*

DOABLE

➜ **Antico Caffé Spinnato** ★ BAR/CAFE If you want to eat a light lunch, or try the best *cassata* in Palermo, you should go here. This bar and cafe is situated on the only pedestrian street in the city. During the weekend it is full of Palermitans with Gucci bags having a lunch *aperitivo* after their shopping tour— join them at Itlay's "Caffe of the Year (2005)"! *Via Principe di Belmonte 107/115.* ☎ *091/329229. www.spinnato.com. Pastries 1€–3€, platters 3€–12€. Daily 7–1am.*

➜ **Antica Focacceria San Francesco** ★★★ SICILIAN This is the best all-around dining bet in Palermo. Everyone who has been here loves it, from tourists to born-and-bred Palermo locals. A friend of mine ate breakfast, lunch, and dinner here the 3 days she spent in Palermo and never once got tired of it. You can eat in the fancier part upstairs with a view over the piazza, or take a simpler table by the entrance, or just order takeaway. All the traditional local dishes are represented, such as *sfincione, pane con milza,* focaccias, and the legendary pasta with sardines and fennel. For less adventurous palates, you can also choose from a wide range of pastas and entrees *not* made with questionable animal parts or fishy-fish. *Via Alessandro Paternostro 58 (Piazza San Francesco).* ☎ *091/320264. www.afsf.it. Sandwiches 3€–5€, pastas 4.50€–6€. Wed–Mon 9am–4pm and 5:30pm–midnight.*

➜ **Mi manda Picone** ★★ WINE BAR Next door to the Foccaceria San Francesco

SICILY

lies this wine bar and restaurant that is perfect for informal dinners. It is small and family-run, and always filled with couples or groups of friends. *Via Alessandro Paternostro 59 (Piazza San Francesco).* ☎ *091/6160660. Platters 8€–13€, wine 3.50€–7.50€ per glass. Mon–Sat 7pm–1am.*

Partying

Around the Piazza Olivella, in between Via Maqueda and Via Roma, lies a handful of small and cozy small places where you can have your *aperitivo* or come after dinner for a long drink and listen to live music. You'll pay from 2€–8€ for a glass of wine, depending on how fancy the place is; 4€ or 5€ for a beer, and 5€ on up for a cocktail in most places.

➔ **Cortile Patania** ★ This is a place where you can spend your whole afternoon if you want. It is relaxing and comfortable with sofas around the tables and if you are into backgammon, there's that, too. The hip factor is not high, but it could be nice just being your uncool self for a moment, could it not? On Wednesday a vegetarian buffet is served from 8pm, on Thursdays they have live jazz music after dinner, and on Sundays they serve American brunch. *Via G. Patania 34 (Piazza Olivella).* ☎ *091/7434772. Tues–Sun until 3am.*

➔ **I Candelai** ★★ Off Via Maqueda you will find Via dei Candelai, which is totally abandoned during the daytime. But after dinner this road is chock-full of students and other young locals, who throng the pubs here every night. The sweet smell of pot smoke lies as heavy on this street as the smog on Via Maqueda. I Candelai is one of the most popular dance and live music clubs in Palermo—on Fridays and Sundays, the place becomes a crowded complex packed with gyrating 20-year-olds. *Via dei Candelai 65 (Via Maqueda).* ☎ *091/327151. www.candelai.it. Fri–Sat 8pm–no set closing time. Cover 4€–10€.*

➔ **I Grilli** ★★ This is one of the best hangouts in Palermo, and there are cute bartenders, to boot! They have a pretty good *aperitivo* buffet with different kinds of pizza sliced up into tiny pieces. After dinner the DJ plays house music and on Fridays and Saturdays there is live jazz music. *Largo Cavalieri di Malta 11 (next to the church of San Domenico).* ☎ *091/6111243. Tues–Sun until 3am.*

➔ **Kursaal Kalhesa** A book shop, coffee shop, wine bar, and restaurant with a garden outside. During the evening the garden fills up with young intellectuals that use literature conversations as an excuse to drink wine. (Kind of like Oprah's Book Club goes to Sicily . . .) The place is decorated with some very impressive architecture. *Foro Italico (Umberto I) 21.* ☎ *091/6162111. www.kursaalkalhesa.it. Tues–Sat 11:30am–1:30am; Sun 6:30pm–1:30am.*

➔ **LúLú Bar** ★ The cooler neighbor of Cortile Patania. It will be empty before dinner, but after dinner, and especially on Saturdays and Sundays, the young and hot people from Palermo come here to drink and listen to music. There's live music on Sunday nights. *Via San Basilio 37 (Piazza Olivella).* ☎ *333/7851373. Open Wed–Mon until 3am.*

Sightseeing

The "four corners" of the city, the **Quattro Canti di Città** ★, is in the heart of the old town, at the junction of Corso Vittorio Emanuele and Via Maqueda. The ruling Spanish of the 17th century influenced the design of this grandiose baroque square, replete with fountains and statues. From here you can walk to **Piazza Bellini** ★, the most attractive square.

Opening onto this square is **Santa Maria dell'Ammiraglio (La Martorana),** which was erected in 1143. Also fronting the square is **San Cataldo** (1160), in the Arab-Byzantine style. Here, too, is the late-16th-century

Santa Caterina, attached to a vast Dominican monastery constructed in 1310. The church contains interesting 18th-century multicolored marble ornamentation.

Adjoining the square is **Piazza Pretoria,** dominated by a fountain designed in Florence in 1554 for a villa but acquired by Palermo about 20 years later. A short walk will take you to **Piazza di Cattedrale** and the Duomo.

MTV **Best** → **The Capuchin Crypt (Catacombe dei Cappuccini)** ★★★ The elderly monk who watches over the site will greet you as he gestures toward the cool and dark stairway that leads to the crypt. And what a crypt it is!! It feels more like the set for *Night of the Living Dead* or Michael Jackson's "Thriller" than a religious environment. No horror movie or haunted house can compete with this crypt filled with thousands of bodies dressed up to their toes and suspended by hooks on the walls. The bodies, in various levels of decay, stare down at you and look like they are ready to grab you! The crypt dates back to 1599, when the local priests mummified a holy monk for all to see. In time the locals decided that they wanted their relatives remembered in this same way. Soon there were hundreds of corpses. Some of the deceased wrote wills, specifying the clothes in which they wanted to be buried. Some dandies even went so far as to ask to have their outfits changed from time to time! If you are not so freaked out by this that you neglect to read the signs, you'll see that the crypt is divided into categories: Men, Women, Virgins, Children, Priests, Monks, and Professionals. The Professionals Hall includes writers, lawyers, and at least one American. As you leave, you can purchase some freaky postcards of your favorite corpses from the crypt. You can always send them to people you hate. Otherwise, visitors to the crypt shouldn't need souvenirs, as the weeklong nightmares should keep the memories fresh

in your mind for a long time. This is not a tour for the easily frightened. However, it is an absolute must for fans of horror movies, the macabre, and mummies, and, of course, morticians. *Piazza Cappuccini 1.* ☎ *091/212117. Tues–Sun 9am–noon and 3–5pm. Admission 2€.*

FREE → **Chiesa della Martorana/San Cataldo** ★★ This church, named for Eloisa Martorana, who in 1194 founded a nearby Benedictine convent, is worth a visit for its Byzantine mosaics. In 1143, the church was founded at the request of George of Antioch, an admiral in the fleet of Roger II. Today this Norman church is concealed behind a baroque façade. You enter through a portico-cum–bell tower that, although constructed free-standing, was connected to the church in the 1500s. The first two bays of the church were added in the 1500s and frescoed in the 1600s. The **mosaics** ★★ are stunning, created along strict Byzantine lines. Two panels evoke George of Antioch at the feet of the Madonna and Roger II receiving the crown from Christ. Other subjects depict a trio of Archangels (Gabriel, Raphael, and Michael) and, in the register below, eight prophets. *Piazza Bellini 2, adjacent to Piazza Pretoria.* ☎ *091/6161692. Free admission. La Martorana: Mon–Sat 9:30am–1pm and 3:30–6:30pm; Sun 8:30am–1pm. San Cataldo: Tues–Sat 9am–5pm; Sat–Sun 9am–1pm. Bus: 101 or 102.*

→ **Galleria Regionale della Sicilia** ★★★ This is the greatest gallery of regional art in Sicily and one of Italy's finest art galleries. It's in the **Palazzo Abatellis** ★, which is itself an architectural treasure, a Catalan-Gothic structure with a Renaissance overlay designed by Matteo Carnelivari in 1490. The superb collection of Sicilian sculpture and paintings shows the evolution of the arts in Sicily from the 13th to the 18th century. On the main floor sculpture predominates.

SICILY

Beyond room 2, the former chapel is dominated by the gallery's most celebrated work, the **Triumph of Death** ★★★, dating from 1449 and of uncertain attribution, although sometimes attributed to Pisanello. In all its gory magnificence, a horseback-riding skeleton, representing Death, tramples his victims. The second masterpiece of the gallery lies at the end of the corridor exhibiting Arabic ceramics in room 4, the white marble, slanty-eyed bust of **Eleanara di Aragona** ★★ or Eleanora of Aragon by Francesco Laurana, who created it in the 15th century. This was Laurana's masterpiece.

The second-floor galleries are filled mainly with paintings from the Sicilian school, including a spectacular **Annunciation** ★★, the creation of Antonello da Messina. This masterpiece of his hangs in room 11. In the salon of Flemish paintings rest the celebrated **Triptych of Malvagna** ★★ from 1510, the creation of Mabuse, whose real name was Jean Gossaert. *Piazza Olivella 24.* ☎ *091/6116805. Admission 4.50€. Tues–Sat 8:30am–6:15pm; Sun 9am–1pm. Bus: 101, 102, 103, 104, or 107.*

➜ **Il Duomo** ★★ East meets West in this curious spectacle of a cathedral. It was built in the 12th century on the foundation of an earlier basilica that had been converted into a mosque by the Arabs. The impressive Gothic "porch" on the southern front was built in the 15th century. But the cupola, added in the late 18th century, detracts from the overall appearance, and the interior was revamped at the same time, resulting in a glaring incongruity in styles. Graced with a Latin cross plan, the interior has a nave and two side aisles, divided by pillars. The only section that the restorers left alone were the **apses** ★, which still retain their impressive geometric design. The pantheon of royal tombs includes that of the Holy Roman Emperor Frederick II, in red porphyry under a canopy of marble. Visits are not allowed

during Masses. *Piazza di Cattedrale, Corso Vittorio Emanuele.* ☎ *091/334373. Duomo: free admission (donation appreciated); Crypt: 1€; treasury: 1€. Mon–Sat 8:30am–5:30pm. Bus: 103, 104, 108, 110, 118, or 139.*

➜ **Museo Archeologico Regionale** ★★★ This is one of the grandest archaeological museums in all Italy, stuffed with artifacts from prehistoric times until the Roman era. Spread over several buildings, the oldest from the 13th century, the museum's collection includes major Sicilian finds from the Phoenician, Punic, Greek, Roman, and Saracen periods, with several noteworthy treasures from Egypt. Even though some of the exhibitions appear shabby and the museum is definitely not state of the art, its treasures are worth wading through the dust. You pass through small **cloisters** ★ on the ground floor, centered around a lovely hexagonal 16th-century fountain bearing a statue of Triton. In room 3 is some rare Phoenician art, including a pair of sarcophagi in the shape of human beings that date from the 5th century B.C.

The most important pieces, in room 13, are the **metopes of Selinunte** ★★. These finds were unearthed at the temples of Selinunte, once one of the major cities of Magna Graecia. The Selinunte sculptures are remarkable for their beauty, casting a light on the brilliance of Siceliot sculpture in general.

In room 7 is found a remarkable and rare series of large Roman bronzes, including the most impressive, a supremely realistic **bronze Ram** ★★, a Hellenistic work from Syracuse. It's certainly worth the climb up the steps. Another notable work here is **Hercules Killing the Stag** ★, discovered at Pompeii, a Roman copy of a Greek original from the 3rd century B.C. In room 8 the most remarkable sculpture is **Satyr Filling a Drinking Cup** ★, a Roman copy of a Praxitelean original. *Piazza Olivella 24.*

☎ 091/6116805. Admission 4.50€. Tues–Sat 8:30am–6:15pm; Sun 9am–1pm. Bus: 101, 102, 103, 104, or 107.

FREE → **Oratory of the Rosary of St. Dominic (Oratorio del Rosario di San Domenico)** ★★★ Palermo's most splendid oratory is a gem of stucco decoration by Giacomo Serpotta (1652–1732), a romp of cherubs. Serpotta excelled in the use of marble and polychrome, but it was in stucco that he earned his greatest fame. He worked on this oratory, his masterpiece, from 1714 to 1717. Serpotta depicted the Joyful Mysteries of the Rosary, on the left and rear walls, although some of these are the work of Pietro Novelli. Themes throughout the oratory are wide-ranging, depicting a Flagellation to an Allegories of the Virtues. Serpotta also depicted scenes from the Apocalypse of St. John. Particularly graphic is a depiction of a writhing Devil falling from Heaven. At the high altar is a masterpiece by Anthony Van Dyck, *Madonna of the Rosary* (1628). Illustrating the Coronation of the Virgin, the ceiling was frescoed by Pietro Novelli. Because of ongoing restoration, visits are now extremely limited. *Via dei Bambinai.* ☎ 091/332779. Free admission. Mon 3–6pm; Tues–Fri 9am–1pm and 3–5:30pm; Sat 9am–1pm. Bus: 107.

→ **Palazzo dei Normanni** ★★ /**Cappella Palatina** ★★★ This is Palermo's greatest attraction and Sicily's finest treasure trove. Allow 1¹/₂ hours and visit this site if you have to skip all the rest. The history goes back to the days of the Arab emirs and their harems around the 9th century, but they in time abandoned the site. Discovered by the conquering Normans, the palace was restored and turned into a sumptuous residence. Today it is the seat of Sicily's semiautonomous regional government. If you enter from Piazza Indipendenza you'll be directed to the Cappella Palatina, representing the apex of the Arabo-Norman collective genius and built from 1130 to 1140 by Roger II when it was adorned with Byzantine mosaics. You'd have to travel to Istanbul or Ravenna to encounter mosaics such as this. The whole cycle constitutes the largest cycle of Islamic paintings to survive to the present day.

At the entrance to the nave is a royal throne encrusted in mosaics. Note the towering **Paschal Candelabrum** ★ carved with figures, wild animals, and acanthus leaves, a masterpiece that has come down from the 12th century. Covering the central nave is a honeycomb stalactite wooden **muqarnas ceiling** ★★, a masterpiece and the creation of Arab artisans brought in from North Africa. They depicted scenes from daily life, including animal hunts and dances. Expect tight security as you wander around the **Royal Apartments** ★★ above, because this is still a seat of government. On some days you may not gain entrance at all. When visits are possible, you enter Salone d'Ercole from 1560, the chamber of the Sicilian Parliament. (The guides are terribly obnoxious and do not know a word of English, but swallow your pride because it is the only way to see the palace.) The most intriguing room of the apartments is the Sala di Ruggero II, where King Roger himself slumbered. The room is decorated with 12th-century mosaics like the chapel just visited. *Piazza del Parlamento.* ☎ 091/7054317. Admission 5€. Mon–Sat 8:30am–noon and 2–5pm; Sun 8am–noon. Bus: 104, 105, 108, 109, 110, 118, 304, or 309.

MTV Best → **San Giovanni degli Eremiti** ★★ This is one of the most famous of all the Arabo-Norman monuments still standing in Palermo. It is certainly the most romantic building remaining from the heyday of Norman Palermo. It is on the western edge of the Albergheria district. Since 1132, this church with its series of five red domes has remained one of the most characteristic landmarks on the Palermo skyline. In an atmosphere appropriate for the recluse it honors, St. John of the Hermits (now deconsecrated), with its twin-columned cloister, is one of the most idyllic spots in Palermo. A medieval veil hangs heavy in the gardens, with their citrus blossoms and flowers, especially on a hot summer day as you wander around in the cloister. A single nave divides the simple interior into two bays, surmounted by a dome. A small cupola surmounts the presbytery. The right-hand apse is covered by one of the red domes. Surrounding the left-hand apse is a bell tower with pointed windows, and it too is crowned by one of the church's smallest red domes. The small late **Norman cloister** ★, with a Moorish cistern in the center, was part of the original Benedictine monastery that once stood here. The cloister is a blessed oasis of calm in Palermo and is one of the best make-out spots in town. (So, find yourself a cute young monk, and get busy!) *Via dei Benedettini 3.* ☎ *091/6515019. Admission 4.50€, 2€ students. Mon–Sat 9am–1pm and 3–7pm; Sun 9am–1pm. Bus: 109 or 318.*

FREE → **Santa Cita/Oratorio del Rosario di Santa Cita** ★★★ The oratory is a far greater artistic treasure than the church. The church that stood here in 1943 when Allied bombs rained down on it had itself been rebuilt between 1586 and 1603. Only a glimmer of its former self, it still contains a lovely marble **chancel arch** ★ by Antonello Gagini. Look for it in the presbytery. Gagini from 1517 to 1527 created other sculptures in the church but they are damaged. In the second chapel left of the choir is a sarcophagus of Antonio Scirotta, also the creation of Gagini. To the right of the presbytery is the lovely **Capella del Rosario** ★, with its polychrome marquetry and intricate stucco work that's like lace. The sculpted reliefs here are by Gioacchino Vitaliano. On the left side of the church is the oratory, the real reason to visit. The oratory is entered through the church. It was the crowning achievement of Giacomo Serpotta, who worked on it between 1686 and 1718. Serpotta was the leading baroque decorator of his day.

His cherubs and angels romp with abandon, a delight as they climb onto the window frames or spread garlands in their path. They can also be seen sleeping, eating, or hugging their knees deep in thought. *Via Valverde 3.* ☎ *091/332779. Free admission (donation appreciated). Mon–Fri 9am–noon. Bus: 107.*

MTV Best FREE → **Santa Maria dello Spasimo** ★ This amazing Gothic church was almost completely destroyed, together with everything else in the Kalsa quarter, during World War II. What remains is a gigantic shell without a roof, with two trees growing inside. The church is now open as a cultural attraction, but in the past it has served as a theater, a hospital, a warehouse, and a garbage dump. According to legend, the Renaissance painter Raphael was commissioned to create a *Madonna dello Spasimo* for this church, but the boat delivering the painting sank on its way to Sicily. The painting was miraculously saved and was sent to the court of Spain. Today it hangs in the Prado museum. *Via dello Spasimo 35. Free.*

→ **Villa Malfitano** ★★ One of Palermo's great villas, built in the Liberty style, lies in a spectacular garden. The villa was built in 1886 by Joseph Whitaker, grandson of the famous English gentleman and wine merchant Ingham, who moved to Sicily in 1806 and made a fortune producing marsala wine. Whitaker arranged to have trees shipped to Palermo from all over the world, and he planted them around his villa. These included such rare species as Dragon's Blood, an enormous banyan tree that is the only example found in Europe. High society in Palermo flocked here for lavish parties, and royalty from Great Britain visited. The villa today is lavishly furnished, with antiques and artifacts from all over the world. The *Sala d'Estate* (Summer Room) is particularly stunning, with *trompe l'oeil* frescoes covering both the walls and the ceiling. *Via Dante 167.* ☎ *091/6816133. Admission 6€. Mon–Sat 9am–1pm. Bus: 103, 106, 108, 122, 134, 164, or 824.*

For Some Modern Art: Expa & KalsArt

Expa Galleria dell'Architettura is a new cultural space dedicated to contemporary architecture and design. Expa (which stands for exhibition in Palermo) is in the atmospheric old stables of the late-Gothic Palazzo Cefalà; how the defunct structures have been reclaimed and made into a forum for modern art and architecture is a fascinating example of the urban rebirth.

From July to September Expa organizes a range of very hip cultural happenings in the Kalsa under the name **Kals'Art.** The festival features art exhibitions, performances, music, and experimental art. Scuderie di Palazzo Cefalà. Via Alloro 97. ☎ **091/617-0319.** www.expa.org.

→ **The Zisa** ★★ **The Cuba** ★ These fortresslike buildings were constructed under the Norman king William I, both by workers from the Islamic school of architecture. They were closely connected to surrounding parks. The most important hall of **The Zisa** (from the Arabic word *aziz,* or "splendor") is called Sala della Fontana and is magnificently decorated and contains a fountain, canal, and basins into which the water flows. Of the 12th-century **Cuba,** all that remains are the external walls with their giant arches. The interior is made up of only one floor and organized around a central space with a fountain. *Castello Zisa: Piazza Guglielmo il Buono. ☎ 091/6520269. Mon–Sat 9am–6:30pm; Sun 9am–1pm. The Cuba: Corso Calatafimi 100. ☎ 091/5900299. Mon–Sat 9am–6:30pm; Sun 9am–1pm. Admission: The Zisa 3€, and the Cuba 2€.*

Shopping

We love shopping, but we never waste our time in Palermo on boutique-hopping—there is so much else to do and see! There is nothing here that you cannot buy in other cities, but if you must, there are three main streets for shopping: Via Maqueda, Via Roma, and Via della Libertà. Via Maqueda is full of small, inexpensive shops that all sell the same stuff: tops and jeans decorated with sequins

Walking over to Via Roma, you will find the bigger shops like Max & Co, Benetton, Sisley, etc. On Via della Libertà, the more exclusive shops include Chanel, MaxMara, and Louis Vuitton, among others. Giglio on Via della Libertà 44 sells all designer clothes under one roof. For unique pieces of interior design and clothing, check out **Officine Achab 9,** in the Kalsa at Via Alloro 13 (☎ **091/6161849;** Mon–Sat 9am–1pm and 4–7:30pm).

STREET MARKETS

As we've mentioned before, no physical remains of Palermo's Islamic period are preserved, but if you want to take a magic carpet ride back in time, just visit the MTV Best **street markets.** Today, the markets still preserve their souklike Arab features in their customs of selling and buying (i.e., howling in a burlesque way), colors, odors, and sheer density of vendors' stands!

The three large historical markets are Vucciria, Capo, and Ballarò. The **Vucciria** ★★, whose name comes from the French *boucherie* ("butcher's shop"), runs from Via Argenteria to Piazza Garraffello. Navigating the yelps of the eager vendors, you can find meat, vegetables, fruit, and fresh fish at the Vucciria. The smells are overpowering yet indescribable since they're all mixed together. The Vucciria at sunset is quite a photogenic spectacle: huge sparkling lamps illuminate every counter, casting light on the meat, tuna fish, and olives. The painter Renato Guttuso describes the life of the market in his famous painting *La Vucciria* (1974).

The market of **Ballarò** ★★ runs from Piazza Casa Professa to Corso Tukory and is the most visited market by residents of

Taking a Break . . . and a Bath

Take a half-day off from the traffic and the chaos, and walk into harmony and stillness of a **Turkish bath** ★★. During the Muslim years, the city was full of *hammam*, or Turkish baths. Today there is just one (newly opened), next to the Politeama Theater. Baths and treatment rooms are soothingly lit, with slabs of white and gray marble kept warm by the presence of steam. Services offered include steam bath with soaps from Morocco, peeling treatments, and Jacuzzi hydro-massage. Massages (with actual massage therapists, as opposed to the water-jet tubs) should be booked at least 2 days in advance. The hammam is open Monday to Saturday from 10am to 11pm, last entry at 9pm. The hammam is open to the ladies on odd-numbered days; while even-numbered days are reserved for men. Entrance to the hammam costs 30€; massage and other special treatments cost extra. Via Torrearsa 17 D. ☎ 091/320783. www. hammam.pa.it.

Palermo. **Il Capo** begins where Via Carini and Via Beati Paoli meet. This is also a lively food market, although less abundant than the Vucciria or Ballarò. The markets are open all day, but if you come in midday, you run the risk of finding many stands deserted as vendors have left for a long lunch break.

Day Trips from Palermo

Monreale: Stunning Mosaics

The town of Monreale is 10km (6¼ miles) from Palermo, up Monte Caputo and on the edge of the Conca d'Oro plain. In Palermo, take bus no. 389, departing from Piazza Indipendenza, which drops you off at Monreale's Piazza Vittorio Emanuele 40 minutes later, depending on traffic. During the day, three buses per hour leave for Monreale, costing 1€ one-way.

The Normans under William II founded a Benedictine monastery at Monreale in the 1170s. Eventually a great cathedral was built near the monastery's ruins. Like the Alhambra in Granada, Spain, the **Chiostro del Duomo di Monreale** ★★, Piazza Guglielmo il Buono (☎ 091/6404413), has a relatively drab façade, but the interior is virtually bedazzled with shimmering mosaics of biblical scenes—some of the most spectacular anywhere in Italy. The mosaics have a definite Eastern look despite the Western-style robed Christ reigning over his kingdom.

On the north and west façades are two bronze doors depicting biblical stories in relief. Located next to the cathedral, the splendid cloister is enough to make Monreale famous, with 228 spiral columns inlaid with mosaic tiles. Admission to the cathedral is free; if you visit the cloisters, there's a charge of 4.50€. The cathedral is open daily 8am to 6pm. From May to September, the cloister is open daily 8am to 6pm. October to April it is open daily 8am to 12:30pm and 3:30 to 6pm.

You can also visit the **treasury** for 2.05€, and the **terraces**, 1.55€. They're open daily 9:30am to 12:30pm and 3:30 to 5:30pm. The terraces are actually the rooftop of the church, from which you'll be rewarded with a view of the cloisters.

Before or after your visit to Monreale, drop in at **Bar Italia,** Piazza Vittorio Emanuele (☎ 091/6402421), near the Duomo. The plain cookies are wonderfully flavorful and fresh; if you go early in the morning, order one of the freshly baked croissants and a cup of cappuccino, Monreale's best.

Cefalú: a Picturesque Fishing Village

Another good day-trip destination lies 81km (50 miles) east of Palermo, where the fishing village of **Cefalù** ★★ is tucked onto every inch of a spit of land underneath an awesome crag called the *Rocca* (fortress). The village is known for its Romanesque cathedral, an outstanding achievement of Arab-Norman architecture (see below). Its beaches, its medley of architectural styles, and its narrow streets were captured in the Oscar-winning *Cinema Paradiso*. An appropriate location for such a movie, Cefalù is a little paradise all its own. Although it has become a well-known vacation spot, in part due to the nearby Club Med, the town's *centro storico* retains its old-world appeal.

Female travelers should be mindful of the aggressive, yet totally harmless, local men—they can be intensely curious about foreign visitors. You can tour the town in half a day and spend the rest of the time enjoying life on the beach.

GETTING THERE

From Palermo, 36 **trains** make the 1-hour trip daily, costing 4€ one-way. For information and schedules in Palermo, call ☎ **892021. SAIS,** Via Balsamo 20 (☎ **091/6171141**), runs **buses** between Palermo and Cefalù, costing from 4.20€ one-way for the 1¹⁄₂-hour trip. If you're **driving,** follow Route 113 east from Palermo to Cefalù. Driving time is about 1¹⁄₂ hours. You'll have to park at the top of the Rocca and then join lines of visitors walking up and down the narrow, steep streets near the water. You'll pass a lot of forgettable shops. In the past few years, it seems that half of the denizens of Cefalù have become trinket peddlers and souvenir hawkers.

You'll find the **tourist office** at Corso Ruggero 77 (☎ **0921/421050**), open Monday

Mondello Lido

The City's Beach Retreat

When the summer sun burns hot, and when old men on the square seek a place in the shade and bambini tire of their toys, it's beach weather. For Palermo residents, that means **Mondello,** 12km (7½ miles) east. Before this beachfront town started attracting the wealthy of Palermo, it was a fishing village (and still is), and you can see rainbow-colored fishing boats bobbing in the harbor. A good sandy beach stretches for about 2.4km (1½ miles), and it's filled to capacity on a July or August day. Some women traveling alone find Mondello more inviting and less intimidating than Palermo. In summer, an express **bus** (no. 6, "Beallo") goes to Mondello from the train station in Palermo.

to Saturday 8am to 2pm and 3:30 to 7:30pm, and Sunday 9am to 1pm.

SIGHTSEEING

Make a beeline to Cefalù's Duomo first thing in the morning so that you can avoid the tour bus hordes. Resembling a military fortress, the **Duomo** ★★, Piazza del Duomo, off Corso Ruggero (☎ **0921/922021**), was built by Roger II to fulfill a vow he'd made when faced with a possible shipwreck. Construction began in 1131, and, in time, two square towers rose, curiously placed between the sea and a rocky promontory. The architectural line of the cathedral boasts a severe elegance that has earned it a position in many art history books. The interior, which took a century to complete, overwhelms you with 16 Byzantine and Roman columns supporting towering capitals. The horseshoe arches are one of the island's best examples of the Saracen influence on Norman architecture. The celebrated **mosaic** ★ of *Christ the Pantocrator*, one of

Sleeping in an Art Installation on the Sicilian Sea

If you are into modern art and architecture, you need to check out the **Atelier Sul Mare** ★★, a museum-cum-hotel in the tiny fishing village of Castel di Tusa, about 1 hour from Palermo by train. Every room is a life-sized diorama that has been dreamed up by international artists and design teams. The rooms don't have numbers but instead names like *The Prophet: Homage to Pier Paolo Pasolini* or *On a Paper Boat I Set Sail* and each has a fully conceptualized theme—the sea outside, seen from big panoramic windows, is the only proof of your basic world outside; the rest of your furnishings are the physical manifestations of an artist's vision. Note that this is not the most comfortable or luxurious place you'll ever stay—hey, cushions get in the way of the *concept,* man—but how many chances in life will you get to sleep inside an art installation? If a night in one of the "art rooms" proves to be a bit intense, you can break away and take a morning swim on the beach outside the hotel, where the water is crystal clear. After a night and morning here, head back Palermo or Cefalù, since there's not much else to do in Tusa. Via Cesare Battisti, 4, Castel sul Mare. ☎ **0921/334295.** www.ateliersulmare.com. "Art rooms" from 80€ per person per night, "standard" rooms from 60€ per person per night.

only three on Sicily, in the dome of the cathedral apse is alone worth the trip. The nearby mosaic of the *Virgin with Angels and the Apostles* is a well-preserved work from 1148. In the transept is a statue of the Madonna. Roger's plan to have a tomb placed in the Duomo was derailed by the authorities at Palermo's cathedral, where he rests today. Admission is free, and the church is open daily 8am to noon and 3:30 to 7pm. In the off season it is open daily 8am to noon and 3:30 to 6pm.

Before leaving town, try to visit the **Museo Mandralisca** ★, Via Mandralisca 13 (☎ **0921/421547**), opposite the cathedral. It has an outstanding art collection, including the 1470 portrait of an unknown by Antonello da Messina. Some art critics have journeyed all the way from Rome just to stare at this handsome work, and it's often featured on Sicilian tourist brochures. Admission is 4.15€, and the museum's open daily 9am to 7pm.

Agrigento & the Valley of the Temples

129km (80 miles) S of Palermo, 175km (109 miles) SE of Trapani, 217km (135 miles) W of Siracusa

Agrigento's Valley of the Temples is one of the most memorable and evocative sights of the ancient world. Greek colonists from Gela (Caltanissetta) called this area Akragas when they established a beachhead in the 6th century B.C. In time, the settlement grew to become one of the most prosperous cities in Magna Graecia. A great deal of that growth is attributed to the despot Phalaris, who ruled

from 571 to 555 B.C. and is said to have roasted his victims inside a brass bull. He eventually met the same fate.

Empedocles (ca. 490–430 B.C.), the Greek philosopher and politician (also considered by some the founder of medicine in Italy), was the most famous son of Akragas. He formulated the theory that matter consists of four elements (earth, fire, water, and air), modified by the agents love and strife. In modern times the town produced playwright Luigi Pirandello (1867–1936), who won the Nobel Prize for literature in 1934.

Like nearby Selinunte, the city was attacked by war-waging Carthaginians, beginning in 406 B.C. In the 3rd century B.C., the city changed hands between the Carthaginians and the Romans until it finally succumbed to Roman domination by 210 B.C. It was then known as Agrigentium.

The modern part of Agrigento occupies a hill, and the narrow casbahlike streets show the influence of the conquering Saracens. Heavy Allied bombing during World War II necessitated much rebuilding. The result is, for the most part, uninspired and not helped by all the cement factories in the area. But below the town stretch the long reaches of the Valley of the Temples (Valle dei Templi), where you'll see some of the greatest Greek ruins in the world.

Visit Agrigento for its past, not for the modern incarnation. Once you've been awed by the ruined temples, you can visit the *centro storico,* with its tourist boutiques hawking postcards and T-shirts, and enjoy people-watching at a cafe along Via Atenea. When it gets too hot (as it so often does), flee to a beach at nearby San Leone.

Getting There

Most people do the Valley of the Temples as a day trip from Palermo. The **train** takes 1¹/₂ hours and costs 7€ one-way. There are 14 trains daily. The main rail station, **Stazione Centrale,** Piazza Marconi (☎ 892021), is downhill from Piazzale Aldo Moro and Piazza Vittorio Emanuele. From Syracuse by rail, you must first take one of four daily trains to Catania; the 6-hour trip costs 16€ one-way. Three trains a day make the trip from Ragusa to Agrigento at a cost of 9.20€ one-way. This is an extremely awkward connection as you have to change trains at Gela and then at Canicattì. Depending on the train, the trip can last from 5 to 9 hours.

Cuffaro (☎ 0922/403150) runs four **buses** per day from Palermo; the trip takes 2 hours and costs 7.20€ one-way. The company also has service from Syracuse; the trip takes 5 hours and costs 16€ one-way.

By **car** from Syracuse, take SS115 through Gela. From Palermo, cut southeast along S121, which becomes S188 and S189 before it finally reaches Agrigento and the Mediterranean. Allow about 2¹/₂ hours for this jaunt.

Tourist Office

The **tourist** office is at Piazzale Aldo Moro 7 (☎ 0922/20454) open Sunday to Friday 8am to 1pm and 3 to 8pm; Saturday 8am to 1pm. There is another Tourist Office at Via Empedocle 73 (☎ 0922/20391) open Monday to Friday 8am to 2:30pm and Wednesday 3:30 to 7pm.

Wandering Among The Ruins

Many writers are fond of suggesting that the Greek ruins in the **Valle dei Templi** ★★★ be viewed at dawn or sunset, when their mysterious aura is indeed heightened. Regrettably, you can't get very close at those times. Instead, search them out under the cobalt-blue Sicilian sky. The backdrop is idyllic, especially in spring, when the striking almond trees blossom into pink.

Ticket booths are at the west and east entrances (☎ 0922/497341); tickets cost 4.50€ for adults. Hours are daily 8:30am to 7pm.

Board a bus or climb into your car to investigate. Riding out the Strada Panoramica, you'll first approach (on your left) the **Temple of Juno (Tempio di Giunone)** ★★, erected sometime in the mid–5th century B.C., at the peak of a construction boom honoring the deities. Many of its Doric columns have been restored. As you climb the blocks, note the remains of a cistern as well as a sacrificial altar in front. The temple affords good views of the entire valley.

SICILY

A Day Trip to Erice

Established some 3,000 years ago, **Erice** ★★ is an enchanting medieval city. From its thrilling mountaintop setting, two sheer cliffs drop 755m (2,476 ft.) to open up vistas across the plains of Trapani and down the west coast of Sicily. On a clear day, you can see Cape Bon in Tunisia, but this Sicilian aerie is often shrouded in a mist that only adds to the mystique (or, in winter, the misery; temperatures can plummet below Sicilian norms and snow and hail are not uncommon).

Erice is a lovely place to spend an afternoon wandering the medieval streets, with their baroque balconies and flowering vines, and drinking in the vistas. The southwest corner of town contains the Villa Balio gardens, originally laid out in the 19th century. Beyond the gardens, a path winds along the cliff edge up to Erice's highest point, the **Castello di Venere** ★, today little more than crumbling Norman-era walls surrounding the sacred site where a temple to Venus once stood. Piercing the walls are several windows and doorways with spectacular views across the countryside.

Erice is noted for its pastries. Stop off at **Pasticceria Grammatica**, via Vittoria Emanuele 14, near Piazza Umberto (☎ 0923/869390), to sample sugary almond treats kissed with lemon or citrus juices.

Rail passengers from the rest of the island arrive at Trapani, which is 14km (8⅓ miles) to the southeast. You then board an AST **bus** (☎ 0923/21021) that departs from Piazza Montalto in Trapani, heading for Erice. Service is daily year-round from 6:40am to 7:30pm, the trip lasting 50 minutes and costing 2.50€ one-way. If you're driving, follow the A29dir from Palermo or Segesta to the first Trapani exit, then continue along the switchback road up the mountain.

The **Temple of Concord (Tempio della Concordia)** ★★★, which you'll come to next, ranks along with the Temple of Hephaestus (the Theseion) in Athens as the best-preserved Greek temple in the world. With 13 columns on its side, 6 in front, and 6 in back, the temple was built in the *peripteral hexastyle*. You'll see the clearest example in Sicily of what an inner temple was like. In the late 6th century A.D., the pagan structure was transformed into a Christian church, which might have saved it for posterity, although today it has been stripped down to its classical purity.

The **Temple of Hercules (Tempio di Ercole)** ★★ is the oldest, dating from the 6th century B.C. Badly ruined (only eight pillars are standing), it once ranked in size with the Temple of Zeus. At one time the temple sheltered a celebrated statue of Hercules.

The infamous Gaius Verres, the Roman magistrate who became an especially bad governor of Sicily, attempted to steal the image as part of his temple-looting tear on the island. Astonishingly, you can still see signs of black searing from fires set by long-ago Carthaginian invaders.

The **Temple of Jove or Zeus (Tempio di Giove)** ★ was the largest in the valley, similar in some respects to the Temple of Apollo at Selinunte, until it was ruined by an earthquake. It even impressed Goethe. In front of the structure was a large altar. The giant on the ground was one of several *telamones* (atlases) used to support the edifice. Carthaginian slave labor built what was then the largest Greek temple in the world and one of the most remarkable.

The so-called **Temple of Castor and Pollux (Tempio di Dioscuri)**, with four

Doric columns intact, is composed of fragments from different buildings. At various times it has been designated as a temple honoring Castor and Pollux, the twin sons of Leda and deities of seafarers; Demeter (Ceres), the goddess of marriage, of the fertile earth, and of Corn Flakes (cereal); or Persephone, the daughter of Zeus who became the symbol of spring. Note that on some maps, this temple is called Tempio di Castore e Polluce. The temples can usually be visited daily from 8:30am until 1 hour before sunset.

City bus nos. 1, 2, and 3 run to the valley from the train station in Agrigento.

Syracuse (Siracusa): An Undiscovered Island of Cool

56km (35 miles) SE of Catania

Seaside Siracusa ★★, with its Greek ruins and ridiculously lovely historic island, has always been a popular summer resort, but only recently has it begun to draw large numbers of international tourists. In Siracusa's picturesque old town, Ortigia island, the piazzas are like outdoor living rooms with places to eat and drink at every turn. As a younger, hipper population increasingly favors Siracusa, the town is doing its best to keep up: Restaurants and bars are getting chicer, and lots of new hotels and B&Bs are springing up on Ortigia. The price for all this is still very low, so I recommend going there soon, before Siracusa turns into another VIP-town for the rich and famous like Taormina, Capri, or Sardinia's Costa Smeralda.

Getting There

BY AIR

Siracusa does not have its own airport, but the airport of Catania is not far away. From Rome or Milan, there are several flights a day to Catania. The Italian budget airline **Wind Jet** (www.volawindjet.it) offers tickets from 100€ round-trip. Keep in mind, however, that low fare equals low comfort and low service. Other companies that serve Catania from mainland Italy Air One (www.flyairone.it, from 110€ round-trip) and Alitalia (www.alitalia.com, from 160€ round-trip).

From Catania airport Interbus (www.interbus.it) has air-conditioned coaches that take about an hour to reach Siracusa, or you could rent a car. If you're in a group of three or more, I would strongly recommend renting a car, so that you are free to leave Siracusa for a day on the beach or to visit other small villages in the region. At the Catania airport you will find all the major car-rental companies. If you are a good planner, you should book a car in advance; it will cost less and you will not have to waste precious time at the airport haggling over the rental agreement.

BY TRAIN

You can get to Siracusa by train, but it's usually faster to take a bus. The train from Palermo to Siracusa takes 6 to 7 hours and you have to change trains at least one time, usually in Catania. There are good train connections between Palermo and Catania, but Catania train station is not a place you want to spend more than 10 minutes. For more about trains to Siracusa, check out **www.trenitalia.com**.

BY BUS

From Catania, 20 Interbus **buses** daily make the 1¼-hour trip to Siracusa. The one-way fare is 4.50€. Phone **Interbus** (☎ **0931/66710** in Siracusa, or 095-539306 in Catania) for information and schedules.

BY CAR

Driving in Sicily is not as horrid as it may sound. This part of Sicily is less crowded by industries than the northern coast around Palermo, therefore there is less traffic and not so many trucks on the road (even though we had to pass 1 hr. behind a truck filled with watermelons getting smoked by the black clouds of diesel—very charming). What may hold up traffic are tractors filled with fruits, vegetables, or if you are unlucky, manure. If you are staying in the old part of Siracusa, on the island of Ortigia, it might be difficult to find a place to park. As in almost all Italian cities, the old town is closed for cars without a special permit. You could ask the hotel if they have a garage or a private parking you can use. Otherwise there are parking spaces on Riva della Posta and on the Lungomare d´Ortigia where you pay by the hour. From Catania airport, it's easy to find you way to Siracusa (it's about 50 km (31 miles), less than 1 hr. away). Since the airport is south of Catania (away from the worst of the urban traffic), you can easily get on the highway E 45 towards Siracusa. The first part of the highway is quite narrow but after 20 km (12 miles) it turns into a standard highway.

Siracusa Orientation

The city is basically divided in two parts: the "modern" city (referred to as *la città*) and the old town that lies on an island called **Ortigia.** Ortigia is reached by two bridges, Ponte Umbertino and Ponte Santa Lucia. The main roads that cut through the whole city and reach Ortigia are **Corso Umberto I** and its parallel, **Via Malta.** These two roads and **Corso Gelone,** which leads to the Archeological Park and to the church of Madonna delle Lacrime, meet up at the **Foro Siracusano,** a park in the middle of the city. The railway station is at the western end of Corso Umberto I. Most of the budget hotels are found here. In Ortigia the small roads and alleys require no long-winded orientation. No matter which way you wander, you will always end up by the sea or on the main piazza, Piazza del Duomo.

Tourist Office

The **APT** (official tourist board) is at Via San Sebastiano 43 (north of Ortigia, off Corso Gelone; ☎ 0931/481-200). There are also three independent tourist agencies on Ortigia. **Syrako** is on Via Ruggero Settimo 19 (Largo Porta Marina; ☎ 0931/24133; www. syrako.it). **A.A.T.** is on Via della Maestranza 33 (☎ 0931/464255). They can help you rent a car, give you information about transporta- tion to the airport, or arrange guided tours. The third tourist information agency is in the **Antico Mercato D´Ortigia** on Via Tento 2 (Largo XXV Luglio; ☎ 0931/449201; www.antico mercato.it). Other than information they have an Internet cafe, ATM, bike rental, and luggage deposit.

Recommended Websites

○ **www.apt-siracusa.it** The official web- site of the Siracusa tourist board, with a hotel search, restaurant listings, and useful cultural background information.

○ **www.sicilyweb.com** On this site you will find a good deal of historical informa- tion about almost all Sicilian towns and cities.

Syracuse **NUTS & BOLTS**

ATMs *Bancomats* can be a problem to find in Ortigia. There is one on Largo XXV Luglio, the modern-ish piazza you come to after crossing the bridge from the mainland. There's another *bancomat* in the Antico Mercato D´Ortigia. You should have plenty of cash on you at all times to cover bars, restaurants, monument admissions, buses, and taxis. Most hotels and B&Bs take credit cards, but be sure to ask ahead of time.

Emergencies   In an emergency, call the *polizia* at ☎ 113; for nonemergencies (like lost or stolen property), use ☎ 0931/495111 or visit the main police station (*questura*) at Viale Scala Greca 248 (way north of the city). You can also turn to Italy's Army police force, the **Carabinieri,** to report emergencies or other disturbances of the peace. Call the Carabinieri at ☎ 112 for emergencies only; for nonemergencies, call ☎ 0931/65176. Their station (*caserma*) is at Piazza S. Giuseppe 6 (Ortigia). To report a fire, a gas leak, or a grandma stuck in an elevator, dial ☎ 115 or ☎ 0931/481911, for the *vigili del fuoco* (fire department), based at Via Von Platen Augusto 33 (north of the city).

For medical emergencies, call an ambulance at ☎ 118, or visit the *pronto soccorso* (emergency room, where you will not be charged for treatment, regardless of your insurance status) at **Ospedale Generale Provinciale,** Via Testaferrata (Via Gelone), ☎ 0931/68555.

The *polizia municipale,* who handle dog bites and parking tickets and are the bane of every Italian driver's existence, are at Via Molo 2, ☎ 0931/451150.

Since Siracusa is by the sea, you might see a drunken Dane falling off the pier or canoeing into a yacht; in that case, you would want to call the coast guard, **Capitaneria del Porto,** ☎ 0931/481011.

Internet points   Since Sicily is almost 30 years behind the rest of Italy in most aspects; do not expect to find a hotel with Wi-Fi in the room. Better to leave your iBook at home and go with good old postcard writing instead. If, however, you absolutely have to blog or check your e-mail every day, you can look up an Internet point. There aren't many on Ortigia, but you can try the **Net Café** in Antico Mercato D´Ortigia, Via Tento 2, near Largo XXV Luglio (☎ 0931/449201; www.anticomercato.it), or **Il Fermento,** an Internet cafe and wine bar, at Via del Crocefisso 44 (☎ 0931/449139). Otherwise, the strip of Corso Umberto (on the mainland) that's closer to Ortigia has a few cafes and bars with Internet terminals that sometimes work. Ask around.

Sleeping

In August, try to book your accommodations well in advance, or you might find yourself sleeping in Dionysus's Ear. If all else fails, you can almost always scrounge something up in the budget hotel corridor of Corso Umberto, which leads down from the train station. Alternatively, give the **tourist board** folks a holler at ☎ 0931/481-200.

CHEAP

→ **Belvedere San Giacomo** ★ This small, enchanting B&B is right by the sea, on the third floor in a newly renovated building. There is no elevator—but don't worry—luggage is pulled up with a crane outside the building! The B&B is a huge apartment divided into bedrooms, some with bathrooms and some with a shared bathroom in the hall. Living room, kitchen, and terrace are for everyone staying in the B&B to use. The price is between 25€–35€/person but the price is negotiable, especially if you're not here in August. The owner, Antonio Disco, is prepared to give a lower price if you stay for more than 3 days. Rooms are immaculately kept and decorated with some nice personal touches; some have a spectacular view over the sea and air-conditioning. *Belvedere San Giacomo 1 (the piazza between Via Nizza and Via dei Tolomei, by the sea).* ☎ *348/9044985 (cellphone). www.b&b-sangiacomo.too.it. No credit cards.*

➔**Casa Vacanze Aretusa** ★★ Rent your own flat and feel like a real citizen of Siracusa! The 17th-century building lies in a small picturesque alley between Fontana Aretusa and Piazza del Duomo. The apartments are as lovely as the alley, with warm colors, antique furniture, and wooden-beam ceilings. The units are all completely renovated and very comfortable, fully equipped with bathroom, air conditioning, cooking area and bed linens. On the roof there is a terrace with a view over the rooftops and the Siracusa bay. This is a perfect place for couples to stay—or if you are coming with your parents! *Vicolo Zuccalà 1 (Largo Aretusa).* ☎ *0931/492870 or 335/269209 (cellphone). www.residenceriviera.it. 1-room apt (sleeps 2) 77€, 1-room apt (sleeps 3) 89€, 2-room apt (sleeps 4) 105€.*

➔**Hotel Centrale** If everything in your price range on Ortigia and the Milano (below) is booked, try the Centrale. This is a bare-bones choice on the budget hotel strip that leads down from the train station toward the center of town. There's just enough small-town charm to keep it from being totally dreary, though, and it's only a 15-minute walk from here to the heart of Ortigia. *Corso Umberto 141.* ☎ *0931/60528. Double 60€.*

➔**Hotel Milano** Only resort to this guy if the Ortigia places are full. Even closer to the train station but slightly more handsome than the Centrale, the Milano is a good budget choice with such unusual amenities (for this price range) as A/C and TV. It's about a 20-minute walk to Ortigia from here, which can definitely get old if you're in town for a few days. *Corso Umberto 10.* ☎ *0931/66981. Double 60€.*

➔**Olimpo Residence** Like the Casa Vacanze Aretusa (above), this is an apart-ment-hotel, only less expensive, less cozy, and less picturesque. Staying here with your friends is like living in a student's apartment, but without books to read or papers to write! A lot of young people come here since it is so cheap; even the girls working at the desk seem like bored students who have to work during the summer holidays. The apartments are spartan but clean and comfortable and situated in the heart of Ortigia. *Via del Crocefisson 12/14 (via Roma).* ☎ *0931/449081 or 338/3664065 (cellphone). www.olimporesidence.it. 1-room apt 45€–80€/night, 2-room apt 300€–450€/week.*

DOABLE

➔**Caol Ishka Hotel** ★★ This hotel is out-side the center of Siracusa, on the bank of the river Anapo beside the Fiume Ciane nat-ural reserve. It's a combination of tradition and high design, which goes for the rooms as well as the food served in their restaurant. It could be wonderful staying here if you are into nature, but you'll feel isolated if you do not have a car. If you are escaping with your lover, it's perfect—you could lock yourselves into these high-concept rooms and peek out once or twice a day to eat the fusion dishes served at the hotel restaurant (even though living on love would be the best and cheapest diet). They have weekend offers that com-bine double room with dinner. *Via Elorina (crossing Via Pantanelli).* ☎ *0931/69057. www.caolishka.com. Double from 190€. Includes breakfast.*

SPLURGE

➔**Hotel des Étrangers et Miramare** ★★ Get indulgent and check in at this exclusive hotel on the Passeggio Adorno right on the seaside. The property has a fitness center, massage facilities, and a roof garden with a restaurant. If you stay here you should be prepared to mingle with cocky Englishmen and newlyweds. But if you have the euros to foot the bill, this is an excellent splurge. Go ahead, flirt with the bartender in the roof garden bar. The rooms are beautifully fur-nished, although quite small, and some have a sea view. *Passeggio Adorno 10/12 (Largo Aretusa).* ☎ *0931/62671. Single 110€–130€, double 190€–230€. Breakfast included.*

Eating

CAFES & SNACKS

As a rule of thumb, when you're having coffee and a pastry, Espresso standing up at bar will run you around .75€–.90€; cappuccino standing up at the bar: .90€–1.10€; pastry standing up at bar 1€–1.50€; prices double when you sit down at any bar; prices triple when you sit down at fancy places.

→ **Gran Caffè del Duomo** ★★ Have a lemon granita or a sandwich overlooking the beautiful Duomo at this classy, nice bar, with prices that are rather low despite it being a tourist hub. *Piazza Duomo 18/19.* ☎ *0931/ 21544. www.grancaffedelduomo.com.*

→ **Maugeri** ★ This pastry shop is a perfect place to come after dinner for dessert and coffee. There are no seats, so the coffee is taken standing. Buy the homemade cassata or cannoli and enjoy them by the fountain of Aretusa, just a few meters away. *Largo Aretusa.* ☎ *0931/22006.*

→ **Midolo & Boscarino** ★★ Have breakfast with the Syracusans at this coffee bar, just off Ortigia on the main drag of Corso Umberto. Order a brioche (sweet bun) with *granita di mandorle* (almond paste) and a *caffellatte.* I promise, it is the best basic Italian breakfast you'll ever have—and for only 3€. *Corso Umberto 86.*

→ **Sciué Sciué** ★ *Sciué sciué* means "hurry, hurry" in Neapolitan. This hole-in-the-wall, hidden away in an alley far from the big piazzas, offers fast food to anyone lucky enough to stumble upon it. The owner is an old lady from Naples who came to Siracusa 20 years ago because of the violence in Naples. She makes a perfect quick lunch or snack, with all the warmth that you'd expect from a woman from the south of Italy. Her *arancini* (deep-fried rice ball, filled with cheese and vegetables) are great. She also makes very good pies and sandwiches. This is

a simple place but with a wonderful personality and a big heart, and it's cheap! *Via Santa Teresa 8 (Lungomare d'Ortigia).* ☎ *0931/ 445074.*

CHEAP

→ **Enoteca Solaria** ★★ WINE BAR "A dinner without wine is like a day without sun." Those are the words of Enzo Italia, the owner of this prestigious little vineria. But do be prepared for some politics with your wine. Enzo is an ex-hippie and anarchist, who will offer an anti-Bush manifesto as soon as he finds out you are American. After having approved your political stance Enzo will serve you the best wines from Sicily. A bottle of wine costs from 10€–15€; the meal is secondary to the *vino* but well made. Steak with salad is 8€, plates with ham and cheese are about 5€; and all types of *bruschettas* are 1€. *Via Roma 86. www.enotecasolaria.com.* ☎ *0931/463007.*

→ **Il Blue** ★ LIGHT FARE/*APERITIVO* This suave spot is where the cool Syracusans hang out. The outdoor tables are surrounded with cushioned benches and soft textiles moving softly in the breeze. It is the place your summer fling will take you to show you off to his friends. Make sure you wear your shortest skirt and glossiest lipstick, that way you will get more points (and more free drinks) than last week's fling. You can enjoy an *aperitivo* and a light dinner, or come after dinner showing off your tanned and oiled legs. Try the house "sushi"—plates with raw fish from the region, or the selected ham and cheeses for around 10€. Ask the waiter to recommend a wine from the region, it will be served from their own cantina. *Via Nizza 50/52 (Piazza San Giuseppe).* ☎ *0931/442052. Daily until 2:30am.*

→ **Machu Picchu** ★★ LIGHT FARE/*APERITIVO* Tired of tourist traps? Just wanna chill? Take a walk to the other side of Ortigia, away from the crowded piazzas. On Via dei Tolomei you will find Machu Picchu with its

"Siracusa (You're a Fine Girl)"

Don't mean to question Siracusa's honor or anything, but the girl has seen her fair share of Mediterranean seafaring bedfellows. The ancient Greeks landed and settled in here as early as 734 B.C. After them, the Phoenicians, the Moors, the Normans, and the Spanish all did their stints in Siracusa before sailing off. Today, the fine city has outgrown her wilder youth, and is happily married to Sicily. She's a 2,800-year-old mixture of old houses from the 15th century, some buildings from the 1920s (with their cold, fascist-inspired architecture), and here and there, columns and ruins from the Magna Grecia period (7th century B.C.).

Siracusa saw her glory days around the 5th century B.C., when the tyrant Dionysius I ruled the city. At the age of 23, he started to turn the city into one of the world's largest. He defended Siracusa from the Carthaginians and dreamed of making Sicily into the political center of the world, instead of Greece. The island of Ortigia became a fortress for him and his legionnaires, while he let the city grow onto the mainland, surrounded by a 22km-long (17-mile) wall. Remains of this era can be seen in the archeological park of Neapolis (see below).

terrace in front of the sea. This is the preferred hangout of the well-dressed, well-behaved, wannabes who frequent the island. The place is great, with comfortable, white-cushioned chairs, chill-out music and excellent food. Just remember to bring your newly bought Prada sunglasses even if the sun is going down. *Via dei Tolomei 11 (by the sea).* ☎ *0931/21887. Daily until 2:30am. Pasta from 8 €, fish and meat dishes from 8 €.*

SPLURGE

➜ **Trattoria La Foglia** ★★ SEAFOOD/VEGETARIAN Some Siracusani say this is a tourist trap, because of the prices, but you won't find it expensive if you've just come from the mainland, or more upmarket resort towns like Taormina or the Aeolian Islands. In any case, the food is fabulous, especially if you are a vegetarian. La Foglia serves only vegetarian and fish dishes. Coming into the restaurant is like coming home to granny's house; the room is furnished like a living room and all the tables are set differently. Don't expect a party evening if you choose to eat here—the atmosphere is more of a warm and familiar kind. You'll find homemade ravioli

from 10€, fish dishes from 15€, and dishes with vegetables for 12.50€. *Via Copodieci, 29 (Via Roma). www.lafoglia.it.* ☎ *0931/66233.*

Partying

If Ortigia sometimes seems like a sleepy island during the day, it definitely gets fired up after dinner. On the Passegio Adorno and around Largo Aretusa the young and the bold meet up to make further plans for the night. If you feel like after-dinner drinks there are tons of great bars open until 2 or 3am in summer.

Generally speaking, a glass of wine will set you back anywhere from 2€ to 8€ depending on whether you're drinking the house wine and how fancy the place is; a beer will cost 4€ or 5 €, and a cocktail from 5€ on up.

➜ **Lunganotte** ★ This is definitely a tourist trap. If you see an Italian here, he or she is certainly a tourist as well. The good thing is that you have a wonderful view over the sea, and they have the most delicious watermelon daiquiris. One of the most popular make-out spots in Siracusa is right in front of this bar. But if you are more of a viewer than a doer, this is the first row to a great spectacle—of young Italians picking up Swedish girls with that wildly original line, *"Ciao bellissima." Via Lungomare Alfeo 23.* ☎ *0931/64200.*

➜ **Peter Pan** ★★ Not fancy, but a cool place nonetheless. It feels almost like a university pub—small and overcrowded—with a friendly vibe that makes it easy to feel at home and strike up conversations with new people. After being here 2 nights in a row, you are already part of the crowd, and the bartender will greet you when you run into him in town during the day. *Via Castello Maniace 46/48 (Largo Aretusa).* ☎ *0931/468937.*

➜ **Vecchio Pub** This is supposed to be the oldest pub of Siracusa, opened in 1979 . . . a statement that seems pretty ironic considering the city was built way before Christ was born. Anyway, it is a typical "English pub" with typical young foreign tourists getting wasted on Heineken and shots of suspicious-looking, candy-colored liquor. There is a backyard garden where you can have a sandwich or a salad for lunch or a light dinner before pumping your body full of alcohol. *Via delle Vergini 9 (between Largo Aretusa and Piazza del Duomo).* ☎ *0931/464693. Daily until 2am.*

Sightseeing

ORTIGIA

Just walking around city/island of **Ortigia** is a treat. Every alley has its own scenery, its own little church and its own surprises. During the sleepy hours from 1–4pm, when people close their shops for lunch and siesta, walking around is like eavesdropping on the town—you hear the slam of pots and pans from apartments above, you smell the aromas of onions and fried fish, or you hear the low voice of a mother putting her baby to sleep. These are the real noises and odors of a Sicilian town, and even though it is so hot that your soles of your shoes are melting, you should make a point of sneaking around

---

Presto, change-o! The Myth of Ortigia

Once upon a time on ancient Olympus, the god Zeus had a crush on Astoria, the mother of Apollo and Artemis, and he wouldn't leave her alone. Finally, in order to escape him, Astoria turned herself into a quail, then into an island off Sicily—and then, eventually, into an up-and-coming hipster neighborhood in Queens (New York City!). (Wish you could pull such handy self-transformations when you need to blow off aggressive Italian men today!!) The name *Ortigia* in fact means "quail" and if you look at it from the correct angle, Siracusa's island is shaped like a bird.

---

during these hours just to get close to the real life of Siracusa.

FREE ➜ **The Duomo** ★★★ Before becoming a Christian cathedral, the Duomo used to be the Greek temple of Athena. Coming inside you can see the columns that are the remains of the temple. The mosaics and windows in the Duomo are from the Norman period. After an earthquake in 1693 (when a large number of buildings and churches were destroyed around this area), the façade was reconstructed with Corinthian columns and three new entrances. *Piazza del Duomo. Daily 8am–noon and 4–7pm. Free admission.*

➜ **Castello Maniace** ★ If you like military architecture, the 13th-century Maniace fort is sure to please. It was built on the eastern-most point of the island (to protect Ortigia from intruders) with a standard-issue square footprint and towers in each corner. The fort was built during the reign of Frederick II but was dedicated to a Byzantine general, Giorgio Maniace who, some years earlier, had

SICILY

Summer Culture

The Ortigia Festival

Every summer in July the Ortigia theater foundation organizes a high-quality cultural festival (www.ortigia festival.it) in the archeological park of Neapolis and in the Castello Maniace fortress. Last year Peter Greenaway set up his multimedia project "Tulse Luper a Siracusa," and the Nobel Prize winner of literature, Derek Walcott, presented his *Odyssey*. The English cult band Tiger Lillies also performed.

wrested control of Sicily from the Muslims. *Via Castello Maniace.* ☎ *0931/464420. Daily 8:30am–1:30pm. Admission 2€.*

➜ **Fonte Aretusa** ★★ One of the dreamiest little spots in Siracusa is this freshwater fountain surrounded by papyrus trees, on the north side of Ortigia. The myth says that Aretusa turned herself into this fountain to escape from the underground river, Alfeo. It is impressive to see a freshwater spring only a couple of meters from the sea. The beauty and myth of the Fonte Aretusa are sung by Virgil, Pindar, Milton, and many others. *Largo di Fonte Aretusa.*

➜ **Piazza del Duomo** ★★★ Even better than the Duomo by itself, this phenomenally gorgeous square is the real heart of Ortigia and without a doubt one of the most beautiful piazzas in all of Italy. (Yep, we said "in all of Italy.") The ebullient, wonderfully maintained space looks like something Franco Zeffirelli might have dreamed up for a stage production of some happy-ending Sicilian love story. Coming here at sunset is like finding a treasure: the beige limestones of the Duomo and the surrounding baroque palaces light up in intense, glowing tones of pink and gold.

OFF ORTIGIA

➜ **Archeological Park of Neapolis** ★★ Siracusa's main attraction is its ancient **Greek theater** ★★; it's among the biggest of its kind in the world and dates back to the 5th century B.C. The theater has a diameter of 140m (459 ft.) and originally had 67 rows of seats; today only 46 rows remain. On this very stage, the Greek tragedist Aeschylus produced his play *The Persians* for the first time in 473 B.C. Around the corner from the Greek theater there are (much less impressive) remains from a Roman amphitheater and some Roman houses, but if you are tired of ruins, you can easily skip that and go visit **Dionysius's Ear** ★★! Dionysius's Ear is a huge and spectacular artificial cave in a lush and rocky, primordial landscape that looks like something out of the film *Jurassic Park* (or the 1970s low-budget dinosaur-era TV show, *Land of the Lost*). Even though there are no dinosaurs (bummer), the legend of the cave is scary enough. Shaped like a gigantic, pointy ear, the cave has an extraordinary way of amplifying even the softest sound. It is said that the tyrant Dionysius I threw his prisoners into the cave and then listened to their every curse and whisper while he spied on them from the rock ledges above. You can go deep into the cave and imagine yourself being prisoner there—but you start to feel freaked out after a few minutes. *Parco Archeologico, entrance from Via Romagnoli or Via Latomia del Paradiso (Corso Gelone).* ☎ *0931/66206. Daily 9am to 2 hours before the sunset. Admission 6€, 18–24 years 3€.*

Playing Outside

In Siracusa, by the Lungomare di Ortigia, you can relax on a comfy lounge just a few steps from the water on **Lido Maniace** ★ (www.lidomaniace.it), a sunbathing deck with a cocktail bar and jet-ski and canoe rental. It's perfect for a lazy Sunday afternoon when you want to go for a dip but don't feel like leaving the comforts of lovely Ortigia. There's a fee charged for sun beds, umbrella, and water-sports.

The seaside resorts south of Siracusa can easily be reached, by car, bus, or by ferries that leave from the port of Ortigia to the **island of Maddalena** about every hour. The most famous beaches are **Arenella** ★★ (9km/5¹/₂ miles from Siracusa; Contrada Arenella; ☎ 0931/715025), with sandy and rocky beaches; and **Fontane Bianche** ★ (15 km/9¹/₃ miles from Siracusa; Via Mazzarò 1; ☎ 0931/790900), a beautiful bay with fine limestone cliffs and clear water. Along both beaches there are a handful of establish-ments with lounges and umbrellas, bar and pizzeria, sport activities and entertainment, and disco during the night. The price for the use of a sun bed and umbrella is about 6€ a day.

Buses to Arenella (no. 23) and Fontane Bianche (nos. 21 and 22) depart almost every hour from Riva della Posta in Siracusa (near Ponte Umbertino). Visit the Syrako informa-tion center, Via Ruggero Settimo 19 (www.syrako.it) for information about bus and boat tours, diving expeditions, and other excursions.

Shopping

If you want to buy gifts or souvenirs, the most typical products of Siracusa are handcrafts like papyrus, ceramics, and jewelry.

Sebastian Brancato ★★ is a Syracusan artist who manufactures and decorates papyrus paper, much like ancient Egyptian papyrus. In Mr. Brancato's workshop you can watch the papyrus-making process and buy blank paper or pieces that he has painted. He's at Via Ruggero Settimo 24 (☎ **333/4141632** [cellphone]; Mon–Sun 8:30am–1:30pm and 3–8pm).

For jewelry made from coral and amber from the nearby river Simeto, check out **Reoro,** Via Landolina 17 (☎ **0931/465454;** Mon 4:30–8:30pm, Tues–Sat 9:30am–1:30pm

and 4:30–8:30pm). Pick up some Mafia para-phernalia (or tell your friends that's what it is) at **Bazar delle Cose Vecchie** ★ a hit-or-miss Sicilian antiques shop at Via Consiglio Regionale 7-30-40 (☎ **0931/24191;** Tues–Sat 10am–9pm, Sun–Mon 5–9pm).

At **Il Gusto dei Sapori Smarriti** ("The Taste of Lost Flavors"), you can find pack-aged Sicilian gourmet items to bring home to your friends and family. It's at Piazza Cesare Battisti 4 (☎ **0931/60069;** Mon–Sat 7am–2:30pm).

A Day Trip from Siracusa: Baroque Noto—The Stone Garden

Noto is famous for two things: its baroque architecture and its marzipan. It's an easy daytrip from Siracusa.

The ancient town of Noto totally col-lapsed during the earthquake of 1693 and was completely rebuilt over the next century by a number of architects, who created an urban baroque style that became one of a kind. The new town center was given the nickname "Stone Garden" and the puffed-up appellation "the Chief Town of the Baroque of Val di Noto." The main street, Corso Vittorio Emanuele, cuts right through the town, interrupted by three piazzas with three impressive churches: first is the Piazza dell'Immacolata with the church of San Francesco, in the middle lies the Piazza del Municipio (Noto's main piazza and site of the Duomo—in 1996 the cupola of the Duomo collapsed and restoration is still going on), and by the end of the Corso Vittorio Emanuele, you reach Piazza XVI Maggio with the church of San Domenico.

Noto epitomizes Sicilian baroque: It's a bizarre, confusing, and overwhelming mix-ture of human and fantasy figures that pop out of the building façades. On Via Nicolaci, look for the over-the-top balconies that are decorated with angels, beasts, flowers, and babies.

The Best Pastry Shop in Sicily?

....

If you want cream on top of the baroque cake, you have to head towards Via Ducezio and **Mandorlo in Fiore** ★★★, the best pastry shop in Sicily! "Almond in Bloom" is famous for its *cassata* (a type of ice cream), which they deliver all over Italy. Inside the shop, the colors of elaborately worked marzipan glow in the counter. There are hundreds of different cakes, biscuits, and candied fruits to choose from, but I have only one thing to say—get the cassata. It is the best in the world! And when it comes to the cassata, I never exaggerate. Via Ducezio 2 (by the church of Santa Carmine). ☎ 0931/836615.

GETTING THERE

You can reach Noto by **Interbus** (☎ 0931/66710), which offers 13 buses per day from Siracusa; the trip takes 50 minutes and costs 3€ one-way (though the buses stop running at 7pm, so don't plan on staying late). Noto can also be reached by **train** (usually nine per day) heading southwest from Siracusa. The ride takes 30 minutes and costs 2.75€ one-way. For schedules, call ☎ 892021.

If you have a car, you can spend the evening and have dinner here. Noto turns into the set of the most romantic film imaginable during the sunset hours. There are also some good places to eat.

The **tourist office** is at Piazza XVI Maggio, Villetta Ercole, in front of San Domenico church (☎ 0931/573779). Pick up a map and some tips about exploring the town on foot. From March to October, office hours are Monday to Saturday 8am to 2pm and 3:30 to 6:30pm, Sunday 9am to 1pm; November to February, hours are Monday to Friday 8am to 2pm and 3:30 to 6:30pm, Saturday 8:30am to 1:30pm.

SIGHTSEEING

Mercifully, traffic has been diverted away from Noto's heart, to protect its fragile buildings. Your best approach is through the monumental **Royal Gate (Porta Reale),** crowned by three symbols—a dog, a swan, and a tower, representing the town's former allegiance to the Bourbon monarchy. From here, take **Corso Vittorio Emanuele,** going through the **old patricians' quarter.** The rich-looking, honey-colored buildings along this street are some of the most captivating on the island. This street will take you to the three most important piazzas.

You arrive first at **Piazza Immacolata,** dominated by the baroque façade of **San Francesco all'Immacolata** (☎ 0931/835279), which still contains notable artworks rescued from a Franciscan church in the old town. Notable works include a painted wooden *Madonna and Child* (1564), believed to be the work of Antonio Monachello. The church is open daily 8:30am to noon and 4 to 7:30pm; admission is free. Immediately to the left stands the **St. Salvador Monastery (Monastero del Santissimo Salvatore),** characterized by an elegant tower, its windows adorned with wrought-iron balconies. When it reopens, it will contain a minor collection of religious art and artifacts.

The next square is **Piazza Municipio** ★, the most majestic of the trio. It's dominated by the **Palazzo Ducezio** (☎ 0931/98611), a graceful town hall with curvilinear elements enclosed by a classical portico, the work of architect Vincenzo Sinatra (no relation to Ol' Blue Eyes). The upper section of this palace was added as late as the 1950s. Its most beautiful room is the Louis XI–style Hall of Representation (Salone di Rappresentanza), decorated with gold and stucco. On the vault is a Mazza fresco representing the mythological figure of Ducezio founding Neas (the ancient name of Noto).

On one side of the square, a broad flight of steps leads to the **Duomo,** flanked by two horseshoe-shape hedges. The cathedral was inspired by models of Borromini's churches in Rome and completed in 1776. In 1996, the dome collapsed, destroying a large section of the nave, and it's still under repair. The date of completion for the extensive renovations is uncertain. On the far side of the cathedral is the **Palazzo Villadorata,** graced with a classic façade. Its six **extravagant balconies** ★★ are supported by sculpted buttresses of horses, griffins, and grotesque bald and bearded figures with chubby-cheeked cherubs at their bellies. The palazzo is divided into 90 rooms, the most beautiful the Yellow Hall (Salone Giallo), the Green Hall (Salone Verde), and the Red Hall (Salone Rosso), with their frescoed domes from the 18th century. The charming Feasts Hall (Salone delle Feste) is dominated by a fresco representing mythological scenes. In one of its aisles, the palazzo contains a *pinacoteca* (picture gallery) with antique manuscripts, rare books, and portraits of noble families.

The final square is **Piazza XVI Maggio,** dominated by the convex façade of its **Chiesa di San Domenico** ★, with two tiers of columns separated by a high cornice. The interior is filled with polychrome marble altars and is open daily 8am to noon and 2 to 5pm. Directly in front of the church is a

public garden, the **Villetta d'Ercole,** named for its 18th-century fountain honoring Hercules.

Right off Corso Vittorio Emanuele is one of Noto's most fascinating streets, **Via Nicolaci** ★, lined with magnificent baroque buildings.

Noto in summer also is known for some fine **beaches** nearby; the best are 6km ($3^3/_4$ miles) away at **Noto Marina.** You can catch a bus at the Giardini Pubblici in Noto. The one-way fare is 1.50€.

While wandering the streets, you'll find nothing finer on a hot day than one of the highly praised cones from **Corrado Costanza,** Via Silvio Spaventa 7–9 (☎ 0931-835243), open Thursday to Tuesday 7am to 2pm and 4 to 11:30pm. It enjoys local renown for its gelato, the best in the area. The gelati come in various flavors and are often made with fresh fruit.

A Nice Place to Eat in Noto

A bit off the main tourist drag, **Trattoria del Crocifisso** ★★ serves Sicilian specialties to a crowd of mostly locals. They also have a small bar at the entrance where you can take your *aperitivo* and wait for your table. A meal with wine starts at 20€. Via Principe Umberto 48. ☎ **0931/571151.** www.trattoriadel crocifisso.it. Thurs–Tues for dinner.

Taormina: Perched on the Edge of a Volcano

250km (155 miles) E of Palermo

Taormina's ★★ relaxed vibe, mild climate, and spectacular setting, on the edge of a cliff overlooking the Ionian Sea, with Mt Etna looming in the background, makes it one of the most sublime places to go on vacation. But with all its attractive qualities, Taormina

was bound to be exploited by international tourism. Hordes of holidaymakers ascend to the medieval town, packing the main street, Corso Umberto, from April to October.

Out of season, Taormina quiets down considerably. In spite of the summer crowds,

Tourist Office

The **tourist office** is in the Palazzo Corvaja, Piazza Santa Caterina (☎ 0942/23243), open Monday to Saturday 8am to 2pm and 4 to 7pm.

Taormina is still charming and well worth a visit—just don't expect to have it to yourself! It's filled with intimate piazzas and palazzi dating from the 15th to the 19th centuries. There are restaurants for every day of the week, and countless stores selling everything from designer handbags to cheap souvenirs and trinkets. Taormina tourists tend to be a bit older, so what passes for nightlife in town might seem a bit tame, but there are few better ways to spend a Sicilian summer evening than catching an opera in the open-air Teatro Greco-Romano. If you're still set on partying, the loud and lively resort of Giardini, below Taormina, has a bunch of nightclubs right on the water. During the day, escape the throngs by going on one of the many adventure excursions within easy reach of Taormina—like hanging out at the beaches below town (Taormina itself isn't on the beach), or climbing Mt. Etna.

Getting There

You can make **rail** connections on the Messina line south. It's possible to board a train in Rome for the 8-hour trip to Messina, where you make connections on to Taormina. Call ☎ 892021 for schedules. There are 26 trains a day from both Messina and Catania; trips from both towns take 1 to 1¹/₂ hours and cost 3.08€ one-way. The Sicilian Gothic train station for **Taormina/Giardini-Naxos** is a mile from the heart of the resort, below the town. Buses run uphill from the station every 15 to 45 minutes (schedules vary throughout the year), daily 9am to 9pm; a one-way ticket costs 1.50€. You can also take a taxi for 10€ and up.

In addition, you can take the train as far as Messina and then hop a Taormina-bound **bus.** There are 15 a day, taking 1¹/₂ hours and costing 3€ one-way. More details are available by calling **Interbus** at ☎ 0942/625301.

By **car** from Messina, head south along A18. From Catania, continue north along A18. If you're arriving by car, the main parking lot is **Lumbi Parking,** Contrada Lumbi, which is signposted off the Taormina Nord Autostrada junction. There is another garage at **Mazzarò Parking** along Via Nazionale in Mazzarò, in the vicinity of the cable-car station lying off the coastal road. For 24-hour parking, count on paying anywhere from 12€ to 15€.

Getting Around

Once you've arrived in Taormina, everything in town is accessible on foot. Corso Umberto is the main east-west drag, and most of Taormina is built within 200m (656 ft.) above or below it. North of Corso Umberto, the hillside becomes inhospitably steep; south of Corso Umberto, the high terrace on which Taormina is perched abruptly gives way to the sparkling Ionian Sea below. The town's dramatic, elevated position means that you can't walk to the beach, but you can avail yourself of the inexpensive, frequently running cable car or bus to the sandy shores at Mazzarò, Isola Bella, and Giardini.

Sleeping

Most of Taormina's cheaper hotels are located east or west of the main town nucleus, which is fine—distances here are short enough, and roads are level enough to make staying "on the outskirts" perfectly convenient. Don't bother with splurging on one of Taormina's fancier hotels; your hotel mates will only be middle-aged Germans who wear too much perfume when they go out at night. If you're looking to shack up with the truly fabulous of Taormina, head for the hills, where the chic and carefree own or rent

Taormina

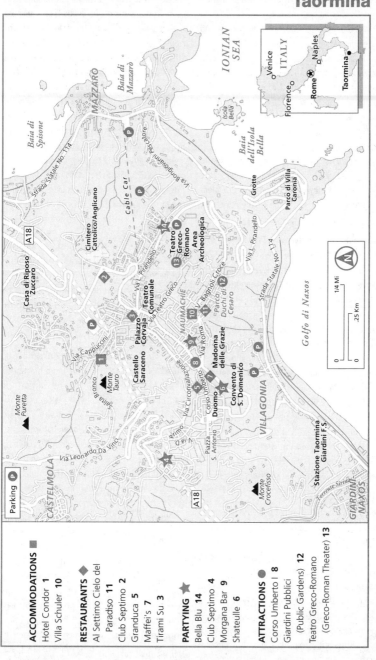

ACCOMMODATIONS ■
Hotel Condor 1
Villa Schuler 10

RESTAURANTS ◆
Al Settimo Cielo del
  Paradiso 11
Club Septimo 2
Granduca 5
Maffei's 7
Tirami Su 3

PARTYING ★
Bella Blu 14
Club Septimo 4
Morgana Bar 9
Shateulle 6

ATTRACTIONS ●
Corso Umberto I 8
Giardini Pubblici
  (Public Gardens) 12
Teatro Greco-Romano
  (Greco-Roman Theater) 13

Parking ℗

holiday villas nestled against eastern Sicily's stunning landscape.

When traveling to Taormina in July and especially August, you should try to book as far in advance as possible, as the budget lodging tends to fill up quickly. If you're coming primarily to hit the beach, at least in July and August, then consider staying at Mazzarò, 5km (3 miles) from the center, and trekking up the hill for the shopping, nightlife, and dining.

If you're driving to the top of Taormina to a hotel, call ahead to see what arrangements can be made for your car. Also ask for clear directions because the narrow one-way streets are bewildering once you get here.

CHEAP

→ **Hotel Condor** ★ This aptly named inn boasts soaring views over Taormina's plunging hillsides to the sea. Unlike its namesake, however, this pensione is neither bird of prey nor scavenger, offering instead mercifully priced accommodations to the weary budget traveler. The 1970s-style rooms are small but clean and bright, with light-colored marble terrazzo floors and blue bedspreads recalling the sand and sea. Breakfast (and other meals, for those too lazy to eat elsewhere) is served on a panoramic terrace jutting out from the side of the hotel. All rooms have A/C, TV, telephone, and hair dryer. *Via Dietro Cappuccini 25.* ☎ *0942/23124. www.condorhotel.com. Double 76€–98€.*

DOABLE/SPLURGE

→ **Villa Schuler** ★ Filled with the fragrance of bougainvillea and jasmine, this hotel offers style and comfort at a good price. Family owned and run, it sits high above the Ionian Sea, with views of Mt. Etna and the Bay of Naxos. The hotel is a 2-minute stroll from Corso Umberto I and about a 15-minute walk from the cable car to the beach. The guest rooms are comfortably furnished, with well-maintained bathrooms with tub/shower combinations, and many have a small balcony or terrace with a view of the sea. Breakfast can be served in your room or taken on a terrace with a panoramic sea view. The most luxurious way to stay here is to book the garden villa suite with its own private access. It's spacious and beautifully furnished, with two bathrooms (one with a Jacuzzi). The villa comes with a kitchenette, patio, private garden, and veranda, and costs from 220€ per day for two, including breakfast. *Piazzetta Bastione, Via Roma.* ☎ *0942/23481. www.villaschuler.com. Double 116€–130€, junior suite 130€–170€. Amenities: Bar; dry cleaning; laundry service; library; lounge; room service (24-hr.). In-room: A/C, TV, hair dryer, safe.*

Eating

Taormina has plenty of honest, reasonable, excellent-quality restaurants. Even the places that look like full-on tourist traps don't charge you an arm and a leg for mediocre food, and they don't skimp on portions or abundant carafes of house wine.

CHEAP

→ **Al Settimo Cielo del Paradiso** ★ SICILIAN/ITALIAN   It's far from being the most famous or popular restaurant in Taormina, but in some ways, it's our undisputed favorite, thanks to a high-altitude view that seems to sweep out over half of Sicily, superb food, and a sense of chic. To reach it, you'll take an elevator from the marble-floored lobby of the also-recommended hotel, then dine on a rooftop. Salvatore Martorana is the owner and impresario here, orchestrating dishes that are likely to include well-crafted versions of pennette or risotto with salmon; succulent salads of grilled giant prawns served with a limoncello sauce; *involtini* (spiral pasta) with grilled swordfish layered with vegetables and herbs; and a wide selection of very fresh fish prepared any way you want. There's a catch here. You must enter the restaurant between 8 and 9pm, as it has the shortest opening times of any place along the coast. *On the top floor of the Hotel Villa Paradiso, Via Roma 2.* ☎ *0942/23922. Reservations recommended. Main courses 8€–15€. Daily 1–2pm and 7:30–9pm.*

➔**Tirami Su** ✦ SICILIAN   This is one of the most frequently praised inexpensive restaurants in Taormina, drawing appreciative comments from a wide variety of residents and visitors, as well as managers of hotels in cities as far away as Messina. It's small, it's basic-looking, and it lies beside a noisy commercial street that's so busy and so impossibly narrow that you might fear for your life as you approach or leave it, especially if you've had too much wine. Within an environment accented with murals, and tables and shelves loaded down with the bounty of a Sicilian harvest, you'll enjoy dishes that include a filet of beef with mushrooms and cream sauce; *involtini* of swordfish, a savory fish soup, and a Palermo-style entrecôte with croquette potatoes. The spaghetti with seafood that's served here is, according to the raves of overfed and fully satisfied diners, incredibly wonderful. We concur with that assessment. *Via Costantino Patricio.* ☎ *0942/24803. Reservations recommended. Pizzas 5€–9€; main courses 7.50€–14€. Wed–Mon 12:30–3pm and 7:30pm–midnight.*

DOABLE

➔**Club Septimo** ✦ INTERNATIONAL/ ITALIAN/MEDITERRANEAN   In addition to its excellent cuisine, this restaurant and club offers a sweeping view of Taormina and the Ionian Sea and is framed with reproductions of ancient Roman columns. In the center of Taormina, 200m (656 ft.) from the Greek Amphitheater, this is a ritzy place, especially if you get a table on the terrace overlooking the Ionian Sea. The setting is one of the most beautiful in Taormina, with large terraces and age-old trees and lots of planting. Menus present classic and modern cuisine ideas almost in equal measure. Among the more stimulating dishes recently sampled were

Music & Theater Festivals in Taormina

The Greek Theater (see below) offers **theatrical performances** from July to September. In addition, churches and other venues are the settings for a **summer festival of classical music** from May to September. Each July an **international film festival** is held in the theater. For more information about the festivals, visit www.taormina-arte.com and www.taorminafilmfest.it.

swordfish with a surprise addition of mussels and "other creatures of the sea," served with sliced potatoes and given an aromatic touch with saffron. Small shrimp were spiced up with strong-tasting but flavorful Sicilian cheese and sautéed lightly in an olive oil sauce. *Via San Pancrazio 50.* ☎ *0942/625522. Reservations required. Main courses 8€–16€. June–Sept daily 7:30pm–midnight (or later).*

➔**Granduca** ✦ ITALIAN/SICILIAN   This is the most atmospheric choice in town, and it serves an excellent, carefully executed cuisine. You enter into an antiques store with potted plants and art objects. Even more alluring is the terrace with its panoramic views. In fair weather, request a table in the beautiful gardens. The competent cookery always focuses on the quality of its ingredients. Our favorite pasta here is spaghetti *alla Norma* (with tomato sauce, eggplant, and ricotta cheese). If you want something truly Sicilian, ask for pasta with sardines. Pasta also comes with a savory kettle of freshly caught mussels and clams. The best meat dish is *involtini alla Siciliana,* or grilled meat rolls, and at night you can make a selection of various pizzas baked to perfection in a wood-fired oven. *Corso Umberto I 172.* ☎ *0942/ 24983. Reservations recommended. Main*

SICILY

courses 8€–15€. *Daily 12:30–3pm and 7:30pm–midnight.*

➜ **Maffei's** ★ SICILIAN/SEAFOOD Maffei's is small, with only 10 tables, but it serves the best fish in Taormina. Every day the chef selects the freshest fish at the market, and you can tell him how you'd like it prepared. We often choose the house specialty, swordfish *alla messinese,* braised with tomato sauce, black olives, and capers. The *fritto misto* (a mixed fish fry with calamari, shrimp, swordfish, and sea bream) is superbly light because it's prepared with a virgin olive oil. Among the desserts are velvety lemon mousse and crepes flambé stuffed with vanilla cream. *Via San Domenico de Guzman 1.* ☎ *0942/24055. Reservations required. Main courses 10€–18€. Daily noon–3pm and 7pm–midnight. Closed Jan to mid-Feb.*

Partying

There are some decent clubs in Taormina (though most are in the form of piano bars frequented by rhythm-challenged couples and the odd sleazeball old guy trawling for young flesh), but Taormina is not exactly Ibiza when it comes to partying. Instead, evenings are often better spent lingering over dinner (and maybe doing some tipsy shopping after) and going to bed early. But if that veal chop smothered in marsala isn't enough liver damage for the day, there's plenty of partying to be done down the hill, at the beach community of Giardini. If you're up for an adventure, try to befriend the young, rich northern Italians who vacation in and around Taormina, and then hitch a ride to their fabulous villa parties in the towns nearby. Yeah, it could be a bitch finding your way back the next morning, but isn't this what vacation stories are made of?

As for clubs in Taormina itself, **Bella Blu** ★, Guardiola Vecchia (☎ *0942/24239*), caters to a high-energy European crowd. At the

Club Septimo ★, Via San Pancrazio 50 (☎ *0942/625522*), a sweeping view of the town and the sea is framed with reproductions of Roman columns, and the interior has all the strobe and ultraviolet lights you might want. This one charges a cover ranging from 8€ to 13€. **Shateulle** ★, Piazza Garibaldi (☎ *0942/626175*), occupies a site on an intimate-looking piazza several steps downhill from Corso Umberto I. Although most of the youngish guests opt for seats outside, some venture into the chrome-and-mirror-trimmed bar inside. Year-round, it's open daily 5pm to 4am. **Morgana Bar** ★★, Scesa Morgana 4 (☎ *0942/620056*), is named after the seductive fairy (Morgan la Fée) of Camelot days, who lured valiant knights to their doom, and is an ultrahip, cutting-edge bar that's tucked into one of the narrow alleyways running downhill from the Corso Umberto I. Centered around a semicircular bar top, it flows out onto a candlelit terrace.

Sightseeing

➜ **Corso Umberto I** ★★ The east-west-running main drag of Taormina is a sight in itself, and one you'll be seeing a lot of, even if you're only in town for a short stay. Corso Umberto is pedestrianized in the heart of the old city, with busy cross streets and quiet alleys leading off of it uphill (north) and downhill (south) to hidden shops and restaurants. The midpoint of Corso Umberto is where you can stop, sigh, and drink in the breathtaking sea view from Largo IX Aprile, with its pink stone pavement. Travel the full half-mile length of Corso Umberto to its western end, and you'll find the lovely baroque Fontana Monumentale and Taormina's Duomo (cathedral), the church of San Nicola, built in the 12th century but tweaked a lot over the next few centuries.

➜ **Giardini Pubblici (Public Gardens)** ★ Taormina's shady and rustic public gardens make for a great, and surprising, detour when you get tired of wandering back and forth on the main drag, Corso Umberto I. Unlike many Italian gardens, which sprawl out over acres and acres, this park is beautifully manageable in size, and although it's on some steep land, easy to explore thanks to gentle stairs and ramps. And did I mention the shade? The two weird, gingerbread-y houses you see here are the Victorian follies designed by the eccentric British woman, a Miss Florence Trevelyan, who bought this land back in 1882 and made it a park. *Via Bagnoli Croce.*

📺 **Best** → **Teatro Greco-Romano (Greco-Roman Theater)** ★★★ Lodged against the town's steep southern slope, with sweeping views of the Ionian Sea and Mt. Etna's smoking cap, Taormina's ancient Greek theater is one hell of a place for drama. Despite the name, this was not a wrestling venue; instead, it was a 5,000-spectator-capacity theater where fratricide, sex, and good old-fashioned gouging out of eyes were acted out nightly, in plays like Sophocles's *Oedipus Rex* and Euripides's *Medea* 2,500 years ago. Later, in the Roman period, the stage was modified so that gladiator battles and other bloodsports—the Romans' preferred form of entertainment—could be held in the theater. (Woody Allen also recognized the dramatic force of the place; he set the vertiginous chorus scenes of *Mighty Aphrodite* in these very ruins.) You can tour the semicircular theater during the day, but for a very memorable night, try to get tickets to one of the concerts or operas staged here in summer, during the Taormina Arte festival. (The night we saw the Sicilian opera, *Cavalleria Rusticana,* performed here, the tenor got mad at the conductor for rushing his aria and stormed offstage in the middle of the finale, at which point the disgruntled people in the audience threw tomatoes at him. It was rad, and so Sicilian, but more to the point:

Why had these people brought tomatoes to the opera?!?) *Via del Teatro Greco.* ☎ *0942/ 23220. Apr–Sept daily 9am–7pm; Oct–Mar daily 9am–4pm. Admission 4.50€, 2€ ages 18–25; tickets for performances 15€–70€.*

Playing Outside

SWIMMING

Many visitors to Taormina come for the beach, although the sands aren't exactly at the resort. To reach the best and most popular beach, the **Lido Mazzarò** ★★, you have to go south of town via a cable car (☎ **0942/ 23605**) that leaves from Via Pirandello every 15 minutes. A one-way ticket costs 1.60€. This beach is one of the best equipped in Sicily, with bars, restaurants, and hotels. You can rent beach chairs, umbrellas, and watersports equipment at various kiosks from the beginning of April to October. The dense concentration of beach clubs occupies every square inch of sand, but swim away from the shore a bit, and you'll find the sea is gorgeous and clean. To the right of Lido Mazzarò, past the Capo Sant'Andrea headland, is the region's prettiest cove, where twin crescents of beach sweep from a sand spit out to the miniscule **Isola Bella** islet. You can walk here in a minute from the cable car, but it's more fun to paddle a boat from Mazzarò around Capo Sant'Andrea, which hides a few grottoes with excellent light effects on the seaward side.

North of Mazzarò are the long wide beaches of **Spisone** and **Letojanni,** more developed but less crowded than Giardini, the large built-up resort beach south of Isola Bella. With tons of beach clubs playing the summer's hottest European dance hits, **Giardini** ★★ is where most young people come to deplete their bottles of sunscreen.

In addition to the cable car, there's a local bus (1€ one way/75-min ticket) that leaves Taormina for Mazzarò, Spisone, and

Letojanni, and another that heads down the coast to Giardini; you can catch it outside the town gate on Via Pirandello.

HIKING

➜ **Alcantara Gorge** ★ To see some beautiful rapids and waterfalls, head outside of town to the **Gole dell'Alcantara** ★ (☎ **0942/985010**), a series of gorges. Uncharacteristically for Sicily, the waters are extremely cold (but quite refreshing in Aug). During most conditions, it's possible to walk up the river from May to September (when the water level is low), although you must inquire about current conditions before you do. From the parking lot, take an elevator partway into the scenic abyss and then continue on foot. You're likely to get wet, so take your bathing suit. If you don't have appropriate shoes, you can rent rubber boots at the entrance. Allow at least an hour for the hike of the gorge, plus at least another hour for getting there and back. From October to April, only the entrance is accessible, but the view is always panoramic. It costs 2.50€ to enter the gorge, which is open daily from 9am to 5pm. If you're driving, head up SS185 some 17km (11 miles)

from Taormina. To get there by bus, take **Interbus** (☎ **0942/625301;** www.interbus.it) for the 20-minute trip departing from Taormina at 9:30am. There's only one bus back, which leaves at 2:30pm. The round-trip fare is 4.50€. You can also go by taxi from Taormina, but you'll have to negotiate the fare with your driver. If you'd like a taxi, call **Franco Nunzio** at ☎ **0942/51094.**

Shopping

You can't go too far in Taormina without finding brightly colored accessories for the beach—the shops along Corso Umberto have bathing suits, sarongs, and flip-flops at all price ranges. (So, if you somehow "lose" your bikini top after that late-night dip at Giardini, there are tons of shops in Taormina that can hook you up.) As in lots of resort towns, the smarty-pants shop owners here keep their stores open until midnight or later, since they know there's always a good traffic of liquor-filled, carefree vacationers on the prowl after dinner. Indeed, one of the greatest purchases I ever made is the soccer-ball-print Moschino Cheap & Chic handbag I acquired one saucy night in Taormina.

Mt. Etna: Still Blowing Its Top

Looming menacingly over the coast of eastern Sicily, ⭐ ⓑ**Best** **Mt. Etna** ★ ★ ★ is the highest and largest active volcano in Europe—and we do mean active. The peak changes in size over the years but is currently in the neighborhood of 3,292m (10,798 ft.). Etna has been active in modern times (in 1928, the little village of Mascali was buried under its lava), and eruptions in 1971, 1992, 2001, and 2003 rekindled Sicilians' fears.

Etna has figured prominently in history and in Greek mythology. Empedocles, the 5th-century-B.C. Greek philosopher, is said to have jumped into its crater as a sign that he was being delivered directly to Mt.

Olympus to take his seat among the gods. It was under Etna that Zeus crushed the multi-headed, viper-riddled dragon Typhoeus, thereby securing domination over Olympus. Hephaestus, the god of fire and blacksmiths, made his headquarters in Etna, aided by the single-eyed Cyclops.

The Greeks warned that when Typhoeus tried to break out of his prison, lava erupted and earthquakes cracked the land. That must mean that the monster nearly escaped on March 11, 1669, one of the most violent eruptions ever—it destroyed Catania, about 27km (17 miles) away.

OKKIO! It's a Very Active Volcano

Always get the latest report from the tourist office before setting out for a trip to Mt. Etna. Adventurers have been killed by a surprise "belch" (volcanic explosion). In October 2003, Mt. Etna continued to menace eastern Sicily, erupting again and spewing columns of ash that blackened the skies as far away as Africa, as rivers of steaming lava flowed down its volcanic slopes. Crews with bulldozers diverted lava and saved the town of Linguaglossa on the mountain's northern face. Although Mt. Etna has had no major eruptions since, it remains one of the world's most active volcanoes, with sporadic gas, steam, and ash emissions from its summit. In event of emergency, call **Alpine Aid Etna North** (☎ 095/643-300) or Alpine Aid Etna South (☎ 095/914-141).

Getting There

You can visit Mt. Etna as a day trip from various towns and cities: **Catania** is the closest. (Etna is 31km/19 miles north of Catania and 60km/37 miles south of Messina). A tour from Catania, lasting 3 hours, 20 minutes, costs 6€ per person. Inquire at the office at the train station in Catania, Via Caronda 350 (☎ 095/730-62-55; Mon–Sat 9am–7pm).

You can also consider a package tour from Taormina. Contact **CST,** Corso Umberto I 101 (☎ 0942/625301) for tickets and information daily from 6:40am to 8:30pm. Buses run from June to October only; a one-way trip costs 70€ per person. The tour features a guide and a Jeep excursion to the crater; food is not included in the price. From June to August, departures are daily at 3:45pm returning at midnight. In September, tours leave at 3:15pm, returning at 11pm, and in October there is a departure at 2:15pm with a return at 10:30pm.

If you have a car, you can drive yourself. One of the easiest approaches is via E45 south from Messina or Taormina to Acireale. From here, you can approach by following the signs west going via the little towns of Aci Sant'Antonio and Viagrande, continuing west until you reach the Nicolosi. Allow about 45 minutes from Acireale to Nicolosi. At Nicolosi, you can book one of the official guides from **Funivia del Etna** (☎ 095/

911158). From Nicolosi, the road winds its way up to **Rifugio Sapienza,** the starting point for all expeditions to the crater.

Tour Information

To get more information about visiting Mt. Etna, contact the **Parco Regionale dell'Etna,** Via Etnea 107, Nicolosi (☎ 095/914-588) or the base camp of Grande Albergo del Parco, Contrada Serra La Nave, Ragalna (☎ 095/911-500).

Climbing the Slopes

From Rifugio Sapienza, it's possible to hike up to the **Torre del Filosofo (Philosopher's Tower),** at 2,920m (9,578 ft.). The trip here and back takes about 5 hours. At the tower you'll have a panoramic sweep of Etna, with its peaks and craters hissing with steam. This is a difficult hike and not for the faint of heart. The climb is along ashy, pebbly terrain, and once you reach the tower, you have another risky 2-hour hike to the craters. Because the craters can erupt unexpectedly (as they did in the early 1990s, killing 11), *all guided tours to the craters have been suspended*—if you insist on going all the way, you'll have to do it alone. On the return from the Philosopher's Tower to Rifugio Sapienza, you'll pass Valle de Bove, the original crater of Etna. Note that there are no snack shacks once you hit the mountain, so don't forget to bring food if you're planning on being up there for a while.

SICILY

A Quick Look at Catania

Somehow Catania, the closest major town, has learned to live with Etna, but the volcano's presence is felt everywhere. For example, in certain parts of the city you'll find hardened remains of lava flows, all a sickly purple color. Grottoes in weird shapes, almost fantasy-like, line the shores, and boulderlike islands rise from the water.

Catania's present look, earning for it the title of the "baroque city," stems from just after the 1693 earthquake, when the Camastra duke, with several architects and artists, decided to rebuild the city in the baroque style. This reconstruction took the whole 18th century. The most famous artists involved were Alonzo Di Benedetto, Antonino and Francesco Battaglia, Giovanni Vaccarini, and Stefano Ittar. Fragments of solidified black lava were used (first by the Romans and then until the end of the 19th century) in the construction of walls. This lava, and the way it was positioned into the masonry, gave added strength to the walls.

Most rushed visitors today pass through only on their way to or from Catania's airport, second in importance in Sicily only to Palermo's. Flights on Alitalia, including those from Rome, arrive at **Aeroporto Fontanarossa** (☎ 095-340505), 5km (3 miles) south of the city center. From here, you can take the Alibus (or a taxi) into the Catania train station. If you're heading for Taormina, you can catch a train there (nine times a day) for 3€ one-way. However, there is a bus just outside the airport gate that will take you to Taormina in about an hour, costing about 4€. It's much more convenient than getting to the train station.

Aeolian Islands (Isole Eolie)

Lipari: 30km (19 miles) N of Milazzo; Stromboli: 81km (50 miles) N of Milazzo; Vulcano: 20km (12 miles) N of Milazzo

Just off the northeast coast of Sicily lies an archipelago—the **Aeolian Islands** ★★★—that American visitors like Dustin Hoffman and Al Pacino have called the "Hawaii of the Mediterranean." You've never heard of the Aeolian Islands? Likewise, they're unfamiliar with you. Americans are a rare sight on this island chain, which, like Hawaii, consists of dramatic volcanic terrain and smoking or lava-spewing craters. Unlike Hawaii, the Aeolians are a well-kept secret, unmarred by mass international tourism, and known almost exclusively to Italians.

Lipari ★ is the most populated of the *isole Eolie* and has the most bargain hotels and restaurants, but vacationers here tend to be older, or families with small children.

Stromboli ★★ is the most dramatic, with its perpetually smoking volcanic cone and nightly lava showers; **Vulcano** ★ also has a dramatic crater and volcanic mud-baths.

Panarea ★★★ is by far the most fun for young people, attracting international yacht-setters and less wealthy party people alike with its casually chic village, secluded coves, and hip nightlife. The other islands in the archipelago, Filicudi, Alicudi, and Salina (where *Il Postino* was filmed) are sleepy and rustic, with few tourist-oriented facilities (e.g., where new-agey Italians might go in summer for a yoga retreat and other holistic things, staying in accommodations that function as goatherders' lodges the rest of the year).

The Aeolian Islands

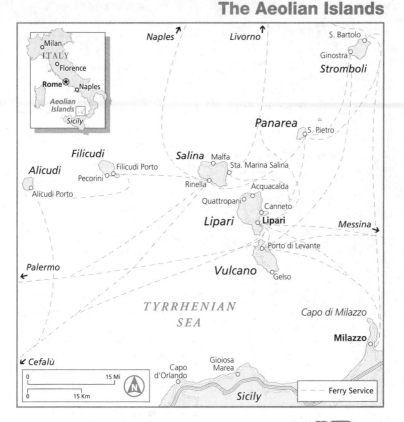

Naples ↗

Livorno ↑

S. Bartolo

Ginostra

Stromboli

Panarea ○ S. Pietro

ITALY
○ Milan
○ Florence
Rome ⊕ ○ Naples
Aeolian Islands
Sicily

Filicudi ○
Salina Malfa
○ Sta. Marina Salina

Alicudi
Filicudi Porto ○
Pecorini ○○
Rinella ○
Acquacalda

○ Alicudi Porto
Quattropani ○ Canneto

Lipari ○ **Lipari**

Messina ↘

○ Porto di Levante

Palermo
←

Vulcano ○ Gelso

*TYRRHENIAN
SEA*

Capo di Milazzo

Milazzo ○

↙ Cefalù

0 ———— 15 Mi

0 ———— 15 Km

Capo
d'Orlando ○

Gioiosa
Marea ○

Sicily

‑ ‑ ‑ Ferry Service

Tourist season runs from May to October (which means that from Nov–Apr, hydrofoil and ferry service is scant, and most restaurants, hotels, and vacation-related services will be closed). Crowds swell to overflowing in August, the traditional Italian vacation month, when hotels are at their most expensive, and quite hard to come by if you don't book well in advance. Note that almost all accommodations rates in the Aeolians are quoted **per person,** per night, breakfast included.

Panarea

There's something magical and blessed about this tiny speck of land surrounded by historic seas and active volcanoes. 📺 Best **Panarea** is glamorous, unpretentious, and hedonistic, attracting young and beautiful people in their early 20s to mid-30s from June to September. Holidaymakers here a mix of down-to-earth Sicilians and cosmopolitan Italians from Milan, Turin, and Rome, who may work in fashion, finance, and film, many of whom will be more than willing to practice their English with you while you grind away at the open-air *discoteca* at the Hotel Raya. What makes Panarea so special is that it's still an insider place, and some of my fellow Italy insiders will probably be annoyed that I'm sharing the secret of Panarea in this book. If word gets out, please don't tell 'em I sent you.

One Day at the Beach, Three Outfits

As with any Italian beach destination, Panarea has a very specific dress code despite its laid-back, island vibe. First, your **day outfit** is what you wear to the beach or on a boat trip—bathing suit, cover-up, and flip-flops. When you get back from your seafaring adventures in the afternoon, it's time to go back to the hotel and change into your *aperitivo* outfit—bathing suit, cover-up, and flip-flops. (Note that it is essential that the components of *aperitivo* outfit be different from day outfit.) Finally, once you've had a few drinks and snacks at the port, return to the hotel, shower, and change into your **evening outfit**—any casual ensemble of gauzy fabrics, flat sandals, and ethnic-looking accessories will do the trick for dinner and getting your freak on at the Raya disco.

THE BEST OF PANAREA

Best Way to Pretend You're Columbus

Circumnavigating the island—as a total boating novice—in a **rental *barchetta***. Drop anchor, enjoy an on-board picnic, and dive into gorgeous coves, never having to contend with waves or swells in the open sea. Live to tell the harrowing tale of how you guided your vessel back into port after guzzling wine with the crew of the *Pinta* and the *Santa Maria*.

Best Way to Burn Off Cannoli Calories

Pounding the 2m-wide (6½-ft.) pavement on the panoramic, 20-minute walk from the port to Caletta dei Zimmari beach.

Best Place to Find One-Night Romance

Who cares if you don't speak Italian and they don't speak English? The music blaring under the stars at the **Hotel Raya Discoteca** is too loud to make any words intelligible anyway. Scope your bronzed and linen-shirted quarry from the sidelines, and then make your move. . . . In summer, people come to Panarea to hook up. See p. 709.

Best Hangover Cure

Slurping down a smoothie at the **Bar del Porto**. See p. 708.

GETTING THERE

We normally recommend the ferry when you're traveling to Italy's islands, since they're cheaper and have open-air decks where you can walk around, but in this case, Panarea's distance from the closest major port means that the **hydrofoil** will save you a lot of valuable travel time.

The easiest way to reach Panarea, and the rest of the Aeolian Islands, is by hydrofoil from Milazzo, on the northeastern coast of Sicily. Milazzo consists of its depressing industrial marina, a godforsaken lineup of waterfront restaurants, and not much more, so plan to arrive here from somewhere else (there are regular buses from Taormina, Catania, and Messina), and sail to the island the same day. Hydrofoils operated by **Siremar** (☎ **081/844-9297** or toll-free in Italy only ☎ 892-123; www.siremar.it) take about 2 hours to reach Panarea from Milazzo, including stops at Vulcano and Lipari en route for about 12€-14€, depending on the season. (Compare with almost 4 hr. with the conventional ferry!)

You can also get to Panarea from mainland Italy—**SNAV** (☎ **081/428-5555**; www.snav.it) hydrofoils sail from Naples-Mergellina once per day. Trip time to Panarea is 4½ hours and it costs 76€ one-way.

GETTING AROUND

One thing's for sure, you don't have to worry about getting lost on Panarea. The whole island measures a scant 5 sq. km (2 sq. miles),

SICILY

and the village of **San Pietro,** which surrounds the port, is pretty much where everything's at, in terms of lodging, dining, and partying. From the port area, you can walk to the beach at Cala dei Zimmari (20 minutes along a pretty road, with red rocks, prickly pears, and sea views that will make you stop and say, "Woo hoo, I'm on a very exclusive island off Sicily!" at least once along the way). Everything else you might want to visit—secluded coves, the uninhabited western shore of the island, or swimming locales that are separate islands altogether—are reached by sea, either via group water taxi, or, better yet, via Panarea's ubiquitous small, inexpensive rental motorboats that you pilot yourself. See "Playing Outside," p. 709.

SLEEPING
Doable
➜**Camere alla Caletta** ★ Under the same management as Oasi da Pina (see below), but a bit farther away from the port, this yellow-and-whitewashed Aeolian-style structure has terraces with *epulere* (columns) and *bisuoli* (benches made of local stone). Airy, spare, but comfortable rooms have bath, A/C, minibar, TV, fan, and hair dryer. *Località Caletta.* ☎ *090/983-324. www.dapina.com. 80€–120€ per person.*

➜**Hycesia** ★★ With cane furniture and tile floors in soft blues, this is a soothing place to stay in the heart of San Pietro, the village directly behind the port. The hotel's in-house restaurant, also called Hycesia, is one of the most deservedly popular places to eat on Panarea, so if you stay here, you'll get on a priority list for the highly coveted tables here. *Via di San Pietro.* ☎ *090/983-041. www.hycesia.it. 45€–120€ per person, depending on the season.*

➜**Oasi da Pina** ★★ One of the more "distant" hotels from the port (it's a whole 5-min. walk), the "Oasis" is indeed a tranquil spot. Rooms are very comfortably furnished (without being too elegant for the beach-vacation atmosphere of Panarea), with bold, hand-painted ceramic tiles on the walls and floor. All rooms come with A/C, TV, minibar, and TV. The landscape design makes the most of small area, creating a resort-y feel with its natural rock environment, grassy grounds, curvy pool, and rattan loungers. Also on the premises, there's a bar, a geothermic Jacuzzi tub, two restaurants, a minimarket, and rental office for scooters and electric cars. The management also rents apartments and rooms farther up the hill (see Camere alla Caletta, above). *Via di San Pietro.* ☎ *090/983-324. www.dapina.com. 80€–120€ per person.*

Splurge
➜**Hotel Quartara** ★★ In the tangle of narrow lanes on the hill behind the port, this is an enchanting place to stay. Asian-inspired rooms are done up in soothing tones of gray and blue that have a way of cooling your sunburn even if the aloe you bought at the local *farmacia* doesn't. Each unit has its own private sitting area in front of the room entrance, and all guests can avail of the wonderful roof solarium, with comfy loungers and views over the water to Stromboli. *Via di San Pietro 15.* ☎ *090/983-027. www.quartara hotel.com. Double 65€–190€.*

EATING
The food is amazing on Panarea. Even beach snack-shacks and simple hotel restaurants will have your tastebuds screaming for more seafood and tomatoes. The only place to steer clear of is the overpriced and overrated restaurant at the Hotel Raya.

Snacks
➜**Bar at Caletta dei Zimmari** ★ This is a no-frills snack bar adjacent to the beach at Caletta dei Zimmari, with sandwiches and prepackaged Algida ice creams you'll come to know and love in Italy, but it also happens to be home of the best tomato-and-garlic *bruschetta* I've ever tasted. *Mamma mia,*

SICILY

there is just something about Sicilian produce. *Beach at Caletta dei Zimmari.*

MTV Best ➔ **Bar del Porto** ★ Located right opposite the hydrofoil landing, this snack bar serves the busy port community of dock workers, fishermen, and day-trippers. It's also a convenient spot where you can pick up a sandwich to take on boat trips around the island. Feeling a bit rough after that all-nighter at the Raya Discoteca? Have the Bar del Porto make you a fresh fruit smoothie—your hangover will back down in 5 minutes flat once you've soaked up all those pesticide-free nutrients. (I swear, I've never experienced anything so effective.) By night, the bar sees its share of chic customers settle in for an *aperitivo* at its harbor-facing outside tables. *Piazza del Porto.*

Doable

➔ **Hycesia** ★★★ Even before you board your hydrofoil to Panarea, call and make a dinner reservation at Hycesia. I'm not kidding. The setting isn't particularly glamorous, and there's no sea view, but it's a perfect Panarean courtyard, enclosed by white-washed stone walls and wooden trellises. To start, try the lobster salad with *pachino* (Sicilian cherry tomatoes—of a sweetness that's incredible); for your primo, the pasta with squid ink and fresh ricotta is fantastic (as is the island specialty, pasta with sea urchins), then move onto a secondo of seared tuna with four types of vinegar, mint, and lemon. *Via di San Pietro.* ☎ *090/983-041. Daily for dinner. Reservations essential. Primi 10€–15€; secondi 15€–18€.*

➔ **La Risacca** ★★★ Soft sea breezes temper the warm Sicilian summer nights in this pavilion-style dining room overlooking the port. Rich woods, local ceramics, stone benches, and cushions in south Asian fabrics give La Risacca a chic, pared-down colonial feel. As for the food, which comes largely from the sea, just let them bring you the house specialties. A local tomato-and–sea urchin

pasta, *pasta ai ricci di mare,* sounded strange at first, but was recommended so irrefutably by our waiter that we had to order it—an explosion of balanced flavor, with no weird texture or intense fishy taste, that sea urchin pasta was probably the most amazing seafood pasta we've ever had. The menu also offers secondi of simply and exquisitely prepared fish, such as tuna and swordfish, caught that morning in the waters off Panarea. And for those of you who think it's cool to have guacamole mixed right at your table in a Mexican restaurant, wait until you order the cannoli at La Risacca! Cannoli here are not so much a dessert as a dramatic tour de force, as each component of this quintessentially Sicilian treat is assembled right in front of you (by a hot Sicilian waiter, no less) and served with sexy flair. For the setting, the food, the service, and the price tag, this is one of the most memorable meals we've had, anywhere. *Via di San Pietro.* ☎ *090/983-277. Daily for dinner. Reservations recommended. Primi 10€–15€; secondi 15€–18€.*

PARTYING

The whole island is a party, and the island is small, so you won't have to look too hard to find a place to kick back, drink, dance, and have fun. The stretch of storefronts along the port include several bars that are packed at *aperitivo* hour. After dinner, all and sundry head to the discoteca at the Hotel Raya, so if you spotted a hottie on the beach that afternoon, he's sure to be there, showered, ironed, and three sheets to the wind.

➔ **Bridge** ★ *APERITIVO* If you want to party with the coolest kids on Panarea, you'd better make yourself a fixture at this *aperitivo* bar (an ex-bridge club), overlooking the port. The best thing about this place is that you have a prime view of new arrivals at the hydrofoil landing, so while you shake your booty in your bikini top and sarong, you can vamp for the luggage-toting *arrivistes* and pretend that you've partying on Panarea all summer, dahling! (Let's just hope you have the tan to back it up.) *Via Porto.* ☎ *339/217-2605.*

🎵 **Best** →**Raya** ★★ DISCOTECA For the full-on open-air, Mediterranean summer dance club experience, the *discoteca* at the Hotel Raya is pretty much the only game in town. (The hotel itself and in-house restaurant, by the way, are overpriced and overrated, so just come for the party after dinner.) It's also a great place to find a summer fling: Who cares if you don't speak Italian and they don't speak English? The music blaring under the stars here is too loud to make any words intelligible anyway. Scope your bronzed and linen-shirted quarry from the sidelines, and then make your move. Via di San Pietro. ☎ **090/983013.** www.hotelraya.it. Daily 10pm–5am.

SIGHTSEEING

It might come as a relief to know that there's nothing cultural you have to see on Panarea. Yeah, there's the requisite archaeological site, the *Villaggio Preistorico* ("Prehistoric Village," a Bronze Age settlement with a few rings of yellowish stone preserved) on the western end of the island, near the beach at Cala Junco. Unless you're a Smurf, in which case the ruins here will look like Stonehenge, the *Villagio Preistorico* is totally missable as Italian archaeological sites go. So, hit the beach, so that *you'll* be a tanned sight worth seeing at *aperitivo* hour instead!

PLAYING OUTSIDE
Boating

🎵 **Best** Getting your own *barchetta* ("little boat") is de rigueur for exploring Panarea's petite perimeter. Indeed, navigating the calm waters around Italy's lesser-known islands at the helm of your own small motorboat is one of life's most glorious pleasures, permitting you to drop anchor and jump in the deep green-blue sea wherever you please. Rental outfits couldn't care less if you don't have

any boating experience—they'll just take one look at you, and after sizing you up, set you up with the simplest craft they think you can handle and give you a quick-and-dirty lesson on how to troubleshoot any outboard motor issues.

Panarea is tiny, and its waters are calm, so everyone ends up renting the cheapest and easiest option, a 3m (10-ft.) wooden *gozzo,* which comes with a lightweight fabric sun shade. Half-day rentals, which start at 60€, give you plenty of time to circumnavigate the island, with several stops for swimming in gorgeous coves, where the only other people you're likely to encounter are debonair Italian captains-of-industry who will invite you aboard their sleek cigarette boats and offer you champagne and mozzarella. The tricky part is bringing your ship back into port after all that sun and booze. . . .

Boat rental agencies, including **Eolie Mare** (☎ **388/9810100**), **Panarea Service** (☎ **338/4093772**), and **Da Diego** (☎ **338/2931533**), are all over Panarea's bustling little port—just look for the bobbing, light-blue hulls and *NOLEGGIO* (rental) signs. As with vehicle rentals anywhere, you'll have to sign a legal waiver, and bring your boat back with a full tank (there's a fuel station at the port), or pay a surcharge. In the unlikely event you run into mechanical problems, Panarea is so small and friendly that any passing boat will stop to help you, and if they can't get you on your way, they'll call your agency, who will "rescue" you within 20 minutes.

If, on the other hand, you don't have the time, budget, or desire to rent your own small craft, the port at Panarea also has plenty of larger motorboats which function as group water-taxis to the island's hard-to-access coves and beaches. These shuttles, operated by the same agencies as listed above, will also take you to Basiluzzo, Lisca Bianca, and the other *isolotti* ("little islands") which tend to be packed with day-trippers and not nearly as pleasant as the swimming spots along the shores of Panarea itself.

Swimming

➜ **Cala Junco** ★★ A bit farther west of Caletta Zimmari, on the southern side of the island, Cala Junco (pronounced "*Yoon*-ko") consists of huge, light-gray boulders that are weathered to such a smooth texture that it can be more comfortable to prop yourself up against these rounded rocks than in the sand or a beach chair. The protected cove off Cala Junco has dark and clear Mediterranean green-blue waters, with plenty of spots where you can grip the rock walls, rest, and dive down to explore the fish-filled reefs. No facilities. Use of beach: free. Access by 40-min. walk from town (not recommended) or by water taxi from port, about 5€.

➜ **Caletta dei Zimmari** ★ A relaxed and panoramic walk south from the port and main town of Panarea takes you to Caletta dei Zimmari, the only real stretch of sandy shore on the island. It's also one of few swimming spots you don't need a boat to access, which makes it a good option when you only have half a morning of beach time before you have to catch the hydrofoil. Caletta dei Zimmari can get crowded, by Panarea standards (which really isn't very crowded), and the water here, while clean and calm, is a wide bay of sandy shallows, not the fabulous, deep emerald coves you'll find elsewhere on the island. The no-frills snack bar nearby has toilets, changing rooms, and astonishingly delicious tomato *bruschetta*. Use of beach: free. Access by 20-min. walk from town.

➜ **Islands off Panarea** ★ Between 500m and 2km (1,640 ft.–1¼ mile) off the coast of Panarea, Lisca Bianca, Dattilo, Formiche, I Panarelli, and Bottaro, and Basiluzzo are rock outcroppings in the middle of the sea, marketed as fantastic swimming destinations by the water taxi companies that serve them. With the exception of Basiluzzo, whose virgin coves have towering, awesomely striated limestone walls, the *isolotti* off Panarea are too tiny for the crowds of swimmers that are dumped there throughout the day. It's worth the trip only if you feel like going for a boat ride, not if you feel like lounging at the beach.

SHOPPING

Panarea is full of ethnic-chic little boutiques where you can pick up vaguely Indian- or Southeast Asian–looking gear, from sarongs to cool wrist cuffs with seashells sewn on. Even if you don't stay at the hotel, you should pay a visit to the **Hotel Raya boutique,** Via di San Pietro (☎ **090/983013;** www.hotel raya.it) and pick up a white T-shirt, emblazoned with the words HOTEL RAYA PANAREA in aqua and a simple, nondorky graphic of a sting ray. This souvenir of your exclusive Italian island getaway will be a great gym shirt for years to come.

Vulcano

Vulcano ★, the island closest to the mainland, the ancient Thermessa, figured heavily in the mythologies of the region. The still-active **Vulcano della Fossa** was thought to be not only the home of Vulcan but also the gateway to Hades. Thucydides, Siculus, and Aristotle each recorded eruptions. Three dormant craters also exist on the island, but a climb to the rim of the active **Gran Cratere (Big Crater)** ★★★ draws the most attention. It hasn't erupted since 1890, but one look inside the sulfur-belching hole makes you understand how it could've inspired the hellish legends surrounding it. The 418m (1,371 ft.) peak is an easier climb than the one on Stromboli, taking just about an hour—though it's just as hot, and the same precautions prevail. Avoid midday, load up on sunscreen and water, and wear good hiking shoes.

Here the risks of mounting a volcano aren't addressed by legislation, so you can make the climb without a guide. Breathing the sulfuric air at the summit has its risks, though, because the steam is tainted with numerous toxins. To get to the peak from Porto Levante, the main port, follow Via Piano away from the sea for about 200m (656 ft.) until you see the first of the *CRATERE* signs, and then follow the marked trail.

The **Laghetto di Fanghi,** famous free mud baths that reputedly cure every known ailment, are along Via Provinciale a short way from the port. Be warned that the mud discolors everything from cloth to jewelry, which is one explanation for the prevalent nudity. Expect to encounter muddy pools brimming with naked, package-tour Germans. Within sight, the *acquacalda* features hot-water jets that act as a natural Jacuzzi. Either can scald you if you step or sit on the vents that release the heat, so take care if you decide to enter.

The island offers one of the few smooth sandy beaches in the entire chain, the **Spiaggia Sabbie Nere (Black Sands Beach),** with dark sand so hot in the midday sun that thongs or wading shoes are suggested if you plan to while away your day along the shore. You can find the beach by following signs posted along Via Ponente.

A knowledge of street names is worthless, really, because there are no signs. Not to worry—the locals who gather at the dock are friendly and experienced at giving directions to tongue-tied foreign visitors, especially because all they ever have to point out are the paths to the crater, the mud baths, and the beach. You'll need to spend little time in the village center itself. This is a drab 1970s eyesore filled with souvenir shops and fast-food snack bars.

SLEEPING

Doable

➔ **Hotel Eolian** ★ Opening onto Ponente Bay, this hotel consists of a series of white-sided stucco bungalows in a garden studded with palms and tropical plants. None opens onto a view of the water—that's reserved for the restaurant and bar—but most guests spend their days beside the sea anyway. The hotel was built in keeping with the typical Aeolian style of architecture, with a main building surrounded by several bungalows. All the buildings are set in a luxuriant Mediterranean garden. From the restaurant and bar you can enjoy a panoramic view of some of the other islands, including Lipari, Salina, and Filicudi. You can walk down from the terrace of the bar to reach the beach where you can indulge in various watersports or else rent small boats to discover some of the remote and more romantic parts of the Vulcano coastline. A thermal sulphurous pool was installed in 2001, and it's said to aid bodies with poor circulation. Bedrooms are furnished in a very minimalist way, each room medium in size with a tiled bathroom with a shower unit. Only two accommodations are equipped with bathtubs. *Via Porto Levante.* ☎ *090/9852151. www.eolianhotel.com. Double per person 124€–176€, 148€–214€ with half board. Rates include breakfast. Closed Oct–Apr.*

Splurge

➔ **Les Sables Noirs** ★★ This is the most elegant place to stay on Vulcano, offering surprising luxury in this remote outpost. Overlooking a black sandy beach, its bedrooms also front a panoramic sweep of the Bay of Ponente. The resort evokes the aura of the Caribbean with its stucco and bamboo. You get both style and excellent service here. Accommodations are spacious and comfortably furnished, each decorated in a typical Mediterranean style, many of them opening onto a wide flowering balcony. All have tiled bathrooms, about half with showers, the other with bathtubs. A special feature here is the **restaurant,** which serves not only impressive regional specialties but opens onto a panoramic terrace in front of the beach. *Via Porto di Ponente.* ☎ *090/9850. www.framonhotels.com. Double 186€, suite 340€. Closed Oct–Mar.*

SICILY

EATING

→ **Vincenzino** SICILIAN/AEOLIAN   This is the most appealing of the trattorie near the ferry port. Known for its hefty portions and affordable prices, it serves clients in a rustic setting, feeding them well with large portions of mainly fish dishes. You might begin with spaghetti Vincenzino with crayfish, capers, and a tomato sauce. Sometimes fish is shaped into roulades, particularly the swordfish, or else it might appear in a seafood salad. We're especially fond of the risotto *alla pescatora,* with crayfish, mussels, and other sea creatures. Another good choice is the house-style macaroni with ricotta, eggplant, fresh tomatoes, and herbs. From October to March, the menu is limited to a simple array of platters from the bar. *Via Porto di Levante.* ☎ *090/ 9852016. Reservations recommended. Main courses 8€–10€; fixed-price menu 15€. Daily noon–3pm and 7–10pm.*

Lipari

Homer called it "a floating island, a wall of bronze and splendid smooth sheer cliffs." The offspring of seven volcanic eruptions, **Lipari** ★ is the largest of the Aeolians. Lipari is also the name of the island's only real town. It's the administrative headquarters of the Aeolian Islands (except autonomous Salina). The town sits on a plateau of red volcanic rock on the southeastern shore, framed by two beaches, Marina Lunga, which functions as the harbor, and Marina Corta.

Its dominant feature is a 16th-century **Spanish castle,** within the walls of which lies a 17th-century cathedral featuring a 16th-century Madonna and an 18th-century silver statue of San Bartolomeo. There's also an **archaeological park** where stratified clues about continuous civilizations dating from 1700 B.C. have been uncovered.

Excellent artifacts from the Stone and Bronze ages, as well as relics from Greek and Roman acropolises that once stood here, are housed next door in the former bishop's palace, now the **Museo Archeologico Eoliano** ★★, Via del Castello (☎ **090/ 9880174**), one of Sicily's major archaeological museums. It houses one of the world's finest Neolithic collections. The oldest discoveries date from 4200 B.C. Lustrous red ceramics, known as the "Diana style," come from the last Neolithic period, 3000 to 2500 B.C. Other exhibits are reconstructed necropolises from the Middle Bronze Age and a 6th-century A.D. depiction of Greek warships. Some 1,200 pieces of painted terra cotta from the 4th and 3rd centuries B.C., including stone theatrical masks, are on exhibit. The museum also houses the only Late Bronze Age (8th-c. B.C.) necropolis found in Sicily. It's open daily 9am to 1:30pm and 3 to 7pm. Admission is 4.50€.

The most popular **beaches** are at **Canneto,** about a 20-minute walk north of Lipari on the eastern coast, and, just north of it, **Spiaggia Bianca** (named for the white sand, an oddity among the region's black sands). To reach the beach from Canneto, take the waterfront road, climb the stairs of Via Marina Garibaldi, and then veer right down a narrow cobbled path for about 297m (974 ft.).

Acquacalda (Hot Water) is the island's northernmost city, but nobody likes to go on its beaches (the black sand is rocky and unpleasant for walking or lying on). The town is also known for its obsidian and pumice quarries. West of Acquacalda at Quattropani, you can make a steep climb to the **Duomo de Chiesa Barca,** where the point of interest isn't the cathedral but the panoramic view from the church grounds. On the west coast, 4km (2¹⁄₂ miles) from Lipari, the island's other great view is available by making another steep climb to the **Quattrocchi Belvedere.**

Twenty-nine kilometers (18 miles) of road circle the island, connecting all its villages and attractions. Buses run by Lipari's **Autobus Urso Guglielmo,** 9 Via Cappuccini (☎ 090/9811262), make 10 circuits of the island per day. Tickets costing 1.55€ are purchased onboard from the driver. Urso buses also operate tours of the island in summer from the beginning of July until the end of September. Three buses at a time leave at 9:30am, 11:30am, and 5pm, costing 3.70€ for the circuit. Along the way you'll pass the highlights of Lipari's scenery. It's also possible to summon one of the independently operated taxis, most of which are found at Marina Corta.

SLEEPING

Doable

➜ **Hotel Carasco** ★★ This hotel enjoys the most dramatic location in Lipari, with its own private stretch of rocks opening onto the sea. There are panoramic views from its bougainvillea-draped pool. Carasco consists of two buildings linked by an addition, sitting on its lonely bluff by the sea. The cool interior contrasts with the bright heat of the outdoors; it has brown terra-cotta floors and dark-wood furniture upholstered in dark fabrics. Each well-furnished bedroom comes with a ceiling fan and rustic artifacts, with an emphasis on comfort. This hotel opened in 1971 and has stayed up-to-date ever since. Try, if possible, for a room with one of the private balconies. Bathrooms are in fine condition and equipped with shower or tub. *Porto delle Genti, 98055 Lipari.* ☎ *090/9811605. www.carasco.it. Half board 70€–120€ per person. Closed Oct 13–Easter.*

Splurge

➜ **Villa Meligunis** ★★ This first-class hotel is as good as it gets in the Aeolian Islands. A restored 18th-century villa with additions, it represents the epitome of Aeolian hospitality. Less than 45m (148 ft.) from the ferry docks, this appealingly contemporary hotel rose from a cluster of 17th-century fishermen's

cottages at Marina Corta. Its architectural style is Spanish Mediterranean, with a dramatic rooftop terrace overlooking the bay. It's furnished with every comfort, with stylish charm from its lovely fountain to its wrought-iron bedsteads that fashion photographers have used as a backdrop. The guest rooms are comfortably furnished with summery pieces and remain relatively uncluttered, each with a well-maintained bathroom with either a tub or a shower. The hotel's name derives from the ancient Greek designation for Lipari, Meligunia. The on-site restaurant serves excellent regional specialties. *Via Marte 7, 98055 Lipari.* ☎ *090/9812426. www.villameligunis.it. Double 120€–290€ double, suite 195€–365€.*

EATING

➜ **E Pulera** ★★ SICILIAN/AEOLIAN Owned by the same family that owns the Filippino (see below), this restaurant emphasizes its Aeolian origins. Artifacts and maps of the islands fashioned from ceramic tiles are scattered about. Some tables occupy a terrace with a view of a flowering lawn where you'll probably want to linger. Specialties include a delightful version of *zuppe di pesce alla pescatora* (fishermen's soup), *bocconcini di pesce spada* (swordfish ragout), and risotto with crayfish or squid in its own ink. Other good choices are a rich assortment of seafood antipasti that's usually laden with basil and garlic, *roulade* of eggplant, and herb-laden versions of roasted lamb. We were recently served one of the most delightful pasta dishes we'd ever tasted in the Aeolian Islands: fettuccine with yellow pumpkin, shrimp, and wild fennel. *Via Isabella Vainiches.* ☎ *090/9811158. Reservations recommended. Main courses 10€–13€. Daily 8pm–midnight. Closed Oct–May 15.*

➜ **Filippino** ★★ SICILIAN/AEOLIAN It's a pleasant surprise to find such a fine restaurant in such a remote location. Filippino has

SICILY

thrived in the heart of town, near Town Hall, since 1910, when it was opened by the ancestors of the family that runs it today. You'll dine in one of two large rooms or on an outdoor terrace ringed with flowering shrubs and potted flowers. Menu items are based on old-fashioned Sicilian recipes and prepared with flair. Try the *maccheroni* stuffed with stone bass or with mozzarella, prosciutto, and ricotta baked in the oven. Veal scaloppine is tempting when cooked in Malvasia wine, and the array of fresh fish is broad. We especially enjoyed the *cupolette di pesce spada* with basil ("little dome" of swordfish) and the eggplant *caponata*. *Piazza Mazzini.* ☎ *090/9811002. Reservations required July– Aug. Main courses 6€–10€. Daily noon– 2:30pm and 7:30–10:30pm. Closed Mon Oct–Mar.*

→ **La Nassa** ★ SICILIAN/AEOLIAN   At this enchanting family-run restaurant, the delectable cuisine of Donna Teresa matches the enthusiasm of her son Bartolo, who has thousands of interesting stories to tell. The food is the most genuine and fresh you can find on the island, prepared respecting both antique traditions and modern taste. After the *sette perle* ("seven pearl") appetizer, a combination of fresh fish, sweet shrimp, and spices, you can try the fish roulades, or any kind of fish you like, cooked in every possible way to satisfy your request. Local favorites include *sarago, cernia,* and *dentice,* as delicate in texture as their names are untranslatable. If you are more in a meat mood (not likely after you've seen the restaurant's boats coming back with delicious, just-caught fish), you can opt for Teresa's sausages seasoned with Aeolian herbs. *Via G. Franza 41.* ☎ *090/9811319. Reservations recommended. Main courses 8€–18€. Daily July–Sept for lunch and dinner; Fri–Wed May–June for lunch and dinner. Closed Nov–Easter.*

Stromboli

The most distant island in the archipelago, **Stromboli** ★★ achieved notoriety and became a household word in the U.S. in 1950 with the release of the Roberto Rossellini cinéma vérité film starring Ingrid Bergman. The American public was far more interested in the "illicit" affair between Bergman and Rossellini than in the film. Although the affair was tame by today's standards, it temporarily ended Bergman's American film career, and she was denounced on the Senate floor. People today are more likely to know "Stromboli" as the name of countless Italian-American pizza and calzone joints.

The entire surface of Stromboli is the cone of a sluggish but active volcano. Puffs of smoke can be seen during the day. At night on the **Sciara del Fuoco (Slope of Fire)** ★★, lava glows on its way down to meet the sea with a loud hiss and a cloud of steam—a memorable vision that might leave you feeling a little too vulnerable.

In fact, the island can serve as a fantasyland for those who have volcano-mania. The main attraction is a steep, difficult climb to the lip of the 915m (3,000-ft.) **Gran Cratere** ★★★. The view of bubbling pools of ooze (which glow with heat at night) is accompanied by rising clouds of steam and a sulfuric stench. The journey is a 3-hour hike best taken in early morning or late afternoon to avoid the worst of the brutal sunshine—and even then it requires plenty of sunscreen and water and a good pair of shoes. The law states that you can climb the slope only with a guide. The island's authorized guide company is **Guide Alpine Autorizzate** (☎ **090/986211**), which charges 15€ per person to scale the volcano. Guides lead groups on a 3-hour trip up the mountain, leaving at 5pm and returning at 11pm. The trip down takes only 2 hours but you're allowed an hour at the rim.

In spite of the volcano and its sloped terrain, there are two settlements. **Ginostra** is on the southwestern shore, little more than a cluster of summer homes with 15 year-round residents. **Stromboli** is on the northeastern shore, a conglomeration of the villages of Ficogrande, San Vincenzo, and Piscita, where the only in-town attraction is the black-sand beach.

SLEEPING

Doable

➜ **La Locanda del Barbablu** ★ This is a quirky choice, a charming isolated Aeolian inn with only a few rooms, standing against turn-of-the-20th-century breakfronts. Rooms are small but comfortably furnished, often with four-poster beds encrusted with cherubs and mother-of-pearl inlay. There's a wide terrace opening onto dramatic views of the volcano and the sea. It's worthwhile to dine in the **restaurant** even if you're not a guest. The cuisine is inventive, offering dishes such as filet of tuna baked in cloves and cinnamon and flavored with hot peppers. *Via Vittorio Emanuele 17–19, 98050 Stromboli.* ☎ *090/986118. Double 120€–240€. Closed Nov–Feb.*

➜ **La Sirenetta–Park Hotel** ★★ This is a well-maintained government-rated four-star hotel, with white-tile floors and walls offset by contemporary dark-wood furniture and trim. The rooms each possess a quality mattress and a small tiled bathroom. Natural wicker furnishings upholstered with blue floral prints grace the public areas. A large terrace overlooks the sea. *Via Marina 33, 98050 Ficogrande (Stromboli).* ☎ *090/986025. www.lasirenetta.it. Double 140€–256€ in summer; 180€–300€ with half board. Rates include breakfast. Off-season discounts. Closed Nov 1 to mid-Mar.*

EATING

➜ **Il Canneto** AEOLIAN   This is a typical island restaurant constructed in the old style

A Stromboli Bar

As the sun sets and the volcano lights the sky, everybody heads for the island's most popular bar, **Bar Ingrid,** at Piazza San Vicenzo (☎ **090/986385**).

with white walls and dark tables of solid wood. Among the local trattorie, it's one of the more reliable joints but nothing fancy. The specialty of the kitchen is always fish caught in local waters. A delectable pasta is large macaroni with minced swordfish or a whitefish cooked in a light tomato sauce with fresh herbs. Most diners opt for the mixed grilled fish based on the catch of the day. Swordfish roulades are also prepared with a certain flair here. The summer diners are often more exotic than the fish on the platters. *Via Roma 64.* ☎ *090/986014. Reservations recommended. Main courses 9€–15€. Daily 7–11pm. Closed Oct–Mar.*

➜ **Punta Lena** ★ AEOLIAN   The island's best cuisine is served at this old Aeolian house that's been tastefully converted into a 17-seat restaurant, with a terrace opening onto the sea. The restaurant lies on the beach, a 10-minute walk from the center of town. Most of the local cuisine is based on the use of fresh fish, and there is a genuine effort here to cook with fresh products whenever possible. We recently dropped by to sample their spaghetti *Stromboliana* made with fresh anchovies, wild fennel, fresh mint, and tomatoes, the pasta topped with toasted croutons. Except for the unnecessary croutons, this was an excellent dish, as was the gnocchi *alla Saracena* with whitefish, capers, olives, and tomatoes. The chef loves spaghetti as much as Rudolph Valentino did, and that pasta also appears with freshly caught little shrimp and sautéed zucchini. Your best bet is to stick to whatever the fishermen brought in that day—just ask one of the friendly waiters. The restaurant also stocks the island's widest selection of wines. Fish is served grilled, stewed, or *en papillote* (in paper casing).

Marina Ficogrande. ☎ *090/986204. Reservations recommended. Main courses 8€–15€. Daily noon–2:30pm and 7–11pm. Closed Nov 1–Mar 31.*

Appendix: Italy in Depth

The Etruscans

Of all the early inhabitants of Italy, the most significant were the Etruscans. But who were they? No one knows, and the many inscriptions that they left behind (mostly on graves) are of no help because the Etruscan language has never been deciphered by modern scholars. It's thought they arrived on the eastern coast of Umbria several centuries before Rome was built, around 800 B.C. Their religious rites and architecture show an obvious contact with Mesopotamia; the Etruscans might have been refugees from Asia Minor who traveled west about 1200 to 1000 B.C. Within 2 centuries, they had subjugated Tuscany and Campania and the Villanova tribes who lived there.

While the Etruscans were building temples at Tarquinia and Caere (present-day Cerveteri), the few nervous Latin tribes who remained outside their sway were gravitating to Rome, then little more than a village of sheepherders. As Rome's power grew, however, it increasingly profited from the strategically important Tiber crossing, where the ancient Salt Way (Via Salaria) turned northeastward toward the central Apennines.

From their base at Rome, the Latins remained free of the Etruscans until about 600 B.C. But the Etruscan advance was inexorable, and although the Latin tribes concentrated their forces at Rome for a last stand, they were swept away by the sophisticated Mesopotamian conquerors. The new overlords introduced gold tableware and jewelry, bronze urns and terra-cotta statuary, and the best of Greek and Asia Minor art and culture. They also made Rome the governmental seat of all Latium. Roma is an Etruscan name, and the kings of Rome had Etruscan names: Numa, Ancus, Tarquinius, and even Romulus.

The Estruscans ruled until the Roman revolt around 510 B.C., and by 250 B.C. the Romans and their Campania allies had vanquished the Etruscans, wiping out their language and religion. However, many of the former rulers' manners and beliefs remained and were assimilated into the culture. Even today, certain Etruscan customs and bloodlines are believed to exist in Italy, especially in Tuscany.

The best places to see the legacy left by these mysterious people are in Cerveteri and Tarquinia, outside Rome. Especially interesting is the Etruscan necropolis, just 6.4km (4 miles) southeast of Tarquinia, where thousands of tombs have been discovered. To learn more about the Etruscans, visit the Museo Nazionale di Villa Giulla in Rome.

The Roman Republic

After the Roman Republic was established in 510 B.C., the Romans continued to increase their power by conquering neighboring communities in the highlands and forming alliances with other Latins in the lowlands. They gave to their Latin allies, and then to conquered peoples, partial or complete Roman citizenship, with the obligation of military service. Citizen colonies were set up as settlements of Roman farmers, and many of the famous cities of Italy originated as colonies. For the most part, these colonies were fortified and linked to Rome by military roads.

The stern Roman republic was characterized by a belief in the gods, the necessity of learning from the past, the strength of the family, education through reading books and performing public service, and, most importantly, obedience. The all-powerful Senate presided as Rome defeated rival powers one after the other and grew to rule the Mediterranean. The Punic Wars with Carthage in the 3rd century B.C. cleared away a major obstacle, although people said later that Rome's breaking of its treaty with Carthage (which led to that city's total destruction) put a curse on Rome.

No figure was more towering during the republic than Julius Caesar, the charismatic conqueror of Gaul—"the wife of every husband and the husband of every wife." After defeating the last resistance of the Pompeiians in 45 B.C., he came to Rome and was made dictator and consul for 10 years. By then he was almost a king. Conspirators led by Marcus Junius Brutus stabbed him to death in the Senate on March 15, 44 B.C. "Beware the ides of March."

Marc Antony, a Roman general, assumed control by seizing Caesar's papers and wealth. Intent on expanding the Republic, Antony met with Cleopatra at Tarsus in 41 B.C. She seduced him, and he stayed in Egypt for a year. When Antony eventually returned to Rome, still smitten with Cleopatra, he made peace with Caesar's willed successor, Octavius, and, through the pacts of Brundisium, soon found himself married to Octavius's sister, Octavia. This marriage, however, didn't prevent him from marrying Cleopatra in 36 B.C. The furious Octavius gathered western legions and defeated Antony at the Battle of Actium on September 2, 31 B.C. Cleopatra fled to Egypt, followed by Antony, who committed suicide in disgrace a year later. Cleopatra, unable to seduce his successor and thus retain her rule of Egypt, followed suit with the help of an asp.

Dateline

- **Bronze Age** Celts, Teutonic tribes, and others from the Mediterranean and Asia Minor inhabit the peninsula.
- **1000 B.C.** Large colonies of Etruscans settle in Tuscany and Campania, quickly subjugating many of the Latin inhabitants of the peninsula.
- **800 B.C.** Rome begins to take shape, evolving from a strategically located shepherds' village into a magnet for Latin tribes fleeing the Etruscans.
- **600 B.C.** Etruscans occupy Rome, designating it the capital of their empire. The city grows rapidly, and a major seaport opens at Ostia.
- **510 B.C.** The Latin tribes, still centered in Rome, revolt against the Etruscans. Alpine Gauls attack from the north, and Greeks living in Sicily destroy the Etruscan navy.
- **250 B.C.** The Romans, allied with the Greeks, Phoenicians, and native Sicilians, defeat the Etruscans. Rome flourishes and begins the accumulation of a vast empire.
- **49 B.C.** Italy (through Rome) controls the entire Mediterranean world.
- **44 B.C.** Julius Caesar is assassinated. His successor, Augustus, transforms Rome from a city of brick into a city of marble.

The Roman Empire

By 49 B.C., Italy ruled the entire Mediterranean world, either directly or indirectly, because all political, commercial, and cultural pathways led straight to Rome. The potential for wealth and glory to be found in Rome lured many people, draining other Italian communities of human resources. Foreign imports, especially agricultural imports, hurt local farmers and landowners. Municipal governments faltered, and civil wars ensued. Public order was restored by the Caesars (planned by Julius but brought to fruition under Augustus). On the eve of the birth of Christ, Rome was a mighty empire whose generals had brought the Western world under the sway of Roman law and civilization.

Born Gaius Octavius in 63 B.C., Augustus, the first Roman emperor, reigned from 27 B.C. to A.D. 14. His reign, called "the golden age of Rome," led to the Pax Romana, 2 centuries of peace. He had been adopted by, and eventually became the heir of, his great-uncle Julius Caesar. In Rome you can still visit the remains of the Forum of Augustus, built before the birth of Christ, and the Domus Augustana, where the imperial family lived on Palatine Hill.

The emperors, whose succession started with Augustus's principate after the death of Julius Caesar, brought Rome to new, almost giddy, heights. Augustus transformed the city from brick to marble, much the way Napoleon III transformed Paris many centuries later. But success led to corruption. The emperors wielded autocratic power, and the centuries witnessed a steady decay in the ideals and traditions on which the empire had been founded. The army became a fifth column of barbarian mercenaries, the tax collector became the scourge of the countryside, and for every good emperor (Augustus, Claudius, Trajan, Vespasian, and Hadrian, to name a few) there were three or four debased heads of state (Caligula, Nero, Domitian, Caracalla, and others).

After Augustus died (by poison, perhaps), his widow, Livia—a crafty social climber who had divorced her first husband to marry Augustus—set up her son, Tiberius, as ruler through a series of intrigues and poisonings. A long series of murders ensued, and Tiberius, who ruled during Pontius Pilate's trial and crucifixion of Christ, was eventually murdered in an uprising of landowners. In fact, murder was so common that a short time later, Domitian (A.D. 81–96) became so obsessed with the possibility of assassination that he had the walls of his palace covered in mica so that he could see behind him at all times. (He was killed anyway.)

Excesses and scandal ruled the day: Caligula (a bit overfond of his sister, Drusilla)

APPENDIX: ITALY IN DEPTH

■ **3rd century A.D.** Rome declines under a series of incompetent and corrupt emperors.

■ **4th century A.D.** Rome is fragmented politically as administrative capitals are established in such cities as Milan and Trier, Germany.

■ **A.D. 395** The empire splits; Constantine establishes a "New Rome" at Constantinople (Byzantium). The Goths successfully invade Rome's northern provinces.

■ **410–55** Rome is sacked by barbarians.

■ **475** Rome falls, leaving only the primate of the Catholic Church in control. The pope slowly adopts many of the powers once reserved for the Roman emperor.

■ **800** Charlemagne is crowned Holy Roman Emperor by Pope Leo III.

Italy dissolves into a series of small warring kingdoms.

■ **Late 11th century** The popes function like secular princes with private armies.

■ **1065** The Holy Land falls to the Muslim Turks; the Crusades are launched.

■ **1303–77** The Papal Schism occurs; the pope and his entourage move from Rome to Avignon, France.

continues

appointed his horse a lifetime member of the Senate, lavished money on foolish projects, and proclaimed himself a god. Caligula's successor, his uncle Claudius, was deceived and publicly humiliated by one of his wives, the lascivious Messalina (he had her killed for her trouble); he was then poisoned by his final wife, his niece Agrippina, to secure the succession of Nero, her son by a previous marriage. Nero's thanks was later to murder not only his mother but also his wife, Claudius's daughter, and his rival, Claudius's son. The disgraceful Nero was removed as emperor while visiting Greece; he committed suicide with the cry, "What an artist I destroy."

By the 3rd century A.D., corruption had become so prevalent there were 23 emperors in 73 years. How bad were things? So bad that Caracalla, to secure control of the empire, had his brother Geta slashed to pieces while Geta was lying in his mother's arms. Rule of the empire changed hands so frequently that news of the election of a new emperor commonly reached the provinces together with a report of that emperor's assassination.

The 4th-century reforms of Diocletian held the empire together, but at the expense of its inhabitants, who were reduced to tax units. Diocletian reinforced imperial power while paradoxically weakening Roman dominance and prestige by dividing the empire into east and west halves and establishing administrative capitals at outposts such as Milan and Trier, Germany. He instituted not only heavy taxes but also a socioeconomic system that made professions hereditary. This edict was so strictly enforced that the son of a silversmith could be tried as a criminal if he attempted to become a sculptor instead.

Constantine became emperor in A.D. 306, and in 330 he made Constantinople (or Byzantium) the new capital of the Empire, moving the administrative functions away from Rome altogether, partly because the menace of possible barbarian attack in the West had increased greatly. Constantine took the best Roman artisans, politicians, and public figures with him, creating a city renowned for its splendor, intrigue, jealousies, and passion. Constantine was the first Christian emperor, allegedly converting after he saw the True Cross in the heavens, accompanied by the legend "In This Sign Shall You Conquer." He then defeated the pagan Maxentius and his followers in battle.

The Empire Falls

The eastern and western sections of the Roman Empire split in 395, leaving Italy without the support it had once received from east of the Adriatic. When the Goths moved toward Rome in the early 5th century, citizens

- **1377** The papacy returns to Rome.
- **1443** Brunelleschi's dome caps the Duomo in Florence as the Renaissance bursts into full bloom.
- **1469–92** Lorenzo il Magnifico rules in Florence as the Medici patron of Renaissance artists.
- **1499** Leonardo da Vinci completes *The Last Supper* in Milan.
- **1508** Michelangelo begins work on the Vatican's Sistine Chapel.
- **1527** Rome is sacked by Charles V of Spain, who is crowned Holy Roman Emperor the following year.
- **1796–97** Napoleon's series of invasions arouses Italian nationalism.
- **1861** The Kingdom of Italy is established.
- **1915–18** Italy enters World War I on the side of the Allies.
- **1922** Fascists march on Rome; Benito Mussolini becomes premier.
- **1929** A concordat between the Vatican and the Italian government is signed, delineating the rights and responsibilities of each party.
- **1935** Italy invades Abyssinia (Ethiopia).

in the provinces, who had grown to hate and fear the cruel bureaucracy set up by Diocletian and followed by succeeding emperors, welcomed the invaders. And then the pillage began.

Rome was first sacked by Alaric, king of the Visigoths, in August 410. The populace made no attempt to defend the city (other than trying vainly to buy him off, a tactic that had worked 3 years before); most people simply fled into the hills or headed to their country estates if they were rich. The feeble Western emperor Honorius hid out in Ravenna the entire time.

More than 40 troubled years passed. Then Attila the Hun invaded Italy to besiege Rome. Attila was dissuaded from attacking, thanks largely to a peace mission headed by Pope Leo I in 452. Yet relief was short-lived: In 455, Gaiseric the Vandal carried out a 2-week sack that was unparalleled in its pure savagery. The empire of the West lasted for only another 20 years; finally, in 476, the sacks and chaos ended the once-mighty city, and Rome was left to the popes, under the nominal auspices of an exarch from Byzantium (Constantinople).

The last would-be Caesars to walk the streets of Rome were both barbarians: The first was Theodoric, who established an Ostrogoth kingdom at Ravenna from 493 to 526; the second was Totila, who held the last chariot races in the Circus Maximus in 549. Totila was engaged in an ongoing battle with Belisarius, the general of the Eastern emperor Justinian, who sought to regain Rome for the Eastern Empire. The city changed hands several times, recovering some of its ancient pride by bravely resisting Totila's forces, but eventually it was entirely depopulated by the continuing battles.

Christianity, a new religion that created a new society, was probably founded in Rome about a decade after the death of Jesus. Gradually gaining strength despite early persecution, it was finally accepted as the official religion. The best way today to relive the early Christian era is to visit Rome's Appian Way and its Catacombs, along Via Appia Antica, built in 312 B.C. According to Christian tradition, it was here that an escaping Peter encountered the vision of Christ. The Catacombs of St. Callixtus form the first cemetery of the Christian community of Rome.

The Middle Ages

A ravaged Rome entered the Middle Ages, its once-proud population scattered and unrecognizable in rustic exile. A modest population started life again in the swamps of the Campus Martius, while the seven hills, now without water because the aqueducts were cut, stood abandoned and crumbling.

- **1936** Italy signs "Axis" pact with Germany.
- **1940** Italy invades Greece.
- **1943** U.S. Gen. George Patton lands in Sicily and soon controls the island.
- **1945** Mussolini is killed by a mob in Milan; World War II ends.
- **1946** The Republic of Italy is established.
- **1957** The Treaty of Rome, establishing the European Community (EC), is signed by six nations.
- **1960s** The country's economy grows under the EC, but the impoverished south lags behind.
- **1970s** Italy is plagued by left-wing terrorism; former premier Aldo Moro is kidnapped and killed.
- **1980s** Political changes in Eastern Europe induce Italy's strong Communist Party to modify its program and even to change its name; the Socialists head their first post-1945 coalition government.
- **1994** A conservative coalition, led by Silvio Berlusconi, wins general elections.
- **1995** Following the resignation of Berlusconi, treasury minister Lamberto Dini is named prime minister to head the transitional government.

continues

After the fall of the Western Empire, the pope took on more imperial powers, yet there was no political unity. Decades of rule by barbarians and then by Goths were followed by takeovers in different parts of the country by various strong warriors, such as the Lombards. Italy became divided into several spheres of control. In 731, Pope Gregory II renounced Rome's dependence on Constantinople and thus ended the twilight era of the Greek exarch who had nominally ruled Rome.

Papal Rome turned toward Europe, where the papacy found a powerful ally in Charlemagne, a king of the barbarian Franks. In 800, he was crowned emperor by Pope Leo III. The capital that he established at Aachen (Aix-la-Chapelle in French) lay deep within territory known to the Romans a half-millennium before as the heart of the barbarian world. Although Charlemagne pledged allegiance to the church and looked to Rome and its pope as the final arbiter in most religious and cultural affairs, he launched northwestern Europe on a course toward bitter political opposition to the meddling of the papacy in temporal affairs.

The successor to Charlemagne's empire was a political entity known as the Holy Roman Empire (962–1806). The new empire defined the end of the Dark Ages but ushered in a period of long, bloody warfare. The Lombard leaders battled Franks. Magyars from Hungary invaded northeastern Lombardy and, in turn, were defeated by the increasingly powerful Venetians. Normans gained military control of Sicily in the 11th century, divided it from the rest of Italy, and altered forever the island's racial and ethnic makeup and its architecture. As Italy dissolved into a fragmented collection of city-states, the papacy fell under the power of Rome's feudal landowners. Eventually, even the process for choosing popes came into the hands of the increasingly Germanic Holy Roman emperors, although this balance of power would very soon shift.

Rome during the Middle Ages was a quaint rural town. Narrow lanes with overhanging buildings filled many areas, such as the Campus Martius, that had once been showcases of imperial power. Great basilicas were built and embellished with golden-hued mosaics. The forums, mercantile exchanges, temples, and theaters of the Imperial Era slowly disintegrated and collapsed. The decay of ancient Rome was assisted by periodic earthquakes, centuries of neglect, and, in particular, the growing need for building materials. Rome receded into a dusty provincialism. As the seat of the Roman Catholic church, the state was almost completely controlled by priests, who had an insatiable need for new churches and convents.

■ **1996** Dini steps down as prime minister, and President Scalfaro dissolves both houses of parliament. In general elections, the center-left coalition known as the Olive Tree sweeps both the Senate and the Chamber of Deputies.

■ **1997–98** Twin earthquakes hit Umbria, killing 11 people and destroying precious frescos in Assisi's basilica. Romano Prodi survives a neo-Communist challenge and continues to press for budget cuts in an effort to "join Europe."

■ **1999** The euro technically becomes the official currency of Italy and other E.U. nations.

■ **2000** Italy welcomes Jubilee visitors in the wake of political discontent.

■ **2001** Billionaire media magnate Silvio Berlusconi is elected prime minister, winning by a landslide and leading the right wing to sweeping victory.

■ **2002** Euro notes are introduced into circulation, and lire begin to be withdrawn from circulation over a transition period.

■ **2003** Italy assumes presidency of E.U.

■ **2006** Italy's *Azzuri* win the FIFA World Cup for the fourth time in a dramatic shootout over France.

By the end of the 11th century, the popes shook off control of the Roman aristocracy, rid themselves of what they considered the excessive influence of the emperors at Aachen, and began an aggressive expansion of church influence and acquisitions. The deliberate organization of the church into a format modeled on the hierarchies of the ancient Roman Empire put it on a collision course with the empire and the other temporal leaders of Europe. The result was an endless series of power struggles.

The southern half of the country took a different road when, in the 11th century, the Normans invaded southern Italy, wresting control from the local strongmen and, in Sicily, from the Muslim Saracens who had occupied the region throughout the Dark Ages. To the south, the Normans introduced feudalism, a repressive social system that discouraged individual economic initiative, and whose legacy accounts for the social and economic differences between north and south that persist to this day.

In the mid–14th century, the Black Death ravaged Europe, killing a third of Italy's population. Despite such setbacks, the northern Italian city-states grew wealthy from Crusade booty, trade with one another and with the Middle East, and banking. These wealthy principalities and pseudorepublics ruled by the merchant elite flexed their muscles in the absence of a strong central authority.

The Renaissance

The story of Italy from the dawn of the Renaissance in the 15th century to the Age of Enlightenment in the 17th and 18th centuries is as varied and fascinating as that of the rise and fall of the empire. The papacy soon became essentially a feudal state, and the pope was a medieval (later Renaissance) prince engaged in many of the worldly activities that brought criticism on the church in later centuries. The 1065 fall of the Holy Land

to the Turks catapulted the papacy into the forefront of world politics, primarily because of the Crusades, many of which the popes directly caused or encouraged (but most of which were judged military and economic disasters). During the 12th and 13th centuries, the bitter rivalries that rocked Europe's secular and spiritual bastions took their toll on the Holy Roman Empire, which grew weaker as city-states, buttressed by mercantile and trade-related prosperity, grew stronger and as France emerged as a potent nation in its own right. Each investiture of a new bishop to any influential post resulted in endless jockeying for power among many factions.

These conflicts reached their most visible impasse in 1303 during the Great Schism, when the papacy was moved to the French city of Avignon. For more than 70 years, until 1377, viciously competing popes (one in Rome, another under the protection of the French kings in Avignon) made simultaneous claims to the legacy of St. Peter, underscoring as never before the degree to which the church was both a victim and a victimizer in the temporal world of European politics.

The seat of the papacy was eventually returned to Rome, where successive popes were every bit as interesting as the Roman emperors they had replaced. The great families (Barberini, Medici, Borgia) enhanced their status and fortunes impressively when one of their sons was elected pope. For a look at life during this tumultuous period, you can visit Rome's Castel Sant'Angelo, which became a papal residence in the 14th century.

Despite the centuries that had passed since the collapse of the Roman Empire, the age of siege wasn't yet over. In 1527, Charles V, king of Spain, carried out the worst sack of Rome ever. To the horror of Pope Clement VII (a Medici), the entire city was brutally pillaged by the man who was to be crowned Holy Roman Emperor the next year.

During the years of the Renaissance, the Reformation, and the Counter-Reformation, Rome underwent major physical changes. The old centers of culture reverted to pastures and fields, and great churches and palaces were built with the stones of ancient Rome. This construction boom, in fact, did far more damage to the temples of the Caesars than any barbarian sack had done. Rare marbles were stripped from the imperial baths and used as altarpieces or sent to lime kilns. So enthusiastic was the papal destruction of Imperial Rome that it's a miracle anything is left.

This era is best remembered because of its art. The great ruling families, especially the Medicis in Florence, the Gonzagas in Mantua, and the Estes in Ferrara, not only reformed law and commerce but also sparked a renaissance in art. Out of this period arose such towering figures as Leonardo da Vinci and Michelangelo. Many visitors come to Italy to view what's left of the art and glory of that era—everything from Michelangelo's Sistine Chapel at the Vatican to his statue of *David* in Florence, from Leonardo's *Last Supper* in Milan to the Duomo in Florence, graced by Brunelleschi's dome.

A United Italy

The 19th century witnessed the final collapse of the Renaissance city-states, which had existed since the end of the 13th century. These units, eventually coming under the control of a *signore* (lord), were essentially regional states, with mercenary soldiers, civil rights, and assistance for their friendly neighbors. Some had attained formidable power under such *signori* as the Estes in Ferrara, the Medicis in Florence, and the Viscontis and Sforzas in Milan.

During the 17th, 18th, and 19th centuries, turmoil continued through a succession of many European dynasties. Napoleon made a bid for power in Italy beginning in 1796, fueling his war machines with what was considered a relatively easy victory. During the Congress of Vienna (1814–15), which followed Napoleon's defeat, Italy was once again divided among many factions: Austria was given Lombardy and Venetia, and the Papal States were returned to the pope. Some duchies were put back into the hands of their hereditary rulers, and southern Italy and Sicily went to a Bourbon dynasty. One historic move, which eventually contributed to the unification of Italy, was the assignment of the former republic of Genoa to Sardinia (which, at the time, was governed by the House of Savoy).

Political unrest became a fact of Italian life, at least some of it encouraged by the rapid industrialization of the north and the almost total lack of industrialization in the south. Despite those barriers, in 1861, thanks to the brilliant efforts of patriots Camillo Cavour (1810–61) and Giuseppe Garibaldi (1807–82), the Kingdom of Italy was proclaimed and Victor Emmanuel (Vittorio Emanuele) II of the House of Savoy, king of Sardinia, became the head of the new monarchy.

Garibaldi, the most respected of all Italian heroes, must be singled out for his efforts, which included taking Sicily, returning to the mainland and marching north to meet Victor Emmanuel II at Teano, and finally declaring a unified Italy (with the important exception of Rome itself). It must have seemed especially sweet to a man whose efforts at unity had caused him to flee the country fearing for his life on four occasions. It's a tribute to the tenacity of this red-bearded hero that he never gave up, even in the early 1850s, when he was forced to wait out one of his exiles as a candle maker on Staten Island in New York.

Although the hope, promoted by Europe's theocrats and some of its devout Catholics, of attaining one empire ruled by the pope and the church had long ago faded, there was still a fight, followed by generations of hard feelings, when the Papal States—a strategically and historically important principality under the pope's temporal jurisdiction—were confiscated by the new Kingdom of Italy.

The establishment of the kingdom, however, didn't signal a complete unification of Italy because Rome was still under papal control and Venetia was still held by Austria. This was partially resolved in 1866, when Venetia joined the rest of Italy after the Seven Weeks' War between Austria and Prussia; in 1871, Rome became the capital of the newly formed country. The Vatican, however, didn't yield its territory to the new order, despite guarantees of nonintervention proffered by the government, and relations between the pope and the country of Italy remained rocky.

The Rise Of *Il Duce* & World War II

On October 28, 1922, Benito Mussolini, who had started his Fascist Party in 1919, knew the time was ripe for change. He gathered 50,000 supporters for a march on Rome. Inflation was soaring and workers had just called a general strike, so rather than recognizing a state under siege, King Victor Emmanuel II recognized Mussolini as the new government leader. In 1929, *Il Duce* defined the divisions between the Italian government and the Vatican by signing a concordat granting political and fiscal autonomy to Vatican City. The agreement also made Roman Catholicism the official state religion—but that designation was removed in 1978 by a revision of the concordat.

Impressions
....

It is not impossible to govern Italians. It is merely useless.
....
                                    Benito Mussolini

During the Spanish Civil War (1936–39), Mussolini's support of Franco's Fascist party, whose members had staged a coup against the democratically elected government of Spain, helped encourage the formation of the "Axis" alliance between Italy and Nazi Germany. Despite having outdated military equipment, Italy added to the general horror of the era by invading Abyssinia (Ethiopia) in 1935. In 1940, Italy invaded Greece through Albania, and, in 1942, it sent thousands of Italian troops to assist Hitler in his disastrous campaign along the Russian front. In 1943, Allied forces, under the command of U.S. Gen. George Patton and British Gen. Bernard Montgomery, landed in Sicily and quickly secured the island as they prepared to move north toward Rome.

In the face of likely defeat and humiliation, Mussolini was overthrown by his cabinet (Grand Council). The Allies made a separate deal with Victor Emmanuel III, who had collaborated with the Fascists during the previous 2 decades and now easily shifted allegiances. A politically divided Italy watched as battalions of fanatical German Nazis released Mussolini from his Italian jail cell to establish the short-lived Republic of Salò, headquartered on the edge of Lake Garda. Mussolini had hoped for a groundswell of popular opinion in favor of Italian Fascism, but events quickly proved this to be nothing more than a futile dream.

In April 1945, with almost a half-million Italians rising in a mass demonstration against him and the German war machine, Mussolini was captured by Italian partisans as he fled to Switzerland. Along with his mistress, Claretta Petacci, and several other of his intimates, he was shot and strung upside-down from the roof of a Milan gas station.

The Postwar Years

Disaffected with the monarchy and its identification with the fallen Fascist dictatorship, Italy's citizens voted in 1946 for the establishment of a republic. The major political party that emerged following World War II was the Christian Democratic Party, a right-of-center group whose leader, Alcide De Gasperi (1881–1954), served as premier until 1953. The second-largest party was the Communist Party; however, by the mid-1970s, it had abandoned its revolutionary program in favor of a democratic form of "Eurocommunism" (in 1991, the Communists even changed their name to the Democratic Party of the Left).

Even though after the war Italy had been stripped of all its overseas colonies, it quickly succeeded in rebuilding its economy, in part because of U.S. aid under the Marshall Plan (1948–52). By the 1960s, as a member of the European Community (founded in Rome in 1957), Italy had become one of the world's leading industrialized nations, prominent in the manufacture of automobiles and office equipment.

But the country continued to be plagued by economic inequities between the prosperous industrialized north and the economically depressed south. It suffered an unprecedented flight of capital (frequently aided by Swiss banks only too willing to accept discreet deposits from wealthy Italians) and an increase in bankruptcies, inflation (almost 20% during much of the 1970s), and unemployment.

During the late 1970s and early 1980s, Italy was rocked by the rise of terrorism, instigated both by neo-Fascists and by left-wing intellectuals from the Socialist-controlled universities of the north.

The 1990s & Into the New Millennium

By the late 19th century, the Mafia had become a kind of shadow government in the south; even to this day, it still controls a number of politicians, national officials, and even judges, although the influence of the *Cosa Nostra* is declining. In the early 1990s,

the Italians reeled as many leading politicians were accused of wholesale corruption. As a result, a newly formed right-wing group, led by media magnate Silvio Berlusconi, swept to victory in 1994's general elections. Berlusconi became prime minister at the head of a coalition government. However, in December 1994, he resigned as prime minister after the federalist Northern League Party defected from his coalition and he lost his parliamentary majority. Treasury Minister Lamberto Dini, a nonpolitical banker with international financial credentials, was named to replace Berlusconi.

Dini signed on merely as a transitional player in the topsy-turvy political game. His austere measures enacted to balance Italy's budget, including cuts in pensions and health care, weren't popular among the mostly blue-collar workers or the influential labor unions. Aware of a predicted defeat in a no-confidence vote, Dini stepped down. His resignation in January 1996 left beleaguered Italians shouting *"Basta!"* (Enough!). This latest reshuffling in Italy's political deck prompted President Oscar Scalfaro to dissolve both houses of parliament.

Once again the Italians were faced with forming a new government. The elections of April 1996 proved a shocker, not only for the defeated politicians but also for the victors. The center-left coalition known as the Olive Tree, led by Romano Prodi, swept both the Senate and the Chamber of Deputies. The Olive Tree, whose roots stem from the old Communist Party, achieved victory by shifting toward the center and focusing its campaign on a strong platform protecting social benefits and supporting Italy's bid to become a solid member of the European Union.

Prodi carried through on his commitment when he announced a stringent budget for 1997, in a bid to be among the first countries to enter the monetary union. That year saw further upheavals in the Prodi government as he continued to push ahead with cuts to the country's generous social-security system. By autumn, though, Prodi was forced to submit his resignation when he lost critical support in Parliament from the Communist Refounding Party, which balked at pension and welfare cuts in the 1998 budget. The party eventually backed off with its demands, and Prodi was returned to office, where he pledged to see legislation for a 35-hour work-week passed by 2001.

In September 1997, twin earthquakes (5.7 and 5.6 on the Richter scale), with an epicenter just outside Assisi, struck within hours of each other. Umbria sustained considerable damage, especially in Acciano and Assisi, where 11 people were killed and another 13,000 were forced to take refuge in tents. The following 11 days of aftershocks and tremors hindered the recovery effort by the Italian government and relief organizations, and poured salt in the wounds of those left wondering what to do. One of the victims of these quakes was the Basilica of St. Francis in Assisi, where vaults collapsed and magnificent frescoes were reduced to dust.

On the political front, Massimo D'Alema became the first former Communist to lead a Western European government in October 1998, when he formed Italy's 56th postwar government. He replaced departing prime minister Romano Prodi.

As 1999 neared its end, Italy rushed to complete its myriad renovation and restoration projects so that everything would be perfect for the Jubilee. The big financial news of 1999 was Italy's entrance under the euro umbrella.

Italy spent all of 2000 welcoming Jubilee Year visitors from around the world, but everything wasn't a celebration. At the time, there was popular disillusionment with the costs of E.U. membership, and the predicted weakness of the euro against the U.S. dollar and the British pound.

In the spring of 2000, Giuliano Amato, former prime minister and onetime Socialist, returned to power as the leader of Italy's 58th government since the war. For a year, he presided over an unwieldy coalition of a dozen political parties, ranging from former Communists to former Christian Democrats.

The richest man in Italy, billionaire media tycoon Silvio Berlusconi, swept to victory in May 2001 as prime minister, winning with right-wing support. Calling for a "revolution" in Italy, Berlusconi has promised 1.5 million new jobs, pension hikes, epic tax cuts, anti-crime bills, and beefed-up public works projects.

In 2002, Italians officially abandoned their long-beloved lire and began trading in euros along with their neighbors to the north, including France and Germany, a total of 12 countries (but not Britain). As the new currency went into effect, counterfeiters and swindlers had a field day. But in general, especially among businesses, the transition went relatively smoothly.

In 2003, Italy was often propelled into world headlines. Italy assumed the presidency of the European Union. At the same time Prime Minister Silvio Berlusconi triggered an uproar in the European Parliament. Responding to a heckling German member of Parliament, Martin Schulz, Berlusconi suggested he might be perfect as a Nazi concentration camp guard in a forthcoming film. This insensitive remark touched off a "cultural war" between Italy and Germany.

On other fronts, the Italian Parliament sent troops to Iraq after Baghdad was occupied by American forces, an event ending in tragedy when 18 service personnel were killed, Italy's highest military deaths since World War II.

In other developments in 2003, Gianni Angelli, the FIAT executive, died in Turin at the age of 81. He was the most famous Italian in the world. The House of Savoia, the former rulers of the kingdom of Italy, were

APPENDIX: ITALY IN DEPTH

allowed to return after 57 years of exile in Switzerland.

Right before Christmas in 2004, Prime Minister Silvio Berlusconi received a present from judges in Milan. In a corruption trial that had dragged on for 4 years, he was absolved of all alleged crimes, including such serious charges as buying off judges. Berlusconi blamed the charges on "vindictive left-wing prosecutors." Judges ruled that there was "some substance to one of the allegations— that is, funneling $434,404 into the private bank account of a judge—but noted that the statute of limitations had run out.

As much of the world watched and prayed, Pope John Paul II died on April 2, 2005, at the age of 84, ending a reign of 26 years as pope. Worldwide mourning was proclaimed among Catholics. On April 20, a new pope, Joseph Cardinal Ratzinger, was elected by his fellow cardinals. The Vatican's hardliner on church doctrine took the papal throne as Benedict the 16th. In 2006, Italy rejoiced as their beloved *Azzuri* won the FIFA World Cup for the fourth time, in a dramatic shootout over France.

A Taste of Italy

Italians are among the world's greatest cooks. Just ask any one of them. Despite the unification of Italy, regional tradition still dominates the various kitchens, from Rome to Lombardy, from the Valle d'Aosta to Sicily. The term "Italian cuisine" has little meaning unless it's more clearly defined as Neapolitan, Roman, Sardinian, Sicilian, Venetian, Piedmontese, Tuscan, or whatever. Each region has a flavor and a taste of its own, as well as a detailed repertoire of local dishes.

Food has always been one of life's great pleasures for the Italians. This has been true even from the earliest days: To judge from the lifelike banquet scenes found in Etruscan tombs, the Etruscans loved food and took delight in enjoying it. The Romans became famous for their never-ending banquets and for their love of exotic treats, such as flamingo tongues.

Although culinary styles vary, Italy abounds in trattorie specializing in local dishes—some of which are a delight for carnivores, such as the renowned *bistecca alla fiorentina* (cut from flavorful Chianina beef and then charcoal-grilled and served with a fruity olive oil). Other dishes, especially those found at the antipasto buffet, would appeal to every vegetarian's heart: peppers, greens, onions, pastas, beans, tomatoes, and fennel.

Incidentally, except in the south, Italians don't use as much garlic in their food as many foreigners seem to believe. Most Italian dishes, especially those in the north, are butter-based. And spaghetti and meatballs isn't an Italian dish, although certain restaurants throughout the country have taken to serving it "for homesick Americans."

Cuisines Around The Country

Rome is the best place to introduce yourself to Italian cuisine because it boasts specialty restaurants representing every region. Throughout your Roman holiday, you'll encounter such specialties as *zuppa di pesce* (a soup or stew of various fish, cooked in white wine and flavored with herbs), *cannelloni* (tube-shaped pasta baked with any number of stuffings), *riso col gamberi* (rice with shrimp, peas, and mushrooms, flavored with white wine and garlic), *scampi alla griglia* (grilled prawns, one of the best-tasting, albeit expensive, dishes in the city), *quaglie col risotto e tartufi* (quail with rice and truffles), *lepre alla cacciatore* (hare flavored with tomato sauce and herbs), *zabaglione* (a creamy dessert made with sugar, egg yolks, and Marsala), *gnocchi alla romana* (potato-flour dumplings with a meat sauce, covered with grated cheese), *abbacchio* (baby spring

Impressions

In Italy, the pleasure of eating is central to the pleasure of living. When you sit down to dinner with Italians, when you share their food, you are sharing their lives.

Fred Plotkin
Italy for the Gourmet Traveler (1996)

lamb, often roasted over an open fire), *saltimbocca alla romana* (literally "jump-in-your-mouth"—thin slices of veal with sage, ham, and cheese), *fritto alla romana* (a mixed fry likely to include everything from brains to artichokes), *carciofi alla romana* (tender artichokes cooked with herbs such as mint and garlic, flavored with white wine), *fettuccine all'uovo* (egg noodles with butter and cheese), *zuppa di cozze* (a hearty bowl of mussels cooked in broth), *fritto di scampi e calamaretti* (baby squid and prawns, fast-fried), *fragoline* (wild strawberries, in this case from the Alban Hills), and *finocchio* (fennel, a celerylike raw vegetable with the flavor of anisette, often eaten as a dessert or in a salad).

From Rome, it's on to **Tuscany,** where you'll encounter the hearty cuisine of the Tuscan hills. The main ingredient for almost any meal is the superb local olive oil, adored for its low acidity and lovely flavor. In Italy's south, the olives are gathered only after they've fallen off the trees, but here they're handpicked off the trees so that they won't get bruised (ensuring lower acidity and milder aroma). Typical Tuscan pastas are *pappardelle* and *penne* mingled with a variety of sauces, many of which are tomato-based. Tuscans are extremely fond of strong cheeses such as Gorgonzola, fontina, and parmigiano. Meat and fish are prepared simply and might seem undercooked, although locals would argue that it's better to let the inherent flavor of the ingredients survive the cooking process.

The next major city to visit is **Venice,** where the cookery is typical of the **Venezia**

district. Long ago it was called "tasty, straightforward, and homely" by one food critic, and we concur. Two of the most typical dishes are *fegato alla veneziana* (liver and onions) and *risi e bisi* (rice and fresh peas). Seafood figures heavily in the Venetian diet, and grilled fish is often served with the bitter red radicchio, a lettuce that comes from Treviso.

In **Lombardy,** of which **Milan** is the center, the cookery is more refined and flavorful. No dish here is more famous than *cotoletta alla milanese* (cutlets of tender veal dipped in egg and bread crumbs and fried in olive oil until they're a golden brown)—the Viennese call it Wiener schnitzel. *Osso buco* is the other great dish of Lombardy; this is cooked with the shin bone of veal in a ragout sauce and served on rice and peas. *Risotto alla milanese* is also a classic—rice that can be dressed in almost any way, depending on the chef's imagination. It's often flavored with saffron and butter, to which chicken giblets have been added, and it's seemingly always served with heaps of *Parmigiano-Reggiano* cheese. *Polenta,* a cornmeal mush that's "more than mush," is the staff of life in some parts of northeastern Italy and is eaten in lieu of pasta.

The cooking in the **Piedmont,** of which **Turin** is the capital, and the **Aosta Valley** is different from that in the rest of Italy. Victuals here are said to appeal to strong-hearted men returning from a hard day's work in the mountains. You get such dishes as *bagna cauda,* a sauce made with olive oil, garlic, butter, and anchovies, in which you dip uncooked fresh vegetables. *Fonduta* is also celebrated: It's made with melted fontina cheese, butter, milk, egg yolks, and, for an elegant touch, white truffles.

Liguria, whose chief town is **Genoa,** turns to the sea for a great deal of its cuisine, as reflected by its version of bouillabaisse, a *burrida* flavored with spices. But its most famous food item is *pesto,* a sauce made with fresh basil, garlic, cheese, and walnuts, which is used to dress pasta, fish, and many other dishes.

Emilia-Romagna, with such towns as **Modena, Parma, Bologna, Ravenna,** and **Ferrara,** is one of the great gastronomic centers. Rich in produce, its school of cooking produces many notable pastas now common around Italy: *tagliatelle, tortellini,* and *cappelletti* (larger than tortellini and made in the form of "little hats"). Tagliatelle, of course, are long strips of macaroni, and tortellini are little squares of dough stuffed with chopped pork, veal, or whatever. Equally popular is *lasagna,* which by now everybody has heard of. In Bologna, it's often made by adding finely shredded spinach to the dough. The best-known sausage of the area is *mortadella,* and equally famous is a *cotoletta alla bolognese* (veal cutlet fried with a slice of ham or bacon). The distinctive and famous cheese *Parmigiano-Reggiano* is a product of Parma and also Reggio Emilia. *Zampone* (stuffed pig's foot) is a specialty of Modena. Parma is also known for its ham, which is fashioned into air-cured *prosciutto di Parma.* Served in wafer-thin slices, it's deliciously sweet and hailed by gourmets as the finest in the world.

Much of the cookery of **Campania** (spaghetti with clam sauce, pizzas, and so forth), with **Naples** as its major city, is already familiar to North Americans because so many Neapolitans moved to the New World and opened restaurants. Mozzarella, or buffalo cheese, is the classic cheese of this area. Mixed fish fries, done a golden brown, are a staple of nearly every table.

Sicily has a distinctive cuisine, with good, strong flavors and aromatic sauces. A staple of the diet is *maccheroni con le sarde* (spaghetti with pine seeds, fennel, spices, chopped sardines, and olive oil). Fish is good and fresh in Sicily (try swordfish). Among meat dishes, you'll see *involtini siciliani* (rolled meat with a stuffing of egg, ham, and cheese cooked in bread crumbs) on the menu. A *caponata* is a special way of cooking eggplant in a flavorful tomato sauce. The desserts and homemade pastries are excellent, including *cannoli,* cylindrical pastry cases stuffed with ricotta and candied fruit (or chocolate). Their ice creams, called *gelati,* are among the best in Italy.

And Some *Vino* to Wash It All Down . . .

Italy is the largest wine-producing country in the world; as far back as 800 B.C. the Etruscans were vintners. It's said that more soil is used in Italy for the cultivation of grapes than for the growing of food. Many Italian farmers produce wine just for their own consumption or for their relatives in "the big city." However, it wasn't until 1965 that laws were enacted to guarantee regular consistency in wine making. Wines regulated by the government are labeled "DOC" (*Denominazione di Origine Controllata*). If you see "DOCG" on a label (the "G" means *garantita*), that means even better quality control.

THE VINEYARDS OF ITALY

Following traditions established by the ancient Greeks, Italy produces more wine than any other nation. More than 1.6 million hectares (4 million acres) of soil are cultivated as vineyards, and recently there has been an increased emphasis on recognizing vintages from lesser-known growers who might or might not be designated as working within a zone of controlled origin and name. (It's considered an honor, and usually a source of profit, to own vines within a DOC. Vintners who are presently limited to marketing their products as unpretentious table wines—*vino di tavola*—often expend great efforts lobbying for an elevated status as a DOC.)

Italy's wine producers range from among the most automated and technologically sophisticated in Europe to low-tech, labor-intensive family plots that turn out just a few hundred bottles per year. You can sometimes save money by buying directly from a producer (the signs beside the highway of any wine-producing district will advertise VENDITA DIRETTA). Not only will you avoid paying the retailer's markup, but you also might get a glimpse of the vines that produced the vintage that you carry home with you.

Useful vocabulary words for such endeavors are *bottiglieria* (a simple wine shop) and *enoteca* (a more upscale shop where many vintages, from several growers, are displayed and sold like magazines in a bookstore). In some cases, you can buy a glass of the product before you buy the bottle, and platters of cold cuts or cheeses are sometimes available to offset the tang (and alcoholic effects) of the wine.

REGIONAL WINES

Here we've cited only a few popular wines. Rest assured that there are hundreds more, and you'll have a great time sampling them to find your own favorites.

Latium: In this major wine-producing region, many of the local wines come from the Castelli Romani, the hill towns around Rome. Horace and Juvenal sang the praises of Latium wines even in imperial times. These wines, experts agree, are best drunk when young, and they're most often white, mellow, and dry (or "demi-sec"). There are seven types, including **Falerno** (straw yellow in color) and **Cecubo** (often served with roast meat). Try also **Colli Albani** (straw yellow with amber tints, served with both fish and meat). The golden yellow wines of **Frascati** are famous, produced in both a

demi-sec and a sweet variety, the latter served with dessert.

Tuscany: Tuscan wines rank with some of the finest reds in France. **Chianti** is the best known, and it comes in several varieties. The most highly regarded is **Chianti Classico,** a lively ruby-red wine mellow in flavor with a bouquet of violets. A good label is Antinori. A lesser known but remarkably fine Tuscan wine is **Brunello di Montalcino,** a brilliant garnet red served with roasts and game. The ruby-red, almost purple, **Vino Nobile di Montepulciano** has a rich, rugged body; it's a noble wine that's aged for 4 years. The area around San Gimignano produces a light, sweet white wine called **Vernaccia.** While you're in Tuscany, order the wonderful dessert wine called **Vin Santo,** which tastes almost like sherry and is usually accompanied by biscotti that you dunk into your glass.

Emilia-Romagna: The sparkling **Lambrusco** of this region is, by now, best known by Americans, but this wine can be of widely varying quality. Most of it is a brilliant ruby red. Be more experimental, and try such wines as the dark ruby red **Sangiovese** (with a delicate bouquet) and the golden yellow **Albana,** somewhat sweet. **Trebbiano,** generally dry, is best served with fish.

The Veneto: From this rich breadbasket in northeastern Italy come such world-famous wines as **Bardolino** (a light ruby red often served with poultry), **Valpolicella** (produced in "ordinary quality" and "superior dry," best served with meats), and **Soave** (beloved by W. Somerset Maugham), which has a pale amber color with a light aroma and a velvety flavor. Also try one of the **Cabernets,** either the ruby-red **Cabernet di Treviso** (ideal with roasts and game) or the even deeper ruby-red **Cabernet Franc,** which has a marked herbal bouquet and is served with roasts.

Friuli—Venezia Giulia: This area attracts those who enjoy a "brut" wine with a trace of flint. From classic grapes come **Merlot,** deep ruby in color, and several varieties of **Pinot,** including **Pinot Grigio,** whose color ranges from straw yellow to gray-pink (good with fish). Also served with fish, the **Sauvignon** has a straw-yellow color and a delicate bouquet.

Lombardy: These wines are justly renowned—and, if you don't believe us, would you instead take the advice of Leonardo da Vinci, Pliny, and Virgil? These great men have sung the praise of this wine-rich region bordered by the Alps to the north and the Po River to the south. To go with the tasty, refined cuisine of the Lombard kitchen are such wines as **Frecciarossa** (a pale straw-yellow color with a delicate bouquet—order it with fish), **Sassella** (bright ruby red—order it with game, red meat, and roasts), and the amusingly named **Inferno** (a deep ruby red with a penetrating bouquet—order it with meats).

The Piedmont: The finest wines in Italy, mostly red, are said to be produced on the vine-clad slopes of the Piedmont. Of course, **Asti Spumante,** the color of straw with an abundant champagnelike foam, is the prototype of Italian sparkling wines. While traveling through this area of northwestern Italy, you'll want to sample **Barbaresco** (brilliant ruby red with a delicate flavor—order it with red meats), **Barolo** (also brilliant ruby red, best when it mellows into a velvety old age), **Cortese** (pale straw yellow with green glints—order it with fish), and **Gattinara** (an intense ruby-red beauty in youth that changes with age). Piedmont is also the home of **vermouth,** a white wine to which aromatic herbs and spices, among other ingredients, have been added; it's served as an aperitif.

Liguria: This area doesn't have as many wine-producing regions as other parts of Italy, yet it grows dozens of different grapes. These are made into such wines as **Dolceacqua** (lightish ruby red, served with

hearty food) and **Vermentino Ligure** (pale yellow with a good bouquet, often served with fish).

Campania: From the volcanic soil of Vesuvius, the wines of Campania have been extolled for 2,000 years. Homer praised the glory of **Falerno,** straw yellow in color. Neapolitans are fond of ordering a wine known as **Lacrima Christi ("tears of Christ")** to accompany many seafood dishes. It comes in amber, red, and pink. With meat dishes, try the dark mulberry-color **Gragnano,** which has a faint bouquet of faded violets. The reds and whites of Ischia and Capri are also justly renowned.

Sicily: The wines of Sicily, called a "paradise of the grape," were extolled by the ancient poets, including Martial. Caesar himself lavished praise on **Mamertine** when it was served at a banquet honoring his third consulship. **Marsala,** an amber wine served with desserts, is the most famous wine of Sicily; it's velvety and fruity and sometimes used in cooking, as in veal Marsala. The wines made from grapes grown in the volcanic soil of Etna come in both red and white varieties. Also try the **Corvo Bianco di Casteldaccia** (straw yellow, with a distinctive bouquet) and the **Corvo Rosso di Casteldaccia** (ruby red, almost garnet, full-bodied and fruity).

Other Drinks

Italians drink other libations as well. Their most famous drink is **Campari,** bright red in color and flavored with herbs; it has a quinine bitterness to it. It's customary to serve it with ice cubes and soda.

Limoncello, a bright yellow drink made by infusing pure alcohol with lemon zest, has become Italy's second-most popular drink. It has long been a staple in the lemon-producing region along the Amalfi Coast in Capri and Sorrento, and recipes for the sweetly potent concoction have been passed down by families there for generations. About a decade ago, restaurants in Sorrento, Naples, and Rome started making their own versions. Visitors to those restaurants as well as the Sorrento peninsula began singing limoncello's praises and requesting bottles to go. Now it's one of the most up-and-coming liqueurs in the world, thanks to heavy advertising promotions.

Beer, once treated as a libation of little interest, is still far inferior to wines produced domestically, but foreign beers, especially those of Ireland and England, are gaining great popularity with Italian youth, especially in Rome. This popularity is mainly because of atmospheric pubs, which now number more than 300 in Rome alone, where young people linger over a pint and a conversation. Most pubs are in the Roman center, and many are licensed by Guinness and its Guinness Italia operations. In a city with 5,000 watering holes, 300 pubs might seem like a drop, but because the clientele is young, the wine industry is trying to devise a plan to keep that drop from becoming a steady stream of Italians who prefer grain to grapes.

High-proof **grappa** is made from the "leftovers" after the grapes have been pressed. Many Italians drink this before or after dinner (some put it into their coffee). It's an acquired taste—to an untrained foreign palate, it often seems rough and harsh.

INDEX

INDEX

Notes

Notes

Notes

YOU DON'T HAVE TO BE ON CAMPUS TO WATCH mtvU.

MTVU **Über**™

MUSIC ABOVE ALL - IN YOUR CONTROL

Streaming 24/7, 1000s of music videos, student-produced content and more.

LOG ON TO mtvU.com